International Mortality Statistics

International Mortality Statistics

MICHAEL ALDERSON

Facts On File, Inc.
119 West 57 Street, New York, NY 10019

International Mortality Statistics

First published in the United States of America in 1981 by Facts on File Inc.

Library of Congress in Cataloguing in Publication Data

Alderson, Michael.
International Mortality Statistics

Includes bibliographical references.
1. Mortality – Statistics. I. Title

HB1321.A43 312′.2 80-22536
ISBN 0-87196-514-3

Typeset by Leaper & Gard Ltd, Bristol
Printed in Great Britain by
St Edmundsbury Press, Bury St Edmunds, Suffolk

Contents

1 Introduction .. 3

1.1 Aim .. 3
1.1.1 Coverage .. 3
1.1.2 The validity of the data .. 3
1.1.3 European and world history, 1901-75 .. 4
1.1.4 Published trends in mortality statistics .. 4
1.1.5 Statistical methods used in the present work .. 4
1.1.6 Alignment of the International Classification of Disease .. 4

1.2 Uses of Mortality Statistics .. 5
1.2.1 Descriptive studies .. 5
1.2.2 Generation of hypotheses .. 5
1.2.3 Hypothesis testing .. 5
1.2.4 Evaluation of public health measures .. 5
1.2.5 Descriptive studies – specific suggestions .. 6
1.2.6 Generation of hypotheses – specific suggestions .. 6
1.2.7 Evaluation of public health measures – specific suggestions .. 6

References .. 7

Appendix .. 8
Official departments responsible for mortality statistics in each of the countries for which data have been provided

2 Validity of mortality statistics .. 13

2.1 Validity of Census Data .. 13

2.2 Validity of Mortality Data .. 14
2.2.1 Is the death registered? .. 14
2.2.2 Is information missing? .. 15
2.2.3 Accuracy of cause of death data .. 16
2.2.4 Accuracy of clinical diagnosis .. 16
2.2.5 Comparisons of clinical and autopsy diagnosis .. 17
2.2.6 Comparisons between death certificates and reviews of detailed case histories .. 18

2.2.7 Certification .. 19
2.2.8 Classification of cause of death .. 22
2.2.9 Coding of cause of death .. 23
2.2.10 Problems with specific diseases .. 24

2.3 Registration Systems in Different Countries .. 34
2.3.1 Australia .. 34
2.3.2 Austria .. 35
2.3.3 Belgium .. 35
2.3.4 Bulgaria .. 35
2.3.5 Canada .. 35
2.3.6 Chile .. 35
2.3.7 Czechoslovakia .. 36
2.3.8 Denmark .. 36
2.3.9 Eire .. 36
2.3.10 Finland .. 36
2.3.11 France .. 36
2.3.12 Greece .. 37
2.3.13 Hungary .. 37
2.3.14 Iceland .. 37
2.3.15 Italy .. 37
2.3.16 Japan .. 37
2.3.17 Netherlands .. 37
2.3.18 New Zealand .. 38
2.3.19 Norway .. 38
2.3.20 Poland .. 38
2.3.21 Portugal .. 38
2.3.22 Romania .. 38
2.2.23 Spain .. 38
2.3.24 Sweden .. 39
2.3.25 Switzerland .. 39
2.3.26 Turkey .. 39
2.3.27 UK – England and Wales .. 39
2.3.28 UK – Northern Ireland .. 39
2.3.29 UK– Scotland .. 39
2.3.30 US .. 40
2.3.31 Yugoslavia .. 40
40

2.4 Indicators of Validity of Mortality Statistics .. 40
2.4.1 Number of doctors per 10,000 population .. 40
2.4.2 Proportion of the population in rural areas .. 41
2.4.3 Percentage of certificates issued by Medical Practitioners .. 41
2.4.4 The percentage of all certificates from ill-defined causes .. 41

References .. 42

Table 2.1 Number of doctors/10,000 population in different countries during the 20th century .. 48
Table 2.2 Percentage of population classified as living in rural areas in different countries during the 20th century .. 49
Table 2.3 Percentage of death certificates signed by doctors in different countries during the 20th century .. 50

Table 2.4 Percentage of certificates from ill-defined causes in different countries in the 20th century 51

3 European and world history, 1901–75 55

3.1 The Effects of Wars 55

3.2 Migration 56

3.3 Notes on Countries Involved 57
3.3.1 Australia 57
3.3.2 Austria 57
3.3.3 Belgium 58
3.3.4 Bulgaria 58
3.3.5 Canada 58
3.3.6 Chile 58
3.3.7 Czechoslovakia 59
3.3.8 Denmark 59
3.3.9 Eire 59
3.3.10 Finland 59
3.3.11 France 59
3.3.12 Greece 60
3.3.13 Hungary 60
3.3.14 Iceland 60
3.3.15 Italy 60
3.3.16 Japan 61
3.3.17 Netherlands 61
3.3.18 New Zealand 61
3.3.19 Norway 62
3.3.20 Poland 62
3.3.21 Portugal 62
3.3.22 Romania 62
3.3.23 Spain 63
3.3.24 Sweden 63
3.3.25 Switzerland 63
3.3.26 Turkey 63
3.3.27 UK – England and Wales 63
3.3.28 UK – Northern Ireland 63
3.3.29 UK – Scotland 63
3.3.30 US 64
3.3.31 Yugoslavia 64

References 64

Table 3.1 Estimated war deaths in two world wars 66
Table 3.2 Immigration and emigration per thousand population for various countries this century 67

4 Published trends in mortality statistics 71

4.1 General Publications 71

4.2 Data for Individual Countries 72
4.2.1 Canada 72
4.2.2 Czechoslovakia 72
4.2.3 Finland 72
4.2.4 France 72
4.2.5 Italy 72
4.2.6 Japan 72
4.2.7 Netherlands 72
4.2.8 New Zealand 73
4.2.9 Norway 73
4.2.10 Portugal 73
4.2.11 United Kingdom – England and Wales 73
4.2.12 US 73
4.2.13 Yugoslavia 74

References 74

5 Statistical method 79

5.1 Handling Population Data 79

5.2 Handling Data on Deaths 80

5.3 Age Specific Numbers of Deaths 81

5.4 Standardisation of the Rates 81

5.5 Death Rates for Certain Causes of Death 83
5.5.1 Deaths in infancy 83
5.5.2 Acute infectious disease 84
5.5.3 Congenital abnormalities 84
5.5.4 Maternal mortality 84
5.5.5 Plague and yellow fever 84

5.6 Presentation of the Material 84

References 84

Appendix 86
Source of mortality statistics for each of the countries for which data have been provided

6 Alignment of the revisions of the International Classification of Diseases 91

6.1 Various Approaches that have been used 91

6.2 The Selected Approach 91

6.3 Notes 92

Reference 97

Appendix 99
Alignment of the 8 revisions of the International Classification of Diseases

Cause of Death Tables 111

Numerical Index to Cause of Death Tables 515

Alphabetical Index to Cause of Death Tables 521

1 – Introduction

Contents

		Page
1.1	**Aim**	3
1.1.1	Coverage	3
1.1.2	The validity of the data	3
1.1.3	European and world history, 1901-75	4
1.1.4	Published trends in mortality statistics	4
1.1.5	Statistical methods used in the present work	4
1.1.6	Alignment of the international classification of disease	4
1.2	**Uses of Mortality Statistics**	5
1.2.1	Descriptive studies	5
1.2.2	Generation of hypotheses	5
1.2.3	Hypothesis testing	5
1.2.4	Evaluation of public health measures	5
1.2.5	Descriptive studies: specific suggestions	6
1.2.6	Generation of hypotheses: specific suggestions	6
1.2.7	Evaluation of public health measures: specific suggestions	6
	References	7
	Appendix	8
	Official departments responsible for mortality statistics in each of the countries for which data have been provided	

1

Introduction

This chapter presents the aim and coverage of this work; five sub-sections then indicate the material covered in the chapters 2-6. The final section presents some ideas on the potential uses of mortality statistics.

1.1 Aim

This book gives serial mortality of the 20th century for European and other selected countries in tabular form by sex, calendar period, cause of death and country.

The material should be of interest to individuals (including both specialists and those without detailed knowledge of this field) wishing to examine the long-term trends in mortality within a particular country, or to make comparisons between patterns of mortality in different countries during the present century. Section 1.2 of this chapter gives some specific suggestions about the uses to which the data might be put.

1.1.1 Coverage

Data have been included for all those countries in Europe for which they have been available in a continuous sequence throughout this century, or at least for a greater part of it. This includes: Austria, Belgium, Bulgaria, Czechoslovakia, Denmark, Eire, Finland, France, Greece, Hungary, Iceland, Italy, Netherlands, Norway, Poland, Portugal, Romania, Spain, Sweden, Switzerland, UK – England and Wales, Northern Ireland, Scotland and Yugoslavia. In addition, a number of other developed countries have been included: Australia, Canada, Chile, Japan, New Zealand, Turkey and US. This covers the main countries for which data are available for the 20th century. For the majority of the countries the material was available from the beginning of the century; other countries did not publish national data by cause until later in the second or third decades of the century. The method of indicating availability of data on the statistical tables is discussed in section 5.6 (see page 84).

The data are tabulated for 178 causes of death, which have been selected to provide continuity over the greatest period of time. The national data for many countries have been published by varying combinations of the International Classification of Diseases (ICD) – a classification that has been regularly revised at about 10-year intervals throughout the century. Chapter 6 discusses the problems of the alignment of the classification and indicates exactly how this has been achieved in the present work. A double scheme has been used, first by following certain specific causes as far as possible from the present day; second, broader causes were followed forwards from the beginning of the century using combinations of specific categories of death for later years. In addition to trying to identify as many specific causes of death as are feasible, the tables also provide certain broader causes based on a varying number of combinations of specific causes. The appendix to chapter 6 sets out the detail of the method on alignment.

1.1.2 The validity of the data

No attempt is made to provide interpretation of the data that are presented. However, chapter 2 discusses in some detail aspects of the validity of the data. This begins with consideration of census data and is then followed by a lengthy section on mortality data. The various sources of error are covered, including the accuracy of clinical diagnosis, with some historical material on the development of medical knowledge during this century. Particular attention is paid to published studies that have quantified the degree of error in mortality statistics. Sub-sections deal with the problems of specific diseases, in the order of the main chapters in the International Classification of Disease.

The different countries for which data are presented vary in their registration system at local and national level.

The third section of chapter 2 discusses very briefly the development of national registration in each of the 31 countries.

There are various indicators of the validity of mortality statistics: the proportion of doctors in a population, the proportion of the population living in rural areas, the percentage of death certificates issued by medical practitioners and the percentage of all certificates that are from ill-defined causes of death. The final section of chapter 2 deals with each of these problems in turn, and presents some statistics on the trends of these indicators for the 31 countries throughout this century.

1.1.3 European and world history, 1901–75

War has an appreciable effect on the quality of mortality statistics. This is due to the distorting effect from the large numbers of deaths that may occur in sub-groups of the population; the major shifts in national boundaries that occur; and subsequent forced or voluntary migration of large numbers of poulations. Chapter 3 discusses European and world history; there is a brief general section for each of the 31 countries and then specific comments on the effect of war and migration. Tables on war deaths and immigration and emigration statistics are provided in order to show the effect of these upon the populations. The published statistics on migration are difficult to interpret due to many errors and biases in the material and caution is urged when studying these figures.

1.1.4 Published trends in mortality statistics

Chapter 4 reviews publications that have appeared in the past on trends in mortality statistics. This begins with general articles that have covered either one disease for many countries, or patterns of mortality for several countries. Further sections in the chapter then deal with specific publications that have appeared for each of the participating countries. It is interesting to note that this chapter is relatively short compared with the preceding ones – an indication of the limited amount of material that has been published in detail on international trends in mortality. (This point is, of course, a major justification for the present work.) It must be acknowledged that more limited trend data are also buried in many of the official government publications for each of the countries. However, these data are of limited value for the potential user, because of their incomplete coverage and their relative inaccessibility.

1.1.5 Statistical methods used in the present work

Chapter 5 explains the methods that have been used in handling the data. The chapter is divided into five subsections. The first section discusses the way the population data have been assembled; the second deals with the basic data that have been accumulated on mortality for each of the countries. The third section discusses the source of age-specific numbers of deaths and the production of age-specific death rates by cause which are then used to age-standardize all the tabulated data. The fourth section discusses why and how age-standardization of mortality statistics has been carried out; various methods of standardization are reviewed. The reasons for selecting the indirect method are also explained. The fifth section of chapter 5 describes the method of presentation of the data in the tables.

An appendix to this chapter lists the official departments responsible for handling mortality statistics in each of the countries, while an appendix to chapter 5 indicates the sources of data used to compile the statistical tables.

1.1.6 Alignment of the International Classification of Disease

The International Classification of Disease (ICD) has been revised at approximately 10-yearly intervals throughout the century. Chapter 6 deals with the problems of alignment of the classification, and indicates exactly the way that this has been done.

The general philosophy has been that by spelling out the different codes that have been aligned for different decades this century (or different revisions of the ICD) the user can see how the data have been handled. For many causes (whether relatively specific or broad) pragmatic decisions have had to be taken, to achieve 'alignment'.

The appendix to chapter 6 shows the detail of the codes that have been used; some causes had a major discrepancy from one ICD revision to another with an increment or decrement of up to 50 per cent in the numbers of deaths from one revision to another. However, the data have still been considered as a usable alignment if: the cause is of interest; there has been major trend in the death rate throughout the century; and it is felt that the inadequate fit does not destroy the use of presented data. This latter point is a matter of subjective judgment. When there has been discontinuity from one revision to another, attention has been drawn to this in section 2.2.8, and the actual codes used are spelt out in chapter 6. A number of broad causes of death, incorporating two or more specific causes have been provided in the tables. Users may also aggregate other causes if they wish to use broader categories other than those that are specifically presented in this work. Aggregation of specific causes is only satisfactory for those tables that have been standardized using rates for the same standard populations. This point is discussed in chapter 5, section 5.4.

1.2 Uses of Mortality Statistics

This section gives a brief indication of the categories of use to which mortality statistics may be put. This topic has been dealt with at greater length by Alderson (1974 and 1977). Four rather different classes of use are described and then a few specific examples of the types of application of the present material are provided.

1.2.1 Descriptive studies

Many authors agree that one application is for the general description of a range of health problems. Usually it is suggested that the data can be presented to show the variation by person, place, or time. The statistics presented in this book are age-adjusted indices by causes for different countries, which have been aggregated into five-year calendar periods. No analyses are included by age, marital status, occupation, place of birth, locality within country, or specific calendar years. (Such tabulations are available in some of the national publications from which the present data were derived; they do not usually permit examination of permutations of all these variates or cover as wide a range of causes of death has have been presented here.) The tables will permit examination of the patterns of mortality, looking for variation between the sexes, from one country to another and over a period of 75 years. Such material will illustrate the trends in disease and the changing character of medical problems throughout this century.

1.2.2 Generation of hypotheses

The probing of variation hinted at in the previous section is a prerequisite to the more detailed exploration that can occur with the simultaneous examination of two or more sets of data. For example, the trends in laryngeal cancer can be examined in relation to national per capita estimates of cigarette consumption. Such studies are often referred to as 'correlation studies', but this term (with implications of a specific statistical analysis) is not the most appropriate label. Various ways of examining such sets of data may be used:

1. graphic representation of time trends in two or more variates;
2. scatter diagrams, for example, plotting points for each country in relation to the mortality for the cause and estimated population exposure to a particular environmental agent;
3. statistical analyses, exploring the strength of the association between mortality and the putative environmental factor (multivariate analysis may be suitable to adjust for the influence of various confounding factors).

Alderson (1980) has recently reviewed the application of such studies as a tool for generating hypotheses. All the warnings about quality of data must be considered (see chapter 2). It must be emphasized that the (statistical) examination of multiple associations can reveal many spurious results as well as a few genuine 'leads'. The biological plausibility must also be considered, as well as the possible biases in the data. The results should be used to generate hypotheses which require testing by other approaches.

1.2.3 Hypothesis testing

If a hypothesis is put forward as a result of work other than through the method indicated in the previous subsection, it may be suitable for a test using mortality statistics. For example, if clinical and pathological experience suggests that patients with peptic ulcer are at higher risk of developing gastric cancer than the general population, examination of the male and female mortality from these two conditions for different countries provides a simple probe of the hypothesis. In certain circumstances such a study may provide a powerful test of the hypothesis; for example, Stolley (1972) demonstrated a significant positive correlation between increased mortality from asthma and national sales of a particular type of medicated aerosol used for treatment. However, it will be more usual to require data derived from individuals rather than national populations to test aetiological hypotheses.

1.2.4 Evaluation of public health measures

If alteration in mortality is (one of) the expected result(s) of a particular public health measure or campaign, this can be readily studied at local or national level. Innovation in case of special groups, such as pregnant women, can be monitored by the trends in overall and cause specific mortality. Again, such an approach only provides a general background statistic for examining progress; the errors and biases in the data have to be considered. Zeighami *et al.* (1979) warned about the problem created when examining mortality for a specific cause, if the all-cause mortality rates were very different in the populations being studied.

1.2.5 Descriptive studies: specific suggestions

Each of the specific (major) causes of death, the subtotals of combinations of causes, and the totals at the level of ICD chapters may be examined. The basic material has been presented; however, for an appropriate descriptive study the examination and presentation of the data warrants further detailed consideration of the errors and biases in the data for each country and the validity of the alignment for the given cause being examined.

The controversy over the trends for ischaemic heart disease are discussed in the next chapter (see page 30). The tables provide a wider range of material than has previously been probed by one author and warrants detailed examination of this issue.

The opportunity provided for looking at the trends in infectious disease, and testing whether the degree of decrease shown for the majority of countries has been paralleled in all countries is rather different. Such probing of the material leads on to generation of hypotheses.

1.2.6 Generation of hypotheses: specific suggestions

Association of diseases. The following examples indicate topics that have already been examined in other ways: trends in peptic ulcer and gastric ulcer by sex and country; trends in respiratory tuberculosis and lung cancer; and trends in liver/gall bladder disease and liver cancer.

Association of disease with various environmental factors. An appreciable proportion of malignant disease is ascribed to 'environmental factors' (either generated by personal behaviour or from an external environment of home, leisure or work). A number of recent studies (see Alderson 1980 for review) have explored the interassociations between recent mortality by cancer site and a range of data on environmental factors.

Some of the queries about the interpretation of these studies may be resolved by the major increase in power provided by looking at trends in the association of these two categories of data over time.

Though the emphasis of such work has been on malignant disease, the exploration of trends in ischaemic heart disease might be equally interesting; change in mortality from alimentary, renal or arthritic conditions could also be related to indices of environmental factors.

Hypothesis testing. The tables should be used as a resource for fairly swift (and simple) exploration of trends of interrelationships suggested by other work. For example, if other work indicates that a particular disease may be generated after about 15 years of individual exposure to hair dyes, data would require retrieval on the potential exposure in different countries – such material then is related to the cause of death data provided in this book.

There has been considerable interest in the influence of both smoking and drinking alcohol upon the risk of malignant and other chronic diseases. Data could be retrieved on per capita consumption of cigarettes in different countries and consumption of alcoholic beverages (beer, wines, or spirits) for a varying length of time (for some countries the material is available throughout the century). These 'environmental' data could be related to mortality from cancer and other chronic disease that are thought definitely and possibly to be related to smoking or drinking alcohol. Such analyses should permit the exploration of discrepancies in the fit of the data to estimate the relative contribution of these and other factors and to explore whether the list of 'related' diseases needs expanding or contracting.

1.2.7 Evaluation of public health measures: specific suggestions

The statistics provided should facilitate specific probes of the impact upon mortality of national measures to control particular diseases. This requires knowledge of such measures, the validity of data on their promulgation, and the likelihood of mortality as a realistic measure of impact of the campaign. However, an indication of the class of studies is

* relation of water fluoride levels to overall mortality and specific causes suggested as occurring as adverse effects of this agent;
* impact of alteration of iodine in the diet on death from thyroid diseases and thyroid cancer;
* change in mortality from diseases subject to major early detection programmes;
* effect of alternative forms of delivery of medical care (where these have been instituted across the country) upon mortality for (potentially) fatal conditions, for example, relating spread of hospital intensive coronary care facilities to mortality from ischaemic heart disease.

References

Alderson, M.R. (1974). *Central government routine health statistics, vol. 2. Review of UK Statistical sources* (ed. W.F. Maunder), Heinemann, London.

—— (1977). *An introduction of epidemiology*. Revised reprint. Macmillan, London.

—— (1980). *Epidemiology's contribution to studies on cancer aetiology.* **In press.**

Stolley, P.D. (1972). Why the United States was spared an epidemic of deaths due to asthma. *Amer. Rev. Resp. Dis.,* **105**, 883-890.

Zeighami, E., Sohler, K.B. and Deal, R.B. (1979). Estimators of relative risk – a life table simulation. *J. Chron. Dis.*, **32**, 589-598.

1 – Appendix

Official departments responsible for mortality statistics in each of the countries for which data have been provided

Australia
Information Services
Australian Bureau of Statistics
P O Box 10
Belconnen
ACT 2616
Australia

Austria
Head: Division of Population Statistics
Central Statistical Office
Neue Hofburg
Vienna 1014
Austria

Belgium
Chief of Section Demographic Statistics
National Institute of Statistics
Leuvenseweg 44
1000 Brussels
Belgium

Bulgaria
Division of Population Statistics
Ministry of Information and Statistics
Sophia
Bulgaria

Canada
Director
Health Division
Statistics Canada
Ottawa Ontario
KLA 0T6
Canada

Chile
Chief: Division of Special Studies and Coordination
National Institute for Statistics
Casilla 7597 Correa 3
Santiago
Chile

Czechoslovakia
Chief of International Statistics Division
Federal Statistics Bureau
Sokolovská 142
Karlin
Prague 8
Czechoslovakia

Denmark
Chief Statistician
Board of Health
Store Kongensgade 1
1264 Copenhagen K
Denmark

Eire

The Director
General Statistics Office
Ardee Road
Dublin 6
Eire

Finland

Head of Division
Population Statistics
Central Statistical Office
Helsinki
Finland

France

Head, Section for Statistical Information on Morbidity and Mortality
National Institute for Health and Medical Research
44 Chemin de Ronde
La Vasinet 78-110
Paris
France

Greece

Director of Statistical Service
Department of National Health
17 Aristotelous St.
Athens
Greece

Hungary

Head: Population Statistics Department
Central Statistical Office
5-7 Keleti Karoly Street
Budapest H-1525
Hungary

Iceland

Head: Division of Population Statistics
Statistical Bureau of Iceland
Reijkavik
Iceland

Italy

Chief of Health Statistics
Central Institute of Statistics
Viale Liege 11
00198 Rome
Italy

Japan

Director of Health and Welfare Statistics and Information Department
Ministry of Health and Welfare
Tokyo
Japan

Netherlands

Head of the Department for Health Statistics
Central Statistics Bureau
428 Prinses Beatrixlaan
P O Box 959
2270 AZ Voorburg
Netherlands

New Zealand

Chief Health Statistician
National Health Statistics Centre
Department of Health
89 Courtenay Place
Wellington
New Zealand

Norway

Chief: Division 1
Central Bureau of Statistics
Dronningens Gate 16
Oslo 1
Norway

Poland

Chief: International Statistics Division
Central Statistical Office
Al. Niepodleglosci 208
00-925 Warsaw
Poland

Portugal

Chief: Division of Demography
Institute of National Statistics
Av Rovisco Pais
Lisbon
Portugal

Romania

Head of Division of Health Statistics
Ministry of Health
Str. Alecu Constantinescu Nr 9 sector 7
Of. Postal 1
Bucharest
Romania

Spain

Head of Division of Health Statistics
National Institute of Statistics
Avde Del Generalisimo 91
Madrid – 16
Spain

Sweden

Head: Division of Population Statistics
National Central Bureau of Statistics
Fack
S-102 50 Stockholm
Sweden

Switzerland

Head of Division of Population Statistics
Federal Bureau of Statistics
Hallwylstrasse 15
3003 Bern
Switzerland

Turkey

Head of Division
Population Statistics
State Institute of Statistics
Ankara
Turkey

UK: England and Wales

Chief Medical Statistician
Office of Population Censuses and Surveys
St Catherines House
10 Kingsway
London WC2B 6JP
England

UK: Northern Ireland

Registrar General
General Register Office
Fermanagh House
Ormeau Avenue
Belfast
BT2 8HX
Northern Ireland

UK: Scotland

Registrar General
Registrar General's Office
New Register House
Edinburgh 2
Scotland

USA

Director of National Centre for Health Statistics
Public Health Service
Health Resources Administration
Department of Health Education and Welfare
Hyattsville
Maryland 29782
USA

Yugoslavia

Director of Division of Health Statistics
State Institute for Statistics
Belgrade
Yugoslavia

2 – Validity of mortality statistics

Contents

2.1 **Validity of Census Data** 13

2.2 **Validity of Mortality Data** 14
2.2.1 Is the death registered? 14
2.2.2 Is information missing? 15
2.2.3 Accuracy of cause of death data 16
2.2.4 Accuracy of clinical diagnosis 16
2.2.5 Comparisons of clinical and autopsy diagnosis 17
2.2.6 Comparisons between death certificates and reviews of detailed case histories 18
2.2.7 Certification 19
2.2.8 Classification of the cause of death 22
2.2.9 Coding of the cause of death 23
2.2.10 Problems with specific diseases 24

2.3 **Registration Systems in Different Countries** 34
2.3.1 Australia 34
2.3.2 Austria 35
2.3.3 Belgium 35
2.3.4 Bulgaria 35
2.3.5 Canada 35
2.3.6 Chile 35
2.3.7 Czechoslovakia 36
2.3.8 Denmark 36
2.3.9 Eire 36
2.3.10 Finland 36
2.3.11 France 36
2.3.12 Greece 37
2.3.13 Hungary 37
2.3.14 Iceland 37
2.3.15 Italy 37
2.3.16 Japan 37
2.3.17 Netherlands 37

2.3.18 New Zealand 38
2.3.19 Norway 38
2.3.20 Poland 38
2.3.21 Portugal 38
2.3.22 Romania 38
2.3.23 Spain 38
2.3.24 Sweden 39
2.3.25 Switzerland 39
2.3.26 Turkey 39
2.3.27 UK: England and Wales 39
2.3.28 UK: Northern Ireland 39
2.3.29 UK: Scotland 40
2.3.30 USA 40
2.3.31 Yugoslavia 40

2.4 **Indicators of Validity of Mortality Statistics** 40
2.4.1 Number of doctors per 10,000 population 40
2.4.2 Proportion of the population in rural areas 41
2.4.3 Percentage of certificates issued by Medical Practitioners 41
2.4.4 The percentage of all certificates from ill-defined causes 41

References 42

Table 2.1 Number of doctors/10,000 population in different countries during the 20th century 48
Table 2.2 Percentage of population classified as living in rural areas in different countries during the 20th century 49
Table 2.3 Percentage of death certificates signed by doctors in different countries during the 20th century 50
Table 2.4 Percentage of certificates from ill-defined causes in different countries in the 20th century 51

2

Validity of mortality statistics

An essential consideration in handling mortality statistics is the validity of the data. This chapter discusses a number of relevant points, and ends with some conclusions about the applications and limitations of the material that is presented in the tables.

It is essential that the points raised in this chapter are carefully considered before attempting to interpret any trends in disease for one country or variation in disease between countries. If due caution is given to the points raised in this chapter, the material may be of considerable value. There are two separate aspects to the calculation of mortality rates: the population estimates which are required as denominators for the rates, and the cause of death for individuals who have died.

This chapter opens with brief consideration of the validity of population estimates and then turns to a number of different factors influencing the validity of the cause of death. After this there is a brief comment on the registration system existing in each of the countries. There are a number of pointers to the validity of the mortality statistics and these are discussed in the fourth section: the number of doctors per 10,000 population; the percentage of the population living in rural areas; the percentage of death certificates issued by medical practitioners; and the percentage of certificates that are ascribed to ill-defined, unknown, and senility as causes of death.

2.1 Validity of census data

Pascua (1949) reviewed the mortality trends in Europe during the first half of this century. He stated that it cannot be definitely asserted that the population censuses were of the same standard for each of the countries. Pascua makes the general point that it is quite likely that the internal efficiency of the administration responsible for taking the census for several countries is not equal to that in the majority of other countries (he does not then specifically indicate to which of the countries this comment refers). A separate issue is that different techniques can be used to calculate population estimates in the inter-censal years and these might theoretically influence the calculation of mortality rates. This point is discussed in section 5.1.

Pascua suggested that in some countries the population estimates may be out by as much as 500,000 persons. In particular he calls attention to the quality of the data for Portugal at the beginning of the century; and inflation of the population estimates for Italy and Spain in the 1940s which may have led to an artificial reduction in the death rates. However, he indicates that this is unlikely to be of sufficient magnitude to influence the general conclusions drawn from the data.

Preston, *et al.* (1972) pointed out that, in the absence of fraud, the census counts tend to be low rather than high and that certain groups are likely to be under-enumerated. This is particularly true for children below the age of 5 (especially infants), transients, and those at ages of high mobility. In addition, there is likely to be variation in the validity of reported age at different age groups; an excess of people report themselves as 18, 21, or 65. Persons between the ages of 21 and 65 often under-report their true age, while those over 65 may inflate their age. Preston *et al.* suggested that US censuses have been shown to be of substantial accuracy, but not as complete as those for England and Wales.

When considering the relationship of population estimates to counts of numbers of individuals dying in a country, it is important to know whether both data relate to the same 'population'. Pascua (1949) pointed out that a particular problem occurs with Finland, where the definitions are different for the two sets of data. Before 1936 the number of *de facto* deaths are not known; the earliest statistics related to *de jure* deaths, including incomplete statistics on nationals dying abroad. Pascua suggested that it would not be appropriate to relate *de jure* deaths to the *de jure* population, and, though ideal, it was not possible to relate *de facto* deaths to *de facto* population; the solution had to be the use of *de jure* deaths and *de facto* population. Further comments on this issue are given in section 2.3.

Pascua (1950) suggested that the census estimates were equally reliable for the two sexes, and that any difference that did occur would have only introduced very minor errors into the calculated death rates. This comment referred particularly to the total male and total female populations; errors within age-specific groups of the population might be more misleading. (The method of handling the data for this work makes this issue only relevant to the age-specific data that have been used to calculate standard rates – see section 5.3.)

A report from the United Nations (1952a) discussed various accuracy tests for census data. A comparison of numbers for adjacent age groups and also for the sex ratio within age groups was applied to data from the *Demographic Yearbook*. In 102 countries, the age distributions were considered reasonably reliable for 43 of them, fairly unreliable for 34, and quite unreliable for 25. Other countries were excluded from this analysis because of war mortality and discontinuous migration.

Benjamin and Carrier (1954) examined the quality of the demographic statistics of England and Wales. Using a variety of ways of cross-checking census data they suggested that the quality had improved in the first half of the 20th century. A simple issue to test is the over- or underestimation of the final digit in age. They observed a decrease in deficiency of ages ending in 7 for males from −6.1 to −2.3 per cent and for females of −5.7 to −2.3 per cent from 1911 to 1931. The post-1950 census enumeration survey in the US suggested that there had been an undercount of 1.4 per cent of the total population, with 1.2 per cent white and 3.2 per cent non-white deficiencies. However, Coale (1955) suggested that the post-census check was affected by the same problems as the census itself.

2.2 Validity of mortality data

The primary concern often expressed when considering mortality statistics is the validity of the data on cause of death. There are a number of factors that influence the validity and this section discusses them and includes a review of the relevant literature.

The sub-sections have been arranged in a logical order, beginning with consideration of whether the death is registered or information is omitted at registration. The chain of events leading from diagnosis to published statistics are then discussed, indicating various studies that have commented on the validity of data (from comparison of either clinical diagnosis and autopsy, or case histories and death certificates). The process of certification itself, the classification of disease that is used, and the coding of the cause of death can all influence the validity of the material.

The next sub-section then discusses published comments about a range of specific diseases. The section ends with the description of the registration system as it exists in different countries.

2.2.1 Is the death registered?

Pascua (1949) commented that under-registration of mortality had been a well-known fact in some periods of history and that registration of deaths has not been equally complete for all countries. A corollary of this is that variation in mortality rates at one point in time between countries may be a reflection of the efficiency of registration, while change over time (with increasing mortality) may indicate improvement in registration rather than alteration of actual mortality rates. Though this point should be considered, in general, registration of mortality is complete in the countries considered in this work. (Some specific comments are provided on the registration system in different countries in sub-sections 2.3.1–2.3.31.)

Pascua (1949) commented that some mortality figures seemed to lack authenticity and that this particularly applied to data for nations around the period of time covered by the two World Wars. Denmark, Holland, Norway, Spain and Switzerland show very little influence of the First World War on their official statistics; Norway, Sweden, Portugal, Spain and Switzerland showed very little effect from the Second World War. The other European countries were all influenced to a greater or less degree. In addition, Spain showed variation from the abnormal effects of war conditions in the period 1936–41.

Pascua (1949) calculated crude death rates (from published data on population estimates and numbers of deaths) for each country in the first half of this century. He pointed out that these figures did not always agree with the stated rates in official publications. This was thought to be due to a number of small corrections in the basic figures of deaths or population estimates which were often not sufficiently explained in the official text of tables or commentaries upon them. The crude mortality rates for Portugal at the beginning of the century were less than 20 per 1,000 in the first decade but then far higher for a 20-year period. Pascua suggested that problems of the extension and efficiency of registration of deaths was probably the reason for this.

A specific problem is due to the diverse definitions of stillbirth used in different countries and the repercussions of this on the statistics generated. Variation in classification of some early neonatal deaths can influence the counts of livebirths and deaths occurring in the first week of life.

The Health Committee of the League of Nations discussed this issue and drafted a definition of stillbirth in 1925. However, in the following 25 years little standardization occurred, although this has been remedied to a degree by the 6th revision of the International Classification of Disease published in 1948. Pascua (1947-8) provided details of the then existing different definitions of stillbirth used in 16 European and 7 other countries. He drew specific attention to the problem of Spain and Belgium.

Using additional material not normally included in the official statistics Pascua suggested that the published birth rate in Spain was approximately 0.8 per cent lower than it should be and this results in a gross overstatement of the official stillbirth ratio by roughly one-third. In addition, the infant mortality rate is about 5 per cent less than it should be, the maternal mortality rate is increased by about 0.8 per cent when properly reckoned, and the crude death rate for Spain is 1.2 per cent lower than it should be.

A comparable situation existed for Belgium. Stowman (1947-8) suggested that the data for stillbirths were also unreliable for France, where infants dying before their birth was registered are counted as stillborn. This might have occurred in the Netherlands, particularly in the first 30 years of this century.

The important general point is that if there is any tendency to consider a liveborn infant who dies shortly after birth as a 'stillbirth', the number of deaths to living persons is underestimated and this underestimation particularly influences the calculation of first-week, first-month, and first-year deaths. To a much lesser degree it also lowers the overall mortality. If the number of livebirths is used as a denominator in the calculation of maternal mortality these statistics will also be inaccurate due to the artificially lowered number of livebirths. When studying deaths in the newborn it has been suggested that stillbirths and first-week deaths should be counted together, and presented at a rate per 1,000 total births – live plus still; this gets over any artificial re-allocation of livebirths to stillbirths. (Such a suggestion would be of no value if the 'stillbirth' was not registered.)

Dean (1979) obtained 2,000 names of men and women from burial records in parishes in the west of Ireland in 1971. These were checked against the register of births and deaths: 6.5 per cent had been neither certified nor registered and a further 7.5 per cent had been registered but not certified. A follow-up was being repeated to see if registration and certification had improved.

2.2.2 Is information missing?

A particular problem occurs when deaths are registered for individuals whose age is unknown. In particular, deaths of persons abroad or military personnel are also sometimes referred to as deaths of 'age unknown', e.g. this is suggested to occur for Norway and for some data for Finland (Pascua, 1949). Finland, Ireland, Sweden and Switzerland use a system for assigning the deaths to the age group considered to be the most probable.

Pascua (1949) suggested that the extremely low or zero proportion officially quoted as 'age unknown' for France indicated that some form of redistribution must be officially carried out. He concluded that even if the deaths of unknown age could be separated into the presumed age at death and included in the appropriate age groups their number would be too small to modify any substantial feature of the evolution of mortality in Europe during this century. Though this point needs to be considered, it is not much of a problem as far as the bulk of the data presented in this book. Since a technique of age standardization (see chapter 5, section 5.4) has been used for most countries the data have only been handled as the total number of deaths at all ages. However, the process of standardization required the calculation of age-specific standard rates. If the age distribution of the individuals contributing to these standard rates had been erroneous it is possible that this might have created some distortion in the figures. There was no evidence from the data used by age that this was in any way an appreciable problem or contributing error.

Rarely will the cause of death not be declared at death registration (this will be particularly in deaths thought to be due to natural occurrences, that occur in remote rural areas). If the fact of death is registered but not the cause of death this would create a distortion in the calculation of cause-specific mortality. Aubenque *et al.* (1978) described a method where a regression technique could be used to distribute the deaths of cause unknown through all the specific causes. Such a method is apparently in use in France, but where the proportion of deaths of cause unknown are very small it makes extremely little difference to the overall calculated cause-specific rates. (Rather than use some sophisticated correction technique it would presumably be more important to try to get an estimated cause of death for all deaths.)

2.2.3 Accuracy of cause of death data

Any data collection system may be inaccurate. The problem of inaccuracy is best discussed by first considering the separate steps in the chain leading to the production of mortality statistics. These steps are:

1. Conversion of basic information about the patient into the diagnosis made by the clinician.
2. Completion of the death certificate to transcription onto the death notification.
3. Classification of the underlying cause of death to coding of the underlying cause of death to the national processing system.
4. Publication of mortality statistics and interpretation of these.

Graunt was the first constructive critic of medical statistical data (Greenwood, 1948). He examined the accuracy of his sources of data and attempted to correct some errors in classification. Farr, the first medical statistician to the Registrar General in England, was aware that the accuracy of mortality statistics depended on the precision of diagnosis, correct completion of the death certificate, validity of the classification of diseases, and careful compilation of the tabulations. From his time, a number of investigations have been carried out which throw light on the possible sources of error in mortality statistics.

Section 2.2.4 presents some comments on the development of diagnostic facilities and recognition of clinical syndromes. This is followed by sections 2.2.5 and 2.2.6 which discuss the wide range of studies that have been carried out to check on the validity of the basic medical information; further sections deal with the problems of certification, classification and coding of the cause of death.

2.2.4 Accuracy of clinical diagnosis

The stage of development of medical knowledge and the availability of diagnostic facilities together influence the precision of clinical (and autopsy) diagnosis. It is important to consider the influence of these factors in determining the validity of mortality statistics throughout the present century, from one country to another, and from the centre of population to the most isolated rural communities. No hard data arc available on the relative spread of medical knowledge and facilities in the countries involved in the present study, but the following points warrant consideration.

The quality of clinical diagnosis steadily improved in the 18th and 19th century with descriptions of syndromes, documentation of clinical examination method, and relation of history and clinical findings to the macroscopic appearance at autopsy. An example of this advance was the treatise by Laënnec (1819) in which he described the stethoscope and art of auscultation.

The identification of infectious diseases was founded on clinical observation long before the development of bacteriology in the 19th century (and subsequently virology). Solid, malignant tumours and their natural history had been noted before morbid anatomy permitted detailed study; both Hodgkin's disease and leukaemia were clearly described in the 19th century. The major endocrine abnormalities, deficiency diseases, allergic phenomena, respiratory disease, peptic ulcer, cirrhosis, gallstones, nephritis, and diseases of pregnancy had all been described by the end of the 19th century. Cardiovascular disease has been the subject of considerable advance in the 20th century, though angina had been described long before. Herrick (1912) resolved a number of problems of definition of ischaemic heart disease.

The classification and recognition of diseases of early infancy have changed markedly over the past 40 years. This does not invalidate the statistics presented here, as problems following birth may be distinguished fairly crudely from the other categories of fatal illness in the first year of life. Anyone wishing to explore the development of clinical science should consult a text on classic descriptions of disease (such as Major, 1965).

There have been extensive additions over the past 150 years to the diagnostic methods for confirming clinical diagnosis. Pasteur provided a great stimulus to bacteriology in the first half of the 19th century when he conclusively proved that agents of putrefaction did not develop *de novo*. Towards the end of the 19th century differential strains began to be used to examine organisms in tissue; a range of serological tests were also developed (for example, Wasserman reported his diagnostic test for syphilis in 1906).

The diagnostic facilities offered by clinical chemistry are a recent development in the history of medicine, with the following milestones:

* electrochemistry was applied first to the assay of calcium in 1934;
* electrophoreses was developed for clinical use in the 1930s;
* the application of immunochemistry rapidly expanded as a diagnostic tool from the late 1950s;
* the developments of microtechniques and automation of analyses have occurred in the past 20 years.

Roentgen discovered x-rays in 1895; in a few years this

was followed by the use of x-rays for study of disease. Though initially used for studying abnormality of bones and the presence of foreign bodies, this was soon extended to other diseases, particularly in the chest. Double contrast methods of examining the stomach and large intestine were developed in the 1920s and 1930s. A dye was found which was excreted in the bile and provided shadows of the gall bladder. Renal stones were also detected shortly after the discovery of x-rays; retrograde urography was initiated in 1904 and exretion urography in 1929. Contrast media had been injected into veins of subjects in the 1920s and by 1939 a technique had been achieved which was suitable for visualizing all four chambers of the heart.

Work in Germany and the US in 1947–8 provided the physical basis for radio-isotope scanning, which was being clinically tested by 1950 in the US. This was followed shortly afterwards by studies of the brain and thyroid. In 1957, a scintillation camera with improved resolution was developed. Clinical applications for investigating the kidneys, spleen, and pancreas occurred in the early 1960s. The electrocardiograph was developed at the end of the 19th century. Chest leads were introduced in the 1930s in place of the three limb leads of Einthoven; this was followed in the 1940s by use of the augmented unipolar limb leads – resulting in the standard 12-lead ECG, which is the present conventional recording.

Morgagni, working in the early part of the 18th century, put the scientific study of gross morbid anatomy on a firm foundation (see Major, 1965). His principle contribution was to correlate post-mortem findings with symptoms exhibited before death by the patient. It was not until the 19th century that improvements in the microscope – especially the development of achromatic lenses – enabled it to be used with advantage.

By the end of the 19th century, great improvements had been made in the compound microscope and the embedding of tissues in wax was perfected so that thin sections could be cut. A range of specific stains were developed. Since the 1950s the electron microscope has been used to study biopsy and surgical specimens; although contributing to the definition of certain renal disease and malignant tumours, it has principally served as a research rather than diagnostic tool.

The development of antisepsis and anaesthetics in the middle of the 19th century led to a major extension of the use of operative surgery for diagnosis and treatment. For example, the first gastrectomy was performed in 1878. The extension of alimentary, genitourinary, gynaecological, and then thoracic surgery in the early part of the 20th century improved the quality of diagnosis both from the naked eye examination of the focus of disease and the greater opportunity for obtaining specimens for histological examination.

2.2.5 Comparisons of clinical and autopsy diagnosis

This section describes a number of studies that have compared clinical diagnosis and autopsy findings. Obviously, such deaths are not necessarily representative of all deaths. (There may be a tendency to perform an autopsy when the diagnosis has not been satisfactorily established; those patients dying in hospital may have very different conditions from those dying at home.)

Jackson (1896) published a report in a comparison of autopsy records over an 18-month period with clinical histories – based on a consecutive series of 100 cases where mention had been made of a pathological lesion in the heart. He concluded that the autopsy findings bore a moderately close correspondence to the clinical diagnosis.

Cabot (1912) carried out a similar type of study on 3,000 autopsies at the Massachusetts General Hospital. He drew up a table showing the percentage of diagnostic success for various causes of death. He found that diabetes mellitus heading the list had 95 per cent clinical success, while at the bottom acute nephritis had only 18 per cent success. He emphasized that some diagnoses were relatively inaccessible under the present diagnostic methods. Since this time a number of comparable studies were carried out: *Journal of the American Medical Association*, 1914; Swartout, 1934; Swartout and Webster, 1940; Pohlen and Emerson, 1942; Pohlen and Emerson, 1943; James, Patton and Heslin, 1955 (a number of other studies only looked at specific causes of death and this material is referred to in sub-sections 2.2.10.1-2.2.10.13).

The first large-scale comparison of diagnosis before and after post-mortem for persons dying in English hospitals was carried out in 1955 and reported by the Registrar General (1958). Further data were presented on the mortality for the 10 participating hospitals by Heasman (1962). A more extensive study was reported by Heasman and Lipworth (1966); their material was based on a large number of deaths occurring in 75 hospitals in England and Wales. The report indicated considerable variation between the clinical and autopsy diagnoses. In the final analysis, the numbers in many of the different cause groups were broadly comparable, as some of the discrepancies were self-cancelling due to cross-transfer of deaths. The Heasman and Lipworth study was restricted to patients dying in hospital, who all had an autopsy. It is not clear whether the level of accuracy of the clinical diagnosis is the same for patients who die in hospital and have an autopsy; in hospital but do not have an autopsy, and outside hospital who do not have an autopsy.

It is not possible to extrapolate from these findings an interpretation of the accuracy of certified cause of death for all deaths occurring in the country. A total of 9,501 deaths were examined, and in only 45.3 per cent was the same underlying cause of death given as a result of the investigation, compared with the original clinical diagnosis. However, the discrepancy for broad categories was much smaller: 183 patients were coded as dying from malignant disease clinically and 182 by the pathologuists; for pneumonia and bronchitis, the original number of deaths was 718, and the pathologists ascribed 719 to this condition.

A similar study was reported by Waldron and Vickerstaff (1977) based on an analysis of 1,126 patients having autopsies in the hospitals in the Birmingham region. They found that in 47.5 per cent the clinical diagnosis was confirmed; in 26.4 per cent there was partial agreement, and in 26.1 per cent, the clinical and pathological diagnoses disagreed. They again emphasized that estimates of the numbers dying for certain conditions, such as malignant disease, was little changed after autopsy, even though many individual patients had had their original diagnosis changed. This last study was initiated partly because it had been observed that the necropsy rates in the United Birmingham Hospitals were decreasing (Waldron and Vickerstaff, 1975). Two other studies in Britain (Cameron *et al*., 1977; Gau, 1977) indicated that this was a general phenomenon. It was suggested that if there is a general decline in the use of autopsy this may lead to a decrease in the validity of mortality statistics. A rather different point was put by the *Journal of the American Medical Association* (1965), which questioned the value of the routine autopsy and emphasized that the more done the better was an outmoded view.

Beadenkopf *et al.* (1965) compared the demographic characteristics of deaths in Albany New York 1955–9 with those occurring in the Albany Medical Center Hospital and those coming to autopsy. The following factors increasing the likelihood of having an autopsy: younger age, female, cause of death not heart disease, Protestant or Catholic, US born, Negroes, divorced and non-local residence. This degree of selection may bias the comparability of mortality statistics.

2.2.6 Comparisons between death certificates and review of detailed case histories

Another way of enquiring into the validity of mortality statistics is to investigate the diagnostic evidence supporting medical certificates. Moriyama *et al.* (1958) sent enquiries to certifiers of 1,837 deaths in Pennsylvania in 1956. The questionnaire asked for information about diagnostic methods, the certifier's certainty of the diagnosis, and whether he would consider revising the death certificate if his opinion had changed.

There was a response from 96 per cent of the certifiers. It was suggested that the support for the diagnosis varied with different conditions; 65 per cent of subjects dying from malignant disease were thought to have had a solidly established diagnosis but only one-third of those dying from 'cardiovascular-renal disease'. It also appeared for certain conditions, that there was a greater support for the diagnosis in males, and that the quality of the diagnostic information decreased with advancing age, particularly over 65. It was also suggested that there was a lower support for the diagnosis for patients dying in rural areas.

Resulting from this consideration of major variation in death rates from cardiovascular disease and arteriosclerotic heart disease in different countries throughout the world, a major project examining the supporting information for the diagnosis for patients dying was mounted through the Pan-American Sanitary Bureau (Puffer *et al.*, 1965; Puffer and Griffith, 1967). For 10 cities in Central and South America and the cities of San Francisco and Bristol, detailed records were obtained for deaths occurring over a two-year period in persons aged 15–74. For each death the interviewed contacted the next-of-kin and obtained an indication of the medical care. Particulars were then sought from hospital and treating practitioners. Where possible all written material was examined by a doctor in each location, and if there was any doubt, the treating clinician was approached to comment upon the diagnostic material. For sudden deaths, the next-of-kin was interviewed by the research team doctor; if a coroner's autopsy had occurred, particulars were obtained.

A total of 43,298 deaths were investigated in the 12 cities; in Riberiao Preto only 1,016 deaths were included, while in five of the cities over 4,000 deaths were involved. When deaths were excluded from one broad group of causes because of the acquisition of detailed information, the numbers were often counter-balanced by deaths transferred to the group. Thus the effect on death rates resulting from the use of detailed information in most instances were small.

For the 12 cities combined, the group of infective and parasitic disease was increased by 5 per cent, while tuberculosis was increased by 6 per cent. The number of deaths from malignant neoplasm was also increased by 5 per cent. For cardiovascular disease, respiratory disease and digestive disease there was a decrease of 1, 13 and 6 per cent respectively.

The largest change was for maternal causes of death

where there was an addition of 35 per cent; accidents and violence only increased by 2 per cent. It was concluded that for the majority of cities the official death rates for broad groups of causes were probably acceptable indicators of health problems. However, for epidemiological purposes their value was more limited, since even with small differences between the numbers of original and final assignments, change between the two assignments often involved relatively many deaths. Thus for broad groups of causes these changes were numerous despite relatively small net increases or decreases.

Where individual divisions of broad groups of causes were considered, far more changes occurred with the use of additional information, with less tendency to counterbalancing in the final results. For example, a large increase in specific forms of cardiovascular disease (such as hypertensive and rheumatic heart disease) and maligant neoplasms (by site) were noted. It was suggested that comparisons of the results from this study were difficult to make with other reported work because of variation in the design, selection of population, and the method employed. It was concluded that in every participating city medical certification could be improved and it was suggested that a record linkage system to ensure the use of available hospital and autopsy information in generating mortality statistics be devised.

Alderson (1965) used the data from the first year's deaths in the above study in Bristol for a more detailed examination of the accuracy of death certification. There were 2,247 deaths for investigation, and it was suggested that in 70 per cent of these the initial codings were correct, in 20 per cent a minor alteration was required, and in 10 per cent a major alteration. The three variables on the certificate – the certifier, the cause of death, and the particulars of the deceased – were examined to see which factors might be associated with a particularly high rate of revision of the diagnosis. Statistically significant excess changes were associated with: certificates signed by hospital doctors, or doctors recently qualified; deaths in non-teaching hospitals; increasing age of the deceased and respiratory disease.

The support for the diagnosis was graded into five levels; it was shown, where the diagnosis was poorly supported, no change could be made to an alternative diagnosis because of lack of positive evidence. However, where a certificate was incorrect the author classified the errors into five types and examine the cause of the error. In 6 per cent of the certificates the wording was in the wrong order and resulted in difficulty in identifying the underlying cause of death; in 13 per cent, the wording was incomplete, often omitting a specific known cause of death; in 3 per cent, the certificates were issued before an autopsy, which gave fresh information and changed the final opinion of the underlying cause of death. In 5 per cent, the certifier revised his diagnosis when the case history was reviewed, while in 3 per cent, there was a difference of opinion as to the correct cause of death.

Pole *et al.* (1977) compared mortality rates with incidence rates derived from a register of acute myocardial infarction in Perth, Australia. The incidence rate was lower in elderly women than the mortality; they felt this was probably due to the less stringent criteria for the certified cause of death than the diagnostic requirements for their register. No detail was provided of certified deaths not included in the register.

A study group in London (Clarke and Whitfield, 1978) compared detailed hospital material including autopsy reports with the death certificates for 191 persons under the age of 50 dying in hospitals. They reported that in 39 cases there was a major discrepancy between the sources of information, and in a further 54 per cent a minor but important difference. Others suggested (Adelstein, 1978; Griffith, 1978) that the degree of discrepancies identified had been rather over-emphasized in their study.

2.2.7 Certification

Lewis (1915) observed that between 1894 and 1914 both the numbers of deaths from senility and diphtheria had steadily dropped. He pointed out that the reasons for this decrease are different. It was very likely that diphtheria had in fact decreased; however, the reduction in the number of deaths ascribed to senility might be from spurious accuracy where certifiers were giving myocardial and arteriosclerotic reasons as cause of death without specific evidence.

In the 1930s and 1940s there was a move towards adopting medical certification forms designed to record the physician's opinion of the sequence of events so that contributing causes could be evaluated. A US committee (World Health Organization, 1947) examined the influence of such certificates. They suggested that there had been relatively limited development of definitive rules of procedure for selecting the main cause of death; many countries had no rules at all, or only a few general ones. Others had adopted a comprehensive set of rigid rules as used by the UK, or the US.

The 6th Decennial Revision Conference of the International Classification of Disease (World Health Organization, 1948) established international agreement for a uniform medical certificate and rules of procedure for selection and classification of causes of death. The new procedure was based on the principle that the certifying practitioner was the best person to designate the underlying cause, and he was the best person to determine the conditions which lead directly to death (stating any antecedent conditions which gave rise to the direct cause). With certain exceptions the physician's statement is accepted for statistical tabulation – only where consistency is threatened by obvious vagaries in reporting is this general rule set aside and other ones implemented. An instruction book for physicians on the use of the international form of medical certificate of cause of death was prepared (World Health Organization, 1952a).

Dunn (1949) discussed with approval the introduction of the 6th revision of the ICD and the international form for certification. He stressed that it is important that the attending physician, who knows most about the facts of death, fills in the certificate to show the proper relationship of the various conditions involved in the death. A few years later, Dunn (1955) suggested that in the US approximately 20 per cent of death certificates were obviously incorrectly completed.

Stocks (1935) discussed the increase in deaths from various causes that occurred during a major flu epidemic in England. For every 100 deaths coded to influenza (including 73 with specified respiratory complications) there were an additional 190 excess deaths over the expected figures. He suggested that an appreciable proportion of these were secondary to influenza (particularly in the elderly or those with myocardial disease). He felt that the certificates had probably incorrectly omitted the influenza.

Moriyama (1956) referred to the difficulty in coding when the physicians had a concept of the primary cause of death different from the underlying cause of death. In the US, the certifier in the 1930s had been asked to identify the principle of fundamental cause of death; in 1939 they had been requested to underline the cause which should be coded statistically. In 1948, the 'English' pattern was adopted in which the sequence of events was recorded; however, examination in 1950 had suggested about one-quarter of the certificates were not internally consistent.

Angrist (1958) discussed certification from the medico-legal point of view. He recommended that doctors should consult an expert in certification whenever they were in doubt about the completion of the cause of death; there was often confusion between the primary cause of death and the disease causing it. He said it was important to define the main disease, and the contributing and complicating causes. Angrist advocated that the evidence for the diagnosis and the degree of certainty should be recorded.

The *Demographic Year Book* (United Nations, 1957) pointed out that a death may be registered

1. following an autopsy (which would presumably identify the true cause of death);
2. if an autopsy was not performed but the decedent was treated prior to death by a medical attendant, the reported cause should reflect the opinion of that physician;
3. the body may be examined, but not autopsied by a physician, who may question persons who saw the death;
4. the physician or other medically trained person may question witnesses without seeing the body;
5. witnesses may in certain circumstances give the cause of death without the benefit of medical advice or questioning.

These five sources of information may constitute five quite different degrees of accuracy. In some countries, 'medically certified' means that the certificate has been signed by a doctor; this can represent four of the five possibilities. In other countries, the same category may mean that the subject was attended by a doctor prior to death. Despite these limitations the percentage certification by physicians does provide an index on the quality of the cause of death statistics (this issue is discussed further in sub-section 2.4.3).

Periodically it is suggested that when the certifying practitioner hands the certificate to the next-of-kin, or otherwise where the document is not confidential there may be a psychological restriction on the certifier using certain diagnostic terms.

In New York, a confidential method of reporting the cause of death was used from the beginning of 1947. Jacobson (1948) studied the hospital case notes for individuals who had died from five conditions (alcoholism, syphilis, pueperal infection, diabetes, and appendicitis). All these conditions were understated to a certain amount, and he suggested there was no indication that better statistics had been obtained from the use of the confidential certificate.

Isotalo (1960) described an enhanced certificate that had just been introduced in Finland, where the certifier was asked to provide information on the evidence supporting the diagnosis. A few years later, an expert committee on health statistics (WHO, 1967a) discussed various epidemiological methods for the study of chronic diseases. Among other things, they advocated that 'WHO and national bodies should initiate trials with different forms of death certificates designed to elicit more complete information on the pathological conditions present at death'. The advisability of dropping the distinction between 'underlying cause' and other conditions contributing or present at the time of death should also be investigated.

In a number of countries where the certificate is inadequate for a precise classification of the cause of death, the certifying practitioner may be asked for more precise information. For example, in 1945 the general register office in England and Wales made 13,944 enquiries; though this only represented about 2 per cent of all deaths, it yielded results that appreciably improved the statistics. As well as this type of enquiry, a number of countries also have the system where the practitioner can identify that at a later stage he may be in a position to provide further information. This is particularly used by the certifier when the initial certificate is issued prior to an autopsy. In England in 1960 there were about 25,000 certificates so marked (about 5 per cent of all the deaths); replies were received to 80 per cent of the enquiries sent out.

In many countries, some system of legal enquiry is initiated for deaths due to accident and violence. The mechanisms for certifying the cause of death varies. Often the legal certificate will only be issued after there has been an autopsy or an inquest. Further particulars about variation between different countries are given in sub-section 2.2.3. A special enquiry was carried out in England in the 1960s, and a report was subsequently published (Brodrick, 1971). This suggested that doctors should be legally obliged not to provide a death certificate in certain circumstances but to report deaths to an appropriate authority so that the cause could be further investigated and more accurately settled. This might have led to more post-mortems before the issue of official death certificates. This report has not been translated into practice and reference has already been made to the declining proportion of deaths when an autopsy is performed.

In certain circumstances. legislation in many countries permits lay reporting of the cause of death. This is particularly relevant to countries with high mortality and a relative dearth of medical practitioners in rural areas. A WHO (1974) report indicated that it was preferable to have formal lay reporting, with appropriate guidance, rather than failure to document any cause of death for a proportion of deaths. Some countries limit the publication of the cause of death statistics to those deaths where medical attendance has occurred. Such statistics avoid the unreliable element that may occur with the use of laymen's medical diagnoses. However, these statistics are limited in their usefulness because they cannot be related to the population from which the deaths arose, nor are they representative of deaths occurring in the general population.

The mortality statistics published by WHO for different countries may be rather misleading as insufficient specificity of the source of data is provided. The Registrar General in England periodically produces a table which shows the deaths classified by an abbreviated cause list, by sex and method of certification. This distinguishes deaths: reported to the coroner; where post-mortem occurs without inquest; where inquest occurs with or without post-mortem; deaths certified by medical practitioner with or without autopsy, and with or without mention of operation or other examination on the certificate; and the number certified. In 1965 (Registrar General, 1967) the proportion uncertified was extremely small – only 610 male deaths out of a total of 282,328, and 423 female deaths out of a total of 267,051.

Reid and Rose (1964) prepared a number of case histories and circulated these to hospital physicians in Norway, the UK and the US; the physicians were asked to complete a standard death certificate for each history. There was a consistent allocation of the underlying cause of death to major categories between the three national sets of certifiers; within some of these groups there were divergencies. The Americans allocated 24 per cent of the histories to arteriosclerotic heart disease compared with 13.8 per cent by the Norwegians. The British doctors allocated 18.3 per cent of the histories to chronic bronchitis and emphysema compared with 10.6 per cent the Norwegians. This study indicated the variation in certification practice between the groups of doctors in different countries, in a 'test' situation.

Gordon (1959) pointed out that, according to death certificates completed for all deaths in Ilford in a 3-year period, hypertension was less common among those dying with coronary disease than among those dying from all (other) causes. He suggested this was partly due to diagnostic fashion. This report was circulated by the local coroner to pathologists in the locality. Subsequently, the proportion of deaths certified from coronary heart disease following coroner's autopsy in which hypertension was mentioned rose from 4.5 to 32.5 per cent; in the community in general, the figure had dropped from 13.1 per cent to 10.0 per cent. This is compatible with a specific effect on the earlier paper on certification practice (Gordon, 1967).

Bourke and Hall (1968) examined the age of doctors certifying deaths from five causes outside hospital in Eire in 1963. They suggested that older doctors were more likely to certify deaths from 'other myocardial infarction' in males and deaths from 'senility without mention of psychoses' in both sexes. This was not a result of the older doctors having older patients and was thought to indicate use of outmoded terminology.

Netsky and Miyaji (1976) referred to the belief in Japan that extensive use of an organ may cause disease; a clinician flatters the family when diagnosing cerebral haemorrhage as the sudden illness of the father.

2.2.8 Classification of the cause of death

The need for a uniform classification of the cause of death has long been recognized and the first statistical congress held in Brussels in 1853 requested Dr Farr of England and Dr d'Espine of Switzerland to prepare lists of diseases sitable for classification (see United Nations, 1951). They submitted two separate lists to a second congress in 1855 and a compromise was adopted; this was revised over the next 30 years but not generally followed as a standard in different countries.

In 1898, the American Public Health Association recommended that a revised list was produced for the beginning of each decennium to reflect appropriate developments in medical science and statistical procedure. This was approved by the International Institute of Statistics in 1899 and six revisions were made in conferences convened by the French Government (these occurred in 1900, 1909, 1920, 1929, 1938 and 1948). The first three revisions followed an agenda prepared by Bertillon; after his death in 1922, a joint committee of the International Institute of Statistics and the League of Nations Health Organization were responsible. In 1946, the interim commission of the WHO took this over and the 6th revision held in 1948 was carried out by an expert committee reporting to the World Health Assembly. This adopted regulations regarding nomenclature with respect to disease and cause of death.

The principles of classification have followed those initially laid down by Farr. Each succeeding revision of the international list has reflected advances in medical science by adding categories of new disease entities; more and more emphasis has also been given to the aetiology of disease. It has not been found practicable to shift the classification completely to an aetiological base. The 6th revision represented a rather sweeping change because it served a dual purpose of classifying cause of illness as well as cause of death. However, the general structure of the old classification was preserved. The 7th revision conference in 1955 introduced very minor changes whilst the 8th revision involved more marked alteration in the classification at the conference in 1965.

Bunle (1954) discussed the use of the international short-lists for 1909, 1920 and 1929. He indicated that those of 1909 and 1920 were little different, but the 1929 revision introduced an 'other' category for each of the eight different chapters in the classification – instead of pooling all others as the earlier classifications have done in a final 'dustbin' category.

Throughout this century, major revisions in the international classification have particularly resulted in the following:

Revision	Changes
3rd	1. Acute miliary tuberculosis was transferred to respiratory TB at the 3rd revision.
4th	1. Brain tumours were transferred to neoplasms from the nervous system.
5th	1. Criminal abortion was transferred to complications of pregnancy from accidental deaths.
	2. Aortic aneurysm was transferred from 'aneurysm' to syphilis.
6th	1. Various infectious diseases were transferred from the organ system involved to infectious disease.
	2. Malnutrition above one year was moved from accident to deficiency disease.
	3. Rheumatism unqualified was transferred to joint disease from acute rheumatic fever.
	4. Pneumonia and diarrhoea in the first four weeks of life were transferred to certain diseases in early infancy from the categories pneumonia and diarrhoea.
	5. Tachycardia, oedema, cardiac failure, dropsy, and certain other vague terms were transferred from other diseases of the heart to ill-defined conditions.
	6. Gastritis and duodenitis were combined to form a new category in diarrhoeal diseases.
	7. Pulmonary oedema due to heart disease was transferred from respiratory to other and unspecified heart disease.
	8. Bronchiectasis was separated from chronic bronchitis.
	9. Interstitial nephritis was transferred from chronic nephritis into a residual category.
	10. Jaundice of the newborn was transferred to ill-defined conditions from certain diseases of early infancy.
	11. Uraemia was transferred from unspecified nephritis to ill-defined conditions.
7th	1. Only very minor modifications were made and the classification really remained similar to the 6th.
8th	1. Diarrhoeal diseases were moved from the alimentary to infectious disease chapter.
	2. Cerebrovascular disease was transferred from diseases of the nervous system and sense organs to the diseases of the circulatory system.

Revision **Changes**

8th–cont. 3. A fourth digit sub-division was provided for cerebrovascular disease and ischaemic heart disease in order to show an association with hypertension.

4. The former section diseases peculiar to early infancy was merged with the supplemental classification on causes of stillbirth to form a new section on certain causes of perinatal morbidity and mortality.

5. The circumstances surrounding certain accidents such as falls and fire were altered so that they could be coded in the classification.

Buren (1939) lists a large number of changes in the first four revisions of the ICD and the USA manual of joint causes of death that have created difficulty with assessing trends in mortality. He suggested that it was sometimes preferable to follow causes forward from an early revision rather than attempt to work backwards from the latest revision.

Dunn and Shackley (1944) presented the first set of bridge tables for the USA, with data for 1940 coded according to the 4th and 5th revisions of the ICD. About 25 per cent of the 200 detailed causes showed variation of 5 per cent or more, but use of broader cause groups reduced the effect of classification change (e.g. the specific sub-divisions for heart disease changed greatly but there was an overall loss of 2.9 per cent for all heart disease).

The history of the revision of the ICD and detailed discussion of the 8th revision have been provided by Moriyama (1966) and Robb-Smith (1969). The intention of the revisions of the classification is to allow for alteration in medical knowledge over time. Every change in classification does pose problems when trying to get comparability over a period of time. The way this has been tackled for the present work is described in chapter 6. Clarke and Whitfield (1979) discussed the accuracy of mortality statistics for haemolytic disease of the newborn as a specific example of the problems that can occur due to the organization of the classification. They suggested that the deaths coded to this condition were appreciably inflated; in about one-quarter of the cases death was not due to haemolytic disease of any type, but the mention of hydrops without other stated cause is classified under the 8th revision with haemolytic disease of the newborn. This is a numerically small cause of death, but indicates the way in which the classification (and its associated coding rules) can artificially introduce error into the statistics by misaligning certain sub-groups of disease.

2.2.9 Coding of the cause of death

In the 1900 revision of the international classification, Bertillon suggested rules for determining the 'primary' cause of death where two disorders were included on the certificate – the most important was that 'if one of the two diseases is not an immediate and frequent complication of the other, the death should be classified under the head of the primary disease'. In other instances, a more commonly fatal disease, a communicable disease, or an acute disease were accorded priority. Huber (1927) discovered that Bertillon's recommendations were nominally followed in many countries; the main variations were in England, Scotland, and New Zealand where a priority system was in effect which gave precedence to violent causes, infectious causes, and then the most dangerous causes.

Huber suggested that elsewhere selection procedures were quite relaxed and little attempt was made to ensure compliance with the stated principles. At that time a rigid set of selection principles was in effect in the US and several other countries followed her lead. There were national variations; Sweden and Norway showed an exceptionally strong preference for assigning infectious and parasitic disease as the cause of death while New Zealand and Australia displayed assignments close to the average for all countries.

A study was carried out in 1935 (US Bureau for Census, 1938) which involved certificates for 1,032 cases each containing from two to five causes of death. These certificates were submitted to statistical offices of various countries with the request that they be classified according to the selection procedure usually followed. Data were included for 18 countries in the report. Even though the results were tabulated by broad cause, the analysis showed marked differences; for example, Norway had assigned 29.5 per cent of the certificates to infectious and parasitic disease while Turkey had only assigned 12.1 per cent.

Deporte (1941) reported that a new certificate of the English pattern was introduced into the US in 1940 and he had investigated the effect on certification practice. Out of 500 certificates, 370 quoted two or more causes. The physicians choice (by order of the items) was in disagreement with the rules in 171; of these certificates, 105 seemed in a logical sequence (i.e. the rules were probably wrong) and in 66, the statements were not in a logical order.

Around 1947, between 50 and 70 per cent of death certificates for Australia, Denmark, England and Wales, New Zealand, Switzerland and the US listed more than one cause of death; in contrast, in France and Greece 15 per cent contained multiple causes. Thurber Fales and Moriyama (1949) reported another study of the US

Committee on Joint Causes of Death. Over 10,000 certificates were coded first using the US joint cause procedure, modification of this procedure and the English method.

Comparison of the coded results using the modified US and England systems showed that for 95 per cent of the assignments the causes of death were in agreement. When compensating errors were included, the comparability was 97 per cent. These results suggested that the arbitrary selection of the primary cause of death using the manual of joint causes of death was not primarily responsible for the apparent discrepancy between cause of death assignments and clinical interpretation of the diseases present.

A major change was introduced for the 6th revision of the ICD, when the coder was instructed to accept the opinions of the attending physician for the underlying cause. The physician was assisted in delineating the underlying cause by the introduction of the new form of death certificate which was uniform in different countries for the first time. This asked for the sequence of conditions, connected by the phrase 'as a consequence of' for each separate entry. The physician's opinion was to stand unless the sequence of morbid conditions appeared illogical or improbable – he was either then queried by sending a request for further information or an arbitrary coding rule was applied.

Moriyama (1956) estimated that the physicians' judgement was not reflected in the coding for only about 5 per cent of the assignments. This change from arbitrary coding rules to physician's judgement introduces some of the most serious problems of comparability in countries where multiple cause deaths form a high percentage of the total. The total number of deaths for cardiovascular disease, neoplasm, infectious and parasitic disease, violence and certain diseases of early infancy changed by less than 5 per cent. However, arteriosclerotic heart disease lost a large number of deaths to cerebrovascular lesions; in England and Wales and in the US deaths from bronchitis doubled. In some countries, nephritis doubled, diabetes lost one-third to one-half, and maternal mortality lost about one-tenth of the deaths.

A study of coding differences was carried out by the World Health Organization (WHO, 1967b). A sample of 1,000 completed death certificates (written in English) was circulated to Czechoslovakia, Denmark, England, Finland, Netherlands and Sweden. In each of the participating countries these certificates were coded according to normal national practice and the results returned to WHO. The selection rule that was employed for each case was indicated, and it was also stated for each certificate whether or not a query would have been sent to the certifying physician. All the certificates were also coded by the WHO centre for classification of disease. The extent of agreement from country to country was appreciable; the agreement was lowest for the two Czechoslovakia coders and highest for those in Finland.

The bulk of discrepancies appeared to be caused by differences in national practice rather than individual coding. Considerable disagreement occurred for infective and parasitic disease, other heart disease, hypertension, pneumonia, nephritis, and infection of the newborn. National differences in the interpretation of selection rules were at the root of most of the coding discrepancies. There were apparently considerable divergencies between the coders on the extent to which they were prepared to accept the statement of the certifying doctor. Acceptance or rejection of the certifier's statement was the crux of variation in the coding. The report made some suggestions about how these coding problems could be resolved in the next revision of the ICD.

Because of the increase in proportion of certificates that mention more than one cause, suggestions have periodically been made that multiple cause coding should be introduced. Farr (1854) had suggested that at some period it would be right to investigate double causes of death. Since this time a number of studies of the issue have been explored; in Canada, England, the US, and other countries steps are now taken to multiple cause code at least a sample of all death certificates. Cohen and Steinitz (1969) emphasized that contributory causes might be more subject to biases in identification and certification and that clearer definition was required before extended use of such items.

Abramson *et al.* (1971) compared autopsy findings with 476 death certificates to check on the identification of disease present at the time of death. They found marked limitations in the reporting of cerebrovascular and heart disease, peptic ulcer, and liver cirrhosis. Malignant disease was reported fairly consistently, but not the specific site involved. However, the published data that had been used for this book has been based upon single-cause coding. The topic of multiple cause coding has been reviewed by Alderson (1974).

2.2.10 Problems with specific diseases

An indication of the concern of the limitations of the material is provided in a report by the United Nations (1963) which proposed that data on cause of death might be usefully grouped into five main categories:

infectious and parasitic diseases;
cancer;
cardiovascular disease and bronchitis over the age of 5;

violence;
other causes.

Use of such broad categories can be justified in an attempt to avoid the difficulties with finer sub-grouping where there has been change in diagnostic fashion, diagnostic accuracy, terminology, and transfer between categories for other reasons. However, aggregation to this extent may conceal very different trends for various diseases; it will also involve conditions with quite different aetiologies.

This section presents a brief view of articles that have referred to the difficulty of interpreting mortality trends for particular conditions. Obviously, a major element of selection has taken place in providing these brief notes which are meant to indicate the problems rather than provide an exhaustive review of the relevant literature. There are a number of general points that need to be considered. A joint United Nations/WHO meeting (WHO, 1970) pointed out that at that time only about 34 per cent of the world's population was covered by routine mortality statistics. It stressed the importance of extending this coverage and (for existing systems) the need to build in some routine evaluation of the data. The meeting suggested it was important to check the completeness of the data, the representativeness, the accuracy of the non-diagnostic and diagnostic data.

The following comments attempt to distinguish validation studies carried out on specific diseases, comments on the validity of the data made from internal examination of the material, or from general knowledge rather than from specific studies. The diseases are ordered according to the ICD.

Infective and parasitic diseases

Cholera. Stocks (1950) suggested that it was doubtful whether all the deaths ascribed to this condition at the beginning of the century were genuine; he therefore combined cholera with dysentery and unspecific diarrhoea.

Diphtheria. A WHO report (1951a) pointed out that in 1938 pseudomembraneous angina and croup of several organs may have been allocated elsewhere, if not specifically designated as diphtheria. This was a new shift away from the disease category. Improved bacteriological diagnosis may also have caused different allocation of some conditions.

Malaria. In reviewing the trends over the first half of this century (WHO, 1950b), it was pointed out that there had been very slight changes in the classification and it was not thought they had introduced any major heterogeneity into the statistical series. Perhaps improvement in the quality of diagnosis was a more important source of change but the impact of this was uncertain; this may have shifted more spurious conditions out of the specific malaria rubric than vice versa. There may have been a tendency with some deaths to code to complications thus losing malaria deaths.

Measles. A WHO report (1950) suggested that the exclusion of German measles in the 6th revision may have moved out some deaths, but the mortality from German measles was very low compared with that for measles and was unlikely to have appreciably altered the figures. There was also the tendency, where terminal bronchopneumonia is the cause of death, that the rules of allocation result in the death being coded to bronchopneumonia rather than measles. It was not possible to quantify the extent of this.

Scarlet fever. A WHO report (1954a) reviewed the trends over the first half of the century and noted that the 4th revision had moved puerperal scarlet fever from the specific scarlet fever category to infections during childbirth. This is a very small change and unlikely to have altered the general comparability of the rubric. Perhaps more important is the tendency with alteration in coding rules for complications of bronchopneumonia, nephritis, heart disease, and pleurisy to be coded to these latter conditions rather than the underlying scarlet fever. It was not possible to quantify this aspect.

Syphilis. There have been a number of changes in the classification which create problems. The 1st and 2nd revisions did not sub-divide syphilis in the detailed list; the 3rd introduced five sub-divisions which were reduced to three in the 4th. Over this whole period the sum total for syphilis was not affected though the parts are difficult to align. The 5th revision considerably enlarged the concept of syphilis by adding to the main clinical manifestations tabes dorsalis, general paralysis of the insane, aneurysm of the aorta, and other forms of circulatory disease. The 6th revision altered the numbering but not the content of the section. The major change introduced by the 5th revision can be overcome by identifying the specific conditions which were tabulated in other parts of earlier classifications.

The other issue to remember is that syphilis was always considered a shameful disease and very likely to be under-reported in open certificates. Hare (1972) commented on the problems of disentangling the factors of validity of the data against alteration in innate virulence of the organism, prevention, or treatment. He drew attention to the problem of certifying a disease such as syphilis, and the alteration in death registration and classification systems.

Martin (1972) described the conquest of general paralysis; he presented statistics on the number of deaths from 1911-69. He emphasized that the aetiology was not defined at the beginning of the century, but did not question the validity of the statistics.

Tuberculosis. Ash (1915) reviewed the diagnoses from a series of 198 autopsies carried out on patients dying in a consumptive hospital in the US. Twenty-three (11.6 per cent) of these were proved to be deaths from conditions other than tuberculosis, emphasizing the difficulty in achieving appropriate clinical diagnosis. Of the 23, 7 had been recognized clinically as non-tuberculosis prior to death. Springett (1950) in a major review of mortality rates from tuberculosis for a number of countries in the 19th and 20th century, pointed out that the accuracy of certification may have changed over this time but the technique of analysis (age-specific rates over time or cohort rates) would both be vitiated by the underlying errors. He did not quantify the likely error in the data. Springett (1971) pointed out that tuberculosis mortality rates were useful indices of the distribution of the disease up until the middle of the present century; with improved therapy and a drop in case-fatality, mortality becomes less and less meaningful as a measure of distribution of the disease.

Horwitz and Palmer (1954) examined the histories of 314 individuals notified as active tuberculosis in Denmark who died within a year of notification. In only 174 was tuberculosis identified as the underlying cause of death on the death certificate. In reviewing the material and comparison with national data they suggest that about 108 deaths might have been expected from other causes leaving the overall excess from tuberculosis as 206; the actual certification underestimated this figure by 32.

Typhus. The terminology has rather altered from the expressions coded to thus rubric in 1900. In 1920, Mexican typhus was included and from 1938, other rickettsioses such as endemic typhus, rocky mountain spotted fever, trench fever and others. A WHO report (1951) concluded that these had not introduced any major variation in the contents of the statistical series over the first half of this century.

Typhoid and paratyphoid. A WHO report (1951) pointed out that the diagnostic criteria had altered during the first half of the century and it was not clear to what extent variation in facilities in different countries had influenced the precision of the diagnosis. It concluded that it was questionable what proportion of deaths from this disease might have been left in the more general category of diarrhoea and enteritis.

Whooping cough. A WHO report (1951c) suggested that the classification had not introduced any appreciable difference this century. The rules for coding might have altered the proportion dying with associated bronchitis and bronchial pneumonia, where whooping cough had not been identified as the underlying cause of death.

Meningococcal meningitis. Lambert (1973) contrasted trends in England and Wales over a 20-year period for notifications, hospital in-patient spells, and deaths. There was a decrease for the earlier period and then an increase for the latest data for the three sets of statistics. He commented that the extent of agreement of the figures from these three sources was considerable and supported the validity of the data.

Neoplasms

Many reports have been published examining the validity of mortality statistics for malignant disease over this century; two reviews from WHO (1952b, 1955a) have examined long-term trends. Greenwood and Wood (1914) examined this issue. They particularly looked at the trends in the end of the 19th and early 20th century for 'accessible' and 'inaccessible' sites. They concluded that it was incorrect to state that the recorded incidence of cancer was not a consequence of genuinely increased incidence (though referring to incidence, they are dealing with mortality data).

MacDonald (1938) compared the death notification with particulars from private practitioners or hospitals for a sample of deaths from cancer. Details were only obtained for one-third of the cancer deaths initially identified. Review suggested that the site was appropriate in 78.2 per cent (of 2,033 deaths); this varied from 99.1 per cent agreement in breast cancer to 17.5 per cent in liver cancer (when secondaries had been certified as the primary site). Dorn and Horn (1941) reviewed the diagnostic particulars for over 13,000 death certificates mentioning malignant disease and suggested digestive disease tract certification was accurate, while skin, brain and bone were least accurate.

Lilienfeld *et al.* (1972) in discussing mortality in the US pointed out that three of the most important factors that influence cancer mortality are age, sex, and colour. They suggested that these factors can be assumed to be associated with variation in population, enumeration, diagnostic accuracy, or case-fatality, and that the relative influence of these influences may be determined (though they do not spell out exactly how this can be done).

Ehrlich *et al.* (1975) reviewed 1,212 consecutive autopsies in a major Israeli hospital: malignant disease diagnosed clinically was confirmed in 226, though the site was discrepant in 30; 43 clinical diagnoses were not confirmed; 28 previously unrecognized malignancies were detected at autopsy. They found that advanced age, non-European ethnic origin, short terminal hospitalization, and limited investigation contributed to failed clinical diagnosis.

Lung cancer. Once they examined this issue, Kennaway (1936) provided no specific conclusion as to whether the trends were valid, because of the difficulty in determining the influence of improved diagnosis and fashions in diagnosis.

A WHO report (1952c) suggested that the 5th revision was responsible for a jump in deaths from lung cancer. The Registrar General (1957a) and Gilliam (1955) examined English and American statistics and discussed the difference there would have been to the trends in lung cancer mortality with varying levels of diagnostic error. They concluded that the major changes in mortality were genuine rather than a reflection of diagnostic shift.

McKenzie (1956) contrasted diagnostic data with certificates for lung cancer mortality. In the majority there was an established or corroborated diagnosis; and even in those over 74 at death, he thought the diagnosis should have been changed for only 3 per cent. A WHO report (1955a) also examined trends from respiratory cancers; particular comment was made about the difficulty in aligning detailed with short-lists of the ICD and various national lists.

In a follow-up study of asbestos workers, Newhouse and Wagner (1969) identified 436 deaths; further information was available from autopsy reports in 74 and histological specimens in 84. Review of the cause of death slightly increased the lung cancer deaths from 39 to 42 and there was marked increase in mesothelioma deaths (pleural from 1 to 6 and peritoneal from 4 to 14). Gastrointestinal tumours were reduced from 14 to 7.

Uterine cancer. Weiss (1978) reviewed the mortality from cancer of the uterus and concluded that there was appreciable under-reporting of a specific corpus cancer because an appreciable number are coded as uterine cancer NOS. He suggested there was reason to believe that the gross under-reporting of the specific site had altered over time and was decreasing in the latest data. Another important issue is the appropriateness of the denominator (see Alderson and Donnan, 1978); with increasing frequency of hysterectomy for non-malignant conditions, the proportion of women who can develop malignant disease of the uterus will decline.

Hodgkin's disease. This would have been included under leukaemia in 1900. At the 2nd revision, Hodgkin's disease was identified specifically as one of the conditions to be included under this heading. In the 3rd revision a separate code was allocated to Hodgkin's disease; in the 4th this was moved from the chapter of general diseases to diseases of the blood and blood forming organs; in the 5th revision, Hodgkin's disease was uniquely identified within the chapter infective and parasitic disease (aleukaemia was still identified under leukaemia and split off from its previous alignment with Hodgkin's disease). At the 6th revision both leukaemia and Hodgkin's disease were moved into the neoplasm chapter.

A WHO report (1955b) showed the difficulty in interpreting the trends because of these major changes in classification. In addition, there are the problems of diagnostic validity. This makes interpretation of the data over a long time period extremely difficult.

Endocrine, nutritional, and metabolic diseases

Addison's disease. Mason *et al.* (1968) checked the medical histories of 51 patients certified as dying from Addison's disease. Six had been wrongly certified (though from this kind of study one does not know how many certified to other causes should have in fact been certified to Addison's disease). Twenty-nine of the patients had tuberculosis disease of the adrenal, but this had only been identified on the death certificate in 19. In 30 of the subjects the diagnosis had been unsuspected prior to death and only identified at autopsy (thus suggesting the decrease in the autopsy frequency would result in an appreciable number of these cases being missed).

Asthma. Inman and Adelstein (1969) reviewed the trend in asthma mortality in England and Wales for 1959-68. They discussed various reasons for the rise and then decrease in asthma mortality and argued that this was a real increase rather than a spurious result of changes in diagnosis or classification. The rules by which asthma is classified had changed; since 1958, where asthma is mentioned, but bronchitis also appears in the certificate, bronchitis will be coded rather than the asthma. They felt that the observed trends were not a result of the 'technical' factors.

Diabetes. The 2nd revision transferred diabetes insipidus from this rubric. In the 5th revision, diabetic pigmentary cirrhosis was excluded and in the 6th revision, renal diabetes was also excluded. The diagnostic category was gradually refined and some deaths would have been shifted out of the diagnostic group diabetes. A WHO report (1955c) suggested this would have only very slight effect on the overall mortality figures. More important are the rules of selection which have varied over time and between countries.

Trowell (1974) points out that in the period 1920–39 diabetes held high priority as classification for the underlying cause in England (perhaps only 10 per cent of the diabetic deaths were coded to some other disease when two conditions were mentioned). The 5th revision introduced the major change in rules of selection and this resulted in a one-third drop in diabetic deaths in England and Wales. Trowell also suggested that at times of war there might be some individuals recruited into the armed forces with diabetes. If they died they did not become included in the mortality statistics. (However, because the forces were predominantly fit, one would assume that with an appreciable proportion of the adult male population in the forces the civilian mortality rates would 'rise'.)

Trowell suggested that the presence of mild diabetes and other major diseases in persons over the age of 74 may result in some certification to diabetes that was not really appropriate. However, he concluded that despite the limitations of the death certificate and its handling, the statistics were sufficiently valid to use with care.

Warren and Corfield (1973) suggested that for most European countries and the US and Canada there may have been greater awareness of diabetes from screening and other studies, and this might have altered diagnostic practice and death certification. In a specific review of the condition in Norway in 1956–65, Ustvedt and Olsen (1977) suggested that it is possible that change in certification practice had occurred but they thought that this was unlikely.

Tokuhata *et al.* (1975) sent enquiries to certifiers of 311 decedents in Pennsylvania, USA, and found that 8 per cent had diabetes diagnosed prior to death, which was not mentioned on the certificates. In addition, 74 per cent of certificates mentioning diabetes identified some other underlying cause. The authors suggest that the extent of the diabetes is underestimated, due to failure to recognize that the stated underlying cause is often secondary to the diabetes.

Thyroid disease. Greenwald in a series of papers (1965, 1967, 1968, 1970, 1973) has reviewed mortality from exophthalmic goitre in Australia, Canada, Netherlands, Norway, Sweden, Switzerland, UK and US. He pointed out since 1920, the pathological conditions included under exophthalmic goitre may have increased; the 6th revision re-aligned the rubric from exophthalmic goitre to thyrotoxicosis with or without goitre. The fatality of this condition may have altered over the time and also the diagnostic facilities. However, there are divergent age specific trends over time and he concluded that the data are valid rather than a reflection of technical aspects.

Diseases of the nervous system and sense organs

Cerebrovascular disease has now been transferred to the cardiovascular system in the 8th revision of the ICD. Florey *et al.* (1969) compared clinical records and autopsy material with diagnoses for a large sample of deaths from cerebrovascular disease in the US. For 607 cases who definitely had some form of cerebrovascular disease 74 per cent of the certificates agreed with the diagnosis obtained from the total clinical material. It was suggested that cerebral haemorrhage was over-diagnosed at the expense of thrombo-embolism on the death certificates.

Kruger *et al.* (1967) drew attention to the successive revisions of the ICD, which had changed the definitions of both haemorrhagic and occlusive cerebrovascular disease and had failed to distinguish non-specific cerebrovascular disease. Because of these problems, they suggested that consistent classification could not be obtained and therefore mounted a specific study to recode data to provide a uniform set of statistics. Acheson and Sanderson (1978) showed that the 8th revision may have led to a false impression of the rate of fall of cerebral haemorrhage due to the revisions that were included.

Bronte-Stewart and Pickering (1959) suggested that the clinical methods of distinguishing haemorrhage from thrombosis were not sufficiently reliable for the data to be analysed. Acheson (1960) discussed the clinical problems of diagnosis in relation to cerebrovascular disease and emphasized the shortcomings of the published data. The 5th revision added the supplementary heading of hemiplegia which also created some problems (there may be a tendency to use this general term even though a more specific diagnosis was available).

A further complication is the relationship with hypertension and the national laws and practices on the completion of the certificate and coding. Larsson (1967) suggested that mortality statistics were perhaps more reliable for cerebrovascular disease compared with many other conditions, though he advocated combining all forms of cerebrovascular disease in order to study trends.

Following an examination of multiple cause coding of Swedish data, he suggested there was considerable underestimate of the occurrence of the cerebrovascular disease in the three largest cities and one county in Sweden.

Acheson *et al.* (1973) compared death certificates with medical records for US veterans dying with strokes and 'control' deaths. Mortality from strokes was higher in Georgia than in five western states, but there was no evidence that the quality of care and certification was contributing to this difference.

Epilepsy. This condition has been identified in the ICD since the beginning of the century, and there is no problem with classification. The real problem is likely to be the variation in allocating underlying cause of death where epilepsy is associated with accidents; the procedure may have varied over time and between countries (WHO, 1955d).

Multiple sclerosis. Kurland and Moriyama (1951) pointed out that in 1947 if a death certificate used the expression 'cerebral sclerosis' the coding rules had allocated this to multiple sclerosis. A detailed enquiry of 284 death certificates indicated that the vast majority were cases of cerebro-arteriosclerosis. Though this was a very small proportion of the total deaths from cerebro-arteriosclerosis, it was an appreciable proportion of the deaths coded to disseminated sclerosis (284 out of a total of 1,583). Following this, the rules of allocation were amended.

Kurland and Moriyama also reported an autopsy study which showed that out of 33 clinical diagnoses of multiple sclerosis 10 were disproved on autopsy but 11 from other diagnoses were transferred to the same condition (thus providing compensating errors). There was also the problem that in 1940 about 15 per cent of certificates mentioning disseminated sclerosis were assigned to associated causes. This allocation rule altered with the 6th revision, and may have led to a rise in deaths coded to multiple sclerosis.

Acheson (1972) and Agramoff and Goldberg (1974) have discussed the validity of the diagnosis of multiple sclerosis and suggested that mortality statistics underestimate the numbers of individuals dying with this condition. Agramoff and Goldberg believed that quite a large proportion of the deaths principally due to this condition did not have it specified on the death certificate.

Paralysis agitans. This was identified as a specific condition in the 4th revision (forming one of the sub-sections of other diseases of the nervous system). However, some countries had identified it earlier on as a specific cause in their own coding system (e.g. New Zealand from 1885).

Parkinson's disease. Brown and Knox (1972) discussed the trends in this condition; they felt that many patients, though suffering from this, were certified as dying from other causes. Duvoisin and Yahr (1972) pointed out that Brown and Knox had ignored some very major problems in the handling of the data. The coding system did not differentiate paralysis agitans that was due to post-encepahlitic Parkinsonism. Also, the rules for allocation in 1921-39 gave encaphalitis lethargica a high degree of preference over paralysis agitans. These rules for allocation were then changed with the 1940 revision of the ICD, which resulted in an appreciable drop in the proportion of deaths certified as paralysis agitans. Duvoisin and Yahr conclude that analysis of mortality data over a long period for this condition is extremely difficult due to the changing statistical practice as well as quality of the diagnosis.

Diseases of the circulatory system

This is one of the conditions on which many studies have been carried out, examining the validity of mortality statistics in different ways.

Jackson (1896) identified consecutive autopsies where a pathological lesion of the heart had been observed. He compared 100 autopsy results with the clinical history and suggested there was in fact 'moderately close correspondence' between the two sets of data.

Woolsey and Moriyama (1948) examined the factors associated with the trends in heart disease mortality in the US for 1900-45. They indicated that there had been improvement in clinical diagnosis; reduced tendency to certify ill-defined heart disease when the underlying illness was not known; alteration in the ICD, particularly the introduction of disease of coronary arteries in the 4th and transfer of cardio-renal deaths to chronic nephritis in the 5th revision and alteration in priority in joint cause allocation in the US in 1925. Using a very broad category of cardiovascular-renal-senility rubric they show no evidence of increase or decrease due to compensating changes within these rubrics.

Kuller *et al.* (1967) examined data for a representative sample of deaths in Baltimore in 1964-5. For those where the underlying cause of death was arterio-sclerotic heart disease, they suggested that 452 were correct and only 26 were incorrect. There were also 498 deaths coded to other causes, and there was no evidence on review of all information that any of these were definitely due to arteriosclerotic heart disease.

Moriyama *et al.* (1966) sent questionnaires to the

certifiers for a national sample of deaths from cardiovascular disease. There was only an 87 per cent response and there was no check whether there was relevant data they did not learn about other than through the responses. They considered that for 53 per cent the diagnosis of death had been a reasonable inference or better (some were reasonably supported and others well established). The majority of the remaining deaths should have been attributed elsewhere in the broad cause 'cardiovascular-renal' disease. They used their data to argue for a rather different system of handling mortality statistics, with the emphasis on multiple cause.

Stocks (1969) presented some of the specific results from the Inter-American Study of Mortality (this has been discussed in section 2.2.6). There was considerable variation in the mortality rates in the different countries and he concluded that these could not be explained by variation in practice of the official coders.

Stocks examined the probability of variation in completeness of recognition of coronary involvement or the mention in the medical records of specific symptoms and signs of these diseases. After an internal comparison of the data, he suggested that such factors were unlikely to be causing the difference and concluded that it was extrinsic factors (such as differences in smoking and physical activity) responsible for the differences in cardio-vascular mortality rates.

Robb-Smith (1967) published a major review on the enigma of coronary heart disease during this century. He dicusses the difficulties of interpreting national mortality statistics and shows different practices in the terminology used in different countries. In the UK and US chronic valvular disease of unknown aetiology was rarely certified, but it was a relatively frequent term in Italy and Japan. He concluded that there was abundant evidence (but did not quote this) that change in diagnostic semantics is one of the factors in the increased prevalence of ischaemic heart disease. He also identified differences in the trends in mortality within sex and age groups (this makes one think that some general factor such as this could not account for these trends). He also commented that, due to alteration in the classification, deaths that had in the earlier part of the century been coded to nephitis were now classified to hypertension. There had also been major problems in the UK with alteration in the rules of precedence in 1940.

Another specific example of certification practice has been shown by McMichael (1979). He stated that in France, patients having coronary artery disease who subsequently die of heart failure tend to be certified as suffering from chronic myocarditis rather than having the coronary disease identified. Only by summing the two causes of death are comparable rates to other Western countries obtained.

Benjamin (1968) drew attention to the 10 per cent decrease in deaths from heart disease that occurred in 1940 after the change in the assignment rules. He also supported the suggestion of using broad groups when making comparisons and advocated that heart disease, other diseases of the circulatory system, intracranial lesions of vascular origin, nephritis and bronchitis should all be pooled together. He acknowledged this was a very large group but suggested that separation was unlikely to achieve any real increase in definition.

To study the time trend of ischaemic heart disease in Canada from 1901–61, Anderson and LeRiche (1970) tabulated data for Ontario from original death certificates and coroner's records. They used three diagnostic groups: (i) angina pectoris, arteriosclerotic heart disease, and coronary thrombosis; (ii) (i) plus heart failure, myocarditis cardiac dropsy, and organic heart disease, and (iii) (ii) plus rheumatic heart disease, chronic nephitis, cardio-renal disease, asthma, indigestion, hypertension, and apoplexy. These were thought to provide upper and lower estimate limits of true IHD mortality. Anderson and LeRiche concluded from similar trends in these data that there had been a genuine increase in IHD.

Lambert (1975) reviewed mortality from hypertensive disease for 47 countries for 1950–71. He dealt at some length with difficulty created in interpreting the data due to a wide variety of extraneous influences. The 8th revision of the ICD had resulted in halving the mortality from hypertensive disease (with transfer to chronic ischaemic heart disease). Completeness of registration was not thought to be a problem and there was no clear evidence that availability of diagnostic facilities influenced the statistics; choice of terminology, coding practice, and classification change caused discontinuity but he concluded the main trends demonstrated real changes in mortality from this condition.

Beral (1976), in examining the cardiovascular mortality in young women, suggested that it was unlikely that diagnostic fashion could account for the trends in this disease. This point was made after examining the internal evidence of the trends over time in different age groups in 21 countries.

Clayton *et al.* (1977) examined the trend in heart disease in England and Wales in 1950–73 and suggested that considerable transfer had occurred during this period between myocardial degeneration, hypertensive disease, and ischaemic heart disease. They suggested a regrouping of the ICD categories to make useful international comparisons. However, Wald and Mann (1977) disputed these conclusions, advocating that the decrease in hypertensive mortality was partly due to actual reduction in fatality from improved treatment for this condition. They supported this argument by pointing to the difference in the trends in men and women.

Cooper *et al.* (1978) discussed the influence of the 8th revision of the ICD; they suggested that about 15 per cent more deaths were assigned to coronary heart disease under the 8th revision, partly from transfer from the previous category of other myocardial degeneration and from preference in classifying deaths mentioning hypertension. (About half the deaths previously assigned to hypertensive heart disease were transferred to the category chronic ischaemic heart disease.)

Guberan (1979) presented data on cardiovascular mortality for Switzerland for 1951-76. He used four sub-divisions and all deaths from circulatory disease, suggesting that such broad categories avoided problems from changing diagnostic habits. The Swiss data were compared with similar statistics for 13 other developed countries.

Deutscher *et al.* (1971) emphasized the different estimates that can be given of age and sex trends for various cardiovascular diseases and diabetes if morbidity rather than mortality rates are studied. They suggested that this is partly due to the different case-fatality rates for various age and sex sub-groups of the population. It must be remembered that alteration in case-fatality will be reflected in mortality trends.

Diseases of the respiratory system

Markush (1968) reported a study cross-checking the diagnostic particulars for a sample of deaths in the US. There were 2,356 deaths in a random sample and 837 with respiratory disease mentioned in Part I or Part II of the certificate. Markush concluded that the prevalence of chronic respiratory disease at death was more than nine times greater than its underlying cause death rate. Severe chronic respiratory disease present at the time of death was only listed on the death certificates in about half the patients. It appeared that the US vital statistics would under-estimate the contribution of chronic respiratory disease.

In a further publication of this work, Markush (1969) found evidence that diagnostic custom by the certifier tended to exaggerate differences which they already believed existed. This custom might include certifying 'popular' diseases, with a compensatory decreases in other conditions.

A more restrictive study on a specific sample of deaths coming to autopsy at two hospitals in Denver was reported by Mitchell *et al.* (1971). They compared the reported death certificate diagnosis with the data from autopsy. It appeared that chronic bronchitis and emphysema were moderately under-reported in these deaths; where chronic obstructive airways disease was present, about 76 per cent had chronic bronchitis or emphysema mentioned on the death certificate. There were also patients in whom an autopsy was not performed and where established chronic airways obstruction existed prior to death, yet this was not mentioned on the death certificate.

Hewitt (1956) examined the mortality patterns of London Boroughs in 1950-2. There was no evidence from internal analysis of the data of a tendency by London doctors to confuse various specific respiratory disease groups. He also concluded that there was no concrete evidence that respiratory disease was identified in these patients, when they might have been referred to as cardiovascular deaths with more limited diagnostic facilities.

The Office of Health Economics (1963) reviewed the trend in pneumonia and other respiratory disease in England in the middle of the 19th century. There was some suggestion that a change in certification might have been responsible for the trends, as the increase in respiratory death rates of the over 75s has been associated with a decreasing proportion of deaths certified to old age and senility. However, there was no levelling-off in the respiratory disease rates despite the fact that the proportion of ill-defined death certificates was now stable.

Diseases of the digestive system

Morris and Titmus (1944) examined the trends in mortality from peptic ulcer in England and Wales for the period 1911-42. They concentrated particularly on statistics from 1921-41, because they felt that before this time the statistics were less reliable. However, they felt that, compared with other causes of death, the data were more likely to be dependable. (They referred to the usual hospital care preceded by the history and a dramatic form of death.)

Susser and Stein (1962) reviewed the mortality statistics for peptic ulcer for England and Wales over the first 60 years of this century. They discussed the possibility that diagnostic factors, fashions of diagnosis, and uneven distribution of treatment might be responsible for some fluctuations in the data; however, having carried out cohort analyses of data for males and females they concluded that these factors were unlikely to be influencing the trends. In a further publication with data for a number of countries, Susser (1967) felt that the material was valid, though difficult to interpret because of the relatively low fatality rate during the later period.

Benjamin (1968) again discussed a point of reduced

case fatality with modern treatment but still suggested that peptic ulcer was worth examining as a discreet cause. He advocated that other digestive diseases might then profitably be combined into one broad group to obtain comparable data.

Meade *et al.* (1968) reviewed the mortality from various causes among doctors in the period 1947-65. They suggested that alteration in access to radiology was unlikely to have had an influence on the statistics from duodenal ulcer in this period, and from examination of the material they could find no evidence that there had been changes in terminology used in certifying death over the period.

Trapnell and Duncan (1975) reviewed the epidemiology of acute pancreatitis. They discussed mortality statistics and suggested that they were the only reliable measure of the distribution of this disease in the community.

Diseases of genito-urinary system

The 6th revision of the ICD introduced a number of changes into the classification of diseases. The most important was the transfer of arteriosclerotic kidney into the circulatory diseases (it had been classified with chronic nephritis in the 5th). In 1949, the effect of this was to transfer 69 per cent of the male and 64 per cent of the female deaths in England and Wales from chronic nephritis to the circulatory group (Registrar General, 1957b). Albumenuria was also transferred out of the chapter into that of symptoms and ill-defined conditions.

Kessner and Florey (1967) examined the mortality trends for acute and chronic nephritis and infection of the kidney comparing data for England, Wales and the US. They suggested there had been a drop in chronic nephritis from the classification change but also a decrease in the incidence of acute nephritis and a smaller proportion of people developing chronic forms of this disease. They felt there had been a genuine increase in infections of the kidney rather than a shift in diagnostic fashion.

Waters (1958a) disputed this latter finding and suggested that the increase in infection was predominantly from a switch in diagnosis from chronic nephritis. He also suggested that there may have been a switch from hyperplasia of the prostate to infections. In the absence of hard data there was further disagreement in the literature between these authors (Florey and Kessner, 1968; Waters, 1968b).

Rosenheim (1968) suggested that improvement in radiology had resulted in improved detections of chronic pyelonephritis, especially in children and young adults. Hamtoft and Mosbech (1968) contrasted the trends in Denmark with those in England; though they acknowledged that changes in terminology and coding had affected the trends, they felt that some increase in mortality from infective renal disease had occurred in women (perhaps due to phenacetin abuse).

Hansen and Susser (1971) re-examined the data for the UK and US. They concluded that the cohort effects they identified argued against either diagnostic fashion or better recognition of kidney disease in the period 1880-1930. They also felt the subsequent decline in death rate was unlikely to be due to alteration in diagnostic facilities or coding. (Better recognition would have produced an overall rise in kidney disease they suggest, while the actual trend was a fall.) They suggested the data did reflect a genuine change after mentioning the questions about unreliability.

Ueda *et al.* (1976) analysed 270 autopsies for deaths occurring in a population study in Japan. They identified a range of renal diseases and associated pathology and showed how mortality statistics under-estimated the prevalence of hypertensive renal disease, since nephrosclerosis was rarely diagnosed on a clinical basis.

For a number of years there has been interest in endemic nephropathy in the Balkans (see *Lancet*, 1973). This rather specific disease, influencing only portions of these countries, is an example of an interesting problem that cannot be adequately studied by routine mortality statistics, as it is lost within the classification of other more general conditions.

Complications of pregnancy, childbirth, and the puerperium

A WHO report (1954b) discussed the comparability of trends for maternal mortality. The 6th revision introduced breaks in the continuity of the data, and the report suggested that though overall maternal mortality provided a reasonable trend, analysis by specific cause was difficult over time.

The detailed statistical review of the Lane Report provided no comment about the validity of abortion statistics during this century. However, attention has already been drawn to the ICD revision that introduced discontinuity. Beral (1979) drew attention to the spectacular decline of maternal mortality in England and Wales this century and advocated use of net reproductive mortality (a sum of abortion; complications of pregnancy, delivery and the puerperium; estimated deaths from contraception). She discussed the difficulties of establishing the mortality from the last of these three components.

Diseases of the musculoskeletal system and connective tissue

Logan (1963) drew attention to the deficiencies in mortality statistics in relation to rheumatic complaints, conditions which are rarely fatal, and for which mortality statistics are a relatively poor indicator of the community burden from this disease.

The WHO Working Group (Regional Office for Europe, 1972) acknowledged limitations in the data but maintained they were still of some interest. They pointed out that the challenge was to identify ways in which the data could be improved. Wood and Benn (1972) drew attention to the difficulty introduced by the 8th revision, which transferred diffuse diseases of the connective tissue to the musculoskeletal system chapter. However, they reported a comparison of international data for 31 countries, though they emphasized the difficulty of interpreting this material. It is because of some of these difficulties that major population surveys have been carried out for this condition (see for example, Lawrence *et al.*, 1961).

Barker and Gardner (1974) discussed the distribution of Paget's disease and pointed out that as the mortality was low, variation in death rates would be influenced by many factors, including death certification practice. They did not have any data to demonstrate the extent of this.

Congenital abnormalities

Weatherall and Haskey (1976) showed that the major reduction in infant mortality over the past 100 years has left congenital malformations as the single largest cause of infant loss. They also emphasized that the number of children who died because of malformations gives no measure of the incidence, as there are major variations in the case fatality with type of malformation. They have no data on the actual validity of mortality statistics.

Certain causes of perinatal mortality

Stowman (1947–8) discussed the downward trend of infant mortality. He and a number of authors have drawn attention to the problem raised earlier (see section 2.2.1) of the variation in the registration of stillbirth and early neonatal deaths. This obviously influences the numerator and denominator in calculation of infant mortality. There are also other problems within the early neonatal period; some countries count first-day deaths as those occurring within 24 hours, and other countries those occurring on the same day as birth. Another variation is in defining neonatal; England and Wales count death in the first four weeks of life, while many nations include deaths in the first calendar month from birth. The numerator may be related to births in the year in which the death occurs, or may be 'related to births' which take into account alteration in the birth rate from month to month. (Stowman concluded that this was not warranted.)

Fedrick and Butler (1972) examined the causes of death of nearly 12,000 neonatal deaths in the UK in 1958. They found that there was the greatest accuracy for infants dying of anencephaly and rhesus incompatibility, and lowest agreement for major renal malformations and pulmonary lesions. They suggested that the prime reasons for these discrepancies was the quality of the statement made by the certifying doctor and the coding system. This latter point is supported by Clarke and Whitfield (1979).

A particular problem is the certification of 'cot deaths', where clinical appraisal and detailed investigation after death may still lead to inadequate explanation of the underlying pathology. This issue has been reviewed by a number of authors (see for example *Lancet*, 1975).

Accidents, poisonings, and violence

Turkel (1955) analysed 400 consecutive coroner's cases reported in San Francisco. Out of the 232 where death was presumed natural, autopsy showed that eight were violent deaths, while in six an unsuspected contagious cause was identified. For those in whom there was thought to be evidence of violence or trauma it was found that 51 were from natural causes at autopsy, while in 12 the influence of violence was unestablished.

Norman (1962) in a WHO report on road traffic accidents showed that there was variation in the definition of a 'fatal accident'. In Belgium, an accident was only so classified if death occurred at the site of the accident, while in the UK deaths occurring within 30 days following an accident were included. Such variation obviously influences the statistics. An advisory group (WHO, 1957) commented on the problems associated with accident mortality statistics. A special report was mentioned for France where it had been estimated that there were 4,000 road deaths annually reported by physicians' death certificates; when information was also collected from the police it was estimated that approximately 8,000 road fatalities had occurred. In Belgium, efforts were made to improve the quality of the death certificate; it was mentioned that often the physician would be aware of the lesions and clinical features, but unaware of the circumstances of the accident. Thus special attempts were made to acquire this information. England's system is rather different: all deaths from accident are reported to the coroner (providing these are so identified), and the cause of death is ascertained following inquest, with an autopsy where this is thought necessary.

Backett (1965) in a WHO report on home accidents showed that many countries do not classify their accidents by place of accident, thus creating problems in identifying the toll from home accidents. Because of this, special enquiries were made in the early 1960s to identify deaths from home accidents in member countries.

Schilling (1966) in a special examination of the hazards from trawler fishing showed that deaths at sea were not registered through the same system as deaths occurring on land amongst fishermen. Thus in the UK the Registrar General's published statistics of mortality rates for fishermen were grossly deficient for those causes of death occurring at sea.

Brooke and Atkinson (1974) in a WHO report on suicide and attempted suicide reviewed the systems for certifying suicide in 24 countries. With the exception of Switzerland, the majority of the countries used some form of legal assessment. There appeared to be little uniformity in who made the decision whether the death was from suicide, and whether this individual made the decision himself, by agreement with medical and chemical experts, or via the verdict of a jury. Even in a particular location, it seems that there were different ways of arriving at a decision. They suggested that both the quantity and depth of evidence on which decisions are based may also differ, both within and between countries. Autopsies might be carried out by pathologists with different backgrounds and training.

There were also different methods in the various countries for recording an 'open' verdict or amending a decision. The decision may include 'probably suicide' and statistical systems dealt with this in different ways. The report advocated the Swiss system of an anonymous confidential document for statistical purposes which was separate from the death certificate required for burial purposes. They suggested that this might alter the suicide rate in such countries as Ireland, where there were religious constraints on identifying suicide.

Oliver and Hetzel (1973) analysed trends in suicide in Australia; they suggested that 'accidental death due to ingestion of therapeutic substances' or 'undetermined deaths' in the 8th revision conceal a large number of suicides, constituting the major part of deaths from this cause.

2.3 Registration systems in different countries

A brief review of the development of registration was provided by a report of the Regional Office for Europe (1962). This showed that systematic vital registration in Europe had its origin in the parish register of christenings, weddings and burial that were maintained in Western Europe from the 15th century onwards. In most countries these registers were superseded early in the 19th century by civil registers of vital events kept for purely legal purposes. It was only in the 19th century that vital records were made into regular statistical publications. In all European countries registration of vital events is compulsory and based on a registration law. An informant is responsible for providing the appropriate information at local registration offices which are usually under the control of a central agency. Statistical compilation of the records is generally the function of a distinct statistical agency. A survey carried out in Europe (Regional Office for Europe, 1962) indicated that in 22 countries the central statistical service was responsible for mortality statistics, in two countries a statistical agency of the central health authority, and responsibility was shared in Turkey. Tables in the report indicate for each of the countries:

1. the level (local, regional, or central) from which inquiries are directed to the certifier in cases of doubt about the cause of death;
2. the supplementary information recorded about the fatal sequence, contributory causes of death, injury or pregnancy if appropriate, diagnostic evidence, details about the certifier;
3. the form used for reporting cause of death;
4. individuals responsible for certifying the cause of death in various circumstances;
5. the channels for statistical reporting on the cause of death.

The following notes have used a sequence of statistical handbooks published by the League of Nations (1924-30) as a source of background information and a number of other specific publications. They indicate the major differences in the various countries contributing towards the present volume.

2.3.1 Australia

Following a conference of state and commonwealth statisticians in 1906, the Bertillon classification was adopted for coding cause of death. Prior to 1966 the statistics excluded deaths occurring in full-blooded Aborigines (and they were not included in the population estimates used to calculate rates). A WHO report (1952d) showed that this applied back to 1901.

The place of usual residence was used for tabulation rather than the place of death, while the date of registration (rather than the date of death) was used. Usually there was only an interval of a few days; where this was over 10 years the deaths are excluded from the statistics.

2.3.2 Austria

The General Sanitary Law, 1870, made registration of deaths obligatory (League of Nations, 1925c). The declaration of the occurrence of death had to be accompanied by a certificate signed by a practitioner in attendance on the deceased in their last illness giving the fact and cause of death. In the 1920s, the primary and immediate cause of death were recorded in Latin terminology. In the absence of an attending doctor an official medical officer examined the body and if unable to certify the precise cause of death an autopsy may be sanctioned by superior administrative authority. The certificate was a public document.

Until 1937, the Ministry of Culture (including Health) was responsible for national mortality statistics; it then came under the Central Statistical Office. Initially a transscript was forwarded from the local registrar; since 1953 a photocopy has been sent. Coding is carried out in the central office by trained staff under medical supervision.

2.3.3 Belgium

Registration of deaths has been compulsory in Belgium since 1803 and it is usually done within 24 hours (League of Nations, 1924b). The registrar (or in large urban areas, the civil doctor) is responsible for examining the body to check the fact of death. There is no legal provision for the cause of death to be verified, but medical practitioners, and in their absence others having knowledge of the cause of death, are urged to provide this information. A circular from the Ministry of Interior of 1866 was still in force requesting this information in the 1920s. Generally, the attendant leaves a sealed note with the family which is handed in when the declaration is made of the fact of death. This document goes to the local Bureau of Statistics of Hygiene, which has the responsibility for consolidating the data for a period and forwarding these to the Central Statistical Bureau. The cause of death statistics are coded locally.

The present system for registration now follows WHO guidance, but a three-part form is used with the cause of death being recorded on section C; this is handled separately, to safeguard confidentiality. The civil code specifies those violent deaths which require specific police investigation. These causes do not correspond exactly to deaths classified as from external cause in the ICD.

2.3.4 Bulgaria

In the earlier part of the century mortality statistics were not published. When they began in 1927, they only related to towns, even so the proportion without medical certification of the cause of death was appreciable. A central system for coding and processing the data has been the responsibility of a section of the Central Statistical Office.

Certification was predominantly by medical practitioner by the 1960s, though it was permissible by paramedical personnel in remote areas of the country. Individual certificates are sent to the central statistic services for tabulation.

2.3.5 Canada

The foundation of the vital statistics system was in ecclesiastical registration dating from 1610 (League of Nations, 1930). The British North American Act of 1867 provided for registration of vital events; the Vital Statistics Act became effective on 1/1/1920 and compulsory registration was made obligatory. Quebec did not report to the national system until 1926. Qualified medical practitioners in attendance are required to notify the fact of death to the divisional registrar and a medical certificate must be signed by the attending doctor giving the cause of death. In the 1920s each medical practitioner was provided with suggestions on certifying death. If the certificate is thought to be incomplete it is returned to the certifier so the registrar can obtain additional information from relatives. If a coroner holds an inquest, he is responsible for providing the cause of death. The District Registrar copies the information and forwards this at monthly intervals to the Province Registrar.

The registration area covered the mainland from 1920, though deaths for Yukon and Northwest territories were not always provided in the same detail. They represent less than 0.5 per cent of the deaths in 1943. Newfoundland was included in the national data from 1949.

2.3.6 Chile

Civil registration existed from the beginning of the 20th century; births were registered separately from still births. The proportion of deaths having cause certified by doctors was initially low (e.g. 22 per cent in 1911), but this rose steadily during the first half century. There was major variation from one province to another.

The particulars are recorded at local level by civil registrars, who are responsible for recording and coding the information. This is sent weekly to the Central Statistics Institute, for processing.

2.3.7 Czechoslovakia

From 1919 to 1924 the Western Province followed the Austrian regulations and the Eastern Province, former Hungarian regulations (League of Nations, 1927a). At this time the distribution of doctors in the country was very uneven, with a very much higher proportion of uncertified deaths in Slovakia. A uniform system was introduced on 1 January 1925 with declaration of the fact of death required within 48 hours. It was the duty of the attending medical officer to complete the certificate of cause of death and provide this to the informant; this may be opened by the registrar during registration. Laymen were appointed post-mortem examiners in rural areas, but their certificate must be inspected and signed by the official physician. Since 1955 physicans must examine all persons. The local registrars provide consolidated data to the Federal Office for Statistics at monthly intervals; the data are coded and processed there.

2.3.8 Denmark

Data were provided for the urban population on mortality from 1876; from 1921, cause of death was registered throughout the country (League of Nations, 1926a). Usually this was certified by physicians. If a person was more than 2 km away from the nearest doctor, a layman could provide a certificate which had to be verified later by a physician. Outside Copenhagen the clergy were responsible for the system; inside Copenhagen the Municipal Office was responsible. Special certificates were used for reporting violent deaths. Even recently civil or medico-legal certificates could be issued in rural areas by lay coroners, though the majority of deaths are certified by physicians.

In 1966 a new confidential certificate was introduced. The data are processed by the statistics division of the National Health Service, where completed registers of deaths now exist, cross-indexed by date of birth, date of death, and locality.

2.3.9 Eire

Deaths had been registered compulsorily from 1864, with obligatory certification of the cause of death (League of Nations, 1929a). Following partition, an order was passed in 1923 confirming the vital statistics system, but there was no appreciable change in that for mortality. The functions of the Registrar General of Ireland were transferred to the Minister of France initially, in whose department the Registrar General was located. There was a system of local registrars who forwarded data at quarterly intervals to the Registrar General. Today, the Central Statistics Office handles the material on behalf of the Ministry of Health.

From 1960-7 the statistics excluded deaths in Eire of non-residents, but from 1968 they have been included. Before 1970, deaths were tabulated by year of registration, but then (to comply with UN requirements) year of occurrence was used. About 200 deaths annually are registered more than a year after occurrence; these are excluded from the statistics.

2.3.10 Finland

Deaths have been registered in Finland compulsorily since 1749; the declaration was made by local clergy using special forms, except in some suspected homicide cases, when an autopsy was required. In 1893 death certificates were introduced for use in the towns; in 1936 they became compulsory for the whole country, though in some special cases the death certificate could be issued by the police authorities.

The published statistics include individuals dying abroad, providing they were included in the population register at the time of death.

2.3.11 France

Registration of the fact of death has been compulsory since 1803, and initially the mayor at each locality was responsible (League of Nations, 1927b). The declaration of death was followed by personal examination of the corpse by the registrar or some other official. Initially, there was no legal enactment demanding certification of the cause of death, though this was advocated by the French Penal Code, which prescribed that the medical practitioner must not under any circumstances divulge information he required during the performance of his professional duties. From 1885, the information of the cause of death was provided for the main cities in France (population over 10,000); by 1906, the statistics covered the whole country but were not published by sex or age. From 1911, more detailed statistics were made available by age and from 1925, information was provided for the National Statistical System on cause of death by age and sex. In 1937, a circular made the declaration of cause of death confidential, and this was recorded on a separate sheet. From 1950, the information was classified by place of residence, and in 1955 the international certificate was introduced. All deaths are certified by either the treating doctor, or the Civilian Medical Officer.

In the early part of the century in rural districts certification was frequently by lay persons (in 1913, 27 per cent of all deaths in persons over 15 were certified by lay people, and 49 per cent in people dying in rural areas).

Deaths in the period 1940-5 exclude war deaths and also deaths among prisoners-of-war dying in Germany.

Aubenque *et al.* (1978) state that the certificate as issued is usually used to identify the cause of death. When there is evidence that the doctor has made an error of certification the rules of selection of the principle cause of death from the WHO regulations are followed.

When the cause of death is indeterminate, death may be without a certified cause, with a cause that is purely symptomatic, or whether death is attributed to senility. In the period 1925-36 about 25 to 30 per cent of deaths fell into these categories; this gradually decreased to 16 per cent in the period 1945-9 and 7 per cent in the period 1970-4. A method has been used to allocate the deaths where the cause was not specified in the same proportion as the distribution by known causes, taking age and sex into account.

2.3.12 Greece

In the 1920s, the local mayors and presidents of communes were responsible for compiling quarterly tables of deaths in their area. The cause of death was analysed, but was not always recorded precisely and was sometimes omitted.

Problems with the statistical services resulted in inability to publish mortality statistics in 1939-45.

The local administrations are still responsible for collecting the basic information. The informant must have a certificate from a physician or the body has to be visited by an official. The Department's Bureau of Statistics collate and verify the information and forward it to the National Statistical Office for coding and analysis.

2.3.13 Hungary

Compulsory registration has been in force since 1894. The physician fills in the Death Certificate which will be sent to the local Registrar. If the deceased was an inpatient in a hospital, the hospital administration fill in the Statistical Record of Death and this would be sent to the local Registrar together with the Death Certificate. If the person has died at home, it is the Registrar's responsibility to fill in the Statistical Record of Death. Then the local Registrar sends a copy of the Death Certificate and the Statistical Record of Death to the local branch of Central Statistical Office (this is generally at County level). This local branch mails a copy to the Central Statistical Office, Budapest, monthly.

2.3.14 Iceland

From 1911 to 1950, if death occurred within the vicinity of a doctor, he was responsible for providing a certificate of the cause of death (League of Nations, 1926,a). Elsewhere this was the pastor's duty. A yearly list of burials and causes of death was sent to the District Physician, who forwarded them to the Central Statistics Office. Since 1951, a medical certificate must be in the hand of the pastor before any burial can take place. The pastors forward these certificates every 3 months to the Statistical Bureau.

2.3.15 Italy

There have been problems with the national published data, because of variation in the metropolitan territory initially contributing the material, and the exclusion of 'zones of operation' during the two World Wars (World Health Organization, 1952e).

2.3.16 Japan

Minor changes were introduced in 1900 in the method of data collection. The mayors or headmen of cities, wards, towns, and villages prepared monthly returns which were forwarded to the Central Bureau of Statistics (of the Imperial Cabinet). Stillbirths were excluded from the deaths, and deaths were tabulated by the place of death.

From 1935, deaths occurring to residents temporarily overseas and foreigners dying in Japan were included in the statistics. Following the Second World War a Ministry of Welfare (subsequently Health and Welfare) was established; this became responsible for analysing the national mortality data from 1960.

A WHO report (1952) showed that for 1901-50 the data for Japan excluded Okinawa.

2.3.17 Netherlands

Death registration has been compulsory since 1815, with the communal registrar being the sole competent authority (League of Nations, 1924a) for recording details about the deceased and issuing a burial permit. All deaths are certified by medical practitioners. If death occurs without medical attendance, the body has to be seen by the local civil medical officer. The cause of death certificate is placed in a sealed envelope, which is not opened by the local Registrar but forwarded to the Central Bureau of Statistics for classification and compilation of statistics. The Division of Health Statistics is responsible for maintaining confidentiality of these data, which is greatly facilitated by the parallel system for handling the basic particulars about each death and the cause of death.

Only one cause of death was inserted on the certificate, until the recommended WHO form of certificate was adopted.

2.3.18 New Zealand

Initially, the registrar general was responsible for centrally processing mortality statistics for the country. Deaths have to be registered within three days in towns and seven days elsewhere. The annual statistics relate to deaths registered in the year (i.e. not by date of death).

In March 1949, a medical statistics branch was formed in the National Health Institute; this became responsible for the compilation and analysis of mortality and morbidity data. The death certificates were all forwarded monthly to the medical statistician for inspection and then processing.

From 1928 a system was introduced where certificates which lacked necessary diagnostic information were referred back to the certifying practitioner for further information. More recently, post-mortem reports, cancer registration records, or even summaries of hospital admission are used to check the diagnoses.

Though death certificates were not required by law from a medical practitioner for a death of a Maori, the standard of registration and certification steadily improved: in 1955 the annual mortality statistics provided tables combining deaths for European and Maoris for the first time.

2.3.19 Norway

All deaths must be notified to the Probate Court (in rural districts "lensmannen") in the municipality where the deaths occurred before burial can take place. In urban districts medical examination of the body is compulsory. If a medical certificate is not presented, "lensmannen" is obliged to issue a "certificate to the public health officer". The public health officer in the municipality where the death occurred is required to scrutinise the information of cause of death stated on the certificates. Initially cause of death statistics were provided by the local health officers, but from 1928 individual records were sent to the Central Bureau of Statistics.

A system exists for cross-checking all supplementary information. Deaths from cancer are matched against cancer registration particulars; additional information is also collected where there have been autopsies or deaths from violence. The particulars are reviewed by the medical consultant to the Central Bureau of Statistics.

2.3.20 Poland

The Central Statistical Office was set up in 1918 by official decree as an independent governmental organ, based on the administrative system formerly existing in the Polish provinces in Austria, Prussia and Russia. Registrars at local level were responsible for collecting the particulars for each person dying. The cause of death was certified where possible by physicians, though the development of the medical services in rural areas was limited. The Second World War also resulted in deliberate destruction of administrative systems and medical care provision.

Certification was predominantly by medical practitioner by the 1960s, though it was permissible by paramedical personnel in remote areas of the country. Individual certificates are sent to the Central Statistical Services for tabulation.

2.3.21 Portugal

Registration has been in force since 1886 and became compulsory in 1911 (League of Nations, 1926b). The attending medical practitioner is required by law to submit a certificate of the cause of death (both primary and contributory conditions). The certifying practitioner is responsible for coding the cause of the death at the time of completion of the certificate. In the absence of an attending practitioner, the local medical officer of health or appointed doctor acts in that capacity to provide a 'probable' cause of death. At monthly intervals the data are transcribed by the local medical officers and forwarded via the District Offices to the Statistical Division at the Department of Health in Lisbon.

This system changed in 1929 with data collection by the Civil Registration Offices; material are sent weekly to the Central Statistical Office, which is responsible for processing, tabulation, and publication of statistics.

2.3.22 Romania

Mortality statistics have been published since 1930, relying on local registration and where possible, medical certification of the cause of death. The Regional Office for Europe (1962) states that certification was, without exception, made by physicians; the data are forwarded to the Central Statistical Services for tabulation.

2.3.23 Spain

Death registration has been compulsory since 1871 League of Nations, 1925b). Since 1874, the attending medical practitioner has been required to submit a death certificate giving the cause of death. For sudden and accidental deaths a magistrate orders an autopsy by the judicial medical officer, which is usually carried out in the presence of another doctor. When ill-defined causes of death are recorded the central authorities in Madrid may correspond with the certifying physician to identify further information. The certificates are forwarded via the statistical bureau in the province with summaries going to the Central Statistical Office. From 1901-71 the cause of death has been coded at province level, since 1972 central coding has occurred.

2.3.24 Sweden

Since 1831 clergy have had to inscribe the cause of death in epidemics and for certain other causes (League of Nations, 1926a). In towns it became the medical officer's duty to provide a certificate which was then entered into the register by clergy. In 1891, arrangements were made to deal with the deaths occurring without medical attendance. Since then practically all deaths in urban areas have a stated cause quoted. The provincial medical officer is responsible for reviewing the causes of death transcribed by the pastor and classifying these as either proved or surmised.

A WHO report (1952f) showed that in northern Sweden an appreciable proportion of certificates were still issued by the parsons without medical information. A doctor will complete the certificate if they have attended the patient during their last illness or examined the body after death; otherwise the clergy are responsible, though they may discuss the probable cause of death with a doctor (and record this on the certificate). When the Central Bureau code the underlying cause of death they distinguish those which are thought reliable from probable.

The annual statistics include persons registered as resident and those who die abroad; if notification of death occurs after the deadline for processing, they are excluded from the figures. The WHO guidelines were adopted in 1949 and a new form for medical certification was introduced in 1971.

2.3.25 Switzerland

Uniform registration throughout the country was decreed in 1874 (League of Nations, 1928). The entry must mention the cause of death according to that provided on the death certificate either from the attending physician, or in the absence of treatment, the doctor specifically called in to verify the fact of death. A confidential death system was introduced in 1900, with improvement in the quality of the data. The doctor is responsible for sending this information direct to the Central Statistical Office. For violent deaths the information goes to the medical jurist to complete.

The WHO guidelines were adopted in 1948. This created some difficulty, due to the new approach to selection of the underlying cause of death.

2.3.26 Turkey

Mortality data in Turkey are collected by the State Institute of Statistics; they have been available since 1931. Until the end of 1949, these statistics were collected from all provincial centres and published for selected 'important' provinces. Until 1950, they were collected and published for all province centres; since 1957 mortality data include all province and district centres. (A province centre is a city with or without surrounding rural area, a district centre is a town surrounded by villages and rural areas.)

When a death occurs in a province or district centre, a 'burial permit' is completed. Its medical information part is completed by a doctor and a copy of the 'burial permit' is sent to the State Institute of Statistics (by Directorates of Health in provincial centres; and from the Office of Medical Officer of Health in district centres). The mortality statistics derived from these data are issued by the Institute.

2.3.37 UK – England and Wales

Since 1839, the nearest relative or other informant has had the legal duty to declare the death to the registrar for the district in which the death occurred. The informant is usually responsible for obtaining the cause of death certificate from the attending physician and presenting this to the local registrar. This information has to be provided by Act of 1874 (it was initially an optional provision). Persons found dead, or violent deaths, are reported to the coroner who may or may not order an autopsy or hold an inquest before issuing a certificate of the cause of death (League of Nations, 1925a).

When an ambiguous or unsatisfactory cause of death is provided an inquiry is made to the certifying practitioner. At the beginning of the century the certificate asked for the primary and secondary (contributory) cause of death; this was expanded and was the forerunner of the WHO model certificate. The data are coded centrally (though deaths are registered in the district in which they occur and are coded to the district of residence).

2.3.28 UK – Northern Ireland

By 1864 a system existed comparable to that in England

and Wales. After partition of Ireland in 1922 the Registrar General's Office was established in Belfast and became responsible for registration throughout Northern Ireland.

2.3.29 UK – Scotland

Registration of death has been compulsory since 1855 (League of Nations, 1929b). The certification of the cause of death was made obligatory under the same legislation. This certificate is not confidential and may be submitted by hand by the relative to the registrar. The local registrars send details weekly to the Central Office.

2.3.30 USA

The Bureau of the Census began the annual collection of mortality statistics in 1900 with 10 participating states, the District of Columbia and a number of cities in non-registration states. The 11 jurisdictions were in the north-eastern US and contained 26.2 per cent of the population; the proportion of urban residents was considerably higher than in the country as a whole. By 1910, the registration states had increased to 51.4 per cent of the total population, but only 12.3 per cent of the non-white population. Coverage had risen to 80.9 per cent of the total and 66.1 per cent of the non-white populations by 1920. In 1933 the entire US was included.

The District Registrar collects the information on each death and sends it to the State Health Department where it is checked. Copies are then forwarded to the National Centre for Health Statistics. In cooperation with the States, the National Centre is responsible for central processing of mortality statistics. Standard death certificates have been used since the introduction of registration areas; these have been periodically revised, the last change was in 1978.

In the 1950s there was still considerable variation from state to state in the percentage of deaths with ill-defined or unknown cause (from 0.1 per cent to 10 per cent).

2.3.31 Yugoslavia

This uses a decentralized coding system in the six constituent republics of Yugoslavia. No further details have been provided.

2.4 Indicators of validity of mortality statistics

It has been suggested that there are four factors that influence and reflect upon the validity of cause of death mortality statistics. These are the number of doctors per 10,000 population, the proportion of the population in urban and rural areas, the percentage of certificates signed by medical practitioners, and the percentage of certificates coded to ill-defined conditions.

Each of these is now briefly discussed and tables are provided, indicating the trend in these parameters during the present century for all the countries involved in this study.

2.4.1 Number of doctors per 10,000 population

It is self-evident that the ratio of doctors to the population will be related to the provision of medical care, and probably the degree of investigation prior to certification of death. When the number of doctors per 10,000 is very low, there may be an increasing proportion of certificates that are not signed by medically qualified persons. WHO has collected a considerable amount of data on world trends in medical manpower. A review article (Doan, 1974) has provided a comprehensive review of the data from 1950–70, based on a WHO questionnaire on health manpower sent annually to member countries.

A strict definition of 'medically qualified' was used (all graduates of a medical school or faculty actually working in the country in any medical field – practice, teaching, administration, research or laboratory). However, study of the data revealed the defectiveness of the information for a number of countries; some reported those individuals on the medical register (not all of whom would be in practice, and some of them might be working abroad); others identified only personnel in government services or personnel working in hospitals.

The trend in the doctor-population ratio is not as important as the structural trend in the medical profession that had occurred at the same time; variation by age, sex, sector of activity, and geographic location has far-reaching effects on medical care. The concentration of medical manpower in the urban areas may have been taking place in a number of countries at a faster rate than the concentration of the rest of the population.

Another WHO contribution (Gilliand and Galland, 1977) suggests that 'medical density' was probably the most reliable of the sets of information collected by WHO, though the definition of physician varied. Both Gilliand and Gallano (1977) and Estok (1978) have emphasized the caution required in interpreting available statistics for different countries.

Table 2.1 provides statistics on the ratio of doctor to population at various times in the present century. The footnotes of this table indicate some of the problems in interpreting these statistics.

2.4.2 Proportion of the population in rural areas

A number of authors have discussed the relative advantage of mortality rates in rural areas compared with urban ones (e.g. Farr, 1843; Greenwood, 1936; Martin, 1956). However, these authors do not comment on the impact of the provision of services upon the accuracy of mortality rates by cause in urban and rural areas. Sub-section 2.4.1 indicated that the proportion of doctors in urban areas may be different to the proportion of population in urban areas. In addition, there may be major variation in the provision of diagnostic facilities which would readily influence the validity of the mortality statistics. A WHO report (1967b) showed that the proportion of autopsies carried out in various localities in four countries increased with the size of the population in these localities. For example, in Czechoslovakia 60 per cent of people dying in relatively small aggregations of population had autopsy, 71 per cent in medium size aggregations had autopsy, and 87 per cent in large urban aggregations had autopsy. Similar trends were shown for England and Wales, Finland, and Sweden.

Federici *et al.* (1976) showed that there are a considerable number of difficulties in studying urban/rural mortality differentials and their variation over time. Specific problems with mortality statistics are:

1. the urban and rural localities are classified on the basis of criteria that vary from country to country and that can change over time;
2. in many countries the data are given for place of death and not place of residence.

These authors pointed out that it is difficult to arrive at a definition of categories of urban and rural, and that such a definition does not lend itself to statistical recording. The categories used can change from time to time as structural changes occur in society. Industrialization of countries does not just involve shifting the population from small to large towns and from less populated to intensely populated areas; social, cultural, and economic structures of the whole population may change. Adoption of one criteria rather than another may change the meaning of urban and rural, and greatly alter the content of any statistics. This will seriously prejudice the comparability of published material.

Three United Nations Reports (1952b, 1960 and 1971) have been used as sources of data; each warns of the limitations of the available data for different countries. Table 2.2 presents statistics from these and other sources. The footnotes indicate the main qualifications in attempting to interpret these statistics.

2.4.3 Percentage of certificates issued by medical practitioners

Reference has already been made in section 2.3 that not all certificates are provided by medical practitioners. In many countries it is quite usual to have certificates issued by lay persons in certain circumstances; the degree of checking of the cause of death data will vary from country to country. Table 2.3 gives statistics indicating the percentage of certificates signed by medical practitioners. However, there are problems of comparability of the data. For example, in England and Wales deaths from violent causes are reported to the coroner and he only issues the cause of death after an inquest. A simple examination of the percentage of certificates not issued by medical practitioners may be misleading, as deaths from violence will have been carefully imvestigated and in many cases the cause of death will only have been identified after an autopsy is performed. It is the proportion of the 'uncertified' of deaths that are of real interest as an indication of the validity of the data. Published statistics do not usually differentiate between certificates provided by coroners, and other forms of lay certification. An indication of the way in which the percentage not certified by medical practitioners may be misleading is the statistics for England and Wales in 1965: 81.3 per cent of all certificates were issued by medical physicans; 18.5 per cent were issued by coroners, and only 0.2 per cent were uncertified. The data thus indicate that Table C requires careful interpretation; in particular, the information provided in sub-sections 2.3.1–2.3.31 requires consideration.

2.4.4 The percentage of all certificates from ill-defined causes

The ICD has always allowed for causes that are 'ill-defined'. The actual designation of the various rubrics has changed over time, but are usually thought to include deaths from unknown causes, ill-defined causes, and from senility. When the proportion of deaths ascribed to these rubrics are large and then decrease, there will automatically be an increase in specific causes. A WHO report (1952c) showed that the percentage assigned to these rubrics diminished considerably during the first half of the 20th century for many countries – this may be due to better certification. It is not possible to say what proportion of causes would have been transferred from the general rubrics to specific ones at any given time if the quality of data had been better.

The report suggested that one of the major contributing factors to the rise in recorded mortality from malignant neoplasms might be the gradual transfer from the ill-defined categories. Another WHO report (1955e), suggested that a general indication of the degree of perfection of diagnosis of cause of death is given by variation in the numerical importance of the rubrics for senility and ill-defined causes. To explore this issue, the report presented some statistics (in 1936 it used the categories senility, unspecified, and ill-defined causes; for the post-war years the rubrics 'senility' without mention of psychoses, ill-defined, and unknown causes were used).

Preston *et al.* (1972) drew attention to the important trend in the declining proportion of deaths assigned to ill-defined and unknown causes. They suggested that below the age of 65 the bias from this trend was likely to be small; for example, in England and Wales this had only altered from 1.8 per cent in the period 1848–72, to 0 per cent in 1956–7. However, over the age of 65 the picture is much less satisfactory. They also suggest that for certain countries the problem was more marked even in younger people. Preston (1976) used a number of statistical techniques to examine the mortality patterns of various countries by cause. He suggested that there was consistent and compelling statistical evidence that most of the decline from other and unknown causes should be attributed to transfer to specific cardiovascular disease.

Preston argued that poor diagnostic coding practices had often obscured the important decline from this cause. After making adjustments to the recorded level of mortality from other and unknown causes, he suggested that cardiovascular disease had had a mortality decline equivalent to that of the respiratory diseases. This suggestion is somewhat at variance to the other authors who have studied this issue.

There are rather different interpretations when looking at the proportion of deaths ascribed to ill-defined causes, and the absolute numbers or rates for this category. Also, when examining the trend over time it is difficult to distinguish how much of the variation in ill-defined categories of death are due to deaths becoming more precisely diagnosed and certified; those being certified to more specific categories, in the absence of clear medical information (i.e. spurious diagnostic accuracy); and decrease due to an actual diminution of the numbers of individuals genuinely dying from ill-defined conditions.

Table 2.4 provides some statistics of the percentage of deaths from all causes occurring in the 'ill-defined categories'.

References

Abramson, J.H., Sacks, M.I., and Cahana, E. (1971). Death certificate data as an indication of the presence of certain common diseases at death. *J. Chron. Dis.*, **24**, 417–31.

Acheson, E.D. (1972). The epidemiology of multiple sclerosis in *Multiple Sclerosis, A Reappraisal*, pp. 3–80 (eds. D. McAlpine, E.C. Lumsden and E.D. Acheson) 2nd edn. Churchill Livingstone, Edinburgh.

Acheson, R.M. (1960). Mortality from cerebrovascular accidents and hypertension in the Republic of Ireland. *Brit. J. Prev. Soc. Med.*, **14**, 139–47.

Acheson, R.M., Nefzger, M.D. and Heyman, A. (1973). Mortality from stroke among veterans in Georgia and 5 Western states. *J. Chron. Dis.*, **26**, 405-15.

Acheson, R. and Sanderson, C. (1978). Strokes: social class and geography. *Population Trends*, **12**, 13–17.

Adelstein, A.M. (1978). Death certification and epidemiological research. *Brit. Med. J.*, **2**, 1229-30.

Agranoff, B.W. and Goldberg, D. (1974). Diet and the geographical distribution of multiple sclerosis. *Lancet*, **2**, 1061-6.

Alderson, M.R. (1965). The accuracy of certification of death, and the classification of the underlying cause of death from the death certification (MD thesis, London University).

—— (1974). *Central Government Routine Health Statistics. Vol. 2 Review of UK Statistical Sources* (ed. W.F. Maunder), Heinemann, London.

Alderson, M.R. and Donnan, S. (1978). Hysterectomy rates and their influence upon mortality from carcinoma of the cervix. *J. Epidem. Comm. Hlth.*, **32**, 175–7.

Anderson, T.W. and Le Riche, W.H. (1970). Ischaemic heart disease and sudden death, 1901-61. *Brit. J. Prev. Soc. Med.*, **24**, 1-9.

Angtist, A. (1958). Certified cause of death – analysis and recommendations. *J. Amer. Med. Assoc.*, **166**, 2148–53.

Ash, J.E. (1915). The pathology of mistaken diagnoses in a hospital for advanced tuberculosis. *J. Amer. Med. Assoc.*, **64**, 11-15.

Aubenque, M., Damiani, P. and DeRuffe, L. (1978). La mortalité per cause en France de 1925 a 1974. *J. de la Societé de Statistique de Paris.*, **3**, 1–20.

Backett, E.M. (1965). Domestic accidents, Public Health Papers No. 26. World Health Organization, Geneva.

Barker, D.J.P. and Gardner, M.J. (1974). Distribution of Paget's disease in England, Wales and Scotland and a possible relationship with Vitamin D deficiency in childhood. *Brit. J. Prev. Soc. Med.*, **28**, 226-32.

Beadenkopf, W.G., Polan, A.K., Marks, R.U. and Tornatore, L.M. (1965). Some demographic characteristics of an autopsied population. *J. Chron. Dis.*, **18**, 333-51.

Benjamin, B. (1968). *Health and Vital Statistics*. Allen and Unwin, London.

Benjamin, B. and Carrier, N.H. (1954). An evaluation of the quality of demographic statistics in England and Wales in Vol. 4 *Proceedings of the World Population Conference*, pp. 37--61, United Nations, New York.

Beral, V. (1976). Cardiovascular-disease mortality trends and oral contraceptive use in young women. *Lancet*, **2**, 1047-52.

—— (1979). Reproductive mortality. *Brit. Med. J.*, **2**, 632-4.

Bourke, G.H. and Hall, M.A. (1968). A study of some certified causes of death and age of the certifying doctor. *J. Irish Med. Assoc.*, **61**, 115-22.

Brodrick, N. (1971). Report of the committee on death certification and coroners. Cmnd 4810. HMSO, London.

Bronte-Stewart, B. and Pickering, G.W. (1959). Cardiovascular diseases in *Medical Surveys and Clinical Trials* (ed. L.J. Witts), pp. 238-60, Oxford University Press, London.

Brooke, E.M. and Atkinson, M. (1974). Ascertainment of deaths from suicide in *Suicide and Attempted Suicide: Public Health Papers No. 58*, pp. 15-70. World Health Organization, Geneva.

Brown, E.L. and Knox, E.G. (1972). Epidemiological approach to Parkinson's disease. *Lancet*, **1**, 974-6.

Bunle, H. (1954). *Le mouvement natural de la population dans le monde de 1906 à 1936*. L'institut National d'etudes Demographiques, Paris.

Nuren, G.H. van (1939). Some things you can't prove by mortality statistics. *US Bureau of Census: Vital Statistics Special Reports*, **12**, 195-210.

Cabot, R.C. (1912). Diagnostic pitfalls identified during a study of 3,000 autopsies. *J. Amer. Med. Assoc.*, **59**, 2295-8.

Cameron, H.M., McGoogan, E,, Clarke, J. and Wilson, B.A. (1977). Trends in hospital necropsy rates: Scotland 1961-74. *Brit. Med. J.*, **1**, 1577-80.

Clarke, C. and Whitfield, A.G.W. (1978). Death certification and epidemiological research. *Brit. Med. J.*, **2**, 1063-5.

Clarke, C. and Whitfield, A.G.W. (1979). Deaths from rhesus haemolytic disease in England and Wales in 1977; accuracy of records and assessment of anti-D prophylaxis. *Brit. Med. J.*, **1**, 1665-9.

Clayton, D.G., Taylor, D. and Shaper, A.G. (1977). Trends in heart disease in England and Wales, 1950-1973. *Health Trends*, **9**, 1-6.

Coale, A.J. (1955). The population of the United States in 1950 classified by age, sex, and color – a revision of census figures. *J. Amer. Stat. Assoc.*, **50**, 16-54.

Cohen, J. and Steinitz, R. (1969). Underlying and contributory causes of death of adult males in two districts. *J. Chron. Dis.*, **22**, 17-24.

Cooper, R., Stamler, J., Dyer, A. and Garside, D. (1978). The decline in mortality from coronary heart disease, USA, 1968-1975. *J. Chron. Dis.*, **31**, 709-20.

Dean, G. (1979). *Annual Report 1978*, Medico-social research Board, Dublin.

Deporte, J.V. (1941). Mortality statistics and the physician. *Amer. J. Publ. Hlth.*, **31**, 1051-6.

Deutscher, S., Robertson, W.B.C. and Smith, A.P. (1971). Age and sex trends in ischaemic heart disease, cerebrovascular disease, hypertension, and diabetes. *Brit. J. Prev. Soc. Med.*, **25**, 84-93.

Doan, B.D.H. (1974). World trends in medical power, 1950-70. *World Hlth Stats. Rep.*, **27**, 84-108.

Dorn, H.F. and Horn, J.I. (1941). The reliability of certificates of death from cancer. *Amer. J. Hyg.*, **34**, 12-23.

Dunn, H.L. (1949). The doctor and the new international list of diseases and causes of death. *J. Amer. Med. Assoc.*, **140**, 520-2.

Dunn, H.L. (1955). 1956 revisions of standard birth and death certificates. *J. Amer. Med. Assoc.*, **159**, 1184-6.

Dunn, H.L. and Schakley, W. (1944). Comparison of cause-of-death assignments by the 1929 and 1938 Revisions of the International Lists: Deaths in the United States, 1940. United States, Bureau of the Census. Vital Statistics – Special Reports *19*: 155-277.

Duvoisin, R.C. and Yahr, M.D. (1972). Epidemiological approach to Parkinson's disease. *Lancet*, **1**, 1400-1.

Ehrlich, D., Li-Sik, M. and Modan, B. (1975). Some factors affecting the accuracy of cancer diagnosis. *J. Chron. Dis.*, **28**, 359-64.

Estok, S. (1978). Quality and uniformity of health manpower statistics. *World Hlth. Stats. Rep.*, **31**, 134-42.

Farr, W. (1843). Causes of the high mortality in town districts, in *5th Annual Report of the Registrar General of Births, Marriages and Deaths in England*, pp. 406-35. HMSO, London.

—— (1854). Letter to the Registrar General in *13th Annual Report of the Registrar General of Births, Deaths and Marriages in England*, p. 129. HMSO, London.

Federici, N. de Sarno Prignano, A., Pasquali, P., Cariani, G. and Natale, M. (1976). Urban/rural differences in mortality, 1950-70. *World Hlth. Stats. Rep.*, **29**, 249-378.

Federick, J. and Butler, N.R. (1972). Accuracy of registered causes of neonatal deaths in 1958. *Brit. J. Prev. Soc. Med.*, **26**, 101-5.

Florey, C. du V. and Kessner, D.M. (1968). Mortality

trends of renal disease. *Lancet*, **1**, 817.

Florey, C. du V., Senter, M.G. and Acheson, R.M. (1969). A study of the validity of the diagnosis of stroke in mortality data. *Amer. J. Epidem.*, **89**, 15-24.

Gau, G. (1977). The ultimate audit. *Brit. Med. J.*, **1**, 1580-2.

Gilliam, A.G. (1955). Trends of mortality attributed to carcinoma of the lung. *Cancer*, **8**, 1130-6.

Gilliand, P. and Gallano, R. (1977). Outline on international comparison of public health, based on data collected by the World Health Organization. *World Hlth Stats. Rep.*, **30**, 227-42.

Gordon, I. (1959). The certification of death, with special reference to coronary disease (III). *Medical Officer*, **102**, 237-8.

—— (1967). The value of death certification (V). *Medical Officer*, **117**, 67-70.

Greenwald, I. (1965). The significance of the increased mortality from exophthalmic goitre in Australia after 1923. *Med. J. Aust.*, **1**, 836-7.

—— (1967). Studies of exophthalmic goitre, I, II, III. *J. Chron. Dis.*, **20**, 255-68.

—— (1968). Studies of exophthalmic goitre IV: Great Britain 1919-64. *J. Chron. Dis.*, **21**, 483-91.

—— (1970). Studies of exophthalmic goitre, V. *J. Chron. Dis.*, 22, 811-17.

—— (1973). Studies of exophthalmic goitre, VI. *J. Chron. Dis.*, **26**, 719-36.

Greenwood, M. (1936). English death rates, past, present and future. *J. Roy. Stat. Soc.*, **99**, 674-707.

—— (1948). *Medical Statistics from Graunt to Farr*. Cambridge University Press, Cambridge.

Greenwood, M. and Wood, F. (1914). On changes in the recorded mortality from cancer and their possible interpretations. *Proc. Roy. Soc. Med.*, **7**, 119-52.

Griffith, W.G. (1978). Death certificates and epidemiological research. *Brit. Med. J.*, **2**, 1366.

Guberan, E. (1979). Surprising decline of cardiovascular mortality in Switzerland: 1951-76. *J. Epid. Comm. Hlth.*, **33**, 114-20.

Hamtoft, H. and Mosbech, J. (1968). Mortality trends of renal diseases. *Lancet*, **1**, 751-2.

Hansen, H. and Susser, M. (1971). Historic trends in deaths from chronic kidney disease in the United States and Britain. *Amer. J. Epid.*, **93**, 413-24.

Hare, E.H. (1972). Conquest of General Paralysis. *Brit. Med. J.*, **2**, 418.

Heasman, M.A. (1962). Accuracy of death certification. *Proc. Roy. Soc. Med.*, **55**, 733-40.

Heasman, M.A. and Lipworth, L. (1966). Accuracy of certification of cause of death. *General Register Office* Studies on Medical and Population Subjects No. 20. HMSO, London.

Herrick, J.B. (1912). Clinical features of sudden obstruction of the coronary arteries. *J. Amer. Med. Assoc.*, **59**, 2015-20.

Hewitt, D. (1956). Mortality in the London boroughs, 1950-52 with special reference to respiratory disease. *Brit. J. Prev. Soc. Med.*, **10**, 45-57.

Horwitz, O. and Palmer, C.E. (1964). Epidemiological basis of tuberculosis eradication. *Bull. Wld. Hlth. Org.*, **30**, 609-21.

Huber, M. (1926). Report on methods of issuing certificates of death and its causes. *Bull. Inst. Int. Statist.*, **22**, 23-66.

Inman, W.H.W. and Adelstein, A.M. (1969). Rise and fall of asthma mortality in England and Wales in relation to use of pressurised aerosols. *Lancet*, **2**, 279-85.

Isotalo, A. (1960). Medico-legal aspects of medical certification of cause of death. *Bull. Wld. Hlth. Org.*, **23**, 811-811-14.

Jackson, H. (1896). An examination of one hundred cases of disease of the heart collected from the autopsy records Boston City Hospital. *Boston Med. Surg. J.*, **134**, 501-5.

Jacobson, P.H. (1948). Relative efficiency of open and confidential method of reporting cause of death. *Amer. J. Publ. Hlth.*, **38**, 789-807.

James, G., Patton, R.E. and Heslin, A.S. (1955). Accuracy of cause of death statements on death certificates. *Publ. Hlth. Rep. (Wash.)*, **70**, 39-51.

Journal of American Medical Association (1914). Clinical diagnosis and necropsy findings in Bellevue. *J. Amer. Med. Assoc.*, **62**, 1279-80.

Journal of American Medical Association (1965). What about the autopsy? *J. Amer. Med. Assoc.*, **193**, 172-3.

Kennaway, N.M. and Kennaway, E.L. (1936). A study of the incidence of cancer of the lung and larynx. *J. Hyg. (Camb.)*, **36**, 236-67.

Kessner, D.M. and Florey, C. du V. (1967). Mortality trends for acute and chronic nephritis and infections of the kidney. *Lancet*, **2**, 979-82.

Krueger, D.E., Williams, J.L., Paffenbarger, R.S. (1967). Trends in death rates from cerebrovascular disease in Memphis, Tennessee, 1920-1960. *J. Chron. Dis.*, **20**, 129-37.

Kuller, L., Lilienfeld, A. and Fisher, R. (1967). Quality of death certificate diagnosis of arteriosclerotic heart disease. *Public Hlth. Report*, **82**, 339-46.

Kurland, L.T. and Moriyama, I.M. (1951). Certification of multiple sclerosis as a cause of death. *J. Amer. Med. Assoc.*, **145**, 725-8.

Laënnec, R.Y.H. (1819). *A treatise on the diseases of the chest and on medical auscultation*. (trans: J. Forbes,

1830), Wood, New York.

Lambert, P.M. (1973). Recent trends in meningococcal infection. *Community Med.,* **129**, 279-81.

—— (1975). Hypertensive disease, study on mortality. *Wld. Hlth. Stat. Rep.,* **28**, 401-17.

Lancet (1973). Endemic nephropathy. *Lancet,* **1**, 472.

Larsson, T. (1967). Mortality from cerebrovascular disease. in *Thule International Symposia on Stroke* (eds. A. Engel and T. Larsson), pp. 15-40. Nordiska Bokhandelns, Stockholm.

Lawrence, J.S., Laine, V.A.I. and de Graaff, R. (1961). The epidemiology of Rheumatoid Arthritis in Northern Europe. *Proc. Roy. Soc. Med.,* **54**, 454-62.

League of Nations (1924a), *Kingdom of Netherlands – Statistical Handbook No. 1*, League of Nations Organization, Geneva.

—— (1924b). *Kingdom of Belgium – Statistical Handbook No. 2*, League of Nations Health Organization, Geneva.

—— (1925a). *England and Wales – Statistical Handbook No. 3*, League of Nations Health Organization, Geneva.

—— (1925b). *Kingdom of Spain – Statistical Handbook No. 4*, League of Nations Health Organization, Geneva.

—— (1925c). *Republic of Austria – Statistical Handbook No. 5*, League of Nations Health Organization, Geneva.

—— (1926a). *Scandinavian Countries and Baltic Republics – Statistical Handbook No. 6*, League of Nations Health Organization, Geneva.

—— (1926b). *Republic of Portugal – Statistical Handbook No. 7*, League of Nations Health Organization, Geneva.

—— (1927a). *Republic of Czechoslovakia – Statistical Handbook No. 8*, League of Nations Health Organization, Geneva.

—— (1927b). *French Republic – Statistical Handbook No. 9*, League of Nations Health Organization, Geneva.

—— (1927c). *Hungary – Statistical Handbook No. 10*, League of Nations Health Organization, Geneva.

—— (1928). *Switzerland – Statistical Handbook No. 12*, League of Nations Health Organization, Geneva.

—— (1929a). *Ireland – Statistical Handbook No. 11*, League of Nations Health Organization, Geneva.

—— (1929b). *Scotland – Statistical Handbook No. 13*, League of Nations Health Organization, Geneva.

—— (1930). *Canada – Statistical Handbook No. 14*, League of Nations Health Organization, Geneva.

Lewis, J.S. (1915). Diagnoses and certificates of death. *J. Amer. Med. Assoc.,* **65**, 1441-7.

Lilienfeld, A.M., Levin, M.L. and Kessler, I.I. (1972). *Cancer in the United States*, Harvard University Press, Cambridge, Mass.

Logan, W.P.O. (1963). *Epidemiological studies of rheumatoid arthritis*, EURO-213. 2/7. WHO Regional Office for Europe, Copenhagen.

MacDonald, E.J. (1938). Accuracy of the cancer death records. *Amer. J. Publ. Hlth.,* **28**, 818-24.

McKenzie, A. (1956). Diagnosis of cancer of lung and stomach. *Brit. Med. J.,* **2**, 204-7.

McMichael, J. (1979). French wine and death certificates. *Lancet,* **1**, 1186-7.

Major, R.H. (1965). *Classic descriptions of disease*, 3rd edn. Thomas, Springfield.

—— (1969). National chronic respiratory disease mortality study. *J. Chron. Dis.,* **21**, 737-48.

Martin, J.P. (1972). Conquest of general paralysis. *Brit. Med. J.,* **3**, 159-60.

Martin, W.J. (1956). A study of sex, age, and regional differences in the advantage of rural over urban mortality. *Brit. J. Prev. Soc. Med.,* **10**, 88-91.

Mason, A.S., Meade, T.W., Lee, J.A.H. and Morris, J.N. (1968). Epidemiological and clinical picture of Addison's disease. *Lancet,* **2**, 744-7.

Meade, T.W., Arie, T.H.D., Brewis, M., Bond, D.J. and Morgan, J.N. (1968). Recent history of ischaemic heart disease and duodenal ulcer in doctors. *Brit. Med. J.,* **3**, 701-4.

Mitchell, R.A., Maisel, J.C., Dart, G.A. and Silvers, G.W. (1971). The accuracy of the death certificate in reporting cause of death in adults. *Amer. Rev. Resp. Dis.,* **101**, 844-50.

Moriyama, I.M. (1956). Development of the present concept of cause of death. *Amer. J. Publ. Hlth.,* **46**, 436-41.

—— (1966). The eighth revision of the International Classification of Diseases. *Amer. J. Publ. Hlth.,* **56**, 1277-80.

Moriyama, I.M., Baum, W.S., Haenszel, W.M., Mattison, B.F. (1958). Inquiry into diagnostic evidence supporting medical certifications of death. *Amer. J. Publ. Hlth.,* **48**, 1376-87.

Moriyama, I.M. Dawber, T.R. and Kannel, W.B. (1966). Evaluation of diagnostic information supporting medical certification of deaths from cardiovascular disease in epidemiological approaches to the study of cancer and other chronic diseases. National Cancer Institute (Bethesda) US Department of Health, Education and Welfare, Washington DC. Monograph 19.

Morris, J.N. and Titmuss, R.M. (1944). Epidemiology of peptic ulcer – vital statistics. *Lancet,* **2**, 841-5.

Netsky, M.G. and Miyaji, T. (1976). Prevalence of cerebral haemorrhage and thrombosis in Japan: study of the major causes of death. *J. Chron. Dis.,* **29**, 711-21.

Newhouse, M.L. and Wagner, J.C. (1969). Validation of death certificates in asbestos workers. *Brit. J. Indust. Med.*, **26**, 302-7.

Norman, L.G. (1962). *Road traffic accidents.* Public Health Papers No. 12. World Health Organization, Geneva.

Office of Health Economics (1963). *Pneumonia in decline*. Office of Health Economics, London.

Oliver, R.G. and Hetzel, B.S. (1973). An analysis of recent trends in suicide rates in Australia. *Int. J. Epidem.*, **2**, 91-101.

Pascua, M. (1947-8). Diversity of stillbirth definitions and some statistical repercussions. *Epidemiological and Vital Statistics Report,* **1**, 210-22.

—— (1949). Evolution of mortality in Europe during the 20th century. *Epidemiological and Vital Statistics Report,* **2**, 64-80.

—— (1950). Evolution of mortality in Europe during the 20th century. *Epidemiological and Vital Statistics Report,* **3**, 30-62.

Pohlen, K. and Emerson, H. (1942). Errors in clinical statements of causes of death. *Amer. J. Publ. Hlth.*, **32**, 251-60.

—— and —— (1943). Errors in clinical statements of causes of death. *Amer. J. Publ. Hlth.*, **33**, 505-16.

Pole, D.J., McCall, M.G., Reader, R. and Woodings, T. (1977). Incidence and mortality of acute myocardial infarctions in Perth, Western Australia. *J. Chron. Dis.*, **30**, 19-27.

Preston, S.H. (1976). *Mortality Patterns in National Populations with Special Reference to Cause of Death*, Academic Press, New York.

Preston, S.H., Keyfitz, N., Schoen, R. (1972). *Causes of Death. Life Tables for National Populations*, Seminar Press, New York.

Puffer, R.R. and Griffith, W.G. (1967). *Patterns of Urban Mortality*, Pan American Health Organization, Washington.

Puffer, R.R., Griffiths, G.W., Curiel, D. and Stocks, P. (1965). International collaborative research on mortality in *Trends in the Study of Morbidity and Mortality,* pp. 113-30. Public Health Papers No. 27. WHO, Geneva.

Regional Office for Europe (1962). *Mortality Statistics*, WHO Regional Office for Europe, Copenhagen.

—— (1972). Studies on chronic rheumatoid arthritis and their relation to rheumatic complaints as a public health problem. *EURO 2133.* WHO Regional Office for Europe, Copenhagen.

Registrar General (1957a). Cancer of the Lung. *Statistical Review for England and Wales 1955, part III, Commentary*, 134-42. HMSO, London.

—— (1957b). Genito-urinary diseases. *Statistical Review for England and Wales, 1955, part III Commentary*, 150-60. HMSO, London.

—— (1958). Certification of cause of death. *Statistical Review of England and Wales 1956, part III*, 182-92. HMSO, London.

—— (1967). *Statistical Review of England and Wales for 1965, part I, Tables, Medical*, 428-9. HMSO, London.

Reid, D.D. and Rose, G.A. (1964). Assessing the comparability of mortality statistics. *Brit. Med. J.*, **2**, 1437-9.

Robb-Smith, A.H.T. (1967). *The Enigma of Coronary Heart Disease*, Lloyd-Duke, London.

—— (1969). The eighth revision of the International Classification of Diseases, *Health Trends,* **1**, 6-9.

Rosenheim, M. (1968). Mortality trends of renal diseases. *Lancet,* **1**, 299.

Schilling, R.S.F. (1966). Trawler fishing: an extreme occupation. *Proc. Roy. Soc. Med.*, **59**, 405-10.

Springett, V.H. (1950). A comparative study of tuberculosis mortality rates. *J. Hyg.*, **48**, 361-95.

—— (1971). Tuberculosis control in Britain 1945-1970-1995, *Tubercule,* **52**, 136-47.

Stocks, P. (1935). The effect of influenzal epidemics on the certified causes of death. *Lancet,* **2**, 286-95.

—— (1950). Fifty years of progress as shown by vital statistics. *Brit. Med. J.*, **1**, 54-7.

—— (1969). Heart disease mortality in cities of Latin America and in cities and regions of England and Wales. *Bull. Wld. Hlth. Org.*, **40**, 409-23.

Stowman, K. (1947-8). Downward trend of infant mortality persists. *Epid. Vit. Stat. Rep.*, **1**, 188-94.

Susser, M. (1967). Causes of peptic ulcer. *J. Chronic Dis.*, **20**, 435-56.

Susser, M. and Stein, Z. (1962). Civilisation and peptic ulcer. *Lancet,* **1**, 115-19.

Swartout, H.O. (1934). Ante-mortem and post-mortem diagnosis. *New Engl. J. Med.*, **211**, 539-42.

Swartout, H.O. and Webster, R.G. (1940). To what degree are mortality statistics dependable? *Amer. J. Publ. Hlth.*, **30**, 811-15.

Thurber Fales, W. and Moriyama, I.M. (1949). International adoption of principles of morbidity and mortality classifications. *Amer. J. Publ. Hlth.*, **39**, 31-6.

Tokuhata, G.K., Miller, W., Digon, E., and Hartman, T. (1975). Diabetes mellitus: an underestimated public health problem. *J. Chron. Dis.*, **28**, 23-35.

Trapnell, J.E. and Duncan, E.H.L. (1975). Patterns of incidence in acute pancreatitis. *Brit. Med. J.*, **2**, 179-83.

Trowell, H. (1974). Diabetes mellitus death rates in England and Wales 1920-70 and food supplies. *Lancet,* **2**, 998-1002.

Turkel, H.W. (1955). Evaluating a medico-legal office. *J. Amer. Med. Assoc.*, **158**, 1485-9.

Ueda, K., Omae, T., Hirota, Y., Takeshite, M., Hiyoshi, Y., Nakamura, Y. and Katsuki, S. (1976). Epidemiological and clinico-pathological study on renal disease observed in the autopsy cases in Hiayama population, Kyushu Island, Japan. *J. Chron. Dis.*, **29**, 159-73.

United Nations (1951). Development of statistics of causes of death, in *Demographic Yearbook, 1951*, pp. 18-26. United Nations, New York.

—— (1952a). Accuracy tests for census age distributions tabulated in five-year and ten-year groups. *Pop. Bull.*, **2**, 59-79.

—— (1952b). *Demographic Yearbook, 1952*. United Nations, New York.

—— (1957). Migration in *Demographic Yearbook, 1957*, pp. 606-17. United Nations, New York.

—— (1960). *Demographic Yearbook, 1960*. United Nations, New York.

—— (1963). The situation and recent trends of mortality in the world. *Pop. Bull.*, **6**, 1-145.

—— (1971). *Demographic Yearbook, 1971*. United Nations, New York.

US Bureau for Census (1938). Classification of Joint Causes of Death. *Vital Statistics – Special Reports*, **5**, 385-469.

Ustvedt, H.J. and Olsen, E. (1977). Incidence of diabetes mellitus in Oslo, Norway, 1956-65. *Brit. J. Prev. Soc. Med.*, **31**, 251-7.

Wald, N.J. and Mann, J.I. (1977). Deaths from ischaemic heart disease. *Brit. Med. J.*, **2**, 772-3.

Waldron, H.A. and Vickerstaff, L. (1977). *Intimations of quality: ante-mortem and post-mortem diagnosis*. Nuffield Provincial Hospitals Trust, London.

Warren, M.D. and Corfield, A. (1973). Mortality from diabetes. *Lancet*, **1**, 1511-12.

Waters, W.E. (1968a). Trends in mortality from nephritis and infections of the kidney in England and Wales. *Lancet*, **1**, 241-3.

—— (1968b). Mortality trends of renal disease. *Lancet*, **1**, 1091-2.

Weatherall, J.A.C. and Haskey, J.C. (1976). Surveillance of malformations. *Brit. Med. Bull.*, **32**, 39-44.

Weiss, N.A. (1978). Assessing the risks from menopausal oestrogen use. *J. Chron. Dis.*, **31**, 705-8.

Wood, P.H.N. and Benn, R.T. (1972). Digest of data on the rheumatic diseases. *Ann. Rheum. Dis.*, **31**, 72-7.

Woolsey, T.D. and Moriyama, I.M. (1948). Statistical studies of heart disease II Important factors in heart disease mortality trends. *Public Health Reports*, **63**, 1247-73.

World Health Organization (1947). *Problem of joint causes of death*. Final report of the US Committee on Joint Causes of Death. IC/MS/11, Rev. 2, World Health Organization, Geneva.

—— (1948). *Manual of the International Statistical Classification of Diseases, Injuries and Cause of Death*, vol. I and II, World Health Organization, Geneva.

—— (1951a). Evaluation of mortality in the 20th century – diphtheria. *Epid. Vit. Stats. Rep.*, **4**, 92-111.

—— (1951b). Evaluation of mortality in the 20th century – malaria. *Epid. Vit. Stats. Rep.*, **4**, 125-30.

—— (1951c). Evaluation of mortality in the 20th century – typhus. *Epid. Vit. Stats. Rep.*, **4**, 133-7.

—— (1952a). *Medical certification of cause of death*. World Health Organization, Geneva.

—— (1952b). Cancer mortality. *Epid. Vit. Stats. Rep.*, **5**, 1-144.

—— (1952c). Cancer mortality – method. *Epid. Vit. Stats. Rep.*, **6**, 1-8.

—— (1952d). Cancer mortality – Australia. *Epid. Vit. Stats. Rep.*, **5**, 117-24.

—— (1952e). Cancer mortality – Italy. *Epid. Vit. Stats. Rep.*, **5**, 56-62.

—— (1952f). Cancer mortality – Sweden. *Epid. Vit. Stats. Rep.*, **5**, 77-82.

—— (1954a). Scarlet fever mortality. *Epid. Vit. Stats. Rep.*, **7**, 301-3.

—— (1954b). Maternal mortality. *Epid. Vit. Stats. Rep.*, **7**, 37-83.

—— (1955a). Mortality from malignant disease. *Epid. Vit. Stats. Rep.*, **8**, 211-86.

—— (1955b). Mortality from Hodgkin's Disease. *Epid. Vit. Stats. Rep.*, **8**, 89-95.

—— (1955c). Mortality from diabetes. *Epid. Vit. Stats. Rep.*, **8**, 467-512.

—— (1955d). Mortality from epilepsy. *Epid. Vit. Stats. Rep.*, **8**, 169-93.

—— (1955e). Deaths from ill-defined diseases. *Epid. Vit. Stats. Rep.*, **8**, 216 and 278-85.

—— (1957). *Accidents in childhood*. Technical Report Series, No. 118. World Health Organization, Geneva.

—— (1967a). *Epidemiological Methods in the Study of Chronic Diseases*, Technical Report Series, No. 365. World Health Organization, Geneva.

—— (1967b). The accuracy and comparability of death statistics. *WHO Chronicle*, **21**, 11-17.

—— (1970). *Programmes of analysis of mortality trends and levels*. Report of a joint UN/WHO meeting. Technical Report Series No. 440. World Health Organization, Geneva.

—— (1974). *Methodology and application of lay reporting of perinatal and maternal morbidity and mortality*. WHO/HS/Nat. Com./74.323. WHO, Geneva.

Table 2.1 Number of Doctors/10,000 Population in Different Countries during the 20th Century

	1901–	1906–	1911–	1916–	1921–	1926–	1931–	1936–	1941–	1946–	1951–	1956–	1961–	1966–	1971–
Australia	–	.	8.8	.	7.3		6.3	.	.	9.8	10.7	13.3	13.8	.	13.9
Austria	.	.	.	10.7	11.4	12.1	.	.	.	15.9	18.2	18.3	18.1	18.5	20.9
Belgium	5.4	5.7	5.9	5.6	5.9	6.7	7.4	7.9	8.5	9.7	11.2	12.8	14.6	15.4	18.9
Bulgaria	–	–	–	–	–	3.2	4.2	4.8	4.7	7.1	11.5	14.0	16.6	18.6	21.5
Canada	.	.	.	.	8.3	9.2	.	.	.	10.2	10.7	11.0	13.0	14.6	17.1
Chile	–	–	.	.	.	.	.	.	.	3.6	5.0	5.5	4.7	5.0	4.3
Czechoslovakia	–	–	–	.	4.7	5.3	6.4	.	.	9.2	12.8	16.1	18.5	21.0	23.9
Denmark	.	.	6.1	6.2	6.3	7.1	7.4	8.6	9.4	10.4	11.2	12.3	13.5	14.4	16.3
Eire	–	–	–	–	.	.	.	.	.	9.9		10.5	10.4	10.2	12.1
Finland	1.5	1.2	1.9	2.1	2.3	2.7	3.1	3.6	3.9	4.2	5.3	6.0	7.2	9.2	12.6
France	4.1	4.7	5.1	.	5.6	6.0	6.2	6.5	6.4	7.8	10.2	10.8	12.4	13.4	14.7
Greece	–	–	–	–	5.6	7.8	.	.	.	9.6	10.8	12.5	14.1	16.2	20.4
Hungary	–	–	–	6.9	5.8	8.3	10.0	11.9	14.3	10.5	12.4	13.9	15.7	19.5	22.8
Iceland	–	–	5.8	8.7	8.6	9.8	11.3	11.7	12.3	12.7	12.7	12.8	13.5	14.5	16.3
Italy	.	.	.	.	.	7.5	.	.	.	12.2	13.8	15.9	17.0	18.1	19.9
Japan	8.1	7.7	8.2	8.3	7.2	7.5	8.0	8.4	.	9.2	10.6	10.8	10.9	11.3	11.6
Netherlands	–	–	4.9	5.1	5.3	5.7	6.4	7.3	7.5	8.0	10.0	10.6	11.3	11.8	14.0
New Zealand	.	.	10.4	8.4	8.5	9.2	9.3	9.3	11.0	11.8	13.3	14.1	14.5	15.6	17.7
Norway	4.5	4.6	4.6	4.6	4.9	7.5	6.6	7.4	8.3	10.5	11.0	11.8	12.7	13.8	17.2
Poland	–	–	–	–	–	2.4	3.4	3.7		3.2	3.8	7.2	10.2	13.0	15.6
Portugal	.	.	.	.	.	.	.	.	.	6.5	7.5	8.0	8.5	9.1	12.7
Romania	–	–	–	–	–	–	.	.	6.3	9.0	10.3	13.4	13.3	13.6	13.1
Spain	.	.	.	.	.	.	.	.	.	10.1	11.0	11.8	12.6	13.4	15.5
Sweden	–	–	2.3	2.8	3.3	3.7	4.3	4.9	5.4	6.5	8.0	9.5	11.0	13.6	16.3
Switzerland	6.0	6.8	.	7.0	7.7	8.3	8.8	8.8	9.0	13.0	13.6	13.5	13.1	14.2	17.9
Turkey	–	–	–	–	–	–	0.8	1.0	1.3	2.3	3.3	4.0	3.5	3.5	4.5
UK England and Wales										8.7	9.0	10.5	11.5	12.2	13.1
Northern Ireland	9.0	9.1	9.2	9.5	10.4	11.5	11.6	12.3	13.9	10.4	11.4	11.9	11.9	13.3	15.1
Scotland										10.6	11.5	11.8	12.3	13.0	16.7
USA	.	.	.	.	13.2	12.6	.	.	.	13.3	14.9	15.0	14.8	15.3	18.2
Yugoslavia	–	–	–	–	.	3.7	3.6	3.6	.	3.1	5.1	6.2	8.4	9.9	11.8

Symbols used in tables:
– No mortality statistics are presented in this quinquennium for the country
. Data are not available for this item for this quinquennium
Note: See discussion of this topic in the text, p. 40

Table 2.2: Percentage of Population Classified as Living in Rural Areas in Different Countries during the 20th Century

	1900	1910	1920	1930	1940	1950	1960	1970
Australia	–	.	.	36	.	31	18	14
Austria	.	.	.	55	.	51	50	48
Belgium	25	22	22	20	.	19	15	12
Bulgaria	–	–	80	79	.	75	62	48
Canada	62	55	50	46	46	37	30	.
Chile	–	–	–	51	48	40	32	24
Czechoslovakia	–	.	.	53	.	49	52	.
Denmark	62	60	57	58	55	53	54	55
Eire	–	–	68	64	61	59	54	48
Finland	89	87	86	81	77	68	61	49
France	59	56	54	49	48	47	37	30
Greece	–	–	64	69	68	63	57	.
Hungary	–	66	65	64	62	62	56	51
Iceland	–	66	56	44	36	25	19	15
Italy	.	.	.	.	48	.	52	.
Japan	.	.	82	76	62	62	36	28
Netherlands	–	.	.	.	20	29	22	11
New Zealand	.	.	.	.	.	27	24	18
Norway	72	71	70	62	.	68	68	57
Poland	–	–	76	73	.	63	52	48
Portugal	.	.	.	81	.	69	77	74
Romania	–	–	–	79	.	77	68	59
Spain	.	.	.	.	.	39	35	25
Sweden	–	.	.	.	63	52	27	19
Switzerland	.	.	.	64	62	57	49	42
Turkey	–	–	–	76	76	75	68	61
UK England and Wales	.	.	.	20	.	19	20	22
Northern Ireland	–	–	.	.	47	47	45	44
Scotland	.	.	.	31	.	29	29	29
USA	60	54	49	44	43	36	30	26
Yugoslavia	–	–	.	78	.	81	72	.

Symbols used in this table:
– no mortality statistics are presented in this quinquennium for this country
. data are not available for this item for this quinquennium

NOTE: See discussion of this topic in the text, p. 41.

The data are for the censuses nearest to the year identified in the column headings.

Table 2.3 Percentage of Death Certificates Signed by Doctors in Different Countries during the 20th Century

	1901–	1906–	1911–	1916–	1921–	1926–	1931–	1936–	1941–	1946–	1951–	1956–	1961–	1966–	1971-5
Australia	–	88	89	90	90	.	.	.	.	.	100	100	100	.	.
Austria	.	.	.	.	.	97	98	98	.	.	100	100	100	100	.
Belgium	.	.	.	.	.	.	.	.	.	.	100	100	100	.	.
Bulgaria	–	–	–	–	–	.	.	.	.	.	100	100	100	.	.
Canada	.	.	.	.	.	.	.	.	.	.	.	83	80	77	.
Chile	–	–	22	23	37	48	.	.	.	.	70	72	77	81	.
Czechoslovakia	–	–	–	.	68	.	.	.	.	.	100	100	100	100	.
Denmark	99	94	95	96	95	97	100	100	99	99	100	100	100	100	100
Eire	–	–	–	–	74	76	81	83	86	88	90	93	96	98	99
Finland	.	.	32	43	42	53	60	65	73	77	91	100	100	100	100
France	.	70	71	77	72	76	79	86	86	87	92	98	98	97	99
Greece	–	–	–	–	.	.	.	.	.	.	83	87	91	92	99
Hungary	–	–	–	62	73	78	81	.	.	.	97	99	100	100	100
Iceland	–	–	32	43	42	53	60	63	67	77	100	100	99	99	99
Italy	.	.	.	.	.	.	.	.	.	.	100	100	100	100	.
Japan	.	.	.	.	.	.	.	.	.	.	100	100	100	.	.
Netherlands	93	93	95	96	97	.	.	.	.	.	100	100	99	99	99
New Zealand	–	.	.	.	.	.	.	.	.	.	.	.	86	82	83
Norway	.	.	.	.	.	.	.	.	.	.	100	100	100	100	100
Poland	–	–	–	–	–	46	.	.	.	.	57	65	78	89	94
Portugal	.	.	.	.	.	.	.	.	.	.	78	87	96	97	98
Romania	–	–	–	–	–	–	.	.	.	.	100	100	100	100	100
Spain	100	100	100	100	100	100	100	.	100	100	100	100	100	100	100
Sweden	–	–	.	.	44	51	57	61	.	.	91	100	100	.	.
Switzerland	97	97	98	98	97	98	99	99	99	100	100	100	100	100	.
Turkey	–	–	–	–	–	–	.	.	.	.	57	52	52	.	.
UK England and Wales	.	.	.	.	.	88	89	.	.	85	86	84	83	81	79
Northern Ireland	–	–	–	–	88	91	93	94	96	97	95	91	88	87	84
Scotland	97	98	98	98	99	99	100	100	100	100	100	100	100	100	100
USA	.	.	.	.	.	.	.	.	.	.	.	.	.	.	.
Yugoslavia	–	–	–	–	.	.	.	.	.	.	66	46	54	.	.

Symbols used in this table:
– indicates no mortality statistics are presented in this quinquennium for this country
. indicates data not available for this item for this quinquennium
NOTE: See discussion of this topic in the text, p. 41

SERIAL MORTALITY TABLES FOR VARIOUS COUNTRIES 1901-1975

TABLE 2.4 PERCENTAGE OF CERTIFICATES FROM ILL DEFINED CAUSES IN DIFFERENT COUNTRIES IN THE 20TH CENTURY

	1901-	1906-	1911-	1916-	1921-	1926-	1931-	1936-	1941-	1946-	1951-	1956-	1961-	1966-	1971-75
1 AUSTRALIA	-	10.21	10.19	10.59	9.24	7.04	5.78	4.54	4.07	3.28	1.93	1.26	.75	.61	.71
2 AUSTRIA	.	.	.	.	-	.	9.38	9.04	-	.	6.32	2.54	3.51	1.83	1.67
3 BELGIUM	29.91	28.77	26.30	28.53	24.33	21.04	16.83	18.96	18.27	16.67	14.09	12.48	8.41	7.15	8.75
4 BULGARIA	-	-	-	-	-	.	.	.	.	.	.	.	5.80	5.30	5.97
5 CANADA	13.75	14.39	12.25	7.90	6.86	3.78	2.90	2.07	2.22	2.11	1.58	1.16	.80	.68	.98
6 CHILE	-	22.62	26.74	17.96	15.20	14.35	7.95	7.63	8.35	7.62	9.95	9.30	7.89	6.13	7.89
7 CZECHOSLOVAKIA	-	-	-	23.58	22.55	16.40	14.06	12.70	7.65	8.36	8.84	4.30	2.42	1.61	1.17
8 DENMARK	8.75	9.24	10.68	12.78	15.88	14.96	9.48	8.63	8.59	3.71	1.89	1.33	1.31	1.28	2.04
9 EIRE	-	-	-	-	25.05	21.99	17.71	16.31	16.19	15.49	12.23	8.68	6.35	3.09	1.59
10 FINLAND	.	.	.	.	.	24.11	19.65	12.73	10.59	12.59	6.70	3.03	1.35	.58	.28
11 FRANCE	7.63	22.19	21.68	22.02	.	.	.	.	14.45	17.75	18.16	15.43	14.08	11.59	8.51
12 GREECE	-	-	-	-	.	21.37	18.55	17.74	-	-	-	23.40	17.43	13.25	11.58
13 HUNGARY	-	-	-	18.45	17.10	16.34	16.80	16.35	17.39	17.41	15.54	6.04	2.47	.60	.18
14 ICELAND	-	-	30.55	27.79	26.35	24.40	24.01	25.19	.	.	4.76	3.26	1.86	1.57	1.32
15 ITALY	7.57	7.33	7.68	8.66	9.39	7.82	7.18	7.27	9.72	8.11	8.38	5.53	4.27	3.51	3.31
16 JAPAN	23.60	17.66	12.60	11.66	10.78	10.31	10.49	10.84	-	8.82	10.86	10.84	9.35	7.66	6.03
17 NETHERLANDS	17.37	17.92	16.73	15.15	14.52	10.80	10.41	9.29	11.42	7.08	5.44	4.30	3.79	3.35	4.00
18 NEW ZEALAND	-	10.01	8.86	8.94	8.54	5.79	3.75	2.81	3.10	1.62	1.00	.65	.55	.54	.40
19 NORWAY	15.97	16.57	20.44	18.89	18.85	18.09	16.87	14.84	14.17	13.36	7.99	6.99	6.35	5.71	5.00
20 POLAND	-	-	-	-	-	-	-	-	-	-	29.80	21.66	14.93	10.58	8.71
21 PORTUGAL	.	.	47.50	44.54	40.97	17.61	.	.	.	.	17.23	16.09	14.23	15.31	15.80
22 ROMANIA	-	-	-	-	-	-	-	.	-	.	-	6.11	.64	.29	.19
23 SPAIN	9.52	9.51	9.20	8.30	8.77	8.24	9.56	9.53	9.57	10.04	14.05	15.24	11.77	9.70	6.11
24 SWEDEN	-	-	.	.	.	.	13.74	11.71	10.23	8.93	6.06	3.00	1.20	.80	.47
25 SWITZERLAND	9.55	-	8.37	-	9.00	6.63	7.07	5.72	4.25	2.86	1.95	1.48	1.64	1.71	1.27
26 TURKEY	-	-	-	-	-	-	7.23	5.42	6.81	6.16	7.16	8.02	7.58	7.27	7.64
27 UK ENGLAND AND WALES	12.84	11.91	8.35	7.18	6.57	4.72	3.90	3.60	3.57	2.70	1.66	1.51	1.09	.72	.61
28 UK NORTHERN IRELAND	-	-	-	-	14.03	12.88	10.63	10.11	9.19	7.74	5.62	3.48	.60	.38	.59
29 UK SCOTLAND	11.00	9.06	8.22	7.69	8.20	7.23	6.28	5.38	5.22	4.10	2.80	1.34	.86	.52	.39
30 USA	6.82	4.73	2.86	2.52	2.68	2.67	2.41	2.18	2.15	1.85	1.42	1.18	1.24	1.30	1.52
31 YUGOSLAVIA	-	-	-	-	.	.	.	.	-	-	19.42	23.87	25.36	27.08	23.05

\- NO MORTALITY DATA ARE PRESENTED IN THIS QUINQUENNIUM FOR THIS COUNTRY

. NO MORTALITY DATA ARE AVAILABLE FOR THIS ITEM

0 VALUE<0.5

3 – European and world history, 1901–75

Contents

		Page
3.1	**The Effects of Wars**	55
3.2	**Migration**	56
3.3	**Notes on Countries Involved**	57
3.3.1	Australia	57
3.3.2	Austria	57
3.3.3	Belgium	58
3.3.4	Bulgaria	58
3.3.5	Canada	58
3.3.6	Chile	58
3.3.7	Czechoslovakia	59
3.3.8	Denmark	59
3.3.9	Eire	59
3.3.10	Finland	59
3.3.11	France	59
3.3.12	Greece	60
3.3.13	Hungary	60
3.3.14	Iceland	60
3.3.15	Italy	60
3.3.16	Japan	61
3.3.17	Netherlands	61
3.3.18	New Zealand	61
3.3.19	Norway	62
3.3.20	Poland	62
3.3.21	Portugal	62
3.3.22	Romania	62
3.3.23	Spain	63
3.3.24	Sweden	63
3.3.25	Switzerland	63
3.3.26	Turkey	63
3.3.27	UK: England and Wales	63
3.3.28	UK: Northern Ireland	63

3.3.29 UK: Scotland .. 63
3.3.30 US .. 64
3.3.31 Yugoslavia .. 64

References .. 64

Table 3.1 Estimated war deaths in two world wars .. 66
Table 3.2 Immigration and emigration per thousand population for various countries this century .. 67

3

European and world history, 1901–75

This chapter is provided as an indication of the influence of warfare, boundary changes and migration upon the mortality patterns of the countries. It is not possible in this kind of work to provide comprehensive details of all aspects of these issues. The notes that follow should serve as a warning of the extent to which these important population changes have affected the various countries. Some general notes are provided and then brief particulars about each of the countries.

3.1 The effects of wars

During this century Europe has been involved in two major world wars and a series of other confrontations. In particular there has been: the Second Balkan War, 1912-13; the First World War which involved the majority of European and some other countries from 1914-18; the Russian-Polish War of 1920; the war between Turkey and Greece of 1919-22; the expansion of Germany in 1936-9; the Second World War from 1939-45 which again involved the majority of European countries; and the development of the 'Iron Curtain' across Europe in 1948.

It is important to consider some of the changes associated with these wars because of their impact on the population structure both during and after these events. The material and human cost of the First World War was immense and the political and social consequences were incalculable. Some indication of this problem is given by:

* the identification of the military who were killed (who will be predominantly fit males aged 15 to 40);
* the number of civilians who were killed – this was a much more powerful influence in the Second than in the First World War;
* the forced migration that occurred during or after a war; and
* the major alterations in national boundaries, which were particularly marked after the First World War and resulted in the delineation of new 'countries'.

The frontier settlements of 1919-24 left vast numbers under alien rule; this was followed by the mass movement of refugees. In addition to these mass movements Berend and Ranki (1974) emphasized the utter economic chaos that ensued in Eastern Europe following the War, with particularly severe disruption of industry and agriculture, which was severe in all countries and left the whole of Poland devastated. These different changes have a major impact on the (estimates of) patterns of mortality of the countries.

A particularly tragic aspect of the Second World War was the mass extermination of the Jews in many countries by the Third Reich. Table 3.1 provides an indication of the numbers killed in the two world wars in the different countries which have mortality statistics presented in the statistical tables. In the First World War it is estimated that over 5 million were killed, and in the Second World War over 11 million (not including the 5 million Jews who were murdered). Notes are provided in section 2.3 which indicate the extent to which war has been a major influence for each of the European and other countries involved in the present mortality study. The statistics on war deaths and migration as a result of warfare have been obtained from Gilbert (1966 and 1970) and Lichtheim (1972).

Though statistics were available for the German Empire from 1901, the changes of boundaries after the Second World War (irrespective of the deaths during both World Wars and minor boundary changes after the first) were such that it was concluded that a sequence of mortality statistics for the period 1901-75 would be of no value. This is the only major omission of a European country.

3.2 Migration

Migration can occur as indicated in section 3.1 (during or following a war). However, there have also been major population shifts during the present century which have been from three other different reasons. There have been returning expatriates and other nationals migrating from 'former colonies' of the European colonial powers. (Colonial empires flourished in the period 1815-1914 an and then steadily declined in the 20th century, though at certain times appreciable numbers of individuals from European countries will have worked abroad.)

At certain periods of this century there have been major movements of workers migrating from one European country to another. Rather different from these two has been the emigration of individuals from European countries to the Americas and Australasia. A report from the UN (1953) pointed out that international movements of people in varying proportions may have profound effects on the crude death rates of both the receiving and sending countries, since there are direct biological relations between mortality and sex and age. (Immigration may also have important effects on the birth rates.) What these effects will be depends on the manner and extent to which the migrants enter the normal family formation of the population to which they go.

A UN report (1953) pointed out that data on emigration and immigration are scattered throughout a wide variety of official publications. These sources are often difficult to use for various reasons: change in the title of publications; change in form and designation of tables; interruptions in the publication; changes in definition or gaps in the series (e.g. in large libraries). There is also the difficulty of measuring or closely defining permanent movement of persons from one country to another. This partly depends on the various methods of collecting information (such as passport and visa statistics, frontier control, transport agency statistics and population registers). There are special problems due to different procedures for recording intercontinental and continental movements, different degrees of control and supervision exercised over nationals and various aliens and that some statistics are deliberately restricted (for example, to emigration of nationals, immigration of aliens, migration to and from certain countries, movements by sea only etc.).

One of the greatest difficulties is the definition. Fundamentally, the most significant item to be counted is persons leaving one country who have been permanently resident entering another country to establish permanent or semi-permanent residence. It is not easy to distinguish these individuals from the usually more numerous passengers and travellers leaving and arriving under conditions involving temporary change of location. In addition, a tourist may change his mind and set up residence permanently in a country he finds attractive. This is even more likely to happen to a person on business, or a student. Conversely, someone arriving and intending to stay permanently may change his mind and leave before 12 months (a period conventionally considered to constitute permanence). For an island such as the UK it may seem easy to record all passengers arriving or leaving, but there are difficulties, particularly since the advent of air transport.

The actual count of migrants is far more difficult than enumeration of a static population. The classification by sex, and age may present problems – age is particularly subject to mis-statement. In addition, there may be changes in definitions, methods of collection, and classification of the data. All these pose problems, let alone the errors that can occur in compilation and tabulation of the data. All these factors together lead to problems in obtaining international comparability of the data.

A United Nations report (1971) stressed that in Europe, a greater diversity of methods prevail, which reflect the particular difficulty of collecting migration data in a continent due to multiplicity of frontiers crossed by travellers each year. The definitions used correspond, where possible, to those advocated in the 1953 recommendations of the UN.

The report pointed out that long-term immigrants depend on the identification of this aspect by the traveller, who may subsequently change his plans or intentions. Furthermore, clandestine movements are known to occur across certain frontiers which escape statistical recording, unless provision is made for this when such individuals' status is ultimately regularized.

The *Demographic Yearbook, 1974* (United Nations, 1975) presents data for various countries. The statistics aggregate counts of

1. individuals who are thought to be long-term migrants (used instead of permanent to designate more than one year's duration;
2. short-term movements, i.e. temporary or less than one year; and
3. various forms of frontier traffic (this includes visitors, transit visitors, cruise ship visitors, residents returning after a stay abroad, and one or two other special categories).

Because of the problems of definition, the major categories or types of arrival and departure are not shown separately. Though the table is headed 'International migration', its real title perhaps should be 'International arrivals and departures' as long-term migrants are grouped with other visitors. The impact of this major change can be illustrated by Italy; the previous publication recorded 7,610 immigrants and 39,300 emigrants in 1969. In the new publication for the latest available year 22,964,000 'arrivals' are recorded. It will no longer be possible to assess the extent of migration.

Limited notes are included in section 2.3 for each individual country to cover these aspects of migration. The brief commentary tries to indicate whether it is the fit and healthy who have been leaving or moving into a country, or other groups as well (for instance, the elderly and young children moving with migrant workers). Statistics on the extent of migration are provided in Table 3.2.

The International Labour Office (1959) has produced a detailed analysis of international migration for 1945-57, including refugees, other political migrants and economic migrants. This suggested that the immediate post-war political migration was of unprecedented scale, while economic migration has been of a more stable nature. These latter movements were less than the scale before and after the First World War.

Beijer (1971) drew attention to the change in migrant patterns. Earlier in the century it had been from countries with high population density and high industrial level to those with low density and development. More recently, movement has been to countries with high industrial development but shortage of manpower; this 'brain drain' influenced the characteristics of the migrants.

Jaffe (1971) emphasized the unprecedented movement of a million Europeans from Africa to Europe in the 1960s. At the same time there were major shifts from the Caribbean islands to the UK and from Latin America to North America. Though these new movements involved relatively small numbers, they were in different directions to the historical flows of migration.

3.3 Notes on countries involved

The following notes provide a brief comment about major historical items relevant to demographic changes in each of the countries involved in the present work. Apart from general points the impact of death from warfare and extent of migration are touched upon. These comments should be read in conjunction with the statistics presented in Tables 3.1 and 3.2 at the end of this chapter.

The countries are listed in alphabetical order and the number for each country is the same as the number identifying the countries in the main statistical tables.

3.3.1 Australia

Colonization of Australia began at the end of the 18th century, after the American War of Independence. Initially the settlers confined themselves to a narrow coastal tract near the present Sydney (to seaward of the Blue Mountains). During the 19th century the population grew and spread; Queensland was the last colony to be proclaimed in 1859. The six colonies were federated into the Commonwealth of Australia in 1901: the population was then nearly 5 million, with 65 per cent living in the capital cities of the six states. In 1910, the Northern Territory was realigned in the Commonwealth, splitting off from Southern Australia.

Deaths from warfare. Though troops fought in both world wars of the present century no foreign armies invaded or bombarded Australia and its boundaries have been stable.

Migration. There has been appreciable migration into Australia throughout this century, particularly of workers who had been medically checked and their families.

3.3.2 Austria

At the end of the 19th century the major power in central Europe was the Austro-Hungarian alliance, which had established a flourishing economic system by 1914. As a result of the First World War the Austro-Hungarian empire was radically reshaped, with Austria one of the new countries formed. This remained an independent country until March 1938 when it was annexed by Germany. Following the Second World War, the country was divided into zones controlled by the Americans, British, French and Russians; Vienna was within the Russian zone, but was one of the cities that was divided into four separate occupation zones. When the 'Iron Curtain' was created in 1948 this separated the eastern Russian zone from the other three portions of Austria. However, the occupying troops were evacuated in 1955 and Austria once more became an independent neutral county.

Deaths from warfare. There are no available statistics for battle deaths in the First World War among the population that became Austria. During the Second World War there were 230,000 deaths among service people, and 104,000 among civilians. Included in this second figure was an estimated 60,000 Jews who were murdered (out of a total Jewish population of 70,000).

Migration. During the Second World War 80,000 Germans migrated from northern Italy into Austria, 118,000 from Romania, and 36,000 from Yugoslavia. In the period 1945–7 a further 50,000 migrated from Romania to Austria and 250,000 from Yugoslavia.

3.3.3 Belgium

Belgium had been accorded a policy of neutrality in 1831 by the five great European powers and it remained an independent nation from that time. In 1914 it was invaded by the Germans and liberated into eastern Belgium by movement of the boundary in 1919; this boundary then became stable, until the Second World War. In 1940, the country was again invaded by Germany and remained occupied until late in 1944. There was no alteration in the Belgian boundary following the 1948 reshaping of Europe.

Deaths from warfare. During the First World War there were 44,000 deaths among servicemen. In the Second World War there were 12,000 among the military and 16,000 among civilians. During the Second World War it is estimated that 28,000 Jews in Belgium were murdered (out of a total Jewish population of 85,000).

Migration. There was no major migration of Germans into or out of Belgium during the War, but 500,000 Belgians were compelled to move to Germany to work under forced labour during the latter portion of the Second World War.

3.3.4 Bulgaria

The northern portion of Bulgaria was freed from Turkish domination in 1878 and the central portion freed in 1885. As a result of the Second Balkan War a further portion in the south was liberated from Turkey in 1913. However, there was then conflict between Bulgaria, Serbia, and Romania. Bulgaria was defeated. In 1913 a small portion north-east of Bulgaria (Dobrudza) was assigned to Romania. There was no further alteration in the boundary until the Second World War.

In 1941, Hitler imposed the Vienna Pact upon the Bulgarians, which threw open its territories to German forces. At the same time the whole of Macedonia was annexed and southern Dobrudza was again recovered under an agreement signed with Romania and the Soviet Union. In 1944 an armistice was signed between Bulgaria, the Soviet Union, US and the UK. After the Second World War the treaty was confirmed and the union of Dobrudza with Bulgaria remained.

Deaths from warfare. In the First World War there were 90,000 deaths, and in the Second World War 10,000 deaths among the military and 10,000 among civilians. In addition, 40,000 Jews were murdered (out of an estimated Jewish population of 48,000).

Migration. During the Second World War there was no specific migration of Germans or other nationals.

3.3.5 Canada

The boundaries of British Canada were initially fixed by negotiation after the American War of Independence. The Dominion of Canada was established by the British North America Act of 1867 when it only embraced the four provinces of Quebec, Ontario, New Brunswick and Nova Scotia. This Dominion, enlarged by the western provinces and the Maritimes was given legislative autonomy by the Statute of Westminster in 1931. Newfoundland remained separate until 1949.

Deaths from warfare. Although it sent troops to fight in both World Wars, the boundaries of Canada have remained intact during the present century. In the Second World War, 31,000 Canadian troops were killed.

Migration. During this century there has been major growth in population due to emigration, particularly from Europe. Jones (1971) presented data on immigration: the proportion of foreign born was 22 per cent in 1911, but reduced to 16 per cent in 1961. About 1 per cent of the population are new immigrants each year, although the percentage remaining is not directly available. The immigrants are predominantly in their 20s and 30s; post-war selection of skilled workers has occurred.

3.3.6 Chile

Chile became an independent nation in 1810; it was involved in the War of the Pacific from 1879–82, emerging victorious over Bolivia and Peru. Chile then acquired the Bolivian provinces of Autofagasto and Tarapaca and the Peruvian provinces of Tacua and Arica. During the 19th century the population nearly trebled in size. In 1929 Tacua was returned to Peru, but the other provinces were retained.

Deaths from warfare. Although there were occasional periods of unrest during the 20th century no serious warlike action occurred until 1973 when the late president Allende was defeated by the armed forces and carabineros combined.

Migration. There has been no forced migration as in Europe, while the general flow of immigrants and emigrants has been less than in many of the other countries involved in this book.

3.3.7 Czechoslovakia

Czechoslovakia was one of the countries formed after the First World War from a portion of the original Austro-Hungarian Empire. Austria and Hungary were separated to the south, and to the north-east, some of the previous Empire was ceded to Poland. In October 1938 the fringe of Czechoslovakia adjacent to Germany was 'evacuated' (the areas initially ceded to Germany were those where over 50 per cent of the inhabitants were German). The following month the eastern portion of the country was identified as autonomous from Germany (Slovakia), while a south eastern portion of this was ceded to Hungary.

In March 1939 the complete dissolution and subjugation of Czechoslovakia occurred, and the whole country was declared a German protectorate. Following the Second World War the original boundaries of Czechoslovakia were restored, apart from a small portion to the east of the country, which was annexed by Russia.

Deaths from warfare. During the Second World War there were 50,000 deaths among the military and 220,000 deaths among civilians. In addition, it is estimated that 60,000 out of 81,000 Jews were murdered.

Migration. Approximately 3,500,000 Germans are estimated to have migrated from Czechoslovakia into West Germany in the period 1945-7.

3.3.8 Denmark

Following the defeat of Napoleon, Denmark was identified as an independent country in 1815. It was attacked by Germany in 1864 and lost the provinces of Schleswig and Holstein. Denmark was not involved in the First World War, but as a result of it retained the two provinces in 1919 that it had lost in 1864. The boundary then remained stable until the Second World War; Denmark was invaded by Germany in March 1940, and remained occupied until 1944. Following the Second World War the 1937 frontier was reconfirmed.

Death from warfare. As a result of the Second World War it is estimated that some 3,000 military and civilians were killed, while some 100 Jews out of a population of 6,000 were murdered.

Migration. There was no major migration of Germans during or after the Second World War. Compared with the other European countries the migration has been slight from year to year.

3.3.9 Eire

The stormy history of Ireland in the early part of this century culminated in the Anglo-Irish treaty which was signed in December 1921. The Irish Free State then came into being, with status similar to the Dominion of Canada. Civil war then broke out in the Free State, which continued until 1923. In 1937 a new constitution came into force and the links between Eire and the UK were severed.

Deaths from warfare. Eire remained neutral throughout the Second World War.

Migration. The population of Ireland was halved between 1841 and 1911, due to a very high emigration following the potato famines and late marriage of many who remained. Table 3.2 shows the relatively modest changes that have subsequently occurred.

3.3.10 Finland

In 1915 Finland became a Grand Duchy of Russia, and remained so until the Bolshevik revolution and the civil war with the nationalists. In 1919 an independent country was identified. In 1939 Russia invaded Finland which accepted terms in March 1940. In 1941 the UK declared war in Finland; following further fighting the Finns again sued for an armistice with the Russians in 1944. Following the Second World War the eastern portion of Finland was annexed by Russia.

Deaths from warfare. During the Second World War it is estimated that a total of 85,000 military and civilian deaths occurred.

Migration. It is likely that a considerable shift of population occurred after the eastern Korelian boundary had been moved at the end of the Second World War – one estimate suggests that 410,000 Finns crossed back into Finland.

3.3.11 France

In August 1914 Germany declared war on France and the eastern portion of France was a battleground throughout the First World War. Until the armistice in November 1918 the eastern strip of France was occupied by German forces. As a result of the settlement, Germany lost the zone of Alsace-Lorraine, which became part of France. The boundary then remained stable until September 1939 when France declared war on Germany. The invasion of France occurred in the summer of 1940 and after a decisive series of battles the French government asked for an armistice. From 1940 to 1945 the northern and western portion of France was occupied by German forces, with the Vichy Republic in the south and east of France. In 1944, France was liberated and following the settlement at the end of the Second World War its original boundaries restored.

Deaths from warfare. It is estimated that in the First World War there were a total of 1,400,000 battle casualties; in the Second World War 211,000 military and 108,000 civilians were killed. In addition, 65,000 out of a total population of 300,000 Jews were murdered.

Migration. During the Second World War about 4,000 Germans in France migrated to East Germany, while in the period 1945-7 it is estimated that 400,000 Germans migrated from France into Western Germany.

3.3.12 Greece

The southern portion of Greece was freed from Turkish domination in 1830. A major portion of the central zone of Greece was given autonomy in 1897 as a result of the Greek-Turkish war. Following the Second Balkan War, a further portion of Greece in the north was freed from Turkish domination in 1913. Greece was involved in the First World War in 1917-18; following this, a small portion of Bulgaria was ceded to Greece. There was a further Turkish-Greek war from 1919-22; Greece occupied a northern portion of Turkey from 1919-22 but at the end of hostilities they withdrew. In 1940 Greece was invaded by Italy and in 1941 by Germany; it remained an occupied country until it was liberated in 1944. From 1946-9 there was a civil war with bitter fighting between the monarchists and parties of the Left, particularly in the north of the country. In 1946 the monarchy was restored, and remained for the next 20 years.

Deaths from warfare. In the First World War there were 5,000 deaths of military personnel and in the Second World War 73,000 military and 140,000 civilian deaths. At the same time it is estimated that about some 60,000 Jews out of 67,000 were murdered.

Migration. See Table 3.2.

3.3.13 Hungary

This is another of the new states that were created from the former Austro-Hungarian Empire in 1918. In 1941, Hungary joined the war on the side of the Germans and was one of the forces which then invaded Yugoslavia. It remained a co-operating power with the Axis until 1945. Following the Second World War, Hungary's pre-war boundaries were restored.

Deaths from warfare. It is estimated that in the Second World War 410,000 military and 280,000 civilians were killed. In addition, approximately 200,000 Jews out of a total population of 710,000 were murdered.

Migration. Following the Second World War approximately 200,000 Germans living in Hungary migrated in 1945-7 to West Germany.

3.3.14 Iceland

This country was under the rule of Denmark, but during the 19th century Icelandic nationalism began to emerge. Partial home rule commenced in 1904, and full sovereignty was granted under the Danish king in 1918. When Denmark was invaded by the Germans in 1940, first British and American troops occupied Iceland. In 1944 its ties with Denmark were finally severed and Iceland became a republic.

Deaths from warfare. Iceland has not been involved in the major war activities.

Migration. See Table 3.2.

3.3.15 Italy

Italian unity was complete only in 1870, and initially Italy became part of the triple alliance with Germany and Austria. However, rapprochement with Britain and France occurred at the beginning of the 20th century, and in 1915 Italy entered the First World War on the side of the allies. As a result of the treaty signed following the First World War, a small area in the north-west was ceded to Italy (these were two separate zones from the Austro-Hungarian Empire). One of these zones, Fiume, was the scene of further fighting, however, this was finally given to Italy in 1924.

In June 1940 Italy declared war on France and the UK and invaded Greece. Italian forces were involved in fighting in the north of Greece and subsequently in North Africa. In September 1943, Italy surrendered and in October declared war on Germany. Following the armistice, a small area in the north-east of Italy adjacent to Trieste was occupied by the British and US from 1945-55; it was subsequently absorbed into Yugoslavia.

Deaths from warfare. It is estimated that 615,000 military were killed in the First World War and 830,000 military and 80,000 civilians in the Second World War. In addition, 9,000 out of a population of 120,000 Jews were murdered.

Migration. During the Second World War about 80,000 Germans migrated from Northern Italy to Austria. After the War, about 140,000 Italians moved from the Trieste area of Yugoslavia into northern Italy.

3.3.16 Japan

Modern Japan established its new constitution in 1888, and introduced a Council of Ministers and Diet in the succeeding years. A war with Russia was fought and won in 1904-5, but there were no boundary changes. In 1910 Korea was occupied, and in 1915 China was attacked and partly overrun. Following the Washington conference of 1921 Japan withdrew from the Shantung area it had occupied. In 1931, Manchuria was occupied, and in 1936 the conquest of nationalist China commenced. Fighting continued in China and in 1941 Indochina was occupied.

At the end of 1941 Pearl Harbour in Hawaii was attacked by Japanese planes and the US entered the war. Fighting continued until the summer of 1945 when Japan surrendered after two atomic bombs had been dropped. America occupied Japan from 1945-52; by this time the Japanese had given up all territories outside the main island complex of Japan.

Deaths from warfare. Very few soldiers were killed in the First World War, but over 2 million military personnel and civilians are thought to have been killed in the Second World War.

Migration. War did not result in massive population movement as in Europe, but the pressure of overcrowding on the main islands has led to a steady exodus of emigrants. They have chiefly moved to Hawaii, and North and South America.

3.3.17 Netherlands

From 1839 until the early part of the 20th century the boundaries of the Netherlands were stable. This country remained neutral during the First World War, and was not involved in fighting until May 1940 when it was invaded and rapidly overrun by the Germans. The country was eventually liberated in 1945 and following the Second World War the original frontier restored.

Deaths from warfare. It is estimated that 12,000 military deaths occurred and 198,000 civilians were killed in the Second World War. At the same time, 104,000 out of a total 140,000 Jews were murdered.

Migration. During the Second World War there was considerable deportation of forced labour from the Netherlands into Germany. The Netherlands has always been heavily populated in the 20th century and despite reclamation of land from the North Sea there has been a steady emigration of surplus population to the Americas and Australasia. In the 1960s there has also been major migration from previous colonies back to the Netherlands.

3.3.18 New Zealand

Cook circumnavigated New Zealand in 1769, and at the end of that century migrants from Europe began to arrive. In 1840 the British authorities sent Captain William Hobson as the first Governor; a treaty was signed in which the Maoris ceded sovereignty to the British Crown and New Zealand became a colony. During the second half of the 19th century there were spasmodic 'wars' between the settlers and Maoris. These petered out, without any particular decisive battle fought.

In 1800 there were about 200,000 Maoris in New Zealand, but their numbers were markedly reduced during the 19th century by internal tribal fighting, warfare with the settlers, and disease. By 1900 only 30,000 remained – however, their numbers have again increased and in 1971 reached 228,000 – 9 per cent of the total population. This is one of the highest rates of natural increase in the world.

Deaths from warfare. Although troops fought with their British allies during both World Wars in the present century, no foreign armies have reached New Zealand – whose boundaries have remained intact. No aerial bombardment occurred. In the First World War 17,000 troops were killed overseas and in the Second World War 12,000 troops were killed.

Migration. There has been a steady flow of immigrants to New Zealand throughout this century, particularly from Western Europe.

3.3.19 Norway

Sweden and Norway had been united under a French king from 1815, but this voluntary union was dissolved in 1905.

Norway was not involved in the First World War, but was invaded in April 1940 by the Germans and remained occupied until near the end of the war. The boundaries of Norway have not changed throughout the present century.

Deaths from warfare. It is estimated that there were approximately 6,000 military and 3,000 civilian deaths during the Second World War, with no documented deliberate extermination of Jews in Norway.

Migration. See Table 3.2.

3.3.20 Poland

Poland emerged as an independent nation following the First World War. As a result of treaties in 1919 it was formed predominantly from the former territory of Imperial Russia, from territory ceded from Germany and from territory of the former Austro-Hungarian Empire.

There was a Russian-Polish war in 1920 which again resulted in alteration of the boundary. Poland invaded Russia but was repulsed, and finally a boundary was drawn considerably to the east of the line that had been proposed in December 1919. In addition, further territory from Lithuania was seized by Poland. A small portion of Germany to the south-west of Poland was ceded to Poland after a plebiscite in 1921.

Poland was invaded by Germany in September 1939 and partitioned later that month as a result of the Russo-German treaty. In June 1941, Germany declared war on Russia and for most of the remainder of the war Poland was occupied by German forces. At the end of the Second World War the boundaries were again redrawn; the eastern boundary of Poland moved to the west, with a considerable portion of the country occupied by Russia. At the same time the western boundary moved west with annexation of an area from Germany. The southern portion of East Prussia was also annexed by Poland.

Deaths from warfare. It is estimated that in the Second World War 320,000 Polish military deaths occurred and 3,000,000 civilians were killed. In addition, 2,600,000 Jews were murdered out of a total Jewish population of 3,000,000 in Poland.

Migration. The patterns of migration were complex during and after the Second World War, partly due to the extensive alterations in the boundaries. During the period 1940-4, 163,000 Germans moved from the former territory of Poland into the eastern portion of the German Reich (in addition 135,000 moved from the Baltic States, 350,000 from Russia and 96,000 from Romania into the same zone of the Reich).

After the Second World War the boundaries of Poland moved to the west; a total of over 5 million Germans from this new country of Poland were expelled and they moved to West Germany in the period 1945-7.

3.3.21 Portugal

Portugal has been a stable nation since 1834 when civil war ended and a monarchy remained. In 1910 the king abdicated and a republic was proclaimed. In 1916 Portugal entered the First World War and sent an expeditionary force to fight in France against Germany. No direct fighting has occurred on Portuguese land during this century and the boundary has remained unchanged.

Deaths from warfare. It is estimated that there were 7,000 deaths of military personnel in the First World War; Portugal did not fight during the Second World War.

Migration. There have been three rather different forms of migration during this century. In 1910 there was a major emigration out of the country of families going to Brazil. In the 1960s the balance of migration was inwards, particularly of families returning from the former colonial possessions. At the same time workers moved from Portugal to other European countries, especially Spain. In the 1970s there was again a reversal of the migration of workers from Portugal into Europe, particularly with the return of families who had been resident in the western portion of Spain in the preceding years.

3.3.22 Romania

Romania had been a possession of the Turkish Empire from the 14th to the 19th centuries. Moldavia became autonomous in 1822 and also Wallachia. A further portion of Romania became independent in 1879 after a major defeat of Turkey.

As a result of the Second Balkan War a small portion of Bulgaria was ceded to Romania. In 1916 the country was overrun by the central powers (Germany, Austro-Hungary, Bulgaria, and Turkey). At the end of the First World War the boundaries of Romania were extended to the north and west by land taken from the former Austro-Hungarian Empire, and from the north and east by land taken from the Russian Empire.

During the Second World War Romania co-operated with the Axis countries, but as early as 1940 a portion of the north-west region was ceded to the USSR. In 1944 the country was liberated, and following the Second World War the boundary was confirmed – a portion of the territory to the north and east was ceded to the USSR (this was the area of Bessarabia, which had been acquired in 1919). At the same time a small portion of the country to the south and east was ceded to Bulgaria.

Deaths from warfare. It is estimated that there were 335,000 Romanians killed in the First World War and 300,000 military and 280,000 civilians killed in the Second World War. This was in addition to an estimated 750,000 Jews who were murdered out of a total Jewish population of 1 million.

Migration. During the Second World War about 118,000 Germans migrated from Romania to Austria and a further 50,000 in the period 1945-7. In addition, just under 100,000 migrated in 1939-44 from Romania to the eastern portion of the German Reich (territory which was incorporated in Poland in 1945).

3.3.23 Spain

Spain had become an independent country at the beginning of the 19th century. In 1931, the king was dethroned and a Spanish Republic declared; in 1936, civil war began and continued for two years. There have been no boundary changes throughout this century.

Deaths from warfare. The country was not involved in the First World War. During the civil war there was bitter fighting throughout Spain, and it is estimated that over 1 million people were killed in this period (not including the international brigades who were involved – volunteers from a number of countries fighting against troops from Germany and Italy). Spain remained neutral throughout the Second World War.

Migration. See Table 3.2.

3.2.24 Sweden

Sweden had been united with Norway during the 19th century but this union was dissolved in 1905. Sweden has not been involved in either of the two major wars this century and her boundaries have not altered at all.

Migration. See Table 3.2.

3.3.25 Switzerland

Switzerland, which was an independent nation at the beginning of this century, has remained free from the wars that have been fought across Europe throughout this period. Its boundaries have remained intact throughout this period.

Migration. See Table 3.2.

3.2.26 Turkey

The large Ottoman Empire began to contract in the later portion of the 19th century, following defeat of Turkey by the Russians and release of portions of Bulgaria, Romania, and Serbia. Following the Balkan War of 1913 the Empire again contracted markedly with independence of further portions of Albania, Bulgaria, Greece, and Serbia. Turkey was then involved in the First World War and subsequently in fighting with Greece in 1919-22. The Greek forces were finally defeated in 1922 and the pre-war boundaries restored. During the Second World War, Turkey remained neutral until 23 February 1945; the limited involvement in the war did not result in any change of boundary.

Deaths from warfare. In the First World War nearly a third of a million Turkish troops lost their lives. There were no appreciable number of deaths in the 1919-22 hostilities with Greece or the limited involvement with the Second World War.

Migration. Major shifts of population occurred in the early 1920s, with nearly 2 million people leaving Turkey for Greece, Bulgaria, and other parts of Europe. At the same time, about 500,000 migrated from Greece, Bulgaria, and Romania to Turkey.

3.3.27/29 UK

The UK has been involved in both the major World Wars this century. However, the country has not been involved as part of the battlefield, and the external and internal boundaries of the UK (i.e. the mainland of England, Scotland and Wales) have not altered throughout the century.

When the Anglo-Irish treaty was signed in December 1921, the six counties of Ulster (Antrim, Armagh, Down, Fermanagh, Londonderry, and Tyrone) opted out of the Irish measure; they were given partial autonomy as Northern Ireland while retaining their representation in Parliament.

Deaths from warfare. It is estimated that there were a total of 947,000 military deaths during the First World War (this includes troops from the UK and the Empire). During the Second World War there were nearly 500,000 deaths among the military and civilian population of the UK.

Migration. The Registrar General (1966) discussed migration statistics for England and Wales and emphasized the problems of estimating inward and outward movements between the censuses.

3.3.30 US

Following the American War of Independence in 1776, the 13 colonies broke free from trans-atlantic political ties. During the 19th century further territory was purchased, ceded, or annexed from Britain, France, and Spain. As new territories were settled and organized into states they could apply for admission to the union. This process was completed for the 48 coterminous states with the admission of Arizona and New Mexico in 1912. Alaska was purchased from the Russians in 1867 and Hawaii was annexed in 1898, though they only became the 49th and 50th states in 1959.

Deaths from warfare. The US became involved in both world wars, losing 116,000 troops in the first and 292,000 in the second. No invasion or aerial bombardment occurred and the US boundaries have remained stable during this century, apart from the addition of states joining the Union.

Migration. Though there have been no forced migrations across the boundaries of the US due to war, there have been major moves of emigrants to the country during this century. Table 3.2 indicates the extent of this: migrants have come from Europe, South and Central America and Asia. Jones (1971) showed that immigration had slowed by the middle of the century, when there was about 0.12 per cent of the population arriving each year. Emigration was thought to be significant: the immigrants were selected for occupational skill (rather than an ethnic basis which had been an earlier criteria).

3.3.31 Yugoslavia

Yugoslavia is one of the nations that emerged following the First World War. It was formed from a portion of the Austro-Hungarian Empire, and the countries of Serbia (including a portion of Macedonia) and Montenegro. In April 1941, Yugoslavia was invaded predominantly by Germany, but also by Hungarian and Italian forces. It capitulated after a brief fight and remained occupied for the greater portion of the Second World War.

The boundaries were confirmed following the end of the Second World War, with no appreciable change, apart from the disputed area in the north-west of Yugoslavia, adjacent to Italy. The monarchy was abolished in 1945. Although it became communist, Yugoslavia remained outside the 'Iron Curtain' countries from 1948 onwards.

Deaths from warfare. It is estimated that 410,000 military personnel and 1,280,000 civilians were killed in the Second World War. In addition, 58,000 out of the total of 70,000 Jews were murdered.

Migration. During the Second World War, about 36,000 Germans returned from Yugoslavia to Austria. In the period 1945-7 a further 250,000 moved back into Austria from north-east Yugoslavia and 140,000 to Italy.

References

Beijer, G. (1971). Migration to, from, and within Europe. 2554-72 International Population Conference Report, Vol. 4, International Union for the Scientific Study of the Population, Liege.

Berend, I.T. and Ranki, G. (1974). *Economic development in East-central Europe in the 19th and 20th centuries*. Columbia University Press, New York.

Gilbert, M. (1966). *Modern History Atlas*, Weidenfeld and Nicolson, London.

—— (1970). *First World War Atlas*, Weidenfeld and Nicolson, London.

International Labour Office (1959). *International Migration, 1945-57*. ILO, Geneva.

Jaffe, A.J. (1971). Amount and structure of international migrations, in *International Population Conference*, Vol. IV. International Union for the Scientific Study of Population, Liege, pp. 2525-35, London, 1969.

Jones, L.W. (1971). The amount and structure of immigration into Canada and the United States, in *International Population Conference Report*, Vol. IV. International Union for the Scientific Study of the Population, Liege, pp. 2583-94, London, 1969.

Lichtheim, J. (1972). *Europe in the twentieth century*. Weidenfeld and Nicolson, London.

Registrar General (1966). *Statistical Review for England and Wales for 1963, part III. Commentary*, pp. 28-38. HMSO, London.

United Nations (1953). *Sex and age of international migrants: statistics for 1918-47*. United Nations, New York.

—— (1971). International migration, in *Demographic Yearbook, 1970*, pp. 748-53, United Nations, New York.

—— (1975). International migration, in *Demographic Yearbook, 1974*, pp. 290-4, United Nations, New York.

Table 3.1 Estimated War Deaths in Two World Wars

	Military 1914–18	Military, civilian 1939–45	Jews murdered 1939–45
Australia	54,000	29,000	0
Austria	n.a.	334,000	60,000
Austro-Hungary	1,290,000	n.a.	n.a.
Belgium	44,000	28,000	28,000
Bulgaria	90,000	20,000	40,000
Canada	51,000	31,000	0
Chile	0	0	0
Czechoslovakia	n.a.	270,000	60,000
Denmark	0	3,000	100
Eire	n.a.	0	0
Finland	n.a.	85,000	0
France	1,400,000	319,000	65,000
Greece	5,000	213,000	60,000
Hungary	n.a.	690,000	200,000
Iceland	0	0	0
Italy	615,000	910,000	9,000
Japan	300	2,000,000	0
Montenegro	3,000	n.a.	n.a.
Netherlands	0	210,000	104,000
New Zealand	17,000	12,000	0
Norway	0	9,000	0
Poland	n.a.	3,320,000	2,600,000
Portugal	7,000	0	0
Romania	335,000	580,000	750,000
Serbia	45,000	n.a.	n.a.
Spain	0	0	0
Sweden	0	0	0
Switzerland	0	0	0
Turkey	325,000		0
UK	796,000	460,000	0
US	116,000	292,000	0
Yugoslavia	n.a.	1,690,000	58,000

n.a. = not applicable, i.e. country did not exist as separate state.

Sources: Gilbert (1966), Gilbert (1970), Lichtheim (1972).

Table 3.2 Immigration and Emigration per Thousand Population for Various Countries this Century

	1901-	1906-	1911-	1916-	1921-	1926-	1931-	1936-	1941-	1946-	1951-	1956-	1961-	1066-	1971-
Australia	–	3/3	5/3	2/2	5/3	7/3	2/2	2/1	1/1	9/3	12/3	12/4	14/6	17/8	16/10
Austria	.	.	.	.	1/1	5/1	./0	.	.	2/0	.	.	1/0	1/2	1/1
Belgium	5/4	5/5	3/3	3/3	5/4	6/4	3/2	2/1	1/1	4/3	5/4	6/4	8/4	6/4	7/4
Bulgaria	–	–	–	–	–	.	0/2	0/3	0/0	.	./0	0/0	0/0	0/0	./1
Canada	25/.	33/.	37/.	12/.	11/.	15/.	2/.	1/.	1/.	6/.	11/.	10/.	5/.	9/.	8/2
Chile	–	–	–	–	–	–	.	.	.	.	.	.	0/.	.	0/0
Czechoslovakia	–	–	–	./2	1/3	0/2	./0	./1	.	.	.	0/0	0/0	0/1	0/0
Denmark	./3	./3	./2	./1	./2	./2	3/1	3/3	1/1	5/7	4/5	5/6	6/6	2/2	7/7
Eire	–	–	–	–	1/8	1/8	1/0	0/0	.	.	.	0/1	0/1	.	.
Finland	0/6	1/5	1/3	0/1	0/2	./1	./0	./0	16/0	26/1	./2	./1	0/0	1/1	3/3
France	.	.	.	.	.	.	.	.	.	.	0/.	2/.	3/4	2/4	./12
Greece	–	–	–	–	./2	./1	3/4	2/2	.	.	.	./4	./11	./7	3/4
Hungary	–	–	–	.	0/0	2/1	0/0	0/0	0/0	0/0	.	.	.	.	.
Iceland	–	–	.	.	.	.	.	.	.	.	.	.	3/5	4/6	6/6
Italy	4/8	6/9	6/6	2/2	2/4	1/2	1/1	0/0	0/.	0/1	1/3	1/2	0/1	0/1	2/2
Japan	./0	0/0	0/0	0/0	0/0	0/0	0/0	./0	12/4	17/2	.	.	2/2	5/5	7/7
Netherlands	–	–	6/5	6/4	6/6	7/6	6/5	4/5	1/4	6/6	4/6	4/5	4/3	5/4	6/3
New Zealand	–	40/31	36/29	21/18	10/1	7/2	1/2	3/1	1/1	9/4	12/4	10/5	13/6	11/10	19/14
Norway	./9	./7	./4	5/1	1/3	0/3	./0	./0	.	./0	./1	3/1	3/4	4/3	5/3
Poland	–	–	–	–	–	./6	./1	./3	.	.	.	.	./1	.	0/0
Portugal	./5	./7	./9	3/5	3/5	2/5	./1	1/2	0/0	1/2	./4	./4	./6	./11	./11
Romania	–	–	–	–	–	–	.	0/0	.	.	.	.	.	.	.
Spain	.	./7	./6	2/3	2/3	2/2	1/1	0/0	0/0	0/1	1/2	1/2	1/1	0/2	0/2
Sweden	–	–	1/3	1/1	1/2	1/2	1/0	1/0	1/0	4/1	4/2	3/2	4/2	5/3	4/4
Switzerland	./1	./1	./1	./1	./1	./1	./0	2/0	2/0	1/1	./1	./0	3/3	0/4	.
Turkey	–	–	–	–	–	–	.	.	.	0/.	.	.	0/0	0/0	.
UK	.	.	2/6	1/2	1/4	1/3	1/0	1/1	.	1/3	1/3	1/2	2/3	4/6	4/4
US	9/.	11/3	9/3	2/1	4/1	2/1	0/0	0/0	0/0	1/0	1/0	2/0	2/.	2/.	2/.
Yugoslavia	–	–	–	–	0/1	0/1	0/0	0/0	.	.	.	.	.	.	.

Symbols used in tables:
– indicates no mortality statistics are presented in this quinquennium for this country
indicates data are not available for this item for this quinquennium

4 – Published trends in mortality statistics

Contents

		Page
4.1	**General Publications**	71
4.2	**Data for Individual Countries**	72
4.2.1	Canada	72
4.2.2	Czechoslavakia	72
4.2.3	Finland	72
4.2.4	France	72
4.2.5	Italy	72
4.2.6	Japan	72
4.2.7	Netherlands	72
4.2.8	New Zealand	73
4.2.9	Norway	73
4.2.10	Portugal	73
4.2.11	UK – England and Wales	73
4.2.12	US	73
4.2.13	Yugoslavia	73
	References	74

4

Published trends in mortality statistics

This section briefly highlights a number of publications which have presented trends in mortality statistics either for specific countries or for a range of countries. Before starting this work, the literature was reviewed to see whether consolidated data had already been presented.

It was concluded that there was interest in the presentation of trend data for countries by cause, but that no previous publication had handled the data in the degree and depth of material that has been made available here. Obviously, the intention of making the data available is that they will serve specific uses. A WHO conference on vital and health statistics (WHO, 1974) confirmed that statistics of cause of death remained one of the most important elements of health statistics, which in many countries still served as the main basis for establishing health policies.

It is not the place of this brief note to discuss the uses to which mortality statistics may be put, but these have been indicted in section 1.2 and reviewed in some detail by Alderson (1974, and 1977).

4.1 General publications

From 1920 to 1923 the League of Nations (Health Organization) published *Epidemiological Intelligence*. Seven issues were published and they contained some limited material on mortality statistics.

From 1923 to 1938 the League of Nations published an "Annual Epidemiological Report and Corrected Statistics of Notifiable Diseases". This title indicates the emphasis on notifiable disease: data are included on causes of death from 31 infectious diseases, vital statistics by country, and a table showing the mortality from certain causes for individual countries. This table was updated each year and showed trends.

The last major publication in this series (League of Nations, 1941) contained crude mortality rates for the period 1911-35 for 51 countries for all causes, infant mortality, 10 infectious diseases, puerperal sepsis, and ill-defined diseases. In addition, some material was published on deaths for 14 causes for large towns in certain countries.

Bunle (1954) reviewed the "Movement of Population" in the world from 1906 to 1936, using a short-list of 30 causes of death for 31 countries; the number of deaths by cause and country were presented for persons of all ages combined.

A major series of articles examining the mortality for European countries was published in the first few years after the formation of WHO. Pascua (1949) presented the crude mortality for European countries for the period 1900-50. Pascua (1950) then extended this with an examination of age-specific mortality (for all causes combined) again for European countries during the 20th century.

The third part of this general review of European mortality (Pascua, 1951) presented mortality by cause. This publication was restricted to a consideration of deaths from eight specific infectious diseases. Subsequently, a number of other WHO reports have presented data on specific causes of death, providing trends over various time periods; many have already been referred to in various sub-sections of chapter 2 in the section Problems with specific diseases (2.2.10). The most extensive review was on malignant disease (WHO, 1952). These reports are extremely interesting, but are scattered in a number of different publications; none of them cover the range of countries, calendar periods, and causes of death which have been tackled in this book.

A report from the United Nations (1963) examined trends of mortality for the world; only two groups of countries were used from the beginning of the century (England and Wales, and the US). Eleven others were studied over the period 1936-56, using a list of 50 causes of death; it was suggested that more comprehensive data were not available or valid.

Perhaps the most extensive publication (Preston *et al.*,

1972) provides material for 47 countries, though usually for a shorter time scale than covered in this book and only uses 11 broad causes. It differs from this book because data are presented by cause, sex, and age.

Ovcarov and Bystrova (1978) present mortality trends 1950–73 for nine broad causes for males and females in the age range 35-64 for 18 countries. Some data were age-standardized, while others were presented as age-specific rates. (It seems rather extraordinary that in this 138-page report that was only passing reference to the problems of change in classification and one sentence on the preference in diagnosis for these causes where a combination has led to death.)

In addition to these general reviews, more restricted ones have been provided; for example, Härö (1966) reviewed the mortality in Scandinavia for 1948–64. The data are given by age and sex, but not tabulated by cause.

4.2 Data for individual countries

Material has been published for a number of individual countries; the following notes make very brief comments about these references.

4.2.1 Canada

A general review of mortality for 1950–72 has been produced by Statistics Canada (1976): this included age-standardized rates by sex for 21 causes for each year 1950–72. In addition to this general report, a number of special reviews have covered particular causes of death (accidents, 1950-64; cancer, 1950-63 and 1960–73; cardiovascular renal mortality, 1950-68; infant mortality, 1950-64; suicide, 1950-68).

4.2.2 Czechoslavakia

Srb and Haas (1956) published a report on mortality statistics by cause of death. This presented limited data for each year for the period 1919-48 for the 17 chapters in the ICD. The cause data were for persons with no tabulation by age.

4.2.3 Finland

Strommer (1969) reviewed the demographic transition in Finland using crude mortality and infant mortality rates for the period 1887-1965. Considerable comment was made about the variation in births, marriages, fertility, and deaths, but there was no reference to deaths by cause. Kannisto (1947) presented data for Finland on variation in expectation of life, competing causes, and years of life lost. Again, this provided no detailed analysis of mortality data over time by cause.

4.2.4 France

Aubenque *et al.* (1978) briefly reviewed the mortality by cause for 1925–74. They presented mortality rates by sex and 5-year calendar periods for 6 broad age groups and 14 causes of death.

4.2.5 Italy

Perhaps the most extensive historical trend data have been published for Italy (Institute Centrale di Statistica, 1958). This report tabulated data by cause of death for the period 1887–1955. An attempt was made to align the causes to the 6th revision 150 list. For various causes of death the time span for which this could be done varied; some were only available for the period 1933–55, but other causes covered the full span 1887–1955. This major undertaking of alignment of the causes of death appears to be unique compared with that provided by other countries. The report is divided into two sections: Part I is tabulated by age and sex and Part II by region of country.

4.2.6 Japan

Netsky and Miyaki (1977) presented limited data on the leading causes of death in Japan for 1920–65; no reference was made to more detailed material on trends, other than from examination of annual reports of the Ministry of Health.

Segi *et al.* (1955) presented different sets of statistics on cancer in Japan for the period 1900-54. For the longer time trend the material was chiefly given as crude rates by sex for a broad list of sites. For the 1940s and 1950s data were presented as age- and sex-specific rates and more specific sites were available. Further publications followed from these workers. The most extensive material for Japan was in Segi *et al.* (1965) which provided age- and sex-specific rates for sites for the period 1899–1962.

4.2.7 Netherlands

A report was published (Central Bureau voor de Statistiek, 1957) showing the mortality trend of the country for the period 1921–55. This special report presented data by sex, age, and single calendar year, for 14 broad causes of death. A compendium of health statistics of the Netherlands (Centraal Bureau voor de Statistiek, 1974) presented limited data on trends in crude mortality rates for persons 1900-72 for: tuberculosis, other infectious and parasitic diseases; malignancy of the respiratory system, digestive organs, and other sites; ischaemic, and other heart disease; respiratory disease; disease of the digestive system.

4.2.8 New Zealand

The annual publication *Mortality and Demographic Data* has had the same general format since 1963. Each issue selects certain specific causes of death and presents trend data (for about a 20-year period) with appropriate special analysis and comment.

4.2.9 Norway

An extensive publication covers trends in mortality by cause for the period 1856-1955 (Statistisk Sentralbyra, 1961). Data are presented graphically by sex, age, and cause. Rates have been calculated for 12 age groups and causes that vary in their specificity (as can be expected infectious diseases were more specifically identified over this period than some other diseases.) A companion volume (Statistick Sentralbyra, 1966) analysed infant mortality in Norway for the period 1901-63. A more recent publication (Statistick Sentralbyra, 1974) has examined the mortality trends in Norway for 1951-70. In addition to presenting data by underlying cause, tabulations have been provided showing the associated causes of death. The data are given by age, sex, and calendar period; the specificity of the cause group varies, but for some problems a three-digit ICD cause is tabulated.

4.2.10 Portugal

Soares and Da Motta (1950) reviewed the mortality in Portugal (continent plus islands) for the period 1902-52. The numbers and rates for persons dying from all causes and for eight infectious diseases were presented graphically with a commentary by the authors.

4.2.11 UK – England and Wales

Stocks (1950) has reviewed the mortality in England and Wales in the first 50 years of the present century. This short but interesting publication only presented data for a very limited number of causes of death. In a more extensive historical examination, Logan (1950-51) reviewed the trends in mortality in England and Wales for the period 1848-1947. He chose disease groups of importance numerically, which had not undergone great classification, diagnostic or certification change, and which were published (at least at intervals) during the 100 year span. The tables included 37 causes of death (including seven with sub-divisions), with proportionate rates for males and females and seven age groups.

Campbell (1965) presented trends in mortality for England and Wales for 1931-61, by cause, sex, and age. The main material was graphical and included infectious disease (four sub-divisions); malignancy (seven sub-divisions); leukaemia; vascular lesions of the CNS; cardiovascular disease (nine sub-divisions); respiratory disease (three sub-divisions); pregnancy, childbirth, and puerperal disease; congenital malformations; and accidents (three sub-divisions).

4.2.12 US

Linder and Grove (1943) presented mortality statistics for the registration area of the US for 1900-40 by age, sex, and race. The number of causes tabulated varied, but there were 58 in the table by sex. Grove and Hetzel (1968) brought this work up to 1960 and produced some data for the complete period. The most detailed cause table (which contained death rates for persons with no age or sex split) was divided into the different ICD revisions, with rates being given for each cause in the full list of the ICD. No attempt was made to align the causes from one revision to the next.

Erdhardt and Berlin (1974) edited "Mortality and Morbidity in the United States", which provided some data on mortality trends in the US. This volume is interesting for the detailed discussions on a number of aspects of use of mortality statistics. It is of limited value as a source for specific data on mortality trends by cause. However, 11 companion volumes in this series provide more detailed data on trends by cause for specific diseases (often by age and sex) for varying periods in the present century. The following are the volumes, listed in order of the International Classification: tuberculosis – Lovell, 1969; venereal disease – Brown *et al.*, 1970; infectious disease – Dauer, Korns, and Schuman, 1968; cancer – Lilienfeld, Levin and Kessler, 1972; mental disorders – Kramer *et al.* 1972; neurology and organ disorders – Kurland, Kurtzke, and Goldberg, 1973; cardiovascular diseases – Moriyama, Krueger and Stamler, 1971; digestive diseases – Mendeloff and Dunn, 1971; maternal mortality – Shapiro, Schlesinger, and Nesbitt, 1968; rheumatic diseases – Cobb, 1971; accidents – Iskrant and Joliet, 1969.

The trend data on cardiovascular disease has been extended by Cooper *et al.* (1978), who presented material for 1940-76.

4.2.13 Yugoslavia

Vukovich (1971) has looked at the mortality in Yugoslavia by age and region. He pointed out the importance of considering the health status of the population and the previous history of the population (living conditions, health care etc.). However, no detailed data has been published on trends in mortality by cause for this country.

References

Alderson, M.R. (1974). *Routine Central Government Health Statistics*, Heinemann, London.

—— (1977). *An Introduction to Epidemiology*, Macmillan, London.

Aubenque, M., Damiani, P. and Deruffe, L. (1978). La mortalité par cause en France de 1925 a 1974. *J. de la Société de Statistique de Paris*, **3**, 1-20.

Brown, W.J., Donoghue, J.F., Aznick, N.W., Blount, J.H., Ewen, N.H., Jones, O.G. (1970). *Syphilis and other venereal diseases*, Harvard University Press, Cambridge, Mass.

Bunle, H. (1954). *Le mouvement naturel de la population dans le monde de 1906 à 1936*, L'institut National d'etudes Demographiques, Paris.

Campbell, H. (1965). Changes in mortality trends in England and Wales, 1931-1961, *Vital and Health Statistics*, Ser 3. No. 3: 1-49. US National Center for Health Statistics.

Centraal Bureau Voor de Statistiek (1957). *De sterfte in Nederland naar geslacht, leeftijd en doodsoorzaken, 1921-1955*, Uitgenersmaatschappij W. de Haan N.V., Zeist.

—— (1974). *Compendium gezandheidsstatistiek Nederland, 1974*, Staatsuitgenerij, 's – Gravenhage.

Cobb, S. (1971). *The Frequency of the Rheumatic Diseases*, Harvard University Press, Cambridge, Mass.

Cooper, R., Stamler, J., Dyer, A. and Garside, D. (1978). The decline in mortality from coronary heart disease, USA, 1968-75. *J. Chron. Dis.*, **31**: 709-20.

Dauer, C.C., Korns, R.F., Schuman, L.M. (1968). *Infectious Diseases*, Harvard University Press, Cambridge, Mass.

Erhardt, C.L. and Berlin, J.E. (1974). *Mortality and Morbidity in the United States*, Harvard University Press, Cambridge, Mass.

Grove, R.P. and Hetzel, A.M. (1968). *Vital statistics rates in the United States, 1940-60*, US Department of Health, Education, and Welfare, Washington.

Härö, A.S. (1966). Kuolleisuns Suomessa ja muissa pobjoismaissa, 1948-1964. *Duodecim*, **82**, 1136-51.

Instituto Centrale Di Statistica (1958). *Cause di morte 1887-1955*, Instituto Centrale di Statistica, Rome.

Iskrant, A.P. and Joliet, P.V. (1968). *Accidents and Homicide*, Harvard University Press, Cambridge, Mass.

Kannisto, V. (1947). *The causes of death as demographical factors in Finland*. pp. 9-148 Syskunn 27 Päiränä, Helsinki.

Kramer, M., Pollock, E.S., Redick, R.W., Locke, B.Z. (1972). *Mental disorders/suicide*, Harvard University Press, Cambridge, Mass.

Kurland, L.T., Kurtzke, J.F., Goldberg, I.D. (1973). *Epidemiology of neurologic and sense organ disorders*, Harvard University Press, Cambridge, Mass.

League of Nations (1941). *Epidemiology Reports, 1938*. League of Nations Health Organization, Geneva.

Lilienfeld, A.M., Levin, M.L. and Kessler, I.I. (1972). *Cancer in the United States*, Harvard University Press, Cambridge, Mass.

Linder, F.E. and Grove, R.D. (1943). *Vital Statistics Rates in the United States, 1900-40*. Bureau of Census, Washington.

Logan, W.P.D. (1950). Mortality in England and Wales from 1848 to 1947. *Population Studies*, **4**, 132-178.

Lovell, A.M. (1969). *Tuberculous morbidity and mortality and its control*, Harvard University Press, Cambridge, Mass.

Medeloff, A.I. and Dunn, J.P. (1971). *Digestive diseases*. Harvard University Press, Cambridge, Mass.

Moriyama, I.M., Krueger, D.E. and Stamler, J. (1971). *Cardiovascular diseases in the United States*, Harvard University Press, Cambridge, Mass.

Netsky, M.G. and Miyaki, T. (1976). Prevalence of cerebral haemorrhage and thrombosis in Japan: study of the major causes of death. *J. Chron. Dis.*, **29**, 711-712.

Ovcarov, V.K. and Bystrova, V.A. (1978). Present trends in mortality in the age group 35-64 in selected developed countries between 1950 and 1973. *WHO. Stat. Quarterly*, **31**, 208-346.

Pascua, M. (1949). Evolution of mortality in Europe during the 20th century. *Epid. Vit. Stat. Rep.*, **2**, 64-80.

—— (1950). Evolution of mortality in Europe during the 20th century. *Epid. Vit. Stat. Rep.*, **3**, 30-62.

—— (1951). Evolution of mortality in Europe during the 20th century. *Epid. Vit. Stat. Rep.*, **4**, 36-137.

Preston, S.H., Keyfitz, N., Schoen, R. (1972). *Causes of*

Death: Life Tables for National Populations, Seminar Press, New York.

Segi, M., Fukushima, I., Fujsaku, S., Honma, H., Mikami, Y., Kurihara, M., and Saito, S. (1955). *Cancer mortality statistics in Japan, 1900–1954*, Tohaku University, Sendai.

Segi, M., Kurihara, M. and Matsuyama, T. (1965). *Cancer mortality in Japan, 1899–1965*, Tohoku University, Sendai.

Shapiro, S., Schlesinger, E.R. and Nesbitt, R.E.L. (1968). *Infant, perinatal, maternal, and childhood mortality in the United States*. Harvard University Press, Cambridge, Mass.

Soares, C. and Cayolla da Motta, L. (1954). Evoluçao das taxas de mortalidade e de morbilidade, de alguma doenças infectocontagiosas em Portugal 1902-1952. *Boletim dos Servicos de Saúde Pública*, **1**, 254–78.

Srb, V. and Haas, V. (1956). *Statistics of Cause of Death from Different Classifications*, State Statistics Office, Prague.

Statistics Canada (1976). *General mortality, 1950–72*, Statistics Canada, Ottawa.

Statistisk Sentralbyra (1961). *Dφdeligheten og dens arsaker i Norge, 1856-1955*, Statistisk Sentralbyra, Oslo.

—— (1966). *Dφdelighet blant spedbarn i Norge 1901-1963*. Statistick Sentralbyra, Oslo.

—— (1974). *Dφdelighet sutvikeling og dφdsarsaks – mφnster, 1951-70*. Statistick Sentralbyra, Oslo.

Stocks, P. (1950). Fifty years of progress as shown by vital statistics. *Brit. Med. J.*, **1**, 54-57.

Strommer, A. (1969). *The Demographic transition in Finland*. Publication of the Population Research Institute, series A: 13: 9-103. Tornico, 1969.

United Nations (1963). The situation and recent trends of mortality in the world. *Pop. Bull.*, **6**: 1-145.

Vukovic, Z. (1971). *Some public health aspects of ageing*. Report to the European Social Research Committee.

World Health Organization (1952). Cancer mortality. *Epid. Vit. Stats. Rep.*, **5**, 1-144.

—— (1974). New approaches in health statistics. *Technical Report Series, 559*. World Health Organization, Geneva.

5 – Statistical method

Contents

		Page
5.1	**Handling Population Data**	79
5.2	**Handling Data on Deaths**	80
5.3	**Age-Specific Numbers of Deaths**	81
5.4	**Standardization of the Rates**	81
5.5	**Death Rates for Certain Causes of Death**	83
5.5.1	Deaths in infancy	83
5.5.2	Acute infectious disease	84
5.5.3	Congenital abnormalities	84
5.5.4	Maternal mortality	84
5.5.5	Plague and yellow fever	84
5.6	**Presentation of the Material**	84
	References	84
	Appendix Source of mortality statistics for each of the countries for which data have been provided	86

5

Statistical method

This chapter discusses the various statistical methods used in assembling and processing data. It begins with a consideration of how the population estimates have been assembled and how the numbers of deaths have been handled including the use of interpolation. A specific problem occurs where the data on numbers of deaths for the standard population are not available for the five year age group for which it is desired; a section discusses how this is dealt with.

The arguments for standardization are then presented, and the various mathematical techniques which might be used briefly reviewed and, a specification of the actual method that has been used for this work is given. The chapter ends with a discussion of the standard format that has been used to present the data, noting the characteristics of the layout selected.

A general point to consider is that all the material has been grouped into quinquennia, beginning with 1901-5, 1906-10, 1911-15, etc. Though the primary data were generally available by calendar year, it has been necessary to group the data for ease of presentation. It is also suggested that five year rates provide a more appropriate picture of the long-term trends for causes involving small numbers of deaths.

5.1 Handling population data

Population estimates from periodic censuses were used to provide estimates of the populations throughout the period 1901-50. These were used to provide estimates of the mid-year population for each of the specified quinquennia. As the year of the census rarely corresponded to the mid-year of the quinquennia a log-linear interpolation was performed to provide estimates of the mid-quinquennial population.

Pascua (1950) drew attention to the problem where a number of deaths was available for broad age groups and the material had to be split. He suggested that this could be done by three different methods:

a graphic adjustment on an arithmetic scale;
a graphic adjustment on a logarithmic scale for rates;
an algebraic process fitting a polynomial of the fourth order.

He presented results from these three approaches and showed that the simplest procedure gave results that were fairly close to those obtained from the other two. This supports the approach that has been used in this book. Sometimes census data were not always available for a time beyond the boundaries of the overall period 1901-50 and thus some extrapolation was required to provide an estimate of the first or last quinquennia. For the period 1951-75 the population estimates were provided on the computer tapes obtained from the World Health Organization (WHO, 1975).

Population estimates were required for five-year age groups from the age 0 to 85+. For some countries at certain periods during the century census data have not been published by five-year age groups. Where this occurs, interpolation was required to provide the best estimate of the population in five-year age groups. From the next available calendar periods providing five-year age group data, a log-linear interpolation was used to give an initial estimate for the cell where only ten-year age group population figures were available. The ratio of these preliminary estimates were then used to split the published ten-year figures into estimates for the two five-year groups. Having split the census data into the appropriate five-year age groups, the standard interpolation discussed in the previous paragraph was applied to convert the data from census years to mid-quinquennial estimates.

The population estimates have been checked in various ways. The first check was an arithmetic sum check of the age-specific counts against the all-age figure fed in independently from the published material. The census data have then been plotted to check for any discontinuities (a visual check is a more satisfactory way of identifying steps in the data from one quinquennia to another).

Care has been taken to check that the population estimates match the population for which mortality have been provided; in particular, some countries in the earlier part of the century only published mortality statistics by sex and cause for urban areas, or a restricted registration area within the country. Other countries restricted their data to certain sub-groups of the population (e.g. the separate publication of cause of death data for white and non-white in US). A further check of the combined death and population data has been the calculation of crude mortality rates over the century, which have again been examined for discontinuity.

The population from whom the deaths are obtained can change rapidly for two main reasons: alteration of national boundaries and expansion of the registration area from which the deaths are recorded. In the former cases it is usual that the mortality statistics have not been published around the time of major boundary change (particularly due to the exigencies of war). Where the registration area suddenly alters, it was vital to check that the population estimates used for the year before and after the change are the appropriate ones. Where such a change occurred within one of the standard quinquennia used throughout this book, the general approach was that the deaths for each of the five years have been summed and also the population estimates for each of the years in the quinquennia. This usually provided appropriate statistics to obtain an average index of mortality for the five-year period. However, where the imbalance between the two sub-sets of data was so great that the ratio of the number of deaths in the two portions of the quinquennia differed by more than 1 : 10, the larger number of deaths was inflated to produce a quinquennial estimate, rather than using a weighted estimate from all the data. The appropriate registration area population estimate was then used.

5.2 Handling data on deaths

The appendix to this chapter indicates the sources of data for the number of deaths for each of the countries. Because the technique of indirect standardization has been selected (see section 5.4) the data abstracted from the publications of each country were restricted to the total number of deaths by sex and cause. For most of the countries and most of the causes the data are available for males and females. There are 12 causes for which data are only presented for one of the sexes. This includes 11 causes where the death can only occur in one sex. The other is cancer of the breast. Since this disease is relatively rare in males compared with females, only the female data have been presented. The full index to the statistical tables clearly shows these causes that only relate to one sex) page 515.

Seven of the countries only published deaths by cause of persons in the early part of this century. This material has been utilized to generate additional tables of the trend in mortality of persons to provide longer trends than would have been available by sex for these countries. The following countries were involved: Austria 1929–37; Canada (Ontario) 1901–20; France 1901–21; Romania 1948 and 1956; Turkey 1931–56; Yugoslavia 1924–9.

After review of these data, it was decided to align the cause lists to provide 20 tables by cause. This restriction was for two reasons: first, the number of countries that presented "person" data were limited; and second, a restrictive cause list was generally used for the countries publishing such data. These 20 causes are identified in the full index to the statistical tables (see page 515).

Sometimes data on the number of deaths were only available for one, two, three, or four years within a quinquennia. These data were taken as a best estimate of mortality from the particular cause throughout the whole quinquennia; they have been inflated by the appropriate factor so that they represent deaths in the five years (e.g. if data were available for two years, this was multiplied by a factor of 2.5). This deficiency in the published data may be for a number of reasons.

1. Failure to publish a report for a particular year, particularly due to problems created by war.
2. The data were not presented by sex for all five years within a quinquennia, in which case the data by sex were used as a basis for the estimates of mortality.
3. A country switched from publishing deaths by a short cause list to a long list part-way through the quinquennia. The data from the long list were used as an estimate of the mortality by cause throughout the quinquennia.
4. The change in the classification of the ICD was aligned wherever possible to provide continuity from one revision to another, but in certain circumstances this was not possible and led to a cause only being identified part-way through a quinquennia.
5. Irrespective of the date of the revision conference, various countries may have adopted a new revision

at different times after it became available.

Publications of mortality statistics for the US included separate tables for white and non-white from 1914 onwards; in that year 10 per cent of the total deaths occurred among the non-white population. Consideration was given to tabulating these data separately; however, Johnson (1974) found that only 65 per cent of a sample of the US population gave themselves the same racial designation on re-survey a year after initial questioning. Because of these doubts about the validity of the data, the US statistics refer to the country as a whole.

5.3 Age-specific numbers of deaths

Because a technique of indirect standardization has been used (see section 5.4), it was only necessary to abstract age-specific counts of deaths by cause for the "standard population". Because the predominant alignment of the revisions of the ICD have been against the 7th revision A list, it was decided to use death rates for the A 150 list from the 7th revision as the standard.

A special interest in a much more detailed examination of English mortality trends necessitated the preparation of age-specific data for England and Wales for the complete period 1901-75. This made this country an appropriate choice for the standard population. For 137 causes there were over 500 deaths for males plus females in the period 1951-75; these data have been used to generate standard age-specific rates.

For the remaining causes (all of which were classified in the third revision of the ICD) the data for England and Wales for 1921-30 were examined. For 16 of these, there were again over 500 deaths for males and females combined in this calendar period. Therefore, these data have been used again to generate age-specific rates. The numbers of deaths were small for the remaining causes of death (for example, from rabies). A search was made of all other countries to identify a suitable source of an appreciable number of deaths to calculate stable age-specific rates. Data for four causes were obtained from Italy, four causes from Japan, and one each from Spain and US. Two causes remained for which the numbers were generally very low, but fluctuated from one year to another – plague and yellow fever. Since the interest with these causes is really on the absolute numbers of deaths rather than in age-standardized index, rates were not calculated. The index to the statistical tables (see page 515) identifies the source of standard rates for each cause. Section 5.5 describes those 15 causes of death for which standardization was not appropriate.

5.4 Standardization of the rates

Alderson (1977) emphasized that some method is required for comparing the force of mortality for different localities, where the proportion of the elderly varies (there is a direct influence of the age distribution of different populations upon their crude death rates).

One approach to the problem is to examine the mortality by specific age groups. Although this enables direct comparisons to be made irrespective of any variation in age distribution, it can result in the presentation of a large amount of material (if, for example, the age-specific mortality rates for 15 five-year age groups are examined). This would create a problem in the preparation and presentation of the material, and the sheer number of separate sets of data creates difficulties in their interpretation. Cox (1976) pointed out that the development of any index will result in some loss of efficiency, depending on how completely the index represents all the attributes of the constituent data. He suggested that no single-figure index could express all the qualities of the group of data it represents and that some information will be lost by the amalgamation of the detailed figures. He provides a good general review of the various indexes that might be used, and goes on to provide examples of the various uses to which such indexes might be put.

Practical considerations weighed heavily in the decisions about the approach used for this book. A review of various techniques is now given to indicate that the selected method has scientific backing. There is a long history to the use of age-adjusted mortality figures. This stems from a major piece of work by Chadwick (1842) in which the author used a fallacious index of health in different localities in the UK – he used the mean age of death, and Neison (1844) showed that this index was distorted by the age distribution of the populations concerned and proposed a method of age adjustment. Farr (1859) used the method of age adjustment for handling the published mortality statistics for England and Wales; the procedure he applied has not greatly changed since then.

Yule (1934) discussed in detail the two main ways of calculating age-adjusted mortality rates – the direct and indirect methods. He pointed out that the direct method was impossible to apply where the data for the specific populations were not tabulated by age (i.e. where only an all-age mortality figure was available). He also pointed out that if the numbers of deaths for the cause of interest were relatively small for any given population the age-specific rates would be "untrustworthy" and this might contribute a high standard error and distort the directly standardized rate. For these reasons the direct method would be inappropriate. (Although different authors differ in their terminology, the convention is adopted here of referring to the indirectly standardized index as the Standardized Mortality Ratio – SMR.) Gaffey (1976) wrote a brief critique of the SMR, he showed that there is essentially no relationship between the value of the SMR and life expectancy of a population and that the size of the SMR is not generally equal to the size of the relative risk of death of the specific populations. He emphasized that some of the questions of method had not benefitted from the same attention as had been given to criticism of the way of choosing a standard population in calculating a SMR.

Pascua (1949), who has produced one of the major works on international comparisons of trends in mortality, came out very strongly against the use of a process of standardization. He seemed to be particularly concerned that the standard population may be so divergent from that of the constituent nations at different times that the data becomes fictitious or misleading. He particularly challenged the appropriateness of the use of the England and Wales population for 1901, which had been used as a standard population for international comparisons produced by the League of Nations. Pascua strongly supported the restriction of international comparisons to an examination of age- and sex-specific rates; although this is an ideal, the volume of material (and sometimes the absence of age specific numbers of deaths) rule out this approach for this work.

Kilpatrick (1962) has drawn attention for the need to check whether the age-specific rates are heterogenous. If there is variation in the relative risk of mortality at different age groups between the specific population and the standard population then age standardization will produce a distorting effect. Kilpatrick also carried out a comparison of four different techniques, for producing an age-adjusted index (Standardized Mortality Ratio, Comparative Mortality Figure, Yule's index, and Yerushalmy's index). He concluded that the SMR was the most appropriate and efficient index to use for general purposes (it has the smallest standard error).

Gail (1978) emphasized the same point of considering the constancy of the relative risk over the age range. He described the application of a particular test of heterogeneity for indirect Standardized Mortality Ratios and went on to provide an example of use of this technique for finding aetiological relationships in certain forms of vital statistics.

Kalton (1968) demonstrated the use of standardization as a technique to control the influence of "extraneous variables" when analysing various sets of data (he was particularly concerned with the use of this technique in analysis of survey data). Osborn (1975) discussed "a multiplicative model" for the analysis of vital statistics rates. These papers are probing issues beyond the basic relevance of producing an index for comparative purposes as required in this work.

A number of other techniques have been suggested. Yule (1934) advocated the development of a rather different index. Yerushalmy (1951) suggested that observed or expected deaths were of little relevance to the epidemiologist and that age-adjusted rates were inappropriate as the principle concern was considering the actual death rates occurring in different populations. For these reasons he proposed his own index.

Hakama (1970) presented a parametric approach to the development of an age-adjusted incidence rate for malignant disease. The foundation of this appeared to be his suggestion that the incidence curve approximates to the Gaussian curve. This did not seem to agree with the data he actually presented for four sites of malignancy, and his approach has not been generally accepted.

Breslow and Day (1975) proposed a method for refining and extending the technique of indirect standardization, but this seemed more specifically directed to the analysis of relative frequency data than to replacing the conventional SMR for incidence (or mortality) data.

Day (1976) reviewed the techniques for age standardization and suggested they should be replaced (as far as cancer incidence was concerned) by a cumulative rate, which was generated from the sum of the age-specific incidence rates over the age range 0–74. This technique was advocated since it avoided the arbitrariness of selecting a standard population and also used simpler calculations.

Gentleman and Forbes (1977) used age-specific data by cause and country and calculated the variation in the probability of dying from a particular cause for the different countries. Their algebraic approach generated a form of age-standardized index, but again one that was only appropriate if age-specific rates were available.

Lilienfeld and Pyne (1979) reviewed various techniques used to adjust for age and suggested the index of mortality, "The relative risk index". Again, this required age-specific data; these were combined over each of the age cells using weights for the different age groups. They compared their index with the SMR (and other equivalent indexes) and suggested there are advantages in their approach.

In conclusion, because data for some countries, particularly at the beginning of the century only provide deaths for all ages an approach such as indirect standardization is required. Even where age-specific data were available (for the majority of countries and for the majority of the time span this was true), the sheer volume of the material would have ruled out its presentation in the present work – it would have increased the size of the tables by something like a factor of 18.

At the outset of the work the above indexes were reviewed and discussions held with a number of colleagues working in this field; it was decided to use the conventional indirect SMR. This was applicable for the material available, and it was a technique that was familiar to many people who would be examining and using the data. This seemed preferable to the use of one of the techniques discussed above. A general point should be considered – providing the relative risk is constant over the age groups, these indices will all give very similar results.

The standard rates that have been used have been based on deaths of persons (i.e. pooling the data for males plus females except for the 12 causes for which sex-specific data are only applicable). This meant that these rates were based on large numbers of deaths and one can immediately compare the SMRs for the two sexes for any given cause.

The reader examining the main statistical tables has no way of immediately judging the likely random variation of the SMRs that have been tabulated. An important general point is that random variation is not a major problem in interpreting trends in mortality by cause at the national level; the numbers of deaths upon which trends are based are often large, while there are many other sources of discontinuity in the numbers of deaths coded to a particular cause.

However, some of the users will not be able to judge the numbers of deaths involved (from their own knowledge), but may wish to estimate them. The following indicate how the raw data can be regenerated using the additional statistics presented in the final two tables.

1. Standard rates by cause. As already indicated, these have been specially calculated for each cause for persons, by age. Table 179 presents the rates for each of the 163 causes of death which required standardization.

2. Population estimates for each country. For each of the 15 quinquennia involved, an estimate of the population for each country has been produced for 18 age groups and the two sexes. These are given in Table 180, together with the average annual livebirths in each quinquennium.

The following calculations can be readily performed:

$$\text{Expected deaths (E)} = \text{Standard rate} \times \text{population}$$

$$\text{Observed deaths (E)} = \frac{\text{SMR} \times \text{Expected deaths}}{n}$$

(n is the factor used to generate the specific cause table.)

$$\text{Test of O} - \text{E}, X^2 = \frac{(\text{O} - \text{E})^2}{\text{E}}$$

$$\text{Combined SMR} = \frac{\text{O}_1 + \text{O}_2}{\text{E}_1 + \text{E}_2}$$

(Where $_1$ relates to cause $_1$ and $_2$ relates to cause $_2$.)

5.5 Death rates for certain causes of death

For certain causes of death age standardization is not necessarily appropriate; deaths in infancy, certain acute infectious diseases, congenital abnormalities, and maternal mortality. For each of these categories of death the following sub-sections describe more appropriate ways of handling the data. These are the only causes included in the present work where rates have been calculated by methods other than age standardization. This section ends with a comment about plague and yellow fever – the two causes for which the tables show absolute numbers of deaths rather than rates.

5.5.1 Deaths in infancy

Perinatal mortality includes stillbirths and first week deaths. Stillbirths were not clearly identified for many countries before the war and there were major problems about their ascertainment and diagnostic validity, so no attempt has been made to tackle this topic here. There are a number of causes of death that occur predominantly in the first week, first month, or first year of life.

Examination of relevant causes of death for males in England and Wales in 1951-75 showed that the following percentage of all deaths from the cause occurred under the age of one year: birth injuries, 100 per cent; post-natal asphyxia and atelectasis, 99.9 per cent; birth injuries, post-natal asphyxia and atelectasis, 100 per cent; infections of the newborn, 100 per cent; haemolytic disease of the newborn, 99.2 per cent; all diseases of the newborn, 99.9 per cent.

For these conditions it is most appropriate to use either the total of live plus stillbirths or livebirths as the denominator in calculating rates. In the absence of valid estimates of stillbirths for each of the countries during this century and because the deaths obtained have not been abstracted by age (and the early part of the century were not available separately tabulated for different periods within the first year of life), livebirths have been used as the denominator.

5.5.2 Acute infectious disease

Certain infectious diseases cause deaths predominantly in the younger age group. Again, England and Wales data were examined. The following percentages of all deaths from the cause occurred under 5 years of age: diphtheria (1921-9), 48.7 per cent; scarlet fever (1921-9), 46.8 per cent; measles (1951-74), 71.4 per cent; whooping cough (1951-74), 95.7 per cent. On the basis of these figures, it has been decided that whooping cough is the only infectious disease which was best not presented as an SMR. Death rates from whooping cough have been calculated with the estimated population aged 0-4 as the denominator.

5.5.3 Congenital Abnormalities

Spina bifida and meningocele are the only fatal congenital abnormality in this work which predominantly cause deaths under the age of 1 (90.5 per cent of all deaths from spina bifida in England and Wales 1951-74 were under the age of 1). The data for this are presented as rates using livebirths as the denominator. SMRs have been calculated for the remaining categories of congenital abnormalities.

5.5.4 Maternal mortality

For the three previous categories of cause of death the deaths occur at particular ages and thus the appropriateness of SMRs was reviewed. Maternal mortality occurs in women predominantly in the age range 15-44. However, a more appropriate index of "persons at risk" is the number of pregnancies occurring in the community. The denominator usually used today is total births (live plus stillbirths). Livebirths have been used as a denominator in this book because of the reasons discussed under deaths in infancy. This applies to all complications of pregnancy, childbirth and the puerperium, including deaths from abortion.

5.5.5 Plague and yellow fever

Deaths from these two conditions are very rare, yet when they do occur they may be in an epidemic rather than isolated deaths. It was therefore decided to aggregate the absolute number of deaths in each country for each quinquennium and present these absolute numbers.

5.6 Presentation of the material

A standard format has been selected for all tables. Generally, the data are presented by calendar period and country for any particular cause. The tables are usually available for (1) males, and (2) females, and as previously mentioned, for 12 diseases a table is provided for only one sex. For 20 conditions the data are presented for persons (because primary publications for some countries only provided data for persons).

For some countries the data were not available for the early part of the century. Even if mortality statistics have been published at the beginning of the century, some countries used a much more restricted cause list than others and therefore specific countries may not contribute to the early portion of a particular cause table.

The data have been so adjusted that the age-standardized index is only presented in whole numbers; no decimals appear on the tables. If a particular value for any cell is less than 0.5 this has been presented as 0. Two other symbols were used on the tables: if the data were not published for any country for a particular calendar period a - is inserted; if some data were published, but the specific cause is not available a . is used. The point of distinguishing these two is that a - indicates that even for a broad cause for that country and that calendar period no data will appear, while . indicates that though the material may be missing for a specific cause it may appear on one of the adjacent tables providing a broader cause group.

To retain the most appropriate range of results, for diseases that have radically altered in their force of mortality the base to which the data has been standardized may be 100, or only 10, or 1,000. The base has been selected so that the appropriate trends may be shown for all the countries and that the majority of figures fall in the range 9999-0.9. The footnote to each statistical table indicates which base has been used.

References

Alderson, M.R. (1977). *An Introduction to Epidemiology*. Macmillan, London.

Breslow, N.E. and Day, N.E. (1975). Indirect standardization and multiplicative models for rates with reference to the age adjustment of cancer incidence and relative frequency data. *J. Chron. Dis.*, **28**, 289-303.

Chadwick, E. (1842). Report on the sanitary condition of the labouring population of Great Britain. Reprinted Edinburgh University Press, Edinburgh, 1965.

Cox, P.R. (1976). Methods of summary and comparison, in *Demography*, pp 294-323, Cambridge University Press, London.

Day, N.E. (1976). "A new measure of age standardized incidence: the cumulative rate" in *Cancer Incidence in Five Continents* (ed. Waterhouse, J., Muir, C., Correa, P., and Powell J). pp 443-445, International Agency for Research on Cancer, Lyon.

Farr, W. (1859). Method of comparing the local rates of mortality with the standard rate in *Twentieth Annual Report of the Registrar General of Births, Deaths and Marriages in England*. pp 174-176, HMSO, London.

Gaffey, W.R. (1976). A critique of the Standardized Mortality Ratio. *J. Occup. Med.*, **18**, 157-60.

Gail, M. (1978). The analysis of heterogeneity for indirect Standardized Mortality Ratios. *J. Roy. Statist. Soc. A*, **141**, 224-34.

Gentleman, J.F. and Forbes, W.F. (1977). The identification of environmental factors in various disease processes by analysing the variation in disease-specific mortality rates. *J. Chron. Dis.*, **30**, 477-87.

Hakama, M. (1970). Age-adjustment of incidence rates in cancer epidemiology. *Acta. Path. Microbiol. Scand. Suppl.* 213.

Johnson, C.E. (1974). Consistency of reporting of ethnic origin in the current population survey. Technical paper No. 31, US Bureau of Census, Washington.

Kalton, G. (1968). Standardization: a technique to control for extraneous variables. *Applied Statist.*, **17**, 118-36.

Kilpatrick, S.J. (1962). Occupational mortality indices. *Population Studies*, **16**, 175-87.

Lilienfeld, D.E. and Pyne, D.A. (1979). On indices of mortality: deficiencies, validity, and alternatives. *J. Chron. Dis.*, **32**, 463-68.

Neison, F.G.P. (1844). On a method for conducting enquiries into the comparative sanitary condition of various districts, with illustrations, derived from numerous places in Great Britain at the period of the last census. *J. Stat. Soc.*, **7**, 40-68.

Osborn, J. (1975). A multiplicative model for the analysis of Vital Statistics rates. *Appl. Statist.*, **24**, 74-84.

Pascua, M. (1949). Evolution of mortality in Europe during the 20th century. *Epid. Vit. Stat. Rep.*, **2**, 64-80.

—— (1950). Evolution of mortality in Europe during the 20th century. *Epid. Vit. Stat. Rep.*, **3**, 30-62.

World Health Organization (1975). Users' guide to standardized computer tape transcripts. *World Health Statistics Report*, **28**, 221-231.

Yerushalmy, J. (1951). A mortality index for use in place of the age-adjusted death rate. *Amer. J. Publ. Hlth.*, **41**, 907-22.

Yule, G.U. (1934). On some points relating to Vital Statistics more especially statistics of occupational mortality. *J. Roy. Statist. Soc.*, **97**, 1-72.

5 – Appendix

Source of mortality statistics for each of the countries for which data have been provided

	Years
Australia	
Commonwealth vital statistics	1907-49
Austria	
Movement of population	1901-37
Belgium	
Annual statistics	1901-53
Bulgaria	
Movement of the population	1927-44
Statistical yearbook of Bulgaria	1960-3
Canada	
Report of the registrar general for Ontario	1901-20
Vital statistics	1921-49
Chile	
Demography	1932-54
Czechoslavakia	
Movement of population	1919-27
	1931-4
Statistical yearbook	1937
Movement of population	1942
Movement of population	1944-52
Denmark	
Causes of death	1900-50
Eire	
Annual report of the registrar general	1921-49
Finland	
Movement of the population	1901-51
France	
Vital statistics of towns	1911
	1921
Causes of deaths	1925-49
Greece	
Movement of the population	1921-38
Vital statistics	1956-60
Hungary	
Movement of the population	1919-30
Annual statistics	1931-42
Annual statistics	1948-54
Iceland	
Vital statistics	1911-60
Italy	
Cause of death, 1887-1955	1901-50
Japan	
Movement of the population	1901-36
Vital statistics	1949
Netherlands	
Deaths	1901-49
New Zealand	
Vital statistics	1910-47
Medical statistics	1948-9
Norway	
Health statistics	1901-50
Poland	
Provided by the Central Statistical Office	1946-54

	Years
Vital statistics	1955-8
Portugal	
Movement of population	1901-27
Annual demographic statistics	1929-54
Romania	
Provided by Ministry of Health	1948
	1956
Spain	
Movement of population	1901-50
Sweden	
Cause of death statistics	1911-50
Switzerland	
Movement of population	1901-50
Turkey	
Health statistics yearbook	1931-74
UK: England and Wales	
Annual report of the registrar general	1901-49
UK: Northern Ireland	
Annual report of the registar general	1922-49
UK: Scotland	
Annual report of the registrar general	1901-49
US	
Mortality statistics	1901-49
Yugoslavia	
Statistical yearbook	1938-39
Vital statistics	1951-60

6 – Alignment of the revisions of the International Classification of Disease

Contents

		Page
6.1	**Various approaches that have been used**	91
6.2	**The selected approach**	91
6.3	**Notes**	92
	Reference	97
	Appendix Alignment of the eight revisions of the International Classification of Diseases	98

6

Alignment of the revisions of the International Classification of Disease

The alignment of the various revisions of the ICD have been carried out so that mortality rates may be provided for various causes of death throughout the major portion of this century. There are many reasons for difficulty in interpreting mortality statistics, and one of them is the revisions that occur in the ICD. This issue has already been discussed (see section 2.2.8) and the purpose of the alignment discussed in this chapter is to provide trend data that are not overtly misleading due to the discontinuity introduced by each of the classification revisions.

6.1 Various approaches that have been used

Authors have varied between highly specific and very general aggregations of data in examining trends. One extreme is the US publication (Grove and Hetzel, 1943) that presented data on mortality statistics during this century, which were merely tabulated for each revision of the ICD. The numbers of death were presented for each of the detailed lists but no attempt was made to indicate which codes in the different revisions could be aligned. This approach seems of little value in presenting the historical sequence as it leaves the individual user with the major task of aligning the data.

At the other extreme is the suggestion that trend data for mortality statistics is only valid if it uses a broad a cause as "cardio-respiratory-renal disease". Again, this suggestion will not result in the production of statistics that can serve any very useful purpose. It is suggested that if the classification alignment results in trend data being produced for a broad cause that incorporates diseases with very different aetiological factors then examination of the trend data is of limited value.

To meet some of the uses discussed in section 1.8 there is a need to provide data at the level that distinguishes diseases with different aetiology. A number of special studies were reviewed in chapter 4, but none have spanned the first 75 years of this century, and in particular none have aligned the various revisions of the ICD to the non-standard national classifications used by many countries for the first 50 years of this century.

These publications have been examined to see the way in which different authors have tackled this problem. This, together with examination of detailed aspects of the classifications at each revision, the bridge tables where they have been produced, and the numbers of deaths in the various specific rubrics have led to the production of an alignment of the first eight revisions of the ICD.

6.2 The selected approach

Bearing in mind the considerations raised in the preceding section, the alignment developed has two rather different approaches.

One is to try to produce a continuous sequence for a particular cause of death right from the year 1901. This approach is particularly suited to some of the infectious diseases, which were clearly diagnosed at the beginning of the century, and for which unique code numbers have existed in each revision of the ICD.

A much greater problem occurs for those diseases that were less clearly defined in the early part of the century, and where there have been major changes in the classification. For these diseases the approach has been to select a rubric or group of rubrics based on the 7th revision A list and follow them back through earlier revisions providing the best fit for as long a time span as possible. One of the reasons for using the A list for the 7th revision is that a major source of data for this work has been the WHO mortality tapes for the period 1951-75; for the majority of the different countries these data are coded by the 150 A lists.

In general, the specific causes that have been identified

in this work have been classified into three categories:

1. satisfactory, where there is a good fit throughout the time period;
2. moderate discontinuity, where the fit from one classification to another may have introduced mis-alignment of + or – 10 per cent in the deaths included;
3. major discrepancy, where the alignment from one revision to another is decidedly poor, but the condition is thought to be one of general interest and the variation in mortality throughout the century has been large compared with the discontinuity introduced by any particular revision of the ICD. (In some of the latter categories the revision may have introduced a different of ± 50 per cent in the numbers of deaths ascribed to the cause, but it is suggested that such an effect introduces a step in the trend of the SMRs that still does not grossly distort the overall trend in mortality.)

Where appropriate, as well as identifying specific conditions the alignment has provided grouped conditions (for example, the specific forms of tuberculosis are identified, but also all tuberculosis). In addition, the data have usually been aggregated at the level of an ICD chapter. This point requires careful observation, as there is double counting of the deaths in these sub-group totals. Individual users of the material may also produce their own sub-groups, remembering that these are only valid where the causes being aggregated have been indirectly standardized to the same standard population (this point is discussed in section 5.4).

6.3 Notes

The following notes indicate that particular conditions for which there has been difficulty in producing an aligned classification. The notes are set out in the order in which the data appear in the statistical tables; it follows the arrangement of the ICD 7th revision A list. The number of the statistical table is given in parentheses after each sub-heading in the following notes.

Tuberculosis – respiratory system (Table I). The second revision included under rubric 28 both acute phthisis and generalized miliary tuberculosis. These were split by a sub-division of the code 29, and where possible 29a has been included under respiratory tuberculosis and 29a under tuberculosis – all other causes. If the sub-divisions are not available all deaths coded to 29 have been included under respiratory. The 8th revision first identified "Late effects of respiratory tuberculosis" in the detailed list. This was not included in the A list respiratory category, although it represented about 20 per cent of respiratory deaths. The 7-8 alignment is therefore poor.

Tuberculosis – "alimentary" (3). The rubrics used cover tuberculosis of the intestines, peritoneum, and mesenteric glands. Tuberculosis of the upper alimentary tract (a very rare site to be involved) is included in all tuberculosis, but not separately identified.

Tuberculosis – bones and joints (4). The first revision included in 32 "white tumour". This is thought to be equivalent to a cold abscess and has been included under the bone and joint category.

Syphilis (8-12). The 6th revision introduced a new category "early syphilis" which has not been previously distinguished. Prior to the 5th revision the central nervous system manifestations were not included under syphilis, but can still be separately identified as tabes dorsalis and general paralysis of the insane. In the 3rd revision, tabes dorsalis is also identified as locomotor ataxi, and in the 2nd revision only has the latter diagnosis.

There is a particular problem with syphlitic aneurysm. This was classified with disease of the arteries from the 1st to 4th revision and then in the 5th revision coded as a manifestation of syphilis – even if it was not specified as due to syphilis. From the 7th revision it has been coded as a cardiovascular condition unless specified as due to syphilis. The alignment may therefore be poor.

"Gonoccocal infection" (13). This line provides a query due to the variation in the classification of lymphogranuloma venereum. In the 6th, 7th, and 8th revisions this is lost in other infectious disease, but appears in earlier revisions in the line. It is, however, only a small component of the deaths (in 1941 it was responsible in England and Wales for 1 death in comparison with 32 from gonorrhea). Before the 5th revision, the entry also included a small proportion of deaths from other venereal conditions.

"Venereal disease" (14). This line provides a relatively good fit, apart from minor discontinuity created by variation in classification of lymphogranuloma venereum.

The 5th revision entry has a contribution of deaths from conditions other than syphilis and gonorrhea that does not appear in the two preceding lines. There is not strict compatability between the 5th and 6th classification entries.

Paratyphoid fever (16). The 6th revision separated food poisoning into other salmonella infections and food poisoning excluding salmonella. In the period 1950–7, the latter category were only about 10 per cent of the deaths in the former. This small segment has not been included in the 6-8th revisions, but has been transferred from violent deaths in the 5th and earlier versions to include the numerically important other salmonella infections that were grouped with food poisoning.

Cholera (18). In the earlier part of this century Asiatic and cholera nostras were given adjacent codes. In the 8th revision cholera nostras no longer appears in the infection section but was transferred to alimentary disease. Cholera nostras has therefore been removed throughout the century from this section and is included in "All alimentary diseases".

Diarrhoea (no specific table). Typhoid, para-typhoid, cholera, brucellosis, and dysentery can be followed through the classifications from the 1st to the 8th revision. There is probably some degree of overlap with the other diarrhoeal diseases that are coded in alimentary disease. This is likely to be more a problem of diagnosis than classification.

Septicemia/pyemia (23). In the 5th, 4th, and 2nd revisions these conditions were identified as sub-divisions of a particular rubric. Where possible, the sub-divisions have been identified, otherwise the main rubric provides an acceptable alignment. The full rubric contains gas gangrene in revisions 1-5 and vaccinia in revisions 1-3.

Meningococcal infections (26). These can be identified from the 1st revision through to the 8th revision. The bridge tables suggest this alignment is satisfactory. Although there are major swings in the numbers of deaths throughout the century, there is no indication that this is due to variation in the classification.

Poliomyelitis and infectious encephalitis including late effects (31). The alignment from the 3rd revision through to the 7th seems reasonably robust. Late effects of poliomyelitis were distinguished from acute poliomyelitis and not retrievable in the A list of the 8th revision which meant that an entry for this period was not possible. In the 2nd revision poliomyelitis only formed a portion of a broader category, so again, no entry is possible.

Hepatitis infections (35). This is not available before the 6th revision as it is included in a part coded to alimentary disease.

Hyatid disease (39). The 3rd and earlier revisions identified deaths from liver disease in a separate code, but cannot be retrieved from a more general code. There is no indication that this created discontinuity in the general alignment from the 1st to 8th revisions, as the deaths from non-liver hydatid disease are a small component of the total.

Malignant neoplasm – buccal cavity and pharynx (42). In the 3rd, 2nd, and 1st revisions, pharynx was not included in this rubric; this line is therefore a relatively poor fit. In 1921 there were about eight times as many deaths from buccal cavity as pharynx. Though there is discontinuity in the classification, this line is retained throughout the century as it still indicates the major drop in deaths that have occurred for buccal cavity cancer.

Malignant neoplasm – alimentary tract (42–49). There were major changes in the classification, one of which has already been referred to: the combination of pharynx with the upper alimentary tract in the first three revisions. In addition, the alignment of the stomach and the large bowel is impossible before the 4th revision because of the very broad code used for the digestive organs. There is a bad bridge between the 5th and 6th revisions as the former includes pancreas, liver, and other digestive organs in addition to the alimentary tract. (This title covers different anatomical sites to those included in "Tuberculosis of the alimentary tract".)

Malignant neoplasm – larynx (50). In the 5th revision the code included trachea; however, in 1975 there were 587 deaths from laryngeal cancer and only 20 from trachea. This suggests that the location of the specific site trachea is not crucial to the alignment of the larynx. To overcome this defect, a broader cause line is also provided including larynx, trachea, bronchus and lung. In the 5th revision this category in the detailed list also included respiratory disease unspecified; however, in 1948 there were over 5,000 deaths from the complete rubric of which none were classified to respiratory unspecified. This suggests that rubric 47 of the 5th revision is satisfactory, if 47a and b are not separately available.

Malignant neoplasm – female genital organs (57). From the 3rd to the 1st revision there was one rubric covering all these sites. Unfortunately, the A list for the 6-8th revisions has aligned ovarian and other genital cancers in the broad category "all other neoplasms". The line therefore cannot be carried through to the latest calendar period.

Malignant neoplasm – bone and connective tissue (60). The 8th revision separated connective tissue from bone in the A list; the numbers involved are such that the bridge is unusable. However, an entry is provided for the 5th-7th revisions.

Leukaemia and aleukaemia (62). From the 5th revision and earlier this had been classified with diseases of the blood. The codes identifying this cause can be transferred from the other chapters and a reasonable alignment made.

Hodgkin's disease (63). Several changes have occurred in this diagnosis and its location in various parts of the classification during this century. An alignment was provided for the 2nd-5th revisions. Unfortunately, Hodgkin's disease is then not separately identified in the subsequent A lists.

Malignant neoplasm – all forms (65). This is an attempt to produce an overall summary code. There is the problem with Hodgkin's disease and leukaemia, which have been transferred from other sections of the classification before the 6th revision.

Neoplasm – benign and unspecified (66). In the earlier part of the century some of these sites were scattered elsewhere in the classification. An attempt has been made to identify the various locations to which they would be coded. The line should provide an adequate fit for these causes.

Avitaminosis and other deficiency states (71). The 5th-8th revisions include steatorrhoea and the 4th-8th osteomalacia. However, these conditions only provide a small proportion of the total rubric used and although they create misalignment in the category it is suggested that this is still satisfactory as a "broad fit." There is a poor bridge particularly between the 4th and 5th revisions. In the 3rd revision osteomalacia is classified with other diseases of bone and cannot be separated.

Allergic disorders, all other endocrine, metabolic and blood diseases (73). Asthma and hayfever were transferred to a part code of the respiratory disease in the 8th revision. Therefore it was felt impossible to provide an entry for the broader group of causes for the 8th revision. In the 3rd and 2nd revisions hayfever is missing (later being classified with asthma); the number of deaths from hayfever are very small compared with asthma and their loss in these earlier revisions can be ignored.

The number of separate conditions that are classified within this line are large, but many of them have relatively small numbers of deaths in any one year. The detailed allocations from the 2nd edition through to the 7th have been examined, and it is suggested that the alignment provides a usable category. The fit for other specific categories of thyroid disease is poor, but these contribute a small loss to the total line (22 out of 2,500 deaths in males, and 130 out of 3,000 deaths in females in the 5th revision).

Mental illness (75). It was found impossible to provide adequate lines for psychoses, psychoneuroses, and disorders of personality. These have been combined into Mental Illness, which also includes some deaths from alcoholism and drug addiction.

Vascular lesions affecting central nervous system (78). Despite the major change in the 8th classification, the bridge between the 7th-8th revisions is good. The alignment between the 5th and 4th revision is not perfect, as in the earlier revision cerebrovascular lesions associated with arteriosclerosis had been coded in a separate (but identifiable) section. An important point about this rubric is that it was affected by changes in the coding rules in 1940.

Meningitis – non-meningococcal (79). The data for the last revision are only available through a part code. While the 3rd revision excludes a small proportion of deaths coded to "bell's mania". The 6th-8th revisions included deaths from *H. influenza meningitis*, which represents about 10 per cent of the deaths in this rubric.

Otitis media and mastoiditis (83). In the 6th and subsequent revisions, diseases of the external ear and some other miscellaneous ear diseases were included with middle-ear diseases. The number of deaths that are lost in other diseases of the sense organs however are small compared with those remaining in this rubric (in 1951, 9 deaths were lost in males out of a total of 257 deaths from middle-ear disease). There are major changes in the numbers of deaths from the 3rd to the 8th revisions, which are thought to represent genuine alterations in mortality rather than classification change.

Eye and ear – all diseases (84). This broader category is also missing the small component of external-ear disease.

Rheumatic fever (87). The 8th revision intermediate list lost a proportion of deaths to chronic rheumatic heart disease, but this discontinuity is small compared with the major drop in deaths from the condition throughout the present century. The line is therefore considered usable. In the 4th and earlier revisions it is possible that some acute cardiac manifestations will have been coded to heart disease rather than rheumatic fever.

Heart disease – chronic rheumatic (88). Again a discontinuity between the 7th and 8th revision causes distortion on this line, with transfer of some of the deaths in the 8th revision to arteriosclerotic and degenerative heart disease (the deaths transferred form a small fraction of the latter line and will cause no appreciable discontinuity to it).

For earlier revisions there are some variations in classification, but examination of the bridge tables and the numbers of deaths in individual specific rubrics suggest that lines have been derived that are usable, considering the major variation in death rates from this condition during this century.

Heart disease – arteriosclerotic and degenerative (89). There has been change in nomenclature and classification during this century, but a usable line has been derived after examination of bridge tables and specific numbers of deaths in the different categories. There is a bad bridge between the 4th and 5th classifications, due to the exclusion of "Functional heart disease" and "other heart disease" from the 5th and subsequent revisions (these categories represented less than 3 per cent of the deaths included in this cause in 1947). Major variation is likely to come from diagnostic and certification practice rather than amendment in the classification over the whole period.

Hypertensive disease (92). There is a major discontinuity between the 5th and 6th revisions. In the later classification hypertensive disease was coded to "high blood pressure" but also distributed among a range of other heart conditions (which had large numbers of deaths). Although the transfer from these other conditions involved only a small proportion, they are responsible for major discrepancy in the alignment. This is one of the few causes of death where the 7th revision differed from the 6th.

Arteries – all diseases (93). There is discontinuity between the 7th and 8th revisions, with a scatter of an appreciable number of deaths through a wide range of rubrics in the later classification. The overall alignment is satisfactory. In the V, IV, and III revisions aneurysm has been included, when subsequently they were coded within syphilis – even if not specified as due to this. Gangrene has been included in this line, even when coded as senile gangrene. However, it is felt that this still provides an acceptable alignment throughout the century. Again, problems of diagnosis and certification are probably responsible for considerable variation rather than discontinuity in the classification.

Influenza (99). This condition was classified within infectious disease in the list to the 5th revision; in the 6th onwards it has been located within respiratory disease. A new code also appeared in the 6th revision – for *H. infuenzae* infection; this is not separately available in the A list. The number of deaths are small compared with those coded to flu (about 2 per cent in an epidemic year).

Pneumonia – lobar (100). This is available from the 2nd to the 7th revision inclusive.

Pneumonia – broncho (101). This is available from the 1st to the 7th revision.

Pneumonia – all forms (103). Due to the combination of the lobar and bronchopneumonia in the 8th revision A list it is only possible to include this latter period for the broader category of pneumonia.

Bronchitis – chronic and unqualified (105). This includes bronchiectasis in the 2nd–5th revisions; this was handled in a different way from the 6th to the 8th revision, and cannot be separately distinguished in the A lists. However, bronchiectasis was responsible for about 1/120th of the deaths from bronchitis in England and Wales in 1950, and therefore provides no appreciable discontinuity from its removal.

Bronchitis – all forms (106). There is a poor bridge from the 7th to 8th revisions as the latter combined acute bronchitis with acute upper respiratory infections (an addition of about 5 per cent to acute bronchitis) and also emphysema and asthma were combined with chronic bronchitis (an addition of about 10 per cent to chronic bronchitis). However, this cause is provided as a number of countries did not distinguish acute from chronic bronchitis in their tables published in the earlier part of the century.

Empyema and lung abscess (108). Adequate alignment is obtained by bringing together sub-divisions of detailed list codes for the 2nd–5th revisions.

Gastritis and duodenitis (115). In the 2nd and 3rd revision these rubrics are broader, including other diseases such as perforation of the stomach. This does not distort the overall totals for this line. The bridge between the 5th and 6th revisions is poor, but cannot be improved with the available codes.

Gastro-enteritis and colitis (119). This alignment could not be continued in the 8th revision due to transfer of major components into the infectious disease chapter.

Biliary calculi (122). This combined with cholecystitis in the 6th, 7th, and 8th revisions. However, it can be uniquely identified in the earlier classifications back to the 1st revision and is thus provided for the 1st–5th revisions.

Cholelithiasis and cholecystitis (123). The 6th revision A list excludes other diseases of the gall bladder and bile ducts. These are separately distinguished in the detailed lists for the 5th and 4th revisions; using the sub-divisions of these codes (127A or 128:1) provides a good alignment.

Nephritis – acute (126). The England and Wales data showed a doubling in the number of deaths from the 7th to 8th revision (80–170 deaths). This was thought to be due to a change in coding practice rather than the classification. In the 3rd and earlier revision, unspecified nephritis was allocated to acute in persons under the age of 10.

Nephritis – chronic, other and unspecified (127). The 6th revision detailed list separated sub-acute from chronic nephritis, though these were combined in the A list. In the 3rd and earlier lists "nephritis unspecified" was allocated to "chronic nephritis" in persons over 10 years of age.

Kidney – infections (129). The alignment of the rubrics from the 6th to 8th revision seems adequate, though diagnostic and certification practice may have contributed to recent trends (see sub-section 2.2.10. page 32). Part of the detailed list rubric used for the 5th and 4th appears to give appropriate alignment. The other portion of the latter codes is transferred to hydronephrosis and is lost in the other diseases of the kidney from the 6th revision onwards.

Kidney and ureter – all diseases excluding calculi (130). A small anomally occurs with the location of chyluria. This appears to be classified in the line for the 2nd, 3rd, 4th, and 5th revisions (though the index to the 4th and 5th suggests it is located in the "Other diseases due to Helminths").

Prostrate – hyperplasia (132). In the 5th revision, hypertrophy accounted for 5,273 deaths in 1941 in England and Wales, while other diseases of the prostrate only accounted for 220 (i.e. less than 5 per cent). In the earlier revisions these two rubrics were combined, but it is suggested that the alignment is satisfactory.

Abortion (137). The bridge tables suggest there is acceptable alignment between the 5th to 8th revisions. A very small inconsistency occurs with deaths from abortion with toxaemia but no sepsis; these are included in the 5th and 8th revisions, but coded in toxaemia in the 6th and 7th revisions. Prior to this, a proportion of abortions were classified under suicide, homicide or other forms of violence. It is impossible to determine the magnitude of deaths lost to these other categories. However, because of the interest in examining the trends in abortion the line has been maintained from the 2nd revision through to the 8th. It is a poor alignment and this must be considered; it reflects the deaths that were ascribed to abortion excluding those coded to violent deaths in the earlier part of this century.

Arthritis and spondylitis (140). The terminology used for this condition has changed over the present century. In the 1st revision, rheumatoid arthritis and gout were coded together; from the 2nd onwards gout is an allergic disease. In the 3rd and 4th revisions, rheumatoid and osteoarthritis were combined. The 5th revision separated rheumatoid arthritis and other chronic arthritic rheumatism; these were then identified from the 6th revision onwards as rheumatoid arthritis and (separately) osteoarthritis. It is not possible to distinguish these two latter conditions in the 6th–8th A lists. It is felt that the line provided on arthritis and spondylitis is a reasonable alignment.

Rheumatism – muscular and unspecified (141). Terminology has changed since the 2nd revision, but again it is felt that the alignment was satisfactory.

Congenital malformations – "cardiovascular" (148). There is a poor bridge between the 5th and earlier revisions. Before the 5th it is only possible to identify abnormalities to the heart; an additional 10 per cent of deaths from abnormalities of vessels are missing.

Newborn – postnatal asphyxia and atelectasis (151). There is a poor bridge between the 7th and 8th revisions. The 8th uses a broader range of terms, but the numerically important one is derived from the comparable code in the 7th revision (this provides about 90 per cent, while the main source of other deaths is ill-defined diseases of infancy).

Newborn – haemolytic disease (154). The bridge tables, and earlier classification suggests that this alignment is adequate, with negligible variation despite changing terminology.

Ill-defined and unknown causes (158). This is obviously a category where the terminology used and the diagnostic criteria will have varied markedly throughout the century. However, it is suggested that this line should be included, defining the specific ICD rubrics used for each revision. This provides an estimate of those "conditions" which were not thought to be sufficiently specified to link to any particular system or aetiology.

An example is gangrene, which appears in the 1st to 3rd revisions; subsequently, it is aligned to the disease of artieries in the 5th revision. It has been decided to extract it from the ill-defined conditions for the earlier revisions and locate it with vascular disease. Rather different are the terms "infantile convulsions age less than 5", and "amputation". These are much vaguer diagnostic categories, with a wide range of possible aetiologies. They have therefore been included with those other deaths identified as "ill-defined".

Accidents – motor vehicles (160). The alignment from the 5th to the 8th revision seems acceptable. Before this a proportion of deaths involving motor vehicles and other transport were included in deaths from accidental falls. The alignment cannot therefore be carried back before the 5th revision (and also accidental falls only goes as far as the 5th revision).

Accidents – poisoning (163). During the century the classification has radically altered, due to the exposure to new chemicals and the hazards these pose for accidental poisoning. However, it is suggested that the categories utilized provide an indication of the development of this problem during this century. Reference has already been made to the location of food poisoning from the 5th revision and earlier with this section (this has been transferred to "paratyphoid" in our alignment).

Accidents – falls (164). There is a poor bridge between the 5th and 6th revision; the former does not include falls in mines and quarries.

Accidents – "fire and heat" (165). The classification changed between the 5th and 6th revisions, and again between the 7th and 8th revisions. In the latter there is a relatively poor bridge with about one-fifth of the deaths in the 7th revision coded elsewhere in the 8th revision. For example, the detailed list of the 8th revision moved accidents due to blasting materials (E 923.1), which is not available in the A list that has been used. However, the line is retained as the best available.

Accidents – firearms (166). In the 8th revision there was some variation due to the legal aspects of coding the deaths caused by firearms (deaths were transferred from an accidental category to self-inflicted). The line is retained as being the best estimate of accidental gunshot wounds.

Accidents – drowning and submersion (167). Again, there is legal variation in the 8th revision, with separate classification of those deaths where it is undetermined whether the death was accidental or intentional. This led to 35 per cent reduction in deaths of males and 48 per cent reduction in England and Wales. Again, the line is retained as the best estimate that is available from the data.

Homicide and injury purposely inflicted by other persons (not in war) (172). The identification of both infanticide and execution varied during the century, but the number of deaths involved are small compared with the total, and it is suggested that the alignment is adequate.

Reference

Grove, R.P. and Hetzel, A.M. (1968). *Vital statistics rates in the United States, 1940–60.* US Department of Health, Education, and Welfare, Washington, D.C.

6 Appendix Alignment of the 8 Revisions of the International Classification of Diseases

DE No.	Cause	Revisions 8th 1965		7th 1955		6th 1948		5th 1938		4th 1929			3rd 1920		2nd 1909	1st 1901
		ICD No.	A	A	B	A	B	Det.	Abbr.	Det.	Inter.	Abbr.	Det.	Abbr.	Det.	Det.
1	Tuberculosis – respiratory system	010–012	6	1	1	1	1	13	6	23	11	10	31	13	28, 29a, (or 28, 29)	26, 27
2	Tuberculosis – Meninges and central nervous system	013	7	2		2		14		24			32	14	30	28
3	Tuberculosis – "alimentary"	014	8	3		3		15		25			33		31	29
4	Tuberculosis – Bones and joints	015	9	4		4		16, 17		26, 27			34, 35		32, 33	30, 32
5	Tuberculosis – all other forms	016–019	10	5		5		18–22		28–32			36, 37		34, 35 (or 29b, 34, 35)	31, 33–35
6	Tuberculosis – non-respiratory	013–019	7, 8, 9, 10	2, 3, 4, 5	2	2, 3, 4, 5	2	14–22	7	24–32	12	11	32–37	14, 15	30–35 (or 29b, 30–35)	28–35
7	Tuberculosis – all forms	010–019	6–10	1–5	1, 2	1–5	1, 2	13–22	6, 7	23–32	11, 12	10, 11	31–37	13–15	28–35	26–35
8	Tabes dorsalis	–	–	8	–	8	–	30(a)	–	80	31	–	72	–	62	62
9	General paralysis of the insane	–	–	9	–	9	–	30(b)	–	83	33	–	76	–	67	67
10	Syphilis – CNS	094	36	8, 9	–	8, 9	–	30(a) 30(b)	–	80, 83	31, 33	21	72, 76	–	62, 67	62, 67
11	Syphilis – all other	092–3, 095–7	37	10		10		30(c), 30db, dc, dd		34(b, c)			38		37	36
12	Syphilis – all forms	090–097	34–37	6, 7, 8, 9, 10	3	6, 7, 8, 9, 10	3	30	9	34, 80, 83	13, 31 33	12, 21	38, 72, 76	–	37, 62, 67	36, 62,
13	"Gonococcal infection"	098	38	11		11		25		35		13	39, 40		38(b)	37, 38
14	"Venereal disease"	090–098	34–38	6–11	–	6–11		25, 30, 44a	–	34–35, 80, 83	13, 31 33	–	38–40, 72, 76	–	37, 38, 62, 67	36–38, 62, 67
15	Typhoid fever	001	2	12	4	12	4	1	–	1			1(a)			
16	Paratyphoid fever and other salmonella infections	002–3	3	13	–	13		2, 177		2, 177			1(b), 175			

17	Typhoid and paratyphoid	001–003	2, 3	12, 13	–	12, 13	–	1, 2, 177	1	1, 2, 177	1	1	1, 175	1	1, 164	
18	Cholera	000	1	14	5	14	5	4		12			14	10	12	12
19	Brucellosis – (undulant fever)	023	13	15		15		5					4		3	3
20	Dysentery – all forms	004, 006	4	16	6	16	6	27		3	9		16		14	14
21	Scarlet fever	–	–	17	–	17	–	8	3		5	5	8	6	7	7
22	Erysipelas	035	18	19	–	19		11		5			21		18	18
23	Septicaemia/pyaemia	–	–	20	–	20	–	24a, b, d (or 24)	–	36(a, b) (or 36)	14	–	41	–	20AB (or 20)	20
24	Diphtheria	032	15	21	8	21	8	10	5	0	7	7	10	8	9	9
25	Whooping cough	033	16	22	9	22	9	9	4	9	6	6	9	7	8	8
26	Meningococcal infections	036	19	23	10	23	10	6		18			24		61A, B	61 pt. 2
27	Plague	020	11	24	11	24	11	3	2	14	10	9	17		15	15
28	Leprosy	030	14	25		25		23		33			20		17	17
29	Tetanus	037	20	26		26		12		22			29		24	72
30	Anthrax	022	12	27		27		7		20			27		22	22
31	Poliomyelitis and infectious encephalitis including late effects	–	–	28–30	–	28–30	–	36, 37		16, 17	–	–	22, 23	–	–	–
32	Smallpox	050	24	31	13	31	13	34	11	6	3	3	6	4	5	5
33	Measles	055	25	32	14	32	14	35	12	7	4	4	7	5	6	6
34	Yellow fever	060	26	33		33		38(a)		37			18		16	16
35	Hepatitis – infectious	070	28	34		34										
36	Rabies	–	–	35		35		38(b)		21			28		23	23
37	Typhus and other rickettsial diseases	080–083	30	36	15	36	15	39	13	3	2	2	2	2	2	2
38	Malaria	084	31	37	16	37	16	28	8	38	15	13	5	3	4	4
39	Hydatid disease	122	40	39		39		41		41			121		112	111
40	Ankylostomiasis	126	42	41		41		40		40			115		106	
41	Infections – all forms	000–007, 010–136	1, 4 6–44	1–43	–	1–43	–	1–32, 34–43, 44a, c, d,		1–10, 12–44, 80, 83,	1–7, 9–17, 31, 33	1–7, 9–14, 21	1–10, 12–14, 16–42,		1–9, 11 12, 14– 25, 28–	1–9, 11, 12, 14– 24, 26–

6 Appendix *(continued)*

DE No.	Cause	Revisions 8th 1965		7th 1955		6th 1948		5th 1938		4th 1929			3rd 1920		2nd 1909	1st 1901
		ICD No.	A	A	B	A	B	Det.	Abbr.	Det.	Inter.	Abbr.	Det.	Abbr.	Det.	Det.
41	Infections – *(continued)*							177		177			72, 76, 115, 116, 121, 130, 175		35, 37, 38, 61A, B, 62, 67, 112, 121, 106, 107, 164	38, 61 pt. 2, 62, 67, 72, 107, 111
42	Malignant neoplasm – buccal cavity and pharynx	140–149	45	44		44		45		45			43		39	39
43	Malignant neoplasm – oesophagus	150	46	45		45		46(a)		46(a)						
44	Malignant neoplasm – stomach	151	47	46		46		46(b)		46(b)						
45	Malignant neoplasm – buccal cavity, pharnyx, oesophagus and stomach	140–151	45–47	44–46		44–46		45, 46a, b		45, 46a, b			43, 44		39, 40	39, 40
46	Malignant neoplasm – intestine excluding rectum	152, 153	48	47		47		46(c)								
47	Malignant neoplasm – rectum	154	49	48		48		46(d)		46(c)						
48	Malignant neoplasm – intestine and rectum	152–154	48, 49	47, 48		47, 48		46c, d					45		41	41
49	Malignant neoplasm – "alimentary tract"	140–154	45–49	44–48		44–48		45, 46		45, 46			43–45		39–41	39–41
50	Malignant neoplasm – larynx	161	50	49		49		47(a)								
51	Malignant neoplasm – trachea, bronchus and lung, not specified as secondary	162	51	50		50		47(b)		47						
52	Malignant neoplasm – larynx, trachea, bronchus and lung	161, 162	50, 51	49, 50		49, 50		47a, b (or 47)		47						
53	Malignant neoplasm – breast	174	54	51		51		50		50			47		43	43
54	Malignant neoplasm – cervix uteri	180	55	52		52		48(a)								
55	Malignant neoplasm – uterus, other and unspecified	181, 182	56	53		53		48(b)								

56	Malignant neoplasm – uterus	180–182	55, 56	52, 53		52, 53		48		48						
57	Malignant neoplasm – female genital organs							48, 49		48, 49			46		42	42
58	Malignant neoplasm – prostrate	185	57	54		54		51(b)								
59	Malignant neoplasm – skin	172, 173	53	55		55		53		52			48		44	44
60	Malignant neoplasm – bone and connective tissue			56		56		55b								
61	Malignant neoplasm – all solid tumours	140–199	45–58	44–57		44–57		45–55		45–53			43–49		39-45	39-45
62	Leukaemia and aleukaemia	204–207	59	58		58		74		72a (or 72a, b(2)) 1935–			65(a)		53A	
63	Hodgkin's disease							44b		72b (or 72b (1)) 1935–			65(b)		53B	
64	Lymphosarcoma and other neoplasms of lymphatic and haemotopoietic system	200–203, 208, 209	60	59		59										
65	Malignant neoplasm – all forms	140–209	45–60	44–59	18	44–59	18	44b, 45–55, 74		45–53, 72			43–49, 65		39-45, 53	39–45, 53
66	Neoplasm – benign and unspecified	210–239	61	60	19	60	19	56, 57	16	54, 55	19	16	50, 84 (2), 137, 139		46, 74c, 129, 131	
67	Neoplasm – all forms	140–239	45–61	44–60	18, 19	44–60	18, 19	44b, 45–57, 74		45–55, 72	18, 19, pt. 27	15, 16, pt. 20	43–50, 65, 84(2), 137, 139	–	39–46, 53, 74(c) 129, 131	
68	Goitre – non-toxic	240, 241	62	61		61		63(a)		66(a)			60b: 3			
69	Thyrotoxicosis with or without goitre	242	63	62		62		63(b)		66(b)			60(a)		51	51
70	Diabetes mellitus	250	64	63	20	63	20	61	18	59	22	18	57		50	50
71	Avitaminosis and other deficiency states	260–269	65	64		64		66a, b: 2 67–71		60–64	23		53–56		26, 27, 36, 49	25, 49
72	Anaemias	280–285	67	65	21	65	21	73		71	26		58		54	54
73	Allergic disorders, all other endocrine, metabolic and blood diseases			66		66		60, 62 63c, d, e,		58, 65, 66c, d, e,			52:3, 59, 60b(1), 2,		48c, 52, 55, 74B,	

6 Appendix *(continued)*

DE No.	Cause	Revisions 8th 1965 ICD No.	8th 1965 A	7th 1955 A	7th 1955 B	6th 1948 A	6th 1948 B	5th 1938 Det.	5th 1938 Abbr.	4th 1929 Det.	4th 1929 Inter.	4th 1929 Abbr.	3rd 1920 Det.	3rd 1920 Abbr.	2nd 1909 Det.	1st 1901 Det.
73	Allergic disorders *(continued)*							64, 65, 66b:1, 3, 72, 75, 76, 112		67–70, 73, 74 112			61–64, 69, 105		84A, 96, 116, 88	
74	Allergic disorders, endocrine, metabolic and blood diseases	240–289	62–68	61–66		61–66		60–73, 75, 76, 112		58–71, 73, 74, 112 (-63:2 (if available)			52:3, 53-64, 69, 105		26, 27, 36, 48c, 49–52, 54, 55, 74B, 84A, 88, 96, 116	
75	Mental illness	290–309	69, 70	67, 68		67, 68		77, 79b, c, 84b, c, d 162b		75, 76, 84, 162a			66, 68, 77, 164:1		56, 59, 68, 154A	
76	Mental deficiency	310–315	71	69		69		84(a)								
77	Mental illness – all forms	290–309, 310–315	69–71	67–69		67–69		77, 79b, c, 84, 162b								
78	Vascular lesions affecting central nervous system	430–438	85	70	22	70	22	83	22	82, 97:1, 97:2			74, 75, 83, 91b: 1	18	64–66, 82a	
79	Meningitis – non-meningococcal	320	72	71	23	71	23	81	21	79	30		71	17	61c	61 pt. 1
80	Multiple sclerosis	340	73	72		72		87(d)		87(d)			84:3			
81	Epilepsy	345	74	73		73		85		85	35		78		69	69
82	Organs of vision – all diseases	360–369, 374–375	75–77	74–76		74–76		88		88			85		75	75
83	Otitis media and mastoiditis	381–383	78	77		77		89		89			86		76	76
84	Eye and ear – all diseases	360–369, 374, 375, 381–383	75–78	74–77		74–77		88, 89		88, 89	37		85, 86		75, 76	75, 76

85	Nervous system and sense organs – all diseases	320–389, 430–438	72–79, 85	70–78	–	70–78		80–83, 85, 87b, c, d, e, 88, 89		78, 79, 81, 82, 85, 87b, c, d, e, 97:1, 2			70, 71, 73–75, 78, 82, 83, 84:1, 3, 4, 5, 85, 86, 91b:1		60, 61c, 63–66, 69, 73, 74A, D, 75, 76, 82A	
86	Mental illness and diseases of the nervous system	290–389, 430–438	69–79, 85	67–78		67–78		77, 79b, c, 80–85, 87b, c, d, e, 88, 89, 162b		75, 76, 78, 79, 81, 82, 84, 85, 87b, c, d, e, 88, 89, 97:1, 2, 162a			66, 68, 70, 71, 73–75, 77, 78, 82, 83, 84:1, 3, 4, 5, 85, 86, 91b:1, 164:1		56, 59, 60, 61c, 63–66, 68, 69, 73, 74A, D, 75, 76, 82A, 154A	
87	Rheumatic fever	390–392	80	79	24	79	24	58, 87a, 90a		56, 87a			51, 81		47, 72	47, 73
88	Heart disease – chronic rheumatic	393–398	81	80	25	80	25	92b, (or 92b:1) 93b, 95b		92:2, 3, 4, 5			90:2, 3, 4			
89	Heart disease – arteriosclerotic and degenerative	410–414	83	81	26	81	26	92a, c, 93c, d, 94		92:1, 93(b), c, 94, 95			89, 90:1, 5–9			
90	Heart – all diseases	393–398, 410–414, 420–429	81, 83, 84	80–82	25–27	80–82	25–27	90b, 91–95	24	90–95	38–43	24	87–90	19	77–80, 85(a)	77–80
91	Heart disease and acute rheumatism	390–398, 410–414, 420–429	80, 81, 83, 84	79–82	24–27	79–82	24–27	58, 87a, 90–95		56, 87a, 90–95			51, 81, 87–90		47, 72, 77–80, 85a	47, 73, 77–80
92	Hypertensive disease	400–404	82	83, 84	28, 29	83, 84		102		102			96			
93	Arteries – all diseases	440–448	86	85		85		96–99		96, 97:3, 98, 99			91a, b:2, c, 151		81, 82B, 142	81, 142
94	Circulatory system – all diseases	400–404, 440–448, 450–458	82, 86–88	83–86		83–86		96–103, 111a		96, 97:3, 98–103, 111:2			91a, b:2, c, 92–96, 151		81, 82B, 83, 84B, 85, 142	81–83, 85, 86, 142
95	Cardio-vascular disease	393–398, 400–404, 410–414, 420–429, 440–448, 450–458	81–84, 86–88	80–86		80–86		90b, 91–103, 111a		90–96, 97:3, 98–103, 111:2			87–90, 91a, b:2, c, 92–96, 151		77–81, 82B, 83, 84B, 85, 142	77–86, 142

6 Appendix *(continued)*

DE No.	Cause	Revisions														
		8th 1965		7th 1955		6th 1948		5th 1938		4th 1929			3rd 1920		2nd 1909	1st 1901
		ICD No.	A	A	B	A	B	Det.	Abbr.	Det.	Inter.	Abbr.	Det.	Abbr.	Det.	Det.
96	Cardio-vascular disease and vascular lesions affecting central nervous system	393–398, 400–404, 410–414, 420–438, 440–448, 450–458	81–88	70, 80–86		70, 80–86		83, 90b, 91–103, 111a		82, 90–103, 111:2			74, 75, 83, 87–96, 151		64–66, 77–83, 84B, 85, 142	
97	Circulatory disease and acute rheumatism	390–398, 400–404, 410–414, 420–429, 440–448, 450–458	80–84, 86–88	79–86		79–86		58, 87a, 90–103, 111a		56, 87a, 90–96, 97:3, 98–103, 111:2			51, 81 87–90, 91a, b:2, c, 92–96, 151		47, 72, 77–81, 82B, 83, 84B, 85, 142	47, 73, 77–83, 85, 86, 142
98	Respiratory infections – acute upper	460–466	89	87		87										
99	Influenza	470–474	90	88	30	88	30	33	10	11	8	8	11	9	10	10
100	Pneumonia – lobar			89		89		108		108			101a		92A	
101	Broncho – pneumonia			90		90		107		107			100		91	92
102	Pneumonia – primary atypical, other and unspecified			91		91		109		109			101b		92B	
103	Pneumonia – all forms	480–486	91, 92	89–91	31	89–91	31	107–109	27	107–109	48	27	100, 101	22	91, 92	92, 93
104	Bronchitis – acute			92		92		106a		106a			99a		89 if available	
105	Bronchitis – chronic and unqualified			93		93		106b, c		106b, c			99b, c, d		90 if available	
106	"Bronchitis" – all forms	460–466, 490–493	89, 93	87, 92, 93		87, 92, 93		106		106	47	26	99	20, 21	89, 90	90, 91
107	Tonsils and adenoids – hypertrophy	500	94	94		94				115:3			109:1		100A	
108	Empyema and lung abscess	510, 513	95	95		95		110a, 114c, d		110:1, 114b:1, 2			102:1, 104, 107b, c		93A, 95	

109	Pleurisy			96		96		110b		110:2			102:2		93B	
110	Respiratory disease – all forms	460-519	89-96	87-97		87-97		33, 104-111b, c, 113, 114, 115b, c		11, 104-110, 111:1, 113, 114, 115:2, 3			11, 97-104, 106, 107, 109:1		10, 86, 87, 89-95, 97-98, 100A	10, 87, 88, 90-96, 98, 99
111	Teeth and supporting structures – all diseases	520–525	97	98		98		115(a)		115(1)			108(1)		99(a)	
112	Stomach – ulcer	–	–	99		99		117(a)		117(a)			111(a)		102	103
113	Duodenum – ulcer	–	–	100		100		117(b)		117(b)			111(b)		104H 105H	
114	Peptic ulcer	531-533	98	99, 100	33	99, 100	33	117		117	51		111		102, 104H, 105H	
115	Gastritis and duodenitis	535	99	101		101		118		118			112		103	104
116	Stomach and duodenum – all diseases	531-533, 535	98, 99	99-101		99-101		117, 118		117, 118			111, 112		102, 103, 104H, 105H	
117	Appendicitis	540-543	100	102	34	102	34	121	30	121	54	30	117	26	108	118
118	Intestinal obstruction and hernia	550-553, 560	101	103	35	103	35	122		122	55		118	27	109	108
119	Gastro-enteritis and colitis excluding diarrhoea of the newborn			104		104		119, 120, 123a	29	119, 120, 123:2	52, 53	29	15, 113, 114	25	13, 104 (a-g), 105 (a-g)	13, 105, 106
120	Gastritis, duodenitis, enteritis and colitis			101, 104	36	101, 104	36	118-120, 123a		118-120, 123:2			15, 112-114		13, 103, 104 (a-g), 105 (a-g)	13, 104, 105, 106
121	Cirrhosis of liver	571	102	105	37	105	37	124		124	56		122		113	112
122	Biliary calculi							126		126			123		114	113
123	Cholelithiasis and cholecystitis	574, 575	103	106		106		126, 127a		126, 127:1						
124	Liver and biliary passages – all diseases	571, 574, 575	102, 103	105, 106		105, 106		124, 126 127	31	124, 126, 127	56, 57	31	122, 123	28	113, 114	112, 113
125	Alimentary disease – all forms	008, 009, 520-577	5, 97-104	98-107		98-107		115a, d, 116-129	29-32	115:1, 4, 116-129	51-58	29-32	15, 108, 109:2, 110-114, 117-120, 122-127		13, 99, 100B, C, 101-105, 108-111, 113-115, 117, 118	13, 100-106, 108-110, 112-114, 116-118
126	Nephritis – acute	580	105	108		108		130		130			128		119	119

6 Appendix *(continued)*

DE No.	Cause	Revisions: 8th 1965		7th 1955		6th 1948		5th 1938		4th 1929			3rd 1920		2nd 1909	1st 1901
		ICD No.	A	A	B	A	B	Det.	Abbr.	Det.	Inter.	Abbr.	Det.	Abbr.	Det.	Det.
127	Nephritis – chronic, other and unspecified	581–584	106	109		109		131, 132		131, 132			129		120	120
128	Nephritis and nephrosis	580–584	105, 106	108, 109	38	108, 109	38	130–132	33	130–132	59	33	128, 129	29	119, 120	119, 120
129	Kidney – infections	590	107	110		110		133(a)		133(a)						
130	Kidney – all diseases excluding calculi	580–584, 590	105–107	108–110		108–110		130–133		130–133	59–60		128, 129, 131		119, 120, 122	119, 120, 122
131	Urinary system – calculi	592, 594	108	111		111		134		134			132		123	122
132	Prostrate – "hyperplasia"	600	109	112	39	112	39	137(a)		137			135		126	125
133	Genito-urinary system – all diseases	580–584, 590–607, 610–629	105–111	108–114		108–114		130–139	33–34	130–139	59–65	33–34	128, 129, 131–136, 138, 140–142		119, 120, 122–128, 130, 132, 133	119–128, 130, 132, 133
134	Pregnancy, childbirth and the puerperium – sepsis	670, 671, 673	116	115		115		147	35	145	68	35	146	31	137	137
135	Pregnancy and the puerperium – toxaemias	636–639	112	116		116		114, 148		146, 147	69		148		138	138
136	Pregnancy and childbirth – haemorrhage	632, 651–653	113	117		117		143, 146		144	67		144		134(b), 135	
137	Abortion	640–645	114, 115	118, 119		118, 119		140, 141		140, 141			143(a)		134(a)	
138	Pregnancy, childbirth and the puerperium – complications	630–645, 650–662, 670–678	112–118	115–120	40	115–120	40	140–150	35, 36	140–150	66–70	35, 36	143–150	31, 32	134–141	134–141
139	Skin and subcutaneous tissue – infections	680–686	119	121		121		151, 152		151, 152	71		152, 153		143, 144	143, 144
140	Arthritis and spondylitis	710–715	121	122		122		59a, b, 156a		57:2 156a			52:2, 156		48B, 147	

141	Rheumatism – muscular and unspecified	716–718	122	123		123		59c		57:1			52:1		48A	
142	Osteomyelitis and periostitis	720	123	124		124		154		154			155(1)			
143	Ankylosis and acquired musculoskeletal deformities	727, 735–8	124	125		125										
144	Bones and joints – all diseases	710–718, 720–727, 735–738	121– 124	122– 125		122– 125		59, 154–156		57, 154–156 (+63:2 if available)	21, 72		52:1, 2 155, 156, 158		48A, B, 146, 147, 149	47, 48, 146, 147, 149
145	Skin diseases	680–686, 690–709, 721–726, 728–734	119, 120, 125	121, 126		121, 126		151–153		151–153	71		152–154		143–145	143–145
146	Skin, musculoskeletal system and connective tissue – all diseases	680–686, 690–718, 720–738	119– 125	121– 126		121– 126		59, 151–156	17, 37	57, 151–156 (+63:2 if available)	71–72	17, 37	52:1, 2, 152–156, 158		48A, B, 143–147, 149	47, 48, 143–147, 149
147	Congenital malformations – spina bifida and meningocele	741	126	127		127		157(b)		157(b)						
148	Congenital malformations – "cardio-vascular"	746–747	127, 128	128		128		157c, 157ib		157(c)			159(2)		150(c)	
149	Congenital malformations – all forms	740–759	126– 130	127– 129	41	127– 129	41	157		157	73		159		150	150
150	Newborn – birth injuries	764–768, 772	131	130		130		160		160			161(2)		152(c)	
151	Newborn – post-natal asphyxia and atelectasis	776	134	131		131		161(a)		161(a)			162(2)		152(b)	
152	Newborn – birth injuries, post-natal asphyxia and atelectasis	764–768, 772, 776	131, 134	130, 131	42	130, 131	42	160, 161(a)		160, 161(a)			161(2), 162(2)		152(b), 152(c)	
153	Newborn – infections			132	43	132	43	161(c)		161C:1, 2						
154	Newborn – haemolytic disease	774, 775	133	133		133		161e		161(b)			160(2)		151(c)	
155	Newborn – all diseases	760–779	131– 135	130– 135	42– 44	130– 135	42– 44	158–161		158–161	74–77		160–162		151, 152	151–152
156	Newborn – diseases and congenital malformations	740–779	126– 135	127– 135	41– 44	127– 135	41– 44	157–161	38	157–161	73–77	38	159–162	33	150–152	150–152

6 Appendix *(continued)*

DE No.	Cause	Revisions 8th 1965		7th 1955		6th 1948		5th 1938		4th 1929			3rd 1920		2nd 1909	1st 1901
		ICD No.	A	A	B	A	B	Det.	Abbr.	Det.	Inter.	Abbr.	Det.	Abbr.	Det.	Det.
157	Senility without mention of psychosis	794	136	136		136		162a, c	39	162b	78	39	164(2)		154B	154
158	Ill-defined and unknown causes of mortality	780–793, 795–796	137	137		137		86, 199, 200		86, 199 200			79, 80, 157, 204, 205		70, 71, 148, 187–189	70, 71, 148, 173, 177–179
159	Senility, ill-defined, and unknown causes of mortality	780–796	136, 137	136, 137	45	136, 137	45	86, 162a, c, 199, 200		86, 162b, 199, 200			79, 80, 157, 164(2), 204, 205		70, 71, 148, 154B, 187–189	70, 71, 148, 154, 173, 177–179
160	Accidents – motor vehicle	E810–E823	138	138	47	138	47	170	42							
161	Accidents – other transport	E800–807, E825–845	139	139		139		169, 171–173								
162	Accidents – all transport	E800–E845	138, 139	138, 139		138, 139		169–173								
163	Accidents – poisoning	E850–E877	140	140		140		78, 79a, d, 178, 179		77, 178, 179			66, 176, 177, 181		57, 58, 165, 168	57, 58, 174, 175
164	Accidents – falls	E880–E887	141	141		141		186								
165	Accidents – "fire and heat"	E890–E899	142	143, 144		143, 144		180, 181		180, 181			178, 179		166, 167	
166	Accidents – firearms	E922	144	145		145		184		184			183		170	
167	Accidents – drowning and submersion	E910	143	146		146		183		183			182		169	172
168	Accidents – other than motor vehicles	E800–E807, E825–E949, E980–E989	139–146, 149	139–147	48	139–147		78, 79a, d, 169, 171–176, 178–195								
169	Accidents – all forms	E800–E949, E980–E989	138–146,	138–147	47–48	138–147	47–48	78, 79a, d, 169–176, 178–195		77, 176, 178–195	81, 82, 84		67, 163, 176–189, 192–196, 201–203		57, 58, 153, 165–181, 185, 186	57, 59, 153, 164–172, 174–176
170	Suicide and self-inflicted injury	E950–E959	147	148	49	148	49	163, 164	40	163–171	79	40	165–174	36	155–163	155–163

171	Accidents – all non-traffic and suicide	E850–877, 880–887, 890–949, 980–989	140– 147, 149	140– 148		140– 148		78, 79a, d, 163, 164, 174–176, 178–195						
172	Homicide and injury purposely inflicted by other persons (not in war)	E960–E978	148	149		149		165–168, 198	172–175, 198	80, 84	41	197–200		182–184	
173	War injury	E990–E999	150	150		150		196, 197	196, 197	83		190, 191			
174	Homicide and war injury	E960–978, 990–999	148, 150	149, 150	50	149, 150	50	165–168, 196–198	172–175, 196–198			190, 191, 197–200			
175	Accidents – all violence excluding suicide	E800–949, 960–999	138– 146, 148– 150	138– 147, 149, 150	47, 48, 50	138– 147, 149, 150	47, 48, 50	78, 79a,d,41–43 165–176, 178–198	77, 172–176, 178–198	80–84	41, 42	67, 163, 176–203		57, 58, 153, 165–186	57, 59, 153, 164–172, 174–176
176	Homicide, suicide and war injury	E950–978, E990–999	147, 148, 150	148– 150	49, 50	148– 150	49, 50	163–168, 40, 41 196–198	163–175, 196–198	79, 80, 83, 84		165–174, 190–191, 197–200			
177	Accidents and violence – all forms	E800–807, 810–823, 825–845, 850–877, 880–887, 890–978, 980–999	138– 150	138– 150	47– 50	138– 150	47– 50	78, 79a,d,40–43 163–176, 178–198	77, 163–176, 178–198	79–84	40–42	67, 163, 165–174, 176–203	35–36	57, 58, 153, 155–163, 168–186	57, 59, 153, 155–172, 174–176

Cause of Death Tables

SERIAL MORTALITY TABLES FOR VARIOUS COUNTRIES 1901-1975

TABLE 1 : TUBERCULOSIS - RESPIRATORY SYSTEM : MALES

	1901-	1906-	1911-	1916-	1921-	1926-	1931-	1936-	1941-	1946-	1951-	1956-	1961-	1966-	1971-75
1 AUSTRALIA	-	16778	15244	14010	12363	10749	8438	7291	6749	5409	2786	1422	967	464	187
2 AUSTRIA	.	.	.	.	-	-	-	-	-	12781	6976	5007	4415	3156	1985
3 BELGIUM	22623	21132	19701	18377	13619	11884	11237	10204	13276	8522	5462	4069	2886	1865	1115
4 BULGARIA	-	-	-	-	-	42670	31451	26284	28024	26157	12433	3461	3159	2537	1613
5 CANADA	-	-	-	-	11580	11515	9658	8161	7442	5748	2579	1307	892	626	285
6 CHILE	-	64165	60787	58600	53646	54530	53632	54283	52100	48018	20163	14840	13376	9805	6334
7 CZECHOSLOVAKIA	-	-	-	52686	35206	34258	26149	21013	23942	17742	11246	6873	3897	2314	1367
8 DENMARK	35467	29254	23558	24310	12084	9186	7498	5261	4717	3489	1523	747	582	295	203
9 EIRE	-	-	-	-	19994	17436	15580	14808	16805	12968	6632	3539	2756	1894	1023
10 FINLAND	60042	56092	53978	52448	42354	39471	33899	35961	38699	31548	12625	8294	4439	2061	812
11 FRANCE	-	-	-	-	24851	25719	22407	21428	21339	11782	7312	5087	3645	2259	1187
12 GREECE	-	-	-	-	30964	30863	28059	23323	-	-	-	4287	3519	2505	1385
13 HUNGARY	-	-	-	58444	50514	36089	27942	22846	24409	18582	10205	6863	5907	4532	2726
14 ICELAND	-	-	19100	20463	21525	22031	19000	13553	9102	4785	1520	833	240	407	206
15 ITALY	.	.	.	.	20959	16957	13492	11417	15206	10087	5150	4147	3314	2045	1248
16 JAPAN	29041	31017	30977	32480	30405	31234	33061	36585	-	30389	15582	9332	6139	4092	2642.
17 NETHERLANDS	28184	25484	21719	25290	14206	11309	7680	5690	9927	4424	1651	732	404	224	156
18 NEW ZEALAND	-	12713	11601	11066	9534	7905	6210	6298	6100	5030	3247	1625	881	656	256
19 NORWAY	37060	34235	32350	30994	28289	22467	17843	12863	10969	7358	2898	1430	799	417	107
20 POLAND	-	-	-	-	-	-	-	-	-	-	.	10979	10894	7980	4437
21 PORTUGAL	23158	22330	26503	29867	31815	38604	34129	30708	30931	30505	17136	12422	8632	6272	3338
22 ROMANIA	-	-	-	-	-	-	-	-	-	-	-	7545	6228	4811	2643
23 SPAIN	32300	28646	25541	28849	26047	23651	20735	21866	21835	21164	9492	5818	4671	3128	1978
24 SWEDEN	-	-	27170	25628	20415	17186	14573	11183	9788	5649	2482	1381	938	682	485
25 SWITZERLAND	37215	37215	28918	28918	21527	18316	14554	11541	11059	7876	3997	2763	1822	1285	979
26 TURKEY	-	-	-	-	-	-	-	-	-	-	-	17673	11609	7551	4512
27 UK ENGLAND AND WALES	30484	25615	24196	22714	17734	15413	12959	10700	10426	7749	3973	1939	1219	677	377
28 UK NORTHERN IRELAND	-	-	-	-	20799	16921	14925	12539	12276	9672	4350	2146	1439	773	525
29 UK SCOTLAND	32942	28978	23926	20700	16090	13159	11362	10525	10381	10580	4893	2554	1765	921	553
30 USA	55428	37099	30738	25858	15858	13574	10849	9189	7767	5944	2832	1636	1136	702	365
31 YUGOSLAVIA	-	-	-	-	-	-	-	-	-	-	.	12000	8122	4632	3038

- NO MORTALITY DATA ARE AVAILABLE FOR EVEN A BROADER GROUP OF CAUSES FOR THIS DISEASE

. MORTALITY DATA ARE PRESENTED FOR A BROADER GROUP OF CAUSES FOR THIS DISEASE

0 VALUE<0.5

THE STANDARD MORTALITY RATIOS WERE DERIVED WITH A FACTOR OF 1000

SERIAL MORTALITY TABLES FOR VARIOUS COUNTRIES 1901-1975

TABLE 1 : TUBERCULOSIS - RESPIRATORY SYSTEM : FEMALES

	1901-	1906-	1911-	1916-	1921-	1926-	1931-	1936-	1941-	1946-	1951-	1956-	1961-	1966-	1971-75
1 AUSTRALIA	-	15749	13090	10825	9276	7984	5914	4699	3706	2488	878	379	236	107	55
2 AUSTRIA	.	.	.	.	-	-	-	-	-	6228	2902	1603	1147	793	500
3 BELGIUM	20114	18564	17107	17926	12989	10732	8551	6395	6801	3904	1573	885	519	349	218
4 BULGARIA	-	-	-	-	-	39087	25799	19665	19282	17044	7559	1651	1344	869	516
5 CANADA	-	-	-	-	12900	14749	11198	8810	6965	4843	1607	624	374	256	113
6 CHILE	-	65402	63689	62717	55271	59634	54662	52165	47707	41367	14955	9036	7052	4727	2634
7 CZECHOSLOVAKIA	-	-	-	48273	32031	30132	20625	15926	14459	10275	5424	2831	1478	827	491
8 DENMARK	23743	22953	18380	18329	14329	11198	8412	5292	3951	2732	1004	426	222	142	94
9 EIRE	-	-	-	-	21070	18471	15902	14480	16143	12043	4762	1935	1266	757	386
10 FINLAND	58094	53510	51541	45073	37855	37826	29909	27381	23915	15418	5100	2883	1406	680	376
11 FRANCE	-	-	-	-	17005	17464	12916	10820	10530	5638	2802	1631	1124	697	422
12 GREECE	-	-	-	-	24713	24348	20036	15342	-	-	-	1686	1102	724	399
13 HUNGARY	-	-	-	60215	50193	35930	24845	19272	18211	10996	4712	2573	1924	1322	830
14 ICELAND	-	-	23710	25303	25248	27285	20679	13430	13135	5400	1336	591	309	214	197
15 ITALY	.	.	.	.	21944	17873	13016	9973	10416	6088	2334	1348	839	464	291
16 JAPAN	29820	32938	31876	33893	29039	28005	27631	30795	-	22220	10594	5289	2909	1705	953
17 NETHERLANDS	25979	25229	22257	27652	16155	12970	8258	5678	7955	3371	1091	396	182	111	76
18 NEW ZEALAND	-	12095	12059	10899	8970	6970	5502	4751	3685	3463	1787	827	410	292	114
19 NORWAY	39192	37510	33237	31131	29162	22358	16843	10918	7495	4635	1544	600	376	193	42
20 POLAND	-	-	-	-	-	-	-	-	-	-	.	4156	3519	2234	1188
21 PORTUGAL	16654	15117	17231	19020	19756	25380	21572	18792	18857	17041	8184	4748	2561	1537	701
22 ROMANIA	-	-	-	-	-	-	-	-	-	-	-	3691	2659	1605	725
23 SPAIN	26518	24358	21508	25317	21282	18426	14429	13699	13405	12326	4928	2469	1646	882	532
24 SWEDEN	-	-	28404	25472	20385	17903	14778	10322	7963	4372	1478	710	414	293	217
25 SWITZERLAND	35171	35171	27868	27868	21223	17700	13359	9557	8444	5406	2132	1224	754	551	373
26 TURKEY	-	-	-	-	-	-	-	-	-	-	-	10360	5882	3373	1812
27 UK ENGLAND AND WALES	20878	17748	16331	16362	12568	10462	8451	6437	5321	4200	1519	559	321	190	111
28 UK NORTHERN IRELAND	-	-	-	-	23049	18593	14249	11512	10309	7596	2450	914	470	278	223
29 UK SCOTLAND	28760	24532	20254	17671	13433	10610	8541	7529	7863	7893	2612	987	526	315	186
30 USA	47006	30686	24488	22017	14917	12414	8853	6714	4872	3122	1161	558	355	216	120
31 YUGOSLAVIA	-	-	-	-	-	-	-	-	-	-	.	7196	4200	1854	1258

- NO MORTALITY DATA ARE AVAILABLE FOR EVEN A BROADER GROUP OF CAUSES FOR THIS DISEASE

. MORTALITY DATA ARE PRESENTED FOR A BROADER GROUP OF CAUSES FOR THIS DISEASE

0 VALUE<0.5

THE STANDARD MORTALITY RATIOS WERE DERIVED WITH A FACTOR OF 1000

SERIAL MORTALITY TABLES FOR VARIOUS COUNTRIES 1901-1975

TABLE 1 : TUBERCULOSIS - RESPIRATORY SYSTEM : PERSONS

	1901-	1906-	1911-	1916-	1921-	1926-	1931-	1936-	1941-	1946-	1951-	1956-	1961-	1966-	1971-75
1 AUSTRALIA	-	16307	14246	12509	10887	9415	7207	6010	5233	3946	1816	890	592	280	119
2 AUSTRIA	.	.	.	.	-	.	14062	12303	-	9119	4679	3075	2551	1803	1132
3 BELGIUM	21354	19832	18380	18146	13299	11303	9871	8257	9959	6143	3416	2383	1624	1052	632
4 BULGARIA	-	-	-	-	-	40888	28639	22975	23624	21544	9961	2530	2227	1682	1051
5 CANADA	.	10493	13210	11862	12195	13032	10387	8470	7213	5307	2100	969	632	437	196
6 CHILE	-	54792	62260	60693	54475	57140	54159	53199	49843	44579	17452	11819	10073	7145	4381
7 CZECHOSLOVAKIA	-	-	-	50326	33508	32052	23200	18301	18870	13742	8118	4698	2592	1511	892
8 DENMARK	28838	25690	20625	20922	13267	10241	7974	5277	4322	3099	1255	581	395	215	146
9 EIRE	-	-	-	-	20528	17949	15738	14647	16476	12508	5701	2733	2000	1315	697
10 FINLAND	59029	54752	52709	48594	40000	38608	31778	31337	30631	22616	8417	5277	2752	1293	569
11 FRANCE	53401	29423	27030	22644	20631	21278	17286	15651	15385	8388	4818	3183	2263	1405	772
12 GREECE	-	-	-	-	27779	27536	23953	19235	-	-	-	3618	2920	2041	1099
13 HUNGARY	-	-	-	59361	50348	36006	26327	20976	21156	14488	7236	4544	3751	2793	1696
14 ICELAND	-	-	21652	23125	23552	24875	19901	13488	11222	5104	1425	710	275	309	201
15 ITALY	.	.	.	.	21465	17433	13243	10660	12683	7970	3653	2658	1992	1197	735
16 JAPAN	29433	31981	31428	33191	29711	29585	30282	33617	-	26087	12957	7205	4439	2832	1746
17 NETHERLANDS	27043	25352	21997	26504	15206	12160	7975	5684	8918	3884	1363	558	289	165	114
18 NEW ZEALAND	-	12436	11810	10987	9263	7451	5862	5528	4873	4231	2504	1216	639	467	182
19 NORWAY	38205	35999	32828	31068	28757	22409	17310	11833	9140	5932	2193	999	579	300	73
20 POLAND	-	-	-	-	-	-	-	-	-	-	.	8138	6838	4831	2655
21 PORTUGAL	19598	18366	21388	23860	25136	31296	27189	24113	24270	23131	12180	8184	5283	3643	1873
22 ROMANIA	-	-	-	-	-	-	-	.	-	.	-	5477	4319	3100	1621
23 SPAIN	29289	26404	23434	27011	23558	20899	17384	17481	17309	16396	7011	4002	3032	1912	1199
24 SWEDEN	-	-	27828	25545	20399	17564	14680	10736	8845	4991	1966	1036	668	481	346
25 SWITZERLAND	36143	36143	28361	28361	21364	17986	13912	10476	9652	6544	2992	1933	1245	889	653
26 TURKEY	-	-	-	-	-	-	27657	24006	29091	21168	15432	14023	8767	5521	3218
27 UK ENGLAND AND WALES	25457	21496	20017	19309	14959	12751	10532	8387	7520	5813	2632	1184	729	412	232
28 UK NORTHERN IRELAND	-	-	-	-	21987	17804	14570	11998	11224	8576	3335	1483	917	506	362
29 UK SCOTLAND	30687	26587	21960	19075	14666	11792	9849	8916	9020	9120	3647	1693	1082	586	350
30 USA	51225	33986	27725	23993	15400	13007	9866	7958	6313	3609	1973	1077	726	443	234
31 YUGOSLAVIA	-	-	-	-	62180	75891	50706	42675	-	-	.	9402	6015	3144	2086

\- NO MORTALITY DATA ARE AVAILABLE FOR EVEN A BROADER GROUP OF CAUSES FOR THIS DISEASE

. MORTALITY DATA ARE PRESENTED FOR A BROADER GROUP OF CAUSES FOR THIS DISEASE

0 VALUE<0.5

THE STANDARD MORTALITY RATIOS WERE DERIVED WITH A FACTOR OF 1000

SERIAL MORTALITY TABLES FOR VARIOUS COUNTRIES 1901-1975

TABLE 2 : TUBERCULOSIS - MENINGES AND CENTRAL NERVOUS SYSTEM : MALES

	1901-	1906-	1911-	1916-	1921-	1926-	1931-	1936-	1941-	1946-	1951-	1956-	1961-	1966-	1971-75
1 AUSTRALIA	-	1477	1461	1290	998	950	639	473	307	183	103	24	18	12	15
2 AUSTRIA	.	.	.	.	-	-	-	-	-	.	326	194	98	46	34
3 BELGIUM	3181	3005	2800	3144	3347	3229	.	.	.	.	349	179	73	44	26
4 BULGARIA	-	-	-	-	-	10130	.	.	.	.	.	.	191	88	67
5 CANADA	-	-	-	-	1517	1634	1493	1364	1279	925	378	106	41	23	10
6 CHILE	-	569	686	658	886	3218	4459	5051	5540	5263	1531	866	608	364	288
7 CZECHOSLOVAKIA	-	-	-	3082	2845	3040	2337	1631	1458	1647	485	174	69	27	16
8 DENMARK	9897	7810	6046	5737	4035	2958	1932	1154	833	531	91	16	12	0	6
9 EIRE	-	-	-	-	2984	2496	2987	3116	4442	3562	1668	476	140	77	53
10 FINLAND	-	-	-	-	.	.	.	.	5185	3573	820	126	33	12	16
11 FRANCE	-	-	-	-	4383	4148	.	.	3941	2851	1176	342	170	95	81
12 GREECE	-	-	-	-	4216	5383	5472	4853	-	-	-	395	227	116	103
13 HUNGARY	-	-	-	4418	5215	5523	4933	4187	4411	.	457	229	88	36	23
14 ICELAND	-	-	9857	11000	11875	11000	9111	5222	2600	1500	.	.	0	0	0
15 ITALY	.	.	.	.	5045	4359	3204	2746	2970	2327	834	357	175	90	47
16 JAPAN	2659	3403	3390	3548	2911	2665	3004	3605	-	2089	1194	434	179	72	38
17 NETHERLANDS	6176	6034	5068	6247	4458	3185	2374	1573	1765	791	201	33	15	8	13
18 NEW ZEALAND	-	1941	1633	1781	1806	1130	1278	748	846	592	467	126	47	4	8
19 NORWAY	10546	9590	8675	7874	7860	6667	4412	3060	2147	1085	230	24	31	18	7
20 POLAND	-	-	-	-	-	-	-	-	-	-	.	410	242	82	39
21 PORTUGAL	.	.	2111	2174	2793	4204	.	.	.	.	2430	1553	705	450	232
22 ROMANIA	-	-	-	-	-	-	-	-	-	-	-	1073	533	315	136
23 SPAIN	3938	3374	2708	3304	3187	3537	3634	3709	4094	4827	2313	770	370	143	84
24 SWEDEN	-	-	5624	5361	4574	3760	2721	1772	1235	535	118	39	20	15	8
25 SWITZERLAND	8225	8225	6003	6003	3849	3101	2448	1751	1493	1025	381	130	57	46	42
26 TURKEY	-	-	-	-	-	-	-	-	-	-	-	2601	1219	606	329
27 UK ENGLAND AND WALES	5927	5368	4573	4016	2969	2496	2147	1696	2004	1131	355	69	48	35	25
28 UK NORTHERN IRELAND	-	-	-	-	4474	4126	3894	3138	3670	2276	800	148	53	34	0
29 UK SCOTLAND	8128	9566	7208	5231	4378	3830	3165	3085	3379	2100	561	119	35	35	14
30 USA	4593	3541	3018	2361	1367	1021	662	448	322	259	136	52	35	23	18
31 YUGOSLAVIA	-	-	-	-	-	-	-	-	-	-	.	.	447	225	137

- NO MORTALITY DATA ARE AVAILABLE FOR EVEN A BROADER GROUP OF CAUSES FOR THIS DISEASE

. MORTALITY DATA ARE PRESENTED FOR A BROADER GROUP OF CAUSES FOR THIS DISEASE

0 VALUE<0.5

THE STANDARD MORTALITY RATIOS WERE DERIVED WITH A FACTOR OF 100

SERIAL MORTALITY TABLES FOR VARIOUS COUNTRIES 1901-1975

TABLE 2 : TUBERCULOSIS - MENINGES AND CENTRAL NERVOUS SYSTEM : FEMALES

	1901-	1906-	1911-	1916-	1921-	1926-	1931-	1936-	1941-	1946-	1951-	1956-	1961-	1966-	1971-75
1 AUSTRALIA	-	1491	1470	1140	943	854	626	436	362	230	104	31	17	17	7
2 AUSTRIA	.	.	.	.	-	-	-	-	-	.	324	188	83	48	24
3 BELGIUM	3139	2821	2651	2792	3552	3214	.	.	.	.	314	131	46	23	20
4 BULGARIA	-	-	-	-	-	11187	.	.	.	.	.	.	116	71	45
5 CANADA	-	-	-	-	1377	1681	1518	1390	1350	967	351	87	47	20	16
6 CHILE	-	609	537	443	759	2916	4047	4616	5157	5025	1325	797	557	298	233
7 CZECHOSLOVAKIA	-	-	-	2885	2347	2697	2041	1418	1464	1605	424	180	70	40	20
8 DENMARK	9524	6933	5564	5441	3798	2921	1963	989	744	405	74	16	9	6	6
9 EIRE	-	-	-	-	2757	2543	3120	2977	3855	3491	1637	339	136	97	38
10 FINLAND	-	-	-	-	.	.	.	.	4294	3160	756	140	51	27	13
11 FRANCE	-	-	-	-	3528	3544	.	.	3343	2500	963	262	140	71	50
12 GREECE	-	-	-	-	3719	4585	4809	3988	-	-	-	377	189	98	80
13 HUNGARY	-	-	-	3996	4748	5027	4558	4057	4188	.	495	241	88	33	26
14 ICELAND	-	-	10429	9125	11500	11111	8444	4444	1800	1455	.	.	0	0	0
15 ITALY	.	.	.	.	5148	4256	3234	2768	2923	2489	905	377	187	91	54
16 JAPAN	2569	3450	3388	3538	2765	2497	2685	3116	-	2165	1206	429	173	75	41
17 NETHERLANDS	5191	5377	4858	5944	4203	3061	2166	1599	1893	881	204	51	17	8	15
18 NEW ZEALAND	-	1688	1706	1815	1768	1433	942	1019	1026	511	460	120	39	50	0
19 NORWAY	10223	8975	8019	7256	6977	6062	4128	2681	1721	970	236	28	16	11	11
20 POLAND	-	-	-	-	-	-	-	-	-	-	.	320	185	62	32
21 PORTUGAL	.	.	1991	2069	2607	3552	.	.	.	.	1820	1491	583	300	140
22 ROMANIA	-	-	-	-	-	-	-	-	-	-	-	1013	485	275	128
23 SPAIN	3548	3114	2479	2972	2852	3140	3247	3251	3889	4636	2128	666	320	128	75
24 SWEDEN	-	-	5276	5186	4266	3566	2546	1461	1080	455	113	46	18	10	18
25 SWITZERLAND	8753	8753	6146	6146	4160	3444	2274	1648	1648	1074	369	91	42	35	31
26 TURKEY	-	-	-	-	-	-	-	-	-	-	-	2272	1220	566	280
27 UK ENGLAND AND WALES	5193	4807	4047	3595	2596	2204	1916	1551	1780	1083	341	79	41	31	22
28 UK NORTHERN IRELAND	-	-	-	-	3859	3773	3295	2768	3394	2133	781	151	107	26	52
29 UK SCOTLAND	7010	8336	6107	4969	3774	3397	2765	2669	3672	2218	560	76	40	24	25
30 USA	4123	3229	2724	2083	1208	888	555	390	267	217	109	45	29	18	13
31 YUGOSLAVIA	-	-	-	-	-	-	-	-	-	-	.	.	461	192	125

- NO MORTALITY DATA ARE AVAILABLE FOR EVEN A BROADER GROUP OF CAUSES FOR THIS DISEASE

. MORTALITY DATA ARE PRESENTED FOR A BROADER GROUP OF CAUSES FOR THIS DISEASE

0 VALUE<0.5

THE STANDARD MORTALITY RATIOS WERE DERIVED WITH A FACTOR OF 100

SERIAL MORTALITY TABLES FOR VARIOUS COUNTRIES 1901-1975

TABLE 3 : TUBERCULOSIS - ALIMENTARY : MALES

	1901-	1906-	1911-	1916-	1921-	1926-	1931-	1936-	1941-	1946-	1951-	1956-	1961-	1966-	1971-75
1 AUSTRALIA	-	4085	2835	2660	1530	1108	944	552	345	217	114	36	16	19	0
2 AUSTRIA	.	.	.	.	-	-	-	-	-	.	485	288	125	129	87
3 BELGIUM	.	.	.	.	.	.	.	.	.	.	380	218	92	51	34
4 BULGARIA	-	-	-	-	-	.	.	.	.	.	.	.	68	46	43
5 CANADA	-	-	-	-	2860	3344	2276	1829	1149	635	165	85	34	20	10
6 CHILE	-	3750	2766	4879	3768	5693	6284	6273	5660	4338	1636	947	384	387	210
7 CZECHOSLOVAKIA	-	-	-	6126	3970	3649	2756	1687	1415	1149	412	190	83	119	35
8 DENMARK	.	.	.	.	.	.	.	.	.	.	69	46	18	8	0
9 EIRE	-	-	-	-	9167	7691	6171	4944	5099	3403	1458	449	159	145	56
10 FINLAND	-	-	-	-	.	.	.	.	4513	2772	622	330	108	52	10
11 FRANCE	-	-	-	-	.	.	.	.	2460	1162	530	270	154	91	53
12 GREECE	-	-	-	-	.	7890	6770	5314	-	-	-	222	180	45	28
13 HUNGARY	-	-	-	4371	4104	2714	4659	3526	3550	.	383	243	144	59	56
14 ICELAND	-	-	.	.	.	.	.	.	.	.	.	.	0	0	0
15 ITALY	.	.	.	.	.	.	4422	3202	3648	1759	607	279	145	59	23
16 JAPAN	24629	26284	31037	36544	37574	34232	31389	33954	-	6714	3163	1086	389	177	96
17 NETHERLANDS	13827	11757	9371	10396	5370	3742	2657	1599	2275	756	145	40	29	14	3
18 NEW ZEALAND	-	3500	2409	2542	1667	1586	1156	1118	806	563	277	98	18	50	31
19 NORWAY	6630	5813	5160	5434	6036	4690	2951	1879	700	395	100	59	44	0	0
20 POLAND	-	-	-	-	-	-	-	-	-	-	.	203	158	119	59
21 PORTUGAL	.	.	.	.	.	.	.	.	.	.	2122	1050	497	266	159
22 ROMANIA	-	-	-	-	-	-	-	-	-	-	-	792	353	119	45
23 SPAIN	25646	19182	13390	14834	11272	8532	6423	6241	4651	3397	1703	827	417	184	69
24 SWEDEN	-	-	.	.	.	.	.	.	.	.	199	91	56	29	9
25 SWITZERLAND	10789	10789	7559	7559	5038	3578	2540	1598	1165	577	360	167	46	64	34
26 TURKEY	-	-	-	-	-	-	-	-	-	-	-	3443	1251	564	565
27 UK ENGLAND AND WALES	23163	17095	13217	9957	6025	3899	2561	1753	1934	844	281	113	66	42	34
28 UK NORTHERN IRELAND	-	-	-	-	11429	9077	7148	4464	4714	2966	194	129	152	59	29
29 UK SCOTLAND	29833	28068	22868	17191	13186	8414	4806	2926	2202	1035	336	128	42	17	50
30 USA	10202	7876	6829	5343	3347	2637	1538	929	576	292	81	41	32	26	14
31 YUGOSLAVIA	-	-	-	-	-	-	-	-	-	-	.	.	198	110	40

- NO MORTALITY DATA ARE AVAILABLE FOR EVEN A BROADER GROUP OF CAUSES FOR THIS DISEASE

. MORTALITY DATA ARE PRESENTED FOR A BROADER GROUP OF CAUSES FOR THIS DISEASE

0 VALUE<0.5

THE STANDARD MORTALITY RATIOS WERE DERIVED WITH A FACTOR OF 100

SERIAL MORTALITY TABLES FOR VARIOUS COUNTRIES 1901-1975

TABLE 3 : TUBERCULOSIS - ALIMENTARY : FEMALES

	1901-	1906-	1911-	1916-	1921-	1926-	1931-	1936-	1941-	1946-	1951-	1956-	1961-	1966-	1971-75
1 AUSTRALIA	-	5016	3782	3163	2109	1320	810	576	422	169	82	26	4	14	3
2 AUSTRIA	.	.	.	.	-	-	-	-	-	.	589	295	209	131	105
3 BELGIUM	.	.	.	.	.	.	.	.	.	.	336	200	97	71	36
4 BULGARIA	-	-	-	-	-	.	.	.	.	.	.	.	117	97	41
5 CANADA	-	-	-	-	4607	4793	3695	2732	1846	857	276	89	29	15	16
6 CHILE	-	1846	3246	5552	3625	6805	7107	8253	7535	5386	1795	901	457	392	183
7 CZECHOSLOVAKIA	-	-	-	5948	4191	3819	2788	1880	1458	1360	388	232	103	82	35
8 DENMARK		.	.	.	.	.	.	.	.	.	93	70	57	38	15
9 EIRE	-	-	-	-	9593	9448	7632	6294	6514	3634	1296	443	114	125	80
10 FINLAND	-	-	-	-	.	.	.	.	4149	2398	758	362	198	68	81
11 FRANCE	-	-	-	-	.	.	.	.	2577	1212	510	197	137	76	43
12 GREECE	-	-	-	-	.	9779	7993	6079	-	-	-	251	100	54	17
13 HUNGARY	-	-	-	4318	4259	2898	5874	4560	4046	.	526	249	159	61	58
14 ICELAND	-	-	.	.	.	.	.	.	.	.	.	.	0	0	0
15 ITALY	.	.	.	.	.	.	6145	4707	4626	2546	755	302	133	63	31
16 JAPAN	39189	44823	56309	68580	67543	58538	49784	53831	-	12225	5138	1725	602	276	123
17 NETHERLANDS	14035	12967	11008	12671	7709	5085	4039	2464	3252	1195	325	114	31	10	18
18 NEW ZEALAND	-	6000	3895	4136	3120	1750	1645	1294	703	610	167	38	68	16	0
19 NORWAY	6885	6434	5607	6390	5935	5266	3397	2167	1130	744	221	33	31	19	9
20 POLAND	-	-	-	-	-	-	-	-	-	-	.	178	141	106	31
21 PORTUGAL	.	.	.	.	.	.	.	.	.	.	1814	1074	449	286	157
22 ROMANIA	-	-	-	-	-	-	-	-	-	-	-	640	367	156	44
23 SPAIN	24730	20245	15174	18106	13096	10682	7386	6821	5346	4149	1981	966	450	156	88
24 SWEDEN	-	-	.	.	.	.	.	.	.	.	243	82	68	41	34
25 SWITZERLAND	14333	14333	10762	10762	6356	4957	3616	2442	1874	1092	469	290	100	86	41
26 TURKEY	-	-	-	-	-	-	-	-	-	-	-	3368	1176	493	440
27 UK ENGLAND AND WALES	19486	14824	11049	8976	5415	3586	2426	1586	1551	761	262	104	73	39	28
28 UK NORTHERN IRELAND	-	-	-	-	11043	10931	8931	5433	5156	2281	714	56	108	26	25
29 UK SCOTLAND	25379	25162	20243	16701	11236	7487	4598	2926	2458	1313	397	221	154	151	67
30 USA	12423	9717	8330	6476	4284	3181	1879	1110	669	323	80	34	27	18	10
31 YUGOSLAVIA	-	-	-	-	-	-	-	-	-	-	.	.	264	118	50

- NO MORTALITY DATA ARE AVAILABLE FOR EVEN A BROADER GROUP OF CAUSES FOR THIS DISEASE

. MORTALITY DATA ARE PRESENTED FOR A BROADER GROUP OF CAUSES FOR THIS DISEASE

0 VALUE<0.5

THE STANDARD MORTALITY RATIOS WERE DERIVED WITH A FACTOR OF 100

SERIAL MORTALITY TABLES FOR VARIOUS COUNTRIES 1901-1975

TABLE 4 : TUBERCULOSIS - BONES AND JOINTS : MALES

	1901-	1906-	1911-	1916-	1921-	1926-	1931-	1936-	1941-	1946-	1951-	1956-	1961-	1966-	1971-75
1 AUSTRALIA	-	1011	1726	1635	1444	1087	939	692	635	366	176	104	45	16	12
2 AUSTRIA	.	.	.	.	-	-	-	-	-	.	605	326	213	153	78
3 BELGIUM	.	.	.	.	.	.	.	.	.	.	397	277	89	98	42
4 BULGARIA	-	-	-	-	-	.	.	.	.	.	.	.	320	195	118
5 CANADA	-	-	-	-	1784	1291	1475	1271	956	539	189	75	48	30	17
6 CHILE	-	.	.	.	1021	1287	2568	2942	2982	2223	379	434	251	120	87
7 CZECHOSLOVAKIA	-	-	-	7073	5405	4807	4155	3557	3507	2439	1028	683	252	104	59
8 DENMARK	.	.	.	.	.	.	.	.	.	.	122	38	18	34	16
9 EIRE	-	-	-	-	4868	4705	4092	3500	3733	2592	1155	490	253	111	59
10 FINLAND	-	-	-	-	.	.	.	.	3770	2913	926	299	184	143	21
11 FRANCE	-	-	-	-	.	.	.	.	2072	958	414	304	208	113	64
12 GREECE	-	-	-	-	.	1302	3409	2876	-	-	-	166	110	88	35
13 HUNGARY	-	-	-	5317	5060	4703	4089	3541	3600	.	855	656	329	166	111
14 ICELAND	-	-	.	.	.	.	.	.	.	.	.	.	0	0	0
15 ITALY	.	.	.	.	.	5374	3847	2981	3115	1795	600	315	156	90	76
16 JAPAN	.	.	.	.	4599	4759	4974	5444	-	4956	2226	765	277	125	71
17 NETHERLANDS	.	.	.	.	2222	1813	1939	1361	2591	1136	226	134	76	41	20
18 NEW ZEALAND	-	.	.	.	2190	1175	1068	979	922	826	523	183	132	62	45
19 NORWAY	6557	6484	5200	4261	3411	2692	2143	1835	1313	907	443	161	75	28	7
20 POLAND	-	-	-	-	-	-	-	-	-	-	.	721	506	257	100
21 PORTUGAL	.	.	.	.	.	.	.	.	.	.	973	560	327	222	102
22 ROMANIA	-	-	-	-	-	-	-	-	-	-	-	824	486	147	66
23 SPAIN	.	.	.	.	.	.	2151	2084	1954	1445	660	349	212	117	70
24 SWEDEN	-	-	.	.	.	.	1900	1278	1273	661	208	90	75	29	21
25 SWITZERLAND	14196	14196	11395	11395	3660	3354	4192	3357	2741	1353	594	401	199	169	161
26 TURKEY	-	-	-	-	-	-	-	-	-	-	-	1338	638	282	135
27 UK ENGLAND AND WALES	.	.	2952	3286	2396	1817	1687	1286	1271	642	296	137	103	47	29
28 UK NORTHERN IRELAND	-	-	-	-	4321	3333	.	.	.	732	568	227	130	106	61
29 UK SCOTLAND	.	.	4932	4154	3907	2657	2355	1758	1331	939	476	207	112	52	23
30 USA	.	.	.	.	1539	1215	1025	764	535	318	107	50	34	20	13
31 YUGOSLAVIA	-	-	-	-	-	-	-	-	-	-	.	.	611	222	67

- NO MORTALITY DATA ARE AVAILABLE FOR EVEN A BROADER GROUP OF CAUSES FOR THIS DISEASE

. MORTALITY DATA ARE PRESENTED FOR A BROADER GROUP OF CAUSES FOR THIS DISEASE

0 VALUE<0.5

THE STANDARD MORTALITY RATIOS WERE DERIVED WITH A FACTOR OF 100

SERIAL MORTALITY TABLES FOR VARIOUS COUNTRIES 1901-1975

TABLE 4 : TUBERCULOSIS - BONES AND JOINTS : FEMALES

	1901-	1906-	1911-	1916-	1921-	1926-	1931-	1936-	1941-	1946-	1951-	1956-	1961-	1966-	1971-75
1 AUSTRALIA	-	779	1185	1033	972	654	615	576	530	266	146	52	35	20	9
2 AUSTRIA	.	.	.	.	-	-	-	-	-	.	957	461	282	167	109
3 BELGIUM	.	.	.	.	.	.	.	.	.	.	275	173	83	41	37
4 BULGARIA	-	-	-	-	-	.	.	.	.	.	.	.	252	182	107
5 CANADA	-	-	-	-	1378	1064	1192	958	633	421	192	74	30	25	15
6 CHILE	-	.	.	.	544	989	1740	1945	2033	1565	208	349	202	122	85
7 CZECHOSLOVAKIA	-	-	-	6478	5155	4178	3974	3843	3298	2671	1392	829	300	112	73
8 DENMARK	.	.	.	.	.	.	.	.	.	.	152	76	49	46	5
9 EIRE	-	-	-	-	3688	3073	2887	2571	2990	1825	922	333	115	124	64
10 FINLAND	-	-	-	-	.	.	.	.	2570	1891	590	407	205	110	32
11 FRANCE	-	-	-	-	.	.	.	.	1498	683	367	246	179	105	56
12 GREECE	-	-	-	-	.	1171	2587	2605	-	-	-	173	106	58	30
13 HUNGARY	-	-	-	5250	4237	4112	3059	2630	3057	.	684	641	327	146	118
14 ICELAND	-	-	.	.	.	.	.	.	.	.	.	.	0	0	0
15 ITALY	.	.	.	.	.	4630	3388	2780	2935	1541	493	250	127	71	61
16 JAPAN	.	.	.	.	4046	3930	3909	4408	-	3975	2077	780	311	152	78
17 NETHERLANDS	.	.	.	.	1930	1639	1883	1475	3551	1482	409	117	70	33	30
18 NEW ZEALAND	-	.	.	.	1465	865	881	617	566	487	382	107	72	22	30
19 NORWAY	4129	3740	2553	2568	2447	1714	1041	856	705	533	244	117	109	32	12
20 POLAND	-	-	-	-	-	-	-	-	-	-	.	599	498	240	131
21 PORTUGAL	.	.	.	.	.	.	.	.	.	.	509	323	197	140	76
22 ROMANIA	-	-	-	-	-	-	-	-	-	-	-	718	419	105	75
23 SPAIN	.	.	.	.	.	.	1519	1389	1282	978	563	247	179	86	51
24 SWEDEN	-	-	.	.	.	.	1140	1030	728	393	191	54	53	6	14
25 SWITZERLAND	15754	15754	12850	12850	4202	3409	4574	3007	3117	1567	826	417	210	123	114
26 TURKEY	-	-	-	-	-	-	-	-	-	-	-	1079	588	283	47
27 UK ENGLAND AND WALES	.	.	2046	2029	1629	1142	1029	732	703	419	187	115	73	44	26
28 UK NORTHERN IRELAND	-	-	-	-	3594	3100	.	.	.	1522	627	192	148	70	85
29 UK SCOTLAND	.	.	3423	3333	2618	2114	1578	1057	963	525	315	95	102	54	65
30 USA	.	.	.	.	1014	820	663	478	323	189	68	32	22	15	11
31 YUGOSLAVIA	-	-	-	-	-	-	-	-	-	-	.	.	593	166	51

- NO MORTALITY DATA ARE AVAILABLE FOR EVEN A BROADER GROUP OF CAUSES FOR THIS DISEASE

. MORTALITY DATA ARE PRESENTED FOR A BROADER GROUP OF CAUSES FOR THIS DISEASE

0 VALUE<0.5

THE STANDARD MORTALITY RATIOS WERE DERIVED WITH A FACTOR OF 100

SERIAL MORTALITY TABLES FOR VARIOUS COUNTRIES 1901-1975

TABLE 5 : TUBERCULOSIS - ALL OTHER FORMS : MALES

	1901-	1906-	1911-	1916-	1921-	1926-	1931-	1936-	1941-	1946-	1951-	1956-	1961-	1966-	1971-75
1 AUSTRALIA	-	10175	5290	4902	.	4851	2898	2772	2357	1620	900	490	287	870	902
2 AUSTRIA	.	.	.	.	-	-	-	-	-	.	2899	2246	1703	2065	2161
3 BELGIUM	.	.	.	.	.	.	.	.	.	.	1764	1267	767	561	747
4 BULGARIA	-	-	-	-	-	.	.	.	.	.	.	.	522	780	675
5 CANADA	-	-	-	-	8112	8660	6467	5281	4601	3123	1588	699	520	867	1215
6 CHILE	-	.	.	.	12296	16785	18154	15855	18510	15823	4409	3781	3297	2519	2811
7 CZECHOSLOVAKIA	-	-	-	11675	8898	8033	5480	4797	3406	4172	2011	1162	827	581	483
8 DENMARK	.	.	.	.	.	.	.	.	.	.	920	662	325	900	2402
9 EIRE	-	-	-	-	15994	18955	12258	12325	12404	9911	3885	1532	866	998	2301
10 FINLAND	-	-	-	-	.	.	.	.	4584	3420	3333	2084	856	2898	6846
11 FRANCE	-	-	-	-	.	.	.	.	10186	6785	3930	2416	1707	1348	1271
12 GREECE	-	-	-	-	.	13839	7583	5972	-	-	-	564	318	237	3035
13 HUNGARY	-	-	-	10954	11630	9362	8555	7016	8371	.	3308	1954	1161	2126	6634
14 ICELAND	-	-	.	.	.	.	.	.	.	.	.	.	417	0	357
15 ITALY	.	.	.	.	.	.	.	.	.	.	2044	1172	925	1062	679
16 JAPAN	.	.	.	.	12311	10592	10455	10531	-	11550	6611	2478	1237	753	396
17 NETHERLANDS	.	.	.	.	19965	14017	10588	10510	12850	6591	1699	872	449	566	1355
18 NEW ZEALAND	-	.	.	.	6646	5909	5641	5024	3668	3720	2941	796	824	1708	4071
19 NORWAY	16630	15036	19278	20162	21569	15581	11865	10898	9012	6554	2927	1382	1051	2304	3662
20 POLAND	-	-	-	-	-	-	-	-	-	-	.	2081	837	540	1307
21 PORTUGAL	.	.	.	.	.	.	.	.	.	.	3178	2961	1749	1204	800
22 ROMANIA	-	-	-	-	-	-	-	-	-	-	-	2831	1652	1006	680
23 SPAIN	.	.	.	.	.	.	11219	10047	10035	8889	4098	2423	1742	1528	933
24 SWEDEN	-	-	.	.	.	.	.	.	.	.	1633	835	709	1286	2805
25 SWITZERLAND	17052	17052	19246	19246	24620	22604	16213	12049	10930	7719	5021	2923	2174	1803	1377
26 TURKEY	-	-	-	-	-	-	-	-	-	-	-	3256	1299	536	0
27 UK ENGLAND AND WALES	.	.	23673	21061	14634	11399	8095	6590	5179	3392	1708	852	546	1730	1869
28 UK NORTHERN IRELAND	-	-	-	-	23386	20063	.	.	.	3611	2577	1066	390	1179	1567
29 UK SCOTLAND	.	.	32792	27851	20294	15990	11044	9442	9110	3959	2000	881	655	1630	2561
30 USA	.	.	.	.	6847	5573	3893	3212	2718	2161	1223	624	424	807	754
31 YUGOSLAVIA	-	-	-	-	-	-	-	-	-	-	.	.	1584	1958	3738

- NO MORTALITY DATA ARE AVAILABLE FOR EVEN A BROADER GROUP OF CAUSES FOR THIS DISEASE

. MORTALITY DATA ARE PRESENTED FOR A BROADER GROUP OF CAUSES FOR THIS DISEASE

0 VALUE<0.5

THE STANDARD MORTALITY RATIOS WERE DERIVED WITH A FACTOR OF 1000

SERIAL MORTALITY TABLES FOR VARIOUS COUNTRIES 1901-1975

TABLE 5 : TUBERCULOSIS - ALL OTHER FORMS : FEMALES

	1901-	1906-	1911-	1916-	1921-	1926-	1931-	1936-	1941-	1946-	1951-	1956-	1961-	1966-	1971-75
1 AUSTRALIA	-	8275	4615	3800	.	4230	2657	2026	2103	1361	706	344	179	347	361
2 AUSTRIA	.	.	.	.	-	-	-	-	-	.	3053	2047	1557	1552	1158
3 BELGIUM	.	.	.	.	.	.	.	.	.	.	1129	870	482	419	343
4 BULGARIA	-	-	-	-	-	.	.	.	.	.	.	.	490	457	327
5 CANADA	-	-	-	-	7615	8152	6330	5335	4467	2761	1307	520	270	515	703
6 CHILE	-	.	.	.	9367	15362	17289	16640	19089	15080	4462	3028	2296	2100	1962
7 CZECHOSLOVAKIA	-	-	-	9338	7367	6749	4472	3739	3817	3605	1751	1164	683	513	432
8 DENMARK	.	.	.	.	.	.	.	.	.	.	1049	387	248	591	1302
9 EIRE	-	-	-	-	15479	15502	11459	10699	11157	8549	2810	956	680	496	1019
10 FINLAND	-	-	-	-	.	.	.	.	2644	1620	2359	1171	826	1444	2214
11 FRANCE	-	-	-	-	.	.	.	.	6535	4130	2245	1201	875	719	632
12 GREECE	-	-	-	-	.	11156	5293	4061	-	-	-	353	272	138	817
13 HUNGARY	-	-	-	12231	12165	10889	7197	5118	6611	.	2457	1552	952	1247	2447
14 ICELAND	-	-	.	.	.	.	.	.	.	.	.	.	0	0	1333
15 ITALY	.	.	.	.	.	.	.	.	.	.	1628	830	528	536	363
16 JAPAN	.	.	.	.	11391	8975	8296	8793	-	10672	5986	2111	1015	562	343
17 NETHERLANDS	.	.	.	.	19249	13200	9831	9237	12653	6518	1682	589	387	339	823
18 NEW ZEALAND	-	.	.	.	5287	5361	5080	3886	4110	3544	1728	811	327	1103	1678
19 NORWAY	15275	11739	14675	15714	16596	10529	7163	7011	5133	4506	1521	714	712	981	1967
20 POLAND	-	-	-	-	-	-	-	-	-	-	.	1130	534	332	408
21 PORTUGAL	.	.	.	.	.	.	.	.	.	.	2264	1443	962	647	467
22 ROMANIA	-	-	-	-	-	-	-	-	-	-	-	1501	870	551	368
23 SPAIN	.	.	.	.	.	.	9088	7901	7291	6628	2961	1650	1126	886	528
24 SWEDEN	-	-	.	.	.	.	.	.	.	.	966	551	372	743	1600
25 SWITZERLAND	13808	13808	17540	17540	22860	19556	11875	8204	8136	5307	3763	2320	1156	1154	904
26 TURKEY	-	-	-	-	-	-	-	-	-	-	-	1872	767	372	26
27 UK ENGLAND AND WALES	.	.	18229	16356	11148	8480	5758	4501	3468	2272	1043	587	400	807	772
28 UK NORTHERN IRELAND	-	-	-	-	23662	17458	.	.	.	3980	2162	611	207	1071	965
29 UK SCOTLAND	.	.	24389	20439	16269	12536	8379	7987	7774	3103	1445	595	398	825	1106
30 USA	.	.	.	.	5973	4785	3251	2388	1924	1423	738	333	247	403	357
31 YUGOSLAVIA	-	-	-	-	-	-	-	-	-	-	.	.	1049	1017	1420

- NO MORTALITY DATA ARE AVAILABLE FOR EVEN A BROADER GROUP OF CAUSES FOR THIS DISEASE

. MORTALITY DATA ARE PRESENTED FOR A BROADER GROUP OF CAUSES FOR THIS DISEASE

0 VALUE<0.5

THE STANDARD MORTALITY RATIOS WERE DERIVED WITH A FACTOR OF 1000

SERIAL MORTALITY TABLES FOR VARIOUS COUNTRIES 1901-1975

TABLE 6 : TUBERCULOSIS - NON-RESPIRATORY : MALES

	1901-	1906-	1911-	1916-	1921-	1926-	1931-	1936-	1941-	1946-	1951-	1956-	1961-	1966-	1971-75
1 AUSTRALIA	-	14301	11654	10589	7761	7476	5217	4039	3118	1962	1056	470	264	512	517
2 AUSTRIA	.	.	.	.	-	-	-	-	-	10546	4292	2353	1542	1535	1439
3 BELGIUM	32250	29286	26802	30129	29586	25933	19308	16090	17818	12094	3914	1656	786	581	558
4 BULGARIA	-	-	-	-	-	54191	40694	36937	42321	37444	16682	2442	1547	920	716
5 CANADA	-	-	-	-	13212	13682	11394	9710	8139	5488	2304	832	466	554	681
6 CHILE	-	38365	10484	11115	12147	25913	33086	34634	37102	33033	12654	6208	4391	2955	2595
7 CZECHOSLOVAKIA	-	-	-	28375	22573	21818	16923	12823	11184	9759	4815	2048	992	609	402
8 DENMARK	58402	48596	36667	35836	23910	17330	13092	7718	6008	3561	935	484	244	544	1370
9 EIRE	-	-	-	-	30000	28771	24644	23218	27224	20839	9151	3039	1271	983	1458
10 FINLAND	-	-	-	-	34711	38440	33434	32973	26703	18902	5802	2025	825	1737	3715
11 FRANCE	-	-	-	-	23556	24060	19076	17389	21196	12849	6095	2774	1737	1184	1015
12 GREECE	-	-	-	-	26698	31586	31195	26350	-	-	-	1815	1075	577	1978
13 HUNGARY	-	-	-	28823	31154	29401	27862	22928	24095	18546	8730	2629	1376	1517	3909
14 ICELAND	-	-	59048	70000	65833	67692	59286	34138	20000	10833	2750	444	200	0	179
15 ITALY	.	.	.	.	.	.	.	.	.	.	4608	2188	1262	961	598
16 JAPAN	31748	41533	48285	53891	51440	46794	45989	50768	-	23208	12139	4345	1802	886	474
17 NETHERLANDS	56941	43298	35176	42371	31211	22207	17029	12908	16595	7610	1834	731	387	378	779
18 NEW ZEALAND	-	13800	13358	13857	13003	9037	8783	6790	5968	5016	3702	1069	714	974	2140
19 NORWAY	.	.	48105	44845	44371	35044	23829	17961	12714	7769	2785	1056	781	1349	2053
20 POLAND	-	-	-	-	-	-	-	-	-	-	.	3309	1870	905	948
21 PORTUGAL	22363	20051	21649	23521	26828	33061	30222	27798	26391	25310	16579	7853	3816	2424	1319
22 ROMANIA	-	-	-	-	-	-	-	-	-	-	-	6281	3241	1678	852
23 SPAIN	48419	39757	31667	34734	28600	26395	24938	24196	23755	23680	11202	4598	2558	1485	859
24 SWEDEN	-	-	36350	34668	29622	24636	15235	10292	8624	4269	1611	748	590	825	1659
25 SWITZERLAND	59699	59699	47403	47403	32447	27505	25374	19136	14558	8916	4701	2535	1590	1344	1085
26 TURKEY	-	-	-	-	-	-	-	-	-	-	-	16190	7158	3414	1905
27 UK ENGLAND AND WALES	59868	50146	40623	34893	24043	18357	14184	10896	10801	6113	2401	902	598	1127	1162
28 UK NORTHERN IRELAND	-	-	-	-	39447	33766	28629	22222	22426	14338	4412	1342	630	874	905
29 UK SCOTLAND	79914	80878	64050	49227	38929	29523	21473	18017	17315	9648	3392	1138	609	1042	1495
30 USA	39569	29187	22261	17253	12185	9481	6390	4600	3424	2464	1209	563	384	527	471
31 YUGOSLAVIA	-	-	-	-	-	-	-	-	-	-	.	6216	3031	2006	2415

- NO MORTALITY DATA ARE AVAILABLE FOR EVEN A BROADER GROUP OF CAUSES FOR THIS DISEASE

. MORTALITY DATA ARE PRESENTED FOR A BROADER GROUP OF CAUSES FOR THIS DISEASE

0 VALUE<0.5

THE STANDARD MORTALITY RATIOS WERE DERIVED WITH A FACTOR OF 1000

SERIAL MORTALITY TABLES FOR VARIOUS COUNTRIES 1901-1975

TABLE 6 : TUBERCULOSIS - NON-RESPIRATORY : FEMALES

	1901-	1906-	1911-	1916-	1921-	1926-	1931-	1936-	1941-	1946-	1951-	1956-	1961-	1966-	1971-75
1 AUSTRALIA	-	14135	11728	9434	7266	6580	4571	3425	3068	1797	896	347	185	264	224
2 AUSTRIA	.	.	.	.	-	-	-	-	-	11136	5137	2431	1625	1335	964
3 BELGIUM	29128	26683	25360	28294	27957	24606	15579	12746	13213	8089	2655	1172	563	404	321
4 BULGARIA	-	-	-	-	-	58912	39076	32804	36554	35086	15675	2611	1272	731	456
5 CANADA	-	-	-	-	13543	14633	12355	10282	8557	5502	2174	685	336	363	445
6 CHILE	-	33789	8181	8954	9921	24508	30740	33594	36118	31484	11574	5416	3713	2497	1970
7 CZECHOSLOVAKIA	-	-	-	25661	20059	19301	15106	12034	11052	9313	4713	2295	1007	591	413
8 DENMARK	48910	38916	30566	31101	23070	18523	12843	7296	6124	3311	1021	408	272	440	779
9 EIRE	-	-	-	-	28190	26658	24325	21953	25216	19043	8007	2164	953	773	786
10 FINLAND	-	-	-	-	27511	29573	24509	25126	19855	14049	4665	1782	991	1056	1394
11 FRANCE	-	-	-	-	18250	19053	14048	12925	16073	9520	4280	1737	1149	765	579
12 GREECE	-	-	-	-	23257	28555	27592	22537	-	-	-	1598	835	427	692
13 HUNGARY	-	-	-	27906	28921	27700	25424	20916	21819	15036	6809	2441	1288	1031	1675
14 ICELAND	-	-	52083	52400	60000	60690	47097	25625	15714	9474	1905	870	0	0	690
15 ITALY	.	.	.	.	.	.	.	.	.	.	4422	1937	1004	652	428
16 JAPAN	42858	58790	67967	78886	73831	64072	57485	63135	-	26598	13341	4696	1889	914	489
17 NETHERLANDS	50194	39718	33583	40829	31318	22130	16983	13128	18773	8592	2195	682	360	253	540
18 NEW ZEALAND	-	18605	13983	14494	12252	9522	7720	6625	6163	4327	2771	913	419	752	910
19 NORWAY	.	.	39350	38059	36585	28661	18849	13495	8878	6111	1893	641	604	641	1174
20 POLAND	-	-	-	-	-	-	-	-	-	-	.	2353	1494	719	491
21 PORTUGAL	17923	15963	18651	19352	22093	27119	24798	23246	22582	21272	12734	6124	2680	1527	823
22 ROMANIA	-	-	-	-	-	-	-	-	-	-	-	4946	2535	1248	651
23 SPAIN	45220	39006	31492	36018	27839	24998	22306	20863	20816	20888	9598	3736	2023	1037	608
24 SWEDEN	-	-	31540	29405	24982	21437	13263	8309	6689	3704	1247	553	382	494	1023
25 SWITZERLAND	63707	63707	50805	50805	34190	28136	23794	16966	14458	8361	4393	2290	1095	959	767
26 TURKEY	-	-	-	-	-	-	-	-	-	-	-	13421	6571	3034	1492
27 UK ENGLAND AND WALES	50327	42466	33130	28726	19530	14696	11140	8328	8036	4819	1779	740	475	623	553
28 UK NORTHERN IRELAND	-	-	-	-	36582	32536	26619	19527	20720	12350	4539	993	653	753	782
29 UK SCOTLAND	65359	68085	51906	43040	31698	24735	17520	14794	16392	8699	2827	816	573	719	832
30 USA	35460	27053	21054	16027	11479	8709	5632	3834	2688	1836	833	363	259	297	250
31 YUGOSLAVIA	-	-	-	-	-	-	-	-	-	-	.	5701	2757	1353	1187

- NO MORTALITY DATA ARE AVAILABLE FOR EVEN A BROADER GROUP OF CAUSES FOR THIS DISEASE

. MORTALITY DATA ARE PRESENTED FOR A BROADER GROUP OF CAUSES FOR THIS DISEASE

0 VALUE<0.5

THE STANDARD MORTALITY RATIOS WERE DERIVED WITH A FACTOR OF 1000

SERIAL MORTALITY TABLES FOR VARIOUS COUNTRIES 1901-1975

TABLE 7 : TUBERCULOSIS - ALL FORMS : MALES

	1901-	1906-	1911-	1916-	1921-	1926-	1931-	1936-	1941-	1946-	1951-	1956-	1961-	1966-	1971-75
1 AUSTRALIA	-	16361	14650	13451	11626	10237	7943	6801	6204	4886	2521	1275	857	472	239
2 AUSTRIA	49861	47102	44246	53484	-	-	-	-	-	.	5587	4621	3993	2917	1905
3 BELGIUM	24192	22450	20820	20165	16001	13959	12418	11058	13930	9034	5240	3722	2581	1678	1034
4 BULGARIA	-	-	-	-	-	44561	32924	27923	30180	27824	13048	3308	2921	2301	1484
5 CANADA	-	-	-	-	11845	11868	9935	8403	7550	5707	2535	1230	822	614	347
6 CHILE	-	59258	51330	49788	45955	49210	49841	50714	49389	45307	18803	13268	11700	8526	5657
7 CZECHOSLOVAKIA	-	-	-	48814	33206	32294	24694	19719	22004	16522	10262	6143	3466	2063	1225
8 DENMARK	39394	32507	25704	26198	13998	10467	8358	5631	4909	3500	1435	708	532	331	373
9 EIRE	-	-	-	-	21534	19181	16958	16073	18383	14167	7020	3461	2524	1751	1092
10 FINLAND	-	-	-	-	41111	39306	33825	35495	36786	29484	11514	7297	3875	2012	1240
11 FRANCE	-	-	-	-	24663	25474	21920	20843	21319	11937	7130	4744	3362	2099	1162
12 GREECE	-	-	-	-	30244	30986	28586	23825	-	-	-	3902	3147	2216	1473
13 HUNGARY	-	-	-	53721	47432	35027	27927	22858	24361	18577	9981	6228	5249	4098	2896
14 ICELAND	-	-	26033	28626	29014	29740	25714	16851	10800	5766	1714	769	233	341	201
15 ITALY	25144	25441	23828	26671	22175	19424	15144	12666	16020	10499	5067	3853	3008	1884	1153
16 JAPAN	29495	32782	33905	36138	34076	33968	35321	39058	-	29116	14987	8520	5459	3600	2313
17 NETHERLANDS	33103	28525	24001	28156	17019	13086	9177	6824	10979	4933	1680	732	401	247	250
18 NEW ZEALAND	-	12890	11887	11517	10089	8083	6601	6372	6080	5028	3319	1536	854	708	556
19 NORWAY	.	.	35042	33334	30941	24482	18780	13647	11233	7420	2881	1375	796	555	391
20 POLAND	-	-	-	-	-	-	-	-	-	-	.	9709	9444	6880	3900
21 PORTUGAL	23022	21939	25671	28792	30973	37667	33469	30218	30176	29655	17044	11691	7866	5665	3027
22 ROMANIA	-	-	-	-	-	-	-	-	-	-	-	7348	5776	4339	2369
23 SPAIN	34968	30492	26552	29808	26463	24102	21421	22239	22140	21560	9760	5628	4343	2875	1806
24 SWEDEN	-	-	28668	27080	21862	18324	14670	11053	9618	5448	2356	1290	889	702	651
25 SWITZERLAND	40900	40900	31871	31871	23221	19715	15708	12255	11491	8029	4101	2730	1787	1294	994
26 TURKEY	-	-	-	-	-	-	-	-	-	-	-	17391	10772	6771	4023
27 UK ENGLAND AND WALES	35437	29636	26866	24635	18716	15858	13139	10729	10480	7513	3746	1790	1129	743	491
28 UK NORTHERN IRELAND	-	-	-	-	23741	19576	17060	14024	13841	10400	4359	2020	1312	789	584
29 UK SCOTLAND	41070	37805	30585	25318	19723	15706	12903	11648	11413	10441	4669	2344	1592	939	692
30 USA	52890	35835	29386	24481	15272	12928	10161	8494	7112	5414	2582	1468	1017	674	382
31 YUGOSLAVIA	-	-	-	-	-	-	-	-	-	-	19757	11959	7312	4220	2942

- NO MORTALITY DATA ARE AVAILABLE FOR EVEN A BROADER GROUP OF CAUSES FOR THIS DISEASE

. MORTALITY DATA ARE PRESENTED FOR A BROADER GROUP OF CAUSES FOR THIS DISEASE

0 VALUE<0.5

THE STANDARD MORTALITY RATIOS WERE DERIVED WITH A FACTOR OF 1000

SERIAL MORTALITY TABLES FOR VARIOUS COUNTRIES 1901-1975

TABLE 7 : TUBERCULOSIS - ALL FORMS : FEMALES

	1901-	1906-	1911-	1916-	1921-	1926-	1931-	1936-	1941-	1946-	1951-	1956-	1961-	1966-	1971-75
1 AUSTRALIA	-	15466	12856	10592	8950	7762	5706	4506	3611	2385	881	374	228	132	81
2 AUSTRIA	42286	40002	34315	41890	-	-	-	-	-	.	2658	1719	1215	870	566
3 BELGIUM	21577	19871	18415	19514	15215	12769	9575	7311	7717	4497	1726	926	526	357	233
4 BULGARIA	-	-	-	-	-	42295	27906	21698	21880	19704	8736	1793	1333	849	508
5 CANADA	-	-	-	-	13007	14729	11387	9043	7215	4947	1697	634	368	273	165
6 CHILE	-	59463	53369	52847	46975	53190	50313	48849	45642	39619	14357	8391	6444	4322	2518
7 CZECHOSLOVAKIA	-	-	-	44790	30195	28477	19782	15332	13957	10132	5319	2753	1410	793	480
8 DENMARK	27797	25510	20289	20306	15704	12325	9081	5588	4272	2817	1006	423	229	185	193
9 EIRE	-	-	-	-	22167	19733	17181	15609	17510	13105	5260	1970	1217	759	449
10 FINLAND	-	-	-	-	36218	36537	29076	27037	23298	15205	5033	2717	1344	736	521
11 FRANCE	-	-	-	-	17184	17693	13078	11118	11311	6187	3015	1646	1128	707	445
12 GREECE	-	-	-	-	24472	25050	21279	16511	-	-	-	1673	1063	680	441
13 HUNGARY	-	-	-	55137	46865	34648	24934	19519	18746	11589	5019	2554	1834	1282	949
14 ICELAND	-	-	28503	29618	30833	32486	25052	15268	13546	6025	1429	636	259	179	276
15 ITALY	28173	27748	25533	27551	22937	20246	14784	11500	11807	7141	2643	1434	863	492	311
16 JAPAN	31993	37252	37941	41519	36763	34249	32768	36338	-	22967	11053	5195	2753	1586	885
17 NETHERLANDS	30040	27652	24139	29816	18615	14436	9631	6829	9630	4187	1261	440	209	133	145
18 NEW ZEALAND	-	13150	12384	11494	9501	7375	5837	5030	4051	3594	1941	841	412	365	238
19 NORWAY	.	.	34227	32252	30340	23334	17151	11307	7700	4851	1595	606	409	258	206
20 POLAND	-	-	-	-	-	-	-	-	-	-		3874	3209	2008	1084
21 PORTUGAL	16860	15254	17459	19073	20130	25659	22088	19499	19445	17701	8888	4958	2580	1536	719
22 ROMANIA	-	-	-	-	-	-	-	-	-	-	-	3880	2641	1553	714
23 SPAIN	29544	26729	23118	27034	22333	19480	15679	14814	14546	13630	5632	2659	1702	905	544
24 SWEDEN	-	-	28897	26082	21084	18432	14556	10032	7781	4276	1446	688	410	322	331
25 SWITZERLAND	39728	39728	31434	31434	23177	19244	14444	10237	9216	5829	2457	1378	804	610	429
26 TURKEY	-	-	-	-	-	-	-	-	-	-	-	10917	6007	3311	1753
27 UK ENGLAND AND WALES	25739	21719	18991	18261	13621	11086	8837	6703	5700	4287	1556	584	343	253	174
28 UK NORTHERN IRELAND	-	-	-	-	25131	20734	16129	12709	11866	8312	2764	926	498	351	307
29 UK SCOTLAND	34826	31649	25348	21658	16257	12750	9875	8593	9098	8009	2643	962	533	374	280
30 USA	45152	30098	23931	21042	14362	11824	8353	6278	4544	2928	1111	528	340	229	140
31 YUGOSLAVIA	-	-	-	-	-	-	-	-	-	-	14108	7909	3979	1778	1247

- NO MORTALITY DATA ARE AVAILABLE FOR EVEN A BROADER GROUP OF CAUSES FOR THIS DISEASE

MORTALITY DATA ARE PRESENTED FOR A BROADER GROUP OF CAUSES FOR THIS DISEASE

0 VALUE<0.5

THE STANDARD MORTALITY RATIOS WERE DERIVED WITH A FACTOR OF 1000

SERIAL MORTALITY TABLES FOR VARIOUS COUNTRIES 1901-1975

TABLE 7 : TUBERCULOSIS - ALL FORMS : PERSONS

	1901-	1906-	1911-	1916-	1921-	1926-	1931-	1936-	1941-	1946-	1951-	1956-	1961-	1966-	1971-75
1 AUSTRALIA	-	15949	13816	12100	10344	9042	6852	5667	4913	3634	1688	816	534	296	157
2 AUSTRIA	45930	43419	39091	47466	-	20046	16355	12880	-	.	3941	2978	2412	1748	1138
3 BELGIUM	22871	21145	19594	19832	15602	13359	10972	9144	10750	6700	3393	2243	1486	971	603
4 BULGARIA	-	-	-	-	-	43433	30427	24811	26004	23716	10861	2530	2106	1558	983
5 CANADA	21065	13471	13128	12092	12389	13215	10624	8709	7389	5337	2122	935	594	440	253
6 CHILE	-	59362	52363	51342	46475	51243	50082	49761	47467	42372	16495	10735	8963	6330	4005
7 CZECHOSLOVAKIA	-	-	-	46669	31601	30259	22079	17387	17711	13108	7614	4324	2359	1378	822
8 DENMARK	32869	28570	22650	22875	14895	11439	8734	5609	4581	3149	1214	561	375	255	278
9 EIRE	-	-	-	-	21848	19455	17068	15846	17949	13639	6144	2713	1862	1246	763
10 FINLAND	-	-	-	-	38557	37858	31308	30950	29455	21617	7908	4754	2473	1304	840
11 FRANCE	54039	30256	27736	23410	20647	21295	17158	15556	15817	8767	4861	3040	2139	1339	773
12 GREECE	-	-	-	-	27309	27960	24854	20086	-	-	-	3354	2639	1817	1173
13 HUNGARY	-	-	-	54453	47139	34830	26370	21114	21420	14816	7307	4247	3405	2575	1841
14 ICELAND	-	-	27388	29167	30000	31224	25361	16010	12238	5900	1568	701	246	258	239
15 ITALY	26682	26619	24701	27121	22566	19850	14956	12057	13806	8726	3781	2568	1864	1138	702
16 JAPAN	30750	35024	35930	38843	35439	34111	34017	37666	-	25890	12923	6775	4037	2539	1557
17 NETHERLANDS	31522	28075	24072	29008	17836	13776	9409	6827	10291	4551	1465	581	302	188	195
18 NEW ZEALAND	-	13007	12115	11506	9807	7739	6226	5704	5050	4297	2618	1180	627	530	391
19 NORWAY	.	.	34604	32754	30619	23870	17915	12410	9376	6077	2212	976	595	400	294
20 POLAND	-	-	-	-	-	-	-	-	-	-	.	6696	6030	4219	2360
21 PORTUGAL	19665	18283	21163	23436	24996	31063	27209	24316	24284	23134	12548	7987	4960	3381	1748
22 ROMANIA	-	-	-	-	-	-	-	37731	-	27810	-	5492	4103	2855	1490
23 SPAIN	32150	28529	24762	28367	24309	21673	18376	18263	18073	17294	7523	4023	2917	1811	1127
24 SWEDEN	-	-	28790	26550	21450	18381	14611	10524	8670	4845	1888	980	642	506	435
25 SWITZERLAND	40287	40287	31640	31640	23197	19462	15031	11173	10270	6845	3216	2002	1257	926	691
26 TURKEY	-	-	-	-	-	-	27721	25054	29945	24099	17438	14176	8417	5096	2938
27 UK ENGLAND AND WALES	30371	25499	22691	21226	15986	13297	10827	8548	7765	5757	2551	1131	701	476	319
28 UK NORTHERN IRELAND	-	-	-	-	24474	20186	16571	13333	12787	9300	3510	1433	875	553	435
29 UK SCOTLAND	37718	34506	27790	23360	17870	14124	11283	10010	10165	9123	3565	1587	1009	627	464
30 USA	49027	33046	26752	22809	14828	12388	9270	7391	5822	3323	1827	981	662	437	252
31 YUGOSLAVIA	-	-	-	-	-	-	-	-	-	-	16702	9778	5527	2916	2038

\- NO MORTALITY DATA ARE AVAILABLE FOR EVEN A BROADER GROUP OF CAUSES FOR THIS DISEASE

. MORTALITY DATA ARE PRESENTED FOR A BROADER GROUP OF CAUSES FOR THIS DISEASE

0 VALUE<0.5

THE STANDARD MORTALITY RATIOS WERE DERIVED WITH A FACTOR OF 1000

SERIAL MORTALITY TABLES FOR VARIOUS COUNTRIES 1901-1975

TABLE 8 : TABES DORSALIS : MALES

	1901-	1906-	1911-	1916-	1921-	1926-	1931-	1936-	1941-	1946-	1951-	1956-	1961-	1966-	1971-75
1 AUSTRALIA	-	2909	3924	3587	3065	2071	1544	1271	743	542	249	149	67	51	.
2 AUSTRIA	.	.	.	.	-	-	-	-	-	.	738	437	289	150	.
3 BELGIUM	.	.	.	.	.	.	9211	10368	.	.	402	308	107	99	.
4 BULGARIA	-	-	-	-	-	.	.	.	.	.	.	.	36	41	.
5 CANADA	-	-	-	-	1538	1438	1203	925	726	383	147	89	59	31	.
6 CHILE	-	0	467	773	261	633	870	833	746	400	298	180	120	112	.
7 CZECHOSLOVAKIA	-	-	-	3412	3160	3237	3249	2343	.	.	640	584	319	268	.
8 DENMARK	3600	4375	3684	3714	1300	1039	753	548	.	.	134	79	33	20	.
9 EIRE	-	-	-	-	881	512	371	253	.	.	117	65	22	0	.
10 FINLAND	-	-	-	-	-	.	.	.	1169	781	436	195	143	45	.
11 FRANCE	-	-	-	-	.	.	.	.	579	327	267	169	124	101	.
12 GREECE	-	-	-	-	.	56	144	70	-	-	-	140	79	110	.
13 HUNGARY	-	-	-	.	.	.	5058	3944	3482	.	1290	804	469	150	.
14 ICELAND	-	-	.	.	.	.	.	.	.	.	.	.	0	200	.
15 ITALY	-	-	-	-	-	-	-	-	-	-	395	269	170	94	.
16 JAPAN	.	4848	4380	4591	4343	4007	3379	3529	-	1631	1271	745	384	224	.
17 NETHERLANDS	2869	2324	2840	3070	2650	2497	1688	1386	1643	717	410	231	182	140	.
18 NEW ZEALAND	-	2250	3700	2227	2417	2571	1394	1436	800	675	236	121	82	0	.
19 NORWAY	0	176	1415	909	1085	742	433	479	304	241	113	55	74	50	.
20 POLAND	-	-	-	-	-	-	-	-	-	-	.	38	57	49	.
21 PORTUGAL	-	-	-	-	-	-	.	.	.	.	389	275	148	78	.
22 ROMANIA	-	-	-	-	-	-	-	-	-	-	-	232	188	71	.
23 SPAIN	1111	1143	1227	1692	1462	1362	1342	1044	.	.	331	175	129	110	.
24 SWEDEN	-	-	.	.	.	.	384	269	162	81	70	36	15	6	.
25 SWITZERLAND	3187	3187	2401	2401	1462	953	.	.	.	.	259	284	166	130	.
26 TURKEY	-	-	-	-	-	-	-	-	-	-	-	24	0	5	16
27 UK ENGLAND AND WALES	3865	3742	4587	4325	3910	3663	2849	2013	1036	521	318	183	89	51	.
28 UK NORTHERN IRELAND	-	-	-	-	1542	1533	2000	1324	.	0	351	368	175	58	.
29 UK SCOTLAND	3710	4054	4213	3632	3196	2745	2138	1680	927	700	355	241	132	79	.
30 USA	7920	6813	6038	4604	3519	2528	1684	1139	697	398	122	65	42	28	.
31 YUGOSLAVIA	-	-	-	-	-	-	-	-	-	-	.	.	140	123	.

\- NO MORTALITY DATA ARE AVAILABLE FOR EVEN A BROADER GROUP OF CAUSES FOR THIS DISEASE

. MORTALITY DA¯A ARE PRESENTED FOR A BROADER GROUP OF CAUSES FOR THIS DISEASE

0 VALUE<0.5

THE STANDARD MORTALITY RATIOS WERE DERIVED WITH A FACTOR OF 100

SERIAL MORTALITY TABLES FOR VARIOUS COUNTRIES 1901-1975

TABLE 8 : TABES DORSALIS : FEMALES

	1901-	1906-	1911-	1916-	1921-	1926-	1931-	1936-	1941-	1946-	1951-	1956-	1961-	1966-	1971-75
1 AUSTRALIA	-	5000	8358	6500	5368	4655	2394	1807	628	1468	234	172	155	141	.
2 AUSTRIA	.	.	.	.	-	-	-	-	-	.	3460	2303	1570	908	.
3 BELGIUM	.	.	.	.	.	.	70870	82887	.	.	1304	1337	725	412	.
4 BULGARIA	-	-	-	-	-	.	.	.	.	.	.	.	105	92	.
5 CANADA	-	-	-	-	5660	3352	3564	2241	2052	865	223	197	87	94	.
6 CHILE	-	0	625	2553	1000	2222	2167	1940	2667	882	521	522	74	160	.
7 CZECHOSLOVAKIA	-	-	-	19180	16501	17132	14784	12469	.	.	1838	2151	1002	661	.
8 DENMARK	10000	6667	10714	9677	5854	3523	2632	1942	.	.	500	382	172	0	.
9 EIRE	-	-	-	-	1739	1047	674	136	.	.	316	104	102	0	.
10 FINLAND	-	-	-	-	-	.	.	.	2887	2476	862	775	138	412	.
11 FRANCE	-	-	-	-	.	.	.	.	2766	1077	1171	804	680	479	.
12 GREECE	-	-	-	-	.	667	500	220	-	-	-	348	346	419	.
13 HUNGARY	-	-	-	.	.	.	23158	20497	13814	.	4370	3683	1206	926	.
14 ICELAND	-	-	.	.	.	.	.	.	.	.	.	.	0	0	.
15 ITALY	-	-	-	-	-	-	-	-	-	-	1184	679	483	409	.
16 JAPAN	.	24849	20797	18798	15803	13678	11811	9313	-	4783	3888	2291	1030	582	.
17 NETHERLANDS	8764	6260	8321	10286	8487	8631	6310	4190	5439	1984	1172	849	372	433	.
18 NEW ZEALAND	-	0	19333	3889	1429	4615	3750	3947	652	1415	1333	152	278	0	.
19 NORWAY	0	833	4603	2537	2500	3158	2073	1136	526	289	443	157	213	0	.
20 POLAND	-	-	-	-	-	-	-	-	-	-	.	167	322	302	.
21 PORTUGAL	-	-	-	-	-	-	.	.	.	.	1046	1163	249	333	.
22 ROMANIA	-	-	-	-	-	-	-	-	-	-	-	1386	546	216	.
23 SPAIN	6567	5340	7639	9490	8537	5910	5722	4856	.	.	1346	633	509	339	.
24 SWEDEN	-	-	.	.	.	.	1833	1350	651	340	275	142	0	0	.
25 SWITZERLAND	13837	13837	10568	10568	8571	3084	.	.	.	.	1628	1361	657	283	.
26 TURKEY	-	-	-	-	-	-	-	-	-	-	-	0	0	0	56
27 UK ENGLAND AND WALES	7385	7691	7430	5733	6605	5940	5118	3748	2105	1046	748	475	300	228	.
28 UK NORTHERN IRELAND	-	-	-	-	3704	2059	1765	4276	.	0	870	625	0	0	.
29 UK SCOTLAND	8333	7217	5146	5321	5254	3566	3714	3444	1479	1397	802	352	236	111	.
30 USA	24795	20731	19470	14974	10928	7306	4526	2827	1664	888	303	157	107	50	.
31 YUGOSLAVIA	-	-	-	-	-	-	-	-	-	-	.	.	524	489	.

- NO MORTALITY DATA ARE AVAILABLE FOR EVEN A BROADER GROUP OF CAUSES FOR THIS DISEASE
. MORTALITY DATA ARE PRESENTED FOR A BROADER GROUP OF CAUSES FOR THIS DISEASE
0 VALUE<0.5
THE STANDARD MORTALITY RATIOS WERE DERIVED WITH A FACTOR OF 1000

SERIAL MORTALITY TABLES FOR VARIOUS COUNTRIES 1901-1975

TABLE 9 : GENERAL PARALYSIS OF THE INSANE : MALES

	1901-	1906-	1911-	1916-	1921-	1926-	1931-	1936-	1941-	1946-	1951-	1956-	1961-	1966-	1971-75
1 AUSTRALIA	-	6012	5178	5007	4090	2893	2249	1725	1263	757	332	149	54	26	.
2 AUSTRIA	.	.	.	.	-	-	-	-	-	.	571	260	179	160	.
3 BELGIUM	.	.	.	.	.	.	.	.	.	.	504	370	206	162	.
4 BULGARIA	-	-	-	-	-	.	.	.	.	.	.	.	72	65	.
5 CANADA	-	-	-	-	3105	2241	2477	2316	2131	1315	433	274	147	60	.
6 CHILE	-	846	1030	912	2183	1461	1286	1495	1078	940	484	331	118	79	.
7 CZECHOSLOVAKIA	-	-	-	50	76	188	.	.	.	.	897	492	311	259	.
8 DENMARK	.	.	.	.	.	.	1882	1612	.	.	272	135	126	26	.
9 EIRE	-	-	-	-	1598	1098	673	709	.	.	156	74	38	0	.
10 FINLAND	-	-	-	-	-	.	.	4381	2770	1587	500	443	201	150	.
11 FRANCE	-	-	-	-	.	.	.	.	2145	796	543	341	202	131	.
12 GREECE	-	-	-	-	.	1920	1757	1405	-	-	-	236	201	49	.
13 HUNGARY	-	-	-	.	.	.	6644	5944	5655	.	923	435	198	110	.
14 ICELAND	-	-	.	.	.	.	.	.	.	.	.	.	0	0	.
15 ITALY	-	-	-	-	-	-	-	-	-	-	731	518	331	180	.
16 JAPAN	.	.	.	.	5546	5983	5444	5702	-	3948	3039	1712	1080	682	.
17 NETHERLANDS	4477	4699	4924	5333	3519	2486	2245	2027	2205	782	353	327	192	124	.
18 NEW ZEALAND	-	7800	6074	5258	4171	4100	2543	1577	1228	524	456	111	103	59	.
19 NORWAY	0	213	2078	2588	2514	1273	1262	1272	1500	532	180	60	41	22	.
20 POLAND	-	-	-	-	-	-	-	-	-	-	.	203	167	148	.
21 PORTUGAL	-	-	-	-	-	-	.	.	.	.	844	693	538	332	.
22 ROMANIA	-	-	-	-	-	-	-	-	-	-	-	596	352	104	.
23 SPAIN	2682	3113	4207	4614	4195	4476	4262	4399	.	.	1279	1174	827	628	.
24 SWEDEN	-	-	.	.	.	.	937	700	494	286	96	62	24	14	.
25 SWITZERLAND	.	.	.	.	3239	2686	.	.	2000	1210	422	369	153	222	.
26 TURKEY	-	-	-	-	-	-	-	-	-	-	-	209	220	202	178
27 UK ENGLAND AND WALES	11216	10054	9788	8012	5964	4524	3105	2144	1485	672	278	160	82	64	.
28 UK NORTHERN IRELAND	-	-	-	-	2867	3947	2538	1756	.	698	348	85	184	49	.
29 UK SCOTLAND	7626	9028	8957	7597	6567	4366	3132	2298	1529	840	449	372	243	128	.
30 USA	13963	9121	10361	9222	8845	6364	4889	4207	3896	2280	543	199	73	37	.
31 YUGOSLAVIA	-	-	-	-	-	-	-	-	-	-	.	.	171	85	.

- NO MORTALITY DATA ARE AVAILABLE FOR EVEN A BROADER GROUP OF CAUSES FOR THIS DISEASE

. MORTALITY DATA ARE PRESENTED FOR A BROADER GROUP OF CAUSES FOR THIS DISEASE

0 VALUE<0.5

THE STANDARD MORTALITY RATIOS WERE DERIVED WITH A FACTOR OF 100

SERIAL MORTALITY TABLES FOR VARIOUS COUNTRIES 1901-1975

TABLE 9 : GENERAL PARALYSIS OF THE INSANE : FEMALES

	1901-	1906-	1911-	1916-	1921-	1926-	1931-	1936-	1941-	1946-	1951-	1956-	1961-	1966-	1971-75
1 AUSTRALIA	-	13971	9798	10171	7101	5494	4241	4128	2980	1715	828	259	157	119	.
2 AUSTRIA	.	.	.	.	-	-	-	-	-	.	2770	1846	1047	767	.
3 BELGIUM	.	.	.	.	.	.	.	.	.	.	1741	2019	676	546	.
4 BULGARIA	-	-	-	-	-	.	.	.	.	.	.	.	84	304	.
5 CANADA	-	-	-	-	8322	8292	8819	7484	6282	3526	1470	812	281	129	.
6 CHILE	-	5000	5942	7714	7867	6173	5843	5204	3945	3484	2222	1605	865	595	.
7 CZECHOSLOVAKIA	-	-	-	309	516	838	.	.	.	.	4084	2073	1410	1404	.
8 DENMARK	.	.	.	.	.	.	6860	8244	.	.	1111	323	743	310	.
9 EIRE	-	-	-	-	1375	1584	769	943	.	.	833	0	91	0	.
10 FINLAND	-	-	-	-	-	.	.	24034	8413	5185	1689	1975	1243	434	.
11 FRANCE	-	-	-	-	.	.	.	.	12386	4529	3139	1914	1054	988	.
12 GREECE	-	-	-	-	.	6953	6630	8547	-	-	-	810	984	497	.
13 HUNGARY	-	-	-	.	.	.	24079	23347	18359	.	2525	1834	899	140	.
14 ICELAND	-	-	.	.	.	.	.	.	.	.	.	.	0	0	.
15 ITALY	-	-	-	-	-	-	-	-	-	-	2722	1718	1117	766	.
16 JAPAN	.	.	.	.	15844	16539	16649	17320	-	12840	8772	4704	3295	2107	.
17 NETHERLANDS	18919	15760	17692	15355	11000	7376	6490	5904	5870	2808	1444	898	946	861	.
18 NEW ZEALAND	-	25000	15000	9231	1935	5946	5682	5686	1897	1563	1250	897	0	538	.
19 NORWAY	0	694	4079	4938	3721	2308	3674	4151	5130	1040	741	67	124	0	.
20 POLAND	-	-	-	-	-	-	-	-	-	-	.	1539	1252	722	.
21 PORTUGAL	-	-	-	-	-	-	.	.	.	.	6780	3576	2938	1307	.
22 ROMANIA	-	-	-	-	-	-	-	-	-	-	-	4258	1831	463	.
23 SPAIN	17555	19721	28846	28042	25245	24732	23835	23413	.	.	7362	6664	4427	3857	.
24 SWEDEN	-	-	.	.	.	.	2183	2521	1385	1201	559	182	85	88	.
25 SWITZERLAND	.	.	.	.	12171	9571	.	.	8006	4742	1827	1244	857	758	.
26 TURKEY	-	-	-	-	-	-	-	-	-	-	-	1852	1745	2115	2375
27 UK ENGLAND AND WALES	33095	27427	20720	14177	11449	9253	7701	6463	4199	2194	918	571	310	245	.
28 UK NORTHERN IRELAND	-	-	-	-	3333	7857	7143	4891	.	2041	755	1091	509	0	.
29 UK SCOTLAND	18750	20156	19559	16828	14387	11152	9717	7460	3932	2558	2027	952	498	202	.
30 USA	65872	35015	42154	35278	28953	20359	15112	12360	11433	6914	1691	700	292	126	.
31 YUGOSLAVIA	-	-	-	-	-	-	-	-	-	-	.	.	591	323	.

\- NO MORTALITY DATA ARE AVAILABLE FOR EVEN A BROADER GROUP OF CAUSES FOR THIS DISEASE

. MORTALITY DATA ARE PRESENTED FOR A BROADER GROUP OF CAUSES FOR THIS DISEASE

0 VALUE<0.5

THE STANDARD MORTALITY RATIOS WERE DERIVED WITH A FACTOR OF 1000

SERIAL MORTALITY TABLES FOR VARIOUS COUNTRIES 1901-1975

TABLE 10 : SYPHILIS - CNS : MALES

	1901-	1906-	1911-	1916-	1921-	1926-	1931-	1936-	1941-	1946-	1951-	1956-	1961-	1966-	1971-75
1 AUSTRALIA	-	6461	6308	6018	4969	3444	2623	2070	1402	897	399	201	80	63	47
2 AUSTRIA	.	.	.	.	-	-	-	-	-	.	869	458	310	189	69
3 BELGIUM	.	.	.	.	.	.	.	.	.	.	616	459	217	165	64
4 BULGARIA	-	-	-	-	-	.	3727	4254	.	.	.	.	77	59	16
5 CANADA	-	-	-	-	3335	2573	2621	2326	2056	1222	413	258	146	71	48
6 CHILE	-	647	1084	1157	1920	1527	1520	1658	1278	980	552	364	160	80	42
7 CZECHOSLOVAKIA	-	-	-	1983	1868	2010	.	.	.	.	1061	717	426	270	110
8 DENMARK	.	.	.	.	.	.	1882	1547	.	.	283	147	112	60	36
9 EIRE	-	-	-	-	1712	1115	719	674	.	.	185	94	41	7	13
10 FINLAND	-	-	-	-	-	.	.	.	2857	1695	640	458	238	112	79
11 FRANCE	-	-	-	-	.	.	2968	2487	2521	791	565	355	225	127	77
12 GREECE	-	-	-	-	.	1505	1429	1110	-	-	-	261	198	109	126
13 HUNGARY	-	-	-	.	.	.	8046	6857	6361	.	1453	804	428	221	181
14 ICELAND	-	-	.	.	.	.	.	.	.	.	.	.	0	125	0
15 ITALY	-	-	-	-	-	-	-	-	-	-	785	550	350	205	85
16 JAPAN	.	.	.	.	6751	6993	6223	6530	-	4060	3122	1768	1063	629	288
17 NETHERLANDS	5093	4942	5444	5878	4246	3360	2706	2362	2646	1015	509	382	252	164	68
18 NEW ZEALAND	-	8000	6800	5436	4636	4627	2763	2060	1413	798	484	155	125	63	89
19 NORWAY	.	.	2391	2457	2526	1385	1205	1246	1299	544	202	77	75	37	61
20 POLAND	-	-	-	-	-	-	-	-	-	-	.	184	164	160	101
21 PORTUGAL	-	-	-	-	-	-	2652	2911	3051	2664	1727	693	497	297	89
22 ROMANIA	-	-	-	-	-	-	-	-	-	-	-	599	382	139	74
23 SPAIN	2727	3082	3976	4561	4098	4259	4077	4007	.	.	1176	1001	701	514	359
24 SWEDEN	-	-	.	.	.	.	931	684	466	261	113	68	27	12	14
25 SWITZERLAND	.	.	.	.	.	.	2299	1633	1607	.	472	446	214	203	107
26 TURKEY	-	-	-	-	-	-	-	-	-	-	-	186	178	164	150
27 UK ENGLAND AND WALES	11113	9983	10360	8788	6910	5625	4049	2820	1730	815	398	229	115	80	41
28 UK NORTHERN IRELAND	-	-	-	-	3075	3920	3096	2121	.	508	468	286	239	100	42
29 UK SCOTLAND	8153	9448	9428	8064	6959	4951	3638	2736	1703	1047	549	422	261	122	48
30 USA	15529	11064	11630	9924	9008	6454	4794	3924	3402	1970	481	188	79	62	43
31 YUGOSLAVIA	-	-	-	-	-	-	-	-	-	-	.	.	213	192	86

- NO MORTALITY DATA ARE AVAILABLE FOR EVEN A BROADER GROUP OF CAUSES FOR THIS DISEASE

. MORTALITY DATA ARE PRESENTED FOR A BROADER GROUP OF CAUSES FOR THIS DISEASE

0 VALUE<0.5

THE STANDARD MORTALITY RATIOS WERE DERIVED WITH A FACTOR OF 100

SERIAL MORTALITY TABLES FOR VARIOUS COUNTRIES 1901-1975

TABLE 10 : SYPHILIS - CNS : FEMALES

	1901-	1906-	1911-	1916-	1921-	1926-	1931-	1936-	1941-	1946-	1951-	1956-	1961-	1966-	1971-75
1 AUSTRALIA	-	13882	12439	11793	8613	6942	4656	4211	2632	2159	755	295	209	208	205
2 AUSTRIA	.	.	.	.	-	-	-	-	-	.	4149	2767	1734	952	311
3 BELGIUM	.	.	.	.	.	.	.	.	.	.	2065	2278	936	833	638
4 BULGARIA	-	-	-	-	-	.	12500	11667	.	.	.	.	126	381	101
5 CANADA	-	-	-	-	9735	8349	8860	7043	5974	3175	1231	723	260	227	129
6 CHILE	-	4118	5058	7586	6957	6200	5909	5246	4632	3268	2047	1561	714	480	290
7 CZECHOSLOVAKIA	-	-	-	11381	10000	10598	.	.	.	.	4160	2836	1647	1122	467
8 DENMARK	.	.	.	.	.	.	6750	7356	.	.	1121	469	643	362	154
9 EIRE	-	-	-	-	2054	1799	972	765	.	.	790	65	129	126	0
10 FINLAND	-	-	-	-	-	.	.	.	8072	5363	1786	1944	1004	494	311
11 FRANCE	-	-	-	-	.	.	16844	12832	11195	3922	2961	1853	1169	739	350
12 GREECE	-	-	-	-	.	5712	5336	6581	-	-	-	809	935	454	459
13 HUNGARY	-	-	-	.	.	.	31972	29871	22096	.	4500	3587	1398	920	657
14 ICELAND	-	-	.	.	.	.	.	.	.	.	.	.	0	0	0
15 ITALY	-	-	.	-	-	-	-	-	-	-	2734	1674	1109	653	299
16 JAPAN	.	.	.	.	21168	20664	19677	18736	-	12631	8984	4929	3118	1854	905
17 NETHERLANDS	19473	15598	18296	17708	13321	10657	8656	6947	7668	3294	1781	1176	917	739	243
18 NEW ZEALAND	-	20000	22143	9394	2308	7234	6607	6667	1842	2035	1735	741	170	465	559
19 NORWAY	.	.	5769	5182	4274	3629	3955	3724	4103	941	811	146	221	0	37
20 POLAND	-	-	-	-	-	-	-	-	-	-	.	1272	1137	773	448
21 PORTUGAL	-	-	-	-	-	-	18733	19175	21353	16098	9950	3349	2304	1152	369
22 ROMANIA	-	-	-	-	-	-	-	-	-	-	-	4041	1699	539	349
23 SPAIN	17439	18351	26684	27120	24321	22315	21437	20532	.	.	6287	5306	3552	2886	2407
24 SWEDEN	-	-	.	.	.	.	2716	2675	1412	1088	577	220	61	56	104
25 SWITZERLAND	.	.	.	.	.	.	8100	6758	6276	.	2332	1742	1023	912	773
26 TURKEY	-	-	-	-	-	-	-	-	-	-	-	1454	1350	1627	1859
27 UK ENGLAND AND WALES	30559	25764	20362	14294	12639	10535	8847	7076	4373	2238	1125	704	409	293	170
28 UK NORTHERN IRELAND	-	-	-	-	4667	7143	6316	6250	.	1515	1081	1169	366	230	110
29 UK SCOTLAND	19231	19641	18023	15979	14039	10551	9532	7629	3799	2730	1967	903	505	283	247
30 USA	65758	39249	44225	36274	28990	20119	14354	11158	9681	5730	1437	609	277	175	151
31 YUGOSLAVIA	-	-	-	-	-	-	-	-	-	-	.	.	755	781	381

- NO MORTALITY DATA ARE AVAILABLE FOR EVEN A BROADER GROUP OF CAUSES FOR THIS DISEASE

. MORTALITY DATA ARE PRESENTED FOR A BROADER GROUP OF CAUSES FOR THIS DISEASE

0 VALUE<0.5

THE STANDARD MORTALITY RATIOS WERE DERIVED WITH A FACTOR OF 1000

SERIAL MORTALITY TABLES FOR VARIOUS COUNTRIES 1901-1975

TABLE 11 : SYPHILIS - ALL OTHER : MALES

	1901-	1906-	1911-	1916-	1921-	1926-	1931-	1936-	1941-	1946-	1951-	1956-	1961-	1966-	1971-75
1 AUSTRALIA	-	7058	6394	5571	3902	4169	.	.	5954	5336	2585	1709	911	377	117
2 AUSTRIA	.	.	.	.	-	-	-	-	-	.	2741	1908	812	688	309
3 BELGIUM	.	.	.	.	.	.	.	.	.	.	1555	998	488	356	131
4 BULGARIA	-	-	-	-	-	.	.	.	.	.	.	.	330	155	39
5 CANADA	-	-	-	-	6171	6548	.	.	.	3043	1871	1291	763	346	96
6 CHILE	-	7474	11301	24156	28789	48304	.	15217	9549	8109	5018	3419	2159	1126	439
7 CZECHOSLOVAKIA	-	-	-	.	.	.	.	.	.	.	3157	2277	1380	550	139
8 DENMARK	.	.	.	.	.	.	.	.	.	.	2274	1179	750	424	119
9 EIRE	-	-	-	-	.	.	.	.	.	.	1093	430	234	89	76
10 FINLAND	-	-	-	-	-	.	.	.	.	.	3667	4105	2324	930	395
11 FRANCE	-	-	-	-	.	.	.	.	.	3445	2659	1917	1624	665	82
12 GREECE	-	-	-	-	.	3502	3346	.	-	-	-	225	131	99	50
13 HUNGARY	-	-	-	.	.	.	.	.	.	.	2372	1618	1163	616	314
14 ICELAND	-	-	.	.	.	.	.	.	.	.	.	.	227	612	0
15 ITALY	-	-	-	-	-	-	-	-	-	-	3594	2319	1257	507	192
16 JAPAN	.	.	.	.	.	.	.	.	-	4081	3304	2175	1475	586	152
17 NETHERLANDS	3350	3105	3288	3432	.	.	.	.	.	3025	1946	1327	817	546	172
18 NEW ZEALAND	-	.	.	.	2778	3768	.	.	.	5987	2817	1005	392	322	126
19 NORWAY	.	.	.	.	.	.	.	.	.	.	2863	2181	1304	583	169
20 POLAND	-	-	-	-	-	-	-	-	-	-	.	415	545	558	188
21 PORTUGAL	-	-	-	-	-	-	.	.	.	.	2654	1626	1526	879	236
22 ROMANIA	-	-	-	-	-	-	-	-	-	-	-	1146	1300	475	128
23 SPAIN	4904	5762	5384	5757	5578	4260	2094	1896	.	.	3339	2401	1815	462	87
24 SWEDEN	-	-	.	.	.	.	.	.	.	.	996	527	368	194	45
25 SWITZERLAND	.	.	.	.	.	.	.	.	.	.	1847	1104	666	320	262
26 TURKEY	-	-	-	-	-	-	-	-	-	-	-	97	22	27	77
27 UK ENGLAND AND WALES	.	.	9052	8537	5567	5214	3709	4127	5147	4346	3356	2315	1584	764	156
28 UK NORTHERN IRELAND	-	-	-	-	.	.	.	.	.	3443	2561	2373	1114	535	190
29 UK SCOTLAND	.	.	.	.	.	.	.	.	.	2887	1841	1219	671	403	77
30 USA	.	13593	13791	17188	.	.	.	.	.	5830	3748	2365	1768	713	123
31 YUGOSLAVIA	-	-	-	-	-	-	-	-	-	-	.	.	1551	546	184

- NO MORTALITY DATA ARE AVAILABLE FOR EVEN A BROADER GROUP OF CAUSES FOR THIS DISEASE

. MORTALITY DATA ARE PRESENTED FOR A BROADER GROUP OF CAUSES FOR THIS DISEASE

0 VALUE<0.5

THE STANDARD MORTALITY RATIOS WERE DERIVED WITH A FACTOR OF 1000

SERIAL MORTALITY TABLES FOR VARIOUS COUNTRIES 1901-1975

TABLE 11 : SYPHILIS - ALL OTHER : FEMALES

	1901-	1906-	1911-	1916-	1921-	1926-	1931-	1936-	1941-	1946-	1951-	1956-	1961-	1966-	1971-75
1 AUSTRALIA	-	5556	4679	3598	2283	2076	.	.	1802	1420	720	434	312	129	43
2 AUSTRIA	.	.	.	.	-	-	-	-	-	.	1429	1021	499	335	190
3 BELGIUM	.	.	.	.	.	.	.	.	.	.	826	533	281	161	75
4 BULGARIA	-	-	-	-	-	.	.	.	.	.	.	.	128	65	27
5 CANADA	-	-	-	-	2926	3906	.	.	.	750	524	361	238	115	43
6 CHILE	-	5784	9068	17540	22317	35826	.	6633	3664	2296	1813	996	635	340	51
7 CZECHOSLOVAKIA	-	-	-	.	.	.	.	.	.	.	1505	1103	629	342	90
8 DENMARK	.	.	.	.	.	.	.	.	.	.	922	615	359	262	122
9 EIRE	-	-	-	-	.	.	.	.	.	.	406	116	41	30	19
10 FINLAND	-	-	-	-	-	.	.	.	.	.	1408	1483	973	485	168
11 FRANCE	-	-	-	-	.	.	.	.	.	1495	1151	823	702	299	53
12 GREECE	-	-	-	-	.	1514	1756	.	-	-	-	48	43	41	24
13 HUNGARY	-	-	-	.	.	.	.	.	.	.	1030	842	503	260	133
14 ICELAND	-	-	.	.	.	.	.	.	.	.	.	.	0	0	0
15 ITALY	-	-	-	-	-	-	-	-	-	-	1346	857	444	173	64
16 JAPAN	.	.	.	.	.	.	.	.	-	1566	1183	792	560	266	79
17 NETHERLANDS	2201	2471	2274	2278	.	.	.	.	.	934	588	548	288	205	76
18 NEW ZEALAND	-	.	.	.	1075	1827	.	.	.	2390	767	365	83	75	68
19 NORWAY	.	.	.	.	.	.	.	.	.	.	850	677	367	215	126
20 POLAND	-	-	-	-	-	-	-	-	-	-	.	223	320	243	104
21 PORTUGAL	-	-	-	-	-	-	.	.	.	.	577	522	517	298	51
22 ROMANIA	-	-	-	-	-	-	-	-	-	-	-	659	551	226	39
23 SPAIN	3598	4091	3494	3831	3455	2457	624	634	.	.	1317	1005	769	203	24
24 SWEDEN	-	-	.	.	.	.	.	.	.	.	389	225	178	96	33
25 SWITZERLAND	.	.	.	.	.	.	.	.	.	.	713	542	323	170	147
26 TURKEY	-	-	-	-	-	-	-	-	-	-	-	21	26	5	89
27 UK ENGLAND AND WALES	.	.	5432	4882	3076	2409	1231	1335	1806	1516	1138	876	729	379	92
28 UK NORTHERN IRELAND	-	-	-	-	.	.	.	.	.	1958	846	1064	536	315	53
29 UK SCOTLAND	.	.	.	.	.	.	.	.	.	774	564	371	248	151	52
30 USA	.	9114	8461	9093	.	.	.	.	.	1967	1194	801	604	240	49
31 YUGOSLAVIA	-	-	-	-	-	-	-	-	-	-	.	.	878	345	131

- NO MORTALITY DATA ARE AVAILABLE FOR EVEN A BROADER GROUP OF CAUSES FOR THIS DISEASE

. MORTALITY DATA ARE PRESENTED FOR A BROADER GROUP OF CAUSES FOR THIS DISEASE

0 VALUE<0.5

THE STANDARD MORTALITY RATIOS WERE DERIVED WITH A FACTOR OF 1000

SERIAL MORTALITY TABLES FOR VARIOUS COUNTRIES 1901-1975

TABLE 12 : SYPHILIS - ALL FORMS : MALES

	1901-	1906-	1911-	1916-	1921-	1926-	1931-	1936-	1941-	1946-	1951-	1956-	1961-	1966-	1971-75
1 AUSTRALIA	-	15369	14723	13696	10788	8654	7451	6708	7278	5888	2804	1742	892	438	178
2 AUSTRIA	.	.	.	.	-	-	-	-	-	5763	4088	2331	1150	860	385
3 BELGIUM	.	.	.	.	.	.	9175	8227	2784	1573	1924	1526	737	541	207
4 BULGARIA	-	-	-	-	-	.	9082	9922	8732	4300	1644	599	491	231	59
5 CANADA	-	-	-	-	10097	9267	9811	9562	9296	5268	2234	1480	871	399	154
6 CHILE	-	7130	10896	21528	26473	41853	54254	44169	30036	18891	7456	4736	3093	1884	746
7 CZECHOSLOVAKIA	-	-	-	5266	6701	7388	.	.	7401	7825	4892	3145	1949	931	297
8 DENMARK	12928	11795	11739	13240	4345	3732	4798	4332	4946	2140	2357	1213	801	450	151
9 EIRE	-	-	-	-	3382	2368	1586	1834	2228	1808	1222	523	264	85	83
10 FINLAND	-	-	-	-	-	.	.	10446	8894	5816	4239	4208	2356	960	448
11 FRANCE	-	-	-	-	.	.	5094	4571	4587	3643	3210	2159	1702	750	180
12 GREECE	-	-	-	-	.	5106	4730	3738	-	-	-	568	409	258	225
13 HUNGARY	-	-	-	.	.	.	17011	14992	14218	7291	4965	2579	1621	846	527
14 ICELAND	-	-	1053	0	.	400	741	690	1563	556	500	435	192	690	0
15 ITALY	-	-	-	-	-	-	-	-	-	-	4696	2917	1675	760	298
16 JAPAN	.	26607	26655	25094	26179	27001	23266	22926	-	11197	7932	4557	2858	1447	558
17 NETHERLANDS	10288	9839	10707	11497	9114	9154	7994	7220	7703	4740	2465	1681	1070	722	245
18 NEW ZEALAND	-	14546	12043	10573	8885	10354	8363	8864	7407	6504	3171	1095	535	359	235
19 NORWAY	2808	2750	6186	5368	5072	3415	3388	4109	5377	3627	2785	1970	1224	546	230
20 POLAND	-	-	-	-	-	-	-	-	-	-	.	693	765	770	335
21 PORTUGAL	-	-	-	-	-	-	23401	19088	13598	10000	6120	4547	2417	1475	403
22 ROMANIA	-	-	-	-	-	-	-	-	-	-	-	1850	1656	609	218
23 SPAIN	8127	9392	10440	11647	10793	9898	9546	9067	7917	5765	5035	3684	2596	1150	601
24 SWEDEN	-	-	.	.	.	.	2872	2327	1679	1116	1026	549	359	182	58
25 SWITZERLAND	9374	9374	8594	8594	11200	9318	7640	5906	5392	3585	2299	1596	881	588	388
26 TURKEY	-	-	-	-	-	-	-	-	-	-	-	451	307	286	359
27 UK ENGLAND AND WALES	24486	20986	23176	20431	15096	12842	9949	8086	7179	5011	3439	2300	1507	764	198
28 UK NORTHERN IRELAND	-	-	-	-	6507	8000	6591	5564	6021	4837	2825	2410	1301	594	220
29 UK SCOTLAND	18863	21494	20094	17386	14464	10664	7869	5867	6052	4138	2372	1649	957	528	140
30 USA	.	30678	28871	29151	24706	21351	19152	18934	14774	9318	3903	2285	1621	702	170
31 YUGOSLAVIA	-	-	-	-	-	-	-	-	-	-	.	2480	1658	770	290

- NO MORTALITY DATA ARE AVAILABLE FOR EVEN A BROADER GROUP OF CAUSES FOR THIS DISEASE

. MORTALITY DA‾A ARE PRESENTED FOR A BROADER GROUP OF CAUSES FOR THIS DISEASE

0 VALUE<0.5

THE STANDARD MORTALITY RATIOS WERE DERIVED WITH A FACTOR OF 1000

SERIAL MORTALITY TABLES FOR VARIOUS COUNTRIES 1901-1975

TABLE 12 : SYPHILIS - ALL FORMS : FEMALES

	1901-	1906-	1911-	1916-	1921-	1926-	1931-	1936-	1941-	1946-	1951-	1956-	1961-	1966-	1971-75
1 AUSTRALIA	-	6626	5704	4728	3183	2760	1830	1716	2008	1574	732	423	302	153	74
2 AUSTRIA	.	.	.	.	-	-	-	-	-	3201	2087	1283	685	434	209
3 BELGIUM	.	.	.	.	.	.	6682	6336	1850	1093	895	795	376	256	156
4 BULGARIA	-	-	-	-	-	.	3137	3636	2643	1776	892	296	180	116	47
5 CANADA	-	-	-	-	3858	4472	4697	4048	3538	1781	661	428	257	134	61
6 CHILE	-	5366	8240	15574	19396	30439	38733	30637	18739	10060	3463	2004	1265	927	289
7 CZECHOSLOVAKIA	-	-	-	3210	4093	4286	.	.	3528	3757	2248	1462	881	499	143
8 DENMARK	6260	6099	5680	5889	2932	2180	2233	2178	2703	1042	977	604	405	273	138
9 EIRE	-	-	-	-	764	835	585	400	902	835	518	117	61	43	16
10 FINLAND	-	-	-	-	-	.	.	4945	3097	2039	1605	1603	977	492	187
11 FRANCE	-	-	-	-	.	.	2804	2302	2182	1657	1493	976	767	358	93
12 GREECE	-	-	-	-	.	2085	2073	1746	-	-	-	170	213	107	91
13 HUNGARY	-	-	-	.	.	.	8066	7440	5750	3411	2122	1256	627	352	207
14 ICELAND	-	-	385	0	.	303	0	263	732	227	0	192	0	0	0
15 ITALY	-	-	-	-	-	-	-	-	-	-	1853	1084	580	260	102
16 JAPAN	.	20035	19768	17791	15128	13045	10750	9855	-	4341	2626	1436	943	505	201
17 NETHERLANDS	4648	4316	4541	4474	3839	3608	3031	2474	2680	2069	857	650	380	287	105
18 NEW ZEALAND	-	4242	4893	2909	1527	2724	2166	2460	2115	2450	921	438	128	139	154
19 NORWAY	2020	1899	2660	1977	1473	1462	1308	1516	1979	1386	865	603	343	183	123
20 POLAND	-	-	-	-	-	-	-	-	-	-	.	411	472	348	168
21 PORTUGAL	-	-	-	-	-	-	13095	10385	7992	5767	2963	2128	1070	667	130
22 ROMANIA	-	-	-	-	-	-	-	-	-	-	-	1144	710	271	84
23 SPAIN	5590	6135	6870	7204	6465	5315	4797	4522	3682	2568	2322	1709	1180	590	359
24 SWEDEN	-	-	.	.	.	.	1054	358	610	477	422	225	168	92	47
25 SWITZERLAND	4875	4875	4203	4203	4842	3724	3210	2582	2540	1496	961	710	430	286	241
26 TURKEY	-	-	-	-	-	-	-	-	-	-	-	284	229	253	384
27 UK ENGLAND AND WALES	10334	8123	7531	6190	4435	3569	2837	2411	2368	1714	1148	854	685	366	104
28 UK NORTHERN IRELAND	-	-	-	-	2283	2005	1919	1861	2165	1754	887	1065	539	300	60
29 UK SCOTLAND	7281	7204	6596	5762	4569	3090	2591	1799	1831	1286	797	459	289	179	78
30 USA	.	13693	13553	12910	10418	9168	8040	7524	5267	3224	1255	778	562	237	66
31 YUGOSLAVIA	-	-	-	-	-	-	-	-	-	-	.	1225	886	419	171

- NO MORTALITY DATA ARE AVAILABLE FOR EVEN A BROADER GROUP OF CAUSES FOR THIS DISEASE

. MORTALITY DATA ARE PRESENTED FOR A BROADER GROUP OF CAUSES FOR THIS DISEASE

0 VALUE<0.5

THE STANDARD MORTALITY RATIOS WERE DERIVED WITH A FACTOR OF 1000

SERIAL MORTALITY TABLES FOR VARIOUS COUNTRIES 1901-1975

TABLE 13 : GONOCOCCAL INFECTION : MALES

	1901-	1906-	1911-	1916-	1921-	1926-	1931-	1936-	1941-	1946-	1951-	1956-	1961-	1966-	1971-75
1 AUSTRALIA	-	.	.	.	664	681	610	467	175	122	108	74	23	64	0
2 AUSTRIA	.	.	.	.	-	-	-	-	-	.	.	.	.	.	.
3 BELGIUM	.	.	.	.	.	.	.	.	.	.	0	29	115	115	0
4 BULGARIA	-	-	-	-	-	.	.	.	.	.	.	.	.	.	.
5 CANADA	-	-	-	-	895	1290	1082	1230	894	199	140	68	13	25	39
6 CHILE	-	4839	.	.	2294	1782	1989	1939	762	437	400	230	467	125	74
7 CZECHOSLOVAKIA	-	-	-	233	129	493	.	.	0	207	32	39	20	0	0
8 DENMARK	.	.	.	.	.	.	.	.	.	.	180	0	0	55	0
9 EIRE	-	-	-	-	1648	885	1416	708	263	0	0	0	87	0	0
10 FINLAND	-	-	-	-	-	.	.	.	.	.	120	61	61	124	64
11 FRANCE	-	-	-	-	.	.	.	.	311	139	0	0	0	22	16
12 GREECE	-	-	-	-	.	1323	451	793	-	-	-	33	64	62	92
13 HUNGARY	-	-	-	.	.	.	210	300	149	.	.	.	.	.	.
14 ICELAND	-	-	.	.	.	.	.	.	.	.	.	.	0	0	0
15 ITALY	-	-	-	-	-	-	-	-	-	-	85	176	287	35	10
16 JAPAN	.	1799	1590	1137	806	663	563	593	-	337	170	154	39	27	2
17 NETHERLANDS	148	167	.	.	176	431	752	449	461	362	164	160	151	144	20
18 NEW ZEALAND	-	0	12046	426	980	943	926	702	323	352	345	103	94	91	86
19 NORWAY	.	.	.	.	.	.	.	.	.	.	152	0	72	0	68
20 POLAND	-	-	-	-	-	-	-	-	-	-	.	.	.	.	.
21 PORTUGAL	-	-	-	-	-	-	.	.	.	.	302	0	0	0	63
22 ROMANIA	-	-	-	-	-	-	-	-	-	-	-	.	.	.	.
23 SPAIN	1890	979	.	.	.	.	590	1456	513	299	336	237	140	72	0
24 SWEDEN	-	-	.	.	.	.	.	.	.	.	74	112	72	0	34
25 SWITZERLAND	2446	2446	3893	3893	.	.	.	.	.	.	437	104	0	44	0
26 TURKEY	-	-	-	-	-	-	-	-	-	-	-	65	43	35	56
27 UK ENGLAND AND WALES	728	607	600	805	977	1717	1492	1219	977	369	228	511	298	98	28
28 UK NORTHERN IRELAND	-	-	-	-	541	638	.	.	.	0	0	741	175	167	170
29 UK SCOTLAND	2135	220	.	.	894	1080	857	1130	.	263	0	155	0	0	0
30 USA	.	.	.	.	1767	1906	2020	1615	692	240	139	137	94	41	26
31 YUGOSLAVIA	-	-	-	-	-	-	-	-	-	-	.	.	.	.	.

- NO MORTALITY DATA ARE AVAILABLE FOR EVEN A BROADER GROUP OF CAUSES FOR THIS DISEASE

. MORTALITY DATA ARE PRESENTED FOR A BROADER GROUP OF CAUSES FOR THIS DISEASE

0 VALUE<0.5

THE STANDARD MCRTALITY RATIOS WERE DERIVED WITH A FACTOR OF 1000

SERIAL MORTALITY TABLES FOR VARIOUS COUNTRIES 1901-1975

TABLE 13 : GONOCOCCAL INFECTION : FEMALES

	1901-	1906-	1911-	1916-	1921-	1926-	1931-	1936-	1941-	1946-	1951-	1956-	1961-	1966-	1971-75
1 AUSTRALIA	-	.	.	.	94	268	213	122	296	0	28	0	0	0	20
2 AUSTRIA	.	.	.	.	-	-	-	-	-	.	.	.	.	.	.
3 BELGIUM	.	.	.	.	.	.	.	.	.	.	74	29	0	57	0
4 BULGARIA	-	-	-	-	-	.	.	.	.	.	.	.	.	.	.
5 CANADA	-	-	-	-	1245	1947	2031	1333	673	94	16	14	0	26	13
6 CHILE	-	1000	.	.	1572	629	1551	1218	613	268	0	258	189	49	0
7 CZECHOSLOVAKIA	-	-	-	110	142	422	.	.	104	133	0	19	58	0	0
8 DENMARK	.	.	.	.	.	.	.	.	.	.	0	0	0	0	0
9 EIRE	-	-	-	-	345	367	556	187	180	87	0	0	0	0	0
10 FINLAND	-	-	-	-	-	.	.	.	.	.	114	0	58	0	0
11 FRANCE	-	-	-	-	.	.	.	.	178	46	0	0	0	5	5
12 GREECE	-	-	-	-	.	398	227	0	-	-	-	0	62	60	60
13 HUNGARY	-	-	-	.	.	.	319	435	144	.	.	.	.	.	.
14 ICELAND	-	-	.	.	.	.	.	.	.	.	.	.	0	0	0
15 ITALY	-	-	-	-	-	-	-	-	-	-	39	252	240	5	15
16 JAPAN	.	415	296	238	247	205	170	230	-	84	59	24	12	0	2
17 NETHERLANDS	73	291	.	.	177	233	568	361	738	146	24	0	0	0	0
18 NEW ZEALAND	-	0	1250	2273	625	196	0	0	0	0	116	0	0	0	0
19 NORWAY	.	.	.	.	.	.	.	.	.	.	76	0	0	0	0
20 POLAND	-	-	-	-	-	-	-	-	-	-	.	.	.	.	.
21 PORTUGAL	-	-	-	-	-	-	.	.	.	.	0	28	0	0	29
22 ROMANIA	-	-	-	-	-	-	-	-	-	-	-	.	.	.	.
23 SPAIN	1316	399	.	.	.	.	487	793	237	231	161	93	119	15	0
24 SWEDEN	-	-	.	.	.	.	.	.	.	.	75	113	0	0	0
25 SWITZERLAND	1818	1818	2862	2862	.	.	.	.	.	.	52	0	0	0	0
26 TURKEY	-	-	-	-	-	-	-	-	-	-	-	72	48	98	43
27 UK ENGLAND AND WALES	428	749	596	607	719	630	606	397	199	53	12	0	0	0	6
28 UK NORTHERN IRELAND	-	-	-	-	0	833	.	.	.	0	0	0	0	0	0
29 UK SCOTLAND	54	106	.	.	426	376	541	481	.	249	50	49	0	0	0
30 USA	.	.	.	.	8235	10374	8873	4720	2035	534	95	44	21	16	15
31 YUGOSLAVIA	-	-	-	-	-	-	-	-	-	-	.	.	.	.	.

- NO MORTALITY DATA ARE AVAILABLE FOR EVEN A BROADER GROUP OF CAUSES FOR THIS DISEASE

. MORTALITY DATA ARE PRESENTED FOR A BROADER GROUP OF CAUSES FOR THIS DISEASE

0 VALUE<0.5

THE STANDARD MORTALITY RATIOS WERE DERIVED WITH A FACTOR OF 1000

SERIAL MORTALITY TABLES FOR VARIOUS COUNTRIES 1901-1975

TABLE 14 : "VENEREAL DISEASE" : MALES

	1901-	1906-	1911-	1916-	1921-	1926-	1931-	1936-	1941-	1946-	1951-	1956-	1961-	1966-	1971-75
1 AUSTRALIA	-	15323	14700	13743	10812	8680	7469	6708	7253	5859	2793	1736	887	442	176
2 AUSTRIA	.	.	.	.	-	-	-	-	-	.	3656	2313	1147	852	382
3 BELGIUM	.	.	.	.	.	.	.	.	.	.	2307	1514	741	546	205
4 BULGARIA	-	-	-	-	-	.	.	.	.	.	.	.	406	229	61
5 CANADA	-	-	-	-	10165	9401	9887	9649	9341	5254	2233	1476	864	398	157
6 CHILE	-	8362	11478	22042	26864	41946	54240	44288	30095	18870	6827	4750	3183	1898	756
7 CZECHOSLOVAKIA	-	-	-	5256	6658	7397	.	.	7333	8336	4470	3120	1934	923	295
8 DENMARK	.	.	.	.	.	.	.	.	.	.	2355	1201	793	451	150
9 EIRE	-	-	-	-	3542	2451	1730	1895	2235	1790	1210	518	271	84	82
10 FINLAND	-	-	-	-	-	.	.	.	8846	5774	4220	4181	2344	967	452
11 FRANCE	-	-	-	-	.	.	.	.	3898	3623	3179	2139	1686	745	180
12 GREECE	-	-	-	-	.	5288	4761	3828	-	-	-	567	413	262	231
13 HUNGARY	-	-	-	.	.	.	16883	14900	14096	.	4169	2555	1606	838	522
14 ICELAND	-	-	.	.	.	.	.	.	.	.	.	.	189	690	0
15 ITALY	-	-	-	-	-	-	-	-	-	-	4663	2911	1692	757	297
16 JAPAN	.	29810	26719	25085	26114	26907	23183	22855	-	11174	7896	4541	2838	1438	554
17 NETHERLANDS	10223	9779	10630	11457	9062	9140	8037	7219	7712	4755	2463	1685	1078	732	245
18 NEW ZEALAND	-	14546	14177	10528	8963	10409	8405	8874	7374	6479	3188	1098	544	369	245
19 NORWAY	.	.	.	.	.	.	.	.	.	.	2775	1950	1219	541	234
20 POLAND	-	-	-	-	-	-	-	-	-	-	.	691	760	764	335
21 PORTUGAL	-	-	-	-	-	-	.	.	.	.	6039	4505	2395	1462	407
22 ROMANIA	-	-	-	-	-	-	-	-	-	-	-	1834	1641	603	216
23 SPAIN	8381	9460	10410	11678	10796	9910	9556	9205	7921	5756	5037	3684	2591	1148	596
24 SWEDEN	-	-	.	.	.	.	.	.	.	.	1024	554	362	181	60
25 SWITZERLAND	9715	9715	9154	9154	.	.	.	.	.	.	2328	1592	874	587	385
26 TURKEY	-	-	-	-	-	-	-	-	-	-	-	467	316	292	370
27 UK ENGLAND AND WALES	24931	20897	23195	20530	15111	12959	10040	8151	7213	5005	3431	2330	1524	767	198
28 UK NORTHERN IRELAND	-	-	-	-	6533	8017	.	.	.	3722	2799	2472	1311	610	238
29 UK SCOTLAND	19138	21347	20093	17495	14478	10715	7904	5954	.	3915	2349	1651	948	523	139
30 USA	31619	25544	28991	29242	24788	21463	19272	18979	14728	9263	3885	2281	1617	700	172
31 YUGOSLAVIA	-	-	-	-	-	-	-	-	-	-	2795	2810	1643	763	288

\- NO MORTALITY DATA ARE AVAILABLE FOR EVEN A BROADER GROUP OF CAUSES FOR THIS DISEASE

. MORTALITY DATA ARE PRESENTED FOR A BROADER GROUP OF CAUSES FOR THIS DISEASE

0 VALUE<0.5

THE STANDARD MORTALITY RATIOS WERE DERIVED WITH A FACTOR OF 1000

SERIAL MORTALITY TABLES FOR VARIOUS COUNTRIES 1901-1975

TABLE 14 : "VENEREAL DISEASE" : FEMALES

	1901-	1906-	1911-	1916-	1921-	1926-	1931-	1936-	1941-	1946-	1951-	1956-	1961-	1966-	1971-75
1 AUSTRALIA	-	6575	5709	4827	3170	2777	1842	1714	2034	1570	728	419	299	151	75
2 AUSTRIA	.	.	.	.	-	-	-	-	-	.	1864	1274	678	429	207
3 BELGIUM	.	.	.	.	.	.	.	.	.	.	1089	790	372	257	154
4 BULGARIA	-	-	-	-	-	.	.	.	.	.	.	.	125	114	46
5 CANADA	-	-	-	-	4057	4773	4979	4203	3602	1789	657	426	255	136	62
6 CHILE	-	5565	8388	15667	19606	30290	38758	30631	18858	10143	3399	2042	1295	930	287
7 CZECHOSLOVAKIA	-	-	-	3195	4073	4302	.	.	3506	4026	2073	1450	878	495	141
8 DENMARK	.	.	.	.	.	.	.	.	.	.	967	599	401	270	136
9 EIRE	-	-	-	-	795	867	639	415	912	836	513	116	61	42	16
10 FINLAND	-	-	-	-	-	.	.	.	3197	2060	1604	1587	974	487	185
11 FRANCE	-	-	-	-	.	.	.	.	2049	1644	1479	966	760	354	92
12 GREECE	-	-	-	-	.	2131	2089	1729	-	-	-	168	217	112	95
13 HUNGARY	-	-	-	.	.	.	8035	7426	5712	.	1699	1245	621	348	205
14 ICELAND	-	-	.	.	.	.	.	.	.	.	.	.	0	0	0
15 ITALY	-	-	-	-	-	-	-	-	-	-	1840	1099	597	258	103
16 JAPAN	.	21779	19636	17668	15035	12963	10683	9808	-	4317	2611	1426	936	500	199
17 NETHERLANDS	4616	4326	4536	4443	3831	3609	3084	2500	2775	2077	852	644	376	284	104
18 NEW ZEALAND	-	4242	5134	3333	1623	2730	2149	2439	2099	2429	926	434	127	137	153
19 NORWAY	.	.	.	.	.	.	.	.	.	.	864	597	340	181	122
20 POLAND	-	-	-	-	-	-	-	-	-	-	.	407	468	345	166
21 PORTUGAL	-	-	-	-	-	-	.	.	.	.	2638	2111	1060	660	132
22 ROMANIA	-	-	-	-	-	-	-	-	-	-	-	1133	704	268	83
23 SPAIN	5756	6134	6860	7212	6441	5306	4820	4582	3676	2572	2318	1703	1182	586	355
24 SWEDEN	-	-	.	.	.	.	.	.	.	.	424	232	167	91	46
25 SWITZERLAND	5111	5111	4565	4565	.	.	.	.	.	.	957	703	426	283	239
26 TURKEY	-	-	-	-	-	-	-	-	-	-	-	298	238	272	390
27 UK ENGLAND AND WALES	10323	8172	7627	6283	4489	3609	2874	2427	2366	1702	1137	846	678	363	103
28 UK NORTHERN IRELAND	-	-	-	-	2261	2087	.	.	.	1957	878	1056	533	297	60
29 UK SCOTLAND	7223	7153	6604	5801	4584	3108	2627	1833	.	1081	794	459	286	178	77
30 USA	15683	12113	14048	14162	11745	10744	9252	8077	5474	3260	1254	775	559	236	66
31 YUGOSLAVIA	-	-	-	-	-	-	-	-	-	-	1326	1134	881	415	169

- NO MORTALITY DATA ARE AVAILABLE FOR EVEN A BROADER GROUP OF CAUSES FOR THIS DISEASE

MORTALITY DATA ARE PRESENTED FOR A BROADER GROUP OF CAUSES FOR THIS DISEASE

0 VALUE<0.5

THE STANDARD MORTALITY RATIOS WERE DERIVED WITH A FACTOR OF 1000

SERIAL MORTALITY TABLES FOR VARIOUS COUNTRIES 1901-1975

TABLE 15 : TYPHOID FEVER : MALES

	1901-	1906-	1911-	1916-	1921-	1926-	1931-	1936-	1941-	1946-	1951-	1956-	1961-	1966-	1971-75
1 AUSTRALIA	-	.	.	.	5153	3025	1404	839	317	103	52	13	4	4	0
2 AUSTRIA	.	.	.	.	-	-	-	-	-	2204	533	250	120	25	6
3 BELGIUM	.	.	.	.	.	.	.	.	.	.	149	76	51	18	9
4 BULGARIA	-	-	-	-	-	.	.	.	.	.	.		10	15	5
5 CANADA	-	-	-	-	7536	6477	3309	2388	1101	347	107	43	16	4	6
6 CHILE	-	.	.	.	.	.	16498	18584	16463	14697	4425	3448	2290	1283	826
7 CZECHOSLOVAKIA	-	-	-	24050	10323	8656	6260	6156	17340	3184	780	284	82	50	6
8 DENMARK	9151	5502	2560	3382	1343	991	635	218	314	192	29	9	0	9	17
9 EIRE	-	-	-	-	4587	3918	2927	2275	1681	568	174	31	16	30	0
10 FINLAND	-	-	-	-	-	.	.	2055	3115	1529	119	61	19	0	0
11 FRANCE	-	-	-	-	.	.	.	.	2879	1332	363	165	100	77	38
12 GREECE	-	-	-	-	.	.	15793	15733	-	-	-	601	166	64	19
13 HUNGARY	-	-	-	20309	16957	17921	17803	8921	4722	.	471	166	76	41	24
14 ICELAND	-	-	.	.	.	.	.	.	.	.	0	0	0	0	0
15 ITALY	.	.	.	.	.	.	.	.	.	.	1470	585	228	119	79
16 JAPAN	.	.	15537	21750	23782	15571	12858	10931	-	806	241	74	21	8	2
17 NETHERLANDS	.	.	.	.	2923	1530	957	425	2281	459	37	31	14	0	0
18 NEW ZEALAND	-	.	.	.	.	738	472	457	136	567	106	57	17	0	0
19 NORWAY	.	.	.	.	.	636	1024	413	556	130	25	12	0	0	0
20 POLAND	-	-	-	-	-	-	-	-	-	-	.	408	171	57	14
21 PORTUGAL	.	.	.	.	.	.	.	.	.	.	1696	969	529	300	319
22 ROMANIA	-	-	-	-	-	-	-	-	-	-	-	186	117	66	22
23 SPAIN	.	.	.	.	.	.	11730	19803	10598	5751	1995	801	432	165	98
24 SWEDEN	-	-	.	.	.	.	.	.	.	.	18	6	0	0	0
25 SWITZERLAND	.	.	.	.	1658	1526	.	.	.	.	106	108	60	21	20
26 TURKEY	-	-	-	-	-	-	-	-	-	-	-	6429	2140	889	300
27 UK ENGLAND AND WALES	.	.	.	.	1289	863	481	372	173	71	17	7	10	4	1
28 UK NORTHERN IRELAND	-	-	-	-	2951	2570	.	.	.	161	96	31	31	0	0
29 UK SCOTLAND	.	.	.	.	1270	640	541	423	256	76	35	9	0	0	0
30 USA	.	.	.	.	.	5776	4059	2057	585	194	45	22	10	5	3
31 YUGOSLAVIA	-	-	-	-	-	-	-	-	-	-	.	595	222	105	56

- NO MORTALITY DATA ARE AVAILABLE FOR EVEN A BROADER GROUP OF CAUSES FOR THIS DISEASE

. MORTALITY DATA ARE PRESENTED FOR A BROADER GROUP OF CAUSES FOR THIS DISEASE

0 VALUE<0.5

THE STANDARD MORTALITY RATIOS WERE DERIVED WITH A FACTOR OF 1000

SERIAL MORTALITY TABLES FOR VARIOUS COUNTRIES 1901-1975

TABLE 15 : TYPHOID FEVER : FEMALES

	1901-	1906-	1911-	1916-	1921-	1926-	1931-	1936-	1941-	1946-	1951-	1956-	1961-	1966-	1971-75
1 AUSTRALIA	-	.	.	.	3852	1898	870	475	250	59	44	27	0	7	0
2 AUSTRIA	.	.	.	.	-	-	-	-	-	3170	793	257	106	95	0
3 BELGIUM	.	.	.	.	.	.	.	.	.	.	129	60	18	35	13
4 BULGARIA	-	-	-	-	-	.	.	.	.	.	.	.	10	10	0
5 CANADA	-	-	-	-	5330	5348	2633	1785	795	318	59	37	0	8	2
6 CHILE	-	.	.	.	.	.	12970	13427	12811	10374	4063	2522	2003	873	494
7 CZECHOSLOVAKIA	-	-	-	24139	10304	8702	5782	5965	15212	2937	843	292	82	43	11
8 DENMARK	6920	3718	1644	2716	1181	650	454	117	225	99	10	0	0	0	0
9 EIRE	-	-	-	-	3596	2746	2343	1336	1696	425	60	62	47	15	0
10 FINLAND	-	-	-	-	-	.	.	1320	3295	1173	168	94	9	0	17
11 FRANCE	-	-	-	-	.	.	.	.	4012	1710	268	99	63	44	36
12 GREECE	-	-	-	-	.	.	17872	17630	-	-	-	568	162	88	5
13 HUNGARY	-	-	-	21429	17608	16460	15304	6962	3607	.	291	167	63	27	19
14 ICELAND	-	-	.	.	.	.	.	.	.	.	0	0	0	0	0
15 ITALY	.	.	.	.	.	.	.	.	.	.	1755	630	220	118	69
16 JAPAN	.	.	13687	19262	21764	14483	12203	10726	-	828	214	55	18	7	3
17 NETHERLANDS	.	.	.	.	2139	891	580	251	1788	275	32	54	18	0	0
18 NEW ZEALAND	-	.	.	.	.	305	371	404	437	214	172	59	18	0	15
19 NORWAY	.	.	.	.	.	484	453	274	211	90	0	0	0	0	0
20 POLAND	-	-	-	-	-	-	-	-	-	-	.	357	155	48	10
21 PORTUGAL	.	.	.	.	.	.	.	.	.	.	1338	619	295	212	210
22 ROMANIA	-	-	-	-	-	-	-	-	-	-	-	149	116	35	14
23 SPAIN	.	.	.	.	.	.	11829	15717	11236	5905	1813	732	334	124	77
24 SWEDEN	-	-	.	.	.	.	.	.	.	.	6	6	11	5	0
25 SWITZERLAND	.	.	.	.	1312	1031	.	.	.	.	132	55	101	27	0
26 TURKEY	-	-	-	-	-	-	-	-	-	-	-	7025	2919	1066	330
27 UK ENGLAND AND WALES	.	.	.	.	1129	747	391	305	126	59	16	9	5	5	3
28 UK NORTHERN IRELAND	-	-	-	-	2195	2760	.	.	.	606	60	0	0	0	0
29 UK SCOTLAND	.	.	.	.	1319	644	370	346	153	39	16	16	8	0	0
30 USA	.	.	.	.	.	4450	3072	1501	409	137	34	17	7	5	2
31 YUGOSLAVIA	-	-	-	-	-	-	-	-	-	-	.	696	286	81	48

\- NO MORTALITY DATA ARE AVAILABLE FOR EVEN A BROADER GROUP OF CAUSES FOR THIS DISEASE

. MORTALITY DATA ARE PRESENTED FOR A BROADER GROUP OF CAUSES FOR THIS DISEASE

0 VALUE<0.5

THE STANDARD MORTALITY RATIOS WERE DERIVED WITH A FACTOR OF 1000

SERIAL MORTALITY TABLES FOR VARIOUS COUNTRIES 1901-1975

TABLE 16 : PARATYPHOID FEVER AND OTHER SALMONELLA INFECTIONS : MALES

	1901-	1906-	1911-	1916-	1921-	1926-	1931-	1936-	1941-	1946-	1951-	1956-	1961-	1966-	1971-75
1 AUSTRALIA	-	.	.	.	3407	2207	1932	1272	618	419	449	202	184	320	415
2 AUSTRIA	.	.	.	.	-	-	-	-	-	1648	1213	612	341	225	111
3 BELGIUM	.	.	.	.	.	.	.	.	.	.	192	637	688	857	828
4 BULGARIA	-	-	-	-	-	.	.	.	.	.	.	.	306	465	1247
5 CANADA	-	-	-	-	2658	2759	1855	1439	1217	955	164	277	328	211	168
6 CHILE	-	.	.	.	.	.	12857	10282	7555	5386	2662	1536	1136	1119	1326
7 CZECHOSLOVAKIA	-	-	-	3156	3084	2222	2732	1879	6186	4826	744	602	432	336	371
8 DENMARK	.	.	.	.	.	.	1437	270	457	143	634	346	332	120	116
9 EIRE	-	-	-	-	11441	3311	600	331	0	861	67	206	69	340	855
10 FINLAND	-	-	-	-	-	.	.	4361	12171	6044	1842	1040	470	318	222
11 FRANCE	-	-	-	-	.	.	.	.	3980	2462	509	166	126	137	192
12 GREECE	-	-	-	-	.	.	12581	15432	-	-	-	410	243	23	111
13 HUNGARY	-	-	-	.	.	.	457	636	111	.	323	330	140	116	492
14 ICELAND	-	-	.	.	.	.	.	.	.	.	.	.	0	0	0
15 ITALY	.	.	.	.	.	.	.	.	.	.	756	538	314	174	236
16 JAPAN	.	.	5479	7090	7753	6063	5157	5064	-	509	171	105	51	40	23
17 NETHERLANDS	.	.	.	.	569	854	921	691	1566	779	507	2018	3000	1714	1399
18 NEW ZEALAND	-	.	.	.	.	0	972	263	380	872	686	714	403	75	207
19 NORWAY	.	.	.	.	.	2188	963	350	592	247	59	55	157	101	49
20 POLAND	-	-	-	-	-	-	-	-	-	-	.	149	852	1099	635
21 PORTUGAL	.	.	.	.	.	.	.	.	.	.	127	195	213	525	578
22 ROMANIA	-	-	-	-	-	-	-	-	-	-	-	86	99	667	1023
23 SPAIN	.	.	.	.	.	.	11278	10873	8752	4403	1088	717	427	252	202
24 SWEDEN	-	-	.	.	.	.	.	.	.	.	2091	358	222	189	460
25 SWITZERLAND	.	.	.	.	1038	895	.	.	.	.	622	811	922	1130	540
26 TURKEY	-	-	-	-	-	-	-	-	-	-	-	1371	257	322	178
27 UK ENGLAND AND WALES	.	.	.	.	995	1106	708	773	555	791	604	483	266	246	327
28 UK NORTHERN IRELAND	-	-	-	-	0	1724	.	.	.	0	1045	294	422	411	400
29 UK SCOTLAND	.	.	.	.	1867	1894	1202	837	482	442	683	277	233	543	310
30 USA	.	.	.	.	.	4740	3630	2972	2091	1114	163	231	224	211	199
31 YUGOSLAVIA	-	-	-	-	-	-	-	-	-	-	.	.	258	179	369

- NO MORTALITY DATA ARE AVAILABLE FOR EVEN A BROADER GROUP OF CAUSES FOR THIS DISEASE

. MORTALITY DATA ARE PRESENTED FOR A BROADER GROUP OF CAUSES FOR THIS DISEASE

0 VALUE<0.5

THE STANDARD MORTALITY RATIOS WERE DERIVED WITH A FACTOR OF 1000

SERIAL MORTALITY TABLES FOR VARIOUS COUNTRIES 1901-1975

TABLE 16 : PARATYPHOID FEVER AND OTHER SALMONELLA INFECTIONS : FEMALES

	1901-	1906-	1911-	1916-	1921-	1926-	1931-	1936-	1941-	1946-	1951-	1956-	1961-	1966-	1971-75
1 AUSTRALIA	-	.	.	.	1719	1667	1318	895	552	481	317	265	203	302	335
2 AUSTRIA	.	.	.	.	-	-	-	-	-	2177	1700	848	189	258	162
3 BELGIUM	.	.	.	.	.	.	.	.	.	.	156	240	700	667	732
4 BULGARIA	-	-	-	-	-	.	.	.	.	.	.	.	242	321	833
5 CANADA	-	-	-	-	1972	2835	1875	1260	1150	853	155	198	243	230	165
6 CHILE	-	.	.	.	.	.	11850	7844	6568	5098	1444	1347	739	967	1121
7 CZECHOSLOVAKIA	-	-	-	3396	2540	1895	2036	1863	3203	2138	587	514	451	323	354
8 DENMARK	.	.	.	.	.	.	2787	725	343	277	614	335	200	154	112
9 EIRE	-	-	-	-	8333	1329	556	280	206	272	342	69	69	272	915
10 FINLAND	-	-	-	-	-	.	.	4731	15803	8775	880	1441	921	202	316
11 FRANCE	-	-	-	-	.	.	.	.	3644	2473	584	150	104	140	167
12 GREECE	-	-	-	-	.	.	13611	13532	-	-	-	333	158	43	83
13 HUNGARY	-	-	-	.	.	.	499	272	104	.	487	299	108	124	481
14 ICELAND	-	-	.	.	.	.	.	.	.	.	.	.	1111	0	0
15 ITALY	.	.	.	.	.	.	.	.	.	.	884	518	267	155	182
16 JAPAN	.	.	4760	6954	6406	4802	3915	4035	-	599	202	72	25	16	5
17 NETHERLANDS	.	.	.	.	585	701	627	468	1209	1175	456	1502	1678	1510	1048
18 NEW ZEALAND	-	.	.	.	.	0	1000	263	247	284	196	88	80	148	340
19 NORWAY	.	.	.	.	.	1655	759	197	311	237	57	107	153	98	47
20 POLAND	-	-	-	-	-	-	-	-	-	-	.	167	476	732	354
21 PORTUGAL	.	.	.	.	.	.	.	.	.	.	339	194	147	209	481
22 ROMANIA	-	-	-	-	-	-	-	-	-	-	-	106	113	398	575
23 SPAIN	.	.	.	.	.	.	10695	9906	7387	3827	1179	717	375	178	137
24 SWEDEN	-	-	.	.	.	.	.	.	.	.	1097	125	241	69	291
25 SWITZERLAND	.	.	.	.	398	813	.	.	.	.	414	704	651	1012	471
26 TURKEY	-	-	-	-	-	-	-	-	-	-	-	982	678	341	223
27 UK ENGLAND AND WALES	.	.	.	.	888	1016	651	679	476	611	403	411	193	218	322
28 UK NORTHERN IRELAND	-	-	-	-	0	2064	.	.	.	725	1111	676	649	253	0
29 UK SCOTLAND	.	.	.	.	1215	2000	1484	1212	830	143	641	350	138	448	276
30 USA	.	.	.	.	.	3393	2917	2375	1887	809	156	162	152	161	136
31 YUGOSLAVIA	-	-	-	-	-	-	-	-	-	-	.	.	198	177	261

- NO MORTALITY DATA ARE AVAILABLE FOR EVEN A BROADER GROUP OF CAUSES FOR THIS DISEASE

. MORTALITY DATA ARE PRESENTED FOR A BROADER GROUP OF CAUSES FOR THIS DISEASE

0 VALUE<0.5

THE STANDARD MORTALITY RATIOS WERE DERIVED WITH A FACTOR OF 1000

SERIAL MORTALITY TABLES FOR VARIOUS COUNTRIES 1901-1975

TABLE 17 : TYPHOID AND PARATYPHOID : MALES

	1901-	1906-	1911-	1916-	1921-	1926-	1931-	1936-	1941-	1946-	1951-	1956-	1961-	1966-	1971-75
1 AUSTRALIA	-	1572	1421	722	486	289	149	91	37	16	12	5	4	6	7
2 AUSTRIA	.	.	.	.	-	-	-	-	-	.	47	32	16	6	2
3 BELGIUM	1392	1038	935	722	408	292	173	113	130	77	18	18	17	17	15
4 BULGARIA	-	-	-	-	-	612	924	458	208	133	41	8	6	9	22
5 CANADA	-	-	-	-	673	586	307	223	112	45	12	8	7	4	3
6 CHILE	-	16427	4477	5584	4763	2515	1592	1725	1503	1318	343	313	210	126	91
7 CZECHOSLOVAKIA	-	-	-	2068	915	761	568	545	1547	401	63	34	14	10	7
8 DENMARK	.	.	.	.	.	.	77	23	34	18	14	7	6	3	3
9 EIRE	-	-	-	-	576	381	253	194	139	62	16	6	3	9	15
10 FINLAND	-	-	-	-	-	.	.	243	461	229	41	23	10	5	4
11 FRANCE	-	-	-	-	342	358	258	192	276	153	39	17	11	9	7
12 GREECE	-	-	-	-	2499	2100	1597	1568	-	-	-	57	18	6	4
13 HUNGARY	-	-	-	.	.	.	1493	755	395	230	69	19	9	5	11
14 ICELAND	-	-	1522	1000	1185	310	258	59	0	0	.	.	0	0	0
15 ITALY	3032	2357	2140	2050	1715	1556	1072	831	1033	562	135	58	24	13	11
16 JAPAN	1153	1255	1385	1930	2112	1400	1159	997	-	76	23	8	3	1	1
17 NETHERLANDS	864	632	443	625	253	142	95	47	216	51	12	38	54	30	24
18 NEW ZEALAND	-	633	546	337	244	128	55	42	18	62	21	17	9	1	4
19 NORWAY	569	396	271	315	169	116	101	40	56	15	3	2	3	2	1
20 POLAND	-	-	-	-	-	-	-	-	-	-	.	36	29	23	12
21 PORTUGAL	1661	1415	1293	1697	1843	1744	1350	1531	1689	822	196	84	47	34	36
22 ROMANIA	-	-	-	-	-	-	-	-	-	-	-	17	11	17	19
23 SPAIN	3820	2832	2229	2554	2109	1620	1166	1833	1029	553	184	79	43	18	12
24 SWEDEN	-	-	404	520	201	93	60	49	29	27	39	7	4	3	8
25 SWITZERLAND	482	482	259	259	156	142	77	40	61	18	20	23	21	21	11
26 TURKEY	-	-	-	-	-	-	-	-	-	-	-	560	183	79	28
27 UK ENGLAND AND WALES	1214	797	530	233	124	90	52	44	24	20	12	9	6	5	6
28 UK NORTHERN IRELAND	-	-	-	-	248	242	182	106	78	45	26	8	10	7	7
29 UK SCOTLAND	1724	1405	466	237	137	85	65	49	29	14	15	6	4	10	6
30 USA	5023	3068	1880	1214	790	553	399	221	84	35	7	6	5	4	4
31 YUGOSLAVIA	-	-	-	-	-	-	-	-	-	-	.	.	23	12	11

- NO MORTALITY DATA ARE AVAILABLE FOR EVEN A BROADER GROUP OF CAUSES FOR THIS DISEASE

. MORTALITY DATA ARE PRESENTED FOR A BROADER GROUP OF CAUSES FOR THIS DISEASE

0 VALUE<0.5

THE STANDARD MOFTALITY RATIOS WERE DERIVED WITH A FACTOR OF 100

SERIAL MORTALITY TABLES FOR VARIOUS COUNTRIES 1901-1975

TABLE 17 : TYPHOID AND PARATYPHOID : FEMALES

	1901-	1906-	1911-	1916-	1921-	1926-	1931-	1936-	1941-	1946-	1951-	1956-	1961-	1966-	1971-75
1 AUSTRALIA	-	1043	792	522	350	186	94	55	30	13	9	7	4	6	6
2 AUSTRIA	.	.	.	.	-	-	-	-	-	.	77	37	12	13	3
3 BELGIUM	1267	944	746	648	367	236	155	101	106	70	15	9	15	15	15
4 BULGARIA	-	-	-	-	-	735	857	450	213	106	23	2	5	6	15
5 CANADA	-	-	-	-	477	493	251	170	85	41	8	6	4	5	3
6 CHILE	-	15702	4430	5478	4386	2248	1278	1253	1181	952	299	233	179	89	60
7 CZECHOSLOVAKIA	-	-	-	2077	904	758	516	527	1314	334	58	33	15	9	7
8 DENMARK	.	.	.	.	.	.	85	22	25	13	12	6	4	3	2
9 EIRE	-	-	-	-	442	250	203	115	144	40	11	6	5	6	17
10 FINLAND	-	-	-	-	-	.	.	189	542	249	29	33	17	4	7
11 FRANCE	-	-	-	-	415	467	322	235	366	185	33	11	7	6	6
12 GREECE	-	-	-	-	2349	2123	1775	1694	-	-	-	53	16	8	2
13 HUNGARY	-	-	-	.	.	.	1283	584	301	192	51	19	7	4	10
14 ICELAND	-	-	1040	1231	393	400	125	29	0	0	.	.	20	0	0
15 ITALY	3304	2517	2093	2552	2091	1816	1214	983	1404	726	160	61	23	12	9
16 JAPAN	928	1076	1218	1718	1917	1285	1081	961	-	79	21	6	2	1	0
17 NETHERLANDS	697	492	287	439	188	86	59	29	169	43	11	31	31	27	19
18 NEW ZEALAND	-	453	378	250	187	74	48	38	40	23	18	6	3	3	7
19 NORWAY	396	290	225	328	141	74	50	26	23	12	1	2	3	2	1
20 POLAND	-	-	-	-	-	-	-	-	-	-	.	32	21	17	7
21 PORTUGAL	1451	1260	1144	1512	1761	1635	1349	1482	1707	843	137	55	27	21	26
22 ROMANIA	-	-	-	-	-	-	-	-	-	-	-	14	12	10	11
23 SPAIN	4040	2927	2336	2601	2169	1694	1164	1475	1059	556	170	73	34	13	9
24 SWEDEN	-	-	282	380	152	69	60	32	32	22	21	3	5	2	5
25 SWITZERLAND	405	405	210	210	116	99	46	42	36	19	18	17	20	21	9
26 TURKEY	-	-	-	-	-	-	-	-	-	-	-	601	254	94	31
27 UK ENGLAND AND WALES	838	536	342	185	109	79	44	37	19	16	9	8	4	5	6
28 UK NORTHERN IRELAND	-	-	-	-	182	272	133	83	60	43	25	12	12	5	0
29 UK SCOTLAND	1230	1014	367	204	130	87	56	49	27	6	13	8	3	8	5
30 USA	3523	2140	1385	955	655	441	305	165	66	25	6	4	3	3	3
31 YUGOSLAVIA	-	-	-	-	-	-	-	-	-	-	.	.	27	10	8

- NO MORTALITY DATA ARE AVAILABLE FOR EVEN A BROADER GROUP OF CAUSES FOR THIS DISEASE

. MORTALITY DATA ARE PRESENTED FOR A BROADER GROUP OF CAUSES FOR THIS DISEASE

0 VALUE<0.5

THE STANDARD MORTALITY RATIOS WERE DERIVED WITH A FACTOR OF 100

SERIAL MORTALITY TABLES FOR VARIOUS COUNTRIES 1901-1975

TABLE 18 : CHOLERA : MALES

	1901-	1906-	1911-	1916-	1921-	1926-	1931-	1936-	1941-	1946-	1951-	1956-	1961-	1966-	1971-75
1 AUSTRALIA	-	0	0	0	0	0	0	0	0	0	0	0	0	0	0
2 AUSTRIA	0	150	7070	900	-	-	-	-	-	.	0	0	0	0	0
3 BELGIUM	690	940	0	650	0	.	.	.	.	.	0	0	0	0	0
4 BULGARIA	-	-	-	-	-	0	.	.	.	.	.	.	0	0	0
5 CANADA	-	-	-	-	0	0	0	0	20	0	0	0	0	0	0
6 CHILE	-	0	0	0	0	.	.	0	90	160	0	0	0	0	0
7 CZECHOSLOVAKIA	-	-	-	.	.	.	.	.	0	30	0	0	0	10	0
8 DENMARK	0	230	0	0	0	0	.	.	.	.	0	0	0	0	0
9 EIRE	-	-	-	-	0	0	0	0	0	0	0	0	0	0	0
10 FINLAND	160	1590	720	1170	200	0	.	.	0	0	0	0	0	0	0
11 FRANCE	-	-	-	-	290	70	.	.	0	0	0	0	0	0	0
12 GREECE	-	-	-	-	680	740	.	.	-	-	-	0	0	0	0
13 HUNGARY	-	-	-	70	60	0	0	0	0	.	0	0	0	0	0
14 ICELAND	-	-	.	.	.	.	.	.	.	.	0	0	0	0	0
15 ITALY	-	-	-	-	-	-	-	-	-	-	0	0	0	0	60
16 JAPAN	22870	10850	5570	29420	2430	290	0	0	-	0	0	0	0	0	0
17 NETHERLANDS	40	400	0	0	0	0	0	20	0	0	0	0	0	0	0
18 NEW ZEALAND	-	0	0	0	0	0	0	0	0	0	0	0	0	0	70
19 NORWAY	0	100	0	0	0	0	80	0	70	0	0	0	0	0	0
20 POLAND	-	-	-	-	-	-	-	-	-	-	.	0	0	0	0
21 PORTUGAL	0	0	0	0	0	0	.	.	.	.	0	0	0	0	740
22 ROMANIA	-	-	-	-	-	-	-	-	-	-	-	0	0	0	0
23 SPAIN	270	20	200	0	20	0	0	0	0	0	0	0	0	0	0
24 SWEDEN	-	-	120	230	70	0	0	0	0	0	0	0	0	0	0
25 SWITZERLAND	0	0	0	0	0	0	.	.	.	.	0	0	0	0	0
26 TURKEY	-	-	-	-	-	-	-	-	-	-	-	0	0	320	20
27 UK ENGLAND AND WALES	0	10	0	0	0	0	0	0	0	0	0	0	0	0	0
28 UK NORTHERN IRELAND	-	-	-	-	0	0	.	.	.	0	0	0	0	0	140
29 UK SCOTLAND	0	0	.	.	.	.	.	.	.	0	0	0	0	0	0
30 USA	.	0	0	0	0	0	.	0	0	0	0	0	0	0	0
31 YUGOSLAVIA	-	-	-	-	-	-	-	-	-	-	.	0	0	0	0

- NO MORTALITY DATA ARE AVAILABLE FOR EVEN A BROADER GROUP OF CAUSES FOR THIS DISEASE

. MORTALITY DA‾A ARE PRESENTED FOR A BROADER GROUP OF CAUSES FOR THIS DISEASE

0 VALUE<0.5

THE STANDARD MORTALITY RATIOS WERE DERIVED WITH A FACTOR OF 100000

SERIAL MORTALITY TABLES FOR VARIOUS COUNTRIES 1901-1975

TABLE 18 : CHOLERA : FEMALES

	1901-	1906-	1911-	1916-	1921-	1926-	1931-	1936-	1941-	1946-	1951-	1956-	1961-	1966-	1971-75
1 AUSTRALIA	-	0	0	0	0	0	0	0	0	0	0	0	0	0	0
2 AUSTRIA	0	70	2560	660	-	-	-	-	-	.	0	0	0	0	0
3 BELGIUM	370	920	0	1050	0	.	.	.	.	.	0	0	0	0	0
4 BULGARIA	-	-	-	-	-	0	.	.	.	.	.	.	0	0	0
5 CANADA	-	-	-	-	0	0	0	0	0	0	0	0	0	0	0
6 CHILE	-	0	0	0	0	.	.	0	0	0	0	0	0	0	0
7 CZECHOSLOVAKIA	-	-	-	.	.	.	.	.	0	30	0	0	0	0	0
8 DENMARK	0	0	0	0	0	0	.	.	.	.	0	0	0	0	0
9 EIRE	-	-	-	-	0	0	0	0	0	0	0	0	0	0	0
10 FINLAND	480	740	280	330	120	0	.	.	0	0	0	0	0	0	0
11 FRANCE	-	-	-	-	120	50	.	.	0	0	0	0	0	0	0
12 GREECE	-	-	-	-	460	450	.	.	-	-	-	0	0	0	0
13 HUNGARY	-	-	-	130	0	0	0	0	0	.	0	0	0	0	0
14 ICELAND	-	-	.	.	.	.	.	.	.	.	0	0	0	0	0
15 ITALY	-	-	-	-	-	-	-	-	-	-	0	0	0	0	30
16 JAPAN	17710	6580	3250	21260	1410	210	0	0	-	0	0	0	0	0	0
17 NETHERLANDS	0	310	0	0	0	0	0	0	0	0	0	0	0	0	0
18 NEW ZEALAND	-	0	0	0	0	0	0	0	0	0	0	0	0	0	0
19 NORWAY	0	0	0	0	0	0	0	0	0	0	0	0	0	0	0
20 POLAND	-	-	-	-	-	-	-	-	-	-	.	0	0	0	0
21 PORTUGAL	0	0	0	0	0	0	.	.	.	.	0	0	0	0	580
22 ROMANIA	-	-	-	-	-	-	-	-	-	-	-	0	0	0	0
23 SPAIN	80	0	270	0	10	0	0	0	0	0	0	0	0	0	0
24 SWEDEN	-	-	0	70	0	0	0	0	0	0	0	0	0	0	0
25 SWITZERLAND	0	0	0	0	0	0	.	.	.	.	0	0	0	0	0
26 TURKEY	-	-	-	-	-	-	-	-	-	-	-	0	0	330	20
27 UK ENGLAND AND WALES	0	0	0	0	0	0	0	0	0	0	0	0	0	0	0
28 UK NORTHERN IRELAND	-	-	-	-	0	0	.	.	.	0	0	0	0	0	0
29 UK SCOTLAND	0	0	.	.	.	.	.	.	.	0	0	0	0	0	0
30 USA	.	0	0	0	0	0	.	0	0	0	0	0	0	0	0
31 YUGOSLAVIA	-	-	-	-	-	-	-	-	-	-	.	0	0	0	0

\- NO MORTALITY DATA ARE AVAILABLE FOR EVEN A BROADER GROUP OF CAUSES FOR THIS DISEASE

. MORTALITY DATA ARE PRESENTED FOR A BROADER GROUP OF CAUSES FOR THIS DISEASE

0 VALUE<0.5

THE STANDARD MORTALITY RATIOS WERE DERIVED WITH A FACTOR OF 100000

SERIAL MORTALITY TABLES FOR VARIOUS COUNTRIES 1901-1975

TABLE 19 : ERUCELLOSIS (UNDULANT FEVER) : MALES

	1901-	1906-	1911-	1916-	1921-	1926-	1931-	1936-	1941-	1946-	1951-	1956-	1961-	1966-	1971-75
1 AUSTRALIA	-	0	0	0	162	0	0	245	0	105	0	263	240	73	265
2 AUSTRIA	.	.	.	.	-	-	-	-	-	.	206	120	0	0	114
3 BELGIUM	.	.	.	.	.	.	.	.	.	.	225	87	86	84	165
4 BULGARIA	-	-	-	-	-	.	.	.	.	.	.	.	0	0	0
5 CANADA	-	-	-	-	0	541	2013	1790	1148	721	418	106	145	0	40
6 CHILE	-	8065	16301	3582	560	0	.	0	1848	2885	0	0	0	0	109
7 CZECHOSLOVAKIA	-	-	-	.	.	.	0	0	0	0	345	129	122	233	0
8 DENMARK	.	.	.	.	.	.	8845	7289	3205	602	382	0	172	0	0
9 EIRE	-	-	-	-	0	0	0	278	1120	836	0	1166	593	1466	565
10 FINLAND	-	-	-	-	-	.	.	.	251	0	0	0	0	0	0
11 FRANCE	-	-	-	-	.	.	.	.	5550	4072	1565	1114	761	618	491
12 GREECE	-	-	-	-	.	1846	2903	.	-	-	-	1768	413	292	829
13 HUNGARY	-	-	-	.	.	.	104	0	0	.	0	87	84	80	308
14 ICELAND	-	-	.	.	.	.	.	.	.	.	.	.	0	0	0
15 ITALY	-	-	-	-	10944	9325	10803	12123	11113	14385	5998	2632	1485	760	347
16 JAPAN	.	.	.	.	0	0	0	0	-	62	153	75	39	18	16
17 NETHERLANDS	0	171	158	146	0	122	112	0	485	276	253	157	145	68	0
18 NEW ZEALAND	-	0	0	0	0	645	592	1667	535	616	0	391	1071	0	302
19 NORWAY	.	.	.	.	.	0	317	0	0	258	0	0	0	0	0
20 POLAND	-	-	-	-	-	-	-	-	-	-	.	85	127	172	53
21 PORTUGAL	-	-	-	-	-	-	.	.	.	.	1124	641	725	935	725
22 ROMANIA	-	-	-	-	-	-	-	-	-	-	-	0	0	44	41
23 SPAIN	3459	2301	11960	14835	23565	31405	37000	43538	31514	23491	11719	4308	2385	1836	1426
24 SWEDEN	-	-	.	.	.	.	1642	777	123	116	111	0	0	0	0
25 SWITZERLAND	.	.	.	.	.	.	4086	1840	3107	3309	1043	648	446	138	131
26 TURKEY	-	-	-	-	-	-	-	-	-	-	-	0	105	0	86
27 UK ENGLAND AND WALES	.	.	213	204	97	46	303	457	348	234	93	54	52	84	0
28 UK NORTHERN IRELAND	-	-	-	-	0	0	.	.	.	0	0	0	0	592	0
29 UK SCOTLAND	.	.	.	.	.	.	.	.	.	0	0	333	329	164	0
30 USA	.	0	93	24	38	558	1576	2050	1537	974	361	137	119	36	4
31 YUGOSLAVIA	-	-	-	-	-	-	-	-	-	-	.	.	0	0	0

\- NO MORTALITY DATA ARE AVAILABLE FOR EVEN A BROADER GROUP OF CAUSES FOR THIS DISEASE

. MORTALITY DATA ARE PRESENTED FOR A BROADER GROUP OF CAUSES FOR THIS DISEASE

0 VALUE<0.5

THE STANDARD MORTALITY RATIOS WERE DERIVED WITH A FACTOR OF 10000

SERIAL MORTALITY TABLES FOR VARIOUS COUNTRIES 1901-1975

TABLE 19 : BRUCELLOSIS (UNDULANT FEVER) : FEMALES

	1901-	1906-	1911-	1916-	1921-	1926-	1931-	1936-	1941-	1946-	1951-	1956-	1961-	1966-	1971-75
1 AUSTRALIA	-	0	0	0	0	0	0	126	116	0	287	87	78	0	0
2 AUSTRIA	.	.	.	.	-	-	-	-	-	.	0	192	0	0	0
3 BELGIUM	.	.	.	.	.	.	.	.	.	.	0	0	78	0	0
4 BULGARIA	-	-	-	-	-	.	.	.	.	.	.	.	251	0	0
5 CANADA	-	-	-	-	0	501	1196	1432	764	410	184	163	0	0	0
6 CHILE	-	4839	3385	4651	272	0	.	267	1179	907	0	139	0	111	0
7 CZECHOSLOVAKIA	-	-	-	.	.	.	0	0	0	0	309	58	0	0	51
8 DENMARK	.	.	.	.	.	.	3218	4104	1222	769	365	0	0	0	0
9 EIRE	-	-	-	-	0	0	0	292	285	283	0	877	292	0	0
10 FINLAND	-	-	-	-	-	.	.	.	441	629	0	0	0	0	0
11 FRANCE	-	-	-	-	.	.	.	.	2884	1624	831	310	264	280	212
12 GREECE	-	-	-	-	.	1266	699	.	-	-	-	1097	187	264	755
13 HUNGARY	-	-	-	.	.	.	0	230	439	.	0	0	0	0	136
14 ICELAND	-	-	.	.	.	.	.	.	.	.	.	.	0	0	0
15 ITALY	-	-	-	-	10628	9672	9934	8388	8658	8404	3903	1514	763	286	190
16 JAPAN	.	.	.	.	0	0	60	0	-	0	33	49	0	0	7
17 NETHERLANDS	874	163	0	0	0	0	0	100	470	177	162	75	0	64	0
18 NEW ZEALAND	-	0	0	0	0	0	613	559	0	595	0	0	347	0	291
19 NORWAY	.	.	.	.	.	0	289	0	513	0	0	0	0	0	0
20 POLAND	-	-	-	-	-	-	-	-	-	-	.	0	0	25	47
21 PORTUGAL	-	-	-	-	-	-	.	.	.	.	2406	91	353	698	345
22 ROMANIA	-	-	-	-	-	-	-	-	-	-	-	0	0	0	0
23 SPAIN	2826	1938	12461	15009	22429	23859	21588	22440	15382	11373	5922	2063	1618	762	729
24 SWEDEN	-	-	.	.	.	.	1026	860	234	334	0	0	0	0	0
25 SWITZERLAND	.	.	.	.	.	.	2099	2550	2414	1948	2458	143	132	124	117
26 TURKEY	-	-	-	-	-	-	-	-	-	-	-	0	111	0	96
27 UK ENGLAND AND WALES	.	.	24	23	43	40	191	252	156	117	65	31	0	15	29
28 UK NORTHERN IRELAND	-	-	-	-	0	0	.	.	.	0	0	0	0	0	0
29 UK SCOTLAND	.	.	.	.	.	.	.	.	.	0	0	143	141	0	0
30 USA	.	121	116	37	20	394	1034	1382	894	596	177	77	57	20	34
31 YUGOSLAVIA	-	-	-	-	-	-	-	-	-	-	.	.	0	41	0

- NO MORTALITY DATA ARE AVAILABLE FOR EVEN A BROADER GROUP OF CAUSES FOR THIS DISEASE

. MORTALITY DATA ARE PRESENTED FOR A BROADER GROUP OF CAUSES FOR THIS DISEASE

0 VALUE<0.5

THE STANDARD MORTALITY RATIOS WERE DERIVED WITH A FACTOR OF 10000

SERIAL MORTALITY TABLES FOR VARIOUS COUNTRIES 1901-1975

TABLE 20 : DYSENTERY- ALL FORMS : MALES

	1901-	1906-	1911-	1916-	1921-	1926-	1931-	1936-	1941-	1946-	1951-	1956-	1961-	1966-	1971-75
1 AUSTRALIA	-	9164	7689	5308	5179	5000	2695	1792	1939	933	938	426	248	221	154
2 AUSTRIA	5066	1167	8503	73705	-	-	-	-	-	953	103	72	222	82	13
3 BELGIUM	.	.	.	.	.	.	.	.	.	.	173	92	60	49	39
4 BULGARIA	-	-	-	-	-	.	.	.	.	.	.	.	1516	869	518
5 CANADA	-	-	-	-	9057	3370	3564	3889	3400	1288	713	509	205	96	69
6 CHILE	-	27255	50611	40809	32986	26364	15359	10687	6777	4923	3330	3544	2524	1564	984
7 CZECHOSLOVAKIA	-	-	-	56790	17927	3147	2872	7786	5658	493	271	295	290	192	41
8 DENMARK	267	124	110	0	0	32	.	.	773	95	135	21	62	0	19
9 EIRE	-	-	-	-	901	890	67	98	586	351	195	203	172	205	0
10 FINLAND	40429	10080	12820	36101	2774	645	346	.	2531	742	199	134	25	0	23
11 FRANCE	-	-	-	-	.	.	.	.	2666	699	380	236	186	102	55
12 GREECE	-	-	-	-	.	92392	78142	65317	-	-	-	4376	2226	489	22
13 HUNGARY	-	-	-	54924	37058	15960	25626	22097	15965	8381	10195	2090	978	397	139
14 ICELAND	-	-	10000	0	.	0	1000	2000	.	.	0	0	0	0	0
15 ITALY	-	-	-	-	7091	4019	3104	2095	2443	826	500	316	152	76	22
16 JAPAN	53498	45030	43616	44365	41279	53770	65242	72675	-	44344	37569	10133	2445	329	39
17 NETHERLANDS	738	371	497	619	520	253	588	653	15170	1209	349	205	78	40	30
18 NEW ZEALAND	-	6667	2083	3269	1217	3333	1397	2381	1147	867	693	409	210	40	0
19 NORWAY	2083	761	583	1187	736	369	577	536	2914	275	0	81	52	49	0
20 POLAND	-	-	-	-	-	-	-	-	-	-	.	930	300	75	30
21 PORTUGAL	-	-	-	-	-	-	.	.	.	.	11435	390	336	13	112
22 ROMANIA	-	-	-	-	-	-	-	-	-	-	-	1448	556	1057	1323
23 SPAIN	63277	32555	19159	19192	17367	11214	4765	4925	4605	1615	1084	647	364	106	15
24 SWEDEN	-	-	339	1226	330	263	332	173	279	55	26	25	12	23	32
25 SWITZERLAND	829	829	356	356	651	337	.	.	.	.	103	19	89	50	47
26 TURKEY	-	-	-	-	-	-	-	-	-	-	-	3200	1601	1264	523
27 UK ENGLAND AND WALES	2962	2208	2608	5561	1378	949	890	912	1345	497	283	165	156	88	55
28 UK NORTHERN IRELAND	-	-	-	-	449	270	0	84	331	397	677	672	144	210	204
29 UK SCOTLAND	.	.	851	1378	751	967	1066	1883	2688	720	538	197	293	156	155
30 USA	37194	21035	13727	14703	9081	7371	6156	6069	3908	1891	1398	673	456	198	114
31 YUGOSLAVIA	-	-	-	-	-	-	-	-	-	-	.	4732	1668	649	277

- NO MORTALITY DATA ARE AVAILABLE FOR EVEN A BROADER GROUP OF CAUSES FOR THIS DISEASE

. MORTALITY DATA ARE PRESENTED FOR A BROADER GROUP OF CAUSES FOR THIS DISEASE

0 VALUE<0.5

THE STANDARD MORTALITY RATIOS WERE DERIVED WITH A FACTOR OF 1000

SERIAL MORTALITY TABLES FOR VARIOUS COUNTRIES 1901-1975

TABLE 20 : DYSENTERY- ALL FORMS : FEMALES

	1901-	1906-	1911-	1916-	1921-	1926-	1931-	1936-	1941-	1946-	1951-	1956-	1961-	1966-	1971-75
1 AUSTRALIA	-	6054	5220	3438	3739	4408	2122	1515	1868	799	771	252	237	250	91
2 AUSTRIA	4055	1058	2488	52380	-	-	-	-	-	618	81	67	54	21	0
3 BELGIUM	.	.	.	.	.	.	.	.	.	.	109	46	36	43	17
4 BULGARIA	-	-	-	-	-	.	.	.	.	.	.	.	1388	753	631
5 CANADA	-	-	-	-	7881	3538	3661	3727	2912	1181	552	309	204	57	61
6 CHILE	-	23462	44232	36331	30405	25204	12399	9310	6642	3508	2653	3316	1857	932	633
7 CZECHOSLOVAKIA	-	-	-	47898	15577	3083	2217	5759	4805	485	218	458	349	203	53
8 DENMARK	0	0	88	81	0	59	.	.	929	113	86	61	38	0	34
9 EIRE	-	-	-	-	862	414	238	270	164	226	165	201	167	0	32
10 FINLAND	36667	7472	9823	23468	2006	269	653	.	1755	474	163	0	0	0	0
11 FRANCE	-	-	-	-	.	.	.	.	1703	325	151	80	67	44	19
12 GREECE	-	-	-	-	.	81810	69233	57447	-	-	-	4289	2681	766	49
13 HUNGARY	-	-	-	52633	30742	13200	20693	17119	12005	5881	7415	1852	801	407	151
14 ICELAND	-	-	20000	1111	.	1000	6364	5455	.	.	0	0	0	0	0
15 ITALY	-	-	-	-	5447	3268	2393	1435	1286	545	359	184	79	37	11
16 JAPAN	48863	43638	44316	47542	45663	58391	69181	76159	-	42797	37713	10939	2495	313	39
17 NETHERLANDS	593	273	73	288	141	172	304	365	10408	1068	229	186	16	8	0
18 NEW ZEALAND	-	5333	2048	2872	748	1500	1591	2740	1667	838	435	351	161	0	34
19 NORWAY	1620	583	727	1093	1154	146	103	259	1939	227	54	0	0	23	43
20 POLAND	-	-	-	-	-	-	-	-	-	-	.	890	229	64	48
21 PORTUGAL	-	-	-	-	-	-	.	.	.	.	8578	208	167	82	20
22 ROMANIA	-	-	-	-	-	-	-	-	-	-	-	930	391	885	982
23 SPAIN	57841	29533	16300	16458	14802	9654	4509	4092	3446	1278	1012	484	362	87	16
24 SWEDEN	-	-	269	724	199	128	291	118	250	13	37	47	11	21	10
25 SWITZERLAND	615	615	196	196	495	370	.	.	.	.	72	0	93	0	14
26 TURKEY	-	-	-	-	-	-	-	-	-	-	-	2946	1429	1135	598
27 UK ENGLAND AND WALES	2085	1915	2391	3366	1125	616	523	645	935	272	179	142	113	52	35
28 UK NORTHERN IRELAND	-	-	-	-	202	0	240	305	438	144	403	197	63	244	60
29 UK SCOTLAND	.	.	297	703	425	474	574	1780	2279	535	492	299	162	176	47
30 USA	39551	23653	15002	15063	8961	7338	5541	5459	3356	1388	1150	524	319	122	60
31 YUGOSLAVIA	-	-	-	-	-	-	-	-	-	-	.	4246	1377	478	205

- NO MORTALITY DATA ARE AVAILABLE FOR EVEN A BROADER GROUP OF CAUSES FOR THIS DISEASE

. MORTALITY DATA ARE PRESENTED FOR A BROADER GROUP OF CAUSES FOR THIS DISEASE

0 VALUE<0.5

THE STANDARD MORTALITY RATIOS WERE DERIVED WITH A FACTOR OF 1000

SERIAL MORTALITY TABLES FOR VARIOUS COUNTRIES 1901-1975

TABLE 21 : SCARLET FEVER : MALES

	1901-	1906-	1911-	1916-	1921-	1926-	1931-	1936-	1941-	1946-	1951-	1956-	1961-	1966-	1971-75
1 AUSTRALIA	-	422	322	481	256	611	340	220	136	31	9	2	3	0	.
2 AUSTRIA	3267	2972	3144	1776	-	-	-	-	-	279	77	29	16	8	.
3 BELGIUM	3994	5544	5662	2172	1481	693	1054	657	476	200	54	23	8	0	.
4 BULGARIA	-	-	-	-	-	1426	955	3344	3317	780	241	39	28	12	.
5 CANADA	-	-	-	-	1795	1386	806	714	386	102	55	18	4	5	.
6 CHILE	-	653	316	184	338	1722	203	662	129	45	72	69	69	16	.
7 CZECHOSLOVAKIA	-	-	-	1237	3711	1246	1244	1199	575	392	27	11	4	0	.
8 DENMARK	3178	1860	3206	1291	539	217	468	451	482	48	8	8	0	6	.
9 EIRE	-	-	-	-	836	1032	1118	1263	340	96	79	0	0	0	.
10 FINLAND	-	-	-	-	-	837	915	1640	827	131	42	21	4	0	.
11 FRANCE	-	-	-	-	510	553	358	208	169	97	25	10	4	3	.
12 GREECE	-	-	-	-	3162	3315	4981	389	-	-	-	6	12	10	.
13 HUNGARY	-	-	-	7653	10464	1599	885	562	649	642	164	61	8	3	.
14 ICELAND	-	-	794	2090	.	132	2051	128	235	0	.	.	0	0	.
15 ITALY	1653	3032	3420	2065	2497	2123	1260	245	79	60	20	11	9	7	.
16 JAPAN	7	146	75	49	73	129	186	229	-	10	21	16	10	4	.
17 NETHERLANDS	995	1215	788	1466	288	571	261	224	295	42	42	10	4	2	.
18 NEW ZEALAND	-	355	563	648	304	575	95	105	162	23	0	0	0	0	.
19 NORWAY	1695	1243	1330	930	178	384	390	352	855	143	15	0	5	0	.
20 POLAND	-	-	-	-	-	-	-	-	-	-	.	68	27	15	.
21 PORTUGAL	547	440	255	225	100	215	180	251	93	37	31	24	9	12	.
22 ROMANIA	-	-	-	-	-	-	-	-	-	-	-	63	15	18	.
23 SPAIN	1981	3290	1351	1371	764	511	586	441	127	80	58	29	21	10	.
24 SWEDEN	-	-	1816	2202	630	527	383	869	526	38	8	0	0	4	.
25 SWITZERLAND	1622	1622	720	720	279	322	347	313	100	93	26	14	10	15	.
26 TURKEY	-	-	-	-	-	-	-	-	-	-	-	10	16	7	7
27 UK ENGLAND AND WALES	.	.	2332	1257	1190	741	753	403	138	35	21	7	2	0	.
28 UK NORTHERN IRELAND	-	-	-	-	2392	1199	1926	1627	193	70	12	0	0	0	.
29 UK SCOTLAND	.	.	4778	2221	2703	1454	2208	876	221	50	0	0	3	0	.
30 USA	6825	4881	2888	1394	1303	838	843	480	136	32	16	4	2	2	.
31 YUGOSLAVIA	-	-	-	-	-	-	-	-	-	-	.	.	15	6	.

\- NO MORTALITY DATA ARE AVAILABLE FOR EVEN A BROADER GROUP OF CAUSES FOR THIS DISEASE

. MORTALITY DATA ARE PRESENTED FOR A BROADER GROUP OF CAUSES FOR THIS DISEASE

0 VALUE<0.5

THE STANDARD MORTALITY RATIOS WERE DERIVED WITH A FACTOR OF 1000

SERIAL MORTALITY TABLES FOR VARIOUS COUNTRIES 1901-1975

TABLE 21 : SCARLET FEVER : FEMALES

	1901-	1906-	1911-	1916-	1921-	1926-	1931-	1936-	1941-	1946-	1951-	1956-	1961-	1966-	1971-75
1 AUSTRALIA	-	531	402	757	370	833	518	254	205	29	11	5	3	0	.
2 AUSTRIA	3240	3196	3298	1800	-	-	-	-	-	239	108	42	11	0	.
3 BELGIUM	3731	5348	5157	1962	1540	733	977	603	342	215	51	20	2	0	.
4 BULGARIA	-	-	-	-	-	1335	1159	3825	2828	525	237	23	18	6	.
5 CANADA	-	-	-	-	1813	1412	743	748	348	101	45	16	3	3	.
6 CHILE	-	974	341	177	442	2473	267	848	167	48	41	81	86	32	.
7 CZECHOSLOVAKIA	-	-	-	1009	3578	1280	1280	1182	632	359	44	10	0	0	.
8 DENMARK	3402	1888	2996	1103	712	186	591	529	740	113	0	0	0	0	.
9 EIRE	-	-	-	-	1064	1167	1257	1379	310	100	71	6	6	0	.
10 FINLAND	-	-	-	-	-	745	756	1495	935	87	33	11	0	0	.
11 FRANCE	-	-	-	-	437	587	432	258	218	128	27	13	6	5	.
12 GREECE	-	-	-	-	2911	3106	4793	370	-	-	-	7	11	21	.
13 HUNGARY	-	-	-	7865	10564	1643	1101	601	597	649	156	68	12	0	.
14 ICELAND	-	-	833	2813	.	411	4933	267	247	0	.	.	0	0	.
15 ITALY	1548	2878	3172	2012	2374	2070	1275	269	114	72	18	13	7	6	.
16 JAPAN	11	142	85	47	83	136	216	213	-	16	23	17	9	7	.
17 NETHERLANDS	797	1140	798	1502	292	596	262	201	307	52	50	4	3	5	.
18 NEW ZEALAND	-	588	711	1266	498	862	358	121	332	24	7	0	11	0	.
19 NORWAY	1513	889	1250	809	97	383	341	534	1030	206	0	11	0	8	.
20 POLAND	-	-	-	-	-	-	-	-	-	-	.	67	25	20	.
21 PORTUGAL	559	486	231	254	158	306	259	262	113	28	23	27	16	0	.
22 ROMANIA	-	-	-	-	-	-	-	-	-	-	-	56	17	28	.
23 SPAIN	1974	3309	1342	1474	836	553	651	492	106	87	55	27	14	12	.
24 SWEDEN	-	-	1828	2178	581	482	418	811	454	79	8	0	0	0	.
25 SWITZERLAND	1719	1719	843	843	369	393	360	404	139	141	27	4	10	10	.
26 TURKEY	-	-	-	-	-	-	-	-	-	-	-	17	21	11	15
27 UK ENGLAND AND WALES	.	.	2330	1289	1275	776	881	401	151	45	40	7	3	0	.
28 UK NORTHERN IRELAND	-	-	-	-	2496	1438	1992	1569	302	85	48	0	11	0	.
29 UK SCOTLAND	.	.	5224	2411	2870	1716	2329	888	162	44	11	4	0	0	.
30 USA	6672	5052	2877	1382	1426	859	931	490	132	26	17	7	2	1	.
31 YUGOSLAVIA	-	-	-	-	-	-	-	-	-	-	.	.	22	4	.

- NO MORTALITY DATA ARE AVAILABLE FOR EVEN A BROADER GROUP OF CAUSES FOR THIS DISEASE

. MORTALITY DATA ARE PRESENTED FOR A BROADER GROUP OF CAUSES FOR THIS DISEASE

0 VALUE<0.5

THE STANDARD MORTALITY RATIOS WERE DERIVED WITH A FACTOR OF 1000

SERIAL MORTALITY TABLES FOR VARIOUS COUNTRIES 1901-1975

TABLE 22 : ERYSIPELAS : MALES

	1901-	1906-	1911-	1916-	1921-	1926-	1931-	1936-	1941-	1946-	1951-	1956-	1961-	1966-	1971-75
1 AUSTRALIA	-	6403	9108	6382	6201	6571	3805	2850	1142	356	80	54	99	30	0
2 AUSTRIA	.	.	.	.	-	-	-	-	-	4201	1649	1069	333	958	780
3 BELGIUM	.	.	.	.	.	.	.	.	.	.	396	252	162	48	32
4 BULGARIA	-	-	-	-	-	.	.	.	.	.	.	.	56	41	57
5 CANADA	-	-	-	-	14322	17611	10305	6262	1511	416	201	168	76	45	17
6 CHILE	-	30508	11263	11325	6033	13001	10974	12090	7088	3007	399	1158	5827	687	290
7 CZECHOSLOVAKIA	-	-	-	17945	15167	16185	21235	15257	16429	6543	1210	614	462	230	242
8 DENMARK	31695	29452	20816	19850	10703	9679	.	.	.	.	455	176	330	93	60
9 EIRE	-	-	-	-	5882	5118	6372	3706	1378	911	207	53	53	0	0
10 FINLAND	-	-	-	-	-	.	.	22968	19451	2908	514	291	228	173	42
11 FRANCE	-	-	-	-	.	.	.	.	2562	869	351	273	132	65	55
12 GREECE	-	-	-	-	.	17316	22256	16088	-	-	-	326	84	136	18
13 HUNGARY	-	-	-	21418	22136	27621	25317	15810	9761	.	1073	816	611	197	186
14 ICELAND	-	-	.	.	.	.	.	.	.	.	.	.	0	0	0
15 ITALY	42670	39347	30687	23992	21785	17508	19100	12313	6166	2815	804	382	275	140	39
16 JAPAN	.	30074	23651	28789	43350	45872	44138	42172	-	4833	2677	1586	590	206	111
17 NETHERLANDS	13932	14906	13745	19364	9038	11907	9049	6580	10750	2672	994	633	283	145	264
18 NEW ZEALAND	-	10638	5917	3936	4026	3650	935	2667	765	0	83	150	139	0	187
19 NORWAY	22578	17377	17498	17275	10330	14648	10046	6177	8927	1400	432	310	164	115	75
20 POLAND	-	-	-	-	-	-	-	-	-	-	.	204	198	163	83
21 PORTUGAL	-	-	-	-	-	-	.	.	.	.	2227	791	582	488	187
22 ROMANIA	-	-	-	-	-	-	-	-	-	-	-	279	234	107	147
23 SPAIN	25538	22390	21726	17734	13703	10939	10487	9035	4658	1746	664	585	276	109	77
24 SWEDEN	-	-	19428	20207	14004	22256	14582	7952	3056	900	456	324	247	71	218
25 SWITZERLAND	16478	16478	12370	12370	12230	10983	9882	4366	2204	1383	533	590	479	332	522
26 TURKEY	-	-	-	-	-	-	-	-	-	-	-	1136	325	108	19
27 UK ENGLAND AND WALES	21971	16084	16098	10796	10201	12475	14669	6081	1413	557	149	61	47	36	13
28 UK NORTHERN IRELAND	-	-	-	-	7031	12031	.	.	.	0	0	121	116	0	111
29 UK SCOTLAND	31451	21238	21997	14993	19202	18512	19331	8784	1837	794	101	0	0	32	0
30 USA	41595	30681	24771	19564	14277	13284	9116	4072	894	246	118	64	39	23	15
31 YUGOSLAVIA	-	-	-	-	-	-	-	-	-	-	.	.	329	132	56

- NO MORTALITY DATA ARE AVAILABLE FOR EVEN A BROADER GROUP OF CAUSES FOR THIS DISEASE

. MORTALITY DATA ARE PRESENTED FOR A BROADER GROUP OF CAUSES FOR THIS DISEASE

0 VALUE<0.5

THE STANDARD MORTALITY RATIOS WERE DERIVED WITH A FACTOR OF 10000

SERIAL MORTALITY TABLES FOR VARIOUS COUNTRIES 1901-1975

TABLE 22 : ERYSIPELAS : FEMALES

	1901-	1906-	1911-	1916-	1921-	1926-	1931-	1936-	1941-	1946-	1951-	1956-	1961-	1966-	1971-75
1 AUSTRALIA	-	6547	9255	6164	7890	7351	3918	3011	1151	388	295	197	102	66	12
2 AUSTRIA	.	.	.	.	-	-	-	-	-	4994	2132	778	897	1095	1147
3 BELGIUM	.	.	.	.	.	.	.	.	.	.	533	355	202	193	49
4 BULGARIA	-	-	-	-	-	.	.	.	.	.	.	.	51	168	121
5 CANADA	-	-	-	-	14763	16507	10043	5264	1176	406	301	95	74	84	22
6 CHILE	-	16612	10132	9133	6042	10173	12066	11210	6041	2193	369	1145	4750	507	451
7 CZECHOSLOVAKIA	-	-	-	15504	14011	14779	18979	13549	14188	6108	2059	1510	927	684	368
8 DENMARK	18113	22592	16174	14857	11117	10072	.	.	.	.	1025	487	328	328	178
9 EIRE	-	-	-	-	5993	4910	4971	4313	1862	532	565	102	50	146	47
10 FINLAND	-	-	-	-	-	.	.	22179	17312	3728	951	777	242	226	242
11 FRANCE	-	-	-	-	.	.	.	.	2365	926	469	315	157	79	87
12 GREECE	-	-	-	-	.	15415	18824	13860	-	-	-	527	366	200	60
13 HUNGARY	-	-	-	18225	19571	24512	21582	14098	7232	.	1325	1110	487	265	355
14 ICELAND	-	-	.	.	.	.	.	.	.	.	.	.	0	0	0
15 ITALY	38526	35006	28157	21984	19841	15131	15890	11080	5635	2813	816	562	305	228	94
16 JAPAN	.	25971	20935	25044	36264	37323	36189	33060	-	4353	2259	1422	633	167	115
17 NETHERLANDS	12871	15320	13270	18856	9226	11893	9033	7286	9790	3417	1183	853	441	446	517
18 NEW ZEALAND	-	7692	4895	5477	2993	2644	974	1595	749	350	391	139	125	116	161
19 NORWAY	18019	15219	16667	15086	8217	12015	9475	6522	7723	2916	729	276	183	101	223
20 POLAND	-	-	-	-	-	-	-	-	-	-	.	268	292	168	205
21 PORTUGAL	-	-	-	-	-	-	.	.	.	.	2422	892	694	658	223
22 ROMANIA	-	-	-	-	-	-	-	-	-	-	-	377	250	122	80
23 SPAIN	25985	23177	21939	18134	13456	9654	9562	8543	4815	1650	655	491	308	93	54
24 SWEDEN	-	-	18843	17726	13239	22825	15561	10042	3267	1405	742	335	206	47	203
25 SWITZERLAND	15402	15402	11620	11620	8876	8837	10046	6332	2868	1532	588	564	364	288	740
26 TURKEY	-	-	-	-	-	-	-	-	-	-	-	1704	254	186	20
27 UK ENGLAND AND WALES	18920	13382	12415	8308	8100	9521	10906	4469	1268	456	123	44	49	41	19
28 UK NORTHERN IRELAND	-	-	-	-	6469	12727	.	.	.	0	107	0	0	0	88
29 UK SCOTLAND	24666	18174	16809	11356	14962	13608	15050	7012	1843	903	218	52	74	24	0
30 USA	33367	23688	20618	16587	12896	11756	7878	3483	842	238	102	63	47	25	20
31 YUGOSLAVIA	-	-	-	-	-	-	-	-	-	-	.	.	386	171	79

- NO MORTALITY DATA ARE AVAILABLE FOR EVEN A BROADER GROUP OF CAUSES FOR THIS DISEASE

. MORTALITY DATA ARE PRESENTED FOR A BROADER GROUP OF CAUSES FOR THIS DISEASE

0 VALUE<0.5

THE STANDARD MORTALITY RATIOS WERE DERIVED WITH A FACTOR OF 10000

SERIAL MORTALITY TABLES FOR VARIOUS COUNTRIES 1901-1975

TABLE 23 : SEPTICAEMIA PYAEMIA : MALES

	1901-	1906-	1911-	1916-	1921-	1926-	1931-	1936-	1941-	1946-	1951-	1956-	1961-	1966-	1971-75
1 AUSTRALIA	-	1326	1691	1353	1227	1003	848	705	564	295	295	415	226	223	.
2 AUSTRIA	.	.	.	.	-	-	-	-	-	.	505	360	242	167	.
3 BELGIUM	.	.	.	.	.	.	.	.	.	.	742	660	502	608	.
4 BULGARIA	-	-	-	-	-	.	.	.	.	.	.	.	263	212	.
5 CANADA	-	-	-	-	2275	2375	1098	676	250	123	264	195	162	145	.
6 CHILE	-	385	3862	2139	2490	3897	5134	4538	3322	1963	491	677	614	1498	.
7 CZECHOSLOVAKIA	-	-	-	6025	5914	3716	260	416	3792	1554	338	245	177	144	.
8 DENMARK	2490	2170	2518	2213	1450	1239	1956	2233	1632	974	347	301	198	214	.
9 EIRE	-	-	-	-	1592	2362	2128	1618	1653	671	314	235	322	259	.
10 FINLAND	-	-	-	-	-	7693	7049	6707	6422	2944	679	421	295	257	.
11 FRANCE	-	-	-	-	.	.	.	.	4386	2398	1089	650	625	754	.
12 GREECE	-	-	-	-	.	3931	5862	7076	-	-	-	666	658	637	.
13 HUNGARY	-	-	-	.	.	.	3287	2548	2259	1426	320	207	135	52	.
14 ICELAND	-	-	.	.	.	.	.	.	.	.	.	.	545	364	.
15 ITALY	-	-	-	-	-	5264	4931	4205	4387	2529	1027	837	658	567	.
16 JAPAN	.	2152	2715	3387	4400	5759	2490	0	-	732	623	467	380	282	.
17 NETHERLANDS	2860	2929	2977	3994	3522	2685	2028	1362	1913	733	356	233	193	216	.
18 NEW ZEALAND	-	2182	1741	1774	1343	792	851	620	494	263	311	481	342	373	.
19 NORWAY	3570	3969	4252	4514	3390	5633	5181	5234	3121	1067	508	330	243	381	.
20 POLAND	-	-	-	-	-	-	-	-	-	-	.	2582	1496	1033	.
21 PORTUGAL	-	-	-	-	-	-	.	.	.	.	1453	1098	473	290	.
22 ROMANIA	-	-	-	-	-	-	-	-	-	-	-	2682	916	402	.
23 SPAIN	3703	3254	3376	4543	5406	5787	7317	10284	8661	4350	1953	1394	950	859	.
24 SWEDEN	-	-	5127	5860	5287	7586	7032	5975	3406	1431	270	341	326	355	.
25 SWITZERLAND	1199	1199	1418	1418	1219	1737	1995	1693	1415	643	345	313	218	358	.
26 TURKEY	-	-	-	-	-	-	-	-	-	-	-	1873	894	1102	2181
27 UK ENGLAND AND WALES	952	877	1090	923	883	1222	1191	756	539	226	117	101	125	111	.
28 UK NORTHERN IRELAND	-	-	-	-	1250	1462	1415	1530	1493	743	382	449	171	465	.
29 UK SCOTLAND	1515	1552	1434	1416	1132	1467	1520	1327	1108	578	289	204	214	254	.
30 USA	4285	2373	1716	885	659	536	421	560	469	184	248	440	569	654	.
31 YUGOSLAVIA	-	-	-	-	-	-	-	-	-	-	.	.	401	407	.

- NO MORTALITY DATA ARE AVAILABLE FOR EVEN A BROADER GROUP OF CAUSES FOR THIS DISEASE
. MORTALITY DATA ARE PRESENTED FOR A BROADER GROUP OF CAUSES FOR THIS DISEASE
0 VALUE<0.5
THE STANDARD MORTALITY RATIOS WERE DERIVED WITH A FACTOR OF 100

SERIAL MORTALITY TABLES FOR VARIOUS COUNTRIES 1901-1975

TABLE 23 : SEPTICAEMIA PYAEMIA : FEMALES

	1901-	1906-	1911-	1916-	1921-	1926-	1931-	1936-	1941-	1946-	1951-	1956-	1961-	1966-	1971-75
1 AUSTRALIA	-	14483	18085	13205	10851	8400	5870	6221	4444	1701	2205	3197	1830	1682	.
2 AUSTRIA	.	.	.	.	-	-	-	-	-	.	4589	3096	2415	725	.
3 BELGIUM	.	.	.	.	.	.	.	.	.	.	6456	5332	3434	6002	.
4 BULGARIA	-	-	-	-	-	.	.	.	.	.	.	.	2347	2796	.
5 CANADA	-	-	-	-	18212	17846	8170	4219	2175	1258	1778	1491	1277	899	.
6 CHILE	-	1750	41888	10564	25777	33805	59793	54766	40144	25369	7761	9487	6776	13031	.
7 CZECHOSLOVAKIA	-	-	-	53502	49898	31293	1802	2554	28444	13352	2907	1761	1754	881	.
8 DENMARK	24464	19000	20000	19857	12944	12120	20838	19045	15140	9957	3197	2530	1940	1457	.
9 EIRE	-	-	-	-	13359	16415	15220	13459	13659	4379	3099	2071	2267	2841	.
10 FINLAND	-	-	-	-	-	77327	69227	56684	57913	26130	7184	4113	2480	1544	.
11 FRANCE	-	-	-	-	.	.	.	.	40495	21845	10541	6525	6443	6854	.
12 GREECE	-	-	-	-	.	39036	52493	56844	-	-	-	6907	6170	6589	.
13 HUNGARY	-	-	-	.	.	.	29021	20655	15051	12240	3440	2010	1318	261	.
14 ICELAND	-	-	.	.	.	.	.	.	.	.	.	.	4546	3636	.
15 ITALY	-	-	-	-	-	51498	46120	41189	43527	26492	10050	7597	6283	5077	.
16 JAPAN	.	19566	24413	30057	37811	50076	20783	0	-	7345	6155	4505	3858	2944	.
17 NETHERLANDS	26021	24012	25000	33929	30155	20461	16032	10804	14733	6601	3712	2548	1504	1946	.
18 NEW ZEALAND	-	17000	22308	11754	8730	8088	6056	4026	3068	1361	2131	3088	2583	2516	.
19 NORWAY	23926	25362	26761	32770	29733	41622	38312	40245	25058	8824	3093	3415	3395	3348	.
20 POLAND	-	-	-	-	-	-	-	-	-	-	.	19639	11979	8633	.
21 PORTUGAL	-	-	-	-	-	-	.	.	.	.	12347	10587	3659	2387	.
22 ROMANIA	-	-	-	-	-	-	-	-	-	-	-	25665	8814	4059	.
23 SPAIN	31903	27457	27104	37175	44170	47398	61406	77386	71284	39592	18339	13051	8663	7488	.
24 SWEDEN	-	-	38854	39661	39753	66698	63723	49880	29746	15567	3134	2518	2719	3234	.
25 SWITZERLAND	10386	10386	11600	11600	13861	18000	18287	14709	11013	4791	2908	1920	1772	2368	.
26 TURKEY	-	-	-	-	-	-	-	-	-	-	-	27680	11570	11933	18594
27 UK ENGLAND AND WALES	6181	5949	5445	4831	5203	6863	6429	4325	3725	1637	1034	696	855	975	.
28 UK NORTHERN IRELAND	-	-	-	-	9636	10294	11029	10000	10411	4805	2716	2410	2386	2150	.
29 UK SCOTLAND	14618	12070	10039	10977	9157	9655	11515	9259	8252	5387	1861	1068	1460	2147	.
30 USA	50187	20521	11593	6669	5466	4751	3529	4474	3450	1552	1871	3254	4495	5103	.
31 YUGOSLAVIA	-	-	-	-	-	-	-	-	-	-	.	.	4029	3674	.

- NO MORTALITY DATA ARE AVAILABLE FOR EVEN A BROADER GROUP OF CAUSES FOR THIS DISEASE

. MORTALITY DATA ARE PRESENTED FOR A BROADER GROUP OF CAUSES FOR THIS DISEASE

0 VALUE<0.5

THE STANDARD MORTALITY RATIOS WERE DERIVED WITH A FACTOR OF 1000

SERIAL MORTALITY TABLES FOR VARIOUS COUNTRIES 1901-1975

TABLE 24 : DIPTHERIA : MALES

	1901-	1906-	1911-	1916-	1921-	1926-	1931-	1936-	1941-	1946-	1951-	1956-	1961-	1966-	1971-75
1 AUSTRALIA	-	9942	14483	12992	9216	7082	7139	5863	4003	1260	505	48	18	7	16
2 AUSTRIA	26741	13916	18114	16694	-	-	-	-	-	8784	1903	336	107	7	0
3 BELGIUM	19161	13622	14225	18519	7720	5616	7010	7527	10698	3842	525	471	91	26	17
4 BULGARIA	-	-	-	-	-	6384	12012	12362	8216	9181	3872	359	85	19	0
5 CANADA	-	-	-	-	13025	8629	3291	3059	2625	910	131	41	30	28	16
6 CHILE	-	9067	5781	5096	2960	3092	5859	3294	3957	3318	2231	3242	2203	432	449
7 CZECHOSLOVAKIA	-	-	-	10157	7749	7720	17765	15649	19422	6077	1357	469	86	18	4
8 DENMARK	15235	10410	7789	9649	9222	4992	3380	2140	4673	880	41	0	0	0	0
9 EIRE	-	-	-	-	9260	9361	12350	10103	9525	1685	344	222	55	0	0
10 FINLAND	-	-	-	-	-	5512	9226	10128	19722	5275	128	9	0	0	0
11 FRANCE	-	-	-	-	5227	7660	6270	4670	8685	2626	334	113	43	19	9
12 GREECE	-	-	-	-	5592	6188	6566	4446	-	-	-	1478	739	114	6
13 HUNGARY	-	-	-	16251	10973	14815	13972	4419	2261	6477	969	246	148	11	6
14 ICELAND	-	-	12448	5859	10662	1384	678	1024	313	536	231	0	0	0	0
15 ITALY	12703	14754	10847	11435	8231	8276	7614	6394	6980	3466	2011	1304	359	133	14
16 JAPAN	8906	9282	8821	6473	5492	5777	6439	5684	-	1302	859	858	161	16	7
17 NETHERLANDS	12299	6918	6090	9125	4038	4015	2602	1028	25427	6533	1060	285	3	3	3
18 NEW ZEALAND	-	7561	6469	14144	5678	5351	2963	1670	2026	956	184	32	0	14	0
19 NORWAY	11533	15396	13569	21673	5567	1993	1360	397	16376	2526	121	0	13	0	12
20 POLAND	-	-	-	-	-	-	-	-	-	-	.	1285	326	38	1
21 PORTUGAL	8066	9167	8251	9139	9689	14644	12892	9157	10115	4344	2729	1750	1916	437	187
22 ROMANIA	-	-	-	-	-	-	-	-	-	-	-	436	94	17	4
23 SPAIN	23193	16948	21866	16551	10676	5991	5099	10742	3913	2193	1340	708	437	43	11
24 SWEDEN	-	-	14006	23004	6269	3253	1031	289	2039	416	21	0	0	0	14
25 SWITZERLAND	17795	17795	13149	13149	8539	5606	3452	1350	3901	3232	218	200	105	40	0
26 TURKEY	-	-	-	-	-	-	-	-	-	-	-	5981	2924	805	229
27 UK ENGLAND AND WALES	19036	14900	13880	14318	9812	9518	9889	9375	5156	602	58	15	7	8	1
28 UK NORTHERN IRELAND	-	-	-	-	8604	6716	8512	7997	6396	935	0	0	0	0	0
29 UK SCOTLAND	13282	15849	17617	15485	11771	10829	9989	10833	6592	763	84	18	9	9	0
30 USA	49368	29146	20753	16022	12430	7226	4450	2299	1202	623	140	46	23	15	6
31 YUGOSLAVIA	-	-	-	-	-	-	-	-	-	-	.	1812	588	247	57

- NO MORTALITY DATA ARE AVAILABLE FOR EVEN A BROADER GROUP OF CAUSES FOR THIS DISEASE

. MORTALITY DATA ARE PRESENTED FOR A BROADER GROUP OF CAUSES FOR THIS DISEASE

0 VALUE<0.5

THE STANDARD MORTALITY RATIOS WERE DERIVED WITH A FACTOR OF 10000

SERIAL MORTALITY TABLES FOR VARIOUS COUNTRIES 1901-1975

TABLE 24 : DIPTHERIA : FEMALES

	1901-	1906-	1911-	1916-	1921-	1926-	1931-	1936-	1941-	1946-	1951-	1956-	1961-	1966-	1971-75
1 AUSTRALIA	-	10017	15401	13818	8774	6760	7297	5657	3981	1099	470	72	38	0	14
2 AUSTRIA	24792	17841	17338	16664	-	-	-	-	-	8632	1750	274	161	27	7
3 BELGIUM	17786	15367	12117	16061	6852	5549	6560	6765	10454	3074	492	460	78	22	0
4 BULGARIA	-	-	-	-	-	6627	10217	12800	8197	6591	3295	389	127	13	0
5 CANADA	-	-	-	-	13514	8513	3519	3206	2340	872	149	47	31	16	13
6 CHILE	-	7515	5352	4872	2581	2786	5342	3437	3677	3133	1941	2776	2254	506	513
7 CZECHOSLOVAKIA	-	-	-	8956	6607	7223	18571	14634	16797	5537	1243	579	111	26	4
8 DENMARK	13654	10037	8277	9684	8249	4784	2898	2487	5671	1114	11	0	0	0	0
9 EIRE	-	-	-	-	9709	10243	15448	11087	9670	1783	173	318	114	14	0
10 FINLAND	-	-	-	-	-	4393	8576	10601	21268	4889	218	19	0	0	0
11 FRANCE	-	-	-	-	4319	7336	6138	4536	9568	2658	351	118	43	10	8
12 GREECE	-	-	-	-	5004	5256	6018	3602	-	-	-	1470	708	149	23
13 HUNGARY	-	-	-	15205	10163	14414	14159	4243	2083	6295	938	255	176	24	6
14 ICELAND	-	-	10000	5306	16858	2158	1053	1064	977	563	0	0	0	0	0
15 ITALY	11782	13042	9234	10050	7261	7261	6860	5991	6544	3070	1913	1308	352	141	17
16 JAPAN	7774	8007	7662	5708	4712	5382	5943	5039	-	1104	790	795	162	18	6
17 NETHERLANDS	11860	6809	6204	9026	3817	3701	2515	1006	25743	6026	1217	296	7	0	0
18 NEW ZEALAND	-	8235	7630	14868	6447	5515	2929	2003	2243	1435	134	17	30	0	0
19 NORWAY	11354	15098	13906	20669	5866	2222	1408	362	18970	2859	128	28	0	0	0
20 POLAND	-	-	-	-	-	-	-	-	-	-	.	1113	356	40	2
21 PORTUGAL	7870	7773	6729	8793	8027	12739	11307	8221	8781	3868	2457	1984	1866	417	279
22 ROMANIA	-	-	-	-	-	-	-	-	-	-	-	417	110	18	7
23 SPAIN	22518	16375	20616	15159	9837	5293	4674	10788	3793	2114	1288	567	384	47	14
24 SWEDEN	-	-	13217	24778	6375	3423	1331	421	2147	434	22	8	8	0	0
25 SWITZERLAND	16591	16591	13055	13055	8227	5341	3251	1307	4628	3550	473	159	27	0	0
26 TURKEY	-	-	-	-	-	-	-	-	-	-	-	5820	3077	815	261
27 UK ENGLAND AND WALES	19618	15627	14430	15305	10422	10249	10531	9836	5341	647	75	17	9	1	1
28 UK NORTHERN IRELAND	-	-	-	-	9619	7799	9558	9104	7451	812	127	0	0	0	0
29 UK SCOTLAND	14127	15950	17357	16007	11109	11266	11015	12550	6773	1043	68	10	0	9	0
30 USA	48305	27286	19939	15216	12100	6917	4324	2077	1067	545	109	44	21	14	4
31 YUGOSLAVIA	-	-	-	-	-	-	-	-	-	-	.	1723	638	253	37

- NO MORTALITY DATA ARE AVAILABLE FOR EVEN A BROADER GROUP OF CAUSES FOR THIS DISEASE
. MORTALITY DATA ARE PRESENTED FOR A BROADER GROUP OF CAUSES FOR THIS DISEASE
0 VALUE<0.5
THE STANDARD MORTALITY RATIOS WERE DERIVED WITH A FACTOR OF 10000

SERIAL MORTALITY TABLES FOR VARIOUS COUNTRIES 1901-1975

TABLE 24 : DIPTHERIA : PERSONS

	1901-	1906-	1911-	1916-	1921-	1926-	1931-	1936-	1941-	1946-	1951-	1956-	1961-	1966-	1971-75
1 AUSTRALIA	-	9979	14931	13395	8999	6924	7217	5762	3992	1182	488	60	28	4	15
2 AUSTRIA	25768	18378	17726	16679	-	14080	19411	16107	-	8709	1828	306	134	17	4
3 BELGIUM	18480	16001	13143	17248	7291	5583	6786	7146	10576	3465	509	466	85	24	8
4 BULGARIA	-	-	-	-	-	6504	11129	12578	8207	7906	3588	373	106	16	0
5 CANADA	31269	18151	23567	24910	13266	8572	3404	3131	2485	891	140	44	31	22	15
6 CHILE	-	8296	5568	4985	2772	2940	5603	3365	3818	3226	2086	3010	2229	469	481
7 CZECHOSLOVAKIA	-	-	-	9560	7182	7473	18164	15147	18126	5811	1301	523	98	22	4
8 DENMARK	14441	10222	8034	9666	8739	4889	3141	2311	5164	995	26	0	0	0	0
9 EIRE	-	-	-	-	9481	9794	13874	10584	9596	1733	260	269	84	7	0
10 FINLAND	-	-	-	-	-	4961	8905	10362	20473	5088	172	14	0	0	0
11 FRANCE	18228	10275	9432	10438	4775	7499	6205	4603	9123	2642	342	116	43	14	9
12 GREECE	-	-	-	-	5308	5733	6298	4034	-	-	-	1399	739	136	14
13 HUNGARY	-	-	-	15730	10570	14616	14065	4332	2173	6387	954	250	162	17	6
14 ICELAND	-	-	11253	5589	13696	1764	862	1043	638	549	119	0	0	0	0
15 ITALY	12250	13912	10054	10755	7754	7777	7242	6195	6766	3272	1963	1306	356	137	16
16 JAPAN	8347	8654	8249	6095	5105	5581	6193	5365	-	1205	825	827	162	17	6
17 NETHERLANDS	12081	6864	6146	9076	3930	3861	2559	1018	25581	6285	1137	290	5	2	2
18 NEW ZEALAND	-	7892	7039	14500	6055	5431	2946	1833	2133	1191	160	24	14	7	0
19 NORWAY	11445	15250	13735	21180	5714	2106	1384	380	17648	2689	124	14	7	0	6
20 POLAND	-	-	-	-	-	-	-	-	-	-	.	1222	340	39	2
21 PORTUGAL	7970	8479	7498	8968	8868	13703	12111	8698	9461	4110	2595	1865	1892	427	232
22 ROMANIA	-	-	-	-	-	-	-	.	-	.	-	427	102	17	6
23 SPAIN	22860	16667	21253	15861	10258	5644	4888	10765	3854	2154	1315	639	411	45	13
24 SWEDEN	-	-	13618	23875	6321	3337	1179	354	2092	425	21	4	4	0	7
25 SWITZERLAND	17194	17194	13103	13103	8384	5475	3353	1329	4259	3388	343	180	67	21	0
26 TURKEY	-	-	-	-	-	-	3457	2936	2755	2162	3510	5906	2995	809	244
27 UK ENGLAND AND WALES	19331	15268	14155	14811	10115	9881	10207	9603	5248	624	66	16	8	5	1
28 UK NORTHERN IRELAND	-	-	-	-	9105	7250	9028	8542	6914	875	62	0	0	0	0
29 UK SCOTLAND	13702	15899	17487	15745	11442	11046	10499	11685	6681	901	76	14	5	9	0
30 USA	48839	28225	20350	15623	12267	7074	4388	2189	1135	467	125	45	22	15	5
31 YUGOSLAVIA	-	-	-	-	18934	23794	26615	22449	-	-	.	1768	612	250	48

- NO MORTALITY DATA ARE AVAILABLE FOR EVEN A BROADER GROUP OF CAUSES FOR THIS DISEASE

. MORTALITY DATA ARE PRESENTED FOR A BROADER GROUP OF CAUSES FOR THIS DISEASE

0 VALUE<0.5

THE STANDARD MORTALITY RATIOS WERE DERIVED WITH A FACTOR OF 10000

SERIAL MORTALITY TABLES FOR VARIOUS COUNTRIES 1901-1975

TABLE 25 : WHOOPING COUGH : MALES

	1901-	1906-	1911-	1916-	1921-	1926-	1931-	1936-	1941-	1946-	1951-	1956-	1961-	1966-	1971-75
1 AUSTRALIA	-	9197	5285	5306	4957	4812	3676	2726	2128	599	200	63	20	24	9
2 AUSTRIA	36303	9466	8825	5970	-	-	-	-	-	2935	1789	765	305	125	29
3 BELGIUM	36678	31925	29961	20593	19620	13038	9139	6474	5027	3221	940	364	147	57	17
4 BULGARIA	-	-	-	-	-	8871	5017	2983	2387	2894	6043	1024	216	117	23
5 CANADA	-	-	-	-	7285	8258	6293	5330	3518	1394	721	273	105	46	20
6 CHILE	-	38258	40700	43256	35480	30014	30313	24670	16795	14563	6928	5448	2006	726	674
7 CZECHOSLOVAKIA	-	-	-	10650	12815	16583	5477	2791	4701	4180	2359	618	39	11	7
8 DENMARK	23915	22640	18591	26523	10224	8978	7251	4584	3439	2024	604	346	103	29	11
9 EIRE	-	-	-	-	13543	11383	7839	6516	7029	5052	2061	802	140	99	36
10 FINLAND	-	-	-	-	-	15870	10683	8798	5998	2769	592	229	79	11	0
11 FRANCE	-	-	-	-	5285	4203	3050	2996	3009	2274	1048	659	307	129	37
12 GREECE	-	-	-	-	8008	12118	13658	16338	-	-	-	1160	673	240	89
13 HUNGARY	-	-	-	8145	8884	4817	3987	3506	3185	3069	2874	546	108	17	16
14 ICELAND	-	-	24074	19643	2333	26875	17419	333	7353	1395	800	175	0	0	0
15 ITALY	13169	11350	11485	10332	7723	6854	4934	4315	3053	2573	816	468	298	147	53
16 JAPAN	3404	5206	6329	7557	8817	9353	9999	9838	-	6410	1633	292	64	9	4
17 NETHERLANDS	14794	12762	12471	11475	7886	7480	4338	3578	3961	2505	645	165	10	7	4
18 NEW ZEALAND	-	10848	4528	3801	2202	3244	2364	1424	1662	658	417	287	77	13	13
19 NORWAY	11542	12097	8477	6573	6686	4225	2758	1553	1903	1677	532	354	114	24	0
20 POLAND	-	-	-	-	-	-	-	-	-	-	.	896	432	150	24
21 PORTUGAL	12890	9466	9595	9615	10748	11038	9950	9713	9138	6397	2535	1360	749	287	147
22 ROMANIA	-	-	-	-	-	-	-	-	-	-	-	1615	1972	669	230
23 SPAIN	28826	14028	15696	24912	6582	4098	4214	4130	2664	2126	1608	580	292	63	18
24 SWEDEN	-	-	11509	10070	7404	4172	2572	1507	1523	746	240	48	34	7	0
25 SWITZERLAND	14893	14893	10791	10791	6707	4104	3206	2877	2022	1684	679	362	170	38	42
26 TURKEY	-	-	-	-	-	-	-	-	-	-	-	1398	711	319	128
27 UK ENGLAND AND WALES	24126	20878	17431	14019	12727	10548	6687	4361	3465	1612	579	137	76	43	25
28 UK NORTHERN IRELAND	-	-	-	-	20884	13923	10000	8793	5893	3715	992	582	256	217	0
29 UK SCOTLAND	37405	30986	34577	25641	28359	16878	13769	8474	6015	2240	809	227	49	100	28
30 USA	14725	11890	9157	9664	6712	5931	4425	3168	2038	661	257	91	40	15	3
31 YUGOSLAVIA	-	-	-	-	-	-	-	-	-	-	.	4120	1370	704	328

\- NO MORTALITY DATA ARE AVAILABLE FOR EVEN A BROADER GROUP OF CAUSES FOR THIS DISEASE

. MORTALITY DATA ARE PRESENTED FOR A BROADER GROUP OF CAUSES FOR THIS DISEASE

0 VALUE<0.5

THE STANDARD MORTALITY RATIOS WERE DERIVED WITH A FACTOR OF 10000

SERIAL MORTALITY TABLES FOR VARIOUS COUNTRIES 1901-1975

TABLE 25 : WHOOPING COUGH : FEMALES

	1901-	1906-	1911-	1916-	1921-	1926-	1931-	1936-	1941-	1946-	1951-	1956-	1961-	1966-	1971-75
1 AUSTRALIA	-	10543	6821	6526	5830	6354	4622	3779	2669	1026	252	98	36	21	19
2 AUSTRIA	13291	11330	10544	7050	-	-	-	-	-	4279	1867	866	252	117	53
3 BELGIUM	34854	31142	25423	17810	19372	13813	8320	5732	5118	2918	786	386	165	54	12
4 BULGARIA	-	-	-	-	-	12250	7254	4658	3568	4695	7790	1488	429	176	19
5 CANADA	-	-	-	-	8584	9226	7279	6119	4124	1653	824	366	112	38	35
6 CHILE	-	46846	51470	54280	43224	36821	36613	30775	20526	17898	8725	6365	2292	837	837
7 CZECHOSLOVAKIA	-	-	-	11844	14455	19547	6551	3540	5592	4961	2710	754	37	19	0
8 DENMARK	27829	27228	19966	27399	10821	10458	8000	4872	3835	2683	900	355	97	10	34
9 EIRE	-	-	-	-	16799	13222	8733	8737	8278	5687	2191	600	186	65	63
10 FINLAND	-	-	-	-	-	18972	13718	10012	9188	3772	817	354	61	22	0
11 FRANCE	-	-	-	-	6411	5123	3479	3570	3742	2635	1176	714	369	161	58
12 GREECE	-	-	-	-	9414	14565	17119	20852	-	-	-	1701	1014	378	175
13 HUNGARY	-	-	-	9597	10599	5718	4844	4471	3581	3516	3320	639	132	31	28
14 ICELAND	-	-	24000	33846	714	25000	23667	0	9091	1220	1277	189	0	0	0
15 ITALY	17532	15341	14835	13685	10184	8969	6571	5800	4201	3571	1003	561	316	144	75
16 JAPAN	4058	6643	8363	10174	11461	12147	13043	12325	-	8675	2163	388	66	8	3
17 NETHERLANDS	18551	17016	15593	14318	9656	9276	5467	4732	4735	3255	740	189	62	0	0
18 NEW ZEALAND	-	14737	5724	5194	2508	3614	3557	1948	2108	1066	588	165	40	41	67
19 NORWAY	14452	13777	11345	7871	7556	5330	3493	2291	2283	1847	550	213	67	0	13
20 POLAND	-	-	-	-	-	-	-	-	-	-	.	1052	546	157	27
21 PORTUGAL	14531	11260	11199	12229	12604	13939	13461	12679	11448	8297	3526	1700	858	417	199
22 ROMANIA	-	-	-	-	-	-	-	-	-	-	-	2091	2601	915	306
23 SPAIN	36146	18213	19902	31358	8387	5708	5782	5647	3864	3193	1959	698	349	55	17
24 SWEDEN	-	-	14461	12505	8676	5576	3274	1581	1733	731	251	79	15	23	0
25 SWITZERLAND	18614	18614	12936	12936	7447	5786	3333	4097	2797	2121	623	313	194	47	27
26 TURKEY	-	-	-	-	-	-	-	-	-	-	-	1815	968	439	157
27 UK ENGLAND AND WALES	28805	26145	22017	18096	15617	13333	8890	5425	4741	2189	713	185	80	41	35
28 UK NORTHERN IRELAND	-	-	-	-	24708	16400	13345	12338	8459	4357	1317	442	162	257	83
29 UK SCOTLAND	46097	38398	40512	30666	34138	19281	16407	10804	7593	2681	997	283	68	71	20
30 USA	18369	14546	11128	11718	8012	7116	5425	3641	2361	799	301	115	42	17	9
31 YUGOSLAVIA	-	-	-	-	-	-	-	-	-	-	.	5449	1793	826	379

- NO MORTALITY DATA ARE AVAILABLE FOR EVEN A BROADER GROUP OF CAUSES FOR THIS DISEASE

. MORTALITY DATA ARE PRESENTED FOR A BROADER GROUP OF CAUSES FOR THIS DISEASE

0 VALUE<0.5

THE STANDARD MORTALITY RATIOS WERE DERIVED WITH A FACTOR OF 10000

SERIAL MORTALITY TABLES FOR VARIOUS COUNTRIES 1901-1975

TABLE 26 : MENINGOCOCCAL INFECTIONS : MALES

	1901-	1906-	1911-	1916-	1921-	1926-	1931-	1936-	1941-	1946-	1951-	1956-	1961-	1966-	1971-75
1 AUSTRALIA	-	33333	43416	13117	3317	1837	872	739	8708	2406	3011	1212	703	576	479
2 AUSTRIA	.	.	.	.	-	-	-	-	-	1566	595	367	358	731	607
3 BELGIUM	.	.	.	.	11606	10271	.	.	.	.	948	749	525	986	1555
4 BULGARIA	-	-	-	-	-	.	.	.	.	.	.	.	769	387	674
5 CANADA	-	-	-	-	3298	6625	3428	2559	3092	1216	1460	946	460	493	820
6 CHILE	-	.	.	.	50	73	205	279	16296	2330	618	508	487	313	149
7 CZECHOSLOVAKIA	-	-	-	1145	1517	2306	1160	1216	1730	981	1162	700	521	207	175
8 DENMARK	.	.	.	.	.	.	3647	2536	8138	3349	659	433	375	355	913
9 EIRE	-	-	-	-	1523	1645	2013	3932	3585	2539	2270	1672	463	482	1041
10 FINLAND	-	-	-	-	-	.	.	8177	7758	4154	983	621	461	1349	1572
11 FRANCE	-	-	-	-	.	.	.	.	1734	2110	1218	804	602	425	539
12 GREECE	-	-	-	-	.	2128	2018	3698	-	-	-	623	307	1005	1244
13 HUNGARY	-	-	-	.	.	.	756	888	5894	.	1110	477	382	413	265
14 ICELAND	-	-	.	.	.	.	.	.	.	.	1500	2727	4583	1667	2174
15 ITALY	432	286	1482	5814	624	518	848	1966	2808	1272	791	1000	1213	1549	822
16 JAPAN	.	2708	1013	2499	2329	748	1361	2141	-	968	583	471	253	84	17
17 NETHERLANDS	.	.	395	5057	2144	2256	2144	1916	1888	2262	1334	1014	596	854	688
18 NEW ZEALAND	-	30833	26129	36565	10935	1135	1250	1929	7826	1367	2782	1655	1186	1143	371
19 NORWAY	1923	1042	6178	3754	2034	1963	1845	2063	4570	2554	1111	649	464	854	2397
20 POLAND	-	-	-	-	-	-	-	-	-	-	.	392	406	465	301
21 PORTUGAL	15045	3781	7829	10523	-	-	.	.	.	.	2021	1779	3801	2819	3882
22 ROMANIA	-	-	-	-	-	-	-	-	-	-	-	526	493	616	446
23 SPAIN	416	444	1158	2025	2209	1190	695	1142	1654	1972	1467	1725	2393	1766	3388
24 SWEDEN	-	-	6768	5892	3276	4318	1931	1515	1279	284	329	469	766	764	754
25 SWITZERLAND	5320	5320	3303	3303	2598	3315	3230	4000	2643	1351	1060	819	1604	1547	1337
26 TURKEY	-	-	-	-	-	-	-	-	-	-	-	1350	281	162	46
27 UK ENGLAND AND WALES	563	877	5801	9505	2536	4059	8737	8685	8664	2622	1883	1082	821	679	1098
28 UK NORTHERN IRELAND	-	-	-	-	1262	2403	.	.	.	1027	1918	1275	625	828	1852
29 UK SCOTLAND	112	27803	6925	9051	6360	11578	13104	11955	10022	3854	2282	1335	950	1375	1395
30 USA	.	1495	5097	6664	2884	8492	5336	4180	4427	1848	1783	996	945	987	534
31 YUGOSLAVIA	-	-	-	-	-	-	-	-	-	-	.	2543	1953	1898	1809

- NO MORTALITY DATA ARE AVAILABLE FOR EVEN A BROADER GROUP OF CAUSES FOR THIS DISEASE

. MORTALITY DATA ARE PRESENTED FOR A BROADER GROUP OF CAUSES FOR THIS DISEASE

0 VALUE<0.5

THE STANDARD MORTALITY RATIOS WERE DERIVED WITH A FACTOR OF 1000

SERIAL MORTALITY TABLES FOR VARIOUS COUNTRIES 1901-1975

TABLE 26 : MENINGOCOCCAL INFECTIONS : FEMALES

	1901-	1906-	1911-	1916-	1921-	1926-	1931-	1936-	1941-	1946-	1951-	1956-	1961-	1966-	1971-75
1 AUSTRALIA	-	27154	32191	7860	2271	1196	941	506	6099	1872	2798	1032	516	390	259
2 AUSTRIA	.	.	.	.	-	-	-	-	-	1151	415	329	252	808	425
3 BELGIUM	.	.	.	.	10410	9026	.	.	.	.	865	686	321	929	1725
4 BULGARIA	-	-	-	-	-	.	.	.	.	.	.	.	597	459	547
5 CANADA	-	-	-	-	2459	5005	2564	1594	2271	831	1044	728	313	399	623
6 CHILE	-	.	.	.	50	55	120	149	11754	1958	587	447	453	284	135
7 CZECHOSLOVAKIA	-	-	-	1123	889	1183	794	692	1447	759	1075	618	277	146	116
8 DENMARK	.	.	.	.	.	.	2811	1374	6250	2767	560	223	433	365	793
9 EIRE	-	-	-	-	1319	986	1250	3014	2687	2000	1502	1013	351	436	1111
10 FINLAND	-	-	-	-	-	.	.	5655	7079	3386	720	447	348	942	1301
11 FRANCE	-	-	-	-	.	.	.	.	1080	1590	820	516	436	342	388
12 GREECE	-	-	-	-	.	1284	1385	2935	-	-	-	535	253	610	1101
13 HUNGARY	-	-	-	.	.	.	580	821	5000	.	749	316	212	254	152
14 ICELAND	-	-	.	.	.	.	.	.	.	.	1053	1429	3913	1304	1364
15 ITALY	491	215	746	3500	472	422	509	1330	2216	973	579	686	904	1240	762
16 JAPAN	.	2473	719	1588	1598	467	840	1319	-	704	404	284	157	59	27
17 NETHERLANDS	.	.	242	3320	1804	1679	1783	1201	1315	1745	1356	863	470	786	558
18 NEW ZEALAND	-	30909	21356	26080	6993	667	1000	667	7580	1471	2176	1338	894	592	255
19 NORWAY	2000	887	5610	2915	1333	1962	1165	1321	3390	1614	1028	456	509	343	1695
20 POLAND	-	-	-	-	-	-	-	-	-	-	.	350	294	308	238
21 PORTUGAL	11531	3667	6037	8863	-	-	.	.	.	.	1372	1354	2865	1760	3241
22 ROMANIA	-	-	-	-	-	-	-	-	-	-	-	485	399	420	283
23 SPAIN	344	534	1033	1702	1905	975	537	888	1542	1741	1298	1523	1872	1254	2674
24 SWEDEN	-	-	4837	4482	2085	2884	1451	970	904	261	178	268	676	683	853
25 SWITZERLAND	3800	3800	2042	2042	2123	2228	1972	3200	2678	1364	893	723	1162	1069	1128
26 TURKEY	-	-	-	-	-	-	-	-	-	-	-	1138	252	96	26
27 UK ENGLAND AND WALES	473	704	3514	4693	2021	2886	6154	6485	6660	2237	1613	928	634	541	916
28 UK NORTHERN IRELAND	-	-	-	-	294	1024	.	.	.	2098	1197	828	641	793	1154
29 UK SCOTLAND	131	22849	4388	6237	4257	8259	9139	8652	7821	2490	1799	1033	882	538	976
30 USA	.	1100	3312	4655	2081	4879	3097	2422	2605	1401	1429	825	754	789	431
31 YUGOSLAVIA	-	-	-	-	-	-	-	-	-	-	.	2039	1281	1491	1550

- NO MORTALITY DATA ARE AVAILABLE FOR EVEN A BROADER GROUP OF CAUSES FOR THIS DISEASE

. MORTALITY DATA ARE PRESENTED FOR A BROADER GROUP OF CAUSES FOR THIS DISEASE

0 VALUE<0.5

THE STANDARD MORTALITY RATIOS WERE DERIVED WITH A FACTOR OF 1000

SERIAL MORTALITY TABLES FOR VARIOUS COUNTRIES 1901-1975

TABLE 27 : PLAGUE : MALES

	1901-	1906-	1911-	1916-	1921-	1926-	1931-	1936-	1941-	1946-	1951-	1956-	1961-	1966-	1971-75
1 AUSTRALIA	-	70	1	0	52	0	0	0	0	0	0	0	0	0	0
2 AUSTRIA	.	.	.	.	-	-	-	-	-	.	0	0	0	0	0
3 BELGIUM	.	.	.	.	.	.	.	.	.	.	0	0	0	0	0
4 BULGARIA	-	-	-	-	-	.	0	0	0	0	0	0	0	0	0
5 CANADA	-	-	-	-	0	0	0	0	0	0	0	0	0	0	0
6 CHILE	-	680	316	83	11	5	52	0	1	4	1	0	0	0	0
7 CZECHOSLOVAKIA	-	-	-	.	.	.	47	5	0	0	0	0	0	0	0
8 DENMARK	.	.	.	.	.	.	.	.	.	.	0	0	0	0	0
9 EIRE	-	-	-	-	0	0	0	0	0	0	0	0	0	0	0
10 FINLAND	-	-	-	-	-	.	.	.	.	.	0	0	0	0	0
11 FRANCE	-	-	-	-	.	.	3	0	5	0	0	0	0	0	0
12 GREECE	-	-	-	-	.	28	0	0	-	-	-	0	0	0	0
13 HUNGARY	-	-	-	.	.	.	0	0	0	0	0	0	0	0	0
14 ICELAND	-	-	.	.	.	.	.	.	0	0	0	0	0	0	0
15 ITALY	-	-	-	-	-	-	-	-	-	-	0	0	0	0	0
16 JAPAN	.	551	60	44	36	6	0	0	-	0	0	0	0	0	0
17 NETHERLANDS	0	0	0	0	0	0	0	0	0	0	0	0	0	0	0
18 NEW ZEALAND	-	5	1	0	0	0	0	0	0	0	0	0	0	0	0
19 NORWAY	.	.	0	0	0	1	0	0	0	0	0	0	0	0	0
20 POLAND	-	-	-	-	-	-	-	-	-	-	.	0	0	0	0
21 PORTUGAL	-	-	-	-	-	-	211	78	36	15	0	0	0	0	0
22 ROMANIA	-	-	-	-	-	-	-	-	-	-	-	0	0	0	0
23 SPAIN	16	3	2	6	14	22	8	0	0	0	0	0	0	0	0
24 SWEDEN	-	-	.	.	.	.	0	0	0	0	0	0	0	0	0
25 SWITZERLAND	0	0	0	0	0	0	.	.	.	.	0	0	0	0	0
26 TURKEY	-	-	-	-	-	-	-	-	-	-	-	0	0	0	0
27 UK ENGLAND AND WALES	14	3	5	17	0	1	0	0	0	0	0	0	1	0	0
28 UK NORTHERN IRELAND	-	-	-	-	0	0	0	0	0	0	0	0	0	0	0
29 UK SCOTLAND	2	0	.	.	.	.	.	.	.	0	0	0	0	0	0
30 USA	.	1	9	24	24	2	3	1	2	2	0	1	4	4	0
31 YUGOSLAVIA	-	-	-	-	-	-	-	-	-	-	.	0	0	0	0

- NO MORTALITY DATA ARE AVAILABLE FOR EVEN A BROADER GROUP OF CAUSES FOR THIS DISEASE

. MORTALITY DATA ARE PRESENTED FOR A BROADER GROUP OF CAUSES FOR THIS DISEASE

SERIAL MORTALITY TABLES FOR VARIOUS COUNTRIES 1901-1975

TABLE 27 : PLAGUE : FEMALES

	1901-	1906-	1911-	1916-	1921-	1926-	1931-	1936-	1941-	1946-	1951-	1956-	1961-	1966-	1971-75
1 AUSTRALIA	-	24	0	0	20	0	0	0	0	0	0	0	0	0	0
2 AUSTRIA	.	.	.	.	-	-	-	-	-	.	0	0	0	0	0
3 BELGIUM	.	.	.	.	.	.	.	.	.	.	0	0	0	0	0
4 BULGARIA	-	-	-	-	-	.	0	0	0	0	0	0	0	0	0
5 CANADA	-	-	-	-	0	0	0	0	0	0	0	0	0	0	0
6 CHILE	-	420	215	51	10	0	0	0	1	0	0	0	0	0	0
7 CZECHOSLOVAKIA	-	-	-	.	.	.	45	0	0	2	0	0	0	0	0
8 DENMARK	.	.	.	.	.	.	.	.	.	.	0	0	0	0	0
9 EIRE	-	-	-	-	0	0	0	0	0	0	0	0	0	0	0
10 FINLAND	-	-	-	-	-	.	.	.	.	.	0	0	0	0	0
11 FRANCE	-	-	-	-	.	.	0	0	0	0	0	0	0	0	0
12 GREECE	-	-	-	-	.	8	0	0	-	-	-	0	0	0	0
13 HUNGARY	-	-	-	.	.	.	0	0	0	0	0	0	0	0	0
14 ICELAND	-	-	.	.	.	.	.	.	0	0	0	0	0	0	0
15 ITALY	-	-	-	-	-	-	-	-	-	-	0	0	0	0	0
16 JAPAN	.	371	22	36	37	2	0	0	-	0	0	0	0	0	0
17 NETHERLANDS	0	0	0	0	0	0	0	0	0	0	0	0	0	0	0
18 NEW ZEALAND	-	0	0	0	0	0	0	0	0	0	0	0	0	0	0
19 NORWAY	.	.	0	0	0	0	0	0	0	0	0	0	0	0	0
20 POLAND	-	-	-	-	-	-	-	-	-	-	.	0	0	0	0
21 PORTUGAL	-	-	-	-	-	-	224	71	34	15	0	0	0	0	0
22 ROMANIA	-	-	-	-	-	-	-	-	-	-	-	0	0	0	0
23 SPAIN	3	0	0	7	12	24	9	0	0	0	0	0	0	0	0
24 SWEDEN	-	-	.	.	.	.	0	0	0	0	0	0	0	0	0
25 SWITZERLAND	0	0	0	0	0	0	.	.	.	.	0	0	0	0	0
26 TURKEY	-	-	-	-	-	-	-	-	-	-	-	0	0	0	0
27 UK ENGLAND AND WALES	1	3	1	4	0	0	0	0	0	0	0	0	0	0	0
28 UK NORTHERN IRELAND	-	-	-	-	0	0	0	0	0	0	0	0	0	0	0
29 UK SCOTLAND	1	0	.	.	.	.	.	.	.	0	0	0	0	0	0
30 USA	.	0	5	4	10	1	0	2	1	0	0	1	0	0	4
31 YUGOSLAVIA	-	-	-	-	-	-	-	-	-	-	.	0	0	0	0

- NO MORTALITY DATA ARE AVAILABLE FOR EVEN A BROADER GROUP OF CAUSES FOR THIS DISEASE

. MORTALITY DATA ARE PRESENTED FOR A BROADER GROUP OF CAUSES FOR THIS DISEASE

SERIAL MORTALITY TABLES FOR VARIOUS COUNTRIES 1901-1975

TABLE 27 : PLAGUE : PERSONS

	1901-	1906-	1911-	1916-	1921-	1926-	1931-	1936-	1941-	1946-	1951-	1956-	1961-	1966-	1971-75
1 AUSTRALIA	-	94	1	0	72	0	0	0	0	0	0	0	0	0	0
2 AUSTRIA	.	.	.	.	-	-	-	-	-	.	0	0	0	0	0
3 BELGIUM	.	.	.	.	.	.	.	.	.	.	0	0	0	0	0
4 BULGARIA	-	-	-	-	-	.	0	0	0	0	0	0	0	0	0
5 CANADA	-	-	-	-	0	0	0	0	0	0	0	0	0	0	0
6 CHILE	-	1100	531	134	21	5	52	0	2	4	1	0	0	0	0
7 CZECHOSLOVAKIA	-	-	-	.	.	.	92	5	0	2	0	0	0	0	0
8 DENMARK	.	.	.	.	.	.	.	.	.	.	0	0	0	0	0
9 EIRE	-	-	-	-	0	0	0	0	0	0	0	0	0	0	0
10 FINLAND	-	-	-	-	-	.	.	.	.	.	0	0	0	0	0
11 FRANCE	-	-	-	-	.	.	3	0	5	0	0	0	0	0	0
12 GREECE	-	-	-	-	.	36	0	0	-	-	-	0	0	0	0
13 HUNGARY	-	-	-	.	.	.	0	0	0	0	0	0	0	0	0
14 ICELAND	-	-	.	.	.	.	.	.	0	0	0	0	0	0	0
15 ITALY	-	-	-	-	-	-	-	-	-	-	0	0	0	0	0
16 JAPAN	.	922	82	80	73	8	0	0	-	0	0	0	0	0	0
17 NETHERLANDS	0	0	0	0	0	0	0	0	0	0	0	0	0	0	0
18 NEW ZEALAND	-	5	1	0	0	0	0	0	0	0	0	0	0	0	0
19 NORWAY	.	.	0	0	0	1	0	0	0	0	0	0	0	0	0
20 POLAND	-	-	-	-	-	-	-	-	-	-	.	0	0	0	0
21 PORTUGAL	-	-	-	-	-	-	435	149	70	30	0	0	0	0	0
22 ROMANIA	-	-	-	-	-	-	-	-	-	-	-	0	0	0	0
23 SPAIN	19	3	2	13	26	46	17	0	0	0	0	0	0	0	0
24 SWEDEN	-	-	.	.	.	.	0	0	0	0	0	0	0	0	0
25 SWITZERLAND	0	0	0	0	0	0	.	.	.	.	0	0	0	0	0
26 TURKEY	-	-	-	-	-	-	-	-	-	-	-	0	0	0	0
27 UK ENGLAND AND WALES	15	6	6	21	0	1	0	0	0	0	0	0	1	0	0
28 UK NORTHERN IRELAND	-	-	-	-	0	0	0	0	0	0	0	0	0	0	0
29 UK SCOTLAND	3	0	.	.	.	.	.	.	.	0	0	0	0	0	0
30 USA	.	1	14	28	34	3	3	3	3	2	0	2	4	4	4
31 YUGOSLAVIA	-	-	-	-	-	-	-	-	-	-	.	0	0	0	0

- NO MORTALITY DATA ARE AVAILABLE FOR EVEN A BROADER GROUP OF CAUSES FOR THIS DISEASE

. MORTALITY DATA ARE PRESENTED FOR A BROADER GROUP OF CAUSES FOR THIS DISEASE

SERIAL MORTALITY TABLES FOR VARIOUS COUNTRIES 1901-1975

TABLE 28 : LEPROSY : MALES

	1901-	1906-	1911-	1916-	1921-	1926-	1931-	1936-	1941-	1946-	1951-	1956-	1961-	1966-	1971-75
1 AUSTRALIA	-	907	683	364	324	265	269	294	227	167	76	69	25	82	48
2 AUSTRIA	.	.	.	.	-	-	-	-	-	.	0	0	0	0	0
3 BELGIUM	.	.	.	.	.	.	.	.	.	.	0	0	0	0	0
4 BULGARIA	-	-	-	-	-	.	.	.	.	.	.	.	20	0	0
5 CANADA	-	-	-	-	24	30	42	19	12	5	5	4	0	0	0
6 CHILE	-	0	0	27	0	.	89	120	74	129	0	26	0	0	0
7 CZECHOSLOVAKIA	-	-	-	.	.	.	962	1167	0	9	0	0	0	0	0
8 DENMARK	.	.	.	.	.	.	.	.	.	.	0	0	0	0	0
9 EIRE	-	-	-	-	0	0	0	0	0	0	0	0	0	0	0
10 FINLAND	-	-	-	-	-	.	.	.	21	0	19	18	0	0	0
11 FRANCE	-	-	-	-	.	.	.	.	43	31	14	16	11	8	6
12 GREECE	-	-	-	-	.	.	386	327	-	-	-	306	240	183	135
13 HUNGARY	-	-	-	.	.	.	0	0	0	.	0	0	0	0	0
14 ICELAND	-	-	4000	5000	1000	3000	1000	500	.	.	.	.	0	0	0
15 ITALY	-	-	-	-	-	-	-	-	-	-	45	34	35	35	9
16 JAPAN	.	10933	8581	7132	4781	3574	2594	2026	-	341	192	43	16	7	4
17 NETHERLANDS	52	59	81	62	67	51	65	17	24	37	14	13	6	5	10
18 NEW ZEALAND	-	0	0	0	0	0	0	0	0	0	0	0	0	0	25
19 NORWAY	2852	2964	1862	1323	818	657	132	95	22	60	0	0	0	0	0
20 POLAND	-	-	-	-	-	-	-	-	-	-	.	0	0	0	2
21 PORTUGAL	-	-	-	-	-	-	.	.	.	.	755	283	118	0	0
22 ROMANIA	-	-	-	-	-	-	-	-	-	-	-	0	0	4	0
23 SPAIN	1272	1084	1052	1229	718	803	839	728	574	537	284	155	185	96	38
24 SWEDEN	-	-	292	197	148	58	22	31	10	0	8	0	0	0	0
25 SWITZERLAND	.	.	.	.	20	55	.	.	.	.	0	0	12	11	0
26 TURKEY	-	-	-	-	-	-	-	-	-	-	-	486	168	55	7
27 UK ENGLAND AND WALES	.	.	11	34	14	13	15	15	14	1	1	0	0	4	4
28 UK NORTHERN IRELAND	-	-	-	-	0	0	.	.	.	0	0	0	0	0	0
29 UK SCOTLAND	.	.	.	.	.	.	.	.	.	0	0	0	0	0	0
30 USA	.	54	50	58	63	50	59	66	47	18	7	7	7	5	2
31 YUGOSLAVIA	-	-	-	-	-	-	-	-	-	-	.	.	0	0	0

- NO MORTALITY DATA ARE AVAILABLE FOR EVEN A BROADER GROUP OF CAUSES FOR THIS DISEASE

. MORTALITY DATA ARE PRESENTED FOR A BROADER GROUP OF CAUSES FOR THIS DISEASE

0 VALUE<0.5

THE STANDARD MORTALITY RATIOS WERE DERIVED WITH A FACTOR OF 100

SERIAL MORTALITY TABLES FOR VARIOUS COUNTRIES 1901-1975

TABLE 28 : LEPROSY : FEMALES

	1901-	1906-	1911-	1916-	1921-	1926-	1931-	1936-	1941-	1946-	1951-	1956-	1961-	1966-	1971-75
1 AUSTRALIA	-	556	1373	678	588	1923	787	1010	1009	917	299	68	61	335	306
2 AUSTRIA	.	.	.	.	-	-	-	-	-	.	0	0	0	0	0
3 BELGIUM	.	.	.	.	.	.	.	.	.	.	0	0	58	0	0
4 BULGARIA	-	-	-	-	-	.	.	.	.	.	.	.	0	0	67
5 CANADA	-	-	-	-	405	0	0	70	0	0	0	0	0	0	0
6 CHILE	-	0	0	0	0	.	213	577	1754	403	735	124	0	0	0
7 CZECHOSLOVAKIA	-	-	-	.	.	.	6983	5208	0	0	0	0	0	0	0
8 DENMARK	.	.	.	.	.	.	.	.	.	.	0	0	0	0	0
9 EIRE	-	-	-	-	0	0	0	0	0	0	0	0	0	0	0
10 FINLAND	-	-	-	-	-	.	.	.	175	333	308	0	0	0	0
11 FRANCE	-	-	-	-	.	.	.	.	374	65	50	12	12	33	11
12 GREECE	-	-	-	-	.	.	3677	3519	-	-	-	2677	3162	2635	1392
13 HUNGARY	-	-	-	.	.	.	0	0	0	.	0	0	0	0	0
14 ICELAND	-	-	20000	20000	10000	0	20000	0	.	.	.	.	0	0	0
15 ITALY	-	-	-	-	-	-	-	-	-	-	235	281	331	184	113
16 JAPAN	.	41838	32291	26769	19284	13882	9588	8509	-	1330	775	207	67	20	12
17 NETHERLANDS	0	0	0	118	0	98	179	81	152	142	0	59	54	50	47
18 NEW ZEALAND	-	0	0	0	0	0	0	0	0	0	0	0	0	0	0
19 NORWAY	19677	23125	23235	11667	10263	3000	3256	851	600	556	0	0	0	0	0
20 POLAND	-	-	-	-	-	-	-	-	-	-	.	0	0	0	0
21 PORTUGAL	-	-	-	-	-	-	.	.	.	.	5385	2117	694	0	66
22 ROMANIA	-	-	-	-	-	-	-	-	-	-	-	89	0	31	0
23 SPAIN	6878	5992	5809	6325	4530	4905	5433	4111	3482	3650	1704	1200	1039	551	419
24 SWEDEN	-	-	1342	1047	1000	947	700	191	89	168	0	75	0	0	0
25 SWITZERLAND	.	.	.	.	0	159	.	.	.	.	0	0	0	0	0
26 TURKEY	-	-	-	-	-	-	-	-	-	-	-	3286	642	370	0
27 UK ENGLAND AND WALES	.	.	20	0	0	48	29	0	0	0	12	0	22	11	11
28 UK NORTHERN IRELAND	-	-	-	-	0	0	.	.	.	0	0	0	0	0	0
29 UK SCOTLAND	.	.	.	.	.	.	.	.	.	0	0	0	0	0	0
30 USA	.	382	105	305	141	217	153	217	271	134	28	26	27	32	3
31 YUGOSLAVIA	-	-	-	-	-	-	-	-	-	-	.	.	0	0	0

- NO MORTALITY DATA ARE AVAILABLE FOR EVEN A BROADER GROUP OF CAUSES FOR THIS DISEASE

. MORTALITY DATA ARE PRESENTED FOR A BROADER GROUP OF CAUSES FOR THIS DISEASE

0 VALUE<0.5

THE STANDARD MORTALITY RATIOS WERE DERIVED WITH A FACTOR OF 1000

SERIAL MORTALITY TABLES FOR VARIOUS COUNTRIES 1901-1975

TABLE 29 : TETANUS : MALES

	1901-	1906-	1911-	1916-	1921-	1926-	1931-	1936-	1941-	1946-	1951-	1956-	1961-	1966-	1971-75
1 AUSTRALIA	-	8215	7950	6789	5603	4918	5719	3759	3163	3193	2561	1462	678	209	138
2 AUSTRIA	.	.	.	.	-	-	-	-	-	6402	3959	3028	1813	1526	872
3 BELGIUM	.	.	.	.	3471	2986	.	.	.	.	1531	1230	1286	653	248
4 BULGARIA	-	-	-	-	-	.	.	.	.	.	.	.	1239	1029	777
5 CANADA	-	-	-	-	1997	1430	1308	1030	458	439	326	141	142	102	37
6 CHILE	-	0	1954	2219	2306	1675	2117	1971	2954	2514	2881	2368	1523	1075	904
7 CZECHOSLOVAKIA	-	-	-	9847	10015	8901	6508	4631	8509	5883	3569	1914	979	1033	604
8 DENMARK	16405	23646	17019	12832	10188	7246	4986	4613	4526	3598	1442	794	372	170	42
9 EIRE	-	-	-	-	2899	2651	2575	2074	2373	1549	1254	906	662	408	97
10 FINLAND	-	-	-	-	-	.	.	.	1453	1364	536	288	321	23	68
11 FRANCE	-	-	-	-	.	.	.	.	7856	6844	4230	2820	1770	1236	1035
12 GREECE	-	-	-	-	.	9372	9894	9115	-	-	-	6208	4295	1890	797
13 HUNGARY	-	-	-	.	.	.	9454	8329	10924	.	6409	4249	2002	1602	1089
14 ICELAND	-	-	.	.	.	.	.	.	.	.	.	.	0	0	0
15 ITALY	6809	5170	5500	5909	6818	6178	5619	5244	6811	5735	3726	2758	1984	1075	672
16 JAPAN	.	14768	13271	15108	15034	12949	10238	8356	-	6098	4483	2534	1706	883	383
17 NETHERLANDS	3302	3934	3371	2591	2288	2385	1871	1754	2235	1738	971	544	304	160	77
18 NEW ZEALAND	-	3500	3832	3879	3071	4203	2708	1477	2157	2334	2079	2026	667	36	67
19 NORWAY	2511	1826	2958	2619	2077	1053	1429	1321	1621	1184	280	291	361	160	0
20 POLAND	-	-	-	-	-	-	-	-	-	-	.	2679	1452	735	409
21 PORTUGAL	-	-	-	-	-	-	.	.	.	.	12408	10355	9142	5728	3185
22 ROMANIA	-	-	-	-	-	-	-	-	-	-	-	7014	1801	821	309
23 SPAIN	14407	11324	8682	8782	8548	6992	6371	6683	6364	6496	5009	4056	3333	1993	882
24 SWEDEN	-	-	2852	3027	1930	1907	1358	1054	916	1020	480	362	94	104	13
25 SWITZERLAND	3922	3922	2861	2861	1072	844	1218	1043	4054	3861	2166	1545	813	486	185
26 TURKEY	-	-	-	-	-	-	-	-	-	-	-	13732	6368	3348	2676
27 UK ENGLAND AND WALES	2384	2468	2106	1818	1599	1543	1198	1067	953	672	462	205	147	86	34
28 UK NORTHERN IRELAND	-	-	-	-	3229	1667	.	.	.	1163	1212	662	567	136	66
29 UK SCOTLAND	3189	1840	1969	1518	1030	1255	944	1123	1054	903	675	186	141	101	20
30 USA	19347	11386	8033	5954	5557	4415	3311	2255	1595	1086	681	497	342	155	58
31 YUGOSLAVIA	-	-	-	-	-	-	-	-	-	-	.	.	7663	4504	1768

\- NO MORTALITY DATA ARE AVAILABLE FOR EVEN A BROADER GROUP OF CAUSES FOR THIS DISEASE

. MORTALITY DATA ARE PRESENTED FOR A BROADER GROUP OF CAUSES FOR THIS DISEASE

0 VALUE<0.5

THE STANDARD MORTALITY RATIOS WERE DERIVED WITH A FACTOR OF 1000

SERIAL MORTALITY TABLES FOR VARIOUS COUNTRIES 1901-1975

TABLE 29 : TETANUS : FEMALES

	1901-	1906-	1911-	1916-	1921-	1926-	1931-	1936-	1941-	1946-	1951-	1956-	1961-	1966-	1971-75
1 AUSTRALIA	-	3499	3341	2860	2154	1747	1677	1337	1291	1336	838	703	338	188	132
2 AUSTRIA	.	.	.	.	-	-	-	-	-	3474	2069	1690	1181	978	614
3 BELGIUM	.	.	.	.	2120	1607	.	.	.	.	874	809	498	359	157
4 BULGARIA	-	-	-	-	-	.	.	.	.	.	.	.	1052	617	504
5 CANADA	-	-	-	-	972	748	495	442	227	157	112	36	38	39	9
6 CHILE	-	149	659	491	1256	574	800	779	1388	1170	2135	1446	826	642	477
7 CZECHOSLOVAKIA	-	-	-	6342	5700	5835	3734	2701	5021	3920	1794	1365	892	1042	691
8 DENMARK	6961	10455	8333	6923	5000	3468	1760	2216	1731	2010	865	448	152	105	0
9 EIRE	-	-	-	-	830	1119	909	916	1076	590	667	393	461	69	66
10 FINLAND	-	-	-	-	-	.	.	.	743	882	213	135	43	64	21
11 FRANCE	-	-	-	-	.	.	.	.	5026	4081	2710	1968	1443	1128	1045
12 GREECE	-	-	-	-	.	4595	5667	5370	-	-	-	3759	2908	1350	820
13 HUNGARY	-	-	-	.	.	.	4114	4466	5134	.	4301	2770	1683	1304	1238
14 ICELAND	-	-	.	.	.	.	.	.	.	.	.	.	0	0	0
15 ITALY	2671	2354	1975	2279	3122	2753	2430	2226	3870	4015	2997	2493	1900	1240	1066
16 JAPAN	.	11477	9979	10953	10316	8717	7002	6015	-	3254	2294	1351	852	414	202
17 NETHERLANDS	1379	1566	1288	1038	660	773	544	457	763	676	407	190	118	56	31
18 NEW ZEALAND	-	1111	714	734	1312	606	1079	272	769	1191	1055	625	638	146	169
19 NORWAY	727	454	595	796	956	361	318	379	436	258	185	58	28	27	51
20 POLAND	-	-	-	-	-	-	-	-	-	-	.	1885	1160	598	397
21 PORTUGAL	-	-	-	-	-	-	.	.	.	.	7494	6987	5603	3930	2580
22 ROMANIA	-	-	-	-	-	-	-	-	-	-	-	4925	1338	684	354
23 SPAIN	6918	5879	4335	3865	3878	2932	2623	2848	2933	2881	2494	2420	1774	1304	922
24 SWEDEN	-	-	1184	1100	760	469	299	264	319	332	231	153	95	26	13
25 SWITZERLAND	2325	2325	1621	1621	705	470	535	383	1755	1634	1049	692	653	284	178
26 TURKEY	-	-	-	-	-	-	-	-	-	-	-	11459	7050	3414	2516
27 UK ENGLAND AND WALES	766	707	541	426	494	443	316	265	315	218	196	91	68	50	27
28 UK NORTHERN IRELAND	-	-	-	-	1500	1200	.	.	.	746	217	426	137	263	65
29 UK SCOTLAND	1307	867	603	407	505	467	403	239	406	214	194	134	76	19	38
30 USA	8718	4932	3470	2642	2261	1625	1398	1020	789	611	412	291	208	127	64
31 YUGOSLAVIA	-	-	-	-	-	-	-	-	-	-	.	.	5179	3112	1221

- NO MORTALITY DATA ARE AVAILABLE FOR EVEN A BROADER GROUP OF CAUSES FOR THIS DISEASE

. MORTALITY DATA ARE PRESENTED FOR A BROADER GROUP OF CAUSES FOR THIS DISEASE

0 VALUE<0.5

THE STANDARD MORTALITY RATIOS WERE DERIVED WITH A FACTOR OF 1000

SERIAL MORTALITY TABLES FOR VARIOUS COUNTRIES 1901-1975

TABLE 30 : ANTHRAX : MALES

	1901-	1906-	1911-	1916-	1921-	1926-	1931-	1936-	1941-	1946-	1951-	1956-	1961-	1966-	1971-75
1 AUSTRALIA	-	603	625	468	365	55	75	116	86	39	18	16	15	0	0
2 AUSTRIA	.	.	.	.	-	-	-	-	-	.	0	22	22	0	0
3 BELGIUM	.	.	.	.	.	.	.	.	.	.	42	33	16	0	0
4 BULGARIA	-	-	-	-	-	.	.	.	.	.	.	.	98	55	34
5 CANADA	-	-	-	-	264	0	0	0	0	0	11	0	0	8	0
6 CHILE	-	57059	33352	26923	21134	17115	10978	11796	13599	6426	980	865	1119	363	278
7 CZECHOSLOVAKIA	-	-	-	375	748	598	478	217	135	156	0	48	11	0	11
8 DENMARK	200	0	170	0	319	299	.	.	0	0	0	0	0	0	0
9 EIRE	-	-	-	-	133	321	314	206	0	103	0	0	0	0	0
10 FINLAND	-	-	-	-	-	.	.	.	0	0	0	0	0	0	0
11 FRANCE	-	-	-	-	.	.	.	.	72	31	22	11	0	0	3
12 GREECE	-	-	-	-	.	16328	13432	10042	-	-	-	270	155	91	69
13 HUNGARY	-	-	-	5771	6390	4262	2913	1930	1250	.	0	0	32	30	0
14 ICELAND	-	-	.	.	.	.	.	.	.	.	.	.	0	0	0
15 ITALY	5985	5046	3830	3963	3595	2660	2296	1602	1147	631	117	39	22	15	0
16 JAPAN	.	9	0	6	87	148	104	189	-	0	2	10	0	0	3
17 NETHERLANDS	1342	721	407	295	49	136	84	77	18	0	0	0	0	13	0
18 NEW ZEALAND	-	333	0	147	133	120	112	0	0	0	0	0	0	0	0
19 NORWAY	240	233	0	0	67	64	180	56	.	.	0	0	0	0	0
20 POLAND	-	-	-	-	-	-	-	-	-	-	.	0	53	49	5
21 PORTUGAL	-	-	-	-	-	-	.	.	.	.	626	318	115	19	0
22 ROMANIA	-	-	-	-	-	-	-	-	-	-	-	283	217	67	38
23 SPAIN	13498	12805	7698	8699	6866	4337	3839	4054	2054	1260	344	165	149	60	28
24 SWEDEN	-	-	.	.	.	.	.	.	.	.	21	0	0	0	0
25 SWITZERLAND	3182	3182	2248	2248	2857	2607	.	.	.	.	0	0	0	0	25
26 TURKEY	-	-	-	-	-	-	-	-	-	-	-	1953	894	313	235
27 UK ENGLAND AND WALES	425	382	323	393	230	137	115	99	63	18	21	17	13	9	12
28 UK NORTHERN IRELAND	-	-	-	-	0	0	.	.	.	0	0	0	0	0	0
29 UK SCOTLAND	170	243	156	302	73	179	.	.	.	0	31	0	0	30	0
30 USA	.	411	250	422	207	95	56	49	47	16	6	3	1	0	0
31 YUGOSLAVIA	-	-	-	-	-	-	-	-	-	-	.	.	159	52	32

- NO MORTALITY DATA ARE AVAILABLE FOR EVEN A BROADER GROUP OF CAUSES FOR THIS DISEASE

. MORTALITY DATA ARE PRESENTED FOR A BROADER GROUP OF CAUSES FOR THIS DISEASE

0 VALUE<0.5

THE STANDARD MORTALITY RATIOS WERE DERIVED WITH A FACTOR OF 1000

SERIAL MORTALITY TABLES FOR VARIOUS COUNTRIES 1901-1975

TABLE 30 : ANTHRAX : FEMALES

	1901-	1906-	1911-	1916-	1921-	1926-	1931-	1936-	1941-	1946-	1951-	1956-	1961-	1966-	1971-75
1 AUSTRALIA	-	57	207	37	33	0	0	0	0	0	0	0	0	0	0
2 AUSTRIA	.	.	.	.	-	-	-	-	-	.	0	0	0	0	0
3 BELGIUM	.	.	.	.	.	.	.	.	.	.	39	0	0	0	14
4 BULGARIA	-	-	-	-	-	.	.	.	.	.	.	.	47	0	33
5 CANADA	-	-	-	-	59	19	17	0	0	13	0	0	0	0	0
6 CHILE	-	29143	20615	14011	14573	9023	6897	5992	6715	3146	461	612	492	160	74
7 CZECHOSLOVAKIA	-	-	-	369	425	198	248	98	61	20	0	22	10	10	0
8 DENMARK	0	0	0	0	49	46	.	.	0	0	0	0	0	0	0
9 EIRE	-	-	-	-	68	55	109	0	53	0	0	0	0	0	0
10 FINLAND	-	-	-	-	-	.	.	.	0	0	0	0	0	0	0
11 FRANCE	-	-	-	-	.	.	.	.	83	7	3	3	0	0	0
12 GREECE	-	-	-	-	.	9270	8831	6449	-	-	-	302	71	17	78
13 HUNGARY	-	-	-	3118	3128	2289	1343	1210	826	.	0	0	0	0	0
14 ICELAND	-	-	.	.	.	.	.	.	.	.	.	.	0	0	0
15 ITALY	3443	2852	1707	2009	1969	1405	1046	761	561	278	60	24	3	8	0
16 JAPAN	.	18	24	3	86	58	77	53	-	0	4	2	0	2	3
17 NETHERLANDS	375	451	279	155	24	0	0	0	0	0	0	0	0	0	0
18 NEW ZEALAND	-	0	0	0	0	0	0	0	0	0	0	0	0	0	0
19 NORWAY	0	0	0	0	0	0	55	0	.	.	0	0	0	0	0
20 POLAND	-	-	-	-	-	-	-	-	-	-	.	27	15	5	0
21 PORTUGAL	-	-	-	-	-	-	.	.	.	.	628	188	16	16	0
22 ROMANIA	-	-	-	-	-	-	-	-	-	-	-	106	57	8	14
23 SPAIN	7988	6735	4655	4941	4062	2546	2118	2353	1378	604	175	75	42	35	13
24 SWEDEN	-	-	.	.	.	.	.	.	.	.	0	0	0	0	0
25 SWITZERLAND	1529	1529	940	940	760	878	.	.	.	.	0	0	0	0	0
26 TURKEY	-	-	-	-	-	-	-	-	-	-	-	1164	486	279	140
27 UK ENGLAND AND WALES	63	48	27	56	12	27	11	20	10	3	0	0	0	0	3
28 UK NORTHERN IRELAND	-	-	-	-	0	127	.	.	.	0	0	0	0	0	0
29 UK SCOTLAND	38	37	70	0	65	0	.	.	.	0	0	0	0	0	26
30 USA	.	68	82	38	41	25	17	13	5	11	0	0	1	0	0
31 YUGOSLAVIA	-	-	-	-	-	-	-	-	-	-	.	.	110	54	36

- NO MORTALITY DATA ARE AVAILABLE FOR EVEN A BROADER GROUP OF CAUSES FOR THIS DISEASE

. MORTALITY DATA ARE PRESENTED FOR A BROADER GROUP OF CAUSES FOR THIS DISEASE

0 VALUE<0.5

THE STANDARD MORTALITY RATIOS WERE DERIVED WITH A FACTOR OF 1000

SERIAL MORTALITY TABLES FOR VARIOUS COUNTRIES 1901-1975

TABLE 31 : POLIOMYELITIS AND INFECTIOUS ENCEPHALITIS (INCLUDING LATE EFFECTS) : MALES

	1901-	1906-	1911-	1916-	1921-	1926-	1931-	1936-	1941-	1946-	1951-	1956-	1961-	1966-	1971-75
1 AUSTRALIA	-	.	.	.	.	2286	1809	2042	1156	1904	2979	688	671	238	.
2 AUSTRIA	.	.	.	.	-	-	-	-	-	3631	2042	2318	393	200	.
3 BELGIUM	.	.	.	.	.	.	574	587	805	760	840	625	323	195	.
4 BULGARIA	-	-	-	-	-	.	.	.	.	.	.	.	553	471	.
5 CANADA	-	-	-	-	3418	3948	2560	2030	1594	2000	3008	1285	634	509	.
6 CHILE	-	.	.	.	.	.	763	468	1074	1275	3295	2733	2231	1767	.
7 CZECHOSLOVAKIA	-	-	-	1695	1956	1789	1420	1301	1965	1452	1758	1305	797	823	.
8 DENMARK	.	.	.	.	.	.	3046	2331	4210	1946	3385	784	985	1285	.
9 EIRE	-	-	-	-	2040	2421	1707	1496	2892	2110	1505	1257	452	400	.
10 FINLAND	-	-	-	-	-	539	833	44	4131	2769	2252	2370	948	679	.
11 FRANCE	-	-	-	-	.	.	.	.	1290	1288	1729	1426	885	496	.
12 GREECE	-	-	-	-	.	.	1705	1727	-	-	-	2040	608	261	.
13 HUNGARY	-	-	-	.	.	.	1033	767	1020	.	837	1167	288	241	.
14 ICELAND	-	-	.	.	.	3500	14762	4546	2083	4444	.	.	0	256	.
15 ITALY	-	-	-	-	4459	3302	2215	2318	2475	1779	2093	3156	1696	741	.
16 JAPAN	.	.	.	.	4319	3163	2892	2918	-	5554	2840	2639	1794	1905	.
17 NETHERLANDS	.	.	.	.	1519	1576	953	724	2531	1070	926	769	298	172	.
18 NEW ZEALAND	-	.	.	.	.	1128	1978	2069	1920	2171	2580	1619	502	284	.
19 NORWAY	1741	1583	6035	1378	1535	1960	2286	1902	6781	4493	4824	1650	587	482	.
20 POLAND	-	-	-	-	-	-	-	-	-	-	.	669	231	274	.
21 PORTUGAL	-	-	-	-	-	-	.	.	.	.	1415	2148	2442	1595	.
22 ROMANIA	-	-	-	-	-	-	-	-	-	-	-	693	898	5	.
23 SPAIN	.	.	.	.	.	.	1306	1151	996	831	1255	1995	1612	938	.
24 SWEDEN	-	-	8877	1702	2346	1819	4978	5771	5796	3188	2599	907	977	705	.
25 SWITZERLAND	575	575	2468	2468	3562	2688	2567	4228	5739	4471	4223	2227	900	557	.
26 TURKEY	-	-	-	-	-	-	-	-	-	-	-	1017	929	1460	413
27 UK ENGLAND AND WALES	.	.	.	.	3659	4474	3348	3074	2582	2999	1774	1213	706	492	.
28 UK NORTHERN IRELAND	-	-	-	-	4185	3913	.	.	.	4134	2077	1369	769	704	.
29 UK SCOTLAND	.	.	.	.	3607	4271	3184	3114	2931	3358	1762	1298	784	465	.
30 USA	.	.	.	.	3793	3202	2520	2120	2085	2277	2216	911	577	510	.
31 YUGOSLAVIA	-	-	-	-	-	-	-	-	-	-	.	.	933	482	.

- NO MORTALITY DATA ARE AVAILABLE FOR EVEN A BROADER GROUP OF CAUSES FOR THIS DISEASE

. MORTALITY DATA ARE PRESENTED FOR A BROADER GROUP OF CAUSES FOR THIS DISEASE

0 VALUE<0.5

THE STANDARD MORTALITY RATIOS WERE DERIVED WITH A FACTOR OF 1000

SERIAL MORTALITY TABLES FOR VARIOUS COUNTRIES 1901-1975

TABLE 31 : POLIOMYELITIS AND INFECTIOUS ENCEPHALITIS (INCLUDING LATE EFFECTS) : FEMALES

	1901-	1906-	1911-	1916-	1921-	1926-	1931-	1936-	1941-	1946-	1951-	1956-	1961-	1966-	1971-75
1 AUSTRALIA	-	.	.	.	.	2244	1481	1378	949	1163	1942	474	485	287	.
2 AUSTRIA	.	.	.	.	-	-	-	-	-	2378	1147	1402	291	155	.
3 BELGIUM	.	.	.	.	.	.	442	466	646	482	539	460	202	148	.
4 BULGARIA	-	-	-	-	-	.	.	.	.	.	.	.	456	378	.
5 CANADA	-	-	-	-	2835	3235	2015	1477	1113	1145	1912	872	510	348	.
6 CHILE	-	.	.	.	.	.	543	376	807	989	2207	2059	1883	1681	.
7 CZECHOSLOVAKIA	-	-	-	1986	1792	1855	1176	1022	1083	1025	1298	1013	741	560	.
8 DENMARK	.	.	.	.	.	.	2475	1621	2878	1488	2139	621	546	1373	.
9 EIRE	-	-	-	-	2091	2327	1512	1207	1964	1905	946	841	624	405	.
10 FINLAND	-	-	-	-	-	493	862	70	3217	2010	1822	1644	622	464	.
11 FRANCE	-	-	-	-	.	.	.	.	997	818	1145	941	646	455	.
12 GREECE	-	-	-	-	.	.	1179	1345	-	-	-	1357	392	277	.
13 HUNGARY	-	-	-	.	.	.	908	600	703	.	364	810	218	184	.
14 ICELAND	-	-	.	.	.	5238	10000	2174	2500	3333	.	.	833	0	.
15 ITALY	-	-	-	-	3792	2926	1875	1848	1910	1520	1651	2439	1332	650	.
16 JAPAN	.	.	.	.	4200	3163	2827	2827	-	4858	2394	2303	1716	1938	.
17 NETHERLANDS	.	.	.	.	1336	1311	680	679	1785	881	658	504	235	103	.
18 NEW ZEALAND	-	.	.	.	.	2148	1524	1329	1521	2065	1596	1056	509	333	.
19 NORWAY	1106	925	4380	828	939	1241	1418	1254	4269	2429	3156	937	569	434	.
20 POLAND	-	-	-	-	-	-	-	-	-	-	.	422	186	207	.
21 PORTUGAL	-	-	-	-	-	-	.	.	.	.	1023	1596	1943	1222	.
22 ROMANIA	-	-	-	-	-	-	-	-	-	-	-	531	773	17	.
23 SPAIN	.	.	.	.	.	.	1092	931	793	590	1097	1424	1214	716	.
24 SWEDEN	-	-	6652	1041	1383	1193	3857	3716	3365	1891	1574	855	899	618	.
25 SWITZERLAND	476	476	2045	2045	3360	2170	2153	3075	3589	2766	2544	1718	728	351	.
26 TURKEY	-	-	-	-	-	-	-	-	-	-	-	954	766	1064	346
27 UK ENGLAND AND WALES	.	.	.	.	3338	4082	3044	2555	1886	2352	1386	903	547	452	.
28 UK NORTHERN IRELAND	-	-	-	-	4462	3934	.	.	.	2809	1465	1155	699	338	.
29 UK SCOTLAND	.	.	.	.	3396	3990	2477	2508	2102	2710	1527	1083	833	650	.
30 USA	.	.	.	.	3436	2836	2025	1546	1454	1522	1610	693	499	418	.
31 YUGOSLAVIA	-	-	-	-	-	-	-	-	-	-	.	.	705	387	.

- NO MORTALITY DATA ARE AVAILABLE FOR EVEN A BROADER GROUP OF CAUSES FOR THIS DISEASE

. MORTALITY DATA ARE PRESENTED FOR A BROADER GROUP OF CAUSES FOR THIS DISEASE

0 VALUE<0.5

THE STANDARD MORTALITY RATIOS WERE DERIVED WITH A FACTOR OF 1000

SERIAL MORTALITY TABLES FOR VARIOUS COUNTRIES 1901-1975

TABLE 32 : SMALLPOX : MALES

	1901-	1906-	1911-	1916-	1921-	1926-	1931-	1936-	1941-	1946-	1951-	1956-	1961-	1966-	1971-75
1 AUSTRALIA	-	4	4	1	3	2	1	0	0	0	0	0	0	0	0
2 AUSTRIA	6	35	318	130	-	-	-	-	-	.	0	0	0	0	0
3 BELGIUM	1603	92	105	82	44	25	.	.	.	12	0	0	1	0	0
4 BULGARIA	-	-	-	-	-	0	0	0	0	0	0	0	0	0	0
5 CANADA	-	-	-	-	57	18	9	2	0	0	0	0	0	0	0
6 CHILE	-	10998	6352	106	6931	33	4	4	6	0	1	0	0	0	0
7 CZECHOSLOVAKIA	-	-	-	1789	193	9	0	0	2	1	0	0	0	0	0
8 DENMARK	10	10	5	0	3	0	.	.	0	0	0	0	0	0	0
9 EIRE	-	-	-	-	0	0	0	0	0	0	0	0	0	0	0
10 FINLAND	216	156	133	1535	14	0	5	400	1	0	0	0	0	0	0
11 FRANCE	-	-	-	-	32	18	7	3	1	1	1	0	0	0	0
12 GREECE	-	-	-	-	741	27	21	13	-	-	-	0	0	0	0
13 HUNGARY	-	-	-	.	.	.	0	0	0	0	0	0	0	0	0
14 ICELAND	-	-	.	.	.	.	.	.	0	0	0	0	0	0	0
15 ITALY	-	-	-	-	-	-	-	-	-	-	0	0	0	0	0
16 JAPAN	17	241	14	124	44	14	6	3	-	1	0	0	0	0	0
17 NETHERLANDS	19	6	2	4	0	7	0	0	1	0	1	0	0	0	0
18 NEW ZEALAND	-	0	0	0	0	0	0	0	0	0	0	0	0	0	0
19 NORWAY	12	22	4	0	0	0	2	0	0	0	0	0	0	0	0
20 POLAND	-	-	-	-	-	-	-	-	-	-	.	0	0	0	0
21 PORTUGAL	2580	4377	489	6786	1173	245	948	266	131	62	2	0	0	0	0
22 ROMANIA	-	-	-	-	-	-	-	-	-	-	-	0	0	0	0
23 SPAIN	2828	2130	1406	1874	742	47	2	194	25	1	0	0	0	0	0
24 SWEDEN	-	-	2	18	1	1	0	0	0	0	0	0	2	0	0
25 SWITZERLAND	42	42	9	9	12	2	0	0	0	.	0	0	0	0	0
26 TURKEY	-	-	-	-	-	-	-	-	-	-	-	1	0	0	1
27 UK ENGLAND AND WALES	378	8	5	7	6	16	2	0	0	3	1	0	1	0	0
28 UK NORTHERN IRELAND	-	-	-	-	0	0	0	0	0	0	0	0	0	0	0
29 UK SCOTLAND	407	5	13	94	16	1	0	0	.	0	0	0	0	0	0
30 USA	866	44	41	59	92	28	6	5	1	1	0	0	0	0	0
31 YUGOSLAVIA	-	-	-	-	-	-	-	-	-	-	.	0	0	0	5

- NO MORTALITY DATA ARE AVAILABLE FOR EVEN A BROADER GROUP OF CAUSES FOR THIS DISEASE

. MORTALITY DATA ARE PRESENTED FOR A BROADER GROUP OF CAUSES FOR THIS DISEASE

0 VALUE<0.5

THE STANDARD MORTALITY RATIOS WERE DERIVED WITH A FACTOR OF 1000

SERIAL MORTALITY TABLES FOR VARIOUS COUNTRIES 1901-1975

TABLE 32 : SMALLPOX : FEMALES

	1901-	1906-	1911-	1916-	1921-	1926-	1931-	1936-	1941-	1946-	1951-	1956-	1961-	1966-	1971-75
1 AUSTRALIA	-	28	21	0	9	9	0	9	0	0	0	0	0	0	0
2 AUSTRIA	81	260	3647	1729	-	-	-	-	-	.	0	0	0	0	0
3 BELGIUM	14370	834	780	732	333	300	.	.	.	67	0	0	0	0	0
4 BULGARIA	-	-	-	-	-	0	0	0	0	0	0	0	0	0	0
5 CANADA	-	-	-	-	464	129	71	15	0	0	0	0	0	0	0
6 CHILE	-	80423	52544	772	65105	264	20	9	35	10	46	6	0	0	0
7 CZECHOSLOVAKIA	-	-	-	23019	2058	50	0	0	69	13	0	0	0	0	0
8 DENMARK	244	91	88	0	16	0	.	.	0	0	0	0	0	0	0
9 EIRE	-	-	-	-	0	0	0	0	0	0	0	0	0	0	0
10 FINLAND	2122	1589	905	9307	47	31	15	3704	0	0	0	0	0	0	0
11 FRANCE	-	-	-	-	543	236	77	11	14	5	19	0	0	0	1
12 GREECE	-	-	-	-	8513	299	285	171	-	-	-	0	0	0	0
13 HUNGARY	-	-	-	.	.	.	0	0	31	0	0	0	0	0	0
14 ICELAND	-	-	.	.	.	.	.	.	0	0	0	0	0	0	0
15 ITALY	-	-	-	-	-	-	-	-	-	-	0	0	0	0	1
16 JAPAN	110	1917	123	1072	373	121	48	37	-	0	2	0	0	0	0
17 NETHERLANDS	299	48	62	37	0	81	0	0	0	10	5	0	0	0	0
18 NEW ZEALAND	-	0	0	0	0	0	0	0	0	0	0	0	0	0	0
19 NORWAY	62	267	0	39	0	0	0	0	0	17	0	0	0	0	0
20 POLAND	-	-	-	-	-	-	-	-	-	-	.	0	9	0	0
21 PORTUGAL	23890	37408	4281	58137	9776	2286	8752	2692	1087	551	6	0	0	0	0
22 ROMANIA	-	-	-	-	-	-	-	-	-	-	-	0	0	0	0
23 SPAIN	25672	19030	12890	16524	6588	477	28	1596	206	4	0	0	0	0	0
24 SWEDEN	-	-	9	122	0	10	10	0	10	9	0	0	18	0	0
25 SWITZERLAND	373	373	21	21	104	0	0	0	0	.	0	0	0	0	0
26 TURKEY	-	-	-	-	-	-	-	-	-	-	-	0	0	0	0
27 UK ENGLAND AND WALES	2435	41	38	53	32	121	14	2	5	18	14	1	25	0	1
28 UK NORTHERN IRELAND	-	-	-	-	0	0	0	0	0	0	0	0	0	0	0
29 UK SCOTLAND	2195	31	137	761	111	12	0	0	.	341	0	0	0	0	0
30 USA	5130	259	299	395	641	172	38	31	6	5	0	0	0	0	0
31 YUGOSLAVIA	-	-	-	-	-	-	-	-	-	-	.	0	0	0	37

- NO MORTALITY DATA ARE AVAILABLE FOR EVEN A BROADER GROUP OF CAUSES FOR THIS DISEASE

. MORTALITY DATA ARE PRESENTED FOR A BROADER GROUP OF CAUSES FOR THIS DISEASE

0 VALUE<0.5

THE STANDARD MORTALITY RATIOS WERE DERIVED WITH A FACTOR OF 10000

SERIAL MORTALITY TABLES FOR VARIOUS COUNTRIES 1901-1975

TABLE 32 : SMALLPOX : PERSONS

	1901-	1906-	1911-	1916-	1921-	1926-	1931-	1936-	1941-	1946-	1951-	1956-	1961-	1966-	1971-75
1 AUSTRALIA	-	34	31	5	18	13	4	4	0	0	0	0	0	0	0
2 AUSTRIA	70	305	3413	1518	-	0	0	0	-	.	0	0	0	0	0
3 BELGIUM	15203	878	910	775	387	272	.	.	.	96	0	0	3	0	0
4 BULGARIA	-	-	-	-	-	0	0	0	0	0	0	0	0	0	0
5 CANADA	523	189	159	250	520	154	82	20	0	0	0	0	0	0	0
6 CHILE	-	95284	58059	915	67212	295	30	24	48	5	27	3	0	0	0
7 CZECHOSLOVAKIA	-	-	-	20479	1997	70	2	0	46	13	0	0	0	0	0
8 DENMARK	175	93	68	0	24	0	.	.	0	0	0	0	0	0	0
9 EIRE	-	-	-	-	0	0	0	0	0	0	0	0	0	0	0
10 FINLAND	2144	1574	1118	12344	94	15	30	3855	7	0	0	0	0	0	0
11 FRANCE	20344	2702	662	506	432	210	72	20	10	7	15	0	0	0	1
12 GREECE	-	-	-	-	7953	285	249	151	-	-	-	0	0	0	0
13 HUNGARY	-	-	-	.	.	.	0	0	16	0	0	0	0	0	0
14 ICELAND	-	-	.	.	.	.	.	.	0	0	0	0	0	0	0
15 ITALY	-	-	-	-	-	-	-	-	-	-	0	0	0	0	1
16 JAPAN	141	2168	132	1158	407	129	54	33	-	3	3	0	0	0	0
17 NETHERLANDS	247	52	42	40	0	73	0	0	3	5	5	0	0	0	2
18 NEW ZEALAND	-	0	0	0	0	0	0	0	0	0	0	0	0	0	0
19 NORWAY	93	246	20	19	0	0	10	0	0	9	0	0	0	0	0
20 POLAND	-	-	-	-	-	-	-	-	-	-	.	0	6	0	0
21 PORTUGAL	24839	40563	4582	62935	10739	2367	9113	2678	1198	584	15	0	0	0	0
22 ROMANIA	-	-	-	-	-	-	-	.	-	.	-	0	0	0	0
23 SPAIN	26971	20166	13473	17624	7003	472	26	1766	230	7	0	0	2	0	0
24 SWEDEN	-	-	14	149	5	10	5	0	5	4	0	0	18	0	0
25 SWITZERLAND	395	395	57	57	112	7	0	0	0	.	0	0	0	0	0
26 TURKEY	-	-	-	-	-	-	156	16	1081	0	10	3	0	0	7
27 UK ENGLAND AND WALES	3094	60	41	60	44	140	16	2	2	22	13	2	17	0	1
28 UK NORTHERN IRELAND	-	-	-	-	0	0	0	0	0	0	0	0	0	0	0
29 UK SCOTLAND	3131	42	132	852	135	12	0	0	.	171	0	0	0	0	0
30 USA	6911	352	354	495	781	227	51	39	9	6	0	0	0	0	0
31 YUGOSLAVIA	-	-	-	-	331	3	0	0	-	-	.	0	0	0	44

- NO MORTALITY DATA ARE AVAILABLE FOR EVEN A BROADER GROUP OF CAUSES FOR THIS DISEASE

. MORTALITY DATA ARE PRESENTED FOR A BROADER GROUP OF CAUSES FOR THIS DISEASE

0 VALUE<0.5

THE STANDARD MORTALITY RATIOS WERE DERIVED WITH A FACTOR OF 10000

SERIAL MORTALITY TABLES FOR VARIOUS COUNTRIES 1901-1975

TABLE 33 : MEASLES : MALES

	1901-	1906-	1911-	1916-	1921-	1926-	1931-	1936-	1941-	1946-	1951-	1956-	1961-	1966-	1971-75
1 AUSTRALIA	-	957	2611	1481	886	1103	557	595	539	359	174	99	76	61	36
2 AUSTRIA	8902	6112	7880	3584	-	-	-	-	-	723	386	302	150	108	65
3 BELGIUM	14818	15278	12469	5913	6020	4600	2540	1641	889	613	328	204	145	66	42
4 BULGARIA	-	-	-	-	-	1375	899	833	830	742	632	431	343	114	55
5 CANADA	-	-	-	-	1732	2388	1089	1517	712	615	394	207	145	52	28
6 CHILE	-	8912	12100	14688	13752	12339	6137	4409	3127	1846	2878	5885	7785	2801	892
7 CZECHOSLOVAKIA	-	-	-	5399	5261	7128	2030	1552	1213	1191	891	595	413	254	49
8 DENMARK	5500	5612	2941	2838	1607	2296	1471	564	350	396	179	93	48	33	40
9 EIRE	-	-	-	-	4015	4138	3457	1875	1067	886	500	167	197	115	68
10 FINLAND	-	-	-	-	-	1274	902	.	461	341	167	164	33	31	45
11 FRANCE	-	-	-	-	3607	2979	1578	1033	553	561	298	263	125	61	43
12 GREECE	-	-	-	-	4730	4143	2818	2699	-	-	-	436	213	109	41
13 HUNGARY	-	-	-	3012	5027	2244	1387	823	565	526	707	873	547	169	33
14 ICELAND	-	-	.	.	714	2143	0	4000	875	444	818	154	308	308	0
15 ITALY	7672	10909	8920	6212	6115	5404	3101	1975	1008	861	427	326	225	161	82
16 JAPAN	2059	2039	3406	4793	7099	6006	4879	2627	-	1475	1895	912	456	240	157
17 NETHERLANDS	13333	8480	7136	6000	3136	3840	1437	950	582	507	310	132	80	45	20
18 NEW ZEALAND	-	77	1362	1932	808	397	453	1263	333	168	394	161	98	153	44
19 NORWAY	3136	2049	1819	1503	1160	526	740	426	759	218	137	158	65	36	41
20 POLAND	-	-	-	-	-	-	-	-	-	-	.	258	306	215	132
21 PORTUGAL	10931	6808	3683	6871	4334	8069	7057	5267	3921	1945	877	1058	1235	998	726
22 ROMANIA	-	-	-	-	-	-	-	-	-	-	-	578	525	695	482
23 SPAIN	25178	14372	11702	9873	9316	7309	5669	4588	1884	1179	784	495	552	180	104
24 SWEDEN	-	-	3556	2274	1564	1221	620	554	291	136	104	52	34	23	14
25 SWITZERLAND	6267	6267	3009	3009	1152	1294	756	582	203	132	211	82	60	30	45
26 TURKEY	-	-	-	-	-	-	-	-	-	-	-	2153	1313	848	619
27 UK ENGLAND AND WALES	13206	12283	14664	9431	6065	5200	4065	2016	1008	438	243	75	107	67	26
28 UK NORTHERN IRELAND	-	-	-	-	5982	6097	6623	4118	972	763	173	49	80	54	100
29 UK SCOTLAND	12310	14030	13783	11806	12055	7038	5734	3444	931	566	160	91	115	101	28
30 USA	6173	5576	3870	4022	2532	2045	1518	628	493	226	130	101	74	23	8
31 YUGOSLAVIA	-	-	-	-	-	-	-	-	-	-	.	3730	3275	1127	329

- NO MORTALITY DATA ARE AVAILABLE FOR EVEN A BROADER GROUP OF CAUSES FOR THIS DISEASE

. MORTALITY DATA ARE PRESENTED FOR A BROADER GROUP OF CAUSES FOR THIS DISEASE

0 VALUE<0.5

THE STANDARD MORTALITY RATIOS WERE DERIVED WITH A FACTOR OF 100

SERIAL MORTALITY TABLES FOR VARIOUS COUNTRIES 1901-1975

TABLE 33 : MEASLES : FEMALES

	1901-	1906-	1911-	1916-	1921-	1926-	1931-	1936-	1941-	1946-	1951-	1956-	1961-	1966-	1971-75
1 AUSTRALIA	-	898	2283	1243	802	967	588	562	568	411	164	84	78	86	28
2 AUSTRIA	8733	5950	8062	3505	-	-	-	-	-	649	405	280	140	89	46
3 BELGIUM	13797	13529	10434	4588	5395	4318	2182	1372	727	592	306	175	107	73	32
4 BULGARIA	-	-	-	-	-	1463	851	1019	824	766	615	455	358	158	58
5 CANADA	-	-	-	-	1844	2338	1067	1440	753	600	439	231	151	85	18
6 CHILE	-	9464	12380	15324	13829	12121	6039	4398	3110	2038	3031	5788	7907	2718	816
7 CZECHOSLOVAKIA	-	-	-	5694	5012	7060	2016	1487	1177	1198	975	635	431	245	58
8 DENMARK	4905	4676	3000	2041	1560	2081	1293	470	442	432	129	84	96	39	9
9 EIRE	-	-	-	-	3806	4155	3522	2092	1321	905	462	226	222	148	132
10 FINLAND	-	-	-	-	-	1256	809	.	451	394	212	186	60	32	10
11 FRANCE	-	-	-	-	3702	2841	1511	924	552	550	334	265	115	74	47
12 GREECE	-	-	-	-	4358	3980	2943	2744	-	-	-	458	191	103	41
13 HUNGARY	-	-	-	2945	4800	2278	1384	902	588	603	636	850	570	140	23
14 ICELAND	-	-	.	.	1333	1429	0	4571	1571	222	700	83	154	0	0
15 ITALY	7299	10456	8551	6149	5898	5056	2911	1756	941	845	443	318	246	185	85
16 JAPAN	2131	2114	3572	5107	7538	6332	5066	2701	-	1569	2068	927	450	232	152
17 NETHERLANDS	12638	7742	6627	5644	2641	3353	1383	760	478	519	301	111	75	54	24
18 NEW ZEALAND	-	0	1269	1507	733	347	423	1137	274	124	298	161	78	76	58
19 NORWAY	3134	2171	1807	1463	1044	537	779	353	677	295	198	160	45	38	38
20 POLAND	-	-	-	-	-	-	-	-	-	-	.	258	331	215	135
21 PORTUGAL	9779	6062	3329	6462	4290	7864	6946	5292	3556	1677	860	920	1203	940	681
22 ROMANIA	-	-	-	-	-	-	-	-	-	-	-	571	565	677	439
23 SPAIN	24683	14073	11521	9416	9160	7276	5592	4338	1881	1213	830	508	547	195	77
24 SWEDEN	-	-	3467	2296	1521	1095	556	576	267	136	94	58	45	9	9
25 SWITZERLAND	5955	5955	2891	2891	1214	1371	837	630	257	186	173	93	51	51	33
26 TURKEY	-	-	-	-	-	-	-	-	-	-	-	2428	1584	1038	819
27 UK ENGLAND AND WALES	12146	11369	13558	8533	5392	4697	3688	1846	930	409	214	76	121	63	31
28 UK NORTHERN IRELAND	-	-	-	-	6339	4857	6597	4348	1171	675	208	26	83	101	35
29 UK SCOTLAND	12107	13186	12814	10964	10722	6605	5314	3059	988	518	245	102	116	72	33
30 USA	5783	5281	3745	3904	2387	1949	1439	610	520	243	138	102	88	21	9
31 YUGOSLAVIA	-	-	-	-	-	-	-	-	-	-	.	4123	3615	1157	399

- NO MORTALITY DATA ARE AVAILABLE FOR EVEN A BROADER GROUP OF CAUSES FOR THIS DISEASE

. MORTALITY DATA ARE PRESENTED FOR A BROADER GROUP OF CAUSES FOR THIS DISEASE

0 VALUE<0.5

THE STANDARD MORTALITY RATIOS WERE DERIVED WITH A FACTOR OF 100

SERIAL MORTALITY TABLES FOR VARIOUS COUNTRIES 1901-1975

TABLE 34 : YELLOW FEVER : MALES

	1901-	1906-	1911-	1916-	1921-	1926-	1931-	1936-	1941-	1946-	1951-	1956-	1961-	1966-	1971-75
1 AUSTRALIA	-	0	0	0	0	0	0	0	0	0	0	0	0	0	0
2 AUSTRIA	.	.	.	.	-	-	-	-	-	.	0	0	0	0	0
3 BELGIUM	.	.	.	.	.	.	.	.	.	.	0	0	0	0	0
4 BULGARIA	-	-	-	-	-	.	.	.	.	.	.	.	0	0	0
5 CANADA	-	-	-	-	0	0	0	1	.	0	0	0	0	0	0
6 CHILE	-	0	278	6	0	.	.	0	1	1	0	0	0	0	0
7 CZECHOSLOVAKIA	-	-	-	.	.	.	15	35	.	.	0	0	0	0	0
8 DENMARK	.	.	.	.	.	.	.	.	.	.	0	0	0	0	0
9 EIRE	-	-	-	-	0	0	0	0	.	.	0	0	0	0	0
10 FINLAND	-	-	-	-	-	.	.	.	.	.	0	0	0	0	0
11 FRANCE	-	-	-	-	.	.	.	.	.	0	0	0	0	0	0
12 GREECE	-	-	-	-	.	.	.	.	-	-	-	0	0	0	0
13 HUNGARY	-	-	-	.	.	.	0	0	0	.	0	0	0	0	0
14 ICELAND	-	-	.	.	.	.	.	.	.	.	.	.	0	0	0
15 ITALY	-	-	-	-	-	-	-	-	-	-	0	0	0	0	2
16 JAPAN	.	.	.	.	7	3	1	0	-	0	0	0	0	0	0
17 NETHERLANDS	0	0	0	0	0	0	0	0	0	0	0	0	0	0	0
18 NEW ZEALAND	-	0	0	0	0	0	0	0	.	0	0	0	0	0	0
19 NORWAY	.	.	.	.	.	0	0	0	.	.	0	0	0	0	0
20 POLAND	-	-	-	-	-	-	-	-	-	-	.	0	0	0	0
21 PORTUGAL	-	-	-	-	-	-	-	-	-	-	0	0	0	0	0
22 ROMANIA	-	-	-	-	-	-	-	-	-	-	-	0	0	0	0
23 SPAIN	24	120	7	0	2	1	0	0	.	.	0	0	0	0	0
24 SWEDEN	-	-	.	.	.	.	0	0	0	0	0	0	0	0	0
25 SWITZERLAND	.	.	.	.	.	.	.	.	.	.	0	0	0	0	0
26 TURKEY	-	-	-	-	-	-	-	-	-	-	-	0	0	0	4
27 UK ENGLAND AND WALES	.	.	0	0	0	1	0	0	0	0	0	0	0	0	0
28 UK NORTHERN IRELAND	-	-	-	-	0	0	.	.	.	0	0	0	0	0	0
29 UK SCOTLAND	.	.	.	.	.	.	.	.	.	0	0	0	0	0	0
30 USA	.	0	0	3	1	0	.	.	.	0	0	0	0	0	0
31 YUGOSLAVIA	-	-	-	-	-	-	-	-	-	-	.	.	0	0	0

- NO MORTALITY DATA ARE AVAILABLE FOR EVEN A BROADER GROUP OF CAUSES FOR THIS DISEASE

. MORTALITY DATA ARE PRESENTED FOR A BROADER GROUP OF CAUSES FOR THIS DISEASE

SERIAL MORTALITY TABLES FOR VARIOUS COUNTRIES 1901-1975

TABLE 34 : YELLOW FEVER : FEMALES

	1901-	1906-	1911-	1916-	1921-	1926-	1931-	1936-	1941-	1946-	1951-	1956-	1961-	1966-	1971-75
1 AUSTRALIA	-	0	0	0	0	0	0	0	0	0	0	0	0	0	0
2 AUSTRIA	.	.	.	.	-	-	-	-	-	.	0	0	0	0	0
3 BELGIUM	.	.	.	.	.	.	.	.	.	.	0	0	0	0	0
4 BULGARIA	-	-	-	-	-	.	.	.	.	.	.	.	0	0	0
5 CANADA	-	-	-	-	0	0	0	0	.	0	0	0	0	0	0
6 CHILE	-	0	89	4	0	.	.	1	1	0	0	0	0	0	0
7 CZECHOSLOVAKIA	-	-	-	.	.	.	11	20	.	.	0	0	0	0	0
8 DENMARK	.	.	.	.	.	.	.	.	.	.	0	0	0	0	0
9 EIRE	-	-	-	-	0	0	0	0	.	.	0	0	0	0	0
10 FINLAND	-	-	-	-	-	.	.	.	.	.	0	0	0	0	0
11 FRANCE	-	-	-	-	.	.	.	.	.	0	0	0	0	0	1
12 GREECE	-	-	-	-	.	.	.	.	-	-	-	0	0	0	0
13 HUNGARY	-	-	-	.	.	.	0	0	0	.	0	0	0	0	0
14 ICELAND	-	-	.	.	.	.	.	.	.	.	.	.	0	0	0
15 ITALY	-	-	-	-	-	-	-	-	-	-	0	0	0	0	0
16 JAPAN	.	.	.	.	5	2	1	0	-	0	0	0	0	0	0
17 NETHERLANDS	0	0	0	0	0	0	0	0	0	0	0	0	0	0	0
18 NEW ZEALAND	-	0	0	0	0	0	0	0	.	0	0	0	0	0	0
19 NORWAY	.	.	.	.	.	0	0	0	.	.	0	0	0	0	0
20 POLAND	-	-	-	-	-	-	-	-	-	-	.	0	0	0	0
21 PORTUGAL	-	-	-	-	-	-	.	.	.	.	0	0	0	0	0
22 ROMANIA	-	-	-	-	-	-	-	-	-	-	-	0	0	0	0
23 SPAIN	3	0	0	0	1	2	0	0	.	.	0	0	0	0	0
24 SWEDEN	-	-	.	.	.	.	0	0	0	0	0	0	0	0	0
25 SWITZERLAND	.	.	.	.	.	.	.	.	.	.	0	0	0	0	0
26 TURKEY	-	-	-	-	-	-	-	-	-	-	-	0	0	0	0
27 UK ENGLAND AND WALES	.	.	0	1	0	0	0	0	0	0	0	0	0	0	0
28 UK NORTHERN IRELAND	-	-	-	-	0	0	.	.	.	0	0	0	0	0	0
29 UK SCOTLAND	.	.	.	.	.	.	.	.	.	0	0	0	0	0	0
30 USA	.	0	0	0	1	0	.	.	.	0	0	0	0	0	0
31 YUGOSLAVIA	-	-	-	-	-	-	-	-	-	-	.	.	0	0	0

- NO MORTALITY DATA ARE AVAILABLE FOR EVEN A BROADER GROUP OF CAUSES FOR THIS DISEASE

. MORTALITY DATA ARE PRESENTED FOR A BROADER GROUP OF CAUSES FOR THIS DISEASE

SERIAL MORTALITY TABLES FOR VARIOUS COUNTRIES 1901-1975

TABLE 35 : HEPATITIS, INFECTIOUS : MALES

	1901-	1906-	1911-	1916-	1921-	1926-	1931-	1936-	1941-	1946-	1951-	1956-	1961-	1966-	1971-75
1 AUSTRALIA	-	.	.	.	.	.	.	.	.	.	1524	1348	1180	667	590
2 AUSTRIA	.	.	.	.	-	-	-	-	-	.	181	238	771	607	426
3 BELGIUM	.	.	.	.	.	.	.	.	.	.	1125	1414	1612	1531	980
4 BULGARIA	-	-	-	-	-	.	.	.	.	.	.	.	4122	3381	2482
5 CANADA	-	-	-	-	.	.	.	.	.	1023	1424	1267	1280	833	667
6 CHILE	-	.	.	.	.	.	.	.	.	.	1980	2361	1652	2101	2005
7 CZECHOSLOVAKIA	-	-	-	.	.	.	.	.	.	.	3016	2342	2231	1993	1853
8 DENMARK	.	.	.	.	.	.	.	.	.	.	947	437	301	108	121
9 EIRE	-	-	-	-	.	.	.	.	.	.	1115	1227	1358	1468	655
10 FINLAND	-	-	-	-	-	.	.	.	2187	1201	1111	571	306	113	131
11 FRANCE	-	-	-	-	.	.	.	.	.	975	814	866	879	1362	2079
12 GREECE	-	-	-	-	.	.	.	.	-	-	-	986	1306	1265	804
13 HUNGARY	-	-	-	.	.	.	.	.	.	.	4804	3825	3472	3521	3018
14 ICELAND	-	-	.	.	.	.	.	.	.	.	.	.	0	0	0
15 ITALY	-	-	-	-	-	-	-	-	-	-	513	1039	1368	1461	1533
16 JAPAN	.	.	.	.	.	.	.	.	-	2031	2540	1264	616	588	2207
17 NETHERLANDS	.	.	.	.	.	.	.	.	.	514	1212	890	491	281	189
18 NEW ZEALAND	-	.	.	.	.	.	.	.	.	1630	1528	2385	1379	1004	872
19 NORWAY	0	0	.	.	.	76	357	167	.	.	755	779	590	201	65
20 POLAND	-	-	-	-	-	-	-	-	-	-	.	862	2051	3032	3116
21 PORTUGAL	-	-	-	-	-	-	.	.	.	.	1987	1297	1873	2207	2030
22 ROMANIA	-	-	-	-	-	-	-	-	-	-	-	12104	10204	5375	3911
23 SPAIN	.	.	.	.	.	.	.	.	.	.	832	757	1168	558	680
24 SWEDEN	-	-	.	.	.	.	16	0	0	26	159	173	88	52	120
25 SWITZERLAND	.	.	.	.	.	.	.	.	2545	1799	2320	3013	2483	2430	1877
26 TURKEY	-	-	-	-	-	-	-	-	-	-	-	18	80	321	56
27 UK ENGLAND AND WALES	.	.	.	.	.	.	.	.	.	1558	1235	1209	974	806	549
28 UK NORTHERN IRELAND	-	-	-	-	.	.	.	.	.	1493	1389	1361	458	1139	1296
29 UK SCOTLAND	.	.	.	.	.	.	.	.	.	952	863	882	703	643	605
30 USA	.	.	.	.	.	.	.	.	.	927	1145	1088	944	887	693
31 YUGOSLAVIA	-	-	-	-	-	-	-	-	-	-	.	.	2636	1956	1407

- NO MORTALITY DATA ARE AVAILABLE FOR EVEN A BROADER GROUP OF CAUSES FOR THIS DISEASE

. MORTALITY DATA ARE PRESENTED FOR A BROADER GROUP OF CAUSES FOR THIS DISEASE

0 VALUE<0.5

THE STANDARD MORTALITY RATIOS WERE DERIVED WITH A FACTOR OF 1000

SERIAL MORTALITY TABLES FOR VARIOUS COUNTRIES 1901-1975

TABLE 35 : HEPATI¯IS, INFECTIOUS : FEMALES

	1901-	1906-	1911-	1916-	1921-	1926-	1931-	1936-	1941-	1946-	1951-	1956-	1961-	1966-	1971-75
1 AUSTRALIA	-	.	.	.	.	.	.	.	.	.	17259	15421	13305	10749	5643
2 AUSTRIA	.	.	.	.	-	-	-	-	-	.	2363	2181	6621	9169	3361
3 BELGIUM	.	.	.	.	.	.	.	.	.	.	11056	13014	17105	15464	9730
4 BULGARIA	-	-	-	-	-	.	.	.	.	.	.	.	25141	19453	16087
5 CANADA	-	-	-	-	.	.	.	.	.	8015	15874	15155	15158	9805	8256
6 CHILE	-	.	.	.	.	.	.	.	.	.	22346	18377	21362	24014	19531
7 CZECHOSLOVAKIA	-	-	-	.	.	.	.	.	.	.	21243	18263	13166	13451	11413
8 DENMARK	.	.	.	.	.	.	.	.	.	.	17600	9006	2456	4942	2188
9 EIRE	-	-	-	-	.	.	.	.	.	.	8182	12766	14371	14076	10169
10 FINLAND	-	-	-	-	-	.	.	.	20655	13647	13537	10225	3288	1657	2116
11 FRANCE	-	-	-	-	.	.	.	.	.	9880	8433	7553	7249	10793	17941
12 GREECE	-	-	-	-	.	.	.	.	-	-	-	6067	10592	7522	5192
13 HUNGARY	-	-	-	.	.	.	.	.	.	.	32494	35678	27451	30638	25389
14 ICELAND	-	-	.	.	.	.	.	.	.	.	.	.	0	4762	4348
15 ITALY	-	-	-	-	-	-	-	-	-	-	4193	7584	9801	8495	8408
16 JAPAN	.	.	.	.	.	.	.	.	-	16183	21735	10770	5604	5278	18550
17 NETHERLANDS	.	.	.	.	.	.	.	.	.	15873	12367	9061	5145	3498	2996
18 NEW ZEALAND	-	.	.	.	.	.	.	.	.	10582	20721	25703	15523	10667	14861
19 NORWAY	0	402	.	.	.	338	1923	904	.	.	12500	5594	7002	3074	591
20 POLAND	-	-	-	-	-	-	-	-	-	-	.	7235	16667	24796	22592
21 PORTUGAL	-	-	-	-	-	-	.	.	.	.	11242	10537	13198	15784	16063
22 ROMANIA	-	-	-	-	-	-	-	-	-	-	-	75351	70479	34271	22320
23 SPAIN	.	.	.	.	.	.	.	.	.	.	6037	6778	8264	4419	5496
24 SWEDEN	-	-	.	.	.	.	0	0	0	0	3252	2957	1753	1158	1004
25 SWITZERLAND	.	.	.	.	.	.	.	.	25641	30435	28885	28013	31089	26862	18625
26 TURKEY	-	-	-	-	-	-	-	-	-	-	-	562	1314	2124	310
27 UK ENGLAND AND WALES	.	.	.	.	.	.	.	.	.	13038	12969	12918	11447	9811	5971
28 UK NORTHERN IRELAND	-	-	-	-	.	.	.	.	.	10274	8696	12651	9770	13115	10695
29 UK SCOTLAND	.	.	.	.	.	.	.	.	.	4870	9494	11503	12481	9855	5263
30 USA	.	.	.	.	.	.	.	.	.	8566	11639	12545	10843	11494	8316
31 YUGOSLAVIA	-	-	-	-	-	-	-	-	-	-	.	.	44439	22435	10205

- NO MORTALITY DATA ARE AVAILABLE FOR EVEN A BROADER GROUP OF CAUSES FOR THIS DISEASE

. MORTALITY DATA ARE PRESENTED FOR A BROADER GROUP OF CAUSES FOR THIS DISEASE

0 VALUE<0.5

THE STANDARD MORTALITY RATIOS WERE DERIVED WITH A FACTOR OF 10000

SERIAL MORTALITY TABLES FOR VARIOUS COUNTRIES 1901-1975

TABLE 36 : RABIES : MALES

	1901-	1906-	1911-	1916-	1921-	1926-	1931-	1936-	1941-	1946-	1951-	1956-	1961-	1966-	1971-75
1 AUSTRALIA	-	0	0	0	0	0	0	0	0	0	0	0	0	0	.
2 AUSTRIA	.	.	.	.	-	-	-	-	-	.	0	0	0	0	.
3 BELGIUM	0	2787	3030	4957	1035	417	.	.	.	.	0	0	0	0	.
4 BULGARIA	-	-	-	-	-	.	.	.	.	.	.	.	0	0	.
5 CANADA	-	-	-	-	87	389	164	0	50	0	0	66	30	0	.
6 CHILE	-	769	461	441	2535	1711	1342	1477	2632	1961	2752	1654	909	0	.
7 CZECHOSLOVAKIA	-	-	-	3977	4208	2135	588	204	.	.	81	0	91	0	.
8 DENMARK	.	.	.	.	.	.	.	.	.	.	0	0	0	0	.
9 EIRE	-	-	-	-	0	0	0	0	.	.	0	0	0	0	.
10 FINLAND	-	-	-	-	-	.	.	.	0	0	0	0	0	0	.
11 FRANCE	-	-	-	-	.	.	.	.	85	0	0	14	0	0	.
12 GREECE	-	-	-	-	.	10535	8261	6081	-	-	-	1705	902	0	.
13 HUNGARY	-	-	-	.	.	.	1643	877	0	.	0	0	0	110	.
14 ICELAND	-	-	.	.	.	.	.	.	.	.	.	.	0	0	.
15 ITALY	-	-	-	-	-	-	-	-	-	-	507	299	279	61	.
16 JAPAN	.	2067	3337	1542	4222	916	91	80	-	1448	92	6	0	0	.
17 NETHERLANDS	0	0	0	0	0	0	0	0	0	123	0	0	201	0	.
18 NEW ZEALAND	-	0	0	0	0	0	0	0	.	0	0	0	0	0	.
19 NORWAY	.	.	.	.	.	222	0	0	.	.	0	0	0	0	.
20 POLAND	-	-	-	-	-	-	-	-	-	-	.	294	114	160	.
21 PORTUGAL	-	-	-	-	-	-	.	.	.	.	0	0	0	0	.
22 ROMANIA	-	-	-	-	-	-	-	-	-	-	-	2185	828	647	.
23 SPAIN	5061	4519	4306	3667	4305	2398	3030	4892	.	.	1067	231	0	0	.
24 SWEDEN	-	-	.	.	.	.	.	.	.	.	0	0	0	0	.
25 SWITZERLAND	84	84	80	80	0	0	.	.	.	.	0	0	0	0	.
26 TURKEY	-	-	-	-	-	-	-	-	-	-	-	12290	4563	4061	2082
27 UK ENGLAND AND WALES	36	17	17	0	0	0	0	0	0	0	15	15	0	0	.
28 UK NORTHERN IRELAND	-	-	-	-	0	0	.	.	.	0	0	0	0	0	.
29 UK SCOTLAND	256	0	0	0	0	130	.	.	.	0	0	0	0	0	.
30 USA	.	3550	2807	1396	1230	1590	1192	1081	.	360	176	61	16	23	.
31 YUGOSLAVIA	-	-	-	-	-	-	-	-	-	-	.	.	315	0	.

- NO MORTALITY DATA ARE AVAILABLE FOR EVEN A BROADER GROUP OF CAUSES FOR THIS DISEASE

. MORTALITY DATA ARE PRESENTED FOR A BROADER GROUP OF CAUSES FOR THIS DISEASE

0 VALUE<0.5

THE STANDARD MORTALITY RATIOS WERE DERIVED WITH A FACTOR OF 1000

SERIAL MORTALITY TABLES FOR VARIOUS COUNTRIES 1901-1975

TABLE 36 : RABIES : FEMALES

	1901-	1906-	1911-	1916-	1921-	1926-	1931-	1936-	1941-	1946-	1951-	1956-	1961-	1966-	1971-75
1 AUSTRALIA	-	0	0	0	0	0	0	0	0	0	0	0	0	0	.
2 AUSTRIA	.	.	.	.	-	-	-	-	-	.	0	0	0	0	.
3 BELGIUM	0	508	501	729	274	8	.	.	.	.	0	0	0	0	.
4 BULGARIA	-	-	-	-	-	.	.	.	.	.	.	.	0	0	.
5 CANADA	-	-	-	-	0	12	0	0	0	0	0	0	3	5	.
6 CHILE	-	0	46	30	85	118	61	34	95	97	90	81	38	14	.
7 CZECHOSLOVAKIA	-	-	-	207	223	33	0	0	.	.	0	9	0	23	.
8 DENMARK	.	.	.	.	.	.	.	.	.	.	0	0	0	0	.
9 EIRE	-	-	-	-	0	0	0	0	.	.	0	0	0	0	.
10 FINLAND	-	-	-	-	-	.	.	.	0	0	0	0	0	0	.
11 FRANCE	-	-	-	-	.	.	.	.	0	0	0	0	1	0	.
12 GREECE	-	-	-	-	.	529	434	250	-	-	-	85	15	18	.
13 HUNGARY	-	-	-	.	.	.	105	77	0	.	0	0	0	0	.
14 ICELAND	-	-	.	.	.	.	.	.	.	.	.	.	0	0	.
15 ITALY	-	-	-	-	-	-	-	-	-	-	9	14	4	0	.
16 JAPAN	.	73	144	73	220	39	3	4	-	67	6	0	0	0	.
17 NETHERLANDS	0	10	0	0	0	0	0	0	0	0	0	0	5	0	.
18 NEW ZEALAND	-	0	0	0	0	0	0	0	.	0	0	0	0	0	.
19 NORWAY	.	.	.	.	.	0	0	0	.	.	0	0	0	0	.
20 POLAND	-	-	-	-	-	-	-	-	-	-	.	0	9	6	.
21 PORTUGAL	-	-	-	-	-	-	.	.	.	.	0	0	0	0	.
22 ROMANIA	-	-	-	-	-	-	-	-	-	-	-	125	46	27	.
23 SPAIN	227	162	174	144	127	115	104	207	.	.	32	6	0	0	.
24 SWEDEN	-	-	.	.	.	.	.	.	.	.	0	0	0	0	.
25 SWITZERLAND	0	0	16	16	16	16	.	.	.	.	0	0	0	0	.
26 TURKEY	-	-	-	-	-	-	-	-	-	-	-	452	182	133	95
27 UK ENGLAND AND WALES	0	0	0	0	0	0	0	0	0	0	0	0	0	4	.
28 UK NORTHERN IRELAND	-	-	-	-	0	0	.	.	.	0	0	0	0	0	.
29 UK SCOTLAND	13	0	0	0	0	0	.	.	.	0	0	0	0	0	.
30 USA	.	133	101	61	52	63	46	53	.	2	10	4	1	1	.
31 YUGOSLAVIA	-	-	-	-	-	-	-	-	-	-	.	.	9	0	.

- NO MORTALITY DATA ARE AVAILABLE FOR EVEN A BROADER GROUP OF CAUSES FOR THIS DISEASE

. MORTALITY DATA ARE PRESENTED FOR A BROADER GROUP OF CAUSES FOR THIS DISEASE

0 VALUE<0.5

THE STANDARD MORTALITY RATIOS WERE DERIVED WITH A FACTOR OF 100

SERIAL MORTALITY TABLES FOR VARIOUS COUNTRIES 1901-1975

TABLE 37 : TYPHUS AND OTHER RICKETTSIAL DISEASES : MALES

	1901-	1906-	1911-	1916-	1921-	1926-	1931-	1936-	1941-	1946-	1951-	1956-	1961-	1966-	1971-75
1 AUSTRALIA	-	0	0	0	.	66	82	175	229	133	39	10	0	8	0
2 AUSTRIA	.	.	.	.	-	-	-	-	-	18	0	0	0	0	0
3 BELGIUM	.	.	.	.	98	0	.	.	.	.	0	5	0	0	0
4 BULGARIA	-	-	-	-	-	1204	392	270	3184	2030	143	0	6	11	0
5 CANADA	-	-	-	-	16	0	0	0	16	8	14	3	0	0	0
6 CHILE	-	0	0	43218	35479	2552	65785	15875	2571	1142	1286	1161	392	178	0
7 CZECHOSLOVAKIA	-	-	-	2309	248	112	69	32	12143	224	20	0	0	3	0
8 DENMARK	0	0	0	0	0	0	.	.	.	.	0	0	0	0	0
9 EIRE	-	-	-	-	646	383	261	145	196	0	0	0	0	0	0
10 FINLAND	-	-	-	-	-	2890	3310	.	126	0	0	0	0	0	0
11 FRANCE	-	-	-	-	112	23	24	24	92	20	13	7	14	9	4
12 GREECE	-	-	-	-	5948	281	242	114	-	-	-	0	0	0	0
13 HUNGARY	-	-	-	4085	639	37	47	49	188	614	20	0	0	0	0
14 ICELAND	-	-	.	.	.	.	.	.	0	0	0	0	0	0	0
15 ITALY	-	-	-	-	-	-	-	-	-	-	13	4	1	3	2
16 JAPAN	24	13	879	112	14	6	6	12	-	237	52	15	5	3	1
17 NETHERLANDS	183	85	9	683	0	0	0	6	33	5	0	0	0	0	11
18 NEW ZEALAND	-	0	0	0	0	0	0	0	0	0	0	0	0	0	0
19 NORWAY	246	0	158	21	60	19	0	17	302	0	0	0	0	12	0
20 POLAND	-	-	-	-	-	-	-	-	-	-	.	38	25	16	2
21 PORTUGAL	1479	1212	678	15564	1003	404	254	164	237	117	31	18	35	18	30
22 ROMANIA	-	-	-	-	-	-	-	-	-	-	-	57	0	0	0
23 SPAIN	1315	1824	792	715	297	80	36	243	4413	117	4	0	0	0	0
24 SWEDEN	-	-	.	.	.	.	8	8	215	27	0	0	0	0	0
25 SWITZERLAND	0	0	0	0	0	0	.	.	.	.	20	19	9	8	15
26 TURKEY	-	-	-	-	-	-	-	-	-	-	-	59	5	4	35
27 UK ENGLAND AND WALES	208	62	28	11	7	1	0	0	7	2	0	2	1	4	1
28 UK NORTHERN IRELAND	-	-	-	-	266	128	0	0	40	0	0	0	0	0	0
29 UK SCOTLAND	792	428	230	280	120	22	0	0	0	0	0	20	0	0	10
30 USA	.	6	12	30	9	26	79	205	399	190	31	16	13	21	35
31 YUGOSLAVIA	-	-	-	-	-	-	-	-	-	-	.	91	34	3	2

- NO MORTALITY DATA ARE AVAILABLE FOR EVEN A BROADER GROUP OF CAUSES FOR THIS DISEASE

. MORTALITY DATA ARE PRESENTED FOR A BROADER GROUP OF CAUSES FOR THIS DISEASE

0 VALUE<0.5

THE STANDARD MORTALITY RATIOS WERE DERIVED WITH A FACTOR OF 1000

SERIAL MORTALITY TABLES FOR VARIOUS COUNTRIES 1901-1975

TABLE 37 : TYPHUS AND OTHER RICKETTSIAL DISEASES : FEMALES

	1901-	1906-	1911-	1916-	1921-	1926-	1931-	1936-	1941-	1946-	1951-	1956-	1961-	1966-	1971-75
1 AUSTRALIA	-	0	0	0	.	26	31	29	100	56	11	15	0	0	4
2 AUSTRIA	.	.	.	.	-	-	-	-	-	8	0	0	0	0	0
3 BELGIUM	.	.	.	.	96	0	.	.	.	.	13	0	5	0	0
4 BULGARIA	-	-	-	-	-	692	161	231	1333	1182	87	15	18	6	0
5 CANADA	-	-	-	-	0	0	0	0	4	4	0	0	3	0	0
6 CHILE	-	0	0	28909	25208	2370	39181	9360	1184	906	1020	1096	395	168	0
7 CZECHOSLOVAKIA	-	-	-	1070	137	93	63	15	3621	105	33	7	0	0	0
8 DENMARK	0	0	0	0	0	0	.	.	.	.	0	0	0	0	0
9 EIRE	-	-	-	-	429	241	204	34	66	17	0	0	0	0	0
10 FINLAND	-	-	-	-	-	2406	2427	.	25	0	0	0	0	0	0
11 FRANCE	-	-	-	-	88	7	24	35	28	17	12	3	6	2	4
12 GREECE	-	-	-	-	4501	313	211	123	-	-	-	0	0	0	0
13 HUNGARY	-	-	-	1321	310	29	44	33	101	463	6	0	0	0	0
14 ICELAND	-	-	.	.	.	.	.	.	0	0	0	0	0	0	0
15 ITALY	-	-	-	-	-	-	-	-	-	-	9	2	2	3	1
16 JAPAN	15	11	405	89	18	4	3	0	-	111	37	14	3	1	0
17 NETHERLANDS	156	36	0	420	7	0	0	0	5	0	0	0	0	8	4
18 NEW ZEALAND	-	0	0	0	0	0	0	0	0	0	0	0	0	0	0
19 NORWAY	177	43	61	0	55	0	0	0	0	0	0	0	0	0	0
20 POLAND	-	-	-	-	-	-	-	-	-	-	.	38	19	3	1
21 PORTUGAL	1257	997	514	12482	635	258	222	157	184	75	55	21	21	15	31
22 ROMANIA	-	-	-	-	-	-	-	-	-	-	-	13	0	0	0
23 SPAIN	1236	1529	792	706	217	48	16	130	2616	74	3	2	0	0	1
24 SWEDEN	-	-	.	.	.	.	0	0	118	0	0	0	0	0	0
25 SWITZERLAND	7	7	0	0	0	0	.	.	.	.	0	9	16	0	0
26 TURKEY	-	-	-	-	-	-	-	-	-	-	-	9	6	19	35
27 UK ENGLAND AND WALES	167	33	22	1	6	2	0	0	0	0	2	0	1	0	0
28 UK NORTHERN IRELAND	-	-	-	-	97	78	38	0	0	0	0	0	0	0	31
29 UK SCOTLAND	679	348	211	242	49	39	19	0	0	9	9	0	0	0	0
30 USA	.	6	9	12	5	10	44	104	213	116	13	9	10	15	15
31 YUGOSLAVIA	-	-	-	-	-	-	-	-	-	-	.	59	21	2	5

- NO MORTALITY DATA ARE AVAILABLE FOR EVEN A BROADER GROUP OF CAUSES FOR THIS DISEASE

. MORTALITY DATA ARE PRESENTED FOR A BROADER GROUP OF CAUSES FOR THIS DISEASE

0 VALUE<0.5

THE STANDARD MORTALITY RATIOS WERE DERIVED WITH A FACTOR OF 1000

SERIAL MORTALITY TABLES FOR VARIOUS COUNTRIES 1901-1975

TABLE 38 : MALARIA : MALES

	1901-	1906-	1911-	1916-	1921-	1926-	1931-	1936-	1941-	1946-	1951-	1956-	1961-	1966-	1971-75
1 AUSTRALIA	-	856	330	450	9	241	221	99	110	58	20	5	2	3	0
2 AUSTRIA	.	.	.	.	-	-	-	-	-	78	36	18	12	0	2
3 BELGIUM	809	640	486	446	274	166	51	66	32	61	23	11	12	9	4
4 BULGARIA	-	-	-	-	-	5500	2514	1907	4021	934	96	22	8	0	0
5 CANADA	-	-	-	-	33	28	16	23	11	5	3	2	3	2	0
6 CHILE	-	1203	1221	1182	959	387	547	2428	7304	4453	0	2	0	0	0
7 CZECHOSLOVAKIA	-	-	-	1013	136	134	25	11	79	40	21	11	1	0	0
8 DENMARK	133	0	0	30	11	36	.	.	4	4	8	4	4	0	10
9 EIRE	-	-	-	-	211	118	128	111	50	33	60	34	11	11	5
10 FINLAND	-	-	-	-	-	.	.	.	47	40	0	8	0	4	0
11 FRANCE	-	-	-	-	331	318	279	189	81	60	35	26	18	13	11
12 GREECE	-	-	-	-	43772	36634	30364	22572	-	-	-	39	2	0	2
13 HUNGARY	-	-	-	.	.	.	40	60	61	62	36	19	4	3	0
14 ICELAND	-	-	.	.	.	.	.	.	0	0	0	0	0	0	0
15 ITALY	13488	5511	4278	10437	5078	3370	2901	1047	1563	448	84	27	25	17	4
16 JAPAN	1053	644	303	269	137	108	53	55	-	70	25	10	5	3	3
17 NETHERLANDS	252	94	69	82	58	38	25	29	26	47	10	16	4	1	6
18 NEW ZEALAND	-	0	47	87	40	37	59	22	0	0	0	7	0	0	0
19 NORWAY	83	315	28	34	59	154	62	157	99	57	49	19	36	21	17
20 POLAND	-	-	-	-	-	-	-	-	-	-	.	13	9	0	1
21 PORTUGAL	4873	2950	1856	2898	1200	1471	1258	1584	2726	488	93	16	2	8	20
22 ROMANIA	-	-	-	-	-	-	-	-	-	-	-	0	0	0	0
23 SPAIN	7429	4842	4021	4537	2906	1467	595	650	2011	276	60	12	0	1	5
24 SWEDEN	-	-	64	27	20	52	17	19	10	17	2	2	4	2	4
25 SWITZERLAND	71	71	49	49	42	32	.	.	.	.	14	10	3	20	24
26 TURKEY	-	-	-	-	-	-	-	-	-	-	-	47	18	14	28
27 UK ENGLAND AND WALES	222	140	127	425	226	94	47	54	31	20	14	4	7	5	7
28 UK NORTHERN IRELAND	-	-	-	-	159	239	42	123	13	13	12	0	12	0	11
29 UK SCOTLAND	146	103	124	323	174	119	44	75	85	44	7	7	7	10	3
30 USA	3290	1380	1242	1473	1193	1257	1376	871	244	69	11	3	3	2	1
31 YUGOSLAVIA	-	-	-	-	-	-	-	-	-	-	.	21	6	0	2

- NO MORTALITY DATA ARE AVAILABLE FOR EVEN A BROADER GROUP OF CAUSES FOR THIS DISEASE

. MORTALITY DATA ARE PRESENTED FOR A BROADER GROUP OF CAUSES FOR THIS DISEASE

0 VALUE<0.5

THE STANDARD MORTALITY RATIOS WERE DERIVED WITH A FACTOR OF 1000

SERIAL MORTALITY TABLES FOR VARIOUS COUNTRIES 1901-1975

TABLE 38 : MALARIA : FEMALES

	1901-	1906-	1911-	1916-	1921-	1926-	1931-	1936-	1941-	1946-	1951-	1956-	1961-	1966-	1971-75
1 AUSTRALIA	-	159	74	193	3	65	33	46	24	11	17	0	0	1	3
2 AUSTRIA	.	.	.	.	-	-	-	-	-	17	4	0	2	0	0
3 BELGIUM	728	464	389	391	189	119	17	26	14	27	5	3	8	0	2
4 BULGARIA	-	-	-	-	-	5073	2681	1520	2607	792	43	5	4	0	0
5 CANADA	-	-	-	-	11	11	5	3	0	0	1	1	0	0	0
6 CHILE	-	324	885	877	603	293	257	1634	5210	2817	0	0	0	0	0
7 CZECHOSLOVAKIA	-	-	-	42	25	33	19	20	27	17	12	2	0	0	0
8 DENMARK	16	0	0	0	20	5	.	.	4	0	0	4	0	0	0
9 EIRE	-	-	-	-	0	12	6	6	0	0	0	0	0	0	0
10 FINLAND	-	-	-	-	-	.	.	.	4	24	4	0	0	0	0
11 FRANCE	-	-	-	-	84	54	37	22	15	8	5	3	3	3	2
12 GREECE	-	-	-	-	44260	37416	32068	23504	-	-	-	14	0	0	2
13 HUNGARY	-	-	-	.	.	.	15	25	22	34	15	5	0	0	0
14 ICELAND	-	-	.	.	.	.	.	.	0	0	0	0	0	0	0
15 ITALY	10902	4182	3441	6379	3847	2411	2007	591	826	267	20	13	6	2	1
16 JAPAN	1023	578	251	202	106	78	26	40	-	5	4	2	0	0	0
17 NETHERLANDS	285	135	59	53	21	29	12	16	20	30	0	0	1	0	1
18 NEW ZEALAND	-	0	0	0	0	13	0	11	0	0	0	0	0	0	0
19 NORWAY	28	349	0	13	0	12	0	0	0	0	0	0	0	0	4
20 POLAND	-	-	-	-	-	-	-	-	-	-	.	7	4	1	0
21 PORTUGAL	3323	2116	1209	1839	717	1166	797	1124	2078	317	66	0	4	2	11
22 ROMANIA	-	-	-	-	-	-	-	-	-	-	-	0	0	0	0
23 SPAIN	6551	4099	3410	3994	2424	1140	447	454	1442	218	45	6	0	1	1
24 SWEDEN	-	-	9	6	11	11	0	0	0	2	0	0	0	2	2
25 SWITZERLAND	19	19	22	22	21	16	.	.	.	.	0	0	0	8	8
26 TURKEY	-	-	-	-	-	-	-	-	-	-	-	44	9	11	24
27 UK ENGLAND AND WALES	26	22	17	13	12	10	5	4	1	2	0	2	2	2	2
28 UK NORTHERN IRELAND	-	-	-	-	0	13	0	0	0	0	0	0	0	0	0
29 UK SCOTLAND	11	4	0	14	14	14	0	10	6	0	0	3	0	6	0
30 USA	3210	1262	1224	1517	1239	1292	1277	769	218	44	5	1	0	1	0
31 YUGOSLAVIA	-	-	-	-	-	-	-	-	-	-	.	27	5	0	1

- NO MORTALITY DATA ARE AVAILABLE FOR EVEN A BROADER GROUP OF CAUSES FOR THIS DISEASE

. MORTALITY DA⁻A ARE PRESENTED FOR A BROADER GROUP OF CAUSES FOR THIS DISEASE

0 VALUE<0.5

THE STANDARD MORTALITY RATIOS WERE DERIVED WITH A FACTOR OF 1000

SERIAL MORTALITY TABLES FOR VARIOUS COUNTRIES 1901-1975

TABLE 39 : HYDATID DISEASE : MALES

	1901-	1906-	1911-	1916-	1921-	1926-	1931-	1936-	1941-	1946-	1951-	1956-	1961-	1966-	1971-75
1 AUSTRALIA	-	5381	4590	3512	3307	2615	3887	2935	2289	2062	1048	1023	607	314	297
2 AUSTRIA	.	.	.	.	-	-	-	-	-	.	134	79	59	194	57
3 BELGIUM	.	.	.	.	.	.	.	.	.	.	37	29	28	69	55
4 BULGARIA	-	-	-	-	-	.	.	.	.	.	.	.	3200	2691	2058
5 CANADA	-	-	-	-	187	15	28	78	24	76	60	26	16	22	27
6 CHILE	-	13056	8783	1709	2783	1106	2367	2948	2966	2298	2711	2693	2758	2918	2983
7 CZECHOSLOVAKIA	-	-	-	91	93	28	116	96	119	39	19	32	30	19	0
8 DENMARK	0	170	0	0	0	0	.	.	.	.	0	0	0	0	0
9 EIRE	-	-	-	-	0	96	47	0	0	0	0	0	0	0	0
10 FINLAND	-	-	-	-	-	.	.	.	0	0	39	0	0	33	0
11 FRANCE	-	-	-	-	.	.	.	.	559	263	178	205	252	245	227
12 GREECE	-	-	-	-	.	2356	3610	4145	-	-	-	2697	2950	2249	1832
13 HUNGARY	-	-	-	.	.	.	415	329	234	.	378	287	207	172	154
14 ICELAND	-	-	76000	54000	43333	26667	18571	13750	11250	3333	.	.	1667	769	0
15 ITALY	-	-	-	-	-	1380	1382	1250	1091	1258	1190	969	876	674	515
16 JAPAN	.	.	.	.	47	68	20	12	-	31	53	36	32	22	20
17 NETHERLANDS	206	201	344	292	246	184	262	241	113	92	84	104	61	23	11
18 NEW ZEALAND	-	3077	7714	3247	2235	2447	4314	4679	3097	3455	2887	1613	947	442	707
19 NORWAY	0	0	.	.	.	0	0	0	.	.	0	38	0	0	0
20 POLAND	-	-	-	-	-	-	-	-	-	-	.	42	37	67	36
21 PORTUGAL	-	-	-	-	-	-	.	.	.	.	938	727	706	744	551
22 ROMANIA	-	-	-	-	-	-	-	-	-	-	-	703	1056	1117	961
23 SPAIN	1617	2611	3547	1965	2298	2293	2527	2538	2084	2018	1741	1551	1687	1441	1361
24 SWEDEN	-	-	.	.	.	.	.	.	.	.	0	17	16	0	15
25 SWITZERLAND	.	.	.	.	.	.	.	.	.	.	369	427	519	506	433
26 TURKEY	-	-	-	-	-	-	-	-	-	-	-	744	1076	946	218
27 UK ENGLAND AND WALES	.	.	252	249	188	234	275	189	174	105	125	85	74	55	52
28 UK NORTHERN IRELAND	-	-	-	-	156	0	.	.	.	0	0	0	0	0	0
29 UK SCOTLAND	.	.	70	101	97	159	31	59	.	138	55	27	54	0	0
30 USA	242	182	137	169	101	99	94	81	65	41	18	20	14	16	8
31 YUGOSLAVIA	-	-	-	-	-	-	-	-	-	-	.	.	853	595	554

- NO MORTALITY DATA ARE AVAILABLE FOR EVEN A BROADER GROUP OF CAUSES FOR THIS DISEASE

. MORTALITY DATA ARE PRESENTED FOR A BROADER GROUP OF CAUSES FOR THIS DISEASE

0 VALUE<0.5

THE STANDARD MORTALITY RATIOS WERE DERIVED WITH A FACTOR OF 1000

SERIAL MORTALITY TABLES FOR VARIOUS COUNTRIES 1901-1975

TABLE 39 : HYDATID DISEASE : FEMALES

	1901-	1906-	1911-	1916-	1921-	1926-	1931-	1936-	1941-	1946-	1951-	1956-	1961-	1966-	1971-75
1 AUSTRALIA	-	6062	4126	3443	780	2294	2357	2463	1686	1637	506	444	403	283	182
2 AUSTRIA	.	.	.	.	-	-	-	-	-	.	243	63	109	77	121
3 BELGIUM	.	.	.	.	.	.	.	.	.	.	0	13	13	25	25
4 BULGARIA	-	-	-	-	-	.	.	.	.	.	.	.	2363	2469	1836
5 CANADA	-	-	-	-	159	117	138	112	38	46	31	63	48	14	26
6 CHILE	-	9730	4974	980	1101	598	2126	2527	2525	1911	2113	2763	2092	2411	2602
7 CZECHOSLOVAKIA	-	-	-	54	114	25	104	0	0	35	17	19	18	9	8
8 DENMARK	0	270	0	0	44	0	.	.	.	.	30	0	0	0	0
9 EIRE	-	-	-	-	62	99	0	49	0	0	0	0	0	0	0
10 FINLAND	-	-	-	-	-	.	.	.	0	35	0	0	0	28	0
11 FRANCE	-	-	-	-	.	.	.	.	336	199	109	122	140	141	164
12 GREECE	-	-	-	-	.	2528	3318	3603	-	-	-	2640	2376	2088	1850
13 HUNGARY	-	-	-	.	.	.	112	436	253	.	133	177	146	221	215
14 ICELAND	-	-	85000	61667	28571	40000	21250	11250	15556	6667	.	.	1667	0	0
15 ITALY	-	-	-	-	-	934	1036	872	822	738	875	751	553	488	388
16 JAPAN	.	.	.	.	33	43	23	12	-	58	31	12	15	11	11
17 NETHERLANDS	98	219	354	187	215	276	217	133	109	103	80	62	69	21	0
18 NEW ZEALAND	-	6364	5410	3000	1750	2111	2323	2037	2992	2559	1736	886	694	479	485
19 NORWAY	0	63	.	.	.	0	0	0	.	.	0	0	0	0	0
20 POLAND	-	-	-	-	-	-	-	-	-	-	.	12	23	29	4
21 PORTUGAL	-	-	-	-	-	-	.	.	.	.	721	593	455	523	575
22 ROMANIA	-	-	-	-	-	-	-	-	-	-	-	408	747	787	803
23 SPAIN	1461	2475	3264	1758	2243	2046	2195	2049	1694	1398	1463	1106	1303	876	895
24 SWEDEN	-	-	.	.	.	.	.	.	.	.	0	0	0	0	15
25 SWITZERLAND	.	.	.	.	.	.	.	.	.	.	227	260	154	269	391
26 TURKEY	-	-	-	-	-	-	-	-	-	-	-	729	1159	1355	422
27 UK ENGLAND AND WALES	.	.	260	198	176	209	191	210	103	112	72	82	53	27	36
28 UK NORTHERN IRELAND	-	-	-	-	0	225	.	.	.	0	0	0	91	0	0
29 UK SCOTLAND	.	.	63	209	58	28	27	130	.	0	0	23	47	0	0
30 USA	178	121	152	130	109	80	89	59	38	12	16	17	11	9	8
31 YUGOSLAVIA	-	-	-	-	-	-	-	-	-	-	.	.	617	619	561

- NO MORTALITY DATA ARE AVAILABLE FOR EVEN A BROADER GROUP OF CAUSES FOR THIS DISEASE
. MORTALITY DATA ARE PRESENTED FOR A BROADER GROUP OF CAUSES FOR THIS DISEASE
0 VALUE<0.5
THE STANDARD MORTALITY RATIOS WERE DERIVED WITH A FACTOR OF 1000

SERIAL MORTALITY TABLES FOR VARIOUS COUNTRIES 1901-1975

TABLE 40 : ANKYLOSTOMIASIS : MALES

	1901-	1906-	1911-	1916-	1921-	1926-	1931-	1936-	1941-	1946-	1951-	1956-	1961-	1966-	1971-75
1 AUSTRALIA	-	.	527	213	450	261	142	52	118	64	174	70	48	29	0
2 AUSTRIA	.	.	.	.	-	-	-	-	-	1071	199	0	0	0	0
3 BELGIUM	.	.	.	.	.	.	.	.	.	.	0	0	0	29	0
4 BULGARIA	-	-	-	-	-	.	.	.	.	.	.	.	0	0	0
5 CANADA	-	-	-	-	0	41	0	0	0	0	0	0	0	0	0
6 CHILE	-	.	236	78	75	140	.	73	159	0	0	0	0	0	0
7 CZECHOSLOVAKIA	-	-	-	41	0	0	118	187	76	0	0	26	0	0	0
8 DENMARK	.	.	.	.	.	.	.	.	.	.	0	0	0	0	0
9 EIRE	-	-	-	-	0	0	0	0	0	0	0	0	0	0	0
10 FINLAND	-	-	-	-	-	.	.	.	.	.	0	0	0	0	0
11 FRANCE	-	-	-	-	.	.	.	.	126	11	0	3	0	3	0
12 GREECE	-	-	-	-	.	57	0	.	-	-	-	23	0	0	0
13 HUNGARY	-	-	-	.	.	.	22	0	0	.	0	0	0	0	0
14 ICELAND	-	-	.	.	.	.	.	.	.	.	.	.	0	0	0
15 ITALY	-	-	-	-	-	-	-	-	-	-	106	27	6	3	3
16 JAPAN	.	13139	10104	7853	4830	3359	2926	2581	-	9574	5811	1919	449	67	9
17 NETHERLANDS	.	.	5548	64	59	0	0	0	0	0	0	0	0	0	0
18 NEW ZEALAND	-	0	0	0	0	0	0	0	0	0	0	74	0	0	0
19 NORWAY	.	.	.	.	.	0	0	0	.	.	0	0	0	0	0
20 POLAND	-	-	-	-	-	-	-	-	-	-	.	58	0	0	6
21 PORTUGAL	-	-	-	-	-	-	.	.	.	.	0	46	0	0	0
22 ROMANIA	-	-	-	-	-	-	-	-	-	-	-	27	0	9	0
23 SPAIN	.	326	624	227	161	146	70	83	55	59	7	0	0	0	10
24 SWEDEN	-	-	.	.	.	.	.	.	.	.	0	0	0	0	0
25 SWITZERLAND	.	.	.	.	.	.	.	.	.	.	0	0	0	0	0
26 TURKEY	-	-	-	-	-	-	-	-	-	-	-	301	0	20	21
27 UK ENGLAND AND WALES	.	.	6	35	0	10	0	0	0	0	0	0	3	6	0
28 UK NORTHERN IRELAND	-	-	-	-	185	148	.	.	.	0	0	0	0	0	0
29 UK SCOTLAND	.	.	.	.	87	123	.	.	.	0	32	0	0	0	0
30 USA	.	137	241	174	161	115	90	78	27	30	19	9	4	3	0
31 YUGOSLAVIA	-	-	-	-	-	-	-	-	-	-	.	.	0	19	0

\- NO MORTALITY DATA ARE AVAILABLE FOR EVEN A BROADER GROUP OF CAUSES FOR THIS DISEASE

. MORTALITY DATA ARE PRESENTED FOR A BROADER GROUP OF CAUSES FOR THIS DISEASE

0 VALUE<0.5

THE STANDARD MORTALITY RATIOS WERE DERIVED WITH A FACTOR OF 10000

SERIAL MORTALITY TABLES FOR VARIOUS COUNTRIES 1901-1975

TABLE 40 : ANKYLOSTOMIASIS : FEMALES

	1901-	1906-	1911-	1916-	1921-	1926-	1931-	1936-	1941-	1946-	1951-	1956-	1961-	1966-	1971-75
1 AUSTRALIA	-	.	440	429	164	385	416	234	69	20	53	140	14	25	11
2 AUSTRIA	.	.	.	.	-	-	-	-	-	555	132	0	14	0	0
3 BELGIUM	.	.	.	.	.	.	.	.	.	.	0	0	0	11	0
4 BULGARIA	-	-	-	-	-	.	.	.	.	.	.	.	0	0	0
5 CANADA	-	-	-	-	0	0	40	0	0	0	0	10	0	0	0
6 CHILE	-	.	151	75	71	0	.	68	147	0	0	0	0	0	0
7 CZECHOSLOVAKIA	-	-	-	35	0	0	100	0	0	0	0	0	0	0	0
8 DENMARK	.	.	.	.	.	.	.	.	.	.	0	0	0	0	0
9 EIRE	-	-	-	-	0	0	0	0	0	0	0	0	0	0	0
10 FINLAND	-	-	-	-	-	.	.	.	.	.	0	0	0	0	0
11 FRANCE	-	-	-	-	.	.	.	.	67	6	0	0	2	7	2
12 GREECE	-	-	-	-	.	165	0	.	-	-	-	0	0	0	0
13 HUNGARY	-	-	-	.	.	.	20	0	0	.	0	14	0	0	0
14 ICELAND	-	-	.	.	.	.	.	.	.	.	.	.	0	0	0
15 ITALY	-	-	-	-	-	-	-	-	-	-	56	29	13	0	0
16 JAPAN	.	10864	8468	7253	4717	3320	2836	2537	-	10366	5872	1943	399	70	16
17 NETHERLANDS	.	.	6794	30	27	0	0	0	19	0	0	0	0	0	0
18 NEW ZEALAND	-	0	244	0	0	0	0	0	0	0	0	0	184	0	0
19 NORWAY	.	.	.	.	.	0	0	0	.	.	0	0	0	0	0
20 POLAND	-	-	-	-	-	-	-	-	-	-	.	0	0	0	0
21 PORTUGAL	-	-	-	-	-	-	.	.	.	.	93	17	0	0	0
22 ROMANIA	-	-	-	-	-	-	-	-	-	-	-	0	0	7	0
23 SPAIN	.	248	445	91	103	40	75	28	39	54	0	0	0	0	0
24 SWEDEN	-	-	.	.	.	.	.	.	.	.	0	0	0	0	0
25 SWITZERLAND	.	.	.	.	.	.	.	.	.	.	0	0	0	0	0
26 TURKEY	-	-	-	-	-	-	-	-	-	-	-	0	0	20	43
27 UK ENGLAND AND WALES	.	.	5	0	0	0	0	0	0	0	0	0	0	0	0
28 UK NORTHERN IRELAND	-	-	-	-	0	0	.	.	.	0	0	0	0	0	0
29 UK SCOTLAND	.	.	.	.	144	34	.	.	.	0	0	0	0	0	0
30 USA	.	112	247	152	150	113	79	63	35	12	8	3	5	3	0
31 YUGOSLAVIA	-	-	-	-	-	-	-	-	-	-	.	.	0	16	15

- NO MORTALITY DATA ARE AVAILABLE FOR EVEN A BROADER GROUP OF CAUSES FOR THIS DISEASE
. MORTALITY DATA ARE PRESENTED FOR A BROADER GROUP OF CAUSES FOR THIS DISEASE
0 VALUE<0.5
THE STANDARD MORTALITY RATIOS WERE DERIVED WITH A FACTOR OF 10000

SERIAL MORTALITY TABLES FOR VARIOUS COUNTRIES 1901-1975

TABLE 41 : INFECTIONS - ALL FORMS : MALES

	1901-	1906-	1911-	1916-	1921-	1926-	1931-	1936-	1941-	1946-	1951-	1956-	1961-	1966-	1971-75
1 AUSTRALIA	-	19492	18684	14891	11830	10414	8103	6811	6293	4570	2676	1420	954	619	433
2 AUSTRIA	44773	38616	39412	49338	-	-	-	-	-	10934	5682	3824	3001	2230	1441
3 BELGIUM	29647	26296	23242	19358	15339	13366	12253	10462	11753	7235	4235	3030	2081	1499	1032
4 BULGARIA	-	-	-	-	-	33012	28046	24260	25613	22244	11577	3254	2631	1981	1380
5 CANADA	-	-	-	-	14019	13493	10022	8606	7218	4926	2519	1325	883	636	453
6 CHILE	-	82561	60515	57925	59471	48534	51745	46030	42374	35285	16100	13412	11929	7962	6000
7 CZECHOSLOVAKIA	-	-	-	43419	29807	28139	22062	18067	21570	13781	8346	4891	2839	1731	1045
8 DENMARK	36427	30681	24368	24795	13547	10613	8594	5980	6002	3719	1786	879	676	476	452
9 EIRE	-	-	-	-	18420	16626	14661	13351	14607	10616	5338	2734	1950	1396	963
10 FINLAND	-	-	-	-	-	31564	26867	29528	30334	21663	8417	5593	2941	1598	1098
11 FRANCE	-	-	-	-	18101	18702	17238	16186	16973	9688	5776	3869	2790	1887	1403
12 GREECE	-	-	-	-	42051	40512	37435	30849	-	-	-	4313	3034	2180	1446
13 HUNGARY	-	-	-	45769	41100	29544	25879	20041	20304	15422	8478	5095	4071	3085	2213
14 ICELAND	-	-	24802	23670	21695	23529	20438	12594	9381	4959	1778	991	641	583	336
15 ITALY	-	-	-	-	-	-	-	-	-	-	4947	3742	2764	1758	1103
16 JAPAN	27754	31962	31859	34801	34814	34178	34476	35820	-	23377	13117	7173	4395	2789	1812
17 NETHERLANDS	29883	25363	21877	25223	15213	12728	8693	6515	12421	5210	1948	1031	620	459	438
18 NEW ZEALAND	-	14930	13575	13593	10012	8175	6404	6287	5885	4653	3219	1752	995	823	688
19 NORWAY	30886	28835	27675	26717	22629	18391	14556	11026	11179	6298	2833	1482	899	639	563
20 POLAND	-	-	-	-	-	-	-	-	-	-	15503	7674	6867	5070	3018
21 PORTUGAL	-	-	-	-	-	-	33524	29637	29016	23993	13749	9513	6754	4702	2852
22 ROMANIA	-	-	-	-	-	-	-	-	-	-	-	6908	5092	3900	2147
23 SPAIN	48392	37858	31877	33784	28491	23809	21192	23585	20653	17252	8400	5114	3954	2570	1842
24 SWEDEN	-	-	24713	24136	17962	15388	12446	9659	8051	4374	2031	1145	859	712	672
25 SWITZERLAND	33723	33723	25693	25693	19033	16247	12910	10143	9758	6819	3692	2534	1686	1308	1062
26 TURKEY	-	-	-	-	-	-	-	-	-	-	-	14529	8410	5280	3488
27 UK ENGLAND AND WALES	37228	30227	28411	24297	18194	15589	12899	10140	9141	6138	3257	1709	1129	760	534
28 UK NORTHERN IRELAND	-	-	-	-	21548	18103	16322	13427	12183	8527	3686	2040	1261	884	802
29 UK SCOTLAND	41732	39956	33784	26938	22771	17125	14264	11746	10230	8137	3751	1980	1352	917	723
30 USA	57161	37987	30305	25543	17532	14608	11570	9442	7378	5148	2613	1574	1191	881	692
31 YUGOSLAVIA	-	-	-	-	-	-	-	-	-	-	19801	11537	6655	3656	2427

\- NO MORTALITY DATA ARE AVAILABLE FOR EVEN A BROADER GROUP OF CAUSES FOR THIS DISEASE

. MORTALITY DATA ARE PRESENTED FOR A BROADER GROUP OF CAUSES FOR THIS DISEASE

0 VALUE<0.5

THE STANDARD MORTALITY RATIOS WERE DERIVED WITH A FACTOR OF 1000

SERIAL MORTALITY TABLES FOR VARIOUS COUNTRIES 1901-1975

TABLE 41 : INFECTIONS - ALL FORMS : FEMALES

	1901-	1906-	1911-	1916-	1921-	1926-	1931-	1936-	1941-	1946-	1951-	1956-	1961-	1966-	1971-75
1 AUSTRALIA	-	16946	15612	12079	9034	8058	5838	4606	3826	2346	1221	632	431	338	258
2 AUSTRIA	36088	33264	30291	40451	-	-	-	-	-	6716	3072	1673	1120	840	528
3 BELGIUM	26489	23400	20114	18010	14205	12054	9623	7388	7183	3991	1679	1042	627	566	477
4 BULGARIA	-	-	-	-	-	31728	23401	19274	18095	15717	7963	2067	1418	906	628
5 CANADA	-	-	-	-	14067	14630	10325	8298	6291	3989	1714	812	503	365	297
6 CHILE	-	77109	60194	58365	57915	50100	48722	43558	38684	30998	13149	9934	8468	5077	3625
7 CZECHOSLOVAKIA	-	-	-	39704	26680	24885	17832	14095	14209	8967	4785	2488	1344	808	506
8 DENMARK	26663	24108	19021	18630	13893	11194	8508	5429	5141	3166	1284	623	400	367	288
9 EIRE	-	-	-	-	18350	16498	14599	12862	13699	9627	3979	1650	1070	738	538
10 FINLAND	-	-	-	-	-	29680	23612	22838	21038	12344	4144	2468	1180	695	541
11 FRANCE	-	-	-	-	13103	13509	10918	9243	9800	5417	2775	1627	1184	890	828
12 GREECE	-	-	-	-	37358	36061	32342	25610	-	-	-	2574	1547	1032	682
13 HUNGARY	-	-	-	46204	40142	28646	22353	16553	15086	9982	4653	2468	1642	1135	870
14 ICELAND	-	-	25230	25625	22044	24915	20639	11424	11292	4783	1663	874	623	253	542
15 ITALY	-	-	-	-	-	-	-	-	-	-	2947	1830	1144	711	467
16 JAPAN	27576	32951	32841	36453	34491	32482	31246	32407	-	19281	10254	4695	2391	1346	807
17 NETHERLANDS	27116	23981	21032	25041	15318	12629	8254	5863	10474	4348	1469	676	370	323	342
18 NEW ZEALAND	-	14654	12802	12593	8679	6775	5193	4500	3948	3237	1945	1045	613	508	451
19 NORWAY	30603	28803	26332	24973	21698	17034	12808	8885	8025	4181	1651	758	518	369	385
20 POLAND	-	-	-	-	-	-	-	-	-	-	9445	3693	2776	1778	1065
21 PORTUGAL	-	-	-	-	-	-	23989	20838	20198	15457	7859	4695	2878	1755	1118
22 ROMANIA	-	-	-	-	-	-	-	-	-	-	-	4200	2773	1846	910
23 SPAIN	43001	33887	28235	30392	24514	19756	16317	16621	14424	11522	5231	2783	1910	1101	872
24 SWEDEN	-	-	23805	22415	16750	14962	11905	8412	6406	3429	1282	692	507	427	427
25 SWITZERLAND	32163	32163	24644	24644	18126	15129	11390	8335	7686	4988	2306	1416	947	758	625
26 TURKEY	-	-	-	-	-	-	-	-	-	-	-	10753	5831	3334	2127
27 UK ENGLAND AND WALES	29028	23544	21040	17997	13379	11030	8800	6440	5174	3548	1486	705	494	375	283
28 UK NORTHERN IRELAND	-	-	-	-	21794	17826	14952	11940	10291	6587	2335	1012	634	551	474
29 UK SCOTLAND	35718	33344	28047	22549	18626	13681	11080	8866	7905	6083	2194	920	600	462	388
30 USA	48315	31700	24625	21521	15449	12481	9077	6567	4508	2774	1290	749	584	471	429
31 YUGOSLAVIA	-	-	-	-	-	-	-	-	-	-	15553	8652	4318	1933	1226

- NO MORTALITY DATA ARE AVAILABLE FOR EVEN A BROADER GROUP OF CAUSES FOR THIS DISEASE

. MORTALITY DATA ARE PRESENTED FOR A BROADER GROUP OF CAUSES FOR THIS DISEASE

0 VALUE<0.5

THE STANDARD MORTALITY RATIOS WERE DERIVED WITH A FACTOR OF 1000

SERIAL MORTALITY TABLES FOR VARIOUS COUNTRIES 1901-1975

TABLE 41 : INFECTIONS - ALL FORMS : PERSONS

	1901-	1906-	1911-	1916-	1921-	1926-	1931-	1936-	1941-	1946-	1951-	1956-	1961-	1966-	1971-75
1 AUSTRALIA	-	18306	17243	13555	10486	9273	6996	5720	5065	3457	1936	1017	685	474	342
2 AUSTRIA	40281	35849	34691	44738	-	19193	16407	12421	-	8600	4225	2613	1935	1438	918
3 BELGIUM	28050	24829	21639	18664	14763	12705	10914	8891	9414	5568	2891	1978	1306	999	733
4 BULGARIA	-	-	-	-	-	32372	25731	21762	21820	18929	9736	2644	2009	1430	994
5 CANADA	22498	15662	17115	20585	14042	14033	10167	8458	6770	4469	2123	1071	692	498	372
6 CHILE	-	79807	60353	58148	58681	52152	50205	44771	40489	33084	14577	11615	10136	6466	4760
7 CZECHOSLOVAKIA	-	-	-	41451	28150	26415	19823	15967	17661	11222	6449	3606	2035	1233	753
8 DENMARK	30998	27026	21384	21354	13728	10916	8549	5696	5559	3436	1528	747	532	419	366
9 EIRE	-	-	-	-	18385	16562	14630	13111	14155	10123	4661	2190	1504	1061	746
10 FINLAND	-	-	-	-	-	30582	25148	25949	25322	16585	6061	3870	1970	1098	788
11 FRANCE	43608	23704	22182	18144	15424	15921	13841	12416	13034	7335	4122	2634	1908	1340	1089
12 GREECE	-	-	-	-	39680	38256	34849	28186	-	-	-	4082	2855	2016	1312
13 HUNGARY	-	-	-	45993	40607	29081	24054	18228	17581	12515	6429	3686	2763	2031	1485
14 ICELAND	-	-	25034	24726	21882	24273	20545	11974	10383	4868	1719	932	632	415	441
15 ITALY	-	-	-	-	-	-	-	-	-	-	3891	2730	1902	1198	762
16 JAPAN	27664	32458	32352	35632	34650	33314	32827	34076	-	21245	11626	5879	3345	2031	1282
17 NETHERLANDS	28461	24654	21444	25130	15267	12678	8469	6184	11431	4771	1704	849	491	388	387
18 NEW ZEALAND	-	14804	13217	13120	9371	7495	5810	5399	4905	3934	2572	1391	799	660	565
19 NORWAY	30736	28818	26962	25792	22135	17672	13631	9898	9525	5193	2220	1106	701	498	470
20 POLAND	-	-	-	-	-	-	-	-	-	-	12204	9928	4643	3278	1951
21 PORTUGAL	-	-	-	-	-	-	28337	24843	24220	19374	10527	6880	4637	3083	1896
22 ROMANIA	-	-	-	-	-	-	-	35522	-	24642	-	5467	3859	2809	1491
23 SPAIN	45611	35802	29990	32030	26426	21690	18621	19875	17334	14187	6691	3859	2855	1780	1322
24 SWEDEN	-	-	24233	23228	17323	15165	12164	9013	7202	3888	1647	912	677	565	544
25 SWITZERLAND	32910	32910	25139	25139	18550	15651	12099	9176	8649	5837	2948	1933	1288	1012	827
26 TURKEY	-	-	-	-	-	-	24481	24306	27202	18471	13642	12669	7143	4342	2840
27 UK ENGLAND AND WALES	32967	26751	24523	20944	15629	13153	10703	8142	6909	4731	2291	1160	782	550	397
28 UK NORTHERN IRELAND	-	-	-	-	21677	17958	15607	12650	11182	7512	2971	1492	926	705	626
29 UK SCOTLAND	38528	36437	30737	24601	20566	15290	12567	10208	8981	7028	2906	1401	939	666	537
30 USA	52739	34916	27546	23579	16513	13565	10340	8011	5937	3156	1935	1147	873	663	551
31 YUGOSLAVIA	-	-	-	-	-	-	-	-	-	-	17529	9998	5411	2741	1788

\- NO MORTALITY DATA ARE AVAILABLE FOR EVEN A BROADER GROUP OF CAUSES FOR THIS DISEASE

. MORTALITY DATA ARE PRESENTED FOR A BROADER GROUP OF CAUSES FOR THIS DISEASE

0 VALUE<0.5

THE STANDARD MORTALITY RATIOS WERE DERIVED WITH A FACTOR OF 1000

SERIAL MORTALITY TABLES FOR VARIOUS COUNTRIES 1901-1975

TABLE 42 : MALIGNANT NEOPLASM - BUCCAL CAVITY AND PHARYNX : MALES

	1901-	1906-	1911-	1916-	1921-	1926-	1931-	1936-	1941-	1946-	1951-	1956-	1961-	1966-	1971-75
1 AUSTRALIA	-	.	58999	62896	58010	50756	49972	40285	31298	26175	17772	14559	14142	16287	17439
2 AUSTRIA	.	.	.	.	-	-	-	-	-	16955	14940	12955	12044	14195	16209
3 BELGIUM	.	.	.	.	.	.	.	.	.	.	11090	11992	12477	11578	11952
4 BULGARIA	-	-	-	-	-	.	.	.	.	.	.	.	8702	8860	7726
5 CANADA	-	-	-	-	32121	30317	38698	35454	32243	27062	20077	18338	17957	18281	18795
6 CHILE	-	9350	6193	3193	2358	7241	10441	8784	9631	9049	8228	8773	9929	9885	11584
7 CZECHOSLOVAKIA	-	-	-	11696	10368	13453	22538	21846	15111	14995	15364	14897	14681	13688	14661
8 DENMARK	.	.	.	.	.	.	.	.	.	.	9559	9756	9259	8133	8586
9 EIRE	-	-	-	-	58884	62648	67720	64510	51553	44213	36881	30138	22880	20454	18228
10 FINLAND	-	-	-	-	-	.	.	.	15780	14237	18614	14748	13543	11417	10376
11 FRANCE	-	-	-	-	.	.	.	.	22217	22666	25545	32355	38723	45943	54580
12 GREECE	-	-	-	-	.	4452	6541	5968	-	-	-	4793	6111	5649	6014
13 HUNGARY	-	-	-	.	.	.	25291	23289	21550	21179	17444	17384	17561	17604	20991
14 ICELAND	-	-	.	.	.	.	.	.	.	.	.	.	9009	10484	10870
15 ITALY	.	.	.	.	.	.	24990	25778	21812	21547	21226	22424	23919	24974	25564
16 JAPAN	.	12391	12770	13147	15096	16544	12587	9660	-	6843	6191	5806	6176	6575	7144
17 NETHERLANDS	33413	26513	23056	21497	19055	18410	19600	18521	15831	12281	8688	7681	7578	7245	8556
18 NEW ZEALAND	-	38889	79261	43510	38997	45028	45477	31379	27517	21082	15465	15364	12020	11993	14391
19 NORWAY	.	.	.	.	.	18239	23937	18294	16691	15392	13657	13155	12579	11891	12955
20 POLAND	-	-	-	-	-	-	-	-	-	-	.	10452	13445	16696	21145
21 PORTUGAL	.	.	.	.	.	.	.	.	.	.	19902	19363	20526	21058	21942
22 ROMANIA	-	-	-	-	-	-	-	-	-	-	-	9275	12052	12112	12473
23 SPAIN	13313	13886	16112	18775	22654	24411	16659	15051	13106	11903	12250	10824	12741	11870	14731
24 SWEDEN	-	-	.	.	.	.	.	.	.	.	8956	9715	9891	9635	10291
25 SWITZERLAND	19034	19034	18699	18699	44938	41506	38026	37710	35807	31403	27108	29395	29903	25716	27414
26 TURKEY	-	-	-	-	-	-	-	-	-	-	-	5047	2765	1960	1286
27 UK ENGLAND AND WALES	.	.	67455	69972	67656	63725	64180	52595	39705	28192	22952	18051	14318	13099	11966
28 UK NORTHERN IRELAND	-	-	-	-	50449	57902	57397	50064	43110	38084	23436	21548	15700	16039	12346
29 UK SCOTLAND	.	.	.	.	67890	60591	63009	55003	48756	36143	28696	21635	16822	15327	12862
30 USA	28814	28291	30654	27466	26904	26680	30187	27787	25934	23729	19744	19926	19684	19900	19564
31 YUGOSLAVIA	-	-	-	-	-	-	-	-	-	-	.	.	10102	10168	13497

- NO MORTALITY DATA ARE AVAILABLE FOR EVEN A BROADER GROUP OF CAUSES FOR THIS DISEASE

. MORTALITY DATA ARE PRESENTED FOR A BROADER GROUP OF CAUSES FOR THIS DISEASE

0 VALUE<0.5

THE STANDARD MORTALITY RATIOS WERE DERIVED WITH A FACTOR OF 10000

SERIAL MORTALITY TABLES FOR VARIOUS COUNTRIES 1901-1975

TABLE 42 : MALIGNANT NEOPLASM - BUCCAL CAVITY AND PHARYNX : FEMALES

	1901-	1906-	1911-	1916-	1921-	1926-	1931-	1936-	1941-	1946-	1951-	1956-	1961-	1966-	1971-75
1 AUSTRALIA	-	.	6528	5451	6560	5143	6498	6273	6456	4876	4791	4935	4863	5068	5189
2 AUSTRIA	.	.	.	.	-	-	-	-	-	4977	4237	3367	3350	3219	2863
3 BELGIUM	.	.	.	.	.	.	.	.	.	.	3675	2830	3523	2522	2786
4 BULGARIA	-	-	-	-	-	.	.	.	.	.	.	.	2911	2813	2639
5 CANADA	-	-	-	-	6112	6240	8452	7229	7147	5954	5190	5133	4921	4980	5522
6 CHILE	-	7407	3569	1243	1046	3793	4660	3991	5225	4066	5521	3808	3554	3677	3477
7 CZECHOSLOVAKIA	-	-	-	2116	2008	2450	5444	4385	3272	4160	4292	4115	4012	3385	2986
8 DENMARK	.	.	.	.	.	.	.	.	.	.	5260	4577	4352	4248	3774
9 EIRE	-	-	-	-	6878	9153	10458	11765	10624	10198	10500	8449	8442	7325	6966
10 FINLAND	-	-	-	-	-	.	.	.	5211	5226	7822	6466	5662	4816	4261
11 FRANCE	-	-	-	-	.	.	.	.	3166	2980	2813	3110	3251	3618	4072
12 GREECE	-	-	-	-	.	2150	2806	2655	-	-	-	1802	2240	2221	2176
13 HUNGARY	-	-	-	.	.	.	6194	5377	4359	3243	3689	3669	3521	3518	4032
14 ICELAND	-	-	.	.	.	.	.	.	.	.	.	.	6202	8333	7500
15 ITALY	.	.	.	.	.	.	4798	5181	4127	3934	3671	3896	3919	3860	3747
16 JAPAN	.	4456	4959	4687	5160	5779	4942	3932	-	3420	2758	2733	2722	2806	2801
17 NETHERLANDS	7608	6437	6229	6189	6519	6361	6163	6607	5406	4928	3856	3700	3450	2838	2925
18 NEW ZEALAND	-	8824	36554	9389	6022	8462	8279	8753	7922	6029	6465	6379	6032	4675	5356
19 NORWAY	.	.	.	.	.	7281	8983	8694	7460	8352	5704	6229	5629	5586	4650
20 POLAND	-	-	-	-	-	-	-	-	-	-	.	3386	3721	4035	4245
21 PORTUGAL	.	.	.	.	.	.	.	.	.	.	3717	4280	4859	4593	4198
22 ROMANIA	-	-	-	-	-	-	-	-	-	-	-	2479	3074	3512	3543
23 SPAIN	2950	3238	3691	4541	5334	5348	3555	3279	2886	2860	2246	2098	2654	2461	2499
24 SWEDEN	-	-	.	.	.	.	.	.	.	.	7579	6694	6724	5344	5171
25 SWITZERLAND	1656	1656	1867	1867	6754	6145	5460	5746	5952	5056	5007	4256	3866	3977	4064
26 TURKEY	-	-	-	-	-	-	-	-	-	-	-	1624	947	777	460
27 UK ENGLAND AND WALES	.	.	8715	9036	8477	8215	9083	8918	7189	6538	7000	6672	6034	5713	5138
28 UK NORTHERN IRELAND	-	-	-	-	9509	8722	10333	11409	10441	10805	9051	7851	9112	8345	6476
29 UK SCOTLAND	.	.	.	.	11012	8213	10682	11068	11292	9192	8344	7854	7252	6745	5290
30 USA	6774	5852	7005	5989	5664	6112	7160	6650	6307	5709	4877	5015	5169	5564	5909
31 YUGOSLAVIA	-	-	-	-	-	-	-	-	-	-	.	.	2269	2358	2757

- NO MORTALITY DATA ARE AVAILABLE FOR EVEN A BROADER GROUP OF CAUSES FOR THIS DISEASE

. MORTALITY DATA ARE PRESENTED FOR A BROADER GROUP OF CAUSES FOR THIS DISEASE

0 VALUE<0.5

THE STANDARD MORTALITY RATIOS WERE DERIVED WITH A FACTOR OF 10000

SERIAL MORTALITY TABLES FOR VARIOUS COUNTRIES 1901-1975

TABLE 43 : MALIGNANT NEOPLASM - OESOPHAGUS : MALES

	1901-	1906-	1911-	1916-	1921-	1926-	1931-	1936-	1941-	1946-	1951-	1956-	1961-	1966-	1971-75
1 AUSTRALIA	-	.	.	.	.	.	16080	15538	13849	11937	11495	9083	9841	10598	12268
2 AUSTRIA	.	.	.	.	-	-	-	-	-	.	15514	13412	12498	13257	11646
3 BELGIUM	.	.	.	.	.	.	.	.	.	.	11528	11109	10775	11113	10897
4 BULGARIA	-	-	-	-	-	.	.	.	.	.	.	.	4917	4250	3380
5 CANADA	-	-	-	-	.	.	9252	9553	9228	8543	9058	8678	9316	9942	10381
6 CHILE	-	.	.	.	.	.	.	17751	16105	20510	26412	27379	28404	32329	31113
7 CZECHOSLOVAKIA	-	-	-	.	.	.	26869	24514	.	.	11485	8341	7866	7148	7921
8 DENMARK	.	.	.	.	.	.	.	.	.	.	11684	9644	8685	7867	8605
9 EIRE	-	-	-	-	.	.	.	.	.	.	12725	12776	15851	14244	15774
10 FINLAND	-	-	-	-	-	.	.	.	23825	26907	26366	22642	17484	14489	11889
11 FRANCE	-	-	-	-	.	.	.	.	.	33098	31059	34623	39703	40996	39575
12 GREECE	-	-	-	-	.	.	.	.	-	-	-	3984	4620	5331	5335
13 HUNGARY	-	-	-	.	.	.	8341	8409	7406	.	8395	7321	7644	7467	7835
14 ICELAND	-	-	.	.	.	.	.	.	.	.	.	.	15951	18132	9406
15 ITALY	.	.	.	.	.	.	9249	9724	9521	10204	11176	11957	12719	13420	13525
16 JAPAN	.	.	23808	24878	25885	25614	25943	25395	-	21714	20952	20844	21655	23043	22455
17 NETHERLANDS	.	.	.	.	.	31409	25226	21848	18847	15235	11320	9999	9166	8610	9214
18 NEW ZEALAND	-	.	.	.	.	20237	17065	16976	16623	13681	12235	10394	10319	12200	13493
19 NORWAY	.	.	.	.	.	13904	17258	17058	14001	13299	10011	8470	8331	7627	7481
20 POLAND	-	-	-	-	-	-	-	-	-	-	.	12325	15507	14345	13161
21 PORTUGAL	.	.	.	.	.	.	.	.	.	.	13835	13919	15229	16288	17918
22 ROMANIA	-	-	-	-	-	-	-	-	-	-	-	5866	5851	5916	5139
23 SPAIN	.	.	.	.	.	.	5871	5340	.	.	7021	8641	10979	12248	14572
24 SWEDEN	-	-	.	.	.	.	.	.	.	.	7900	7774	7608	7587	8567
25 SWITZERLAND	74918	74918	76861	76861	77114	70785	66594	68359	58827	50900	40704	33403	30895	25929	23521
26 TURKEY	-	-	-	-	-	-	-	-	-	-	-	4655	3956	3199	2680
27 UK ENGLAND AND WALES	.	.	.	.	.	.	.	21847	18762	16510	14681	13284	13085	14338	15295
28 UK NORTHERN IRELAND	-	-	-	-	.	.	.	.	.	16625	12743	10795	11043	12092	12444
29 UK SCOTLAND	.	.	.	.	.	.	.	.	.	19590	17267	16409	15888	16826	18486
30 USA	.	.	.	.	.	9213	8963	9588	9733	10517	10679	10807	10939	11042	11534
31 YUGOSLAVIA	-	-	-	-	-	-	-	-	-	-	.	.	6055	6819	7498

- NO MORTALITY DATA ARE AVAILABLE FOR EVEN A BROADER GROUP OF CAUSES FOR THIS DISEASE

. MORTALITY DATA ARE PRESENTED FOR A BROADER GROUP OF CAUSES FOR THIS DISEASE

0 VALUE<0.5

THE STANDARD MORTALITY RATIOS WERE DERIVED WITH A FACTOR OF 10000

SERIAL MORTALITY TABLES FOR VARIOUS COUNTRIES 1901-1975

TABLE 43 : MALIGNANT NEOPLASM - OESOPHAGUS : FEMALES

	1901-	1906-	1911-	1916-	1921-	1926-	1931-	1936-	1941-	1946-	1951-	1956-	1961-	1966-	1971-75
1 AUSTRALIA	-	.	.	.	.	.	4854	5093	4740	4169	3525	3802	4050	4716	5035
2 AUSTRIA	.	.	.	.	-	-	-	-	-	.	3169	2451	2479	2251	1868
3 BELGIUM	.	.	.	.	.	.	.	.	.	.	4301	3419	3169	2915	2983
4 BULGARIA	-	-	-	-	-	.	.	.	.	.	.	.	1690	1637	1442
5 CANADA	-	-	-	-	.	.	4894	4087	4140	3931	3704	3647	3395	3288	3537
6 CHILE	-	.	.	.	.	.	.	9293	8900	10433	12041	14000	15383	16404	14458
7 CZECHOSLOVAKIA	-	-	-	.	.	.	5124	4860	.	.	2607	1763	1537	1629	1534
8 DENMARK	.	.	.	.	.	.	.	.	.	.	5248	4774	4088	3514	3489
9 EIRE	-	-	-	-	.	.	.	.	.	.	8895	9173	9679	11862	11872
10 FINLAND	-	-	-	-	-	.	.	.	17845	19313	18666	16459	13836	10548	9169
11 FRANCE	-	-	-	-	.	.	.	.	.	3603	3430	3440	3560	3502	3317
12 GREECE	-	-	-	-	.	.	.	.	-	-	-	1589	1825	1850	1832
13 HUNGARY	-	-	-	.	.	.	1305	1921	1100	.	2298	1823	1507	1566	1323
14 ICELAND	-	-	.	.	.	.	.	.	.	.	.	.	16316	9434	7627
15 ITALY	.	.	.	.	.	.	2330	2507	2202	2409	2548	2523	2484	2410	2522
16 JAPAN	.	.	7976	8156	8870	8242	7752	7606	-	7101	6876	6799	6502	6287	5494
17 NETHERLANDS	.	.	.	.	.	9697	8326	7801	7070	6114	5128	4035	3792	3885	3422
18 NEW ZEALAND	-	.	.	.	.	9110	7404	6437	6641	5568	7016	4920	5488	5942	6005
19 NORWAY	.	.	.	.	.	6339	7776	6230	4953	4049	3392	2276	2349	2509	2277
20 POLAND	-	-	-	-	-	-	-	-	-	-	.	3597	4085	3363	2967
21 PORTUGAL	.	.	.	.	.	.	.	.	.	.	5230	4572	5122	5827	5532
22 ROMANIA	-	-	-	-	-	-	-	-	-	-	-	1686	1782	1571	1520
23 SPAIN	.	.	.	.	.	.	1510	1864	.	.	1762	2379	3250	3368	3214
24 SWEDEN	-	-	.	.	.	.	.	.	.	.	4180	4019	3201	3090	3156
25 SWITZERLAND	11372	11372	10149	10149	8008	8021	6631	6591	5777	6042	5018	3946	4135	3282	3163
26 TURKEY	-	-	-	-	-	-	-	-	-	-	-	1858	1796	1576	1343
27 UK ENGLAND AND WALES	.	.	.	.	.	.	.	7121	6589	6686	6671	6689	7003	7449	7898
28 UK NORTHERN IRELAND	-	-	-	-	.	.	.	.	.	9664	9048	7469	8359	8446	6755
29 UK SCOTLAND	.	.	.	.	.	.	.	.	.	11051	10349	9083	9257	9654	10452
30 USA	.	.	.	.	.	2802	2610	2620	2480	2651	2607	2618	2636	2802	2955
31 YUGOSLAVIA	-	-	-	-	-	-	-	-	-	-	.	.	1559	1557	1667

- NO MORTALITY DATA ARE AVAILABLE FOR EVEN A BROADER GROUP OF CAUSES FOR THIS DISEASE

. MORTALITY DATA ARE PRESENTED FOR A BROADER GROUP OF CAUSES FOR THIS DISEASE

0 VALUE<0.5

THE STANDARD MORTALITY RATIOS WERE DERIVED WITH A FACTOR OF 10000

SERIAL MORTALITY TABLES FOR VARIOUS COUNTRIES 1901-1975

TABLE 44 : MALIGNANT NEOPLASM - STOMACH : MALES

	1901-	1906-	1911-	1916-	1921-	1926-	1931-	1936-	1941-	1946-	1951-	1956-	1961-	1966-	1971-75
1 AUSTRALIA	-	.	.	.	.	.	20659	18619	16754	15660	13825	11647	9674	8735	7813
2 AUSTRIA	.	.	.	.	-	-	-	-	-	.	27975	27056	25195	22540	19092
3 BELGIUM	.	.	.	.	.	.	.	.	.	.	19825	18487	16847	14541	12284
4 BULGARIA	-	-	-	-	-	.	.	.	.	.	.	.	24378	20635	17787
5 CANADA	-	-	-	-	.	.	19249	18080	17050	15421	14304	12467	10679	9142	7834
6 CHILE	-	.	.	.	.	.	.	22903	40844	40921	47071	41830	37393	34979	32612
7 CZECHOSLOVAKIA	-	-	-	.	.	.	37795	35489	.	.	27581	26339	25575	22949	19530
8 DENMARK	39862	42564	40028	36653	35122	34278	30536	26348	22253	19684	19215	16548	13714	10979	9360
9 EIRE	-	-	-	-	.	.	.	.	.	.	15863	14764	14032	13144	11813
10 FINLAND	-	-	-	-	-	.	.	.	40492	42057	38492	30423	24648	19565	15469
11 FRANCE	-	-	-	-	.	.	.	.	.	17494	16373	15171	13601	11360	9440
12 GREECE	-	-	-	-	.	.	.	.	-	-	-	7975	9249	8594	7863
13 HUNGARY	-	-	-	.	.	.	31048	28348	28244	.	27812	27975	25499	24154	21811
14 ICELAND	-	-	.	.	.	.	.	.	.	.	.	.	28913	21206	19534
15 ITALY	.	.	.	.	.	.	18302	19292	18677	19574	20903	20188	19799	18482	16190
16 JAPAN	.	35769	37523	39043	42490	.	38274	38099	-	40362	41706	42642	41007	38927	34373
17 NETHERLANDS	.	.	.	.	.	41331	33422	31516	28107	25675	22046	19045	17242	15134	12959
18 NEW ZEALAND	-	.	.	.	.	19088	18920	16748	15776	14879	13346	11747	10342	9402	8117
19 NORWAY	35904	36294	37475	36090	38031	35924	35329	32848	31828	31514	23836	18786	15908	14313	11246
20 POLAND	-	-	-	-	-	-	-	-	-	-	.	22719	26350	24426	21329
21 PORTUGAL	.	.	.	.	.	.	.	.	.	.	17383	17608	19268	19906	19964
22 ROMANIA	-	-	-	-	-	-	-	-	-	-	-	20588	22229	19052	17121
23 SPAIN	.	.	.	.	.	.	17489	16410	.	.	15775	16896	17893	16599	15128
24 SWEDEN	-	-	.	.	.	.	.	.	.	.	18297	16492	14092	11157	10063
25 SWITZERLAND	42925	42925	40141	40141	38582	37999	35642	32788	28349	26089	23440	19770	16755	13830	11820
26 TURKEY	-	-	-	-	-	-	-	-	-	-	-	14584	12394	10367	8653
27 UK ENGLAND AND WALES	.	.	.	.	.	.	.	19297	17383	17143	16453	15337	14143	12933	11742
28 UK NORTHERN IRELAND	-	-	-	-	.	.	.	.	.	19200	15725	16532	13668	12789	11420
29 UK SCOTLAND	.	.	.	.	.	.	.	.	.	18735	17735	16526	15088	13550	11921
30 USA	.	.	.	.	.	18075	16207	14901	13142	11668	9415	7749	6293	5126	4314
31 YUGOSLAVIA	-	-	-	-	-	-	-	-	-	-	.	.	12714	13264	13494

- NO MORTALITY DATA ARE AVAILABLE FOR EVEN A BROADER GROUP OF CAUSES FOR THIS DISEASE

. MORTALITY DATA ARE PRESENTED FOR A BROADER GROUP OF CAUSES FOR THIS DISEASE

0 VALUE<0.5

THE STANDARD MORTALITY RATIOS WERE DERIVED WITH A FACTOR OF 10000

SERIAL MORTALITY TABLES FOR VARIOUS COUNTRIES 1901-1975

TABLE 44 : MALIGNANT NEOPLASM - STOMACH : FEMALES

	1901-	1906-	1911-	1916-	1921-	1926-	1931-	1936-	1941-	1946-	1951-	1956-	1961-	1966-	1971-75
1 AUSTRALIA	-	.	.	.	.	.	11230	10586	9986	8866	7766	6165	5265	4696	4049
2 AUSTRIA	.	.	.	.	-	-	-	-	-	.	16787	15902	14571	12942	10300
3 BELGIUM	.	.	.	.	.	.	.	.	.	.	12296	11454	10118	8175	6647
4 BULGARIA	-	-	-	-	-	.	.	.	.	.	.	.	16038	12488	10186
5 CANADA	-	-	-	-	.	.	12390	11107	9677	8557	7522	6334	5115	4374	3695
6 CHILE	-	.	.	.	.	.	.	19087	29428	28653	31024	26186	23651	20421	17450
7 CZECHOSLOVAKIA	-	-	-	.	.	.	25362	22923	.	.	15588	14414	13373	11897	9941
8 DENMARK	26647	27042	26166	26594	26605	25172	23526	20473	17110	13715	12834	10505	8730	6251	5185
9 EIRE	-	-	-	-	.	.	.	.	.	.	11068	10623	9328	9168	7963
10 FINLAND	-	-	-	-	-	.	.	.	25992	25303	22287	17343	13030	10106	7942
11 FRANCE	-	-	-	-	.	.	.	.	.	9783	9102	8319	7241	5988	4849
12 GREECE	-	-	-	-	.	.	.	.	-	-	-	4920	5717	4921	4483
13 HUNGARY	-	-	-	.	.	.	23451	19882	18652	.	16556	15607	13752	12536	10806
14 ICELAND	-	-	.	.	.	.	.	.	.	.	.	.	12786	9125	7718
15 ITALY	.	.	.	.	.	.	12430	12822	12021	11971	12360	11315	10608	9583	8229
16 JAPAN	.	21534	21557	22731	23566	.	20381	19815	-	20866	21227	21586	20811	19808	17459
17 NETHERLANDS	.	.	.	.	.	33613	22144	21330	19590	16989	14114	11282	9388	8187	6447
18 NEW ZEALAND	-	.	.	.	.	10574	10553	9803	8785	8230	7981	6476	5338	4415	3919
19 NORWAY	24813	24877	23353	23812	25196	25536	23642	22200	23269	21970	14563	11436	9122	7870	5909
20 POLAND	-	-	-	-	-	-	-	-	-	-	.	10823	12094	10879	8734
21 PORTUGAL	.	.	.	.	.	.	.	.	.	.	10317	9913	10588	10907	10398
22 ROMANIA	-	-	-	-	-	-	-	-	-	-	-	11880	11934	9161	7759
23 SPAIN	.	.	.	.	.	.	11488	10019	.	.	9634	9831	10312	9351	8472
24 SWEDEN	-	-	.	.	.	.	.	.	.	.	12146	9850	7620	6222	5435
25 SWITZERLAND	28246	28246	26445	26445	24550	24511	22616	20727	19185	16725	15364	12384	10006	8102	6430
26 TURKEY	-	-	-	-	-	-	-	-	-	-	-	8736	7380	6605	5431
27 UK ENGLAND AND WALES	.	.	.	.	.	.	.	11929	10323	10089	9268	8284	7281	6477	5649
28 UK NORTHERN IRELAND	-	-	-	-	.	.	.	.	.	13885	11003	11017	8241	6988	6670
29 UK SCOTLAND	.	.	.	.	.	.	.	.	.	13178	11853	10516	8861	7341	6589
30 USA	.	.	.	.	.	13205	11383	9671	7925	6520	4936	3970	3188	2565	2113
31 YUGOSLAVIA	-	-	-	-	-	-	-	-	-	-	.	.	6895	6767	6509

- NO MORTALITY DATA ARE AVAILABLE FOR EVEN A BROADER GROUP OF CAUSES FOR THIS DISEASE

. MORTALITY DATA ARE PRESENTED FOR A BROADER GROUP OF CAUSES FOR THIS DISEASE

0 VALUE<0.5

THE STANDARD MORTALITY RATIOS WERE DERIVED WITH A FACTOR OF 10000

SERIAL MORTALITY TABLES FOR VARIOUS COUNTRIES 1901-1975

TABLE 45 : MALIGNANT NEOPLASM - BUCCAL CAVITY, PHARYNX, OESOPHAGUS AND STOMACH : MALES

	1901-	1906-	1911-	1916-	1921-	1926-	1931-	1936-	1941-	1946-	1951-	1956-	1961-	1966-	1971-75
1 AUSTRALIA	-	27058	26520	26833	28228	26829	22930	20340	17785	16167	13879	11563	10146	9766	9430
2 AUSTRIA	.	.	.	.	-	-	-	-	-	.	24805	23654	22027	20350	17710
3 BELGIUM	.	.	.	.	.	.	.	.	.	.	17739	16756	15519	13742	12047
4 BULGARIA	-	-	-	-	-	.	.	.	.	.	.	.	19956	17061	14685
5 CANADA	-	-	-	-	22616	22775	19753	18580	17428	15577	14113	12500	11212	10181	9312
6 CHILE	-	18766	13459	16939	16669	24484	.	27804	34038	34682	40090	36338	33277	32034	30259
7 CZECHOSLOVAKIA	-	-	-	29046	31957	37171	34676	32525	.	.	24003	22562	21904	19721	17348
8 DENMARK	.	.	.	.	.	.	.	.	.	.	17147	14855	12529	10237	9171
9 EIRE	-	-	-	-	.	.	.	.	.	.	17489	16002	15181	14034	13036
10 FINLAND	-	-	-	-	-	.	.	.	35572	37048	34726	27717	22494	18013	14442
11 FRANCE	-	-	-	-	.	.	.	.	.	20228	19444	19746	19939	19154	18367
12 GREECE	-	-	-	-	.	8765	9326	.	-	-	-	7068	8252	7820	7306
13 HUNGARY	-	-	-	.	.	.	27165	24934	24534	.	24082	23899	22096	21060	19678
14 ICELAND	-	-	.	.	.	.	.	.	.	.	.	.	25023	19692	17166
15 ITALY	.	.	.	.	.	.	17645	18540	17650	18399	19510	19204	19171	18385	16730
16 JAPAN	.	23963	33031	34370	37478	39321	35610	33383	-	34279	35113	35765	34695	33372	29904
17 NETHERLANDS	40876	35666	40774	39817	38394	37576	30838	28801	25526	22810	19137	16579	15086	13382	11966
18 NEW ZEALAND	-	22034	26339	24238	24383	24378	21317	18238	17062	15318	13394	11911	10508	10074	9530
19 NORWAY	.	.	.	.	.	25155	31518	29058	27683	27214	20779	16701	14459	13085	10859
20 POLAND	-	-	-	-	-	-	-	-	-	-	.	19973	23481	22188	20119
21 PORTUGAL	.	.	.	.	.	.	.	.	.	.	17120	17247	18803	19490	19861
22 ROMANIA	-	-	-	-	-	-	-	-	-	-	-	17313	18827	16445	14908
23 SPAIN	10040	11697	13457	15646	16909	19594	15714	14661	.	.	14144	15081	16366	15489	15007
24 SWEDEN	-	-	.	.	.	.	.	.	.	.	15838	14534	12718	10479	9864
25 SWITZERLAND	45168	45168	43311	43311	44819	43114	40383	38460	33536	30244	26333	22728	20141	16790	15091
26 TURKEY	-	-	-	-	-	-	-	-	-	-	-	12171	10190	8472	7034
27 UK ENGLAND AND WALES	.	.	28881	28647	29411	28878	.	22548	19782	18146	16839	15306	14005	13156	12287
28 UK NORTHERN IRELAND	-	-	-	-	23403	24825	.	.	.	20262	16059	16187	13484	13010	11661
29 UK SCOTLAND	.	.	.	.	28748	30000	.	.	.	20237	18758	17018	15378	14208	12979
30 USA	.	27129	21828	20903	22121	20578	16560	15419	13924	12704	10631	9413	8315	7478	6905
31 YUGOSLAVIA	-	-	-	-	-	-	-	-	-	-	.	.	11478	12014	12619

- NO MORTALITY DATA ARE AVAILABLE FOR EVEN A BROADER GROUP OF CAUSES FOR THIS DISEASE

. MORTALITY DATA ARE PRESENTED FOR A BROADER GROUP OF CAUSES FOR THIS DISEASE

0 VALUE<0.5

THE STANDARD MORTALITY RATIOS WERE DERIVED WITH A FACTOR OF 10000

SERIAL MORTALITY TABLES FOR VARIOUS COUNTRIES 1901-1975

TABLE 45 : MALIGNANT NEOPLASM - BUCCAL CAVITY, PHARYNX, OESOPHAGUS AND STOMACH : FEMALES

	1901-	1906-	1911-	1916-	1921-	1926-	1931-	1936-	1941-	1946-	1951-	1956-	1961-	1966-	1971-75
1 AUSTRALIA	-	16453	16065	16044	15681	14420	9825	9351	8864	7778	6845	5694	5045	4737	4310
2 AUSTRIA	.	.	.	.	-	-	-	-	-	.	13539	12677	11673	10395	8309
3 BELGIUM	.	.	.	.	.	.	.	.	.	.	10261	9410	8435	6834	5718
4 BULGARIA	-	-	-	-	-	.	.	.	.	.	.	.	12614	9925	8153
5 CANADA	-	-	-	-	16363	15967	10895	9688	8611	7617	6726	5817	4841	4274	3856
6 CHILE	-	17165	12404	16932	16515	22671	.	22980	23948	23477	25649	22107	20385	18127	15601
7 CZECHOSLOVAKIA	-	-	-	20106	20579	24956	20411	18424	.	.	12558	11532	10704	9540	8010
8 DENMARK	.	.	.	.	.	.	.	.	.	.	10964	9070	7609	5646	4792
9 EIRE	-	-	-	-	.	.	.	.	.	.	10690	10191	9291	9384	8445
10 FINLAND	-	-	-	-	-	.	.	.	22714	22418	20312	16129	12416	9648	7760
11 FRANCE	-	-	-	-	.	.	.	.	.	8152	7638	7077	6296	5381	4542
12 GREECE	-	-	-	-	.	5961	6074	.	-	-	-	4117	4794	4197	3860
13 HUNGARY	-	-	-	.	.	.	18489	15805	14655	.	13314	12400	10937	10026	8733
14 ICELAND	-	-	.	.	.	.	.	.	.	.	.	.	12656	9091	7683
15 ITALY	.	.	.	.	.	.	10187	10544	9791	9765	10052	9282	8743	7951	6936
16 JAPAN	.	16672	17905	18789	19665	20189	17899	16443	-	17103	17269	17517	16890	16116	14231
17 NETHERLANDS	26526	26366	27545	27674	27558	27372	18517	17874	16339	14191	11768	9458	7969	7017	5647
18 NEW ZEALAND	-	15234	18615	16328	13747	13128	9865	9206	8386	7621	7688	6236	5430	4667	4371
19 NORWAY	.	.	.	.	.	16871	19823	18481	18970	17952	12023	9560	7770	6846	5247
20 POLAND	-	-	-	-	-	-	-	-	-	-	.	9021	10085	9094	7438
21 PORTUGAL	.	.	.	.	.	.	.	.	.	.	8909	8564	9208	9527	9062
22 ROMANIA	-	-	-	-	-	-	-	-	-	-	-	9453	9565	7485	6422
23 SPAIN	6333	7373	8509	10018	10575	12261	9230	8146	.	.	7737	7960	8504	7779	7098
24 SWEDEN	-	-	.	.	.	.	.	.	.	.	10516	8675	6876	5670	5070
25 SWITZERLAND	23131	23131	21605	21605	20354	20269	18572	17169	15905	13996	12811	10330	8527	6978	5709
26 TURKEY	-	-	-	-	-	-	-	-	-	-	-	7012	5912	5278	4327
27 UK ENGLAND AND WALES	.	.	17452	16344	16063	15697	.	10867	9463	9235	8659	7887	7115	6546	5934
28 UK NORTHERN IRELAND	-	-	-	-	16926	17031	.	.	.	13254	10520	10176	8346	7339	6663
29 UK SCOTLAND	.	.	.	.	19284	19787	.	.	.	12437	11282	10040	8760	7625	7035
30 USA	.	24652	19589	18193	17655	15290	9676	8336	6965	5871	4588	3875	3305	2900	2619
31 YUGOSLAVIA	-	-	-	-	-	-	-	-	-	-	.	.	5646	5561	5423

- NO MORTALITY DATA ARE AVAILABLE FOR EVEN A BROADER GROUP OF CAUSES FOR THIS DISEASE

. MORTALITY DATA ARE PRESENTED FOR A BROADER GROUP OF CAUSES FOR THIS DISEASE

0 VALUE<0.5

THE STANDARD MORTALITY RATIOS WERE DERIVED WITH A FACTOR OF 10000

SERIAL MORTALITY TABLES FOR VARIOUS COUNTRIES 1901-1975

TABLE 46 : MALIGNANT NEOPLASM - INTESTINE EXCLUDING RECTUM : MALES

	1901-	1906-	1911-	1916-	1921-	1926-	1931-	1936-	1941-	1946-	1951-	1956-	1961-	1966-	1971-75
1 AUSTRALIA	-	.	.	.	.	.	.	.	11318	10990	10492	10150	9879	10371	11304
2 AUSTRIA	.	.	.	.	-	-	-	-	-	.	9184	7940	8021	9754	10768
3 BELGIUM	.	.	.	.	.	.	.	.	.	.	8840	9602	9970	10416	10575
4 BULGARIA	-	-	-	-	-	.	.	.	.	.	.	.	2594	2769	3170
5 CANADA	-	-	-	-	.	.	.	.	11616	11275	10837	10958	10798	11605	11685
6 CHILE	-	.	.	.	.	.	.	2231	2019	1918	1861	2692	2756	3341	3723
7 CZECHOSLOVAKIA	-	-	-	.	.	.	.	.	.	.	5598	5050	5578	6768	7964
8 DENMARK	.	.	.	.	.	.	.	.	.	.	10045	10203	10958	9567	9772
9 EIRE	-	-	-	-	.	.	.	.	.	.	10466	9646	9603	10416	11864
10 FINLAND	-	-	-	-	-	.	.	.	4128	4743	4102	3944	4220	4703	4511
11 FRANCE	-	-	-	-	.	.	.	.	.	9080	8670	9189	9447	9918	10459
12 GREECE	-	-	-	-	.	.	.	.	-	-	-	2920	3495	3509	4124
13 HUNGARY	-	-	-	.	.	.	.	.	.	.	4496	5253	5617	6884	8781
14 ICELAND	-	-	.	.	.	.	.	.	.	.	.	.	6383	5718	8410
15 ITALY	.	.	.	.	.	.	.	.	3642	3918	4310	5388	6356	7511	8474
16 JAPAN	.	.	.	.	.	.	.	.	-	2084	2009	2252	2580	3097	3830
17 NETHERLANDS	.	.	.	.	.	8149	.	.	9541	8209	7322	7607	8313	8918	9403
18 NEW ZEALAND	-	.	.	.	.	.	.	.	11939	11457	10512	9603	10150	11552	13053
19 NORWAY	.	.	.	.	.	3096	4809	6230	.	.	6501	5905	6452	7405	7290
20 POLAND	-	-	-	-	-	-	-	-	-	-	.	2223	3120	3792	4165
21 PORTUGAL	.	.	.	.	.	.	.	.	.	.	4946	5089	5773	6752	6530
22 ROMANIA	-	-	-	-	-	-	-	-	-	-	-	2593	3079	2823	2790
23 SPAIN	.	.	.	.	.	.	.	.	.	.	3306	4035	4960	4874	5415
24 SWEDEN	-	-	.	.	.	.	.	.	.	.	7668	7583	7860	8302	9513
25 SWITZERLAND	5490	5490	7457	7457	7963	8193	8458	9557	9527	8519	9134	8913	9162	9463	10272
26 TURKEY	-	-	-	-	-	-	-	-	-	-	-	3727	2892	2389	2445
27 UK ENGLAND AND WALES	.	.	.	.	.	.	.	16272	15144	13907	11941	10235	9605	9946	10007
28 UK NORTHERN IRELAND	-	-	-	-	.	.	.	.	.	15692	10801	10633	9530	10604	12057
29 UK SCOTLAND	.	.	.	.	.	.	.	.	.	17326	16109	13357	12930	12205	12077
30 USA	.	.	.	.	.	.	.	10259	10500	10294	9968	10201	10510	10916	11482
31 YUGOSLAVIA	-	-	-	-	-	-	-	-	-	-	.	.	1729	2360	3112

- NO MORTALITY DATA ARE AVAILABLE FOR EVEN A BROADER GROUP OF CAUSES FOR THIS DISEASE

. MORTALITY DATA ARE PRESENTED FOR A BROADER GROUP OF CAUSES FOR THIS DISEASE

0 VALUE<0.5

THE STANDARD MCRTALITY RATIOS WERE DERIVED WITH A FACTOR OF 10000

SERIAL MORTALITY TABLES FOR VARIOUS COUNTRIES 1901-1975

TABLE 46 : MALIGNANT NEOPLASM - INTESTINE EXCLUDING RECTUM : FEMALES

	1901-	1906-	1911-	1916-	1921-	1926-	1931-	1936-	1941-	1946-	1951-	1956-	1961-	1966-	1971-75
1 AUSTRALIA	-	.	.	.	.	.	.	.	12622	12109	11291	10759	10391	10494	10608
2 AUSTRIA	.	.	.	.	-	-	-	-	-	.	7868	6963	7076	7813	8670
3 BELGIUM	.	.	.	.	.	.	.	.	.	.	9617	10316	10370	10404	10083
4 BULGARIA	-	-	-	-	-	.	.	.	.	.	.	.	2182	2510	2850
5 CANADA	-	-	-	-	.	.	.	.	14229	13913	12926	12656	11840	11570	11174
6 CHILE	-	.	.	.	.	.	.	2882	2779	2662	3164	3443	3328	4119	4173
7 CZECHOSLOVAKIA	-	-	-	.	.	.	.	.	.	.	4898	4129	4234	4897	5588
8 DENMARK	.	.	.	.	.	.	.	.	.	.	10666	11103	10881	10153	9479
9 EIRE	-	-	-	-	.	.	.	.	.	.	10138	9854	10020	11449	11704
10 FINLAND	-	-	-	-	-	.	.	.	4188	5467	4207	4302	4595	4577	4833
11 FRANCE	-	-	-	-	.	.	.	.	.	10033	9261	9159	8769	8464	8263
12 GREECE	-	-	-	-	.	.	.	.	-	-	-	2907	3546	3547	3905
13 HUNGARY	-	-	-	.	.	.	.	.	.	.	5002	5569	5975	6918	7944
14 ICELAND	-	-	.	.	.	.	.	.	.	.	.	.	6844	7107	8603
15 ITALY	.	.	.	.	.	.	.	.	3766	3921	4369	5150	5691	6184	6857
16 JAPAN	.	.	.	.	.	.	.	.	-	2254	2007	2172	2417	2835	3274
17 NETHERLANDS	.	.	.	.	.	11236	.	.	12191	9734	8788	8955	9165	9768	9488
18 NEW ZEALAND	-	.	.	.	.	.	.	.	13605	13494	12138	10846	10920	11393	12116
19 NORWAY	.	.	.	.	.	2935	5239	5533	.	.	6168	5920	6232	6844	6860
20 POLAND	-	-	-	-	-	-	-	-	-	-	.	1962	2645	3241	3295
21 PORTUGAL	.	.	.	.	.	.	.	.	.	.	5946	5761	6433	6796	6435
22 ROMANIA	-	-	-	-	-	-	-	-	-	-	-	2475	3242	2596	2686
23 SPAIN	.	.	.	.	.	.	.	.	.	.	3893	4627	5539	5388	5442
24 SWEDEN	-	-	.	.	.	.	.	.	.	.	6863	7504	7334	7243	7896
25 SWITZERLAND	6361	6361	8020	8020	7578	8267	8062	8301	8850	7654	7585	7543	7264	7273	7196
26 TURKEY	-	-	-	-	-	-	-	-	-	-	-	3287	2736	2085	2189
27 UK ENGLAND AND WALES	.	.	.	.	.	.	.	15265	13879	13198	11283	10174	9436	9269	9206
28 UK NORTHERN IRELAND	-	-	-	-	.	.	.	.	.	12768	11181	10772	9234	11134	11667
29 UK SCOTLAND	.	.	.	.	.	.	.	.	.	16676	14897	13095	12160	11919	11301
30 USA	.	.	.	.	.	.	.	11850	11806	11389	10669	10290	10106	9833	9563
31 YUGOSLAVIA	-	-	-	-	-	-	-	-	-	-	.	.	1438	2159	2681

- NO MORTALITY DATA ARE AVAILABLE FOR EVEN A BROADER GROUP OF CAUSES FOR THIS DISEASE

. MORTALITY DATA ARE PRESENTED FOR A BROADER GROUP OF CAUSES FOR THIS DISEASE

0 VALUE<0.5

THE STANDARD MORTALITY RATIOS WERE DERIVED WITH A FACTOR OF 10000

SERIAL MORTALITY TABLES FOR VARIOUS COUNTRIES 1901-1975

TABLE 47 : MALIGNANT NEOPLASM - RECTUM : MALES

	1901-	1906-	1911-	1916-	1921-	1926-	1931-	1936-	1941-	1946-	1951-	1956-	1961-	1966-	1971-75
1 AUSTRALIA	-	.	.	.	.	.	8114	9275	9135	9163	8810	8719	7816	7903	8576
2 AUSTRIA	.	.	.	.	-	-	-	-	-	.	12946	11907	11904	12817	13967
3 BELGIUM	.	.	.	.	.	.	.	.	.	.	14038	13213	13207	12344	11205
4 BULGARIA	-	-	-	-	-	.	.	.	.	.	.	.	5084	5772	6808
5 CANADA	-	-	-	-	.	.	8017	9682	10336	10469	10037	9994	9352	9697	8854
6 CHILE	-		.	.	.	.	.	2293	2262	2142	2825	3682	3138	3402	3646
7 CZECHOSLOVAKIA	-	-	-	.	.	.	10347	10989	.	.	11205	11482	12168	14946	16389
8 DENMARK	.	.	.	.	.	.	.	.	.	.	17476	17319	15986	14413	14452
9 EIRE	-	-	-	-	.	.	.	.	.	.	12121	10907	9996	10083	11169
10 FINLAND	-	-	-	-	-	.	.	.	4946	5866	6288	5997	6918	6763	7803
11 FRANCE	-	-	-	-	.	.	.	.	.	9831	9443	9544	9740	9756	9778
12 GREECE	-	-	-	-	.	.	.	.	-	-	-	627	892	982	958
13 HUNGARY	-	-	-	.	.	.	4262	4956	5271	.	7431	7961	8988	10446	11889
14 ICELAND	-	-	.	.	.	.	.	.	.	.	.	.	3390	7868	5011
15 ITALY	.	.	.	.	.	.	3336	3874	4298	4637	5145	5883	6854	7864	8501
16 JAPAN	.	.	.	.	.	.	4870	5200	-	6147	6043	6132	6498	7138	7873
17 NETHERLANDS	.	.	.	.	.	9968	11509	13339	14495	12761	10542	9803	9492	9590	9798
18 NEW ZEALAND	-	.	.	.	.	9782	12041	12788	13584	10272	10009	10705	10963	10657	12614
19 NORWAY	.	.	.	.	.	4572	7068	6962	.	.	6695	6519	7212	7444	9672
20 POLAND	-	-	-	-	-	-	-	-	-	-	.	3087	4196	5275	7165
21 PORTUGAL	.	.	.	.	.	.	.	.	.	.	5013	4860	5147	5866	8246
22 ROMANIA	-	-	-	-	-	-	-	-	-	-	-	2797	3642	3932	4483
23 SPAIN	.	.	.	.	.	.	2452	2551	.	.	2763	3477	4093	4360	5422
24 SWEDEN	-	-	.	.	.	.	.	.	.	.	8775	9155	9103	8466	9274
25 SWITZERLAND	9848	9848	11860	11860	12989	12872	14315	14490	15189	13933	13204	11612	10881	11332	10396
26 TURKEY	-	-	-	-	-	-	-	-	-	-	-	614	1856	2280	1176
27 UK ENGLAND AND WALES	.	.	.	.	.	.	.	22017	21337	19489	16376	14307	12929	12833	12392
28 UK NORTHERN IRELAND	-	-	-	-	.	.	.	.	.	15998	12948	12189	10676	11306	10454
29 UK SCOTLAND	.	.	.	.	.	.	.	.	.	16470	15217	14155	13183	12812	12276
30 USA	.	.	.	.	.	8054	8511	10027	10130	10251	9141	8406	7527	6936	6109
31 YUGOSLAVIA	-	-	-	-	-	-	-	-	-	-	.	.	4188	5220	6349

- NO MORTALITY DATA ARE AVAILABLE FOR EVEN A BROADER GROUP OF CAUSES FOR THIS DISEASE

. MORTALITY DATA ARE PRESENTED FOR A BROADER GROUP OF CAUSES FOR THIS DISEASE

0 VALUE<0.5

THE STANDARD MORTALITY RATIOS WERE DERIVED WITH A FACTOR OF 10000

SERIAL MORTALITY TABLES FOR VARIOUS COUNTRIES 1901-1975

TABLE 47 : MALIGNANT NEOPLASM - RECTUM : FEMALES

	1901-	1906-	1911-	1916-	1921-	1926-	1931-	1936-	1941-	1946-	1951-	1956-	1961-	1966-	1971-75
1 AUSTRALIA	-	.	.	.	.	.	5587	6532	6702	6101	5227	5336	4794	5068	5014
2 AUSTRIA	.	.	.	.	-	-	-	-	-	.	6863	6736	6978	7256	7604
3 BELGIUM	.	.	.	.	.	.	.	.	.	.	8648	7988	7899	7338	6658
4 BULGARIA	-	-	-	-	-	.	.	.	.	.	.	.	3634	4233	4711
5 CANADA	-	-	-	-	.	.	6586	6569	7036	6903	6382	6407	6032	5804	5060
6 CHILE	-	.	.	.	.	.	.	1388	2605	2662	3555	3160	3033	2974	3245
7 CZECHOSLOVAKIA	-	-	-	.	.	.	5157	5883	.	.	6198	6372	6757	8067	8989
8 DENMARK	.	.	.	.	.	.	.	.	.	.	9350	10113	8855	8497	8485
9 EIRE	-	-	-	-	.	.	.	.	.	.	5598	5830	4907	5712	6106
10 FINLAND	-	-	-	-	-	.	.	.	3970	4524	5154	4805	5753	5388	5610
11 FRANCE	-	-	-	-	.	.	.	.	.	5747	5227	5187	5093	4937	4747
12 GREECE	-	-	-	-	.	.	.	.	-	-	-	581	774	728	825
13 HUNGARY	-	-	-	.	.	.	2956	3598	3999	.	5409	5924	6392	6835	7395
14 ICELAND	-	-	.	.	.	.	.	.	.	.	.	.	3155	3254	3113
15 ITALY	.	.	.	.	.	.	2575	2931	3055	3102	3581	3948	4272	4595	4992
16 JAPAN	.	.	.	.	.	.	3645	3787	-	4378	4402	4599	4710	5135	5341
17 NETHERLANDS	.	.	.	.	.	7445	8628	9023	9924	8892	7115	6459	6182	6162	5720
18 NEW ZEALAND	-	.	.	.	.	10602	7870	8559	7938	7355	6786	6608	6695	6306	7994
19 NORWAY	.	.	.	.	.	3087	4207	4265	.	.	4171	3973	4273	5071	6039
20 POLAND	-	-	-	-	-	-	-	-	-	-	.	2107	3014	3690	4980
21 PORTUGAL	.	.	.	.	.	.	.	.	.	.	3684	3249	3613	4029	5248
22 ROMANIA	-	-	-	-	-	-	-	-	-	-	-	2317	3086	3129	3797
23 SPAIN	.	.	.	.	.	.	2149	2162	.	.	2229	2627	3207	3229	3735
24 SWEDEN	-	-	.	.	.	.	.	.	.	.	5286	4938	5312	5104	5559
25 SWITZERLAND	5958	5958	7114	7114	6719	6644	6509	6779	6971	6533	6383	5985	5119	5540	5408
26 TURKEY	-	-	-	-	-	-	-	-	-	-	-	576	1262	2051	995
27 UK ENGLAND AND WALES	.	.	.	.	.	.	.	10730	10180	9655	8374	7734	7354	7382	7053
28 UK NORTHERN IRELAND	-	-	-	-	.	.	.	.	.	8618	6555	6605	6900	6745	6333
29 UK SCOTLAND	.	.	.	.	.	.	.	.	.	8330	7504	7978	7392	7250	6893
30 USA	.	.	.	.	.	7163	7217	7869	7426	7140	6259	5525	4759	4174	3602
31 YUGOSLAVIA	-	-	-	-	-	-	-	-	-	-	.	.	3134	3770	4700

- NO MORTALITY DATA ARE AVAILABLE FOR EVEN A BROADER GROUP OF CAUSES FOR THIS DISEASE
. MORTALITY DATA ARE PRESENTED FOR A BROADER GROUP OF CAUSES FOR THIS DISEASE
0 VALUE<0.5
THE STANDARD MORTALITY RATIOS WERE DERIVED WITH A FACTOR OF 10000

SERIAL MORTALITY TABLES FOR VARIOUS COUNTRIES 1901-1975

TABLE 48 : MALIGNANT NEOPLASM - INTESTINE AND RECTUM : MALES

	1901-	1906-	1911-	1916-	1921-	1926-	1931-	1936-	1941-	1946-	1951-	1956-	1961-	1966-	1971-75
1 AUSTRALIA	-	5640	6612	7529	8827	9483	.	.	10515	10318	9873	9624	9121	9464	10301
2 AUSTRIA	.	.	.	.	-	-	-	-	-	.	10570	9400	9451	10882	11945
3 BELGIUM	.	.	.	.	.	.	.	.	.	.	10751	10929	11160	11124	10806
4 BULGARIA	-	-	-	-	-	.	.	.	.	.	.	.	3509	3874	4512
5 CANADA	-	-	-	-	7628	8322	.	.	11145	10978	10543	10605	10269	10907	10648
6 CHILE	-	2112	882	622	779	996	.	563	2108	2000	2215	3055	2897	3364	3695
7 CZECHOSLOVAKIA	-	-	-	5850	6351	7469	.	.	.	.	7660	7417	8009	9787	11073
8 DENMARK	.	.	.	.	.	.	.	.	.	.	12775	12815	12803	11346	11489
9 EIRE	-	-	-	-	7014	9423	.	.	.	.	11073	10109	9747	10294	11609
10 FINLAND	-	-	-	-	-	.	.	.	4429	5156	4908	4701	5215	5464	5727
11 FRANCE	-	-	-	-	.	.	.	.	.	9356	8954	9319	9555	9858	10209
12 GREECE	-	-	-	-	.	754	903	.	-	-	-	2080	2541	2581	2962
13 HUNGARY	-	-	-	.	.	.	1570	1824	5719	.	5577	6250	6859	8197	9926
14 ICELAND	-	-	.	.	.	.	.	.	.	.	.	.	5285	6506	7161
15 ITALY	.	.	.	.	.	.	.	.	3928	4182	4617	5570	6539	7641	8484
16 JAPAN	.	2372	2389	2570	2987	3127	3123	.	-	3585	3498	3683	4025	4586	5317
17 NETHERLANDS	6099	6816	7465	7824	8564	8818	.	.	11364	9885	8505	8413	8746	9164	9548
18 NEW ZEALAND	-	8016	7231	8819	10057	11010	.	.	12546	11021	10327	10007	10448	11223	12891
19 NORWAY	.	.	.	.	.	.	.	.	.	.	6572	6130	6730	7420	8167
20 POLAND	-	-	-	-	-	-	-	-	-	-	.	2542	3517	4340	5272
21 PORTUGAL	.	.	.	.	.	.	.	.	.	.	4971	5005	5542	6426	7163
22 ROMANIA	-	-	-	-	-	-	-	-	-	-	-	2668	3286	3232	3414
23 SPAIN	1254	1385	1960	2017	2217	2529	.	.	.	.	3106	3830	4641	4685	5418
24 SWEDEN	-	-	.	.	.	.	5798	6874	7676	7842	8075	8160	8316	8362	9425
25 SWITZERLAND	7096	7096	9079	9079	9815	9919	10619	11377	11614	10513	10632	9905	9794	10151	10318
26 TURKEY	-	-	-	-	-	-	-	-	-	-	-	2580	2510	2349	1978
27 UK ENGLAND AND WALES	.	.	13849	14487	16143	17491	.	18393	17430	15962	13572	11732	10828	11009	10885
28 UK NORTHERN IRELAND	-	-	-	-	9546	11506	.	.	.	15807	11589	11203	9951	10862	11468
29 UK SCOTLAND	.	.	.	.	17473	18055	.	.	.	17011	15781	13650	13023	12429	12150
30 USA	6293	5738	6167	6089	6913	7677	.	10411	10363	10278	9664	9541	9415	9457	9512
31 YUGOSLAVIA	-	-	-	-	-	-	-	-	-	-	.	.	2633	3413	4304

- NO MORTALITY DATA ARE AVAILABLE FOR EVEN A BROADER GROUP OF CAUSES FOR THIS DISEASE

. MORTALITY DATA ARE PRESENTED FOR A BROADER GROUP OF CAUSES FOR THIS DISEASE

0 VALUE<0.5

THE STANDARD MORTALITY RATIOS WERE DERIVED WITH A FACTOR OF 10000

SERIAL MORTALITY TABLES FOR VARIOUS COUNTRIES 1901-1975

TABLE 48 : MALIGNANT NEOPLASM - INTESTINE AND RECTUM : FEMALES

	1901-	1906-	1911-	1916-	1921-	1926-	1931-	1936-	1941-	1946-	1951-	1956-	1961-	1966-	1971-75
1 AUSTRALIA	-	6699	7682	8485	9376	9968	.	.	10447	9902	9066	8771	8342	8511	8564
2 AUSTRIA	.	.	.	.	-	-	-	-	-	.	7498	6880	7040	7609	8280
3 BELGIUM	.	.	.	.	.	.	.	.	.	.	9261	9462	9464	9281	8831
4 BULGARIA	-	-	-	-	-	.	.	.	.	.	.	.	2715	3142	3535
5 CANADA	-	-	-	-	8875	9500	.	.	11589	11340	10527	10369	9717	9464	8943
6 CHILE	-	1995	1232	848	1127	1548	.	584	2715	2662	3308	3339	3221	3700	3832
7 CZECHOSLOVAKIA	-	-	-	5834	5843	6049	.	.	.	.	5376	4954	5162	6062	6836
8 DENMARK	.	.	.	.	.	.	.	.	.	.	10183	10740	10137	9546	9116
9 EIRE	-	-	-	-	5529	6559	.	.	.	.	8475	8382	8152	9351	9658
10 FINLAND	-	-	-	-	-	.	.	.	4108	5121	4555	4487	5021	4875	5119
11 FRANCE	-	-	-	-	.	.	.	.	.	8459	7782	7706	7425	7178	6984
12 GREECE	-	-	-	-	.	792	1154	.	-	-	-	2055	2532	2515	2779
13 HUNGARY	-	-	-	.	.	.	1087	1323	5512	.	5152	5699	6128	6887	7742
14 ICELAND	-	-	.	.	.	.	.	.	.	.	.	.	5496	5701	6596
15 ITALY	.	.	.	.	.	.	.	.	3518	3620	4079	4709	5171	5602	6175
16 JAPAN	.	2048	2065	2326	2439	2768	2681	.	-	3035	2887	3062	3257	3679	4032
17 NETHERLANDS	7098	7268	8166	9402	9645	9844	.	.	11357	9424	8174	8039	8071	8448	8110
18 NEW ZEALAND	-	9490	9870	9457	10862	10841	.	.	11516	11234	10174	9295	9376	9534	10606
19 NORWAY	.	.	.	.	.	.	.	.	.	.	5437	5207	5515	6195	6558
20 POLAND	-	-	-	-	-	-	-	-	-	-	.	2015	2781	3407	3914
21 PORTUGAL	.	.	.	.	.	.	.	.	.	.	5116	4839	5400	5782	6000
22 ROMANIA	-	-	-	-	-	-	-	-	-	-	-	2417	3185	2792	3094
23 SPAIN	1479	1626	2375	2486	2427	2997	.	.	.	.	3283	3894	4684	4597	4817
24 SWEDEN	-	-	.	.	.	.	4566	5573	6046	6389	6285	6563	6593	6460	7042
25 SWITZERLAND	6213	6213	7687	7687	7261	7669	7490	7741	8159	7242	7144	6972	6477	6638	6542
26 TURKEY	-	-	-	-	-	-	-	-	-	-	-	2290	2195	2073	1751
27 UK ENGLAND AND WALES	.	.	12247	12718	13189	13888	.	13597	12519	11898	10216	9281	8675	8580	8420
28 UK NORTHERN IRELAND	-	-	-	-	7974	9437	.	.	.	11239	9486	9247	8379	9527	9715
29 UK SCOTLAND	.	.	.	.	15009	14773	.	.	.	13611	12184	11219	10412	10209	9688
30 USA	7901	8058	8476	8426	8788	9235	.	10548	10197	9829	9052	8544	8149	7765	7388
31 YUGOSLAVIA	-	-	-	-	-	-	-	-	-	-	.	.	2060	2751	3423

- NO MORTALITY DATA ARE AVAILABLE FOR EVEN A BROADER GROUP OF CAUSES FOR THIS DISEASE

. MORTALITY DATA ARE PRESENTED FOR A BROADER GROUP OF CAUSES FOR THIS DISEASE

0 VALUE<0.5

THE STANDARD MORTALITY RATIOS WERE DERIVED WITH A FACTOR OF 10000

SERIAL MORTALITY TABLES FOR VARIOUS COUNTRIES 1901-1975

TABLE 49 : MALIGNANT NEOPLASM - ALIMENTARY TRACT : MALES

	1901-	1906-	1911-	1916-	1921-	1926-	1931-	1936-	1941-	1946-	1951-	1956-	1961-	1966-	1971-75
1 AUSTRALIA	-	17130	17318	17936	19300	18843	19028	17905	16541	15643	12026	10666	9671	9626	9833
2 AUSTRIA	.	.	.	.	-	-	-	-	-	22518	19577	17062	16208	15965	15034
3 BELGIUM	.	.	.	.	.	.	.	.	.	.	14502	14054	13495	12527	11470
4 BULGARIA	-	-	-	-	-	.	.	.	.	.	.	.	12338	10960	9996
5 CANADA	-	-	-	-	15683	16096	17413	17510	17029	15521	12457	11619	10772	10519	9934
6 CHILE	-	10997	7595	9338	9276	13559	20613	16701	21557	22564	22581	20946	19233	18792	18027
7 CZECHOSLOVAKIA	-	-	-	18402	20196	23515	24791	23921	19595	21141	16447	15568	15506	15146	14455
8 DENMARK	.	.	.	.	.	.	.	.	.	.	15119	13907	12657	10752	10251
9 EIRE	-	-	-	-	14339	16218	17591	18336	18764	17306	14503	13254	12647	12292	12372
10 FINLAND	-	-	-	-	-	.	.	.	22577	24252	20998	17126	14551	12245	10438
11 FRANCE	-	-	-	-	.	.	.	.	16862	17835	14579	14908	15124	14840	14572
12 GREECE	-	-	-	-	.	5047	6211	7296	-	-	-	4748	5594	5385	5284
13 HUNGARY	-	-	-	.	.	.	15368	14266	15836	19292	17804	15756	15067	15123	15172
14 ICELAND	-	-	.	.	.	.	.	.	.	.	.	.	15848	13550	12490
15 ITALY	.	.	.	.	.	.	.	.	11163	11809	12605	12878	13305	13396	12903
16 JAPAN	.	16721	18908	19707	21625	22712	22819	23128	-	20219	20609	21020	20584	20101	18536
17 NETHERLANDS	24816	22368	25370	25016	24598	24284	23211	22765	18984	16837	14207	12785	12136	11417	10838
18 NEW ZEALAND	-	15553	17495	17090	17744	17180	19084	17699	14981	13333	11971	11024	10480	10608	11082
19 NORWAY	.	.	.	.	.	16075	20724	19644	18644	18638	14159	11775	10862	10449	9613
20 POLAND	-	-	-	-	-	-	-	-	-	-	.	11969	14319	13986	13280
21 PORTUGAL	.	.	.	.	.	.	.	.	.	.	11507	11592	12671	13457	14003
22 ROMANIA	-	-	-	-	-	-	-	-	-	-	-	10580	11678	10359	9603
23 SPAIN	5986	6951	8174	9390	10160	11742	11230	10649	9865	10589	9045	9880	10940	10485	10562
24 SWEDEN	-	-	.	.	.	.	.	.	.	.	12232	11571	10672	9494	9660
25 SWITZERLAND	27640	27640	27545	27545	28716	27863	26705	25999	23435	21136	19075	16792	15347	13712	12875
26 TURKEY	-	-	-	-	-	-	-	-	-	-	-	7773	6665	5655	4700
27 UK ENGLAND AND WALES	.	.	21962	22136	23316	23648	24256	23222	21225	19028	15326	13649	12534	12163	11638
28 UK NORTHERN IRELAND	-	-	-	-	17028	18698	19902	19359	20220	19674	13977	13865	11842	12013	11572
29 UK SCOTLAND	.	.	.	.	23568	24516	25302	24604	23739	21384	17379	15457	14288	13385	12596
30 USA	4486	6709	14589	14062	15103	15310	15725	15690	15161	13818	10183	9473	8827	8400	8119
31 YUGOSLAVIA	-	-	-	-	-	-	-	-	-	-	.	.	7389	8045	8779

- NO MORTALITY DATA ARE AVAILABLE FOR EVEN A BROADER GROUP OF CAUSES FOR THIS DISEASE

. MORTALITY DATA ARE PRESENTED FOR A BROADER GROUP OF CAUSES FOR THIS DISEASE

0 VALUE<0.5

THE STANDARD MORTALITY RATIOS WERE DERIVED WITH A FACTOR OF 10000

SERIAL MORTALITY TABLES FOR VARIOUS COUNTRIES 1901-1975

TABLE 49 : MALIGNANT NEOPLASM - ALIMENTARY TRACT : FEMALES

	1901-	1906-	1911-	1916-	1921-	1926-	1931-	1936-	1941-	1946-	1951-	1956-	1961-	1966-	1971-75
1 AUSTRALIA	-	11927	12181	12547	12767	12363	12201	12061	11601	10691	7878	7127	6585	6504	6305
2 AUSTRIA	.	.	.	.	-	-	-	-	-	14803	12199	9984	9515	9093	8295
3 BELGIUM	.	.	.	.	.	.	.	.	.	.	9796	9434	8915	7979	7179
4 BULGARIA	-	-	-	-	-	.	.	.	.	.	.	.	8009	6768	6012
5 CANADA	-	-	-	-	12885	12967	13614	13375	12845	11413	8497	7941	7123	6706	6246
6 CHILE	-	10049	7174	9420	9338	12826	18071	14248	17910	18581	15282	13360	12390	11416	10153
7 CZECHOSLOVAKIA	-	-	-	13536	13787	16230	16707	15648	13471	14060	9231	8485	8135	7924	7463
8 DENMARK	.	.	.	.	.	.	.	.	.	.	10601	9847	8787	7468	6819
9 EIRE	-	-	-	-	8839	10288	11163	12011	12754	11979	9656	9344	8757	9369	9013
10 FINLAND	-	-	-	-	-	.	.	.	15345	15867	13011	10734	8989	7436	6537
11 FRANCE	-	-	-	-	.	.	.	.	10967	10765	7705	7371	6826	6227	5697
12 GREECE	-	-	-	-	.	3553	4428	5150	-	-	-	3156	3737	3411	3353
13 HUNGARY	-	-	-	.	.	.	10448	9108	10424	13934	12207	9301	8709	8568	8272
14 ICELAND	-	-	.	.	.	.	.	.	.	.	.	.	9302	7501	7171
15 ITALY	.	.	.	.	.	.	.	.	6842	6913	7281	7156	7078	6853	6579
16 JAPAN	.	9915	10582	11177	11723	12168	12206	12344	-	10605	10610	10802	10553	10334	9485
17 NETHERLANDS	17523	17507	18551	19192	19248	19248	18986	18422	14032	11984	10099	8798	8017	7685	6801
18 NEW ZEALAND	-	12581	14567	13142	12408	11064	12443	12219	9831	9293	8845	7666	7279	6949	7282
19 NORWAY	.	.	.	.	.	11415	14073	13295	13896	13546	8942	7525	6716	6541	5858
20 POLAND	-	-	-	-	-	-	-	-	-	-	.	5783	6706	6457	5798
21 PORTUGAL	.	.	.	.	.	.	.	.	.	.	7145	6831	7432	7780	7635
22 ROMANIA	-	-	-	-	-	-	-	-	-	-	-	6204	6613	5309	4877
23 SPAIN	4094	4722	5678	6540	6809	7973	7909	7325	7208	7659	5664	6066	6723	6293	6033
24 SWEDEN	-	-	.	.	.	.	.	.	.	.	8546	7691	6744	6039	5995
25 SWITZERLAND	15341	15341	15181	15181	14309	14455	13455	12811	12319	10863	10178	8767	7571	6819	6100
26 TURKEY	-	-	-	-	-	-	-	-	-	-	-	4831	4191	3790	3130
27 UK ENGLAND AND WALES	.	.	15043	14667	14734	14860	14989	14393	12943	11976	9385	8539	7846	7500	7103
28 UK NORTHERN IRELAND	-	-	-	-	12786	13520	14446	14235	14714	13869	10038	9742	8362	8363	8092
29 UK SCOTLAND	.	.	.	.	17302	17466	17786	17240	15735	14718	11702	10589	9531	8833	8279
30 USA	4032	6623	14436	13665	13549	13285	12997	12291	11403	9796	6665	6052	5569	5181	4862
31 YUGOSLAVIA	-	-	-	-	-	-	-	-	-	-	.	.	3978	4255	4494

- NO MORTALITY DATA ARE AVAILABLE FOR EVEN A BROADER GROUP OF CAUSES FOR THIS DISEASE

. MORTALITY DATA ARE PRESENTED FOR A BROADER GROUP OF CAUSES FOR THIS DISEASE

0 VALUE<0.5

THE STANDARD MORTALITY RATIOS WERE DERIVED WITH A FACTOR OF 10000

SERIAL MORTALITY TABLES FOR VARIOUS COUNTRIES 1901-1975

TABLE 50 : MALIGNANT NEOPLASM - LARYNX : MALES

	1901-	1906-	1911-	1916-	1921-	1926-	1931-	1936-	1941-	1946-	1951-	1956-	1961-	1966-	1971-75
1 AUSTRALIA	-		.	.	.	.	.	.	.	.	1576	1690	1658	1874	2018
2 AUSTRIA	.	.	.	.	-	-	-	-	-	.	3174	3188	3593	3380	3105
3 BELGIUM	.	.	.	.	.	.	.	.	.	.	3106	3446	3954	4546	4217
4 BULGARIA	-	-	-	-	-	.	.	.	.	.	.	.	3834	3387	3880
5 CANADA	-	-	-	-	.	.	1193	1536	1552	1542	1543	1679	1638	1901	2111
6 CHILE	-	.	.	.	.	.	.	1207	1140	1110	1452	1503	1446	1699	2177
7 CZECHOSLOVAKIA	-	-	-	.	.	.	.	.	.	.	2305	2597	2811	3220	3713
8 DENMARK	.	.	.	.	.	.	.	.	.	.	919	1043	1066	1332	1533
9 EIRE	-	-	-	-	.	.	.	.	.	.	2674	2402	1985	2040	1959
10 FINLAND	-	-	-	-	-	.	.	.	3714	3269	2878	2668	3065	2788	2490
11 FRANCE	-	-	-	-	.	.	.	.	.	9024	8201	8447	9659	10080	10225
12 GREECE	-	-	-	-	.	.	.	.	-	-	-	3664	3867	3986	3902
13 HUNGARY	-	-	-	.	.	.	.	.	.	.	3958	3769	3819	4218	5188
14 ICELAND	-	-	.	.	.	.	.	.	.	.	.	.	980	357	1148
15 ITALY	.	.	.	.	.	.	.	.	.	.	3139	3842	4714	5565	6103
16 JAPAN	.	.	.	.	.	.	.	.	-	1942	1682	1508	1433	1447	1398
17 NETHERLANDS	.	.	.	.	.	2203	2230	1919	2058	1660	1478	1415	1550	1622	1849
18 NEW ZEALAND	-	.	.	.	.	.	.	.	2265	2037	1938	1465	1262	1503	1602
19 NORWAY	.	.	.	.	.	550	965	862	770	789	713	405	583	888	1019
20 POLAND	-	-	-	-	-	-	-	-	-	-	.	1482	2534	3244	3590
21 PORTUGAL	.	.	.	.	.	.	.	.	.	.	4169	4674	4934	5268	4811
22 ROMANIA	-	-	-	-	-	-	-	-	-	-	-	3527	4423	4413	4634
23 SPAIN	.	.	.	.	.	.	.	.	.	.	5375	5799	6277	6650	6834
24 SWEDEN	-	-	.	.	.	.	.	.	.	.	491	492	601	624	714
25 SWITZERLAND	6392	6392	8629	8629	5184	5053	4885	5205	4520	3688	3545	3100	3008	3099	3007
26 TURKEY	-	-	-	-	-	-	-	-	-	-	-	7137	7529	7114	6054
27 UK ENGLAND AND WALES	.	.	.	.	.	.	.	3760	3275	2954	2463	2126	1873	1715	1637
28 UK NORTHERN IRELAND	-	-	-	-	.	.	.	.	.	1571	1549	1620	1579	1456	1629
29 UK SCOTLAND	.	.	.	.	.	.	.	.	.	2586	2188	1973	1910	1803	1783
30 USA	.	.	.	.	.	.	.	1870	1867	1939	1883	1928	1972	2095	2091
31 YUGOSLAVIA	-	-	-	-	-	-	-	-	-	-	.	.	3164	4042	4655

- NO MORTALITY DATA ARE AVAILABLE FOR EVEN A BROADER GROUP OF CAUSES FOR THIS DISEASE
. MORTALITY DATA ARE PRESENTED FOR A BROADER GROUP OF CAUSES FOR THIS DISEASE
0 VALUE<0.5
THE STANDARD MORTALITY RATIOS WERE DERIVED WITH A FACTOR OF 1000

SERIAL MORTALITY TABLES FOR VARIOUS COUNTRIES 1901-1975

TABLE 50 : MALIGNANT NEOPLASM - LARYNX : FEMALES

	1901-	1906-	1911-	1916-	1921-	1926-	1931-	1936-	1941-	1946-	1951-	1956-	1961-	1966-	1971-75
1 AUSTRALIA	-	.	.	.	.	.	.	.	.	.	2856	1813	2010	2098	2186
2 AUSTRIA	.	.	.	.	-	-	-	-	-	.	2446	1789	2118	2112	1835
3 BELGIUM	.	.	.	.	.	.	.	.	.	.	2965	2853	3082	3547	2729
4 BULGARIA	-	-	-	-	-	.	.	.	.	.	.	.	3341	3995	3258
5 CANADA	-	-	-	-	.	.	3958	3723	4028	2934	2362	2848	2280	2151	2850
6 CHILE	-	.	.	.	.	.	.	2567	2755	2428	5005	3433	2300	3093	3593
7 CZECHOSLOVAKIA	-	-	-	.	.	.	.	.	.	.	2864	2387	1853	1853	1830
8 DENMARK	.	.	.	.	.	.	.	.	.	.	2034	1476	1888	1386	2532
9 EIRE	-	-	-	-	.	.	.	.	.	.	8829	9249	8630	7906	9310
10 FINLAND	-	-	-	-	-	.	.	.	7123	7354	3607	2688	1550	1232	1159
11 FRANCE	-	-	-	-	.	.	.	.	.	5637	4463	3410	3622	3326	3437
12 GREECE	-	-	-	-	.	.	.	.	-	-	-	4838	3893	4178	4318
13 HUNGARY	-	-	-	.	.	.	.	.	.	.	4702	4166	3857	4211	3671
14 ICELAND	-	-	.	.	.	.	.	.	.	.	.	.	3509	1587	4286
15 ITALY	.	.	.	.	.	.	.	.	.	.	2728	2794	2876	2709	3031
16 JAPAN	.	.	.	.	.	.	.	.	-	6285	4641	4196	3213	2829	2029
17 NETHERLANDS	.	.	.	.	.	5280	3853	5458	4368	3584	2514	2042	1629	1884	1692
18 NEW ZEALAND	-	.	.	.	.	.	.	.	5600	2821	3264	2116	836	1961	2174
19 NORWAY	.	.	.	.	.	2411	3945	3941	3273	2838	922	276	249	562	934
20 POLAND	-	-	-	-	-	-	-	-	-	-	.	2088	2881	3236	2547
21 PORTUGAL	.	.	.	.	.	.	.	.	.	.	3537	4059	3926	4159	4729
22 ROMANIA	-	-	-	-	-	-	-	-	-	-	-	6317	6600	4706	4635
23 SPAIN	.	.	.	.	.	.	.	.	.	.	3329	4143	3412	3945	3195
24 SWEDEN	-	-	.	.	.	.	.	.	.	.	1253	1164	456	646	683
25 SWITZERLAND	8424	8424	9444	9444	3483	3112	2377	3616	3141	2030	2064	1767	1171	1592	1034
26 TURKEY	-	-	-	-	-	-	-	-	-	-	-	20128	15333	15070	15140
27 UK ENGLAND AND WALES	.	.	.	.	.	.	.	8914	8138	7066	4639	3875	3256	2649	2651
28 UK NORTHERN IRELAND	-	-	-	-	.	.	.	.	.	7973	8317	7011	6014	4655	4885
29 UK SCOTLAND	.	.	.	.	.	.	.	.	.	6477	5081	4683	3531	3402	3456
30 USA	.	.	.	.	.	.	.	2442	2154	2161	1721	1820	1952	2123	2530
31 YUGOSLAVIA	-	-	-	-	-	-	-	-	-	-	.	.	3885	5036	4487

- NO MORTALITY DATA ARE AVAILABLE FOR EVEN A BROADER GROUP OF CAUSES FOR THIS DISEASE

. MORTALITY DATA ARE PRESENTED FOR A BROADER GROUP OF CAUSES FOR THIS DISEASE

0 VALUE<0.5

THE STANDARD MORTALITY RATIOS WERE DERIVED WITH A FACTOR OF 10000

SERIAL MORTALITY TABLES FOR VARIOUS COUNTRIES 1901-1975

TABLE 51 : MALIGNANT NEOPLASM - TRACHEA, BRONCHUS AND LUNG,NOT SPECIFIED AS SECONDARY : MALES

	1901-	1906-	1911-	1916-	1921-	1926-	1931-	1936-	1941-	1946-	1951-	1956-	1961-	1966-	1971-75
1 AUSTRALIA	-	.	.	.	.	.	2001	2435	.	.	5316	7260	9728	11940	13531
2 AUSTRIA	.	.	.	.	-	-	-	-	-	.	12106	14124	15317	16112	16388
3 BELGIUM	.	.	.	.	.	.	.	.	.	.	7991	9722	13301	16299	20419
4 BULGARIA	-	-	-	-	-	.	.	.	.	.	.	.	11168	10531	10666
5 CANADA	-	-	-	-	.	.	1231	1798	1532	2344	5280	6963	8872	11206	13450
6 CHILE	-	.	.	.	.	.	.	1236	1452	2156	4155	3875	4139	4884	5472
7 CZECHOSLOVAKIA	-	-	-	.	.	.	1710	2301	.	.	9578	12295	16099	18248	19406
8 DENMARK	.	.	.	.	.	.	.	.	.	.	5438	7645	10222	12043	14305
9 EIRE	-	-	-	-	.	.	.	.	.	.	4450	6504	8236	10873	12806
10 FINLAND	-	-	-	-	-	.	.	.	5065	8697	13086	15817	17818	19263	19287
11 FRANCE	-	-	-	-	.	.	.	.	.	3160	4161	5849	7502	8879	10342
12 GREECE	-	-	-	-	.	.	.	.	-	-	-	6362	8341	9741	11339
13 HUNGARY	-	-	-	.	.	.	.	.	.	4407	6279	7421	9576	11830	13647
14 ICELAND	-	-	.	.	.	.	.	.	.	.	.	.	3333	4486	4713
15 ITALY	.	.	.	.	.	.	.	.	1873	2968	3598	5537	7640	10174	12464
16 JAPAN	.	.	.	.	.	.	1116	1204	-	798	1242	2452	3461	4413	5427
17 NETHERLANDS	.	.	.	.	.	1205	2129	3296	4420	6031	8332	11066	14691	18330	21376
18 NEW ZEALAND	-	.	.	.	.	2768	2119	2501	2602	4314	6633	8496	10423	12758	13745
19 NORWAY	.	.	.	.	.	260	434	739	1157	1802	2282	3138	3949	5167	6109
20 POLAND	-	-	-	-	-	-	-	-	-	-	.	4814	7055	9835	12527
21 PORTUGAL	.	.	.	.	.	.	.	.	.	.	2357	2360	2952	3680	4314
22 ROMANIA	-	-	-	-	-	-	-	-	-	-	-	5867	7627	8054	8505
23 SPAIN	.	.	.	.	.	.	2602	2636	.	.	2878	4255	5355	6319	7852
24 SWEDEN	-	-	.	.	.	.	.	.	.	.	2858	3830	4800	5710	7233
25 SWITZERLAND	286	286	540	540	983	1746	2336	2982	3715	5158	7503	8803	10121	11965	13697
26 TURKEY	-	-	-	-	-	-	-	-	-	-	-	7160	7583	8125	8021
27 UK ENGLAND AND WALES	.	.	.	.	.	.	4185	5469	6256	9610	13943	17533	19982	21779	22458
28 UK NORTHERN IRELAND	-	-	-	-	.	.	.	3523	3512	5379	7229	10156	11712	14157	15756
29 UK SCOTLAND	.	.	.	.	.	.	3586	4640	6595	10011	13962	18265	21818	24095	25380
30 USA	.	.	.	.	.	.	.	2618	3336	4721	6526	8526	10580	13024	15030
31 YUGOSLAVIA	-	-	-	-	-	-	-	-	-	-	.	.	6070	7465	9153

- NO MORTALITY DATA ARE AVAILABLE FOR EVEN A BROADER GROUP OF CAUSES FOR THIS DISEASE

. MORTALITY DATA ARE PRESENTED FOR A BROADER GROUP OF CAUSES FOR THIS DISEASE

0 VALUE<0.5

THE STANDARD MORTALITY RATIOS WERE DERIVED WITH A FACTOR OF 10000

SERIAL MORTALITY TABLES FOR VARIOUS COUNTRIES 1901-1975

TABLE 51 : MALIGNANT NEOPLASM - TRACHEA, BRONCHUS AND LUNG,NOT SPECIFIED AS SECONDARY : FEMALES

	1901-	1906-	1911-	1916-	1921-	1926-	1931-	1936-	1941-	1946-	1951-	1956-	1961-	1966-	1971-75
1 AUSTRALIA	-	.	.	.	.	.	7210	7890	.	.	9400	9980	12100	15920	20620
2 AUSTRIA	.	.	.	.	-	-	-	-	-	.	15800	18020	17870	19120	21320
3 BELGIUM	.	.	.	.	.	.	.	.	.	.	11080	10850	13070	13570	16440
4 BULGARIA	-	-	-	-	-	.	.	.	.	.	.	.	22470	19270	18250
5 CANADA	-	-	-	-	.	.	6770	7760	6980	7280	10880	10800	13640	17720	24820
6 CHILE	-	.	.	.	.	.	.	7420	8140	10060	15790	13910	14900	16050	14990
7 CZECHOSLOVAKIA	-	-	-	.	.	.	5770	6720	.	.	15890	15970	16710	17450	16840
8 DENMARK	.	.	.	.	.	.	.	.	.	.	12450	14460	18730	23430	29490
9 EIRE	-	-	-	-	.	.	.	.	.	.	13630	16420	19490	26100	37820
10 FINLAND	-	-	-	-	-	.	.	.	6920	10170	13170	11180	11530	11800	12760
11 FRANCE	-	-	-	-	.	.	.	.	.	8980	9540	10220	11260	11450	11550
12 GREECE	-	-	-	-	.	.	.	.	-	-	-	14100	15630	17750	17900
13 HUNGARY	-	-	-	.	.	.	.	.	.	13340	15980	17480	21060	22080	25260
14 ICELAND	-	-	.	.	.	.	.	.	.	.	.	.	15390	23710	31140
15 ITALY	.	.	.	.	.	.	.	.	6150	7740	8540	10490	12440	13980	15450
16 JAPAN	.	.	.	.	.	.	4300	4490	-	2890	4760	9260	12820	15270	17040
17 NETHERLANDS	.	.	.	.	.	4630	6180	8390	10020	10010	9430	9510	10480	10890	12740
18 NEW ZEALAND	-	.	.	.	.	5210	8800	8370	6460	7210	9320	12640	14900	19760	29720
19 NORWAY	.	.	.	.	.	1420	3260	4790	7320	8350	7820	7670	7800	10160	12190
20 POLAND	-	-	-	-	-	-	-	-	-	-	.	9380	11930	14230	15970
21 PORTUGAL	.	.	.	.	.	.	.	.	.	.	6400	6640	7040	8090	9570
22 ROMANIA	-	-	-	-	-	-	-	-	-	-	-	13840	16030	15660	15830
23 SPAIN	.	.	.	.	.	.	4100	4790	.	.	7450	10060	10570	11830	12470
24 SWEDEN	-	-	.	.	.	.	.	.	.	.	10870	11790	12010	14020	17920
25 SWITZERLAND	1740	1740	2350	2350	3260	3410	4850	6260	6120	8080	9380	9480	9340	10120	12630
26 TURKEY	-	-	-	-	-	-	-	-	-	-	-	20360	20030	21060	26420
27 UK ENGLAND AND WALES	.	.	.	.	.	.	11480	13360	12460	16020	18570	21510	26900	33730	41210
28 UK NORTHERN IRELAND	-	-	-	-	.	.	.	16200	15670	16240	13140	18190	17230	23570	29440
29 UK SCOTLAND	.	.	.	.	.	.	16740	16670	20160	22200	21920	24540	29290	36640	46510
30 USA	.	.	.	.	.	.	.	9310	10790	12050	11890	13120	16300	23220	32710
31 YUGOSLAVIA	-	-	-	-	-	-	-	-	-	-	.	.	11110	13070	15200

- NO MORTALITY DATA ARE AVAILABLE FOR EVEN A BROADER GROUP OF CAUSES FOR THIS DISEASE

. MORTALITY DATA ARE PRESENTED FOR A BROADER GROUP OF CAUSES FOR THIS DISEASE

0 VALUE<0.5

THE STANDARD MORTALITY RATIOS WERE DERIVED WITH A FACTOR OF 100000

SERIAL MORTALITY TABLES FOR VARIOUS COUNTRIES 1901-1975

TABLE 52 : MALIGNANT NEOPLASM - LARYNX,TRACHEA,BRONCHUS AND LUNG : MALES

	1901-	1906-	1911-	1916-	1921-	1926-	1931-	1936-	1941-	1946-	1951-	1956-	1961-	1966-	1971-75
1 AUSTRALIA	-	.	.	.	.	.	1941	2361	2667	3941	5633	7554	9938	12148	13733
2 AUSTRIA	.	.	.	.	-	-	-	-	-	9315	12259	14671	15954	16665	16854
3 BELGIUM	.	.	.	.	.	.	.	.	.	.	8707	10493	14122	17215	21109
4 BULGARIA	-	-	-	-	-	.	.	.	.	.	.	.	11994	11240	11522
5 CANADA	-	-	-	-	.	.	1553	2207	2847	4099	5596	7272	9110	11451	13690
6 CHILE	-	.	.	.	.	.	1126	1544	1746	2421	4463	4206	4446	5246	5959
7 CZECHOSLOVAKIA	-	-	-	.	.	.	.	.	3574	5172	9986	12707	16458	18669	19949
8 DENMARK	.	.	.	.	.	.	.	.	.	.	5555	7732	10236	12083	14338
9 EIRE	-	-	-	-	.	.	1149	1421	1867	2876	5165	7067	8609	11178	13022
10 FINLAND	-	-	-	-	-	.	.	.	6022	9408	13550	16138	18197	19518	19456
11 FRANCE	-	-	-	-	.	.	.	.	3086	4714	6585	8291	10261	11752	13271
12 GREECE	-	-	-	-	.	.	1357	1646	-	-	-	7305	9288	10680	12215
13 HUNGARY	-	-	-	.	.	.	2088	2651	3136	.	7476	8336	10441	12756	14828
14 ICELAND	-	-	.	.	.	.	.	.	.	.	.	.	3538	4457	4929
15 ITALY	.	.	.	.	.	.	1170	1490	1801	2880	4458	6557	8866	11586	13977
16 JAPAN	.	.	.	.	.	.	1084	1169	-	1339	1698	2824	3783	4714	5687
17 NETHERLANDS	.	.	.	.	.	1835	2740	3779	4912	6353	8532	11163	14717	18263	21284
18 NEW ZEALAND	-	.	.	.	.	.	.	.	3207	4807	7032	8691	10492	12828	13815
19 NORWAY	.	.	.	.	.	427	728	989	1363	1994	2435	3167	4008	5285	6237
20 POLAND	-	-	-	-	-	-	-	-	-	-	.	5105	7587	10503	13232
21 PORTUGAL	.	.	.	.	.	.	.	.	.	.	3546	3700	4364	5171	5649
22 ROMANIA	-	-	-	-	-	-	-	-	-	-	-	6737	8714	9134	9656
23 SPAIN	.	.	.	.	.	.	2524	2557	2823	3539	4415	5888	7112	8171	9723
24 SWEDEN	-	-	.	.	.	.	.	.	.	.	2922	3865	4838	5727	7230
25 SWITZERLAND	2182	2182	3083	3083	2482	3181	3710	4445	5080	6276	8358	9485	10738	12556	14211
26 TURKEY	-	-	-	-	-	-	-	-	-	-	-	8991	9536	9979	9592
27 UK ENGLAND AND WALES	.	.	.	.	.	.	4061	5530	7059	10224	14273	17648	19943	21637	22269
28 UK NORTHERN IRELAND	-	-	-	-	.	.	1619	2447	.	6180	7492	10347	11840	14170	15773
29 UK SCOTLAND	.	.	.	.	.	.	.	.	.	11817	14207	18310	21735	23910	25148
30 USA	.	.	.	.	.	1567	1820	2711	3666	5167	6904	8861	10867	13274	15215
31 YUGOSLAVIA	-	-	-	-	-	-	-	-	-	-	.	.	6840	8456	10292

- NO MORTALITY DATA ARE AVAILABLE FOR EVEN A BROADER GROUP OF CAUSES FOR THIS DISEASE
. MORTALITY DATA ARE PRESENTED FOR A BROADER GROUP OF CAUSES FOR THIS DISEASE
0 VALUE<0.5
THE STANDARD MORTALITY RATIOS WERE DERIVED WITH A FACTOR OF 10000

SERIAL MORTALITY TABLES FOR VARIOUS COUNTRIES 1901-1975

TABLE 52 : MALIGNANT NEOPLASM - LARYNX,TRACHEA,BRONCHUS AND LUNG : FEMALES

	1901-	1906-	1911-	1916-	1921-	1926-	1931-	1936-	1941-	1946-	1951-	1956-	1961-	1966-	1971-75
1 AUSTRALIA	-	.	.	.	.	.	6990	7650	7840	9330	10000	10240	12360	16080	20660
2 AUSTRIA	.	.	.	.	-	-	-	-	-	13590	15450	18010	17970	19180	21220
3 BELGIUM	.	.	.	.	.	.	.	.	.	.	11680	11420	13650	14290	16810
4 BULGARIA	-	-	-	-	-	.	.	.	.	.	.	.	22810	19920	18700
5 CANADA	-	-	-	-	.	.	7780	8670	10420	10800	11280	11360	13930	17840	24940
6 CHILE	-	.	.	.	.	.	5680	7230	8720	10490	16830	14540	15150	16510	15630
7 CZECHOSLOVAKIA	-	-	-	.	.	.	.	.	14860	17480	16280	16210	16770	17480	16890
8 DENMARK	.	.	.	.	.	.	.	.	.	.	12700	14470	18730	23120	29350
9 EIRE	-	-	-	-	.	.	6220	7840	9540	11360	16070	18920	21700	27850	39660
10 FINLAND	-	-	-	-	-	.	.	.	8900	12120	13880	11660	11660	11820	12720
11 FRANCE	-	-	-	-	.	.	.	.	7020	9140	10680	11010	12090	12190	12340
12 GREECE	-	-	-	-	.	.	4290	6130	-	-	-	15180	16380	18520	18730
13 HUNGARY	-	-	-	.	.	.	8160	8990	10350	.	17230	18230	21610	22710	25630
14 ICELAND	-	-	.	.	.	.	.	.	.	.	.	.	16040	23450	31550
15 ITALY	.	.	.	.	.	.	4670	4910	5930	7510	9130	11040	12960	14400	15940
16 JAPAN	.	.	.	.	.	.	4170	4350	-	4720	6040	10270	13410	15670	17150
17 NETHERLANDS	.	.	.	.	.	6100	7170	9810	11090	10810	9920	9850	10660	11150	12880
18 NEW ZEALAND	-	.	.	.	.	.	.	.	7960	7860	10060	12920	14680	19760	29460
19 NORWAY	.	.	.	.	.	2160	4440	5920	8150	9000	7860	7510	7630	10010	12100
20 POLAND	-	-	-	-	-	-	-	-	-	-	.	9730	12440	14800	16270
21 PORTUGAL	.	.	.	.	.	.	.	.	.	.	7310	7710	8060	9160	10780
22 ROMANIA	-	-	-	-	-	-	-	-	-	-	-	15340	17560	16640	16790
23 SPAIN	.	.	.	.	.	.	3970	4640	5230	6730	8270	11050	11320	12720	13100
24 SWEDEN	-	-	.	.	.	.	.	.	.	.	10920	11790	11770	13770	17550
25 SWITZERLAND	4210	4210	5130	5130	4210	4250	5430	7170	7370	9060	9730	9740	9420	10310	12560
26 TURKEY	-	-	-	-	-	-	-	-	-	-	-	25770	24080	25050	30300
27 UK ENGLAND AND WALES	.	.	.	.	.	.	11130	13500	14610	17760	19470	22070	27090	33490	40710
28 UK NORTHERN IRELAND	-	-	-	-	.	.	10950	11960	.	12350	15400	19870	18620	24320	30080
29 UK SCOTLAND	.	.	.	.	.	.	.	.	.	25260	22840	25250	29480	36560	46110
30 USA	.	.	.	.	.	7110	7400	9200	10820	12340	12060	13280	16410	23150	32460
31 YUGOSLAVIA	-	-	-	-	-	-	-	-	-	-	.	.	11970	14230	16130

- NO MORTALITY DATA ARE AVAILABLE FOR EVEN A BROADER GROUP OF CAUSES FOR THIS DISEASE

. MORTALITY DATA ARE PRESENTED FOR A BROADER GROUP OF CAUSES FOR THIS DISEASE

0 VALUE<0.5

THE STANDARD MORTALITY RATIOS WERE DERIVED WITH A FACTOR OF 100000

SERIAL MORTALITY TABLES FOR VARIOUS COUNTRIES 1901-1975

TABLE 53 : MALIGNANT NEOPLASM - BREAST : FEMALES

	1901-	1906-	1911-	1916-	1921-	1926-	1931-	1936-	1941-	1946-	1951-	1956-	1961-	1966-	1971-75
1 AUSTRALIA	-	5835	6316	6269	.	7705	8269	8491	8934	8782	8263	7834	7863	7987	8221
2 AUSTRIA	.	.	.	.	-	-	-	-	-	5597	5921	6229	6660	7375	7911
3 BELGIUM	.	.	.	.	.	.	.	.	.	.	8077	8192	8569	8929	9487
4 BULGARIA	-	-	-	-	-	.	.	.	.	.	.	.	3664	3787	4562
5 CANADA	-	-	-	-	7719	7867	8739	9428	9449	9383	9187	9319	9556	9547	9613
6 CHILE	-	665	649	588	729	1325	1855	2010	2410	2327	3458	3830	3698	4591	4900
7 CZECHOSLOVAKIA	-	-	-	1994	2130	2690	3238	3509	3381	3776	4862	5304	5692	6180	6849
8 DENMARK	5980	6370	6501	7006	7052	7245	8102	8774	9050	9497	10030	9900	10190	10261	10688
9 EIRE	-	-	-	-	5219	6050	5841	6548	6825	7254	7283	8000	8202	8836	10002
10 FINLAND	-	-	-	-	-	.	.	.	3939	4188	4532	5397	5361	5889	6280
11 FRANCE	-	-	-	-	.	.	.	.	4267	4815	5696	6447	6736	7123	7351
12 GREECE	-	-	-	-	.	1248	1529	1598	-	-	-	1548	2749	3611	4305
13 HUNGARY	-	-	-	.	.	.	3175	3426	3397	3713	4318	4837	5462	6179	7373
14 ICELAND	-	-	.	.	.	.	.	.	.	.	.	.	9217	8024	7954
15 ITALY	.	.	.	.	.	.	4074	4415	4209	4696	5340	5753	6206	6765	7322
16 JAPAN	.	839	917	958	1019	1114	1223	1335	-	1681	1626	1549	1555	1666	1894
17 NETHERLANDS	3824	4382	4993	5323	6325	7988	8501	9527	9459	9554	9514	9645	10169	10908	11110
18 NEW ZEALAND	-	5115	5020	6311	7395	9207	9428	9271	10069	9492	9238	8589	9340	9644	9968
19 NORWAY	2633	2886	2899	3357	4063	4649	5283	5586	5658	5934	7114	6957	6998	7312	7363
20 POLAND	-	-	-	-	-	-	-	-	-	-	.	2222	3608	4508	4966
21 PORTUGAL	.	.	.	.	.	.	.	.	.	.	4337	4489	4864	4975	5581
22 ROMANIA	-	-	-	-	-	-	-	-	-	-	-	2474	3299	3707	4137
23 SPAIN	1420	1565	1890	1915	1909	2298	2244	2155	2230	2163	2355	2729	3652	3898	4632
24 SWEDEN	-	-	.	.	.	.	5009	5899	6264	6726	7387	7628	7956	7690	8451
25 SWITZERLAND	5796	5796	6692	6692	7165	7695	7843	8289	8594	8799	9071	8915	9113	9725	10127
26 TURKEY	-	-	-	-	-	-	-	-	-	-	-	1892	1697	1834	1602
27 UK ENGLAND AND WALES	.	.	8865	9084	9713	10126	10471	10386	9627	9688	9534	9516	9807	10174	10823
28 UK NORTHERN IRELAND	-	-	-	-	7088	7662	7760	7303	7567	8732	7441	7811	7979	9078	9407
29 UK SCOTLAND	.	.	.	.	8748	8836	9097	9411	9169	8792	9097	9467	9571	9980	10365
30 USA	8308	7671	8029	7540	7610	8104	8669	8907	8808	8838	8682	8642	8679	8860	8894
31 YUGOSLAVIA	-	-	-	-	-	-	-	-	-	-	.	.	2980	3539	4196

- NO MORTALITY DATA ARE AVAILABLE FOR EVEN A BROADER GROUP OF CAUSES FOR THIS DISEASE

. MORTALITY DATA ARE PRESENTED FOR A BROADER GROUP OF CAUSES FOR THIS DISEASE

0 VALUE<0.5

THE STANDARD MORTALITY RATIOS WERE DERIVED WITH A FACTOR OF 10000

SERIAL MORTALITY TABLES FOR VARIOUS COUNTRIES 1901-1975

TABLE 54 : MALIGNANT NEOPLASM - CERVIX UTERI : FEMALES

	1901-	1906-	1911-	1916-	1921-	1926-	1931-	1936-	1941-	1946-	1951-	1956-	1961-	1966-	1971-75
1 AUSTRALIA	-	.	.	.	.	.	.	.	.	.	8687	9090	8822	8145	7392
2 AUSTRIA	.	.	.	.	-	-	-	-	-	.	4056	5008	5622	6925	7462
3 BELGIUM	.	.	.	.	.	.	.	.	.	.	6863	6764	6214	5761	5018
4 BULGARIA	-	-	-	-	-	.	.	.	.	.	.	.	3762	3959	4359
5 CANADA	-	-	-	-	.	.	8201	10727	11170	11431	12372	11531	10092	9073	6902
6 CHILE	-	.	.	.	.	.	.	6371	6098	6496	14650	14491	16615	21671	24421
7 CZECHOSLOVAKIA	-	-	-	.	.	.	.	.	.	.	7387	9935	10636	8811	7893
8 DENMARK	.	.	.	.	.	.	.	.	.	.	11739	15835	15527	14770	12488
9 EIRE	-	-	-	-	.	.	.	.	.	.	2956	3415	3821	5739	5554
10 FINLAND	-	-	-	-	-	.	.	.	.	.	5449	7534	8187	7661	5782
11 FRANCE	-	-	-	-	.	.	.	.	.	2827	3288	4177	4149	4016	3692
12 GREECE	-	-	-	-	.	.	.	.	-	-	-	243	652	1059	1417
13 HUNGARY	-	-	-	.	.	.	.	.	.	.	2193	5068	7142	8896	9843
14 ICELAND	-	-	.	.	.	.	.	.	.	.	.	.	9434	13833	8777
15 ITALY	.	.	.	.	.	.	.	.	.	.	2047	2681	2647	2453	1939
16 JAPAN	.	.	.	.	.	.	.	.	-	2183	2364	4796	5344	4397	3519
17 NETHERLANDS	.	.	.	.	.	.	.	.	8008	8421	8987	9041	8644	8039	7257
18 NEW ZEALAND	-	.	.	.	.	.	.	.	11380	11152	10910	10644	9286	8599	8118
19 NORWAY	.	.	.	.	.	.	.	.	1572	2597	10105	9943	8380	8410	7983
20 POLAND	-	-	-	-	-	-	-	-	-	-	.	5109	9010	12399	13380
21 PORTUGAL	.	.	.	.	.	.	.	.	.	.	13261	14120	13542	14058	9959
22 ROMANIA	-	-	-	-	-	-	-	-	-	-	-	11284	11387	13311	14345
23 SPAIN	.	.	.	.	.	.	.	.	.	.	430	525	988	1240	1168
24 SWEDEN	-	-	.	.	.	.	.	.	.	.	4766	7035	8084	7795	6979
25 SWITZERLAND	.	.	.	.	.	.	.	.	.	.	7329	11393	9980	8612	8351
26 TURKEY	-	-	-	-	-	-	-	-	-	-	-	879	173	263	68
27 UK ENGLAND AND WALES	.	.	.	.	.	.	.	10122	9420	9736	11170	10872	10167	9551	8476
28 UK NORTHERN IRELAND	-	-	-	-	.	.	.	.	.	9548	8187	7001	7050	7347	6726
29 UK SCOTLAND	.	.	.	.	.	.	.	.	.	8976	9338	9518	9627	9561	8621
30 USA	.	.	.	.	.	.	.	.	.	15111	13667	12341	10852	8627	6806
31 YUGOSLAVIA	-	-	-	-	-	-	-	-	-	-	.	.	5320	8045	7096

- NO MORTALITY DATA ARE AVAILABLE FOR EVEN A BROADER GROUP OF CAUSES FOR THIS DISEASE

. MORTALITY DATA ARE PRESENTED FOR A BROADER GROUP OF CAUSES FOR THIS DISEASE

0 VALUE<0.5

THE STANDARD MORTALITY RATIOS WERE DERIVED WITH A FACTOR OF 10000

SERIAL MORTALITY TABLES FOR VARIOUS COUNTRIES 1901-1975

TABLE 55 : MALIGNANT NEOPLASM - UTERUS, OTHER AND UNSPECIFIED : FEMALES

	1901-	1906-	1911-	1916-	1921-	1926-	1931-	1936-	1941-	1946-	1951-	1956-	1961-	1966-	1971-75
1 AUSTRALIA	-	.	.	.	.	.	.	.	.	.	15273	12460	9599	8276	7927
2 AUSTRIA	.	.	.	.	-	-	-	-	-	.	49182	43642	36987	33365	26648
3 BELGIUM	.	.	.	.	.	.	.	.	.	.	29819	27175	24299	21534	17201
4 BULGARIA	-	-	-	-	-	.	.	.	.	.	.	.	13018	13070	12168
5 CANADA	-	-	-	-	.	.	39543	35412	29801	24770	17618	14759	12774	11287	9840
6 CHILE	-	.	.	.	.	.	.	56057	59494	59938	43975	34412	26192	20876	15985
7 CZECHOSLOVAKIA	-	-	-	.	.	.	.	.	.	.	34020	22638	17146	16808	17477
8 DENMARK	.	.	.	.	.	.	.	.	.	.	27085	21284	20267	14586	13381
9 EIRE	-	-	-	-	.	.	.	.	.	.	17613	16162	13824	11703	11462
10 FINLAND	-	-	-	-	-	.	.	.	.	.	25274	18405	14500	11818	10292
11 FRANCE	-	-	-	-	.	.	.	.	.	31004	28114	25668	23515	21022	19341
12 GREECE	-	-	-	-	.	.	.	.	-	-	-	15070	17053	13959	13213
13 HUNGARY	-	-	-	.	.	.	.	.	.	.	61047	51585	40340	30748	27796
14 ICELAND	-	-	.	.	.	.	.	.	.	.	.	.	20879	16337	12613
15 ITALY	.	.	.	.	.	.	.	.	.	.	33628	32371	30988	29061	26620
16 JAPAN	.	.	.	.	.	.	.	.	-	65975	56066	39768	30997	26272	21037
17 NETHERLANDS	.	.	.	.	.	.	.	.	21782	19350	14990	12320	12894	13201	10832
18 NEW ZEALAND	-	.	.	.	.	.	.	.	18028	15717	13594	10450	10485	9443	9543
19 NORWAY	.	.	.	.	.	.	.	.	26008	27096	10963	9132	8878	9656	8284
20 POLAND	-	-	-	-	-	-	-	-	-	-	.	23424	24534	20261	13633
21 PORTUGAL	.	.	.	.	.	.	.	.	.	.	15005	12881	12866	11619	14668
22 ROMANIA	-	-	-	-	-	-	-	-	-	-	-	39368	39550	27425	21116
23 SPAIN	.	.	.	.	.	.	.	.	.	.	22921	23945	25686	22375	22492
24 SWEDEN	-	-	.	.	.	.	.	.	.	.	20047	16453	13349	11707	12342
25 SWITZERLAND	.	.	.	.	.	.	.	.	.	.	22602	17115	17353	17801	15471
26 TURKEY	-	-	-	-	-	-	-	-	-	-	-	17639	18968	13106	11236
27 UK ENGLAND AND WALES	.	.	.	.	.	.	.	25494	23642	18329	11088	10366	9965	9510	9329
28 UK NORTHERN IRELAND	-	-	-	-	.	.	.	.	.	22807	16828	13621	11010	9192	10358
29 UK SCOTLAND	.	.	.	.	.	.	.	.	.	19791	18425	14135	11761	9656	8655
30 USA	.	.	.	.	.	.	.	.	.	26270	20171	15955	13564	11694	10564
31 YUGOSLAVIA	-	-	-	-	-	-	-	-	-	-	.	.	20278	15624	16837

- NO MORTALITY DATA ARE AVAILABLE FOR EVEN A BROADER GROUP OF CAUSES FOR THIS DISEASE

. MORTALITY DATA ARE PRESENTED FOR A BROADER GROUP OF CAUSES FOR THIS DISEASE

0 VALUE<0.5

THE STANDARD MORTALITY RATIOS WERE DERIVED WITH A FACTOR OF 10000

SERIAL MORTALITY TABLES FOR VARIOUS COUNTRIES 1901-1975

TABLE 56 : MALIGNANT NEOPLASM - UTERUS : FEMALES

	1901-	1906-	1911-	1916-	1921-	1926-	1931-	1936-	1941-	1946-	1951-	1956-	1961-	1966-	1971-75
1 AUSTRALIA	-	.	.	.	.	.	15748	15111	14567	13131	11033	10296	9102	8193	7588
2 AUSTRIA	.	.	.	.	-	-	-	-	-	25488	21123	19326	17516	17126	14929
3 BELGIUM	.	.	.	.	.	.	.	.	.	.	15265	14367	13056	11785	9692
4 BULGARIA	-	-	-	-	-	.	.	.	.	.	.	.	7039	7217	7168
5 CANADA	-	-	-	-	.	.	18770	19159	17602	16073	14211	12661	11037	9862	7969
6 CHILE	-	.	.	.	.	.	20780	20513	23437	23966	24303	21087	19831	21403	21537
7 CZECHOSLOVAKIA	-	-	-	.	.	.	19786	19783	17598	20468	16719	14487	13023	11800	11511
8 DENMARK	26478	27744	24730	27213	18665	18344	18357	18295	18262	17389	17197	17806	17273	14701	12828
9 EIRE	-	-	-	-	.	.	9355	9231	9730	9033	8360	8139	7558	7984	7799
10 FINLAND	-	-	-	-	-	.	.	.	.	.	12326	11354	10446	9179	7461
11 FRANCE	-	-	-	-	.	.	.	.	12673	12738	12563	12322	11577	10600	9775
12 GREECE	-	-	-	-	.	.	7053	7008	-	-	-	5485	6553	5754	5786
13 HUNGARY	-	-	-	.	.	.	26132	25000	24000	25054	22529	21646	19219	16978	16553
14 ICELAND	-	-	.	.	.	.	.	.	.	.	.	.	13600	14781	10201
15 ITALY	.	.	.	.	.	.	2067	2326	1969	2349	13227	13328	12967	12273	11140
16 JAPAN	.	.	.	.	.	.	27069	26226	-	23852	20629	16726	14125	11925	9613
17 NETHERLANDS	.	.	.	.	.	12881	12755	13085	12761	12205	11103	10215	10191	9948	8596
18 NEW ZEALAND	-	.	.	.	.	16415	14132	12710	13710	12780	11875	10574	9721	8908	8644
19 NORWAY	.	.	10497	10992	12825	12018	12008	10776	10315	11365	10414	9648	8565	8881	8099
20 POLAND	-	-	-	-	-	-	-	-	-	-	.	11448	14471	15223	13472
21 PORTUGAL	.	.	.	.	.	.	.	.	.	.	13878	13679	13298	13167	11697
22 ROMANIA	-	-	-	-	-	-	-	-	-	-	-	21094	21334	18341	16773
23 SPAIN	.	.	.	.	.	.	11300	10277	9550	8914	8371	8878	9882	8915	8990
24 SWEDEN	-	-	.	.	.	.	.	.	.	.	10265	10470	10039	9277	9051
25 SWITZERLAND	19338	19338	17521	17521	16509	14800	14314	14204	14250	13422	12802	13478	12711	12059	11047
26 TURKEY	-	-	-	-	-	-	-	-	-	-	-	6507	6580	4662	3864
27 UK ENGLAND AND WALES	.	.	.	.	.	.	16979	15701	14511	12851	11140	10684	10091	9535	8807
28 UK NORTHERN IRELAND	-	-	-	-	.	.	15311	15149	12997	13656	11323	9424	8517	8041	8104
29 UK SCOTLAND	.	.	.	.	.	.	15458	15721	14566	13054	12627	11211	10421	9597	8634
30 USA	.	.	.	.	.	28088	25974	24771	22517	20040	15967	13637	11836	9756	8212
31 YUGOSLAVIA	-	-	-	-	-	-	-	-	-	-	.	.	10606	10729	10537

- NO MORTALITY DATA ARE AVAILABLE FOR EVEN A BROADER GROUP OF CAUSES FOR THIS DISEASE

. MORTALITY DATA ARE PRESENTED FOR A BROADER GROUP OF CAUSES FOR THIS DISEASE

0 VALUE<0.5

THE STANDARD MORTALITY RATIOS WERE DERIVED WITH A FACTOR OF 10000

SERIAL MORTALITY TABLES FOR VARIOUS COUNTRIES 1901-1975

TABLE 57 : MALIGNANT NEOPLASM - FEMALE GENITAL ORGANS : FEMALES

	1901-	1906-	1911-	1916-	1921-	1926-	1931-	1936-	1941-	1946-	1951-	1956-	1961-	1966-	1971-75
1 AUSTRALIA	-	8591	8135	8129	8398	8394	8481	8365	8087	7798	.	.	.	.	.
2 AUSTRIA		.	.	.	-	-	-	-	-	12987	12159	.	.	.	.
3 BELGIUM	.	.	.	.	.	.	.	.	.	.	.	.	.	.	.
4 BULGARIA	-	-	-	-	-	.	.	.	.	.	.	.	.	.	.
5 CANADA	-	-	-	-	7950	8376	9205	9762	9371	8959	.	.	.	.	.
6 CHILE	-	5233	4098	3702	4057	5669	8524	8606	9759	10318	.	.	.	.	.
7 CZECHOSLOVAKIA	-	-	-	6621	7105	8519	9156	9451	8124	9511	.	.	.	.	.
8 DENMARK	.	.	.	.	.	.	.	.	.	.	.	.	.	.	.
9 EIRE	-	-	-	-	3768	4398	4510	4737	5049	5046	.	.	.	.	.
10 FINLAND	-	-	-	-	-	.	.	.	6389	6223	.	.	.	.	.
11 FRANCE	-	-	-	-	.	.	.	.	5762	5886	.	.	.	.	.
12 GREECE	-	-	-	-	.	2077	2944	2931	-	-	-	.	.	.	.
13 HUNGARY	-	-	-	.	.	.	.	.	.	.	.	.	.	.	.
14 ICELAND	-	-	.	.	.	.	.	.	.	.	.	.	.	.	.
15 ITALY	.	.	.	.	.	.	5228	5528	4969	5195	.	.	.	.	.
16 JAPAN	.	9285	9538	10043	10402	10647	10601	10481	-	.	.	.	.	.	.
17 NETHERLANDS	5518	5744	5602	5867	6550	7105	7610	7914	7856	7714	.	.	.	.	.
18 NEW ZEALAND	-	8019	7068	7699	7425	8317	8730	8057	8615	8290	.	.	.	.	.
19 NORWAY	.	.	.	.	.	4836	6076	5942	6009	6995	.	.	.	.	.
20 POLAND	-	-	-	-	-	-	-	-	-	-	.	.	.	.	.
21 PORTUGAL	.	.	.	.	.	.	.	.	.	.	.	.	.	.	.
22 ROMANIA	-	-	-	-	-	-	-	-	-	-	-	.	.	.	.
23 SPAIN	9733	10425	10476	10528	9930	10158	8948	8186	7511	7061	.	.	.	.	.
24 SWEDEN	-	-	.	.	.	.	10356	11351	11824	12364	.	.	.	.	.
25 SWITZERLAND	.	.	.	.	8483	7785	7401	7839	7983	7945	.	.	.	.	.
26 TURKEY	-	-	-	-	-	-	-	-	-	-	-	.	.	.	.
27 UK ENGLAND AND WALES	.	.	10488	10026	10142	9871	9442	9240	8874	8343	.	.	.	.	.
28 UK NORTHERN IRELAND	-	-	-	-	7024	7463	7659	7955	7492	7668	.	.	.	.	.
29 UK SCOTLAND	.	.	.	.	8982	9103	8468	8698	8268	8002	.	.	.	.	.
30 USA	14001	12060	12181	11799	11552	11980	12082	11973	11331	10716	.	.	.	.	.
31 YUGOSLAVIA	-	-	-	-	-	-	-	-	-	-	.	.	.	.	.

- NO MORTALITY DATA ARE AVAILABLE FOR EVEN A BROADER GROUP OF CAUSES FOR THIS DISEASE

. MORTALITY DATA ARE PRESENTED FOR A BROADER GROUP OF CAUSES FOR THIS DISEASE

0 VALUE<0.5

THE STANDARD MORTALITY RATIOS WERE DERIVED WITH A FACTOR OF 10000

SERIAL MORTALITY TABLES FOR VARIOUS COUNTRIES 1901-1975

TABLE 58 : MALIGNANT NEOPLASM - PROSTATE : MALES

	1901-	1906-	1911-	1916-	1921-	1926-	1931-	1936-	1941-	1946-	1951-	1956-	1961-	1966-	1971-75
1 AUSTRALIA	-	.	.	.	.	.	.	.	.	.	12304	12660	12101	12688	13064
2 AUSTRIA	.	.	.	.	-	-	-	-	-	.	9769	11017	11442	11779	12046
3 BELGIUM	.	.	.	.	.	.	.	.	.	.	11125	11240	13163	12927	12962
4 BULGARIA	-	-	-	-	-	.	.	.	.	.	.	.	5183	5542	5543
5 CANADA	-	-	-	-	.	.	7610	9473	.	10706	10416	10875	11247	11364	12284
6 CHILE	-	.	.	.	.	.	.	2413	3231	4668	6441	7301	7298	8719	10322
7 CZECHOSLOVAKIA	-	-	-	.	.	.	.	.	.	.	6532	7088	7728	8149	9170
8 DENMARK	.	.	.	.	.	.	.	.	.	.	10494	11843	12810	10636	11225
9 EIRE	-	-	-	-	.	.	.	.	.	.	6719	7312	8765	10138	11221
10 FINLAND	-	-	-	-	-	.	.	.	3197	5375	8541	9811	9735	10128	12305
11 FRANCE	-	-	-	-	.	.	.	.	5096	6886	8895	11823	12847	13073	12445
12 GREECE	-	-	-	-	.	.	.	.	-	-	-	3403	3921	4835	5503
13 HUNGARY	-	-	-	.	.	.	.	.	.	.	6991	7993	10425	11707	13017
14 ICELAND	-	-	.	.	.	.	.	.	.	.	.	.	5509	11224	10077
15 ITALY	.	.	.	.	.	.	.	.	2180	3608	5092	6589	7725	8407	8986
16 JAPAN	.	.	.	.	.	.	.	.	-	313	661	1160	1499	1720	1886
17 NETHERLANDS	.	.	.	.	.	.	.	.	9396	9202	10383	10820	11838	12713	12924
18 NEW ZEALAND	-	.	.	.	.	.	.	.	10478	10682	12095	11643	11835	12118	14104
19 NORWAY	.	.	.	.	.	3810	5879	7371	8016	9601	11203	12810	13930	13929	15850
20 POLAND	-	-	-	-	-	-	-	-	-	-	.	2994	5316	7144	7180
21 PORTUGAL	.	.	.	.	.	.	.	.	.	.	7873	7975	9192	10775	11125
22 ROMANIA	-	-	-	-	-	-	-	-	-	-	-	6493	7517	7063	7190
23 SPAIN	.	.	.	.	.	.	.	.	2766	4398	5519	6863	8871	9686	10614
24 SWEDEN	-	-	.	.	.	.	.	.	.	.	10304	13335	15265	14864	17845
25 SWITZERLAND	2126	2126	4225	4225	5628	6787	8264	9822	10725	11223	12143	13111	13611	14548	16233
26 TURKEY	-	-	-	-	-	-	-	-	-	-	-	4272	4976	5138	4774
27 UK ENGLAND AND WALES	.	.	.	.	.	.	.	8647	8334	9036	9478	10082	10282	10122	9986
28 UK NORTHERN IRELAND	-	-	-	-	.	.	.	.	.	8159	8467	9863	10052	10166	10526
29 UK SCOTLAND	.	.	.	.	.	.	.	.	.	9192	9055	10250	10839	9568	9891
30 USA	.	.	.	.	.	.	.	12754	11812	12242	11894	11714	11407	11390	11978
31 YUGOSLAVIA	-	-	-	-	-	-	-	-	-	-	.	.	4661	5802	6417

- NO MORTALITY DATA ARE AVAILABLE FOR EVEN A BROADER GROUP OF CAUSES FOR THIS DISEASE

. MORTALITY DATA ARE PRESENTED FOR A BROADER GROUP OF CAUSES FOR THIS DISEASE

0 VALUE<0.5

THE STANDARD MORTALITY RATIOS WERE DERIVED WITH A FACTOR OF 10000

SERIAL MORTALITY TABLES FOR VARIOUS COUNTRIES 1901-1975

TABLE 59 : MALIGNANT NEOPLASM - SKIN : MALES

	1901-	1906-	1911-	1916-	1921-	1926-	1931-	1936-	1941-	1946-	1951-	1956-	1961-	1966-	1971-75
1 AUSTRALIA	-	26480	32658	38359	38619	33568	31664	31554	33269	30809	25024	29937	32831	34446	35264
2 AUSTRIA	.	.	.	.	-	-	-	-	-	15162	11958	13301	13416	14542	15035
3 BELGIUM	.	.	.	.	.	.	.	.	.	.	12315	12130	10024	13378	10225
4 BULGARIA	-	-	-	-	-	.	.	.	.	.	.	.	11135	11754	11875
5 CANADA	-	-	-	-	25817	19602	19490	19379	17273	14412	12462	13442	13516	13631	13068
6 CHILE	-	3846	4598	2915	4976	2620	6835	3554	6338	6552	5539	6527	6685	8971	8179
7 CZECHOSLOVAKIA	-	-	-	11002	10050	13033	22569	18697	17516	15386	12668	14610	16436	16022	17206
8 DENMARK	.	.	.	.	.	.	.	.	.	.	13584	14338	14910	16507	18436
9 EIRE	-	-	-	-	28386	31008	25481	31579	33946	29462	22835	23156	23200	19791	18354
10 FINLAND	-	-	-	-	-	.	.	.	14648	11570	10375	14605	13824	18157	20407
11 FRANCE	-	-	-	-	.	.	.	.	19260	19097	16392	14368	14099	13501	12124
12 GREECE	-	-	-	-	.	4687	6027	8639	-	-	-	6371	7958	6896	7718
13 HUNGARY	-	-	-	.	.	.	28630	25653	25984	.	14526	17460	17162	16861	19409
14 ICELAND	-	-	.	.	.	.	.	.	.	.	.	.	6349	7143	8974
15 ITALY	.	.	.	.	.	.	18629	19958	16037	14502	15243	13275	12267	12427	11122
16 JAPAN	.	8256	8008	6728	5367	4871	5850	6685	-	7551	6583	6617	6003	5768	5373
17 NETHERLANDS	15653	14420	15963	14446	16084	18302	15865	17552	15130	13547	11277	12134	12090	12425	13429
18 NEW ZEALAND	-	14286	14474	20175	22917	27326	.	.	21806	24924	22966	20714	21357	28013	31426
19 NORWAY	.	.	19097	20198	19953	18004	13527	14088	10321	8456	12046	13515	14561	17521	22750
20 POLAND	-	-	-	-	-	-	-	-	-	-	.	5323	9888	13966	13699
21 PORTUGAL	.	.	.	.	.	.	.	.	.	.	8203	9426	11192	11891	14332
22 ROMANIA	-	-	-	-	-	-	-	-	-	-	-	3736	8073	9300	12842
23 SPAIN	19741	18745	19149	25543	26118	26812	19160	19735	13835	12306	11125	11254	11470	9244	10198
24 SWEDEN	-	-	.	.	.	.	.	.	.	.	9267	11818	12830	14344	16702
25 SWITZERLAND	13938	13938	16127	16127	22478	16722	11801	15249	15928	17086	15488	16255	17466	18693	22141
26 TURKEY	-	-	-	-	-	-	-	-	-	-	-	5543	5491	4897	4076
27 UK ENGLAND AND WALES	.	.	30838	32600	34085	34670	23682	22241	19561	15766	13162	11597	10733	11347	11871
28 UK NORTHERN IRELAND	-	-	-	-	31746	35115	29540	29195	33182	20751	10775	12663	13824	17338	10862
29 UK SCOTLAND	.	.	.	.	10088	25208	19780	18033	15760	13330	15719	15845	14518	12233	15147
30 USA	40218	36608	33898	31592	28208	26206	26256	24368	21711	19602	17417	17355	18275	17680	17868
31 YUGOSLAVIA	-	-	-	-	-	-	-	-	-	-	.	.	10994	10115	11677

- NO MORTALITY DATA ARE AVAILABLE FOR EVEN A BROADER GROUP OF CAUSES FOR THIS DISEASE

. MORTALITY DATA ARE PRESENTED FOR A BROADER GROUP OF CAUSES FOR THIS DISEASE

0 VALUE<0.5

THE STANDARD MORTALITY RATIOS WERE DERIVED WITH A FACTOR OF 10000

SERIAL MORTALITY TABLES FOR VARIOUS COUNTRIES 1901-1975

TABLE 59 : MALIGNANT NEOPLASM - SKIN : FEMALES

	1901-	1906-	1911-	1916-	1921-	1926-	1931-	1936-	1941-	1946-	1951-	1956-	1961-	1966-	1971-75
1 AUSTRALIA	-	12117	18165	21573	22938	19290	18443	16203	20992	18024	16545	16485	17408	18327	17756
2 AUSTRIA	.	.	.	.	-	-	-	-	-	12414	11141	11416	10829	11727	10941
3 BELGIUM	.	.	.	.	.	.	.	.	.	.	11396	9942	7488	8125	6936
4 BULGARIA	-	-	-	-	-	.	.	.	.	.	.	.	8544	9804	8137
5 CANADA	-	-	-	-	12026	12246	12852	13093	9777	10525	8206	8555	9226	9336	8808
6 CHILE	-	2367	5351	3924	4535	3575	6274	5712	5666	6146	6209	4702	5594	6741	7356
7 CZECHOSLOVAKIA	-	-	-	10142	9896	13928	22438	18260	15654	13728	12206	12373	12780	12218	12125
8 DENMARK	.	.	.	.	.	.	.	.	.	.	10515	12388	13162	12456	13533
9 EIRE	-	-	-	-	20341	19364	20108	16622	15825	18614	16820	15841	16047	17550	14856
10 FINLAND	-	-	-	-	-	.	.	.	12080	13932	9068	10817	9058	12232	11734
11 FRANCE	-	-	-	-	.	.	.	.	16361	15565	15122	14203	13609	11638	10563
12 GREECE	-	-	-	-	.	4204	5993	6522	-	-	-	5342	7782	6706	7295
13 HUNGARY	-	-	-	.	.	.	17358	16918	18714	.	10753	14146	13851	13564	15840
14 ICELAND	-	-	.	.	.	.	.	.	.	.	.	.	4167	10000	14607
15 ITALY	.	.	.	.	.	.	13256	13531	10759	10281	10243	9814	9058	8489	7299
16 JAPAN	.	5101	5071	4972	3496	3423	4343	4835	-	4837	5087	5184	4543	4262	3849
17 NETHERLANDS	7860	10180	9817	10562	9853	12933	12199	12869	12235	9524	9983	9135	9024	9147	9470
18 NEW ZEALAND	-	4545	8468	11224	12356	12995	.	.	11658	13869	12681	13680	15859	17520	19271
19 NORWAY	.	.	10627	11472	11111	13071	12469	11350	8280	6156	10627	9572	10818	11085	12404
20 POLAND	-	-	-	-	-	-	-	-	-	-	.	4500	8955	11941	11740
21 PORTUGAL	.	.	.	.	.	.	.	.	.	.	10237	8708	9666	10599	11782
22 ROMANIA	-	-	-	-	-	-	-	-	-	-	-	3835	7449	7338	8963
23 SPAIN	14115	16647	16743	21410	20371	21140	17240	15095	11586	9555	9485	9704	8771	7196	7092
24 SWEDEN	-	-	.	.	.	.	.	.	.	.	6497	7934	9080	9316	10357
25 SWITZERLAND	18087	18087	19319	19319	21812	19865	15012	13969	15694	14100	12527	13573	13638	12733	12358
26 TURKEY	-	-	-	-	-	-	-	-	-	-	-	4558	5161	3866	3981
27 UK ENGLAND AND WALES	.	.	15091	15461	15589	15367	14605	13232	11239	10032	9375	8655	8496	8234	9227
28 UK NORTHERN IRELAND	-	-	-	-	27248	20915	20166	25200	20463	17939	11672	11579	10669	11749	7781
29 UK SCOTLAND	.	.	.	.	5361	13178	12448	13311	11662	9852	10358	10540	10733	11145	11189
30 USA	21381	19824	20575	19335	17900	16978	15521	14973	13014	12534	11188	10946	10649	10132	9803
31 YUGOSLAVIA	-	-	-	-	-	-	-	-	-	-	-	.	8206	8750	9003

- NO MORTALITY DATA ARE AVAILABLE FOR EVEN A BROADER GROUP OF CAUSES FOR THIS DISEASE

. MORTALITY DATA ARE PRESENTED FOR A BROADER GROUP OF CAUSES FOR THIS DISEASE

0 VALUE<0.5

THE STANDARD MORTALITY RATIOS WERE DERIVED WITH A FACTOR OF 10000

SERIAL MORTALITY TABLES FOR VARIOUS COUNTRIES 1901-1975

TABLE 60 : MALIGNANT NEOPLASM - BONE AND CONNECTIVE TISSUE : MALES

	1901-	1906-	1911-	1916-	1921-	1926-	1931-	1936-	1941-	1946-	1951-	1956-	1961-	1966-	1971-75
1 AUSTRALIA	-	.	.	.	.	.	.	.	.	.	12109	11396	11035	11684	.
2 AUSTRIA	.	.	.	.	-	-	-	-	-	.	12679	16514	17451	17655	.
3 BELGIUM	.	.	.	.	.	.	.	.	.	.	18466	17450	16554	15897	.
4 BULGARIA	-	-	-	-	-	.	.	.	.	.	.	.	14725	13518	.
5 CANADA	-	-	-	-	.	.	.	.	.	14871	15223	13317	12690	11319	.
6 CHILE	-	.	.	.	.	.	.	3900	4964	7995	13855	13323	11540	13939	.
7 CZECHOSLOVAKIA	-	-	-	.	.	.	.	.	.	.	16952	17829	18289	15858	.
8 DENMARK	.	.	.	.	.	.	.	.	.	.	12945	13849	11089	9711	.
9 EIRE	-	-	-	-	.	.	.	.	.	.	19404	20376	19275	16109	.
10 FINLAND	-	-	-	-	-	.	.	.	11835	13674	17239	17810	15210	13438	.
11 FRANCE	-	-	-	-	.	.	.	.	.	18252	19316	18941	18887	18241	.
12 GREECE	-	-	-	-	.	.	.	.	-	-	-	9702	18316	16412	.
13 HUNGARY	-	-	-	.	.	.	.	.	.	.	13512	19961	19525	21064	.
14 ICELAND	-	-	.	.	.	.	.	.	.	.	.	.	10606	15068	.
15 ITALY	.	.	.	.	.	.	.	.	.	.	19807	19301	17953	17266	.
16 JAPAN	.	.	.	.	.	.	.	.	-	4942	8429	10633	10843	9436	.
17 NETHERLANDS	.	.	.	.	.	.	.	.	.	18147	18320	15056	13762	13353	.
18 NEW ZEALAND	-	.	.	.	.	.	.	.	.	14438	13368	10238	11450	9109	.
19 NORWAY	40735	37753	16203	15995	17486	14730	11973	11563	.	.	15448	9147	8559	9319	.
20 POLAND	-	-	-	-	-	-	-	-	-	-	.	6210	12006	14804	.
21 PORTUGAL	.	.	.	.	.	.	.	.	.	.	15944	16497	19473	18635	.
22 ROMANIA	-	-	-	-	-	-	-	-	-	-	-	13395	19143	18083	.
23 SPAIN	.	.	.	.	.	.	.	.	.	.	9295	12079	15360	13854	.
24 SWEDEN	-	-	.	.	.	.	.	.	.	.	18423	14683	11089	11186	.
25 SWITZERLAND	.	.	.	.	14732	13308	.	.	.	.	16621	15734	13717	15723	.
26 TURKEY	-	-	-	-	-	-	-	-	-	-	-	2370	3110	4583	2821
27 UK ENGLAND AND WALES	.	.	.	.	.	.	.	15161	17272	14703	14260	12791	11440	10821	.
28 UK NORTHERN IRELAND	-	-	-	-	.	.	.	.	.	27893	16762	14953	8977	11698	.
29 UK SCOTLAND	.	.	.	.	.	.	.	.	.	20505	21388	18696	15996	13734	.
30 USA	.	.	.	.	.	.	.	.	.	15374	13547	12617	11756	11694	.
31 YUGOSLAVIA	-	-	-	-	-	-	-	-	-	-	.	.	12670	12290	.

- NO MORTALITY DATA ARE AVAILABLE FOR EVEN A BROADER GROUP OF CAUSES FOR THIS DISEASE

. MORTALITY DATA ARE PRESENTED FOR A BROADER GROUP OF CAUSES FOR THIS DISEASE

0 VALUE<0.5

THE STANDARD MORTALITY RATIOS WERE DERIVED WITH A FACTOR OF 10000

SERIAL MORTALITY TABLES FOR VARIOUS COUNTRIES 1901-1975

TABLE 60 : MALIGNANT NEOPLASM - BONE AND CONNECTIVE TISSUE : FEMALES

	1901-	1906-	1911-	1916-	1921-	1926-	1931-	1936-	1941-	1946-	1951-	1956-	1961-	1966-	1971-75
1 AUSTRALIA	-	.	.	.	.	.	.	.	.	.	8847	6888	8058	8290	.
2 AUSTRIA	.	.	.	.	-	-	-	-	-	.	9135	10579	10207	11190	.
3 BELGIUM	.	.	.	.	.	.	.	.	.	.	11126	10868	10653	8376	.
4 BULGARIA	-	-	-	-	-	.	.	.	.	.	.	.	10716	9737	.
5 CANADA	-	-	-	-	.	.	.	.	.	11263	9221	8690	8000	7662	.
6 CHILE	-	.	.	.	.	.	.	2950	6280	7189	13842	9968	9530	10327	.
7 CZECHOSLOVAKIA	-	-	-	.	.	.	.	.	.	.	11492	11988	11841	9789	.
8 DENMARK	.	.	.	.	.	.	.	.	.	.	9205	7700	7902	7846	.
9 EIRE	-	-	-	-	.	.	.	.	.	.	12199	10800	10493	12023	.
10 FINLAND	-	-	-	-	-	.	.	.	8714	10100	12044	12903	9995	7937	.
11 FRANCE	-	-	-	-	.	.	.	.	.	12268	12224	11656	11062	10515	.
12 GREECE	-	-	-	-	.	.	.	.	-	-	-	8458	11499	11753	.
13 HUNGARY	-	-	-	.	.	.	.	.	.	.	11216	13099	14378	14150	.
14 ICELAND	-	-	.	.	.	.	.	.	.	.	.	.	18310	6329	.
15 ITALY	.	.	.	.	.	.	.	.	.	.	12802	12205	10598	10026	.
16 JAPAN	.	.	.	.	.	.	.	.	-	3637	5916	6935	7215	6135	.
17 NETHERLANDS	.	.	.	.	.	.	.	.	.	13073	11746	9447	9807	8291	.
18 NEW ZEALAND	-	.	.	.	.	.	.	.	.	5822	10683	7938	7199	6496	.
19 NORWAY	32451	31050	11486	12300	12548	10569	9675	9717	.	.	11816	6119	6783	6490	.
20 POLAND	-	-	-	-	-	-	-	-	-	-	.	5084	8533	9650	.
21 PORTUGAL	.	.	.	.	.	.	.	.	.	.	12772	12067	12734	12169	.
22 ROMANIA	-	-	-	-	-	-	-	-	-	-	-	8759	12327	12310	.
23 SPAIN	.	.	.	.	.	.	.	.	.	.	6652	8448	10813	10184	.
24 SWEDEN	-	-	.	.	.	.	.	.	.	.	12632	12144	8786	7027	.
25 SWITZERLAND	.	.	.	.	12277	11551	.	.	.	.	10367	10314	9257	7279	.
26 TURKEY	-	-	-	-	-	-	-	-	-	-	-	1212	2142	1918	2716
27 UK ENGLAND AND WALES	.	.	.	.	.	.	.	11203	11228	10197	9074	8190	7526	6517	.
28 UK NORTHERN IRELAND	-	-	-	-	.	.	.	.	.	13035	8955	9410	9036	9259	.
29 UK SCOTLAND	.	.	.	.	.	.	.	.	.	12327	13087	10964	8843	8011	.
30 USA	.	.	.	.	.	.	.	.	.	9726	9002	8562	7960	7896	.
31 YUGOSLAVIA	-	-	-	-	-	-	-	-	-	-	.	.	8207	8782	.

- NO MORTALITY DATA ARE AVAILABLE FOR EVEN A BROADER GROUP OF CAUSES FOR THIS DISEASE

. MORTALITY DATA ARE PRESENTED FOR A BROADER GROUP OF CAUSES FOR THIS DISEASE

0 VALUE<0.5

THE STANDARD MORTALITY RATIOS WERE DERIVED WITH A FACTOR OF 10000

SERIAL MORTALITY TABLES FOR VARIOUS COUNTRIES 1901-1975

TABLE 61 : MALIGNANT NEOPLASM - ALL SOLID TUMOURS : MALES

	1901-	1906-	1911-	1916-	1921-	1926-	1931-	1936-	1941-	1946-	1951-	1956-	1961-	1966-	1971-75
1 AUSTRALIA	-	7607	7867	8166	8704	8634	8738	8673	8325	8614	8688	9050	9395	10183	10860
2 AUSTRIA	8188	8935	8968	8563	-	-	-	-	-	12173	13001	13740	14008	14220	14067
3 BELGIUM	4638	5018	5690	5278	5709	6176	6546	7139	7071	7457	9916	11362	12690	13535	14341
4 BULGARIA	-	-	-	-	-	5266	5868	7028	7183	8732	10272	8954	10036	9432	9040
5 CANADA	-	-	-	-	7107	7148	8000	8484	8638	8850	8978	9320	9662	10313	10815
6 CHILE	-	4059	3553	4274	4361	6028	7876	8112	8453	9086	11446	10886	10676	10982	11087
7 CZECHOSLOVAKIA	-	-	-	7226	8114	9163	9763	9734	8571	9658	11325	12055	13513	14305	14809
8 DENMARK	11713	12716	12734	12526	10565	10485	9829	9501	9471	9442	10176	10746	11354	11053	11877
9 EIRE	-	-	-	-	6474	7375	7683	8154	8613	8534	9088	9349	9759	10465	11378
10 FINLAND	-	-	-	-	-	6037	6938	9513	9862	11587	13290	13309	13161	13088	12751
11 FRANCE	-	-	-	-	4449	5466	5677	6585	8183	9712	10454	11379	12430	12976	13427
12 GREECE	-	-	-	-	2130	2868	3697	4371	-	-	-	7339	8077	8559	9049
13 HUNGARY	-	-	-	5639	6495	7491	7888	7609	8093	8678	9189	10261	11093	12162	13394
14 ICELAND	-	-	8934	10799	9653	11054	10526	10414	11854	10625	.	.	9286	9229	9175
15 ITALY	4012	4597	4876	4772	4888	4782	5836	6392	6365	7164	8125	9173	10171	11230	12041
16 JAPAN	5182	5897	6475	6785	7352	7642	7744	7926	-	8316	8792	9681	10059	10251	10105
17 NETHERLANDS	7992	8840	9821	9756	9715	9896	9800	10105	10362	10212	10246	10703	11837	12860	13673
18 NEW ZEALAND	-	7648	7928	7889	8115	8695	8643	8480	8813	9093	9295	9479	10073	10674	11473
19 NORWAY	7548	7429	7962	7964	8709	8755	8983	8828	8384	8827	8664	8481	8602	8994	9525
20 POLAND	-	-	-	-	-	-	-	-	-	-	.	7630	9497	10585	11406
21 PORTUGAL	1853	1803	2074	2223	2604	3690	3681	3874	3803	4028	5883	6988	7727	8470	8951
22 ROMANIA	-	-	-	-	-	-	-	-	-	-	-	8313	9257	8839	8836
23 SPAIN	3526	3941	4440	4746	5094	5744	5955	5763	5454	6072	6928	8139	9145	9442	10216
24 SWEDEN	-	-	7163	7357	7617	7724	8267	8366	8017	7718	8142	8543	8919	8930	10295
25 SWITZERLAND	11966	11966	12394	12394	12502	12323	12390	12878	12352	12067	11990	11823	11865	12074	12650
26 TURKEY	-	-	-	-	-	-	-	-	-	-	-	8299	7958	7464	6568
27 UK ENGLAND AND WALES	7666	7590	9159	9282	10023	10441	10738	10913	10886	11316	11939	12381	12787	13330	13475
28 UK NORTHERN IRELAND	-	-	-	-	7471	8103	8609	8892	9633	10248	9656	10654	10254	11188	11590
29 UK SCOTLAND	7528	8602	9281	9379	10129	10569	10934	11066	11358	12005	12665	13384	14123	14510	14806
30 USA	7608	6444	6408	6429	6978	7384	7744	8277	8488	8917	9054	9390	9778	10339	10838
31 YUGOSLAVIA	-	-	-	-	-	-	-	-	-	-	.	.	6778	7565	8529

- NO MORTALITY DATA ARE AVAILABLE FOR EVEN A BROADER GROUP OF CAUSES FOR THIS DISEASE

. MORTALITY DATA ARE PRESENTED FOR A BROADER GROUP OF CAUSES FOR THIS DISEASE

0 VALUE<0.5

THE STANDARD MCRTALITY RATIOS WERE DERIVED WITH A FACTOR OF 10000

SERIAL MORTALITY TABLES FOR VARIOUS COUNTRIES 1901-1975

TABLE 61 : MALIGNANT NEOPLASM - ALL SOLID TUMOURS : FEMALES

	1901-	1906-	1911-	1916-	1921-	1926-	1931-	1936-	1941-	1946-	1951-	1956-	1961-	1966-	1971-75
1 AUSTRALIA	-	8227	8431	8594	8805	8561	8271	8215	8157	7855	7153	6827	6659	6748	6869
2 AUSTRIA	9096	9642	9422	9619	-	-	-	-	-	9841	9615	9495	9226	9117	8726
3 BELGIUM	5356	5686	6194	6068	6410	6862	7493	7740	7638	7657	8391	8760	8753	8442	8174
4 BULGARIA	-	-	-	-	-	4951	5865	6223	6530	6948	7327	6017	6321	5802	5529
5 CANADA	-	-	-	-	8786	8569	9085	9278	9099	8787	8191	7984	7687	7527	7377
6 CHILE	-	5265	4752	5599	5803	7409	9169	9032	9543	9862	11380	10332	10118	10213	9596
7 CZECHOSLOVAKIA	-	-	-	7284	7613	8596	8875	8695	7792	8409	8501	8225	8245	8200	8156
8 DENMARK	11312	11902	11603	12453	10969	10872	10852	10625	10619	9905	10029	9909	9754	9042	8903
9 EIRE	-	-	-	-	5531	6445	6554	7115	7493	7467	7450	7769	7628	8208	8737
10 FINLAND	-	-	-	-	-	5332	6016	7572	7837	8263	8558	8071	7410	6986	6733
11 FRANCE	-	-	-	-	4472	5556	5525	5937	6984	7459	7564	7525	7418	7145	6883
12 GREECE	-	-	-	-	1951	2828	3590	3909	-	-	-	4771	4981	4937	4983
13 HUNGARY	-	-	-	6292	7277	8507	8698	8163	8237	8223	8075	8411	8367	8476	8871
14 ICELAND	-	-	7232	6748	7635	8329	8396	8953	9122	8726	.	.	8868	8671	8001
15 ITALY	5111	5705	5824	5634	5386	4931	5791	6183	5971	6298	6616	6852	6899	6934	6935
16 JAPAN	4693	5354	5808	6125	6404	6614	6654	6718	-	6845	6842	6996	6926	6743	6369
17 NETHERLANDS	7795	8618	9156	9456	9676	10099	10203	10357	10491	9719	9013	8511	8311	8402	8014
18 NEW ZEALAND	-	8620	8955	8820	8622	8874	8506	8289	8423	8156	7900	7413	7472	7453	7950
19 NORWAY	6516	6691	6685	6958	7712	8136	8308	8036	7788	8034	7792	7236	6825	6839	6715
20 POLAND	-	-	-	-	-	-	-	-	-	-	.	5937	7072	7279	7060
21 PORTUGAL	2042	1983	2244	2335	2738	4015	3854	3914	3534	3744	4977	5442	5727	5912	6035
22 ROMANIA	-	-	-	-	-	-	-	-	-	-	-	6629	6890	6067	5889
23 SPAIN	4118	4493	4839	5072	5185	5571	5337	4935	4781	4929	5294	5878	6288	6204	6277
24 SWEDEN	-	-	6704	6964	7246	7546	7889	8038	7795	7721	7793	7617	7389	7192	7698
25 SWITZERLAND	10422	10422	10488	10488	9791	9654	9545	9656	9545	9112	8758	8340	7882	7720	7462
26 TURKEY	-	-	-	-	-	-	-	-	-	-	-	5310	4791	4440	3969
27 UK ENGLAND AND WALES	10217	9369	9771	9564	9802	9869	9665	9418	8744	8594	8128	7913	7822	7946	8100
28 UK NORTHERN IRELAND	-	-	-	-	8233	8621	8979	8819	9075	9274	8064	8025	7378	7721	7986
29 UK SCOTLAND	9042	10199	10448	10357	10647	10703	10444	10264	9660	9477	9173	8846	8658	8648	8726
30 USA	12119	10154	9834	9447	9392	9542	9486	9381	8980	8594	7886	7423	7138	7016	6956
31 YUGOSLAVIA	-	-	-	-	-	-	-	-	-	-	.	.	4962	5129	5447

- NO MORTALITY DATA ARE AVAILABLE FOR EVEN A BROADER GROUP OF CAUSES FOR THIS DISEASE

. MORTALITY DATA ARE PRESENTED FOR A BROADER GROUP OF CAUSES FOR THIS DISEASE

0 VALUE<0.5

THE STANDARD MORTALITY RATIOS WERE DERIVED WITH A FACTOR OF 10000

SERIAL MORTALITY TABLES FOR VARIOUS COUNTRIES 1901-1975

TABLE 62 : LEUKAEMIA AND ALEUKAEMIA : MALES

	1901-	1906-	1911-	1916-	1921-	1926-	1931-	1936-	1941-	1946-	1951-	1956-	1961-	1966-	1971-75
1 AUSTRALIA	-	4790	5021	6203	7154	4630	5974	7237	7403	10015	11334	13107	14266	14249	14614
2 AUSTRIA	-	-	-	-	-	-	-	-	-	8159	12164	13472	13419	13916	14996
3 BELGIUM	-	-	-	-	-	-	.	.	.	.	10403	12255	13790	14269	14753
4 BULGARIA	-	-	-	-	-	-	-	-	-	-	-	-	11297	10445	10116
5 CANADA	-	-	-	-	3896	3983	5297	6608	8390	9979	12524	13901	15526	15745	16041
6 CHILE	-	.	.	.	.	.	.	3018	3401	4610	7444	8857	8937	9910	9470
7 CZECHOSLOVAKIA	-	-	-	.	.	.	4568	6434	5487	6911	10872	13452	14281	15434	15842
8 DENMARK	-	-	-	-	-	-	8405	10702	12021	14058	15367	18269	19502	17781	17169
9 EIRE	-	-	-	-	1649	2357	2932	2955	4174	5270	7817	9668	12096	13194	13246
10 FINLAND	-	-	-	-	-	-	-	.	5432	8128	10160	13024	15083	14964	16007
11 FRANCE	-	-	-	-	-	-	-	-	3939	6594	10637	12945	14519	15590	16254
12 GREECE	-	-	-	-	-	.	.	.	-	-	-	12988	15113	16419	16125
13 HUNGARY	-	-	-	-	-	-	.	.	.	.	11220	11586	13287	14097	14961
14 ICELAND	-	-	-	-	-	-	-	-	-	-	.	.	15349	12821	13200
15 ITALY	-	-	-	-	-	-	7645	8415	6041	7063	9633	11938	13801	15362	15603
16 JAPAN	-	.	.	.	.	.	.	.	-	4563	5856	7583	8628	9031	9344
17 NETHERLANDS	.	.	.	.	4219	5533	7479	9131	8219	10779	12052	14359	15548	16354	15619
18 NEW ZEALAND	-	.	.	.	.	.	.	9699	8916	12524	13659	14781	15476	14222	16012
19 NORWAY	2134	2153	2262	2850	3219	4482	5017	6218	7909	11434	13711	15291	16373	16811	15157
20 POLAND	-	-	-	-	-	-	-	-	-	-	5203	9302	11152	11922	12643
21 PORTUGAL	-	-	-	-	-	-	-	-	-	-	6970	8154	10527	11828	12485
22 ROMANIA	-	-	-	-	-	-	-	-	-	-	-	7721	9589	10272	10454
23 SPAIN	.	.	.	.	.	.	2034	1649	2356	2777	4550	7108	8685	9248	10173
24 SWEDEN	-	-	.	.	.	.	6004	7437	9413	11853	14112	15633	17533	16287	16300
25 SWITZERLAND	3104	3104	3785	3785	5526	6419	6694	7718	8588	11440	12385	13918	14258	14800	15236
26 TURKEY	-	-	-	-	-	-	-	-	-	-	-	8204	8498	9385	8076
27 UK ENGLAND AND WALES	.	.	3055	2970	3519	4187	4856	6111	6550	8196	10293	11767	12380	13064	13096
28 UK NORTHERN IRELAND	-	-	-	-	2498	3033	.	.	.	8502	9311	11197	13706	13344	13712
29 UK SCOTLAND	.	.	3014	2768	3685	3876	4313	5261	6933	8131	10348	10986	12496	12418	11996
30 USA	.	.	.	.	4314	5330	6821	8688	10698	13017	15524	16758	17100	17294	16718
31 YUGOSLAVIA	-	-	-	-	-	-	-	-	-	-	.	.	9220	10050	9510

\- NO MORTALITY DATA ARE AVAILABLE FOR EVEN A BROADER GROUP OF CAUSES FOR THIS DISEASE

. MORTALITY DATA ARE PRESENTED FOR A BROADER GROUP OF CAUSES FOR THIS DISEASE

0 VALUE<0.5

THE STANDARD MORTALITY RATIOS WERE DERIVED WITH A FACTOR OF 10000

SERIAL MORTALITY TABLES FOR VARIOUS COUNTRIES 1901-1975

TABLE 62 : LEUKAEMIA AND ALEUKAEMIA : FEMALES

	1901-	1906-	1911-	1916-	1921-	1926-	1931-	1936-	1941-	1946-	1951-	1956-	1961-	1966-	1971-75
1 AUSTRALIA	-	3135	3708	4065	5122	4194	4498	5626	6321	7847	8639	9574	9583	9894	9777
2 AUSTRIA	-	-	-	-	-	-	-	-	-	5809	8086	9085	9226	9793	10121
3 BELGIUM	-	-	-	-	-	-	.	.	.	.	8230	8745	9389	9700	10030
4 BULGARIA	-	-	-	-	-	-	-	-	-	-	-	-	7626	7665	7318
5 CANADA	-	-	-	-	3315	3146	4087	5148	6363	8141	8993	10179	10438	10293	10528
6 CHILE	-	.	.	.	.	.	.	1112	2117	3299	5422	6540	7078	7695	7891
7 CZECHOSLOVAKIA	-	-	-	.	.	.	3755	4563	4498	5148	7783	8499	9412	9629	10240
8 DENMARK	-	-	-	-	-	-	5376	7421	8486	9438	11378	11938	12553	10841	11048
9 EIRE	-	-	-	-	1392	1392	2259	2712	3217	3210	6011	6588	7421	7747	7551
10 FINLAND	-	-	-	-	-	-	-	.	3949	5700	7625	9915	11496	12069	10688
11 FRANCE	-	-	-	-	-	-	-	-	2714	4084	6760	8682	9586	10030	10508
12 GREECE	-	-	-	-	-	.	.	.	-	-	-	9566	10451	10429	9776
13 HUNGARY	-	-	-	-	-	-	.	.	.	.	7792	7967	8838	9426	10028
14 ICELAND	-	-	-	-	-	-	-	-	-	-	.	.	8811	10484	12030
15 ITALY	-	-	-	-	-	-	5396	5978	4345	4912	6827	8189	9549	10113	10134
16 JAPAN	-	.	.	.	.	.	.	.	-	2935	3810	5291	6255	6518	6551
17 NETHERLANDS	.	.	.	.	2962	4475	5625	7885	6798	7553	9376	10715	10862	11467	10508
18 NEW ZEALAND	-	.	.	.	.	.	.	6745	6688	9036	9969	12068	11532	11140	10971
19 NORWAY	1520	1220	1904	1627	2414	2695	3066	4506	5042	7412	10331	10777	10656	11946	10253
20 POLAND	-	-	-	-	-	-	-	-	-	-	3177	6321	7835	7984	8518
21 PORTUGAL	-	-	-	-	-	-	-	-	-	-	5706	6278	7560	9003	8659
22 ROMANIA	-	-	-	-	-	-	-	-	-	-	-	5103	6542	6946	6818
23 SPAIN	.	.	.	.	.	.	1331	1215	1631	2150	3388	5003	6343	6796	7159
24 SWEDEN	-	-	.	.	.	.	4041	4717	6764	7901	9944	10988	11681	11436	11542
25 SWITZERLAND	2375	2375	2962	2962	4027	4226	4075	5770	6211	7833	8449	8933	9982	9961	10589
26 TURKEY	-	-	-	-	-	-	-	-	-	-	-	4704	5366	6788	5900
27 UK ENGLAND AND WALES	.	.	2493	2327	2579	3134	3688	4658	4659	5858	7310	8014	8724	8650	8564
28 UK NORTHERN IRELAND	-	-	-	-	1843	2411	.	.	.	6559	5823	7740	7861	8303	8018
29 UK SCOTLAND	.	.	2439	2411	2643	2909	3856	3963	4558	5681	6848	7850	8274	8836	7951
30 USA	.	.	.	.	3208	4094	5140	6379	7739	9143	10683	11280	11174	11294	10636
31 YUGOSLAVIA	-	-	-	-	-	-	-	-	-	-	.	.	6459	7087	6558

- NO MORTALITY DATA ARE AVAILABLE FOR EVEN A BROADER GROUP OF CAUSES FOR THIS DISEASE

. MORTALITY DATA ARE PRESENTED FOR A BROADER GROUP OF CAUSES FOR THIS DISEASE

0 VALUE<0.5

THE STANDARD MORTALITY RATIOS WERE DERIVED WITH A FACTOR OF 10000

SERIAL MORTALITY TABLES FOR VARIOUS COUNTRIES 1901-1975

TABLE 63 : HODGKIN'S DISEASE : MALES

	1901-	1906-	1911-	1916-	1921-	1926-	1931-	1936-	1941-	1946-	1951-	1956-	1961-	1966-	1971-75
1 AUSTRALIA	-	.	.	.	.	13769	12296	15251	11586	12959	.	.	.	.	.
2 AUSTRIA	-	-	-	-	-	-	-	-	-	.	.	.	.	.	.
3 BELGIUM	-	-	-	-	-	-	.	.	.	.	.	.	.	.	.
4 BULGARIA	-	-	-	-	-	-	-	-	-	-	-	-	.	.	.
5 CANADA	-	-	-	-	6811	9355	11123	12508	14907	16411	.	.	.	.	.
6 CHILE	-	.	.	.	.	.	.	9191	7915	7440	.	.	.	.	.
7 CZECHOSLOVAKIA	-	-	-	.	.	.	7961	11029	.	.	.	.	.	.	.
8 DENMARK	-	-	-	-	-	-	15966	16912	.	.	.	.	.	.	.
9 EIRE	-	-	-	-	7424	9697	10165	11523	.	.	.	.	.	.	.
10 FINLAND	-	-	-	-	-	-	-	.	6344	11297	.	.	.	.	.
11 FRANCE	-	-	-	-	-	-	-	-	13823	17704	.	.	.	.	.
12 GREECE	-	-	-	-	-	.	.	.	-	-	-	.	.	.	.
13 HUNGARY	-	-	-	-	-	-	.	.	.	.	.	.	.	.	.
14 ICELAND	-	-	-	-	-	-	-	-	-	-	.	.	.	.	.
15 ITALY	-	-	-	-	-	-	-	-	14899	17269	.	.	.	.	.
16 JAPAN	-	.	.	.	.	.	.	.	-	.	.	.	.	.	.
17 NETHERLANDS	.	.	.	.	8923	14720	12909	17420	15859	17297	.	.	.	.	.
18 NEW ZEALAND	-	.	.	.	.	.	.	22619	15826	18323	.	.	.	.	.
19 NORWAY	.	.	.	.	.	5421	6901	11111	11751	13611	.	.	.	.	.
20 POLAND	-	-	-	-	-	-	-	-	-	-	.	.	.	.	.
21 PORTUGAL	-	-	-	-	-	-	-	-	-	-	.	.	.	.	.
22 ROMANIA	-	-	-	-	-	-	-	-	-	-	-	.	.	.	.
23 SPAIN	.	.	.	.	.	.	2820	2777	19419	18610	.	.	.	.	.
24 SWEDEN	-	-	.	.	.	.	10784	11831	9455	12619	.	.	.	.	.
25 SWITZERLAND	.	.	.	.	.	.	13678	17080	18839	19524	.	.	.	.	.
26 TURKEY	-	-	-	-	-	-	-	-	-	-	-	.	.	.	.
27 UK ENGLAND AND WALES	.	.	10344	10369	12744	14261	16561	15729	17726	18208	.	.	.	.	.
28 UK NORTHERN IRELAND	-	-	-	-	6250	7188	.	.	.	.	.	.	.	.	.
29 UK SCOTLAND	.	.	9107	9683	10853	14263	14789	14739	15968	17301	.	.	.	.	.
30 USA	.	.	.	.	9621	11617	13950	17237	17877	18356	.	.	.	.	.
31 YUGOSLAVIA	-	-	-	-	-	-	-	-	-	-	.	.	.	.	.

- NO MORTALITY DATA ARE AVAILABLE FOR EVEN A BROADER GROUP OF CAUSES FOR THIS DISEASE

. MORTALITY DATA ARE PRESENTED FOR A BROADER GROUP OF CAUSES FOR THIS DISEASE

0 VALUE<0.5

THE STANDARD MORTALITY RATIOS WERE DERIVED WITH A FACTOR OF 10000

SERIAL MORTALITY TABLES FOR VARIOUS COUNTRIES 1901-1975

TABLE 63 : HODGKIN'S DISEASE : FEMALES

	1901-	1906-	1911-	1916-	1921-	1926-	1931-	1936-	1941-	1946-	1951-	1956-	1961-	1966-	1971-75
1 AUSTRALIA	-	.	.	.	.	7876	7569	8365	8713	7851	.	.	.	.	.
2 AUSTRIA	-	-	-	-	-	-	-	-	-	.	.	.	.	.	.
3 BELGIUM	-	-	-	-	-	-	.	.	.	.	.	.	.	.	.
4 BULGARIA	-	-	-	-	-	-	-	-	-	-	-	-	.	.	.
5 CANADA	-	-	-	-	4488	4379	5988	7337	7975	9321	.	.	.	.	.
6 CHILE	-	.	.	.	.	.	.	2669	5405	3588	.	.	.	.	.
7 CZECHOSLOVAKIA	-	-	-	.	.	.	4366	5275	.	.	.	.	.	.	.
8 DENMARK	-	-	-	-	-	-	9387	11974	.	.	.	.	.	.	.
9 EIRE	-	-	-	-	5443	5597	6511	7793	.	.	.	.	.	.	.
10 FINLAND	-	-	-	-	-	-	-	.	4744	5591	.	.	.	.	.
11 FRANCE	-	-	-	-	-	-	-	-	9309	11204	.	.	.	.	.
12 GREECE	-	-	-	-	-	.	.	.	-	-	-	.	.	.	.
13 HUNGARY	-	-	-	-	-	-	.	.	.	.	.	.	.	.	.
14 ICELAND	-	-	-	-	-	-	-	-	-	-	.	.	.	.	.
15 ITALY	-	-	-	-	-	-	-	-	9608	10642	.	.	.	.	.
16 JAPAN	-	.	.	.	.	.	.	.	-	.	.	.	.	.	.
17 NETHERLANDS	.	.	.	.	6522	10989	7810	11707	13075	11878	.	.	.	.	.
18 NEW ZEALAND	-	.	.	.	.	.	.	12590	9091	7839	.	.	.	.	.
19 NORWAY	.	.	.	.	.	3891	5941	6243	7924	11628	.	.	.	.	.
20 POLAND	-	-	-	-	-	-	-	-	-	-	.	.	.	.	.
21 PORTUGAL	-	-	-	-	-	-	-	-	-	-	.	.	.	.	.
22 ROMANIA	-	-	-	-	-	-	-	-	-	-	-	.	.	.	.
23 SPAIN	.	.	.	.	.	.	1768	1921	14778	13503	.	.	.	.	.
24 SWEDEN	-	-	.	.	.	.	6704	9003	6295	7789	.	.	.	.	.
25 SWITZERLAND	.	.	.	.	.	.	11396	12896	16579	12799	.	.	.	.	.
26 TURKEY	-	-	-	-	-	-	-	-	-	-	-	.	.	.	.
27 UK ENGLAND AND WALES	.	.	5430	5235	6352	7353	8129	8084	8465	8513	.	.	.	.	.
28 UK NORTHERN IRELAND	-	-	-	-	6093	6017	.	.	.	.	.	.	.	.	.
29 UK SCOTLAND	.	.	4476	5441	7721	7837	7719	9675	8467	10238	.	.	.	.	.
30 USA	.	.	.	.	5444	6348	8272	10462	11174	10662	.	.	.	.	.
31 YUGOSLAVIA	-	-	-	-	-	-	-	-	-	-	.	.	.	.	.

- NO MORTALITY DATA ARE AVAILABLE FOR EVEN A BROADER GROUP OF CAUSES FOR THIS DISEASE

. MORTALITY DATA ARE PRESENTED FOR A BROADER GROUP OF CAUSES FOR THIS DISEASE

0 VALUE<0.5

THE STANDARD MORTALITY RATIOS WERE DERIVED WITH A FACTOR OF 10000

SERIAL MORTALITY TABLES FOR VARIOUS COUNTRIES 1901-1975

TABLE 64 : LYMPHOSARCOMA AND OTHER NEOPLASMS OF LYMPHATIC AND HAEMATOPOIETIC SYSTEM : MALES

	1901-	1906-	1911-	1916-	1921-	1926-	1931-	1936-	1941-	1946-	1951-	1956-	1961-	1966-	1971-75
1 AUSTRALIA	-	.	.	.	.	.	.	.	.	.	9641	12034	14187	16628	17187
2 AUSTRIA	-	-	-	-	-	-	-	-	-	.	8361	10844	12859	12707	11540
3 BELGIUM	-	-	-	-	-	-	.	.	.	.	8643	10338	10015	12675	14576
4 BULGARIA	-	-	-	-	-	-	-	-	-	-	-	-	8853	8531	9087
5 CANADA	-	-	-	-	.	.	.	.	.	11337	12233	14040	15747	17250	17939
6 CHILE	-	.	.	.	.	.	.	.	.	.	5948	6150	7097	8043	9470
7 CZECHOSLOVAKIA	-	-	-	.	.	.	.	.	.	.	9249	11811	14023	14758	13978
8 DENMARK	-	-	-	-	-	-	.	.	.	.	12960	16669	17899	17416	17618
9 EIRE	-	-	-	-	.	.	.	.	.	.	6592	7702	10559	12092	13262
10 FINLAND	-	-	-	-	-	-	-	.	.	.	7886	10878	13584	15225	17497
11 FRANCE	-	-	-	-	-	-	-	-	.	5644	6119	7714	8576	10004	11589
12 GREECE	-	-	-	-	-	.	.	.	-	-	-	4467	7562	8733	9253
13 HUNGARY	-	-	-	-	-	-	.	.	.	.	6439	7992	9392	11207	12624
14 ICELAND	-	-	-	-	-	-	-	-	-	-	.	.	11818	12917	12595
15 ITALY	-	-	-	-	-	-	-	-	-	-	9878	11475	12625	13129	13057
16 JAPAN	-	.	.	.	.	.	.	.	-	3079	3750	4557	5615	6975	7986
17 NETHERLANDS	.	.	.	.	.	.	.	.	.	10373	11420	13899	15920	16744	17004
18 NEW ZEALAND	-	.	.	.	.	.	.	.	.	13443	13204	16344	15716	17785	20283
19 NORWAY	.	.	.	.	.	.	.	.	.	.	12495	15955	16724	16846	17277
20 POLAND	-	-	-	-	-	-	-	-	-	-	.	3995	6675	7997	8855
21 PORTUGAL	-	-	-	-	-	-	-	-	-	-	4493	4742	6251	8065	6852
22 ROMANIA	-	-	-	-	-	-	-	-	-	-	-	5908	9148	9467	9329
23 SPAIN	.	.	.	.	.	.	.	.	.	.	3148	3863	5620	6015	7459
24 SWEDEN	-	-	.	.	.	.	.	.	.	.	9290	12885	15729	17996	20284
25 SWITZERLAND	.	.	.	.	2830	3155	.	.	3151	3380	11461	13276	14849	15603	17189
26 TURKEY	-	-	-	-	-	-	-	-	-	-	-	4098	3593	4024	3979
27 UK ENGLAND AND WALES	.	.	.	.	.	.	.	.	.	8100	9887	11103	12279	14108	14822
28 UK NORTHERN IRELAND	-	-	-	-	.	.	.	.	.	10830	7640	10094	11088	13620	15343
29 UK SCOTLAND	.	.	.	.	.	.	.	.	.	9637	11032	11957	15456	16974	16172
30 USA	.	.	.	.	.	.	.	.	.	12771	14059	16048	17149	19270	19794
31 YUGOSLAVIA	-	-	-	-	-	-	-	-	-	-	.	.	7972	8412	8063

- NO MORTALITY DATA ARE AVAILABLE FOR EVEN A BROADER GROUP OF CAUSES FOR THIS DISEASE

. MORTALITY DATA ARE PRESENTED FOR A BROADER GROUP OF CAUSES FOR THIS DISEASE

0 VALUE<0.5

THE STANDARD MORTALITY RATIOS WERE DERIVED WITH A FACTOR OF 10000

SERIAL MORTALITY TABLES FOR VARIOUS COUNTRIES 1901-1975

TABLE 64 : LYMPHOSARCOMA AND OTHER NEOPLASMS OF LYMPHATIC AND HAEMATOPOIETIC SYSTEM : FEMALES

	1901-	1906-	1911-	1916-	1921-	1926-	1931-	1936-	1941-	1946-	1951-	1956-	1961-	1966-	1971-75
1 AUSTRALIA	-	.	.	.	.	.	.	.	.	.	6044	7756	9837	11063	12541
2 AUSTRIA	-	-	-	-	-	-	-	-	-	.	5319	7369	7952	8327	8150
3 BELGIUM	-	-	-	-	-	-	.	.	.	.	4640	5809	5700	7543	8409
4 BULGARIA	-	-	-	-	-	-	-	-	-	-	-	-	4242	4704	5009
5 CANADA	-	-	-	-	.	.	.	.	.	6561	7624	9029	10305	11637	12718
6 CHILE	-	.	.	.	.	.	.	.	.	.	2540	3202	3878	5104	5926
7 CZECHOSLOVAKIA	-	-	-	.	.	.	.	.	.	.	5597	6307	8096	8771	8983
8 DENMARK	-	-	-	-	-	-	.	.	.	.	8493	11005	11066	11353	12302
9 EIRE	-	-	-	-	.	.	.	.	.	.	2912	4816	6548	7929	8121
10 FINLAND	-	-	-	-	-	-	-	.	.	.	4212	5809	7912	10208	12302
11 FRANCE	-	-	-	-	-	-	-	-	.	3223	3351	4270	4870	5955	7436
12 GREECE	-	-	-	-	-	.	.	.	-	-	-	2327	3927	4364	5058
13 HUNGARY	-	-	-	-	-	-	.	.	.	.	4002	4508	5633	6756	7944
14 ICELAND	-	-	-	-	-	-	-	-	-	-	.	.	6438	6226	10714
15 ITALY	-	-	-	-	-	-	-	-	-	-	5474	6526	6822	7638	7776
16 JAPAN	-	.	.	.	.	.	.	.	-	1764	2052	2433	2987	3777	4351
17 NETHERLANDS	.	.	.	.	.	.	.	.	.	6463	7449	8557	9949	10946	12076
18 NEW ZEALAND	-	.	.	.	.	.	.	.	.	8717	8405	9423	11960	13207	13157
19 NORWAY	.	.	.	.	.	.	.	.	.	.	8386	8615	9692	12669	12319
20 POLAND	-	-	-	-	-	-	-	-	-	-	.	1872	3015	4012	4551
21 PORTUGAL	-	-	-	-	-	-	-	-	-	-	2078	2517	3268	3890	3291
22 ROMANIA	-	-	-	-	-	-	-	-	-	-	-	2988	4383	4661	4866
23 SPAIN	.	.	.	.	.	.	.	.	.	.	1563	1946	2779	3005	4213
24 SWEDEN	-	-	.	.	.	.	.	.	.	.	6556	9778	10390	12737	14606
25 SWITZERLAND	.	.	.	.	1362	1983	.	.	2011	1796	7966	9067	9160	10206	12020
26 TURKEY	-	-	-	-	-	-	-	-	-	-	-	1834	1801	1880	2222
27 UK ENGLAND AND WALES	.	.	.	.	.	.	.	.	.	4463	5504	6862	7711	9205	10154
28 UK NORTHERN IRELAND	-	-	-	-	.	.	.	.	.	5373	5757	6268	8422	9638	8973
29 UK SCOTLAND	.	.	.	.	.	.	.	.	.	4946	6451	8075	9583	11529	11677
30 USA	.	.	.	.	.	.	.	.	.	8037	8822	10270	11351	12959	13728
31 YUGOSLAVIA	-	-	-	-	-	-	-	-	-	-	.	.	4576	4562	4674

- NO MORTALITY DATA ARE AVAILABLE FOR EVEN A BROADER GROUP OF CAUSES FOR THIS DISEASE

. MORTALITY DATA ARE PRESENTED FOR A BROADER GROUP OF CAUSES FOR THIS DISEASE

0 VALUE<0.5

THE STANDARD MORTALITY RATIOS WERE DERIVED WITH A FACTOR OF 10000

SERIAL MORTALITY TABLES FOR VARIOUS COUNTRIES 1901-1975

TABLE 65 : MALIGNANT NEOPLASM - ALL FORMS: MALES

	1901-	1906-	1911-	1916-	1921-	1926-	1931-	1936-	1941-	1946-	1951-	1956-	1961-	1966-	1971-75
1 AUSTRALIA	-	7210	7467	7793	8333	8307	8441	8448	8100	8461	8800	9274	9704	10523	11187
2 AUSTRIA	-	-	-	-	-	-	-	-	-	.	13036	13644	13957	14165	14015
3 BELGIUM	-	-	-	-	-	-	.	.	.	.	9904	11355	12638	13528	14359
4 BULGARIA	-	-	-	-	-	-	-	-	-	-	-	-	9575	9432	9071
5 CANADA	-	-	-	-	6793	6860	7719	8229	8449	8761	9195	9621	10048	10712	11210
6 CHILE	-	3753	3292	3933	4028	5572	7320	7617	7989	8623	9948	10620	10469	10827	10961
7 CZECHOSLOVAKIA	-	-	-	.	.	.	.	.	.	10145	10811	12089	13552	14352	14812
8 DENMARK	-	-	-	-	-	-	9571	9342	9234	9271	10413	11139	11777	11429	12192
9 EIRE	-	-	-	-	.	.	.	.	.	.	8976	9308	9849	10591	11489
10 FINLAND	-	-	-	-	-	-	-	.	.	.	12990	13215	13237	13218	13008
11 FRANCE	-	-	-	-	-	-	-	-	8007	9443	10322	11307	12367	12956	13448
12 GREECE	-	-	-	-	-	2928	3564	4234	-	-	-	7418	8269	8789	9249
13 HUNGARY	-	-	-	-	-	-	7541	7350	7792	.	9552	10225	11100	12185	13413
14 ICELAND	-	-	-	-	-	-	-	-	-	-	10259	10312	9561	9461	9409
15 ITALY	-	-	-	-	-	-	-	-	-	-	8229	9329	10354	11408	12172
16 JAPAN	-	5932	6062	6352	6785	.	7492	7498	-	7975	8494	9418	9850	10095	10007
17 NETHERLANDS	8778	8371	9308	9245	.	.	.	.	.	11013	10340	10915	12076	13085	13835
18 NEW ZEALAND	-	7281	7660	7539	7807	8355	.	.	.	9953	9553	9863	10425	11018	11906
19 NORWAY	.	.	.	.	.	6707	8613	8538	.	.	8928	8901	9060	9440	9909
20 POLAND	-	-	-	-	-	-	-	-	-	-	.	7557	9453	10538	11357
21 PORTUGAL	-	-	-	-	-	-	-	-	-	-	5907	6948	7766	8560	8987
22 ROMANIA	-	-	-	-	-	-	-	-	-	-	-	8209	9263	8904	8900
23 SPAIN	3336	3733	4194	4478	4799	5412	5634	5444	5318	5901	6721	7961	9015	9325	10126
24 SWEDEN	-	-	.	.	.	.	8005	8147	7861	7669	8342	8865	9350	9392	10744
25 SWITZERLAND	.	.	.	.	.	.	11890	12412	11670	.	11984	11929	12028	12263	12865
26 TURKEY	-	-	-	-	-	-	-	-	-	-	-	8124	7809	7413	6532
27 UK ENGLAND AND WALES	.	.	8695	8821	9561	9996	10320	10523	10541	11015	11829	12324	12760	13347	13507
28 UK NORTHERN IRELAND	-	-	-	-	7112	7726	.	.	.	10783	9582	10652	10380	11327	11771
29 UK SCOTLAND	.	.	8792	8893	.	.	.	.	.	12308	12546	13270	14119	14529	14771
30 USA	.	7509	6148	6173	6716	7148	7554	8137	8401	8948	9409	9823	10230	10828	11293
31 YUGOSLAVIA	-	-	-	-	-	-	-	-	-	-	.	6750	6901	7674	8544

- NO MORTALITY DATA ARE AVAILABLE FOR EVEN A BROADER GROUP OF CAUSES FOR THIS DISEASE

. MORTALITY DATA ARE PRESENTED FOR A BROADER GROUP OF CAUSES FOR THIS DISEASE

0 VALUE<0.5

THE STANDARD MORTALITY RATIOS WERE DERIVED WITH A FACTOR OF 10000

SERIAL MORTALITY TABLES FOR VARIOUS COUNTRIES 1901-1975

TABLE 65 : MALIGNANT NEOPLASM - ALL FORMS: FEMALES

	1901-	1906-	1911-	1916-	1921-	1926-	1931-	1936-	1941-	1946-	1951-	1956-	1961-	1966-	1971-75
1 AUSTRALIA	-	7703	7925	8101	8349	8174	7923	7921	7896	7653	7161	6934	6840	6969	7125
2 AUSTRIA	-	-	-	-	-	-	-	-	-	.	9513	9423	9190	9112	8744
3 BELGIUM	-	-	-	-	-	-	.	.	.	.	8221	8673	8681	8448	8227
4 BULGARIA	-	-	-	-	-	-	-	-	-	-	-	-	6161	5819	5561
5 CANADA	-	-	-	-	8307	8107	8646	8882	8764	8571	8197	8087	7856	7740	7634
6 CHILE	-	4871	4399	5160	5345	6832	8474	8404	8933	9266	9978	9923	9775	9933	9402
7 CZECHOSLOVAKIA	-	-	-	.	.	.	.	.	.	8392	8179	8173	8271	8254	8233
8 DENMARK	-	-	-	-	-	-	10397	10266	10215	9578	10019	9996	9866	9156	9055
9 EIRE	-	-	-	-	.	.	.	.	.	.	7273	7649	7591	8188	8687
10 FINLAND	-	-	-	-	-	-	-	.	.	.	8389	8052	7540	7223	7005
11 FRANCE	-	-	-	-	-	-	-	-	6771	7220	7421	7461	7401	7184	6989
12 GREECE	-	-	-	-	-	2927	3418	3733	-	-	-	4831	5101	5069	5110
13 HUNGARY	-	-	-	-	-	-	8262	7801	7855	.	8327	8276	8296	8449	8873
14 ICELAND	-	-	-	-	-	-	-	-	-	-	8328	8512	8792	8651	8200
15 ITALY	-	-	-	-	-	-	-	-	-	-	6586	6878	6968	7038	7043
16 JAPAN	-	5382	5445	5739	5893	.	6445	6336	-	6524	6567	6781	6770	6637	6309
17 NETHERLANDS	7916	8150	8678	8956	.	.	.	.	.	9918	8973	8576	8433	8563	8202
18 NEW ZEALAND	-	8216	8499	8317	8145	8418	.	.	.	8491	7976	7610	7727	7735	8197
19 NORWAY	.	.	.	.	.	6215	7933	7724	.	.	7878	7370	7007	7136	6964
20 POLAND	-	-	-	-	-	-	-	-	-	-	.	5814	6963	7195	7023
21 PORTUGAL	-	-	-	-	-	-	-	-	-	-	4932	5372	5702	5936	6024
22 ROMANIA	-	-	-	-	-	-	-	-	-	-	-	6463	6799	6047	5883
23 SPAIN	3900	4250	4575	4793	4888	5249	5041	4667	4632	4778	5118	5729	6181	6123	6238
24 SWEDEN	-	-	.	.	.	.	7577	7752	7564	7535	7812	7768	7584	7456	7986
25 SWITZERLAND	.	.	.	.	.	.	9150	9320	8859	.	8725	8377	7975	7851	7674
26 TURKEY	-	-	-	-	-	-	-	-	-	-	-	5158	4705	4438	3980
27 UK ENGLAND AND WALES	.	.	9228	9040	9294	9395	9236	9041	8418	8329	8030	7885	7841	7999	8168
28 UK NORTHERN IRELAND	-	-	-	-	7812	8193	.	.	.	9387	7931	7964	7422	7793	8016
29 UK SCOTLAND	.	.	9856	9787	.	.	.	.	.	9502	9029	8797	8675	8735	8790
30 USA	.	11293	9277	8915	8884	9070	9078	9045	8723	8451	7997	7622	7380	7312	7255
31 YUGOSLAVIA	-	-	-	-	-	-	-	-	-	-	.	5160	4994	5169	5454

- NO MORTALITY DATA ARE AVAILABLE FOR EVEN A BROADER GROUP OF CAUSES FOR THIS DISEASE

. MORTALITY DATA ARE PRESENTED FOR A BROADER GROUP OF CAUSES FOR THIS DISEASE

0 VALUE<0.5

THE STANDARD MORTALITY RATIOS WERE DERIVED WITH A FACTOR OF 10000

SERIAL MORTALITY TABLES FOR VARIOUS COUNTRIES 1901-1975

TABLE 66 : NEOFLASM - BENIGN AND UNSPECIFIED : MALES

	1901-	1906-	1911-	1916-	1921-	1926-	1931-	1936-	1941-	1946-	1951-	1956-	1961-	1966-	1971-75
1 AUSTRALIA	-	.	.	.	.	.	20846	23639	21636	19577	14935	8546	6558	5775	5433
2 AUSTRIA	-	-	-	-	-	-	-	-	-	25968	31084	20983	18953	18852	17072
3 BELGIUM	-	-	-	-	-	-	30841	32122	29350	25391	15642	11410	11005	10582	15245
4 BULGARIA	-	-	-	-	-	-	17899	28863	25039	25641	24410	23262	18231	18008	14944
5 CANADA	-	-	-	-	.	.	20122	24349	9604	8615	8248	6759	6629	6117	5875
6 CHILE	-	.	.	.	.	.	11783	10438	9320	9608	14673	13851	16258	14048	14846
7 CZECHOSLOVAKIA	-	-	-	.	.	.	23083	26406	20043	25253	10218	9722	10456	9878	12008
8 DENMARK	-	-	-	-	-	-	41812	47783	38189	45789	31366	25016	21799	17217	12075
9 EIRE	-	-	-	-	.	12132	15817	21022	17950	19314	16583	15233	15588	12430	7688
10 FINLAND	-	-	-	-	-	-	-	35058	33747	36188	14359	11867	16808	14445	11646
11 FRANCE	-	-	-	-	-	-	30798	31441	28012	28407	32379	31389	32277	32716	30390
12 GREECE	-	-	-	-	-	.	20642	18722	-	-	-	38255	42603	43120	29476
13 HUNGARY	-	-	-	-	-	-	32159	36366	28959	26000	20758	19129	15620	12646	14414
14 ICELAND	-	-	-	-	-	-	-	-	32857	14103	16279	15464	14815	9402	5556
15 ITALY	-	-	-	-	-	-	-	-	-	-	26945	21019	25056	25732	21388
16 JAPAN	-	.	.	.	.	.	18170	18681	-	26464	28232	27439	27053	27852	27082
17 NETHERLANDS	.	.	.	.	.	.	28824	33115	28312	21878	17516	18648	25190	26037	30307
18 NEW ZEALAND	-	.	.	.	.	16213	22968	17672	11389	7727	7644	6174	4290	5690	3919
19 NORWAY	.	.	.	.	.	18152	24506	41910	.	.	14362	12043	10869	13469	23061
20 POLAND	-	-	-	-	-	-	-	-	-	-	.	34743	34147	30574	22520
21 PORTUGAL	-	-	-	-	-	-	38475	25034	21736	23442	20769	4895	4231	4632	2730
22 ROMANIA	-	-	-	-	-	-	-	-	-	-	-	9659	6730	14253	18294
23 SPAIN	.	.	.	.	.	.	18787	29096	40104	53559	33975	12112	7412	5259	2005
24 SWEDEN	-	-	.	.	.	.	48090	54374	58299	65034	28227	21700	23787	19107	8017
25 SWITZERLAND	10059	10059	14746	14746	7271	9162	26284	17585	11618	9385	11732	10592	11228	10564	8713
26 TURKEY	-	-	-	-	-	-	-	-	-	-	-	3847	1335	2094	446
27 UK ENGLAND AND WALES	11066	11967	13713	14783	22126	24119	24021	21062	18011	16388	13812	10294	9936	9859	8859
28 UK NORTHERN IRELAND	-	-	-	-	.	.	20420	23159	37434	24138	10760	7331	11184	9554	9271
29 UK SCOTLAND	22174	21461	22939	16750	.	.	22945	21538	12896	11492	7867	7755	6944	7352	7560
30 USA	.	.	.	.	.	13011	12965	12800	12076	11530	10956	10290	9702	9466	9503
31 YUGOSLAVIA	-	-	-	-	-	-	-	-	-	-	.	27115	25185	23900	12831

- NO MORTALITY DATA ARE AVAILABLE FOR EVEN A BROADER GROUP OF CAUSES FOR THIS DISEASE

. MORTALITY DATA ARE PRESENTED FOR A BROADER GROUP OF CAUSES FOR THIS DISEASE

0 VALUE<0.5

THE STANDARD MORTALITY RATIOS WERE DERIVED WITH A FACTOR OF 10000

SERIAL MORTALITY TABLES FOR VARIOUS COUNTRIES 1901-1975

TABLE 66 : NEOPLASM - BENIGN AND UNSPECIFIED : FEMALES

	1901-	1906-	1911-	1916-	1921-	1926-	1931-	1936-	1941-	1946-	1951-	1956-	1961-	1966-	1971-75
1 AUSTRALIA	-	.	.	.	.	.	28671	30357	26376	22304	15677	10387	7507	6686	5722
2 AUSTRIA	-	-	-	-	-	-	-	-	-	31866	32899	21444	18914	19223	17047
3 BELGIUM	-	-	-	-	-	-	33105	35553	32730	26220	13630	9885	9087	9723	11525
4 BULGARIA	-	-	-	-	-	-	22287	35358	22239	23461	22060	17176	15438	14066	12033
5 CANADA	-	-	-	-	.	.	39889	41270	22478	15150	12064	9715	8070	6553	5617
6 CHILE	-	.	.	.	.	.	15385	15455	13974	11264	15137	15352	16584	14254	14163
7 CZECHOSLOVAKIA	-	-	-	.	.	.	25550	28527	18576	22061	10152	10551	10719	9734	10088
8 DENMARK	-	-	-	-	-	-	53648	58403	49057	51517	36944	26227	23094	15348	13277
9 EIRE	-	-	-	-	.	25303	26056	24260	19780	19486	17217	15595	13425	11122	7289
10 FINLAND	-	-	-	-	-	-	-	34658	33020	30981	12394	12798	14771	13001	11441
11 FRANCE	-	-	-	-	-	-	42402	37796	31460	28237	30780	28377	27129	25660	24287
12 GREECE	-	-	-	-	-	.	18520	17204	-	-	-	26781	28780	27701	18956
13 HUNGARY	-	-	-	-	-	-	35739	38350	33890	25267	18165	16918	15954	12971	17122
14 ICELAND	-	-	-	-	-	-	-	-	40000	17442	21277	22330	11404	10484	10448
15 ITALY	-	-	-	-	-	-	-	-	-	-	30098	21377	22858	20779	15831
16 JAPAN	-	.	.	.	.	.	25151	24191	-	27717	27832	24136	22359	21349	19968
17 NETHERLANDS	.	.	.	.	.	.	35259	32933	31109	24619	20333	19331	24078	25082	27693
18 NEW ZEALAND	-	.	.	.	.	32459	32230	23555	17889	15694	8069	7973	7683	6891	4868
19 NORWAY	.	.	.	.	.	22605	26092	36332	.	.	18481	14355	13498	15540	21074
20 POLAND	-	-	-	-	-	-	-	-	-	-	.	32402	29653	23154	17147
21 PORTUGAL	-	-	-	-	-	-	40514	23326	15690	14702	14923	4294	4750	4600	2176
22 ROMANIA	-	-	-	-	-	-	-	-	-	-	-	8384	4602	10384	12515
23 SPAIN	.	.	.	.	.	.	17115	26345	36470	43535	29113	10068	6321	4473	1713
24 SWEDEN	-	-	.	.	.	.	46969	51488	55342	57787	28198	22408	21818	19842	9906
25 SWITZERLAND	26201	26201	28318	28318	6969	7115	37361	28878	20237	16388	16790	15576	11811	13245	12420
26 TURKEY	-	-	-	-	-	-	-	-	-	-	-	4119	1957	2112	368
27 UK ENGLAND AND WALES	31174	28251	27251	26562	31278	32794	30930	24853	20083	16833	12937	10328	9116	8452	7837
28 UK NORTHERN IRELAND	-	-	-	-	.	.	30000	32324	29254	18005	13790	10236	9261	7219	9020
29 UK SCOTLAND	44306	41193	37330	30323	.	.	31111	29923	20825	14154	10309	8852	7244	6405	6800
30 USA	.	.	.	.	.	34421	31951	30381	25901	19006	14297	11636	10062	9079	8274
31 YUGOSLAVIA	-	-	-	-	-	-	-	-	-	-	.	22277	20010	17148	10152

- NO MORTALITY DATA ARE AVAILABLE FOR EVEN A BROADER GROUP OF CAUSES FOR THIS DISEASE

. MORTALITY DATA ARE PRESENTED FOR A BROADER GROUP OF CAUSES FOR THIS DISEASE

0 VALUE<0.5

THE STANDARD MORTALITY RATIOS WERE DERIVED WITH A FACTOR OF 10000

SERIAL MORTALITY TABLES FOR VARIOUS COUNTRIES 1901-1975

TABLE 67 : NEOPLASM - ALL FORMS : MALES

	1901-	1906-	1911-	1916-	1921-	1926-	1931-	1936-	1941-	1946-	1951-	1956-	1961-	1966-	1971-75
1 AUSTRALIA	-	7193	7399	7703	8244	8281	8647	8693	8316	8638	8898	9262	9654	10447	11096
2 AUSTRIA	-	-	-	-	-	-	-	-	-	11888	12997	13749	14027	14231	14057
3 BELGIUM	-	-	-	-	-	-	6521	7090	6986	7287	9471	11356	12615	13487	14371
4 BULGARIA	-	-	-	-	-	-	-	-	-	-	-	-	9711	9562	9158
5 CANADA	-	-	-	-	6741	6837	7930	8494	8468	8759	9181	9576	9994	10639	11127
6 CHILE	-	3796	3661	4271	4443	5735	7411	7674	8016	8642	10039	10683	10580	10889	11034
7 CZECHOSLOVAKIA	-	-	-	6718	7554	8699	9539	9653	8443	9955	10830	12052	13505	14285	14771
8 DENMARK	-	-	-	-	-	-	10086	9948	9683	9828	10727	11342	11921	11511	12191
9 EIRE	-	-	-	-	6156	7115	8055	8381	8353	8332	9085	9392	9930	10617	11435
10 FINLAND	-	-	-	-	-	-	-	9300	9833	11587	13014	13192	13296	13238	12987
11 FRANCE	-	-	-	-	-	-	-	-	8254	9725	10650	11605	12659	13242	13689
12 GREECE	-	-	-	-	-	3027	3807	4474	-	-	-	7909	8796	9300	9538
13 HUNGARY	-	-	-	-	-	-	7947	7824	8136	8404	8934	10363	11168	12191	13427
14 ICELAND	-	-	-	-	-	-	-	-	-	-	10357	10395	9645	9461	9350
15 ITALY	-	-	-	-	-	-	-	-	-	-	8522	9509	10577	11622	12307
16 JAPAN	-	5845	5976	6264	6772	7089	7387	7708	-	8320	8855	9735	10144	10391	10287
17 NETHERLANDS	8817	8350	9251	9217	9400	9562	9806	10240	10356	10249	10452	11033	12273	13278	14078
18 NEW ZEALAND	-	7274	7666	7492	7746	8418	8610	8462	8679	9102	9524	9805	10328	10933	11781
19 NORWAY	7036	6953	7672	7698	8425	8577	8860	9053	8605	9074	9009	8947	9086	9496	10091
20 POLAND	-	-	-	-	-	-	-	-	-	-	5587	8043	9879	10867	11535
21 PORTUGAL	-	-	-	-	-	-	-	-	-	-	6136	6914	7709	8498	8893
22 ROMANIA	-	-	-	-	-	-	-	-	-	-	-	8233	9222	8989	9047
23 SPAIN	3438	3813	4247	4530	4824	5455	5858	5843	5900	6694	7168	8028	8990	9262	10002
24 SWEDEN	-	-	7316	7504	7896	8132	8612	8843	8613	8516	8632	9049	9552	9525	10707
25 SWITZERLAND	11202	11202	11703	11703	11859	11774	12125	12494	12041	11860	11980	11909	12017	12238	12805
26 TURKEY	-	-	-	-	-	-	-	-	-	-	-	8034	7679	7309	6415
27 UK ENGLAND AND WALES	7162	7133	8786	8925	9774	10228	10538	10685	10649	11095	11858	12295	12719	13296	13441
28 UK NORTHERN IRELAND	-	-	-	-	7045	7700	8251	8558	9461	9942	9600	10602	10392	11300	11734
29 UK SCOTLAND	7236	8204	9049	9032	9763	10260	10668	10797	10993	11657	12476	13188	14012	14424	14667
30 USA	7046	5971	6065	6086	6655	7111	7645	8213	8459	8988	9433	9830	10222	10807	11267
31 YUGOSLAVIA	-	-	-	-	-	-	-	-	-	-	4780	6647	7207	7940	8613

- NO MORTALITY DATA ARE AVAILABLE FOR EVEN A BROADER GROUP OF CAUSES FOR THIS DISEASE

. MORTALITY DATA ARE PRESENTED FOR A BROADER GROUP OF CAUSES FOR THIS DISEASE

0 VALUE<0.5

THE STANDARD MORTALITY RATIOS WERE DERIVED WITH A FACTOR OF 10000

SERIAL MORTALITY TABLES FOR VARIOUS COUNTRIES 1901-1975

TABLE 67 : NEOPLASM - ALL FORMS : FEMALES

	1901-	1906-	1911-	1916-	1921-	1926-	1931-	1936-	1941-	1946-	1951-	1956-	1961-	1966-	1971-75
1 AUSTRALIA	-	8045	8184	8305	8547	8394	8265	8277	8181	7876	7288	6985	6850	6965	7105
2 AUSTRIA	-	-	-	-	-	-	-	-	-	9751	9708	9584	9316	9240	8847
3 BELGIUM	-	-	-	-	-	-	7430	7697	7562	7488	7976	8690	8686	8464	8269
4 BULGARIA	-	-	-	-	-	-	-	-	-	-	-	-	6299	5938	5652
5 CANADA	-	-	-	-	8596	8431	9174	9414	8984	8676	8258	8113	7859	7722	7604
6 CHILE	-	5128	4907	5499	5782	7035	8609	8540	9029	9303	10073	10022	9899	10011	9485
7 CZECHOSLOVAKIA	-	-	-	6857	7128	8253	8720	8633	7653	8456	8240	8207	8306	8274	8258
8 DENMARK	-	-	-	-	-	-	11065	11004	10802	10202	10410	10226	10048	9239	9110
9 EIRE	-	-	-	-	5444	6391	7156	7526	7317	7290	7413	7760	7671	8228	8668
10 FINLAND	-	-	-	-	-	-	-	7522	7893	8312	8451	8124	7646	7305	7065
11 FRANCE	-	-	-	-	-	-	-	-	7076	7506	7734	7736	7657	7420	7207
12 GREECE	-	-	-	-	-	3037	3644	3952	-	-	-	5161	5446	5389	5298
13 HUNGARY	-	-	-	-	-	-	8708	8289	8265	7985	7833	8402	8403	8511	8982
14 ICELAND	-	-	-	-	-	-	-	-	-	-	8523	8720	8830	8678	8232
15 ITALY	-	-	-	-	-	-	-	-	-	-	6935	7088	7191	7228	7161
16 JAPAN	-	5625	5660	5942	6161	6368	6521	6645	-	6890	6929	7067	7021	6868	6517
17 NETHERLANDS	8090	8279	8760	9024	9367	9832	10181	10382	10454	9680	9146	8735	8658	8795	8468
18 NEW ZEALAND	-	8670	8781	8446	8283	8711	8552	8289	8308	8057	7977	7615	7727	7723	8149
19 NORWAY	6099	6312	6647	6853	7557	8034	8200	8142	7961	8251	8029	7467	7095	7247	7146
20 POLAND	-	-	-	-	-	-	-	-	-	-	5037	6238	7313	7431	7166
21 PORTUGAL	-	-	-	-	-	-	-	-	-	-	5076	5356	5689	5917	5970
22 ROMANIA	-	-	-	-	-	-	-	-	-	-	-	6493	6766	6111	5979
23 SPAIN	4127	4459	4744	4952	5003	5378	5236	5010	5131	5376	5480	5793	6183	6100	6175
24 SWEDEN	-	-	6831	7081	7509	7850	8146	8333	8249	8251	8099	7969	7775	7618	8010
25 SWITZERLAND	10067	10067	10186	10186	9296	9209	9583	9613	9468	9036	8840	8478	8028	7924	7737
26 TURKEY	-	-	-	-	-	-	-	-	-	-	-	5139	4655	4397	3915
27 UK ENGLAND AND WALES	9857	9049	9532	9330	9648	9759	9564	9273	8583	8448	8097	7918	7858	8005	8164
28 UK NORTHERN IRELAND	-	-	-	-	8025	8429	8750	8637	8827	8915	8015	7996	7448	7785	8029
29 UK SCOTLAND	9020	10028	10311	10123	10440	10504	10286	10119	9437	9233	9047	8798	8655	8704	8764
30 USA	12159	10031	9711	9287	9260	9443	9461	9391	8993	8613	8091	7681	7418	7337	7269
31 YUGOSLAVIA	-	-	-	-	-	-	-	-	-	-	4377	5225	5225	5350	5524

- NO MORTALITY DATA ARE AVAILABLE FOR EVEN A BROADER GROUP OF CAUSES FOR THIS DISEASE

. MORTALITY DATA ARE PRESENTED FOR A BROADER GROUP OF CAUSES FOR THIS DISEASE

0 VALUE<0.5

THE STANDARD MORTALITY RATIOS WERE DERIVED WITH A FACTOR OF 10000

SERIAL MORTALITY TABLES FOR VARIOUS COUNTRIES 1901-1975

TABLE 67 : NEOPLASM - ALL FORMS : PERSONS

	1901-	1906-	1911-	1916-	1921-	1926-	1931-	1936-	1941-	1946-	1951-	1956-	1961-	1966-	1971-75
1 AUSTRALIA	-	7581	7760	7985	8388	8336	8460	8485	8248	8245	8045	8042	8133	8540	8897
2 AUSTRIA	-	-	-	-	-	10310	10660	11159	-	10673	11105	11313	11228	11222	10879
3 BELGIUM	-	-	-	-	-	-	6993	7406	7287	7393	8656	9888	10428	10658	10893
4 BULGARIA	-	-	-	-	-	-	-	-	-	-	-	-	7901	7646	7305
5 CANADA	4184	3569	4486	4540	7619	7595	8524	8935	8717	8718	8724	8842	8903	9109	9229
6 CHILE	-	4485	4304	4904	5136	6412	8036	8127	8546	8990	10057	10330	10215	10416	10188
7 CZECHOSLOVAKIA	-	-	-	6793	7323	8456	9091	9093	8008	9127	9392	9905	10566	10866	11033
8 DENMARK	-	-	-	-	-	-	10604	10503	10269	10023	10561	10754	10924	10284	10504
9 EIRE	-	-	-	-	5795	6748	7603	7955	7832	7807	8240	8560	8758	9365	9970
10 FINLAND	-	-	-	-	-	-	-	8296	8722	9679	10323	10204	9965	9725	9453
11 FRANCE	7914	4544	4393	3644	-	-	-	-	5682	8436	8942	9330	9715	9810	9874
12 GREECE	-	-	-	-	-	3032	3723	4205	-	-	-	8271	9969	10362	10507
13 HUNGARY	-	-	-	-	-	-	8346	8070	8205	8174	8324	9273	9621	10118	10899
14 ICELAND	-	-	-	-	-	-	-	-	-	-	9365	9503	9215	9046	8758
15 ITALY	-	-	-	-	-	-	-	-	-	-	7658	8181	8699	9154	9400
16 JAPAN	-	5732	5813	6098	6451	6706	6925	7140	-	7544	7811	8285	8442	8461	8201
17 NETHERLANDS	8434	8313	8994	9116	9383	9702	10000	10313	10407	9954	9773	9829	10356	10859	10994
18 NEW ZEALAND	-	7880	8160	7929	7999	8559	8581	8376	8491	8566	8718	8645	8927	9181	9786
19 NORWAY	6529	6605	7112	7235	7949	8279	8499	8555	8254	8628	8482	8153	8018	8277	8477
20 POLAND	-	-	-	-	-	-	-	-	-	-	5268	6515	8392	8877	8987
21 PORTUGAL	-	-	-	-	-	-	-	-	-	-	5517	6008	6541	7003	7203
22 ROMANIA	-	-	-	-	-	-	-	5668	-	3941	-	7262	7854	7387	7341
23 SPAIN	3797	4153	4509	4752	4918	5413	5518	5382	5473	5956	6212	6762	7411	7480	7838
24 SWEDEN	-	-	7050	7273	7685	7979	8362	8598	8420	8377	8352	8479	8609	8504	9247
25 SWITZERLAND	10592	10592	10874	10874	10445	10358	10720	10899	10613	10286	10227	9984	9765	9790	9914
26 TURKEY	-	-	-	-	-	-	3677	4703	4947	4715	4893	6504	6099	5838	5178
27 UK ENGLAND AND WALES	8576	8141	9194	9148	9705	9970	9999	9898	9477	9598	9701	9760	9887	10198	10354
28 UK NORTHERN IRELAND	-	-	-	-	7568	8089	8515	8600	9120	9394	8735	9160	8751	9317	9620
29 UK SCOTLAND	8239	9227	9753	9637	10137	10395	10458	10423	10126	10295	10532	10670	10902	11066	11173
30 USA	9641	7982	7854	7654	7934	8257	8543	8803	8730	7036	8732	8689	8705	8888	9010
31 YUGOSLAVIA	-	-	-	-	-	-	-	-	-	-	4555	5850	6097	6495	6888

- NO MORTALITY DATA ARE AVAILABLE FOR EVEN A BROADER GROUP OF CAUSES FOR THIS DISEASE
. MORTALITY DATA ARE PRESENTED FOR A BROADER GROUP OF CAUSES FOR THIS DISEASE
0 VALUE<0.5
THE STANDARD MORTALITY RATIOS WERE DERIVED WITH A FACTOR OF 10000

SERIAL MORTALITY TABLES FOR VARIOUS COUNTRIES 1901-1975

TABLE 68 : GOITRE - NON-TOXIC : MALES

	1901-	1906-	1911-	1916-	1921-	1926-	1931-	1936-	1941-	1946-	1951-	1956-	1961-	1966-	1971-75
1 AUSTRALIA	-	.	.	.	.	.	.	.	748	678	1069	417	252	58	159
2 AUSTRIA	-	-	-	-	-	-	-	-	-	-	16102	11600	4769	4000	2374
3 BELGIUM	-	-	-	-	-	-	-	-	-	-	909	920	1111	968	733
4 BULGARIA	-	-	-	-	-	-	-	-	-	-	-	-	.	.	.
5 CANADA	-	-	-	-	.	.	3609	3067	1706	1289	1682	688	584	571	278
6 CHILE	-	.	.	.	.	.	.	3846	2326	781	943	476	274	610	337
7 CZECHOSLOVAKIA	-	-	-	-	-	-	4583	4872	.	.	1548	1457	948	1688	769
8 DENMARK	-	-	-	-	-	-	-	-	-	-	1351	610	1136	737	594
9 EIRE	-	-	-	-	-	-	1250	3500	.	.	727	546	926	556	182
10 FINLAND	-	-	-	-	-	-	-	-	-	-	435	1400	727	1000	303
11 FRANCE	-	-	-	-	-	-	-	-	.	735	799	773	637	531	465
12 GREECE	-	-	-	-	-	.	.	.	-	-	-	174	615	621	359
13 HUNGARY	-	-	-	-	-	-	4364	3298	3600	.	7778	4865	2547	966	2181
14 ICELAND	-	-	-	-	-	-	-	-	-	-	-	-	3333	0	0
15 ITALY	-	-	-	-	-	-	-	-	-	-	1821	1658	1449	1051	865
16 JAPAN	-	.	.	.	.	-	4421	3594	-	714	691	586	296	300	181
17 NETHERLANDS	.	.	.	.	-	-	1845	1739	2742	1353	1962	2386	663	657	746
18 NEW ZEALAND	-	.	.	.	.	5882	2632	1364	4000	446	625	1714	1081	513	238
19 NORWAY	0	313	.	.	.	.	.	.	.	.	509	154	282	130	0
20 POLAND	-	-	-	-	-	-	-	-	-	-	.	578	746	1756	781
21 PORTUGAL	-	-	-	-	-	-	-	-	-	-	505	841	840	161	534
22 ROMANIA	-	-	-	-	-	-	-	-	-	-	-	899	0	73	130
23 SPAIN	.	.	.	.	.	.	982	1134	.	.	1879	1429	1131	889	507
24 SWEDEN	-	-	-	-	-	-	-	-	-	-	677	548	380	407	270
25 SWITZERLAND	-	-	-	-	-	-	-	-	-	-	9359	5412	2872	3137	2857
26 TURKEY	-	-	-	-	-	-	-	-	-	-	-	2549	833	2124	5000
27 UK ENGLAND AND WALES	.	.	.	.	2927	2093	2312	1660	998	1213	850	635	262	250	182
28 UK NORTHERN IRELAND	-	-	-	-	.	.	-	-	-	0	3043	435	833	0	0
29 UK SCOTLAND	-	-	.	.	-	-	-	-	.	625	244	476	581	114	330
30 USA	.	.	.	.	.	2190	1703	1199	1071	701	581	424	235	180	112
31 YUGOSLAVIA	-	-	-	-	-	-	-	-	-	-	.	.	661	356	285

\- NO MORTALITY DATA ARE AVAILABLE FOR EVEN A BROADER GROUP OF CAUSES FOR THIS DISEASE

. MORTALITY DATA ARE PRESENTED FOR A BROADER GROUP OF CAUSES FOR THIS DISEASE

0 VALUE<0.5

THE STANDARD MORTALITY RATIOS WERE DERIVED WITH A FACTOR OF 1000

SERIAL MORTALITY TABLES FOR VARIOUS COUNTRIES 1901-1975

TABLE 68 : GOITRE - NON-TOXIC : FEMALES

	1901-	1906-	1911-	1916-	1921-	1926-	1931-	1936-	1941-	1946-	1951-	1956-	1961-	1966-	1971-75
1 AUSTRALIA	-	.	.	.	.	.	.	.	2946	2031	2848	2733	965	543	776
2 AUSTRIA	-	-	-	-	-	-	-	-	-	-	23313	15667	9645	8632	5398
3 BELGIUM	-	-	-	-	-	-	-	-	-	-	6219	5505	4378	2760	2038
4 BULGARIA	-	-	-	-	-	-	-	-	-	-	-	-	.	.	.
5 CANADA	-	-	-	-	.	.	18871	18298	8137	5187	4521	2351	1615	1339	687
6 CHILE	-	.	.	.	.	.	.	6250	4082	4167	1667	1733	1494	1939	909
7 CZECHOSLOVAKIA	-	-	-	-	-	-	8079	10833	.	.	4906	4531	4912	4765	2779
8 DENMARK	-	-	-	-	-	-	-	-	-	-	2927	2857	2647	2368	952
9 EIRE	-	-	-	-	-	-	14600	12255	.	.	5088	3276	1333	1452	1385
10 FINLAND	-	-	-	-	-	-	-	-	-	-	2353	4133	2530	2637	1176
11 FRANCE	-	-	-	-	-	-	-	-	.	3782	2498	2625	1921	1396	1248
12 GREECE	-	-	-	-	-	.	.	.	-	-	-	1714	2641	2346	865
13 HUNGARY	-	-	-	-	-	-	10328	11887	17193	.	19852	18138	7571	3974	6654
14 ICELAND	-	-	-	-	-	-	-	-	-	-	-	-	0	6667	0
15 ITALY	-	-	-	-	-	-	-	-	-	-	4851	4474	3848	2430	1965
16 JAPAN	-	.	.	.	.	-	15864	15894	-	1204	2069	1862	1435	932	652
17 NETHERLANDS	.	.	.	.	-	-	8469	5366	5113	8345	5497	6205	3812	3715	2912
18 NEW ZEALAND	-	.	.	.	.	25000	10526	9091	5385	5000	4722	3171	2889	1600	1111
19 NORWAY	811	1579	.	.	.	.	.	.	.	.	2754	2500	1548	1489	900
20 POLAND	-	-	-	-	-	-	-	-	-	-	.	636	1628	2558	2083
21 PORTUGAL	-	-	-	-	-	-	-	-	-	-	1761	2403	1243	509	1117
22 ROMANIA	-	-	-	-	-	-	-	-	-	-	-	696	0	170	304
23 SPAIN	.	.	.	.	.	.	3009	2757	.	.	3067	2454	2767	1558	1627
24 SWEDEN	-	-	-	-	-	-	-	-	-	-	3800	1818	2131	1520	1189
25 SWITZERLAND	-	-	-	-	-	-	-	-	-	-	15050	10357	6160	4820	3936
26 TURKEY	-	-	-	-	-	-	-	-	-	-	-	3898	2813	5000	6637
27 UK ENGLAND AND WALES	.	.	.	.	9764	8554	10046	7281	5244	4160	2621	1690	1225	910	841
28 UK NORTHERN IRELAND	-	-	-	-	.	.	-	-	-	10870	2593	690	323	909	571
29 UK SCOTLAND	-	-	.	.	-	-	-	-	.	1429	2091	1282	1210	902	638
30 USA	.	.	.	.	.	9846	6937	4874	3451	2671	2325	1418	858	560	349
31 YUGOSLAVIA	-	-	-	-	-	-	-	-	-	-	.	.	1212	1006	771

- NO MORTALITY DATA ARE AVAILABLE FOR EVEN A BROADER GROUP OF CAUSES FOR THIS DISEASE
. MORTALITY DATA ARE PRESENTED FOR A BROADER GROUP OF CAUSES FOR THIS DISEASE
0 VALUE<0.5
THE STANDARD MORTALITY RATIOS WERE DERIVED WITH A FACTOR OF 1000

SERIAL MORTALITY TABLES FOR VARIOUS COUNTRIES 1901-1975

TABLE 69 : THYROTOXICOSIS WITH OR WITHOUT GOITRE : MALES

	1901-	1906-	1911-	1916-	1921-	1926-	1931-	1936-	1941-	1946-	1951-	1956-	1961-	1966-	1971-75
1 AUSTRALIA	-	7220	8462	4730	6275	8953	12536	16426	12634	7151	4118	2939	2520	3139	2937
2 AUSTRIA	-	-	-	-	-	-	-	-	-	-	3960	723	2185	2611	2004
3 BELGIUM	-	-	-	-	-	-	-	-	-	-	4144	3085	2695	2546	2227
4 BULGARIA	-	-	-	-	-	-	-	-	-	-	-	-	3952	2705	2097
5 CANADA	-	-	-	-	17513	25108	22714	23123	28323	13409	6571	4225	2667	1497	1073
6 CHILE	-	0	444	893	0	.	.	0	893	1011	2439	1224	355	630	997
7 CZECHOSLOVAKIA	-	-	-	640	10194	9021	7168	9772	.	.	15618	11487	6643	4811	3179
8 DENMARK	-	-	-	-	-	-	-	-	9850	7915	3710	6634	3153	1975	1598
9 EIRE	-	-	-	-	2365	6486	8527	8085	.	.	4878	3713	3500	2993	3893
10 FINLAND	-	-	-	-	-	-	-	-	8408	8406	7084	5419	4677	6531	4315
11 FRANCE	-	-	-	-	-	-	-	-	.	1893	1283	1187	719	1053	1358
12 GREECE	-	-	-	-	-	.	.	.	-	-	-	1048	717	729	719
13 HUNGARY	-	-	-	-	-	-	9393	7848	10026	.	4230	6068	5004	3096	2791
14 ICELAND	-	-	-	-	-	-	-	-	-	-	-	-	0	0	0
15 ITALY	-	-	-	-	-	-	-	-	-	-	3795	3134	3060	2139	1706
16 JAPAN	-	4015	3329	4651	4519	5056	6092	.	-	2462	1783	1523	1335	1481	1466
17 NETHERLANDS	4912	1772	3102	6261	3385	5533	7711	7589	8790	4327	4160	4876	4716	4940	3567
18 NEW ZEALAND	-	5882	16129	22115	21368	29851	28571	32955	34848	17694	10612	6844	5735	6689	4255
19 NORWAY	0	0	2101	1200	2264	709	1639	3012	4696	2261	2975	2893	2060	2261	1309
20 POLAND	-	-	-	-	-	-	-	-	-	-	.	2231	1639	1818	2214
21 PORTUGAL	-	-	-	-	-	-	-	-	-	-	1292	1905	758	723	1354
22 ROMANIA	-	-	-	-	-	-	-	-	-	-	-	1255	2299	1327	1109
23 SPAIN	3819	2216	2603	2922	2564	2105	1281	911	.	.	1690	2119	1057	1178	439
24 SWEDEN	-	-	-	-	-	-	6073	7332	3497	2232	4734	3258	2676	1862	2836
25 SWITZERLAND	6452	6452	6278	6278	5495	3291	-	-	-	-	1645	1970	2917	4209	4122
26 TURKEY	-	-	-	-	-	-	-	-	-	-	-	1946	1329	1224	1152
27 UK ENGLAND AND WALES	.	.	6193	7157	7763	13186	18682	19623	10343	6275	5229	3940	3313	2610	2336
28 UK NORTHERN IRELAND	-	-	-	-	7547	10526	-	-	-	9677	5357	2367	3911	5376	2094
29 UK SCOTLAND	-	-	4987	8049	5145	8750	12500	14414	10265	6742	3785	2928	3303	2464	1685
30 USA	.	9596	9787	11597	17118	28441	24268	22071	15430	9233	4635	2678	1871	1571	1162
31 YUGOSLAVIA	-	-	-	-	-	-	-	-	-	-	.	.	1804	1701	2305

- NO MORTALITY DATA ARE AVAILABLE FOR EVEN A BROADER GROUP OF CAUSES FOR THIS DISEASE

. MORTALITY DATA ARE PRESENTED FOR A BROADER GROUP OF CAUSES FOR THIS DISEASE

0 VALUE<0.5

THE STANDARD MORTALITY RATIOS WERE DERIVED WITH A FACTOR OF 10000

SERIAL MORTALITY TABLES FOR VARIOUS COUNTRIES 1901-1975

TABLE 69 : THYROTOXICOSIS WITH OR WITHOUT GOITRE : FEMALES

	1901-	1906-	1911-	1916-	1921-	1926-	1931-	1936-	1941-	1946-	1951-	1956-	1961-	1966-	1971-75
1 AUSTRALIA	-	7112	7590	8638	7052	8702	8992	9551	6968	3166	1614	1016	726	930	1160
2 AUSTRIA	-	-	-	-	-	-	-	-	-	-	879	730	817	1152	853
3 BELGIUM	-	-	-	-	-	-	-	-	-	-	1850	1422	916	842	1134
4 BULGARIA	-	-	-	-	-	-	-	-	-	-	-	-	1786	1295	931
5 CANADA	-	-	-	-	13032	13920	10722	11289	10988	6231	2964	1472	733	391	285
6 CHILE	-	0	294	295	0	.	.	76	217	243	544	486	156	411	286
7 CZECHOSLOVAKIA	-	-	-	721	2556	2625	3029	3659	.	.	5393	4975	3490	2730	1935
8 DENMARK	-	-	-	-	-	-	-	-	6039	3670	2197	2584	1444	1018	526
9 EIRE	-	-	-	-	2607	5185	4499	6534	.	.	3253	3070	2371	1743	1828
10 FINLAND	-	-	-	-	-	-	-	-	4027	3124	2275	2448	3181	3123	1845
11 FRANCE	-	-	-	-	-	-	-	-	.	819	704	524	429	437	604
12 GREECE	-	-	-	-	-	.	.	.	-	-	-	240	181	222	195
13 HUNGARY	-	-	-	-	-	-	3668	3378	3959	.	2271	2076	1957	1585	985
14 ICELAND	-	-	-	-	-	-	-	-	-	-	-	-	0	417	0
15 ITALY	-	-	-	-	-	-	-	-	-	-	1820	1453	1253	1093	703
16 JAPAN	-	1233	1369	1805	1951	1954	1811	.	-	1106	961	862	606	550	414
17 NETHERLANDS	2182	1996	2433	3079	2368	4391	4292	5216	4214	2753	2556	1896	2187	1801	1473
18 NEW ZEALAND	-	16154	14865	17273	13702	17339	16939	17804	14059	8859	5321	4048	2601	2358	2143
19 NORWAY	766	480	1263	1495	1750	1730	1421	1818	2313	1312	1730	1115	915	551	493
20 POLAND	-	-	-	-	-	-	-	-	-	-	.	562	915	1013	970
21 PORTUGAL	-	-	-	-	-	-	-	-	-	-	655	627	402	352	295
22 ROMANIA	-	-	-	-	-	-	-	-	-	-	-	377	1616	762	724
23 SPAIN	610	631	582	701	773	704	377	369	.	.	442	411	382	353	330
24 SWEDEN	-	-	-	-	-	-	4654	4385	2550	1474	2261	1142	1008	881	1045
25 SWITZERLAND	2500	2500	3491	3491	3700	2934	-	-	-	-	1054	1067	1379	1632	1897
26 TURKEY	-	-	-	-	-	-	-	-	-	-	-	197	477	188	36
27 UK ENGLAND AND WALES	.	.	5423	5264	6703	9334	11610	11139	5123	3811	2368	1797	1409	1065	993
28 UK NORTHERN IRELAND	-	-	-	-	6198	8212	-	-	-	3409	2488	1962	1569	1856	1411
29 UK SCOTLAND	-	-	5819	4832	6144	6885	6992	6711	4209	3088	1439	1168	813	543	520
30 USA	.	9255	8646	9374	12102	17008	12515	11378	7549	4620	2015	1130	740	499	375
31 YUGOSLAVIA	-	-	-	-	-	-	-	-	-	-	.	.	1011	966	967

- NO MORTALITY DATA ARE AVAILABLE FOR EVEN A BROADER GROUP OF CAUSES FOR THIS DISEASE

. MORTALITY DATA ARE PRESENTED FOR A BROADER GROUP OF CAUSES FOR THIS DISEASE

0 VALUE<0.5

THE STANDARD MORTALITY RATIOS WERE DERIVED WITH A FACTOR OF 1000

SERIAL MORTALITY TABLES FOR VARIOUS COUNTRIES 1901-1975

TABLE 70 : DIABETES MELLITUS : MALES

	1901-	1906-	1911-	1916-	1921-	1926-	1931-	1936-	1941-	1946-	1951-	1956-	1961-	1966-	1971-75
1 AUSTRALIA	-	22793	23921	26317	24812	22096	24012	24228	24087	22544	15644	16096	18648	23446	23578
2 AUSTRIA	-	-	-	-	-	-	-	-	-	7993	8088	8538	11789	17894	15127
3 BELGIUM	-	-	-	-	22493	25192	25355	26614	21363	18181	17767	20292	20423	27870	26126
4 BULGARIA	-	-	-	-	-	-	19005	29855	22214	15228	11633	9676	11165	10344	10055
5 CANADA	-	-	-	-	23803	23646	22806	24670	29750	25831	16303	18059	19718	22344	22959
6 CHILE	-	8044	6999	9482	10758	14201	14615	16248	11079	15300	19751	22789	21489	24415	32276
7 CZECHOSLOVAKIA	-	-	-	11702	13406	17701	20911	22729	15002	12731	12221	13417	19970	18214	17077
8 DENMARK	39242	42776	43792	45181	28325	23722	28738	33069	23991	24996	7183	8743	11655	14683	15153
9 EIRE	-	-	-	-	13554	13923	14102	14557	12171	9696	9223	8376	10038	12529	14248
10 FINLAND	-	-	-	-	-	14675	16584	16826	15996	10967	9351	12947	13311	16258	17792
11 FRANCE	-	-	-	-	-	-	14963	16391	12238	9556	11863	13457	17136	18878	16441
12 GREECE	-	-	-	-	-	9579	10229	11320	-	-	-	10439	18027	24655	28862
13 HUNGARY	-	-	-	7510	7389	8970	10227	10242	11099	7331	6991	9020	9646	8316	6337
14 ICELAND	-	-	4762	2151	3846	6087	6250	2857	2564	2874	6771	2283	5534	4577	4101
15 ITALY	10152	12129	12723	11465	12504	16016	18583	18225	16167	11238	14155	15842	19492	23395	23358
16 JAPAN	-	6396	7377	8683	9827	10712	11650	12213	-	7370	6600	7551	9919	14264	15557
17 NETHERLANDS	19358	22198	24457	25966	25310	27400	23554	22232	18865	11173	12653	14972	15428	16182	13175
18 NEW ZEALAND	-	26866	25161	32891	24350	24852	24871	26597	26745	22348	14431	16667	17198	19266	25418
19 NORWAY	14690	13997	15976	17629	19565	16644	14289	15020	13108	14254	8969	8606	9975	8265	7605
20 POLAND	-	-	-	-	-	-	-	-	-	-	.	6486	8210	11813	12297
21 PORTUGAL	-	-	-	-	-	-	12723	13715	12230	9868	11376	12349	14204	15518	14912
22 ROMANIA	-	-	-	-	-	-	-	-	-	-	-	4770	5521	5037	5693
23 SPAIN	11465	13279	15670	15844	16032	17216	17112	17983	12109	8655	10002	11547	13287	15761	20809
24 SWEDEN	-	-	-	-	-	-	16372	13553	9151	8082	11747	13205	16553	17815	15675
25 SWITZERLAND	18336	18336	19390	19390	19136	19321	21661	21747	13836	12451	16363	15110	21326	25253	27119
26 TURKEY	-	-	-	-	-	-	-	-	-	-	-	13361	12814	14541	13505
27 UK ENGLAND AND WALES	27610	26224	32146	26970	24120	24192	24316	23697	12741	8498	7682	7386	8757	9870	10898
28 UK NORTHERN IRELAND	-	-	-	-	21290	19613	19325	18394	12710	9382	8043	8237	8215	10968	12117
29 UK SCOTLAND	21250	25031	27884	22328	20146	18418	20178	21574	13922	9851	9182	9250	10505	13980	13690
30 USA	44897	39819	40673	38479	36458	35255	37866	38458	36093	31049	21466	21486	23055	25189	23892
31 YUGOSLAVIA	-	-	-	-	-	-	-	-	-	-	.	7750	8522	10244	11787

- NO MORTALITY DATA ARE AVAILABLE FOR EVEN A BROADER GROUP OF CAUSES FOR THIS DISEASE

. MORTALITY DATA ARE PRESENTED FOR A BROADER GROUP OF CAUSES FOR THIS DISEASE

0 VALUE<0.5

THE STANDARD MORTALITY RATIOS WERE DERIVED WITH A FACTOR OF 10000

SERIAL MORTALITY TABLES FOR VARIOUS COUNTRIES 1901-1975

TABLE 70 : DIABETES MELLITUS : FEMALES

	1901-	1906-	1911-	1916-	1921-	1926-	1931-	1936-	1941-	1946-	1951-	1956-	1961-	1966-	1971-75
1 AUSTRALIA	-	30374	33281	36543	38134	37142	42270	42493	43885	39460	25172	22101	22034	24065	21352
2 AUSTRIA	-	-	-	-	-	-	-	-	-	9751	11148	11783	15177	22984	18555
3 BELGIUM	-	-	-	-	21668	28750	35993	39878	27615	27033	31702	36099	35623	48462	43979
4 BULGARIA	-	-	-	-	-	-	15822	24112	18759	14380	12902	9946	12715	12905	11708
5 CANADA	-	-	-	-	29348	31128	34559	36061	46784	40853	23107	23002	23631	24446	23467
6 CHILE	-	6732	5550	7786	8745	13377	13933	13525	11859	16816	18944	21513	20746	23076	28507
7 CZECHOSLOVAKIA	-	-	-	6986	9277	13895	18995	23822	15885	16010	16575	21011	29272	27101	23065
8 DENMARK	16318	23226	28571	28605	26751	27046	34321	42085	34385	35944	9523	9747	11333	15819	15374
9 EIRE	-	-	-	-	10945	11293	12533	13129	12408	11178	10047	10986	12636	14404	16701
10 FINLAND	-	-	-	-	-	11779	14802	19755	13969	11640	13128	19694	22412	24702	24972
11 FRANCE	-	-	-	-	-	-	15306	17714	12771	11441	14856	15530	18297	19754	16964
12 GREECE	-	-	-	-	-	6585	7959	9058	-	-	-	11995	20600	29598	35062
13 HUNGARY	-	-	-	6316	6905	10520	11989	14484	14999	8856	9555	13052	14516	13628	9828
14 ICELAND	-	-	3226	5147	2013	1818	2778	3061	474	5778	5372	9057	6040	2687	6150
15 ITALY	5694	7089	8688	7666	9505	13504	17149	18593	17094	13402	18075	20499	25980	31937	31179
16 JAPAN	-	4297	5453	6562	7304	8498	8993	9064	-	5866	5733	6803	9050	11960	12670
17 NETHERLANDS	18415	22863	28311	29894	36588	44624	45566	42794	29209	21380	26518	29545	27476	26682	19690
18 NEW ZEALAND	-	45695	39412	40891	42774	39802	43300	45796	44235	34374	20599	19565	19597	21874	23715
19 NORWAY	8977	10450	13772	14350	15802	18837	18452	19036	15900	20912	10179	10254	10999	8022	7712
20 POLAND	-	-	-	-	-	-	-	-	-	-	.	7140	10425	15347	16066
21 PORTUGAL	-	-	-	-	-	-	9828	12489	10814	9374	10469	11566	13231	15127	14489
22 ROMANIA	-	-	-	-	-	-	-	-	-	-	-	4789	5684	5475	5928
23 SPAIN	9254	11950	15009	16213	17929	21593	22280	20890	14240	11186	13017	15353	19006	21636	28996
24 SWEDEN	-	-	-	-	-	-	20742	18653	12546	12839	16431	15783	18968	19684	16160
25 SWITZERLAND	12358	12358	15473	15473	17594	21415	25660	27533	18365	19296	23438	20846	27623	31991	32685
26 TURKEY	-	-	-	-	-	-	-	-	-	-	-	13954	14367	17079	15239
27 UK ENGLAND AND WALES	23080	22454	25207	21239	23164	26005	29440	29117	16760	12696	10758	9666	10448	10931	11242
28 UK NORTHERN IRELAND	-	-	-	-	16295	16504	18359	21992	16138	13575	10291	9899	10302	13873	12795
29 UK SCOTLAND	15661	20737	22572	20474	22918	25684	31297	35426	23116	18704	15853	16673	15468	17733	15583
30 USA	43919	43634	46538	45451	48536	51928	57683	61108	58026	48060	29936	27660	27149	27729	24857
31 YUGOSLAVIA	-	-	-	-	-	-	-	-	-	-	.	8072	9236	12517	14332

- NO MORTALITY DATA ARE AVAILABLE FOR EVEN A BROADER GROUP OF CAUSES FOR THIS DISEASE

. MORTALITY DATA ARE PRESENTED FOR A BROADER GROUP OF CAUSES FOR THIS DISEASE

0 VALUE<0.5

THE STANDARD MORTALITY RATIOS WERE DERIVED WITH A FACTOR OF 10000

SERIAL MORTALITY TABLES FOR VARIOUS COUNTRIES 1901-1975

TABLE 71 : AVITAMINOSIS AND OTHER DEFICIENCY STATES : MALES

	1901-	1906-	1911-	1916-	1921-	1926-	1931-	1936-	1941-	1946-	1951-	1956-	1961-	1966-	1971-75
1 AUSTRALIA	-	.	1227	900	500	326	88	41	68	54	371	421	256	311	342
2 AUSTRIA	-	-	-	-	-	-	-	-	-	234	145	168	217	333	213
3 BELGIUM	-	-	-	-	-	-	-	-	-	-	56	40	19	646	1091
4 BULGARIA	-	-	-	-	-	-	-	-	-	-	-	-	21	44	36
5 CANADA	-	-	-	-	771	1339	453	328	.	419	259	234	176	209	319
6 CHILE	-	69	1603	3493	4606	4843	3640	3254	3979	3545	5214	4465	2067	6316	7220
7 CZECHOSLOVAKIA	-	-	-	3856	2777	2340	1393	1026	.	.	186	67	33	27	32
8 DENMARK	9868	8195	3723	3423	601	751	-	-	-	-	139	50	15	41	23
9 EIRE	-	-	-	-	540	378	446	272	247	219	326	205	196	216	153
10 FINLAND	-	-	-	-	-	-	-	673	753	124	80	40	18	56	70
11 FRANCE	-	-	-	-	-	-	-	-	153	107	91	125	201	1074	2004
12 GREECE	-	-	-	-	-	387	447	378	-	-	-	70	81	218	171
13 HUNGARY	-	-	-	2691	2760	2405	1921	1137	776	426	62	64	23	17	38
14 ICELAND	-	-	1500	750	600	400	333	333	-	-	-	-	0	0	0
15 ITALY	-	-	-	-	-	-	-	-	-	-	207	149	78	35	34
16 JAPAN	-	22064	12476	21964	26170	18478	15316	12562	-	7140	3372	1206	490	320	225
17 NETHERLANDS	466	337	2147	3143	974	653	257	369	576	301	113	63	61	68	87
18 NEW ZEALAND	-	444	1837	291	226	103	0	12	42	46	116	97	135	160	108
19 NORWAY	3651	2410	1580	1213	1007	474	275	182	148	52	155	105	93	113	135
20 POLAND	-	-	-	-	-	-	-	-	-	-	.	160	213	128	57
21 PORTUGAL	-	-	-	-	-	-	-	-	-	-	2218	2095	2222	1544	1442
22 ROMANIA	-	-	-	-	-	-	-	-	-	-	-	744	5	15	42
23 SPAIN	.	.	23220	20714	13514	8141	4817	4468	.	.	1202	744	299	132	308
24 SWEDEN	-	-	5129	4849	5157	4447	-	-	-	-	37	27	46	47	38
25 SWITZERLAND	5885	5885	3051	3051	1494	1037	-	-	-	-	114	106	80	101	98
26 TURKEY	-	-	-	-	-	-	-	-	-	-	-	950	319	176	68
27 UK ENGLAND AND WALES	3452	2271	1840	1364	847	669	410	210	87	45	101	82	89	106	116
28 UK NORTHERN IRELAND	-	-	-	-	731	844	691	648	250	160	133	141	167	172	152
29 UK SCOTLAND	1198	1140	846	529	381	279	143	165	126	65	223	264	199	192	201
30 USA	.	1092	1377	1681	1185	1940	1260	978	.	294	224	303	334	398	422
31 YUGOSLAVIA	-	-	-	-	-	-	-	-	-	-	.	.	311	209	270

- NO MORTALITY DATA ARE AVAILABLE FOR EVEN A BROADER GROUP OF CAUSES FOR THIS DISEASE

. MORTALITY DATA ARE PRESENTED FOR A BROADER GROUP OF CAUSES FOR THIS DISEASE

0 VALUE<0.5

THE STANDARD MORTALITY RATIOS WERE DERIVED WITH A FACTOR OF 100

SERIAL MORTALITY TABLES FOR VARIOUS COUNTRIES 1901-1975

TABLE 71 : AVITAMINOSIS AND OTHER DEFICIENCY STATES : FEMALES

	1901-	1906-	1911-	1916-	1921-	1926-	1931-	1936-	1941-	1946-	1951-	1956-	1961-	1966-	1971-75
1 AUSTRALIA	-	.	213	115	79	176	43	32	53	32	293	260	165	267	217
2 AUSTRIA	-	-	-	-	-	-	-	-	-	157	130	100	122	112	107
3 BELGIUM	-	-	-	-	-	-	-	-	-	-	46	24	20	648	1030
4 BULGARIA	-	-	-	-	-	-	-	-	-	-	-	-	32	38	28
5 CANADA	-	-	-	-	622	1011	456	346	.	345	254	203	160	165	264
6 CHILE	-	0	2257	2864	3765	4066	3207	2768	3355	3565	4470	3568	1437	4199	4842
7 CZECHOSLOVAKIA	-	-	-	2883	1791	1549	897	679	.	.	78	54	28	23	30
8 DENMARK	4691	4390	1970	1521	393	364	-	-	-	-	101	48	56	34	36
9 EIRE	-	-	-	-	407	365	341	152	271	187	304	231	201	180	195
10 FINLAND	-	-	-	-	-	-	-	390	366	77	37	20	25	52	51
11 FRANCE	-	-	-	-	-	-	-	-	112	84	69	103	154	1131	2233
12 GREECE	-	-	-	-	-	421	482	321	-	-	-	89	70	192	189
13 HUNGARY	-	-	-	2062	2212	1854	1493	985	763	306	64	43	30	11	22
14 ICELAND	-	-	1200	500	500	143	0	125	-	-	-	-	0	0	0
15 ITALY	-	-	-	-	-	-	-	-	-	-	179	112	53	24	19
16 JAPAN	-	11922	6992	11296	14543	10434	8831	7584	-	5465	2624	944	386	253	183
17 NETHERLANDS	393	407	1899	2484	647	501	229	375	643	313	91	70	45	46	49
18 NEW ZEALAND	-	286	2475	234	143	63	27	0	0	11	141	103	75	108	74
19 NORWAY	2073	1654	1061	523	656	337	182	141	96	66	134	86	66	100	89
20 POLAND	-	-	-	-	-	-	-	-	-	-	.	136	128	62	27
21 PORTUGAL	-	-	-	-	-	-	-	-	-	-	1234	1166	1350	1016	943
22 ROMANIA	-	-	-	-	-	-	-	-	-	-	-	654	2	10	40
23 SPAIN	.	.	17693	15467	9970	5820	3298	3252	.	.	791	469	184	91	200
24 SWEDEN	-	-	3869	3760	4604	4789	-	-	-	-	43	28	18	53	45
25 SWITZERLAND	4560	4560	2608	2608	1120	910	-	-	-	-	151	130	101	92	141
26 TURKEY	-	-	-	-	-	-	-	-	-	-	-	697	267	116	69
27 UK ENGLAND AND WALES	2290	1532	1159	906	490	362	236	134	62	39	85	76	85	106	139
28 UK NORTHERN IRELAND	-	-	-	-	633	760	456	370	226	81	102	96	180	144	268
29 UK SCOTLAND	767	615	502	350	219	199	117	63	83	55	180	155	145	171	190
30 USA	.	1431	2287	3386	2260	3914	2286	1728	.	305	215	265	286	340	385
31 YUGOSLAVIA	-	-	-	-	-	-	-	-	-	-	.	.	178	145	173

- NO MORTALITY DATA ARE AVAILABLE FOR EVEN A BROADER GROUP OF CAUSES FOR THIS DISEASE

. MORTALITY DATA ARE PRESENTED FOR A BROADER GROUP OF CAUSES FOR THIS DISEASE

0 VALUE<0.5

THE STANDARD MORTALITY RATIOS WERE DERIVED WITH A FACTOR OF 100

SERIAL MORTALITY TABLES FOR VARIOUS COUNTRIES 1901-1975

TABLE 72 : ANAEMIAS : MALES

	1901-	1906-	1911-	1916-	1921-	1926-	1931-	1936-	1941-	1946-	1951-	1956-	1961-	1966-	1971-75
1 AUSTRALIA	-	3554	3703	4423	4507	2958	2224	1403	1361	1150	1276	988	966	819	662
2 AUSTRIA	-	-	-	-	-	-	-	-	-	871	653	694	683	825	578
3 BELGIUM	-	-	-	-	-	-	-	-	-	-	874	661	648	693	590
4 BULGARIA	-	-	-	-	-	-	-	-	-	-	-	-	347	316	314
5 CANADA	-	-	-	-	7031	4437	3299	2698	1385	1130	1099	832	772	695	609
6 CHILE	-	454	1561	1713	3481	3266	2189	2358	2833	2969	1934	1211	1100	1777	1844
7 CZECHOSLOVAKIA	-	-	-	1082	1211	1356	964	1026	985	887	564	437	584	443	389
8 DENMARK	3384	4164	5433	5332	3595	3942	-	-	-	-	852	577	519	399	369
9 EIRE	-	-	-	-	3326	3769	3822	3813	3418	2848	2321	1709	1318	1097	1016
10 FINLAND	-	-	-	-	-	-	-	-	-	-	1593	1053	767	678	405
11 FRANCE	-	-	-	-	-	-	-	-	1005	759	578	445	433	471	615
12 GREECE	-	-	-	-	-	3035	2228	2076	-	-	-	1343	1226	1091	872
13 HUNGARY	-	-	-	-	-	-	1003	999	919	1389	905	645	492	503	329
14 ICELAND	-	-	-	-	-	-	-	-	-	-	864	440	571	420	370
15 ITALY	-	-	-	-	-	-	1274	1248	1633	1484	1228	966	784	625	495
16 JAPAN	-	2268	1676	1256	1176	966	836	780	-	1025	1165	963	835	773	702
17 NETHERLANDS	1402	1574	1989	2268	2703	2267	1514	1228	1443	1049	656	595	476	518	456
18 NEW ZEALAND	-	5000	2752	4122	3887	2598	1623	1339	1093	854	1347	869	1035	927	591
19 NORWAY	1326	1459	1411	1353	1740	1402	918	719	1163	1146	837	665	704	545	474
20 POLAND	-	-	-	-	-	-	-	-	-	-	.	865	666	462	345
21 PORTUGAL	-	-	-	-	-	-	-	-	-	-	2254	1340	812	551	530
22 ROMANIA	-	-	-	-	-	-	-	-	-	-	-	575	252	193	159
23 SPAIN	8034	5011	4002	3399	2578	2494	2283	3656	3239	2803	2156	1602	939	896	832
24 SWEDEN	-	-	-	-	-	-	-	-	-	-	903	632	585	499	344
25 SWITZERLAND	3029	3029	3358	3358	-	-	-	-	-	-	957	733	809	620	521
26 TURKEY	-	-	-	-	-	-	-	-	-	-	-	13522	7180	4584	3085
27 UK ENGLAND AND WALES	3534	3511	3678	3742	3798	3084	2795	2402	2099	1263	1062	950	904	829	731
28 UK NORTHERN IRELAND	-	-	-	-	5604	4783	3913	3950	3455	2051	1526	1038	1230	1238	970
29 UK SCOTLAND	5121	5190	5443	5668	5094	3944	2971	2365	2957	2212	1424	1228	1127	897	594
30 USA	5167	4175	3061	3060	3364	2408	1756	1261	1104	907	914	736	709	653	581
31 YUGOSLAVIA	-	-	-	-	-	-	-	-	-	-	.	327	225	243	287

- NO MORTALITY DATA ARE AVAILABLE FOR EVEN A BROADER GROUP OF CAUSES FOR THIS DISEASE

. MORTALITY DATA ARE PRESENTED FOR A BROADER GROUP OF CAUSES FOR THIS DISEASE

0 VALUE<0.5

THE STANDARD MORTALITY RATIOS WERE DERIVED WITH A FACTOR OF 1000

SERIAL MORTALITY TABLES FOR VARIOUS COUNTRIES 1901-1975

TABLE 72 : ANAEMIAS : FEMALES

	1901-	1906-	1911-	1916-	1921-	1926-	1931-	1936-	1941-	1946-	1951-	1956-	1961-	1966-	1971-75
1 AUSTRALIA	-	4415	4326	5042	5192	3699	2633	1691	1706	1445	1684	1330	992	850	628
2 AUSTRIA	-	-	-	-	-	-	-	-	-	1334	1016	769	746	740	535
3 BELGIUM	-	-	-	-	-	-	-	-	-	-	825	581	586	562	518
4 BULGARIA	-	-	-	-	-	-	-	-	-	-	-	-	337	238	270
5 CANADA	-	-	-	-	8205	5199	3988	3319	1630	1324	1138	946	739	642	508
6 CHILE	-	870	3179	3780	4754	4815	3119	3402	3239	3273	2348	1347	1283	1417	1221
7 CZECHOSLOVAKIA	-	-	-	1583	1569	1658	1226	1184	1384	1023	779	580	654	478	371
8 DENMARK	3405	3352	4047	5208	3958	3889	-	-	-	-	1211	665	558	407	324
9 EIRE	-	-	-	-	3861	4095	4713	4810	5074	3995	3183	2452	1568	1342	1055
10 FINLAND	-	-	-	-	-	-	-	-	-	-	1667	1391	791	603	447
11 FRANCE	-	-	-	-	-	-	-	-	876	612	479	351	332	360	426
12 GREECE	-	-	-	-	-	3219	2807	2728	-	-	-	1074	992	971	746
13 HUNGARY	-	-	-	-	-	-	1448	1349	1207	1654	1165	832	583	533	396
14 ICELAND	-	-	-	-	-	-	-	-	-	-	187	517	388	822	364
15 ITALY	-	-	-	-	-	-	1373	1334	1570	1395	1027	772	577	447	341
16 JAPAN	-	2788	2006	1543	1374	1104	901	811	-	991	996	848	722	723	717
17 NETHERLANDS	1526	1956	2286	2518	2992	2713	2040	1494	1725	1402	658	556	368	396	420
18 NEW ZEALAND	-	5902	4273	5850	4735	2977	2141	1565	1206	1075	1639	989	975	870	757
19 NORWAY	1272	1266	1239	1347	1850	1523	1108	825	1287	1165	936	752	630	506	461
20 POLAND	-	-	-	-	-	-	-	-	-	-	.	689	536	400	297
21 PORTUGAL	-	-	-	-	-	-	-	-	-	-	1688	1034	631	383	354
22 ROMANIA	-	-	-	-	-	-	-	-	-	-	-	513	215	150	111
23 SPAIN	12134	8094	6538	5554	3823	3230	2842	3000	2694	2365	1667	1196	760	673	545
24 SWEDEN	-	-	-	-	-	-	-	-	-	-	1117	760	605	488	264
25 SWITZERLAND	4347	4347	4530	4530	-	-	-	-	-	-	1173	811	688	570	552
26 TURKEY	-	-	-	-	-	-	-	-	-	-	-	10796	6438	4411	3249
27 UK ENGLAND AND WALES	4419	3874	3752	3722	3999	3279	3138	2822	2530	1643	1332	1185	1098	975	861
28 UK NORTHERN IRELAND	-	-	-	-	5719	5329	4968	5308	4519	2936	2120	1478	1261	1311	1044
29 UK SCOTLAND	5912	6191	5752	5970	5394	4378	3724	3116	3954	2661	1987	1704	1423	1024	748
30 USA	6244	4867	3802	3761	4023	2775	1876	1357	1116	876	888	646	602	524	452
31 YUGOSLAVIA	-	-	-	-	-	-	-	-	-	-	.	283	200	222	225

- NO MORTALITY DATA ARE AVAILABLE FOR EVEN A BROADER GROUP OF CAUSES FOR THIS DISEASE

. MORTALITY DATA ARE PRESENTED FOR A BROADER GROUP OF CAUSES FOR THIS DISEASE

0 VALUE<0.5

THE STANDARD MORTALITY RATIOS WERE DERIVED WITH A FACTOR OF 1000

SERIAL MORTALITY TABLES FOR VARIOUS COUNTRIES 1901-1975

TABLE 73 : ALLERGIC DISORDERS,ALL OTHER ENDOCRINE,METABOLIC AND BLOOD DISEASES : MALES

	1901-	1906-	1911-	1916-	1921-	1926-	1931-	1936-	1941-	1946-	1951-	1956-	1961-	1966-	1971-75
1 AUSTRALIA	-	12361	17090	15209	13714	12559	9290	8915	8533	8189	14893	12292	11802	12854	.
2 AUSTRIA	-	-	-	-	-	-	-	-	-	-	10100	9944	7076	6458	.
3 BELGIUM	-	-	-	-	-	-	-	-	-	-	17176	13354	6574	7860	.
4 BULGARIA	-	-	-	-	-	-	-	-	-	-	-	-	12011	9480	.
5 CANADA	-	-	-	-	12186	15788	16446	18318	.	18283	15143	11709	11178	9912	.
6 CHILE	-	.	22579	21936	25692	.	.	20507	20970	17769	18465	13524	14794	15964	.
7 CZECHOSLOVAKIA	-	-	-	25697	26330	29057	31346	32257	.	.	26298	21073	19820	11531	.
8 DENMARK	-	-	-	-	-	-	-	-	-	-	6204	4685	5599	11550	.
9 EIRE	-	-	-	-	19905	20076	5654	5657	.	.	24662	18741	14778	17022	.
10 FINLAND	-	-	-	-	-	-	-	17315	22675	22659	13109	11068	9349	10239	.
11 FRANCE	-	-	-	-	-	-	-	-	8792	11993	9025	9502	8207	7674	.
12 GREECE	-	-	-	-	-	.	.	.	-	-	-	19707	30859	26856	.
13 HUNGARY	-	-	-	-	-	-	14896	15171	15540	7317	14133	37500	32908	25724	.
14 ICELAND	-	-	-	-	-	-	-	-	-	-	-	-	5405	7143	.
15 ITALY	-	-	-	-	-	-	-	-	-	-	28987	14789	9730	8117	.
16 JAPAN	-	33900	29118	33868	35082	34793	39405	48221	-	56555	44898	36201	28768	24471	.
17 NETHERLANDS	.	.	8197	9246	7539	10743	10245	11856	.	16368	14291	11110	8688	9407	.
18 NEW ZEALAND	-	14463	20246	15540	11236	10039	8635	7572	.	22360	21401	17454	15196	16810	.
19 NORWAY	2714	4174	14899	14107	14000	14408	14547	15133	.	.	13078	11569	13401	12886	.
20 POLAND	-	-	-	-	-	-	-	-	-	-	.	43307	44009	40940	.
21 PORTUGAL	-	-	-	-	-	-	-	-	-	-	4752	5657	4340	3492	.
22 ROMANIA	-	-	-	-	-	-	-	-	-	-	-	3940	23203	27542	.
23 SPAIN	.	36865	31560	29228	21535	17543	15388	16610	17080	18437	21989	25276	24656	23991	.
24 SWEDEN	-	-	-	-	-	-	-	-	-	-	9662	8696	10966	12137	.
25 SWITZERLAND	19372	19372	20187	20187	23752	22553	-	-	-	-	14705	14491	17114	18354	.
26 TURKEY	-	-	-	-	-	-	-	-	-	-	-	16071	13203	12549	14346
27 UK ENGLAND AND WALES	10282	8919	22371	21369	18476	18707	15168	15899	17318	15563	13436	8420	8152	8580	.
28 UK NORTHERN IRELAND	-	-	-	-	17761	20657	-	-	-	27415	22692	12303	9539	9239	.
29 UK SCOTLAND	-	-	9425	8271	7943	8727	9572	11955	.	14902	12188	8801	7932	7509	.
30 USA	22798	15547	14097	13065	13117	12209	9785	8853	.	10143	12685	11199	10423	9557	.
31 YUGOSLAVIA	-	-	-	-	-	-	-	-	-	-	.	.	10128	6851	.

- NO MORTALITY DATA ARE AVAILABLE FOR EVEN A BROADER GROUP OF CAUSES FOR THIS DISEASE

. MORTALITY DATA ARE PRESENTED FOR A BROADER GROUP OF CAUSES FOR THIS DISEASE

0 VALUE<0.5

THE STANDARD MORTALITY RATIOS WERE DERIVED WITH A FACTOR OF 10000

SERIAL MORTALITY TABLES FOR VARIOUS COUNTRIES 1901-1975

TABLE 73 : ALLERGIC DISORDERS, ALL OTHER ENDOCRINE, METABOLIC AND BLOOD DISEASES : FEMALES

	1901-	1906-	1911-	1916-	1921-	1926-	1931-	1936-	1941-	1946-	1951-	1956-	1961-	1966-	1971-75
1 AUSTRALIA	-	10227	14011	12929	13896	12293	10980	9567	10028	9432	11085	9874	9622	9482	.
2 AUSTRIA	-	-	-	-	-	-	-	-	-	-	5603	5112	3906	4443	.
3 BELGIUM	-	-	-	-	-	-	-	-	-	-	10758	8517	5121	6347	.
4 BULGARIA	-	-	-	-	-	-	-	-	-	-	-	-	7064	6009	.
5 CANADA	-	-	-	-	16957	18525	14609	16413	.	12161	10092	7790	7384	7190	.
6 CHILE	-	.	13416	14182	14410	.	.	17542	18014	15323	11956	10613	11714	12357	.
7 CZECHOSLOVAKIA	-	-	-	22468	21354	22774	27289	25139	11957	11466	15221	12355	10605	6652	.
8 DENMARK	-	-	-	-	-	-	-	-	-	-	5475	4361	4400	9054	.
9 EIRE	-	-	-	-	15167	15248	5456	6265	.	.	17754	13655	11834	12842	.
10 FINLAND	-	-	-	-	-	-	-	24429	18927	16327	7723	8422	8959	8552	.
11 FRANCE	-	-	-	-	-	-	-	-	5662	7261	5453	5946	5453	5532	.
12 GREECE	-	-	-	-	-	.	.	.	-	-	-	10900	17018	14497	.
13 HUNGARY	-	-	-	-	-	-	10764	9747	9628	5182	7588	15578	13247	9848	.
14 ICELAND	-	-	-	-	-	-	-	-	-	-	-	-	2555	8667	.
15 ITALY	-	-	-	-	-	-	-	-	-	-	18692	9629	6378	5582	.
16 JAPAN	-	29774	23226	25658	26459	25359	28157	33935	-	37389	28509	23374	18510	15536	.
17 NETHERLANDS	.	.	6190	6555	5951	8194	8962	9930	.	13409	11210	8542	6646	6989	.
18 NEW ZEALAND	-	11616	16865	17987	13500	11614	7378	9276	.	14998	14113	11350	12073	14542	.
19 NORWAY	2081	3077	12548	12378	12572	13484	12455	13502	.	.	11475	8619	8637	8274	.
20 POLAND	-	-	-	-	-	-	-	-	-	-	.	20036	19653	17739	.
21 PORTUGAL	-	-	-	-	-	-	-	-	-	-	2677	3520	3004	2302	.
22 ROMANIA	-	-	-	-	-	-	-	-	-	-	-	3519	16865	19569	.
23 SPAIN	.	32615	28875	24943	17268	12761	10476	9978	9734	9937	12838	12699	14236	12257	.
24 SWEDEN	-	-	-	-	-	-	-	-	-	-	8276	7207	8353	8269	.
25 SWITZERLAND	23688	23688	22681	22681	29408	29925	-	-	-	-	10618	8867	9530	9687	.
26 TURKEY	-	-	-	-	-	-	-	-	-	-	-	10455	7204	6743	6686
27 UK ENGLAND AND WALES	10178	9932	16348	15029	13617	14222	11969	12390	13395	12985	12080	9144	9691	9546	.
28 UK NORTHERN IRELAND	-	-	-	-	11587	15648	-	-	-	21127	16800	10768	8787	9822	.
29 UK SCOTLAND	-	-	10178	7884	9614	10270	11260	12608	.	14878	13360	10134	9009	8974	.
30 USA	23639	18094	14436	13879	13176	11599	8540	8197	.	7300	7473	6993	7678	7698	.
31 YUGOSLAVIA	-	-	-	-	-	-	-	-	-	-	.	.	5077	3669	.

- NO MORTALITY DATA ARE AVAILABLE FOR EVEN A BROADER GROUP OF CAUSES FOR THIS DISEASE

. MORTALITY DATA ARE PRESENTED FOR A BROADER GROUP OF CAUSES FOR THIS DISEASE

0 VALUE<0.5

THE STANDARD MORTALITY RATIOS WERE DERIVED WITH A FACTOR OF 10000

SERIAL MORTALITY TABLES FOR VARIOUS COUNTRIES 1901-1975

TABLE 74 : ALLERGIC DISORDERS,ENDOCRINE,METABOLIC AND BLOOD DISEASES : MALES

	1901-	1906-	1911-	1916-	1921-	1926-	1931-	1936-	1941-	1946-	1951-	1956-	1961-	1966-	1971-75
1 AUSTRALIA	-	20860	25870	26721	24408	20312	18240	16992	16661	15285	16092	14652	15134	15516	13858
2 AUSTRIA	-	-	-	-	-	-	-	-	-	-	9819	9896	9920	12294	9676
3 BELGIUM	-	-	-	-	-	-	-	-	-	-	17088	15704	12928	16808	16009
4 BULGARIA	-	-	-	-	-	-	-	-	-	-	-	-	10534	7128	5707
5 CANADA	-	-	-	-	30524	27165	23905	24330	20323	18388	16022	14616	14789	14438	13662
6 CHILE	-	13187	19316	23938	29164	29002	29819	26625	26663	25921	30865	25620	21034	28285	30278
7 CZECHOSLOVAKIA	-	-	-	-	-	-	26025	26562	26017	22326	17977	16264	18486	11581	9606
8 DENMARK	-	-	-	-	-	-	-	-	-	-	7602	7081	8467	10978	9641
9 EIRE	-	-	-	-	-	-	15777	17194	19882	17660	18858	14727	13165	11890	10527
10 FINLAND	-	-	-	-	-	-	-	-	-	-	12865	12388	11206	11666	10075
11 FRANCE	-	-	-	-	-	-	-	-	10089	10770	10128	10824	11964	13600	14224
12 GREECE	-	-	-	-	-	16172	16922	18418	-	-	-	15404	23056	17991	15224
13 HUNGARY	-	-	-	-	-	-	16529	15159	14987	10024	11507	22011	19550	11564	4593
14 ICELAND	-	-	-	-	-	-	-	-	-	-	-	-	5785	5672	3514
15 ITALY	-	-	-	-	-	-	-	-	-	-	21217	15167	14098	13308	11995
16 JAPAN	-	62737	42319	61684	73380	-	51698	53053	-	45984	32767	24203	19887	12892	9054
17 NETHERLANDS	18653	15811	20809	24256	-	-	17552	17535	18088	14466	13037	12473	11352	11146	8342
18 NEW ZEALAND	-	26378	27780	28285	22389	21560	-	19965	18405	16289	18128	16394	15970	15189	14586
19 NORWAY	16437	14757	18475	18012	19138	16474	14347	14435	13197	13011	11153	9933	11274	8410	5599
20 POLAND	-	-	-	-	-	-	-	-	-	-	11357	25585	26038	17899	6992
21 PORTUGAL	-	-	-	-	-	-	-	-	-	-	14610	13623	13184	11696	11163
22 ROMANIA	-	-	-	-	-	-	-	-	-	-	-	6072	13486	10311	3377
23 SPAIN	42027	42712	69040	62255	44604	33615	26319	28765	26884	21872	19908	20227	18558	13318	12153
24 SWEDEN	-	-	-	-	-	-	-	-	-	-	10933	10615	12923	12505	9224
25 SWITZERLAND	-	-	-	-	-	-	-	-	-	-	15611	14390	18142	18016	15846
26 TURKEY	-	-	-	-	-	-	-	-	-	-	-	34617	22682	19095	17329
27 UK ENGLAND AND WALES	27298	24365	32581	29382	26217	25160	22906	22084	16945	12767	11204	8673	9046	8391	7923
28 UK NORTHERN IRELAND	-	-	-	-	27425	26987	-	-	-	19297	16074	10817	10127	10020	9135
29 UK SCOTLAND	-	-	25420	22675	-	-	-	-	18061	14931	12080	10390	10282	10199	9045
30 USA	36775	30080	30341	29599	28639	28108	25813	24266	22232	19063	16662	15786	16093	15644	14404
31 YUGOSLAVIA	-	-	-	-	-	-	-	-	-	-	18751	15649	9124	6774	6590

- NO MORTALITY DATA ARE AVAILABLE FOR EVEN A BROADER GROUP OF CAUSES FOR THIS DISEASE

. MORTALITY DATA ARE PRESENTED FOR A BROADER GROUP OF CAUSES FOR THIS DISEASE

0 VALUE<0.5

THE STANDARD MORTALITY RATIOS WERE DERIVED WITH A FACTOR OF 10000

SERIAL MORTALITY TABLES FOR VARIOUS COUNTRIES 1901-1975

TABLE 74 : ALLERGIC DISORDERS, ENDOCRINE, METABOLIC AND BLOOD DISEASES : FEMALES

	1901-	1906-	1911-	1916-	1921-	1926-	1931-	1936-	1941-	1946-	1951-	1956-	1961-	1966-	1971-75
1 AUSTRALIA	-	26029	29329	31779	32323	29895	29856	28213	28455	24539	19587	16903	15832	15483	13033
2 AUSTRIA	-	-	-	-	-	-	-	-	-	-	10634	9827	10681	14347	11326
3 BELGIUM	-	-	-	-	-	-	-	-	-	-	21632	21305	19664	26546	24828
4 BULGARIA	-	-	-	-	-	-	-	-	-	-	-	-	9437	7915	6659
5 CANADA	-	-	-	-	40362	36027	32566	33021	30890	25816	17654	15611	15018	14615	13680
6 CHILE	-	9892	18347	21644	25247	28059	27673	24469	24965	25972	26045	22584	18535	23076	24223
7 CZECHOSLOVAKIA	-	-	-	-	-	-	23064	23970	21244	18646	16950	17287	19814	15866	12894
8 DENMARK	-	-	-	-	-	-	-	-	-	-	9596	8332	8489	11251	9676
9 EIRE	-	-	-	-	-	-	18491	20305	22971	19731	19088	16290	14279	13054	12690
10 FINLAND	-	-	-	-	-	-	-	-	-	-	12671	15444	16055	15822	13965
11 FRANCE	-	-	-	-	-	-	-	-	9337	9557	10120	10378	11456	13706	14618
12 GREECE	-	-	-	-	-	13473	14422	14332	-	-	-	11903	17915	18102	18272
13 HUNGARY	-	-	-	-	-	-	16558	16068	16072	10915	11105	15258	13889	10404	6813
14 ICELAND	-	-	-	-	-	-	-	-	-	-	-	-	4342	6502	4818
15 ITALY	-	-	-	-	-	-	-	-	-	-	18572	15140	15727	16948	15691
16 JAPAN	-	42060	29278	37977	44944	-	34456	35178	-	31623	22118	16694	14094	10231	8025
17 NETHERLANDS	17734	16821	22470	24920	-	-	28487	27443	23355	18958	18447	18287	16301	15646	11583
18 NEW ZEALAND	-	38035	39486	40077	37038	32700	-	33949	30174	23926	19848	16489	16187	15918	14685
19 NORWAY	11130	11361	15619	15093	17050	17556	15838	16041	14576	15860	11660	9925	9882	7287	5563
20 POLAND	-	-	-	-	-	-	-	-	-	-	10491	13502	14462	12828	9071
21 PORTUGAL	-	-	-	-	-	-	-	-	-	-	11079	10664	10723	10201	9758
22 ROMANIA	-	-	-	-	-	-	-	-	-	-	-	5720	10587	8084	3597
23 SPAIN	46796	44073	61941	54920	39498	30633	24810	24244	19858	16368	15588	15075	15965	13587	15422
24 SWEDEN	-	-	-	-	-	-	-	-	-	-	13591	11757	13309	12773	9632
25 SWITZERLAND	-	-	-	-	-	-	-	-	-	-	17990	15264	18179	19293	18710
26 TURKEY	-	-	-	-	-	-	-	-	-	-	-	29005	20197	17597	14903
27 UK ENGLAND AND WALES	24762	22645	27781	25070	25973	27008	28015	27174	19441	15322	13018	10859	11101	9927	9210
28 UK NORTHERN IRELAND	-	-	-	-	24813	26914	-	-	-	21918	16179	12171	11174	12201	10418
29 UK SCOTLAND	-	-	26277	24246	-	-	-	-	24682	20288	16812	15225	13612	12846	10624
30 USA	38754	34848	38492	39957	40184	43698	39175	38075	33519	27048	18674	16893	16806	16391	14707
31 YUGOSLAVIA	-	-	-	-	-	-	-	-	-	-	12743	10412	7131	7407	7839

- NO MORTALITY DATA ARE AVAILABLE FOR EVEN A BROADER GROUP OF CAUSES FOR THIS DISEASE

. MORTALITY DATA ARE PRESENTED FOR A BROADER GROUP OF CAUSES FOR THIS DISEASE

0 VALUE<0.5

THE STANDARD MORTALITY RATIOS WERE DERIVED WITH A FACTOR OF 10000

SERIAL MORTALITY TABLES FOR VARIOUS COUNTRIES 1901-1975

TABLE 75 : MENTAL ILLNESS : MALES

	1901-	1906-	1911-	1916-	1921-	1926-	1931-	1936-	1941-	1946-	1951-	1956-	1961-	1966-	1971-75
1 AUSTRALIA	-	7272	7617	8240	5755	3298	.	.	1697	2281	3495	2770	2638	3848	5218
2 AUSTRIA	-	-	-	-	-	-	-	-	-	.	4150	3798	3552	2372	2650
3 BELGIUM	-	-	-	-	-	-	-	-	-	-	3986	3642	3457	3915	4997
4 BULGARIA	-	-	-	-	-	-	-	-	-	-	-	-	777	756	811
5 CANADA	-	-	-	-	.	.	7371	6342	.	2391	1876	1631	1403	1839	2959
6 CHILE	-	-	.	.	.	.	.	5792	8189	7560	12038	9378	10837	6886	6116
7 CZECHOSLOVAKIA	-	-	-	.	.	.	4923	4529	.	.	1225	1014	1030	431	436
8 DENMARK	-	-	-	-	-	-	.	.	.	.	2631	946	830	1261	1639
9 EIRE	-	-	-	-	.	.	.	.	.	.	1724	720	739	420	572
10 FINLAND	-	-	-	-	-	.	.	-	.	.	2287	877	2124	2943	3860
11 FRANCE	-	-	-	-	-	-	-	-	.	6067	8161	11488	11592	9781	7508
12 GREECE	-	-	-	-	-	.	.	.	-	-	-	1898	2708	2572	2396
13 HUNGARY	-	-	-	.	.	.	.	.	.	.	2889	2882	1871	1678	2314
14 ICELAND	-	-	-	-	-	-	-	-	-	-	-	-	1549	1728	860
15 ITALY	-	-	-	-	-	-	-	-	-	-	4001	2442	2167	1444	978
16 JAPAN	-	.	.	.	.	.	7350	7696	-	5540	4804	4140	3504	2998	2385
17 NETHERLANDS	-	-	.	.	.	.	6118	7510	.	8229	4491	2712	2882	3070	3193
18 NEW ZEALAND	-	.	.	.	.	.	.	.	.	2208	2741	1749	1849	1555	2759
19 NORWAY	4582	4625	-	-	-	-	-	-	.	.	1818	1235	1245	1521	2615
20 POLAND	-	-	-	-	-	-	-	-	-	-	-	.	.	2050	2556
21 PORTUGAL	-	-	-	-	-	-	-	-	-	-	2954	2822	1868	621	916
22 ROMANIA	-	-	-	-	-	-	-	-	-	-	-	1116	458	850	1429
23 SPAIN	-	.	.	.	.	.	4208	5092	.	.	2468	2587	2429	2480	1732
24 SWEDEN	-	-	.	.	.	.	.	.	.	.	1706	1948	1399	2325	2285
25 SWITZERLAND	18791	18791	18078	18078	.	.	.	.	1621	2551	6907	5496	4491	3689	1802
26 TURKEY	-	-	-	-	-	-	-	-	-	-	-	9195	6939	5081	1901
27 UK ENGLAND AND WALES	.	.	7452	6347	5098	5710	3531	2800	1752	1046	965	735	881	935	1162
28 UK NORTHERN IRELAND	-	-	-	-	.	.	.	.	.	1288	1082	623	1166	1918	1609
29 UK SCOTLAND	.	.	.	.	.	.	.	.	.	1763	1079	1304	1277	1651	2805
30 USA	.	.	.	.	.	.	.	.	.	2758	2100	1826	1809	2433	3231
31 YUGOSLAVIA	-	-	-	-	-	-	-	-	-	-	.	.	3510	5468	6174

- NO MORTALITY DATA ARE AVAILABLE FOR EVEN A BROADER GROUP OF CAUSES FOR THIS DISEASE

. MORTALITY DATA ARE PRESENTED FOR A BROADER GROUP OF CAUSES FOR THIS DISEASE

0 VALUE<0.5

THE STANDARD MORTALITY RATIOS WERE DERIVED WITH A FACTOR OF 1000

SERIAL MORTALITY TABLES FOR VARIOUS COUNTRIES 1901-1975

TABLE 75 : MENTAL ILLNESS : FEMALES

	1901-	1906-	1911-	1916-	1921-	1926-	1931-	1936-	1941-	1946-	1951-	1956-	1961-	1966-	1971-75
1 AUSTRALIA	-	3910	3607	3527	2857	2085	.	.	1039	826	1470	1145	1157	1858	2654
2 AUSTRIA	-	-	-	-	-	-	-	-	-	.	2616	1324	1602	1199	1020
3 BELGIUM	-	-	-	-	-	-	-	-	-	-	3872	3815	2922	3162	4324
4 BULGARIA	-	-	-	-	-	-	-	-	-	-	-	-	287	268	228
5 CANADA	-	-	-	-	.	.	5821	4752	.	1438	1137	958	797	772	1071
6 CHILE	-	-	.	.	.	.	.	2395	1680	1561	2498	1831	1718	1172	1313
7 CZECHOSLOVAKIA	-	-	-	.	.	.	4036	3893	.	.	1324	1067	952	439	307
8 DENMARK	-	-	-	-	-	-	.	.	.	.	2771	1189	759	1228	1206
9 EIRE	-	-	-	-	.	.	.	.	.	.	1628	551	466	388	492
10 FINLAND	-	-	-	-	-	.	.	-	.	.	1987	738	2829	2233	2790
11 FRANCE	-	-	-	-	-	-	-	-	.	2439	2873	3596	3843	3482	2602
12 GREECE	-	-	-	-	-	.	.	.	-	-	-	1578	2346	2329	2046
13 HUNGARY	-	-	-	.	.	.	.	.	.	.	2142	1849	1061	760	1091
14 ICELAND	-	-	-	-	-	-	-	-	-	-	-	-	787	792	174
15 ITALY	-	-	-	-	-	-	-	-	-	-	2635	1444	1039	651	363
16 JAPAN	-	.	.	.	.	.	4446	4806	-	4611	4084	3152	2570	2025	1531
17 NETHERLANDS	-	-	.	.	.	.	6317	7597	.	8324	4653	3054	3068	3271	3118
18 NEW ZEALAND	-	.	.	.	.	.	.	.	.	1649	1874	1214	988	1103	584
19 NORWAY	3573	3222	-	-	-	-	-	-	.	.	1753	1007	847	1044	1501
20 POLAND	-	-	-	-	-	-	-	-	-	-	-	.	.	1135	1610
21 PORTUGAL	-	-	-	-	-	-	-	-	-	-	2056	1843	1322	105	426
22 ROMANIA	-	-	-	-	-	-	-	-	-	-	-	588	251	156	377
23 SPAIN	-	.	.	.	.	.	2097	2826	.	.	1604	1515	1488	1209	882
24 SWEDEN	-	-	.	.	.	.	.	.	.	.	1479	1084	858	926	799
25 SWITZERLAND	7802	7802	11282	11282	.	.	.	.	190	200	2507	1338	1191	971	953
26 TURKEY	-	-	-	-	-	-	-	-	-	-	-	4160	3296	2948	642
27 UK ENGLAND AND WALES	.	.	6471	5535	5092	5847	3530	2751	1814	1260	1105	929	881	999	1233
28 UK NORTHERN IRELAND	-	-	-	-	.	.	.	.	.	1344	1542	404	654	845	605
29 UK SCOTLAND	.	.	.	.	.	.	.	.	.	1907	1217	1256	1682	1232	2117
30 USA	.	.	.	.	.	.	.	.	.	1174	776	645	623	743	974
31 YUGOSLAVIA	-	-	-	-	-	-	-	-	-	-	.	.	695	1041	1523

\- NO MORTALITY DATA ARE AVAILABLE FOR EVEN A BROADER GROUP OF CAUSES FOR THIS DISEASE

. MORTALITY DATA ARE PRESENTED FOR A BROADER GROUP OF CAUSES FOR THIS DISEASE

0 VALUE<0.5

THE STANDARD MORTALITY RATIOS WERE DERIVED WITH A FACTOR OF 1000

SERIAL MORTALITY TABLES FOR VARIOUS COUNTRIES 1901-1975

TABLE 76 : MENTAL DEFICIENCY : MALES

	1901-	1906-	1911-	1916-	1921-	1926-	1931-	1936-	1941-	1946-	1951-	1956-	1961-	1966-	1971-75
1 AUSTRALIA	-	.	.	.	.	.	.	.	19731	21053	35616	40370	17713	10485	4693
2 AUSTRIA	-	-	-	-	-	-	-	-	-	.	20947	10875	8621	11695	993
3 BELGIUM	-	-	-	-	-	-	-	-	-	-	46053	38402	49625	28835	20983
4 BULGARIA	-	-	-	-	-	-	-	-	-	-	-	-	32051	17797	25820
5 CANADA	-	-	-	-	.	.	.	.	.	22854	13155	20494	21805	11536	4885
6 CHILE	-	-	.	.	.	.	.	7143	1333	3686	12443	29128	25972	8836	3208
7 CZECHOSLOVAKIA	-	-	-	.	.	.	.	.	.	.	13027	15177	17862	6576	5535
8 DENMARK	-	-	-	-	-	-	.	.	.	.	9886	2662	5556	7394	4301
9 EIRE	-	-	-	-	.	.	.	.	.	.	30570	48128	42857	17526	985
10 FINLAND	-	-	-	-	-	.	.	-	.	.	5091	8088	21933	12453	1205
11 FRANCE	-	-	-	-	-	-	-	-	.	16788	17116	19067	22310	16770	7397
12 GREECE	-	-	-	-	-	.	.	.	-	-	-	4637	9703	11673	4688
13 HUNGARY	-	-	-	.	.	.	.	.	.	.	8696	11545	15926	29926	34574
14 ICELAND	-	-	-	-	-	-	-	-	-	-	-	-	7692	0	0
15 ITALY	-	-	-	-	-	-	-	-	-	-	15717	17837	15459	11908	2787
16 JAPAN	-	.	.	.	.	.	.	.	-	7811	8866	8222	6840	5320	3481
17 NETHERLANDS	-	-	.	.	.	.	.	.	.	55970	48138	43811	17693	12956	12814
18 NEW ZEALAND	-	.	.	.	.	.	.	.	.	67568	27660	40252	70787	3784	1031
19 NORWAY	-	-	-	-	-	-	-	-	.	.	26961	11429	13023	8000	0
20 POLAND	-	-	-	-	-	-	-	-	-	-	-	.	.	24241	21140
21 PORTUGAL	-	-	-	-	-	-	-	-	-	-	54250	50177	24437	10357	9178
22 ROMANIA	-	-	-	-	-	-	-	-	-	-	-	19608	3895	0	0
23 SPAIN	-	.	.	.	.	.	.	.	.	.	19851	18221	21491	24214	5699
24 SWEDEN	-	-	.	.	.	.	.	.	.	.	19071	16010	19370	10682	683
25 SWITZERLAND	.	.	.	.	.	.	.	.	.	.	1418	671	2727	4225	6322
26 TURKEY	-	-	-	-	-	-	-	-	-	-	-	13004	8403	2757	3173
27 UK ENGLAND AND WALES	.	.	.	.	.	.	.	27011	30617	24035	16870	11579	11417	6654	6102
28 UK NORTHERN IRELAND	-	-	-	-	.	.	.	.	.	29070	28736	25843	30108	7143	1020
29 UK SCOTLAND	.	.	.	.	.	.	.	.	.	11785	21959	20067	13505	6472	5782
30 USA	.	.	.	.	.	.	.	.	.	7663	4926	8106	10439	7428	6081
31 YUGOSLAVIA	-	-	-	-	-	-	-	-	-	-	.	.	10124	8042	7131

- NO MORTALITY DATA ARE AVAILABLE FOR EVEN A BROADER GROUP OF CAUSES FOR THIS DISEASE

. MORTALITY DATA ARE PRESENTED FOR A BROADER GROUP OF CAUSES FOR THIS DISEASE

0 VALUE<0.5

THE STANDARD MORTALITY RATIOS WERE DERIVED WITH A FACTOR OF 10000

SERIAL MORTALITY TABLES FOR VARIOUS COUNTRIES 1901-1975

TABLE 76 : MENTAL DEFICIENCY : FEMALES

	1901-	1906-	1911-	1916-	1921-	1926-	1931-	1936-	1941-	1946-	1951-	1956-	1961-	1966-	1971-75
1 AUSTRALIA	-	.	.	.	.	.	.	.	19477	16770	23936	29872	17749	10135	6675
2 AUSTRIA	-	-	-	-	-	-	-	-	-	.	16281	9548	7981	10934	1188
3 BELGIUM	-	-	-	-	-	-	-	-	-	-	36511	46979	45880	26384	14313
4 BULGARIA	-	-	-	-	-	-	-	-	-	-	-	-	13646	14751	22642
5 CANADA	-	-	-	-	.	.	.	.	.	28802	14694	19454	22378	12259	3897
6 CHILE	-	-	.	.	.	.	.	2857	1596	3354	27964	25688	32412	8623	3889
7 CZECHOSLOVAKIA	-	-	-	.	.	.	.	.	.	.	12598	16912	14411	8158	5024
8 DENMARK	-	-	-	-	-	-	.	.	.	.	7722	5039	3371	8961	364
9 EIRE	-	-	-	-	.	.	.	.	.	.	38172	52198	41848	16402	508
10 FINLAND	-	-	-	-	-	.	.	-	.	.	5018	5435	23443	15985	2756
11 FRANCE	-	-	-	-	-	-	-	-	.	17120	18342	20217	24033	15256	10274
12 GREECE	-	-	-	-	-	.	.	.	-	-	-	5102	10693	8560	4110
13 HUNGARY	-	-	-	.	.	.	.	.	.	.	5983	11558	14026	24771	29350
14 ICELAND	-	-	-	-	-	-	-	-	-	-	-	-	0	7692	7692
15 ITALY	-	-	-	-	-	-	-	-	-	-	16456	13715	14028	9436	2939
16 JAPAN	-	.	.	.	.	.	.	.	-	7774	8908	7743	6454	4413	3144
17 NETHERLANDS	-	-	.	.	.	.	.	.	.	62691	50735	47009	12985	13127	7810
18 NEW ZEALAND	-	.	.	.	.	.	.	.	.	36364	37956	59091	54913	5000	0
19 NORWAY	-	-	-	-	-	-	-	-	.	.	19000	14078	7583	2262	444
20 POLAND	-	-	-	-	-	-	-	-	-	-	-	.	.	19939	17302
21 PORTUGAL	-	-	-	-	-	-	-	-	-	-	85561	66261	29932	9773	5331
22 ROMANIA	-	-	-	-	-	-	-	-	-	-	-	17865	2629	0	0
23 SPAIN	-	.	.	.	.	.	.	.	.	.	17843	14930	17004	20458	4814
24 SWEDEN	-	-	.	.	.	.	.	.	.	.	21750	10327	18765	8353	231
25 SWITZERLAND	.	.	.	.	.	.	.	.	.	.	1045	331	3303	3652	5158
26 TURKEY	-	-	-	-	-	-	-	-	-	-	-	7261	5007	1747	1661
27 UK ENGLAND AND WALES	.	.	.	.	.	.	.	27372	25523	22826	15416	10334	10689	6741	5826
28 UK NORTHERN IRELAND	-	-	-	-	.	.	.	.	.	52326	31034	22727	23656	6186	2105
29 UK SCOTLAND	.	.	.	.	.	.	.	.	.	16447	14474	16667	9177	4153	4667
30 USA	.	.	.	.	.	.	.	.	.	5907	3959	6697	9323	6440	4742
31 YUGOSLAVIA	-	-	-	-	-	-	-	-	-	-	.	.	6605	6557	4935

- NO MORTALITY DATA ARE AVAILABLE FOR EVEN A BROADER GROUP OF CAUSES FOR THIS DISEASE

. MORTALITY DATA ARE PRESENTED FOR A BROADER GROUP OF CAUSES FOR THIS DISEASE

0 VALUE<0.5

THE STANDARD MORTALITY RATIOS WERE DERIVED WITH A FACTOR OF 10000

SERIAL MORTALITY TABLES FOR VARIOUS COUNTRIES 1901-1975

TABLE 77 : MENTAL ILLNESS - ALL FORMS : MALES

	1901-	1906-	1911-	1916-	1921-	1926-	1931-	1936-	1941-	1946-	1951-	1956-	1961-	1966-	1971-75
1 AUSTRALIA	-	.	.	.	.	.	1671	1696	1736	2255	3505	2961	2509	3443	4528
2 AUSTRIA	-	-	-	-	-	-	-	-	-	.	3927	3515	3265	2245	2398
3 BELGIUM	-	-	-	-	-	-	-	-	-	-	3835	3662	3607	3814	4726
4 BULGARIA	-	-	-	-	-	-	-	-	-	-	-	-	1088	876	1019
5 CANADA	-	-	-	-	.	.	.	.	2675	2088	1789	1697	1520	1743	2643
6 CHILE	-	-	.	.	.	.	.	6402	8210	7125	9338	7742	8692	5329	4656
7 CZECHOSLOVAKIA	-	-	-	.	.	.	.	.	.	2004	1302	1085	1129	459	450
8 DENMARK	-	-	-	-	-	-	.	.	.	.	2434	873	802	1210	1530
9 EIRE	-	-	-	-	.	.	.	.	.	.	1877	1170	1133	572	517
10 FINLAND	-	-	-	-	-	.	.	-	.	.	1932	865	2135	2683	3348
11 FRANCE	-	-	-	-	-	-	-	-	.	5569	7390	10383	10527	8892	6815
12 GREECE	-	-	-	-	-	.	.	.	-	-	-	1699	2493	2409	2202
13 HUNGARY	-	-	-	.	.	.	4482	3496	4890	.	2592	2644	1839	1820	2435
14 ICELAND	-	-	-	-	-	-	-	-	-	-	-	-	1412	1474	748
15 ITALY	-	-	-	-	-	-	-	-	-	-	3672	2360	2092	1414	902
16 JAPAN	-	.	.	.	.	.	.	.	-	4311	3872	3482	3004	2594	2072
17 NETHERLANDS	-	-	.	.	.	.	.	.	9951	8166	4539	2934	2742	2859	2980
18 NEW ZEALAND	-	.	.	.	.	.	.	.	.	2829	2742	2076	2625	1380	2349
19 NORWAY	-	-	-	-	-	-	-	-	.	.	1917	1225	1251	1452	2356
20 POLAND	-	-	-	-	-	-	-	-	-	-	-	.	472	1808	2490
21 PORTUGAL	-	-	-	-	-	-	-	-	-	-	3405	3205	1960	684	917
22 ROMANIA	-	-	-	-	-	-	-	-	-	-	-	1265	448	724	1221
23 SPAIN	-	.	.	.	.	.	.	.	.	.	2391	2470	2389	2472	1578
24 SWEDEN	-	-	.	.	.	.	.	.	.	.	1727	1915	1446	2218	2110
25 SWITZERLAND	.	.	.	.	.	.	.	.	4473	4065	6057	4848	3991	3308	1680
26 TURKEY	-	-	-	-	-	-	-	-	-	-	-	6717	5140	3745	1487
27 UK ENGLAND AND WALES	.	.	.	.	.	.	.	2403	1899	1202	1045	779	910	905	1106
28 UK NORTHERN IRELAND	-	-	-	-	.	.	.	.	.	1540	1306	867	1400	1762	1415
29 UK SCOTLAND	.	.	3326	3239	.	.	.	.	.	1688	1216	1388	1286	1531	2557
30 USA	.	.	.	.	.	.	.	.	.	2474	1873	1685	1706	2224	2933
31 YUGOSLAVIA	-	-	-	-	-	-	-	-	-	-	.	.	3084	4712	5348

- NO MORTALITY DATA ARE AVAILABLE FOR EVEN A BROADER GROUP OF CAUSES FOR THIS DISEASE

. MORTALITY DATA ARE PRESENTED FOR A BROADER GROUP OF CAUSES FOR THIS DISEASE

0 VALUE<0.5

THE STANDARD MORTALITY RATIOS WERE DERIVED WITH A FACTOR OF 1000

SERIAL MORTALITY TABLES FOR VARIOUS COUNTRIES 1901-1975

TABLE 77 : MENTAL ILLNESS - ALL FORMS : FEMALES

	1901-	1906-	1911-	1916-	1921-	1926-	1931-	1936-	1941-	1946-	1951-	1956-	1961-	1966-	1971-75
1 AUSTRALIA	-	.	.	.	.	.	1292	1188	1154	933	1583	1362	1226	1771	2453
2 AUSTRIA	-	-	-	-	-	-	-	-	-	.	2533	1296	1544	1192	966
3 BELGIUM	-	-	-	-	-	-	-	-	-	-	3456	3884	3046	3125	4140
4 BULGARIA	-	-	-	-	-	-	-	-	-	-	-	-	402	384	424
5 CANADA	-	-	-	-	.	.	.	.	2061	1615	1185	1102	992	826	1004
6 CHILE	-	-	.	.	.	.	.	3193	2744	2520	2563	1986	2046	1105	1122
7 CZECHOSLOVAKIA	-	-	-	.	.	.	.	.	.	1783	1430	1135	999	471	323
8 DENMARK	-	-	-	-	-	-	.	.	.	.	2559	1125	722	1202	1125
9 EIRE	-	-	-	-	.	.	.	.	.	.	1856	1010	818	507	450
10 FINLAND	-	-	-	-	-	.	.	-	.	.	1783	714	2774	2170	2569
11 FRANCE	-	-	-	-	-	-	-	-	.	2381	2789	3478	3741	3353	2507
12 GREECE	-	-	-	-	-	.	.	.	-	-	-	1457	2217	2194	1920
13 HUNGARY	-	-	-	.	.	.	3424	2508	2885	.	1956	1773	1092	896	1229
14 ICELAND	-	-	-	-	-	-	-	-	-	-	-	-	686	790	234
15 ITALY	-	-	-	-	-	-	-	-	-	-	2522	1436	1073	676	358
16 JAPAN	-	.	.	.	.	.	.	.	-	3825	3486	2789	2309	1825	1388
17 NETHERLANDS	-	-	.	.	.	.	.	.	10872	8406	4707	3247	2877	3080	2917
18 NEW ZEALAND	-	.	.	.	.	.	.	.	.	1901	2113	1772	1515	1036	519
19 NORWAY	-	-	-	-	-	-	-	-	.	.	1767	1042	840	983	1392
20 POLAND	-	-	-	-	-	-	-	-	-	-	-	.	102	999	1622
21 PORTUGAL	-	-	-	-	-	-	-	-	-	-	2889	2424	1508	195	436
22 ROMANIA	-	-	-	-	-	-	-	-	-	-	-	753	252	138	336
23 SPAIN	-	.	.	.	.	.	.	.	.	.	1625	1512	1510	1292	844
24 SWEDEN	-	-	.	.	.	.	.	.	.	.	1541	1080	932	920	753
25 SWITZERLAND	.	.	.	.	.	.	.	.	3991	2935	2275	1221	1116	921	922
26 TURKEY	-	-	-	-	-	-	-	-	-	-	-	3320	2653	2324	537
27 UK ENGLAND AND WALES	.	.	.	.	.	.	.	2512	1880	1349	1139	936	894	977	1194
28 UK NORTHERN IRELAND	-	-	-	-	.	.	.	.	.	1861	1702	586	820	824	571
29 UK SCOTLAND	.	.	3838	3610	.	.	.	.	.	1882	1238	1291	1619	1170	2006
30 USA	.	.	.	.	.	.	.	.	.	1099	730	648	657	734	934
31 YUGOSLAVIA	-	-	-	-	-	-	-	-	-	-	.	.	690	994	1407

- NO MORTALITY DATA ARE AVAILABLE FOR EVEN A BROADER GROUP OF CAUSES FOR THIS DISEASE

. MORTALITY DATA ARE PRESENTED FOR A BROADER GROUP OF CAUSES FOR THIS DISEASE

0 VALUE<0.5

THE STANDARD MORTALITY RATIOS WERE DERIVED WITH A FACTOR OF 1000

SERIAL MORTALITY TABLES FOR VARIOUS COUNTRIES 1901-1975

TABLE 78 : VASCULAR LESIONS AFFECTING CENTRAL NERVOUS SYSTEM : MALES

	1901-	1906-	1911-	1916-	1921-	1926-	1931-	1936-	1941-	1946-	1951-	1956-	1961-	1966-	1971-75
1 AUSTRALIA	-	9171	10474	9795	.	.	8047	8075	8578	9423	10984	10871	10462	10947	10641
2 AUSTRIA	12044	12416	11008	10622	-	-	-	-	-	10623	11758	11981	12067	12312	11954
3 BELGIUM	12555	13524	14822	11915	8862	6177	10924	10570	8980	9209	6135	5278	6111	10849	10238
4 BULGARIA	-	-	-	-	-	10591	13492	14573	14500	13889	13071	5818	12455	14714	16528
5 CANADA	-	-	-	-	6923	5521	3600	2232	7970	7820	9025	8937	7780	7319	6921
6 CHILE	-	36834	22624	13293	8318	9254	9801	9231	9992	10285	11208	11160	10785	10492	10413
7 CZECHOSLOVAKIA	-	-	-	8819	9175	10002	8980	8837	7297	7619	8165	9372	9173	11780	14466
8 DENMARK	-	-	-	-	-	-	3897	3663	3531	5482	9599	8603	8613	7316	6388
9 EIRE	-	-	-	-	6268	6428	6785	6812	7126	7536	7545	8511	9307	10252	10420
10 FINLAND	-	-	-	-	-	.	.	8667	9759	10418	13441	13801	13391	13384	11053
11 FRANCE	-	-	-	-	9408	10105	12266	13430	13335	11608	11323	10619	10191	10116	9672
12 GREECE	-	-	-	-	3761	5925	6903	7039	-	-	-	6571	7351	7967	8441
13 HUNGARY	-	-	-	9742	10301	10050	10508	9811	9723	9662	10970	12664	12494	12839	12390
14 ICELAND	-	-	9142	12611	9363	8569	9132	9164	8949	9884	10112	8335	7997	8089	7989
15 ITALY	14377	14075	14464	14845	14951	16454	16252	15716	14231	12708	12996	12917	11879	11149	10268
16 JAPAN	28182	24301	21113	24437	31906	35127	35638	37005	-	20083	24411	26535	27361	25336	20900
17 NETHERLANDS	9238	8841	8170	8470	7813	7398	7257	7067	7161	7086	8316	8291	7859	7591	7031
18 NEW ZEALAND	-	8152	6583	7352	7402	6925	6952	7423	7994	7690	8717	8677	8952	9525	10071
19 NORWAY	5402	5733	6514	6857	7199	7071	.	.	7073	8004	8934	9646	9779	9928	9650
20 POLAND	-	-	-	-	-	-	-	-	-	-	.	4666	4760	3912	4746
21 PORTUGAL	13183	13075	13015	13974	13826	16284	16461	15620	14173	13246	13468	14490	15460	18598	21004
22 ROMANIA	-	-	-	-	-	-	-	-	-	-	-	8019	11732	12695	12168
23 SPAIN	25124	24544	23831	22663	21103	19586	18430	17841	13982	11462	10402	10874	11068	10443	11497
24 SWEDEN	-	-	6953	6360	6565	6976	7193	7809	7298	7619	9449	8977	7835	6604	6231
25 SWITZERLAND	7641	7641	6246	6246	5509	5975	4272	3492	2887	2453	10923	9856	9562	8261	7392
26 TURKEY	-	-	-	-	-	-	-	-	-	-	-	10053	8820	7680	8740
27 UK ENGLAND AND WALES	13101	10506	11770	10664	11278	10773	10723	10769	10139	10194	11632	11377	11024	10504	9568
28 UK NORTHERN IRELAND	-	-	-	-	11097	10699	10394	9896	10727	11022	10730	11176	11194	11051	11981
29 UK SCOTLAND	16854	17665	19413	18399	16339	16025	15725	13955	13467	12839	14210	14375	14273	13197	12987
30 USA	22147	16824	14777	13611	13515	12790	11334	10631	9859	9377	10024	9746	9019	8457	7670
31 YUGOSLAVIA	-	-	-	-	-	-	-	-	-	-	.	6714	7443	8501	8935

- NO MORTALITY DATA ARE AVAILABLE FOR EVEN A BROADER GROUP OF CAUSES FOR THIS DISEASE

. MORTALITY DATA ARE PRESENTED FOR A BROADER GROUP OF CAUSES FOR THIS DISEASE

0 VALUE<0.5

THE STANDARD MORTALITY RATIOS WERE DERIVED WITH A FACTOR OF 10000

SERIAL MORTALITY TABLES FOR VARIOUS COUNTRIES 1901-1975

TABLE 78 : VASCULAR LESIONS AFFECTING CENTRAL NERVOUS SYSTEM : FEMALES

	1901-	1906-	1911-	1916-	1921-	1926-	1931-	1936-	1941-	1946-	1951-	1956-	1961-	1966-	1971-75
1 AUSTRALIA	-	9767	10895	10280	.	.	9225	9611	10370	10765	11654	10834	10182	10282	10132
2 AUSTRIA	9820	10460	9189	9298	-	-	-	-	-	9758	10619	10381	10119	10144	9762
3 BELGIUM	8924	9779	10271	9110	7217	5248	8888	9031	8141	8412	5287	4432	5188	8901	8453
4 BULGARIA	-	-	-	-	-	10137	12118	13073	12473	12233	12252	5905	13529	15081	15790
5 CANADA	-	-	-	-	7641	6292	4046	2356	8994	8859	9463	8891	7632	6560	5851
6 CHILE	-	28862	18786	10831	7026	8031	8287	7967	8463	8697	9873	9108	9075	9006	9160
7 CZECHOSLOVAKIA	-	-	-	7385	7227	7703	7183	7381	5995	6623	7243	8327	7709	9723	11623
8 DENMARK	-	-	-	-	-	-	4625	4185	4193	6047	10378	8689	8113	6531	5397
9 EIRE	-	-	-	-	6781	7580	8104	8326	8757	8799	8642	9395	9789	10305	10411
10 FINLAND	-	-	-	-	-	.	.	10025	10313	11256	13994	14182	12556	11864	9091
11 FRANCE	-	-	-	-	6406	6967	8621	9639	10009	9089	8473	7880	7335	7161	7066
12 GREECE	-	-	-	-	3254	5371	6833	7293	-	-	-	7119	7967	8624	9068
13 HUNGARY	-	-	-	7676	7979	8156	8869	8610	8725	8535	10563	12320	11280	11112	10103
14 ICELAND	-	-	7004	7720	8609	8407	7860	8144	8811	8575	10055	9758	7429	7244	6610
15 ITALY	12064	11888	12310	12412	12195	13184	13191	12870	11598	10874	10610	10266	9218	8525	7965
16 JAPAN	20209	17717	15390	17433	20483	22079	22642	23223	-	15558	17292	17283	17265	16012	13694
17 NETHERLANDS	9968	9560	9173	9428	9327	8766	8437	8074	8000	8784	9374	8849	7844	7113	6320
18 NEW ZEALAND	-	9477	6910	8487	8892	8608	9005	9756	10457	9973	10424	9825	9635	9601	10241
19 NORWAY	4701	5166	6024	6327	6893	7277	.	.	7320	8391	9444	10027	9817	8845	8764
20 POLAND	-	-	-	-	-	-	-	-	-	-	.	3988	4123	3302	3858
21 PORTUGAL	9678	9484	9119	9744	9892	12371	12748	12099	11088	10896	10840	11533	12396	14688	16646
22 ROMANIA	-	-	-	-	-	-	-	-	-	-	-	7351	11654	12198	11208
23 SPAIN	23022	21293	20231	19286	17398	15862	14953	13633	10929	9482	8632	9106	9467	8998	10096
24 SWEDEN	-	-	6620	6327	6743	7234	7488	8294	8068	8507	10311	9464	7666	6259	5645
25 SWITZERLAND	6662	6662	5688	5688	5279	5760	4111	3140	2833	2280	10365	8909	8318	7267	6354
26 TURKEY	-	-	-	-	-	-	-	-	-	-	-	8075	7685	7368	7365
27 UK ENGLAND AND WALES	14116	11367	10659	9598	9811	9322	9322	9494	9354	9734	10515	10172	9692	9167	8616
28 UK NORTHERN IRELAND	-	-	-	-	11206	11507	11279	11679	12200	12917	11698	11553	11469	10604	10889
29 UK SCOTLAND	14486	15037	17104	15440	14220	14338	14463	12495	12519	12678	13714	13390	12852	12209	11112
30 USA	20130	15681	14005	13729	13686	12317	10872	10139	9422	8738	9089	8686	7976	7310	6497
31 YUGOSLAVIA	-	-	-	-	-	-	-	-	-	-	.	6224	6647	7457	7882

- NO MORTALITY DATA ARE AVAILABLE FOR EVEN A BROADER GROUP OF CAUSES FOR THIS DISEASE

. MORTALITY DA¯A ARE PRESENTED FOR A BROADER GROUP OF CAUSES FOR THIS DISEASE

0 VALUE<0.5

THE STANDARD MORTALITY RATIOS WERE DERIVED WITH A FACTOR OF 10000

SERIAL MORTALITY TABLES FOR VARIOUS COUNTRIES 1901-1975

TABLE 78 : VASCULAR LESIONS AFFECTING CENTRAL NERVOUS SYSTEM : PERSONS

	1901-	1906-	1911-	1916-	1921-	1926-	1931-	1936-	1941-	1946-	1951-	1956-	1961-	1966-	1971-75
1 AUSTRALIA	-	9444	10671	10027	-	-	8635	8859	9516	10140	11356	10850	10300	10554	10336
2 AUSTRIA	10848	11366	10025	9906	-	9795	9420	9795	-	10120	11087	11014	10859	10939	10542
3 BELGIUM	10615	11512	12343	10375	7971	5676	9828	9744	8531	8783	5656	4793	5575	9694	9158
4 BULGARIA	-	-	-	-	-	10349	12759	13763	13387	12963	12605	5866	13047	14917	16121
5 CANADA	5663	5922	6256	6183	7276	5900	3820	2293	8476	8335	9247	8914	7702	6906	6310
6 CHILE	-	32545	20577	11990	7632	8598	8984	8546	9160	9417	10476	9999	9816	9651	9696
7 CZECHOSLOVAKIA	-	-	-	8020	8085	8711	7964	8009	6562	7055	7639	8768	8300	10536	12721
8 DENMARK	-	-	-	-	-	-	4292	3944	3885	5782	10013	8649	8341	6878	5821
9 EIRE	-	-	-	-	6538	7034	7472	7591	7967	8186	8112	8974	9566	10281	10415
10 FINLAND	-	-	-	-	-	-	-	9468	10092	10934	13786	14039	12867	12425	9806
11 FRANCE	18126	12454	9869	7365	7681	8291	10137	11187	11335	10075	9569	8906	8382	8224	8000
12 GREECE	-	-	-	-	3496	5635	6867	7194	-	-	-	9018	12134	12811	14002
13 HUNGARY	-	-	-	8660	9081	9050	9636	9167	9185	9034	10740	12468	11789	11821	11018
14 ICELAND	-	-	7827	9613	8904	8470	8363	8549	8867	9123	10079	9141	7681	7620	7225
15 ITALY	13206	12963	13365	13599	13529	14743	14629	14190	12805	11704	11677	11427	10351	9602	8890
16 JAPAN	23849	20781	18065	20699	25663	27881	28358	29245	-	17456	20280	21150	21497	19940	16715
17 NETHERLANDS	9634	9231	8711	8984	8619	8121	7878	7596	7602	7980	8873	8587	7851	7326	6625
18 NEW ZEALAND	-	8713	6725	7865	8101	7735	7961	8591	9252	8875	9629	9306	9339	9569	10171
19 NORWAY	5016	5419	6241	6560	7027	7187	-	-	7212	8222	9217	9856	9800	9316	9141
20 POLAND	-	-	-	-	-	-	-	-	-	-	-	4405	4367	3535	4192
21 PORTUGAL	11190	11023	10773	11515	11519	13970	14241	13490	12305	11835	11852	12672	13584	16191	18324
22 ROMANIA	-	-	-	-	-	-	-	-	-	-	-	7630	11686	12404	11609
23 SPAIN	24031	22805	21880	20826	19061	17494	16445	15402	12203	10294	9344	9817	10119	9584	10661
24 SWEDEN	-	-	6765	6341	6665	7120	7356	8075	7717	8097	9914	9240	7743	6412	5897
25 SWITZERLAND	7107	7107	5932	5932	5377	5852	4179	3290	2856	2353	10599	9301	8826	7665	6763
26 TURKEY	-	-	-	-	-	-	5727	6270	8723	8882	9158	8921	8177	7510	8020
27 UK ENGLAND AND WALES	13632	10960	11133	10049	10430	9934	9910	10026	9676	9922	10959	10636	10189	9653	8960
28 UK NORTHERN IRELAND	-	-	-	-	11157	11145	10880	10865	11533	12056	11269	11390	11353	10785	11317
29 UK SCOTLAND	15448	16104	18042	16648	15096	15043	14996	13110	12915	12745	13918	13785	13400	12575	11786
30 USA	21100	16241	14387	13671	13601	12552	11100	10378	9632	7231	9520	9162	8432	7793	6967
31 YUGOSLAVIA	-	-	-	-	-	-	-	-	-	-	-	6428	6976	7889	8319

- NO MORTALITY DATA ARE AVAILABLE FOR EVEN A BROADER GROUP OF CAUSES FOR THIS DISEASE

. MORTALITY DATA ARE PRESENTED FOR A BROADER GROUP OF CAUSES FOR THIS DISEASE

0 VALUE<0.5

THE STANDARD MORTALITY RATIOS WERE DERIVED WITH A FACTOR OF 10000

SERIAL MORTALITY TABLES FOR VARIOUS COUNTRIES 1901-1975

TABLE 79 : MENINGITIS - NON-MENINGOCOCCAL : MALES

	1901-	1906-	1911-	1916-	1921-	1926-	1931-	1936-	1941-	1946-	1951-	1956-	1961-	1966-	1971-75
1 AUSTRALIA	-	.	.	.	1066	627	440	424	399	215	217	168	131	101	93
2 AUSTRIA	-	-	-	-	-	-	-	-	-	909	579	458	289	294	312
3 BELGIUM	4589	4548	4651	4671	4061	3541	1739	1610	1509	1034	371	153	103	108	83
4 BULGARIA	-	-	-	-	-	1005	-	-	-	-	-	-	137	131	201
5 CANADA	-	-	-	-	738	1057	525	399	450	294	236	142	130	98	88
6 CHILE	-	9351	7575	10996	10511	11515	15524	13421	7320	4464	1519	981	1006	720	568
7 CZECHOSLOVAKIA	-	-	-	3412	2507	1787	1149	927	1158	860	468	245	188	178	189
8 DENMARK	-	-	-	-	-	-	.	.	539	390	183	141	112	125	112
9 EIRE	-	-	-	-	1414	1387	1209	1145	824	529	305	175	155	172	145
10 FINLAND	-	-	-	-	-	.	.	.	597	461	275	243	164	134	140
11 FRANCE	-	-	-	-	3513	3643	-	-	1677	1184	495	285	226	227	198
12 GREECE	-	-	-	-	2239	2044	1991	1863	-	-	-	189	230	164	128
13 HUNGARY	-	-	-	.	.	.	2136	1844	1506	1333	135	322	256	232	242
14 ICELAND	-	-	-	-	-	-	-	-	-	-	167	171	205	159	68
15 ITALY	4782	4147	3611	2618	2175	1345	843	873	788	661	332	277	208	148	128
16 JAPAN	17494	16186	14819	13764	12646	9647	7379	6315	-	919	532	270	171	126	120
17 NETHERLANDS	4009	2346	1940	1426	1078	645	463	347	532	315	170	166	141	135	110
18 NEW ZEALAND	-	.	.	.	901	567	284	371	286	219	225	227	193	185	151
19 NORWAY	1497	1269	1174	1393	915	857	.	.	612	334	191	159	151	99	98
20 POLAND	-	-	-	-	-	-	-	-	-	-	.	812	465	280	203
21 PORTUGAL	2211	2552	2932	3550	3674	3062	-	-	-	-	830	502	329	292	376
22 ROMANIA	-	-	-	-	-	-	-	-	-	-	-	864	492	537	235
23 SPAIN	13080	12693	12056	11875	9693	6498	4785	4180	2891	1906	1010	681	425	246	209
24 SWEDEN	-	-	.	.	.	.	.	.	.	.	145	148	124	111	120
25 SWITZERLAND	1317	1317	658	658	613	621	545	502	505	440	230	185	174	159	158
26 TURKEY	-	-	-	-	-	-	-	-	-	-	-	542	460	398	579
27 UK ENGLAND AND WALES	2595	2121	1550	1218	797	527	417	344	282	167	134	127	124	113	95
28 UK NORTHERN IRELAND	-	-	-	-	1284	1182	1045	582	363	217	132	75	154	171	103
29 UK SCOTLAND	4449	3181	2737	2481	1607	1177	828	596	541	251	174	137	132	132	127
30 USA	6920	3230	1269	743	507	431	328	324	270	189	161	162	162	138	113
31 YUGOSLAVIA	-	-	-	-	-	-	-	-	-	-	.	388	201	234	186

- NO MORTALITY DATA ARE AVAILABLE FOR EVEN A BROADER GROUP OF CAUSES FOR THIS DISEASE

. MORTALITY DATA ARE PRESENTED FOR A BROADER GROUP OF CAUSES FOR THIS DISEASE

0 VALUE<0.5

THE STANDARD MORTALITY RATIOS WERE DERIVED WITH A FACTOR OF 100

SERIAL MORTALITY TABLES FOR VARIOUS COUNTRIES 1901-1975

TABLE 79 : MENINGITIS - NON-MENINGOCOCCAL : FEMALES

	1901-	1906-	1911-	1916-	1921-	1926-	1931-	1936-	1941-	1946-	1951-	1956-	1961-	1966-	1971-75
1 AUSTRALIA	-	.	.	.	753	458	294	270	292	160	135	119	92	87	60
2 AUSTRIA	-	-	-	-	-	-	-	-	-	547	356	307	201	190	182
3 BELGIUM	4063	4018	3694	3780	3605	3047	1424	1239	1265	819	263	101	68	84	60
4 BULGARIA	-	-	-	-	-	629	-	-	-	-	-	-	109	116	136
5 CANADA	-	-	-	-	602	903	410	338	321	238	164	122	91	74	53
6 CHILE	-	8210	7032	10267	9809	10457	13884	11982	6577	3767	1251	759	800	598	468
7 CZECHOSLOVAKIA	-	-	-	2845	2067	1430	891	735	840	657	336	149	133	128	123
8 DENMARK	-	-	-	-	-	-	.	.	393	301	134	99	100	82	82
9 EIRE	-	-	-	-	1221	1323	1009	848	643	410	197	129	125	87	125
10 FINLAND	-	-	-	-	-	.	.	.	430	287	208	161	114	110	80
11 FRANCE	-	-	-	-	2801	2851	-	-	1237	804	321	186	149	145	129
12 GREECE	-	-	-	-	1839	1607	1753	1521	-	-	-	159	183	134	78
13 HUNGARY	-	-	-	.	.	.	1771	1470	1127	1076	121	245	200	155	168
14 ICELAND	-	-	-	-	-	-	-	-	-	-	114	150	116	23	116
15 ITALY	4394	3755	3329	2308	1905	1146	701	670	636	523	255	207	161	110	88
16 JAPAN	16301	15187	14066	13151	12152	9005	6700	5762	-	821	479	227	139	99	93
17 NETHERLANDS	3501	2101	1571	1252	806	483	340	235	369	242	126	111	97	100	79
18 NEW ZEALAND	-	.	.	.	604	427	268	273	186	77	191	190	180	130	125
19 NORWAY	1233	1041	895	920	700	503	.	.	374	214	125	97	99	56	100
20 POLAND	-	-	-	-	-	-	-	-	-	-	.	590	306	181	121
21 PORTUGAL	1816	2095	2492	2968	2977	2553	-	-	-	-	653	369	261	195	256
22 ROMANIA	-	-	-	-	-	-	-	-	-	-	-	628	362	398	178
23 SPAIN	11522	11157	10617	10413	8342	5676	4034	3381	2352	1583	806	528	334	178	152
24 SWEDEN	-	-	.	.	.	.	.	.	.	.	132	107	80	79	80
25 SWITZERLAND	1015	1015	514	514	406	470	382	354	333	225	143	119	105	89	80
26 TURKEY	-	-	-	-	-	-	-	-	-	-	-	462	395	333	577
27 UK ENGLAND AND WALES	2155	1733	1312	1018	636	413	294	250	198	109	89	83	93	81	72
28 UK NORTHERN IRELAND	-	-	-	-	1095	909	846	458	313	134	112	73	105	68	75
29 UK SCOTLAND	3818	2644	2288	2057	1224	987	602	442	349	163	110	118	108	86	92
30 USA	5727	2661	1030	567	386	310	229	212	175	127	112	114	121	97	83
31 YUGOSLAVIA	-	-	-	-	-	-	-	-	-	-	.	319	132	157	130

- NO MORTALITY DATA ARE AVAILABLE FOR EVEN A BROADER GROUP OF CAUSES FOR THIS DISEASE

. MORTALITY DATA ARE PRESENTED FOR A BROADER GROUP OF CAUSES FOR THIS DISEASE

0 VALUE<0.5

THE STANDARD MORTALITY RATIOS WERE DERIVED WITH A FACTOR OF 100

SERIAL MORTALITY TABLES FOR VARIOUS COUNTRIES 1901-1975

TABLE 80 : MULTIPLE SCLEROSIS : MALES

	1901-	1906-	1911-	1916-	1921-	1926-	1931-	1936-	1941-	1946-	1951-	1956-	1961-	1966-	1971-75
1 AUSTRALIA	-	.	.	.	.	.	7861	8017	6363	6350	4253	3440	3632	3139	2494
2 AUSTRIA	-	-	-	-	-	-	-	-	-	.	9352	9519	7838	8009	5711
3 BELGIUM	-	-	-	-	.	.	.	.	.	.	15666	11810	13462	10378	9364
4 BULGARIA	-	-	-	-	-	-	-	-	-	-	-	-	1668	2074	2058
5 CANADA	-	-	-	-	.	.	9001	12660	16198	10995	8480	5881	5816	5757	5806
6 CHILE	-	.	.	.	.	.	.	816	1496	1037	2872	532	527	738	1037
7 CZECHOSLOVAKIA	-	-	-	.	.	.	.	.	.	.	13287	11941	10565	10458	8422
8 DENMARK	-	-	-	-	-	-	.	.	.	.	11982	13413	13973	10051	7809
9 EIRE	-	-	-	-	.	.	.	.	.	.	17813	16577	19122	14233	11535
10 FINLAND	-	-	-	-	-	.	.	.	.	.	5232	7138	5932	4351	4033
11 FRANCE	-	-	-	-	-	-	-	-	.	12898	18715	12742	5103	4521	3727
12 GREECE	-	-	-	-	-	.	.	.	-	-	-	1471	1936	2798	2478
13 HUNGARY	-	-	-	.	.	.	2327	3653	4621	.	6596	6725	7652	6306	6088
14 ICELAND	-	-	-	-	-	-	-	-	-	-	-	-	6557	6154	4286
15 ITALY	-	-	-	-	-	-	-	-	-	-	4038	4325	4321	3553	2820
16 JAPAN	.	.	.	.	.	.	.	.	-	863	598	684	615	669	387
17 NETHERLANDS	.	.	.	.	.	.	.	.	14871	10441	11426	10300	10843	10451	7694
18 NEW ZEALAND	-	.	.	.	.	.	.	3436	9106	6241	6300	4321	3527	4574	4344
19 NORWAY	.	.	.	.	.	.	.	.	.	.	10251	9240	8690	7156	7278
20 POLAND	-	-	-	-	-	-	-	-	-	-	.	5618	9030	10896	9843
21 PORTUGAL	-	-	-	-	-	-	-	-	-	-	8478	10294	10505	10218	7668
22 ROMANIA	-	-	-	-	-	-	-	-	-	-	-	6836	3610	3411	4310
23 SPAIN	.	.	.	.	.	.	10106	7826	.	.	12182	14447	13999	9558	2972
24 SWEDEN	-	-	.	.	.	.	.	.	.	.	5877	6824	7067	5163	7012
25 SWITZERLAND	.	.	.	.	.	.	.	.	.	.	9331	11561	11203	10091	7370
26 TURKEY	-	-	-	-	-	-	-	-	-	-	-	900	842	578	256
27 UK ENGLAND AND WALES	.	.	.	.	12957	13497	12974	14111	12688	9220	8710	8568	8247	7815	7799
28 UK NORTHERN IRELAND	-	-	-	-	.	.	.	.	.	15217	18548	13267	14611	12082	14077
29 UK SCOTLAND	.	.	.	.	.	.	.	.	23620	16805	17611	15685	14272	12482	10644
30 USA	.	.	.	.	.	.	.	.	.	5458	5651	4986	4491	4591	3884
31 YUGOSLAVIA	-	-	-	-	-	-	-	-	-	-	.	.	3404	2942	3431

- NO MORTALITY DATA ARE AVAILABLE FOR EVEN A BROADER GROUP OF CAUSES FOR THIS DISEASE

. MORTALITY DATA ARE PRESENTED FOR A BROADER GROUP OF CAUSES FOR THIS DISEASE

0 VALUE<0.5

THE STANDARD MORTALITY RATIOS WERE DERIVED WITH A FACTOR OF 10000

SERIAL MORTALITY TABLES FOR VARIOUS COUNTRIES 1901-1975

TABLE 80 : MULTIPLE SCLEROSIS : FEMALES

	1901-	1906-	1911-	1916-	1921-	1926-	1931-	1936-	1941-	1946-	1951-	1956-	1961-	1966-	1971-75
1 AUSTRALIA	-	.	.	.	.	.	7295	7371	7620	6497	5380	5262	4778	5481	4974
2 AUSTRIA	-	-	-	-	-	-	-	-	-	.	14002	14013	12271	12095	10534
3 BELGIUM	-	-	-	-	.	.	.	.	.	.	13704	12147	13064	10589	8783
4 BULGARIA	-	-	-	-	-	-	-	-	-	-	-	-	1697	2220	2261
5 CANADA	-	-	-	-	.	.	8289	12806	16116	11919	8106	8236	8614	8110	8323
6 CHILE	-	.	.	.	.	.	.	397	1011	1234	1198	501	357	1160	1414
7 CZECHOSLOVAKIA	-	-	-	.	.	.	.	.	.	.	13188	13595	13375	11296	10256
8 DENMARK	-	-	-	-	-	-	.	.	.	.	12235	14256	13252	10844	8436
9 EIRE	-	-	-	-	.	.	.	.	.	.	15780	19709	17015	14959	15467
10 FINLAND	-	-	-	-	-	.	.	.	.	.	3876	5587	5016	4288	3918
11 FRANCE	-	-	-	-	-	-	-	-	.	10568	16905	13185	6948	6130	5575
12 GREECE	-	-	-	-	-	.	.	.	-	-	-	1301	1444	2143	2082
13 HUNGARY	-	-	-	.	.	.	3546	4165	6390	.	7504	8643	8095	6727	6428
14 ICELAND	-	-	-	-	-	-	-	-	-	-	-	-	9836	0	2817
15 ITALY	-	-	-	-	-	-	-	-	-	-	4150	4113	4409	3979	3821
16 JAPAN	.	.	.	.	.	.	.	.	-	342	410	553	530	535	443
17 NETHERLANDS	.	.	.	.	.	.	.	.	18590	13547	14351	13243	12181	10843	9979
18 NEW ZEALAND	-	.	.	.	.	.	.	2166	6210	7537	7864	8303	7190	9949	7393
19 NORWAY	.	.	.	.	.	.	.	.	.	.	10283	8721	7877	6884	6142
20 POLAND	-	-	-	-	-	-	-	-	-	-	.	5736	8817	10475	9066
21 PORTUGAL	-	-	-	-	-	-	-	-	-	-	6184	6576	8257	7814	5716
22 ROMANIA	-	-	-	-	-	-	-	-	-	-	-	6528	3840	3652	3538
23 SPAIN	.	.	.	.	.	.	8210	7044	.	.	11908	13718	13346	8170	2934
24 SWEDEN	-	-	.	.	.	.	.	.	.	.	7125	7069	6610	5354	6428
25 SWITZERLAND	.	.	.	.	.	.	.	.	.	.	16727	18186	18248	16035	14239
26 TURKEY	-	-	-	-	-	-	-	-	-	-	-	742	681	594	389
27 UK ENGLAND AND WALES	.	.	.	.	12032	13192	13909	13867	12562	10832	11882	11944	11451	11083	11535
28 UK NORTHERN IRELAND	-	-	-	-	.	.	.	.	.	21277	23529	20696	15604	14918	16585
29 UK SCOTLAND	.	.	.	.	.	.	.	.	19946	18302	20621	19325	17126	16304	13443
30 USA	.	.	.	.	.	.	.	.	.	5922	6112	5917	5919	6044	5928
31 YUGOSLAVIA	-	-	-	-	-	-	-	-	-	-	.	.	3748	3897	3518

- NO MORTALITY DATA ARE AVAILABLE FOR EVEN A BROADER GROUP OF CAUSES FOR THIS DISEASE

. MORTALITY DATA ARE PRESENTED FOR A BROADER GROUP OF CAUSES FOR THIS DISEASE

0 VALUE<0.5

THE STANDARD MORTALITY RATIOS WERE DERIVED WITH A FACTOR OF 10000

SERIAL MORTALITY TABLES FOR VARIOUS COUNTRIES 1901-1975

TABLE 81 : EPILEPSY : MALES

	1901-	1906-	1911-	1916-	1921-	1926-	1931-	1936-	1941-	1946-	1951-	1956-	1961-	1966-	1971-75
1 AUSTRALIA	-	2444	3341	3308	2894	2450	2376	2051	2070	1702	1410	1195	1167	1091	1049
2 AUSTRIA	-	-	-	-	-	-	-	-	-	1618	1647	1828	1481	1540	1245
3 BELGIUM	-	-	-	-	.	.	.	.	.	.	1560	1505	1116	1073	973
4 BULGARIA	-	-	-	-	-	-	-	-	-	-	-	-	1478	1326	1320
5 CANADA	-	-	-	-	2915	3077	2414	1894	1635	1498	1224	1316	1135	907	887
6 CHILE	-	2643	3832	3683	3156	.	3244	2945	3065	3125	3960	3717	3845	3085	3129
7 CZECHOSLOVAKIA	-	-	-	2805	2840	2773	2308	2009	1690	1668	1139	1179	1443	1393	1489
8 DENMARK	2327	2193	2037	2266	1939	1829	2170	1639	1620	811	899	765	742	539	506
9 EIRE	-	-	-	-	4180	4489	4496	3930	2970	2669	2122	1691	1516	1278	827
10 FINLAND	-	-	-	-	-	.	.	.	3316	2194	1829	1731	1169	930	887
11 FRANCE	-	-	-	-	-	-	-	-	1224	1078	1165	1177	1040	1056	1103
12 GREECE	-	-	-	-	-	.	2758	2464	-	-	-	1191	1649	1357	1356
13 HUNGARY	-	-	-	62505	57745	37999	2668	2423	2704	1917	1775	1642	1507	1641	1521
14 ICELAND	-	-	1379	2903	1471	1944	1282	952	-	-	-	-	923	1268	921
15 ITALY	-	-	-	-	-	-	2893	2658	3156	1534	1538	1446	1143	930	876
16 JAPAN	.	1546	1517	1567	1402	1346	1263	1342	-	1877	1699	1390	1160	860	634
17 NETHERLANDS	2769	2766	2756	3054	2209	2059	1671	1566	1996	1310	1074	829	801	825	927
18 NEW ZEALAND	-	4400	3662	3844	2597	2994	2189	2632	3560	1800	2169	1310	1376	913	883
19 NORWAY	2595	2612	2812	2778	2711	2214	2257	2155	2156	1780	1895	1511	1322	1496	1204
20 POLAND	-	-	-	-	-	-	-	-	-	-	.	1060	1289	1323	1167
21 PORTUGAL	-	-	-	-	-	-	-	-	-	-	3611	3476	3696	3835	3263
22 ROMANIA	-	-	-	-	-	-	-	-	-	-	-	1329	1241	1075	1156
23 SPAIN	5750	4611	3871	3865	3089	2888	2740	3031	2421	1828	1700	1413	1220	1242	985
24 SWEDEN	-	-	.	.	.	.	2076	1713	1569	1215	1099	860	775	878	1180
25 SWITZERLAND	3760	3760	3660	3660	2769	2488	1862	2361	2163	1737	1280	1069	1021	670	674
26 TURKEY	-	-	-	-	-	-	-	-	-	-	-	1323	1216	1014	796
27 UK ENGLAND AND WALES	6825	5840	5907	6547	4247	4148	3982	3706	3189	1883	1335	1132	1102	1047	1021
28 UK NORTHERN IRELAND	-	-	-	-	4633	3850	3609	3543	2854	2272	1393	1255	1060	1122	985
29 UK SCOTLAND	5259	4969	4797	4734	3372	3490	2692	2426	2645	2230	1736	1413	1424	1062	1003
30 USA	5512	3848	3439	3327	2519	2281	1868	1562	1453	1243	1205	1036	905	867	724
31 YUGOSLAVIA	-	-	-	-	-	-	-	-	-	-	.	.	1532	1411	1303

- NO MORTALITY DATA ARE AVAILABLE FOR EVEN A BROADER GROUP OF CAUSES FOR THIS DISEASE

. MORTALITY DATA ARE PRESENTED FOR A BROADER GROUP OF CAUSES FOR THIS DISEASE

0 VALUE<0.5

THE STANDARD MORTALITY RATIOS WERE DERIVED WITH A FACTOR OF 1000

SERIAL MORTALITY TABLES FOR VARIOUS COUNTRIES 1901-1975

TABLE 81 : EPILEPSY : FEMALES

	1901-	1906-	1911-	1916-	1921-	1926-	1931-	1936-	1941-	1946-	1951-	1956-	1961-	1966-	1971-75
1 AUSTRALIA	-	2231	2454	2806	2421	1980	1545	1297	1525	1322	1152	875	755	814	745
2 AUSTRIA	-	-	-	-	-	-	-	-	-	1300	1360	1205	980	988	662
3 BELGIUM	-	-	-	-	.	.	.	.	.	.	1209	1252	829	820	762
4 BULGARIA	-	-	-	-	-	-	-	-	-	-	-	-	1077	1052	893
5 CANADA	-	-	-	-	2552	2669	1984	1492	1241	1019	1003	888	888	624	565
6 CHILE	-	2445	2467	2252	2132	.	2108	1729	1971	1913	2468	2211	2145	1947	1866
7 CZECHOSLOVAKIA	-	-	-	2375	2094	2045	1917	1467	1312	1276	937	860	1073	993	895
8 DENMARK	1280	1411	1236	1777	1667	1689	1395	1321	1129	630	590	607	365	288	306
9 EIRE	-	-	-	-	3668	3459	3346	3278	2726	2312	1710	1402	1070	821	744
10 FINLAND	-	-	-	-	-	.	.	.	2378	1939	1355	1380	807	694	468
11 FRANCE	-	-	-	-	-	-	-	-	817	703	691	741	636	606	609
12 GREECE	-	-	-	-	-	.	1949	1768	-	-	-	1048	1223	1102	945
13 HUNGARY	-	-	-	44850	42219	28196	1919	1583	1947	1469	1089	1278	1139	1068	906
14 ICELAND	-	-	1613	303	1667	1842	1219	698	-	-	-	-	625	857	533
15 ITALY	-	-	-	-	-	-	1997	1933	2125	1179	1170	1072	848	649	603
16 JAPAN	.	1236	1170	1231	1082	1042	1004	977	-	1332	1165	1023	902	659	502
17 NETHERLANDS	2260	2151	2178	2820	1904	1759	1604	1338	1789	1121	875	684	544	536	627
18 NEW ZEALAND	-	5000	2381	2588	2427	2692	2082	1822	1966	1471	1250	897	921	702	774
19 NORWAY	2024	2028	1971	2053	1927	1785	1700	1341	1522	1365	1414	1076	996	886	961
20 POLAND	-	-	-	-	-	-	-	-	-	-	.	901	1012	990	763
21 PORTUGAL	-	-	-	-	-	-	-	-	-	-	2285	2169	2343	2299	1753
22 ROMANIA	-	-	-	-	-	-	-	-	-	-	-	1146	988	839	847
23 SPAIN	4786	3906	3290	3090	2504	2289	2083	2027	1699	1366	1420	1125	995	912	748
24 SWEDEN	-	-	.	.	.	.	1615	1407	1109	902	789	560	558	461	578
25 SWITZERLAND	2861	2861	2829	2829	2231	1928	1642	1704	1660	1094	1132	569	840	441	536
26 TURKEY	-	-	-	-	-	-	-	-	-	-	-	1004	902	807	689
27 UK ENGLAND AND WALES	5762	5037	4806	4935	3658	3424	3367	2941	2133	1500	1169	926	871	752	738
28 UK NORTHERN IRELAND	-	-	-	-	3811	3355	2790	2683	2379	1454	1172	830	582	835	735
29 UK SCOTLAND	3601	3833	3408	3231	2456	2432	2112	1798	1980	1634	1386	1112	908	929	795
30 USA	4079	3030	2574	2408	1898	1649	1326	1087	1019	809	750	658	572	549	455
31 YUGOSLAVIA	-	-	-	-	-	-	-	-	-	-	.	.	1311	1129	935

- NO MORTALITY DATA ARE AVAILABLE FOR EVEN A BROADER GROUP OF CAUSES FOR THIS DISEASE

. MORTALITY DATA ARE PRESENTED FOR A BROADER GROUP OF CAUSES FOR THIS DISEASE

0 VALUE<0.5

THE STANDARD MORTALITY RATIOS WERE DERIVED WITH A FACTOR OF 1000

SERIAL MORTALITY TABLES FOR VARIOUS COUNTRIES 1901-1975

TABLE 82 : ORGANS OF VISION - ALL DISEASES: MALES

	1901-	1906-	1911-	1916-	1921-	1926-	1931-	1936-	1941-	1946-	1951-	1956-	1961-	1966-	1971-75
1 AUSTRALIA	-	190	234	300	354	430	520	454	302	268	344	386	192	325	224
2 AUSTRIA	-	-	-	-	-	-	-	-	-	.	552	105	49	189	47
3 BELGIUM	-	-	-	-	.	.	.	.	.	.	351	152	126	70	104
4 BULGARIA	-	-	-	-	-	-	-	-	-	-	-	-	.	.	.
5 CANADA	-	-	-	-	894	1242	1183	1544	893	649	170	160	105	175	116
6 CHILE	-	313	563	566	723	726	469	195	315	51	188	280	157	117	182
7 CZECHOSLOVAKIA	-	-	-	.	.	.	399	861	263	197	0	0	0	0	13
8 DENMARK	-	-	-	-	-	-	.	.	.	.	83	78	0	68	33
9 EIRE	-	-	-	-	1260	818	435	366	473	286	109	221	165	164	53
10 FINLAND	-	-	-	-	-	.	.	.	.	.	107	205	148	95	0
11 FRANCE	-	-	-	-	-	-	-	-	243	132	102	212	232	364	515
12 GREECE	-	-	-	-	-	773	424	569	-	-	-	74	159	210	210
13 HUNGARY	-	-	-	.	.	.	.	.	.	.	108	0	0	0	0
14 ICELAND	-	-	-	-	-	-	-	-	-	-	-	-	0	0	0
15 ITALY	-	-	-	-	-	-	12864	12393	9858	6300	175	308	543	119	142
16 JAPAN	.	782	747	585	891	797	734	458	-	427	270	350	159	107	59
17 NETHERLANDS	190	461	234	94	59	273	127	260	436	178	71	276	327	596	628
18 NEW ZEALAND	-	0	400	556	170	313	147	0	0	0	86	310	213	204	520
19 NORWAY	.	.	.	.	.	.	.	.	305	114	53	0	91	42	124
20 POLAND	-	-	-	-	-	-	-	-	-	-	317	323	192	278	77
21 PORTUGAL	-	-	-	-	-	-	-	-	-	-	127	266	135	0	222
22 ROMANIA	-	-	-	-	-	-	-	-	-	-	-	180	0	11	19
23 SPAIN	1661	446	595	488	457	685	399	311	307	242	865	513	231	17	11
24 SWEDEN	-	-	.	.	.	.	.	.	.	.	24	0	21	40	75
25 SWITZERLAND	343	343	334	334	479	347	.	.	.	.	318	330	297	152	201
26 TURKEY	-	-	-	-	-	-	-	-	-	-	-	303	149	261	652
27 UK ENGLAND AND WALES	1269	918	870	986	922	1201	1092	1093	620	376	258	293	277	153	106
28 UK NORTHERN IRELAND	-	-	-	-	204	656	.	.	.	714	130	0	122	116	116
29 UK SCOTLAND	876	1000	980	927	704	645	625	342	356	418	187	292	107	35	35
30 USA	.	486	566	630	512	522	410	269	206	208	242	139	90	114	106
31 YUGOSLAVIA	-	-	-	-	-	-	-	-	-	-	.	.	23	11	30

- NO MORTALITY DATA ARE AVAILABLE FOR EVEN A BROADER GROUP OF CAUSES FOR THIS DISEASE

. MORTALITY DATA ARE PRESENTED FOR A BROADER GROUP OF CAUSES FOR THIS DISEASE

0 VALUE<0.5

THE STANDARD MORTALITY RATIOS WERE DERIVED WITH A FACTOR OF 1000

SERIAL MORTALITY TABLES FOR VARIOUS COUNTRIES 1901-1975

TABLE 82 : ORGANS OF VISION - ALL DISEASES: FEMALES

	1901-	1906-	1911-	1916-	1921-	1926-	1931-	1936-	1941-	1946-	1951-	1956-	1961-	1966-	1971-75
1 AUSTRALIA	-	4167	1523	3687	2905	4120	4348	2736	5962	2353	2372	4159	3963	3320	2506
2 AUSTRIA	-	-	-	-	-	-	-	-	-	.	5084	1386	1077	3000	1274
3 BELGIUM	-	-	-	-	.	.	.	.	.	.	1295	1911	890	279	1068
4 BULGARIA	-	-	-	-	-	-	-	-	-	-	-	-	.	.	.
5 CANADA	-	-	-	-	5923	9051	12140	15134	8405	6987	1607	1386	1497	859	942
6 CHILE	-	3030	6061	8537	8721	4278	4975	3256	3419	1453	1761	2000	2404	2371	1856
7 CZECHOSLOVAKIA	-	-	-	.	.	.	2576	6471	763	1229	0	0	0	0	98
8 DENMARK	-	-	-	-	-	-	.	.	.	.	1953	1444	1645	299	829
9 EIRE	-	-	-	-	16794	6098	8537	4268	5263	2841	3226	532	1031	2010	0
10 FINLAND	-	-	-	-	-	.	.	.	.	.	426	806	1141	1075	1356
11 FRANCE	-	-	-	-	-	-	-	-	2088	1012	872	2312	3279	4044	4455
12 GREECE	-	-	-	-	-	6452	2671	4651	-	-	-	879	1193	1091	1142
13 HUNGARY	-	-	-	.	.	.	.	.	.	.	935	342	163	0	0
14 ICELAND	-	-	-	-	-	-	-	-	-	-	-	-	0	0	0
15 ITALY	-	-	-	-	-	-	82035	74473	57084	39719	2276	3198	3681	1505	867
16 JAPAN	.	6522	8228	8171	7796	7011	5679	6687	-	5206	3186	3631	2510	1529	939
17 NETHERLANDS	2976	3679	1582	1818	1127	1842	3194	4348	3376	4415	5102	4321	4690	5846	7886
18 NEW ZEALAND	-	0	2273	0	1818	1667	0	0	0	0	3279	7143	7643	4734	2778
19 NORWAY	.	.	.	.	.	.	.	.	4278	1500	2830	1739	800	727	346
20 POLAND	-	-	-	-	-	-	-	-	-	-	3765	1420	722	2211	1186
21 PORTUGAL	-	-	-	-	-	-	-	-	-	-	2053	2718	1625	0	2230
22 ROMANIA	-	-	-	-	-	-	-	-	-	-	-	2057	99	0	0
23 SPAIN	18162	6186	6653	4611	3727	5415	2324	2905	2845	2180	6899	2914	1971	191	312
24 SWEDEN	-	-	.	.	.	.	.	.	.	.	0	210	193	522	636
25 SWITZERLAND	5747	5747	4595	4595	3109	6931	.	.	.	.	2649	4805	3476	3382	2227
26 TURKEY	-	-	-	-	-	-	-	-	-	-	-	3082	2381	3276	5576
27 UK ENGLAND AND WALES	9358	8774	7729	7150	7840	10974	10539	10080	7082	4960	4511	4777	4094	2313	1605
28 UK NORTHERN IRELAND	-	-	-	-	1852	8955	.	.	.	0	3448	2198	0	1923	0
29 UK SCOTLAND	7143	12069	3361	4564	6024	5118	7605	4000	4983	6289	4559	2882	3261	771	1728
30 USA	.	5764	5278	5460	4914	4592	3202	2330	1768	1893	2492	1250	996	1294	1274
31 YUGOSLAVIA	-	-	-	-	-	-	-	-	-	-	.	.	780	366	341

- NO MORTALITY DATA ARE AVAILABLE FOR EVEN A BROADER GROUP OF CAUSES FOR THIS DISEASE

. MORTALITY DATA ARE PRESENTED FOR A BROADER GROUP OF CAUSES FOR THIS DISEASE

0 VALUE<0.5

THE STANDARD MORTALITY RATIOS WERE DERIVED WITH A FACTOR OF 10000

SERIAL MORTALITY TABLES FOR VARIOUS COUNTRIES 1901-1975

TABLE 83 : OTITIS MEDIA AND MASTOIDITIS : MALES

	1901-	1906-	1911-	1916-	1921-	1926-	1931-	1936-	1941-	1946-	1951-	1956-	1961-	1966-	1971-75
1 AUSTRALIA	-	420	1938	1954	3436	5165	4767	4544	2921	1934	1117	709	571	418	144
2 AUSTRIA	-	-	-	-	-	-	-	-	-	.	4252	4039	1975	1669	1188
3 BELGIUM	-	-	-	-	.	.	.	.	.	.	2179	1271	602	230	129
4 BULGARIA	-	-	-	-	-	-	-	-	-	-	-	-	1374	1138	690
5 CANADA	-	-	-	-	6931	11994	10538	10492	8038	5972	5215	2612	1416	920	394
6 CHILE	-	267	693	401	812	1093	2217	2423	1874	1076	2423	3563	2696	1960	1200
7 CZECHOSLOVAKIA	-	-	-	2156	2706	5210	6775	7778	9686	10847	4558	2766	1885	1303	731
8 DENMARK	-	-	-	-	-	-	12654	11829	6247	3225	1683	819	953	597	290
9 EIRE	-	-	-	-	3480	4770	5300	4382	3101	2215	1376	727	447	471	292
10 FINLAND	-	-	-	-	-	.	.	.	4716	2265	1161	673	423	550	573
11 FRANCE	-	-	-	-	-	-	-	-	6171	8623	3555	1860	816	363	265
12 GREECE	-	-	-	-	-	1015	1692	2537	-	-	-	348	194	62	74
13 HUNGARY	-	-	-	.	.	.	6242	6585	8610	.	9817	7312	7435	5093	4228
14 ICELAND	-	-	-	-	-	-	-	-	-	-	-	-	0	0	0
15 ITALY	-	-	-	-	-	-	-	-	-	-	1778	1508	1138	771	340
16 JAPAN	.	1387	1630	1943	2223	1883	1973	1939	-	3640	1618	952	465	212	121
17 NETHERLANDS	2564	2067	2607	3152	2290	6011	6043	6598	8707	3907	1730	1486	1307	627	352
18 NEW ZEALAND	-	500	1869	261	1463	4846	4394	5797	4040	2155	2837	2259	1774	365	761
19 NORWAY	.	.	.	.	.	3669	3647	4170	6332	2226	717	631	523	306	245
20 POLAND	-	-	-	-	-	-	-	-	-	-	8990	4501	6535	4393	1867
21 PORTUGAL	-	-	-	-	-	-	-	-	-	-	11084	12903	18393	13986	5752
22 ROMANIA	-	-	-	-	-	-	-	-	-	-	-	6254	5968	4504	1784
23 SPAIN	909	751	796	978	954	713	1515	2099	2114	2366	2834	4580	5969	4607	1156
24 SWEDEN	-	-	.	.	.	.	8571	7119	3024	1109	760	438	308	193	151
25 SWITZERLAND	5350	5350	5907	5907	6047	6532	7756	6592	4122	1711	1242	979	1120	575	454
26 TURKEY	-	-	-	-	-	-	-	-	-	-	-	2878	2681	1336	303
27 UK ENGLAND AND WALES	8759	9191	9383	9207	9592	11175	12784	11128	8763	4935	2601	1505	1108	847	502
28 UK NORTHERN IRELAND	-	-	-	-	7634	6810	.	.	.	3053	1504	1259	1119	403	135
29 UK SCOTLAND	8500	10401	10244	9840	10045	12286	11276	9218	4724	2931	1462	851	553	392	367
30 USA	.	7420	6105	5825	9485	10760	10246	7663	3165	1363	849	646	387	253	187
31 YUGOSLAVIA	-	-	-	-	-	-	-	-	-	-	.	.	4530	1795	1053

- NO MORTALITY DATA ARE AVAILABLE FOR EVEN A BROADER GROUP OF CAUSES FOR THIS DISEASE

. MORTALITY DATA ARE PRESENTED FOR A BROADER GROUP OF CAUSES FOR THIS DISEASE

0 VALUE<0.5

THE STANDARD MORTALITY RATIOS WERE DERIVED WITH A FACTOR OF 1000

SERIAL MORTALITY TABLES FOR VARIOUS COUNTRIES 1901-1975

TABLE 83 : OTITIS MEDIA AND MASTOIDITIS : FEMALES

	1901-	1906-	1911-	1916-	1921-	1926-	1931-	1936-	1941-	1946-	1951-	1956-	1961-	1966-	1971-75
1 AUSTRALIA	-	483	1146	1526	2543	3869	3484	2864	1829	1233	797	516	271	255	104
2 AUSTRIA	-	-	-	-	-	-	-	-	-	.	2626	2277	1178	992	624
3 BELGIUM	-	-	-	-	.	.	.	.	.	.	1271	696	335	121	67
4 BULGARIA	-	-	-	-	-	-	-	-	-	-	-	-	586	793	422
5 CANADA	-	-	-	-	5358	8964	8108	8265	5491	3764	3521	1712	859	604	226
6 CHILE	-	133	267	241	227	693	1509	1575	1385	997	1899	3312	1842	1386	868
7 CZECHOSLOVAKIA	-	-	-	1329	1589	3314	3942	4141	6481	7363	3221	1988	1131	1048	391
8 DENMARK	-	-	-	-	-	-	8348	6667	4592	2438	1435	743	667	459	417
9 EIRE	-	-	-	-	2273	3891	3626	3321	2036	1799	692	563	314	478	296
10 FINLAND	-	-	-	-	-	.	.	.	3113	1404	583	492	559	350	169
11 FRANCE	-	-	-	-	-	-	-	-	4024	5484	2337	1329	455	265	182
12 GREECE	-	-	-	-	-	1266	1400	1548	-	-	-	223	176	24	48
13 HUNGARY	-	-	-	.	.	.	4262	4785	5294	.	7097	4849	5333	3766	3078
14 ICELAND	-	-	-	-	-	-	-	-	-	-	-	-	526	0	0
15 ITALY	-	-	-	-	-	-	-	-	-	-	1043	955	729	512	243
16 JAPAN	.	1132	1246	1473	1580	1424	1489	1592	-	2643	1235	709	314	166	108
17 NETHERLANDS	1445	1783	2124	2462	1486	3742	3534	4333	5675	2833	1104	994	636	444	251
18 NEW ZEALAND	-	1053	1010	463	1102	4194	3150	4148	2517	1796	1698	2034	840	769	623
19 NORWAY	.	.	.	.	.	2257	2548	2698	5442	1917	963	687	376	331	214
20 POLAND	-	-	-	-	-	-	-	-	-	-	5988	2591	4047	2797	1171
21 PORTUGAL	-	-	-	-	-	-	-	-	-	-	11565	9536	13373	9844	3757
22 ROMANIA	-	-	-	-	-	-	-	-	-	-	-	4703	4344	3332	1308
23 SPAIN	738	604	581	743	675	683	1036	1458	1401	1697	2146	3452	4172	3448	825
24 SWEDEN	-	-	.	.	.	.	5670	5596	1874	685	578	377	161	233	68
25 SWITZERLAND	3518	3518	3911	3911	4146	4603	4516	4444	2645	1484	644	405	424	551	347
26 TURKEY	-	-	-	-	-	-	-	-	-	-	-	1749	2323	946	212
27 UK ENGLAND AND WALES	6784	6734	7067	6499	6915	7740	8621	6936	4951	2956	1381	729	750	550	342
28 UK NORTHERN IRELAND	-	-	-	-	4375	4917	.	.	.	1866	882	648	544	260	331
29 UK SCOTLAND	6900	7880	7255	6204	7220	9081	7341	6109	3313	1481	605	338	442	290	221
30 USA	.	5387	4509	4266	7018	7949	7868	5687	2137	910	604	475	303	205	154
31 YUGOSLAVIA	-	-	-	-	-	-	-	-	-	-	.	.	2794	1202	715

- NO MORTALITY DATA ARE AVAILABLE FOR EVEN A BROADER GROUP OF CAUSES FOR THIS DISEASE

. MORTALITY DATA ARE PRESENTED FOR A BROADER GROUP OF CAUSES FOR THIS DISEASE

0 VALUE<0.5

THE STANDARD MORTALITY RATIOS WERE DERIVED WITH A FACTOR OF 1000

SERIAL MORTALITY TABLES FOR VARIOUS COUNTRIES 1901-1975

TABLE 84 : EYE AND EAR - ALL DISEASES : MALES

	1901-	1906-	1911-	1916-	1921-	1926-	1931-	1936-	1941-	1946-	1951-	1956-	1961-	1966-	1971-75
1 AUSTRALIA	-	470	1899	1942	3328	4928	4563	4302	2764	1866	1167	820	605	531	236
2 AUSTRIA	-	-	-	-	-	-	-	-	-	6784	3982	3541	1733	1538	1036
3 BELGIUM	-	-	-	-	.	.	.	.	.	.	2068	1173	585	235	169
4 BULGARIA	-	-	-	-	-	-	-	-	-	-	-	-	1219	1024	626
5 CANADA	-	-	-	-	6794	11585	10161	10214	7656	5683	4778	2429	1320	905	406
6 CHILE	-	375	877	605	1053	1319	2279	2364	1892	1035	2352	3466	2602	1891	1200
7 CZECHOSLOVAKIA	-	-	-	.	.	.	6379	7500	8866	9896	4103	2475	1674	1148	646
8 DENMARK	-	-	-	-	-	-	.	.	.	.	1517	750	818	548	264
9 EIRE	-	-	-	-	3726	4640	4922	4050	2966	2094	1246	746	475	496	282
10 FINLAND	-	-	-	-	-	.	.	.	.	.	1121	709	453	541	510
11 FRANCE	-	-	-	-	-	-	-	-	5513	7588	3167	1734	832	509	511
12 GREECE	-	-	-	-	-	1271	1733	2555	-	-	-	347	250	164	179
13 HUNGARY	-	-	-	.	.	.	.	.	.	10596	11802	6527	6509	4413	3648
14 ICELAND	-	-	-	-	-	-	-	-	-	-	-	-	0	0	0
15 ITALY	-	-	-	-	-	-	-	-	-	-	1666	1485	1274	736	371
16 JAPAN	.	.	.	.	2494	2092	2152	2008	-	3596	1626	1033	497	242	137
17 NETHERLANDS	2448	2105	2504	2936	2128	5618	.	.	8088	3630	1580	1453	1315	857	639
18 NEW ZEALAND	-	454	1897	480	1407	4577	4041	5195	3588	1923	2573	2164	1689	426	935
19 NORWAY	.	.	.	.	.	.	.	.	5732	2017	652	546	498	283	278
20 POLAND	-	-	-	-	-	-	-	-	-	-	8536	4333	6122	4123	1715
21 PORTUGAL	-	-	-	-	-	-	-	-	-	-	10203	11897	16705	12583	5223
22 ROMANIA	-	-	-	-	-	-	-	-	-	-	-	5800	5401	4057	1608
23 SPAIN	1562	887	994	1116	1080	958	1570	2058	2066	2263	2969	4373	5458	4109	1030
24 SWEDEN	-	-	.	.	.	.	.	.	.	.	669	372	272	185	170
25 SWITZERLAND	5094	5094	5581	5581	5757	6105	.	.	.	.	1255	1028	1136	581	500
26 TURKEY	-	-	-	-	-	-	-	-	-	-	-	2857	2604	1366	549
27 UK ENGLAND AND WALES	.	.	9080	8921	9208	10701	12002	10426	7956	4509	2398	1458	1108	817	489
28 UK NORTHERN IRELAND	-	-	-	-	6990	6484	6953	7385	6544	3082	1391	1104	1049	414	179
29 UK SCOTLAND	8301	10125	9938	9494	9562	11495	10504	8433	4381	2795	1383	895	541	362	337
30 USA	.	7067	5881	5650	8973	10101	9509	7042	2939	1321	875	643	388	281	219
31 YUGOSLAVIA	-	-	-	-	-	-	-	-	-	-	.	.	4144	1635	962

- NO MORTALITY DATA ARE AVAILABLE FOR EVEN A BROADER GROUP OF CAUSES FOR THIS DISEASE

. MORTALITY DATA ARE PRESENTED FOR A BROADER GROUP OF CAUSES FOR THIS DISEASE

0 VALUE<0.5

THE STANDARD MORTALITY RATIOS WERE DERIVED WITH A FACTOR OF 1000

SERIAL MORTALITY TABLES FOR VARIOUS COUNTRIES 1901-1975

TABLE 84 : EYE AND EAR - ALL DISEASES : FEMALES

	1901-	1906-	1911-	1916-	1921-	1926-	1931-	1936-	1941-	1946-	1951-	1956-	1961-	1966-	1971-75
1 AUSTRALIA	-	622	1132	1574	2478	3723	3354	2688	1914	1206	820	666	445	400	226
2 AUSTRIA	-	-	-	-	-	-	-	-	-	4342	2678	1959	1027	989	575
3 BELGIUM	-	-	-	-	.	.	.	.	.	.	1135	689	329	116	124
4 BULGARIA	-	-	-	-	-	-	-	-	-	-	-	-	507	677	381
5 CANADA	-	-	-	-	5203	8636	7930	8166	5331	3711	3232	1597	835	571	245
6 CHILE	-	247	499	575	569	823	1616	1606	1434	990	1844	3160	1811	1387	881
7 CZECHOSLOVAKIA	-	-	-	.	.	.	3665	4022	5780	6564	2827	1722	961	876	328
8 DENMARK	-	-	-	-	-	-	.	.	.	.	1344	711	654	396	388
9 EIRE	-	-	-	-	2857	3714	3610	3119	2050	1712	769	509	323	519	249
10 FINLAND	-	-	-	-	-	.	.	.	.	.	539	474	547	359	221
11 FRANCE	-	-	-	-	-	-	-	-	3480	4603	1987	1228	575	474	442
12 GREECE	-	-	-	-	-	1444	1391	1612	-	-	-	240	215	82	108
13 HUNGARY	-	-	-	.	.	.	.	.	.	7199	8225	4226	4512	3119	2515
14 ICELAND	-	-	-	-	-	-	-	-	-	-	-	-	454	0	0
15 ITALY	-	-	-	-	-	-	-	-	-	-	1028	994	824	515	252
16 JAPAN	.	.	.	.	1851	1619	1623	1763	-	2665	1273	811	403	223	142
17 NETHERLANDS	1452	1791	2003	2318	1401	3471	.	.	5255	2754	1230	1092	801	706	675
18 NEW ZEALAND	-	1000	1038	431	1102	3897	2857	3709	2222	1586	1660	2140	1126	918	687
19 NORWAY	.	.	.	.	.	.	.	.	4870	1712	974	675	359	315	196
20 POLAND	-	-	-	-	-	-	-	-	-	-	5622	2408	3638	2548	1064
21 PORTUGAL	-	-	-	-	-	-	-	-	-	-	10309	8510	11681	8451	3307
22 ROMANIA	-	-	-	-	-	-	-	-	-	-	-	4295	3816	2898	1133
23 SPAIN	1479	829	830	887	785	871	1042	1443	1384	1606	2232	3155	3706	2958	716
24 SWEDEN	-	-	.	.	.	.	.	.	.	.	488	325	143	221	96
25 SWITZERLAND	3472	3472	3750	3750	3869	4439	.	.	.	.	696	615	556	658	421
26 TURKEY	-	-	-	-	-	-	-	-	-	-	-	1765	2264	1017	432
27 UK ENGLAND AND WALES	.	.	6791	6207	6576	7400	8074	6517	4593	2768	1411	889	863	589	376
28 UK NORTHERN IRELAND	-	-	-	-	3982	4815	4552	5074	2986	1722	943	671	462	330	276
29 UK SCOTLAND	6627	7719	6738	5812	6757	8311	6847	5541	3124	1612	769	450	560	285	289
30 USA	.	5202	4374	4160	6664	7468	7271	5207	1987	899	657	479	314	247	204
31 YUGOSLAVIA	-	-	-	-	-	-	-	-	-	-	.	.	2510	1075	641

- NO MORTALITY DATA ARE AVAILABLE FOR EVEN A BROADER GROUP OF CAUSES FOR THIS DISEASE

. MORTALITY DATA ARE PRESENTED FOR A BROADER GROUP OF CAUSES FOR THIS DISEASE

0 VALUE<0.5

THE STANDARD MORTALITY RATIOS WERE DERIVED WITH A FACTOR OF 1000

SERIAL MORTALITY TABLES FOR VARIOUS COUNTRIES 1901-1975

TABLE 85 : NERVOUS SYSTEM AND SENSE ORGANS - ALL DISEASES MALES

	1901-	1906-	1911-	1916-	1921-	1926-	1931-	1936-	1941-	1946-	1951-	1956-	1961-	1966-	1971-75
1 AUSTRALIA	-	11014	12117	13132	10774	9357	9316	9100	9416	9854	11245	11029	10457	10873	10563
2 AUSTRIA	-	-	-	-	-	-	-	-	-	11363	12213	12383	12161	12388	11965
3 BELGIUM	-	-	-	-	13435	13670	15407	14303	12324	11339	7425	6096	6905	11005	10325
4 BULGARIA	-	-	-	-	-	-	-	-	-	-	-	-	13197	14023	15658
5 CANADA	-	-	-	-	9604	8716	5627	4144	8958	8527	9531	9151	7991	7477	7146
6 CHILE	-	47538	33337	30932	26254	28939	35842	31068	21995	17691	16639	14235	13918	12597	11828
7 CZECHOSLOVAKIA	-	-	-	14228	13494	13051	11170	10923	10142	9633	8905	9556	9367	11708	14060
8 DENMARK	-	-	-	-	-	-	8001	7594	5960	6309	9723	8741	8666	7354	6529
9 EIRE	-	-	-	-	8212	8647	8968	8695	8476	8472	8784	9290	9894	10625	10761
10 FINLAND	-	-	-	-	-	.	.	11532	10914	11068	13458	13723	13030	13122	11014
11 FRANCE	-	-	-	-	-	-	-	-	13322	12898	13190	12223	11603	11174	10246
12 GREECE	-	-	-	-	-	10136	9512	9262	-	-	-	7936	8702	8882	8889
13 HUNGARY	-	-	-	26254	24945	19645	12911	11847	11458	12861	12035	12853	12552	12827	12485
14 ICELAND	-	-	-	-	-	-	-	-	-	-	-	-	8207	8319	8213
15 ITALY	-	-	-	-	-	-	-	-	-	-	13395	13079	11977	11151	10284
16 JAPAN	52013	47826	43638	44461	50075	48087	45031	44572	-	24531	23871	25168	25597	23586	19511
17 NETHERLANDS	15329	12997	11723	11692	10241	9639	8686	8383	8827	7993	8713	8680	8268	8000	7389
18 NEW ZEALAND	-	10019	9513	9511	9499	8786	7863	8506	8961	8270	9239	9169	9235	9780	10308
19 NORWAY	8099	8025	8303	8712	8661	8787	8494	8778	7883	8394	9169	9729	9842	10044	9738
20 POLAND	-	-	-	-	-	-	-	-	-	-	8652	7366	6369	4951	5405
21 PORTUGAL	-	-	-	-	-	-	-	-	-	-	13119	15309	16096	18580	20401
22 ROMANIA	-	-	-	-	-	-	-	-	-	-	-	9916	11892	12620	12111
23 SPAIN	42546	40992	38934	37062	32554	27509	23724	22247	17154	13689	12337	12288	11890	11105	11602
24 SWEDEN	-	-	8597	7751	7751	8040	9019	9379	8583	8644	9392	8919	7904	6698	6550
25 SWITZERLAND	10745	10745	8793	8793	7785	8169	6205	5369	4536	3771	11262	10306	10073	8851	7720
26 TURKEY	-	-	-	-	-	-	-	-	-	-	-	12226	10697	9808	10001
27 UK ENGLAND AND WALES	19907	15108	16885	15178	14282	13138	12343	12000	10795	10461	11662	11345	11006	10557	9670
28 UK NORTHERN IRELAND	-	-	-	-	14030	13719	13791	12711	12356	11851	11224	11373	11420	11322	12138
29 UK SCOTLAND	26305	24011	22757	21199	19437	18197	17263	15211	14338	13275	14429	14341	14180	13060	12864
30 USA	31441	21677	17355	15749	14809	13918	12072	11133	10125	9473	9991	9679	8956	8481	7752
31 YUGOSLAVIA	-	-	-	-	-	-	-	-	-	-	.	.	8146	8677	8972

- NO MORTALITY DATA ARE AVAILABLE FOR EVEN A BROADER GROUP OF CAUSES FOR THIS DISEASE

. MORTALITY DATA ARE PRESENTED FOR A BROADER GROUP OF CAUSES FOR THIS DISEASE

0 VALUE<0.5

THE STANDARD MORTALITY RATIOS WERE DERIVED WITH A FACTOR OF 10000

SERIAL MORTALITY TABLES FOR VARIOUS COUNTRIES 1901-1975

TABLE 85 : NERVOUS SYSTEM AND SENSE ORGANS - ALL DISEASES FEMALES

	1901-	1906-	1911-	1916-	1921-	1926-	1931-	1936-	1941-	1946-	1951-	1956-	1961-	1966-	1971-75
1 AUSTRALIA	-	10724	11814	12697	10261	9520	9836	10008	10619	10752	11532	10713	9986	10089	9917
2 AUSTRIA	-	-	-	-	-	-	-	-	-	9997	10801	10545	10120	10085	9653
3 BELGIUM	-	-	-	-	10619	10726	11988	11586	10368	9825	6178	5005	5775	9004	8525
4 BULGARIA	-	-	-	-	-	-	-	-	-	-	-	-	14007	14276	14881
5 CANADA	-	-	-	-	9721	8776	5568	3897	9467	9167	9640	8937	7678	6609	5925
6 CHILE	-	37168	27248	25558	21613	23522	28260	24408	17396	13818	13611	10906	10856	10160	9791
7 CZECHOSLOVAKIA	-	-	-	10991	10070	9813	8528	8668	7712	7817	7592	8342	7755	9560	11242
8 DENMARK	-	-	-	-	-	-	7939	7373	6120	6565	10299	8692	8059	6499	5425
9 EIRE	-	-	-	-	8022	9066	9388	9498	9503	9268	9663	9964	10123	10471	10632
10 FINLAND	-	-	-	-	-	.	.	11286	10480	11143	13538	13710	12108	11570	9025
11 FRANCE	-	-	-	-	-	-	-	-	10246	9751	9847	9125	8456	7990	7527
12 GREECE	-	-	-	-	-	8568	8817	8878	-	-	-	8261	9070	9328	9310
13 HUNGARY	-	-	-	19573	18589	15096	10562	9905	9816	10376	10987	12174	11126	10989	10071
14 ICELAND	-	-	-	-	-	-	-	-	-	-	-	-	7759	7190	6782
15 ITALY	-	-	-	-	-	-	-	-	-	-	10794	10299	9232	8486	7928
16 JAPAN	39630	37382	34314	34344	35649	32609	30180	29492	-	18230	17106	16676	16469	15170	12963
17 NETHERLANDS	14175	12368	11577	11720	10870	10181	9349	8832	9072	9263	9513	8961	7983	7317	6490
18 NEW ZEALAND	-	11155	9503	9962	10307	9920	9592	10157	10726	10045	10532	9977	9632	9631	10246
19 NORWAY	6434	6643	7055	7315	7679	8112	8262	8349	7616	8432	9423	9884	9711	8771	8703
20 POLAND	-	-	-	-	-	-	-	-	-	-	5900	5387	4896	3784	4127
21 PORTUGAL	-	-	-	-	-	-	-	-	-	-	10148	11690	12456	14379	15981
22 ROMANIA	-	-	-	-	-	-	-	-	-	-	-	8473	11440	11858	10937
23 SPAIN	37653	34247	31987	30277	25734	21417	18521	16382	12820	10777	9928	9942	9902	9291	10048
24 SWEDEN	-	-	7578	7121	7444	7866	8742	9355	8905	9217	10062	9253	7628	6222	5782
25 SWITZERLAND	8722	8722	7154	7154	6896	7277	5454	4523	3988	3156	10611	9212	8668	7658	6579
26 TURKEY	-	-	-	-	-	-	-	-	-	-	-	9233	8684	8482	8273
27 UK ENGLAND AND WALES	19387	14864	14291	12489	11839	10878	10240	10149	9592	9767	10468	10102	9654	9143	8633
28 UK NORTHERN IRELAND	-	-	-	-	13184	13200	13426	13341	13013	13198	11985	11564	11479	10648	10904
29 UK SCOTLAND	20386	18885	18886	16914	15960	15525	15226	13149	12817	12769	13748	13286	12702	12029	10986
30 USA	27088	19355	15882	15119	14433	12977	11229	10292	9389	8620	8909	8505	7829	7223	6453
31 YUGOSLAVIA	-	-	-	-	-	-	-	-	-	-	.	.	7009	7430	7749

\- NO MORTALITY DATA ARE AVAILABLE FOR EVEN A BROADER GROUP OF CAUSES FOR THIS DISEASE

. MORTALITY DATA ARE PRESENTED FOR A BROADER GROUP OF CAUSES FOR THIS DISEASE

0 VALUE<0.5

THE STANDARD MORTALITY RATIOS WERE DERIVED WITH A FACTOR OF 10000

SERIAL MORTALITY TABLES FOR VARIOUS COUNTRIES 1901-1975

TABLE 86 : MENTAL ILLNESS AND DISEASES OF NERVOUS SYSTEM : MALES

	1901-	1906-	1911-	1916-	1921-	1926-	1931-	1936-	1941-	1946-	1951-	1956-	1961-	1966-	1971-75
1 AUSTRALIA	-	11925	13015	14099	11415	9666	9440	9231	9547	10065	11640	11336	10699	11263	11140
2 AUSTRIA	-	-	-	-	-	-	-	-	-	11396	12512	12733	12476	12541	12146
3 BELGIUM	-	-	-	-	-	-	-	-	-	-	7104	6566	7354	11420	10887
4 BULGARIA	-	-	-	-	-	-	-	-	-	-	-	-	13159	13938	15574
5 CANADA	-	-	-	-	10320	9494	6588	4980	9255	8731	9669	9282	8112	7643	7464
6 CHILE	-	-	34082	31324	26720	29357	35984	31613	23211	18760	18149	15486	15353	13390	12486
7 CZECHOSLOVAKIA	-	-	-	14381	13789	13314	11676	11376	10557	9781	8973	9577	9398	11596	13913
8 DENMARK	-	-	-	-	-	-	8415	8039	6150	6315	9954	8741	8656	7427	6664
9 EIRE	-	-	-	-	8746	9161	9346	8904	8694	8608	8939	9327	9917	10549	10674
10 FINLAND	-	-	-	-	-	5924	7678	-	11143	11063	13563	13635	13171	13349	11373
11 FRANCE	-	-	-	-	-	-	-	-	13448	13217	14147	13672	13078	12388	11139
12 GREECE	-	-	-	-	-	10317	9592	9346	-	-	-	8087	8967	9126	9093
13 HUNGARY	-	-	-	29305	27560	21735	13452	12235	12082	13196	12164	13073	12644	12910	12666
14 ICELAND	-	-	-	-	-	-	-	-	-	-	-	-	8306	8424	8201
15 ITALY	-	-	-	-	-	-	-	-	-	-	13775	13249	12121	11199	10264
16 JAPAN	-	49359	44058	45201	51974	50086	45775	44822	-	24886	24149	25341	25675	23627	19532
17 NETHERLANDS	-	-	11695	11637	10228	9639	9407	9304	10350	9230	9313	9013	8576	8330	7746
18 NEW ZEALAND	-	10258	10092	10070	9896	9099	8002	8548	9028	8309	9533	9358	9519	9847	10524
19 NORWAY	-	-	-	-	-	-	-	-	7911	8379	9329	9768	9883	10113	9947
20 POLAND	-	-	-	-	-	-	-	-	-	-	-	7230	6308	5172	5724
21 PORTUGAL	-	-	-	-	-	-	-	-	-	-	13484	15597	16155	18388	20222
22 ROMANIA	-	-	-	-	-	-	-	-	-	-	-	9963	11768	12531	12113
23 SPAIN	-	40465	38562	36771	32349	27354	28364	27790	17296	13750	12533	12496	12086	11326	11669
24 SWEDEN	-	-	9147	8147	8027	8269	9087	9424	8650	8746	9515	9076	8004	6933	6768
25 SWITZERLAND	13223	13223	11234	11234	10710	11019	7004	5727	5131	4359	12045	10910	10546	9234	7861
26 TURKEY	-	-	-	-	-	-	-	-	-	-	-	13415	11540	10358	10096
27 UK ENGLAND AND WALES	29245	20289	17655	15823	14760	13723	12636	12208	10919	10485	11643	11290	10976	10534	9691
28 UK NORTHERN IRELAND	-	-	-	-	14284	13977	13983	12883	12434	11844	11253	11330	11461	11422	12170
29 UK SCOTLAND	27468	24830	24889	23051	19685	18296	17207	15141	14365	13290	14393	14334	14159	13095	13059
30 USA	33029	23045	18702	16511	15434	14696	12570	11489	10346	9666	10133	9795	9086	8703	8098
31 YUGOSLAVIA	-	-	-	-	-	-	-	-	-	-	7609	7767	8541	9330	9707

- NO MORTALITY DATA ARE AVAILABLE FOR EVEN A BROADER GROUP OF CAUSES FOR THIS DISEASE

. MORTALITY DATA ARE PRESENTED FOR A BROADER GROUP OF CAUSES FOR THIS DISEASE

0 VALUE<0.5

THE STANDARD MCRTALITY RATIOS WERE DERIVED WITH A FACTOR OF 10000

SERIAL MORTALITY TABLES FOR VARIOUS COUNTRIES 1901-1975

TABLE 86 : MENTAL ILLNESS AND DISEASES OF NERVOUS SYSTEM : FEMALES

	1901-	1906-	1911-	1916-	1921-	1926-	1931-	1936-	1941-	1946-	1951-	1956-	1961-	1966-	1971-75
1 AUSTRALIA	-	11177	12125	12981	10493	9655	9889	10039	10633	10730	11600	10759	10022	10209	10149
2 AUSTRIA	-	-	-	-	-	-	-	-	-	9971	10918	10581	10199	10112	9653
3 BELGIUM	-	-	-	-	-	-	-	-	-	-	5953	5512	6144	9334	9011
4 BULGARIA	-	-	-	-	-	-	-	-	-	-	-	-	13849	14113	14720
5 CANADA	-	-	-	-	10176	9177	6311	4514	9653	9283	9676	8971	7715	6636	5991
6 CHILE	-	-	26881	25170	21372	23265	27958	24349	17591	14037	13838	11075	11036	10177	9816
7 CZECHOSLOVAKIA	-	-	-	11004	10095	9889	8958	9076	7826	7924	7698	8389	7789	9487	11123
8 DENMARK	-	-	-	-	-	-	8435	7749	6417	6630	10538	8731	8046	6582	5513
9 EIRE	-	-	-	-	8420	9533	9637	9711	9703	9420	9800	9966	10093	10387	10538
10 FINLAND	-	-	-	-	-	4628	6838	-	10483	11023	13608	13606	12352	11725	9272
11 FRANCE	-	-	-	-	-	-	-	-	10253	9804	10118	9510	8891	8374	7791
12 GREECE	-	-	-	-	-	8564	8777	8874	-	-	-	8362	9278	9525	9461
13 HUNGARY	-	-	-	21405	20096	16312	10959	10156	10127	10487	10995	12260	11122	10959	10104
14 ICELAND	-	-	-	-	-	-	-	-	-	-	-	-	7743	7201	6711
15 ITALY	-	-	-	-	-	-	-	-	-	-	11022	10362	9255	8459	7862
16 JAPAN	-	38713	34263	34429	36826	34021	30671	29641	-	18584	17416	16867	16580	15221	12978
17 NETHERLANDS	-	-	11409	11545	10819	10169	10091	9762	10718	10497	10118	9333	8309	7681	6838
18 NEW ZEALAND	-	11221	9526	9914	10477	10078	9724	10138	10751	10034	10700	10100	9721	9642	10167
19 NORWAY	-	-	-	-	-	-	-	-	7595	8395	9551	9893	9691	8787	8779
20 POLAND	-	-	-	-	-	-	-	-	-	-	-	5297	4827	3882	4313
21 PORTUGAL	-	-	-	-	-	-	-	-	-	-	10451	11892	12497	14184	15803
22 ROMANIA	-	-	-	-	-	-	-	-	-	-	-	8457	11299	11694	10819
23 SPAIN	-	33356	31512	29837	25371	21113	23015	21313	12776	10740	10030	10025	9984	9348	10023
24 SWEDEN	-	-	7772	7282	7595	8014	8847	9396	8947	9290	10144	9277	7653	6267	5808
25 SWITZERLAND	9665	9665	8630	8630	8080	8474	5655	4665	4481	3560	10797	9258	8706	7681	6619
26 TURKEY	-	-	-	-	-	-	-	-	-	-	-	9690	9017	8755	8219
27 UK ENGLAND AND WALES	25711	18283	14974	13072	12368	11531	10574	10385	9732	9824	10482	10091	9644	9153	8682
28 UK NORTHERN IRELAND	-	-	-	-	13551	13516	13677	13561	13087	13166	12063	11475	11428	10611	10825
29 UK SCOTLAND	21085	19423	20270	18175	16061	15593	15182	13093	12800	12781	13727	13281	12755	12024	11121
30 USA	26934	19349	16193	15282	14505	13062	11263	10309	9398	8625	8883	8473	7810	7225	6498
31 YUGOSLAVIA	-	-	-	-	-	-	-	-	-	-	6242	6551	7007	7470	7849

- NO MORTALITY DATA ARE AVAILABLE FOR EVEN A BROADER GROUP OF CAUSES FOR THIS DISEASE

. MORTALITY DATA ARE PRESENTED FOR A BROADER GROUP OF CAUSES FOR THIS DISEASE

0 VALUE<0.5

THE STANDARD MORTALITY RATIOS WERE DERIVED WITH A FACTOR OF 10000

SERIAL MORTALITY TABLES FOR VARIOUS COUNTRIES 1901-1975

TABLE 87 : RHELMATIC FEVER : MALES

	1901-	1906-	1911-	1916-	1921-	1926-	1931-	1936-	1941-	1946-	1951-	1956-	1961-	1966-	1971-75
1 AUSTRALIA	-	12207	15931	14462	16676	14908	12809	15139	9039	6037	5434	1805	1048	646	374
2 AUSTRIA	-	-	-	-	-	-	-	-	-	3528	2410	2850	694	382	238
3 BELGIUM	-	-	-	-	-	-	-	-	-	-	10244	3752	1559	897	369
4 BULGARIA	-	-	-	-	-	-	-	-	-	-	-	-	11525	5443	5431
5 CANADA	-	-	-	-	15025	13307	11382	19014	11926	6743	6805	2011	1039	576	374
6 CHILE	-	59750	68406	80594	73103	55366	53585	40483	27942	26888	5682	4872	2536	2171	1533
7 CZECHOSLOVAKIA	-	-	-	2853	1637	1617	3502	5307	.	5397	4335	2665	2160	1141	66
8 DENMARK	19259	17069	12969	10000	8069	6604	6652	4892	6461	3580	1685	1172	331	289	31
9 EIRE	-	-	-	-	31307	8115	18756	18943	.	.	9067	3810	957	625	400
10 FINLAND	-	-	-	-	-	-	-	-	4118	3230	3445	1197	546	641	458
11 FRANCE	-	-	-	-	-	-	-	-	8966	5580	3924	2378	1353	948	726
12 GREECE	-	-	-	-	-	6489	7555	8365	-	-	-	1947	1544	662	495
13 HUNGARY	-	-	-	-	-	-	2191	2466	1754	1685	3040	1619	718	417	201
14 ICELAND	-	-	2000	5000	3333	3333	4286	4286	-	-	2222	1000	0	0	0
15 ITALY	10377	15241	13304	15039	13170	15521	20681	23411	17099	12539	11491	3761	1996	711	371
16 JAPAN	-	11769	9387	7415	4474	2174	2656	2934	-	4218	3387	3731	2869	1656	982
17 NETHERLANDS	4842	4971	7003	7494	4977	7325	5774	5130	10089	5808	1886	806	393	247	328
18 NEW ZEALAND	-	16667	11692	10139	12279	12326	11539	8421	7113	3929	3386	1958	2000	1035	476
19 NORWAY	14714	12138	14040	11384	8000	7193	4659	4500	-	-	1304	1200	252	202	78
20 POLAND	-	-	-	-	-	-	-	-	-	-	-	.	6235	4557	2178
21 PORTUGAL	-	-	-	-	-	-	-	-	-	-	10149	5257	2635	1564	1461
22 ROMANIA	-	-	-	-	-	-	-	-	-	-	-	.	.	.	.
23 SPAIN	28481	24657	20261	21648	18312	17053	16449	19371	11689	9441	7248	4813	4336	4757	1376
24 SWEDEN	-	-	-	-	-	-	3714	2704	1897	1030	1929	998	361	271	188
25 SWITZERLAND	-	-	-	-	.	.	-	-	-	-	5856	2019	802	322	432
26 TURKEY	-	-	-	-	-	-	-	-	-	-	-	472	110	146	204
27 UK ENGLAND AND WALES	26773	23313	22622	18537	18391	15392	11839	9466	6597	4234	2659	1347	850	289	283
28 UK NORTHERN IRELAND	-	-	-	-	15500	26267	16234	16329	20385	15244	9294	5632	2444	745	408
29 UK SCOTLAND	19699	10438	20573	14983	12388	16678	14576	14452	7942	5588	3672	2476	472	218	459
30 USA	-	34493	24154	17001	12268	9980	7885	5791	4404	3410	3798	2059	1192	720	383
31 YUGOSLAVIA	-	-	-	-	-	-	-	-	-	-	3450	1785	921	737	412

\- NO MORTALITY DATA ARE AVAILABLE FOR EVEN A BROADER GROUP OF CAUSES FOR THIS DISEASE

. MORTALITY DATA ARE PRESENTED FOR A BROADER GROUP OF CAUSES FOR THIS DISEASE

0 VALUE<0.5

THE STANDARD MORTALITY RATIOS WERE DERIVED WITH A FACTOR OF 1000

SERIAL MORTALITY TABLES FOR VARIOUS COUNTRIES 1901-1975

TABLE 87 : RHEUMATIC FEVER : FEMALES

	1901-	1906-	1911-	1916-	1921-	1926-	1931-	1936-	1941-	1946-	1951-	1956-	1961-	1966-	1971-75
1 AUSTRALIA	-	1544	2086	1793	1700	1647	1333	1646	998	571	563	173	83	45	38
2 AUSTRIA	-	-	-	-	-	-	-	-	-	341	277	353	49	60	34
3 BELGIUM	-	-	-	-	-	-	-	-	-	-	1057	454	148	81	21
4 BULGARIA	-	-	-	-	-	-	-	-	-	-	-	-	1478	733	679
5 CANADA	-	-	-	-	1671	1473	1239	1993	1175	605	598	208	98	53	41
6 CHILE	-	6950	10799	12290	10694	8212	6856	5427	3542	3173	695	459	268	195	168
7 CZECHOSLOVAKIA	-	-	-	276	152	147	361	466	.	458	452	251	232	149	1
8 DENMARK	1508	1191	1105	988	948	857	805	586	712	318	161	127	38	37	6
9 EIRE	-	-	-	-	3027	887	1962	2203	.	.	915	385	133	52	25
10 FINLAND	-	-	-	-	-	-	-	-	461	296	308	153	98	35	38
11 FRANCE	-	-	-	-	-	-	-	-	1019	616	370	198	110	83	66
12 GREECE	-	-	-	-	-	554	768	740	-	-	-	243	221	97	73
13 HUNGARY	-	-	-	-	-	-	383	301	251	255	474	148	96	44	17
14 ICELAND	-	-	167	500	167	143	286	125	-	-	111	0	167	154	0
15 ITALY	1272	1423	1233	1432	1398	1693	2243	2603	1955	1337	1210	407	208	81	34
16 JAPAN	-	1537	1189	1038	543	276	374	500	-	529	437	496	412	290	186
17 NETHERLANDS	496	628	570	713	589	845	622	561	1054	582	197	72	28	32	28
18 NEW ZEALAND	-	1455	1458	1403	1200	1305	1239	787	778	327	528	208	167	90	57
19 NORWAY	1430	1348	1383	1165	750	808	439	309	-	-	172	138	45	8	19
20 POLAND	-	-	-	-	-	-	-	-	-	-	-	.	840	647	307
21 PORTUGAL	-	-	-	-	-	-	-	-	-	-	989	476	212	99	136
22 ROMANIA	-	-	-	-	-	-	-	-	-	-	-	.	.	.	.
23 SPAIN	3139	2587	2144	2318	1826	1688	1730	1879	1081	966	860	589	604	677	191
24 SWEDEN	-	-	-	-	-	-	435	288	256	116	268	91	33	23	18
25 SWITZERLAND	-	-	-	-	.	.	-	-	-	-	480	236	113	61	60
26 TURKEY	-	-	-	-	-	-	-	-	-	-	-	66	19	26	20
27 UK ENGLAND AND WALES	2723	2522	2525	2045	2041	1816	1419	1109	670	437	276	125	61	22	22
28 UK NORTHERN IRELAND	-	-	-	-	2141	3238	2185	1735	2506	1663	1264	479	320	109	133
29 UK SCOTLAND	2299	1279	2447	1646	1632	2063	2031	1704	903	762	376	202	56	11	30
30 USA	-	3800	2712	1850	1443	1129	836	625	453	357	353	185	105	64	29
31 YUGOSLAVIA	-	-	-	-	-	-	-	-	-	-	457	207	102	63	40

- NO MORTALITY DATA ARE AVAILABLE FOR EVEN A BROADER GROUP OF CAUSES FOR THIS DISEASE

. MORTALITY DATA ARE PRESENTED FOR A BROADER GROUP OF CAUSES FOR THIS DISEASE

0 VALUE<0.5

THE STANDARD MORTALITY RATIOS WERE DERIVED WITH A FACTOR OF 100

SERIAL MORTALITY TABLES FOR VARIOUS COUNTRIES 1901-1975

TABLE 88 : HEART DISEASE - CHRONIC RHEUMATIC : MALES

	1901-	1906-	1911-	1916-	1921-	1926-	1931-	1936-	1941-	1946-	1951-	1956-	1961-	1966-	1971-75
1 AUSTRALIA	-	.	.	.	.	.	24439	47640	11000	8226	6749	6033	5275	5701	5410
2 AUSTRIA	.	.	.	.	-	-	-	-	-	.	11896	11384	8117	8059	6031
3 BELGIUM	.	.	.	.	.	.	.	.	.	.	4413	2550	1485	1100	1774
4 BULGARIA	-	-	-	-	-	.	.	.	.	.	.	.	14201	12488	7166
5 CANADA	-	-	-	-	.	.	.	.	.	11153	9118	7410	6147	5329	4510
6 CHILE	-	.	.	.	.	.	.	7884	6285	5118	8522	7684	6154	8550	7051
7 CZECHOSLOVAKIA	-	-	-	.	.	.	.	.	.	8804	19351	14581	10579	11140	8882
8 DENMARK	.	.	.	.	.	.	.	.	.	.	3896	3438	3444	3786	4085
9 EIRE	-	-	-	-	.	.	.	.	.	.	9713	8985	7395	8463	8015
10 FINLAND	-	-	-	-	-	-	-	.	.	.	6218	6387	6127	6308	6279
11 FRANCE	-	-	-	-	.	.	.	.	.	1167	1274	1681	1538	2139	2899
12 GREECE	-	-	-	-	.	.	.	.	-	-	-	941	1921	3199	3656
13 HUNGARY	-	-	-	.	.	.	4050	4876	3636	.	4813	4312	3472	4793	6272
14 ICELAND	-	-	.	.	.	.	.	.	.	.	1772	1806	1210	1848	2196
15 ITALY	.	.	.	.	.	.	.	.	.	.	9713	11026	7809	6684	5651
16 JAPAN	.	.	.	.	.	.	.	.	-	5887	3877	4355	4006	3306	2641
17 NETHERLANDS	.	.	.	.	.	.	.	.	.	3685	4161	3825	3711	4272	5703
18 NEW ZEALAND	-	.	.	.	.	.	.	10016	10429	9550	9870	7939	7060	7656	6715
19 NORWAY	.	.	.	.	.	.	.	.	.	.	5576	6845	6962	6161	7764
20 POLAND	-	-	-	-	-	-	-	-	-	-	-	2454	3347	5187	6656
21 PORTUGAL	-	-	-	-	-	-	.	.	.	.	12230	16173	14315	10753	4916
22 ROMANIA	-	-	-	-	-	-	-	-	-	-	-	.	.	.	.
23 SPAIN	.	.	.	.	.	.	.	.	.	.	17631	17060	14706	16056	10814
24 SWEDEN	-	-	.	.	.	.	.	.	.	.	3259	3250	2858	4082	6745
25 SWITZERLAND	.	.	.	.	.	.	.	.	.	.	5323	4260	1429	1219	1831
26 TURKEY	-	-	-	-	-	-	-	-	-	-	-	2486	1868	1211	744
27 UK ENGLAND AND WALES	.	.	.	.	49471	46508	39820	27789	14313	12063	11684	8884	7342	7359	6812
28 UK NORTHERN IRELAND	-	-	-	-	.	.	.	.	.	12027	8949	9335	7627	8832	6696
29 UK SCOTLAND	.	.	.	.	.	.	.	.	11245	10562	9665	8441	7408	7804	5972
30 USA	.	.	.	.	.	.	.	19794	17147	13582	10145	8582	6659	5670	4956
31 YUGOSLAVIA	-	-	-	-	-	-	-	-	-	-	-	7212	7650	5549	3868

- NO MORTALITY DATA ARE AVAILABLE FOR EVEN A BROADER GROUP OF CAUSES FOR THIS DISEASE

. MORTALITY DATA ARE PRESENTED FOR A BROADER GROUP OF CAUSES FOR THIS DISEASE

0 VALUE<0.5

THE STANDARD MORTALITY RATIOS WERE DERIVED WITH A FACTOR OF 10000

SERIAL MORTALITY TABLES FOR VARIOUS COUNTRIES 1901-1975

TABLE 88 : HEART DISEASE - CHRONIC RHEUMATIC : FEMALES

	1901-	1906-	1911-	1916-	1921-	1926-	1931-	1936-	1941-	1946-	1951-	1956-	1961-	1966-	1971-75
1 AUSTRALIA	-	.	.	.	.	.	26296	41211	12936	9881	7319	6242	6043	6427	5550
2 AUSTRIA	.	.	.	.	-	-	-	-	-	.	12088	12423	9628	8823	6805
3 BELGIUM	.	.	.	.	.	.	.	.	.	.	4402	2954	1634	1440	2173
4 BULGARIA	-	-	-	-	-	.	.	.	.	.	.	.	19709	16399	8954
5 CANADA	-	-	-	-	.	.	.	.	.	12192	10040	8376	7108	6029	4734
6 CHILE	-	.	.	.	.	.	.	8436	6591	5215	8492	9777	7617	9140	7100
7 CZECHOSLOVAKIA	-	-	-	.	.	.	.	.	.	11492	23545	18797	13609	13079	10178
8 DENMARK	.	.	.	.	.	.	.	.	.	.	6355	5981	5627	5606	4879
9 EIRE	-	-	-	-	.	.	.	.	.	.	10606	10025	8221	8929	8189
10 FINLAND	-	-	-	-	-	-	-	.	.	.	5612	6905	6246	6617	4976
11 FRANCE	-	-	-	-	.	.	.	.	.	1235	1522	2178	1964	2321	2773
12 GREECE	-	-	-	-	.	.	.	.	-	-	-	670	2163	4208	4105
13 HUNGARY	-	-	-	.	.	.	4398	4895	3448	.	5847	5983	4576	5467	6949
14 ICELAND	-	-	.	.	.	.	.	.	.	.	3371	1646	3166	2542	2477
15 ITALY	.	.	.	.	.	.	.	.	.	.	13051	14894	10075	8477	6752
16 JAPAN	.	.	.	.	.	.	.	.	-	8154	5443	6367	6040	4830	3445
17 NETHERLANDS	.	.	.	.	.	.	.	.	.	5625	5456	5086	4746	5201	5708
18 NEW ZEALAND	-	.	.	.	.	.	.	14850	12467	10875	9989	9465	7715	7863	7002
19 NORWAY	.	.	.	.	.	.	.	.	.	.	6676	8613	9784	8442	9817
20 POLAND	-	-	-	-	-	-	-	-	-	-	-	2329	3754	5648	6898
21 PORTUGAL	-	-	-	-	-	-	.	.	.	.	12580	16719	14399	9800	4792
22 ROMANIA	-	-	-	-	-	-	-	-	-	-	-	.	.	.	.
23 SPAIN	.	.	.	.	.	.	.	.	.	.	21776	22136	20314	21372	15426
24 SWEDEN	-	-	.	.	.	.	.	.	.	.	4018	4727	3755	4965	7169
25 SWITZERLAND	.	.	.	.	.	.	.	.	.	.	6840	5440	1371	1216	1797
26 TURKEY	-	-	-	-	-	-	-	-	-	-	-	2499	2354	1732	722
27 UK ENGLAND AND WALES	.	.	.	.	57221	54803	46787	32475	17084	15901	15442	12382	10740	9775	8858
28 UK NORTHERN IRELAND	-	-	-	-	.	.	.	.	.	14943	11407	12773	10994	11360	9050
29 UK SCOTLAND	.	.	.	.	.	.	.	.	15206	14798	14102	13287	11722	10530	8017
30 USA	.	.	.	.	.	.	.	19121	16279	12647	9537	8310	6986	5895	4828
31 YUGOSLAVIA	-	-	-	-	-	-	-	-	-	-	-	9278	8514	5951	4139

- NO MORTALITY DATA ARE AVAILABLE FOR EVEN A BROADER GROUP OF CAUSES FOR THIS DISEASE

. MORTALITY DATA ARE PRESENTED FOR A BROADER GROUP OF CAUSES FCR THIS DISEASE

0 VALUE<0.5

THE STANDARD MORTALITY RATIOS WERE DERIVED WITH A FACTOR OF 10000

SERIAL MORTALITY TABLES FOR VARIOUS COUNTRIES 1901-1975

TABLE 89 : HEART DISEASE - ARTERIOSCLEROTIC AND DEGENERATIVE : MALES

	1901-	1906-	1911-	1916-	1921-	1926-	1931-	1936-	1941-	1946-	1951-	1956-	1961-	1966-	1971-75
1 AUSTRALIA	-	.	.	.	.	.	11306	12178	16111	17727	16116	16323	17973	18290	16724
2 AUSTRIA	.	.	.	.	-	-	-	-	-	.	9143	10213	10254	9964	9850
3 BELGIUM	.	.	.	.	.	.	.	.	.	.	5925	6219	6364	8394	8438
4 BULGARIA	-	-	-	-	-	.	.	.	.	.	.	.	5878	7179	9714
5 CANADA	-	-	-	-	.	.	.	.	.	15623	15084	15924	16045	15532	14484
6 CHILE	-	.	.	.	.	.	.	3528	2873	3103	3948	5546	6989	6688	6094
7 CZECHOSLOVAKIA	-	-	-	.	.	.	.	.	.	12306	11486	9801	9132	12074	13288
8 DENMARK	.	.	.	.	.	.	.	.	.	.	9724	10889	12383	13736	13543
9 EIRE	-	-	-	-	.	.	.	.	.	.	13223	13386	13904	13247	13732
10 FINLAND	-	-	-	-	-	-	-	.	16815	16400	17096	17084	20020	19990	18414
11 FRANCE	-	-	-	-	.	.	.	.	1960	2177	2515	3420	4027	3912	4096
12 GREECE	-	-	-	-	.	.	.	.	-	-	-	3596	4052	3913	3943
13 HUNGARY	-	-	-	.	.	.	8995	10709	7940	.	8382	9195	10971	11300	10765
14 ICELAND	-	-	.	.	.	.	.	.	.	.	7099	8680	10169	11839	11135
15 ITALY	.	.	.	.	.	.	.	.	.	.	8173	9159	9639	7710	6869
16 JAPAN	.	.	.	.	.	.	.	.	-	3864	3773	3983	4157	3405	2667
17 NETHERLANDS	.	.	.	.	.	.	.	.	.	8890	8339	9057	10126	10177	10007
18 NEW ZEALAND	-	.	.	.	.	.	.	16862	17806	17331	14353	14334	15873	16567	16221
19 NORWAY	.	.	.	.	.	.	.	.	.	.	6621	8939	11097	11731	12216
20 POLAND	-	-	-	-	-	-	-	-	-	-	-	4414	6158	5868	5396
21 PORTUGAL	-	-	-	-	-	-	.	.	.	.	5488	5283	6484	7312	4998
22 ROMANIA	-	-	-	-	-	-	-	-	-	-	-	.	.	.	.
23 SPAIN	.	.	.	.	.	.	.	.	3676	3251	4275	4201	3793	3223	4136
24 SWEDEN	-	-	.	.	.	.	.	.	.	.	9717	10923	12233	12571	13822
25 SWITZERLAND	.	.	.	.	.	.	.	.	.	.	11213	10655	10905	8621	5926
26 TURKEY	-	-	-	-	-	-	-	-	-	-	-	430	107	59	21
27 UK ENGLAND AND WALES	.	.	.	.	6315	8967	12460	15066	12808	14025	14330	14062	14697	14070	13991
28 UK NORTHERN IRELAND	-	-	-	-	.	.	.	.	.	17571	14290	15718	16921	16048	16824
29 UK SCOTLAND	.	.	.	.	.	.	.	.	14366	16232	17321	17677	18522	17190	17433
30 USA	.	.	.	.	.	.	.	16917	16563	17439	17295	17887	18093	17965	16706
31 YUGOSLAVIA	-	-	-	-	-	-	-	-	-	-	-	5442	7421	5152	4603

- NO MORTALITY DATA ARE AVAILABLE FOR EVEN A BROADER GROUP OF CAUSES FOR THIS DISEASE
. MORTALITY DATA ARE PRESENTED FOR A BROADER GROUP OF CAUSES FOR THIS DISEASE
0 VALUE<0.5
THE STANDARD MORTALITY RATIOS WERE DERIVED WITH A FACTOR OF 10000

SERIAL MORTALITY TABLES FOR VARIOUS COUNTRIES 1901-1975

TABLE 89 : HEART DISEASE - ARTERIOSCLEROTIC AND DEGENERATIVE : FEMALES

	1901-	1906-	1911-	1916-	1921-	1926-	1931-	1936-	1941-	1946-	1951-	1956-	1961-	1966-	1971-75
1 AUSTRALIA	-	.	.	.	.	.	8130	7886	10622	10688	8521	8295	8774	8646	7871
2 AUSTRIA	.	.	.	.	-	-	-	-	-	.	6234	6349	5836	5772	5673
3 BELGIUM	.	.	.	.	.	.	.	.	.	.	3507	3297	2977	3686	3630
4 BULGARIA	-	-	-	-	-	.	.	.	.	.	.	.	5435	5935	7535
5 CANADA	-	-	-	-	.	.	.	.	.	9502	8508	8645	8583	8018	7180
6 CHILE	-	.	.	.	.	.	.	2316	1830	1836	2286	3094	4546	4458	4018
7 CZECHOSLOVAKIA	-	-	-	.	.	.	.	.	.	9731	6996	6615	5077	6709	7604
8 DENMARK	.	.	.	.	.	.	.	.	.	.	7103	6968	7180	7763	7267
9 EIRE	-	-	-	-	.	.	.	.	.	.	9917	9394	8772	7439	7143
10 FINLAND	-	-	-	-	-	-	-	.	7621	7555	7826	7830	9030	7974	6653
11 FRANCE	-	-	-	-	.	.	.	.	1160	1153	1220	1710	1944	1730	1816
12 GREECE	-	-	-	-	.	.	.	.	-	-	-	3174	3156	2304	1857
13 HUNGARY	-	-	-	.	.	.	9533	10464	7280	.	6934	7384	8028	7515	6533
14 ICELAND	-	-	.	.	.	.	.	.	.	.	4747	5101	5210	5803	5047
15 ITALY	.	.	.	.	.	.	.	.	.	.	7249	7164	6920	4825	3946
16 JAPAN	.	.	.	.	.	.	.	.	-	3044	2965	2857	2877	2070	1543
17 NETHERLANDS	.	.	.	.	.	.	.	.	.	7252	6293	6056	5799	5004	4560
18 NEW ZEALAND	-	.	.	.	.	.	.	12170	12525	10862	8245	7690	7956	7609	7375
19 NORWAY	.	.	.	.	.	.	.	.	.	.	4299	5285	6145	5819	5573
20 POLAND	-	-	-	-	-	-	-	-	-	-	-	2280	3307	2751	1843
21 PORTUGAL	-	-	-	-	-	-	.	.	.	.	4146	3869	4588	4917	2628
22 ROMANIA	-	-	-	-	-	-	-	-	-	-	-	.	.	.	.
23 SPAIN	.	.	.	.	.	.	.	.	2685	2428	3345	3069	2530	1734	1905
24 SWEDEN	-	-	.	.	.	.	.	.	.	.	7217	7350	7707	7411	7678
25 SWITZERLAND	.	.	.	.	.	.	.	.	.	.	8793	7860	7404	5029	2410
26 TURKEY	-	-	-	-	-	-	-	-	-	-	-	248	85	51	10
27 UK ENGLAND AND WALES	.	.	.	.	5062	7039	9464	10992	9052	9610	8924	8028	7761	6490	6173
28 UK NORTHERN IRELAND	-	-	-	-	.	.	.	.	.	12566	9757	9553	9455	7969	7787
29 UK SCOTLAND	.	.	.	.	.	.	.	.	10594	11668	11197	10738	9994	8454	7965
30 USA	.	.	.	.	.	.	.	11675	10637	10362	9298	9528	9518	9562	8871
31 YUGOSLAVIA	-	-	-	-	-	-	-	-	-	-	-	4786	6410	3685	2566

- NO MORTALITY DATA ARE AVAILABLE FOR EVEN A BROADER GROUP OF CAUSES FOR THIS DISEASE

. MORTALITY DATA ARE PRESENTED FOR A BROADER GROUP OF CAUSES FOR THIS DISEASE

0 VALUE<0.5

THE STANDARD MORTALITY RATIOS WERE DERIVED WITH A FACTOR OF 10000

SERIAL MORTALITY TABLES FOR VARIOUS COUNTRIES 1901-1975

TABLE 90 : HEART - ALL DISEASES : MALES

	1901-	1906-	1911-	1916-	1921-	1926-	1931-	1936-	1941-	1946-	1951-	1956-	1961-	1966-	1971-75
1 AUSTRALIA	-	8231	8993	7981	8133	9231	11303	13285	15297	16382	15361	15593	16876	17338	15933
2 AUSTRIA	8430	9732	11022	12077	-	-	-	-	-	9439	10243	11278	10821	11149	11666
3 BELGIUM	7472	8112	8792	7770	8204	8994	9225	10345	11145	10857	10006	8147	9431	11471	11030
4 BULGARIA	-	-	-	-	-	8758	10509	11856	12979	13170	12917	6941	7231	7472	9631
5 CANADA	-	-	-	-	7285	7950	8936	9650	13344	13905	13947	14515	14485	14086	13345
6 CHILE	-	8793	10574	12368	13738	12530	14915	14941	15461	14626	9672	7152	8160	8109	7318
7 CZECHOSLOVAKIA	-	-	-	6599	6467	8135	8911	10193	11056	11995	12412	11181	9925	12147	12609
8 DENMARK	6499	7536	6418	6278	5310	5653	6620	7455	7114	9923	9851	11147	12075	12786	12472
9 EIRE	-	-	-	-	6925	7671	9342	11785	13388	14491	13308	13470	13910	13884	13831
10 FINLAND	-	-	-	-	-	-	-	14151	16072	15352	16787	16391	19056	19699	18642
11 FRANCE	-	-	-	-	5489	6285	6402	7600	8872	8252	8017	7747	7629	7181	6888
12 GREECE	-	-	-	-	2226	2597	2971	3205	-	-	-	4601	4779	5380	5666
13 HUNGARY	-	-	-	10014	10093	9738	9230	10541	10094	10671	10557	9641	10768	11665	11782
14 ICELAND	-	-	2841	4067	3775	4550	5022	6047	5155	5409	7412	8355	9512	10794	10259
15 ITALY	8594	8570	8801	9132	7496	7735	6827	7332	8219	7885	8298	9322	9861	9870	9607
16 JAPAN	3400	3717	3728	4190	4806	4932	4844	5041	-	5093	4751	4907	4771	4764	4617
17 NETHERLANDS	4123	5058	5418	5754	6025	6168	6671	7550	7826	7875	8100	8758	9886	10344	10594
18 NEW ZEALAND	-	9974	9533	9726	9890	11024	12468	14613	16528	16182	14152	14104	15224	15990	15134
19 NORWAY	3464	3882	3867	4112	4385	3553	3510	3810	4263	5424	7009	8714	10353	11010	11981
20 POLAND	-	-	-	-	-	-	-	-	-	-	-	7855	8337	8961	10139
21 PORTUGAL	-	-	-	-	-	-	8767	8876	9011	8338	8038	7683	6774	7023	6800
22 ROMANIA	-	-	-	-	-	-	-	-	-	-	-	.	.	.	.
23 SPAIN	10118	10886	11280	12064	11483	11429	11569	13154	12218	10480	7213	6280	5580	6741	7731
24 SWEDEN	-	-	4716	4857	5142	5743	3745	4260	4084	4153	9651	10339	11281	11737	12660
25 SWITZERLAND	8554	8554	8270	8270	7260	7377	6854	7137	8263	8494	10851	10387	10632	9903	9060
26 TURKEY	-	-	-	-	-	-	-	-	-	-	-	21697	19269	17799	16968
27 UK ENGLAND AND WALES	10796	8809	9862	9391	8752	10671	13110	14757	12363	13110	13439	13287	13877	13816	13797
28 UK NORTHERN IRELAND	-	-	-	-	9978	10654	11905	13873	14094	16387	14016	15216	16267	16020	16787
29 UK SCOTLAND	12580	13135	9712	9283	8676	9580	11530	14924	13921	15381	16092	16001	16695	16094	16317
30 USA	15278	12740	11845	11153	11372	13340	14551	16332	16853	16655	15962	16318	16389	16333	15399
31 YUGOSLAVIA	-	-	-	-	-	-	-	-	-	-	-	7943	8821	9173	10064

- NO MORTALITY DATA ARE AVAILABLE FOR EVEN A BROADER GROUP OF CAUSES FOR THIS DISEASE

. MORTALITY DATA ARE PRESENTED FOR A BROADER GROUP OF CAUSES FOR THIS DISEASE

0 VALUE<0.5

THE STANDARD MORTALITY RATIOS WERE DERIVED WITH A FACTOR OF 10000

SERIAL MORTALITY TABLES FOR VARIOUS COUNTRIES 1901-1975

TABLE 90 : HEART - ALL DISEASES : FEMALES

	1901-	1906-	1911-	1916-	1921-	1926-	1931-	1936-	1941-	1946-	1951-	1956-	1961-	1966-	1971-75
1 AUSTRALIA	-	7515	7683	6809	6809	7684	8615	9132	10394	10095	8382	8271	8718	8903	8163
2 AUSTRIA	9234	10414	10665	10966	-	-	-	-	-	7372	7495	7445	6490	6922	7096
3 BELGIUM	7216	7766	8046	7752	8031	8626	8753	9162	9091	9044	6805	5051	5706	6571	5985
4 BULGARIA	-	-	-	-	-	7428	9004	9545	9556	9935	10337	6192	6673	6432	7658
5 CANADA	-	-	-	-	6796	7434	7644	7114	9775	9272	8211	8212	8042	7546	6866
6 CHILE	-	7832	10203	12448	14029	12017	13993	14063	13769	12511	7281	4586	5621	5789	5097
7 CZECHOSLOVAKIA	-	-	-	7303	6814	8565	8807	9534	10093	9989	8175	7881	6256	7328	7466
8 DENMARK	5534	6577	5900	6198	5876	5871	6692	6948	6495	8681	7525	7486	7336	7527	6928
9 EIRE	-	-	-	-	6723	7480	8656	10603	11775	11945	10252	9794	9304	8707	7949
10 FINLAND	-	-	-	-	-	-	-	7871	7679	7324	8249	8244	9475	9324	8365
11 FRANCE	-	-	-	-	4586	5132	4987	5677	6421	5956	5427	5057	4751	4303	4113
12 GREECE	-	-	-	-	2224	2517	3023	3244	-	-	-	4028	3832	3963	3910
13 HUNGARY	-	-	-	9775	9411	9570	9244	9905	9397	8895	8745	8057	8111	8000	7472
14 ICELAND	-	-	3346	3043	3241	3372	3632	3507	3993	4035	5000	5071	5192	5543	4909
15 ITALY	11180	11027	11014	11216	9112	9179	7933	8206	8691	8060	7648	7698	7488	7129	6723
16 JAPAN	3134	3692	3695	4086	4333	4262	4042	4044	-	4024	3642	3557	3424	3357	3270
17 NETHERLANDS	4415	5299	5712	5989	6286	6627	6670	7109	7051	7097	6394	6252	6146	5862	5796
18 NEW ZEALAND	-	8387	8450	8263	8554	9288	10342	11152	11959	10512	8667	8197	8332	8111	7487
19 NORWAY	3372	3712	3606	3706	3855	3363	3432	3629	3641	4551	5128	5689	6230	5966	6233
20 POLAND	-	-	-	-	-	-	-	-	-	-	-	4532	4855	4896	4929
21 PORTUGAL	-	-	-	-	-	-	7207	7161	7315	6955	6200	5804	4913	4753	4290
22 ROMANIA	-	-	-	-	-	-	-	-	-	-	-	.	.	.	.
23 SPAIN	11442	11633	11803	12542	11075	10479	10305	10675	9499	8475	5933	4954	4132	4796	5188
24 SWEDEN	-	-	4450	4648	4875	5348	3891	4305	4067	4001	7446	7239	7346	7177	7223
25 SWITZERLAND	10253	10253	9459	9459	8123	7557	7487	7266	7353	7387	8371	7611	7130	6440	5510
26 TURKEY	-	-	-	-	-	-	-	-	-	-	-	15131	14034	13542	13851
27 UK ENGLAND AND WALES	10960	8668	8419	7793	7688	9139	10635	11289	9135	9387	8757	8036	7841	7228	7044
28 UK NORTHERN IRELAND	-	-	-	-	9573	9818	10144	11556	11735	13130	10054	9872	9826	9079	8849
29 UK SCOTLAND	9774	10364	7820	7243	6966	7789	9067	11274	10594	11435	10879	10188	9492	8579	8129
30 USA	12842	10973	10439	10225	10126	11170	11111	11611	11082	10096	8771	8878	8819	8857	8268
31 YUGOSLAVIA	-	-	-	-	-	-	-	-	-	-	-	7360	7602	7245	7695

- NO MORTALITY DATA ARE AVAILABLE FOR EVEN A BROADER GROUP OF CAUSES FOR THIS DISEASE

. MORTALITY DATA ARE PRESENTED FOR A BROADER GROUP OF CAUSES FOR THIS DISEASE

0 VALUE<0.5

THE STANDARD MORTALITY RATIOS WERE DERIVED WITH A FACTOR OF 10000

SERIAL MORTALITY TABLES FOR VARIOUS COUNTRIES 1901-1975

TABLE 90 : HEART - ALL DISEASES : PERSONS

	1901-	1906-	1911-	1916-	1921-	1926-	1931-	1936-	1941-	1946-	1951-	1956-	1961-	1966-	1971-75
1 AUSTRALIA	-	7904	8384	7425	7495	8475	9968	11177	12749	13052	11536	11503	12231	12449	11370
2 AUSTRIA	8860	10096	10831	11480	-	11557	10624	9549	-	8244	8635	8980	8164	8502	8757
3 BELGIUM	7336	7927	8390	7760	8111	8798	8973	9715	10053	9892	8214	6390	7289	8602	8019
4 BULGARIA	-	-	-	-	-	8059	9715	10622	11123	11386	11475	6534	6927	6904	8555
5 CANADA	4483	3336	4408	4557	7047	7699	8305	8410	11594	11619	11060	11298	11130	10557	9698
6 CHILE	-	8281	10377	12410	13891	12257	14422	14470	14549	13483	8374	5721	6741	6812	6063
7 CZECHOSLOVAKIA	-	-	-	6989	6660	8375	8852	9822	10516	10865	10013	9291	7770	9279	9505
8 DENMARK	5908	6949	6102	6229	5619	5771	6659	7184	6785	9266	8620	9198	9509	9873	9331
9 EIRE	-	-	-	-	6820	7572	8988	11183	12563	13188	11737	11556	11456	11085	10604
10 FINLAND	-	-	-	-	-	-	-	10488	11088	10477	11531	11370	13142	13261	12217
11 FRANCE	8001	5910	5586	4735	4975	5626	5584	6473	7413	6870	6441	6089	5837	5372	5139
12 GREECE	-	-	-	-	2225	2555	2998	3225	-	-	-	5591	6560	6961	7305
13 HUNGARY	-	-	-	9889	9737	9650	9237	10201	9718	9684	9538	8742	9240	9530	9231
14 ICELAND	-	-	3147	3449	3455	3844	4194	4537	4474	4622	6042	6522	7137	7910	7324
15 ITALY	9904	9819	9929	10197	8328	8489	7412	7799	8474	7980	7940	8414	8510	8273	7905
16 JAPAN	3257	3704	3710	4135	4550	4565	4401	4488	-	4485	4119	4135	4001	3961	3844
17 NETHERLANDS	4281	5187	5575	5879	6163	6410	6670	7320	7421	7467	7204	7431	7876	7877	7877
18 NEW ZEALAND	-	9297	9060	9063	9263	10189	11425	12884	14201	13250	11240	10896	11371	11477	10701
19 NORWAY	3414	3789	3722	3885	4088	3447	3466	3709	3915	4937	5973	7054	8081	8187	8717
20 POLAND	-	-	-	-	-	-	-	-	-	-	-	6215	6223	6490	6942
21 PORTUGAL	-	-	-	-	-	-	7844	7850	7995	7517	6922	6543	5650	5645	5279
22 ROMANIA	-	-	-	-	-	-	-	17042	-	10896	-	-	-	-	-
23 SPAIN	10807	11284	11561	12321	11261	10901	10855	11734	10653	9312	6458	5498	4732	5600	6232
24 SWEDEN	-	-	4567	4740	4993	5524	3825	4285	4075	4072	8469	8673	9143	9220	9600
25 SWITZERLAND	9478	9478	8934	8934	7749	7479	7214	7211	7744	7859	9424	8779	8583	7856	6938
26 TURKEY	-	-	-	-	-	-	11879	14487	17344	15968	15792	18021	16368	15531	15360
27 UK ENGLAND AND WALES	10882	8735	9045	8482	8146	9797	11693	12759	10481	10934	10652	10105	10160	9703	9570
28 UK NORTHERN IRELAND	-	-	-	-	9757	10197	10945	12623	12810	14621	11820	12194	12572	11951	12030
29 UK SCOTLAND	10937	11514	8607	8097	7691	8554	10127	12837	12004	13098	13054	12556	12335	11443	11170
30 USA	14022	11847	11140	10689	10749	12256	12818	13924	13867	10567	12115	12260	12172	12051	11183
31 YUGOSLAVIA	-	-	-	-	-	-	-	-	-	-	-	7606	8114	8058	8694

- NO MORTALITY DATA ARE AVAILABLE FOR EVEN A BROADER GROUP OF CAUSES FOR THIS DISEASE
. MORTALITY DATA ARE PRESENTED FOR A BROADER GROUP OF CAUSES FOR THIS DISEASE
0 VALUE<0.5
THE STANDARD MORTALITY RATIOS WERE DERIVED WITH A FACTOR OF 10000

SERIAL MORTALITY TABLES FOR VARIOUS COUNTRIES 1901-1975

TABLE 91 : HEART DISEASE AND ACUTE RHEUMATISM : MALES

	1901-	1906-	1911-	1916-	1921-	1926-	1931-	1936-	1941-	1946-	1951-	1956-	1961-	1966-	1971-75
1 AUSTRALIA	-	8427	9248	8208	8384	9436	11462	13457	15385	16432	15405	15596	16869	17326	15919
2 AUSTRIA	-	-	-	-	-	-	-	-	-	9464	10256	11293	10818	11143	11658
3 BELGIUM	-	-	-	-	-	-	-	-	-	-	9913	8171	9436	11469	11024
4 BULGARIA	-	-	-	-	-	-	-	-	-	-	-	-	7350	7520	9675
5 CANADA	-	-	-	-	7510	8143	9084	9885	13472	13967	14007	14521	14480	14077	13334
6 CHILE	-	9852	11864	14035	15298	13705	16045	15789	16020	15142	9764	7234	8193	8135	7333
7 CZECHOSLOVAKIA	-	-	-	6636	6483	8147	8947	10249	.	12666	12447	11198	9938	12147	12597
8 DENMARK	6817	7814	6612	6424	5409	5729	6691	7503	7176	9949	9858	11148	12067	12778	12463
9 EIRE	-	-	-	-	7275	7874	9916	12021	.	.	13377	13491	13907	13877	13822
10 FINLAND	-	-	-	-	-	-	-	-	16110	15378	16814	16384	19038	19681	18625
11 FRANCE	-	-	-	-	-	-	-	-	8752	8298	8046	7762	7635	7183	6888
12 GREECE	-	-	-	-	-	2969	3068	3308	-	-	-	4618	4790	5382	5665
13 HUNGARY	-	-	-	-	-	-	9247	10559	10103	10679	10580	9648	10764	11658	11773
14 ICELAND	-	-	-	-	-	-	-	-	-	-	7429	8357	9501	10783	10248
15 ITALY	8727	8765	8967	9320	7658	7921	7073	7606	8411	8020	8416	9351	9871	9867	9601
16 JAPAN	-	4290	3871	4302	4877	4964	4886	5089	-	5164	4804	4962	4808	4780	4623
17 NETHERLANDS	4190	5124	5513	5856	6088	6263	6740	7606	7942	7936	8111	8757	9880	10336	10587
18 NEW ZEALAND	-	10219	9699	9864	10055	11183	12602	14696	16585	16205	14173	14110	15229	15983	15122
19 NORWAY	3632	4019	4028	4245	4475	3632	3557	3852	-	-	7014	8717	10347	11003	11972
20 POLAND	-	-	-	-	-	-	-	-	-	-	-	7874	8393	9013	10154
21 PORTUGAL	-	-	-	-	-	-	-	-	-	-	8061	7744	6798	7034	6809
22 ROMANIA	-	-	-	-	-	-	-	-	-	-	-	.	.	.	.
23 SPAIN	10522	11242	11570	12372	11741	11668	11796	13419	12367	10595	7298	6332	5622	6785	7737
24 SWEDEN	-	-	-	-	-	-	3779	4282	4098	4159	9660	10338	11274	11730	12652
25 SWITZERLAND	-	-	-	-	7255	7370	-	-	-	-	10899	10396	10630	9897	9055
26 TURKEY	-	-	-	-	-	-	-	-	-	-	-	21655	19227	17764	16938
27 UK ENGLAND AND WALES	11259	9150	10224	9668	9006	10861	13239	14847	12411	13136	13452	13287	13873	13807	13787
28 UK NORTHERN IRELAND	-	-	-	-	10159	10968	12084	14046	14308	16544	14093	15255	16275	16012	16774
29 UK SCOTLAND	12924	13299	10049	9511	8849	9797	11704	15081	13995	15422	16113	16010	16684	16081	16306
30 USA	-	15522	12206	11400	11543	13467	14640	16386	16885	16674	15985	16322	16385	16324	15388
31 YUGOSLAVIA	-	-	-	-	-	-	-	-	-	-	-	7956	8821	9170	10057

- NO MORTALITY DATA ARE AVAILABLE FOR EVEN A BROADER GROUP OF CAUSES FOR THIS DISEASE

. MORTALITY DATA ARE PRESENTED FOR A BROADER GROUP OF CAUSES FOR THIS DISEASE

0 VALUE<0.5

THE STANDARD MORTALITY RATIOS WERE DERIVED WITH A FACTOR OF 10000

SERIAL MORTALITY TABLES FOR VARIOUS COUNTRIES 1901-1975

TABLE 91 : HEART DISEASE AND ACUTE RHEUMATISM : FEMALES

	1901-	1906-	1911-	1916-	1921-	1926-	1931-	1936-	1941-	1946-	1951-	1956-	1961-	1966-	1971-75
1 AUSTRALIA	-	7790	8043	7104	7071	7914	8780	9315	10489	10141	8426	8280	8717	8899	8160
2 AUSTRIA	-	-	-	-	-	-	-	-	-	7394	7511	7464	6489	6921	7094
3 BELGIUM	-	-	-	-	-	-	-	-	-	-	6645	5078	5712	6572	5982
4 BULGARIA	-	-	-	-	-	-	-	-	-	-	-	-	6805	6490	7708
5 CANADA	-	-	-	-	7043	7647	7806	7361	9905	9330	8266	8225	8043	7544	6864
6 CHILE	-	8916	12044	14773	16113	13589	15284	15073	14402	13053	7387	4654	5654	5811	5116
7 CZECHOSLOVAKIA	-	-	-	7333	6825	8573	8838	9574	.	10365	8210	7896	6271	7334	7461
8 DENMARK	5717	6720	6026	6308	5977	5959	6771	7001	6558	8703	7533	7490	7333	7524	6924
9 EIRE	-	-	-	-	7027	7685	9140	10833	.	.	10318	9816	9307	8704	7945
10 FINLAND	-	-	-	-	-	-	-	-	7722	7348	8272	8251	9475	9319	8362
11 FRANCE	-	-	-	-	-	-	-	-	6699	5996	5448	5066	4755	4306	4114
12 GREECE	-	-	-	-	-	2855	3115	3330	-	-	-	4047	3848	3967	3912
13 HUNGARY	-	-	-	-	-	-	9280	9929	9415	8912	8783	8063	8113	7998	7468
14 ICELAND	-	-	-	-	-	-	-	-	-	-	5004	5067	5203	5552	4905
15 ITALY	11340	11204	11163	11388	9277	9371	8179	8482	8887	8187	7757	7727	7498	7130	6720
16 JAPAN	-	4213	3857	4227	4409	4299	4095	4117	-	4099	3700	3618	3470	3386	3285
17 NETHERLANDS	4475	5374	5779	6075	6355	6728	6739	7167	7165	7154	6408	6253	6144	5860	5793
18 NEW ZEALAND	-	8651	8699	8487	8730	9464	10491	11231	12027	10533	8707	8209	8340	8112	7485
19 NORWAY	3515	3845	3742	3821	3926	3438	3469	3653	-	-	5137	5695	6229	5962	6230
20 POLAND	-	-	-	-	-	-	-	-	-	-	-	4554	4916	4956	4952
21 PORTUGAL	-	-	-	-	-	-	-	-	-	-	6133	5845	4928	4758	4297
22 ROMANIA	-	-	-	-	-	-	-	-	-	-	-	.	.	.	.
23 SPAIN	11870	11975	12080	12840	11303	10684	10508	10887	9612	8569	6012	5004	4180	4847	5199
24 SWEDEN	-	-	-	-	-	-	3926	4326	4085	4007	7461	7240	7344	7174	7220
25 SWITZERLAND	-	-	-	-	8118	7553	-	-	-	-	8403	7624	7133	6439	5511
26 TURKEY	-	-	-	-	-	-	-	-	-	-	-	15116	14014	13524	13832
27 UK ENGLAND AND WALES	11413	9019	8756	8051	7924	9328	10767	11380	9182	9413	8771	8039	7840	7225	7041
28 UK NORTHERN IRELAND	-	-	-	-	9799	10165	10363	11725	11981	13287	10151	9903	9843	9081	8852
29 UK SCOTLAND	10084	10525	8134	7443	7154	8012	9274	11432	10666	11489	10900	10195	9489	8574	8126
30 USA	-	13475	10830	10489	10327	11316	11208	11674	11120	10122	8796	8887	8821	8855	8264
31 YUGOSLAVIA	-	-	-	-	-	-	-	-	-	-	-	7373	7604	7244	7691

- NO MORTALITY DATA ARE AVAILABLE FOR EVEN A BROADER GROUP OF CAUSES FOR THIS DISEASE

. MORTALITY DATA ARE PRESENTED FOR A BROADER GROUP OF CAUSES FOR THIS DISEASE

0 VALUE<0.5

THE STANDARD MORTALITY RATIOS WERE DERIVED WITH A FACTOR OF 10000

SERIAL MORTALITY TABLES FOR VARIOUS COUNTRIES 1901-1975

TABLE 92 : HYPERTENSIVE DISEASE : MALES

	1901-	1906-	1911-	1916-	1921-	1926-	1931-	1936-	1941-	1946-	1951-	1956-	1961-	1966-	1971-75
1 AUSTRALIA	-	.	.	.	.	292	554	1037	1506	1992	7391	5508	3731	5368	5211
2 AUSTRIA	-	-	-	-	-	-	-	-	-	.	1999	2033	2447	3467	5728
3 BELGIUM	-	-	-	-	.	.	.	.	.	.	11517	7801	6838	4866	3641
4 BULGARIA	-	-	-	-	-	-	.	.	.	.	.	.	5816	4192	4106
5 CANADA	-	-	-	-	77	50	5526	8798	506	1173	3486	3094	2259	2600	3273
6 CHILE	-	.	.	.	82	31	143	489	735	27	18053	4409	2999	6492	7065
7 CZECHOSLOVAKIA	-	-	-	.	.	.	13	16	145	1875	3378	2988	8848	6886	4377
8 DENMARK	-	-	-	-	-	-	-	-	.	.	1472	1033	847	1380	1976
9 EIRE	-	-	-	-	25	177	1418	2849	2904	4689	6348	5750	4819	7359	6746
10 FINLAND	-	-	-	-	-	.	.	.	7095	7144	1472	935	1737	3221	4726
11 FRANCE	-	-	-	-	-	-	.	.	546	1109	1630	1558	1641	3045	4106
12 GREECE	-	-	-	-	-	199	41	17	-	-	-	994	1185	3069	3913
13 HUNGARY	-	-	-	.	.	.	.	.	.	.	1365	1299	1566	5857	18773
14 ICELAND	-	-	.	.	.	.	.	.	.	.	5539	5777	2439	491	2261
15 ITALY	.	.	.	.	.	.	.	.	.	.	3509	3519	3180	6953	8811
16 JAPAN	-	.	.	.	184	164	178	334	-	9439	7241	6714	6055	8457	9143
17 NETHERLANDS	.	.	.	.	.	.	826	797	954	1716	2226	2040	1801	2431	2664
18 NEW ZEALAND	-	.	.	.	107	320	377	911	654	1839	2947	2749	1879	4456	6003
19 NORWAY	.	.	.	.	.	.	.	.	.	.	1829	1704	1518	2833	4451
20 POLAND	-	-	-	-	-	-	-	-	-	-	.	1960	4223	8000	7860
21 PORTUGAL	-	-	-	-	-	-	.	.	.	.	12034	4953	3200	2386	5661
22 ROMANIA	-	-	-	-	-	-	-	-	-	-	-	.	.	.	.
23 SPAIN	.	.	.	.	.	.	164	482	1018	2206	5360	5880	5329	5526	2946
24 SWEDEN	-	-	.	.	.	.	.	.	.	.	1130	1102	1557	2280	1652
25 SWITZERLAND	.	.	.	.	.	.	.	.	7802	11609	2102	1873	1202	3376	5714
26 TURKEY	-	-	-	-	-	-	-	-	-	-	-	10006	6340	3831	2221
27 UK ENGLAND AND WALES	.	.	.	.	26	265	498	1615	3124	7903	18417	15644	11297	8091	6070
28 UK NORTHERN IRELAND	-	-	-	-	0	1156	.	.	.	5418	5409	4686	3395	5474	6079
29 UK SCOTLAND	.	.	.	.	219	163	337	1007	2511	3608	6616	5009	4141	5507	5075
30 USA	.	.	.	.	113	233	353	490	679	1573	3753	3386	3037	4207	3871
31 YUGOSLAVIA	-	-	-	-	-	-	-	-	-	-	.	2853	336	2620	4337

\- NO MORTALITY DATA ARE AVAILABLE FOR EVEN A BROADER GROUP OF CAUSES FOR THIS DISEASE

. MORTALITY DATA ARE PRESENTED FOR A BROADER GROUP OF CAUSES FOR THIS DISEASE

0 VALUE<0.5

THE STANDARD MORTALITY RATIOS WERE DERIVED WITH A FACTOR OF 10000

SERIAL MORTALITY TABLES FOR VARIOUS COUNTRIES 1901-1975

TABLE 92 : HYPERTENSIVE DISEASE : FEMALES

	1901-	1906-	1911-	1916-	1921-	1926-	1931-	1936-	1941-	1946-	1951-	1956-	1961-	1966-	1971-75
1 AUSTRALIA	-	.	.	.	.	449	666	912	1185	1830	6420	4708	2960	4734	5021
2 AUSTRIA	-	-	-	-	-	-	-	-	-	.	2389	2178	2511	3700	6301
3 BELGIUM	-	-	-	-	.	.	.	.	.	.	11883	9582	8170	5497	3922
4 BULGARIA	-	-	-	-	-	-	.	.	.	.	.	.	7041	5357	5115
5 CANADA	-	-	-	-	100	82	7924	12678	694	1236	3616	3012	2023	2520	3115
6 CHILE	-	.	.	.	37	18	207	309	689	0	16553	4472	3104	6421	7326
7 CZECHOSLOVAKIA	-	-	-	.	.	.	23	19	144	1519	3123	3037	8843	6223	3595
8 DENMARK	-	-	-	-	-	-	-	-	.	.	1678	1197	774	1266	1738
9 EIRE	-	-	-	-	23	138	1084	2924	2984	5256	6716	5332	3962	6637	7047
10 FINLAND	-	-	-	-	-	.	.	.	9633	11350	1525	1240	1849	4184	7525
11 FRANCE	-	-	-	-	-	-	.	.	602	1124	1565	1551	1520	2575	3685
12 GREECE	-	-	-	-	-	85	17	5	-	-	-	930	1330	3421	4282
13 HUNGARY	-	-	-	.	.	.	.	.	.	.	1382	1385	1554	6861	20558
14 ICELAND	-	-	.	.	.	.	.	.	.	.	7572	10645	2559	729	2514
15 ITALY	.	.	.	.	.	.	.	.	.	.	2970	2881	2407	6838	9269
16 JAPAN	-	.	.	.	130	103	107	187	-	8223	6225	5580	5050	7193	8576
17 NETHERLANDS	.	.	.	.	.	.	911	1130	1350	2130	2385	2241	1736	2745	3271
18 NEW ZEALAND	-	.	.	.	40	387	494	1169	916	2143	3201	2246	1714	4340	5778
19 NORWAY	.	.	.	.	.	.	.	.	.	.	1906	1405	1168	2456	4344
20 POLAND	-	-	-	-	-	-	-	-	-	-	.	1688	4857	9146	8858
21 PORTUGAL	-	-	-	-	-	-	.	.	.	.	9234	3786	2632	1815	4047
22 ROMANIA	-	-	-	-	-	-	-	-	-	-	-	.	.	.	.
23 SPAIN	.	.	.	.	.	.	105	383	844	1947	4866	5466	5161	5231	2932
24 SWEDEN	-	-	.	.	.	.	.	.	.	.	1228	1070	1184	2021	1581
25 SWITZERLAND	.	.	.	.	.	.	.	.	9762	14857	2244	1946	1224	4419	7567
26 TURKEY	-	-	-	-	-	-	-	-	-	-	-	9787	6589	4275	2250
27 UK ENGLAND AND WALES	.	.	.	.	14	174	363	1054	2016	5812	14090	12681	9547	6370	4571
28 UK NORTHERN IRELAND	-	-	-	-	0	756	.	.	.	5044	4453	3661	2564	4667	5110
29 UK SCOTLAND	.	.	.	.	148	73	334	874	1586	2765	5098	3912	3088	4645	4464
30 USA	.	.	.	.	84	207	313	497	663	1459	3206	2770	2383	3509	3248
31 YUGOSLAVIA	-	-	-	-	-	-	-	-	-	-	.	3397	364	3313	5513

- NO MORTALITY DATA ARE AVAILABLE FOR EVEN A BROADER GROUP OF CAUSES FOR THIS DISEASE

. MORTALITY DATA ARE PRESENTED FOR A BROADER GROUP OF CAUSES FOR THIS DISEASE

0 VALUE<0.5

THE STANDARD MORTALITY RATIOS WERE DERIVED WITH A FACTOR OF 10000

SERIAL MORTALITY TABLES FOR VARIOUS COUNTRIES 1901-1975

TABLE 93 : ARTERIES - ALL DISEASES : MALES

	1901-	1906-	1911-	1916-	1921-	1926-	1931-	1936-	1941-	1946-	1951-	1956-	1961-	1966-	1971-75
1 AUSTRALIA	-	.	.	.	.	.	16815	16928	13537	11979	13296	14394	15141	15722	15709
2 AUSTRIA	-	-	-	-	-	-	-	-	-	12335	10583	11080	12009	13012	12530
3 BELGIUM	-	-	-	-	.	.	.	.	.	.	52796	53467	58698	15506	11504
4 BULGARIA	-	-	-	-	-	-	.	.	.	.	.	.	11408	11500	16976
5 CANADA	-	-	-	-	.	.	.	.	12138	10606	10322	10030	9953	11553	13064
6 CHILE	-	.	.	.	.	.	.	19634	19761	19741	31096	23873	16805	13443	15610
7 CZECHOSLOVAKIA	-	-	-	.	.	.	.	.	17425	16474	17836	23840	33575	23082	20569
8 DENMARK	6406	6554	5006	5014	1640	2074	-	-	.	.	9561	9870	9243	10005	9754
9 EIRE	-	-	-	-	.	.	.	11631	10222	9440	9408	10904	10920	13875	15234
10 FINLAND	-	-	-	-	-	.	.	30562	20600	17721	14896	10497	12434	14745	17080
11 FRANCE	-	-	-	-	-	-	.	.	16169	14781	13216	11146	10518	10908	10703
12 GREECE	-	-	-	-	-	.	.	.	-	-	-	2338	2973	3159	3373
13 HUNGARY	-	-	-	.	.	.	21918	19464	17864	.	13480	15471	28651	31291	32115
14 ICELAND	-	-	.	.	.	.	.	.	.	.	-	-	5417	5844	5968
15 ITALY	.	.	.	.	.	.	.	.	.	.	11893	12200	11717	11905	12821
16 JAPAN	-	3362	4226	6475	9369	.	.	.	-	5227	4206	3742	3659	3488	3197
17 NETHERLANDS	.	.	.	.	.	.	.	.	15747	12758	10646	9935	9235	8571	9829
18 NEW ZEALAND	-	.	.	.	.	.	.	6691	6907	6631	7873	10152	9777	11330	15009
19 NORWAY	6975	11725	19112	23113	25832	25503	.	.	.	.	9751	7478	6456	5994	6815
20 POLAND	-	-	-	-	-	-	-	-	-	-	.	9162	26848	50939	61110
21 PORTUGAL	-	-	-	-	-	-	.	.	.	.	12807	8739	7739	7328	12645
22 ROMANIA	-	-	-	-	-	-	-	-	-	-	-	.	.	.	.
23 SPAIN	.	.	.	.	.	.	.	.	29484	26127	23657	21346	19776	23157	17772
24 SWEDEN	-	-	.	.	.	.	71048	79569	76721	97327	16605	12498	10030	10109	8929
25 SWITZERLAND	61195	61195	81190	81190	77838	81297	94859	94006	79527	77324	13782	12155	11478	12847	12078
26 TURKEY	-	-	-	-	-	-	-	-	-	-	-	5001	7280	6147	4939
27 UK ENGLAND AND WALES	10708	8314	28704	33228	31603	31049	20942	19519	14896	14449	12446	11563	12330	13499	13460
28 UK NORTHERN IRELAND	-	-	-	-	.	.	.	.	.	11493	7363	8439	10841	12273	12673
29 UK SCOTLAND	10007	10081	.	.	.	.	.	.	13377	11193	11850	12605	13181	13239	13741
30 USA	.	.	.	.	.	.	.	13730	13298	11898	12098	12485	12460	12491	11650
31 YUGOSLAVIA	-	-	-	-	-	-	-	-	-	-	.	.	8712	9355	11495

- NO MORTALITY DATA ARE AVAILABLE FOR EVEN A BROADER GROUP OF CAUSES FOR THIS DISEASE

. MORTALITY DATA ARE PRESENTED FOR A BROADER GROUP OF CAUSES FOR THIS DISEASE

0 VALUE<0.5

THE STANDARD MORTALITY RATIOS WERE DERIVED WITH A FACTOR OF 10000

SERIAL MORTALITY TABLES FOR VARIOUS COUNTRIES 1901-1975

TABLE 93 : ARTERIES - ALL DISEASES : FEMALES

	1901-	1906-	1911-	1916-	1921-	1926-	1931-	1936-	1941-	1946-	1951-	1956-	1961-	1966-	1971-75
1 AUSTRALIA	-	.	.	.	.	.	10842	12129	11199	9968	10165	9873	9951	10477	10090
2 AUSTRIA	-	-	-	-	-	-	-	-	-	9304	7768	8648	8221	8662	8686
3 BELGIUM	-	-	-	-	.	.	.	.	.	.	34660	34524	38485	10222	6726
4 BULGARIA	-	-	-	-	-	-	.	.	.	.	.	.	10429	10445	14799
5 CANADA	-	-	-	-	.	.	.	.	9881	8882	7971	7421	7358	7897	8274
6 CHILE	-	.	.	.	.	.	.	16066	17772	18454	28367	19937	15340	12121	13996
7 CZECHOSLOVAKIA	-	-	-	.	.	.	.	.	14979	13493	15476	21534	29597	19754	16044
8 DENMARK	2885	2984	3139	2553	982	1353	-	-	.	.	9060	8994	8232	8628	7981
9 EIRE	-	-	-	-	.	.	.	7875	6546	6997	6697	7534	8562	10790	11948
10 FINLAND	-	-	-	-	-	.	.	21296	13197	11389	9918	7515	9187	9403	10895
11 FRANCE	-	-	-	-	-	-	.	.	9530	8157	6933	5851	5299	5201	5028
12 GREECE	-	-	-	-	-	.	.	.	-	-	-	1642	2053	2137	2145
13 HUNGARY	-	-	-	.	.	.	15153	13743	13537	.	10507	12855	24290	25654	23663
14 ICELAND	-	-	.	.	.	.	.	.	.	.	-	-	4497	7071	4304
15 ITALY	.	.	.	.	.	.	.	.	.	.	8735	8519	8128	7952	8734
16 JAPAN	-	2062	2782	4191	5260	.	.	.	-	3132	2555	2312	2336	2257	2003
17 NETHERLANDS	.	.	.	.	.	.	.	.	12417	10959	9029	8455	7239	6278	6424
18 NEW ZEALAND	-	.	.	.	.	.	.	5407	5926	5065	5552	6814	6103	6486	8174
19 NORWAY	4269	6707	11203	12692	14845	17081	.	.	.	.	9203	6862	5350	4260	4582
20 POLAND	-	-	-	-	-	-	-	-	-	-	.	6707	20261	37191	44073
21 PORTUGAL	-	-	-	-	-	-	.	.	.	.	6492	4618	4270	4047	7828
22 ROMANIA	-	-	-	-	-	-	-	-	-	-	-	.	.	.	.
23 SPAIN	.	.	.	.	.	.	.	.	19699	18586	18714	16437	17107	18676	14574
24 SWEDEN	-	-	.	.	.	.	55056	62916	61147	75642	14907	11280	8897	8903	7078
25 SWITZERLAND	44425	44425	55392	55392	54259	58130	66823	66889	60340	61169	9202	8142	7675	9000	8104
26 TURKEY	-	-	-	-	-	-	-	-	-	-	-	2611	4663	4315	2817
27 UK ENGLAND AND WALES	6177	4472	12983	15821	14388	15011	11005	10910	9375	9676	8348	7926	8415	8843	8789
28 UK NORTHERN IRELAND	-	-	-	-	.	.	.	.	.	8117	5175	6177	7734	7916	8592
29 UK SCOTLAND	5967	5461	.	.	.	.	.	.	8158	7171	7760	9019	9329	9554	9381
30 USA	.	.	.	.	.	.	.	10510	9948	9098	9184	8901	8832	8332	7269
31 YUGOSLAVIA	-	-	-	-	-	-	-	-	-	-	.	.	7017	7570	9033

- NO MORTALITY DATA ARE AVAILABLE FOR EVEN A BROADER GROUP OF CAUSES FOR THIS DISEASE

. MORTALITY DATA ARE PRESENTED FOR A BROADER GROUP OF CAUSES FOR THIS DISEASE

0 VALUE<0.5

THE STANDARD MORTALITY RATIOS WERE DERIVED WITH A FACTOR OF 10000

SERIAL MORTALITY TABLES FOR VARIOUS COUNTRIES 1901-1975

TABLE 94 : CIRCULATORY SYSTEM - ALL DISEASES : MALES

	1901-	1906-	1911-	1916-	1921-	1926-	1931-	1936-	1941-	1946-	1951-	1956-	1961-	1966-	1971-75
1 AUSTRALIA	-	6666	7270	8274	9505	11859	7287	7664	6433	6015	9387	9124	8682	9657	9504
2 AUSTRIA	-	-	-	-	-	-	-	-	-	7323	7280	7427	8309	9920	10173
3 BELGIUM	-	-	-	-	8860	10692	7609	8236	8753	10327	20903	27200	29393	10045	8032
4 BULGARIA	-	-	-	-	-	-	5463	5709	4672	4055	9731	24198	6035	7440	10086
5 CANADA	-	-	-	-	.	.	.	.	5736	5483	6602	6502	6226	7191	8238
6 CHILE	-	14493	.	.	.	.	.	9788	9960	9824	17321	13478	9623	9254	10072
7 CZECHOSLOVAKIA	-	-	-	.	.	.	.	.	7627	7295	9704	12654	18779	14129	12818
8 DENMARK	-	-	-	-	-	-	-	-	16672	8282	5536	5830	5863	6636	7385
9 EIRE	-	-	-	-	.	.	.	5758	5633	6108	7283	7965	7677	10423	11071
10 FINLAND	-	-	-	-	-	.	.	18700	14859	14386	7630	5240	6909	9044	10723
11 FRANCE	-	-	-	-	-	-	7839	8099	7953	7425	7560	6631	6499	7412	7895
12 GREECE	-	-	-	-	-	.	.	.	-	-	-	1980	2383	3290	3759
13 HUNGARY	-	-	-	2113	2115	2606	9296	8331	7854	5205	6465	7829	13699	17002	23891
14 ICELAND	-	-	.	.	.	.	.	.	2306	3061	-	-	5516	4557	5330
15 ITALY	.	.	.	.	.	.	.	.	.	.	7125	7306	6995	8636	9844
16 JAPAN	-	2579	2994	4034	5292	.	.	.	-	6681	5212	4767	4450	5486	5645
17 NETHERLANDS	8747	8347	.	.	.	.	.	.	7326	6368	5975	5780	5423	5666	6496
18 NEW ZEALAND	-	.	.	.	.	.	.	3734	3433	3803	5182	6475	6382	7957	9328
19 NORWAY	.	.	9264	11098	12300	12310	.	.	6493	5630	5406	4392	3896	4407	5580
20 POLAND	-	-	-	-	-	-	-	-	-	-	.	24751	22942	27477	29625
21 PORTUGAL	-	-	-	-	-	-	8159	8744	7393	6736	9512	6689	5088	4613	9274
22 ROMANIA	-	-	-	-	-	-	-	-	-	-	-	50953	8729	6599	16039
23 SPAIN	12947	14207	.	.	.	.	.	.	14979	13780	14408	13270	12175	13886	10668
24 SWEDEN	-	-	9244	11591	13712	16745	.	.	.	.	8697	7430	6225	7072	5776
25 SWITZERLAND	25733	25733	33731	33731	.	.	41181	42414	37249	38529	8075	7413	7133	8746	9382
26 TURKEY	-	-	-	-	-	-	-	-	-	-	-	13052	10521	9741	9450
27 UK ENGLAND AND WALES	7248	7198	11840	13604	13191	13125	9019	9055	7995	10140	14094	12732	11568	11017	10248
28 UK NORTHERN IRELAND	-	-	-	-	.	.	9204	10434	6419	7403	6176	6450	7469	9019	9945
29 UK SCOTLAND	5892	6711	.	.	.	.	.	.	6893	6682	8733	8388	8531	9602	10322
30 USA	.	.	.	.	.	.	.	6146	6097	6067	7419	7755	7942	8869	8415
31 YUGOSLAVIA	-	-	-	-	-	-	-	-	-	-	.	.	4294	5764	7784

- NO MORTALITY DATA ARE AVAILABLE FOR EVEN A BROADER GROUP OF CAUSES FOR THIS DISEASE

. MORTALITY DATA ARE PRESENTED FOR A BROADER GROUP OF CAUSES FOR THIS DISEASE

0 VALUE<0.5

THE STANDARD MORTALITY RATIOS WERE DERIVED WITH A FACTOR OF 10000

SERIAL MORTALITY TABLES FOR VARIOUS COUNTRIES 1901-1975

TABLE 94 : CIRCULATORY SYSTEM - ALL DISEASES : FEMALES

	1901-	1906-	1911-	1916-	1921-	1926-	1931-	1936-	1941-	1946-	1951-	1956-	1961-	1966-	1971-75
1 AUSTRALIA	-	3374	3941	4496	5848	8082	5075	5768	5480	5256	7640	6835	6186	7273	7159
2 AUSTRIA	-	-	-	-	-	-	-	-	-	6451	6390	6868	6978	7992	8924
3 BELGIUM	-	-	-	-	7074	8158	5823	6001	6345	7792	15818	20167	21575	7939	5847
4 BULGARIA	-	-	-	-	-	-	3297	3769	2476	2487	8044	25715	5756	7465	9479
5 CANADA	-	-	-	-	.	.	.	.	4943	4816	5577	5173	4836	5399	5913
6 CHILE	-	10421	.	.	.	.	.	8035	9121	9304	16016	11702	9039	8745	9584
7 CZECHOSLOVAKIA	-	-	-	.	.	.	.	.	6821	6295	8724	11969	17806	12953	10925
8 DENMARK	-	-	-	-	-	-	-	-	16581	7824	5729	5888	5643	5988	6311
9 EIRE	-	-	-	-	.	.	.	4651	4313	5529	6373	6268	6366	8680	9719
10 FINLAND	-	-	-	-	-	.	.	14878	11746	12085	5874	4521	6049	7735	9831
11 FRANCE	-	-	-	-	-	-	4759	4884	4829	4566	4558	4081	3902	4399	4853
12 GREECE	-	-	-	-	-	.	.	.	-	-	-	1457	1864	2817	3196
13 HUNGARY	-	-	-	1873	1641	2167	6705	6026	6218	3824	5266	7035	12389	15612	21316
14 ICELAND	-	-	.	.	.	.	.	.	2200	2054	-	-	4800	5249	4195
15 ITALY	.	.	.	.	.	.	.	.	.	.	5502	5415	5063	6818	8194
16 JAPAN	-	1891	2294	2922	3402	.	.	.	-	5189	3991	3577	3346	4242	4694
17 NETHERLANDS	6970	6172	.	.	.	.	.	.	6185	5919	5455	5410	4640	4844	5261
18 NEW ZEALAND	-	.	.	.	.	.	.	3327	3189	3458	4443	4892	4639	5769	6524
19 NORWAY	.	.	5782	6512	7584	8735	.	.	5606	4998	5376	4089	3383	3466	4524
20 POLAND	-	-	-	-	-	-	-	-	-	-	.	17173	18003	22445	24114
21 PORTUGAL	-	-	-	-	-	-	4599	5202	4356	4367	5741	4164	3272	2839	6228
22 ROMANIA	-	-	-	-	-	-	-	-	-	-	-	41861	8154	6350	16445
23 SPAIN	11010	11235	.	.	.	.	.	.	9923	9743	11488	10551	10715	11577	8984
24 SWEDEN	-	-	6018	7470	10458	13372	.	.	.	.	8201	6993	5779	6570	4887
25 SWITZERLAND	19499	19499	24080	24080	.	.	31158	32444	30774	34021	6412	5754	5511	7532	8404
26 TURKEY	-	-	-	-	-	-	-	-	-	-	-	9274	7803	7672	7249
27 UK ENGLAND AND WALES	4369	4107	5872	6998	6659	7042	5281	5604	5414	7353	10423	9824	9085	8256	7629
28 UK NORTHERN IRELAND	-	-	-	-	.	.	6743	8676	5290	6282	4812	5110	5831	6705	7413
29 UK SCOTLAND	3885	3952	.	.	.	.	.	.	4594	4872	6335	6474	6544	7749	7910
30 USA	.	.	.	.	.	.	.	4961	4778	4868	5863	5801	5860	6401	5822
31 YUGOSLAVIA	-	-	-	-	-	-	-	-	-	-	.	.	3632	5336	7227

- NO MORTALITY DATA ARE AVAILABLE FOR EVEN A BROADER GROUP OF CAUSES FOR THIS DISEASE

. MORTALITY DATA ARE PRESENTED FOR A BROADER GROUP OF CAUSES FOR THIS DISEASE

0 VALUE<0.5

THE STANDARD MORTALITY RATIOS WERE DERIVED WITH A FACTOR OF 10000

SERIAL MORTALITY TABLES FOR VARIOUS COUNTRIES 1901-1975

TABLE 95 : CARDIO-VASCULAR DISEASE : MALES

	1901-	1906-	1911-	1916-	1921-	1926-	1931-	1936-	1941-	1946-	1951-	1956-	1961-	1966-	1971-75
1 AUSTRALIA	-	.	.	.	8355	9660	10644	12355	13825	14657	15328	15214	15939	16190	14856
2 AUSTRIA	-	-	-	-	-	-	-	-	-	9087	9873	10975	10688	11149	11411
3 BELGIUM	-	-	-	-	8634	9272	8959	9996	10747	10768	11979	11625	12926	11263	10516
4 BULGARIA	-	-	-	-	-	-	-	-	-	-	-	-	6968	7619	9706
5 CANADA	-	-	-	-	9400	10132	10871	12235	12074	12737	13710	13877	13541	13105	12473
6 CHILE	-	9765	10332	12035	13279	12177	14250	14156	14556	13836	10689	8846	8848	8450	7769
7 CZECHOSLOVAKIA	-	-	-	7496	7440	8786	9228	10188	10489	10870	12659	11880	11912	12662	12644
8 DENMARK	-	-	-	-	-	-	-	-	8719	9646	9657	10602	11283	11855	11595
9 EIRE	-	-	-	-	6331	6973	8657	10932	12101	13092	12768	13028	13353	13485	13355
10 FINLAND	-	-	-	-	-	7611	10941	14904	15873	15194	16136	15122	17614	18191	17342
11 FRANCE	-	-	-	-	-	-	-	-	8535	8115	8065	7715	7584	7270	7061
12 GREECE	-	-	-	-	-	2993	3043	3267	-	-	-	4387	4670	5107	5338
13 HUNGARY	-	-	-	8735	8794	8568	9241	10174	9721	9770	9948	9790	11841	12877	13819
14 ICELAND	-	-	2980	3871	3840	4650	4998	5947	-	-	-	-	9050	9946	9405
15 ITALY	8708	9216	9483	9255	7933	7584	7420	8034	8475	7547	8806	9657	10078	9932	9647
16 JAPAN	-	3858	3607	4164	4729	4780	4771	4987	-	5409	4928	5167	5219	5080	4788
17 NETHERLANDS	4895	5608	5977	6565	6455	6997	6806	7472	7743	7696	8014	8502	9338	9645	9887
18 NEW ZEALAND	-	9357	9046	9155	9244	10561	11070	12898	14358	14396	13570	13404	14131	14765	14164
19 NORWAY	3416	4180	4801	5314	5746	5438	5763	5740	4646	5459	7195	8413	9601	10052	10894
20 POLAND	-	-	-	-	-	-	-	-	-	-	10810	10697	10827	12090	13359
21 PORTUGAL	-	-	-	-	-	-	-	-	-	-	9771	8218	7122	7144	7213
22 ROMANIA	-	-	-	-	-	-	-	-	-	-	-	14035	10253	10554	12163
23 SPAIN	10603	11494	12204	13173	12583	12640	12270	13864	12675	11027	8539	7577	6811	7980	8227
24 SWEDEN	-	-	5493	6011	6610	7626	8458	9514	9124	10670	9965	10398	10932	11150	11472
25 SWITZERLAND	11366	11366	12428	12428	11490	12034	12443	12920	13086	13547	10858	10569	10588	9971	9114
26 TURKEY	-	-	-	-	-	-	-	-	-	-	-	20337	17869	16495	15734
27 UK ENGLAND AND WALES	10133	8463	10183	10073	9470	11069	12443	13822	11639	12612	13550	13193	13489	13345	13197
28 UK NORTHERN IRELAND	-	-	-	-	9458	10206	11454	13302	12821	15092	13540	14474	15310	14993	15626
29 UK SCOTLAND	11485	12087	9452	9030	8819	9680	11075	13829	12757	13987	15424	15340	15788	15174	15308
30 USA	14769	12659	11977	11171	11086	12735	13374	14712	15067	15394	16168	16102	15874	15353	14201
31 YUGOSLAVIA	-	-	-	-	-	-	-	-	-	-	7958	6936	8168	8646	9685

- NO MORTALITY DATA ARE AVAILABLE FOR EVEN A BROADER GROUP OF CAUSES FOR THIS DISEASE
. MORTALITY DATA ARE PRESENTED FOR A BROADER GROUP OF CAUSES FOR THIS DISEASE
0 VALUE<0.5
THE STANDARD MORTALITY RATIOS WERE DERIVED WITH A FACTOR OF 10000

SERIAL MORTALITY TABLES FOR VARIOUS COUNTRIES 1901-1975

TABLE 95 : CARDIO-VASCULAR DISEASE : FEMALES

	1901-	1906-	1911-	1916-	1921-	1926-	1931-	1936-	1941-	1946-	1951-	1956-	1961-	1966-	1971-75
1 AUSTRALIA	-	.	.	.	6651	7750	8028	8570	9567	9276	9085	8704	8739	8763	7988
2 AUSTRIA	-	-	-	-	-	-	-	-	-	7217	7480	7814	6986	7386	7419
3 BELGIUM	-	-	-	-	8016	8548	8263	8632	8629	8833	8505	7930	8569	6849	5960
4 BULGARIA	-	-	-	-	-	-	-	-	-	-	-	-	6634	6791	7968
5 CANADA	-	-	-	-	8399	9168	9698	10182	8958	8802	8954	8569	8072	7405	6699
6 CHILE	-	8280	9381	11458	12823	11246	13024	13036	12990	11973	7947	6420	6652	6455	5850
7 CZECHOSLOVAKIA	-	-	-	7530	7100	8696	8710	9302	9545	9181	9854	9008	8651	8437	8066
8 DENMARK	-	-	-	-	-	-	-	-	8205	8536	7964	7744	7372	7393	6819
9 EIRE	-	-	-	-	5979	6594	7859	9712	10520	10863	10113	9774	9368	8897	8260
10 FINLAND	-	-	-	-	-	4442	6494	9056	8366	8126	9297	8665	10030	9495	8615
11 FRANCE	-	-	-	-	-	-	-	-	6333	5718	5361	4997	4709	4358	4246
12 GREECE	-	-	-	-	-	2795	2990	3168	-	-	-	3801	3800	3866	3785
13 HUNGARY	-	-	-	8481	8133	8344	8822	9259	8866	8054	8247	8446	9551	9706	9868
14 ICELAND	-	-	3087	2834	3144	3375	3677	3562	-	-	-	-	5486	5749	4783
15 ITALY	10508	10541	10561	10456	8730	8467	7912	8357	8544	7509	8051	8085	7873	7379	6980
16 JAPAN	-	3649	3461	3892	4062	3934	3791	3841	-	4262	3772	3763	3796	3670	3513
17 NETHERLANDS	4850	5447	5813	6254	6338	6999	6602	6984	6906	7003	6661	6516	6246	5839	5702
18 NEW ZEALAND	-	8093	8042	7822	7894	8809	9182	9846	10497	9668	9080	8377	8206	7850	7320
19 NORWAY	3135	3649	3985	4193	4503	4588	4975	5088	3984	4629	5779	5993	6218	5702	5936
20 POLAND	-	-	-	-	-	-	-	-	-	-	7075	6724	7204	7991	8223
21 PORTUGAL	-	-	-	-	-	-	-	-	-	-	7232	6114	5163	4885	4624
22 ROMANIA	-	-	-	-	-	-	-	-	-	-	-	12129	9762	9552	10498
23 SPAIN	11383	11621	12039	12930	11475	10921	10301	10748	9571	8691	6996	6037	5384	6000	5846
24 SWEDEN	-	-	4722	5137	5843	6738	7525	8468	8100	9112	8187	7923	7709	7307	6810
25 SWITZERLAND	11774	11774	11881	11881	10935	10990	11427	11479	11333	11954	8621	8209	7591	7013	6019
26 TURKEY	-	-	-	-	-	-	-	-	-	-	-	14170	12997	12559	12738
27 UK ENGLAND AND WALES	9837	7863	7995	7661	7517	8789	9739	10332	8503	9038	9045	8347	8059	7409	7148
28 UK NORTHERN IRELAND	-	-	-	-	8657	9128	9565	11073	10655	12218	10051	9827	9788	8844	8597
29 UK SCOTLAND	8782	9285	7315	6760	6711	7436	8448	10217	9575	10358	10662	10173	9505	8603	8090
30 USA	12166	10656	10268	9992	9655	10458	10177	10506	10020	9732	9952	9656	9276	8719	7836
31 YUGOSLAVIA	-	-	-	-	-	-	-	-	-	-	7372	6387	7046	6971	7615

- NO MORTALITY DATA ARE AVAILABLE FOR EVEN A BROADER GROUP OF CAUSES FOR THIS DISEASE

. MORTALITY DATA ARE PRESENTED FOR A BROADER GROUP OF CAUSES FOR THIS DISEASE

0 VALUE<0.5

THE STANDARD MORTALITY RATIOS WERE DERIVED WITH A FACTOR OF 10000

SERIAL MORTALITY TABLES FOR VARIOUS COUNTRIES 1901-1975

TABLE 96 : CARDIO-VASCULAR DISEASE AND VASCULAR LESIONS AFFECTING CENTRAL NERVOUS SYSTEM : MALES

	1901-	1906-	1911-	1916-	1921-	1926-	1931-	1936-	1941-	1946-	1951-	1956-	1961-	1966-	1971-75
1 AUSTRALIA	-	8356	8877	8489	8182	8965	9961	11223	12434	13269	14174	14058	14477	14791	13734
2 AUSTRIA	-	-	-	-	-	-	-	-	-	9495	10377	11244	11059	11463	11558
3 BELGIUM	-	-	-	-	7984	8460	9476	10148	10277	10352	10408	9915	11085	11151	10441
4 BULGARIA	-	-	-	-	-	-	-	-	-	-	-	-	8777	9506	11522
5 CANADA	-	-	-	-	8749	8918	8099	9147	10983	11423	12451	12545	11981	11541	10976
6 CHILE	-	16993	13601	12368	11971	11408	13083	12869	13364	12907	11298	9453	9357	8987	8464
7 CZECHOSLOVAKIA	-	-	-	7841	7893	9105	9163	9831	9645	9955	11541	11215	11189	12428	13131
8 DENMARK	-	-	-	-	-	-	-	-	7333	8530	9641	10062	10561	10624	10178
9 EIRE	-	-	-	-	6314	6827	8158	9832	10765	11592	11344	11795	12249	12604	12556
10 FINLAND	-	-	-	-	-	-	-	13260	14267	13945	15432	14777	16509	16929	15682
11 FRANCE	-	-	-	-	-	-	-	-	9490	9050	8941	8496	8285	8038	7771
12 GREECE	-	-	-	-	-	4085	4080	4298	-	-	-	4975	5392	5878	6180
13 HUNGARY	-	-	-	8997	9188	8958	9576	10078	9722	9742	10218	10552	12015	12867	13435
14 ICELAND	-	-	4599	6180	5308	5697	6107	6813	-	-	-	-	8766	9442	9019
15 ITALY	10206	10502	10804	10739	9800	9950	9783	10094	10018	8930	9929	10532	10562	10259	9814
16 JAPAN	-	8629	8201	9496	11815	12648	12753	13254	-	9198	9986	10746	11023	10416	9062
17 NETHERLANDS	6048	6468	6560	7071	-	5328	6925	7364	7588	7534	8095	8445	8938	9087	9111
18 NEW ZEALAND	-	9335	8991	9078	8867	9604	9988	11456	12671	12603	12262	12124	12733	13359	13072
19 NORWAY	3958	4604	5268	5733	6140	6210	-	-	5303	6147	7666	8746	9649	10018	10558
20 POLAND	-	-	-	-	-	-	-	-	-	-	-	9135	9252	9948	11080
21 PORTUGAL	-	-	-	-	-	-	-	-	-	-	10367	9878	9341	10194	10889
22 ROMANIA	-	-	-	-	-	-	-	-	-	-	-	12461	10641	11119	12164
23 SPAIN	14426	14915	15244	15651	14811	14465	13892	14913	13020	11142	9032	8453	7947	8639	9104
24 SWEDEN	-	-	5889	6106	6598	7450	8116	9054	8632	9848	9826	10014	10094	9917	10044
25 SWITZERLAND	10389	10389	10811	10811	9930	10454	10307	10441	10390	10599	10876	10378	10313	9511	8649
26 TURKEY	-	-	-	-	-	-	-	-	-	-	-	17712	15538	14197	13893
27 UK ENGLAND AND WALES	10908	9004	10596	10226	9434	10163	11993	13019	11240	11965	13036	12706	12829	12585	12221
28 UK NORTHERN IRELAND	-	-	-	-	9892	10336	11171	12396	12263	14008	12777	13580	14199	13929	14643
29 UK SCOTLAND	12890	13544	12048	11467	10778	11339	12295	13862	12945	13679	15098	15081	15383	14645	14685
30 USA	16710	13750	12710	11809	11721	12750	12838	13636	13688	13793	14525	14393	14023	13486	12433
31 YUGOSLAVIA	-	-	-	-	-	-	-	-	-	-	-	-	7976	8607	9486

- NO MORTALITY DATA ARE AVAILABLE FOR EVEN A BROADER GROUP OF CAUSES FOR THIS DISEASE

. MORTALITY DATA ARE PRESENTED FOR A BROADER GROUP OF CAUSES FOR THIS DISEASE

0 VALUE<0.5

THE STANDARD MORTALITY RATIOS WERE DERIVED WITH A FACTOR OF 10000

SERIAL MORTALITY TABLES FOR VARIOUS COUNTRIES 1901-1975

TABLE 96 : CARDIO-VASCULAR DISEASE AND VASCULAR LESIONS AFFECTING CENTRAL NERVOUS SYSTEM : FEMALES

	1901-	1906-	1911-	1916-	1921-	1926-	1931-	1936-	1941-	1946-	1951-	1956-	1961-	1966-	1971-75
1 AUSTRALIA	-	7675	7672	7439	7174	7789	8345	8847	9782	9676	9779	9282	9133	9179	8576
2 AUSTRIA	-	-	-	-	-	-	-	-	-	7899	8327	8511	7842	8145	8068
3 BELGIUM	-	-	-	-	7293	7669	8429	8738	8498	8720	7630	6975	7642	7414	6651
4 BULGARIA	-	-	-	-	-	-	-	-	-	-	-	-	8840	9032	10082
5 CANADA	-	-	-	-	8197	8402	7214	7615	8968	8817	9092	8656	7952	7174	6466
6 CHILE	-	13844	11908	11291	11283	10392	11767	11693	11791	11105	8828	7138	7301	7138	6736
7 CZECHOSLOVAKIA	-	-	-	7492	7133	8433	8303	8788	8599	8407	9246	8825	8397	8786	9041
8 DENMARK	-	-	-	-	-	-	-	-	7127	7865	8616	8000	7574	7157	6427
9 EIRE	-	-	-	-	6196	6862	7926	9338	10042	10302	9710	9670	9484	9285	8854
10 FINLAND	-	-	-	-	-	-	-	9316	8887	8964	10555	10145	10709	10134	8744
11 FRANCE	-	-	-	-	-	-	-	-	7224	6636	6213	5790	5435	5138	5035
12 GREECE	-	-	-	-	-	3797	4026	4282	-	-	-	4700	4935	5165	5236
13 HUNGARY	-	-	-	8270	8093	8294	8834	9087	8828	8181	8864	9484	10017	10088	9932
14 ICELAND	-	-	4141	4156	4629	4748	4823	4823	-	-	-	-	6018	6160	5288
15 ITALY	10919	10898	11025	10976	9654	9728	9329	9571	9365	8414	8740	8675	8239	7693	7251
16 JAPAN	-	6940	6632	7497	8412	8728	8767	8955	-	7263	7381	7388	7409	6984	6258
17 NETHERLANDS	6222	6551	6714	7104	-	5255	7092	7275	7198	7479	7392	7148	6681	6187	5872
18 NEW ZEALAND	-	8651	8278	8269	8244	8756	9135	9822	10486	9750	9445	8773	8598	8331	8120
19 NORWAY	3564	4065	4543	4776	5155	5468	-	-	4896	5657	6780	7095	7203	6567	6713
20 POLAND	-	-	-	-	-	-	-	-	-	-	-	5997	6382	6729	7037
21 PORTUGAL	-	-	-	-	-	-	-	-	-	-	7904	7579	7129	7553	7902
22 ROMANIA	-	-	-	-	-	-	-	-	-	-	-	10857	10268	10263	10690
23 SPAIN	14444	14169	14201	14611	13047	12238	11546	11522	9936	8904	7438	6869	6493	6817	7008
24 SWEDEN	-	-	5241	5462	6088	6874	7515	8420	8091	8948	8764	8342	7697	7019	6488
25 SWITZERLAND	10426	10426	10242	10242	9437	9604	9483	9254	9054	9347	9093	8399	7789	7083	6111
26 TURKEY	-	-	-	-	-	-	-	-	-	-	-	12563	11585	11170	11297
27 UK ENGLAND AND WALES	10952	8792	8701	8174	7796	8354	9627	10108	8732	9227	9446	8848	8509	7895	7555
28 UK NORTHERN IRELAND	-	-	-	-	9342	9767	10027	11235	11069	12406	10501	10299	10248	9327	9228
29 UK SCOTLAND	10306	10823	9932	9078	8717	9280	10056	10827	10369	10986	11491	11049	10419	9593	8925
30 USA	14279	11986	11258	10981	10720	10949	10361	10408	9860	9465	9719	9392	8920	8331	7466
31 YUGOSLAVIA	-	-	-	-	-	-	-	-	-	-	-	-	6938	7102	7687

- NO MORTALITY DATA ARE AVAILABLE FOR EVEN A BROADER GROUP OF CAUSES FOR THIS DISEASE

. MORTALITY DATA ARE PRESENTED FOR A BROADER GROUP OF CAUSES FOR THIS DISEASE

0 VALUE<0.5

THE STANDARD MORTALITY RATIOS WERE DERIVED WITH A FACTOR OF 10000

SERIAL MORTALITY TABLES FOR VARIOUS COUNTRIES 1901-1975

TABLE 97 : CIRCULATORY DISEASE AND ACUTE RHEUMATISM : MALES

	1901-	1906-	1911-	1916-	1921-	1926-	1931-	1936-	1941-	1946-	1951-	1956-	1961-	1966-	1971-75
1 AUSTRALIA	-	8136	8923	8153	8893	9831	10777	12499	13900	14701	15364	15216	15934	16181	14845
2 AUSTRIA	-	-	-	-	-	-	-	-	-	12955	11584	10987	10685	11144	11404
3 BELGIUM	-	-	-	-	-	-	-	-	-	-	13456	11643	12927	11262	10511
4 BULGARIA	-	-	-	-	-	-	-	-	-	-	-	-	7001	7659	9743
5 CANADA	-	-	-	-	9585	10291	12283	13232	12182	12789	13760	13883	13538	13098	12464
6 CHILE	-	10639	11405	13423	14580	13157	15194	16846	15025	14268	10799	8912	8874	8471	7781
7 CZECHOSLOVAKIA	-	-	-	10625	10691	12343	12467	13411	13135	12969	12160	11893	11921	12661	12634
8 DENMARK	-	-	-	-	-	-	-	-	10055	11675	9662	10603	11277	11849	11588
9 EIRE	-	-	-	-	8906	9483	11600	13763	14706	15865	12825	13046	13351	13479	13348
10 FINLAND	-	-	-	-	-	-	-	-	19376	18901	16159	15118	17600	18178	17329
11 FRANCE	-	-	-	-	-	-	-	-	8602	8153	8089	7728	7589	7272	7061
12 GREECE	-	-	-	-	-	3065	3124	3353	-	-	-	4401	4679	5109	5338
13 HUNGARY	-	-	-	-	-	-	9255	10190	9729	13235	12810	9796	11837	12870	13810
14 ICELAND	-	-	-	-	-	-	-	-	-	-	-	-	9041	9937	9397
15 ITALY	13854	14266	14686	14604	13337	13556	13344	13779	13675	12188	8904	9681	10086	9930	9642
16 JAPAN	-	11826	11230	12968	16026	17082	17216	17886	-	5468	4973	5212	5249	5093	4793
17 NETHERLANDS	4946	5661	6056	6649	-	7329	9481	10073	10428	9681	8023	8502	9334	9639	9882
18 NEW ZEALAND	-	12892	12367	12456	10469	11267	13660	15620	17288	16456	13587	13409	14136	14761	14154
19 NORWAY	3555	4293	4933	5423	5819	5501	5800	5773	-	-	7200	8415	9596	10046	10887
20 POLAND	-	-	-	-	-	-	-	-	-	-	-	10709	10871	12130	13368
21 PORTUGAL	-	-	-	-	-	-	-	-	-	-	9867	8268	7142	7153	7220
22 ROMANIA	-	-	-	-	-	-	-	-	-	-	-	14055	10288	10554	12156
23 SPAIN	10922	11775	12446	13430	12797	12838	12459	14084	12799	11121	8608	7618	6845	8016	8231
24 SWEDEN	-	-	-	-	-	-	11144	12412	11823	13479	9972	10398	10927	11145	11467
25 SWITZERLAND	-	-	-	-	13422	14126	-	-	-	-	10898	10577	10586	9965	9111
26 TURKEY	-	-	-	-	-	-	-	-	-	-	-	20304	17836	16468	15711
27 UK ENGLAND AND WALES	15142	12531	10486	10304	9682	11228	12552	13898	11679	12634	13559	13194	13485	13338	13189
28 UK NORTHERN IRELAND	-	-	-	-	13608	14324	15378	17034	16891	18391	13604	14507	15318	14987	15616
29 UK SCOTLAND	17737	18465	16565	15682	14714	15526	16806	18949	17685	17695	15442	15348	15779	15164	15299
30 USA	-	15480	12279	11376	11229	12842	13450	14759	15096	15411	16187	16106	15871	15346	14192
31 YUGOSLAVIA	-	-	-	-	-	-	-	-	-	-	-	-	8169	8644	9679

- NO MORTALITY DATA ARE AVAILABLE FOR EVEN A BROADER GROUP OF CAUSES FOR THIS DISEASE

. MORTALITY DATA ARE PRESENTED FOR A BROADER GROUP OF CAUSES FOR THIS DISEASE

0 VALUE<0.5

THE STANDARD MORTALITY RATIOS WERE DERIVED WITH A FACTOR OF 10000

SERIAL MORTALITY TABLES FOR VARIOUS COUNTRIES 1901-1975

TABLE 97 : CIRCULATORY DISEASE AND ACUTE RHEUMATISM : FEMALES

	1901-	1906-	1911-	1916-	1921-	1926-	1931-	1936-	1941-	1946-	1951-	1956-	1961-	1966-	1971-75
1 AUSTRALIA	-	7056	7364	6608	7167	7941	8166	8723	9647	9315	9121	8710	8739	8760	7985
2 AUSTRIA	-	-	-	-	-	-	-	-	-	10811	9007	7830	6985	7385	7417
3 BELGIUM	-	-	-	-	-	-	-	-	-	-	9740	7952	8572	6849	5958
4 BULGARIA	-	-	-	-	-	-	-	-	-	-	-	-	6671	6839	8009
5 CANADA	-	-	-	-	8602	9343	11303	11244	9067	8850	8999	8580	8073	7403	6697
6 CHILE	-	9176	10908	13391	14557	12554	14100	15595	13519	12426	8059	6473	6678	6473	5864
7 CZECHOSLOVAKIA	-	-	-	10189	9699	11476	11344	12031	11739	10885	9574	9020	8661	8441	8061
8 DENMARK	-	-	-	-	-	-	-	-	9796	10781	7970	7747	7370	7391	6816
9 EIRE	-	-	-	-	8751	9582	11263	13134	13764	14135	10168	9792	9371	8895	8257
10 FINLAND	-	-	-	-	-	-	-	-	12170	12258	9316	8671	10030	9491	8612
11 FRANCE	-	-	-	-	-	-	-	-	6394	5752	5378	5004	4712	4360	4247
12 GREECE	-	-	-	-	-	2852	3066	3240	-	-	-	3817	3813	3870	3787
13 HUNGARY	-	-	-	-	-	-	8852	9279	8881	11141	11004	8450	9551	9703	9864
14 ICELAND	-	-	-	-	-	-	-	-	-	-	-	-	5495	5756	4780
15 ITALY	14818	14803	14990	14936	13149	13266	12738	13082	12800	11500	8141	8109	7881	7379	6978
16 JAPAN	-	9615	9163	10329	11498	11882	11944	12214	-	4324	3821	3814	3834	3693	3525
17 NETHERLANDS	4895	5509	5869	6325	-	7252	9728	9973	9913	9490	6672	6517	6243	5837	5700
18 NEW ZEALAND	-	11944	11439	11413	9238	9673	12524	13413	14343	12340	9113	8386	8212	7851	7318
19 NORWAY	3253	3759	4098	4288	4561	4649	5005	5107	-	-	5787	5998	6217	5699	5934
20 POLAND	-	-	-	-	-	-	-	-	-	-	-	6739	7252	8038	8239
21 PORTUGAL	-	-	-	-	-	-	-	-	-	-	7302	6147	5175	4889	4630
22 ROMANIA	-	-	-	-	-	-	-	-	-	-	-	12152	9800	9551	10493
23 SPAIN	11729	11897	12270	13178	11665	11091	10470	10924	9665	8769	7060	6078	5423	6043	5855
24 SWEDEN	-	-	-	-	-	-	10357	11583	11122	12280	8199	7923	7706	7304	6808
25 SWITZERLAND	-	-	-	-	12829	13058	-	-	-	-	8648	8219	7593	7013	6019
26 TURKEY	-	-	-	-	-	-	-	-	-	-	-	14159	12981	12545	12723
27 UK ENGLAND AND WALES	15184	12253	8276	7876	7713	8947	9849	10409	8542	9060	9056	8350	8058	7407	7146
28 UK NORTHERN IRELAND	-	-	-	-	12959	13640	13908	15492	15328	16081	10131	9852	9802	8845	8600
29 UK SCOTLAND	14317	14903	13810	12549	12045	12844	13893	14922	14253	14076	10680	10179	9502	8599	8088
30 USA	-	13110	10594	10212	9823	10580	10259	10559	10053	9754	9971	9663	9277	8717	7833
31 YUGOSLAVIA	-	-	-	-	-	-	-	-	-	-	-	-	7049	6971	7612

- NO MORTALITY DATA ARE AVAILABLE FOR EVEN A BROADER GROUP OF CAUSES FOR THIS DISEASE

. MORTALITY DATA ARE PRESENTED FOR A BROADER GROUP OF CAUSES FOR THIS DISEASE

0 VALUE<0.5

THE STANDARD MORTALITY RATIOS WERE DERIVED WITH A FACTOR OF 10000

SERIAL MORTALITY TABLES FOR VARIOUS COUNTRIES 1901-1975

TABLE 98 : RESPIRATORY INFECTIONS - ACUTE UPPER : MALES

	1901-	1906-	1911-	1916-	1921-	1926-	1931-	1936-	1941-	1946-	1951-	1956-	1961-	1966-	1971-75
1 AUSTRALIA	-	.	.	.	.	.	.	.	.	.	458	454	432	1162	1207
2 AUSTRIA	-	-	-	-	-	-	-	-	-	.	1593	1575	1661	2766	2769
3 BELGIUM	-	-	-	-	.	.	.	.	.	.	1070	397	200	791	1202
4 BULGARIA	-	-	-	-	-	.	.	.	.	.	.	.	505	1112	1688
5 CANADA	-	-	-	-	.	.	.	.	.	735	582	473	333	462	654
6 CHILE	-	.	.	.	.	.	.	.	.	.	3415	2912	2600	2285	2830
7 CZECHOSLOVAKIA	-	-	-	.	.	.	.	.	.	.	752	552	599	1291	1047
8 DENMARK	.	.	.	.	.	.	.	.	.	.	549	413	208	377	566
9 EIRE	-	-	-	-	.	.	.	.	.	.	337	224	251	1751	2471
10 FINLAND	-	-	-	-	-	-	-	.	.	.	1226	2927	1963	889	807
11 FRANCE	-	-	-	-	.	.	.	.	.	626	453	318	231	390	552
12 GREECE	-	-	-	-	.	.	.	.	-	-	-	909	699	799	919
13 HUNGARY	-	-	-	.	.	.	.	.	.	.	333	420	335	1136	1913
14 ICELAND	-	-	.	.	.	.	.	.	.	.	-	-	0	122	471
15 ITALY	.	.	.	.	.	.	.	.	.	.	725	534	360	2175	2071
16 JAPAN	.	.	.	.	.	.	.	.	-	5339	3698	3426	2174	3161	3078
17 NETHERLANDS	.	.	.	.	.	.	.	.	.	393	452	370	308	369	700
18 NEW ZEALAND	-	.	.	.	.	.	.	.	.	360	714	338	159	1548	1491
19 NORWAY	.	.	.	.	.	.	.	.	.	.	754	602	432	427	318
20 POLAND	-	-	-	-	-	-	-	-	-	-	.	832	609	868	667
21 PORTUGAL	.	.	.	.	.	.	.	.	.	.	670	600	790	467	10252
22 ROMANIA	-	-	-	-	-	-	-	-	-	-	-	597	683	235	385
23 SPAIN	.	.	.	.	.	.	.	.	.	.	478	314	207	3222	3286
24 SWEDEN	-	-	.	.	.	.	.	.	.	.	640	510	406	596	524
25 SWITZERLAND	.	.	.	.	.	.	.	.	.	.	559	573	457	480	654
26 TURKEY	-	-	-	-	-	-	-	-	-	-	-	656	825	688	368
27 UK ENGLAND AND WALES	.	.	.	.	.	.	.	.	.	406	269	193	163	2372	2767
28 UK NORTHERN IRELAND	-	-	-	-	.	.	.	.	.	302	180	105	100	622	1002
29 UK SCOTLAND	.	.	.	.	.	.	.	.	.	357	343	266	320	1493	1718
30 USA	.	.	.	.	.	.	.	.	.	395	406	363	283	523	494
31 YUGOSLAVIA	-	-	-	-	-	-	-	-	-	-	.	.	341	780	716

- NO MORTALITY DATA ARE AVAILABLE FOR EVEN A BROADER GROUP OF CAUSES FOR THIS DISEASE

. MORTALITY DATA ARE PRESENTED FOR A BROADER GROUP OF CAUSES FOR THIS DISEASE

0 VALUE<0.5

THE STANDARD MORTALITY RATIOS WERE DERIVED WITH A FACTOR OF 1000

SERIAL MORTALITY TABLES FOR VARIOUS COUNTRIES 1901-1975

TABLE 98 : RESPIRATORY INFECTIONS - ACUTE UPPER : FEMALES

	1901-	1906-	1911-	1916-	1921-	1926-	1931-	1936-	1941-	1946-	1951-	1956-	1961-	1966-	1971-75
1 AUSTRALIA	-	.	.	.	.	.	.	.	.	.	3220	3220	3238	7869	7058
2 AUSTRIA	-	-	-	-	-	-	-	-	-	.	10666	11802	14210	21742	21449
3 BELGIUM	-	-	-	-	.	.	.	.	.	.	5812	2448	1244	3780	4480
4 BULGARIA	-	-	-	-	-	.	.	.	.	.	.	.	2902	7540	9810
5 CANADA	-	-	-	-	.	.	.	.	.	7745	5126	4235	2516	3391	4173
6 CHILE	-	.	.	.	.	.	.	.	.	.	33274	27431	22365	18954	22408
7 CZECHOSLOVAKIA	-	-	-	.	.	.	.	.	.	.	5986	4436	4223	7896	6444
8 DENMARK	.	.	.	.	.	.	.	.	.	.	4098	4060	1755	4033	3358
9 EIRE	-	-	-	-	.	.	.	.	.	.	2636	1707	1212	16701	19359
10 FINLAND	-	-	-	-	-	-	-	.	.	.	12824	28257	22628	12534	9218
11 FRANCE	-	-	-	-	.	.	.	.	.	3628	2576	1820	1164	2570	3858
12 GREECE	-	-	-	-	.	.	.	.	-	-	-	7785	6771	7656	8347
13 HUNGARY	-	-	-	.	.	.	.	.	.	.	2450	2727	3153	7170	11461
14 ICELAND	-	-	.	.	.	.	.	.	.	.	-	-	1176	2247	4301
15 ITALY	.	.	.	.	.	.	.	.	.	.	6710	4625	2794	16936	16265
16 JAPAN	.	.	.	.	.	.	.	.	-	52919	38165	37346	24715	32586	30695
17 NETHERLANDS	.	.	.	.	.	.	.	.	.	6329	3363	2694	2162	2985	4824
18 NEW ZEALAND	-	.	.	.	.	.	.	.	.	2122	4324	3839	2375	12187	14934
19 NORWAY	.	.	.	.	.	.	.	.	.	.	5753	5552	3260	2537	2738
20 POLAND	-	-	-	-	-	-	-	-	-	-	.	5666	4213	5428	4188
21 PORTUGAL	.	.	.	.	.	.	.	.	.	.	5043	4401	4323	3867	68855
22 ROMANIA	-	-	-	-	-	-	-	-	-	-	-	3552	4232	1603	3353
23 SPAIN	.	.	.	.	.	.	.	.	.	.	3596	2027	1484	24378	26874
24 SWEDEN	-	-	.	.	.	.	.	.	.	.	5385	4276	3203	5467	3782
25 SWITZERLAND	.	.	.	.	.	.	.	.	.	.	4363	3681	3011	3280	4265
26 TURKEY	-	-	-	-	-	-	-	-	-	-	-	5654	5306	5627	1723
27 UK ENGLAND AND WALES	.	.	.	.	.	.	.	.	.	3827	2246	1462	1280	15931	17653
28 UK NORTHERN IRELAND	-	-	-	-	.	.	.	.	.	5693	1305	1089	1154	7527	5836
29 UK SCOTLAND	.	.	.	.	.	.	.	.	.	3705	2728	2071	1772	10808	12102
30 USA	.	.	.	.	.	.	.	.	.	2994	3344	2766	2098	3552	3199
31 YUGOSLAVIA	-	-	-	-	-	-	-	-	-	-	.	.	2928	6536	5217

- NO MORTALITY DATA ARE AVAILABLE FOR EVEN A BROADER GROUP OF CAUSES FOR THIS DISEASE

. MORTALITY DATA ARE PRESENTED FOR A BROADER GROUP OF CAUSES FOR THIS DISEASE

0 VALUE<0.5

THE STANDARD MORTALITY RATIOS WERE DERIVED WITH A FACTOR OF 10000

SERIAL MORTALITY TABLES FOR VARIOUS COUNTRIES 1901-1975

TABLE 99 : INFLUENZA : MALES

	1901-	1906-	1911-	1916-	1921-	1926-	1931-	1936-	1941-	1946-	1951-	1956-	1961-	1966-	1971-75
1 AUSTRALIA	-	3600	2196	16175	3014	2773	3013	1801	955	585	567	698	274	572	319
2 AUSTRIA	-	-	-	-	-	-	-	-	-	1807	1979	2318	1326	1136	644
3 BELGIUM	3967	4187	3894	15481	7144	6453	6474	5098	3877	2574	1497	1836	711	1155	638
4 BULGARIA	-	-	-	-	-	11859	4864	3281	2225	3800	3458	8106	2370	2053	2533
5 CANADA	-	-	-	-	8039	11060	7248	6759	3099	1677	1494	1162	576	574	447
6 CHILE	-	33605	27657	75583	74643	61800	59579	44800	19034	8535	6291	12494	7463	5054	2542
7 CZECHOSLOVAKIA	-	-	-	12632	2226	5152	2420	2612	1161	1259	1158	1172	1322	1289	973
8 DENMARK	4907	4919	2168	29982	4404	5318	4148	2795	881	574	790	970	615	789	548
9 EIRE	-	-	-	-	8655	6847	7456	6850	3690	2442	3540	2243	2040	2288	852
10 FINLAND	-	-	-	-	-	4252	2559	6476	1828	1470	2506	2474	1697	899	1239
11 FRANCE	-	-	-	-	2506	4065	2840	3110	924	1450	1471	2527	1703	2109	1289
12 GREECE	-	-	-	-	15913	16692	19083	14009	-	-	-	2398	2069	1529	829
13 HUNGARY	-	-	-	13229	2450	2501	2120	1778	1736	1234	2168	3490	1944	1213	1395
14 ICELAND	-	-	2530	30000	8020	2679	2520	3369	2222	814	1799	2757	1592	1091	584
15 ITALY	3674	3474	2645	35813	5038	6466	5998	4627	1977	1607	1314	1184	643	1059	507
16 JAPAN	1260	1453	1115	20749	4585	3587	3749	3887	-	463	313	961	812	413	228
17 NETHERLANDS	2598	2542	1719	17103	3914	6539	4611	4383	3491	1971	1873	1884	746	959	661
18 NEW ZEALAND	-	3660	1705	34231	2974	3960	2164	1979	1269	790	703	796	615	561	291
19 NORWAY	892	1369	589	15954	1516	1595	966	941	608	297	267	353	245	645	445
20 POLAND	-	-	-	-	-	-	-	-	-	-	.	1464	761	586	1171
21 PORTUGAL	6206	6984	3433	52252	6678	6720	8222	5012	3209	1486	1782	1608	1112	1102	1530
22 ROMANIA	-	-	-	-	-	-	-	-	-	-	-	6925	2745	1046	900
23 SPAIN	15806	15261	9830	46906	8360	5260	7189	4639	4248	2097	3163	2635	2237	1609	2057
24 SWEDEN	-	-	1249	25807	2190	3006	2245	1433	666	285	570	724	289	355	324
25 SWITZERLAND	3083	3083	25694	25694	6347	7414	7447	5892	2203	1747	2401	3355	1647	1877	1265
26 TURKEY	-	-	-	-	-	-	-	-	-	-	-	1005	239	185	261
27 UK ENGLAND AND WALES	5713	5828	5136	26199	9055	8508	6562	4910	2587	1475	2008	1472	982	1276	513
28 UK NORTHERN IRELAND	-	-	-	-	11695	9744	7728	7585	3743	2432	2724	1652	1210	1518	773
29 UK SCOTLAND	5600	1829	1537	4128	9058	8076	6002	5186	2037	1269	1206	1143	602	1127	625
30 USA	7159	4590	3241	28242	6799	8920	5745	4461	2324	907	632	528	301	349	270
31 YUGOSLAVIA	-	-	-	-	-	-	-	-	-	-	.	3731	2057	1873	717

- NO MORTALITY DATA ARE AVAILABLE FOR EVEN A BROADER GROUP OF CAUSES FOR THIS DISEASE

. MORTALITY DATA ARE PRESENTED FOR A BROADER GROUP OF CAUSES FOR THIS DISEASE

0 VALUE<0.5

THE STANDARD MORTALITY RATIOS WERE DERIVED WITH A FACTOR OF 1000

SERIAL MORTALITY TABLES FOR VARIOUS COUNTRIES 1901-1975

TABLE 99 : INFLUENZA : FEMALES

	1901-	1906-	1911-	1916-	1921-	1926-	1931-	1936-	1941-	1946-	1951-	1956-	1961-	1966-	1971-75
1 AUSTRALIA	-	3690	2454	12535	2959	2501	2694	1441	803	506	441	419	201	373	247
2 AUSTRIA	-	-	-	-	-	-	-	-	-	1522	1496	1563	965	786	477
3 BELGIUM	3489	3695	3394	11796	6413	5971	5611	4145	2964	2041	1359	1515	578	967	526
4 BULGARIA	-	-	-	-	-	9919	4073	2329	1372	2560	2434	6729	2073	1621	1999
5 CANADA	-	-	-	-	8756	11867	7613	6823	3014	1637	1492	1021	580	503	386
6 CHILE	-	30481	23538	70269	68191	56048	52650	40501	17148	7489	5622	10147	6157	4461	2271
7 CZECHOSLOVAKIA	-	-	-	11875	1932	4386	1928	2075	759	902	910	839	978	976	728
8 DENMARK	4863	4527	2205	19551	4156	5274	4244	2793	970	619	884	907	542	736	497
9 EIRE	-	-	-	-	8590	7427	8188	7310	3710	2416	3820	1942	1832	1932	772
10 FINLAND	-	-	-	-	-	3677	2326	4839	1423	1108	2152	2085	1587	889	1001
11 FRANCE	-	-	-	-	2175	3697	2442	2810	793	1284	1285	1994	1498	1625	1081
12 GREECE	-	-	-	-	13441	14413	16441	12269	-	-	-	2208	2169	1587	867
13 HUNGARY	-	-	-	13687	2257	2086	1751	1310	1335	827	1414	2321	1318	784	837
14 ICELAND	-	-	2810	21894	5764	2579	2000	3542	2201	848	1405	2841	1433	1006	978
15 ITALY	3475	3196	2492	43946	4619	5756	5249	3913	1749	1441	1220	999	541	811	436
16 JAPAN	1133	1325	1007	19063	3973	2939	2939	3276	-	372	245	691	571	291	166
17 NETHERLANDS	3035	3241	2048	14229	3938	6485	4708	4472	3585	2043	2018	1756	725	888	571
18 NEW ZEALAND	-	4667	2102	23904	2983	3593	1991	1553	1022	646	580	710	534	357	314
19 NORWAY	1088	1606	842	11762	1412	1731	1076	950	746	350	254	363	271	601	444
20 POLAND	-	-	-	-	-	-	-	-	-	-	.	982	575	455	787
21 PORTUGAL	5174	5722	2862	43708	4871	5302	6207	3837	2354	1115	1282	1240	909	769	1047
22 ROMANIA	-	-	-	-	-	-	-	-	-	-	-	4532	2077	741	696
23 SPAIN	14225	13211	8298	42528	6696	3916	5393	3359	3267	1665	2545	2076	1887	1330	1787
24 SWEDEN	-	-	1378	19365	2344	3089	2529	1539	803	356	684	689	260	358	274
25 SWITZERLAND	3359	3359	17334	17334	5791	6464	6720	4912	2024	1632	2288	2665	1362	1502	994
26 TURKEY	-	-	-	-	-	-	-	-	-	-	-	766	181	175	272
27 UK ENGLAND AND WALES	5373	5614	3894	20932	7291	6723	5350	3599	1916	1143	1581	955	699	887	388
28 UK NORTHERN IRELAND	-	-	-	-	12211	10460	8108	8082	3671	2890	2840	1418	1156	1453	727
29 UK SCOTLAND	4948	1959	1581	3841	7996	6690	5346	4405	1602	1123	1063	853	507	840	475
30 USA	8377	5519	3845	26041	6874	8682	5446	3988	2042	829	546	410	252	284	221
31 YUGOSLAVIA	-	-	-	-	-	-	-	-	-	-	.	3261	1847	1476	629

- NO MORTALITY DATA ARE AVAILABLE FOR EVEN A BROADER GROUP OF CAUSES FOR THIS DISEASE

. MORTALITY DATA ARE PRESENTED FOR A BROADER GROUP OF CAUSES FOR THIS DISEASE

0 VALUE<0.5

THE STANDARD MORTALITY RATIOS WERE DERIVED WITH A FACTOR OF 1000

SERIAL MORTALITY TABLES FOR VARIOUS COUNTRIES 1901-1975

TABLE 100 : PNEUMONIA - LOBAR : MALES

	1901-	1906-	1911-	1916-	1921-	1926-	1931-	1936-	1941-	1946-	1951-	1956-	1961-	1966-	1971-75
1 AUSTRALIA	-	.	.	.	.	.	531	519	350	257	196	157	132	130	.
2 AUSTRIA	-	-	-	-	-	-	-	-	-	.	106	127	103	80	.
3 BELGIUM	2473	2425	2213	2005	2054	2530	2034	1932	1554	882	309	20	18	12	.
4 BULGARIA	-	-	-	-	-	.	.	.	.	.	.	.	59	48	.
5 CANADA	-	-	-	-	682	674	541	526	298	199	109	95	67	67	.
6 CHILE	-	13984	.	.	.	.	228	376	200	177	81	58	132	263	.
7 CZECHOSLOVAKIA	-	-	-	134	160	341	562	562	295	259	268	191	65	53	.
8 DENMARK	1500	1465	1421	1353	797	698	470	325	158	88	70	67	64	45	.
9 EIRE	-	-	-	-	195	227	278	248	196	143	101	72	71	65	.
10 FINLAND	-	-	-	-	-	-	-	.	.	.	187	135	92	104	.
11 FRANCE	-	-	-	-	.	.	.	.	90	99	17	13	8	6	.
12 GREECE	-	-	-	-	.	.	640	520	-	-	-	11	34	39	.
13 HUNGARY	-	-	-	.	.	.	156	187	195	.	95	104	55	39	.
14 ICELAND	-	-	.	.	.	.	.	.	.	.	.	.	94	66	.
15 ITALY	.	.	.	.	.	.	.	.	.	.	59	39	24	16	.
16 JAPAN	.	.	.	.	.	.	2549	2513	-	885	696	574	427	316	.
17 NETHERLANDS	2328	2202	.	.	575	537	403	414	381	184	97	67	34	25	.
18 NEW ZEALAND	-	.	.	.	.	806	478	728	298	219	129	164	144	113	.
19 NORWAY	.	.	.	.	.	820	763	693	428	177	95	56	47	27	.
20 POLAND	-	-	-	-	-	-	-	-	-	-	.	341	173	139	.
21 PORTUGAL	.	.	.	.	.	.	.	.	.	.	340	286	242	191	.
22 ROMANIA	-	-	-	-	-	-	-	-	-	-	-	113	96	76	.
23 SPAIN	2975	2497	.	.	.	.	112	109	105	51	45	43	18	9	.
24 SWEDEN	-	-	.	.	.	.	.	.	.	.	147	109	76	67	.
25 SWITZERLAND	.	.	.	.	.	.	.	.	171	78	38	31	22	14	.
26 TURKEY	-	-	-	-	-	-	-	-	-	-	-	3377	2219	1185	968
27 UK ENGLAND AND WALES	402	501	849	874	772	828	698	555	337	215	167	135	131	106	.
28 UK NORTHERN IRELAND	-	-	-	-	280	358	.	.	.	175	124	138	101	88	.
29 UK SCOTLAND	634	856	.	.	.	.	842	692	374	230	135	146	118	123	.
30 USA	5817	3295	1846	2990	1474	1442	1189	1010	511	294	175	139	106	92	.
31 YUGOSLAVIA	-	-	-	-	-	-	-	-	-	-	.	.	63	14	.

\- NO MORTALITY DATA ARE AVAILABLE FOR EVEN A BROADER GROUP OF CAUSES FOR THIS DISEASE

. MORTALITY DATA ARE PRESENTED FOR A BROADER GROUP OF CAUSES FOR THIS DISEASE

0 VALUE<0.5

THE STANDARD MORTALITY RATIOS WERE DERIVED WITH A FACTOR OF 100

SERIAL MORTALITY TABLES FOR VARIOUS COUNTRIES 1901-1975

TABLE 100 : PNEUMONIA - LOBAR : FEMALES

	1901-	1906-	1911-	1916-	1921-	1926-	1931-	1936-	1941-	1946-	1951-	1956-	1961-	1966-	1971-75
1 AUSTRALIA	-	.	.	.	.	.	373	318	218	156	106	84	75	70	.
2 AUSTRIA	-	-	-	-	-	-	-	-	-	.	67	75	60	38	.
3 BELGIUM	1977	1926	1729	1608	1607	1974	1549	1421	1132	660	210	14	13	10	.
4 BULGARIA	-	-	-	-	-	.	.	.	.	.	.	.	45	36	.
5 CANADA	-	-	-	-	529	523	442	406	214	137	71	59	42	34	.
6 CHILE	-	11687	.	.	.	.	131	150	81	86	43	23	69	149	.
7 CZECHOSLOVAKIA	-	-	-	108	128	269	424	412	209	178	212	142	46	35	.
8 DENMARK	843	904	786	771	570	493	329	212	117	71	53	42	43	25	.
9 EIRE	-	-	-	-	121	139	166	164	131	101	74	57	55	57	.
10 FINLAND	-	-	-	-	-	-	-	.	.	.	134	95	63	54	.
11 FRANCE	-	-	-	-	.	.	.	.	82	88	11	8	6	4	.
12 GREECE	-	-	-	-	.	.	444	358	-	-	-	6	22	30	.
13 HUNGARY	-	-	-	.	.	.	121	127	108	.	57	61	29	23	.
14 ICELAND	-	-	.	.	.	.	.	.	.	.	.	.	107	27	.
15 ITALY	.	.	.	.	.	.	.	.	.	.	40	26	16	10	.
16 JAPAN	.	.	.	.	.	.	1779	1819	-	667	513	402	297	212	.
17 NETHERLANDS	1638	1585	.	.	402	355	276	268	261	145	81	52	25	17	.
18 NEW ZEALAND	-	.	.	.	.	344	269	371	183	162	82	87	82	57	.
19 NORWAY	.	.	.	.	.	613	603	501	289	161	79	55	38	24	.
20 POLAND	-	-	-	-	-	-	-	-	-	-	.	193	107	93	.
21 PORTUGAL	.	.	.	.	.	.	.	.	.	.	202	174	135	106	.
22 ROMANIA	-	-	-	-	-	-	-	-	-	-	-	76	69	54	.
23 SPAIN	2435	2001	.	.	.	.	75	72	67	35	32	30	12	7	.
24 SWEDEN	-	-	.	.	.	.	.	.	.	.	130	83	48	34	.
25 SWITZERLAND	.	.	.	.	.	.	.	.	116	57	23	23	12	8	.
26 TURKEY	-	-	-	-	-	-	-	-	-	-	-	2815	1833	1059	927
27 UK ENGLAND AND WALES	227	274	413	424	364	378	334	253	162	110	86	71	71	60	.
28 UK NORTHERN IRELAND	-	-	-	-	206	228	.	.	.	128	78	75	64	51	.
29 UK SCOTLAND	291	385	.	.	.	.	366	256	172	129	87	83	73	65	.
30 USA	4422	2493	1285	2235	1081	1006	820	656	311	179	99	75	57	47	.
31 YUGOSLAVIA	-	-	-	-	-	-	-	-	-	-	.	.	45	10	.

\- NO MORTALITY DATA ARE AVAILABLE FOR EVEN A BROADER GROUP OF CAUSES FOR THIS DISEASE

. MORTALITY DATA ARE PRESENTED FOR A BROADER GROUP OF CAUSES FOR THIS DISEASE

0 VALUE<0.5

THE STANDARD MORTALITY RATIOS WERE DERIVED WITH A FACTOR OF 100

SERIAL MORTALITY TABLES FOR VARIOUS COUNTRIES 1901-1975

TABLE 101 : BRONCHO-PNEUMONIA : MALES

	1901-	1906-	1911-	1916-	1921-	1926-	1931-	1936-	1941-	1946-	1951-	1956-	1961-	1966-	1971-75
1 AUSTRALIA	-	887	1051	1085	1144	1248	1211	1216	1137	934	565	607	682	715	.
2 AUSTRIA	-	-	-	-	-	-	-	-	-	.	213	293	327	228	.
3 BELGIUM	3340	3245	3787	3513	3493	.	.	.	.	.	527	481	504	506	.
4 BULGARIA	-	-	-	-	-	.	.	.	.	.	.	.	1826	1809	.
5 CANADA	-	-	-	-	1451	1445	1315	1287	1048	859	654	693	594	538	.
6 CHILE	-	1918	2783	2534	5088	10163	14267	15835	15199	14184	11765	9952	7704	5824	.
7 CZECHOSLOVAKIA	-	-	-	701	857	1459	1630	1699	1967	1798	1326	1187	699	719	.
8 DENMARK	5594	5021	3992	4530	3784	3569	2908	2263	1486	1741	511	357	404	438	.
9 EIRE	-	-	-	-	1226	1244	1383	1285	1026	813	497	529	654	682	.
10 FINLAND	-	-	-	-	-	-	-	.	2220	2026	1184	794	555	589	.
11 FRANCE	-	-	-	-	.	.	.	.	1528	1106	570	371	253	196	.
12 GREECE	-	-	-	-	.	3698	3450	2982	-	-	-	675	659	581	.
13 HUNGARY	-	-	-	.	.	.	811	797	687	.	361	385	186	169	.
14 ICELAND	-	-	.	.	.	.	.	.	.	.	.	.	603	772	.
15 ITALY	.	.	.	.	.	.	.	.	.	.	1587	1404	1087	862	.
16 JAPAN	.	2427	2511	3477	3605	3422	2868	2703	-	1216	804	619	409	250	.
17 NETHERLANDS	3397	3269	2657	3371	2424	1951	1498	1204	1100	532	457	327	209	168	.
18 NEW ZEALAND	-	566	774	624	743	719	618	791	668	695	582	880	1159	1012	.
19 NORWAY	.	.	.	.	.	943	1260	1559	1312	1122	662	717	786	787	.
20 POLAND	-	-	-	-	-	-	-	-	-	-	.	345	424	362	.
21 PORTUGAL	.	.	.	.	.	.	.	.	.	.	2246	2894	2905	2727	.
22 ROMANIA	-	-	-	-	-	-	-	-	-	-	-	3458	2109	1888	.
23 SPAIN	2939	3242	3605	5350	4913	5021	5983	5607	4253	2913	2075	1570	1081	848	.
24 SWEDEN	-	-	.	.	.	.	.	.	.	.	611	769	820	944	.
25 SWITZERLAND	3023	3023	3474	3474	1242	1605	941	982	768	577	359	305	304	278	.
26 TURKEY	-	-	-	-	-	-	-	-	-	-	-	5182	4460	3141	2824
27 UK ENGLAND AND WALES	2847	2432	2633	2721	2444	2130	1689	1545	1216	989	980	1144	1399	1433	.
28 UK NORTHERN IRELAND	-	-	-	-	1992	1955	.	.	.	1056	895	859	1007	1034	.
29 UK SCOTLAND	2575	2696	2699	3682	2912	2812	2271	1911	1228	1063	786	890	968	885	.
30 USA	2277	2204	2360	2517	1886	1676	1421	1286	885	619	439	566	559	496	.
31 YUGOSLAVIA	-	-	-	-	-	-	-	-	-	-	.	.	1504	968	.

- NO MORTALITY DATA ARE AVAILABLE FOR EVEN A BROADER GROUP OF CAUSES FOR THIS DISEASE

. MORTALITY DATA ARE PRESENTED FOR A BROADER GROUP OF CAUSES FOR THIS DISEASE

0 VALUE<0.5

THE STANDARD MORTALITY RATIOS WERE DERIVED WITH A FACTOR OF 1000

SERIAL MORTALITY TABLES FOR VARIOUS COUNTRIES 1901-1975

TABLE 101 : BRONCHO-PNEUMONIA : FEMALES

	1901-	1906-	1911-	1916-	1921-	1926-	1931-	1936-	1941-	1946-	1951-	1956-	1961-	1966-	1971-75
1 AUSTRALIA	-	822	943	1038	1030	1071	960	922	891	727	426	405	435	461	.
2 AUSTRIA	-	-	-	-	-	-	-	-	-	.	128	184	209	157	.
3 BELGIUM	2591	2635	2767	2543	2685	.	.	.	.	.	345	303	329	319	.
4 BULGARIA	-	-	-	-	-	.	.	.	.	.	.	.	1451	1435	.
5 CANADA	-	-	-	-	1277	1298	1189	1131	856	702	509	493	413	354	.
6 CHILE	-	1525	2356	2261	4393	8587	12060	13338	12701	11646	9644	7504	5840	4332	.
7 CZECHOSLOVAKIA	-	-	-	498	630	1068	1192	1210	1364	1263	1029	856	548	517	.
8 DENMARK	3494	3529	2764	3235	3236	3266	2507	1966	1339	1618	489	328	355	311	.
9 EIRE	-	-	-	-	1014	1042	1154	1080	864	696	463	444	544	590	.
10 FINLAND	-	-	-	-	-	-	-	.	1419	1341	1028	683	540	520	.
11 FRANCE	-	-	-	-	.	.	.	.	1016	679	357	234	159	122	.
12 GREECE	-	-	-	-	.	2866	2717	2384	-	-	-	529	537	481	.
13 HUNGARY	-	-	-	.	.	.	646	605	492	.	218	253	114	104	.
14 ICELAND	-	-	.	.	.	.	.	.	.	.	.	.	683	864	.
15 ITALY	.	.	.	.	.	.	.	.	.	.	1269	1068	792	591	.
16 JAPAN	.	2066	2159	3068	2964	2695	2207	2036	-	901	577	419	275	170	.
17 NETHERLANDS	2836	2781	2271	2909	2007	1663	1319	1036	1024	511	428	284	161	130	.
18 NEW ZEALAND	-	740	702	607	661	607	499	563	498	521	492	671	862	772	.
19 NORWAY	.	.	.	.	.	870	1250	1597	1331	1254	754	816	869	837	.
20 POLAND	-	-	-	-	-	-	-	-	-	-	.	198	234	204	.
21 PORTUGAL	.	.	.	.	.	.	.	.	.	.	1353	1760	1711	1644	.
22 ROMANIA	-	-	-	-	-	-	-	-	-	-	-	2313	1511	1300	.
23 SPAIN	2544	2699	2879	4304	3638	3480	4071	3649	2800	1974	1455	1111	778	598	.
24 SWEDEN	-	-	.	.	.	.	.	.	.	.	576	714	723	746	.
25 SWITZERLAND	2599	2599	2955	2955	1138	1333	801	833	684	534	312	247	237	211	.
26 TURKEY	-	-	-	-	-	-	-	-	-	-	-	3993	3442	2575	2485
27 UK ENGLAND AND WALES	2324	1989	1826	1781	1612	1359	1096	936	761	655	671	780	1006	1044	.
28 UK NORTHERN IRELAND	-	-	-	-	1521	1487	.	.	.	892	721	669	872	850	.
29 UK SCOTLAND	1711	1842	1844	2454	1813	1758	1501	1264	797	695	570	601	647	641	.
30 USA	2063	2000	2150	2252	1687	1454	1177	1042	668	457	306	362	348	291	.
31 YUGOSLAVIA	-	-	-	-	-	-	-	-	-	-	.	.	1103	689	.

- NO MORTALITY DATA ARE AVAILABLE FOR EVEN A BROADER GROUP OF CAUSES FOR THIS DISEASE

. MORTALITY DATA ARE PRESENTED FOR A BROADER GROUP OF CAUSES FOR THIS DISEASE

0 VALUE<0.5

THE STANDARD MORTALITY RATIOS WERE DERIVED WITH A FACTOR OF 1000

SERIAL MORTALITY TABLES FOR VARIOUS COUNTRIES 1901-1975

TABLE 102 : PNEUMONIA - PRIMARY ATYPICAL, OTHER AND UNSPECIFIED : MALES

	1901-	1906-	1911-	1916-	1921-	1926-	1931-	1936-	1941-	1946-	1951-	1956-	1961-	1966-	1971-75
1 AUSTRALIA	-	.	.	.	.	.	7850	6239	4752	3663	2987	3733	1977	1921	.
2 AUSTRIA	-	-	-	-	-	-	-	-	-	.	12727	11582	7669	5604	.
3 BELGIUM	-	-	-	-	.	.	.	.	.	.	2883	2516	1535	1667	.
4 BULGARIA	-	-	-	-	-	.	.	.	.	.	.	.	285	180	.
5 CANADA	-	-	-	-	16793	11616	6069	4568	4367	3826	2835	3116	2982	3144	.
6 CHILE	-	.	.	.	.	.	90014	77982	41634	31951	17490	12252	7873	4108	.
7 CZECHOSLOVAKIA	-	-	-	76339	64162	64491	36480	27719	28074	20822	3376	2230	1213	846	.
8 DENMARK	.	.	.	.	.	.	.	.	.	.	1055	1296	1377	1383	.
9 EIRE	-	-	-	-	19131	18000	16681	11841	8839	6327	3629	3323	4375	4556	.
10 FINLAND	-	-	-	-	-	48398	43262	.	.	.	2541	2178	1809	2606	.
11 FRANCE	-	-	-	-	.	.	.	.	12145	8695	12366	8498	5341	3341	.
12 GREECE	-	-	-	-	.	.	59921	51001	-	-	-	3018	2168	1771	.
13 HUNGARY	-	-	-	.	.	.	68202	60410	53046	.	23291	19240	5584	2943	.
14 ICELAND	-	-	.	.	.	.	.	.	.	.	.	.	4365	5074	.
15 ITALY	.	.	.	.	.	.	.	.	.	.	2039	1127	828	469	.
16 JAPAN	.	.	.	.	.	.	21624	20126	-	3644	2764	2576	2248	1934	.
17 NETHERLANDS	.	.	.	.	13373	10953	7672	5861	7065	2932	1021	1636	1853	1944	.
18 NEW ZEALAND	-	.	.	.	.	4388	1174	548	490	622	1115	1377	996	1579	.
19 NORWAY	.	.	.	.	.	.	.	.	4678	3939	2324	2834	2993	3861	.
20 POLAND	-	-	-	-	-	-	-	-	-	-	.	19181	12196	5449	.
21 PORTUGAL	.	.	.	.	.	.	.	.	.	.	2272	1505	1441	1557	.
22 ROMANIA	-	-	-	-	-	-	-	-	-	-	-	2577	4131	5248	.
23 SPAIN	.	.	.	.	.	.	17184	17914	15665	9479	4693	3368	2450	1961	.
24 SWEDEN	-	-	.	.	.	.	.	.	.	.	1871	1507	1174	1671	.
25 SWITZERLAND	.	.	.	.	.	.	.	.	10009	6415	3834	3351	2971	2899	.
26 TURKEY	-	-	-	-	-	-	-	-	-	-	-	2159	68	10	16
27 UK ENGLAND AND WALES	.	.	21754	22097	12569	7877	4947	3235	2414	1512	1262	1252	1307	1215	.
28 UK NORTHERN IRELAND	-	-	-	-	20911	16003	.	.	.	2771	2696	1953	2033	1424	.
29 UK SCOTLAND	49731	40916	.	.	.	.	9305	6657	4066	2365	1734	1623	1572	1151	.
30 USA	.	39334	16636	7652	3070	2226	1647	1631	2131	1880	2115	2801	3409	3727	.
31 YUGOSLAVIA	-	-	-	-	-	-	-	-	-	-	.	.	5562	820	.

- NO MORTALITY DATA ARE AVAILABLE FOR EVEN A BROADER GROUP OF CAUSES FOR THIS DISEASE

. MORTALITY DATA ARE PRESENTED FOR A BROADER GROUP OF CAUSES FOR THIS DISEASE

0 VALUE<0.5

THE STANDARD MORTALITY RATIOS WERE DERIVED WITH A FACTOR OF 1000

SERIAL MORTALITY TABLES FOR VARIOUS COUNTRIES 1901-1975

TABLE 102 : PNEUMONIA - PRIMARY ATYPICAL, OTHER AND UNSPECIFIED : FEMALES

	1901-	1906-	1911-	1916-	1921-	1926-	1931-	1936-	1941-	1946-	1951-	1956-	1961-	1966-	1971-75
1 AUSTRALIA	-	.	.	.	.	.	5669	4492	3337	2813	2096	2566	1274	1145	.
2 AUSTRIA	-	-	-	-	-	-	-	-	-	.	9061	7987	5217	3472	.
3 BELGIUM	-	-	-	-	.	.	.	.	.	.	1975	1731	1038	1211	.
4 BULGARIA	-	-	-	-	-	.	.	.	.	.	.	.	185	149	.
5 CANADA	-	-	-	-	15454	10865	5719	4030	3762	3186	2265	2597	2295	2238	.
6 CHILE	-	.	.	.	.	.	76057	65333	34581	26858	12725	9108	5452	3310	.
7 CZECHOSLOVAKIA	-	-	-	67131	53001	51375	28983	22272	20788	15318	2960	1901	1004	693	.
8 DENMARK	.	.	.	.	.	.	.	.	.	.	1081	1205	1300	1134	.
9 EIRE	-	-	-	-	12382	12854	11259	8711	6256	4958	3028	2708	3412	3607	.
10 FINLAND	-	-	-	-	-	33389	30392	.	.	.	2616	2430	1902	2161	.
11 FRANCE	-	-	-	-	.	.	.	.	9537	6947	10336	7108	4594	2899	.
12 GREECE	-	-	-	-	.	.	46241	40346	-	-	-	2351	1808	1495	.
13 HUNGARY	-	-	-	.	.	.	55770	47034	40837	.	18124	14688	4415	2136	.
14 ICELAND	-	-	.	.	.	.	.	.	.	.	.	.	5634	5974	.
15 ITALY	.	.	.	.	.	.	.	.	.	.	1532	849	564	306	.
16 JAPAN	.	.	.	.	.	.	17284	15802	-	3101	2176	1922	1677	1465	.
17 NETHERLANDS	.	.	.	.	11093	8866	6189	4932	5596	2590	847	1325	1496	1589	.
18 NEW ZEALAND	-	.	.	.	.	2758	707	328	431	465	744	978	603	952	.
19 NORWAY	.	.	.	.	.	.	.	.	3215	3456	1984	2650	2935	3768	.
20 POLAND	-	-	-	-	-	-	-	-	-	-	.	12406	7994	3740	.
21 PORTUGAL	.	.	.	.	.	.	.	.	.	.	1536	856	935	875	.
22 ROMANIA	-	-	-	-	-	-	-	-	-	-	-	1899	3309	3886	.
23 SPAIN	.	.	.	.	.	.	12287	12286	10446	6643	3641	2577	1886	1582	.
24 SWEDEN	-	-	.	.	.	.	.	.	.	.	1852	1354	1025	1376	.
25 SWITZERLAND	.	.	.	.	.	.	.	.	8196	5460	3088	2437	2219	1969	.
26 TURKEY	-	-	-	-	-	-	-	-	-	-	-	1872	19	11	13
27 UK ENGLAND AND WALES	.	.	12389	12822	7047	4322	2751	1739	1343	911	792	769	856	821	.
28 UK NORTHERN IRELAND	-	-	-	-	15441	11968	.	.	.	2160	2119	1765	1496	1091	.
29 UK SCOTLAND	28084	25308	.	.	.	.	5741	3777	2144	1560	1129	1062	941	742	.
30 USA	.	32606	14504	6489	2689	1830	1292	1198	1525	1371	1526	1935	2329	2426	.
31 YUGOSLAVIA	-	-	-	-	-	-	-	-	-	-	.	.	4549	618	.

- NO MORTALITY DATA ARE AVAILABLE FOR EVEN A BROADER GROUP OF CAUSES FOR THIS DISEASE

. MORTALITY DATA ARE PRESENTED FOR A BROADER GROUP OF CAUSES FOR THIS DISEASE

0 VALUE<0.5

THE STANDARD MORTALITY RATIOS WERE DERIVED WITH A FACTOR OF 1000

SERIAL MORTALITY TABLES FOR VARIOUS COUNTRIES 1901-1975

TABLE 103 : PNEUMONIA - ALL FORMS : MALES

	1901-	1906-	1911-	1916-	1921-	1926-	1931-	1936-	1941-	1946-	1951-	1956-	1961-	1966-	1971-75
1 AUSTRALIA	-	2316	2590	2551	2470	2525	2055	1913	1544	1217	829	858	773	698	509
2 AUSTRIA	-	-	-	-	-	-	-	-	-	1536	1030	1003	780	731	639
3 BELGIUM	-	-	-	-	.	.	.	.	.	.	629	505	465	509	504
4 BULGARIA	-	-	-	-	-	2710	5852	5390	5640	5814	4418	2230	1473	1517	1476
5 CANADA	-	-	-	-	3025	2654	2010	1860	1387	1096	779	805	685	650	590
6 CHILE	-	16246	15411	19367	22387	17247	17761	18213	14848	13334	9539	8551	6641	5048	3705
7 CZECHOSLOVAKIA	-	-	-	5733	5066	5754	4301	3770	3550	2771	1663	1228	658	698	754
8 DENMARK	.	.	.	.	.	.	.	.	.	.	511	404	436	412	461
9 EIRE	-	-	-	-	2341	2325	2417	1999	1544	1162	672	641	787	967	1147
10 FINLAND	-	-	-	-	-	-	-	.	2479	1981	1288	899	639	822	1005
11 FRANCE	-	-	-	-	1075	1157	1930	1949	1847	1410	1137	759	490	354	300
12 GREECE	-	-	-	-	4843	6296	6897	5781	-	-	-	679	637	631	519
13 HUNGARY	-	-	-	6844	6618	5833	5172	4597	3989	3320	2283	1565	522	364	236
14 ICELAND	-	-	6809	3894	7855	3376	3337	2779	1545	923	1009	827	811	933	967
15 ITALY	7136	6735	6295	7781	5990	6314	5354	5436	3991	2607	1342	1125	859	796	609
16 JAPAN	3999	4406	4910	8361	6989	.	6892	6704	-	2308	1679	1361	990	798	728
17 NETHERLANDS	4404	5010	4060	5217	3343	2785	2071	1746	1709	796	507	408	293	331	400
18 NEW ZEALAND	-	1671	1546	1718	1630	1604	1116	1514	882	806	640	907	1068	1058	778
19 NORWAY	2106	2045	2075	2941	1823	1929	1756	1897	1686	1230	712	731	777	869	1032
20 POLAND	-	-	-	-	-	-	-	-	-	-	.	2048	1367	868	791
21 PORTUGAL	2779	2729	2023	2547	1800	1255	4268	4071	3825	2667	2408	2574	2509	2319	1409
22 ROMANIA	-	-	-	-	-	-	-	-	-	-	-	2861	1922	2082	1726
23 SPAIN	5726	5423	4960	6225	5222	5124	5703	5413	4246	2801	1869	1408	958	724	787
24 SWEDEN	-	-	2272	2191	1560	1677	1733	1782	1056	719	712	755	733	804	369
25 SWITZERLAND	4048	4048	3642	3642	3299	2952	2074	1978	1364	896	530	448	413	419	390
26 TURKEY	-	-	-	-	-	-	-	-	-	-	-	8212	6078	3794	3266
27 UK ENGLAND AND WALES	5411	4379	4545	4625	3629	3132	2439	2028	1433	1059	975	1050	1235	1390	1490
28 UK NORTHERN IRELAND	-	-	-	-	3140	2897	2564	2121	1833	1366	941	885	959	913	1174
29 UK SCOTLAND	6256	5974	5321	6837	4373	4418	3333	2684	1604	1187	828	907	929	974	1004
30 USA	8665	6157	5094	6010	3397	3144	2615	2291	1397	916	650	737	723	699	590
31 YUGOSLAVIA	-	-	-	-	-	-	-	-	-	-	.	2311	1532	979	902

- NO MORTALITY DATA ARE AVAILABLE FOR EVEN A BROADER GROUP OF CAUSES FOR THIS DISEASE

. MORTALITY DATA ARE PRESENTED FOR A BROADER GROUP OF CAUSES FOR THIS DISEASE

0 VALUE<0.5

THE STANDARD MORTALITY RATIOS WERE DERIVED WITH A FACTOR OF 1000

SERIAL MORTALITY TABLES FOR VARIOUS COUNTRIES 1901-1975

TABLE 103 : PNEUMONIA - ALL FORMS : FEMALES

	1901-	1906-	1911-	1916-	1921-	1926-	1931-	1936-	1941-	1946-	1951-	1956-	1961-	1966-	1971-75
1 AUSTRALIA	-	1804	1895	1971	1882	1886	1510	1322	1097	870	546	529	464	410	294
2 AUSTRIA	-	-	-	-	-	-	-	-	-	1050	679	625	477	437	404
3 BELGIUM	-	-	-	-	.	.	.	.	.	.	419	320	301	323	296
4 BULGARIA	-	-	-	-	-	1855	4307	3719	3980	3717	2849	1711	1149	1119	1014
5 CANADA	-	-	-	-	2564	2266	1743	1542	1096	861	585	577	475	415	354
6 CHILE	-	13085	13223	17139	19161	14400	14540	14723	12023	10697	7679	6250	4839	3625	2603
7 CZECHOSLOVAKIA	-	-	-	4672	3893	4265	3145	2718	2451	1953	1265	888	500	478	499
8 DENMARK	.	.	.	.	.	.	.	.	.	.	472	347	369	299	331
9 EIRE	-	-	-	-	1625	1695	1720	1512	1162	925	575	521	624	764	972
10 FINLAND	-	-	-	-	-	-	-	.	1487	1251	1061	745	569	616	676
11 FRANCE	-	-	-	-	712	767	1226	1241	1225	940	794	528	342	237	194
12 GREECE	-	-	-	-	3294	4597	5187	4500	-	-	-	517	504	519	423
13 HUNGARY	-	-	-	5785	5337	4651	4069	3427	2891	2300	1550	1083	351	225	138
14 ICELAND	-	-	2788	1836	3312	1739	1748	1381	1158	783	881	907	917	973	722
15 ITALY	5683	5573	5340	7047	4922	5020	4188	4151	3090	2058	1046	842	615	534	400
16 JAPAN	3063	3553	3996	7096	5590	.	4916	4798	-	1667	1168	889	642	513	463
17 NETHERLANDS	3241	3863	3150	4122	2626	2181	1667	1368	1395	702	452	336	225	252	302
18 NEW ZEALAND	-	1412	1266	1360	1113	1034	738	886	609	596	492	634	745	778	600
19 NORWAY	1631	1581	1545	2233	1380	1557	1548	1685	1431	1252	729	779	809	847	939
20 POLAND	-	-	-	-	-	-	-	-	-	-	.	1138	768	501	445
21 PORTUGAL	1831	1841	1228	1667	1131	813	2671	2494	2265	1625	1427	1517	1434	1346	787
22 ROMANIA	-	-	-	-	-	-	-	-	-	-	-	1889	1362	1388	1147
23 SPAIN	4815	4359	3847	4865	3769	3432	3799	3447	2702	1843	1290	976	676	499	551
24 SWEDEN	-	-	1667	1666	1246	1303	1514	1497	981	719	655	671	618	613	248
25 SWITZERLAND	3372	3372	2935	2935	2602	2116	1526	1448	1072	748	416	330	297	274	249
26 TURKEY	-	-	-	-	-	-	-	-	-	-	-	6347	4641	3102	2881
27 UK ENGLAND AND WALES	3837	3098	2622	2602	2036	1691	1348	1069	804	641	614	670	833	965	1073
28 UK NORTHERN IRELAND	-	-	-	-	2275	2070	1793	1488	1307	1056	718	655	774	731	878
29 UK SCOTLAND	3381	3397	2924	4082	2461	2400	1856	1427	891	730	566	576	591	655	692
30 USA	6707	4825	4024	4699	2694	2378	1920	1613	938	615	419	451	437	402	318
31 YUGOSLAVIA	-	-	-	-	-	-	-	-	-	-	.	1728	1109	674	625

- NO MORTALITY DATA ARE AVAILABLE FOR EVEN A BROADER GROUP OF CAUSES FOR THIS DISEASE

. MORTALITY DATA ARE PRESENTED FOR A BROADER GROUP OF CAUSES FOR THIS DISEASE

0 VALUE<0.5

THE STANDARD MORTALITY RATIOS WERE DERIVED WITH A FACTOR OF 1000

SERIAL MORTALITY TABLES FOR VARIOUS COUNTRIES 1901-1975

TABLE 103 : PNEUMONIA - ALL FORMS : PERSONS

	1901-	1906-	1911-	1916-	1921-	1926-	1931-	1936-	1941-	1946-	1951-	1956-	1961-	1966-	1971-75
1 AUSTRALIA	-	2076	2260	2270	2182	2208	1782	1612	1311	1033	673	673	596	529	380
2 AUSTRIA	-	-	-	-	-	.	2926	2602	-	1256	825	777	594	546	488
3 BELGIUM	-	-	-	-	.	.	.	.	.	.	511	399	370	399	378
4 BULGARIA	-	-	-	-	-	2255	5030	4491	4732	4647	3530	1948	1295	1297	1221
5 CANADA	2297	1714	1577	2178	2796	2462	1878	1702	1242	979	681	688	575	523	456
6 CHILE	-	14568	14259	18203	20699	15747	16054	16356	13338	11921	8539	7274	5642	4261	3091
7 CZECHOSLOVAKIA	-	-	-	5148	4418	4928	3656	3180	2937	2314	1440	1034	564	566	598
8 DENMARK	.	.	.	.	.	.	.	.	.	.	490	374	400	349	387
9 EIRE	-	-	-	-	1966	1995	2054	1748	1347	1040	622	578	699	856	1050
10 FINLAND	-	-	-	-	-	-	-	.	1897	1544	1150	805	596	694	797
11 FRANCE	2953	2064	1763	1676	867	933	1520	1531	1474	1125	928	615	397	279	232
12 GREECE	-	-	-	-	4040	5411	6015	5129	-	-	-	739	859	843	718
13 HUNGARY	-	-	-	6291	5947	5211	4588	3973	3401	2758	1874	1293	423	282	177
14 ICELAND	-	-	4401	2664	5152	2401	2391	1945	1317	843	936	872	870	955	832
15 ITALY	6404	6147	5810	7407	5440	5641	4740	4752	3507	2310	1180	968	720	643	484
16 JAPAN	3497	3956	4430	7696	6240	.	5814	5659	-	1947	1389	1089	789	634	575
17 NETHERLANDS	3781	4396	3575	4635	2964	2468	1860	1548	1545	747	478	370	257	287	344
18 NEW ZEALAND	-	1557	1420	1553	1385	1328	930	1200	743	697	561	759	887	896	674
19 NORWAY	1847	1791	1783	2548	1577	1722	1640	1779	1543	1242	721	757	795	856	979
20 POLAND	-	-	-	-	-	-	-	-	-	-	.	1548	1006	644	577
21 PORTUGAL	2251	2232	1575	2045	1415	999	3333	3138	2897	2049	1817	1935	1860	1726	1028
22 ROMANIA	-	-	-	-	-	-	-	.	-	.	-	2306	1599	1679	1391
23 SPAIN	5257	4860	4362	5489	4427	4184	4628	4285	3356	2243	1527	1152	792	591	647
24 SWEDEN	-	-	1935	1899	1386	1470	1612	1626	1015	719	682	709	670	697	300
25 SWITZERLAND	3685	3685	3251	3251	2905	2477	1761	1675	1197	811	465	379	345	333	305
26 TURKEY	-	-	-	-	-	-	6043	6574	6194	5297	4293	7200	5298	3430	3069
27 UK ENGLAND AND WALES	4595	3710	3460	3473	2718	2303	1808	1470	1062	813	759	817	983	1119	1222
28 UK NORTHERN IRELAND	-	-	-	-	2667	2445	2142	1779	1548	1199	818	756	853	806	995
29 UK SCOTLAND	4596	4482	3929	5232	3264	3253	2484	1959	1190	921	676	711	723	775	804
30 USA	7654	5479	4553	5346	3042	2758	2261	1941	1158	606	526	580	563	528	428
31 YUGOSLAVIA	-	-	-	-	-	-	-	-	-	-	.	1979	1288	802	741

- NO MORTALITY DATA ARE AVAILABLE FOR EVEN A BROADER GROUP OF CAUSES FOR THIS DISEASE

. MORTALITY DATA ARE PRESENTED FOR A BROADER GROUP OF CAUSES FOR THIS DISEASE

0 VALUE<0.5

THE STANDARD MORTALITY RATIOS WERE DERIVED WITH A FACTOR OF 1000

SERIAL MORTALITY TABLES FOR VARIOUS COUNTRIES 1901-1975

TABLE 104 BRONCHITIS - ACUTE: MALES

	1901-	1906-	1911-	1916-	1921-	1926-	1931-	1936-	1941-	1946-	1951-	1956-	1961-	1966-	1971-75
1 AUSTRALIA	-	3146	2822	2401	.	1221	705	559	513	368	313	266	186	179	.
2 AUSTRIA	-	-	-	-	-	-	-	-	-	.	351	350	262	157	.
3 BELGIUM	13848	11580	9181	7699	7665	7557	3290	3008	2888	1642	478	119	115	166	.
4 BULGARIA	-	-	-	-	-	.	.	.	.	.	.	.	55	43	.
5 CANADA	-	-	-	-	813	569	473	287	289	205	191	194	111	109	.
6 CHILE	-	6243	3221	3653	4623	.	.	930	594	411	408	802	907	1083	.
7 CZECHOSLOVAKIA	-	-	-	1670	5036	3572	1049	790	.	.	381	250	265	284	.
8 DENMARK	3558	3493	2789	2495	1392	914	947	887	592	414	287	239	140	343	.
9 EIRE	-	-	-	-	2325	2664	3343	3161	.	.	728	468	402	428	.
10 FINLAND	-	-	-	-	-	-	-	.	.	.	419	249	137	99	.
11 FRANCE	-	-	-	-	.	.	.	.	.	69	55	53	57	58	.
12 GREECE	-	-	-	-	.	.	.	.	-	-	-	79	157	184	.
13 HUNGARY	-	-	-	.	.	.	94	79	135	.	138	215	165	133	.
14 ICELAND	-	-	4819	7582	3700	2000	1000	923	.	.	-	-	578	76	.
15 ITALY	.	.	.	.	.	.	.	.	.	.	566	493	561	445	.
16 JAPAN	24673	23812	11158	10512	6959	5825	3367	2405	-	3555	1939	1312	860	546	.
17 NETHERLANDS	9482	7215	5333	4971	1333	949	585	447	377	332	301	215	102	66	.
18 NEW ZEALAND	-	2646	2875	1988	2278	.	.	1230	945	635	706	563	463	399	.
19 NORWAY	7830	5737	4849	4549	2656	1260	687	651	.	.	105	86	51	42	.
20 POLAND	-	-	-	-	-	-	-	-	-	-	.	307	236	207	.
21 PORTUGAL	15688	15453	11375	15493	10940	6393	.	.	.	.	2194	2048	1578	1046	.
22 ROMANIA	-	-	-	-	-	-	-	-	-	-	-	127	120	30	.
23 SPAIN	35293	36280	33507	33622	27785	21723	8078	6852	.	.	1214	879	623	526	.
24 SWEDEN	-	-	4910	4367	3113	2454	983	898	615	344	246	242	250	225	.
25 SWITZERLAND	7079	7079	3992	3992	.	.	417	297	171	146	154	85	66	49	.
26 TURKEY	-	-	-	-	-	-	-	-	-	-	-	105	327	288	178
27 UK ENGLAND AND WALES	.	.	.	.	6077	4147	2851	3076	3574	2356	1710	1158	994	771	.
28 UK NORTHERN IRELAND	-	-	-	-	10400	8552	.	.	.	779	678	366	357	285	.
29 UK SCOTLAND	.	.	.	.	.	.	.	.	.	1252	1072	876	695	621	.
30 USA	9244	5096	3068	2424	855	490	296	248	162	162	142	148	122	102	.
31 YUGOSLAVIA	-	-	-	-	-	-	-	-	-	-	.	.	365	235	.

- NO MORTALITY DATA ARE AVAILABLE FOR EVEN A BROADER GROUP OF CAUSES FOR THIS DISEASE

. MORTALITY DATA ARE PRESENTED FOR A BROADER GROUP OF CAUSES FOR THIS DISEASE

0 VALUE<0.5

THE STANDARD MORTALITY RATIOS WERE DERIVED WITH A FACTOR OF 1000

SERIAL MORTALITY TABLES FOR VARIOUS COUNTRIES 1901-1975

TABLE 104 : BRONCHITIS - ACUTE: FEMALES

	1901-	1906-	1911-	1916-	1921-	1926-	1931-	1936-	1941-	1946-	1951-	1956-	1961-	1966-	1971-75
1 AUSTRALIA	-	2714	2654	2120	.	1082	773	532	414	259	205	134	115	137	.
2 AUSTRIA	-	-	-	-	-	-	-	-	-	.	237	221	149	64	.
3 BELGIUM	10783	9292	6899	5708	5755	5563	2475	2269	2074	1115	255	87	81	106	.
4 BULGARIA	-	-	-	-	-	.	.	.	.	.	.	.	35	42	.
5 CANADA	-	-	-	-	893	509	473	266	223	156	147	117	76	66	.
6 CHILE	-	5259	2682	3120	3647	.	.	620	455	327	345	533	682	846	.
7 CZECHOSLOVAKIA	-	-	-	1225	3551	2349	672	571	.	.	275	159	176	141	.
8 DENMARK	2407	2568	2124	1999	1252	869	943	980	554	371	217	213	110	214	.
9 EIRE	-	-	-	-	2561	2775	3410	3281	.	.	700	468	367	316	.
10 FINLAND	-	-	-	-	-	-	-	.	.	.	226	199	141	93	.
11 FRANCE	-	-	-	-	.	.	.	.	.	41	33	35	42	34	.
12 GREECE	-	-	-	-	.	.	.	.	-	-	-	64	132	138	.
13 HUNGARY	-	-	-	.	.	.	60	58	67	.	31	102	104	71	.
14 ICELAND	-	-	3652	5433	1942	1438	479	765	.	.	-	-	277	252	.
15 ITALY	.	.	.	.	.	.	.	.	.	.	515	397	429	328	.
16 JAPAN	20359	20537	9314	8600	5573	4721	2726	1922	-	2878	1587	1079	743	473	.
17 NETHERLANDS	7735	6112	4366	4134	1213	908	630	461	424	320	307	188	75	45	.
18 NEW ZEALAND	-	2922	2693	1774	1745	.	.	784	715	580	624	434	304	378	.
19 NORWAY	6357	4785	4034	3647	2219	1053	700	670	.	.	109	56	49	19	.
20 POLAND	-	-	-	-	-	-	-	-	-	-	.	162	133	88	.
21 PORTUGAL	11879	11464	8264	11096	7639	4341	.	.	.	.	1342	1266	928	624	.
22 ROMANIA	-	-	-	-	-	-	-	-	-	-	-	86	80	16	.
23 SPAIN	29209	28401	25695	26197	20537	15830	5883	4774	.	.	900	651	490	361	.
24 SWEDEN	-	-	3686	3168	2401	1759	803	778	506	276	233	223	230	180	.
25 SWITZERLAND	6348	6348	3624	3624	.	.	401	296	208	165	126	63	46	29	.
26 TURKEY	-	-	-	-	-	-	-	-	-	-	-	88	226	225	58
27 UK ENGLAND AND WALES	.	.	.	.	5937	3976	2783	2650	2823	1878	1365	815	664	471	.
28 UK NORTHERN IRELAND	-	-	-	-	11671	9182	.	.	.	1018	711	370	351	165	.
29 UK SCOTLAND	.	.	.	.	.	.	.	.	.	1147	937	705	526	372	.
30 USA	8434	4790	3009	2365	885	520	297	220	130	118	94	92	68	59	.
31 YUGOSLAVIA	-	-	-	-	-	-	-	-	-	-	.	.	259	177	.

- NO MORTALITY DATA ARE AVAILABLE FOR EVEN A BROADER GROUP OF CAUSES FOR THIS DISEASE

. MORTALITY DATA ARE PRESENTED FOR A BROADER GROUP OF CAUSES FOR THIS DISEASE

0 VALUE<0.5

THE STANDARD MORTALITY RATIOS WERE DERIVED WITH A FACTOR OF 1000

SERIAL MORTALITY TABLES FOR VARIOUS COUNTRIES 1901-1975

TABLE 104 : BRONCHITIS - ACUTE: PERSONS

	1901-	1906-	1911-	1916-	1921-	1926-	1931-	1936-	1941-	1946-	1951-	1956-	1961-	1966-	1971-75
1 AUSTRALIA	-	2942	2742	2265	.	1152	739	545	462	311	254	193	146	155	.
2 AUSTRIA	-	-	-	-	-	-	.	.	-	.	285	274	194	99	.
3 BELGIUM	12237	10371	7948	6612	6646	6501	2856	2615	2457	1363	354	101	96	131	.
4 BULGARIA	-	-	-	-	-	.	.	.	.	.	.	.	44	42	.
5 CANADA	4419	2653	2100	1856	853	539	473	277	257	181	169	155	93	86	.
6 CHILE	-	5727	2940	3377	4117	.	.	767	521	367	375	656	785	955	.
7 CZECHOSLOVAKIA	-	-	-	1428	4226	2903	842	670	.	.	323	199	213	200	.
8 DENMARK	2883	2951	2399	2204	1317	890	945	936	572	392	250	225	124	272	.
9 EIRE	-	-	-	-	2448	2722	3378	3222	.	.	714	468	384	368	.
10 FINLAND	-	-	-	-	-	-	-	.	.	.	305	219	139	95	.
11 FRANCE	8691	8110	6937	5333	.	.	.	.	.	52	42	42	47	43	.
12 GREECE	-	-	-	-	.	.	.	.	-	-	-	87	208	228	.
13 HUNGARY	-	-	-	.	.	.	76	68	99	.	79	152	130	97	.
14 ICELAND	-	-	4141	6330	2678	1673	697	831	.	.	-	-	414	172	.
15 ITALY	-	-	-	-	-	-	-	-	-	-	538	440	487	378	.
16 JAPAN	22393	22104	10199	9516	6227	5237	3023	2145	-	3183	1744	1181	794	504	.
17 NETHERLANDS	8558	6632	4823	4532	1270	928	608	454	401	326	304	201	88	54	.
18 NEW ZEALAND	-	2770	2793	1889	2025	.	.	1007	828	607	663	493	376	387	.
19 NORWAY	7038	5223	4406	4056	2416	1146	694	662	.	.	107	69	50	29	.
20 POLAND	-	-	-	-	-	-	-	-	-	-	.	229	176	136	.
21 PORTUGAL	13601	13256	9650	13030	9077	5227	.	.	.	.	1693	1587	1194	794	.
22 ROMANIA	-	-	-	-	-	-	-	.	-	.	-	104	97	22	.
23 SPAIN	32177	32151	29364	29662	23879	18506	6862	5681	.	.	1032	747	546	430	.
24 SWEDEN	-	-	4237	3709	2722	2073	885	833	556	308	239	232	239	201	.
25 SWITZERLAND	6690	6690	3791	3791	.	.	408	296	192	157	138	73	54	37	.
26 TURKEY	-	-	-	-	-	-	.	.	.	-	-	96	274	256	118
27 UK ENGLAND AND WALES	.	.	.	.	5999	4050	2812	2832	3138	2079	1506	951	791	583	.
28 UK NORTHERN IRELAND	-	-	-	-	11086	8892	.	.	.	907	696	368	354	215	.
29 UK SCOTLAND	.	.	.	.	.	.	.	.	.	1192	994	776	594	468	.
30 USA	8828	4941	3038	2394	870	505	296	234	145	111	116	118	92	78	.
31 YUGOSLAVIA	-	-	-	-	-	-	-	-	-	-	.	.	305	202	.

- NO MORTALITY DATA ARE AVAILABLE FOR EVEN A BROADER GROUP OF CAUSES FOR THIS DISEASE

. MORTALITY DATA ARE PRESENTED FOR A BROADER GROUP OF CAUSES FOR THIS DISEASE

0 VALUE<0.5

THE STANDARD MORTALITY RATIOS WERE DERIVED WITH A FACTOR OF 10000

SERIAL MORTALITY TABLES FOR VARIOUS COUNTRIES 1901-1975

TABLE 105 : BRONCHITIS - CHRONIC AND UNQUALIFIED : MALES

	1901-	1906-	1911-	1916-	1921-	1926-	1931-	1936-	1941-	1946-	1951-	1956-	1961-	1966-	1971-75
1 AUSTRALIA	-	9257	9523	8306	.	4669	3301	2718	2389	2230	3386	4659	7841	9360	.
2 AUSTRIA	-	-	-	-	-	-	-	-	-	.	1985	1895	2581	6075	.
3 BELGIUM	21794	18375	15555	12442	11192	11065	7503	6409	6107	4946	5192	4872	4509	4854	.
4 BULGARIA	-	-	-	-	-	.	.	.	.	.	.	.	9675	10435	.
5 CANADA	-	-	-	-	2466	1027	603	572	803	763	1002	1640	2073	2835	.
6 CHILE	-	2807	1226	2617	782	.	.	2191	1773	1660	860	1927	2613	2961	.
7 CZECHOSLOVAKIA	-	-	-	8436	4340	8923	6418	5443	.	.	1889	3419	11519	12718	.
8 DENMARK	9093	8419	6053	5847	4171	4226	3851	3286	2333	671	647	1126	3414	4219	.
9 EIRE	-	-	-	-	20406	16787	13793	12607	.	.	7854	8168	11868	13478	.
10 FINLAND	-	-	-	-	-	-	-	.	.	.	586	1323	3559	4653	.
11 FRANCE	-	-	-	-	.	.	.	.	.	1350	1179	1094	1153	1214	.
12 GREECE	-	-	-	-	.	.	.	.	-	-	-	1081	2471	2605	.
13 HUNGARY	-	-	-	.	.	.	3609	2288	1892	.	741	1257	1464	2431	.
14 ICELAND	-	-	10374	8824	6713	2408	3222	2413	.	.	-	-	1713	1127	.
15 ITALY	.	.	.	.	.	.	.	.	.	.	4934	6494	7981	8268	.
16 JAPAN	9618	10319	22109	23669	20491	14329	13894	14277	-	7693	4155	2131	1454	1084	.
17 NETHERLANDS	10160	8907	7550	7413	6595	7203	4476	4027	3793	2581	2975	3441	3853	4396	.
18 NEW ZEALAND	-	8185	6449	7216	6764	.	.	2948	2469	1905	5611	7211	9574	10116	.
19 NORWAY	8938	7696	5415	4749	3993	2897	2259	1744	.	.	793	824	1057	1248	.
20 POLAND	-	-	-	-	-	-	-	-	-	-	.	655	1019	1848	.
21 PORTUGAL	4901	4698	4812	5426	5384	6866	.	.	.	.	6407	7010	8595	8721	.
22 ROMANIA	-	-	-	-	-	-	-	-	-	-	-	3504	5879	4869	.
23 SPAIN	29364	23467	19611	20721	17483	16637	19633	16765	.	.	8001	6916	6725	5716	.
24 SWEDEN	-	-	2843	2073	1515	1264	745	683	451	375	580	516	782	1037	.
25 SWITZERLAND	14741	14741	11711	11711	4768	4743	4953	4138	2888	1582	1518	1557	2058	2748	.
26 TURKEY	-	-	-	-	-	-	-	-	-	-	-	4066	2871	2148	1943
27 UK ENGLAND AND WALES	.	.	.	.	24408	17456	11161	12115	16079	15734	17263	17230	19090	17623	.
28 UK NORTHERN IRELAND	-	-	-	-	16479	13739	.	.	.	10570	8987	11437	15098	16911	.
29 UK SCOTLAND	.	.	.	.	.	.	.	.	.	11860	10857	13033	16226	15311	.
30 USA	7935	4499	2941	2141	1692	1105	761	682	614	428	404	520	774	956	.
31 YUGOSLAVIA	-	-	-	-	-	-	-	-	-	-	.	.	3934	2374	.

- NO MORTALITY DATA ARE AVAILABLE FOR EVEN A BROADER GROUP OF CAUSES FOR THIS DISEASE

. MORTALITY DATA ARE PRESENTED FOR A BROADER GROUP OF CAUSES FOR THIS DISEASE

0 VALUE<0.5

THE STANDARD MORTALITY RATIOS WERE DERIVED WITH A FACTOR OF 10000

SERIAL MORTALITY TABLES FOR VARIOUS COUNTRIES 1901-1975

TABLE 105 : BRONCHITIS - CHRONIC AND UNQUALIFIED : FEMALES

	1901-	1906-	1911-	1916-	1921-	1926-	1931-	1936-	1941-	1946-	1951-	1956-	1961-	1966-	1971-75
1 AUSTRALIA	-	8256	8439	7532	.	3946	2503	1809	1490	1108	937	869	1033	1193	.
2 AUSTRIA	-	-	-	-	-	-	-	-	-	.	1106	766	876	1835	.
3 BELGIUM	16991	13787	11280	8653	7964	7401	4332	3112	2633	1807	1801	1474	1225	1100	.
4 BULGARIA	-	-	-	-	-	.	.	.	.	.	.	.	5004	5495	.
5 CANADA	-	-	-	-	2965	1115	660	497	548	445	437	495	460	533	.
6 CHILE	-	1695	658	2030	784	.	.	1672	1394	1324	599	1251	1583	1878	.
7 CZECHOSLOVAKIA	-	-	-	6533	3310	6503	4442	3299	.	.	966	1300	3990	4168	.
8 DENMARK	7514	6707	5142	4880	4311	3837	3420	2812	1959	464	423	588	1270	1310	.
9 EIRE	-	-	-	-	20950	17413	14074	11550	.	.	4851	4251	5197	5310	.
10 FINLAND	-	-	-	-	-	-	-	.	.	.	163	213	522	621	.
11 FRANCE	-	-	-	-	.	.	.	.	.	669	542	465	460	434	.
12 GREECE	-	-	-	-	.	.	.	.	-	-	-	852	1900	1961	.
13 HUNGARY	-	-	-	.	.	.	2736	1675	1379	.	355	601	525	840	.
14 ICELAND	-	-	13064	5385	4163	2021	2508	1932	.	.	-	-	776	649	.
15 ITALY	.	.	.	.	.	.	.	.	.	.	3629	3646	3748	3324	.
16 JAPAN	8010	8809	19160	20283	16282	10734	10160	10354	-	5287	2873	1462	1023	713	.
17 NETHERLANDS	8171	7335	6065	5948	5387	5513	3585	3223	3161	1932	1491	1376	1230	1143	.
18 NEW ZEALAND	-	9209	7354	6770	5759	.	.	1487	1216	790	1419	1818	2022	2150	.
19 NORWAY	8521	7877	5617	4885	3924	3547	2647	1821	.	.	750	656	569	477	.
20 POLAND	-	-	-	-	-	-	-	-	-	-	.	351	397	544	.
21 PORTUGAL	3512	3162	2910	3098	2934	3809	.	.	.	.	2978	2980	3806	3546	.
22 ROMANIA	-	-	-	-	-	-	-	-	-	-	-	1998	4145	3330	.
23 SPAIN	24643	18785	15020	15771	11699	10174	12088	9729	.	.	4544	3715	3499	2926	.
24 SWEDEN	-	-	2909	2197	1449	1374	917	707	534	396	449	365	393	541	.
25 SWITZERLAND	15610	15610	11347	11347	4229	4152	4439	3441	2249	1410	921	728	635	652	.
26 TURKEY	-	-	-	-	-	-	-	-	-	-	-	2382	1706	1328	1469
27 UK ENGLAND AND WALES	.	.	.	.	18387	12585	7573	6741	7532	6289	5715	4497	4489	3768	.
28 UK NORTHERN IRELAND	-	-	-	-	17035	13359	.	.	.	7307	4405	4394	4834	5363	.
29 UK SCOTLAND	.	.	.	.	.	.	.	.	.	4869	3883	3389	3903	3178	.
30 USA	9530	5475	3508	2513	1824	1130	680	524	400	243	184	173	203	224	.
31 YUGOSLAVIA	-	-	-	-	-	-	-	-	-	-	.	.	1866	1027	.

- NO MORTALITY DATA ARE AVAILABLE FOR EVEN A BROADER GROUP OF CAUSES FOR THIS DISEASE

. MORTALITY DATA ARE PRESENTED FOR A BROADER GROUP OF CAUSES FOR THIS DISEASE

0 VALUE<0.5

THE STANDARD MORTALITY RATIOS WERE DERIVED WITH A FACTOR OF 10000

SERIAL MORTALITY TABLES FOR VARIOUS COUNTRIES 1901-1975

TABLE 105 : BRONCHITIS - CHRONIC AND UNQUALIFIED : PERSONS

	1901-	1906-	1911-	1916-	1921-	1926-	1931-	1936-	1941-	1946-	1951-	1956-	1961-	1966-	1971-75
1 AUSTRALIA	-	8798	9021	7941	.	4318	2907	2259	1925	1640	2056	2565	4019	4711	.
2 AUSTRIA	-	-	-	-	-	.	.	.	-	.	1472	1222	1546	3458	.
3 BELGIUM	19261	15943	13263	10397	9477	9134	5829	4666	4270	3280	3308	2959	2638	2682	.
4 BULGARIA	-	-	-	-	-	.	.	.	.	.	.	.	7142	7764	.
5 CANADA	3387	2333	3308	2372	2706	1070	630	535	679	607	720	1060	1239	1604	.
6 CHILE	-	2221	928	2310	783	.	.	1914	1570	1480	719	1556	2047	2365	.
7 CZECHOSLOVAKIA	-	-	-	7389	3772	7586	5321	4248	.	.	1367	2209	7138	7702	.
8 DENMARK	8137	7382	5504	5263	4247	4016	3621	3034	2135	562	529	840	2257	2620	.
9 EIRE	-	-	-	-	20687	17110	13937	12074	.	.	6321	6145	8349	9114	.
10 FINLAND	-	-	-	-	-	-	-	.	.	.	328	646	1706	2184	.
11 FRANCE	16942	10819	9330	8089	.	.	.	.	.	945	795	711	729	734	.
12 GREECE	-	-	-	-	.	.	.	.	-	-	-	1246	3244	3402	.
13 HUNGARY	-	-	-	.	.	.	3149	1962	1617	.	524	886	928	1514	.
14 ICELAND	-	-	11975	6780	5206	2180	2803	2131	.	.	-	-	1206	868	.
15 ITALY	-	-	-	-	-	-	-	-	-	-	4215	4905	5583	5417	.
16 JAPAN	8762	9525	20561	21886	18227	12369	11845	12115	-	6343	3437	1756	1213	876	.
17 NETHERLANDS	9096	8068	6760	6638	5959	6320	4012	3609	3464	2242	2199	2352	2447	2613	.
18 NEW ZEALAND	-	8621	6844	7014	6294	.	.	2221	1834	1330	3397	4298	5393	5625	.
19 NORWAY	8765	7795	5527	4824	3955	3258	2475	1787	.	.	769	732	790	821	.
20 POLAND	-	-	-	-	-	-	-	-	-	-	.	493	646	1067	.
21 PORTUGAL	4120	3830	3732	4093	3971	5095	.	.	.	.	4347	4593	5743	5633	.
22 ROMANIA	-	-	-	-	-	-	-	.	-	.	-	2643	4889	3991	.
23 SPAIN	26908	20986	17164	18090	14372	13090	15425	12784	.	.	5987	5051	4863	4102	.
24 SWEDEN	-	-	2879	2142	1478	1325	838	696	496	386	510	435	572	766	.
25 SWITZERLAND	15214	15214	11508	11508	4464	4409	4663	3744	2526	1484	1178	1081	1234	1524	.
26 TURKEY	-	-	-	-	-	-	.	.	.	-	-	3135	2236	1719	1702
27 UK ENGLAND AND WALES	.	.	.	.	21022	14714	9135	9062	11166	10276	10453	9608	10251	9165	.
28 UK NORTHERN IRELAND	-	-	-	-	16780	13533	.	.	.	8816	6455	7474	9255	10222	.
29 UK SCOTLAND	.	.	.	.	.	.	.	.	.	7859	6821	7358	8849	7933	.
30 USA	8755	4990	3224	2326	1758	1118	720	602	504	265	288	333	459	542	.
31 YUGOSLAVIA	-	-	-	-	-	-	-	-	-	-	.	.	2747	1605	.

- NO MORTALITY DATA ARE AVAILABLE FOR EVEN A BROADER GROUP OF CAUSES FOR THIS DISEASE

. MORTALITY DATA ARE PRESENTED FOR A BROADER GROUP OF CAUSES FOR THIS DISEASE

0 VALUE<0.5

THE STANDARD MORTALITY RATIOS WERE DERIVED WITH A FACTOR OF 10000

SERIAL MORTALITY TABLES FOR VARIOUS COUNTRIES 1901-1975

TABLE 106 : "BRONCHITIS" - ALL FORMS : MALES

	1901-	1906-	1911-	1916-	1921-	1926-	1931-	1936-	1941-	1946-	1951-	1956-	1961-	1966-	1971-75
1 AUSTRALIA	-	12350	12104	10436	7154	5650	3802	3111	2763	2457	3621	4721	7515	11520	12829
2 AUSTRIA	-	-	-	-	-	-	-	-	-	3109	2653	2582	3166	7921	6556
3 BELGIUM	-	-	-	-	.	.	.	.	.	.	5695	4753	4356	6597	8066
4 BULGARIA	-	-	-	-	-	4351	2699	2852	2699	1118	963	3133	9127	12039	12099
5 CANADA	-	-	-	-	3233	1619	1107	853	1066	991	1368	1911	2141	4238	5896
6 CHILE	-	12055	5995	7804	7294	5713	5271	3610	2394	2030	3364	4589	5227	6449	7128
7 CZECHOSLOVAKIA	-	-	-	.	.	.	.	.	3238	2710	2243	3610	11130	15966	16127
8 DENMARK	12694	12009	8896	8347	5449	4914	4604	4013	.	.	1091	1429	3368	5378	6960
9 EIRE	-	-	-	-	.	.	.	13946	11320	7993	8137	8097	11414	15726	14956
10 FINLAND	-	-	-	-	-	-	-	.	1067	939	1597	2683	4133	7262	9396
11 FRANCE	-	-	-	-	8149	7919	5294	4012	2330	1579	1291	1167	1198	2286	3270
12 GREECE	-	-	-	-	6111	5368	4923	3956	-	-	-	1406	2681	5241	6164
13 HUNGARY	-	-	-	.	.	.	4129	2817	2161	888	534	1535	1630	4273	7356
14 ICELAND	-	-	.	.	.	.	.	.	2879	1124	-	-	2265	1158	3208
15 ITALY	52939	43723	39813	34776	21344	14511	10774	10603	7740	3943	5405	6689	8085	10414	10194
16 JAPAN	.	.	.	.	.	.	15811	15732	-	14463	8062	4893	3123	4978	5272
17 NETHERLANDS	21128	17138	13497	12879	.	.	.	.	.	3497	3228	3521	3744	5834	8040
18 NEW ZEALAND	-	.	.	.	7882	7103	4192	3534	.	2981	6200	7345	9289	12060	13319
19 NORWAY	.	.	11120	10048	6909	4162	2882	2368	1721	1208	1092	1042	1160	2121	3366
20 POLAND	-	-	-	-	-	-	-	-	-	-	.	1381	1460	5575	9931
21 PORTUGAL	24450	24009	18794	24227	18461	14176	12309	10426	10433	7073	8345	9032	9981	9335	13182
22 ROMANIA	-	-	-	-	-	-	-	-	-	-	-	3569	5768	10815	18434
23 SPAIN	70289	65702	58060	58252	48536	41086	27361	23203	17578	11941	8869	7437	6935	9306	10638
24 SWEDEN	-	-	.	.	.	.	.	.	.	.	994	884	1106	1892	3147
25 SWITZERLAND	.	.	.	.	5414	5805	.	.	.	.	1743	1708	2112	4300	6083
26 TURKEY	-	-	-	-	-	-	-	-	-	-	-	4081	3499	2702	2156
27 UK ENGLAND AND WALES	47314	35114	40140	38874	29115	20529	13301	14408	18644	17098	17883	17256	18791	18770	15794
28 UK NORTHERN IRELAND	-	-	-	-	.	.	15984	14305	12854	10964	9058	10907	14244	17442	15496
29 UK SCOTLAND	47189	38176	37728	35827	28096	23798	18484	17688	13875	12003	11281	13056	15819	16318	14639
30 USA	18537	10321	6409	4896	2557	1577	1031	901	745	666	682	782	952	3849	4620
31 YUGOSLAVIA	-	-	-	-	-	-	-	-	-	-	.	.	4142	4645	6474

- NO MORTALITY DATA ARE AVAILABLE FOR EVEN A BROADER GROUP OF CAUSES FOR THIS DISEASE
. MORTALITY DATA ARE PRESENTED FOR A BROADER GROUP OF CAUSES FOR THIS DISEASE
0 VALUE<0.5
THE STANDARD MORTALITY RATIOS WERE DERIVED WITH A FACTOR OF 10000

SERIAL MORTALITY TABLES FOR VARIOUS COUNTRIES 1901-1975

TABLE 106 : "BRONCHITIS" - ALL FORMS : FEMALES

	1901-	1906-	1911-	1916-	1921-	1926-	1931-	1936-	1941-	1946-	1951-	1956-	1961-	1966-	1971-75
1 AUSTRALIA	-	10972	11004	9450	6762	4859	3163	2253	1833	1312	1205	1059	1188	2116	2608
2 AUSTRIA	-	-	-	-	-	-	-	-	-	1807	1513	1244	1339	2820	2589
3 BELGIUM	-	-	-	-	.	.	.	.	.	.	2146	1527	1259	1540	1914
4 BULGARIA	-	-	-	-	-	3015	1935	1477	1314	539	644	1421	4739	6164	5927
5 CANADA	-	-	-	-	3813	1644	1177	769	763	652	779	761	608	1009	1353
6 CHILE	-	9530	4637	6423	5876	4146	4108	2789	1860	1617	2795	3328	3612	4233	4069
7 CZECHOSLOVAKIA	-	-	-	.	.	.	.	.	2054	1686	1284	1507	4009	5362	5330
8 DENMARK	9735	9202	7192	6804	5409	4515	4212	3690	.	.	754	894	1346	1837	2161
9 EIRE	-	-	-	-	.	.	.	13931	9593	6241	5344	4501	5234	7019	6290
10 FINLAND	-	-	-	-	-	-	-	.	574	430	862	1332	1313	1405	1496
11 FRANCE	-	-	-	-	5354	5169	3209	2314	1306	840	609	519	504	847	1145
12 GREECE	-	-	-	-	4777	4033	3854	3213	-	-	-	1101	2105	3186	3494
13 HUNGARY	-	-	-	.	.	.	3131	2064	1527	535	289	745	679	1591	2767
14 ICELAND	-	-	.	.	.	.	.	.	2254	1281	-	-	1096	982	1483
15 ITALY	51661	42132	38328	34251	20357	13612	10270	9848	6986	3468	4120	3940	4021	4264	3715
16 JAPAN	.	.	.	.	.	.	11843	11653	-	10899	6241	3982	2638	3171	3014
17 NETHERLANDS	17012	14256	10907	10488	.	.	.	.	.	2490	1836	1567	1283	1544	1884
18 NEW ZEALAND	-	.	.	.	7828	6108	3518	2750	.	1521	2182	2315	2298	3384	4058
19 NORWAY	.	.	10164	8953	6272	4497	3254	2464	1908	1236	987	828	672	871	1340
20 POLAND	-	-	-	-	-	-	-	-	-	-	.	728	658	1813	2961
21 PORTUGAL	17680	16917	12724	16134	11831	8715	6982	5849	5673	3977	4402	4347	4714	4099	5928
22 ROMANIA	-	-	-	-	-	-	-	-	-	-	-	2048	4041	7756	13187
23 SPAIN	57631	51308	44399	45337	34950	28134	17954	14436	10817	7167	5319	4226	3827	4931	4941
24 SWEDEN	-	-	.	.	.	.	.	.	.	.	821	696	699	1057	1380
25 SWITZERLAND	.	.	.	.	4575	5129	.	.	.	.	1114	846	722	1139	1531
26 TURKEY	-	-	-	-	-	-	-	-	-	-	-	2528	2100	1784	1457
27 UK ENGLAND AND WALES	44850	33566	32988	30163	23556	15955	9982	9055	10002	7902	6855	5114	4942	4601	3846
28 UK NORTHERN IRELAND	-	-	-	-	.	.	17279	13690	10311	8133	4905	4499	4884	5448	4558
29 UK SCOTLAND	37490	32964	30165	27650	21520	18555	14035	12195	7785	6298	4702	3977	4249	3910	3651
30 USA	18953	10876	6906	5218	2729	1643	964	731	514	413	394	360	336	888	1098
31 YUGOSLAVIA	-	-	-	-	-	-	-	-	-	-	.	.	2111	2087	2714

- NO MORTALITY DATA ARE AVAILABLE FOR EVEN A BROADER GROUP OF CAUSES FOR THIS DISEASE

. MORTALITY DATA ARE PRESENTED FOR A BROADER GROUP OF CAUSES FOR THIS DISEASE

0 VALUE<0.5

THE STANDARD MORTALITY RATIOS WERE DERIVED WITH A FACTOR OF 10000

SERIAL MORTALITY TABLES FOR VARIOUS COUNTRIES 1901-1975

TABLE 107 : TONSILS AND ADENOIDS - HYPERTROPHY : MALES

	1901-	1906-	1911-	1916-	1921-	1926-	1931-	1936-	1941-	1946-	1951-	1956-	1961-	1966-	1971-75
1 AUSTRALIA	-	.	.	.	.	9058	.	.	.	.	1873	1097	519	318	184
2 AUSTRIA	-	-	-	-	-	-	-	-	-	.	515	570	396	312	625
3 BELGIUM	-	-	-	-	.	.	.	.	.	.	581	305	161	313	131
4 BULGARIA	-	-	-	-	-	.	.	.	.	.	.	.	.	.	.
5 CANADA	-	-	-	-	.	368	7522	9073	.	1765	1368	912	430	216	90
6 CHILE	-	.	.	.	.	.	.	.	.	.	0	188	161	144	70
7 CZECHOSLOVAKIA	-	-	-	.	.	.	.	.	.	.	192	0	54	90	18
8 DENMARK	.	.	.	.	.	.	23608	24197	15577	8387	167	274	212	0	0
9 EIRE	-	-	-	-	.	.	.	.	.	.	78	319	159	78	298
10 FINLAND	-	-	-	-	-	-	-	25825	14865	4375	234	114	113	0	58
11 FRANCE	-	-	-	-	.	.	.	.	.	457	306	189	157	111	73
12 GREECE	-	-	-	-	.	.	.	.	-	-	-	279	269	86	84
13 HUNGARY	-	-	-	.	.	.	.	.	.	.	133	255	52	26	0
14 ICELAND	-	-	.	.	.	.	.	.	.	.	-	-	0	0	0
15 ITALY	-	-	-	-	-	-	-	-	-	-	377	444	538	352	111
16 JAPAN	.	.	.	.	.	.	.	.	-	166	89	81	71	68	31
17 NETHERLANDS	.	.	.	.	.	.	.	.	.	487	468	423	419	359	184
18 NEW ZEALAND	-	.	.	.	.	.	.	.	.	1401	1009	498	357	419	79
19 NORWAY	.	.	.	.	.	.	.	.	.	.	363	138	66	0	123
20 POLAND	-	-	-	-	-	-	-	-	-	-	.	20	32	48	24
21 PORTUGAL	.	.	.	.	.	.	.	.	.	.	872	476	574	138	229
22 ROMANIA	-	-	-	-	-	-	-	-	-	-	-	0	0	0	0
23 SPAIN	.	.	.	.	.	.	.	.	.	.	598	186	0	0	7
24 SWEDEN	-	-	.	.	.	.	.	.	.	.	138	34	66	0	0
25 SWITZERLAND	.	.	.	.	.	.	23122	21150	14321	8085	731	492	315	585	531
26 TURKEY	-	-	-	-	-	-	-	-	-	-	-	680	311	130	121
27 UK ENGLAND AND WALES	7969	7110	8468	7963	7767	12373	16883	12541	.	869	657	413	217	82	108
28 UK NORTHERN IRELAND	-	-	-	-	.	.	.	.	.	907	524	0	0	156	0
29 UK SCOTLAND	7070	5812	.	.	.	.	.	.	.	507	450	247	96	143	48
30 USA	8363	6804	.	.	.	.	.	.	.	1513	1127	599	347	213	103
31 YUGOSLAVIA	-	-	-	-	-	-	-	-	-	-	.	.	52	38	73

- NO MORTALITY DATA ARE AVAILABLE FOR EVEN A BROADER GROUP OF CAUSES FOR THIS DISEASE

. MORTALITY DATA ARE PRESENTED FOR A BROADER GROUP OF CAUSES FOR THIS DISEASE

0 VALUE<0.5

THE STANDARD MORTALITY RATIOS WERE DERIVED WITH A FACTOR OF 10000

SERIAL MORTALITY TABLES FOR VARIOUS COUNTRIES 1901-1975

TABLE 107 : TONSILS AND ADENOIDS - HYPERTROPHY : FEMALES

	1901-	1906-	1911-	1916-	1921-	1926-	1931-	1936-	1941-	1946-	1951-	1956-	1961-	1966-	1971-75
1 AUSTRALIA	-	.	.	.	.	9243	.	.	.	.	1410	1060	369	159	275
2 AUSTRIA	-	-	-	-	-	-	-	-	-	.	400	268	317	304	334
3 BELGIUM	-	-	-	-	.	.	.	.	.	.	209	186	0	346	74
4 BULGARIA	-	-	-	-	-	.	.	.	.	.	.	.	.	.	.
5 CANADA	-	-	-	-	.	512	8201	8946	.	2015	1334	818	464	184	56
6 CHILE	-	.	.	.	.	.	.	.	.	.	0	275	236	23	114
7 CZECHOSLOVAKIA	-	-	-	.	.	.	.	.	.	.	153	18	35	68	0
8 DENMARK	.	.	.	.	.	.	29404	22237	17193	6108	221	0	157	0	0
9 EIRE	-	-	-	-	.	.	.	.	.	.	0	406	80	78	225
10 FINLAND	-	-	-	-	-	-	-	28963	19288	3752	55	212	105	52	53
11 FRANCE	-	-	-	-	.	.	.	.	.	297	227	159	73	70	64
12 GREECE	-	-	-	-	.	.	.	.	-	-	-	302	173	111	0
13 HUNGARY	-	-	-	.	.	.	.	.	.	.	0	0	24	49	95
14 ICELAND	-	-	.	.	.	.	.	.	.	.	-	-	0	0	0
15 ITALY	-	-	-	-	-	-	-	-	-	-	354	298	382	231	101
16 JAPAN	.	.	.	.	.	.	.	.	-	82	67	64	56	56	26
17 NETHERLANDS	.	.	.	.	.	.	.	.	.	367	448	381	298	169	145
18 NEW ZEALAND	-	.	.	.	.	.	.	.	.	0	794	502	359	83	158
19 NORWAY	.	.	.	.	.	.	.	.	.	.	215	342	66	63	0
20 POLAND	-	-	-	-	-	-	-	-	-	-	.	0	15	15	37
21 PORTUGAL	.	.	.	.	.	.	.	.	.	.	818	708	766	51	261
22 ROMANIA	-	-	-	-	-	-	-	-	-	-	-	0	0	0	0
23 SPAIN	.	.	.	.	.	.	.	.	.	.	482	176	0	0	7
24 SWEDEN	-	-	.	.	.	.	.	.	.	.	103	0	99	31	0
25 SWITZERLAND	.	.	.	.	.	.	20940	21674	12673	8395	738	603	340	474	308
26 TURKEY	-	-	-	-	-	-	-	-	-	-	-	362	185	223	40
27 UK ENGLAND AND WALES	6827	5543	7207	7041	6838	12949	18720	11462	.	595	488	275	146	72	57
28 UK NORTHERN IRELAND	-	-	-	-	.	.	.	.	.	883	845	0	0	0	0
29 UK SCOTLAND	5231	5700	.	.	.	.	.	.	.	708	324	228	222	88	0
30 USA	7863	6131	.	.	.	.	.	.	.	1305	1052	528	318	144	88
31 YUGOSLAVIA	-	-	-	-	-	-	-	-	-	-	.	.	25	49	94

- NO MORTALITY DATA ARE AVAILABLE FOR EVEN A BROADER GROUP OF CAUSES FOR THIS DISEASE

. MORTALITY DATA ARE PRESENTED FOR A BROADER GROUP OF CAUSES FOR THIS DISEASE

0 VALUE<0.5

THE STANDARD MORTALITY RATIOS WERE DERIVED WITH A FACTOR OF 10000

SERIAL MORTALITY TABLES FOR VARIOUS COUNTRIES 1901-1975

TABLE 108 : EMPYEMA AND LUNG ABSCESS : MALES

	1901-	1906-	1911-	1916-	1921-	1926-	1931-	1936-	1941-	1946-	1951-	1956-	1961-	1966-	1971-75
1 AUSTRALIA	-	.	.	.	.	6675	4259	3924	2658	1921	2454	2118	1288	848	1069
2 AUSTRIA	-	-	-	-	-	-	-	-	-	.	13430	13183	8073	7192	7532
3 BELGIUM	-	-	-	-	.	.	.	.	.	.	6515	4060	4494	3234	1281
4 BULGARIA	-	-	-	-	-	.	.	.	.	.	.	.	4302	3200	2327
5 CANADA	-	-	-	-	.	.	.	.	.	3180	3828	3210	1939	1697	1700
6 CHILE	-	.	.	.	.	.	.	30870	21474	17210	9046	9288	6235	5021	4000
7 CZECHOSLOVAKIA	-	-	-	.	.	.	.	.	.	.	9453	7395	5000	3249	2414
8 DENMARK	.	.	.	.	.	.	.	.	.	.	3458	2800	2693	2740	2685
9 EIRE	-	-	-	-	.	5357	5065	6355	.	.	2817	2329	1774	1084	1137
10 FINLAND	-	-	-	-	-	-	-	.	28643	17125	5041	3954	2465	1947	1750
11 FRANCE	-	-	-	-	.	.	.	.	.	10196	8093	5786	4509	3664	3265
12 GREECE	-	-	-	-	.	.	.	.	-	-	-	3036	2170	2041	1546
13 HUNGARY	-	-	-	.	.	.	.	.	.	.	13433	11995	9608	7139	5887
14 ICELAND	-	-	.	.	.	.	.	.	.	.	-	-	3077	1429	2000
15 ITALY	-	-	-	-	-	-	-	-	-	-	10036	6726	4502	2939	1570
16 JAPAN	.	.	.	.	.	.	.	.	-	19609	12475	9371	7294	5745	4858
17 NETHERLANDS	.	.	.	.	.	.	.	.	6973	2430	1752	1335	959	1014	904
18 NEW ZEALAND	-	.	.	.	.	.	.	10417	7355	5370	2949	2647	1803	2371	769
19 NORWAY	.	.	12579	15783	10925	19282	19588	17333	.	.	1771	1246	898	954	914
20 POLAND	-	-	-	-	-	-	-	-	-	-	.	8066	6669	5551	5054
21 PORTUGAL	.	.	.	.	.	.	.	.	.	.	10156	8303	7765	6137	4921
22 ROMANIA	-	-	-	-	-	-	-	-	-	-	-	11087	11668	10200	12530
23 SPAIN	.	.	.	.	.	.	.	.	.	.	12863	6440	4832	3598	2413
24 SWEDEN	-	-	.	.	.	.	.	.	.	.	1984	1733	1898	1421	1756
25 SWITZERLAND	.	.	.	.	.	.	16090	13031	17340	9942	3828	3458	2954	2369	1886
26 TURKEY	-	-	-	-	-	-	-	-	-	-	-	9385	6609	3811	1159
27 UK ENGLAND AND WALES	.	.	8643	8492	9708	7417	6768	5573	5234	2975	2067	1672	1556	1185	1162
28 UK NORTHERN IRELAND	-	-	-	-	.	.	.	.	.	2083	2476	1682	893	940	1186
29 UK SCOTLAND	.	.	.	.	.	.	.	.	.	2100	1778	1683	1980	1411	1439
30 USA	.	.	.	.	.	.	.	.	.	2764	2269	2406	2276	2605	2649
31 YUGOSLAVIA	-	-	-	-	-	-	-	-	-	-	.	.	3534	2814	1858

- NO MORTALITY DATA ARE AVAILABLE FOR EVEN A BROADER GROUP OF CAUSES FOR THIS DISEASE

. MORTALITY DATA ARE PRESENTED FOR A BROADER GROUP OF CAUSES FOR THIS DISEASE

0 VALUE<0.5

THE STANDARD MORTALITY RATIOS WERE DERIVED WITH A FACTOR OF 1000

SERIAL MORTALITY TABLES FOR VARIOUS COUNTRIES 1901-1975

TABLE 108 : EMPYEMA AND LUNG ABSCESS : FEMALES

	1901-	1906-	1911-	1916-	1921-	1926-	1931-	1936-	1941-	1946-	1951-	1956-	1961-	1966-	1971-75
1 AUSTRALIA	-	.	.	.	.	3240	2313	2208	1069	611	693	893	571	446	349
2 AUSTRIA	-	-	-	-	-	-	-	-	-	.	3977	5370	3109	2514	2863
3 BELGIUM	-	-	-	-	.	.	.	.	.	.	1672	1175	1150	1125	542
4 BULGARIA	-	-	-	-	-	.	.	.	.	.	.	.	965	770	707
5 CANADA	-	-	-	-	.	.	.	.	.	986	2148	1143	713	703	509
6 CHILE	-	.	.	.	.	.	.	13115	11078	7692	3464	5000	2966	2628	2166
7 CZECHOSLOVAKIA	-	-	-	.	.	.	.	.	.	.	4197	3100	1775	1041	819
8 DENMARK	.	.	.	.	.	.	.	.	.	.	1711	732	982	1023	949
9 EIRE	-	-	-	-	.	1590	2069	1709	.	.	1098	895	1065	595	500
10 FINLAND	-	-	-	-	-	-	-	.	9209	3974	1158	1271	888	845	670
11 FRANCE	-	-	-	-	.	.	.	.	.	3126	2409	1861	1304	1179	1148
12 GREECE	-	-	-	-	.	.	.	.	-	-	-	933	980	581	472
13 HUNGARY	-	-	-	.	.	.	.	.	.	.	4000	5006	3786	2786	2545
14 ICELAND	-	-	.	.	.	.	.	.	.	.	-	-	2143	1250	1765
15 ITALY	-	-	-	-	-	-	-	-	-	-	2202	1579	972	674	417
16 JAPAN	.	.	.	.	.	.	.	.	-	5992	3497	2572	2086	1735	1505
17 NETHERLANDS	.	.	.	.	.	.	.	.	2956	1320	837	575	405	437	350
18 NEW ZEALAND	-	.	.	.	.	.	.	2336	2602	1950	1205	1882	1019	1076	823
19 NORWAY	.	.	5784	6340	3726	9343	9737	7918	.	.	651	687	575	175	211
20 POLAND	-	-	-	-	-	-	-	-	-	-	.	3225	2504	1783	1481
21 PORTUGAL	.	.	.	.	.	.	.	.	.	.	2164	2682	2153	1388	1629
22 ROMANIA	-	-	-	-	-	-	-	-	-	-	-	4216	4184	3513	4679
23 SPAIN	.	.	.	.	.	.	.	.	.	.	5819	2081	1689	1350	604
24 SWEDEN	-	-	.	.	.	.	.	.	.	.	797	652	816	723	754
25 SWITZERLAND	.	.	.	.	.	.	11881	9797	8833	4928	1656	988	565	832	477
26 TURKEY	-	-	-	-	-	-	-	-	-	-	-	3561	2256	1654	1016
27 UK ENGLAND AND WALES	.	.	3957	3334	4144	2734	2589	1942	1638	945	853	687	594	515	496
28 UK NORTHERN IRELAND	-	-	-	-	.	.	.	.	.	1852	650	234	735	759	800
29 UK SCOTLAND	.	.	.	.	.	.	.	.	.	1486	757	1051	665	371	715
30 USA	.	.	.	.	.	.	.	.	.	898	749	816	704	848	928
31 YUGOSLAVIA	-	-	-	-	-	-	-	-	-	-	.	.	1059	756	512

\- NO MORTALITY DATA ARE AVAILABLE FOR EVEN A BROADER GROUP OF CAUSES FOR THIS DISEASE

. MORTALITY DATA ARE PRESENTED FOR A BROADER GROUP OF CAUSES FOR THIS DISEASE

0 VALUE<0.5

THE STANDARD MORTALITY RATIOS WERE DERIVED WITH A FACTOR OF 1000

SERIAL MORTALITY TABLES FOR VARIOUS COUNTRIES 1901-1975

TABLE 109 : PLEURISY : MALES

	1901-	1906-	1911-	1916-	1921-	1926-	1931-	1936-	1941-	1946-	1951-	1956-	1961-	1966-	1971-75
1 AUSTRALIA	-	7058	6411	5057	.	4791	3593	3424	2346	1264	176	174	182	154	.
2 AUSTRIA	-	-	-	-	-	-	-	-	-	3692	1547	883	873	1301	.
3 BELGIUM	-	-	-	-	.	.	.	.	.	.	1092	757	715	508	.
4 BULGARIA	-	-	-	-	-	.	.	.	.	.	.	.	210	122	.
5 CANADA	-	-	-	-	.	.	.	.	712	630	336	240	204	210	.
6 CHILE	-	4154	.	.	.	.	.	4079	2488	1895	1765	951	524	404	.
7 CZECHOSLOVAKIA	-	-	-	.	.	.	.	.	.	.	1330	1304	1059	833	.
8 DENMARK	.	.	.	.	.	.	.	.	.	.	299	287	129	79	.
9 EIRE	-	-	-	-	.	3287	2901	2474	.	.	584	540	473	223	.
10 FINLAND	-	-	-	-	-	-	-	.	2675	1744	586	396	114	116	.
11 FRANCE	-	-	-	-	.	.	.	.	.	1275	1007	714	659	609	.
12 GREECE	-	-	-	-	.	.	.	.	-	-	-	491	567	534	.
13 HUNGARY	-	-	-	.	.	.	.	.	.	.	1391	1171	410	151	.
14 ICELAND	-	-	.	.	.	.	.	.	.	.	-	-	0	0	.
15 ITALY	11207	10348	9905	11880	9219	8068	7241	7259	7606	4030	1260	448	315	294	.
16 JAPAN	.	25936	23805	28197	36079	.	.	.	-	3725	1610	808	456	325	.
17 NETHERLANDS	7059	5411	.	.	.	.	.	.	.	423	335	155	93	65	.
18 NEW ZEALAND	-	.	.	.	.	.	.	1786	1396	773	250	306	118	63	.
19 NORWAY	5254	4818	.	.	.	.	.	.	.	.	93	107	56	11	.
20 POLAND	-	-	-	-	-	-	-	-	-	-	.	494	470	303	.
21 PORTUGAL	.	.	.	.	.	.	.	.	.	.	1990	1130	820	773	.
22 ROMANIA	-	-	-	-	-	-	-	-	-	-	-	426	361	275	.
23 SPAIN	9249	7636	.	.	.	.	.	.	.	.	1388	707	450	325	.
24 SWEDEN	-	-	.	.	.	.	2893	3226	1804	805	143	99	103	86	.
25 SWITZERLAND	.	.	.	.	.	.	.	.	.	.	623	244	281	230	.
26 TURKEY	-	-	-	-	-	-	-	-	-	-	-	5619	2568	1477	1225
27 UK ENGLAND AND WALES	.	.	3989	3478	2645	2223	1448	1019	929	458	200	119	118	110	.
28 UK NORTHERN IRELAND	-	-	-	-	.	.	.	.	.	789	391	109	188	50	.
29 UK SCOTLAND	.	.	.	.	.	.	.	.	.	897	463	222	212	172	.
30 USA	9989	6880	.	.	.	.	.	.	.	173	132	104	90	86	.
31 YUGOSLAVIA	-	-	-	-	-	-	-	-	-	-	.	.	118	87	.

- NO MORTALITY DATA ARE AVAILABLE FOR EVEN A BROADER GROUP OF CAUSES FOR THIS DISEASE

. MORTALITY DATA ARE PRESENTED FOR A BROADER GROUP OF CAUSES FOR THIS DISEASE

0 VALUE<0.5

THE STANDARD MORTALITY RATIOS WERE DERIVED WITH A FACTOR OF 100

SERIAL MORTALITY TABLES FOR VARIOUS COUNTRIES 1901-1975

TABLE 109 : PLEURISY : FEMALES

	1901-	1906-	1911-	1916-	1921-	1926-	1931-	1936-	1941-	1946-	1951-	1956-	1961-	1966-	1971-75
1 AUSTRALIA	-	2390	3880	3750	.	2707	1950	1484	1174	575	102	115	97	71	.
2 AUSTRIA	-	-	-	-	-	-	-	-	-	2069	972	610	535	486	.
3 BELGIUM	-	-	-	-	.	.	.	.	.	.	694	440	402	332	.
4 BULGARIA	-	-	-	-	-	.	.	.	.	.	.	.	151	87	.
5 CANADA	-	-	-	-	.	.	.	.	500	431	211	194	136	108	.
6 CHILE	-	2286	.	.	.	.	.	1919	1250	1285	966	453	324	216	.
7 CZECHOSLOVAKIA	-	-	-	.	.	.	.	.	.	.	919	973	675	477	.
8 DENMARK	.	.	.	.	.	.	.	.	.	.	276	178	91	85	.
9 EIRE	-	-	-	-	.	2292	1845	1645	.	.	297	221	126	96	.
10 FINLAND	-	-	-	-	-	-	-	.	1071	746	194	250	85	37	.
11 FRANCE	-	-	-	-	.	.	.	.	.	786	580	460	368	342	.
12 GREECE	-	-	-	-	.	.	.	.	-	-	-	185	314	327	.
13 HUNGARY	-	-	-	.	.	.	.	.	.	.	870	749	224	74	.
14 ICELAND	-	-	.	.	.	.	.	.	.	.	-	-	0	143	.
15 ITALY	7536	6532	6428	6905	6009	5279	4596	4323	3982	2200	763	254	164	152	.
16 JAPAN	.	20180	18796	22611	28752	.	.	.	-	2661	925	422	224	167	.
17 NETHERLANDS	3905	3565	.	.	.	.	.	.	.	493	272	137	57	57	.
18 NEW ZEALAND	-	.	.	.	.	.	.	952	800	582	111	107	105	72	.
19 NORWAY	2829	2835	.	.	.	.	.	.	.	.	91	25	57	25	.
20 POLAND	-	-	-	-	-	-	-	-	-	-	.	381	294	179	.
21 PORTUGAL	.	.	.	.	.	.	.	.	.	.	845	568	413	395	.
22 ROMANIA	-	-	-	-	-	-	-	-	-	-	-	269	206	191	.
23 SPAIN	7738	5591	.	.	.	.	.	.	.	.	781	387	288	205	.
24 SWEDEN	-	-	.	.	.	.	1679	1646	897	381	86	68	96	51	.
25 SWITZERLAND	.	.	.	.	.	.	.	.	.	.	408	208	152	134	.
26 TURKEY	-	-	-	-	-	-	-	-	-	-	-	3889	1853	1099	1115
27 UK ENGLAND AND WALES	.	.	2460	2121	1588	1269	820	538	493	243	93	71	65	60	.
28 UK NORTHERN IRELAND	-	-	-	-	.	.	.	.	.	227	214	169	125	0	.
29 UK SCOTLAND	.	.	.	.	.	.	.	.	.	455	281	164	149	109	.
30 USA	6854	4591	.	.	.	.	.	.	.	103	70	54	44	41	.
31 YUGOSLAVIA	-	-	-	-	-	-	-	-	-	-	.	.	71	23	.

\- NO MORTALITY DATA ARE AVAILABLE FOR EVEN A BROADER GROUP OF CAUSES FOR THIS DISEASE

. MORTALITY DATA ARE PRESENTED FOR A BROADER GROUP OF CAUSES FOR THIS DISEASE

0 VALUE<0.5

THE STANDARD MORTALITY RATIOS WERE DERIVED WITH A FACTOR OF 100

SERIAL MORTALITY TABLES FOR VARIOUS COUNTRIES 1901-1975

TABLE 110 RESPIRATORY DISEASE - ALL FORMS : MALES

	1901-	1906-	1911-	1916-	1921-	1926-	1931-	1936-	1941-	1946-	1951-	1956-	1961-	1966-	1971-75
1 AUSTRALIA	-	2051	2131	2819	1958	1777	1427	1247	1006	814	704	786	794	918	861
2 AUSTRIA	-	-	-	-	-	-	-	-	-	1203	901	845	769	912	661
3 BELGIUM	-	-	-	-	2867	3067	2483	2341	2035	1383	1016	880	814	952	837
4 BULGARIA	-	-	-	-	-	3912	3330	3033	3131	3121	2323	1867	1182	1391	1356
5 CANADA	-	-	-	-	2126	2073	1511	1371	935	702	590	626	562	619	647
6 CHILE	-	10280	9398	14068	15445	12190	12203	11413	8306	6968	5454	4997	3892	2988	2211
7 CZECHOSLOVAKIA	-	-	-	4236	3269	3743	2800	2497	2034	1631	1074	987	1090	1200	1173
8 DENMARK	3905	3642	2878	4506	2287	2169	1840	1432	889	788	379	354	439	530	576
9 EIRE	-	-	-	-	2641	2389	2347	2084	1605	1201	944	861	1069	1328	1306
10 FINLAND	-	-	-	-	-	-	-	2050	1456	1158	952	948	812	902	956
11 FRANCE	-	-	-	-	2221	2562	2233	2260	1832	1301	920	803	641	657	612
12 GREECE	-	-	-	-	4747	4756	4765	3884	-	-	-	595	621	718	671
13 HUNGARY	-	-	-	4381	3677	3141	2858	2496	2173	1892	1484	1239	635	578	564
14 ICELAND	-	-	3885	4146	4513	1914	1854	1661	1067	627	-	-	621	602	663
15 ITALY	-	-	-	-	-	-	-	-	-	-	1013	961	883	951	817
16 JAPAN	4438	4526	4271	6935	5430	5029	4799	4574	-	1831	1205	940	690	654	617
17 NETHERLANDS	3316	3561	2855	4187	2271	2121	1537	1336	1291	695	536	539	465	568	603
18 NEW ZEALAND	-	1705	1479	3290	1462	1464	962	1100	744	613	718	935	1087	1145	1016
19 NORWAY	1877	1715	1554	2754	1297	1227	1054	1089	991	684	432	445	464	560	655
20 POLAND	-	-	-	-	-	-	-	-	-	-	2255	1231	913	869	906
21 PORTUGAL	3106	3135	2393	5725	2808	3064	3254	2878	2632	1806	1726	1700	1687	1581	1344
22 ROMANIA	-	-	-	-	-	-	-	-	-	-	-	2108	1772	2004	1714
23 SPAIN	7276	6830	6036	8546	5470	4881	4631	4160	3308	2236	1707	1320	1040	979	1095
24 SWEDEN	-	-	1827	3044	1331	1394	1089	1056	642	432	422	451	442	509	353
25 SWITZERLAND	3537	3537	4079	4079	2250	2094	1828	1630	1069	762	549	571	496	578	562
26 TURKEY	-	-	-	-	-	-	-	-	-	-	-	4237	3094	1963	1667
27 UK ENGLAND AND WALES	4855	3857	4306	5392	3518	2864	2124	1895	1702	1403	1461	1432	1548	1595	1451
28 UK NORTHERN IRELAND	-	-	-	-	3407	2985	2536	2214	1796	1404	1059	1051	1216	1316	1317
29 UK SCOTLAND	5683	4744	4431	5098	3909	3629	2796	2416	1597	1260	1076	1191	1282	1319	1224
30 USA	5596	3750	2945	4627	2154	2101	1652	1412	876	566	463	551	593	660	630
31 YUGOSLAVIA	-	-	-	-	-	-	-	-	-	-	2747	2241	1053	783	748

\- NO MORTALITY DATA ARE AVAILABLE FOR EVEN A BROADER GROUP OF CAUSES FOR THIS DISEASE

. MORTALITY DA⁻A ARE PRESENTED FOR A BROADER GROUP OF CAUSES FOR THIS DISEASE

0 VALUE<0.5

THE STANDARD MORTALITY RATIOS WERE DERIVED WITH A FACTOR OF 1000

SERIAL MORTALITY TABLES FOR VARIOUS COUNTRIES 1901-1975

TABLE 110 : RESPIRATORY DISEASE - ALL FORMS : FEMALES

	1901-	1906-	1911-	1916-	1921-	1926-	1931-	1936-	1941-	1946-	1951-	1956-	1961-	1966-	1971-75
1 AUSTRALIA	-	1672	1619	2152	1486	1328	1063	857	715	563	379	363	310	330	289
2 AUSTRIA	-	-	-	-	-	-	-	-	-	768	557	482	428	441	339
3 BELGIUM	-	-	-	-	2146	2294	1773	1574	1285	846	496	351	305	358	310
4 BULGARIA	-	-	-	-	-	2885	2439	2003	2048	1930	1487	1309	787	891	831
5 CANADA	-	-	-	-	1985	1924	1397	1210	777	565	433	399	322	301	280
6 CHILE	-	8497	8026	12550	13372	10315	10138	9408	6784	5582	4297	3727	2865	2166	1517
7 CZECHOSLOVAKIA	-	-	-	3450	2448	2768	1978	1700	1365	1106	753	614	551	543	519
8 DENMARK	2518	2493	1918	2981	1927	1900	1560	1199	765	688	322	268	276	279	285
9 EIRE	-	-	-	-	2302	2148	2086	1324	1303	955	765	604	680	819	826
10 FINLAND	-	-	-	-	-	-	-	1280	847	672	647	536	439	423	432
11 FRANCE	-	-	-	-	1517	1763	1450	1482	1232	880	591	497	392	361	313
12 GREECE	-	-	-	-	3438	3570	3633	3019	-	-	-	450	493	531	477
13 HUNGARY	-	-	-	3801	2940	2465	2193	1802	1527	1205	894	764	346	278	248
14 ICELAND	-	-	2146	2525	2124	1117	1045	959	815	546	-	-	602	599	487
15 ITALY	-	-	-	-	-	-	-	-	-	-	756	643	519	497	389
16 JAPAN	3470	3695	3486	5879	4261	3750	3433	3271	-	1310	846	639	462	407	368
17 NETHERLANDS	2520	2782	2212	3281	1800	1702	1266	1083	1054	571	430	352	237	266	267
18 NEW ZEALAND	-	1578	1311	2451	1121	1066	720	706	510	435	412	510	564	591	524
19 NORWAY	1537	1427	1243	2104	1021	1044	950	967	840	685	415	438	438	475	520
20 POLAND	-	-	-	-	-	-	-	-	-	-	1160	660	470	391	389
21 PORTUGAL	2174	2187	1555	4255	1777	1974	2014	1733	1521	1068	998	966	925	856	688
22 ROMANIA	-	-	-	-	-	-	-	-	-	-	-	1361	1243	1408	1160
23 SPAIN	5999	5377	4586	6893	3888	3243	3062	2618	2070	1400	1110	840	656	585	637
24 SWEDEN	-	-	1424	2326	1113	1157	972	894	586	413	383	388	348	367	201
25 SWITZERLAND	3041	3041	3107	3107	1851	1622	1420	1214	798	578	407	368	281	289	253
26 TURKEY	-	-	-	-	-	-	-	-	-	-	-	3210	2331	1592	1468
27 UK ENGLAND AND WALES	4007	3184	2974	3752	2430	1905	1411	1127	944	728	698	613	669	721	713
28 UK NORTHERN IRELAND	-	-	-	-	3082	2640	2189	1870	1387	1121	756	619	687	691	686
29 UK SCOTLAND	3712	3229	2930	3435	2645	2401	1902	1549	921	743	564	506	508	535	528
30 USA	4676	3168	2488	3919	1833	1731	1308	1056	618	386	273	286	277	279	249
31 YUGOSLAVIA	-	-	-	-	-	-	-	-	-	-	2106	1682	725	493	444

- NO MORTALITY DATA ARE AVAILABLE FOR EVEN A BROADER GROUP OF CAUSES FOR THIS DISEASE

. MORTALITY DATA ARE PRESENTED FOR A BROADER GROUP OF CAUSES FOR THIS DISEASE

0 VALUE<0.5

THE STANDARD MORTALITY RATIOS WERE DERIVED WITH A FACTOR OF 1000

SERIAL MORTALITY TABLES FOR VARIOUS COUNTRIES 1901-1975

TABLE 110 : RESPIRATORY DISEASE - ALL FORMS : PERSONS

	1901-	1906-	1911-	1916-	1921-	1926-	1931-	1936-	1941-	1946-	1951-	1956-	1961-	1966-	1971-75
1 AUSTRALIA	-	1875	1890	2500	1729	1557	1246	1049	855	682	526	551	520	579	527
2 AUSTRIA	-	-	-	-	-	1399	1312	1619	-	953	701	629	561	619	457
3 BELGIUM	-	-	-	-	2482	2657	2106	1933	1637	1098	726	581	522	605	523
4 BULGARIA	-	-	-	-	-	3374	2862	2485	2546	2466	1856	1565	967	1118	1070
5 CANADA	2055	1407	1307	1565	2057	2000	1455	1292	857	634	511	510	438	448	441
6 CHILE	-	9339	8678	13276	14362	11203	11111	10349	7495	6227	4833	4299	3327	2536	1826
7 CZECHOSLOVAKIA	-	-	-	3805	2817	3204	2343	2053	1662	1337	894	775	775	811	780
8 DENMARK	3072	2952	2303	3593	2092	2024	1689	1307	824	736	349	308	351	391	412
9 EIRE	-	-	-	-	2465	2264	2213	1952	1451	1075	852	727	862	1053	1044
10 FINLAND	-	-	-	-	-	-	-	1606	1100	868	767	698	584	608	631
11 FRANCE	4398	2930	2569	2902	1822	2107	1783	1807	1477	1049	721	615	487	471	425
12 GREECE	-	-	-	-	4071	4141	4181	3441	-	-	-	655	826	912	861
13 HUNGARY	-	-	-	4080	3293	2787	2507	2127	1827	1513	1155	971	470	404	378
14 ICELAND	-	-	2852	3185	3103	1443	1378	1248	921	581	-	-	611	600	567
15 ITALY	-	-	-	-	-	-	-	-	-	-	872	784	677	688	565
16 JAPAN	3923	4089	3860	6381	4805	4337	4055	3861	-	1539	1004	770	561	514	476
17 NETHERLANDS	2891	3146	2514	3708	2024	1902	1396	1204	1168	630	481	440	343	403	414
18 NEW ZEALAND	-	1650	1404	2906	1301	1272	843	904	625	522	556	705	797	830	733
19 NORWAY	1693	1557	1383	2394	1144	1125	997	1021	907	684	422	441	449	513	579
20 POLAND	-	-	-	-	-	-	-	-	-	-	1611	1647	648	581	592
21 PORTUGAL	2586	2603	1920	4888	2216	2435	2531	2204	1977	1374	1290	1260	1232	1145	949
22 ROMANIA	-	-	-	-	-	-	-	7175	-	3126	-	1683	1470	1663	1398
23 SPAIN	6616	6062	5261	7661	4613	3979	3754	3284	2601	1754	1358	1039	817	749	827
24 SWEDEN	-	-	1603	2646	1210	1263	1025	968	612	422	401	417	391	431	268
25 SWITZERLAND	3269	3269	3541	3541	2026	1828	1597	1395	915	657	468	454	371	408	378
26 TURKEY	-	-	-	-	-	-	3396	3696	3558	-	-	3680	2682	1769	1566
27 UK ENGLAND AND WALES	4413	3504	3560	4468	2903	2320	1718	1454	1262	1010	1009	937	1008	1051	990
28 UK NORTHERN IRELAND	-	-	-	-	3230	2798	2348	2029	1575	1252	892	808	915	952	941
29 UK SCOTLAND	4549	3872	3567	4141	3186	2930	2290	1923	1210	963	779	787	816	837	788
30 USA	5123	3456	2716	4272	1993	1916	1478	1230	743	377	361	407	418	443	406
31 YUGOSLAVIA	-	-	-	-	-	-	-	-	-	-	2387	1923	865	617	574

\- NO MORTALITY DATA ARE AVAILABLE FOR EVEN A BROADER GROUP OF CAUSES FOR THIS DISEASE

. MORTALITY DATA ARE PRESENTED FOR A BROADER GROUP OF CAUSES FOR THIS DISEASE

0 VALUE<0.5

THE STANDARD MORTALITY RATIOS WERE DERIVED WITH A FACTOR OF 1000

SERIAL MORTALITY TABLES FOR VARIOUS COUNTRIES 1901-1975

TABLE 111 : TEETH AND SUPPORTING STRUCTURES - ALL DISEASES : MALES

	1901-	1906-	1911-	1916-	1921-	1926-	1931-	1936-	1941-	1946-	1951-	1956-	1961-	1966-	1971-75
1 AUSTRALIA	-	.	.	.	.	.	.	.	.	.	1278	802	549	406	310
2 AUSTRIA	-	-	-	-	-	-	-	-	-	.	95	111	107	53	0
3 BELGIUM	-	-	-	-	.	.	.	.	.	.	624	361	235	270	0
4 BULGARIA	-	-	-	-	-	-	.	.	.	.	.	.	0	139	0
5 CANADA	-	-	-	-	.	.	.	.	3896	2002	1830	823	515	344	287
6 CHILE	-	.	.	.	.	.	.	0	1229	217	400	530	1032	361	295
7 CZECHOSLOVAKIA	-	-	-	.	.	.	.	.	.	.	157	89	0	28	0
8 DENMARK	.	.	.	.	.	.	.	.	.	.	175	84	159	75	147
9 EIRE	-	-	-	-	.	.	.	.	.	.	1128	128	387	128	0
10 FINLAND	-	-	-	-	-	.	.	.	.	.	214	204	98	94	0
11 FRANCE	-	-	-	-	-	-	.	.	.	97	233	458	163	116	169
12 GREECE	-	-	-	-	-	.	.	.	-	-	-	104	145	90	0
13 HUNGARY	-	-	-	.	.	.	.	.	.	.	0	244	80	0	0
14 ICELAND	-	-	-	-	-	-	-	-	.	.	-	-	0	0	0
15 ITALY	-	-	-	-	-	-	-	-	-	-	555	369	263	213	105
16 JAPAN	.	70610	53890	45503	39930	.	.	.	-	1499	820	641	342	176	149
17 NETHERLANDS	.	.	.	.	.	.	.	.	.	1249	419	427	363	496	208
18 NEW ZEALAND	-	.	.	.	.	.	.	.	.	0	943	1552	315	446	1250
19 NORWAY	.	.	.	.	.	.	.	.	.	.	112	0	0	282	91
20 POLAND	-	-	-	-	-	-	-	-	-	-	.	344	177	557	129
21 PORTUGAL	-	-	-	-	-	-	.	.	.	.	525	199	190	189	236
22 ROMANIA	-	-	-	-	-	-	-	-	-	-	-	0	0	0	0
23 SPAIN	.	.	.	.	.	.	.	.	.	.	656	242	0	0	35
24 SWEDEN	-	-	.	.	.	.	.	.	.	.	102	146	93	87	0
25 SWITZERLAND	.	.	.	.	.	.	.	.	.	.	726	453	693	193	308
26 TURKEY	-	-	-	-	-	-	-	-	-	-	-	568	137	251	493
27 UK ENGLAND AND WALES	.	.	9588	8627	9780	13986	12122	8221	5235	2111	1143	503	302	267	295
28 UK NORTHERN IRELAND	-	-	-	-	.	.	.	.	.	1524	578	1136	0	261	0
29 UK SCOTLAND	.	.	.	.	.	.	.	.	.	786	466	76	149	370	894
30 USA	.	.	.	.	.	.	.	.	.	1892	1329	661	387	235	187
31 YUGOSLAVIA	-	-	-	-	-	-	-	-	-	-	2321	871	164	22	41

- NO MORTALITY DATA ARE AVAILABLE FOR EVEN A BROADER GROUP OF CAUSES FOR THIS DISEASE

. MORTALITY DATA ARE PRESENTED FOR A BROADER GROUP OF CAUSES FOR THIS DISEASE

0 VALUE<0.5

THE STANDARD MORTALITY RATIOS WERE DERIVED WITH A FACTOR OF 10000

SERIAL MORTALITY TABLES FOR VARIOUS COUNTRIES 1901-1975

TABLE 111 : TEETH AND SUPPORTING STRUCTURES - ALL DISEASES : FEMALES

	1901-	1906-	1911-	1916-	1921-	1926-	1931-	1936-	1941-	1946-	1951-	1956-	1961-	1966-	1971-75
1 AUSTRALIA	-	.	.	.	.	.	.	.	.	.	1034	660	175	385	146
2 AUSTRIA	-	-	-	-	-	-	-	-	-	.	306	88	167	41	0
3 BELGIUM	-	-	-	-	.	.	.	.	.	.	380	217	140	169	0
4 BULGARIA	-	-	-	-	-	-	.	.	.	.	.	.	238	133	83
5 CANADA	-	-	-	-	.	.	.	.	2782	1473	958	889	516	257	291
6 CHILE	-	.	.	.	.	.	.	2488	639	312	0	438	378	97	137
7 CZECHOSLOVAKIA	-	-	-	.	.	.	.	.	.	.	93	132	25	0	0
8 DENMARK	.	.	.	.	.	.	.	.	.	.	167	0	0	0	0
9 EIRE	-	-	-	-	.	.	.	.	.	.	889	256	127	373	120
10 FINLAND	-	-	-	-	-	.	.	.	.	.	90	341	163	155	75
11 FRANCE	-	-	-	-	-	-	.	.	.	161	210	246	158	104	150
12 GREECE	-	-	-	-	-	.	.	.	-	-	-	47	176	0	0
13 HUNGARY	-	-	-	.	.	.	.	.	.	.	189	143	69	0	0
14 ICELAND	-	-	-	-	-	-	-	-	.	.	-	-	0	0	0
15 ITALY	-	-	-	-	-	-	-	-	-	-	433	348	360	163	43
16 JAPAN	.	67224	49955	42668	36430	.	.	.	-	1122	583	427	279	201	128
17 NETHERLANDS		.	.	.	.	.	.	.	.	606	258	375	219	116	136
18 NEW ZEALAND	-	.	.	.	.	.	.	.	.	2160	185	833	905	422	782
19 NORWAY	.	.	.	.	.	.	.	.	.	.	0	0	0	175	0
20 POLAND	-	-	-	-	-	-	-	-	-	-	.	99	228	238	77
21 PORTUGAL	-	-	-	-	-	-	.	.	.	.	668	127	121	159	118
22 ROMANIA	-	-	-	-	-	-	-	-	-	-	-	0	0	0	17
23 SPAIN	.	.	.	.	.	.	.	.	.	.	598	174	0	0	10
24 SWEDEN	-	-	.	.	.	.	.	.	.	.	196	140	88	41	0
25 SWITZERLAND	.	.	.	.	.	.	.	.	.	.	425	132	0	225	215
26 TURKEY	-	-	-	-	-	-	-	-	-	-	-	224	144	78	337
27 UK ENGLAND AND WALES	.	.	7784	6754	7441	9088	8803	4846	3404	1461	662	390	189	181	256
28 UK NORTHERN IRELAND	-	-	-	-	.	.	.	.	.	1404	1302	508	0	230	0
29 UK SCOTLAND	.	.	.	.	.	.	.	.	.	340	399	129	125	246	735
30 USA	.	.	.	.	.	.	.	.	.	1447	954	494	372	211	176
31 YUGOSLAVIA	-	-	-	-	-	-	-	-	-	-	1711	1167	63	39	0

- NO MORTALITY DATA ARE AVAILABLE FOR EVEN A BROADER GROUP OF CAUSES FOR THIS DISEASE

. MORTALITY DATA ARE PRESENTED FOR A BROADER GROUP OF CAUSES FOR THIS DISEASE

0 VALUE<0.5

THE STANDARD MORTALITY RATIOS WERE DERIVED WITH A FACTOR OF 10000

SERIAL MORTALITY TABLES FOR VARIOUS COUNTRIES 1901-1975

TABLE 112 : STOMACH - ULCER : MALES

	1901-	1906-	1911-	1916-	1921-	1926-	1931-	1936-	1941-	1946-	1951-	1956-	1961-	1966-	1971-75
1 AUSTRALIA	-	869	1100	1001	.	1745	2051	2254	2209	1968	1832	1667	1148	900	.
2 AUSTRIA	-	-	-	-	-	-	-	-	-	.	1566	1387	1485	1440	.
3 BELGIUM	.	.	.	.	.	.	.	.	.	.	1516	1448	1263	1309	.
4 BULGARIA	-	-	-	-	-	-	.	.	.	.	.	.	1430	1136	.
5 CANADA	-	-	-	-	1593	1782	1933	2081	1858	1388	1119	1045	1023	952	.
6 CHILE	-	250	573	564	480	.	.	2199	3040	3195	3142	2415	2186	2083	.
7 CZECHOSLOVAKIA	-	-	-	1807	1984	2599	2951	3109	.	.	1693	1264	1182	1309	.
8 DENMARK	1250	1906	1901	2621	1532	1928	.	.	.	.	1655	1286	1220	1203	.
9 EIRE	-	-	-	-	2027	2402	2561	2751	.	.	1856	1541	1400	1371	.
10 FINLAND	-	-	-	-	-	.	.	.	.	.	2304	2313	1817	1198	.
11 FRANCE	-	-	-	-	-	-	.	.	.	1122	1043	983	936	863	.
12 GREECE	-	-	-	-	-	.	.	.	-	-	-	1728	1509	1055	.
13 HUNGARY	-	-	-	.	.	.	2917	3378	3708	.	2034	1835	1734	1795	.
14 ICELAND	-	-	1250	1312	1029	1733	1687	3407	.	.	.	.	242	978	.
15 ITALY	.	.	.	.	.	.	.	.	.	.	1577	1406	1355	1251	.
16 JAPAN	.	.	.	.	.	.	9588	9962	-	14128	10527	6810	4690	3647	.
17 NETHERLANDS	1248	1217	1319	1616	1370	1732	2133	2586	3185	1333	1120	1052	863	834	.
18 NEW ZEALAND	-	2231	1487	1475	1032	2159	2019	2003	2239	1753	1490	1375	1028	760	.
19 NORWAY	.	.	.	.	.	1802	2031	2074	.	.	834	711	682	653	.
20 POLAND	-	-	-	-	-	-	-	-	-	-	.	2250	2550	2179	.
21 PORTUGAL	.	.	.	.	.	.	.	.	.	.	4756	3697	2887	2253	.
22 ROMANIA	-	-	-	-	-	-	-	-	-	-	-	2141	1764	974	.
23 SPAIN	3381	3561	3925	4568	4667	5135	4661	6077	.	.	2801	2145	2135	1867	.
24 SWEDEN	-	-	.	.	.	.	.	.	.	.	1522	1231	1275	1263	.
25 SWITZERLAND	2844	2844	3490	3490	2938	3111	3069	2318	2865	2076	1636	1389	1106	1082	.
26 TURKEY	-	-	-	-	-	-	-	-	-	-	-	3826	3404	2757	2389
27 UK ENGLAND AND WALES	1455	1509	2066	2171	2409	3182	3082	3312	2960	2356	2029	1601	1259	1066	.
28 UK NORTHERN IRELAND	-	-	-	-	2633	2582	.	.	.	1557	1398	1378	1274	1141	.
29 UK SCOTLAND	2235	2754	2984	3018	2949	3257	2653	2998	2499	2103	1847	1440	1255	1097	.
30 USA	1842	1832	1968	1940	1976	2259	2182	2251	.	1344	1193	1145	1100	917	.
31 YUGOSLAVIA	-	-	-	-	-	-	-	-	-	-	.	.	1417	1094	.

- NO MORTALITY DATA ARE AVAILABLE FOR EVEN A BROADER GROUP OF CAUSES FOR THIS DISEASE

. MORTALITY DATA ARE PRESENTED FOR A BROADER GROUP OF CAUSES FOR THIS DISEASE

0 VALUE<0.5

THE STANDARD MORTALITY RATIOS WERE DERIVED WITH A FACTOR OF 1000

SERIAL MORTALITY TABLES FOR VARIOUS COUNTRIES 1901-1975

TABLE 112 : STOMACH - ULCER : FEMALES

	1901-	1906-	1911-	1916-	1921-	1926-	1931-	1936-	1941-	1946-	1951-	1956-	1961-	1966-	1971-75
1 AUSTRALIA	-	12078	10653	8147	.	7640	6387	6946	5717	5097	5401	6452	4812	4013	.
2 AUSTRIA	-	-	-	-	-	-	-	-	-	.	6144	5459	5804	6214	.
3 BELGIUM	.	.	.	.	.	.	.	.	.	.	3029	3020	3674	4111	.
4 BULGARIA	-	-	-	-	-	-	.	.	.	.	.	.	4070	3133	.
5 CANADA	-	-	-	-	8007	7528	6790	6073	4279	3211	2997	3643	3729	3691	.
6 CHILE	-	2000	3715	3571	3854	.	.	11792	11233	7889	9147	7732	6762	6016	.
7 CZECHOSLOVAKIA	-	-	-	9412	8579	10250	9042	7444	.	.	3996	3912	3250	4348	.
8 DENMARK	16872	15446	14800	15921	7975	7441	.	.	.	.	6091	5743	6088	6260	.
9 EIRE	-	-	-	-	13723	13897	11636	11605	.	.	6208	6056	6535	6231	.
10 FINLAND	-	-	-	-	-	.	.	.	.	.	4383	4882	5404	4454	.
11 FRANCE	-	-	-	-	-	-	.	.	.	2103	1850	2099	2220	2323	.
12 GREECE	-	-	-	-	-	.	.	.	-	-	-	4999	5582	3699	.
13 HUNGARY	-	-	-	.	.	.	7688	7506	7176	.	4381	4579	4830	5468	.
14 ICELAND	-	-	19753	12360	7216	9346	6034	8661	.	.	.	.	7216	4147	.
15 ITALY	.	.	.	.	.	.	.	.	.	.	3140	2863	2820	2583	.
16 JAPAN	.	.	.	.	.	.	36827	37359	-	45386	34698	23943	16850	13234	.
17 NETHERLANDS	10569	8294	7900	8283	6052	6998	6442	6428	8632	3641	3853	3844	3280	3458	.
18 NEW ZEALAND	-	19588	13793	10423	8827	9554	6863	7068	6429	6475	5694	5630	5095	4236	.
19 NORWAY	.	.	.	.	.	9474	10107	9733	.	.	3797	2822	3622	2935	.
20 POLAND	-	-	-	-	-	-	-	-	-	-	.	5066	5278	5219	.
21 PORTUGAL	.	.	.	.	.	.	.	.	.	.	9577	7792	6688	5795	.
22 ROMANIA	-	-	-	-	-	-	-	-	-	-	-	5382	4784	2734	.
23 SPAIN	14869	15217	15493	16890	15917	15582	12852	13165	.	.	5297	4302	4462	4006	.
24 SWEDEN	-	-	.	.	.	.	.	.	.	.	5660	6232	6525	6814	.
25 SWITZERLAND	19258	19258	18838	18838	14307	12517	10034	8187	9779	7564	6994	6791	5104	4716	.
26 TURKEY	-	-	-	-	-	-	-	-	-	-	-	13087	10516	11544	11179
27 UK ENGLAND AND WALES	28035	20898	17463	14598	11011	10982	9634	8951	7132	6649	6823	6580	5869	5492	.
28 UK NORTHERN IRELAND	-	-	-	-	15900	16234	.	.	.	7931	5520	6051	5955	6432	.
29 UK SCOTLAND	27075	26737	23204	19117	13486	15624	12068	10043	7611	6667	6738	6041	5444	5000	.
30 USA	16157	14490	13611	11614	9379	8429	6477	5435	.	3199	3090	3711	4027	3561	.
31 YUGOSLAVIA	-	-	-	-	-	-	-	-	-	-	.	.	3968	3375	.

- NO MORTALITY DATA ARE AVAILABLE FOR EVEN A BROADER GROUP OF CAUSES FOR THIS DISEASE

. MORTALITY DATA ARE PRESENTED FOR A BROADER GROUP OF CAUSES FOR THIS DISEASE

0 VALUE<0.5

THE STANDARD MORTALITY RATIOS WERE DERIVED WITH A FACTOR OF 10000

SERIAL MORTALITY TABLES FOR VARIOUS COUNTRIES 1901-1975

TABLE 112 : STOMACH - ULCER : PERSONS

	1901-	1906-	1911-	1916-	1921-	1926-	1931-	1936-	1941-	1946-	1951-	1956-	1961-	1966-	1971-75
1 AUSTRALIA	-	10235	10839	9132	.	12689	13540	14677	13656	12036	11336	11054	7755	6171	.
2 AUSTRIA	-	-	-	-	-	-	.	.	-	.	10124	8873	9367	9349	.
3 BELGIUM	-	-	-	-	.	.	.	.	.	.	8447	8055	7544	7911	.
4 BULGARIA	-	-	-	-	-	-	.	.	.	.	.	.	8775	6923	.
5 CANADA	.	.	.	.	12127	12866	13269	13669	11616	8648	7100	7003	6870	6410	.
6 CHILE	-	2237	4674	4559	4303	.	.	16580	20188	19079	19446	15158	13567	12685	.
7 CZECHOSLOVAKIA	-	-	-	13320	13642	17302	18149	17912	.	.	9658	7686	6859	7977	.
8 DENMARK	15134	16885	16482	20032	11338	12903	.	.	.	.	11039	9087	8913	8864	.
9 EIRE	-	-	-	-	16891	18799	18475	19482	.	.	12258	10579	10062	9713	.
10 FINLAND	-	-	-	-	-	.	.	.	.	.	11746	12077	10430	7395	.
11 FRANCE	.	.	.	.	-	-	.	.	.	5814	5288	5148	5007	4762	.
12 GREECE	-	-	-	-	-	.	.	.	-	-	-	13684	14680	10038	.
13 HUNGARY	-	-	-	.	.	.	17841	19794	21043	.	11414	10591	10219	10769	.
14 ICELAND	-	-	16788	12667	8485	12637	10553	19266	.	.	-	-	5014	6733	.
15 ITALY	-	-	-	-	-	-	-	-	-	-	8846	7844	7497	6805	.
16 JAPAN	.	.	.	.	.	.	63704	65575	-	87734	65880	43392	30079	23446	.
17 NETHERLANDS	11459	10102	10384	11997	9682	11931	13581	15752	19768	8275	7357	7001	5772	5674	.
18 NEW ZEALAND	-	21145	14399	12784	9621	15808	13662	13568	14286	11833	10048	9382	7421	5707	.
19 NORWAY	.	.	.	.	.	13279	14657	14642	.	.	5862	4777	5074	4544	.
20 POLAND	-	-	-	-	-	-	-	-	-	-	.	12608	13450	11908	.
21 PORTUGAL	-	-	-	-	-	-	.	.	.	.	24864	19567	15708	12566	.
22 ROMANIA	-	-	-	-	-	-	-	.	-	.	-	12296	10329	5751	.
23 SPAIN	23952	24805	26586	30347	30108	31739	27817	33911	.	.	14827	11498	11624	10205	.
24 SWEDEN	-	-	.	.	.	.	.	.	.	.	10136	9065	9397	9458	.
25 SWITZERLAND	23467	23467	26005	26005	20927	20661	19066	14740	18005	13279	11039	9828	7623	7267	.
26 TURKEY	-	-	-	-	-	-	-	.	.	-	-	24483	21308	19216	17444
27 UK ENGLAND AND WALES	21622	18150	18876	17723	16753	20108	18864	19390	16654	13814	12391	10396	8539	7515	.
28 UK NORTHERN IRELAND	-	-	-	-	20680	20626	.	.	.	11456	9318	9444	8887	8533	.
29 UK SCOTLAND	25070	27076	26034	23874	20431	23023	18412	18754	15122	12826	11711	9506	8314	7349	.
30 USA	17262	16402	16666	15537	14613	15568	14153	13872	.	6487	7247	7275	7161	6001	.
31 YUGOSLAVIA	-	-	-	-	-	-	-	-	-	-	.	.	8330	6626	.

- NO MORTALITY DATA ARE AVAILABLE FOR EVEN A BROADER GROUP OF CAUSES FOR THIS DISEASE

. MORTALITY DATA ARE PRESENTED FOR A BROADER GROUP OF CAUSES FOR THIS DISEASE

0 VALUE<0.5

THE STANDARD MORTALITY RATIOS WERE DERIVED WITH A FACTOR OF 10000

SERIAL MORTALITY TABLES FOR VARIOUS COUNTRIES 1901-1975

TABLE 113 : DLODENUM - ULCER : MALES

	1901-	1906-	1911-	1916-	1921-	1926-	1931-	1936-	1941-	1946-	1951-	1956-	1961-	1966-	1971-75
1 AUSTRALIA	-	.	.	.	.	10204	12846	14553	13733	13918	14047	12620	12129	10314	.
2 AUSTRIA	-	-	-	-	-	-	-	-	-	.	12974	12469	14902	15978	.
3 BELGIUM	.	.	.	.	.	.	.	.	.	.	1932	2346	3103	2325	.
4 BULGARIA	-	-	-	-	-	-	.	.	.	.	.	.	7935	8037	.
5 CANADA	-	-	-	-	10995	11491	13288	16366	14730	13310	11889	12048	11613	9934	.
6 CHILE	-	.	.	.	.	.	.	4583	4279	4746	2039	2758	3527	4337	.
7 CZECHOSLOVAKIA	-	-	-	3301	2933	4630	5823	7367	.	.	7579	6416	6722	8888	.
8 DENMARK	.	.	.	.	.	.	.	.	.	.	9080	6664	6199	8350	.
9 EIRE	-	-	-	-	9878	12265	13717	14005	.	.	10572	10562	9421	9659	.
10 FINLAND	-	-	-	-	-	.	.	.	.	.	4962	5412	4970	4731	.
11 FRANCE	-	-	-	-	-	-	.	.	.	1117	1544	1503	1413	1432	.
12 GREECE	-	-	-	-	-	.	.	.	-	-	-	3486	5681	5845	.
13 HUNGARY	-	-	-	.	.	.	1309	1950	3399	.	4268	5030	6349	6984	.
14 ICELAND	-	-	-	-	-	-	-	-	.	.	.	.	3311	2994	.
15 ITALY	.	.	.	.	.	.	.	.	.	.	12217	12451	14568	14232	.
16 JAPAN	.	.	.	.	.	.	8561	11774	-	11187	9003	6539	5772	5203	.
17 NETHERLANDS	.	.	.	.	3087	4612	6354	10599	15410	8840	11894	9875	7813	7170	.
18 NEW ZEALAND	-	.	.	.	.	18519	16922	18498	19678	16999	16712	17335	12925	8590	.
19 NORWAY	-	.	.	.	.	2462	4467	5845	.	.	4862	5060	4596	5044	.
20 POLAND	-	-	-	-	-	-	-	-	-	-	.	4397	6511	7711	.
21 PORTUGAL	.	.	.	.	.	.	.	.	.	.	18032	15626	15883	17056	.
22 ROMANIA	-	-	-	-	-	-	-	-	-	-	-	10206	9774	9191	.
23 SPAIN	.	.	.	.	.	.	6226	8283	.	.	5027	4865	5988	5621	.
24 SWEDEN	-	-	.	.	.	.	.	.	.	.	14087	10133	8666	8268	.
25 SWITZERLAND	.	.	.	.	6347	7120	7959	6903	8309	7880	7575	8258	9813	7860	.
26 TURKEY	-	-	-	-	-	-	-	-	-	-	-	2004	2694	2432	1645
27 UK ENGLAND AND WALES	.	.	11938	10786	13796	18147	17635	19243	20653	20135	23949	19491	15130	13107	.
28 UK NORTHERN IRELAND	-	-	-	-	12730	17419	.	.	.	13028	16379	13998	13683	10908	.
29 UK SCOTLAND	.	.	.	.	18458	31081	31642	35382	30140	28437	30593	25929	21132	14949	.
30 USA	.	.	.	.	8311	11156	10869	11128	.	12141	12997	13403	12346	9327	.
31 YUGOSLAVIA	-	-	-	-	-	-	-	-	-	-	.	.	12235	10885	.

- NO MORTALITY DATA ARE AVAILABLE FOR EVEN A BROADER GROUP OF CAUSES FOR THIS DISEASE

. MORTALITY DATA ARE PRESENTED FOR A BROADER GROUP OF CAUSES FOR THIS DISEASE

0 VALUE<0.5

THE STANDARD MORTALITY RATIOS WERE DERIVED WITH A FACTOR OF 10000

SERIAL MORTALITY TABLES FOR VARIOUS COUNTRIES 1901-1975

TABLE 113 : DUODENUM - ULCER : FEMALES

	1901-	1906-	1911-	1916-	1921-	1926-	1931-	1936-	1941-	1946-	1951-	1956-	1961-	1966-	1971-75
1 AUSTRALIA	-	.	.	.	.	23560	26120	21430	27210	23390	24780	24130	26520	24990	.
2 AUSTRIA	-	-	-	-	-	-	-	-	-	.	27560	32360	41390	50170	.
3 BELGIUM	.	.	.	.	.	.	.	.	.	.	2830	3620	10940	8690	.
4 BULGARIA	-	-	-	-	-	-	.	.	.	.	.	.	17410	12490	.
5 CANADA	-	-	-	-	29160	29210	28760	33190	30680	27040	22260	28800	29260	26720	.
6 CHILE	-	.	.	.	.	.	.	8260	11150	9980	5950	6280	10200	7380	.
7 CZECHOSLOVAKIA	-	-	-	23720	16600	17830	9390	8460	.	.	12600	12620	13790	18570	.
8 DENMARK	.	.	.	.	.	.	.	.	.	.	17780	17620	21350	24100	.
9 EIRE	-	-	-	-	20200	24780	27110	22550	.	.	21400	21940	26000	27460	.
10 FINLAND	-	-	-	-	-	.	.	.	.	.	5680	10480	10760	12450	.
11 FRANCE	-	-	-	-	-	-	.	.	.	2180	2070	2150	2680	2900	.
12 GREECE	-	-	-	-	-	.	.	.	-	-	-	7840	15030	19010	.
13 HUNGARY	-	-	-	.	.	.	3450	2990	8020	.	7230	9880	14500	20800	.
14 ICELAND	-	-	-	-	-	-	-	-	.	.	.	.	23120	15620	.
15 ITALY	.	.	.	.	.	.	.	.	.	.	15340	17560	22970	25400	.
16 JAPAN	.	.	.	.	.	.	41500	43300	-	48320	31790	21390	15120	13720	.
17 NETHERLANDS	.	.	.	.	10430	12330	14010	16430	19950	15340	20770	25000	21400	19490	.
18 NEW ZEALAND	-	.	.	.	.	33370	30960	39840	31340	22870	38290	45160	35090	25190	.
19 NORWAY	.	.	.	.	.	7180	9470	13920	.	.	13760	12680	16920	18220	.
20 POLAND	-	-	-	-	-	-	-	-	-	-	.	5860	9640	12240	.
21 PORTUGAL	.	.	.	.	.	.	.	.	.	.	31110	28670	34320	32390	.
22 ROMANIA	-	-	-	-	-	-	-	-	-	-	-	20390	18540	17140	.
23 SPAIN	.	.	.	.	.	.	17510	25010	.	.	10750	10760	12260	13970	.
24 SWEDEN	-	-	.	.	.	.	.	.	.	.	30770	29030	26210	29930	.
25 SWITZERLAND	.	.	.	.	18250	17100	15360	12030	14690	17930	22130	24170	25940	29270	.
26 TURKEY	-	-	-	-	-	-	-	-	-	-	-	6670	6740	4650	1290
27 UK ENGLAND AND WALES	.	.	23510	22040	22760	22820	25410	27200	24620	26140	40360	40650	39060	35320	.
28 UK NORTHERN IRELAND	-	-	-	-	25900	36940	.	.	.	11650	27130	37540	35710	45720	.
29 UK SCOTLAND	.	.	.	.	29240	41160	44340	42020	33320	27540	47660	47650	46960	31300	.
30 USA	.	.	.	.	24410	29290	25290	22740	.	23680	25970	31650	34230	27570	.
31 YUGOSLAVIA	-	-	-	-	-	-	-	-	-	-	.	.	19150	25050	.

- NO MORTALITY DATA ARE AVAILABLE FOR EVEN A BROADER GROUP OF CAUSES FOR THIS DISEASE

. MORTALITY DATA ARE PRESENTED FOR A BROADER GROUP OF CAUSES FOR THIS DISEASE

0 VALUE<0.5

THE STANDARD MORTALITY RATIOS WERE DERIVED WITH A FACTOR OF 100000

SERIAL MORTALITY TABLES FOR VARIOUS COUNTRIES 1901-1975

TABLE 114 : PEPTIC ULCER : MALES

	1901-	1906-	1911-	1916-	1921-	1926-	1931-	1936-	1941-	1946-	1951-	1956-	1961-	1966-	1971-75
1 AUSTRALIA	-	.	.	.	12090	15635	18827	20904	20189	18892	18157	16428	13156	10938	9719
2 AUSTRIA	-	-	-	-	-	-	-	-	-	22333	16701	14696	16545	16258	13683
3 BELGIUM	.	.	.	.	.	.	.	.	.	.	10281	9650	8978	9017	8044
4 BULGARIA	-	-	-	-	-	-	.	.	.	.	.	.	12091	11673	10511
5 CANADA	-	-	-	-	15165	16515	18362	20876	18680	15179	12834	12465	12069	10601	8209
6 CHILE	-	.	.	.	3342	6467	11999	15108	19720	20881	17319	15333	14465	14449	13818
7 CZECHOSLOVAKIA	-	-	-	12196	13010	17484	20163	21924	27028	20400	14698	10766	10476	12251	11688
8 DENMARK	.	.	.	.	.	.	16901	17035	15597	18236	14425	10989	10359	11028	9697
9 EIRE	-	-	-	-	17088	20560	22292	24440	18780	17214	16345	14490	13066	13531	13259
10 FINLAND	-	-	-	-	-	.	.	23706	26584	21608	15947	16262	13182	9302	7464
11 FRANCE	-	-	-	-	-	-	.	.	11414	9598	6862	6495	6180	6478	7237
12 GREECE	-	-	-	-	-	14196	21096	23186	-	-	-	11846	11754	10147	7004
13 HUNGARY	-	-	-	.	.	.	17504	20501	23190	20906	16189	13318	13453	14876	15500
14 ICELAND	-	-	-	-	-	-	-	-	.	.	8676	7258	3169	7256	5932
15 ITALY	.	.	.	.	10175	11640	16705	19613	22062	19188	15670	14789	15608	15452	14966
16 JAPAN	.	27671	26344	29899	37354	46598	56727	63538	-	87070	65308	42681	30106	22949	15792
17 NETHERLANDS	.	.	.	.	9565	12478	15738	20653	26719	12476	12840	11342	9139	8444	7438
18 NEW ZEALAND	-	.	.	.	16208	20833	20856	21629	23596	19276	17531	17149	12806	9082	9836
19 NORWAY	7193	8145	10207	10147	13069	13995	14127	15094	14810	9602	7404	6793	6379	6435	6765
20 POLAND	-	-	-	-	-	-	-	-	-	-	.	15333	18242	17091	14054
21 PORTUGAL	.	.	.	.	.	.	.	.	.	.	34544	29780	25238	22221	16094
22 ROMANIA	-	-	-	-	-	-	-	-	-	-	-	17923	15513	10468	8499
23 SPAIN	.	.	.	.	.	.	30212	39487	31793	26168	18862	15003	15560	13739	14009
24 SWEDEN	-	-	13537	14278	16200	17517	17021	16406	13486	12381	16311	12501	11977	12329	13213
25 SWITZERLAND	.	.	.	.	20355	21783	22010	17120	21035	16242	13536	12462	11647	10101	9290
26 TURKEY	-	-	-	-	-	-	-	-	-	-	-	22867	20910	17107	14575
27 UK ENGLAND AND WALES	.	.	18441	18408	21447	28284	27421	29603	28266	24441	24570	19682	15381	13292	11857
28 UK NORTHERN IRELAND	-	-	-	-	22127	24372	28920	28739	24587	19903	16763	15381	14627	12978	11811
29 UK SCOTLAND	.	.	.	.	27117	35840	32638	36617	30778	27452	27075	22192	18570	14434	13530
30 USA	.	.	.	.	15867	19044	18470	19396	18148	14783	13866	13774	12922	9478	6654
31 YUGOSLAVIA	-	-	-	-	-	-	-	-	-	-	.	19853	14806	12937	12094

- NO MORTALITY DATA ARE AVAILABLE FOR EVEN A BROADER GROUP OF CAUSES FOR THIS DISEASE

. MORTALITY DATA ARE PRESENTED FOR A BROADER GROUP OF CAUSES FOR THIS DISEASE

0 VALUE<0.5

THE STANDARD MCRTALITY RATIOS WERE DERIVED WITH A FACTOR OF 10000

SERIAL MORTALITY TABLES FOR VARIOUS COUNTRIES 1901-1975

TABLE 114 : PEPTIC ULCER : FEMALES

	1901-	1906-	1911-	1916-	1921-	1926-	1931-	1936-	1941-	1946-	1951-	1956-	1961-	1966-	1971-75
1 AUSTRALIA	-	.	.	.	5465	5675	5097	5163	4764	4199	4444	5017	4183	4000	3881
2 AUSTRIA	-	-	-	-	-	-	-	-	-	4672	4796	4878	5540	6010	5668
3 BELGIUM	.	.	.	.	.	.	.	.	.	.	2368	1949	2711	2916	3349
4 BULGARIA	-	-	-	-	-	-	.	.	.	.	.	.	3074	3312	3272
5 CANADA	-	-	-	-	6181	5911	5462	5289	4117	3302	2916	3631	3696	3555	2955
6 CHILE	-	.	.	.	2243	3858	5143	5586	7047	5069	5069	4785	4443	4418	4523
7 CZECHOSLOVAKIA	-	-	-	6714	5845	6875	5723	4752	5173	3913	3244	2941	2619	3593	3954
8 DENMARK	.	.	.	.	.	.	5199	4785	4539	4992	4474	4264	4660	4866	4975
9 EIRE	-	-	-	-	9047	9394	8212	7797	6367	4548	4729	4666	5152	5244	5664
10 FINLAND	-	-	-	-	-	.	.	3543	3667	2798	2838	3386	3707	3247	3330
11 FRANCE	-	-	-	-	-	-	.	.	2359	1812	1187	1337	1436	1672	2240
12 GREECE	-	-	-	-	-	5003	6466	6988	-	-	-	3312	4030	4096	2751
13 HUNGARY	-	-	-	.	.	.	4614	4486	4570	3617	3241	3182	3574	4781	5641
14 ICELAND	-	-	-	-	-	-	-	-	.	.	5495	5369	5405	3226	4087
15 ITALY	.	.	.	.	5572	5316	5230	4823	4857	3434	2636	2590	2845	3114	3271
16 JAPAN	.	16031	15285	15820	18911	20332	22783	23875	-	28756	21712	14959	10533	8346	6471
17 NETHERLANDS	.	.	.	.	4052	4701	4472	4595	6058	2928	3336	3551	3030	3051	3426
18 NEW ZEALAND	-	.	.	.	6013	6391	5635	6239	5406	4973	5325	5631	4786	4059	4663
19 NORWAY	6959	7672	8872	8594	7850	7181	6365	6381	5260	3768	2925	2302	2988	2590	2900
20 POLAND	-	-	-	-	-	-	-	-	-	-	.	3241	3571	3758	3620
21 PORTUGAL	.	.	.	.	.	.	.	.	.	.	7505	6034	5687	5065	3822
22 ROMANIA	-	-	-	-	-	-	-	-	-	-	-	4211	3763	2468	2014
23 SPAIN	.	.	.	.	.	.	8364	8948	7240	4958	3638	3064	3235	3227	3524
24 SWEDEN	-	-	10397	8525	9088	9863	7916	6705	4857	4426	4906	5144	5165	5796	6529
25 SWITZERLAND	.	.	.	.	9233	8144	6622	5378	6445	5338	5231	5219	4326	4456	4566
26 TURKEY	-	-	-	-	-	-	-	-	-	-	-	7870	6409	6892	6498
27 UK ENGLAND AND WALES	.	.	11318	9593	7574	7567	6934	6637	5444	5238	6081	5944	5438	5108	5429
28 UK NORTHERN IRELAND	-	-	-	-	10587	11380	10107	9127	6873	6302	4630	5477	5326	5560	5151
29 UK SCOTLAND	.	.	.	.	9354	11237	9361	8062	6183	5324	6424	6009	5616	4728	5291
30 USA	.	.	.	.	6700	6423	5094	4348	3627	3096	3166	3818	4126	3445	2662
31 YUGOSLAVIA	-	-	-	-	-	-	-	-	-	-	.	4541	3316	3847	3984

- NO MORTALITY DATA ARE AVAILABLE FOR EVEN A BROADER GROUP OF CAUSES FOR THIS DISEASE

. MORTALITY DATA ARE PRESENTED FOR A BROADER GROUP OF CAUSES FOR THIS DISEASE

0 VALUE<0.5

THE STANDARD MORTALITY RATIOS WERE DERIVED WITH A FACTOR OF 10000

SERIAL MORTALITY TABLES FOR VARIOUS COUNTRIES 1901-1975

TABLE 115 : GASTRITIS AND DUODENITIS : MALES

	1901-	1906-	1911-	1916-	1921-	1926-	1931-	1936-	1941-	1946-	1951-	1956-	1961-	1966-	1971-75
1 AUSTRALIA	-	557	666	652	468	295	147	94	86	74	15	15	14	11	8
2 AUSTRIA	-	-	-	-	-	-	-	-	-	.	19	17	37	44	30
3 BELGIUM		.	.	.	.	.	.	.	.	.	22	4	11	8	13
4 BULGARIA	-	-	-	-	-	-	.	.	.	.	.	.	9	10	12
5 CANADA	-	-	-	-	865	1036	682	395	227	159	32	21	19	23	19
6 CHILE	-	1027	3520	2953	2657	1891	1467	962	649	397	67	36	42	62	53
7 CZECHOSLOVAKIA	-	-	-	341	379	309	237	217	214	189	74	48	33	19	8
8 DENMARK	.	.	.	.	.	.	.	.	.	.	6	13	12	16	18
9 EIRE	-	-	-	-	1284	1114	963	739	514	361	60	43	17	10	15
10 FINLAND	-	-	-	-	-	.	.	.	.	.	38	31	33	15	23
11 FRANCE	-	-	-	-	-	-	.	.	259	196	7	5	5	6	9
12 GREECE	-	-	-	-	-	624	515	357	-	-	-	11	20	16	11
13 HUNGARY	-	-	-	.	.	.	.	.	.	.	21	24	18	19	22
14 ICELAND	-	-	-	-	-	-	-	-	.	.	-	-	17	0	0
15 ITALY	.	.	.	.	676	557	356	288	195	93	33	30	28	25	27
16 JAPAN	.	10371	7237	5473	4008	2778	2794	2938	-	679	489	362	302	209	140
17 NETHERLANDS	638	686	327	317	274	256	208	178	170	63	7	8	9	9	10
18 NEW ZEALAND	-	880	668	575	300	179	95	64	29	18	9	17	7	15	12
19 NORWAY	1579	992	.	.	.	.	.	.	.	.	12	15	15	9	12
20 POLAND	-	-	-	-	-	-	-	-	-	-	.	36	41	35	22
21 PORTUGAL	.	.	.	.	.	.	.	.	.	.	69	44	39	21	22
22 ROMANIA	-	-	-	-	-	-	-	-	-	-	-	22	1	9	10
23 SPAIN	2806	2166	1613	1453	1037	758	647	619	542	410	55	34	23	31	22
24 SWEDEN	-	-	.	.	.	.	.	.	.	.	14	16	29	32	36
25 SWITZERLAND	.	.	.	.	84	89	.	.	.	.	20	20	15	21	19
26 TURKEY	-	-	-	-	-	-	-	-	-	-	-	14	12	8	14
27 UK ENGLAND AND WALES	350	1008	1285	1045	693	409	255	167	116	59	20	11	10	7	7
28 UK NORTHERN IRELAND	-	-	-	-	1131	928	.	.	.	41	21	6	14	14	14
29 UK SCOTLAND	1593	1643	1491	1234	864	558	334	223	196	166	29	18	15	10	8
30 USA	1784	1353	1595	1052	728	508	335	216	142	75	19	19	22	23	25
31 YUGOSLAVIA	-	-	-	-	-	-	-	-	-	-	.	.	7	7	8

- NO MORTALITY DATA ARE AVAILABLE FOR EVEN A BROADER GROUP OF CAUSES FOR THIS DISEASE

. MORTALITY DATA ARE PRESENTED FOR A BROADER GROUP OF CAUSES FOR THIS DISEASE

0 VALUE<0.5

THE STANDARD MORTALITY RATIOS WERE DERIVED WITH A FACTOR OF 10

SERIAL MORTALITY TABLES FOR VARIOUS COUNTRIES 1901-1975

TABLE 115 : GASTRITIS AND DUODENITIS : FEMALES

	1901-	1906-	1911-	1916-	1921-	1926-	1931-	1936-	1941-	1946-	1951-	1956-	1961-	1966-	1971-75
1 AUSTRALIA	-	582	769	642	457	281	136	83	61	48	13	7	8	7	8
2 AUSTRIA	-	-	-	-	-	-	-	-	-	.	10	9	17	19	8
3 BELGIUM	.	.	.	.	.	.	.	.	.	.	16	3	3	5	5
4 BULGARIA	-	-	-	-	-	-	.	.	.	.	.	.	9	5	5
5 CANADA	-	-	-	-	771	953	576	327	167	86	22	12	11	11	8
6 CHILE	-	853	3137	2945	2561	1693	1262	790	519	310	37	22	27	26	44
7 CZECHOSLOVAKIA	-	-	-	278	311	253	193	142	151	127	57	40	25	12	5
8 DENMARK	.	.	.	.	.	.	.	.	.	.	1	6	6	13	7
9 EIRE	-	-	-	-	1137	1118	918	675	457	265	77	37	16	11	13
10 FINLAND	-	-	-	-	-	.	.	.	.	.	15	13	12	10	7
11 FRANCE	-	-	-	-	-	-	.	.	107	75	3	2	2	2	4
12 GREECE	-	-	-	-	-	335	275	247	-	-	-	13	15	15	8
13 HUNGARY	-	-	-	.	.	.	.	.	.	.	16	22	12	11	13
14 ICELAND	-	-	-	-	-	-	-	-	.	.	-	-	43	0	0
15 ITALY	.	.	.	.	558	456	286	222	141	63	26	20	17	15	13
16 JAPAN	.	10619	7430	5543	4000	2707	2576	2715	-	687	508	390	326	240	173
17 NETHERLANDS	441	490	234	195	144	136	106	77	94	51	5	8	6	6	5
18 NEW ZEALAND	-	1100	665	633	346	125	103	52	39	28	11	9	5	7	6
19 NORWAY	1105	767	.	.	.	.	.	.	.	.	9	13	14	10	6
20 POLAND	-	-	-	-	-	-	-	-	-	-	.	16	20	20	10
21 PORTUGAL	.	.	.	.	.	.	.	.	.	.	55	39	23	13	10
22 ROMANIA	-	-	-	-	-	-	-	-	-	-	-	13	0	3	4
23 SPAIN	2253	1608	1123	979	654	462	356	322	263	176	33	25	18	18	14
24 SWEDEN	-	-	.	.	.	.	.	.	.	.	10	13	21	18	21
25 SWITZERLAND	.	.	.	.	75	64	.	.	.	.	16	12	9	14	10
26 TURKEY	-	-	-	-	-	-	-	-	-	-	-	8	7	6	9
27 UK ENGLAND AND WALES	340	968	1023	827	547	335	214	121	82	45	20	10	8	7	6
28 UK NORTHERN IRELAND	-	-	-	-	1147	818	.	.	.	81	28	13	6	7	5
29 UK SCOTLAND	1443	1411	1220	1075	756	491	302	191	130	100	28	18	16	11	8
30 USA	1992	1423	1528	990	653	429	264	163	97	46	11	10	11	11	12
31 YUGOSLAVIA	-	-	-	-	-	-	-	-	-	-	.	.	6	5	4

- NO MORTALITY DATA ARE AVAILABLE FOR EVEN A BROADER GROUP OF CAUSES FOR THIS DISEASE
. MORTALITY DATA ARE PRESENTED FOR A BROADER GROUP OF CAUSES FOR THIS DISEASE
0 VALUE<0.5
THE STANDARD MORTALITY RATIOS WERE DERIVED WITH A FACTOR OF 10

SERIAL MORTALITY TABLES FOR VARIOUS COUNTRIES 1901-1975

TABLE 116 : STOMACH AND DUODENUM - ALL DISEASES MALES

	1901-	1906-	1911-	1916-	1921-	1926-	1931-	1936-	1941-	1946-	1951-	1956-	1961-	1966-	1971-75
1 AUSTRALIA	-	.	.	.	.	2081	2113	2221	2137	1990	1810	1640	1316	1094	969
2 AUSTRIA	-	-	-	-	-	-	-	-	-	.	1607	1474	1691	1676	1398
3 BELGIUM	6736	6021	5594	5037	4510	3520	.	.	.	.	1049	956	901	900	814
4 BULGARIA	-	-	-	-	-	-	.	.	.	.	.	.	1247	1164	1054
5 CANADA	-	-	-	-	3207	3623	3090	2786	2255	1791	1320	1263	1220	1085	842
6 CHILE	-	.	.	.	6456	5096	4564	3645	3373	2920	2015	1579	1508	1552	1463
7 CZECHOSLOVAKIA	-	-	-	1810	1962	2281	2419	2563	3042	2395	1496	1144	1088	1237	1162
8 DENMARK	.	.	.	.	.	.	.	.	.	.	1427	1102	1039	1112	984
9 EIRE	-	-	-	-	3872	3923	3796	3617	2695	2298	1716	1502	1313	1347	1328
10 FINLAND	-	-	-	-	-	.	.	.	.	.	1636	1654	1353	940	772
11 FRANCE	-	-	-	-	-	-	.	.	1571	1285	687	647	616	646	727
12 GREECE	-	-	-	-	-	2661	3122	3004	-	-	-	1183	1191	1025	708
13 HUNGARY	-	-	-	.	.	.	1718	2013	2277	.	1416	1352	1353	1495	1562
14 ICELAND	-	-	-	-	-	-	-	-	.	.	-	-	345	712	582
15 ITALY	4690	4043	5750	4786	3181	2188	2165	2467	2530	2056	1600	1507	1583	1563	1518
16 JAPAN	30692	26052	17092	13950	11788	10215	11224	12161	-	9909	7371	4867	3508	2633	1808
17 NETHERLANDS	1766	.	.	.	1475	1717	1938	2358	2941	1344	1273	1127	913	846	748
18 NEW ZEALAND	-	.	.	.	2217	2381	2221	2239	2370	1926	1737	1715	1270	921	987
19 NORWAY	3952	2847	.	.	.	.	.	.	.	.	750	695	654	648	685
20 POLAND	-	-	-	-	-	-	-	-	-	-	.	1573	1866	1742	1420
21 PORTUGAL	2744	2117	2129	2175	2253	3663	.	.	.	.	3780	3006	2550	2220	1620
22 ROMANIA	-	-	-	-	-	-	-	-	-	-	-	1800	1526	1044	852
23 SPAIN	.	.	.	.	.	.	4194	5035	4131	3333	1953	1536	1570	1405	1416
24 SWEDEN	-	-	.	.	.	.	.	.	.	.	1627	1256	1228	1268	1362
25 SWITZERLAND	2567	2567	2529	2529	2307	2451	.	.	.	.	1365	1260	1171	1030	947
26 TURKEY	-	-	-	-	-	-	-	-	-	-	-	2266	2072	1691	1457
27 UK ENGLAND AND WALES	4245	3189	4278	3735	3360	3496	3131	3192	2975	2504	2448	1954	1529	1318	1177
28 UK NORTHERN IRELAND	-	-	-	-	4233	4058	.	.	.	1649	1685	1521	1461	1299	1185
29 UK SCOTLAND	.	.	.	.	4247	4520	3788	3985	3366	2991	2710	2212	1850	1436	1344
30 USA	6783	5203	.	.	2960	2829	2429	2295	2039	1589	1396	1388	1309	974	700
31 YUGOSLAVIA	-	-	-	-	-	-	-	-	-	-	.	.	1466	1283	1202

- NO MORTALITY DATA ARE AVAILABLE FOR EVEN A BROADER GROUP OF CAUSES FOR THIS DISEASE

. MORTALITY DATA ARE PRESENTED FOR A BROADER GROUP OF CAUSES FOR THIS DISEASE

0 VALUE<0.5

THE STANDARD MORTALITY RATIOS WERE DERIVED WITH A FACTOR OF 1000

SERIAL MORTALITY TABLES FOR VARIOUS COUNTRIES 1901-1975

TABLE 116 : STOMACH AND DUODENUM - ALL DISEASES FEMALES

	1901-	1906-	1911-	1916-	1921-	1926-	1931-	1936-	1941-	1946-	1951-	1956-	1961-	1966-	1971-75
1 AUSTRALIA	-	.	.	.	.	1092	749	656	578	501	460	505	426	405	397
2 AUSTRIA	-	-	-	-	-	-	-	-	-	.	511	496	575	625	571
3 BELGIUM	5511	4887	4306	3862	3352	2482	.	.	.	.	261	197	272	295	339
4 BULGARIA	-	-	-	-	-	-	.	.	.	.	.	.	338	335	331
5 CANADA	-	-	-	-	2204	2496	1670	1148	724	490	329	380	384	371	305
6 CHILE	-	.	.	.	6069	4286	3382	2304	1830	1171	625	516	496	489	533
7 CZECHOSLOVAKIA	-	-	-	1153	1131	1133	919	735	779	618	397	361	302	374	397
8 DENMARK	.	.	.	.	.	.	.	.	.	.	442	430	469	501	502
9 EIRE	-	-	-	-	2852	2847	2361	1893	1398	894	610	529	536	536	581
10 FINLAND	-	-	-	-	-	.	.	.	.	.	306	356	386	337	339
11 FRANCE	-	-	-	-	-	-	.	.	421	311	122	135	145	168	227
12 GREECE	-	-	-	-	-	1181	1191	1183	-	-	-	349	425	430	286
13 HUNGARY	-	-	-	.	.	.	453	441	449	.	314	351	373	489	578
14 ICELAND	-	-	-	-	-	-	-	-	.	.	-	-	618	316	401
15 ITALY	4300	3711	5230	4471	2751	1374	935	889	738	452	306	291	311	333	345
16 JAPAN	28999	24949	16299	12608	9799	7359	7328	7704	-	4195	3135	2215	1649	1267	957
17 NETHERLANDS	1362	.	.	.	680	723	640	594	769	384	337	363	308	311	345
18 NEW ZEALAND	-	.	.	.	1238	866	739	706	600	539	543	570	479	412	469
19 NORWAY	2943	2316	.	.	.	.	.	.	.	.	304	251	320	273	296
20 POLAND	-	-	-	-	-	-	-	-	-	-	.	348	387	405	374
21 PORTUGAL	1583	1221	909	778	793	1394	.	.	.	.	810	666	602	521	393
22 ROMANIA	-	-	-	-	-	-	-	-	-	-	-	436	370	247	206
23 SPAIN	.	.	.	.	.	.	1501	1487	1206	817	419	348	352	352	373
24 SWEDEN	-	-	.	.	.	.	.	.	.	.	499	528	546	602	680
25 SWITZERLAND	1858	1858	1496	1496	1158	1022	.	.	.	.	542	533	442	464	466
26 TURKEY	-	-	-	-	-	-	-	-	-	-	-	788	643	687	656
27 UK ENGLAND AND WALES	4904	3336	3067	2474	1746	1342	1057	863	678	595	633	602	548	514	544
28 UK NORTHERN IRELAND	-	-	-	-	3084	2596	.	.	.	656	508	562	534	559	516
29 UK SCOTLAND	.	.	.	.	2335	2001	1460	1132	839	705	681	623	582	485	534
30 USA	6776	5046	.	.	1945	1458	997	728	536	390	331	393	427	359	284
31 YUGOSLAVIA	-	-	-	-	-	-	-	-	-	-	.	.	337	388	398

- NO MORTALITY DATA ARE AVAILABLE FOR EVEN A BROADER GROUP OF CAUSES FOR THIS DISEASE

. MORTALITY DATA ARE PRESENTED FOR A BROADER GROUP OF CAUSES FOR THIS DISEASE

0 VALUE<0.5

THE STANDARD MORTALITY RATIOS WERE DERIVED WITH A FACTOR OF 1000

SERIAL MORTALITY TABLES FOR VARIOUS COUNTRIES 1901-1975

TAELE 117 : APPENDICITIS : MALES

	1901-	1906-	1911-	1916-	1921-	1926-	1931-	1936-	1941-	1946-	1951-	1956-	1961-	1966-	1971-75
1 AUSTRALIA	-	10246	10558	9421	9976	11308	11285	10480	7003	4085	2365	1700	1155	628	448
2 AUSTRIA	-	-	-	-	-	-	-	-	-	5000	4785	3971	3236	2765	1912
3 BELGIUM	-	-	6379	5821	7964	10438	9820	8263	6255	3362	1819	1491	1033	608	506
4 BULGARIA	-	-	-	-	-	9533	10605	13070	8769	6186	2605	1629	1637	1436	1101
5 CANADA	-	-	-	-	18132	18365	18504	15071	8774	4202	1982	1445	1020	711	467
6 CHILE	-	2593	3382	4719	4321	3740	4917	4656	3736	2114	1796	1799	1947	1598	1633
7 CZECHOSLOVAKIA	-	-	-	3176	4111	6345	7286	7536	3968	4145	2204	1522	1037	1092	1226
8 DENMARK	.	.	.	.	.	.	12046	11797	8032	4973	3291	2165	1760	1325	889
9 EIRE	-	-	-	-	5701	7268	7204	7086	4397	3214	2086	1569	988	772	772
10 FINLAND	-	-	-	-	-	.	.	.	5689	4246	3090	2339	1686	1362	971
11 FRANCE	-	-	-	-	4072	4493	4756	3825	2578	2270	1975	1493	1103	935	833
12 GREECE	-	-	-	-	3021	3619	4069	4366	-	-	-	655	682	483	278
13 HUNGARY	-	-	-	.	.	.	5884	6823	6189	3667	2024	2004	1924	1607	1621
14 ICELAND	-	-	6111	5500	4546	9565	12000	14815	11333	8788	4054	1905	1277	392	893
15 ITALY	-	-	-	-	4151	5446	7704	8236	6712	5326	3365	2517	1999	1419	1071
16 JAPAN	.	4901	4724	5785	6307	5894	5536	5193	-	4667	2641	1645	1067	782	517
17 NETHERLANDS	3305	3000	3641	3685	4315	5993	6677	5690	4760	3588	1974	1590	1231	1119	797
18 NEW ZEALAND	-	15814	11631	10584	10842	9460	10087	8960	5160	3166	1695	1697	1096	624	582
19 NORWAY	5082	6028	7265	6552	7433	8554	8627	7503	6472	3286	1759	1005	846	673	509
20 POLAND	-	-	-	-	-	-	-	-	-	-	.	1251	1408	1458	1381
21 PORTUGAL	-	-	663	2061	2018	2328	2458	2702	3042	2735	1909	1302	1152	908	771
22 ROMANIA	-	-	-	-	-	-	-	-	-	-	-	596	1007	817	613
23 SPAIN	2865	3294	3748	3667	3641	4165	5000	4136	3601	2611	1674	1144	1036	749	702
24 SWEDEN	-	-	8709	9881	11110	12185	11872	11242	6188	3742	2710	1490	1151	830	751
25 SWITZERLAND	14477	14477	13928	13928	12893	14830	15759	14595	9011	7470	4625	3324	2340	1717	1311
26 TURKEY	-	-	-	-	-	-	-	-	-	-	-	2055	976	693	390
27 UK ENGLAND AND WALES	7416	8472	9741	8783	9377	9091	8836	7717	5220	3494	2409	1835	1194	764	586
28 UK NORTHERN IRELAND	-	-	-	-	9145	8908	10797	8063	6101	4713	1671	1294	1059	647	535
29 UK SCOTLAND	14769	14056	12100	11444	12780	12358	12156	10229	6434	4104	2202	2178	1400	733	516
30 USA	24361	18562	17848	17090	19444	19953	18724	14641	7487	3594	1940	1347	1102	867	568
31 YUGOSLAVIA	-	-	-	-	-	-	-	-	-	-	.	1339	855	599	626

\- NO MORTALITY DATA ARE AVAILABLE FOR EVEN A BROADER GROUP OF CAUSES FOR THIS DISEASE

. MORTALITY DATA ARE PRESENTED FOR A BROADER GROUP OF CAUSES FOR THIS DISEASE

0 VALUE<0.5

THE STANDARD MORTALITY RATIOS WERE DERIVED WITH A FACTOR OF 1000

SERIAL MORTALITY TABLES FOR VARIOUS COUNTRIES 1901-1975

TABLE 117 : APPENDICITIS : FEMALES

	1901-	1906-	1911-	1916-	1921-	1926-	1931-	1936-	1941-	1946-	1951-	1956-	1961-	1966-	1971-75
1 AUSTRALIA	-	7836	7817	6953	7047	6621	6337	5414	3823	2180	1265	930	571	402	322
2 AUSTRIA	-	-	-	-	-	-	-	-	-	3810	3723	2835	2345	1803	1429
3 BELGIUM	-	-	4601	5131	6266	7825	6972	5796	4172	2265	1182	956	720	520	318
4 BULGARIA	-	-	-	-	-	5734	6701	6520	4234	2827	1223	834	767	773	528
5 CANADA	-	-	-	-	13551	13584	12250	9599	5508	2657	1114	725	545	365	272
6 CHILE	-	2000	3225	4631	3897	3522	3760	3254	2409	1457	1139	1094	961	1100	1120
7 CZECHOSLOVAKIA	-	-	-	2299	2733	4724	5188	5535	2815	3128	1787	1161	751	799	830
8 DENMARK	.	.	.	.	.	.	6571	5479	5014	2747	1727	1265	989	757	501
9 EIRE	-	-	-	-	4311	4601	4912	4413	3535	2067	1274	855	745	446	478
10 FINLAND	-	-	-	-	-	.	.	.	4669	2896	1808	1526	1107	881	536
11 FRANCE	-	-	-	-	2357	2831	2834	2159	1523	1244	1101	820	605	552	512
12 GREECE	-	-	-	-	1522	1807	2348	2302	-	-	-	256	273	265	182
13 HUNGARY	-	-	-	.	.	.	3466	4127	4284	2546	1371	1312	1279	1133	1143
14 ICELAND	-	-	3043	2500	4615	3929	5000	6364	4857	3421	1951	444	400	727	500
15 ITALY	-	-	-	-	2929	3822	5085	5359	4554	3455	2048	1497	1169	780	556
16 JAPAN	.	4034	3851	4300	4637	4105	3695	3715	-	3990	2319	1418	846	564	364
17 NETHERLANDS	2359	2184	2519	2448	2214	3770	4219	3519	3033	2294	1219	1096	773	686	483
18 NEW ZEALAND	-	8333	9246	8210	7452	6520	5758	5757	3693	1695	972	980	473	497	329
19 NORWAY	4388	5298	6126	5517	4498	5151	4969	4080	3456	1757	1099	875	428	446	407
20 POLAND	-	-	-	-	-	-	-	-	-	-	.	718	763	964	933
21 PORTUGAL	-	-	436	1147	1185	1007	1473	1407	1667	1348	1050	658	660	535	435
22 ROMANIA	-	-	-	-	-	-	-	-	-	-	-	393	530	417	309
23 SPAIN	2167	2245	2314	2249	2343	2337	2521	2111	1894	1355	897	568	539	396	362
24 SWEDEN	-	-	7484	8888	7985	7455	6611	5833	3440	2111	1277	711	724	590	432
25 SWITZERLAND	10760	10760	10016	10016	8771	10214	10742	8927	5984	4913	3118	2005	1453	878	794
26 TURKEY	-	-	-	-	-	-	-	-	-	-	-	942	467	526	170
27 UK ENGLAND AND WALES	4841	5710	6433	6189	6319	5854	5931	4834	3180	2069	1379	932	732	503	397
28 UK NORTHERN IRELAND	-	-	-	-	5709	6258	6536	5202	3315	2568	815	667	674	409	452
29 UK SCOTLAND	10849	9577	8361	8396	9049	8152	7510	5873	3623	2497	1555	974	806	577	364
30 USA	15535	12901	12856	12779	13539	13839	12205	9249	4907	2184	1047	709	607	473	317
31 YUGOSLAVIA	-	-	-	-	-	-	-	-	-	-	.	671	426	397	357

- NO MORTALITY DATA ARE AVAILABLE FOR EVEN A BROADER GROUP OF CAUSES FOR THIS DISEASE

. MORTALITY DATA ARE PRESENTED FOR A BROADER GROUP OF CAUSES FOR THIS DISEASE

0 VALUE<0.5

THE STANDARD MORTALITY RATIOS WERE DERIVED WITH A FACTOR OF 1000

SERIAL MORTALITY TABLES FOR VARIOUS COUNTRIES 1901-1975

TABLE 118 : INTESTINAL OBSTRUCTION AND HERNIA : MALES

	1901-	1906-	1911-	1916-	1921-	1926-	1931-	1936-	1941-	1946-	1951-	1956-	1961-	1966-	1971-75
1 AUSTRALIA	-	33678	35174	36394	32792	30588	26439	25134	24607	20825	15984	13743	11100	8156	6407
2 AUSTRIA	-	-	-	-	-	-	-	-	-	28054	24231	24018	22264	17191	11054
3 BELGIUM	45341	48182	46674	44521	42659	33465	.	.	.	.	12873	13146	11797	12432	8184
4 BULGARIA	-	-	-	-	-	38557	.	.	.	.	.	.	18171	14821	9166
5 CANADA	-	-	-	-	34647	32158	32436	29543	22461	17725	14179	12796	11920	10032	6979
6 CHILE	-	31311	19678	24521	18523	29085	39001	37512	32409	32774	26881	27359	25391	19144	15621
7 CZECHOSLOVAKIA	-	-	-	24425	30562	33242	29198	27947	23175	21507	22356	17587	16122	13592	11237
8 DENMARK	11293	10359	10194	10591	8703	11410	26975	26557	26962	19570	15680	13465	13420	8125	4810
9 EIRE	-	-	-	-	28531	25712	22809	22740	20820	17806	13702	10632	10743	7528	7155
10 FINLAND	-	-	-	-	-	.	.	.	39959	29467	18218	21857	17534	14650	9641
11 FRANCE	-	-	-	-	22468	26013	.	.	30392	25169	20900	18574	17332	15536	14169
12 GREECE	-	-	-	-	17776	22185	25471	23093	-	-	-	13208	13531	11554	7765
13 HUNGARY	-	-	-	18123	16037	15205	31259	29892	34611	30950	24098	21612	18271	16835	12340
14 ICELAND	-	-	-	-	-	-	-	-	.	.	11688	11494	12183	8796	5882
15 ITALY	-	-	-	-	31376	30814	31883	31280	33100	26065	23586	21551	18854	15488	13083
16 JAPAN	21358	29132	34483	37065	36403	32674	33265	34844	-	32207	24699	19292	15092	10927	7293
17 NETHERLANDS	22938	19501	18387	20043	15217	16484	15551	14951	24634	13879	11946	11619	11678	10607	8630
18 NEW ZEALAND	-	30380	26519	30105	23245	25687	20047	20759	19616	15285	14435	15709	13043	10000	7842
19 NORWAY	32067	30808	27251	27266	24080	25476	21769	22928	27072	13847	12491	10671	11837	8683	7462
20 POLAND	-	-	-	-	-	-	-	-	-	-	.	11077	13029	13258	11181
21 PORTUGAL	29582	26611	23689	24405	23762	27911	.	.	.	.	24982	19130	15215	12179	11563
22 ROMANIA	-	-	-	-	-	-	-	-	-	-	-	22479	24104	16862	9486
23 SPAIN	40974	59846	58667	56537	48009	45101	37438	40199	36214	27481	21490	18529	16274	13555	12395
24 SWEDEN	-	-	24044	26603	19312	19868	19073	18739	19508	14055	13300	12421	11885	9895	7764
25 SWITZERLAND	33960	33960	29491	29491	25326	25047	23081	25113	25712	16035	15747	12616	12979	10413	7233
26 TURKEY	-	-	-	-	-	-	-	-	-	-	-	59291	35900	27223	15718
27 UK ENGLAND AND WALES	42307	36159	38370	39579	35448	35519	35211	29757	23357	17921	14906	13458	12805	9876	8288
28 UK NORTHERN IRELAND	-	-	-	-	40264	31662	23490	21137	23713	19910	13962	12129	11625	8888	8820
29 UK SCOTLAND	50664	39228	38359	37939	35300	32365	29417	26622	25125	19479	18105	16155	16068	11398	7053
30 USA	65125	50500	41955	37948	34527	33976	32127	28959	23435	17511	13112	11456	10966	8726	6166
31 YUGOSLAVIA	-	-	-	-	-	-	-	-	-	-	.	24476	16827	14323	10346

- NO MORTALITY DATA ARE AVAILABLE FOR EVEN A BROADER GROUP OF CAUSES FOR THIS DISEASE
. MORTALITY DATA ARE PRESENTED FOR A BROADER GROUP OF CAUSES FOR THIS DISEASE
0 VALUE<0.5
THE STANDARD MORTALITY RATIOS WERE DERIVED WITH A FACTOR OF 10000

SERIAL MORTALITY TABLES FOR VARIOUS COUNTRIES 1901-1975

TABLE 118 : INTESTINAL OBSTRUCTION AND HERNIA : FEMALES

	1901-	1906-	1911-	1916-	1921-	1926-	1931-	1936-	1941-	1946-	1951-	1956-	1961-	1966-	1971-75
1 AUSTRALIA	-	31206	33930	31531	29516	26273	22971	20160	19758	15838	11574	9741	8534	6994	5573
2 AUSTRIA	-	-	-	-	-	-	-	-	-	23825	20096	20812	18820	15740	11096
3 BELGIUM	36957	38770	39038	35499	36320	30804	.	.	.	.	12641	11864	11346	12762	8128
4 BULGARIA	-	-	-	-	-	14384	.	.	.	.	.	.	9574	7869	5284
5 CANADA	-	-	-	-	28821	24653	25054	22326	17236	13863	10796	10558	10422	8331	6349
6 CHILE	-	25360	16131	19189	13318	20731	25980	24394	25020	22672	19050	19290	19725	16857	15261
7 CZECHOSLOVAKIA	-	-	-	17657	20943	23018	20997	19934	19829	15520	18523	14749	13618	12135	10278
8 DENMARK	10983	10884	11424	11520	8256	9904	21702	22692	23721	16327	13440	11865	12459	8122	3888
9 EIRE	-	-	-	-	24348	21688	17228	19011	19363	13687	12192	10077	8786	7007	6174
10 FINLAND	-	-	-	-	-	.	.	.	19929	13779	10402	15124	13925	12230	7215
11 FRANCE	-	-	-	-	18688	20775	.	.	27981	21198	17534	15476	14562	13561	13250
12 GREECE	-	-	-	-	7318	9514	11987	12870	-	-	-	9174	10186	9946	7889
13 HUNGARY	-	-	-	13472	10747	9562	24101	22446	27401	22219	18275	15310	15199	14601	11112
14 ICELAND	-	-	-	-	-	-	-	-	.	.	11111	13043	10000	11462	5000
15 ITALY	-	-	-	-	21503	20644	20908	20883	23772	16351	15825	14876	13867	11684	10458
16 JAPAN	9407	13586	17810	20002	19831	19106	19695	20901	-	19248	14864	11636	9370	7523	5637
17 NETHERLANDS	23227	21023	18773	20886	15580	15047	14568	14093	24378	10636	9127	9176	9652	9236	7891
18 NEW ZEALAND	-	26190	25392	27907	22947	20810	18336	17986	14177	13016	11344	12491	11697	7406	6134
19 NORWAY	22041	20519	20315	19473	18024	17980	18826	20556	24502	12697	10843	10673	10703	8318	6945
20 POLAND	-	-	-	-	-	-	-	-	-	-	.	6789	8686	9471	8497
21 PORTUGAL	12715	13879	11632	13766	12426	15744	.	.	.	.	13754	11144	8291	7360	7311
22 ROMANIA	-	-	-	-	-	-	-	-	-	-	-	10471	11010	9054	6155
23 SPAIN	25854	36329	33943	34248	28376	26009	24855	27748	23781	18102	14273	13081	13094	11430	10732
24 SWEDEN	-	-	16832	18440	13524	14595	14619	15450	15779	11467	11477	11441	13434	10230	7377
25 SWITZERLAND	30423	30423	26512	26512	21806	21008	20688	21402	21473	13259	11711	9941	9892	8198	5556
26 TURKEY	-	-	-	-	-	-	-	-	-	-	-	21244	13986	13603	9718
27 UK ENGLAND AND WALES	42211	35031	33043	33990	28017	26488	25339	21921	17976	13373	10607	9751	9600	8084	7110
28 UK NORTHERN IRELAND	-	-	-	-	34402	29186	18307	19776	19663	14314	12251	9505	11198	8312	7455
29 UK SCOTLAND	38184	29504	28017	28901	24356	24061	20731	20076	19107	14906	13661	11724	11106	8061	6478
30 USA	63166	49091	39793	34484	31225	30367	28691	25071	20588	15227	10572	9736	9915	7957	5792
31 YUGOSLAVIA	-	-	-	-	-	-	-	-	-	-	.	11041	8619	7549	6683

- NO MORTALITY DATA ARE AVAILABLE FOR EVEN A BROADER GROUP OF CAUSES FOR THIS DISEASE

. MORTALITY DATA ARE PRESENTED FOR A BROADER GROUP OF CAUSES FOR THIS DISEASE

0 VALUE<0.5

THE STANDARD MORTALITY RATIOS WERE DERIVED WITH A FACTOR OF 10000

SERIAL MORTALITY TABLES FOR VARIOUS COUNTRIES 1901-1975

TABLE 119 : GASTRO-ENTERITIS AND COLITIS EXCLUDING DIARRHOEA OF THE NEWBORN : MALES

	1901-	1906-	1911-	1916-	1921-	1926-	1931-	1936-	1941-	1946-	1951-	1956-	1961-	1966-	1971-75
1 AUSTRALIA	-	.	.	.	14431	9263	3604	2777	2395	1465	1300	1043	946	894	.
2 AUSTRIA	-	-	-	-	-	-	-	-	-	6276	2692	2229	1578	1315	.
3 BELGIUM	34436	31745	36063	17323	17885	13140	7237	4110	4481	2927	977	777	630	548	.
4 BULGARIA	-	-	-	-	-	33444	27365	18398	14025	13170	7327	1114	470	757	.
5 CANADA	-	-	-	-	11508	16311	10820	7017	5311	3636	1842	1315	993	722	.
6 CHILE	-	46734	.	.	58564	67782	66537	61288	55940	40998	12799	13551	19845	15579	.
7 CZECHOSLOVAKIA	-	-	-	32231	32842	31995	20142	12613	22925	12645	2320	1556	1085	933	.
8 DENMARK	.	.	.	.	.	.	4249	3040	3349	1865	862	720	642	619	.
9 EIRE	-	-	-	-	6650	9272	6651	6408	10322	5535	1665	1171	982	1528	.
10 FINLAND	-	-	-	-	-	5623	3905	6111	9737	8546	2451	1705	805	665	.
11 FRANCE	-	-	-	-	9313	10953	5771	5911	7273	5405	881	313	201	173	.
12 GREECE	-	-	-	-	27321	38055	37858	29648	-	-	-	2018	1386	854	.
13 HUNGARY	-	-	-	.	.	.	.	.	.	10936	6441	3049	1578	872	.
14 ICELAND	-	-	10633	4706	2043	3200	2804	1429	2320	952	.	.	728	505	.
15 ITALY	82309	74016	56631	58870	56808	51295	35921	28989	26508	15303	6660	3677	2496	1636	.
16 JAPAN	31523	42705	53244	62418	69852	65688	55526	50523	-	20060	11104	5861	3442	1996	.
17 NETHERLANDS	46640	32786	.	.	10407	5903	3281	2163	7823	2562	578	586	711	668	.
18 NEW ZEALAND	-	.	.	.	3348	1850	1321	1073	1495	1095	1642	1366	1057	953	.
19 NORWAY	9184	6203	7949	5226	3906	2611	1844	1741	2469	1414	780	741	680	562	.
20 POLAND	-	-	-	-	-	-	-	-	-	-	.	5177	3666	1787	.
21 PORTUGAL	-	-	-	-	-	-	72818	63967	64880	47788	32876	25689	20468	10673	.
22 ROMANIA	-	-	-	-	-	-	-	-	-	-	-	3439	2669	3486	.
23 SPAIN	99433	94914	.	.	.	.	53416	51669	40140	19625	8496	5077	2946	1489	.
24 SWEDEN	-	-	.	.	.	.	239	223	305	214	593	620	661	672	.
25 SWITZERLAND	33848	33848	17091	17091	8628	5663	3259	2324	2480	1804	1224	1051	982	804	.
26 TURKEY	-	-	-	-	-	-	-	-	-	-	-	40385	23034	15966	14047
27 UK ENGLAND AND WALES	29188	20641	22076	10502	8132	5384	4271	3714	3681	2585	1063	932	955	872	.
28 UK NORTHERN IRELAND	-	-	-	-	8997	9274	8444	8271	8767	3932	2210	1136	818	1042	.
29 UK SCOTLAND	20564	16002	16242	12138	8890	6371	6295	6416	6108	4221	1463	1195	961	1108	.
30 USA	52598	39767	.	.	12195	8291	5248	3963	2585	1435	1181	973	886	761	.
31 YUGOSLAVIA	-	-	-	-	-	-	-	-	-	-	.	.	5833	3317	.

- NO MORTALITY DATA ARE AVAILABLE FOR EVEN A BROADER GROUP OF CAUSES FOR THIS DISEASE
. MORTALITY DATA ARE PRESENTED FOR A BROADER GROUP OF CAUSES FOR THIS DISEASE
0 VALUE<0.5
THE STANDARD MORTALITY RATIOS WERE DERIVED WITH A FACTOR OF 1000

SERIAL MORTALITY TABLES FOR VARIOUS COUNTRIES 1901-1975

TABLE 119 : GASTRO-ENTERITIS AND COLITIS EXCLUDING DIARRHOEA OF THE NEWBORN : FEMALES

	1901-	1906-	1911-	1916-	1921-	1926-	1931-	1936-	1941-	1946-	1951-	1956-	1961-	1966-	1971-75
1 AUSTRALIA	-	.	.	.	12374	7828	3139	2582	2134	1208	1245	903	860	875	.
2 AUSTRIA	-	-	-	-	-	-	-	-	-	3811	1646	1450	1330	1104	.
3 BELGIUM	27003	25371	26968	11440	13434	9980	5161	3092	3313	1939	678	597	498	439	.
4 BULGARIA	-	-	-	-	-	29756	24686	17230	10974	10541	4962	907	409	467	.
5 CANADA	-	-	-	-	9727	13736	8683	5933	4359	2925	1501	1158	910	767	.
6 CHILE	-	40867	.	.	53137	60861	59566	54465	50107	35672	11008	11659	16482	12655	.
7 CZECHOSLOVAKIA	-	-	-	23377	23573	22888	14500	8984	16319	8732	1772	1153	795	702	.
8 DENMARK	.	.	.	.	.	.	2900	2305	2711	1556	933	788	701	692	.
9 EIRE	-	-	-	-	5305	7379	5465	5369	8119	3975	1391	998	933	1218	.
10 FINLAND	-	-	-	-	-	3626	2558	4069	6817	5593	1498	1258	852	698	.
11 FRANCE	-	-	-	-	6053	7039	3713	3976	4496	3172	504	218	148	148	.
12 GREECE	-	-	-	-	26367	37179	37912	29218	-	-	-	2141	1577	1028	.
13 HUNGARY	-	-	-	.	.	.	.	.	.	7561	4351	2263	1170	668	.
14 ICELAND	-	-	6737	3981	1518	1557	1846	1533	1007	539	.	.	762	837	.
15 ITALY	81042	72591	54547	55562	52550	47055	32541	25409	22622	12831	5705	3051	1996	1295	.
16 JAPAN	32696	44284	53741	62774	68344	62598	52413	47653	-	19320	11455	6307	3822	2288	.
17 NETHERLANDS	35467	24592	.	.	7668	4279	2504	1875	6144	1966	598	640	646	698	.
18 NEW ZEALAND	-	.	.	.	2848	1981	1303	1369	1343	918	1426	1228	1041	866	.
19 NORWAY	7621	4967	6373	4350	3041	2107	1548	1449	2402	1130	763	695	769	638	.
20 POLAND	-	-	-	-	-	-	-	-	-	-	.	3217	2260	1088	.
21 PORTUGAL	-	-	-	-	-	-	55984	48149	48436	34902	23153	17870	14228	7278	.
22 ROMANIA	-	-	-	-	-	-	-	-	-	-	-	2514	1901	2414	.
23 SPAIN	92169	85347	.	.	.	.	44295	42163	30993	15387	6552	4098	2267	1219	.
24 SWEDEN	-	-	.	.	.	.	308	317	304	210	595	618	854	680	.
25 SWITZERLAND	24894	24894	11980	11980	5930	4083	2287	1423	1434	1101	974	953	866	810	.
26 TURKEY	-	-	-	-	-	-	-	-	-	-	-	38174	21601	14863	12856
27 UK ENGLAND AND WALES	24145	16630	16673	7738	5737	3835	3050	2641	2505	1834	1011	990	1050	1045	.
28 UK NORTHERN IRELAND	-	-	-	-	7188	7803	6149	6313	5946	2894	1345	1035	888	996	.
29 UK SCOTLAND	16002	12775	12842	8889	6542	4759	4436	4351	4058	2675	1285	1103	1123	1038	.
30 USA	45704	35003	.	.	10386	7043	4506	3365	2124	1146	1003	860	819	753	.
31 YUGOSLAVIA	-	-	-	-	-	-	-	-	-	-	.	.	4577	2651	.

- NO MORTALITY DATA ARE AVAILABLE FOR EVEN A BROADER GROUP OF CAUSES FOR THIS DISEASE

. MORTALITY DATA ARE PRESENTED FOR A BROADER GROUP OF CAUSES FOR THIS DISEASE

0 VALUE<0.5

THE STANDARD MORTALITY RATIOS WERE DERIVED WITH A FACTOR OF 1000

SERIAL MORTALITY TABLES FOR VARIOUS COUNTRIES 1901-1975

TABLE 120 : GASTRITIS, DUODENITIS, ENTERITIS AND COLITIS : MALES

	1901-	1906-	1911-	1916-	1921-	1926-	1931-	1936-	1941-	1946-	1951-	1956-	1961-	1966-	1971-75
1 AUSTRALIA	-	.	.	.	1516	974	388	294	255	162	130	105	95	90	.
2 AUSTRIA	-	-	-	-	-	-	-	-	-	.	230	220	163	140	.
3 BELGIUM	-	-	-	-	.	.	.	.	.	.	95	76	64	55	.
4 BULGARIA	-	-	-	-	-	-	.	.	.	.	.	.	56	77	.
5 CANADA	-	-	-	-	1332	1844	1226	786	576	395	187	133	101	75	.
6 CHILE	-	4772	.	.	6290	7018	6799	6178	5588	4077	1276	1326	1941	1533	.
7 CZECHOSLOVAKIA	-	-	-	3212	3281	3181	2013	1277	2276	1099	347	164	114	98	.
8 DENMARK	.	.	.	.	.	.	.	.	.	.	85	73	66	64	.
9 EIRE	-	-	-	-	987	1193	901	818	1137	633	178	126	100	151	.
10 FINLAND	-	-	-	-	-	.	.	.	.	.	247	173	87	67	.
11 FRANCE	-	-	-	-	-	-	.	.	847	579	87	32	21	18	.
12 GREECE	-	-	-	-	-	4296	3801	2964	-	-	-	198	140	84	.
13 HUNGARY	-	-	-	.	.	.	3316	2137	2151	.	490	302	158	88	.
14 ICELAND	-	-	-	-	-	-	-	-	.	.	65	78	75	49	.
15 ITALY	-	-	-	-	5555	5114	3572	2882	2617	1505	653	364	249	165	.
16 JAPAN	.	7807	6899	7362	7693	7003	6019	5563	-	2100	1191	659	412	254	.
17 NETHERLANDS	4682	3349	.	.	1078	638	372	257	802	265	58	59	71	67	.
18 NEW ZEALAND	-	.	.	.	408	226	154	122	153	111	161	137	104	100	.
19 NORWAY	1318	875	.	.	.	.	.	.	.	.	79	76	70	57	.
20 POLAND	-	-	-	-	-	-	-	-	-	-	.	511	366	182	.
21 PORTUGAL	-	-	-	-	-	-	.	.	.	.	3311	2500	1992	1038	.
22 ROMANIA	-	-	-	-	-	-	-	-	-	-	-	339	259	340	.
23 SPAIN	10345	9758	.	.	.	.	5343	5167	4030	2009	837	500	291	146	.
24 SWEDEN	-	-	.	.	.	.	.	.	.	.	61	65	73	76	.
25 SWITZERLAND	.	.	.	.	857	572	.	.	.	.	124	107	99	83	.
26 TURKEY	-	-	-	-	-	-	-	-	-	-	-	3944	2249	1557	1370
27 UK ENGLAND AND WALES	2918	2256	2453	1281	965	630	483	406	389	267	108	93	95	86	.
28 UK NORTHERN IRELAND	-	-	-	-	1172	1141	.	.	.	194	219	111	83	106	.
29 UK SCOTLAND	2366	1938	1931	1483	1080	762	698	681	645	455	149	121	97	109	.
30 USA	5553	4135	.	.	1366	935	598	443	289	159	119	99	92	80	.
31 YUGOSLAVIA	-	-	-	-	-	-	-	-	-	-	.	831	567	323	.

- NO MORTALITY DATA ARE AVAILABLE FOR EVEN A BROADER GROUP OF CAUSES FOR THIS DISEASE

. MORTALITY DATA ARE PRESENTED FOR A BROADER GROUP OF CAUSES FOR THIS DISEASE

0 VALUE<0.5

THE STANDARD MORTALITY RATIOS WERE DERIVED WITH A FACTOR OF 100

SERIAL MORTALITY TABLES FOR VARIOUS COUNTRIES 1901-1975

TABLE 120 : GASTRITIS, DUODENITIS, ENTERITIS AND COLITIS : FEMALES

	1901-	1906-	1911-	1916-	1921-	1926-	1931-	1936-	1941-	1946-	1951-	1956-	1961-	1966-	1971-75
1 AUSTRALIA	-	.	.	.	13144	8317	3406	2728	2236	1304	1237	891	852	855	.
2 AUSTRIA	-	-	-	-	-	-	-	-	-	.	1424	1424	1334	1126	.
3 BELGIUM	-	-	-	-	.	.	.	.	.	.	656	583	488	431	.
4 BULGARIA	-	-	-	-	-	-	.	.	.	.	.	.	500	464	.
5 CANADA	-	-	-	-	11376	15759	9942	6637	4679	3064	1512	1153	910	776	.
6 CHILE	-	41785	.	.	57590	63079	60815	54765	49890	35380	11134	11365	16065	12352	.
7 CZECHOSLOVAKIA	-	-	-	23381	23655	22831	14551	9076	16194	7642	2534	1233	845	730	.
8 DENMARK	.	.	.	.	.	.	.	.	.	.	903	777	693	705	.
9 EIRE	-	-	-	-	8285	10466	7823	7051	9124	4573	1578	1078	948	1212	.
10 FINLAND	-	-	-	-	-	.	.	.	.	.	1488	1252	858	701	.
11 FRANCE	-	-	-	-	-	-	.	.	5163	3293	493	216	150	150	.
12 GREECE	-	-	-	-	-	41256	37408	23916	-	-	-	2102	1565	1038	.
13 HUNGARY	-	-	-	.	.	.	25911	15854	16344	.	3316	2247	1165	673	.
14 ICELAND	-	-	-	-	-	-	-	-	.	.	1204	806	866	807	.
15 ITALY	-	-	-	-	51271	46756	32249	25170	22242	12560	5576	3001	1975	1293	.
16 JAPAN	.	81213	70694	74662	75856	67153	57003	52746	-	20415	12392	7190	4639	2988	.
17 NETHERLANDS	35495	25091	.	.	7806	4506	2712	2025	6197	2040	592	640	639	688	.
18 NEW ZEALAND	-	.	.	.	3590	2247	1541	1471	1406	965	1408	1211	1018	854	.
19 NORWAY	10590	7075	.	.	.	.	.	.	.	.	762	711	786	640	.
20 POLAND	-	-	-	-	-	-	-	-	-	-	.	3155	2240	1101	.
21 PORTUGAL	-	-	-	-	-	-	.	.	.	.	23020	17344	13771	7042	.
22 ROMANIA	-	-	-	-	-	-	-	-	-	-	-	2465	1835	2335	.
23 SPAIN	95093	86974	.	.	.	.	43805	41629	30672	15361	6413	4024	2239	1189	.
24 SWEDEN	-	-	.	.	.	.	.	.	.	.	603	635	891	713	.
25 SWITZERLAND	.	.	.	.	5940	4126	.	.	.	.	987	954	863	826	.
26 TURKEY	-	-	-	-	-	-	-	-	-	-	-	37158	21010	14452	12505
27 UK ENGLAND AND WALES	24262	18612	18838	9755	7077	4678	3587	2920	2671	1908	1036	983	1033	1025	.
28 UK NORTHERN IRELAND	-	-	-	-	10111	9838	.	.	.	2091	1382	1037	874	980	.
29 UK SCOTLAND	19238	16078	15675	11565	8455	6006	5164	4768	4308	2890	1324	1119	1132	1026	.
30 USA	49487	37017	.	.	11749	7956	5083	3714	2331	1239	999	858	823	755	.
31 YUGOSLAVIA	-	-	-	-	-	-	-	-	-	-	.	6655	4433	2566	.

- NO MORTALITY DATA ARE AVAILABLE FOR EVEN A BROADER GROUP OF CAUSES FOR THIS DISEASE

. MORTALITY DATA ARE PRESENTED FOR A BROADER GROUP OF CAUSES FOR THIS DISEASE

0 VALUE<0.5

THE STANDARD MORTALITY RATIOS WERE DERIVED WITH A FACTOR OF 1000

SERIAL MORTALITY TABLES FOR VARIOUS COUNTRIES 1901-1975

TABLE 121 : CIRRHOSIS OF LIVER : MALES

	1901-	1906-	1911-	1916-	1921-	1926-	1931-	1936-	1941-	1946-	1951-	1956-	1961-	1966-	1971-75
1 AUSTRALIA	-	6369	6661	4859	4105	3836	2906	2806	2384	2826	2832	2902	3017	3574	4860
2 AUSTRIA	-	-	-	-	-	-	-	-	-	4084	7256	11258	13551	16723	18317
3 BELGIUM	8003	8487	8668	6401	6327	6808	.	.	.	.	3290	4267	4611	5279	6172
4 BULGARIA	-	-	-	-	-	7381	.	.	.	.	.	.	2582	3106	3804
5 CANADA	-	-	-	-	1886	2321	2334	2584	2592	3002	2881	3778	3934	4916	7292
6 CHILE	-	11480	5339	4876	3531	5280	6895	9603	13355	14965	18045	23452	35560	36262	35887
7 CZECHOSLOVAKIA	-	-	-	1897	2293	3609	4465	4599	541	1568	3383	4373	5030	7297	9770
8 DENMARK	7196	5447	5659	5741	1362	1309	1317	1265	1265	1451	2360	2601	2713	3014	4418
9 EIRE	-	-	-	-	2067	1951	1456	1429	1090	1000	1035	1129	1399	1478	1596
10 FINLAND	-	-	-	-	-	.	.	.	906	1237	1805	2120	2039	2354	3224
11 FRANCE	-	-	-	-	6816	7032	.	.	4696	6103	13071	15966	18206	19986	19392
12 GREECE	-	-	-	-	3779	4381	5291	6197	-	-	-	7221	9452	9875	8079
13 HUNGARY	-	-	-	.	.	.	3779	4480	3414	3088	3737	4677	4671	5852	7780
14 ICELAND	-	-	-	-	-	-	-	-	.	.	822	1205	1505	1200	734
15 ITALY	11258	11336	10685	9131	9174	9528	9101	8120	6385	6089	8907	10125	13146	16421	18792
16 JAPAN	3722	5528	8779	8675	7197	5935	5786	6058	-	5296	6040	7129	7472	8370	9609
17 NETHERLANDS	4920	4456	3799	3259	2533	2448	2053	1799	1498	1204	1671	1922	1927	1957	2428
18 NEW ZEALAND	-	2927	2809	2550	2115	2132	1727	1887	1235	1213	1454	1543	1454	1846	3126
19 NORWAY	732	843	1295	1100	1280	1196	1185	1156	805	949	1480	1577	1649	1817	1978
20 POLAND	-	-	-	-	-	-	-	-	-	-	.	2085	3272	4545	5902
21 PORTUGAL	81[illegible]1	9055	8491	8782	9903	10682	.	.	.	.	14849	15997	17267	20428	20162
22 ROMANIA	-	-	-	-	-	-	-	-	-	-	-	7869	9808	10859	12027
23 SPAIN	11747	11414	10803	10422	9962	10656	8533	7625	5986	6193	6875	8895	10391	12879	13823
24 SWEDEN	-	-	.	.	.	.	1523	1571	1300	1496	1548	2248	2602	3327	4897
25 SWITZERLAND	11240	11240	8912	8912	6119	7091	10732	8438	6078	6618	8491	8647	9982	10469	9076
26 TURKEY	-	-	-	-	-	-	-	-	-	-	-	8281	6846	5508	4574
27 UK ENGLAND AND WALES	9089	7070	7348	4136	3412	3038	2172	1770	1145	1012	1160	1128	1167	1177	1361
28 UK NORTHERN IRELAND	-	-	-	-	1539	1686	1754	1647	1199	1138	1102	1221	1389	1176	1626
29 UK SCOTLAND	4460	3976	4215	2684	2395	2425	1972	2247	1572	1706	1624	1954	2159	2193	2342
30 USA	17572	13514	11391	7514	5322	5159	5154	5528	5499	6025	6008	6562	7123	8650	9253
31 YUGOSLAVIA	-	-	-	-	-	-	-	-	-	-	.	4425	4871	7471	9258

- NO MORTALITY DATA ARE AVAILABLE FOR EVEN A BROADER GROUP OF CAUSES FOR THIS DISEASE
. MORTALITY DATA ARE PRESENTED FOR A BROADER GROUP OF CAUSES FOR THIS DISEASE
0 VALUE<0.5
THE STANDARD MORTALITY RATIOS WERE DERIVED WITH A FACTOR OF 1000

SERIAL MORTALITY TABLES FOR VARIOUS COUNTRIES 1901-1975

TABLE 121 : CIRRHOSIS OF LIVER : FEMALES

	1901-	1906-	1911-	1916-	1921-	1926-	1931-	1936-	1941-	1946-	1951-	1956-	1961-	1966-	1971-75
1 AUSTRALIA	-	4554	3974	2778	2242	1719	1205	1384	1176	1455	1334	1463	1394	1439	1747
2 AUSTRIA	-	-	-	-	-	-	-	-	-	1555	2365	3486	3841	4748	4968
3 BELGIUM	5599	5815	5978	5078	5205	5528	.	.	.	.	1719	2005	2352	2642	3197
4 BULGARIA	-	-	-	-	-	2969	.	.	.	.	.	.	1286	1636	1625
5 CANADA	-	-	-	-	1353	1636	1722	1711	1765	1785	1693	1958	2075	2478	3067
6 CHILE	-	7845	2324	1942	1825	2472	3153	3823	5770	6169	8008	9852	12626	13536	11763
7 CZECHOSLOVAKIA	-	-	-	815	974	1248	1759	1823	302	962	2012	2501	2585	2970	3352
8 DENMARK	1106	1454	1115	1164	454	409	519	443	2760	1878	2594	3361	3004	2973	2863
9 EIRE	-	-	-	-	696	803	688	530	537	412	569	604	689	849	1036
10 FINLAND	-	-	-	-	-	.	.	.	619	655	1010	1152	1193	992	1083
11 FRANCE	-	-	-	-	3975	3685	.	.	1696	2592	6014	6150	6433	6682	6404
12 GREECE	-	-	-	-	1026	1195	1916	2239	-	-	-	2689	3688	3873	3136
13 HUNGARY	-	-	-	.	.	.	1654	2217	1899	1292	1783	2449	2254	2759	3347
14 ICELAND	-	-	-	-	-	-	-	-	.	.	247	562	909	833	678
15 ITALY	5402	4940	4934	4296	3613	3380	3308	3140	2606	2513	3240	3533	4334	5353	6181
16 JAPAN	1940	3490	6305	6063	4264	2997	2999	3103	-	3396	3677	3967	3622	3364	3238
17 NETHERLANDS	3453	3093	2451	2254	1652	1601	1414	1281	1085	995	1190	1304	1239	1298	1294
18 NEW ZEALAND	-	2154	2382	1562	1448	1424	1160	965	871	997	1117	957	897	955	1445
19 NORWAY	289	350	372	426	486	471	402	530	634	994	1162	1234	1093	1092	1021
20 POLAND	-	-	-	-	-	-	-	-	-	-	.	1326	2141	2699	2891
21 PORTUGAL	3845	3572	3340	3578	3619	4662	.	.	.	.	6705	6756	7496	8639	7716
22 ROMANIA	-	-	-	-	-	-	-	-	-	-	-	4947	6157	5923	6086
23 SPAIN	9069	8577	7813	7348	6609	6639	5046	4434	3519	3577	4134	4625	4838	5486	5461
24 SWEDEN	-	-	.	.	.	.	855	931	1009	1238	1185	1393	1439	1676	1945
25 SWITZERLAND	3257	3257	2481	2481	1846	1790	2385	1859	1501	1708	1952	1757	1963	2200	2280
26 TURKEY	-	-	-	-	-	-	-	-	-	-	-	4502	3759	3163	2790
27 UK ENGLAND AND WALES	6607	5080	4910	2009	1519	1368	950	768	491	530	740	756	820	855	1010
28 UK NORTHERN IRELAND	-	-	-	-	545	712	728	573	741	756	904	1137	1010	1094	1468
29 UK SCOTLAND	2236	2179	2122	1367	1134	971	922	1128	654	861	1031	1365	1341	1239	1459
30 USA	8954	6886	5638	3942	3045	2931	2817	2794	2875	3037	2921	3063	3368	3985	4006
31 YUGOSLAVIA	-	-	-	-	-	-	-	-	-	-	.	2136	2019	2916	3311

\- NO MORTALITY DATA ARE AVAILABLE FOR EVEN A BROADER GROUP OF CAUSES FOR THIS DISEASE

. MORTALITY DATA ARE PRESENTED FOR A BROADER GROUP OF CAUSES FOR THIS DISEASE

0 VALUE<0.5

THE STANDARD MORTALITY RATIOS WERE DERIVED WITH A FACTOR OF 1000

SERIAL MORTALITY TABLES FOR VARIOUS COUNTRIES 1901-1975

TABLE 121 : CIRRHOSIS OF LIVER : PERSONS

	1901-	1906-	1911-	1916-	1921-	1926-	1931-	1936-	1941-	1946-	1951-	1956-	1961-	1966-	1971-75
1 AUSTRALIA	-	5546	5432	3891	3225	2820	2076	2099	1776	2129	2055	2150	2163	2444	3206
2 AUSTRIA	-	-	-	-	-	-	3882	3678	-	2661	4475	6783	7891	9665	10387
3 BELGIUM	6770	7113	7278	5715	5752	6156	.	.	.	.	2448	3046	3381	3831	4527
4 BULGARIA	-	-	-	-	-	5172	.	.	.	.	.	.	1907	2343	2672
5 CANADA	7114	2520	2138	1470	1637	1999	2045	2169	2196	2413	2297	2874	2995	3658	5072
6 CHILE	-	9626	3801	3377	2656	3834	4967	6627	9435	10394	12797	16319	23483	24243	22954
7 CZECHOSLOVAKIA	-	-	-	1316	1584	2335	2999	3091	411	1238	2633	3346	3682	4902	6195
8 DENMARK	3690	3147	3036	3101	880	834	898	836	2042	1673	2482	2998	2866	2992	3585
9 EIRE	-	-	-	-	1383	1378	1076	986	814	706	802	864	1036	1154	1306
10 FINLAND	-	-	-	-	-	.	.	.	745	906	1348	1565	1554	1570	1983
11 FRANCE	10357	8109	7864	5807	5276	5210	.	.	2251	4109	9048	10380	11534	12461	12075
12 GREECE	-	-	-	-	2390	2763	3565	4163	-	-	-	6104	8739	9291	7525
13 HUNGARY	-	-	-	.	.	.	2667	3285	2608	2107	2666	3455	3341	4144	5318
14 ICELAND	-	-	-	-	-	-	-	-	.	.	520	872	1198	1010	705
15 ITALY	8291	8087	7761	6674	6334	6346	6070	5494	4375	4172	5849	6556	8346	10350	11857
16 JAPAN	2814	4494	7522	7343	5680	4404	4328	4510	-	4291	4789	5449	5414	5675	6146
17 NETHERLANDS	4155	3747	3099	2739	2079	2013	1725	1533	1286	1096	1422	1600	1565	1607	1817
18 NEW ZEALAND	-	2585	2618	2095	1801	1791	1450	1429	1051	1102	1280	1238	1161	1374	2231
19 NORWAY	494	577	795	734	848	803	762	819	714	973	1312	1396	1356	1432	1465
20 POLAND	-	-	-	-	-	-	-	-	-	-	.	1718	2633	3503	4196
21 PORTUGAL	5759	6023	5631	5878	6389	7314	.	.	.	.	10207	10752	11760	13769	13146
22 ROMANIA	-	-	-	-	-	-	-	.	-	.	-	6270	7814	8164	8788
23 SPAIN	10353	9928	9238	8824	8206	8520	6657	5891	4644	4758	5355	6528	7332	8805	9210
24 SWEDEN	-	-	.	.	.	.	1168	1234	1148	1361	1359	1803	1994	2460	3336
25 SWITZERLAND	6982	6982	5443	5443	3799	4210	6188	4849	3576	3925	4903	4857	5555	5895	5313
26 TURKEY	-	-	-	-	-	-	8865	11977	13445	7467	6122	6344	5282	4354	3709
27 UK ENGLAND AND WALES	7786	6025	6038	2989	2391	2134	1506	1220	779	745	925	919	972	996	1164
28 UK NORTHERN IRELAND	-	-	-	-	1014	1172	1214	1081	954	935	995	1175	1182	1131	1539
29 UK SCOTLAND	3237	2991	3075	1971	1715	1640	1405	1638	1068	1238	1294	1623	1697	1651	1838
30 USA	13240	10267	8602	5784	4214	4073	4007	4172	4182	3605	4415	4731	5126	6125	6372
31 YUGOSLAVIA	-	-	-	-	-	-	-	-	-	-	.	3165	3305	4976	5996

- NO MORTALITY DATA ARE AVAILABLE FOR EVEN A BROADER GROUP OF CAUSES FOR THIS DISEASE

. MORTALITY DATA ARE PRESENTED FOR A BROADER GROUP OF CAUSES FOR THIS DISEASE

0 VALUE<0.5

THE STANDARD MORTALITY RATIOS WERE DERIVED WITH A FACTOR OF 1000

SERIAL MORTALITY TABLES FOR VARIOUS COUNTRIES 1901-1975

TABLE 122 : BILIARY CALCULI : MALES

	1901-	1906-	1911-	1916-	1921-	1926-	1931-	1936-	1941-	1946-	1951-	1956-	1961-	1966-	1971-75
1 AUSTRALIA	-	6040	5048	5964	6292	6310	6200	6137	5468	4692	.	.	.	.	.
2 AUSTRIA	-	-	-	-	-	-	-	-	-	5942	8282	.	.	.	.
3 BELGIUM	-	-	-	-	.	.	.	.	.	.	.	.	.	.	.
4 BULGARIA	-	-	-	-	-	-	.	.	.	.	.	.	.	.	.
5 CANADA	-	-	-	-	5508	4603	5974	7862	5265	4227	.	.	.	.	.
6 CHILE	-	3401	1653	1606	5189	5356	5309	4330	5569	6343	.	.	.	.	.
7 CZECHOSLOVAKIA	-	-	-	2961	2919	3952	4190	3664	2959	2602	.	.	.	.	.
8 DENMARK	.	.	.	.	.	.	.	.	.	.	.	.	.	.	.
9 EIRE	-	-	-	-	2407	1884	1764	2008	3335	3750	.	.	.	.	.
10 FINLAND	-	-	-	-	-	.	.	.	.	.	.	.	.	.	.
11 FRANCE	-	-	-	-	-	-	.	.	596	619	.	.	.	.	.
12 GREECE	-	-	-	-	-	1888	1490	1408	-	-	-	.	.	.	.
13 HUNGARY	-	-	-	.	.	.	.	.	.	.	.	.	.	.	.
14 ICELAND	-	-	-	-	-	-	-	-	.	.	-	-	.	.	.
15 ITALY	-	-	-	-	-	-	.	.	.	.	.	.	.	.	.
16 JAPAN	.	.	.	.	11095	14166	14108	14527	-	.	.	.	.	.	.
17 NETHERLANDS	2558	2439	3053	3584	4068	4536	4187	4459	3939	5196	.	.	.	.	.
18 NEW ZEALAND	-	4545	7227	5697	4642	5678	4915	4825	3804	3252	.	.	.	.	.
19 NORWAY	2201	3036	4296	4306	6215	5018	4836	4354	3050	2886	.	.	.	.	.
20 POLAND	-	-	-	-	-	-	-	-	-	-	.	.	.	.	.
21 PORTUGAL	-	-	-	-	-	-	.	.	.	.	.	.	.	.	.
22 ROMANIA	-	-	-	-	-	-	-	-	-	-	-	.	.	.	.
23 SPAIN	4124	3858	3658	3521	3425	3099	2915	2613	1789	1358	.	.	.	.	.
24 SWEDEN	-	-	.	.	.	.	.	.	.	.	.	.	.	.	.
25 SWITZERLAND	5006	5006	6792	6792	4316	4414	.	.	3117	4583	.	.	.	.	.
26 TURKEY	-	-	-	-	-	-	-	-	-	-	-	.	.	.	.
27 UK ENGLAND AND WALES	.	.	5946	4930	6133	6190	5834	4747	3222	2873	.	.	.	.	.
28 UK NORTHERN IRELAND	-	-	-	-	2190	2453	.	.	.	.	.	.	.	.	.
29 UK SCOTLAND	.	.	1787	1268	5135	4495	3691	2803	2637	1871	.	.	.	.	.
30 USA	9830	9090	8883	8188	8901	8861	8407	7996	6009	5441	.	.	.	.	.
31 YUGOSLAVIA	-	-	-	-	-	-	-	-	-	-	.	.	.	.	.

- NO MORTALITY DATA ARE AVAILABLE FOR EVEN A BROADER GROUP OF CAUSES FOR THIS DISEASE

. MORTALITY DATA ARE PRESENTED FOR A BROADER GROUP OF CAUSES FOR THIS DISEASE

0 VALUE<0.5

THE STANDARD MORTALITY RATIOS WERE DERIVED WITH A FACTOR OF 10000

SERIAL MORTALITY TABLES FOR VARIOUS COUNTRIES 1901-1975

TABLE 122 : BILIARY CALCULI : FEMALES

	1901-	1906-	1911-	1916-	1921-	1926-	1931-	1936-	1941-	1946-	1951-	1956-	1961-	1966-	1971-75
1 AUSTRALIA	-	15732	13872	14956	16416	16083	15381	14161	10564	8331	.	.	.	.	.
2 AUSTRIA	-	-	-	-	-	-	-	-	-	13816	16625	.	.	.	.
3 BELGIUM	-	-	-	-	.	.	.	.	.	.	.	.	.	.	.
4 BULGARIA	-	-	-	-	-	-	.	.	.	.	.	.	.	.	.
5 CANADA	-	-	-	-	18767	15297	17769	21391	13595	11024	.	.	.	.	.
6 CHILE	-	2830	4089	3509	3485	8845	13665	10529	11229	14814	.	.	.	.	.
7 CZECHOSLOVAKIA	-	-	-	4811	6210	9279	9590	9185	4437	3886	.	.	.	.	.
8 DENMARK	.	.	.	.	.	.	.	.	.	.	.	.	.	.	.
9 EIRE	-	-	-	-	4083	4315	4368	5263	7273	8112	.	.	.	.	.
10 FINLAND	-	-	-	-	-	.	.	.	.	.	.	.	.	.	.
11 FRANCE	-	-	-	-	-	-	.	.	1146	1290	.	.	.	.	.
12 GREECE	-	-	-	-	-	1225	1429	2182	-	-	-	.	.	.	.
13 HUNGARY	-	-	-	.	.	.	.	.	.	.	.	.	.	.	.
14 ICELAND	-	-	-	-	-	-	-	-	.	.	-	-	.	.	.
15 ITALY	-	-	-	-	-	-	.	.	.	.	.	.	.	.	.
16 JAPAN		.	.	.	12822	15683	17146	18001	-	.	.	.	.	.	.
17 NETHERLANDS	7011	8136	8797	10081	12639	16339	15444	14533	11890	15661	.	.	.	.	.
18 NEW ZEALAND	-	9639	15385	14132	15719	16437	13130	11901	9863	8697	.	.	.	.	.
19 NORWAY	3993	6509	6458	7947	11489	12102	10956	10192	7257	6951	.	.	.	.	.
20 POLAND	-	-	-	-	-	-	-	-	-	-	.	.	.	.	.
21 PORTUGAL	-	-	-	-	-	-	.	.	.	.	.	.	.	.	.
22 ROMANIA	-	-	-	-	-	-	-	-	-	-	-	.	.	.	.
23 SPAIN	3240	2955	3237	3556	3866	4329	3955	3253	2700	2075	.	.	.	.	.
24 SWEDEN	-	-	.	.	.	.	.	.	.	.	.	.	.	.	.
25 SWITZERLAND	14654	14654	16676	16676	13396	13435	.	.	8337	12056	.	.	.	.	.
26 TURKEY	-	-	-	-	-	-	-	-	-	-	-	.	.	.	.
27 UK ENGLAND AND WALES	.	.	12749	10073	12737	13424	12606	9573	6787	5609	.	.	.	.	.
28 UK NORTHERN IRELAND	-	-	-	-	5057	6579	.	.	.	.	.	.	.	.	.
29 UK SCOTLAND	.	.	0	0	13650	15276	11214	8778	6475	6099	.	.	.	.	.
30 USA	21487	21253	22587	23181	25569	24265	21350	18005	13335	10647	.	.	.	.	.
31 YUGOSLAVIA	-	-	-	-	-	-	-	-	-	-	.	.	.	.	.

- NO MORTALITY DATA ARE AVAILABLE FOR EVEN A BROADER GROUP OF CAUSES FOR THIS DISEASE

. MORTALITY DATA ARE PRESENTED FOR A BROADER GROUP OF CAUSES FOR THIS DISEASE

0 VALUE<0.5

THE STANDARD MORTALITY RATIOS WERE DERIVED WITH A FACTOR OF 10000

SERIAL MORTALITY TABLES FOR VARIOUS COUNTRIES 1901-1975

TABLE 123 : CHOLELITHIASIS AND CHOLECYSTITIS : MALES

	1901-	1906-	1911-	1916-	1921-	1926-	1931-	1936-	1941-	1946-	1951-	1956-	1961-	1966-	1971-75
1 AUSTRALIA	-	.	.	.	.	.	.	.	.	.	17199	14212	12570	9586	8914
2 AUSTRIA	-	-	-	-	-	-	-	-	-	.	26739	28371	30960	30801	25007
3 BELGIUM	-	-	-	-	.	.	.	.	.	.	10111	11116	10827	11976	12159
4 BULGARIA	-	-	-	-	-	-	.	.	.	.	.	.	7506	8671	7495
5 CANADA	-	-	-	-	.	.	.	.	.	16643	13438	14092	14760	16396	13361
6 CHILE	-	.	.	.	.	.	.	23575	24677	22046	30596	37618	42008	49025	49881
7 CZECHOSLOVAKIA	-	-	-	.	.	.	.	.	.	.	12181	16174	18202	23291	26845
8 DENMARK	27064	35470	27857	26230	29050	27466	.	.	.	.	31846	30153	22789	18626	13140
9 EIRE	-	-	-	-	.	.	.	.	.	.	5294	4545	4240	4274	3558
10 FINLAND	-	-	-	-	-	.	.	.	7828	8880	9927	14437	17962	22739	20315
11 FRANCE	-	-	-	-	-	-	.	.	5465	5403	5348	6855	6665	8397	11905
12 GREECE	-	-	-	-	-	.	.	.	-	-	-	3557	3831	5704	5738
13 HUNGARY	-	-	-	.	.	.	17353	16353	15249	.	14875	16263	21451	22999	26971
14 ICELAND	-	-	-	-	-	-	-	-	.	.	-	-	5634	7407	9890
15 ITALY	-	-	-	-	-	-	22354	23196	16199	13835	12968	12098	14596	17720	18885
16 JAPAN	.	.	.	.	.	.	69419	71350	-	55477	47603	38212	29107	21397	16373
17 NETHERLANDS	.	.	.	.	.	.	.	.	.	21720	18496	18326	17534	16832	15195
18 NEW ZEALAND	-	.	.	.	.	.	.	.	.	19152	15888	15773	16600	9828	8915
19 NORWAY	.	.	.	.	.	11623	14756	14873	.	.	13174	14358	14257	15123	12900
20 POLAND	-	-	-	-	-	-	-	-	-	-	.	5524	9154	12249	11509
21 PORTUGAL	-	-	-	-	-	-	.	.	.	.	14297	12093	11780	10568	7683
22 ROMANIA	-	-	-	-	-	-	-	-	-	-	-	2453	4424	4480	4448
23 SPAIN	.	.	.	.	.	.	6045	5382	13153	11823	13011	7201	8313	7776	5453
24 SWEDEN	-	-	.	.	.	.	.	.	.	.	35402	32758	31699	27443	23326
25 SWITZERLAND	.	.	.	.	15527	17436	.	.	12400	16648	17776	18336	17831	16636	14361
26 TURKEY	-	-	-	-	-	-	-	-	-	-	-	15495	10190	6934	5090
27 UK ENGLAND AND WALES	.	.	.	.	.	.	24038	19889	12924	10168	10793	10256	8524	7201	6171
28 UK NORTHERN IRELAND	-	-	-	-	.	.	.	.	.	11089	4886	7051	6028	9295	5638
29 UK SCOTLAND	.	.	.	.	.	.	22730	18706	.	10332	12413	11982	10849	7908	5394
30 USA	.	.	.	.	.	.	.	.	.	18787	16832	13303	12130	10848	8083
31 YUGOSLAVIA	-	-	-	-	-	-	-	-	-	-	.	.	4084	5450	4590

- NO MORTALITY DATA ARE AVAILABLE FOR EVEN A BROADER GROUP OF CAUSES FOR THIS DISEASE

. MORTALITY DATA ARE PRESENTED FOR A BROADER GROUP OF CAUSES FOR THIS DISEASE

0 VALUE<0.5

THE STANDARD MORTALITY RATIOS WERE DERIVED WITH A FACTOR OF 10000

SERIAL MORTALITY TABLES FOR VARIOUS COUNTRIES 1901-1975

TABLE 123 : CHOLELITHIASIS AND CHOLECYSTITIS : FEMALES

	1901-	1906-	1911-	1916-	1921-	1926-	1931-	1936-	1941-	1946-	1951-	1956-	1961-	1966-	1971-75
1 AUSTRALIA	-	.	.	.	.	.	.	.	.	.	26218	18826	13742	10527	8076
2 AUSTRIA	-	-	-	-	-	-	-	-	-	.	49895	43797	40534	36995	27724
3 BELGIUM	-	-	-	-	.	.	.	.	.	.	22051	19524	18684	18321	17437
4 BULGARIA	-	-	-	-	-	-	.	.	.	.	.	.	9537	10729	9291
5 CANADA	-	-	-	-	.	.	.	.	.	33272	26102	22148	20792	17676	11981
6 CHILE	-	.	.	.	.	.	.	56079	55254	55503	65701	71300	79238	89835	76794
7 CZECHOSLOVAKIA	-	-	-	.	.	.	.	.	.	.	25089	28706	29044	31536	34277
8 DENMARK	30636	47043	60959	54298	67593	70122	.	.	.	.	67027	57419	38104	26607	16729
9 EIRE	-	-	-	-	.	.	.	.	.	.	14198	13962	9122	7731	6995
10 FINLAND	-	-	-	-	-	.	.	.	16600	22002	21991	35510	37067	33025	28165
11 FRANCE	-	-	-	-	-	-	.	.	9747	10320	10364	12170	11905	13420	16200
12 GREECE	-	-	-	-	-	.	.	.	-	-	-	5298	6695	9224	8360
13 HUNGARY	-	-	-	.	.	.	47264	44747	41128	.	38367	39520	37943	37404	41077
14 ICELAND	-	-	-	-	-	-	-	-	.	.	-	-	10345	20202	10811
15 ITALY	-	-	-	-	-	-	39633	40199	30286	28673	26350	23834	24132	24012	24526
16 JAPAN	.	.	.	.	.	.	66887	67627	-	62489	57297	47691	34829	25302	18356
17 NETHERLANDS	.	.	.	.	.	.	.	.	.	66096	46266	37289	29611	24896	19922
18 NEW ZEALAND	-	.	.	.	.	.	.	.	.	38903	28939	23680	18911	10515	10304
19 NORWAY	.	.	.	.	.	21970	29523	28525	.	.	26711	25608	26296	20671	15952
20 POLAND	-	-	-	-	-	-	-	-	-	-	.	12424	19686	24308	20368
21 PORTUGAL	-	-	-	-	-	-	.	.	.	.	16540	13838	11321	10317	8212
22 ROMANIA	-	-	-	-	-	-	-	-	-	-	-	3219	6963	6266	5728
23 SPAIN	.	.	.	.	.	.	7681	6238	18168	16298	16686	11910	13375	12842	10734
24 SWEDEN	-	-	.	.	.	.	.	.	.	.	58057	43308	39680	29973	24434
25 SWITZERLAND	.	.	.	.	39551	41688	.	.	28740	38483	35899	34512	31011	23525	21306
26 TURKEY	-	-	-	-	-	-	-	-	-	-	-	12352	11400	9612	5442
27 UK ENGLAND AND WALES	.	.	.	.	.	.	45496	37635	24675	19254	17273	14066	10796	8294	6719
28 UK NORTHERN IRELAND	-	-	-	-	.	.	.	.	.	26316	15535	15337	10057	8833	7685
29 UK SCOTLAND	.	.	.	.	.	.	58456	49500	.	28322	23609	21576	15400	11820	7221
30 USA	.	.	.	.	.	.	.	.	.	29920	24212	16422	13541	10430	7064
31 YUGOSLAVIA	-	-	-	-	-	-	-	-	-	-	.	.	7408	7555	6701

- NO MORTALITY DATA ARE AVAILABLE FOR EVEN A BROADER GROUP OF CAUSES FOR THIS DISEASE

. MORTALITY DATA ARE PRESENTED FOR A BROADER GROUP OF CAUSES FOR THIS DISEASE

0 VALUE<0.5

THE STANDARD MORTALITY RATIOS WERE DERIVED WITH A FACTOR OF 10000

SERIAL MORTALITY TABLES FOR VARIOUS COUNTRIES 1901-1975

TABLE 124 : LIVER AND BILIARY PASSAGES - ALL DISEASES : MALES

	1901-	1906-	1911-	1916-	1921-	1926-	1931-	1936-	1941-	1946-	1951-	1956-	1961-	1966-	1971-75
1 AUSTRALIA	-	4398	4541	3523	3079	2879	3020	2800	2435	2524	2375	2291	2285	2486	3215
2 AUSTRIA	-	-	-	-	-	-	-	-	-	.	5770	7630	8973	10637	11135
3 BELGIUM	-	-	-	-	.	.	5399	5430	4536	4298	3146	2886	3043	3451	3930
4 BULGARIA	-	-	-	-	-	-	4871	5926	4541	4466	3470	1968	1960	2172	2537
5 CANADA	-	-	-	-	1600	1788	2680	2914	2331	2434	2225	2756	2855	3482	4698
6 CHILE	-	7075	3341	3109	2584	3694	5423	7003	9629	10565	16297	16014	23568	24225	24123
7 CZECHOSLOVAKIA	-	-	-	.	.	.	3422	3538	778	843	2609	3251	3732	5242	6767
8 DENMARK	5491	4723	4542	4528	2005	1908	2533	2392	.	.	2715	2784	2520	2495	2993
9 EIRE	-	-	-	-	.	.	1405	1407	1175	1136	805	819	950	996	1029
10 FINLAND	-	-	-	-	-	.	.	.	1439	1453	1496	1861	1945	2323	2746
11 FRANCE	-	-	-	-	-	-	7735	8546	4600	3747	7672	9346	10576	11520	11129
12 GREECE	-	-	-	-	-	2950	3402	3998	-	-	-	4282	5497	5791	4686
13 HUNGARY	-	-	-	3234	3506	3525	2964	3335	2647	3568	3775	3433	3624	4350	5590
14 ICELAND	-	-	-	-	-	-	-	-	1078	1391	-	-	1098	994	850
15 ITALY	-	-	-	-	-	-	6202	5668	4372	4103	5691	6322	8107	10060	11386
16 JAPAN	.	.	.	.	4382	4904	5630	6448	-	5387	5568	5874	5708	5911	6382
17 NETHERLANDS	3221	2850	2509	2234	.	.	1940	1828	1558	1602	1747	1883	1850	1834	2016
18 NEW ZEALAND	-	.	.	.	1787	1894	1841	1928	1386	1271	1512	1558	1544	1477	2196
19 NORWAY	1510	1626	1059	961	1217	1609	1660	1698	999	1097	1408	1514	1548	1679	1671
20 POLAND	-	-	-	-	-	-	-	-	-	-	.	1519	2387	3250	3983
21 PORTUGAL	-	-	-	-	-	-	8809	9796	9461	9143	9865	10069	10651	12406	12054
22 ROMANIA	-	-	-	-	-	-	-	-	-	-	-	4930	6127	6680	7257
23 SPAIN	7457	7304	6945	6709	6398	6755	11347	9061	4127	4194	4628	5549	6391	7751	8155
24 SWEDEN	-	-	.	.	.	.	.	.	.	.	2418	2703	2856	3062	3707
25 SWITZERLAND	.	.	.	.	4793	5487	.	.	.	.	5696	5761	6463	6644	5693
26 TURKEY	-	-	-	-	-	-	-	-	-	-	-	5974	4774	3716	3013
27 UK ENGLAND AND WALES	.	.	5081	2992	2627	2382	2320	1923	1274	1044	1126	1084	1033	982	1036
28 UK NORTHERN IRELAND	-	-	-	-	.	.	2155	2332	1801	1526	828	991	1043	1069	1162
29 UK SCOTLAND	.	.	.	.	.	.	2132	2185	.	1428	1461	1631	1703	1596	1563
30 USA	11519	9067	7743	5299	3997	4039	4583	4622	4220	4323	4181	4309	4534	5290	5486
31 YUGOSLAVIA	-	-	-	-	-	-	-	-	-	-	.	.	3067	4670	5654

- NO MORTALITY DATA ARE AVAILABLE FOR EVEN A BROADER GROUP OF CAUSES FOR THIS DISEASE

. MORTALITY DATA ARE PRESENTED FOR A BROADER GROUP OF CAUSES FOR THIS DISEASE

0 VALUE<0.5

THE STANDARD MORTALITY RATIOS WERE DERIVED WITH A FACTOR OF 1000

SERIAL MORTALITY TABLES FOR VARIOUS COUNTRIES 1901-1975

TABLE 124 : LIVER AND BILIARY PASSAGES - ALL DISEASES : FEMALES

	1901-	1906-	1911-	1916-	1921-	1926-	1931-	1936-	1941-	1946-	1951-	1956-	1961-	1966-	1971-75
1 AUSTRALIA	-	4026	3539	2906	2701	2347	3282	3116	2520	2377	1903	1651	1385	1258	1303
2 AUSTRIA	-	-	-	-	-	-	-	-	-	.	3685	3894	3941	4238	3870
3 BELGIUM	-	-	-	-	.	.	4596	4607	4147	4062	2570	1981	2122	2248	2472
4 BULGARIA	-	-	-	-	-	-	2436	2971	2319	2078	2061	1301	1277	1385	1318
5 CANADA	-	-	-	-	2308	2198	4035	4303	2958	2525	2096	2073	2077	2150	2180
6 CHILE	-	4693	1673	1434	1373	2183	4664	5061	6336	6692	9096	8733	10673	11651	10087
7 CZECHOSLOVAKIA	-	-	-	.	.	.	2446	2466	960	1142	2276	2661	2727	3054	3388
8 DENMARK	1927	2812	3215	2965	3185	3265	4430	4172	.	.	4405	4434	3376	2824	2278
9 EIRE	-	-	-	-	.	.	1495	1531	1321	1241	969	982	797	812	872
10 FINLAND	-	-	-	-	-	.	.	.	1539	1605	1513	2178	2282	2012	1863
11 FRANCE	-	-	-	-	-	-	4766	4717	2170	1876	3667	3762	3837	3960	3893
12 GREECE	-	-	-	-	-	823	1423	1818	-	-	-	1728	2305	2504	2032
13 HUNGARY	-	-	-	2555	2818	3415	2900	3140	2812	2932	2994	3092	2933	3206	3704
14 ICELAND	-	-	-	-	-	-	-	-	1908	1479	-	-	968	1401	873
15 ITALY	-	-	-	-	-	-	3590	3518	2788	2666	2977	3022	3456	3964	4389
16 JAPAN	.	.	.	.	2729	3094	3923	4542	-	4544	4519	4304	3563	3008	2627
17 NETHERLANDS	2488	2448	2132	2126	.	.	3019	2847	2409	3027	2685	2383	2024	1857	1630
18 NEW ZEALAND	-	.	.	.	2307	2369	2485	2400	2074	1814	1915	1610	1364	1000	1252
19 NORWAY	1196	1307	723	876	1198	1794	1784	1911	1421	1745	1861	1853	1820	1563	1296
20 POLAND	-	-	-	-	-	-	-	-	-	-	.	1292	2069	2582	2504
21 PORTUGAL	-	-	-	-	-	-	4130	4568	4578	4695	4554	4382	4609	5153	4527
22 ROMANIA	-	-	-	-	-	-	-	-	-	-	-	3030	3839	3623	3641
23 SPAIN	5766	5418	4956	4680	4231	4243	7691	6081	2787	2732	3049	3092	3248	3549	3414
24 SWEDEN	-	-	.	.	.	.	.	.	.	.	3276	2745	2627	2314	2194
25 SWITZERLAND	.	.	.	.	3139	3172	.	.	.	.	2679	2527	2491	2272	2207
26 TURKEY	-	-	-	-	-	-	-	-	-	-	-	3228	2702	2254	1856
27 UK ENGLAND AND WALES	.	.	3966	2018	1939	1904	2515	2102	1433	1206	1197	1066	946	842	839
28 UK NORTHERN IRELAND	-	-	-	-	.	.	2932	2695	2337	1932	1204	1322	1008	994	1129
29 UK SCOTLAND	.	.	.	.	.	.	3099	2881	.	1773	1633	1729	1434	1211	1095
30 USA	7065	5831	5185	4215	3876	4010	4723	4177	3511	3102	2700	2419	2433	2582	2388
31 YUGOSLAVIA	-	-	-	-	-	-	-	-	-	-	.	.	1461	1973	2149

- NO MORTALITY DATA ARE AVAILABLE FOR EVEN A BROADER GROUP OF CAUSES FOR THIS DISEASE

. MORTALITY DATA ARE PRESENTED FOR A BROADER GROUP OF CAUSES FOR THIS DISEASE

0 VALUE<0.5

THE STANDARD MORTALITY RATIOS WERE DERIVED WITH A FACTOR OF 1000

SERIAL MORTALITY TABLES FOR VARIOUS COUNTRIES 1901-1975

TABLE 125 : ALIMENTARY DISEASE - ALL FORMS : MALES

	1901-	1906-	1911-	1916-	1921-	1926-	1931-	1936-	1941-	1946-	1951-	1956-	1961-	1966-	1971-75
1 AUSTRALIA	-	8766	8340	6827	5593	4368	3095	2855	2426	2004	1744	1563	1348	1233	1261
2 AUSTRIA	-	-	-	-	-	-	-	-	-	3607	3016	3135	3180	3277	3166
3 BELGIUM	-	-	-	-	6408	6056	4505	3935	4001	2794	1718	1536	1485	1606	1532
4 BULGARIA	-	-	-	-	-	-	8418	8764	6283	6134	3629	1497	1292	1303	1242
5 CANADA	-	-	-	-	5563	6817	5219	4170	3001	2296	1641	1548	1468	1424	1524
6 CHILE	-	14452	15654	18261	19189	21316	20944	19184	17759	13883	8044	7680	10057	8505	7233
7 CZECHOSLOVAKIA	-	-	-	8243	8555	8696	6466	5019	6362	3954	2334	1754	1695	1981	2202
8 DENMARK	4015	3704	3433	2960	1948	1874	3100	2794	2514	2072	1598	1373	1279	1172	1157
9 EIRE	-	-	-	-	3674	2847	3522	3368	3594	2486	1487	1272	1140	1118	1059
10 FINLAND	-	-	-	-	-	4077	3864	3807	4340	3689	1916	1806	1441	1363	1258
11 FRANCE	-	-	-	-	-	-	3975	4026	3732	2960	2594	2699	2830	2982	2905
12 GREECE	-	-	-	-	-	11683	10522	8688	-	-	-	2078	2173	2141	1678
13 HUNGARY	-	-	-	10868	12504	10344	9072	6581	6459	4174	2944	2194	1879	1867	2045
14 ICELAND	-	-	-	-	-	-	-	-	2009	1483	-	-	863	779	687
15 ITALY	-	-	-	-	-	-	-	-	-	-	3581	3016	3031	3066	3084
16 JAPAN	18330	20062	20146	21331	21622	19344	18513	18407	-	9549	6474	4436	3388	2770	2335
17 NETHERLANDS	12226	9125	7767	5456	3749	2845	2312	2078	3440	1733	1225	1198	1148	1141	1089
18 NEW ZEALAND	-	6260	4296	3665	2876	2585	2208	2131	1914	1501	1555	1553	1263	1036	1124
19 NORWAY	4447	3536	3394	2765	2645	2400	2086	2044	2231	1342	1007	934	945	878	869
20 POLAND	-	-	-	-	-	-	-	-	-	-	6134	2821	2395	1988	1839
21 PORTUGAL	-	-	-	-	-	-	18614	16932	16943	12873	9903	8040	6795	5005	3882
22 ROMANIA	-	-	-	-	-	-	-	-	-	-	-	2949	2619	2583	2205
23 SPAIN	27155	25589	24618	25415	23180	20471	15713	15014	11416	6849	4295	3251	2798	2703	2614
24 SWEDEN	-	-	3405	2931	2580	2507	2010	1990	1616	1350	1531	1391	1409	1434	1502
25 SWITZERLAND	10672	10672	6754	6754	4462	4149	4199	3599	3132	2615	2284	2123	2200	2064	1781
26 TURKEY	-	-	-	-	-	-	-	-	-	-	-	14321	8577	6234	5174
27 UK ENGLAND AND WALES	10220	7324	8115	5075	4352	3812	3316	2962	2500	1957	1622	1382	1234	1089	1031
28 UK NORTHERN IRELAND	-	-	-	-	4547	4480	4288	3987	3616	2364	1539	1252	1207	1142	1085
29 UK SCOTLAND	9317	7607	7286	5779	4851	4345	3921	3850	3245	2581	1905	1697	1522	1327	1202
30 USA	18541	14239	10334	8068	5899	5010	4116	3568	2713	2099	1848	1814	1804	1819	1730
31 YUGOSLAVIA	-	-	-	-	-	-	-	-	-	-	5328	4338	2562	2221	2085

- NO MORTALITY DATA ARE AVAILABLE FOR EVEN A BROADER GROUP OF CAUSES FOR THIS DISEASE

. MORTALITY DATA ARE PRESENTED FOR A BROADER GROUP OF CAUSES FOR THIS DISEASE

0 VALUE<0.5

THE STANDARD MORTALITY RATIOS WERE DERIVED WITH A FACTOR OF 1000

SERIAL MORTALITY TABLES FOR VARIOUS COUNTRIES 1901-1975

TABLE 125 : ALIMENTARY DISEASE - ALL FORMS : FEMALES

	1901-	1906-	1911-	1916-	1921-	1926-	1931-	1936-	1941-	1946-	1951-	1956-	1961-	1966-	1971-75
1 AUSTRALIA	-	8437	7982	6247	4859	3531	2373	2069	1682	1307	1087	956	816	757	704
2 AUSTRIA	-	-	-	-	-	-	-	-	-	2315	1959	1855	1761	1675	1466
3 BELGIUM	-	-	-	-	5018	4664	3495	3049	2972	2110	1198	1020	1018	1111	1027
4 BULGARIA	-	-	-	-	-	-	6108	5791	3337	3000	1838	755	702	684	625
5 CANADA	-	-	-	-	4944	5893	4218	3354	2252	1655	1140	1043	987	917	865
6 CHILE	-	12133	13809	16406	17141	18705	18190	16630	15046	11245	5956	5543	6756	5577	4286
7 CZECHOSLOVAKIA	-	-	-	6039	6008	6019	4390	3257	4091	2577	1627	1264	1143	1199	1235
8 DENMARK	2672	2634	2409	2183	1658	1587	2460	2226	2457	1954	1514	1390	1196	1016	831
9 EIRE	-	-	-	-	2852	2193	2661	2469	2718	1642	1035	899	814	771	740
10 FINLAND	-	-	-	-	-	2461	2300	2163	2506	1993	1083	1213	1122	1022	872
11 FRANCE	-	-	-	-	-	-	2503	2459	2250	1698	1419	1316	1289	1303	1309
12 GREECE	-	-	-	-	-	9902	8999	7124	-	-	-	1195	1241	1235	976
13 HUNGARY	-	-	-	8992	9979	8159	6861	4667	4643	2631	1860	1515	1263	1230	1290
14 ICELAND	-	-	-	-	-	-	-	-	1184	825	-	-	834	884	592
15 ITALY	-	-	-	-	-	-	-	-	-	-	2238	1705	1536	1401	1331
16 JAPAN	17304	19182	18992	19973	19416	16554	15522	15418	-	7150	4838	3210	2322	1746	1344
17 NETHERLANDS	9347	7015	6010	4251	2937	2292	1878	1605	2544	1465	1045	1010	934	930	878
18 NEW ZEALAND	-	6485	4347	3507	2730	2201	1701	1635	1332	1062	1128	1102	922	747	747
19 NORWAY	3637	2902	2766	2342	2003	1845	1572	1542	1788	1132	877	837	858	716	683
20 POLAND	-	-	-	-	-	-	-	-	-	-	3549	1637	1395	1193	1082
21 PORTUGAL	-	-	-	-	-	-	12251	10669	10643	7956	5574	4400	3654	2456	1712
22 ROMANIA	-	-	-	-	-	-	-	-	-	-	-	1635	1433	1392	1151
23 SPAIN	23596	21332	19996	20552	18360	15505	11464	10517	7603	4363	2715	1989	1602	1431	1324
24 SWEDEN	-	-	2609	2206	1964	2007	1595	1573	1339	1147	1231	1106	1168	1070	953
25 SWITZERLAND	7489	7489	4515	4515	3046	2718	2507	2179	1881	1637	1317	1217	1173	1051	947
26 TURKEY	-	-	-	-	-	-	-	-	-	-	-	10901	6363	4685	3992
27 UK ENGLAND AND WALES	8899	6223	6032	3693	3009	2525	2201	1815	1428	1116	925	852	830	772	766
28 UK NORTHERN IRELAND	-	-	-	-	3533	3535	3119	2869	2373	1579	998	923	878	838	821
29 UK SCOTLAND	7346	5879	5353	4130	3420	3055	2675	2399	1942	1506	1163	1061	1000	872	849
30 USA	16208	12477	8926	6957	5011	4112	3210	2584	1874	1356	1117	1059	1072	1049	943
31 YUGOSLAVIA	-	-	-	-	-	-	-	-	-	-	3463	2746	1460	1179	1020

- NO MORTALITY DATA ARE AVAILABLE FOR EVEN A BROADER GROUP OF CAUSES FOR THIS DISEASE

. MORTALITY DATA ARE PRESENTED FOR A BROADER GROUP OF CAUSES FOR THIS DISEASE

0 VALUE<0.5

THE STANDARD MORTALITY RATIOS WERE DERIVED WITH A FACTOR OF 1000

SERIAL MORTALITY TABLES FOR VARIOUS COUNTRIES 1901-1975

TABLE 125 : ALIMENTARY DISEASE - ALL FORMS : PERSONS

	1901-	1906-	1911-	1916-	1921-	1926-	1931-	1936-	1941-	1946-	1951-	1956-	1961-	1966-	1971-75
1 AUSTRALIA	-	8613	8172	6551	5240	3961	2739	2460	2046	1643	1394	1235	1056	968	948
2 AUSTRIA	-	-	-	-	-	-	3344	3035	-	2874	2409	2385	2333	2304	2118
3 BELGIUM	-	-	-	-	5679	5332	3977	3470	3461	2434	1433	1250	1223	1324	1240
4 BULGARIA	-	-	-	-	-	-	7229	5774	4730	4457	2660	1102	977	973	913
5 CANADA	6379	5033	5471	3646	5265	6371	4734	3774	2636	1981	1392	1294	1221	1156	1164
6 CHILE	-	13250	14701	17306	18132	19961	19510	17852	16339	12497	6941	6536	8287	6934	5634
7 CZECHOSLOVAKIA	-	-	-	7049	7173	7240	5332	4054	5117	3197	1944	1480	1381	1531	1639
8 DENMARK	3232	3079	2835	2506	1793	1721	2761	2495	2484	2010	1554	1382	1235	1088	976
9 EIRE	-	-	-	-	3253	2512	3084	2916	3150	2059	1257	1080	969	935	888
10 FINLAND	-	-	-	-	-	3198	2999	2882	3296	2709	1427	1457	1252	1160	1026
11 FRANCE	8793	5495	5034	3306	-	-	3147	3133	2875	2223	1903	1877	1907	1970	1941
12 GREECE	-	-	-	-	-	10770	9741	7888	-	-	-	2004	2358	2336	1868
13 HUNGARY	-	-	-	9901	11198	9208	7915	5571	5495	3332	2348	1817	1533	1505	1611
14 ICELAND	-	-	-	-	-	-	-	-	1546	1121	-	-	848	835	636
15 ITALY	-	-	-	-	-	-	-	-	-	-	2854	2298	2200	2123	2081
16 JAPAN	17795	19608	19551	20629	20464	17867	16921	16812	-	8247	5584	3764	2801	2206	1785
17 NETHERLANDS	10710	8016	6846	4827	3327	2559	2088	1834	2978	1594	1132	1100	1035	1027	972
18 NEW ZEALAND	-	6360	4319	3592	2807	2400	1960	1884	1619	1276	1333	1313	1078	876	914
19 NORWAY	4012	3193	3053	2534	2294	2097	1805	1770	1989	1228	937	882	898	790	766
20 POLAND	-	-	-	-	-	-	-	-	-	-	4656	4149	1816	1525	1394
21 PORTUGAL	-	-	-	-	-	-	14996	13342	13330	10072	7388	5925	4974	3519	2615
22 ROMANIA	-	-	-	-	-	-	-	16798	-	4594	-	2218	1957	1917	1617
23 SPAIN	25317	23358	22182	22851	20615	17791	13389	12521	9295	5453	3397	2533	2122	1981	1879
24 SWEDEN	-	-	2970	2535	2245	2236	1786	1767	1469	1243	1373	1240	1280	1237	1200
25 SWITZERLAND	8975	8975	5535	5535	3681	3358	3261	2810	2436	2068	1742	1612	1617	1484	1298
26 TURKEY	-	-	-	-	-	-	10871	12106	12415	-	-	12534	7425	5451	4588
27 UK ENGLAND AND WALES	9532	6748	6975	4314	3611	3099	2695	2318	1888	1479	1219	1071	994	899	872
28 UK NORTHERN IRELAND	-	-	-	-	4004	3974	3664	3393	2950	1946	1245	1070	1023	969	933
29 UK SCOTLAND	8215	6640	6206	4859	4056	3629	3231	3044	2515	1976	1484	1331	1217	1056	988
30 USA	17353	13359	9637	7518	5459	4565	3664	3072	2285	1372	1464	1411	1406	1390	1279
31 YUGOSLAVIA	-	-	-	-	-	-	-	-	-	-	4298	3451	1945	1639	1490

- NO MORTALITY DATA ARE AVAILABLE FOR EVEN A BROADER GROUP OF CAUSES FOR THIS DISEASE

. MORTALITY DATA ARE PRESENTED FOR A BROADER GROUP OF CAUSES FOR THIS DISEASE

0 VALUE<0.5

THE STANDARD MORTALITY RATIOS WERE DERIVED WITH A FACTOR OF 1000

SERIAL MORTALITY TABLES FOR VARIOUS COUNTRIES 1901-1975

TABLE 126 : NEPHRITIS - ACUTE : MALES

	1901-	1906-	1911-	1916-	1921-	1926-	1931-	1936-	1941-	1946-	1951-	1956-	1961-	1966-	1971-75
1 AUSTRALIA	-	13058	12909	11216	12400	10404	7802	7346	6110	4530	2819	1662	1039	1160	1702
2 AUSTRIA	-	-	-	-	-	-	-	-	-	.	1904	1290	911	761	499
3 BELGIUM	.	.	.	.	.	.	.	.	.	.	1639	1529	856	820	432
4 BULGARIA	-	-	-	-	-	.	.	.	.	.	.	.	1314	786	811
5 CANADA	-	-	-	-	17392	13959	10505	8471	6964	4702	3111	1718	1050	709	786
6 CHILE	-	39318	24439	10088	15187	15155	20863	19967	19724	14737	12827	7419	5218	3814	3524
7 CZECHOSLOVAKIA	-	-	-	11745	10202	10765	9485	8297	8132	6347	2296	1654	981	1214	778
8 DENMARK	.	.	.	.	.	.	.	.	.	.	1359	660	500	564	238
9 EIRE	-	-	-	-	16684	20537	21134	18924	16640	12093	4340	2654	1236	996	2007
10 FINLAND	-	-	-	-	-	.	.	.	14962	8704	3746	2475	1424	1085	509
11 FRANCE	-	-	-	-	.	.	.	.	5320	2944	1830	1369	1030	901	348
12 GREECE	-	-	-	-	.	21580	30145	21769	-	-	-	8299	3274	3796	4172
13 HUNGARY	-	-	-	98018	87933	57690	4382	3083	3249	.	1233	1174	699	695	755
14 ICELAND	-	-	6667	36667	20000	4286	8750	11111	.	.	.	.	0	0	0
15 ITALY	.	.	.	.	.	.	27285	27735	29953	13443	5012	3606	2598	1937	931
16 JAPAN	.	.	37395	50925	70794	81031	69730	59458	-	23969	18511	14155	6382	3354	2530
17 NETHERLANDS	18953	14423	12009	14947	9374	7914	4345	4297	7039	3218	1601	1183	863	503	247
18 NEW ZEALAND	-	21429	32368	8929	10978	8039	5455	4622	5625	1673	2738	1774	1379	1111	991
19 NORWAY	.	.	9672	13438	10498	10667	6923	6681	6733	2379	1354	900	719	506	300
20 POLAND	-	-	-	-	-	-	-	-	-	-	.	4433	2842	2598	2149
21 PORTUGAL	.	.	.	.	.	.	.	.	.	.	27796	19842	13498	4874	3358
22 ROMANIA	-	-	-	-	-	-	-	-	-	-	-	7763	4345	2184	2057
23 SPAIN	.	.	58905	59654	50805	44721	27748	32298	25317	16282	8016	5261	3262	2603	3845
24 SWEDEN	-	-	.	.	.	.	4831	5057	4229	2800	1372	974	860	741	137
25 SWITZERLAND	23599	23599	12012	12012	8603	7298	5133	3249	3225	2541	1934	1549	512	453	111
26 TURKEY	-	-	-	-	-	-	-	-	-	-	-	1247	1515	1542	512
27 UK ENGLAND AND WALES	38395	38868	21911	19955	13959	11193	8958	7945	6737	4218	1736	1219	790	958	1700
28 UK NORTHERN IRELAND	-	-	-	-	32162	32065	.	.	.	7692	3982	2174	750	1774	1575
29 UK SCOTLAND	52302	63201	33738	27090	17857	17101	15543	10347	7895	4338	2457	1571	1422	1081	2358
30 USA	56108	45808	40235	28710	22227	17629	13577	10261	7695	5217	3412	1962	1172	1211	1918
31 YUGOSLAVIA	-	-	-	-	-	-	-	-	-	-	.	.	1932	1084	636

- NO MORTALITY DATA ARE AVAILABLE FOR EVEN A BROADER GROUP OF CAUSES FOR THIS DISEASE

. MORTALITY DATA ARE PRESENTED FOR A BROADER GROUP OF CAUSES FOR THIS DISEASE

0 VALUE<0.5

THE STANDARD MORTALITY RATIOS WERE DERIVED WITH A FACTOR OF 1000

SERIAL MORTALITY TABLES FOR VARIOUS COUNTRIES 1901-1975

TABLE 126 : NEPHRITIS - ACUTE : FEMALES

	1901-	1906-	1911-	1916-	1921-	1926-	1931-	1936-	1941-	1946-	1951-	1956-	1961-	1966-	1971-75
1 AUSTRALIA	-	13814	10875	10691	11253	9526	7296	6080	5377	3185	1444	736	641	991	1060
2 AUSTRIA	-	-	-	-	-	-	-	-	-	.	1502	1354	693	567	234
3 BELGIUM	.	.	.	.	.	.	.	.	.	.	1559	1270	698	664	490
4 BULGARIA	-	-	-	-	-	.	.	.	.	.	.	.	1331	665	439
5 CANADA	-	-	-	-	15399	13044	10365	7286	5313	3588	2641	1638	999	613	496
6 CHILE	-	26222	19609	8136	13360	15539	17869	16899	17064	10173	9002	6494	4063	3488	2956
7 CZECHOSLOVAKIA	-	-	-	9975	7488	8081	7969	6023	8696	5619	1627	1184	771	1158	625
8 DENMARK	.	.	.	.	.	.	.	.	.	.	1026	664	416	202	208
9 EIRE	-	-	-	-	13196	19959	16490	15650	14331	9186	3384	2368	1439	1439	1856
10 FINLAND	-	-	-	-	-	.	.	.	10906	5775	3116	2011	889	766	461
11 FRANCE	-	-	-	-	.	.	.	.	3367	2240	1362	1012	832	662	264
12 GREECE	-	-	-	-	.	18632	26940	21281	-	-	-	5940	3529	3542	3771
13 HUNGARY	-	-	-	83636	73466	51749	3781	2569	3046	.	1009	950	766	551	609
14 ICELAND	-	-	10000	21250	15000	8889	10000	3000	.	.	.	.	0	0	556
15 ITALY	.	.	.	.	.	.	26362	27359	27833	13448	4911	3342	2441	1620	831
16 JAPAN	.	.	38385	52138	67666	73814	64196	55501	-	24816	18788	13589	6154	3051	2300
17 NETHERLANDS	17285	12425	10885	12762	7009	6269	4617	3796	5131	3192	1200	923	712	374	164
18 NEW ZEALAND	-	16667	24242	8800	11046	8333	5981	4068	5076	2112	2343	909	453	871	690
19 NORWAY	.	.	9327	12477	9649	8277	5120	5509	4291	1967	1199	848	544	150	334
20 POLAND	-	-	-	-	-	-	-	-	-	-	.	3080	2392	1993	1467
21 PORTUGAL	.	.	.	.	.	.	.	.	.	.	18163	15696	9370	3412	2139
22 ROMANIA	-	-	-	-	-	-	-	-	-	-	-	5672	3872	1646	1562
23 SPAIN	.	.	49459	51477	44309	36815	22815	25460	18070	12311	6753	4299	2682	2016	2945
24 SWEDEN	-	-	.	.	.	.	4775	4223	2990	2695	915	563	549	436	110
25 SWITZERLAND	22237	22237	10256	10256	8498	6079	4409	3397	2760	2088	2000	1243	517	196	167
26 TURKEY	-	-	-	-	-	-	-	-	-	-	-	1572	1165	1555	399
27 UK ENGLAND AND WALES	30177	32331	16795	13846	10567	9237	7312	5922	4741	2871	1044	641	492	582	1153
28 UK NORTHERN IRELAND	-	-	-	-	30488	29029	.	.	.	3478	2031	1128	857	811	1242
29 UK SCOTLAND	42716	51605	23950	19601	14077	14225	12260	9197	6327	4004	2340	1058	627	711	1715
30 USA	50155	40334	35784	25027	19694	14897	11255	8388	6203	3888	2639	1550	869	835	1257
31 YUGOSLAVIA	-	-	-	-	-	-	-	-	-	-	.	.	1715	919	536

- NO MORTALITY DATA ARE AVAILABLE FOR EVEN A BROADER GROUP OF CAUSES FOR THIS DISEASE

. MORTALITY DATA ARE PRESENTED FOR A BROADER GROUP OF CAUSES FOR THIS DISEASE

0 VALUE<0.5

THE STANDARD MORTALITY RATIOS WERE DERIVED WITH A FACTOR OF 1000

SERIAL MORTALITY TABLES FOR VARIOUS COUNTRIES 1901-1975

TABLE 127 : NEPHRITIS - CHRONIC, OTHER AND UNSPECIFIED : MALES

	1901-	1906-	1911-	1916-	1921-	1926-	1931-	1936-	1941-	1946-	1951-	1956-	1961-	1966-	1971-75
1 AUSTRALIA	-	11206	12440	11547	11184	11846	11616	11148	9953	8226	3402	2321	1728	1333	1010
2 AUSTRIA	-	-	-	-	-	-	-	-	-	.	1439	1441	998	1144	756
3 BELGIUM	.	.	.	.	.	.	.	.	.	.	2755	2123	1539	1068	455
4 BULGARIA	-	-	-	-	-	.	.	.	.	.	.	.	1373	1115	810
5 CANADA	-	-	-	-	8270	11726	10898	11466	11798	8693	3304	2104	1396	853	555
6 CHILE	-	1713	2625	4703	5233	7002	9709	8551	8393	7312	2789	2325	2150	1775	1908
7 CZECHOSLOVAKIA	-	-	-	6904	5455	6234	4753	4468	3505	3309	1654	1398	1320	1331	1222
8 DENMARK	.	.	.	.	.	.	.	.	.	.	1133	808	537	377	224
9 EIRE	-	-	-	-	6342	6887	6935	6580	6596	5542	3312	2603	2200	1792	1203
10 FINLAND	-	-	-	-	-	.	.	.	3165	2767	2459	2608	2685	1598	887
11 FRANCE	-	-	-	-	.	.	.	.	11503	8728	2445	1798	1335	908	458
12 GREECE	-	-	-	-	.	9995	10764	11147	-	-	-	2768	2354	2284	1635
13 HUNGARY	-	-	-	.	.	.	5368	4706	4264	.	2664	2064	1355	1169	1072
14 ICELAND	-	-	5114	4375	3491	2931	3071	3669	.	.	.	.	1097	1221	277
15 ITALY	.	.	.	.	.	.	6431	6015	6120	4237	1819	1557	1303	1080	754
16 JAPAN		.	12452	18058	21766	20662	18766	17591	-	6228	4640	3662	2676	1989	1311
17 NETHERLANDS	8554	8575	7776	7423	6196	6044	5292	5018	4192	3123	1788	1369	1206	885	494
18 NEW ZEALAND	-	5668	4311	6462	6202	7108	7722	6870	5143	3830	1723	1171	1158	840	785
19 NORWAY	.	.	5534	5479	4862	5442	5267	4916	3408	2951	1738	1456	1282	1045	658
20 POLAND	-	-	-	-	-	-	-	-	-	-	.	1050	1503	1557	1500
21 PORTUGAL	.	.	.	.	.	.	.	.	.	.	3532	3858	3605	3707	2579
22 ROMANIA	-	-	-	-	-	-	-	-	-	-	-	2569	2246	1453	1242
23 SPAIN	8229	8883	8523	9782	10088	11213	11812	13252	11824	9271	3965	3614	3093	2516	1759
24 SWEDEN	-	-	.	.	.	.	3935	3571	2730	2433	1883	1636	1210	846	596
25 SWITZERLAND	6156	6156	6665	6665	6869	4945	4603	4152	3514	3120	2122	1519	1142	731	565
26 TURKEY	-	-	-	-	-	-	-	-	-	-	-	3463	2395	1706	1245
27 UK ENGLAND AND WALES	8180	7411	9582	7996	6754	7228	7391	6279	5661	4149	2056	1522	1108	850	795
28 UK NORTHERN IRELAND	-	-	-	-	5062	6064	.	.	.	3065	2037	1700	1302	895	885
29 UK SCOTLAND	6420	8632	9349	8904	8048	7516	6510	6191	4607	3734	1770	1438	1100	810	910
30 USA	35342	26864	25688	23073	19674	20573	18081	16601	13746	8715	2482	1667	1278	926	642
31 YUGOSLAVIA	-	-	-	-	-	-	-	-	-	-	.	.	1946	1760	1345

- NO MORTALITY DATA ARE AVAILABLE FOR EVEN A BROADER GROUP OF CAUSES FOR THIS DISEASE

. MORTALITY DATA ARE PRESENTED FOR A BROADER GROUP OF CAUSES FOR THIS DISEASE

0 VALUE<0.5

THE STANDARD MORTALITY RATIOS WERE DERIVED WITH A FACTOR OF 1000

SERIAL MORTALITY TABLES FOR VARIOUS COUNTRIES 1901-1975

TABLE 127 : NEPHRITIS - CHRONIC, OTHER AND UNSPECIFIED : FEMALES

	1901-	1906-	1911-	1916-	1921-	1926-	1931-	1936-	1941-	1946-	1951-	1956-	1961-	1966-	1971-75
1 AUSTRALIA	-	8246	8808	8147	8622	9910	9799	9479	8167	6488	2611	1683	1191	990	842
2 AUSTRIA	-	-	-	-	-	-	-	-	-	.	1230	1012	770	860	614
3 BELGIUM	.	.	.	.	.	.	.	.	.	.	2231	1684	1233	932	424
4 BULGARIA	-	-	-	-	-	.	.	.	.	.	.	.	1148	962	642
5 CANADA	-	-	-	-	7450	11643	11037	11889	11320	8454	3062	1892	1182	700	384
6 CHILE	-	944	2020	3842	4411	5986	8143	8131	7430	6300	2529	2096	1930	1555	1430
7 CZECHOSLOVAKIA	-	-	-	5558	4257	4983	3872	3776	2854	2621	1177	952	976	947	828
8 DENMARK	.	.	.	.	.	.	.	.	.	.	1019	743	472	314	152
9 EIRE	-	-	-	-	4749	5465	5298	5097	4401	3761	2514	1896	1570	1146	776
10 FINLAND	-	-	-	-	-	.	.	.	1999	1929	1732	1997	2112	1233	591
11 FRANCE	-	-	-	-	.	.	.	.	6458	5000	1627	1182	818	586	335
12 GREECE	-	-	-	-	.	8748	9567	10019	-	-	-	2366	2129	2122	1504
13 HUNGARY	-	-	-	.	.	.	4572	3918	3281	.	2077	1615	1027	963	918
14 ICELAND	-	-	2479	2756	3066	2349	2298	2800	.	.	.	.	1065	616	342
15 ITALY	.	.	.	.	.	.	6339	6137	5791	4106	1694	1338	1041	810	573
16 JAPAN	.	.	12231	17568	19739	19126	17962	16991	-	6522	4563	3262	2180	1534	1051
17 NETHERLANDS	9020	9031	8206	8197	7195	7308	6764	6617	4866	3536	1867	1276	1013	706	405
18 NEW ZEALAND	-	4138	3378	4819	5162	7050	7272	6476	4706	3194	1434	818	708	579	609
19 NORWAY	.	.	4292	4347	3866	4131	3796	3294	2300	1910	1300	924	759	549	288
20 POLAND	-	-	-	-	-	-	-	-	-	-	.	786	1054	1092	1027
21 PORTUGAL	.	.	.	.	.	.	.	.	.	.	2819	2542	2351	2262	1583
22 ROMANIA	-	-	-	-	-	-	-	-	-	-	-	1928	1998	1249	927
23 SPAIN	5755	6382	5830	6817	6991	7537	8320	8621	7351	5843	3034	2758	2416	1984	1395
24 SWEDEN	-	-	.	.	.	.	3218	2859	2394	2167	1501	1240	852	516	354
25 SWITZERLAND	5858	5858	5951	5951	6387	4735	4173	4163	3338	3108	2183	1435	963	664	535
26 TURKEY	-	-	-	-	-	-	-	-	-	-	-	2841	1995	1478	989
27 UK ENGLAND AND WALES	6339	5827	6932	5435	5097	5711	5910	4971	4079	3151	1512	991	726	520	528
28 UK NORTHERN IRELAND	-	-	-	-	4430	4619	.	.	.	2970	1938	1134	895	566	489
29 UK SCOTLAND	4663	6258	6760	6002	6161	6281	5731	5546	3929	2975	1521	1067	748	588	734
30 USA	26796	21295	20693	19508	18114	18441	16026	14395	11566	7188	1966	1249	878	618	439
31 YUGOSLAVIA	-	-	-	-	-	-	-	-	-	-	.	.	1751	1478	1109

- NO MORTALITY DATA ARE AVAILABLE FOR EVEN A BROADER GROUP OF CAUSES FOR THIS DISEASE

. MORTALITY DATA ARE PRESENTED FOR A BROADER GROUP OF CAUSES FOR THIS DISEASE

0 VALUE<0.5

THE STANDARD MORTALITY RATIOS WERE DERIVED WITH A FACTOR OF 1000

SERIAL MORTALITY TABLES FOR VARIOUS COUNTRIES 1901-1975

TABLE 128 : NEPHRITIS AND NEPHROSIS : MALES

	1901-	1906-	1911-	1916-	1921-	1926-	1931-	1936-	1941-	1946-	1951-	1956-	1961-	1966-	1971-75
1 AUSTRALIA	-	11322	12469	11527	11258	11760	11395	10934	9738	8019	3369	2284	1689	1323	1050
2 AUSTRIA	-	-	-	-	-	-	-	-	-	.	1464	1433	993	1124	742
3 BELGIUM	3779	4334	4333	4222	3686	4447	6280	6582	6391	5185	2865	2092	1504	1055	454
4 BULGARIA	-	-	-	-	-	6712	5608	4558	5738	4597	4472	2042	1364	1097	810
5 CANADA	-	-	-	-	8827	11862	10875	11293	11522	8465	3293	2081	1376	845	568
6 CHILE	-	4255	4103	5070	5917	7564	10474	9326	9158	7809	3930	2667	2357	1913	2015
7 CZECHOSLOVAKIA	-	-	-	7197	5740	6504	5033	4694	3768	2878	1717	1413	1301	1325	1198
8 DENMARK	9069	8722	8294	7273	4017	3732	3131	2537	2548	1901	1146	800	535	387	225
9 EIRE	-	-	-	-	6919	7653	7725	7260	7146	5901	3367	2605	2149	1749	1247
10 FINLAND	-	-	-	-	-	5443	4706	3838	3872	3127	2536	2601	2611	1568	866
11 FRANCE	-	-	-	-	7308	9006	8991	10329	11952	8420	2413	1775	1319	908	452
12 GREECE	-	-	-	-	8715	9659	11929	11779	-	-	-	3081	2405	2366	1769
13 HUNGARY	-	-	-	9030	7933	5681	5311	4612	4206	3882	2976	2015	1320	1144	1055
14 ICELAND	-	-	5213	6214	4554	3008	3407	4122	3049	2582	1700	1384	1032	1151	261
15 ITALY	8267	8940	9467	9653	8386	7639	7406	7269	7482	4758	1998	1669	1373	1126	763
16 JAPAN	8094	10465	14008	20119	24928	24604	22098	20328	-	7393	5533	4309	2898	2069	1381
17 NETHERLANDS	9330	8937	8038	7882	6389	6157	5237	4977	4357	3128	1778	1359	1187	864	481
18 NEW ZEALAND	-	6623	6019	6611	6482	7167	7593	6742	5170	3711	1780	1205	1171	856	797
19 NORWAY	6049	5412	5778	5950	5194	5742	5360	5014	3591	2920	1718	1426	1252	1016	640
20 POLAND	-	-	-	-	-	-	-	-	-	-	.	1259	1584	1618	1537
21 PORTUGAL	4743	4885	5243	6472	6648	7457	7196	7298	7411	5868	5027	4803	4178	3773	2622
22 ROMANIA	-	-	-	-	-	-	-	-	-	-	-	2873	2366	1495	1288
23 SPAIN	8476	10111	11599	12806	12557	13252	12776	14390	12623	9682	4200	3708	3103	2521	1875
24 SWEDEN	-	-	.	.	.	.	3983	3651	2810	2453	1856	1601	1193	841	572
25 SWITZERLAND	7335	7335	7030	7030	7233	5270	5238	4754	3736	3237	2112	1521	1108	716	541
26 TURKEY	-	-	-	-	-	-	-	-	-	-	-	3305	2334	1695	1195
27 UK ENGLAND AND WALES	10100	9330	10341	8713	7178	7455	7478	6370	5717	4153	2039	1506	1092	855	842
28 UK NORTHERN IRELAND	-	-	-	-	6628	7558	7172	6395	5220	4266	2143	1726	1271	944	923
29 UK SCOTLAND	9390	12109	10869	10013	8633	8075	7026	6426	4788	3767	1807	1446	1117	825	987
30 USA	36599	28015	26569	23413	19828	20399	17819	16240	13406	8520	2534	1684	1272	942	712
31 YUGOSLAVIA	-	-	-	-	-	-	-	-	-	-	.	2926	1945	1720	1304

- NO MORTALITY DATA ARE AVAILABLE FOR EVEN A BROADER GROUP OF CAUSES FOR THIS DISEASE

. MORTALITY DATA ARE PRESENTED FOR A BROADER GROUP OF CAUSES FOR THIS DISEASE

0 VALUE<0.5

THE STANDARD MORTALITY RATIOS WERE DERIVED WITH A FACTOR OF 1000

SERIAL MORTALITY TABLES FOR VARIOUS COUNTRIES 1901-1975

TABLE 128 : NEPHRITIS AND NEPHROSIS : FEMALES

	1901-	1906-	1911-	1916-	1921-	1926-	1931-	1936-	1941-	1946-	1951-	1956-	1961-	1966-	1971-75
1 AUSTRALIA	-	8610	8943	8307	8784	9887	9654	9289	8014	6307	2548	1632	1161	990	854
2 AUSTRIA	-	-	-	-	-	-	-	-	-	.	1243	1029	766	846	595
3 BELGIUM	2302	2786	2812	2632	2579	2833	4387	4360	4027	3498	2132	1663	1207	918	427
4 BULGARIA	-	-	-	-	-	5726	4912	3939	4440	3678	2814	1479	1167	946	632
5 CANADA	-	-	-	-	7942	11729	10997	11622	10975	8176	3038	1878	1172	695	390
6 CHILE	-	2590	3184	4129	5014	6628	8793	8712	8062	6553	3539	2379	2068	1679	1526
7 CZECHOSLOVAKIA	-	-	-	5818	4444	5160	4103	3903	3171	2289	1254	964	965	958	817
8 DENMARK	5015	5000	4970	5103	3783	3373	2716	2117	2181	1744	1019	739	469	308	155
9 EIRE	-	-	-	-	5212	6261	5909	5671	4940	4054	2560	1921	1563	1162	832
10 FINLAND	-	-	-	-	-	4214	3770	3173	2497	2144	1808	1998	2046	1209	584
11 FRANCE	-	-	-	-	4625	5524	5278	5715	6406	4861	1614	1173	819	590	332
12 GREECE	-	-	-	-	7512	8605	10593	10674	-	-	-	2560	2203	2196	1619
13 HUNGARY	-	-	-	7830	6755	5029	4527	3842	3268	2600	2170	1580	1013	942	903
14 ICELAND	-	-	2903	3881	3724	2722	2706	3081	2412	1682	1126	1310	1004	583	352
15 ITALY	7870	8273	9127	9127	8253	7706	7296	7325	7010	4616	1867	1444	1114	852	586
16 JAPAN	8045	10710	13824	19682	22726	22561	20861	19404	-	7660	5430	3866	2406	1618	1119
17 NETHERLANDS	9648	9235	8366	8469	7185	7248	6640	6457	4881	3517	1830	1257	997	689	393
18 NEW ZEALAND	-	4946	4714	5066	5520	7125	7198	6342	4726	3135	1483	823	694	595	613
19 NORWAY	4741	4467	4577	4806	4190	4358	3868	3412	2405	1912	1295	921	748	529	291
20 POLAND	-	-	-	-	-	-	-	-	-	-	.	917	1128	1141	1050
21 PORTUGAL	3097	3048	3533	4557	4606	5231	4648	4730	4645	3599	3386	3262	2729	2323	1612
22 ROMANIA	-	-	-	-	-	-	-	-	-	-	-	2135	2100	1270	961
23 SPAIN	6002	7464	8423	9459	9190	9255	9161	9581	7955	6202	3237	2841	2430	1986	1476
24 SWEDEN	-	-	.	.	.	.	3299	2930	2424	2195	1471	1206	837	512	342
25 SWITZERLAND	6919	6919	6251	6251	6792	5010	4810	4723	3539	3213	2173	1425	940	640	517
26 TURKEY	-	-	-	-	-	-	-	-	-	-	-	2758	1941	1483	950
27 UK ENGLAND AND WALES	7827	7414	7513	5919	5405	5904	5985	5021	4113	3137	1488	974	714	523	559
28 UK NORTHERN IRELAND	-	-	-	-	5886	5989	6068	5628	4512	3607	1943	1133	894	579	528
29 UK SCOTLAND	6969	8968	7774	6792	6612	6724	6089	5742	4055	3028	1563	1067	742	594	782
30 USA	28200	22449	21607	19843	18210	18230	15749	14055	11268	7007	2003	1265	877	630	481
31 YUGOSLAVIA	-	-	-	-	-	-	-	-	-	-	.	2822	1749	1447	1078

- NO MORTALITY DATA ARE AVAILABLE FOR EVEN A BROADER GROUP OF CAUSES FOR THIS DISEASE

. MORTALITY DATA ARE PRESENTED FOR A BROADER GROUP OF CAUSES FOR THIS DISEASE

0 VALUE<0.5

THE STANDARD MORTALITY RATIOS WERE DERIVED WITH A FACTOR OF 1000

SERIAL MORTALITY TABLES FOR VARIOUS COUNTRIES 1901-1975

TABLE 128 : NEPHRITIS AND NEPHROSIS : PERSONS

	1901-	1906-	1911-	1916-	1921-	1926-	1931-	1936-	1941-	1946-	1951-	1956-	1961-	1966-	1971-75
1 AUSTRALIA	-	10071	10824	9998	10068	10851	10540	10113	8865	7143	2939	1939	1406	1143	942
2 AUSTRIA	-	-	-	-	-	-	2472	2478	-	-	1338	1199	859	958	654
3 BELGIUM	3020	3536	3542	3391	3113	3616	5301	5429	5163	4305	2469	1858	1340	979	439
4 BULGARIA	-	-	-	-	-	6212	5255	4241	5067	4118	3600	1746	1260	1018	716
5 CANADA	6558	5859	7109	6819	8406	11798	10933	11452	11257	8323	3166	1979	1272	767	473
6 CHILE	-	3398	3631	4587	5452	7080	9603	9008	8587	7152	3724	2514	2203	1788	1752
7 CZECHOSLOVAKIA	-	-	-	6454	5041	5778	4529	4265	3444	2557	1464	1166	1114	1118	982
8 DENMARK	6725	6570	6370	6018	3893	3542	2912	2317	2357	1819	1080	768	500	345	187
9 EIRE	-	-	-	-	6055	6949	6813	6468	6036	4971	2960	2256	1845	1441	1028
10 FINLAND	-	-	-	-	-	4784	4197	3470	3102	2567	2117	2253	2285	1360	702
11 FRANCE	9534	4775	4838	4016	5835	7090	6934	7742	8802	6384	1953	1427	1028	722	382
12 GREECE	-	-	-	-	8099	9118	11243	11213	-	-	-	3509	3143	3107	2318
13 HUNGARY	-	-	-	8408	7321	5342	4901	4207	3710	3185	2535	1776	1150	1031	969
14 ICELAND	-	-	3899	4895	4086	2847	3016	3543	2700	2096	1392	1344	1017	852	309
15 ITALY	8066	8600	9294	9384	8318	7673	7349	7298	7232	4682	1927	1547	1231	974	664
16 JAPAN	8069	10590	13914	19895	23788	23538	21450	19843	-	7537	5478	4070	2632	1824	1238
17 NETHERLANDS	9497	9093	8209	8187	6801	6719	5959	5738	4626	3329	1805	1306	1087	770	433
18 NEW ZEALAND	-	5875	5428	5891	6023	7147	7399	6542	4944	3416	1626	1005	917	715	697
19 NORWAY	5344	4901	5126	5328	4648	4991	4552	4148	2951	2379	1493	1157	984	754	450
20 POLAND	-	-	-	-	-	-	-	-	-	-	-	1268	1325	1347	1258
21 PORTUGAL	3836	3868	4292	5402	5504	6207	5760	5843	5845	4592	4090	3924	3351	2941	2041
22 ROMANIA	-	-	-	-	-	-	-	-	-	-	-	2468	2220	1371	1109
23 SPAIN	7191	8721	9926	11045	10773	11109	10816	11753	10058	7756	3661	3223	2727	2222	1652
24 SWEDEN	-	-	-	-	-	-	3619	3269	2607	2318	1655	1394	1005	666	448
25 SWITZERLAND	7115	7115	6610	6610	6993	5128	5004	4737	3628	3224	2146	1468	1014	673	527
26 TURKEY	-	-	-	-	-	-	3079	4784	5007	5169	3455	3024	2133	1589	1075
27 UK ENGLAND AND WALES	8914	3328	8810	7188	6208	6605	6657	5622	4795	3582	1727	1201	874	662	677
28 UK NORTHERN IRELAND	-	-	-	-	6231	6720	6584	5988	4839	3915	2035	1402	1063	740	700
29 UK SCOTLAND	8055	10378	9167	8240	7524	7334	6513	6050	4383	3356	1670	1231	902	691	867
30 USA	32355	25270	24138	21656	19030	19328	16790	15142	12320	6193	2257	1462	1060	770	583
31 YUGOSLAVIA	-	-	-	-	-	-	-	-	-	-	-	2869	1837	1570	1180

- NO MORTALITY DATA ARE AVAILABLE FOR EVEN A BROADER GROUP OF CAUSES FOR THIS DISEASE

. MORTALITY DATA ARE PRESENTED FOR A BROADER GROUP OF CAUSES FOR THIS DISEASE

0 VALUE<0.5

THE STANDARD MCRTALITY RATIOS WERE DERIVED WITH A FACTOR OF 1000

SERIAL MORTALITY TABLES FOR VARIOUS COUNTRIES 1901-1975

TABLE 129 : KIDNEY - INFECTIONS : MALES

	1901-	1906-	1911-	1916-	1921-	1926-	1931-	1936-	1941-	1946-	1951-	1956-	1961-	1966-	1971-75
1 AUSTRALIA	-	.	.	.	.	.	.	.	.	.	9122	12138	16625	15447	8347
2 AUSTRIA	-	-	-	-	-	-	-	-	-	.	11172	14368	15974	18503	23063
3 BELGIUM	-	-	-	-	-	-	.	.	.	.	2044	2747	3329	4172	3182
4 BULGARIA	-	-	-	-	-	-	.	.	.	.	.	.	17795	22224	35520
5 CANADA	-	-	-	-	.	.	.	.	.	6669	6674	10449	12756	10802	7125
6 CHILE	-	.	.	.	.	.	.	12152	11876	6551	5703	5640	9210	8394	8711
7 CZECHOSLOVAKIA	-	-	-	.	.	.	.	.	.	.	5744	7981	15700	27537	33253
8 DENMARK	.	.	.	.	.	.	.	.	.	.	13558	22040	24345	21217	16500
9 EIRE	-	-	-	-	.	.	.	.	.	.	3929	5219	9416	10680	10812
10 FINLAND	-	-	-	-	-	-	-	.	10223	6122	4225	10726	22911	24310	15436
11 FRANCE	-	-	-	-	-	-	.	.	.	5439	3622	1527	729	1001	1128
12 GREECE	-	-	-	-	-	.	.	.	-	-	-	2782	4880	7210	4211
13 HUNGARY	-	-	-	.	.	.	9154	11216	3951	.	5392	7192	8048	12445	15863
14 ICELAND	-	-	-	-	-	-	-	-	.	.	-	-	12409	19608	11628
15 ITALY	-	-	-	-	-	-	.	.	.	.	3313	3355	4211	5746	6183
16 JAPAN	-	.	.	.	.	.	.	.	-	6338	3954	2541	3015	3268	3094
17 NETHERLANDS	.	.	.	.	.	.	.	.	.	5234	3620	4593	6298	8013	6169
18 NEW ZEALAND	-	.	.	.	.	.	.	.	.	5419	9052	12721	13856	11028	5787
19 NORWAY	.	.	50117	45791	36521	27282	24017	17887	.	.	5847	8479	11327	12304	12762
20 POLAND	-	-	-	-	-	-	-	-	-	-	.	1036	2634	4934	5559
21 PORTUGAL	-	-	-	-	-	-	.	.	.	.	3489	3088	2743	5496	9723
22 ROMANIA	-	-	-	-	-	-	-	-	-	-	-	2931	3876	5460	7078
23 SPAIN	.	.	.	.	.	.	4025	3666	.	.	2488	2473	3021	3920	3632
24 SWEDEN	-	-	.	.	.	.	.	.	.	.	6568	14873	19211	19854	18365
25 SWITZERLAND	.	.	.	.	.	.	.	.	.	.	5519	6719	10471	11224	10884
26 TURKEY	-	-	-	-	-	-	-	-	-	-	-	15880	7446	6994	9050
27 UK ENGLAND AND WALES	.	.	.	.	.	.	5996	7125	6661	6023	7215	9465	13021	11873	7429
28 UK NORTHERN IRELAND	-	-	-	-	.	.	.	.	.	6871	6950	10239	13745	12790	8782
29 UK SCOTLAND	.	.	.	.	.	.	.	.	.	6596	7407	11103	15174	11245	7689
30 USA	.	.	.	.	.	.	.	.	.	7380	8468	12326	14588	12666	7586
31 YUGOSLAVIA	-	-	-	-	-	-	-	-	-	-	.	.	6334	10200	14522

- NO MORTALITY DATA ARE AVAILABLE FOR EVEN A BROADER GROUP OF CAUSES FOR THIS DISEASE

. MORTALITY DATA ARE PRESENTED FOR A BROADER GROUP OF CAUSES FOR THIS DISEASE

0 VALUE<0.5

THE STANDARD MORTALITY RATIOS WERE DERIVED WITH A FACTOR OF 10000

SERIAL MORTALITY TABLES FOR VARIOUS COUNTRIES 1901-1975

TABLE 129 : KIDNEY - INFECTIONS : FEMALES

	1901-	1906-	1911-	1916-	1921-	1926-	1931-	1936-	1941-	1946-	1951-	1956-	1961-	1966-	1971-75
1 AUSTRALIA	-	.	.	.	.	.	.	.	.	.	7717	12430	21820	21903	12794
2 AUSTRIA	-	-	-	-	-	-	-	-	-	.	9746	12739	15307	19668	22839
3 BELGIUM	-	-	-	-	-	-	.	.	.	.	1686	2471	3695	5025	3796
4 BULGARIA	-	-	-	-	-	-	.	.	.	.	.	.	14472	17041	24239
5 CANADA	-	-	-	-	.	.	.	.	.	4723	4580	7330	9372	8796	5142
6 CHILE	-	.	.	.	.	.	.	9646	7877	3558	3274	5639	7763	9763	11131
7 CZECHOSLOVAKIA	-	-	-	.	.	.	.	.	.	.	4129	6394	12884	22835	28757
8 DENMARK	.	.	.	.	.	.	.	.	.	.	23917	44168	44840	34896	24610
9 EIRE	-	-	-	-	.	.	.	.	.	.	3776	5625	8216	12500	10526
10 FINLAND	-	-	-	-	-	-	-	.	6228	4063	5665	20208	43727	43517	28495
11 FRANCE	-	-	-	-	-	-	.	.	.	865	686	700	544	710	797
12 GREECE	-	-	-	-	-	.	.	.	-	-	-	1852	3750	5390	3280
13 HUNGARY	-	-	-	.	.	.	6696	7291	2895	.	4526	4815	6481	11609	12556
14 ICELAND	-	-	-	-	-	-	-	-	.	.	-	-	27607	32240	33659
15 ITALY	-	-	-	-	-	-	.	.	.	.	2482	2349	2896	3663	3881
16 JAPAN	-	.	.	.	.	.	.	.	-	10060	5611	3792	4566	5296	5609
17 NETHERLANDS	.	.	.	.	.	.	.	.	.	7647	6111	7252	10146	11311	9309
18 NEW ZEALAND	-	.	.	.	.	.	.	.	.	7119	8935	14936	15946	13496	9696
19 NORWAY	.	.	9962	10261	8279	12018	11727	12195	.	.	9739	11421	16625	16228	16554
20 POLAND	-	-	-	-	-	-	-	-	-	-	.	511	2443	4301	4722
21 PORTUGAL	-	-	-	-	-	-	.	.	.	.	1804	1102	1151	3025	4484
22 ROMANIA	-	-	-	-	-	-	-	-	-	-	-	1152	2460	4208	5523
23 SPAIN	.	.	.	.	.	.	2568	2235	.	.	1610	1473	2131	2720	2942
24 SWEDEN	-	-	.	.	.	.	.	.	.	.	8951	16633	22765	21980	17292
25 SWITZERLAND	.	.	.	.	.	.	.	.	.	.	9105	13327	18340	17334	14998
26 TURKEY	-	-	-	-	-	-	-	-	-	-	-	7345	5200	4763	6042
27 UK ENGLAND AND WALES	.	.	.	.	.	.	6191	6646	5570	5232	6264	9037	13377	12435	8766
28 UK NORTHERN IRELAND	-	-	-	-	.	.	.	.	.	7671	5390	7620	13741	16021	10584
29 UK SCOTLAND		.	.	.	.	.	.	.	.	6337	7742	11883	18312	16863	10663
30 USA	.	.	.	.	.	.	.	.	.	6399	6999	10103	12449	11300	7101
31 YUGOSLAVIA	-	-	-	-	-	-	-	-	-	-	.	.	5066	10294	13806

- NO MORTALITY DATA ARE AVAILABLE FOR EVEN A BROADER GROUP OF CAUSES FOR THIS DISEASE

. MORTALITY DATA ARE PRESENTED FOR A BROADER GROUP OF CAUSES FOR THIS DISEASE

0 VALUE<0.5

THE STANDARD MORTALITY RATIOS WERE DERIVED WITH A FACTOR OF 10000

SERIAL MORTALITY TABLES FOR VARIOUS COUNTRIES 1901-1975

TABLE 130 : KIDNEY - ALL DISEASES EXCLUDING CALCULI : MALES

	1901-	1906-	1911-	1916-	1921-	1926-	1931-	1936-	1941-	1946-	1951-	1956-	1961-	1966-	1971-75
1 AUSTRALIA	-	.	9096	8503	8311	8657	8267	7863	6975	5706	2533	1919	1680	1399	976
2 AUSTRIA	-	-	-	-	-	-	-	-	-	2346	1654	1435	1210	1387	1311
3 BELGIUM	-	-	-	-	-	-	.	.	.	.	1814	1441	1080	824	404
4 BULGARIA	-	-	-	-	-	-	.	.	.	.	.	.	1509	1485	1754
5 CANADA	-	-	-	-	6653	8599	7720	7962	7945	5808	2382	1720	1340	928	618
6 CHILE	-	2928	3152	4323	5143	6365	9295	8451	7891	6729	2549	2005	1899	1570	1654
7 CZECHOSLOVAKIA	-	-	-	5254	4179	4618	3603	3407	2913	2644	1312	1203	1393	1816	1939
8 DENMARK	.	.	.	.	.	.	.	.	.	.	1219	1303	1221	1018	748
9 EIRE	-	-	-	-	4820	5359	5398	5167	5045	4138	2283	1838	1703	1498	1186
10 FINLAND	-	-	-	-	-	-	-	.	2953	2319	1856	2105	2507	1853	1092
11 FRANCE	-	-	-	-	-	-	.	.	7493	5634	1690	1200	876	619	329
12 GREECE	-	-	-	-	-	8398	9061	8770	-	-	-	2116	1731	1782	1279
13 HUNGARY	-	-	-	.	.	.	3866	3457	2938	2808	2174	1573	1142	1179	1242
14 ICELAND	-	-	-	-	-	-	-	-	.	.	-	-	1105	1438	585
15 ITALY	-	-	-	-	-	-	.	.	.	.	1425	1207	1039	932	712
16 JAPAN	-	7913	9551	13711	17233	17346	15795	14708	-	5297	3926	3027	2068	1504	1026
17 NETHERLANDS	6547	6319	5679	5612	4593	4393	3798	3662	3194	2318	1286	1041	988	841	530
18 NEW ZEALAND	-	5647	5204	5010	5163	5426	5690	5030	3832	2790	1473	1229	1247	942	723
19 NORWAY	.	.	5506	5468	4653	4683	4318	3877	3000	2408	1313	1218	1209	1095	871
20 POLAND	-	-	-	-	-	-	-	-	-	-	.	893	1161	1251	1211
21 PORTUGAL	-	-	-	-	-	-	.	.	.	.	3467	3316	2854	2670	2051
22 ROMANIA	-	-	-	-	-	-	-	-	-	-	-	2036	1716	1178	1091
23 SPAIN	5819	6959	7994	8857	8701	9209	8972	10103	8962	6902	2887	2543	2139	1781	1348
24 SWEDEN	-	-	.	.	.	.	.	.	.	.	1430	1560	1458	1261	1042
25 SWITZERLAND	.	.	.	.	.	.	.	.	.	.	1575	1225	1087	860	736
26 TURKEY	-	-	-	-	-	-	-	-	-	-	-	2792	1848	1383	1103
27 UK ENGLAND AND WALES	.	.	7308	6173	5115	5277	5296	4561	3991	2952	1577	1309	1166	973	807
28 UK NORTHERN IRELAND	-	-	-	-	4653	5405	5053	4611	3698	3129	1625	1475	1308	1063	907
29 UK SCOTLAND	.	.	7789	7118	6229	5842	5128	4743	3540	2791	1435	1328	1258	930	910
30 USA	25666	19694	18547	16328	13867	14218	12406	11275	9229	5871	1947	1525	1339	1058	729
31 YUGOSLAVIA	-	-	-	-	-	-	-	-	-	-	.	.	1510	1487	1353

- NO MORTALITY DATA ARE AVAILABLE FOR EVEN A BROADER GROUP OF CAUSES FOR THIS DISEASE

. MORTALITY DATA ARE PRESENTED FOR A BROADER GROUP OF CAUSES FOR THIS DISEASE

0 VALUE<0.5

THE STANDARD MORTALITY RATIOS WERE DERIVED WITH A FACTOR OF 1000

SERIAL MORTALITY TABLES FOR VARIOUS COUNTRIES 1901-1975

TABLE 130 : KIDNEY - ALL DISEASES EXCLUDING CALCULI : FEMALES

	1901-	1906-	1911-	1916-	1921-	1926-	1931-	1936-	1941-	1946-	1951-	1956-	1961-	1966-	1971-75
1 AUSTRALIA	-	.	6422	6076	6482	7292	7026	6644	5650	4399	1913	1492	1535	1433	1011
2 AUSTRIA	-	-	-	-	-	-	-	-	-	1636	1286	1120	1055	1278	1255
3 BELGIUM	-	-	-	-	-	-	.	.	.	.	1450	1133	889	759	409
4 BULGARIA	-	-	-	-	-	-	.	.	.	.	.	.	1261	1219	1275
5 CANADA	-	-	-	-	5928	8368	7713	8149	7493	5550	2130	1471	1087	762	436
6 CHILE	-	1708	2373	3444	4170	5499	7637	7631	6823	5605	2098	1779	1636	1444	1389
7 CZECHOSLOVAKIA	-	-	-	4116	3154	3588	2878	2766	2345	2043	924	849	1082	1446	1590
8 DENMARK	.	.	.	.	.	.	.	.	.	.	1510	2079	1955	1507	1042
9 EIRE	-	-	-	-	3515	4315	4031	3937	3455	2770	1749	1410	1281	1195	916
10 FINLAND	-	-	-	-	-	-	-	.	1853	1545	1377	2006	2871	2337	1406
11 FRANCE	-	-	-	-	-	-	.	.	4085	3123	1032	751	523	386	231
12 GREECE	-	-	-	-	-	7151	7773	7694	-	-	-	1718	1539	1586	1130
13 HUNGARY	-	-	-	.	.	.	3242	2796	2259	1847	1556	1193	882	1022	1035
14 ICELAND	-	-	-	-	-	-	-	-	.	.	-	-	1652	1568	1484
15 ITALY	-	-	-	-	-	-	.	.	.	.	1297	1011	812	671	511
16 JAPAN	-	8003	9294	13246	15547	15829	14850	13930	-	5471	3814	2692	1743	1245	924
17 NETHERLANDS	5477	6305	5765	5910	5086	5202	4892	4857	3624	2673	1400	1066	1004	853	596
18 NEW ZEALAND	-	3978	3948	3814	4248	5426	5295	4673	3445	2308	1271	1069	1028	876	744
19 NORWAY	.	.	3276	3441	2976	3215	2888	2611	2024	1655	1176	1003	1093	947	810
20 POLAND	-	-	-	-	-	-	-	-	-	-	.	622	823	890	841
21 PORTUGAL	-	-	-	-	-	-	.	.	.	.	2441	2143	1783	1584	1182
22 ROMANIA	-	-	-	-	-	-	-	-	-	-	-	1446	1457	970	814
23 SPAIN	4106	5068	5725	6441	6249	6296	6292	6579	5524	4321	2151	1877	1624	1356	1038
24 SWEDEN	-	-	.	.	.	.	.	.	.	.	1261	1375	1378	1157	883
25 SWITZERLAND	.	.	.	.	.	.	.	.	.	.	1718	1392	1271	1050	892
26 TURKEY	-	-	-	-	-	-	-	-	-	-	-	2101	1472	1147	835
27 UK ENGLAND AND WALES	.	.	5216	4118	3783	4141	4208	3566	2873	2205	1168	947	953	802	684
28 UK NORTHERN IRELAND	-	-	-	-	4033	4182	4224	4079	3244	2612	1428	996	1073	965	730
29 UK SCOTLAND	.	.	5417	4736	4716	4806	4438	4153	2932	2209	1276	1112	1150	1011	892
30 USA	19483	15546	14905	13711	12645	12658	10928	9709	7685	4772	1538	1173	1013	817	568
31 YUGOSLAVIA	-	-	-	-	-	-	-	-	-	-	.	.	1313	1301	1185

- NO MORTALITY DATA ARE AVAILABLE FOR EVEN A BROADER GROUP OF CAUSES FOR THIS DISEASE

. MORTALITY DATA ARE PRESENTED FOR A BROADER GROUP OF CAUSES FOR THIS DISEASE

0 VALUE<0.5

THE STANDARD MORTALITY RATIOS WERE DERIVED WITH A FACTOR OF 1000

SERIAL MORTALITY TABLES FOR VARIOUS COUNTRIES 1901-1975

TABLE 131 : URINARY SYSTEM - CALCULI : MALES

	1901-	1906-	1911-	1916-	1921-	1926-	1931-	1936-	1941-	1946-	1951-	1956-	1961-	1966-	1971-75
1 AUSTRALIA	-	3606	3787	2779	3111	3622	3981	5216	4403	3520	2729	2351	1997	1905	909
2 AUSTRIA	-	-	-	-	-	-	-	-	-	1952	3349	4515	5681	4760	3720
3 BELGIUM	-	-	-	-	-	-	.	.	.	.	909	714	651	640	788
4 BULGARIA	-	-	-	-	-	-	.	.	.	.	.	.	4153	4666	3589
5 CANADA	-	-	-	-	2386	2726	3249	5076	4548	3226	1922	1789	1628	1183	708
6 CHILE	-	222	1956	848	987	803	701	671	826	625	630	1474	476	654	614
7 CZECHOSLOVAKIA	-	-	-	942	714	1237	2677	3045	1312	798	2322	2752	3058	3866	3383
8 DENMARK	9710	10405	6552	5851	4563	5178	6938	9156	8946	7485	6000	5569	4357	4448	2548
9 EIRE	-	-	-	-	219	731	563	981	745	623	773	653	558	687	324
10 FINLAND	-	-	-	-	-	-	-	.	1041	917	607	656	885	727	976
11 FRANCE	-	-	-	-	-	-	.	.	670	361	372	596	699	694	587
12 GREECE	-	-	-	-	-	2141	2575	2021	-	-	-	1131	1541	1609	1018
13 HUNGARY	-	-	-	.	.	.	2171	3138	2249	1681	2052	3037	3675	4055	3938
14 ICELAND	-	-	-	-	-	-	-	-	.	.	-	-	4000	1818	2083
15 ITALY	-	-	-	-	-	-	3855	4147	3109	3222	2637	2741	3021	2842	2311
16 JAPAN	-	833	565	725	738	874	1123	1232	-	1074	886	906	874	817	562
17 NETHERLANDS	920	1437	1638	986	1252	1756	2850	2914	2004	1992	1874	2158	2304	1955	1639
18 NEW ZEALAND	-	2353	5667	1881	1770	3281	3793	3537	4130	3080	2067	2008	1600	1031	801
19 NORWAY	.	.	2447	2875	2912	1786	2086	1982	1625	1458	1465	1895	1154	1732	1155
20 POLAND	-	-	-	-	-	-	-	-	-	-	.	509	1073	1340	1369
21 PORTUGAL	-	-	-	-	-	-	.	.	.	.	1357	1366	1271	1441	937
22 ROMANIA	-	-	-	-	-	-	-	-	-	-	-	538	1227	1747	1374
23 SPAIN	2424	3065	2958	2042	1990	1725	1371	1425	760	662	724	688	1091	854	703
24 SWEDEN	-	-	.	.	.	.	.	.	.	.	1124	1215	1582	1675	1395
25 SWITZERLAND	1098	1098	1173	1173	763	1608	.	.	1403	1283	1354	1746	1613	1347	920
26 TURKEY	-	-	-	-	-	-	-	-	-	-	-	3478	1960	1235	431
27 UK ENGLAND AND WALES	3660	2988	3328	2963	2941	3165	3389	3197	2402	1850	1711	1406	1172	754	1180
28 UK NORTHERN IRELAND	-	-	-	-	808	726	1240	1606	1429	1389	1402	898	460	1500	874
29 UK SCOTLAND	3238	2107	2417	2675	2284	2832	2422	2924	2806	1641	1549	1426	1211	936	597
30 USA	3379	2936	2932	2643	2828	2927	3535	4316	3587	2550	1848	1755	1587	1067	678
31 YUGOSLAVIA	-	-	-	-	-	-	-	-	-	-	.	.	1252	1050	711

- NO MORTALITY DATA ARE AVAILABLE FOR EVEN A BROADER GROUP OF CAUSES FOR THIS DISEASE

. MORTALITY DATA ARE PRESENTED FOR A BROADER GROUP OF CAUSES FOR THIS DISEASE

0 VALUE<0.5

THE STANDARD MORTALITY RATIOS WERE DERIVED WITH A FACTOR OF 1000

SERIAL MORTALITY TABLES FOR VARIOUS COUNTRIES 1901-1975

TABLE 131 URINARY SYSTEM - CALCULI : FEMALES

	1901-	1906-	1911-	1916-	1921-	1926-	1931-	1936-	1941-	1946-	1951-	1956-	1961-	1966-	1971-75
1 AUSTRALIA	-	14602	16099	10667	17312	17658	18328	23546	20290	16294	13339	11751	10338	12201	5862
2 AUSTRIA	-	-	-	-	-	-	-	-	-	12100	21495	30651	38603	42801	31867
3 BELGIUM	-	-	-	-	-	-	.	.	.	.	4808	4508	4177	6464	5077
4 BULGARIA	-	-	-	-	-	-	.	.	.	.	.	.	25338	32093	22178
5 CANADA	-	-	-	-	10463	11538	16521	22469	15696	14880	10609	9469	9943	8104	4084
6 CHILE	-	0	2479	3750	3984	3321	6061	3976	4420	2171	6667	3436	2813	3745	4321
7 CZECHOSLOVAKIA	-	-	-	1737	2907	3419	9126	13277	8389	6693	13032	20042	22941	27198	28090
8 DENMARK	23232	30841	29600	27941	20112	29974	39474	52339	48577	36765	33222	27928	28320	36933	22879
9 EIRE	-	-	-	-	2098	2801	3571	3252	3385	2030	5583	3828	6279	4328	2832
10 FINLAND	-	-	-	-	-	-	-	.	4460	1092	2395	5244	6579	7357	5714
11 FRANCE	-	-	-	-	-	-	.	.	2832	2105	2494	3015	3499	4030	3934
12 GREECE	-	-	-	-	-	4988	7571	7488	-	-	-	4318	9722	10039	8944
13 HUNGARY	-	-	-	.	.	.	7819	12850	13507	7498	8617	16871	28953	35567	34561
14 ICELAND	-	-	-	-	-	-	-	-	.	.	-	-	27273	12000	22222
15 ITALY	-	-	-	-	-	-	14179	17217	12231	12027	12571	13729	15550	17081	13361
16 JAPAN	-	1672	1957	2708	3183	3747	4743	4711	-	4028	3523	3860	4256	4352	3299
17 NETHERLANDS	7218	8640	9434	7840	10015	15343	20976	23052	20102	13964	16401	15801	19319	15486	13766
18 NEW ZEALAND	-	23077	18056	4706	8911	18487	12857	11043	14815	9174	12791	10239	10123	8427	6186
19 NORWAY	.	.	6969	9635	11912	14956	15804	15617	15349	14807	11753	13743	15815	13433	8403
20 POLAND	-	-	-	-	-	-	-	-	-	-	.	4351	5484	9828	7925
21 PORTUGAL	-	-	-	-	-	-	.	.	.	.	1445	5362	5724	6542	3903
22 ROMANIA	-	-	-	-	-	-	-	-	-	-	-	3176	7260	8800	7738
23 SPAIN	11295	10255	10341	10903	10353	10943	7080	6367	4496	3417	4545	4388	6846	6208	5523
24 SWEDEN	-	-	.	.	.	.	.	.	.	.	7424	9500	14026	15258	13429
25 SWITZERLAND	8012	8012	6176	6176	5701	9451	.	.	7670	8185	12278	12562	12639	7823	7532
26 TURKEY	-	-	-	-	-	-	-	-	-	-	-	4308	3086	4049	3739
27 UK ENGLAND AND WALES	13088	12437	11124	10028	11847	14278	16149	15394	12951	10365	9714	9217	7735	6396	9158
28 UK NORTHERN IRELAND	-	-	-	-	9565	6944	4054	4459	7975	14458	6566	10096	5882	14407	4435
29 UK SCOTLAND	10319	12442	9565	11885	10749	8829	13300	17161	12151	10118	12171	6265	7271	7376	6094
30 USA	10351	11097	12811	11228	14427	16014	19016	22194	18269	13517	11846	12157	11562	8350	5583
31 YUGOSLAVIA	-	-	-	-	-	-	-	-	-	-	.	.	6382	7494	4904

- NO MORTALITY DATA ARE AVAILABLE FOR EVEN A BROADER GROUP OF CAUSES FOR THIS DISEASE

. MORTALITY DATA ARE PRESENTED FOR A BROADER GROUP OF CAUSES FOR THIS DISEASE

0 VALUE<0.5

THE STANDARD MORTALITY RATIOS WERE DERIVED WITH A FACTOR OF 10000

SERIAL MORTALITY TABLES FOR VARIOUS COUNTRIES 1901-1975

TABLE 132 : PROSTATE - "HYPERPLASIA" : MALES

	1901-	1906-	1911-	1916-	1921-	1926-	1931-	1936-	1941-	1946-	1951-	1956-	1961-	1966-	1971-75
1 AUSTRALIA	-	13960	15704	16729	19173	20120	21119	21443	17891	14851	16830	12215	8594	5326	3451
2 AUSTRIA	-	-	-	-	-	-	-	-	-	.	15861	13430	13027	12550	8339
3 BELGIUM	-	-	-	-	-	-	.	.	.	.	8051	9685	6939	6167	3712
4 BULGARIA	-	-	-	-	-	-	.	.	.	.	.	.	12427	11280	6813
5 CANADA	-	-	-	-	20448	24108	25682	30044	18468	14110	9889	7053	5140	3400	1880
6 CHILE	-	769	1916	1379	1866	1897	5278	5770	472	6902	9045	11287	10653	12200	11755
7 CZECHOSLOVAKIA	-	-	-	3656	6250	10720	14392	17861	15696	14492	10685	9686	9450	8573	9576
8 DENMARK	12971	20571	17438	20738	21626	24956	35318	39252	38756	26198	24296	20421	16536	9541	5365
9 EIRE	-	-	-	-	10384	11287	14009	18010	18501	16143	13813	11567	8987	7736	5589
10 FINLAND	-	-	-	-	-	-	-	.	13412	15061	14339	15857	13625	8092	4792
11 FRANCE	-	-	-	-	-	-	.	.	6019	6568	6688	8985	7954	6777	4918
12 GREECE	-	-	-	-	-	3028	3665	3763	-	-	-	3282	6590	6554	4643
13 HUNGARY	-	-	-	.	.	.	6161	7555	8267	7545	10007	10716	9599	9353	8387
14 ICELAND	-	-	-	-	-	-	-	-	.	.	22866	19022	16241	11222	5317
15 ITALY	-	-	-	-	-	-	.	.	.	.	11861	11805	10243	9310	7898
16 JAPAN	-	280	263	364	421	.	588	624	-	1318	1465	1706	1980	2136	1869
17 NETHERLANDS	7499	9599	10285	12864	13947	21407	24680	29699	37007	26824	16101	14634	12298	9616	6991
18 NEW ZEALAND	-	16140	11272	14372	16022	21513	18203	19489	20190	15761	13550	12528	7782	5878	4239
19 NORWAY	.	.	.	.	.	11406	16771	19026	23820	21928	19774	14911	13300	8712	5576
20 POLAND	-	-	-	-	-	-	-	-	-	-	.	1574	4846	5721	4934
21 PORTUGAL	-	-	-	-	-	-	.	.	.	.	6131	5909	5710	6014	3082
22 ROMANIA	-	-	-	-	-	-	-	-	-	-	-	2156	13450	14953	9663
23 SPAIN	1565	1962	0	0	0	0	4691	5145	5351	4970	6072	5498	5493	4105	4766
24 SWEDEN	-	-	.	.	.	.	21026	22212	21272	16078	13902	11897	10410	6519	4199
25 SWITZERLAND	22989	22989	23566	23566	21215	24057	23396	29150	5919	0	18595	16026	15462	12211	7718
26 TURKEY	-	-	-	-	-	-	-	-	-	-	-	37367	25233	17943	9700
27 UK ENGLAND AND WALES	.	.	16672	18545	21741	27471	31880	30871	28260	22631	18335	14158	9812	5943	3814
28 UK NORTHERN IRELAND	-	-	-	-	17604	22212	27029	33501	37738	34177	19134	13935	9261	6124	3834
29 UK SCOTLAND	.	.	17048	19911	20781	23472	24892	26638	29079	23118	17098	14498	10268	6012	3200
30 USA	.	50790	41820	42124	44152	48701	24611	18482	14580	10828	8315	5602	4091	2544	1383
31 YUGOSLAVIA	-	-	-	-	-	-	-	-	-	-	.	7089	7145	6033	5733

- NO MORTALITY DATA ARE AVAILABLE FOR EVEN A BROADER GROUP OF CAUSES FOR THIS DISEASE

. MORTALITY DATA ARE PRESENTED FOR A BROADER GROUP OF CAUSES FOR THIS DISEASE

0 VALUE<0.5

THE STANDARD MORTALITY RATIOS WERE DERIVED WITH A FACTOR OF 10000

SERIAL MORTALITY TABLES FOR VARIOUS COUNTRIES 1901-1975

TABLE 133 : GENITO-URINARY SYSTEM - ALL DISEASES : MALES

	1901-	1906-	1911-	1916-	1921-	1926-	1931-	1936-	1941-	1946-	1951-	1956-	1961-	1966-	1971-75
1 AUSTRALIA	-	6844	7598	7298	7120	7238	6867	6608	5954	4829	2894	2188	1790	1397	985
2 AUSTRIA	-	-	-	-	-	-	-	-	-	3042	2579	2297	2049	2026	1689
3 BELGIUM	-	-	-	-	-	-	3914	4132	3987	3240	2130	1790	1398	1339	1178
4 BULGARIA	-	-	-	-	-	-	3641	4504	4222	3928	3126	1917	1818	1826	1672
5 CANADA	-	-	-	-	5917	7288	6784	7253	6381	4690	2320	1712	1352	998	779
6 CHILE	-	2138	2839	3683	4154	4803	6890	6414	5967	5092	2689	2178	2060	2040	2159
7 CZECHOSLOVAKIA	-	-	-	4040	3410	3927	3473	3535	3010	2457	1711	1557	1672	1949	2043
8 DENMARK	8035	8628	8173	6876	4806	5394	4587	4653	4335	3280	2705	2542	2235	1580	1069
9 EIRE	-	-	-	-	4196	4556	4717	4761	4622	3806	2651	2153	1813	1680	1400
10 FINLAND	-	-	-	-	-	-	-	2855	2811	2511	2073	2322	2468	1742	1043
11 FRANCE	-	-	-	-	-	-	4642	5438	5831	4035	1628	1539	1330	1225	1076
12 GREECE	-	-	-	-	-	5781	6165	5861	-	-	-	1751	1922	2058	1558
13 HUNGARY	-	-	-	4574	4086	3159	2990	2827	2709	2328	2096	1801	1502	1545	1573
14 ICELAND	-	-	-	-	-	-	-	-	2882	2989	-	-	1966	1739	917
15 ITALY	-	-	-	-	-	-	4590	4723	4650	3183	1969	1795	1598	1466	1263
16 JAPAN	-	5995	6693	9353	11829	11980	10975	10253	-	3875	2853	2215	1583	1209	885
17 NETHERLANDS	5096	4982	4554	4592	3930	4295	4127	4318	4437	3250	1995	1808	1664	1458	1207
18 NEW ZEALAND	-	5602	5060	4853	4677	4985	4923	4569	3862	2917	1999	1826	1456	1143	861
19 NORWAY	4270	3909	3862	3974	3655	3992	4073	3950	3701	3181	2284	1905	1763	1400	1052
20 POLAND	-	-	-	-	-	-	-	-	-	-	1421	937	1202	1282	1233
21 PORTUGAL	-	-	-	-	-	-	3071	3111	3148	2478	2506	2586	2223	2121	1546
22 ROMANIA	-	-	-	-	-	-	-	-	-	-	-	1818	2033	1787	1411
23 SPAIN	4743	5396	5959	6489	6258	6550	6293	7021	6213	4818	2353	2076	1800	1590	1417
24 SWEDEN	-	-	3684	3610	3326	3573	3724	3739	3250	2681	1935	1886	1745	1390	1077
25 SWITZERLAND	5224	5224	4893	4893	4886	4180	4255	4440	3989	3200	2316	1963	1901	1597	1181
26 TURKEY	-	-	-	-	-	-	-	-	-	-	-	2789	1842	1361	929
27 UK ENGLAND AND WALES	6525	5650	6622	5919	5180	5496	5685	5141	4631	3541	2405	1925	1522	1144	954
28 UK NORTHERN IRELAND	-	-	-	-	4813	5337	5375	5335	4920	4283	2581	2017	1569	1219	1094
29 UK SCOTLAND	6682	7497	7051	6691	5966	5767	5276	5106	4424	3491	2272	1997	1634	1179	1012
30 USA	18796	14505	13537	11918	10232	10468	9297	8547	6904	4505	1942	1499	1288	1085	894
31 YUGOSLAVIA	-	-	-	-	-	-	-	-	-	-	2367	2312	1462	1378	1281

- NO MORTALITY DATA ARE AVAILABLE FOR EVEN A BROADER GROUP OF CAUSES FOR THIS DISEASE

. MORTALITY DATA ARE PRESENTED FOR A BROADER GROUP OF CAUSES FOR THIS DISEASE

0 VALUE<0.5

THE STANDARD MORTALITY RATIOS WERE DERIVED WITH A FACTOR OF 1000

SERIAL MORTALITY TABLES FOR VARIOUS COUNTRIES 1901-1975

TABLE 133 : GENITO-URINARY SYSTEM - ALL DISEASES : FEMALES

	1901-	1906-	1911-	1916-	1921-	1926-	1931-	1936-	1941-	1946-	1951-	1956-	1961-	1966-	1971-75
1 AUSTRALIA	-	4482	4704	4481	4731	5147	4916	4591	3781	2874	1326	1031	1048	994	725
2 AUSTRIA	-	-	-	-	-	-	-	-	-	1189	1054	952	888	969	904
3 BELGIUM	-	-	-	-	-	-	2408	2423	2165	1806	1019	754	599	636	668
4 BULGARIA	-	-	-	-	-	-	2457	2672	2205	1832	1276	907	864	847	855
5 CANADA	-	-	-	-	4312	5858	5292	5570	4942	3586	1422	1009	772	577	420
6 CHILE	-	1098	1804	2536	3004	3891	5280	5236	4654	3818	1581	1301	1203	1155	1199
7 CZECHOSLOVAKIA	-	-	-	2837	2225	2544	2091	2001	1650	1180	702	648	787	1009	1067
8 DENMARK	4527	4928	4949	4405	3464	3626	2251	2090	1813	1401	1161	1515	1441	1132	800
9 EIRE	-	-	-	-	2298	2781	2659	2568	2245	1774	1136	895	816	824	703
10 FINLAND	-	-	-	-	-	-	-	1729	1334	1058	904	1301	1822	1465	881
11 FRANCE	-	-	-	-	-	-	2362	2564	2646	1870	648	506	413	411	432
12 GREECE	-	-	-	-	-	4726	5008	4854	-	-	-	1087	1055	1178	877
13 HUNGARY	-	-	-	3759	3266	2455	2232	1956	1691	1252	1034	816	677	769	787
14 ICELAND	-	-	-	-	-	-	-	-	1685	1007	-	-	1105	1011	994
15 ITALY	-	-	-	-	-	-	3379	3378	3139	2091	938	757	626	541	457
16 JAPAN	-	6971	7172	9339	10734	10741	9982	9322	-	3715	2546	1778	1169	854	655
17 NETHERLANDS	4244	4074	3776	3851	3341	3513	3349	3340	2519	1854	1022	823	787	742	692
18 NEW ZEALAND	-	3030	3317	2849	3074	3856	3656	3167	2307	1556	962	783	734	633	581
19 NORWAY	2438	2321	2080	2197	1916	2089	1931	1773	1323	1064	780	658	715	611	558
20 POLAND	-	-	-	-	-	-	-	-	-	-	754	542	609	636	594
21 PORTUGAL	-	-	-	-	-	-	2690	2552	2328	1673	1415	1342	1098	975	731
22 ROMANIA	-	-	-	-	-	-	-	-	-	-	-	1130	1008	708	581
23 SPAIN	3504	3905	4403	4728	4430	4321	4099	4220	3517	2719	1390	1186	1011	910	752
24 SWEDEN	-	-	2112	2098	1869	1949	1819	1774	1433	1218	817	885	897	773	595
25 SWITZERLAND	3352	3352	2979	2979	3262	2549	2722	2713	1952	1772	1214	972	932	796	659
26 TURKEY	-	-	-	-	-	-	-	-	-	-	-	1613	1089	821	544
27 UK ENGLAND AND WALES	4094	3608	3655	2935	2678	2888	2899	2433	1911	1445	821	672	654	566	534
28 UK NORTHERN IRELAND	-	-	-	-	2815	2902	2785	2702	2189	1757	920	710	709	685	608
29 UK SCOTLAND	3678	4378	3959	3403	3412	3451	3178	2924	2080	1512	920	780	783	718	665
30 USA	13834	11033	10409	9471	8696	8654	7521	6578	5031	3076	1055	818	715	631	535
31 YUGOSLAVIA	-	-	-	-	-	-	-	-	-	-	1793	1576	854	848	772

- NO MORTALITY DATA ARE AVAILABLE FOR EVEN A BROADER GROUP OF CAUSES FOR THIS DISEASE

. MORTALITY DATA ARE PRESENTED FOR A BROADER GROUP OF CAUSES FOR THIS DISEASE

0 VALUE<0.5

THE STANDARD MORTALITY RATIOS WERE DERIVED WITH A FACTOR OF 1000

SERIAL MORTALITY TABLES FOR VARIOUS COUNTRIES 1901-1975

TABLE 134 : PREGNANCY, CHILDBIRTH AND THE PUERPERIUM - SEPSIS : FEMALES

	1901-	1906-	1911-	1916-	1921-	1926-	1931-	1936-	1941-	1946-	1951-	1956-	1961-	1966-	1971-75
1 AUSTRALIA	-	1506	1615	1751	1674	1890	830	584	535	204	90	67	61	45	26
2 AUSTRIA	2589	2272	1747	1496	-	-	-	-	-	.	217	164	80	45	38
3 BELGIUM	2181	2341	2649	3754	2680	3047	1701	1318	1305	563	214	54	34	17	22
4 BULGARIA	-	-	-	-	-	-	-	-	-	-	.	.	30	40	13
5 CANADA	-	-	-	-	-	1930	1202	985	726	230	92	55	53	44	23
6 CHILE	-	1466	1308	1977	1847	2364	3388	3421	2320	1148	484	351	270	215	230
7 CZECHOSLOVAKIA	-	-	-	1546	1767	2189	1575	1362	627	327	72	73	42	33	19
8 DENMARK	-	-	-	-	1023	1104	.	.	.	.	73	48	20	0	5
9 EIRE	-	-	-	-	1800	1535	1346	943	570	291	130	195	70	83	71
10 FINLAND	.	.	.	.	.	3220	2719	1243	678	162	63	66	40	17	10
11 FRANCE	-	-	-	-	4489	1078	.	.	296	119	61	40	30	29	29
12 GREECE	-	-	-	-	3920	3418	2839	2041	-	-	-	46	20	6	10
13 HUNGARY	-	-	-	1450	1366	1727	1344	1030	644	281	118	77	48	32	51
14 ICELAND	-	-	1399	1228	1792	977	910	822	.	.	.	.	42	46	45
15 ITALY	.	.	.	.	.	1061	1130	883	538	348	114	79	69	44	26
16 JAPAN	1296	1470	1446	1324	1215	889	693	636	-	100	73	56	33	20	17
17 NETHERLANDS	722	702	663	935	717	1046	650	459	469	254	103	74	53	28	16
18 NEW ZEALAND	-	1369	1029	2087	1736	1758	564	651	596	203	61	63	57	71	43
19 NORWAY	1559	1393	1193	1031	739	998	683	589	485	216	61	32	16	21	23
20 POLAND	-	-	-	-	-	-	-	-	-	-	.	48	42	48	34
21 PORTUGAL	2213	2139	1744	2313	1855	1624	.	.	.	.	243	128	73	90	50
22 ROMANIA	-	-	-	-	-	-	-	-	-	-	-	55	60	43	49
23 SPAIN	3562	3598	3242	3337	2859	2157	1964	1719	1050	359	165	96	91	50	34
24 SWEDEN	-	-	1066	1289	1138	1707	909	594	158	35	48	28	4	14	5
25 SWITZERLAND	1948	1948	1656	1656	1579	1197	1509	1206	262	58	180	87	84	61	37
26 TURKEY	-	-	-	-	-	-	-	-	-	-	-	-	-	-	-
27 UK ENGLAND AND WALES	1851	1478	1421	1510	1401	1561	1278	674	368	146	98	64	37	25	18
28 UK NORTHERN IRELAND	-	-	-	-	1246	1594	1669	1073	514	228	188	105	96	43	14
29 UK SCOTLAND	2065	1791	1618	1558	1873	2142	2153	1197	703	128	162	103	90	39	37
30 USA	4488	3706	3483	3136	2732	2467	1533	1172	555	226	65	39	39	39	34
31 YUGOSLAVIA	-	-	-	-	-	-	-	-	-	-	.	.	81	60	36

- NO MORTALITY DATA ARE AVAILABLE FOR EVEN A BROADER GROUP OF CAUSES FOR THIS DISEASE

. MORTALITY DATA ARE PRESENTED FOR A BROADER GROUP OF CAUSES FOR THIS DISEASE

0 VALUE<0.5

THE MORTALITY RATES WERE DERIVED WITH A FACTOR OF 1000000

SERIAL MORTALITY TABLES FOR VARIOUS COUNTRIES 1901-1975

TABLE 135 : PREGNANCY AND THE PUERPERIUM - TOXAEMIAS : FEMALES

	1901-	1906-	1911-	1916-	1921-	1926-	1931-	1936-	1941-	1946-	1951-	1956-	1961-	1966-	1971-75
1 AUSTRALIA	-	680	848	983	1051	1091	1134	956	743	450	225	106	52	52	21
2 AUSTRIA	-	-	-	-	-	-	-	-	-	.	237	159	106	67	46
3 BELGIUM	.	.	.	.	.	.	.	.	.	.	205	122	42	46	19
4 BULGARIA	-	-	-	-	-	-	-	-	-	-	.	.	113	80	39
5 CANADA	-	-	-	-	-	1301	1157	1116	590	338	255	121	58	49	26
6 CHILE	-	420	233	312	236	281	652	694	709	499	398	215	218	219	148
7 CZECHOSLOVAKIA	-	-	-	201	254	331	466	397	261	298	107	70	47	32	19
8 DENMARK	-	-	-	-	.	.	537	708	335	215	132	90	44	44	5
9 EIRE	-	-	-	-	704	717	990	855	598	437	417	251	122	58	18
10 FINLAND	.	.	.	.	.	.	-	.	763	483	435	265	111	61	13
11 FRANCE	-	-	-	-	.	.	.	.	155	187	140	92	46	39	21
12 GREECE	-	-	-	-	.	56	100	95	-	-	-	107	90	48	34
13 HUNGARY	-	-	-	.	.	.	399	341	305	.	251	178	130	95	54
14 ICELAND	-	-	.	.	.	.	.	.	.	.	.	.	127	0	45
15 ITALY	.	.	.	.	.	.	.	.	.	.	449	351	274	186	102
16 JAPAN	.	.	.	.	.	.	800	804	-	566	662	597	392	248	128
17 NETHERLANDS	334	309	314	380	406	388	444	438	261	234	137	115	57	47	26
18 NEW ZEALAND	-	430	413	1197	1256	1211	1241	1059	625	326	197	123	69	58	33
19 NORWAY	.	.	611	626	585	691	655	567	610	438	304	225	78	51	16
20 POLAND	-	-	-	-	-	-	-	-	-	-	.	69	69	50	32
21 PORTUGAL	.	.	.	.	.	.	.	.	.	.	263	221	153	137	86
22 ROMANIA	-	-	-	-	-	-	-	-	-	-	-	113	103	63	31
23 SPAIN	565	559	514	514	398	370	361	307	222	185	152	117	47	47	32
24 SWEDEN	-	-	.	.	.	.	524	482	387	268	210	89	70	24	16
25 SWITZERLAND	461	461	526	526	615	543	609	586	485	373	307	157	87	53	21
26 TURKEY	-	-	-	-	-	-	-	-	-	-	-	-	-	-	-
27 UK ENGLAND AND WALES	.	.	762	819	706	712	818	759	542	338	226	111	59	42	30
28 UK NORTHERN IRELAND	-	-	-	-	902	925	1190	1222	825	370	250	216	78	43	28
29 UK SCOTLAND	.	.	1026	969	1021	1142	1328	1174	760	340	206	105	68	37	37
30 USA	1988	1832	1919	2169	1976	1897	1363	998	610	324	198	94	64	46	29
31 YUGOSLAVIA	-	-	-	-	-	-	-	-	-	-	.	.	103	67	57

- NO MORTALITY DATA ARE AVAILABLE FOR EVEN A BROADER GROUP OF CAUSES FOR THIS DISEASE

. MORTALITY DATA ARE PRESENTED FOR A BROADER GROUP OF CAUSES FOR THIS DISEASE

0 VALUE<0.5

THE MORTALITY RATES WERE DERIVED WITH A FACTOR OF 1000000

SERIAL MORTALITY TABLES FOR VARIOUS COUNTRIES 1901-1975

TABLE 136 : PREGNANCY AND CHILDBIRTH - HAEMORRHAGE : FEMALES

	1901-	1906-	1911-	1916-	1921-	1926-	1931-	1936-	1941-	1946-	1951-	1956-	1961-	1966-	1971-75
1 AUSTRALIA	-	373	.	.	609	682	652	635	379	204	114	81	52	29	9
2 AUSTRIA	-	-	-	-	-	-	-	-	-	.	192	157	84	52	44
3 BELGIUM	.	.	.	.	.	.	.	.	.	.	119	101	46	33	37
4 BULGARIA	-	-	-	-	-	-	-	-	-	-	.	.	117	76	54
5 CANADA	-	-	-	-	-	738	706	624	553	350	188	123	74	41	21
6 CHILE	-	.	.	.	160	349	597	631	644	503	501	446	412	338	189
7 CZECHOSLOVAKIA	-	-	-	173	253	457	582	617	369	337	98	59	41	28	14
8 DENMARK	-	-	-	-	.	.	.	.	354	356	101	27	17	13	0
9 EIRE	-	-	-	-	1002	1071	910	890	679	570	411	195	80	48	32
10 FINLAND	.	.	.	.	.	.	-	.	422	355	234	140	79	33	13
11 FRANCE	-	-	-	-	.	.	.	.	116	140	120	92	60	38	30
12 GREECE	-	-	-	-	.	416	439	422	-	-	-	194	167	86	59
13 HUNGARY	-	-	-	.	.	.	146	104	359	.	128	104	96	86	81
14 ICELAND	-	-	.	.	.	.	.	.	.	.	.	.	169	46	45
15 ITALY	.	.	.	.	.	.	.	.	.	.	309	268	182	135	75
16 JAPAN	.	527	444	514	569	581	619	611	-	465	481	389	254	171	92
17 NETHERLANDS	.	.	.	.	546	549	494	416	375	261	179	117	77	33	18
18 NEW ZEALAND	-	.	.	.	812	452	427	344	389	251	197	120	47	19	33
19 NORWAY	458	353	355	348	408	387	406	301	225	152	115	95	41	33	10
20 POLAND	-	-	-	-	-	-	-	-	-	-	.	80	97	65	36
21 PORTUGAL	.	.	.	.	.	.	.	.	.	.	428	391	327	226	128
22 ROMANIA	-	-	-	-	-	-	-	-	-	-	-	201	219	204	102
23 SPAIN	.	.	.	.	.	.	550	534	419	330	315	267	190	125	67
24 SWEDEN	-	-	.	.	.	.	.	.	.	.	85	55	19	21	9
25 SWITZERLAND	594	594	390	390	663	543	556	498	289	244	148	127	56	38	23
26 TURKEY	-	-	-	-	-	-	-	-	-	-	-	-	-	-	-
27 UK ENGLAND AND WALES	.	.	678	620	536	453	435	452	336	183	113	69	39	20	15
28 UK NORTHERN IRELAND	-	-	-	-	790	797	1094	916	710	443	153	138	54	18	55
29 UK SCOTLAND	.	.	825	805	766	792	934	816	644	375	177	81	51	24	19
30 USA	.	.	.	.	715	744	490	394	389	213	111	73	58	33	20
31 YUGOSLAVIA	-	-	-	-	-	-	-	-	-	-	.	.	156	119	69

- NO MORTALITY DATA ARE AVAILABLE FOR EVEN A BROADER GROUP OF CAUSES FOR THIS DISEASE

. MORTALITY DATA ARE PRESENTED FOR A BROADER GROUP OF CAUSES FOR THIS DISEASE

0 VALUE<0.5

THE MORTALITY RATES WERE DERIVED WITH A FACTOR OF 1000000

SERIAL MORTALITY TABLES FOR VARIOUS COUNTRIES 1901-1975

TABLE 137 : ABORTION : FEMALES

	1901-	1906-	1911-	1916-	1921-	1926-	1931-	1936-	1941-	1946-	1951-	1956-	1961-	1966-	1971-75
1 AUSTRALIA	-	.	.	.	.	323	1615	1450	765	289	153	113	75	32	14
2 AUSTRIA	-	-	-	-	-	-	-	-	-	.	214	154	92	54	44
3 BELGIUM	.	.	.	.	.	.	.	.	.	.	85	47	56	48	25
4 BULGARIA	-	-	-	-	-	-	-	-	-	-	.	.	121	88	110
5 CANADA	-	-	-	-	-	146	713	662	392	174	84	61	46	32	8
6 CHILE	-	.	.	.	.	.	582	1257	1267	601	707	832	938	837	497
7 CZECHOSLOVAKIA	-	-	-	777	466	177	1462	1231	335	242	142	123	59	32	15
8 DENMARK	-	-	-	-	.	.	.	.	.	.	88	122	52	28	3
9 EIRE	-	-	-	-	86	84	234	243	94	55	29	23	6	13	15
10 FINLAND	.	.	.	.	.	.	-	.	1376	424	155	199	87	47	20
11 FRANCE	-	-	-	-	.	.	.	.	186	100	68	70	55	53	38
12 GREECE	-	-	-	-	.	.	339	344	-	-	-	25	11	4	1
13 HUNGARY	-	-	-	.	.	.	1003	1320	1370	687	391	335	214	124	52
14 ICELAND	-	-	.	.	.	.	.	.	.	.	.	.	0	0	0
15 ITALY	.	.	.	.	.	.	.	.	.	.	94	62	46	49	32
16 JAPAN	.	.	.	.	158	152	132	125	-	148	106	76	49	28	13
17 NETHERLANDS	.	.	.	.	138	220	405	352	443	152	46	29	20	21	5
18 NEW ZEALAND	-	.	.	.	.	1313	1458	1014	.	192	125	113	57	32	7
19 NORWAY	12	82	82	174	207	280	.	.	681	128	74	38	6	15	3
20 POLAND	-	-	-	-	-	-	-	-	-	-	.	29	34	28	10
21 PORTUGAL	.	.	.	.	.	.	.	.	.	.	311	232	167	119	79
22 ROMANIA	-	-	-	-	-	-	-	-	-	-	-	262	294	473	925
23 SPAIN	.	.	.	.	.	.	219	286	199	120	75	47	38	25	25
24 SWEDEN	-	-	.	.	.	.	.	.	.	.	57	25	21	10	0
25 SWITZERLAND	714	714	1161	1161	871	745	.	.	.	.	158	96	56	44	30
26 TURKEY	-	-	-	-	-	-	-	-	-	-	-	-	-	-	-
27 UK ENGLAND AND WALES	159	107	134	149	131	103	589	412	448	161	113	76	58	48	25
28 UK NORTHERN IRELAND	-	-	-	-	180	248	415	525	243	87	56	20	18	30	14
29 UK SCOTLAND	213	260	370	539	408	400	517	504	445	164	107	55	57	15	24
30 USA	.	.	.	.	.	1278	1196	780	411	151	67	59	66	41	16
31 YUGOSLAVIA	-	-	-	-	-	-	-	-	-	-	.	.	425	281	119

- NO MORTALITY DATA ARE AVAILABLE FOR EVEN A BROADER GROUP OF CAUSES FOR THIS DISEASE

. MORTALITY DATA ARE PRESENTED FOR A BROADER GROUP OF CAUSES FOR THIS DISEASE

0 VALUE<0.5

THE MORTALITY RATES WERE DERIVED WITH A FACTOR OF 1000000

SERIAL MORTALITY TABLES FOR VARIOUS COUNTRIES 1901-1975

TABLE 138 : PREGNANCY, CHILDBIRTH AND THE PUERPERIUM - COMPLICATIONS : FEMALES

	1901-	1906-	1911-	1916-	1921-	1926-	1931-	1936-	1941-	1946-	1951-	1956-	1961-	1966-	1971-75
1 AUSTRALIA	-	4497	4718	5063	5089	5522	5450	4667	3079	1483	785	533	349	247	121
2 AUSTRIA	-	-	-	-	-	-	-	-	-	2176	1310	956	570	356	232
3 BELGIUM	5821	5736	6492	8470	5529	5883	4894	4006	3685	2096	920	559	303	216	153
4 BULGARIA	-	-	-	-	-	-	-	-	-	-	179	671	635	380	310
5 CANADA	-	-	-	-	-	5660	5051	4561	2856	1461	841	543	371	254	124
6 CHILE	-	6760	6952	7800	7074	6411	8339	8714	6782	4112	3281	2814	2701	2207	1459
7 CZECHOSLOVAKIA	-	-	-	3432	3436	3840	5002	4364	1913	903	417	548	386	252	164
8 DENMARK	-	-	-	-	2269	3093	3813	3173	1927	1106	668	414	195	137	49
9 EIRE	-	-	-	-	4984	4642	4532	3902	2519	1776	1327	886	397	302	215
10 FINLAND	4477	3961	3888	3884	3165	3226	-	4686	4029	1919	1184	881	450	219	92
11 FRANCE	-	-	-	-	11505	2775	2478	1882	1489	926	733	548	381	290	228
12 GREECE	-	-	-	-	7880	6309	5248	4121	-	-	-	713	585	378	265
13 HUNGARY	-	-	-	3089	2952	3324	3712	3742	3267	1891	1107	920	686	487	359
14 ICELAND	-	-	3235	1965	2726	2554	2200	2465	3234	1575	664	507	381	93	180
15 ITALY	2657	2761	2391	2958	2760	2718	2874	2521	1809	1584	1404	1136	896	645	394
16 JAPAN	4222	3912	3119	2905	3033	2775	2681	2652	-	1669	1770	1546	1038	668	375
17 NETHERLANDS	2397	2353	2250	2688	2436	3164	3113	2610	2021	1265	740	513	329	201	116
18 NEW ZEALAND	-	4578	3906	5751	4996	4792	4471	3565	2618	1292	694	553	324	279	198
19 NORWAY	3072	2796	2837	2710	2538	3039	2750	2359	2336	1225	752	511	219	180	88
20 POLAND	-	-	-	-	-	-	-	-	-	-	887	409	379	315	182
21 PORTUGAL	4117	3838	3238	3950	3396	3530	4306	4090	3635	2278	1577	1260	986	787	518
22 ROMANIA	-	-	-	-	-	-	-	-	-	-	-	829	952	995	1273
23 SPAIN	5699	5686	5272	5370	4593	3771	3576	3344	2205	1283	986	762	552	393	275
24 SWEDEN	-	-	2549	2705	2516	3248	3326	2601	1590	780	623	324	189	109	55
25 SWITZERLAND	6079	6079	5893	5893	4877	4276	4496	4007	2311	1656	1193	699	461	313	187
26 TURKEY	-	-	-	-	-	-	-	-	-	-	-	-	-	-	-
27 UK ENGLAND AND WALES	4267	3737	4031	4120	3901	3852	4143	3176	2302	1130	743	453	298	219	143
28 UK NORTHERN IRELAND	-	-	-	-	4630	5144	5542	4888	3197	1633	861	642	349	170	146
29 UK SCOTLAND	5062	5408	5845	6176	6284	6736	6133	4831	3769	1713	854	448	351	193	172
30 USA	10127	8425	7905	8888	7262	7197	6185	4530	2499	1220	604	387	346	251	161
31 YUGOSLAVIA	-	-	-	-	-	-	-	-	-	-	2213	1662	1355	822	361

- NO MORTALITY DATA ARE AVAILABLE FOR EVEN A BROADER GROUP OF CAUSES FOR THIS DISEASE

. MORTALITY DATA ARE PRESENTED FOR A BROADER GROUP OF CAUSES FOR THIS DISEASE

0 VALUE<0.5

THE MORTALITY RATES WERE DERIVED WITH A FACTOR OF 1000000

SERIAL MORTALITY TABLES FOR VARIOUS COUNTRIES 1901-1975

TABLE 139 : SKIN AND SUBCUTANEOUS TISSUE - INFECTIONS : MALES

	1901-	1906-	1911-	1916-	1921-	1926-	1931-	1936-	1941-	1946-	1951-	1956-	1961-	1966-	1971-75
1 AUSTRALIA	-	8846	13099	13718	15308	16348	11299	10055	5074	1523	2303	2643	1565	1205	1040
2 AUSTRIA	-	-	-	-	-	-	-	-	-	10619	3482	4733	3954	2608	1758
3 BELGIUM	-	-	-	-	-	-	.	.	.	.	2530	1863	824	745	381
4 BULGARIA	-	-	-	-	-	-	.	.	.	.	.	.	1681	1089	1078
5 CANADA	-	-	-	-	12157	15507	12849	9983	4149	1463	2938	2789	1304	1056	697
6 CHILE	-	4333	15068	35694	8800	17764	20173	20909	13892	5011	4713	7891	7355	10392	9576
7 CZECHOSLOVAKIA	-	-	-	37257	37850	36758	28953	20321	23651	15355	5941	4697	1338	1045	605
8 DENMARK	.	.	.	.	.	.	.	.	.	.	654	1400	526	580	438
9 EIRE	-	-	-	-	11618	10647	11387	12135	10110	3989	2379	2000	1463	878	766
10 FINLAND	-	-	-	-	-	-	-	.	.	.	1376	1634	694	262	498
11 FRANCE	-	-	-	-	-	-	.	.	8561	3744	2233	1329	981	757	659
12 GREECE	-	-	-	-	-	8962	8698	8000	-	-	-	807	942	1066	555
13 HUNGARY	-	-	-	-	-	-	31435	28430	38526	.	7494	7760	2918	1590	1086
14 ICELAND	-	-	-	-	-	-	-	-	.	.	-	-	1818	0	0
15 ITALY	-	-	-	-	-	-	-	-	-	-	3564	3498	1712	1137	778
16 JAPAN	-	34123	32817	32513	32039	28175	25312	25053	-	13207	7182	6113	2890	1215	711
17 NETHERLANDS	10182	9493	8142	11541	7209	12793	11411	13920	27202	6038	3093	2452	1446	802	688
18 NEW ZEALAND	-	4444	8800	8571	9355	11176	8000	6145	3587	1667	1600	5971	2067	1859	920
19 NORWAY	80	461	8806	9493	6597	6291	.	.	8984	1373	955	1079	996	463	386
20 POLAND	-	-	-	-	-	-	-	-	-	-	.	3803	4314	4096	2634
21 PORTUGAL	-	-	-	-	-	-	.	.	.	.	9926	6279	7036	5042	1260
22 ROMANIA	-	-	-	-	-	-	-	-	-	-	-	2380	4545	3650	2647
23 SPAIN	27012	25963	18831	15815	13802	12460	12240	16690	17104	6118	2815	2357	1196	1012	415
24 SWEDEN	-	-	.	.	.	.	.	.	.	.	682	876	795	685	276
25 SWITZERLAND	9125	9125	5858	5858	12825	14759	19350	14839	11561	3878	2300	2159	1494	900	985
26 TURKEY	-	-	-	-	-	-	-	-	-	-	-	6537	4537	2621	1577
27 UK ENGLAND AND WALES	16067	14562	18405	18810	17085	18088	19398	15389	7389	2774	1747	1337	1088	672	575
28 UK NORTHERN IRELAND	-	-	-	-	11961	12813	.	.	.	3378	1628	1035	1539	532	851
29 UK SCOTLAND	14674	16166	23333	21394	24818	25652	25041	22140	12821	3838	1672	1841	872	828	574
30 USA	19179	12250	10690	10147	8443	7474	6563	4777	2039	819	1015	1402	1220	1057	914
31 YUGOSLAVIA	-	-	-	-	-	-	-	-	-	-	.	.	2413	917	632

- NO MORTALITY DATA ARE AVAILABLE FOR EVEN A BROADER GROUP OF CAUSES FOR THIS DISEASE

. MORTALITY DATA ARE PRESENTED FOR A BROADER GROUP OF CAUSES FOR THIS DISEASE

0 VALUE<0.5

THE STANDARD MORTALITY RATIOS WERE DERIVED WITH A FACTOR OF 1000

SERIAL MORTALITY TABLES FOR VARIOUS COUNTRIES 1901-1975

TABLE 139 : SKIN AND SUBCUTANEOUS TISSUE - INFECTIONS : FEMALES

	1901-	1906-	1911-	1916-	1921-	1926-	1931-	1936-	1941-	1946-	1951-	1956-	1961-	1966-	1971-75
1 AUSTRALIA	-	7080	7895	10744	12295	11500	9195	7935	4537	1162	1979	2388	1534	948	755
2 AUSTRIA	-	-	-	-	-	-	-	-	-	6627	2933	3876	2627	2116	1312
3 BELGIUM	-	-	-	-	-	-	.	.	.	.	2110	1240	676	443	397
4 BULGARIA	-	-	-	-	-	-	.	.	.	.	.	.	1581	1044	458
5 CANADA	-	-	-	-	8497	10265	7669	6930	2647	1058	2226	2188	952	530	672
6 CHILE	-	2188	4323	31579	4528	14624	12513	10693	8371	3893	4074	6310	5000	7631	7661
7 CZECHOSLOVAKIA	-	-	-	25627	27070	27708	21443	14839	19000	13299	4372	3857	1216	844	488
8 DENMARK	.	.	.	.	.	.	.	.	.	.	334	1727	765	614	535
9 EIRE	-	-	-	-	7465	4633	7303	8268	6738	2798	1549	1751	978	783	583
10 FINLAND	-	-	-	-	-	-	-	.	.	.	1622	1750	1056	549	398
11 FRANCE	-	-	-	-	-	-	.	.	5154	2134	1509	974	798	769	592
12 GREECE	-	-	-	-	-	6988	7994	6754	-	-	-	1010	1246	1005	866
13 HUNGARY	-	-	-	-	-	-	23390	21119	27465	.	5344	5886	2378	1542	667
14 ICELAND	-	-	-	-	-	-	-	-	.	.	-	-	833	0	0
15 ITALY	-	-	-	-	-	-	-	-	-	-	2834	2899	1494	1011	714
16 JAPAN	-	30163	27689	27207	26257	21285	19377	20126	-	9764	5463	4315	2279	947	598
17 NETHERLANDS	7244	6271	6285	7209	4243	6608	6032	7542	16841	3179	1991	1975	1119	834	758
18 NEW ZEALAND	-	5000	7143	5714	7857	8125	6944	4878	3368	676	1481	4423	1429	1309	837
19 NORWAY	0	530	6329	5549	4795	4444	.	.	5292	1535	1176	753	888	712	570
20 POLAND	-	-	-	-	-	-	-	-	-	-	.	2320	3127	3054	1837
21 PORTUGAL	-	-	-	-	-	-	.	.	.	.	4705	4423	5244	4310	1007
22 ROMANIA	-	-	-	-	-	-	-	-	-	-	-	2338	3628	2667	2113
23 SPAIN	21164	18832	12954	9991	9411	7265	7402	9664	9954	4126	1876	1596	840	645	432
24 SWEDEN	-	-	.	.	.	.	.	.	.	.	688	681	805	570	264
25 SWITZERLAND	4735	4735	2500	2500	7103	6974	8659	7444	5904	3131	1302	1219	1087	840	706
26 TURKEY	-	-	-	-	-	-	-	-	-	-	-	4375	3256	1568	913
27 UK ENGLAND AND WALES	10105	8531	10646	10108	9394	9742	11039	7929	4401	1571	1498	1062	935	776	677
28 UK NORTHERN IRELAND	-	-	-	-	7119	7945	.	.	.	4167	1188	748	974	574	787
29 UK SCOTLAND	9868	9875	16305	13205	13971	13028	14899	12508	7401	2725	1367	1167	989	1097	780
30 USA	12792	7940	6302	5934	5249	5008	4354	3184	1323	587	677	1027	915	754	685
31 YUGOSLAVIA	-	-	-	-	-	-	-	-	-	-	.	.	2213	754	558

- NO MORTALITY DATA ARE AVAILABLE FOR EVEN A BROADER GROUP OF CAUSES FOR THIS DISEASE
. MORTALITY DATA ARE PRESENTED FOR A BROADER GROUP OF CAUSES FOR THIS DISEASE
0 VALUE<0.5
THE STANDARD MORTALITY RATIOS WERE DERIVED WITH A FACTOR OF 1000

SERIAL MORTALITY TABLES FOR VARIOUS COUNTRIES 1901-1975

TABLE 140 : ARTHRITIS AND SPONDYLITIS : MALES

	1901-	1906-	1911-	1916-	1921-	1926-	1931-	1936-	1941-	1946-	1951-	1956-	1961-	1966-	1971-75
1 AUSTRALIA	-	.	.	.	.	.	12388	12131	10270	8171	6646	7641	7077	8556	9136
2 AUSTRIA	-	-	-	-	-	-	-	-	-	.	3923	2732	5164	6699	4362
3 BELGIUM	-	-	-	-	-	-	.	.	.	.	4193	4785	5061	5164	4150
4 BULGARIA	-	-	-	-	-	-	.	.	.	.	.	.	609	861	906
5 CANADA	-	-	-	-	.	.	10246	8212	.	6486	5719	5019	4887	5368	4843
6 CHILE	-	.	.	.	.	.	.	6098	4936	4686	12036	9258	5123	5210	4153
7 CZECHOSLOVAKIA	-	-	-	.	.	.	.	.	.	.	6759	4183	3132	2613	1610
8 DENMARK	.	.	.	.	.	.	.	.	.	.	1393	2280	3814	4682	4700
9 EIRE	-	-	-	-	.	.	.	.	.	.	19629	20559	12780	8973	10593
10 FINLAND	-	-	-	-	-	-	-	.	.	.	10584	8357	7250	9796	9307
11 FRANCE	-	-	-	-	-	-	.	.	3412	2972	3070	4216	3910	4441	4040
12 GREECE	-	-	-	-	-	.	.	.	-	-	-	4058	5523	3863	1943
13 HUNGARY	-	-	-	.	.	.	3803	4692	6676	.	6936	8478	5664	3389	2926
14 ICELAND	-	-	-	-	-	-	-	-	.	.	-	-	2410	0	943
15 ITALY	-	-	-	-	-	-	.	.	.	.	8349	5665	3684	2311	2172
16 JAPAN	-	.	.	.	.	.	18300	18599	-	13317	10977	10307	9663	9980	8050
17 NETHERLANDS	.	.	.	.	.	.	.	.	.	7969	5847	5695	4501	4609	3937
18 NEW ZEALAND	-	.	.	.	.	.	.	.	.	11696	10933	9864	8540	8333	10911
19 NORWAY	3083	2277	.	.	.	2231	2680	2263	.	.	4428	4048	4399	4034	5408
20 POLAND	-	-	-	-	-	-	-	-	-	-	.	.	14445	11995	9295
21 PORTUGAL	-	-	-	-	-	-	.	.	.	.	2972	3812	2788	2706	1272
22 ROMANIA	-	-	-	-	-	-	-	-	-	-	-	474	0	100	413
23 SPAIN	.	.	.	.	.	.	12363	15521	13851	9615	5580	5017	4345	3318	2762
24 SWEDEN	-	-	.	.	.	.	.	.	.	.	8082	4792	5619	4058	6322
25 SWITZERLAND	77905	77905	59062	59062	44313	44023	.	.	.	.	8255	4653	5607	10457	11636
26 TURKEY	-	-	-	-	-	-	-	-	-	-	-	153	448	677	129
27 UK ENGLAND AND WALES	23144	18797	19959	21403	23290	30223	31695	27810	13239	9093	6421	6903	6576	6640	6459
28 UK NORTHERN IRELAND	-	-	-	-	.	.	.	.	.	18072	12185	8264	5968	6555	6989
29 UK SCOTLAND	22348	18811	.	.	.	.	.	.	.	3916	6817	8750	8311	6497	6034
30 USA	.	.	.	.	.	.	.	.	.	4378	3988	3659	3844	3461	3088
31 YUGOSLAVIA	-	-	-	-	-	-	-	-	-	-	.	.	701	940	1192

- NO MORTALITY DATA ARE AVAILABLE FOR EVEN A BROADER GROUP OF CAUSES FOR THIS DISEASE

. MORTALITY DATA ARE PRESENTED FOR A BROADER GROUP OF CAUSES FOR THIS DISEASE

0 VALUE<0.5

THE STANDARD MORTALITY RATIOS WERE DERIVED WITH A FACTOR OF 10000

SERIAL MORTALITY TABLES FOR VARIOUS COUNTRIES 1901-1975

TABLE 140 : ARTHRITIS AND SPONDYLITIS : FEMALES

	1901-	1906-	1911-	1916-	1921-	1926-	1931-	1936-	1941-	1946-	1951-	1956-	1961-	1966-	1971-75
1 AUSTRALIA	-	.	.	.	.	.	20766	17736	16031	14355	11029	11332	9594	10548	11958
2 AUSTRIA	-	-	-	-	-	-	-	-	-	.	7475	5595	9130	12282	8770
3 BELGIUM	-	-	-	-	-	-	.	.	.	.	6701	7899	6992	6892	6674
4 BULGARIA	-	-	-	-	-	-	.	.	.	.	.	.	1066	1287	1616
5 CANADA	-	-	-	-	.	.	14758	10573	.	12090	9822	9137	8716	7903	7277
6 CHILE	-	.	.	.	.	.	.	9289	6536	6801	15003	13837	8434	8431	7495
7 CZECHOSLOVAKIA	-	-	-	.	.	.	.	.	.	.	11283	9309	7972	6767	3481
8 DENMARK	.	.	.	.	.	.	.	.	.	.	2708	5256	9970	11480	9013
9 EIRE	-	-	-	-	.	.	.	.	.	.	30389	29784	20590	12416	15297
10 FINLAND	-	-	-	-	-	-	-	.	.	.	17270	15504	16224	17270	15008
11 FRANCE	-	-	-	-	-	-	.	.	4766	3777	4475	6222	5827	7023	6500
12 GREECE	-	-	-	-	-	.	.	.	-	-	-	7031	8615	6422	4868
13 HUNGARY	-	-	-	.	.	.	6001	6292	8260	.	12026	15107	11320	7332	6078
14 ICELAND	-	-	-	-	-	-	-	-	.	.	-	-	2941	2632	3101
15 ITALY	-	-	-	-	-	-	.	.	.	.	13961	9214	5825	3780	3781
16 JAPAN	-	.	.	.	.	.	22675	21993	-	19956	17578	17371	16738	19105	18055
17 NETHERLANDS	.	.	.	.	.	.	.	.	.	15826	13555	10223	8998	8797	8137
18 NEW ZEALAND	-	.	.	.	.	.	.	.	.	18559	18319	16464	13087	15380	20284
19 NORWAY	5603	4274	.	.	.	3655	4716	4016	.	.	8891	6677	7755	8161	10598
20 POLAND	-	-	-	-	-	-	-	-	-	-	.	.	20584	18888	14778
21 PORTUGAL	-	-	-	-	-	-	.	.	.	.	1803	2836	2341	2289	973
22 ROMANIA	-	-	-	-	-	-	-	-	-	-	-	841	21	118	1198
23 SPAIN	.	.	.	.	.	.	11757	13315	12133	9767	5547	4538	4907	4468	3873
24 SWEDEN	-	-	.	.	.	.	.	.	.	.	21344	13284	10553	8098	12999
25 SWITZERLAND	74186	74186	59094	59094	46279	43495	.	.	.	.	12038	6819	7956	17253	20441
26 TURKEY	-	-	-	-	-	-	-	-	-	-	-	119	609	845	151
27 UK ENGLAND AND WALES	36059	33337	35096	39743	41741	52152	52752	46644	21235	16429	12136	12880	12196	11587	11973
28 UK NORTHERN IRELAND	-	-	-	-	.	.	.	.	.	26201	17998	15523	10314	14027	11874
29 UK SCOTLAND	25031	26912	.	.	.	.	.	.	.	12016	16558	21528	15667	11346	10502
30 USA	.	.	.	.	.	.	.	.	.	7240	6105	5655	5428	4868	4161
31 YUGOSLAVIA	-	-	-	-	-	-	-	-	-	-	.	.	1120	998	1563

- NO MORTALITY DATA ARE AVAILABLE FOR EVEN A BROADER GROUP OF CAUSES FOR THIS DISEASE

. MORTALITY DATA ARE PRESENTED FOR A BROADER GROUP OF CAUSES FOR THIS DISEASE

0 VALUE<0.5

THE STANDARD MORTALITY RATIOS WERE DERIVED WITH A FACTOR OF 10000

SERIAL MORTALITY TABLES FOR VARIOUS COUNTRIES 1901-1975

TABLE 141 : RHEUMATISM - MUSCULAR AND UNSPECIFIED : MALES

	1901-	1906-	1911-	1916-	1921-	1926-	1931-	1936-	1941-	1946-	1951-	1956-	1961-	1966-	1971-75
1 AUSTRALIA	-	.	.	.	.	.	4059	2596	672	552	638	443	319	879	609
2 AUSTRIA	-	-	-	-	-	-	-	-	-	10415	4102	194	459	436	334
3 BELGIUM	-	-	-	-	-	-	.	.	.	.	37951	4798	3211	2236	1280
4 BULGARIA	-	-	-	-	-	-	.	.	.	.	.	.	131	230	292
5 CANADA	-	-	-	-	.	.	.	.	.	4072	1471	627	511	452	757
6 CHILE	-	.	.	.	.	.	.	17824	15280	21467	58503	50456	29680	16209	8812
7 CZECHOSLOVAKIA	-	-	-	.	.	.	.	.	.	.	1538	680	213	136	50
8 DENMARK	.	.	.	.	.	.	.	.	.	.	0	73	134	433	685
9 EIRE	-	-	-	-	.	.	.	.	.	.	21803	8568	3793	1807	1251
10 FINLAND	-	-	-	-	-	-	-	.	.	.	0	0	122	657	688
11 FRANCE	-	-	-	-	-	-	.	.	.	6548	5502	4033	2483	1729	1037
12 GREECE	-	-	-	-	-	.	.	.	-	-	-	4652	3959	2249	733
13 HUNGARY	-	-	-	.	.	.	241	351	527	.	484	997	429	70	322
14 ICELAND	-	-	-	-	-	-	-	-	.	.	-	-	0	0	0
15 ITALY	-	-	-	-	-	-	.	.	.	.	1250	414	148	145	169
16 JAPAN	-	.	.	.	.	.	.	.	-	13393	7349	3924	2837	2599	2332
17 NETHERLANDS	.	.	.	.	.	.	.	.	.	5077	1930	1790	2506	3083	2818
18 NEW ZEALAND	-	.	.	.	.	.	.	.	.	0	0	0	327	785	1495
19 NORWAY	.	.	12591	12966	12458	6260	.	.	.	.	308	184	0	301	587
20 POLAND	-	-	-	-	-	-	-	-	-	-	.	8521	6367	4487	998
21 PORTUGAL	-	-	-	-	-	-	.	.	.	.	18157	14506	8392	103	1042
22 ROMANIA	-	-	-	-	-	-	-	-	-	-	-	0	0	48	82
23 SPAIN	.	.	.	.	.	.	.	.	.	.	15073	12889	9741	9163	2772
24 SWEDEN	-	-	.	.	.	.	.	.	.	.	498	81	222	101	216
25 SWITZERLAND	.	.	.	.	.	.	.	.	.	.	243	218	262	773	640
26 TURKEY	-	-	-	-	-	-	-	-	-	-	-	32643	9660	5512	2945
27 UK ENGLAND AND WALES	25396	14265	15894	16840	14110	6673	3263	2360	1882	818	217	229	241	471	677
28 UK NORTHERN IRELAND	-	-	-	-	.	.	.	.	.	6452	3958	1047	504	976	721
29 UK SCOTLAND	35605	31688	.	.	.	.	.	.	.	2333	975	365	359	277	660
30 USA	.	.	.	.	.	.	.	.	.	568	365	170	198	423	643
31 YUGOSLAVIA	-	-	-	-	-	-	-	-	-	-	.	.	4840	856	160

- NO MORTALITY DATA ARE AVAILABLE FOR EVEN A BROADER GROUP OF CAUSES FOR THIS DISEASE

. MORTALITY DATA ARE PRESENTED FOR A BROADER GROUP OF CAUSES FOR THIS DISEASE

0 VALUE<0.5

THE STANDARD MORTALITY RATIOS WERE DERIVED WITH A FACTOR OF 10000

SERIAL MORTALITY TABLES FOR VARIOUS COUNTRIES 1901-1975

TABLE 141 : RHEUMATISM - MUSCULAR AND UNSPECIFIED : FEMALES

	1901-	1906-	1911-	1916-	1921-	1926-	1931-	1936-	1941-	1946-	1951-	1956-	1961-	1966-	1971-75
1 AUSTRALIA	-	.	.	.	.	.	5388	3892	727	290	518	275	236	544	745
2 AUSTRIA	-	-	-	-	-	-	-	-	-	22510	6504	160	199	668	332
3 BELGIUM	-	-	-	-	-	-	.	.	.	.	24684	5479	3719	3377	1440
4 BULGARIA	-	-	-	-	-	-	.	.	.	.	.	.	748	301	137
5 CANADA	-	-	-	-	.	.	.	.	.	5837	1873	697	569	554	901
6 CHILE	-	.	.	.	.	.	.	21531	25036	29066	56933	49866	31165	18566	11388
7 CZECHOSLOVAKIA	-	-	-	.	.	.	.	.	.	.	2764	1275	331	90	80
8 DENMARK	.	.	.	.	.	.	.	.	.	.	73	64	112	493	907
9 EIRE	-	-	-	-	.	.	.	.	.	.	12475	7390	2388	1164	1106
10 FINLAND	-	-	-	-	-	-	-	.	.	.	0	0	439	195	745
11 FRANCE	-	-	-	-	-	-	.	.	.	7190	6403	4919	3120	1842	1015
12 GREECE	-	-	-	-	-	.	.	.	-	-	-	6135	4601	2444	913
13 HUNGARY	-	-	-	.	.	.	375	367	1812	.	186	1428	395	173	306
14 ICELAND	-	-	-	-	-	-	-	-	.	.	-	-	0	0	0
15 ITALY	-	-	-	-	-	-	.	.	.	.	1433	494	149	213	248
16 JAPAN	-	.	.	.	.	.	.	.	-	13934	8792	5660	4488	4434	4723
17 NETHERLANDS		.	.	.	.	.	.	.	.	12456	5619	2838	4156	5614	5075
18 NEW ZEALAND	-	.	.	.	.	.	.	.	.	0	332	0	379	803	956
19 NORWAY		.	19562	20056	18230	22140	.	.	.	.	748	224	67	469	661
20 POLAND	-	-	-	-	-	-	-	-	-	-	.	9405	8724	5925	1624
21 PORTUGAL	-	-	-	-	-	-	.	.	.	.	17072	11107	6141	66	882
22 ROMANIA	-	-	-	-	-	-	-	-	-	-	-	0	0	17	150
23 SPAIN		.	.	.	.	.	.	.	.	.	17208	13616	10366	10768	3856
24 SWEDEN	-	-	.	.	.	.	.	.	.	.	779	104	185	541	570
25 SWITZERLAND		.	.	.	.	.	.	.	.	.	177	156	320	1009	918
26 TURKEY	-	-	-	-	-	-	-	-	-	-	-	29271	11673	6889	5083
27 UK ENGLAND AND WALES	31950	19708	17316	17365	13652	6556	3670	2138	1786	751	156	136	155	383	650
28 UK NORTHERN IRELAND	-	-	-	-	.	.	.	.	.	4076	5474	795	738	1186	632
29 UK SCOTLAND	47821	39670	.	.	.	.	.	.	.	1979	1543	1131	593	333	306
30 USA	.	.	.	.	.	.	.	.	.	509	421	159	198	573	741
31 YUGOSLAVIA	-	-	-	-	-	-	-	-	-	-	.	.	5279	1005	116

\- NO MORTALITY DATA ARE AVAILABLE FOR EVEN A BROADER GROUP OF CAUSES FOR THIS DISEASE

. MORTALITY DATA ARE PRESENTED FOR A BROADER GROUP OF CAUSES FOR THIS DISEASE

0 VALUE<0.5

THE STANDARD MORTALITY RATIOS WERE DERIVED WITH A FACTOR OF 10000

SERIAL MORTALITY TABLES FOR VARIOUS COUNTRIES 1901-1975

TABLE 142 : OSTEOMYELITIS AND PERIOSTITIS : MALES

	1901-	1906-	1911-	1916-	1921-	1926-	1931-	1936-	1941-	1946-	1951-	1956-	1961-	1966-	1971-75
1 AUSTRALIA	-	.	.	.	.	.	26242	21491	9607	3030	2703	2927	2333	1164	1101
2 AUSTRIA	-	-	-	-	-	-	-	-	-	.	7023	7043	4847	3861	2941
3 BELGIUM	-	-	-	-	-	-	.	.	.	.	1633	1512	746	1054	648
4 BULGARIA	-	-	-	-	-	-	.	.	.	.	.	.	2904	1349	1441
5 CANADA	-	-	-	-	.	.	14770	15676	7153	2568	1799	1795	758	857	851
6 CHILE	-	.	.	.	.	.	4881	7556	1531	584	2586	2908	2500	2350	2135
7 CZECHOSLOVAKIA	-	-	-	.	.	.	18115	19718	22545	15789	3734	3860	1701	1818	1342
8 DENMARK	31053	19500	21818	20417	23919	21923	12738	11222	11429	2778	603	1371	1061	571	884
9 EIRE	-	-	-	-	.	.	25263	27564	26456	9390	4588	3214	1905	952	1163
10 FINLAND	-	-	-	-	-	-	-	.	17722	8313	2874	3043	1837	1471	849
11 FRANCE	-	-	-	-	-	-	.	.	5424	1981	1979	1207	971	687	535
12 GREECE	-	-	-	-	-	.	17114	18229	-	-	-	1675	1238	441	478
13 HUNGARY	-	-	-	.	.	.	21539	22099	32143	.	9111	8678	5737	3797	3025
14 ICELAND	-	-	-	-	-	-	-	-	.	.	-	-	0	0	2000
15 ITALY	-	-	-	-	-	-	.	.	.	.	4093	3151	1630	1132	626
16 JAPAN	-	.	.	.	.	.	.	.	-	7380	5144	3495	1917	1131	702
17 NETHERLANDS	.	.	.	.	.	.	13478	12613	17176	4809	2992	1875	1815	1395	850
18 NEW ZEALAND	-	.	.	.	.	32258	23636	21111	12250	4167	4444	5763	2969	1029	1667
19 NORWAY	.	.	.	.	.	6875	8676	5069	8077	3647	2198	808	1509	974	513
20 POLAND	-	-	-	-	-	-	-	-	-	-	.	1770	3119	3227	2400
21 PORTUGAL	-	-	-	-	-	-	.	.	.	.	5220	3834	3575	2905	1127
22 ROMANIA	-	-	-	-	-	-	-	-	-	-	-	2875	3437	1721	1328
23 SPAIN	.	.	.	.	.	.	8004	7992	9043	4201	3798	3732	2659	1536	728
24 SWEDEN	-	-	.	.	.	.	.	.	.	.	1493	981	1272	816	775
25 SWITZERLAND	40000	40000	25449	25449	22222	20823	17667	16042	13981	5439	3089	2932	2123	2076	2249
26 TURKEY	-	-	-	-	-	-	-	-	-	-	-	6124	2892	1477	2430
27 UK ENGLAND AND WALES	27524	11149	.	.	18607	18646	17316	14287	10083	4033	2247	1641	1094	845	782
28 UK NORTHERN IRELAND	-	-	-	-	.	.	.	.	.	4546	2500	1622	1316	750	1250
29 UK SCOTLAND	49655	50659	.	.	.	.	27523	20877	16016	4488	2539	1591	1691	797	719
30 USA	.	.	.	.	.	14180	13397	10878	4784	1856	1265	1168	1092	969	820
31 YUGOSLAVIA	-	-	-	-	-	-	-	-	-	-	.	.	2354	1457	795

- NO MORTALITY DATA ARE AVAILABLE FOR EVEN A BROADER GROUP OF CAUSES FOR THIS DISEASE

. MORTALITY DATA ARE PRESENTED FOR A BROADER GROUP OF CAUSES FOR THIS DISEASE

0 VALUE<0.5

THE STANDARD MORTALITY RATIOS WERE DERIVED WITH A FACTOR OF 1000

SERIAL MORTALITY TABLES FOR VARIOUS COUNTRIES 1901-1975

TABLE 142 : OSTEOMYELITIS AND PERIOSTITIS : FEMALES

	1901-	1906-	1911-	1916-	1921-	1926-	1931-	1936-	1941-	1946-	1951-	1956-	1961-	1966-	1971-75
1 AUSTRALIA	-	.	.	.	.	.	10486	9563	5444	1471	1130	1519	1217	744	863
2 AUSTRIA	-	-	-	-	-	-	-	-	-	.	3275	2581	2500	1888	1554
3 BELGIUM	-	-	-	-	-	-	.	.	.	.	883	987	526	735	595
4 BULGARIA	-	-	-	-	-	-	.	.	.	.	.	.	1042	681	638
5 CANADA	-	-	-	-	.	.	9688	8443	3577	1129	1129	818	617	560	639
6 CHILE	-	.	.	.	.	.	3068	3684	385	987	1191	1104	1500	1542	935
7 CZECHOSLOVAKIA	-	-	-	.	.	.	10269	8148	16406	9748	1620	1974	1292	947	680
8 DENMARK	16250	11923	8276	13226	14390	8954	6264	6804	5619	1565	807	672	616	692	465
9 EIRE	-	-	-	-	.	.	11688	16883	14125	5366	3488	1954	2135	440	526
10 FINLAND	-	-	-	-	-	-	-	.	6842	3786	1622	1429	1181	519	629
11 FRANCE	-	-	-	-	-	-	.	.	2525	882	873	508	418	430	357
12 GREECE	-	-	-	-	-	.	8117	8990	-	-	-	1239	539	646	546
13 HUNGARY	-	-	-	.	.	.	10574	12216	13370	.	8000	5524	2343	2256	1671
14 ICELAND	-	-	-	-	-	-	-	-	.	.	-	-	0	0	0
15 ITALY	-	-	-	-	-	-	.	.	.	.	2113	1668	765	605	275
16 JAPAN	-	.	.	.	.	.	.	.	-	5730	3208	2081	1266	720	489
17 NETHERLANDS	.	.	.	.	.	.	7801	6570	8756	3102	1480	948	1088	745	1149
18 NEW ZEALAND	-	.	.	.	.	15517	11563	8611	7073	2394	1930	2969	1127	1039	1325
19 NORWAY	.	.	.	.	.	3513	4359	3855	3933	2188	1078	818	840	231	362
20 POLAND	-	-	-	-	-	-	-	-	-	-	.	1371	1353	1263	1193
21 PORTUGAL	-	-	-	-	-	-	.	.	.	.	4367	2295	1954	1264	507
22 ROMANIA	-	-	-	-	-	-	-	-	-	-	-	2032	1805	1531	797
23 SPAIN	.	.	.	.	.	.	4161	4207	4755	2568	2536	2503	1814	1120	454
24 SWEDEN	-	-	.	.	.	.	.	.	.	.	553	601	675	507	368
25 SWITZERLAND	31902	31902	11017	11017	10106	9495	8207	6195	5203	1985	1689	1296	1117	1320	939
26 TURKEY	-	-	-	-	-	-	-	-	-	-	-	3359	2857	1310	2575
27 UK ENGLAND AND WALES	20235	7976	.	.	7364	8041	7343	5614	4256	1713	1127	1032	544	640	647
28 UK NORTHERN IRELAND	-	-	-	-	.	.	.	.	.	2778	1463	1395	667	417	600
29 UK SCOTLAND	34314	29346	.	.	.	.	9219	7778	5578	2208	1375	719	454	978	576
30 USA	.	.	.	.	.	7254	6450	4813	2161	930	685	654	703	628	614
31 YUGOSLAVIA	-	-	-	-	-	-	-	-	-	-	.	.	1299	822	480

- NO MORTALITY DATA ARE AVAILABLE FOR EVEN A BROADER GROUP OF CAUSES FOR THIS DISEASE

. MORTALITY DATA ARE PRESENTED FOR A BROADER GROUP OF CAUSES FOR THIS DISEASE

0 VALUE<0.5

THE STANDARD MORTALITY RATIOS WERE DERIVED WITH A FACTOR OF 1000

SERIAL MORTALITY TABLES FOR VARIOUS COUNTRIES 1901-1975

TABLE 143 : ANKYLOSIS AND ACQUIRED MUSCULOSKELETAL DEFORMITIES : MALES

	1901-	1906-	1911-	1916-	1921-	1926-	1931-	1936-	1941-	1946-	1951-	1956-	1961-	1966-	1971-75
1 AUSTRALIA	-	.	.	.	.	.	.	.	.	.	2451	4867	3968	2545	6000
2 AUSTRIA	-	-	-	-	-	-	-	-	-	.	16473	7821	4839	17895	5155
3 BELGIUM	-	-	-	-	-	-	.	.	.	.	19149	9312	16016	9506	7836
4 BULGARIA	-	-	-	-	-	-	.	.	.	.	.	.	1323	6829	1376
5 CANADA	-	-	-	-	.	.	.	.	.	6557	6105	6905	5023	9053	9393
6 CHILE	-	.	.	.	.	.	.	.	.	.	19417	12903	7692	6875	12281
7 CZECHOSLOVAKIA	-	-	-	.	.	.	.	.	.	.	20325	14239	16049	4058	3056
8 DENMARK	.	.	.	.	.	.	.	.	.	.	4587	840	1563	11111	12676
9 EIRE	-	-	-	-	.	.	.	.	.	.	5000	6329	13924	1266	6098
10 FINLAND	-	-	-	-	-	-	-	.	.	.	1266	10588	1087	3093	2941
11 FRANCE	-	-	-	-	-	-	.	.	.	8551	6092	5076	6656	7387	11641
12 GREECE	-	-	-	-	-	.	.	.	-	-	-	3297	3000	5556	2500
13 HUNGARY	-	-	-	.	.	.	.	.	.	.	9467	5286	7083	13672	13755
14 ICELAND	-	-	-	-	-	-	-	-	.	.	-	-	0	0	0
15 ITALY	-	-	-	-	-	-	.	.	.	.	6434	2573	4330	2510	6228
16 JAPAN	-	.	.	.	.	.	.	.	-	1361	1089	2064	2047	837	1005
17 NETHERLANDS	.	.	.	.	.	.	.	.	.	6977	25410	17037	6397	11875	32353
18 NEW ZEALAND	-	.	.	.	.	.	.	.	.	0	6122	3636	5000	11111	11940
19 NORWAY	.	.	.	.	.	.	.	.	.	.	2326	1064	3922	4587	2679
20 POLAND	-	-	-	-	-	-	-	-	-	-	.	9217	6873	26348	12482
21 PORTUGAL	-	-	-	-	-	-	.	.	.	.	29762	30168	5729	513	19000
22 ROMANIA	-	-	-	-	-	-	-	-	-	-	-	0	0	0	0
23 SPAIN	.	.	.	.	.	.	.	.	.	.	1692	0	0	0	2457
24 SWEDEN	-	-	.	.	.	.	.	.	.	.	12042	2415	9009	6303	4781
25 SWITZERLAND	.	.	.	.	.	.	.	.	.	.	5172	2362	8633	11921	7453
26 TURKEY	-	-	-	-	-	-	-	-	-	-	-	1818	1143	3057	4525
27 UK ENGLAND AND WALES	.	.	.	.	.	.	.	.	.	5251	9035	8947	10641	10323	10605
28 UK NORTHERN IRELAND	-	-	-	-	.	.	.	.	.	16667	11765	0	13889	13514	13158
29 UK SCOTLAND	.	.	.	.	.	.	.	.	.	0	9016	7143	4688	5385	15152
30 USA	.	.	.	.	.	.	.	.	.	5882	6709	6540	5253	5871	5545
31 YUGOSLAVIA	-	-	-	-	-	-	-	-	-	-	.	.	1309	2179	0

- NO MORTALITY DATA ARE AVAILABLE FOR EVEN A BROADER GROUP OF CAUSES FOR THIS DISEASE

. MORTALITY DATA ARE PRESENTED FOR A BROADER GROUP OF CAUSES FOR THIS DISEASE

0 VALUE<0.5

THE STANDARD MORTALITY RATIOS WERE DERIVED WITH A FACTOR OF 10000

SERIAL MORTALITY TABLES FOR VARIOUS COUNTRIES 1901-1975

TABLE 143 : ANKYLOSIS AND ACQUIRED MUSCULOSKELETAL DEFORMITIES : FEMALES

	1901-	1906-	1911-	1916-	1921-	1926-	1931-	1936-	1941-	1946-	1951-	1956-	1961-	1966-	1971-75
1 AUSTRALIA	-	.	.	.	.	.	.	.	.	.	3139	8696	6597	8359	5587
2 AUSTRIA	-	-	-	-	-	-	-	-	-	.	26906	10788	8462	16304	8621
3 BELGIUM	-	-	-	-	-	-	.	.	.	.	12774	11224	13141	9091	9510
4 BULGARIA	-	-	-	-	-	-	.	.	.	.	.	.	4808	8811	1240
5 CANADA	-	-	-	-	.	.	.	.	.	6780	8824	9949	9292	10721	13870
6 CHILE	-	.	.	.	.	.	.	.	.	.	4464	11511	2500	7263	8763
7 CZECHOSLOVAKIA	-	-	-	.	.	.	.	.	.	.	14216	20811	12935	11416	4264
8 DENMARK	.	.	.	.	.	.	.	.	.	.	4237	2326	2113	7097	10714
9 EIRE	-	-	-	-	.	.	.	.	.	.	9877	19512	10588	0	7692
10 FINLAND	-	-	-	-	-	-	-	.	.	.	0	8036	4098	4615	2878
11 FRANCE	-	-	-	-	-	-	.	.	.	5721	4986	7612	9371	10556	15938
12 GREECE	-	-	-	-	-	.	.	.	-	-	-	3349	6897	3937	4225
13 HUNGARY	-	-	-	.	.	.	.	.	.	.	0	6250	13993	14688	**25581**
14 ICELAND	-	-	-	-	-	-	-	-	.	.	-	-	0	0	16667
15 ITALY	-	-	-	-	-	-	.	.	.	.	9831	3622	4640	4680	8050
16 JAPAN	-	.	.	.	.	.	.	.	-	2402	1125	2405	2597	1598	1880
17 NETHERLANDS		.	.	.	.	.	.	.	.	6637	33591	21453	10494	16620	33417
18 NEW ZEALAND	-	.	.	.	.	.	.	.	.	0	9615	5000	8955	12329	7595
19 NORWAY	.	.	.	.	.	.	.	.	.	.	4082	6604	3448	3937	8271
20 POLAND	-	-	-	-	-	-	-	-	-	-	.	14234	11622	25060	8342
21 PORTUGAL	-	-	-	-	-	-	.	.	.	.	32258	34199	4435	391	7547
22 ROMANIA	-	-	-	-	-	-	-	-	-	-	-	0	0	0	0
23 SPAIN	.	.	.	.	.	.	.	.	.	.	1499	0	0	0	4331
24 SWEDEN	-	-	.	.	.	.	.	.	.	.	7692	4405	6883	9594	6780
25 SWITZERLAND	.	.	.	.	.	.	.	.	.	.	7042	1923	9195	23158	12981
26 TURKEY	-	-	-	-	-	-	-	-	-	-	-	2679	0	2252	4327
27 UK ENGLAND AND WALES	.	.	.	.	.	.	.	.	.	6758	8236	9009	9982	9337	13010
28 UK NORTHERN IRELAND	-	-	-	-	.	.	.	.	.	29412	2564	12195	18605	21739	14583
29 UK SCOTLAND	.	.	.	.	.	.	.	.	.	3378	5229	1863	5325	13483	25668
30 USA	.	.	.	.	.	.	.	.	.	5715	6641	5648	5924	6792	8165
31 YUGOSLAVIA	-	-	-	-	-	-	-	-	-	-	.	.	1965	1414	0

- NO MORTALITY DATA ARE AVAILABLE FOR EVEN A BROADER GROUP OF CAUSES FOR THIS DISEASE

. MORTALITY DATA ARE PRESENTED FOR A BROADER GROUP OF CAUSES FOR THIS DISEASE

0 VALUE<0.5

THE STANDARD MORTALITY RATIOS WERE DERIVED WITH A FACTOR OF 10000

SERIAL MORTALITY TABLES FOR VARIOUS COUNTRIES 1901-1975

TABLE 144 : BONES AND JOINTS - ALL DISEASES : MALES

	1901-	1906-	1911-	1916-	1921-	1926-	1931-	1936-	1941-	1946-	1951-	1956-	1961-	1966-	1971-75
1 AUSTRALIA	-	3605	3014	3333	3681	3160	2966	2586	1665	1148	764	866	775	867	919
2 AUSTRIA	-	-	-	-	-	-	-	-	-	1780	966	587	712	859	552
3 BELGIUM	-	-	-	-	-	-	.	.	.	.	871	760	704	654	494
4 BULGARIA	-	-	-	-	-	-	.	.	.	.	.	.	204	179	166
5 CANADA	-	-	-	-	3395	2479	1999	1968	1267	849	693	596	518	580	548
6 CHILE	-	7885	.	.	1459	1442	2007	2172	1789	1685	3828	3226	1934	1348	958
7 CZECHOSLOVAKIA	-	-	-	3396	3282	3414	3150	3302	3866	2836	950	655	441	341	220
8 DENMARK	2703	2226	2011	1801	1616	1668	2239	2267	2328	1207	171	271	400	511	543
9 EIRE	-	-	-	-	5722	5513	5637	4916	4803	3474	3035	2426	1470	940	1088
10 FINLAND	-	-	-	-	-	-	-	3117	2691	1643	1092	952	744	982	911
11 FRANCE	-	-	-	-	-	-	.	.	854	594	650	642	538	541	483
12 GREECE	-	-	-	-	-	2354	2289	1998	-	-	-	672	747	494	240
13 HUNGARY	-	-	-	2606	2255	1701	1502	1582	2249	1589	1222	1242	817	531	465
14 ICELAND	-	-	-	-	-	-	-	-	.	.	-	-	213	0	168
15 ITALY	-	-	-	-	-	-	2711	2927	2195	1031	1025	682	429	275	256
16 JAPAN	-	4813	5129	5221	6078	5647	4404	4144	-	2221	1599	1282	1086	1057	857
17 NETHERLANDS	4782	4128	.	.	1501	1980	1673	1822	2258	1134	869	754	631	671	659
18 NEW ZEALAND	-	.	.	.	1280	1375	2172	1746	1347	846	1214	1167	940	877	1174
19 NORWAY	985	880	1229	1213	946	904	860	631	1342	988	518	411	475	436	548
20 POLAND	-	-	-	-	-	-	-	-	-	-	1384	1045	1443	1557	1047
21 PORTUGAL	-	-	-	-	-	-	.	.	.	.	1526	1352	842	391	300
22 ROMANIA	-	-	-	-	-	-	-	-	-	-	-	200	179	98	106
23 SPAIN	40507	35576	.	.	.	.	1730	2044	1902	1233	1386	1224	967	796	421
24 SWEDEN	-	-	9755	8086	6632	4099	1180	1150	951	834	863	486	605	429	632
25 SWITZERLAND	9390	9390	7655	7655	5760	5369	4582	3919	3511	3005	914	569	646	1115	1203
26 TURKEY	-	-	-	-	-	-	-	-	-	-	-	1816	658	413	331
27 UK ENGLAND AND WALES	5663	3601	3864	4024	4122	4400	4253	3647	2029	1276	723	738	693	697	689
28 UK NORTHERN IRELAND	-	-	-	-	4899	4856	3851	3599	2810	1951	1443	863	676	724	772
29 UK SCOTLAND	7556	6608	4718	3923	3501	2781	3118	2483	1917	1043	810	902	856	653	667
30 USA	13231	7841	2992	3102	1753	1721	1614	1352	962	679	462	418	426	398	366
31 YUGOSLAVIA	-	-	-	-	-	-	-	-	-	-	1914	650	411	209	153

- NO MORTALITY DATA ARE AVAILABLE FOR EVEN A BROADER GROUP OF CAUSES FOR THIS DISEASE

. MORTALITY DATA ARE PRESENTED FOR A BROADER GROUP OF CAUSES FOR THIS DISEASE

0 VALUE<0.5

THE STANDARD MORTALITY RATIOS WERE DERIVED WITH A FACTOR OF 1000

SERIAL MORTALITY TABLES FOR VARIOUS COUNTRIES 1901-1975

TABLE 144 : BONES AND JOINTS - ALL DISEASES : FEMALES

	1901-	1906-	1911-	1916-	1921-	1926-	1931-	1936-	1941-	1946-	1951-	1956-	1961-	1966-	1971-75
1 AUSTRALIA	-	3541	2742	3559	3753	3108	2835	2449	1925	1629	1076	1133	953	1042	1173
2 AUSTRIA	-	-	-	-	-	-	-	-	-	1934	1092	655	965	1280	903
3 BELGIUM	-	-	-	-	-	-	.	.	.	.	1058	1062	885	854	736
4 BULGARIA	-	-	-	-	-	-	.	.	.	.	.	.	196	194	184
5 CANADA	-	-	-	-	3811	2417	2216	1794	1353	1117	1055	929	874	805	782
6 CHILE	-	9064	.	.	1554	1562	1947	2215	1872	2120	3900	3530	2220	1692	1274
7 CZECHOSLOVAKIA	-	-	-	4337	3441	3188	3321	3348	3739	2894	1272	1067	839	698	362
8 DENMARK	1266	1199	779	1367	1394	2174	4179	4521	3988	1499	299	514	941	1120	922
9 EIRE	-	-	-	-	5881	6119	5757	5800	5687	4002	3532	3208	2108	1200	1492
10 FINLAND	-	-	-	-	-	-	-	2991	2543	2061	1613	1484	1544	1604	1430
11 FRANCE	-	-	-	-	-	-	.	.	689	529	770	853	733	785	713
12 GREECE	-	-	-	-	-	1694	1722	1866	-	-	-	989	1045	739	523
13 HUNGARY	-	-	-	2447	2025	1363	1089	1180	1458	1453	1554	1690	1191	817	725
14 ICELAND	-	-	-	-	-	-	-	-	.	.	-	-	265	236	350
15 ITALY	-	-	-	-	-	-	2702	2936	2427	1200	1453	938	583	395	396
16 JAPAN	-	3572	3755	3631	4901	4949	3827	3525	-	2715	2122	1909	1763	1946	1865
17 NETHERLANDS	4723	4186	.	.	2019	2710	2303	2499	3599	1917	1688	1182	1097	1161	1156
18 NEW ZEALAND	-	.	.	.	2311	2158	2159	1806	1715	1158	1786	1630	1280	1517	1959
19 NORWAY	971	866	1347	1373	1179	1038	996	900	1484	1330	899	673	753	789	1041
20 POLAND	-	-	-	-	-	-	-	-	-	-	1040	1118	1841	2134	1493
21 PORTUGAL	-	-	-	-	-	-	.	.	.	.	1308	1028	604	264	180
22 ROMANIA	-	-	-	-	-	-	-	-	-	-	-	172	84	79	149
23 SPAIN	32512	27310	.	.	.	.	1358	1511	1422	1094	1427	1161	1012	965	571
24 SWEDEN	-	-	7591	6428	5151	3603	1837	1941	1947	1829	2018	1249	1019	818	1254
25 SWITZERLAND	8988	8988	7980	7980	5305	4900	4422	4045	4237	3562	1192	684	815	1753	1990
26 TURKEY	-	-	-	-	-	-	-	-	-	-	-	1495	738	468	417
27 UK ENGLAND AND WALES	6372	4725	4523	4906	4983	5604	5455	4763	2388	1750	1183	1251	1176	1133	1196
28 UK NORTHERN IRELAND	-	-	-	-	5790	5008	5492	4815	3421	2957	1957	1546	1067	1427	1187
29 UK SCOTLAND	6677	6038	4448	3869	3670	3027	2635	2399	1913	1275	1646	2039	1488	1135	1086
30 USA	11387	7141	2710	2690	1694	1638	1545	1372	1127	869	625	567	552	520	468
31 YUGOSLAVIA	-	-	-	-	-	-	-	-	-	-	1747	476	415	180	167

- NO MORTALITY DATA ARE AVAILABLE FOR EVEN A BROADER GROUP OF CAUSES FOR THIS DISEASE

. MORTALITY DATA ARE PRESENTED FOR A BROADER GROUP OF CAUSES FOR THIS DISEASE

0 VALUE<0.5

THE STANDARD MORTALITY RATIOS WERE DERIVED WITH A FACTOR OF 1000

SERIAL MORTALITY TABLES FOR VARIOUS COUNTRIES 1901-1975

TABLE 145 : SKIN DISEASES : MALES

	1901-	1906-	1911-	1916-	1921-	1926-	1931-	1936-	1941-	1946-	1951-	1956-	1961-	1966-	1971-75
1 AUSTRALIA	-	33464	29086	29276	31028	31085	22227	19007	11344	5935	15031	16010	12923	10471	8518
2 AUSTRIA	-	-	-	-	-	-	-	-	-	18561	9539	11879	9055	9961	7824
3 BELGIUM	-	-	-	-	-	-	.	.	.	.	9355	8104	6364	6756	7170
4 BULGARIA	-	-	-	-	-	-	.	.	.	.	.	.	4282	3489	3338
5 CANADA	-	-	-	-	29950	35430	25650	20513	10054	6757	12947	13100	10039	8548	7039
6 CHILE	-	8808	39454	70445	27886	44168	45503	43554	26123	10991	18838	22446	23812	27507	25049
7 CZECHOSLOVAKIA	-	-	-	74472	73467	77383	65643	54384	45878	28997	13623	10595	5095	3732	3054
8 DENMARK	87109	82971	82911	91279	69778	81736	49271	41993	.	.	4153	6852	5958	5948	5693
9 EIRE	-	-	-	-	27344	28393	27281	27506	23667	11237	12132	13189	12125	9434	8025
10 FINLAND	-	-	-	-	-	-	-	6023	8370	3179	4598	7332	7441	6299	6061
11 FRANCE	-	-	-	-	-	-	.	.	21323	11743	12793	11093	11311	10581	11161
12 GREECE	-	-	-	-	-	21810	22010	19736	-	-	-	6963	7781	7646	7052
13 HUNGARY	-	-	-	-	-	-	79355	70467	69766	50177	24534	20971	8111	5145	5138
14 ICELAND	-	-	-	-	-	-	-	-	.	.	-	-	6849	2469	1099
15 ITALY	-	-	-	-	-	-	-	-	-	-	11570	13023	10545	8079	5429
16 JAPAN	-	68477	67177	64944	63150	55564	50218	48944	-	38167	22631	19824	12853	9356	8306
17 NETHERLANDS	23242	21847	19189	23608	16105	28091	23046	27112	49320	15376	11792	11857	11747	10021	7512
18 NEW ZEALAND	-	15000	21951	21467	31630	42637	16135	13669	10211	7112	14064	20507	13978	10384	8925
19 NORWAY	3721	6138	22030	21346	16080	7773	5950	8030	18028	5061	9783	9674	7965	7092	6028
20 POLAND	-	-	-	-	-	-	-	-	-	-	26650	16783	11986	11124	8734
21 PORTUGAL	-	-	-	-	-	-	.	.	.	.	17669	12184	12847	9695	4211
22 ROMANIA	-	-	-	-	-	-	-	-	-	-	-	6318	8831	7790	6788
23 SPAIN	59191	54157	44490	39674	33528	29979	26160	34019	34300	15868	15635	12163	8687	6443	4679
24 SWEDEN	-	-	3264	4032	3833	3344	4199	3616	3555	3897	6407	5362	6391	5200	4874
25 SWITZERLAND	44146	44146	40593	40593	31543	34302	41761	33057	25441	11155	10507	10754	10339	7571	9313
26 TURKEY	-	-	-	-	-	-	-	-	-	-	-	13198	9262	5735	3383
27 UK ENGLAND AND WALES	56386	47675	53323	49608	43836	42701	39861	32494	18661	9791	11767	9776	9730	8190	8436
28 UK NORTHERN IRELAND	-	-	-	-	29882	33649	33929	34267	23617	10700	12690	9061	13078	7132	4931
29 UK SCOTLAND	45561	47040	51806	45481	53116	49835	47162	42407	28701	13050	12711	10852	8531	7236	6596
30 USA	41903	28967	25178	22728	19049	16161	14226	10566	5959	5088	9286	10091	10099	9065	8559
31 YUGOSLAVIA	-	-	-	-	-	-	-	-	-	-	13615	14297	6700	3779	3199

- NO MORTALITY DATA ARE AVAILABLE FOR EVEN A BROADER GROUP OF CAUSES FOR THIS DISEASE

. MORTALITY DATA ARE PRESENTED FOR A BROADER GROUP OF CAUSES FOR THIS DISEASE

0 VALUE<0.5

THE STANDARD MORTALITY RATIOS WERE DERIVED WITH A FACTOR OF 10000

SERIAL MORTALITY TABLES FOR VARIOUS COUNTRIES 1901-1975

TABLE 145 : SKIN DISEASES : FEMALES

	1901-	1906-	1911-	1916-	1921-	1926-	1931-	1936-	1941-	1946-	1951-	1956-	1961-	1966-	1971-75
1 AUSTRALIA	-	31019	21981	24253	27137	24596	19751	16553	10864	6010	13136	14907	11715	10273	9938
2 AUSTRIA	-	-	-	-	-	-	-	-	-	12217	8444	10825	8064	9712	8525
3 BELGIUM	-	-	-	-	-	-	.	.	.	.	9546	6682	5542	7239	7080
4 BULGARIA	-	-	-	-	-	-	.	.	.	.	.	.	5290	4891	3804
5 CANADA	-	-	-	-	23905	27099	17437	15084	7746	6210	10783	12103	9875	9216	9620
6 CHILE	-	6161	19671	61227	19278	34183	28699	22823	18107	9029	15792	19571	19223	25776	29648
7 CZECHOSLOVAKIA	-	-	-	52091	53267	58934	53082	45491	35433	23868	12155	9953	5206	4021	3364
8 DENMARK	50685	54707	46889	56939	50382	58752	36388	32953	.	.	4882	7155	5494	7204	8310
9 EIRE	-	-	-	-	20632	17439	21597	21823	17562	10047	10456	12468	11622	11408	10712
10 FINLAND	-	-	-	-	-	-	-	4614	6698	2421	5622	8259	5386	6204	7924
11 FRANCE	-	-	-	-	-	-	.	.	11904	6878	10031	10982	11850	11111	12398
12 GREECE	-	-	-	-	-	18519	19910	16635	-	-	-	7141	9357	9731	11179
13 HUNGARY	-	-	-	-	-	-	61626	55359	50069	34465	19162	18092	9277	5923	5199
14 ICELAND	-	-	-	-	-	-	-	-	.	.	-	-	3529	2105	2830
15 ITALY	-	-	-	-	-	-	-	-	-	-	9869	11422	10272	8764	7125
16 JAPAN	-	59950	57167	54463	51728	42500	37954	38549	-	27359	16627	15711	12324	11973	13122
17 NETHERLANDS	16817	15620	15828	16739	12220	17747	14179	16780	33824	10143	11051	11382	9744	9173	11043
18 NEW ZEALAND	-	14286	19485	17188	26133	25000	14845	11351	7488	5034	12879	20055	10706	11791	13595
19 NORWAY	2175	3477	16126	13802	12252	7518	5495	5442	12871	5927	8804	8262	8280	7310	10363
20 POLAND	-	-	-	-	-	-	-	-	-	-	18790	12503	9526	9506	7702
21 PORTUGAL	-	-	-	-	-	-	.	.	.	.	8570	8532	9222	7879	4408
22 ROMANIA	-	-	-	-	-	-	-	-	-	-	-	5538	7195	6094	7023
23 SPAIN	47774	38616	31659	26570	22771	18402	17639	20307	21655	11477	13150	10464	7820	6571	5705
24 SWEDEN	-	-	3026	3481	3613	2766	4346	3779	4010	4103	6230	5438	5236	6773	8264
25 SWITZERLAND	28553	28553	29514	29514	18163	19560	24041	21746	18114	11351	9577	8840	8247	10442	10784
26 TURKEY	-	-	-	-	-	-	-	-	-	-	-	10341	6926	3983	1776
27 UK ENGLAND AND WALES	48467	40363	39648	34467	29512	27618	26611	19028	11881	7457	10077	8619	8696	10227	13362
28 UK NORTHERN IRELAND	-	-	-	-	26263	22874	20190	19887	15301	7679	11001	6631	10559	10150	10284
29 UK SCOTLAND	36918	36540	39892	32842	32938	29886	32367	27289	17556	10258	8762	8001	7170	7683	9034
30 USA	30247	21506	18587	16244	14477	12813	11011	8638	5553	5448	8348	9526	10221	11485	11750
31 YUGOSLAVIA	-	-	-	-	-	-	-	-	-	-	11704	9908	6926	4185	4722

- NO MORTALITY DATA ARE AVAILABLE FOR EVEN A BROADER GROUP OF CAUSES FOR THIS DISEASE

. MORTALITY DATA ARE PRESENTED FOR A BROADER GROUP OF CAUSES FOR THIS DISEASE

0 VALUE<0.5

THE STANDARD MORTALITY RATIOS WERE DERIVED WITH A FACTOR OF 10000

SERIAL MORTALITY TABLES FOR VARIOUS COUNTRIES 1901-1975

TABLE 146 : SKIN, MUSCULOSKELETAL SYSTEM AND CONNECTIVE TISSUE - ALL DISEASES : MALES

	1901-	1906-	1911-	1916-	1921-	1926-	1931-	1936-	1941-	1946-	1951-	1956-	1961-	1966-	1971-75
1 AUSTRALIA	-	3484	2965	3146	3419	3137	2639	2288	1435	908	1084	1184	1000	945	890
2 AUSTRIA	-	-	-	-	-	-	-	-	-	1812	961	837	792	915	647
3 BELGIUM	-	-	-	-	-	-	3908	3834	3993	2629	1756	781	676	663	586
4 BULGARIA	-	-	-	-	-	-	3001	3194	2732	2517	940	1072	301	251	236
5 CANADA	-	-	-	-	3212	2962	2252	2005	1153	774	954	907	731	700	616
6 CHILE	-	4514	4276	4723	2161	2909	3259	3240	2189	1403	2900	2755	2148	2016	1686
7 CZECHOSLOVAKIA	-	-	-	5215	5098	5339	4663	4248	4184	2591	1203	829	470	354	255
8 DENMARK	5479	5051	4870	5139	3982	4517	3408	3103	1329	693	274	445	482	546	554
9 EIRE	-	-	-	-	4468	4391	4427	4023	3803	2509	2272	1962	1362	942	967
10 FINLAND	-	-	-	-	-	-	-	1982	1853	1042	807	855	744	829	781
11 FRANCE	-	-	-	-	-	-	1518	1355	1408	837	915	839	787	758	747
12 GREECE	-	-	-	-	-	2276	2250	1988	-	-	-	682	760	609	435
13 HUNGARY	-	-	-	-	-	-	4333	3977	4314	3084	1754	1607	814	524	485
14 ICELAND	-	-	-	-	-	-	-	-	385	256	-	-	419	108	144
15 ITALY	-	-	-	-	-	-	-	-	-	-	1082	947	695	501	376
16 JAPAN	-	5743	5854	5803	6189	5605	4694	4497	-	2971	1907	1600	1175	1003	846
17 NETHERLANDS	3672	3251	1781	2054	1550	2350	1953	2213	3430	1311	1003	939	863	812	698
18 NEW ZEALAND	-	2500	3819	2757	2657	2670	1926	1583	1209	789	1297	1549	1140	947	1052
19 NORWAY	721	792	1659	1620	1237	849	745	706	1541	782	713	646	609	550	570
20 POLAND	-	-	-	-	-	-	-	-	-	-	1982	1334	1333	1362	972
21 PORTUGAL	-	-	-	-	-	-	4147	4692	4273	2233	1807	1293	1036	641	351
22 ROMANIA	-	-	-	-	-	-	-	-	-	-	-	391	486	392	352
23 SPAIN	24939	18545	3500	3073	2599	2295	2127	2649	2580	1390	1464	1221	925	731	441
24 SWEDEN	-	-	5651	4747	3929	2482	855	815	699	647	770	507	619	466	573
25 SWITZERLAND	7176	7176	6100	6100	4597	4514	4404	3656	3100	2204	972	783	810	964	1090
26 TURKEY	-	-	-	-	-	-	-	-	-	-	-	1569	789	490	334
27 UK ENGLAND AND WALES	6089	4458	4537	4447	4238	4343	4139	3479	1962	1152	913	838	810	748	753
28 UK NORTHERN IRELAND	-	-	-	-	4079	4213	3654	3526	2617	1576	1368	881	945	720	654
29 UK SCOTLAND	6940	6452	4931	4206	4311	3749	3809	3237	2321	1154	1005	979	855	683	664
30 USA	9096	5567	2775	2724	1822	1674	1529	1223	803	606	662	671	676	616	576
31 YUGOSLAVIA	-	-	-	-	-	-	-	-	-	-	1661	1002	526	283	226

- NO MORTALITY DATA ARE AVAILABLE FOR EVEN A BROADER GROUP OF CAUSES FOR THIS DISEASE

. MORTALITY DATA ARE PRESENTED FOR A BROADER GROUP OF CAUSES FOR THIS DISEASE

0 VALUE<0.5

THE STANDARD MORTALITY RATIOS WERE DERIVED WITH A FACTOR OF 1000

SERIAL MORTALITY TABLES FOR VARIOUS COUNTRIES 1901-1975

TABLE 146 : SKIN, MUSCULOSKELETAL SYSTEM AND CONNECTIVE TISSUE - ALL DISEASES : FEMALES

	1901-	1906-	1911-	1916-	1921-	1926-	1931-	1936-	1941-	1946-	1951-	1956-	1961-	1966-	1971-75
1 AUSTRALIA	-	3332	2485	3031	3276	2817	2457	2105	1565	1191	1177	1284	1046	1036	1097
2 AUSTRIA	-	-	-	-	-	-	-	-	-	1642	991	828	901	1156	883
3 BELGIUM	-	-	-	-	-	-	3146	2900	3249	2159	1432	901	750	801	725
4 BULGARIA	-	-	-	-	-	-	2356	2146	1792	1655	809	1189	337	318	265
5 CANADA	-	-	-	-	3159	2550	2004	1668	1100	901	1065	1051	923	855	859
6 CHILE	-	5067	3215	4401	1736	2462	2392	2247	1843	1546	2813	2794	2081	2103	2042
7 CZECHOSLOVAKIA	-	-	-	4720	4266	4368	4183	3868	3656	2481	1218	1037	708	577	352
8 DENMARK	2953	3096	2490	3265	2979	3774	3947	3997	2292	866	378	598	779	956	885
9 EIRE	-	-	-	-	4297	4305	4276	4314	4077	2778	2493	2390	1713	1175	1316
10 FINLAND	-	-	-	-	-	-	-	1894	1733	1277	1164	1205	1121	1196	1170
11 FRANCE	-	-	-	-	-	-	818	766	877	594	866	953	918	919	930
12 GREECE	-	-	-	-	-	1765	1842	1776	-	-	-	872	999	837	769
13 HUNGARY	-	-	-	-	-	-	3308	3070	2988	2304	1707	1740	1083	725	642
14 ICELAND	-	-	-	-	-	-	-	-	638	658	-	-	302	225	321
15 ITALY	-	-	-	-	-	-	-	-	-	-	1256	1023	768	594	526
16 JAPAN	-	4659	4634	4444	5024	4632	3813	3675	-	2725	1916	1760	1530	1621	1629
17 NETHERLANDS	3373	3021	1915	2283	1665	2296	1914	2142	3505	1526	1439	1164	1045	1059	1134
18 NEW ZEALAND	-	2039	2746	2282	2810	2310	1862	1518	1304	882	1575	1790	1191	1373	1707
19 NORWAY	644	674	1462	1377	1199	915	805	749	1400	1019	891	737	784	765	1039
20 POLAND	-	-	-	-	-	-	-	-	-	-	1413	1176	1461	1635	1191
21 PORTUGAL	-	-	-	-	-	-	2437	2809	2783	1838	1301	953	739	484	289
22 ROMANIA	-	-	-	-	-	-	-	-	-	-	-	335	352	302	381
23 SPAIN	20107	14229	2903	2511	1965	1572	1536	1737	1744	1117	1379	1112	915	836	571
24 SWEDEN	-	-	4483	3839	3120	2198	1246	1284	1300	1239	1441	959	817	761	1081
25 SWITZERLAND	6304	6304	5809	5809	3790	3635	3564	3259	3226	2553	1095	767	819	1461	1616
26 TURKEY	-	-	-	-	-	-	-	-	-	-	-	1278	717	436	306
27 UK ENGLAND AND WALES	6000	4679	4274	4263	4098	4385	4276	3569	1893	1337	1112	1092	1050	1088	1253
28 UK NORTHERN IRELAND	-	-	-	-	4440	3848	4005	3623	2626	2038	1599	1176	1062	1256	1122
29 UK SCOTLAND	5877	5551	4244	3611	3506	3010	2891	2538	1847	1171	1328	1528	1171	985	1011
30 USA	7597	4864	2322	2204	1582	1478	1348	1150	880	730	714	730	750	784	765
31 YUGOSLAVIA	-	-	-	-	-	-	-	-	-	-	1493	700	535	282	296

- NO MORTALITY DATA ARE AVAILABLE FOR EVEN A BROADER GROUP OF CAUSES FOR THIS DISEASE

. MORTALITY DATA ARE PRESENTED FOR A BROADER GROUP OF CAUSES FOR THIS DISEASE

0 VALUE<0.5

THE STANDARD MORTALITY RATIOS WERE DERIVED WITH A FACTOR OF 1000

SERIAL MORTALITY TABLES FOR VARIOUS COUNTRIES 1901-1975

TABLE 147 : CONGENITAL MALFORMATIONS - SPINA BIFIDA AND MENINGOCELE : MALES

	1901-	1906-	1911-	1916-	1921-	1926-	1931-	1936-	1941-	1946-	1951-	1956-	1961-	1966-	1971-75
1 AUSTRALIA	-	.	.	.	.	.	.	.	181	154	211	191	166	128	170
2 AUSTRIA	.	.	.	.	-	-	-	-	-	.	240	213	160	117	80
3 BELGIUM	.	.	.	.	.	.	.	.	.	.	280	270	207	172	94
4 BULGARIA	-	-	-	-	-	.	.	.	.	.	.	.	148	216	146
5 CANADA	.	.	.	.	.	.	489	573	517	499	587	308	352	291	215
6 CHILE	.	.	.	.	.	.	.	16	33	45	72	62	58	130	129
7 CZECHOSLOVAKIA	.	.	.	.	.	.	170	147	.	.	137	137	157	117	50
8 DENMARK	-	-	-	-	257	198	-	-	-	-	257	207	180	85	66
9 EIRE	-	-	-	-	.	.	544	577	961	1288	684	602	621	385	497
10 FINLAND	-	-	-	-	-	.	.	-	.	.	251	185	146	44	72
11 FRANCE	-	-	-	-	.	.	.	.	.	89	113	109	105	94	71
12 GREECE	-	-	-	-	-	.	.	.	-	-	-	105	79	59	18
13 HUNGARY	-	-	-	.	.	.	213	264	234	.	482	578	446	390	300
14 ICELAND	-	-	.	.	.	.	.	.	-	-	.	.	254	0	90
15 ITALY	-	-	-	-	-	-	281	304	271	322	341	278	214	121	87
16 JAPAN	-	.	.	.	.	.	.	.	-	52	49	38	28	29	23
17 NETHERLANDS	.	.	.	.	.	.	453	627	593	484	425	306	243	194	152
18 NEW ZEALAND	-	.	.	.	.	255	290	551	843	683	243	266	211	191	182
19 NORWAY	.	.	154	130	184	240	.	.	.	.	221	168	159	114	124
20 POLAND	-	-	-	-	-	-	-	-	-	-	-	214	282	204	102
21 PORTUGAL	-	-	-	-	-	-	-	-	-	-	160	188	187	220	89
22 ROMANIA	-	-	-	-	-	-	-	-	-	-	-	222	220	211	132
23 SPAIN	.	.	.	.	.	.	92	84	.	.	87	93	88	63	55
24 SWEDEN	-	-	.	.	.	.	.	.	.	.	249	169	133	82	96
25 SWITZERLAND	61	61	58	58	.	.	.	.	.	.	338	256	245	92	121
26 TURKEY	-	-	-	-	-	-	-	-	-	-	-	-	-	-	-
27 UK ENGLAND AND WALES	.	.	.	.	.	.	677	775	757	508	576	485	314	288	405
28 UK NORTHERN IRELAND	-	-	-	-	.	.	.	.	.	470	688	655	572	548	776
29 UK SCOTLAND	.	.	.	.	.	.	.	.	1238	814	589	600	544	372	535
30 USA	.	.	.	.	.	306	325	508	834	628	175	136	147	114	85
31 YUGOSLAVIA	-	-	-	-	-	-	-	-	-	-	.	.	81	87	52

- NO MORTALITY DATA ARE AVAILABLE FOR EVEN A BROADER GROUP OF CAUSES FOR THIS DISEASE
. MORTALITY DATA ARE PRESENTED FOR A BROADER GROUP OF CAUSES FOR THIS DISEASE
0 VALUE<0.5
THE MORTALITY RATES WERE DERIVED WITH A FACTOR OF 1000000

SERIAL MORTALITY TABLES FOR VARIOUS COUNTRIES 1901-1975

TABLE 147 : CONGENITAL MALFORMATIONS - SPINA BIFIDA AND MENINGOCELE : FEMALES

	1901-	1906-	1911-	1916-	1921-	1926-	1931-	1936-	1941-	1946-	1951-	1956-	1961-	1966-	1971-75
1 AUSTRALIA	-	.	.	.	.	.	.	.	202	188	254	254	212	161	242
2 AUSTRIA	.	.	.	.	-	-	-	-	-	.	358	296	226	110	80
3 BELGIUM	.	.	.	.	.	.	.	.	.	.	413	320	238	185	119
4 BULGARIA	-	-	-	-	-	.	.	.	.	.	.	.	250	230	167
5 CANADA	-	-	-	-	-	.	654	725	724	647	798	432	475	406	279
6 CHILE	.	.	.	.	.	.	.	8	46	33	72	90	71	138	138
7 CZECHOSLOVAKIA	-	-	-	.	.	.	177	235	.	.	193	215	211	147	88
8 DENMARK	-	-	-	-	300	251	-	-	-	-	296	316	259	145	79
9 EIRE	-	-	-	-	.	.	568	788	598	840	875	913	842	632	656
10 FINLAND	-	-	-	-	-	.	.	-	.	.	273	282	183	72	49
11 FRANCE	-	-	-	-	.	.	.	.	.	114	130	134	125	101	77
12 GREECE	-	-	-	-	-	.	.	.	-	-	-	84	97	86	28
13 HUNGARY	-	-	-	.	.	.	289	333	296	.	762	621	569	552	413
14 ICELAND	-	-	.	.	.	.	.	.	-	-	.	.	42	278	90
15 ITALY	-	-	-	-	-	-	348	385	341	409	468	373	270	144	102
16 JAPAN	-	.	.	.	.	.	.	.	-	70	56	46	34	35	33
17 NETHERLANDS	.	.	.	.	.	.	541	735	758	644	658	453	377	291	162
18 NEW ZEALAND	-	.	.	.	.	474	306	594	943	811	285	320	255	285	410
19 NORWAY	.	.	154	158	231	240	.	.	.	.	256	232	200	153	101
20 POLAND	-	-	-	-	-	-	-	-	-	-	-	245	373	264	127
21 PORTUGAL	-	-	-	-	-	-	-	-	-	-	180	184	219	221	84
22 ROMANIA	-	-	-	-	-	-	-	-	-	-	-	229	272	231	192
23 SPAIN	.	.	.	.	.	.	100	103	.	.	92	83	84	62	68
24 SWEDEN	-	-	.	.	.	.	.	.	.	.	326	245	149	76	104
25 SWITZERLAND	46	46	25	25	.	.	.	.	.	.	479	334	288	176	119
26 TURKEY	-	-	-	-	-	-	-	-	-	-	-	-	-	-	-
27 UK ENGLAND AND WALES	.	.	.	.	.	.	969	1085	1107	723	810	660	492	419	572
28 UK NORTHERN IRELAND	-	-	-	-	.	.	.	.	.	571	993	1028	837	773	804
29 UK SCOTLAND	.	.	.	.	.	.	.	.	1437	1097	950	766	713	604	752
30 USA	.	.	.	.	.	389	371	547	959	711	235	176	195	154	111
31 YUGOSLAVIA	-	-	-	-	-	-	-	-	-	-	.	.	119	105	77

- NO MORTALITY DATA ARE AVAILABLE FOR EVEN A BROADER GROUP OF CAUSES FOR THIS DISEASE
. MORTALITY DATA ARE PRESENTED FOR A BROADER GROUP OF CAUSES FOR THIS DISEASE
0 VALUE<0.5
THE MORTALITY RATES WERE DERIVED WITH A FACTOR OF 1000000

SERIAL MORTALITY TABLES FOR VARIOUS COUNTRIES 1901-1975

TABLE 148 : CONGENITAL MALFORMATIONS - "CARDIO-VASCULAR" : MALES

	1901-	1906-	1911-	1916-	1921-	1926-	1931-	1936-	1941-	1946-	1951-	1956-	1961-	1966-	1971-75
1 AUSTRALIA	-	.	.	.	.	.	.	.	11522	10696	10516	11013	10796	8922	7790
2 AUSTRIA	-	-	-	-	-	-	-	-	-	.	8495	10052	9731	9785	8739
3 BELGIUM	-	-	-	-	-	-	-	-	-	-	9482	10369	9419	8904	7660
4 BULGARIA	-	-	-	-	-	.	.	.	.	.	.	.	6125	5779	6986
5 CANADA	-	-	-	-	13615	14946	12288	12709	.	12869	11542	12587	11571	9213	8145
6 CHILE	-	.	.	.	.	.	.	100	62	255	12773	8071	7394	7267	8128
7 CZECHOSLOVAKIA	-	-	-	.	.	.	2497	3481	.	.	9231	9358	10769	10478	11899
8 DENMARK	-	-	-	-	-	-	.	.	.	.	.	.	.	.	.
9 EIRE	-	-	-	-	.	.	5903	8026	.	.	12231	12781	13377	11410	10436
10 FINLAND	-	-	-	-	-	-	-	.	.	.	5959	9789	10347	8385	8886
11 FRANCE	-	-	-	-	.	.	.	.	.	8302	7522	9216	10151	9113	8313
12 GREECE	-	-	-	-	.	.	.	.	-	-	-	6135	9032	10861	10596
13 HUNGARY	-	-	-	.	.	.	3660	4608	4246	.	14382	10758	11502	12904	11879
14 ICELAND	-	-	-	-	-	-	-	-	.	.	.	.	14089	7292	6859
15 ITALY	-	-	-	-	-	-	5189	7287	7534	9628	9867	10045	10476	9944	8885
16 JAPAN	.	.	.	.	.	.	.	.	-	5803	5135	5193	6197	7520	7670
17 NETHERLANDS	.	.	.	.	.	.	10552	11438	10948	10664	11015	11952	12316	10785	8674
18 NEW ZEALAND	-	.	.	.	.	15768	12307	17166	14965	13865	11162	12372	11658	10361	9251
19 NORWAY	.	.	.	.	.	.	.	.	.	.	7876	8897	10780	9293	8468
20 POLAND	-	-	-	-	-	-	-	-	-	-	.	7939	8684	9276	11151
21 PORTUGAL	.	.	-	-	-	-	.	.	.	.	.	.	.	.	.
22 ROMANIA	-	-	-	-	-	-	-	-	-	-	-	4928	6487	9129	7894
23 SPAIN	.	.	.	.	.	.	.	.	.	.	.	.	.	.	.
24 SWEDEN	-	-	-	-	-	-	.	.	.	.	.	.	.	.	.
25 SWITZERLAND	.	.	.	.	.	.	.	.	10648	11002	11089	11397	11874	10115	8529
26 TURKEY	-	-	-	-	-	-	-	-	-	-	-	169	384	473	28
27 UK ENGLAND AND WALES	.	.	8770	8646	8741	9313	10213	11329	13434	11873	10111	11614	12302	10495	9906
28 UK NORTHERN IRELAND	-	-	-	-	.	.	.	.	.	12785	11781	10814	11945	10875	9425
29 UK SCOTLAND	.	.	.	.	6886	8919	.	.	10354	10133	9347	10544	11022	11045	9002
30 USA	23234	23360	21141	20475	18067	15035	12413	11836	13767	13183	11132	11944	11037	9404	8321
31 YUGOSLAVIA	-	-	-	-	-	-	-	-	-	-	.	.	3981	5125	6029

- NO MORTALITY DATA ARE AVAILABLE FOR EVEN A BROADER GROUP OF CAUSES FOR THIS DISEASE

. MORTALITY DATA ARE PRESENTED FOR A BROADER GROUP OF CAUSES FOR THIS DISEASE

0 VALUE<0.5

THE STANDARD MORTALITY RATIOS WERE DERIVED WITH A FACTOR OF 10000

SERIAL MORTALITY TABLES FOR VARIOUS COUNTRIES 1901-1975

TABLE 148 : CONGENITAL MALFORMATIONS - "CARDIO-VASCULAR" : FEMALES

	1901-	1906-	1911-	1916-	1921-	1926-	1931-	1936-	1941-	1946-	1951-	1956-	1961-	1966-	1971-75
1 AUSTRALIA	-	.	.	.	.	.	.	.	11127	9183	8202	9445	9066	7872	6245
2 AUSTRIA	-	-	-	-	-	-	-	-	-	.	6317	8094	8227	7972	6889
3 BELGIUM	-	-	-	-	-	-	-	-	-	-	6076	8683	7801	6517	6120
4 BULGARIA	-	-	-	-	-	.	.	.	.	.	.	.	4392	4658	5483
5 CANADA	-	-	-	-	9692	11171	8822	9805	.	9924	9648	10260	9418	8223	6835
6 CHILE	-	.	.	.	.	.	.	50	138	128	10252	6785	6350	6366	7095
7 CZECHOSLOVAKIA	-	-	-	.	.	.	1615	2208	.	.	8347	8090	9548	8903	8755
8 DENMARK	-	-	-	-	-	-	.	.	.	.	.	.	.	.	.
9 EIRE	-	-	-	-	.	.	5130	6309	.	.	9739	9514	11782	9324	7979
10 FINLAND	-	-	-	-	-	-	-	.	.	.	5035	8424	8727	8015	7506
11 FRANCE	-	-	-	-	.	.	.	.	.	6232	6045	7552	7826	7594	6930
12 GREECE	-	-	-	-	.	.	.	.	-	-	-	4899	8221	8610	8453
13 HUNGARY	-	-	-	.	.	.	2762	3206	3271	.	10869	8281	9897	10375	9763
14 ICELAND	-	-	-	-	-	-	-	-	.	.	.	.	9747	5776	5618
15 ITALY	-	-	-	-	-	-	4134	5885	6183	7697	7926	8135	8804	8489	7614
16 JAPAN	.	.	.	.	.	.	.	.	-	5584	4563	4945	5915	6830	6869
17 NETHERLANDS	.	.	.	.	.	.	8279	9093	9031	8810	9612	10616	10993	8981	7667
18 NEW ZEALAND	-	.	.	.	.	8987	10870	13090	11950	13449	9035	10258	8955	8423	6825
19 NORWAY	.	.	.	.	.	.	.	.	.	.	7603	7999	9302	7268	7044
20 POLAND	-	-	-	-	-	-	-	-	-	-	.	6186	6802	7788	9350
21 PORTUGAL	.	.	-	-	-	-	.	.	.	.	.	.	.	.	.
22 ROMANIA	-	-	-	-	-	-	-	-	-	-	-	4308	5350	7629	6599
23 SPAIN	.	.	.	.	.	.	.	.	.	.	.	.	.	.	.
24 SWEDEN	-	-	-	-	-	-	.	.	.	.	.	.	.	.	.
25 SWITZERLAND	.	.	.	.	.	.	.	.	8816	8605	8463	9502	10005	8055	6651
26 TURKEY	-	-	-	-	-	-	-	-	-	-	-	64	380	548	16
27 UK ENGLAND AND WALES	.	.	6647	6476	6384	7175	7192	7911	10154	9860	8649	9572	10198	8775	8309
28 UK NORTHERN IRELAND	-	-	-	-	.	.	.	.	.	7973	9185	10948	10410	8663	9306
29 UK SCOTLAND	.	.	.	.	5382	5436	.	.	7878	7888	7931	9047	9894	8779	7873
30 USA	16581	17419	15437	14862	13323	11207	9466	9035	10511	10243	8852	9902	9126	7795	6887
31 YUGOSLAVIA	-	-	-	-	-	-	-	-	-	-	.	.	3114	4590	4743

- NO MORTALITY DATA ARE AVAILABLE FOR EVEN A BROADER GROUP OF CAUSES FOR THIS DISEASE

. MORTALITY DATA ARE PRESENTED FOR A BROADER GROUP OF CAUSES FOR THIS DISEASE

0 VALUE<0.5

THE STANDARD MORTALITY RATIO WERE DERIVED WITH A FACTOR OF 10000

SERIAL MORTALITY TABLES FOR VARIOUS COUNTRIES 1901-1975

TABLE 149 : CONGENITAL MALFORMATIONS - ALL FORMS : MALES

	1901-	1906-	1911-	1916-	1921-	1926-	1931-	1936-	1941-	1946-	1951-	1956-	1961-	1966-	1971-75
1 AUSTRALIA	-	6580	9069	9243	9961	10624	10051	10437	10125	9519	10463	10344	9569	8890	8429
2 AUSTRIA	-	-	-	-	-	-	-	-	-	8371	8088	10176	9566	9344	7942
3 BELGIUM	-	-	-	-	-	-	-	-	-	-	8835	11057	10014	9916	8431
4 BULGARIA	-	-	-	-	-	.	.	.	.	.	.	.	5976	6270	6734
5 CANADA	-	-	-	-	12812	12511	12035	12774	15854	14589	12806	12174	10734	9040	8528
6 CHILE	-	8166	18806	2049	7169	3680	1674	1971	2701	3580	6539	6381	6166	7353	9024
7 CZECHOSLOVAKIA	-	-	-	2220	2418	3162	3126	3321	7059	8467	8730	8500	9732	9298	9846
8 DENMARK	-	-	-	-	-	-	.	.	.	.	.	.	.	.	.
9 EIRE	-	-	-	-	4732	5801	7754	10826	17194	17738	13304	14183	15369	12612	11624
10 FINLAND	-	-	-	-	-	-	-	.	8471	8680	7112	9591	9331	7163	7850
11 FRANCE	-	-	-	-	.	.	.	.	4851	8163	7262	8343	8543	7605	6593
12 GREECE	-	-	-	-	.	6063	8886	7635	-	-	-	4915	7014	8716	8890
13 HUNGARY	-	-	-	1710	2168	2574	4370	5307	5251	7985	10957	11358	11720	13151	11958
14 ICELAND	-	-	-	-	-	-	-	-	.	.	7692	8531	10119	5900	7109
15 ITALY	-	-	-	-	-	-	5462	7237	7017	8578	8546	8478	8648	8024	7883
16 JAPAN	.	1447	1559	1919	2805	3855	4461	4966	-	5895	4645	4589	5200	5725	5709
17 NETHERLANDS	11362	5935	5852	6871	6632	9697	11046	12208	13034	12000	11426	11399	10666	9714	7498
18 NEW ZEALAND	-	6466	9652	10300	11688	11953	11402	14249	12714	12033	10900	11200	10244	9572	9152
19 NORWAY	708	433	1190	1148	1363	1844	1596	2146	4393	5709	8039	8520	9421	7812	7259
20 POLAND	-	-	-	-	-	-	-	-	-	-	.	9152	8823	9592	11244
21 PORTUGAL	.	.	-	-	-	-	.	.	.	.	.	.	.	.	.
22 ROMANIA	-	-	-	-	-	-	-	-	-	-	-	7353	6390	8901	7420
23 SPAIN	.	.	.	.	.	.	.	.	.	.	.	.	.	.	.
24 SWEDEN	-	-	-	-	-	-	.	.	.	.	.	.	.	.	.
25 SWITZERLAND	9084	9084	6736	6736	5321	5074	6385	7951	11843	11502	11013	11211	11449	9163	8917
26 TURKEY	-	-	-	-	-	-	-	-	-	-	-	947	1237	1239	527
27 UK ENGLAND AND WALES	12017	12854	9582	9458	9674	10538	11937	12999	15289	12792	10784	11770	11183	9472	9162
28 UK NORTHERN IRELAND	-	-	-	-	6885	9311	10704	13378	16975	12966	14265	13814	14156	12542	11082
29 UK SCOTLAND	10220	12307	10744	9543	10326	10651	11897	13079	14235	13440	11692	12691	13068	11121	9568
30 USA	18059	16575	14930	14424	13144	11500	10290	10142	11714	11695	10484	10270	9235	8202	7340
31 YUGOSLAVIA	-	-	-	-	-	-	-	-	-	-	2024	3390	4241	4905	5453

- NO MORTALITY DATA ARE AVAILABLE FOR EVEN A BROADER GROUP OF CAUSES FOR THIS DISEASE

. MORTALITY DATA ARE PRESENTED FOR A BROADER GROUP OF CAUSES FOR THIS DISEASE

0 VALUE<0.5

THE STANDARD MORTALITY RATIOS WERE DERIVED WITH A FACTOR OF 10000

SERIAL MORTALITY TABLES FOR VARIOUS COUNTRIES 1901-1975

TABLE 149 : CONGENITAL MALFORMATIONS - ALL FORMS : FEMALES

	1901-	1906-	1911-	1916-	1921-	1926-	1931-	1936-	1941-	1946-	1951-	1956-	1961-	1966-	1971-75
1 AUSTRALIA	-	5197	6926	7796	8152	8262	7839	8642	9514	8432	8669	9042	8330	7949	7924
2 AUSTRIA	-	-	-	-	-	-	-	-	-	6861	6744	8271	7879	7521	6404
3 BELGIUM	-	-	-	-	-	-	-	-	-	-	7230	9667	8781	7891	7077
4 BULGARIA	-	-	-	-	-	.	.	.	.	.	.	.	5335	5281	5905
5 CANADA	-	-	-	-	10526	10778	10112	11162	14073	12850	11994	11112	10013	8580	7607
6 CHILE	-	5882	16954	1915	6415	3420	1265	1545	2158	2678	5310	5312	5156	6517	7677
7 CZECHOSLOVAKIA	-	-	-	1592	2055	2638	2482	2604	5383	6973	7537	7588	8595	7894	7618
8 DENMARK	-	-	-	-	-	-	.	.	.	.	.	.	.	.	.
9 EIRE	-	-	-	-	4320	5530	6565	9133	13320	14209	12233	13798	15347	12335	11203
10 FINLAND	-	-	-	-	-	-	-	.	6400	7153	6202	8615	7939	7044	7222
11 FRANCE	-	-	-	-	.	.	.	.	3706	6194	5833	6703	6730	6425	5573
12 GREECE	-	-	-	-	.	6126	8247	7448	-	-	-	3901	5980	7197	7603
13 HUNGARY	-	-	-	1187	1587	1945	3834	4303	3991	6710	9653	9341	10419	11204	10576
14 ICELAND	-	-	-	-	-	-	-	-	.	.	8129	7692	6240	5956	5574
15 ITALY	-	-	-	-	-	-	4781	6345	6130	7332	7498	7404	7575	6896	6697
16 JAPAN	.	1242	1117	1388	2013	2704	3226	3790	-	4890	3731	3981	4552	4925	5000
17 NETHERLANDS	9349	5162	5064	5264	5732	7830	10187	10953	11432	11216	11375	10960	10180	8539	6740
18 NEW ZEALAND	-	3476	8231	8300	9258	9132	9789	11732	10463	11819	8861	9539	8625	8628	9031
19 NORWAY	405	403	1078	954	1314	1634	1370	1990	3786	4098	7026	7730	8097	6704	6170
20 POLAND	-	-	-	-	-	-	-	-	-	-	.	7857	7796	8398	9787
21 PORTUGAL	.	.	-	-	-	-	.	.	.	.	.	.	.	.	.
22 ROMANIA	-	-	-	-	-	-	-	-	-	-	-	6780	5428	7727	6274
23 SPAIN	.	.	.	.	.	.	.	.	.	.	.	.	.	.	.
24 SWEDEN	-	-	-	-	-	-	.	.	.	.	.	.	.	.	.
25 SWITZERLAND	6523	6523	4783	4783	3914	4244	5533	6536	9208	10130	9702	9603	9888	8158	7078
26 TURKEY	-	-	-	-	-	-	-	-	-	-	-	922	1332	1360	539
27 UK ENGLAND AND WALES	9027	9888	7505	7583	7603	8368	9456	10575	12519	10856	9864	10766	10257	8547	8552
28 UK NORTHERN IRELAND	-	-	-	-	6674	7716	9041	13635	14360	11318	13883	16098	14403	13164	11708
29 UK SCOTLAND	8155	10247	9033	8132	8449	8268	9269	11010	11575	11150	11369	12145	12244	10268	9617
30 USA	13638	12990	11617	11249	10302	9358	8592	8459	9964	9884	8991	8790	8071	7211	6407
31 YUGOSLAVIA	-	-	-	-	-	-	-	-	-	-	1705	2828	3559	4441	4646

- NO MORTALITY DATA ARE AVAILABLE FOR EVEN A BROADER GROUP OF CAUSES FOR THIS DISEASE

. MORTALITY DATA ARE PRESENTED FOR A BROADER GROUP OF CAUSES FOR THIS DISEASE

0 VALUE<0.5

THE STANDARD MORTALITY RATIO WERE DERIVED WITH A FACTOR OF 10000

SERIAL MORTALITY TABLES FOR VARIOUS COUNTRIES 1901-1975

TABLE 150 : NEWBORN - BIRTH INJURIES : MALES

	1901-	1906-	1911-	1916-	1921-	1926-	1931-	1936-	1941-	1946-	1951-	1956-	1961-	1966-	1971-75
1 AUSTRALIA	-	.	.	.	.	1642	1900	2407	2237	2060	1866	1803	1575	958	496
2 AUSTRIA	.	.	.	.	-	-	-	-	-	2677	2845	2904	2620	2329	2317
3 BELGIUM	.	.	.	.	.	.	.	.	.	.	1635	1736	1365	1101	675
4 BULGARIA	-	-	-	-	-	.	.	.	.	.	.	.	2164	2309	2043
5 CANADA	-	-	-	-	-	2662	2838	2497	2763	2539	2129	1854	1567	968	403
6 CHILE	-	.	.	.	.	.	2565	3605	2073	1684	1997	1862	1803	1623	1195
7 CZECHOSLOVAKIA	-	-	-	.	.	.	.	.	3854	4539	2715	2291	1750	1355	780
8 DENMARK	-	-	-	-	.	.	1786	1789	1390	1573	1998	1542	1506	1059	974
9 EIRE	-	-	-	-	.	.	551	721	.	.	1925	1882	1335	648	597
10 FINLAND	-	-	-	-	-	.	.	-	1312	1677	1621	1373	1398	1018	556
11 FRANCE	-	-	-	-	.	.	.	.	315	918	1329	1469	1415	986	455
12 GREECE	-	-	-	-	-	.	222	198	-	-	-	389	802	615	575
13 HUNGARY	-	-	-	.	.	.	534	791	857	1226	3153	4588	5309	5788	4963
14 ICELAND	-	-	.	.	.	.	.	.	-	-	.	.	932	974	718
15 ITALY	-	-	-	-	-	-	.	.	.	.	1490	1826	1609	1207	623
16 JAPAN	-	.	.	.	.	.	115	108	-	341	425	590	670	545	382
17 NETHERLANDS	.	.	.	.	.	.	1984	2047	2195	2531	2910	2258	1772	1232	790
18 NEW ZEALAND	-	.	.	.	.	1495	1764	1940	1745	2039	1874	1704	1192	765	515
19 NORWAY	179	128	.	.	.	.	.	.	803	1043	1303	1469	1135	768	494
20 POLAND	-	-	-	-	-	-	-	-	-	-	-	1232	1874	1772	1929
21 PORTUGAL	-	-	-	-	-	-	-	-	-	-	1123	1086	1336	1536	918
22 ROMANIA	-	-	-	-	-	-	-	-	-	-	-	752	2275	3950	628
23 SPAIN	.	.	.	.	.	.	20	17	188	286	305	411	470	385	420
24 SWEDEN	-	-	.	.	.	.	.	.	.	.	1777	1596	1270	1079	802
25 SWITZERLAND	2375	2375	2830	2830	2479	2565	2420	3061	2316	.	1882	1401	1016	569	164
26 TURKEY	-	-	-	-	-	-	-	-	-	-	-	-	-	-	-
27 UK ENGLAND AND WALES	440	574	677	696	867	1045	1368	1639	1537	1669	1749	1560	1405	941	623
28 UK NORTHERN IRELAND	-	-	-	-	.	.	783	1065	1399	1465	1465	1140	1192	742	347
29 UK SCOTLAND	514	738	.	.	385	817	1281	1999	1928	1838	1756	1727	1615	1264	1242
30 USA	2198	2212	2598	2439	2876	3098	5354	5063	2378	2132	1820	1556	1321	742	423
31 YUGOSLAVIA	-	-	-	-	-	-	-	-	-	-	.	.	1330	1514	1306

\- NO MORTALITY DATA ARE AVAILABLE FOR EVEN A BROADER GROUP OF CAUSES FOR THIS DISEASE

. MORTALITY DATA ARE PRESENTED FOR A BROADER GROUP OF CAUSES FOR THIS DISEASE

0 VALUE<0.5

THE MORTALITY RATES WERE DERIVED WITH A FACTOR OF 1000000

SERIAL MORTALITY TABLES FOR VARIOUS COUNTRIES 1901-1975

TABLE 150 : NEWBORN - BIRTH INJURIES : FEMALES

	1901-	1906-	1911-	1916-	1921-	1926-	1931-	1936-	1941-	1946-	1951-	1956-	1961-	1966-	1971-75
1 AUSTRALIA	-	.	.	.	.	1049	1227	1491	1446	1357	1175	1201	1069	601	269
2 AUSTRIA	.	.	.	.	-	-	-	-	-	1665	1738	1775	1620	1392	1469
3 BELGIUM	.	.	.	.	.	.	.	.	.	.	860	1005	763	649	446
4 BULGARIA	-	-	-	-	-	.	.	.	.	.	.	.	1218	1386	1154
5 CANADA	-	-	-	-	-	1735	1678	1531	1662	1608	1343	1179	1062	657	258
6 CHILE	-	.	.	.	.	.	2168	3048	1578	1203	1419	1249	1249	1010	811
7 CZECHOSLOVAKIA	-	-	-	.	.	.	.	.	2892	3371	1686	1309	1013	836	448
8 DENMARK	-	-	-	-	.	.	925	1116	748	858	1112	897	759	598	647
9 EIRE	-	-	-	-	.	.	338	572	.	.	1104	1121	797	559	297
10 FINLAND	-	-	-	-	-	.	.	-	787	1047	948	942	839	627	360
11 FRANCE	-	-	-	-	.	.	.	.	189	591	827	946	880	582	284
12 GREECE	-	-	-	-	-	.	182	138	-	-	-	249	458	319	360
13 HUNGARY	-	-	-	.	.	.	307	475	487	720	1927	2829	3418	3959	3262
14 ICELAND	-	-	.	.	.	.	.	.	-	-	.	.	381	371	224
15 ITALY	-	-	-	-	-	-	.	.	.	.	936	1064	993	694	363
16 JAPAN	-	.	.	.	.	.	72	92	-	240	284	400	429	340	249
17 NETHERLANDS	.	.	.	.	.	.	1222	1266	1333	1494	1663	1341	976	721	441
18 NEW ZEALAND	-	.	.	.	.	766	983	1203	1179	1164	1062	1072	865	441	301
19 NORWAY	142	111	.	.	.	.	.	.	467	690	896	689	694	543	299
20 POLAND	-	-	-	-	-	-	-	-	-	-	-	730	1101	994	1066
21 PORTUGAL	-	-	-	-	-	-	-	-	-	-	822	735	885	1006	588
22 ROMANIA	-	-	-	-	-	-	-	-	-	-	-	486	1355	2537	387
23 SPAIN	.	.	.	.	.	.	15	11	147	200	188	232	252	246	257
24 SWEDEN	-	-	.	.	.	.	.	.	.	.	1072	936	894	728	478
25 SWITZERLAND	1435	1435	1816	1816	1619	1620	1583	1867	1789	.	1197	885	619	399	121
26 TURKEY	-	-	-	-	-	-	-	-	-	-	-	-	-	-	-
27 UK ENGLAND AND WALES	289	388	452	438	530	658	810	963	952	982	1017	937	858	564	367
28 UK NORTHERN IRELAND	-	-	-	-	.	.	439	658	825	907	778	766	722	341	229
29 UK SCOTLAND	308	543	.	.	244	541	905	1242	1258	1099	1024	975	976	815	683
30 USA	1367	1395	1582	1529	1771	1921	3838	3635	1487	1332	1152	1024	871	481	280
31 YUGOSLAVIA	-	-	-	-	-	-	-	-	-	-	.	.	830	875	760

- NO MORTALITY DATA ARE AVAILABLE FOR EVEN A BROADER GROUP OF CAUSES FOR THIS DISEASE

. MORTALITY DATA ARE PRESENTED FOR A BROADER GROUP OF CAUSES FOR THIS DISEASE

0 VALUE<0.5

THE MORTALITY RATES WERE DERIVED WITH A FACTOR OF 1000000

SERIAL MORTALITY TABLES FOR VARIOUS COUNTRIES 1901-1975

TABLE 151 : NEWBORN - POSTNATAL ASPHYXIA AND ATELECTASIS : MALES

	1901-	1906-	1911-	1916-	1921-	1926-	1931-	1936-	1941-	1946-	1951-	1956-	1961-	1966-	1971-75
1 AUSTRALIA	-	.	.	.	.	.	1142	1068	990	828	1499	1325	1449	1423	1046
2 AUSTRIA	.	.	.	.	-	-	-	-	-	.	1113	771	871	1185	2008
3 BELGIUM	.	.	.	.	.	.	.	.	.	.	922	1008	758	1010	982
4 BULGARIA	-	-	-	-	-	.	.	.	.	.	.	.	802	1052	1747
5 CANADA	-	-	-	-	-	.	399	489	727	958	2001	2062	1787	1834	1925
6 CHILE	-	.	.	.	.	.	.	2841	2395	1803	1724	1435	2010	3138	4570
7 CZECHOSLOVAKIA	-	-	-	.	.	.	.	.	.	.	1205	1711	2789	3058	2820
8 DENMARK	-	-	-	-	.	.	.	.	.	.	2283	2753	2826	2459	1780
9 EIRE	-	-	-	-	.	.	641	730	.	.	1779	2083	1821	2064	2442
10 FINLAND	-	-	-	-	-	.	.	-	.	.	1003	1740	2738	2133	1602
11 FRANCE	-	-	-	-	.	.	.	.	.	225	294	426	567	1183	1619
12 GREECE	-	-	-	-	-	.	.	.	-	-	-	473	1849	2465	3092
13 HUNGARY	-	-	-	.	.	.	357	466	316	.	831	866	1295	2024	3869
14 ICELAND	-	-	.	.	.	.	.	.	-	-	.	.	1737	1113	1930
15 ITALY	-	-	-	-	-	-	.	.	.	.	1280	1546	2226	2421	3121
16 JAPAN	-	.	.	.	.	.	.	.	-	235	178	196	372	662	723
17 NETHERLANDS	.	.	.	.	.	.	.	.	.	443	592	645	749	1086	1402
18 NEW ZEALAND	-	.	.	.	.	.	.	.	.	1794	1848	1544	1400	1449	1123
19 NORWAY	77	39	.	.	.	.	.	.	.	.	803	1114	1363	1325	705
20 POLAND	-	-	-	-	-	-	-	-	-	-	-	654	1278	1630	1896
21 PORTUGAL	-	-	-	-	-	-	-	-	-	-	564	723	1274	1675	1541
22 ROMANIA	-	-	-	-	-	-	-	-	-	-	-	553	600	2585	3311
23 SPAIN	.	.	.	.	.	.	213	115	.	.	282	225	244	289	564
24 SWEDEN	-	-	.	.	.	.	.	.	.	.	1352	1840	1693	1418	1406
25 SWITZERLAND	.	.	.	.	.	.	.	.	.	.	2565	2516	2517	2048	2071
26 TURKEY	-	-	-	-	-	-	-	-	-	-	-	-	-	-	-
27 UK ENGLAND AND WALES	809	963	1011	918	890	827	1025	1201	1253	1806	2199	2178	1825	1867	2095
28 UK NORTHERN IRELAND	-	-	-	-	.	.	.	.	.	2049	3021	2580	2841	2848	2440
29 UK SCOTLAND	776	912	.	.	.	.	.	.	.	2104	2734	3286	2977	2085	2348
30 USA	.	.	.	.	.	.	.	.	.	2260	2526	2713	2571	2857	2796
31 YUGOSLAVIA	-	-	-	-	-	-	-	-	-	-	.	.	1113	1188	1348

- NO MORTALITY DATA ARE AVAILABLE FOR EVEN A BROADER GROUP OF CAUSES FOR THIS DISEASE

. MORTALITY DATA ARE PRESENTED FOR A BROADER GROUP OF CAUSES FOR THIS DISEASE

0 VALUE<0.5

THE MORTALITY RATES WERE DERIVED WITH A FACTOR OF 1000000

SERIAL MORTALITY TABLES FOR VARIOUS COUNTRIES 1901-1975

TABLE 151 : NEWBORN - POSTNATAL ASPHYXIA AND ATELECTASIS : FEMALES

	1901-	1906-	1911-	1916-	1921-	1926-	1931-	1936-	1941-	1946-	1951-	1956-	1961-	1966-	1971-75
1 AUSTRALIA	-	.	.	.	.	.	809	769	730	594	1104	977	980	922	677
2 AUSTRIA	.	.	.	.	-	-	-	-	-	.	611	521	604	732	1389
3 BELGIUM	.	.	.	.	.	.	.	.	.	.	587	677	545	671	580
4 BULGARIA	-	-	-	-	-	.	.	.	.	.	.	.	499	751	1121
5 CANADA	-	-	-	-	-	.	272	298	519	664	1309	1328	1141	1189	1261
6 CHILE	-	.	.	.	.	.	.	2565	1970	1439	1375	1067	1600	2348	3282
7 CZECHOSLOVAKIA	-	-	-	.	.	.	.	.	.	.	872	1115	1868	1881	1671
8 DENMARK	-	-	-	-	.	.	.	.	.	.	1574	1792	1888	1625	1111
9 EIRE	-	-	-	-	.	.	533	576	.	.	1267	1316	1277	1300	1295
10 FINLAND	-	-	-	-	-	.	.	-	.	.	655	1276	1765	1401	935
11 FRANCE	-	-	-	-	.	.	.	.	.	187	209	291	402	766	1077
12 GREECE	-	-	-	-	-	.	.	.	-	-	-	346	1170	1452	2074
13 HUNGARY	-	-	-	.	.	.	244	300	236	.	570	596	901	1453	2880
14 ICELAND	-	-	.	.	.	.	.	.	-	-	.	.	1525	881	1167
15 ITALY	-	-	-	-	-	-	.	.	.	.	885	1117	1545	1710	2091
16 JAPAN	-	.	.	.	.	.	.	.	-	182	131	145	252	422	457
17 NETHERLANDS	.	.	.	.	.	.	.	.	.	277	429	431	520	718	930
18 NEW ZEALAND	-	.	.	.	.	.	.	.	.	1452	1305	1168	972	960	691
19 NORWAY	49	29	.	.	.	.	.	.	.	.	560	778	875	816	442
20 POLAND	-	-	-	-	-	-	-	-	-	-	-	487	885	1107	1221
21 PORTUGAL	-	-	-	-	-	-	-	-	-	-	472	558	896	1203	1024
22 ROMANIA	-	-	-	-	-	-	-	-	-	-	-	414	396	1590	2031
23 SPAIN	.	.	.	.	.	.	165	91	.	.	198	141	147	195	356
24 SWEDEN	-	-	.	.	.	.	.	.	.	.	984	1272	1170	902	833
25 SWITZERLAND	.	.	.	.	.	.	.	.	.	.	2009	1795	1707	1397	1297
26 TURKEY	-	-	-	-	-	-	-	-	-	-	-	-	-	-	-
27 UK ENGLAND AND WALES	581	702	692	652	672	587	692	866	886	1224	1441	1428	1194	1198	1274
28 UK NORTHERN IRELAND	-	-	-	-	.	.	.	.	.	1545	2153	1683	1854	1607	1560
29 UK SCOTLAND	573	712	.	.	.	.	.	.	.	1265	1841	2072	1693	1410	1419
30 USA	.	.	.	.	.	.	.	.	.	1482	1682	1849	1753	1907	1864
31 YUGOSLAVIA	-	-	-	-	-	-	-	-	-	-	.	.	758	821	933

- NO MORTALITY DATA ARE AVAILABLE FOR EVEN A BROADER GROUP OF CAUSES FOR THIS DISEASE

. MORTALITY DATA ARE PRESENTED FOR A BROADER GROUP OF CAUSES FOR THIS DISEASE

0 VALUE<0.5

THE MORTALITY RATES WERE DERIVED WITH A FACTOR OF 1000000

SERIAL MORTALITY TABLES FOR VARIOUS COUNTRIES 1901-1975

TABLE 152 : NEWBORN - BIRTH INJURIES,POSTNATAL ASPHYXIA AND ATELECTASIS : MALES

	1901-	1906-	1911-	1916-	1921-	1926-	1931-	1936-	1941-	1946-	1951-	1956-	1961-	1966-	1971-75
1 AUSTRALIA	-	.	.	.	.	.	3042	3475	3227	2888	3365	3128	3024	2381	1542
2 AUSTRIA	.	.	.	.	-	-	-	-	-	.	4052	3675	3491	3514	4325
3 BELGIUM	.	.	.	.	.	.	.	.	.	.	2557	2744	2123	2111	1657
4 BULGARIA	-	-	-	-	-	.	.	.	.	.	.	.	2972	3361	3790
5 CANADA	-	-	-	-	-	.	3236	2986	3489	3496	4130	3916	3354	2802	2328
6 CHILE	-	.	.	.	.	.	.	6047	4468	3487	3404	3297	3812	4762	5765
7 CZECHOSLOVAKIA	-	-	-	.	.	.	.	.	.	3546	3792	4002	4540	4413	3600
8 DENMARK	-	-	-	-	.	.	.	.	.	.	4281	4295	4332	3517	2754
9 EIRE	-	-	-	-	.	.	1192	1451	.	.	3704	3965	3156	2712	3040
10 FINLAND	-	-	-	-	-	.	.	-	.	.	2623	3113	4136	3151	2157
11 FRANCE	-	-	-	-	.	.	.	.	.	1224	1623	1895	1982	2169	2074
12 GREECE	-	-	-	-	-	.	.	.	-	-	-	862	2651	3081	3667
13 HUNGARY	-	-	-	.	.	.	891	1257	1173	.	4960	5454	6604	7812	8832
14 ICELAND	-	-	.	.	.	.	.	.	-	-	1422	1985	2669	2087	2648
15 ITALY	-	-	-	-	-	-	.	.	.	.	2770	3372	3835	3629	3744
16 JAPAN	-	.	.	.	.	.	.	.	-	576	603	786	1042	1208	1105
17 NETHERLANDS	.	.	.	.	.	.	.	.	.	3189	3502	2904	2522	2318	2192
18 NEW ZEALAND	-	.	.	.	.	.	.	.	.	4036	3722	3249	2592	2215	1639
19 NORWAY	.	.	.	.	.	.	.	.	.	.	2106	2583	2497	2093	1200
20 POLAND	-	-	-	-	-	-	-	-	-	-	-	1886	3152	3402	3825
21 PORTUGAL	-	-	-	-	-	-	-	-	-	-	1471	1809	2610	3211	2459
22 ROMANIA	-	-	-	-	-	-	-	-	-	-	-	1305	2875	6535	3938
23 SPAIN	.	.	.	.	.	.	332	207	.	.	587	636	714	675	984
24 SWEDEN	-	-	.	.	.	.	.	.	.	.	3129	3436	2962	2497	2208
25 SWITZERLAND	.	.	.	.	.	.	.	.	.	.	4447	3917	3533	2616	2236
26 TURKEY	-	-	-	-	-	-	-	-	-	-	-	-	-	-	-
27 UK ENGLAND AND WALES	1249	1537	1688	1614	1756	1872	2392	2840	2790	3475	3947	3738	3230	2808	2718
28 UK NORTHERN IRELAND	-	-	-	-	.	.	.	.	.	3595	4486	3720	4033	3590	2787
29 UK SCOTLAND	1290	1650	.	.	.	.	.	.	.	4070	4490	5013	4593	3349	3590
30 USA	.	.	.	.	.	.	.	.	.	4320	4346	4269	3893	3599	3219
31 YUGOSLAVIA	-	-	-	-	-	-	-	-	-	-	.	1928	2443	2702	2654

- NO MORTALITY DATA ARE AVAILABLE FOR EVEN A BROADER GROUP OF CAUSES FOR THIS DISEASE

. MORTALITY DATA ARE PRESENTED FOR A BROADER GROUP OF CAUSES FOR THIS DISEASE

0 VALUE<0.5

THE MORTALITY RATES WERE DERIVED WITH A FACTOR OF 1000000

SERIAL MORTALITY TABLES FOR VARIOUS COUNTRIES 1901-1975

TABLE 152 : NEWBORN - BIRTH INJURIES,POSTNATAL ASPHYXIA AND ATELECTASIS : FEMALES

	1901-	1906-	1911-	1916-	1921-	1926-	1931-	1936-	1941-	1946-	1951-	1956-	1961-	1966-	1971-75
1 AUSTRALIA	-	.	.	.	.	.	2036	2260	2176	1951	2279	2178	2048	1524	946
2 AUSTRIA	.	.	.	.	-	-	-	-	-	.	2465	2296	2225	2124	2858
3 BELGIUM	.	.	.	.	.	.	.	.	.	.	1448	1682	1308	1320	1027
4 BULGARIA	-	-	-	-	-	.	.	.	.	.	.	.	1693	2137	2276
5 CANADA	-	-	-	-	-	.	1950	1829	2181	2272	2652	2507	2203	1846	1519
6 CHILE	-	.	.	.	.	.	.	5419	3548	2642	2486	2316	2849	3358	4093
7 CZECHOSLOVAKIA	-	-	-	.	.	.	.	.	.	2221	2713	2424	2881	2717	2118
8 DENMARK	-	-	-	-	.	.	.	.	.	.	2686	2689	2647	2223	1758
9 EIRE	-	-	-	-	.	.	872	1148	.	.	2371	2437	2074	1859	1592
10 FINLAND	-	-	-	-	-	.	.	-	.	.	1603	2218	2604	2028	1294
11 FRANCE	-	-	-	-	.	.	.	.	.	827	1037	1238	1282	1347	1361
12 GREECE	-	-	-	-	-	.	.	.	-	-	-	595	1628	1771	2434
13 HUNGARY	-	-	-	.	.	.	551	776	723	.	3067	3425	4319	5412	6142
14 ICELAND	-	-	.	.	.	.	.	.	-	-	1422	1013	1907	1252	1391
15 ITALY	-	-	-	-	-	-	.	.	.	.	1821	2182	2538	2404	2455
16 JAPAN	-	.	.	.	.	.	.	.	-	422	415	544	681	763	706
17 NETHERLANDS	.	.	.	.	.	.	.	.	.	1822	2092	1772	1496	1439	1371
18 NEW ZEALAND	-	.	.	.	.	.	.	.	.	2904	2368	2240	1837	1401	991
19 NORWAY	.	.	.	.	.	.	.	.	.	.	1457	1466	1569	1358	741
20 POLAND	-	-	-	-	-	-	-	-	-	-	-	1218	1986	2101	2287
21 PORTUGAL	-	-	-	-	-	-	-	-	-	-	1082	1293	1780	2209	1612
22 ROMANIA	-	-	-	-	-	-	-	-	-	-	-	900	1751	4127	2418
23 SPAIN	.	.	.	.	.	.	241	156	.	.	387	373	400	441	613
24 SWEDEN	-	-	.	.	.	.	.	.	.	.	2056	2208	2064	1630	1311
25 SWITZERLAND	.	.	.	.	.	.	.	.	.	.	3207	2680	2326	1796	1418
26 TURKEY	-	-	-	-	-	-	-	-	-	-	-	-	-	-	-
27 UK ENGLAND AND WALES	870	1089	1144	1089	1203	1246	1502	1829	1839	2205	2458	2365	2052	1762	1641
28 UK NORTHERN IRELAND	-	-	-	-	.	.	.	.	.	2553	2931	2449	2576	1947	1789
29 UK SCOTLAND	881	1254	.	.	.	.	.	.	.	2322	2865	3047	2669	2225	2102
30 USA	.	.	.	.	.	.	.	.	.	2789	2834	2873	2624	2388	2144
31 YUGOSLAVIA	-	-	-	-	-	-	-	-	-	-	.	1195	1589	1695	1692

- NO MORTALITY DATA ARE AVAILABLE FOR EVEN A BROADER GROUP OF CAUSES FOR THIS DISEASE

. MORTALITY DATA ARE PRESENTED FOR A BROADER GROUP OF CAUSES FOR THIS DISEASE

0 VALUE<0.5

THE MORTALITY RATES WERE DERIVED WITH A FACTOR OF 1000000

SERIAL MORTALITY TABLES FOR VARIOUS COUNTRIES 1901-1975

TABLE 153 : NEWBORN - INFECTIONS : MALES

	1901-	1906-	1911-	1916-	1921-	1926-	1931-	1936-	1941-	1946-	1951-	1956-	1961-	1966-	1971-75
1 AUSTRALIA	-	.	.	.	.	.	.	.	45	30	570	427	369	352	.
2 AUSTRIA	.	.	.	.	-	-	-	-	-	.	1474	1449	939	725	.
3 BELGIUM	.	.	.	.	.	.	.	.	.	.	901	599	535	619	.
4 BULGARIA	-	-	-	-	-	.	.	.	.	.	.	.	3532	3089	.
5 CANADA	-	-	-	-	-	.	.	.	.	1185	977	840	595	459	.
6 CHILE	-	.	.	.	.	.	.	207	352	327	6288	6194	7039	7094	.
7 CZECHOSLOVAKIA	-	-	-	.	.	.	.	.	.	3575	2453	1674	1356	1151	.
8 DENMARK	-	-	-	-	.	.	.	.	.	.	161	218	163	198	.
9 EIRE	-	-	-	-	.	.	.	.	.	.	1117	1634	1194	811	.
10 FINLAND	-	-	-	-	-	.	.	-	.	.	1206	755	433	370	.
11 FRANCE	-	-	-	-	.	.	.	.	.	1052	639	351	271	251	.
12 GREECE	-	-	-	-	-	.	.	.	-	-	-	1751	2283	2658	.
13 HUNGARY	-	-	-	.	.	.	.	.	.	.	3136	2957	2241	1645	.
14 ICELAND	-	-	.	.	.	-	.	.	-	-	569	211	212	232	.
15 ITALY	-	-	-	-	-	-	.	.	.	.	2402	2369	1949	1706	.
16 JAPAN	-	.	.	.	.	.	.	.	-	1989	2065	1946	1177	576	.
17 NETHERLANDS	.	.	.	.	.	.	.	.	.	383	450	411	394	347	.
18 NEW ZEALAND	-	.	.	.	.	.	.	.	.	384	444	579	399	381	.
19 NORWAY	.	.	.	.	.	.	.	.	.	.	275	381	297	270	.
20 POLAND	-	-	-	-	-	-	-	-	-	-	-	2741	2661	1693	.
21 PORTUGAL	-	-	-	-	-	-	-	-	-	-	2585	3521	3609	3237	.
22 ROMANIA	-	-	-	-	-	-	-	-	-	-	-	4391	4190	3632	.
23 SPAIN	.	.	.	.	.	.	.	.	.	.	1490	1331	1239	1138	.
24 SWEDEN	-	-	.	.	.	.	.	.	.	.	271	237	209	249	.
25 SWITZERLAND	.	.	.	.	.	.	.	.	.	.	699	710	359	340	.
26 TURKEY	-	-	-	-	-	-	-	-	-	-	-	-	-	-	-
27 UK ENGLAND AND WALES	.	.	.	.	.	.	139	128	125	219	879	716	554	459	.
28 UK NORTHERN IRELAND	-	-	-	-	.	.	.	.	.	1075	820	864	542	593	.
29 UK SCOTLAND	.	.	.	.	.	.	.	.	.	1106	1049	821	592	650	.
30 USA	.	.	.	.	.	.	.	.	.	626	621	692	632	540	.
31 YUGOSLAVIA	-	-	-	-	-	-	-	-	-	-	.	4999	3367	1817	.

- NO MORTALITY DATA ARE AVAILABLE FOR EVEN A BROADER GROUP OF CAUSES FOR THIS DISEASE

. MORTALITY DATA ARE PRESENTED FOR A BROADER GROUP OF CAUSES FOR THIS DISEASE

0 VALUE<0.5

THE MORTALITY RATES WERE DERIVED WITH A FACTOR OF 1000000

SERIAL MORTALITY TABLES FOR VARIOUS COUNTRIES 1901-1975

TABLE 153 : NEWBORN - INFECTIONS : FEMALES

	1901-	1906-	1911-	1916-	1921-	1926-	1931-	1936-	1941-	1946-	1951-	1956-	1961-	1966-	1971-75
1 AUSTRALIA	-	.	.	.	.	.	.	.	46	20	396	313	269	227	.
2 AUSTRIA	.	.	.	.	-	-	-	-	-	.	1017	1083	653	484	.
3 BELGIUM	.	.	.	.	.	.	.	.	.	.	649	390	342	470	.
4 BULGARIA	-	-	-	-	-	.	.	.	.	.	.	.	2733	2366	.
5 CANADA	-	-	-	-	-	.	.	.	.	880	689	619	411	321	.
6 CHILE	-	.	.	.	.	.	.	201	278	256	5180	4870	5668	5807	.
7 CZECHOSLOVAKIA	-	-	-	.	.	.	.	.	.	2774	1754	1135	903	793	.
8 DENMARK	-	-	-	-	.	.	.	.	.	.	166	191	121	95	.
9 EIRE	-	-	-	-	.	.	.	.	.	.	812	1098	688	666	.
10 FINLAND	-	-	-	-	-	.	.	-	.	.	874	462	319	310	.
11 FRANCE	-	-	-	-	.	.	.	.	.	819	503	271	188	188	.
12 GREECE	-	-	-	-	-	.	.	.	-	-	-	1557	1948	2176	.
13 HUNGARY	-	-	-	.	.	.	.	.	.	.	2291	2171	1578	1194	.
14 ICELAND	-	-	.	.	.	.	.	.	-	-	237	169	212	46	.
15 ITALY	-	-	-	-	-	-	.	.	.	.	1801	1831	1482	1370	.
16 JAPAN	-	.	.	.	.	.	.	.	-	1667	1740	1585	972	458	.
17 NETHERLANDS	.	.	.	.	.	.	.	.	.	265	286	248	259	202	.
18 NEW ZEALAND	-	.	.	.	.	.	.	.	.	320	300	379	258	243	.
19 NORWAY	.	.	.	.	.	.	.	.	.	.	227	213	234	140	.
20 POLAND	-	-	-	-	-	-	-	-	-	-	-	2028	1900	1205	.
21 PORTUGAL	-	-	-	-	-	-	-	-	-	-	1927	2690	2786	2347	.
22 ROMANIA	-	-	-	-	-	-	-	-	-	-	-	3370	3338	2855	.
23 SPAIN	.	.	.	.	.	.	.	.	.	.	1073	960	986	848	.
24 SWEDEN	-	-	.	.	.	.	.	.	.	.	216	138	188	127	.
25 SWITZERLAND	.	.	.	.	.	.	.	.	.	.	503	490	232	274	.
26 TURKEY	-	-	-	-	-	-	-	-	-	-	-	-	-	-	-
27 UK ENGLAND AND WALES	.	.	.	.	.	.	101	98	91	138	579	462	373	351	.
28 UK NORTHERN IRELAND	-	-	-	-	.	.	.	.	.	672	590	589	397	335	.
29 UK SCOTLAND	.	.	.	.	.	.	.	.	.	820	646	511	401	387	.
30 USA	.	.	.	.	.	.	.	.	.	465	441	492	448	408	.
31 YUGOSLAVIA	-	-	-	-	-	-	-	-	-	-	.	4271	2935	1599	.

\- NO MORTALITY DATA ARE AVAILABLE FOR EVEN A BROADER GROUP OF CAUSES FOR THIS DISEASE

. MORTALITY DATA ARE PRESENTED FOR A BROADER GROUP OF CAUSES FOR THIS DISEASE

0 VALUE<0.5

THE MORTALITY RATES WERE DERIVED WITH A FACTOR OF 1000000

SERIAL MORTALITY TABLES FOR VARIOUS COUNTRIES 1901-1975

TABLE 154 : NEWBORN - HAEMOLYTIC DISEASE : MALES

	1901-	1906-	1911-	1916-	1921-	1926-	1931-	1936-	1941-	1946-	1951-	1956-	1961-	1966-	1971-75
1 AUSTRALIA	-	.	.	.	.	.	383	326	306	187	461	311	266	220	128
2 AUSTRIA	.	.	.	.	-	-	-	-	-	.	454	453	336	247	114
3 BELGIUM	.	.	.	.	.	.	.	.	.	.	355	294	196	166	71
4 BULGARIA	-	-	-	-	-	.	.	.	.	.	.	.	144	142	83
5 CANADA	-	-	-	-	-	.	528	459	.	542	517	447	349	215	70
6 CHILE	-	.	.	.	.	.	.	74	384	1275	327	377	382	415	282
7 CZECHOSLOVAKIA	-	-	-	.	.	.	.	.	.	.	229	158	121	85	98
8 DENMARK	-	-	-	-	204	295	.	.	.	.	392	311	222	192	85
9 EIRE	-	-	-	-	.	.	241	387	.	.	595	503	442	340	197
10 FINLAND	-	-	-	-	-	.	.	-	.	.	406	298	141	111	69
11 FRANCE	-	-	-	-	.	.	.	.	.	371	350	263	174	102	63
12 GREECE	-	-	-	-	-	.	.	.	-	-	-	949	663	282	75
13 HUNGARY	-	-	-	.	.	.	319	308	541	.	418	496	329	209	331
14 ICELAND	-	-	.	.	.	.	.	.	-	-	.	.	339	232	90
15 ITALY	-	-	-	-	-	-	.	.	.	.	326	295	305	311	227
16 JAPAN	-	.	.	.	.	.	.	.	-	7	19	43	89	109	57
17 NETHERLANDS	.	.	.	.	.	.	.	.	.	403	430	302	222	160	53
18 NEW ZEALAND	-	.	.	.	.	.	.	.	.	555	444	343	283	195	106
19 NORWAY	.	.	.	.	.	.	.	.	.	.	259	156	122	135	94
20 POLAND	-	-	-	-	-	-	-	-	-	-	-	140	253	201	137
21 PORTUGAL	-	-	-	-	-	-	-	-	-	-	331	312	379	354	234
22 ROMANIA	-	-	-	-	-	-	-	-	-	-	-	111	332	445	267
23 SPAIN	.	.	.	.	.	.	241	195	.	.	123	138	146	153	106
24 SWEDEN	-	-	.	.	.	.	.	.	.	.	232	127	132	116	55
25 SWITZERLAND	248	248	280	280	557	725	.	.	512	591	570	398	236	185	116
26 TURKEY	-	-	-	-	-	-	-	-	-	-	-	-	-	-	-
27 UK ENGLAND AND WALES	.	.	510	470	427	336	318	351	435	467	375	257	210	173	82
28 UK NORTHERN IRELAND	-	-	-	-	.	.	.	.	.	571	486	478	403	286	125
29 UK SCOTLAND	.	.	.	.	.	.	.	.	.	385	447	349	273	232	90
30 USA	.	.	.	.	.	.	.	.	.	427	374	295	237	156	73
31 YUGOSLAVIA	-	-	-	-	-	-	-	-	-	-	.	.	161	185	178

- NO MORTALITY DATA ARE AVAILABLE FOR EVEN A BROADER GROUP OF CAUSES FOR THIS DISEASE

. MORTALITY DATA ARE PRESENTED FOR A BROADER GROUP OF CAUSES FOR THIS DISEASE

0 VALUE<0.5

THE MORTALITY RATES WERE DERIVED WITH A FACTOR OF 1000000

SERIAL MORTALITY TABLES FOR VARIOUS COUNTRIES 1901-1975

TABLE 154 : NEWBORN - HAEMOLYTIC DISEASE : FEMALES

	1901-	1906-	1911-	1916-	1921-	1926-	1931-	1936-	1941-	1946-	1951-	1956-	1961-	1966-	1971-75
1 AUSTRALIA	-	.	.	.	.	.	198	203	182	102	280	252	228	174	81
2 AUSTRIA	.	.	.	.	-	-	-	-	-	.	301	273	244	156	76
3 BELGIUM	.	.	.	.	.	.	.	.	.	.	232	202	137	136	62
4 BULGARIA	-	-	-	-	-	.	.	.	.	.	.	.	117	79	67
5 CANADA	-	-	-	-	-	.	342	338	.	293	329	317	276	188	65
6 CHILE	-	.	.	.	.	.	.	77	298	1012	300	254	265	299	206
7 CZECHOSLOVAKIA	-	-	-	.	.	.	.	.	.	.	123	118	86	81	68
8 DENMARK	-	-	-	-	129	230	.	.	.	.	203	154	111	114	27
9 EIRE	-	-	-	-	.	.	167	251	.	.	414	360	394	302	200
10 FINLAND	-	-	-	-	-	.	.	-	.	.	216	173	94	89	52
11 FRANCE	-	-	-	-	.	.	.	.	.	194	210	151	121	70	43
12 GREECE	-	-	-	-	-	.	.	.	-	-	-	640	480	229	67
13 HUNGARY	-	-	-	.	.	.	175	201	365	.	349	245	217	175	246
14 ICELAND	-	-	.	.	.	.	.	.	-	-	.	.	254	93	90
15 ITALY	-	-	-	-	-	-	.	.	.	.	189	184	199	214	158
16 JAPAN	-	.	.	.	.	.	.	.	-	8	15	30	58	64	31
17 NETHERLANDS	.	.	.	.	.	.	.	.	.	241	260	196	182	137	58
18 NEW ZEALAND	-	.	.	.	.	.	.	.	.	577	357	280	192	146	73
19 NORWAY	.	.	.	.	.	.	.	.	.	.	163	143	84	75	85
20 POLAND	-	-	-	-	-	-	-	-	-	-	-	80	147	133	90
21 PORTUGAL	-	-	-	-	-	-	-	-	-	-	253	179	245	242	182
22 ROMANIA	-	-	-	-	-	-	-	-	-	-	-	72	186	300	148
23 SPAIN		.	.	.	.	.	140	105	.	.	86	95	98	105	67
24 SWEDEN	-	-	.	.	.	.	.	.	.	.	116	114	86	99	36
25 SWITZERLAND	223	223	254	254	491	428	.	.	313	347	326	275	195	128	80
26 TURKEY	-	-	-	-	-	-	-	-	-	-	-	-	-	-	-
27 UK ENGLAND AND WALES	.	.	314	271	244	191	178	209	260	314	276	241	184	149	82
28 UK NORTHERN IRELAND	-	-	-	-	.	.	.	.	.	336	319	380	289	231	104
29 UK SCOTLAND	.	.	.	.	.	.	.	.	.	336	291	233	210	166	109
30 USA	.	.	.	.	.	.	.	.	.	296	280	255	211	132	58
31 YUGOSLAVIA	-	-	-	-	-	-	-	-	-	-	.	.	108	123	116

- NO MORTALITY DATA ARE AVAILABLE FOR EVEN A BROADER GROUP OF CAUSES FOR THIS DISEASE

. MORTALITY DATA ARE PRESENTED FOR A BROADER GROUP OF CAUSES FOR THIS DISEASE

0 VALUE<0.5

THE MORTALITY RATES WERE DERIVED WITH A FACTOR OF 1000000

SERIAL MORTALITY TABLES FOR VARIOUS COUNTRIES 1901-1975

TABLE 155 : NEWBORN - ALL DISEASES : MALES

	1901-	1906-	1911-	1916-	1921-	1926-	1931-	1936-	1941-	1946-	1951-	1956-	1961-	1966-	1971-75
1 AUSTRALIA	-	13495	16189	16780	15513	14602	13100	12535	11357	9070	8058	7050	6643	6054	5057
2 AUSTRIA	23190	21846	16631	12390	-	-	-	-	-	18858	15815	13205	10918	9195	7993
3 BELGIUM	9600	10715	12498	15516	11259	10593	10917	10448	12018	9595	9026	10654	8457	7102	5515
4 BULGARIA	-	-	-	-	-	.	.	.	.	.	.	.	8584	5572	4730
5 CANADA	-	-	-	-	-	22525	19426	16358	13646	11879	10465	9431	8729	6927	4506
6 CHILE	-	16410	28352	54026	50325	32732	35482	37323	32789	28451	30975	29189	22003	15325	11823
7 CZECHOSLOVAKIA	-	-	-	31271	32485	27968	28240	24497	15891	11642	8855	7114	6684	7143	6875
8 DENMARK	-	-	-	-	15163	16708	13011	12746	11808	9978	9312	8278	7383	5686	3958
9 EIRE	-	-	-	-	14874	15402	15182	15792	16432	12957	12071	10906	8379	5727	4802
10 FINLAND	-	-	-	-	-	18108	15434	-	12269	11122	10218	7374	7057	5253	3693
11 FRANCE	-	-	-	-	.	.	.	.	9507	10670	11260	8117	6356	4807	3081
12 GREECE	-	-	-	-	-	10623	11513	11156	-	-	-	8950	10759	9616	7475
13 HUNGARY	-	-	-	47778	43087	34972	31820	26155	24592	22338	14937	14975	13406	13207	12877
14 ICELAND	-	-	7955	6877	6543	6010	8799	8052	-	-	5831	5405	5296	5426	4129
15 ITALY	-	-	-	-	-	-	15522	15771	17468	14927	16509	14699	12690	10426	8621
16 JAPAN	-	19691	18872	21113	21565	20167	20416	22946	-	13977	13253	10268	7074	4589	3292
17 NETHERLANDS	11421	9969	9136	8486	7447	9811	9948	8804	9623	7760	7103	5518	5183	4409	3435
18 NEW ZEALAND	-	16237	18074	18298	13464	11583	10473	10071	9370	8157	7820	6977	6193	5010	4292
19 NORWAY	9097	9831	9542	10350	9821	11827	11107	9920	7666	7505	6620	6100	5651	4786	3638
20 POLAND	-	-	-	-	-	-	-	-	-	-	-	11163	11041	9019	6791
21 PORTUGAL	-	-	-	-	-	-	-	-	-	-	17852	18714	15132	12780	6836
22 ROMANIA	-	-	-	-	-	-	-	-	-	-	-	13064	9390	10039	4659
23 SPAIN	3662	6698	7907	10123	9577	8624	11945	11907	11570	9220	11395	9554	7189	4437	2627
24 SWEDEN	-	-	42301	43087	42226	44794	13993	12416	9254	7898	7103	6441	5527	4531	3297
25 SWITZERLAND	22796	22796	19350	19350	12751	12351	12048	12175	10939	10856	10083	8433	7184	5614	3615
26 TURKEY	-	-	-	-	-	-	-	-	-	-	-	-	-	-	-
27 UK ENGLAND AND WALES	13021	13165	20764	18789	16503	13909	14663	13900	11914	9770	8710	7579	6550	5287	4519
28 UK NORTHERN IRELAND	-	-	-	-	19121	17596	18469	18509	17424	12062	10792	8808	8548	6797	5463
29 UK SCOTLAND	11304	12682	21579	20825	20343	19188	18701	17747	16267	11873	10295	9231	7952	5813	5126
30 USA	30079	23261	23023	20233	17106	16440	14065	13044	11345	10404	9516	9226	8900	7533	5670
31 YUGOSLAVIA	-	-	-	-	-	-	-	-	-	-	27705	17059	18585	11991	7297

- NO MORTALITY DATA ARE AVAILABLE FOR EVEN A BROADER GROUP OF CAUSES FOR THIS DISEASE

. MORTALITY DATA ARE PRESENTED FOR A BROADER GROUP OF CAUSES FOR THIS DISEASE

0 VALUE<0.5

THE MORTALITY RATES WERE DERIVED WITH A FACTOR OF 1000000

SERIAL MORTALITY TABLES FOR VARIOUS COUNTRIES 1901-1975

TABLE 155 : NEWBORN - ALL DISEASES : FEMALES

	1901-	1906-	1911-	1916-	1921-	1926-	1931-	1936-	1941-	1946-	1951-	1956-	1961-	1966-	1971-75
1 AUSTRALIA	-	10418	12229	12463	11447	10769	9697	9250	8349	6584	5873	5221	4767	4149	3489
2 AUSTRIA	17138	17215	13074	9806	-	-	-	-	-	14383	11627	9798	7994	6439	5690
3 BELGIUM	8237	8859	10261	12385	8872	8741	8511	8211	9290	7328	6528	7450	6076	4815	3778
4 BULGARIA	-	-	-	-	-	.	.	.	.	.	.	.	5924	3735	2930
5 CANADA	-	-	-	-	-	16730	13947	11914	9457	8347	7142	6600	6049	4876	3225
6 CHILE	-	13535	24209	48770	44992	27866	30873	32651	28719	24632	25649	23921	17692	11917	9089
7 CZECHOSLOVAKIA	-	-	-	24556	25288	21875	22169	19053	12312	8704	6070	4638	4374	4806	4688
8 DENMARK	-	-	-	-	10697	12356	9061	9026	7819	6913	6174	5525	4788	3662	2569
9 EIRE	-	-	-	-	11535	11601	11494	12604	12136	10025	8363	6934	5627	4025	2904
10 FINLAND	-	-	-	-	-	13436	11884	-	9251	8255	7186	5296	4787	3650	2330
11 FRANCE	-	-	-	-	.	.	.	.	6916	7803	8190	5835	4549	3340	2174
12 GREECE	-	-	-	-	-	9964	10770	11003	-	-	-	8071	8662	7365	5612
13 HUNGARY	-	-	-	38979	34739	27661	24782	20284	18566	16714	10832	10614	9389	9576	9201
14 ICELAND	-	-	5420	5322	5608	4657	5082	5012	-	-	4362	3082	4534	2968	2827
15 ITALY	-	-	-	-	-	-	12912	12733	14305	11982	12995	11178	9420	7566	6119
16 JAPAN	-	17324	16626	18231	18308	16950	17074	19050	-	11667	10979	8122	5310	3246	2267
17 NETHERLANDS	8644	7403	6663	6208	5287	6934	6732	6097	6584	5139	4558	3621	3354	3001	2312
18 NEW ZEALAND	-	11894	12762	13897	10021	8264	7146	7602	6787	5845	5441	4996	4218	3379	2753
19 NORWAY	7232	7542	7455	7877	7464	8294	7932	7215	5779	5043	4642	4135	3882	3259	2298
20 POLAND	-	-	-	-	-	-	-	-	-	-	-	8090	7680	6154	4389
21 PORTUGAL	-	-	-	-	-	-	-	-	-	-	13705	14616	11448	9484	4853
22 ROMANIA	-	-	-	-	-	-	-	-	-	-	-	9979	6955	6795	2866
23 SPAIN	2880	5225	6179	7994	7503	6819	9284	9537	9149	7131	8775	7108	5276	3338	1791
24 SWEDEN	-	-	56302	58299	59583	62512	10238	9041	6631	5563	4924	4348	3962	2990	2144
25 SWITZERLAND	17313	17313	14796	14796	9725	8803	8960	8747	8301	7725	7376	5845	4971	3883	2480
26 TURKEY	-	-	-	-	-	-	-	-	-	-	-	-	-	-	-
27 UK ENGLAND AND WALES	10031	10143	15662	14018	12244	10149	10570	10121	8567	6773	5915	5147	4421	3632	2983
28 UK NORTHERN IRELAND	-	-	-	-	13967	13160	12976	13645	12936	8709	7313	6398	5532	4540	4055
29 UK SCOTLAND	8754	9575	16275	15594	14805	13992	13805	12832	11476	8372	6950	5919	5045	3953	3376
30 USA	22638	17463	17381	14942	12611	12072	10270	9484	8084	7284	6724	6588	6271	5313	4060
31 YUGOSLAVIA	-	-	-	-	-	-	-	-	-	-	22326	13822	15509	9661	5128

- NO MORTALITY DATA ARE AVAILABLE FOR EVEN A BROADER GROUP OF CAUSES FOR THIS DISEASE

. MORTALITY DATA ARE PRESENTED FOR A BROADER GROUP OF CAUSES FOR THIS DISEASE

O VALUE<0.5

THE MORTALITY RATES WERE DERIVED WITH A FACTOR OF 1000000

SERIAL MORTALITY TABLES FOR VARIOUS COUNTRIES 1901-1975

TABLE 156 : NEWBORN - DISEASES AND CONGENITAL MALFORMATIONS : MALES

	1901-	1906-	1911-	1916-	1921-	1926-	1931-	1936-	1941-	1946-	1951-	1956-	1961-	1966-	1971-75
1 AUSTRALIA	-	22490	25990	24918	23990	22753	18277	18839	18175	14980	13435	12225	11095	10308	8781
2 AUSTRIA	-	-	-	-	-	-	-	-	-	27072	21439	20674	16859	13658	11155
3 BELGIUM	-	-	-	-	-	-	-	-	-	-	14874	16716	13417	11292	8909
4 BULGARIA	-	-	-	-	-	29561	37898	30041	35874	44657	26892	7742	12029	8934	8028
5 CANADA	-	-	-	-	30151	33267	28411	25008	24356	21604	18218	16353	13882	10458	8101
6 CHILE	-	29250	53699	98760	92913	61191	52664	58461	52051	47156	53793	49024	32924	20346	17001
7 CZECHOSLOVAKIA	-	-	-	68770	64112	44796	30501	22145	27058	19115	13824	10747	11350	11437	12457
8 DENMARK	-	-	-	-	-	-	19520	20103	21161	16081	14048	13362	13076	9614	7627
9 EIRE	-	-	-	-	20400	20809	21123	22962	27556	22430	18873	17731	15198	10921	9798
10 FINLAND	-	-	-	-	-	-	-	20354	18014	17641	14090	11777	11523	8362	6919
11 FRANCE	-	-	-	-	13289	13651	13578	13349	15485	20226	15779	12567	10585	8208	5814
12 GREECE	-	-	-	-	16915	16231	20275	18261	-	-	-	12583	14907	14419	11438
13 HUNGARY	-	-	-	98781	83834	55436	44784	35999	33870	32471	23555	19683	18820	21173	20506
14 ICELAND	-	-	-	-	-	-	-	-	13293	10486	9934	9614	9669	8066	7527
15 ITALY	-	-	-	-	-	-	22116	23896	23070	22335	22468	21071	19059	14940	12581
16 JAPAN	23189	27349	29713	32723	33558	31329	31260	33141	-	20180	15648	13259	10430	7635	5910
17 NETHERLANDS	20566	16203	14533	13889	12328	15688	15766	14890	16053	13971	12197	10600	9915	8470	6239
18 NEW ZEALAND	-	23379	27519	26731	20861	18108	16164	17779	16586	16074	13584	12792	11022	9267	8108
19 NORWAY	-	-	12323	13535	12866	14419	11743	10493	10270	11242	10514	10124	10017	8359	6552
20 POLAND	-	-	-	-	-	-	-	-	-	-	19070	16788	15077	13764	12541
21 PORTUGAL	23088	22351	-	-	-	-	28460	26454	27941	26394	25125	27211	22273	18380	11714
22 ROMANIA	-	-	-	-	-	-	-	-	-	-	-	18898	12340	18193	7855
23 SPAIN	22669	24870	24154	25375	23136	18756	21934	19800	19407	14833	15706	13771	10530	7064	5423
24 SWEDEN	-	-	-	-	-	-	17006	16705	16562	13096	10419	10309	9982	7893	6442
25 SWITZERLAND	34883	34883	26653	26653	18926	17075	16878	17121	20568	18634	15503	14173	13209	9713	7086
26 TURKEY	-	-	-	-	-	-	-	-	-	-	-	26571	24072	20040	17316
27 UK ENGLAND AND WALES	23585	23662	30973	27475	24076	22050	22256	21610	20854	16734	13541	13539	12086	9322	8025
28 UK NORTHERN IRELAND	-	-	-	-	28881	25510	26830	28658	29760	19338	17965	15812	15649	12312	9881
29 UK SCOTLAND	20181	22448	33303	31671	32403	28354	27503	26863	25575	20269	16240	16115	14343	10525	8757
30 USA	43794	34548	32757	28529	24512	22192	19752	19410	18990	18293	15899	15144	13386	11263	8944
31 YUGOSLAVIA	-	-	-	-	-	-	-	-	-	-	39350	22693	24989	15994	10704

- NO MORTALITY DATA ARE AVAILABLE FOR EVEN A BROADER GROUP OF CAUSES FOR THIS DISEASE

. MORTALITY DATA ARE PRESENTED FOR A BROADER GROUP OF CAUSES FOR THIS DISEASE

0 VALUE<0.5

THE STANDARD MORTALITY RATIOS WERE DERIVED WITH A FACTOR OF 10000

SERIAL MORTALITY TABLES FOR VARIOUS COUNTRIES 1901-1975

TABLE 156 : NEWBORN - DISEASES AND CONGENITAL MALFORMATIONS : FEMALES

	1901-	1906-	1911-	1916-	1921-	1926-	1931-	1936-	1941-	1946-	1951-	1956-	1961-	1966-	1971-75
1 AUSTRALIA	-	18014	20463	19601	18538	17440	14110	14709	15027	12165	10468	9837	8746	7967	6984
2 AUSTRIA	-	-	-	-	-	-	-	-	-	21345	16444	15980	12997	10161	8459
3 BELGIUM	-	-	-	-	-	-	-	-	-	-	11330	12768	10537	8323	6791
4 BULGARIA	-	-	-	-	-	25602	30901	24669	29055	35940	19046	5860	9070	6611	5789
5 CANADA	-	-	-	-	23410	25719	21370	19310	18394	16519	13952	12697	10825	8413	6526
6 CHILE	-	24175	46753	90443	84038	52614	46181	51771	46136	41141	44898	40525	26706	16295	13578
7 CZECHOSLOVAKIA	-	-	-	55012	50893	35695	24302	17446	21456	14899	10366	7994	8484	8549	9090
8 DENMARK	-	-	-	-	-	-	14307	15188	14930	11658	10311	9842	9358	6798	5607
9 EIRE	-	-	-	-	16560	16580	16716	19193	21145	18093	14557	13232	12231	9095	7563
10 FINLAND	-	-	-	-	-	-	-	16007	14408	14181	10621	9305	8593	6716	5346
11 FRANCE	-	-	-	-	10530	10628	10346	10058	11543	15177	11967	9517	7994	6274	4562
12 GREECE	-	-	-	-	16995	16312	19617	18638	-	-	-	11859	12646	11681	9271
13 HUNGARY	-	-	-	82205	68687	44324	35447	28423	26066	25251	18204	14905	14498	16591	16000
14 ICELAND	-	-	-	-	-	-	-	-	10426	8843	8610	6697	7757	5490	5552
15 ITALY	-	-	-	-	-	-	19013	20044	19655	18729	18594	16875	15071	11528	9644
16 JAPAN	20948	24950	26740	28782	28805	26534	26430	27930	-	17421	13381	11001	8322	5900	4591
17 NETHERLANDS	16036	12495	11107	10530	9379	11783	11957	11511	12236	10714	9525	8403	7760	6622	4928
18 NEW ZEALAND	-	17322	20572	21145	16226	13583	12147	14226	12815	12943	10205	9948	8291	7192	6447
19 NORWAY	-	-	10011	10678	10200	10567	8756	8059	8186	7950	8174	7794	7710	6412	4846
20 POLAND	-	-	-	-	-	-	-	-	-	-	15982	13017	11492	10410	9292
21 PORTUGAL	18541	17925	-	-	-	-	23120	21533	23265	21381	20122	22054	17768	14336	8786
22 ROMANIA	-	-	-	-	-	-	-	-	-	-	-	15368	9738	13370	5584
23 SPAIN	18055	20085	19080	20473	18239	15098	17406	16090	15905	12047	12543	10586	8099	5604	4230
24 SWEDEN	-	-	-	-	-	-	13049	12838	12474	9826	8048	7814	7942	5955	5136
25 SWITZERLAND	26298	26298	20341	20341	14629	12634	13097	12861	15963	14270	12300	10799	10094	7579	5374
26 TURKEY	-	-	-	-	-	-	-	-	-	-	-	25559	22330	18384	15908
27 UK ENGLAND AND WALES	17754	17989	23586	20828	18313	16557	16619	16502	15925	12705	10425	10535	9430	7358	6408
28 UK NORTHERN IRELAND	-	-	-	-	22264	19863	19903	23092	23469	15124	14126	14104	12346	10235	8875
29 UK SCOTLAND	15862	17466	25710	24335	24200	21085	20730	20313	18973	15282	12577	12097	10815	8390	7194
30 USA	33416	26597	25367	21701	18754	17039	15120	14839	14457	13756	12085	11589	10236	8679	7004
31 YUGOSLAVIA	-	-	-	-	-	-	-	-	-	-	32796	19309	21790	13680	8131

- NO MORTALITY DATA ARE AVAILABLE FOR EVEN A BROADER GROUP OF CAUSES FOR THIS DISEASE

. MORTALITY DATA ARE PRESENTED FOR A BROADER GROUP OF CAUSES FOR THIS DISEASE

0 VALUE<0.5

THE STANDARD MORTALITY RATIOS WERE DERIVED WITH A FACTOR OF 10000

SERIAL MORTALITY TABLES FOR VARIOUS COUNTRIES 1901-1975

TABLE 157 : SENILITY WITHOUT MENTION OF PSYCHOSIS : MALES

	1901-	1906-	1911-	1916-	1921-	1926-	1931-	1936-	1941-	1946-	1951-	1956-	1961-	1966-	1971-75
1 AUSTRALIA	-	2536	2984	3112	2367	1634	1118	849	735	499	232	131	64	36	25
2 AUSTRIA	-	-	-	-	-	-	-	-	-	-	891	247	291	127	101
3 BELGIUM	3568	3731	3787	4061	3419	3217	2565	2434	2262	1857	1192	885	340	214	228
4 BULGARIA	-	-	-	-	-	1306	-	-	-	-	-	-	388	381	541
5 CANADA	-	-	-	-	974	568	342	236	208	147	83	53	34	17	13
6 CHILE	-	809	1029	2110	2372	1759	1581	1437	1334	1279	1152	792	626	698	486
7 CZECHOSLOVAKIA	-	-	-	8214	6386	4846	3766	3169	1970	1384	1003	493	280	192	135
8 DENMARK	2404	2578	2553	2964	2787	2592	1335	1090	981	372	152	88	59	20	13
9 EIRE	-	-	-	-	7469	6430	5415	5311	5209	4536	1369	811	563	278	147
10 FINLAND	-	-	-	-	-	6048	4398	3237	3267	2965	1249	445	169	56	21
11 FRANCE	-	-	-	-	3215	3392	-	-	1798	1296	1046	698	536	288	147
12 GREECE	-	-	-	-	3092	2992	2160	1845	-	-	-	1352	907	714	483
13 HUNGARY	-	-	-	10218	8442	6171	5412	4446	4200	4306	3086	950	333	73	20
14 ICELAND	-	-	3455	3281	2784	2400	2436	2056	-	-	.	.	57	31	14
15 ITALY	3346	3210	3077	3214	2911	2499	1764	1666	1848	1188	948	608	420	306	248
16 JAPAN	3369	2999	2614	3070	4072	4496	4655	5013	-	2812	2426	1770	1191	773	475
17 NETHERLANDS	2797	2452	2108	2137	1673	1082	1038	872	833	459	249	157	102	68	60
18 NEW ZEALAND	-	2271	1844	2091	1671	1143	669	522	578	228	87	55	37	22	11
19 NORWAY	2353	2307	2347	2483	2216	1691	1307	1027	712	681	321	217	169	109	88
20 POLAND	-	-	-	-	-	-	-	-	-	-	5261	3384	1848	1218	915
21 PORTUGAL	1835	2024	.	.	.	.	-	-	-	-	2342	2197	1689	1814	1736
22 ROMANIA	-	-	-	-	-	-	-	-	-	-	-	.	.	.	.
23 SPAIN	1352	2296	2495	2703	2327	2066	1923	2159	1606	1321	930	734	561	449	264
24 SWEDEN	-	-	-	-	-	-	1677	1444	1147	955	487	215	74	36	16
25 SWITZERLAND	1943	1943	1548	1548	1345	1027	941	699	458	281	214	125	78	41	26
26 TURKEY	-	-	-	-	-	-	-	-	-	-	-	2187	1387	831	699
27 UK ENGLAND AND WALES	2964	2074	2594	2185	1670	1120	815	721	572	360	200	156	104	55	28
28 UK NORTHERN IRELAND	-	-	-	-	4276	3653	2438	2525	2246	1767	645	361	23	9	6
29 UK SCOTLAND	2556	2094	2150	1956	1868	1500	1148	907	679	410	229	107	53	32	18
30 USA	1445	828	549	361	293	240	189	159	143	95	39	21	14	8	5
31 YUGOSLAVIA	-	-	-	-	-	-	-	-	-	-	.	.	1643	1249	923

- NO MORTALITY DATA ARE AVAILABLE FOR EVEN A BROADER GROUP OF CAUSES FOR THIS DISEASE

. MORTALITY DATA ARE PRESENTED FOR A BROADER GROUP OF CAUSES FOR THIS DISEASE

0 VALUE<0.5

THE STANDARD MORTALITY RATIOS WERE DERIVED WITH A FACTOR OF 100

SERIAL MORTALITY TABLES FOR VARIOUS COUNTRIES 1901-1975

TABLE 157 : SENILITY WITHOUT MENTION OF PSYCHOSIS : FEMALES

	1901-	1906-	1911-	1916-	1921-	1926-	1931-	1936-	1941-	1946-	1951-	1956-	1961-	1966-	1971-75
1 AUSTRALIA	-	2238	2549	2602	1938	1389	974	781	580	445	207	120	67	36	23
2 AUSTRIA	-	-	-	-	-	-	-	-	-	-	709	206	244	114	89
3 BELGIUM	3118	3330	3226	3593	3047	2924	2455	2434	2221	1943	1119	863	351	227	216
4 BULGARIA	-	-	-	-	-	319	-	-	-	-	-	-	388	400	559
5 CANADA	-	-	-	-	1078	671	395	271	238	170	91	62	32	21	15
6 CHILE	-	913	1178	2425	2674	2066	1893	1722	1533	1504	1193	753	547	564	426
7 CZECHOSLOVAKIA	-	-	-	8594	6190	4703	3489	2862	1775	1248	1058	509	278	185	129
8 DENMARK	1833	2043	2103	2252	2483	2376	1425	1173	1036	388	171	95	56	22	11
9 EIRE	-	-	-	-	6992	6290	5316	5197	4883	4022	1302	803	531	251	143
10 FINLAND	-	-	-	-	-	5713	4213	3123	2836	2528	1097	400	151	46	17
11 FRANCE	-	-	-	-	2704	2888	-	-	1642	1115	923	640	493	277	154
12 GREECE	-	-	-	-	3183	3150	2650	2466	-	-	-	1616	1071	828	560
13 HUNGARY	-	-	-	10048	8046	5992	5139	4244	3961	3932	2842	916	316	73	20
14 ICELAND	-	-	3239	3358	2719	2295	2084	2057	-	-	.	.	99	68	22
15 ITALY	3891	3679	3467	3619	3040	2512	1810	1703	1858	1215	934	611	409	293	236
16 JAPAN	3534	3461	3024	3612	4379	4567	4630	4895	-	2258	2031	1515	1116	795	521
17 NETHERLANDS	2708	2435	2065	2146	1671	1189	1115	984	952	502	270	174	114	73	64
18 NEW ZEALAND	-	2301	1640	1847	1458	1005	539	467	492	237	96	63	39	24	13
19 NORWAY	2292	2217	2219	2371	2186	1792	1443	1161	780	754	400	253	186	124	96
20 POLAND	-	-	-	-	-	-	-	-	-	-	4181	2642	1550	1045	768
21 PORTUGAL	1851	1960	.	.	.	.	-	-	-	-	2142	1961	1579	1594	1553
22 ROMANIA	-	-	-	-	-	-	-	-	-	-	-	.	.	.	.
23 SPAIN	1811	2626	2655	2814	2347	2069	1884	1972	1486	1199	792	704	521	416	287
24 SWEDEN	-	-	-	-	-	-	1784	1552	1209	1039	527	245	90	43	18
25 SWITZERLAND	2002	2002	1479	1479	1301	965	895	716	479	312	212	125	82	47	31
26 TURKEY	-	-	-	-	-	-	-	-	-	-	-	2325	1594	1111	932
27 UK ENGLAND AND WALES	3661	2516	2176	1801	1418	971	734	626	500	338	192	154	104	60	36
28 UK NORTHERN IRELAND	-	-	-	-	4147	3594	2416	2709	2366	1792	637	355	23	9	6
29 UK SCOTLAND	2407	1983	1979	1720	1734	1439	1135	871	617	398	236	125	64	32	20
30 USA	1643	951	638	431	351	278	197	155	137	90	38	21	14	8	6
31 YUGOSLAVIA	-	-	-	-	-	-	-	-	-	-	.	.	1491	1143	834

- NO MORTALITY DATA ARE AVAILABLE FOR EVEN A BROADER GROUP OF CAUSES FOR THIS DISEASE
. MORTALITY DATA ARE PRESENTED FOR A BROADER GROUP OF CAUSES FOR THIS DISEASE
0 VALUE<0.5
THE STANDARD MORTALITY RATIOS WERE DERIVED WITH A FACTOR OF 100

SERIAL MORTALITY TABLES FOR VARIOUS COUNTRIES 1901-1975

TABLE 158 : ILL-DEFINED AND UNKNOWN CAUSES OF MORTALITY : MALES

	1901-	1906-	1911-	1916-	1921-	1926-	1931-	1936-	1941-	1946-	1951-	1956-	1961-	1966-	1971-75
1 AUSTRALIA	-	424	311	282	244	181	91	70	56	39	39	31	20	31	53
2 AUSTRIA	12388	11561	9051	8088	-	-	-	-	-	1241	562	115	145	93	96
3 BELGIUM	4419	3843	3366	3515	2579	1873	1076	1665	1519	890	668	592	609	599	737
4 BULGARIA	-	-	-	-	-	491	581	411	827	669	1136	723	227	174	227
5 CANADA	-	-	-	-	398	217	165	105	116	88	83	62	42	42	77
6 CHILE	-	6747	7877	5529	4397	3588	1636	1557	1643	1123	1571	979	722	370	613
7 CZECHOSLOVAKIA	-	-	-	2292	1926	995	426	236	280	174	193	65	32	21	18
8 DENMARK	654	584	482	457	402	295	276	279	255	91	50	45	81	109	197
9 EIRE	-	-	-	-	806	573	427	326	302	192	281	176	126	58	18
10 FINLAND	-	-	-	-	-	645	407	371	284	217	96	66	50	36	24
11 FRANCE	-	-	-	-	5450	2610	3165	3319	2014	1464	1320	1074	986	876	638
12 GREECE	-	-	-	-	2767	1878	1710	1270	-	-	-	761	550	359	359
13 HUNGARY	-	-	-	942	726	539	523	337	448	213	101	36	17	4	3
14 ICELAND	-	-	3053	2186	2187	1417	1242	1178	203	119	.	.	78	81	85
15 ITALY	257	133	86	353	257	27	82	48	330	125	235	89	70	61	76
16 JAPAN	4121	2728	1555	1560	1189	909	785	748	-	317	308	277	215	173	120
17 NETHERLANDS	1586	1655	1356	1310	879	667	526	480	1340	409	304	258	261	253	321
18 NEW ZEALAND	-	402	335	263	128	62	58	20	12	10	27	11	17	26	24
19 NORWAY	216	168	710	684	496	646	631	587	801	546	342	406	462	473	484
20 POLAND	-	-	-	-	-	-	-	-	-	-	.	621	450	288	273
21 PORTUGAL	7834	8182	9686	12817	8837	2424	1618	1271	1413	1118	907	632	420	458	514
22 ROMANIA	-	-	-	-	-	-	-	-	-	-	-	186	54	29	18
23 SPAIN	2017	1472	1171	1111	966	673	804	953	787	606	1011	974	607	482	306
24 SWEDEN	-	-	751	580	386	242	129	52	32	19	138	62	27	32	27
25 SWITZERLAND	1123	1123	881	881	798	490	578	395	255	129	45	42	96	132	94
26 TURKEY	-	-	-	-	-	-	-	-	-	-	-	438	324	306	320
27 UK ENGLAND AND WALES	1576	1080	472	347	220	121	98	70	47	17	8	7	8	10	26
28 UK NORTHERN IRELAND	-	-	-	-	328	276	129	113	96	70	75	34	39	26	57
29 UK SCOTLAND	1283	955	632	548	502	433	387	344	384	285	186	66	55	31	29
30 USA	1369	650	258	278	242	271	244	224	190	152	127	110	120	140	168
31 YUGOSLAVIA	-	-	-	-	-	-	-	-	-	-	.	.	1576	1949	1732

- NO MORTALITY DATA ARE AVAILABLE FOR EVEN A BROADER GROUP OF CAUSES FOR THIS DISEASE

. MORTALITY DATA ARE PRESENTED FOR A BROADER GROUP OF CAUSES FOR THIS DISEASE

0 VALUE<0.5

THE STANDARD MORTALITY RATIOS WERE DERIVED WITH A FACTOR OF 10

SERIAL MORTALITY TABLES FOR VARIOUS COUNTRIES 1901-1975

TABLE 158 : ILL-DEFINED AND UNKNOWN CAUSES OF MORTALITY : FEMALES

	1901-	1906-	1911-	1916-	1921-	1926-	1931-	1936-	1941-	1946-	1951-	1956-	1961-	1966-	1971-75
1 AUSTRALIA	-	297	209	198	149	96	39	28	25	19	20	16	11	18	27
2 AUSTRIA	10955	10053	7888	7423	-	-	-	-	-	1146	466	71	110	65	57
3 BELGIUM	3684	3198	2598	2617	2031	1542	896	955	942	597	463	404	432	436	563
4 BULGARIA	-	-	-	-	-	397	474	319	578	430	902	723	216	152	188
5 CANADA	-	-	-	-	308	155	105	68	82	72	64	40	25	25	44
6 CHILE	-	6088	7525	5144	4054	3223	1405	1344	1116	791	1428	898	640	324	535
7 CZECHOSLOVAKIA	-	-	-	2068	1664	845	348	185	200	121	212	68	32	18	13
8 DENMARK	381	355	322	298	304	218	159	154	142	53	32	30	45	67	121
9 EIRE	-	-	-	-	753	534	382	290	238	156	201	120	90	44	12
10 FINLAND	-	-	-	-	-	471	281	182	110	93	72	50	31	20	11
11 FRANCE	-	-	-	-	4278	2044	2406	2439	1377	1028	898	729	645	597	437
12 GREECE	-	-	-	-	2474	1701	1576	1125	-	-	-	561	412	281	295
13 HUNGARY	-	-	-	942	715	507	407	255	320	127	59	21	7	2	2
14 ICELAND	-	-	2357	1876	1726	1217	1042	861	172	144	.	.	35	40	50
15 ITALY	271	137	87	371	222	25	58	38	264	105	159	48	36	31	40
16 JAPAN	3771	2556	1470	1459	1111	838	690	631	-	244	232	196	140	106	69
17 NETHERLANDS	1235	1385	1125	1049	701	505	379	310	416	206	153	125	118	126	168
18 NEW ZEALAND	-	328	257	171	80	36	23	7	7	5	19	6	11	24	24
19 NORWAY	149	116	601	569	406	511	495	427	587	372	218	236	231	218	204
20 POLAND	-	-	-	-	-	-	-	-	-	-	.	503	370	199	141
21 PORTUGAL	6948	7199	8631	11408	7481	1945	1320	961	1076	854	660	472	290	263	256
22 ROMANIA	-	-	-	-	-	-	-	-	-	-	-	149	53	29	17
23 SPAIN	1933	1353	1062	996	830	570	695	655	541	450	805	838	521	387	211
24 SWEDEN	-	-	699	517	348	212	111	36	18	9	75	34	15	17	11
25 SWITZERLAND	977	977	739	739	618	411	402	275	176	80	29	30	59	79	54
26 TURKEY	-	-	-	-	-	-	-	-	-	-	-	362	273	255	261
27 UK ENGLAND AND WALES	1170	783	322	229	137	72	59	42	25	10	4	4	5	8	18
28 UK NORTHERN IRELAND	-	-	-	-	258	225	101	88	78	44	54	26	33	28	45
29 UK SCOTLAND	897	669	521	391	313	263	232	191	192	135	97	33	27	18	16
30 USA	1182	552	207	228	198	218	187	160	127	92	72	63	67	74	84
31 YUGOSLAVIA	-	-	-	-	-	-	-	-	-	-	.	.	1461	1691	1471

- NO MORTALITY DATA ARE AVAILABLE FOR EVEN A BROADER GROUP OF CAUSES FOR THIS DISEASE

. MORTALITY DATA ARE PRESENTED FOR A BROADER GROUP OF CAUSES FOR THIS DISEASE

0 VALUE<0.5

THE STANDARD MORTALITY RATIOS WERE DERIVED WITH A FACTOR OF 10

SERIAL MORTALITY TABLES FOR VARIOUS COUNTRIES 1901-1975

TABLE 159 : SENILITY, ILL-DEFINED AND UNKNOWN CAUSES OF MORTALITY : MALES

	1901-	1906-	1911-	1916-	1921-	1926-	1931-	1936-	1941-	1946-	1951-	1956-	1961-	1966-	1971-75
1 AUSTRALIA	-	2890	3011	3051	2381	1667	1081	826	707	482	255	159	84	74	96
2 AUSTRIA	-	-	-	-	-	-	-	-	-	-	999	353	427	219	195
3 BELGIUM	11270	10128	9039	9257	7111	5800	3872	4533	4033	2756	1841	1447	957	825	963
4 BULGARIA	-	-	-	-	-	-	-	-	-	-	-	-	618	547	787
5 CANADA	-	-	-	-	1544	867	564	363	349	258	197	136	85	67	100
6 CHILE	-	13527	16272	12936	11172	9264	4901	4654	4791	3559	3472	2866	2202	1423	2017
7 CZECHOSLOVAKIA	-	-	-	11087	8895	5839	3862	3010	2105	1589	1245	516	285	194	141
8 DENMARK	3331	3308	3001	3280	2978	2644	1537	1325	1194	444	195	129	138	132	202
9 EIRE	-	-	-	-	7587	6290	5178	4880	4765	4009	1537	915	639	311	151
10 FINLAND	-	-	-	-	-	6117	4343	3318	3187	2794	1187	486	228	106	58
11 FRANCE	-	-	-	-	-	-	-	-	4158	3009	2599	1890	1622	1247	819
12 GREECE	-	-	-	-	-	5712	4324	3262	-	-	-	2159	1441	1040	802
13 HUNGARY	-	-	-	10052	8205	6019	5380	4268	4243	3946	2758	863	312	69	22
14 ICELAND	-	-	8813	6827	6347	4400	4069	3452	-	-	360	291	160	134	109
15 ITALY	3187	2842	2666	3270	2853	2123	1610	1485	2063	1197	1139	644	454	342	306
16 JAPAN	12083	8206	5322	5731	6118	5815	5566	5714	-	2922	2603	1979	1373	942	593
17 NETHERLANDS	5860	5179	4259	4140	2940	2055	1748	1508	2933	1080	648	465	403	345	395
18 NEW ZEALAND	-	2638	2141	2186	1605	1058	655	473	509	209	113	62	54	54	47
19 NORWAY	2326	2226	2961	3070	2572	2262	1886	1585	1551	1233	667	619	628	579	619
20 POLAND	-	-	-	-	-	-	-	-	-	-	7802	4044	2403	1511	1212
21 PORTUGAL	-	-	18839	24212	17282	6116	-	-	-	-	3602	2910	2083	2240	2230
22 ROMANIA	-	-	-	-	-	-	-	-	-	-	-	1159	104	47	29
23 SPAIN	4829	4809	4409	4422	3810	3004	3094	3465	2679	2123	2429	2125	1358	1044	634
24 SWEDEN	-	-	-	-	-	-	1634	1342	1054	867	588	257	93	63	40
25 SWITZERLAND	3944	3944	2998	2998	2589	1744	1789	1222	776	428	247	162	186	195	128
26 TURKEY	-	-	-	-	-	-	-	-	-	-	-	2928	1954	1446	1314
27 UK ENGLAND AND WALES	5918	3651	3069	2450	1776	1137	843	718	558	335	185	146	101	61	55
28 UK NORTHERN IRELAND	-	-	-	-	4093	3489	2259	2295	2022	1571	658	359	68	40	78
29 UK SCOTLAND	4940	3820	3101	2696	2504	2042	1642	1333	1176	755	444	176	115	67	51
30 USA	3647	1892	928	818	694	676	564	485	405	303	214	169	166	167	184
31 YUGOSLAVIA	-	-	-	-	-	-	-	-	-	-	4722	4453	3885	4156	3504

- NO MORTALITY DATA ARE AVAILABLE FOR EVEN A BROADER GROUP OF CAUSES FOR THIS DISEASE

. MORTALITY DATA ARE PRESENTED FOR A BROADER GROUP OF CAUSES FOR THIS DISEASE

0 VALUE<0.5

THE STANDARD MORTALITY RATIOS WERE DERIVED WITH A FACTOR OF 100

SERIAL MORTALITY TABLES FOR VARIOUS COUNTRIES 1901-1975

TABLE 159 : SENILITY, ILL-DEFINED AND UNKNOWN CAUSES OF MORTALITY : FEMALES

	1901-	1906-	1911-	1916-	1921-	1926-	1931-	1936-	1941-	1946-	1951-	1956-	1961-	1966-	1971-75
1 AUSTRALIA	-	2400	2452	2476	1853	1314	882	709	538	412	207	125	71	51	46
2 AUSTRIA	-	-	-	-	-	-	-	-	-	-	729	254	320	158	126
3 BELGIUM	8600	7830	6646	6791	5380	4592	3313	3330	3084	2405	1459	1152	696	571	638
4 BULGARIA	-	-	-	-	-	-	-	-	-	-	-	-	554	513	708
5 CANADA	-	-	-	-	1423	820	497	330	319	248	165	106	58	45	53
6 CHILE	-	10476	13618	11212	9747	7850	4235	3959	3367	2726	2923	2144	1575	1042	1421
7 CZECHOSLOVAKIA	-	-	-	10547	7851	5289	3488	2710	1804	1470	1277	529	283	185	129
8 DENMARK	2174	2272	2257	2353	2555	2351	1445	1218	1081	405	187	116	94	79	107
9 EIRE	-	-	-	-	7086	6127	5048	4784	4445	3594	1376	842	565	269	141
10 FINLAND	-	-	-	-	-	5576	4028	2953	2605	2301	1044	413	170	63	27
11 FRANCE	-	-	-	-	-	-	-	-	2829	1982	1676	1209	974	706	450
12 GREECE	-	-	-	-	-	5272	4413	3595	-	-	-	2063	1372	1014	761
13 HUNGARY	-	-	-	9936	7890	5834	4969	3996	3856	3554	2538	829	290	68	20
14 ICELAND	-	-	5865	5303	4511	3459	3004	2710	-	-	374	221	126	101	66
15 ITALY	3560	3248	3011	3633	2914	2167	1631	1526	1959	1195	1012	598	405	295	250
16 JAPAN	9850	7515	5152	5647	5857	5451	5139	5205	-	2296	2084	1577	1152	828	541
17 NETHERLANDS	4708	4303	3527	3440	2489	1778	1513	1289	1429	739	431	298	228	188	207
18 NEW ZEALAND	-	2537	1844	1821	1344	900	492	410	432	212	107	62	46	45	37
19 NORWAY	2198	2100	2634	2742	2390	2132	1789	1462	1264	1035	568	445	372	297	270
20 POLAND	-	-	-	-	-	-	-	-	-	-	5531	3011	1841	1154	835
21 PORTUGAL	-	-	13810	17530	11828	4431	-	-	-	-	2705	2284	1721	1700	1652
22 ROMANIA	-	-	-	-	-	-	-	-	-	-	-	1012	80	35	20
23 SPAIN	4936	4533	4008	3985	3286	2621	2600	2564	1971	1597	1630	1551	1012	759	463
24 SWEDEN	-	-	-	-	-	-	1719	1439	1109	943	548	254	96	53	25
25 SWITZERLAND	3496	3496	2454	2454	2026	1417	1318	974	631	368	220	142	131	114	73
26 TURKEY	-	-	-	-	-	-	-	-	-	-	-	2618	1826	1390	1246
27 UK ENGLAND AND WALES	5485	3439	2350	1877	1411	937	716	602	473	315	179	145	100	62	46
28 UK NORTHERN IRELAND	-	-	-	-	3910	3390	2241	2454	2128	1584	626	346	53	34	46
29 UK SCOTLAND	3485	2750	2491	2035	1929	1601	1291	997	765	500	312	144	83	44	31
30 USA	3316	1730	881	747	630	586	447	355	285	196	120	89	83	75	73
31 YUGOSLAVIA	-	-	-	-	-	-	-	-	-	-	4219	3645	3073	3001	2431

- NO MORTALITY DATA ARE AVAILABLE FOR EVEN A BROADER GROUP OF CAUSES FOR THIS DISEASE

. MORTALITY DATA ARE PRESENTED FOR A BROADER GROUP OF CAUSES FOR THIS DISEASE

0 VALUE<0.5

THE STANDARD MORTALITY RATIOS WERE DERIVED WITH A FACTOR OF 100

SERIAL MORTALITY TABLES FOR VARIOUS COUNTRIES 1901-1975

TABLE 159 : SENILITY, ILL-DEFINED AND UNKNOWN CAUSES OF MORTALITY : PERSONS

	1901-	1906-	1911-	1916-	1921-	1926-	1931-	1936-	1941-	1946-	1951-	1956-	1961-	1966-	1971-75
1 AUSTRALIA	-	2662	2743	2765	2113	1485	977	764	616	443	227	139	76	60	64
2 AUSTRIA	-	-	-	-	-	-	2192	1900	-	-	837	291	358	179	148
3 BELGIUM	9797	8853	7679	7838	6130	5115	3556	3861	3509	2565	1617	1271	800	668	755
4 BULGARIA	-	-	-	-	-	-	-	-	-	-	-	-	582	527	741
5 CANADA	3131	2279	2001	1081	1482	843	530	346	334	253	180	120	71	54	72
6 CHILE	-	11835	14820	12006	10404	8495	4536	4269	3996	3093	3164	2435	1828	1196	1663
7 CZECHOSLOVAKIA	-	-	-	10777	8292	5519	3642	2832	1931	1520	1264	524	284	188	133
8 DENMARK	2585	2640	2527	2690	2739	2480	1486	1266	1132	423	191	122	114	102	146
9 EIRE	-	-	-	-	7314	6201	5107	4828	4591	3785	1451	875	598	287	146
10 FINLAND	-	-	-	-	-	5804	4157	3097	2826	2479	1094	438	189	77	37
11 FRANCE	3107	6131	5369	4663	-	-	-	-	2484	2350	2006	1445	1187	875	563
12 GREECE	-	-	-	-	-	5474	4371	3430	-	-	-	2635	2472	1637	1332
13 HUNGARY	-	-	-	9989	8033	5918	5154	4118	4030	3725	2633	844	299	68	21
14 ICELAND	-	-	6898	5847	5175	3801	3389	2979	-	-	369	248	140	115	84
15 ITALY	3427	3049	2844	3459	2885	2147	1621	1507	2006	1196	1068	617	425	313	270
16 JAPAN	10820	7829	5230	5686	5973	5609	5321	5419	-	2535	2281	1725	1233	870	561
17 NETHERLANDS	5219	4692	3853	3754	2693	1905	1622	1390	2127	897	532	376	307	257	285
18 NEW ZEALAND	-	2594	2009	2020	1481	981	574	441	469	210	110	62	50	49	40
19 NORWAY	2254	2155	2776	2882	2467	2187	1830	1514	1385	1118	611	521	481	414	410
20 POLAND	-	-	-	-	-	-	-	-	-	-	6378	4085	2037	1275	959
21 PORTUGAL	-	-	15875	20227	13985	5082	-	-	-	-	3023	2505	1850	1884	1848
22 ROMANIA	-	-	-	-	-	-	-	-	-	-	-	1071	89	39	23
23 SPAIN	4885	4658	4181	4171	3504	2776	2795	2911	2241	1794	1925	1763	1142	865	526
24 SWEDEN	-	-	-	-	-	-	1682	1396	1085	909	566	255	95	57	31
25 SWITZERLAND	3700	3700	2686	2686	2257	1548	1506	1073	689	391	231	150	152	145	93
26 TURKEY	-	-	-	-	-	-	1913	1638	2304	1842	2042	2744	1878	1414	1277
27 UK ENGLAND AND WALES	5694	3540	2636	2102	1552	1014	764	646	505	322	181	146	100	61	49
28 UK NORTHERN IRELAND	-	-	-	-	3988	3432	2248	2384	2082	1578	640	351	59	36	57
29 UK SCOTLAND	4042	3156	2720	2278	2142	1766	1424	1124	918	598	363	156	95	52	37
30 USA	3472	1807	904	781	661	629	502	415	340	195	161	123	118	112	114
31 YUGOSLAVIA	-	-	-	-	-	-	-	-	-	-	4433	3973	3394	3449	2841

- NO MORTALITY DATA ARE AVAILABLE FOR EVEN A BROADER GROUP OF CAUSES FOR THIS DISEASE

. MORTALITY DATA ARE PRESENTED FOR A BROADER GROUP OF CAUSES FOR THIS DISEASE

0 VALUE<0.5

THE STANDARD MORTALITY RATIOS WERE DERIVED WITH A FACTOR OF 100

SERIAL MORTALITY TABLES FOR VARIOUS COUNTRIES 1901-1975

TABLE 160 : ACCIDENTS - MOTOR VEHICLE : MALES

	1901-	1906-	1911-	1916-	1921-	1926-	1931-	1936-	1941-	1946-	1951-	1956-	1961-	1966-	1971-75
1 AUSTRALIA	-	.	.	.	.	.	.	.	15126	23872	31908	31551	32172	35484	34366
2 AUSTRIA	.	.	.	.	-	-	-	-	-	8212	9007	35503	30171	39419	43709
3 BELGIUM	.	.	.	.	.	.	.	.	.	.	14435	20211	25574	31422	31511
4 BULGARIA	-	-	-	-	-	.	.	4787	8169	.	.	.	6894	16814	16334
5 CANADA	-	-	-	-	.	.	.	.	15823	19484	24834	27020	29670	31685	32122
6 CHILE	-	.	.	.	.	.	.	2248	1578	1671	5061	10290	9601	23168	21089
7 CZECHOSLOVAKIA	-	-	-	.	.	.	.	.	9872	9674	10184	16177	18912	25281	24115
8 DENMARK	.	.	.	.	.	.	.	.	4500	10314	15968	19459	22075	26778	22880
9 EIRE	-	-	-	-	.	.	.	6856	2793	5109	8334	10159	12448	17061	23491
10 FINLAND	.	.	.	.	.	.	.	.	.	.	12538	18719	26834	27887	26280
11 FRANCE	-	-	-	-	.	.	.	.	2414	4307	17598	24301	27298	30092	28469
12 GREECE	-	-	-	-	.	.	.	.	-	-	-	6373	11349	14701	17011
13 HUNGARY	-	-	-	.	.	.	.	.	.	6091	7410	9685	11787	15593	21960
14 ICELAND	-	-	.	.	.	.	.	.	12920	10427	10596	10463	12724	14928	14286
15 ITALY	.	.	.	.	.	.	.	.	.	.	17907	22984	28453	29541	30283
16 JAPAN	.	.	.	.	.	.	.	.	-	4703	7338	13937	21286	24300	21359
17 NETHERLANDS	.	.	.	.	.	.	9456	9373	6194	10142	14668	19381	22720	26780	24693
18 NEW ZEALAND	-	.	.	.	.	21516	12394	16935	11861	15738	21099	20898	22039	26082	28478
19 NORWAY	.	.	.	.	.	.	.	.	6585	4894	7408	10901	13097	15255	15510
20 POLAND	-	-	-	-	-	-	-	-	-	-	.	6782	10267	13779	14925
21 PORTUGAL	.	.	.	.	.	.	.	.	.	.	20634	10858	16606	25345	39775
22 ROMANIA	-	-	-	-	-	-	-	-	-	-	-	.	.	.	.
23 SPAIN	.	.	.	.	.	.	.	.	1055	1338	5092	8505	12696	15674	18088
24 SWEDEN	-	-	3624	3251	4690	7981	7133	9246	4691	9136	15992	16693	19006	17958	16385
25 SWITZERLAND	.	.	.	.	.	.	15763	12388	4091	14236	22283	27996	29224	28785	29025
26 TURKEY	-	-	-	-	-	-	-	-	-	-	-	11720	14747	16596	14863
27 UK ENGLAND AND WALES	.	.	.	.	.	.	.	19335	16270	11693	13066	15407	17091	16022	14803
28 UK NORTHERN IRELAND	-	-	-	-	.	.	11200	11943	13455	9891	13706	14269	15420	19612	25752
29 UK SCOTLAND	.	.	1607	3076	6458	14285	.	.	19511	11912	13306	15062	17631	18870	19146
30 USA	.	.	.	.	.	.	.	32490	27196	29121	30427	28207	28430	32320	28496
31 YUGOSLAVIA	-	-	-	-	-	-	-	-	-	-	.	.	.	18727	.

- NO MORTALITY DATA ARE AVAILABLE FOR EVEN A BROADER GROUP OF CAUSES FOR THIS DISEASE

. MORTALITY DATA ARE PRESENTED FOR A BROADER GROUP OF CAUSES FOR THIS DISEASE

0 VALUE<0.5

THE STANDARD MORTALITY RATIOS WERE DERIVED WITH A FACTOR OF 10000

SERIAL MORTALITY TABLES FOR VARIOUS COUNTRIES 1901-1975

TABLE 160 : ACCIDENTS - MOTOR VEHICLE : FEMALES

	1901-	1906-	1911-	1916-	1921-	1926-	1931-	1936-	1941-	1946-	1951-	1956-	1961-	1966-	1971-75
1 AUSTRALIA	-	.	.	.	.	.	.	.	4194	5005	7522	9136	10217	12056	11484
2 AUSTRIA	.	.	.	.	-	-	-	-	-	2454	1926	7622	7947	10928	12208
3 BELGIUM	.	.	.	.	.	.	.	.	.	.	3471	5209	6920	10363	10855
4 BULGARIA	-	-	-	-	-	.	.	1131	1565	.	.	.	1650	4120	4328
5 CANADA	-	-	-	-	.	.	.	.	4675	5896	8184	9020	10352	11407	11650
6 CHILE	-	.	.	.	.	.	.	175	195	241	1113	2081	1775	4597	4275
7 CZECHOSLOVAKIA	-	-	-	.	.	.	.	.	3413	2392	2034	3187	4373	6526	7206
8 DENMARK	.	.	.	.	.	.	.	.	1474	2801	4529	5785	7900	10220	9177
9 EIRE	-	-	-	-	.	.	.	1743	813	1498	1901	2957	3646	5249	6726
10 FINLAND	.	.	.	.	.	.	.	.	.	.	3490	5088	7515	9482	9187
11 FRANCE	-	-	-	-	.	.	.	.	696	1037	3897	5878	7858	9461	8957
12 GREECE	-	-	-	-	.	.	.	.	-	-	-	1786	2681	4041	5366
13 HUNGARY	-	-	-	.	.	.	.	.	.	1401	1570	1669	2174	3904	5806
14 ICELAND	-	-	.	.	.	.	.	.	2703	3881	4069	3557	6039	3994	6003
15 ITALY	.	.	.	.	.	.	.	.	.	.	2991	4031	5848	6688	7716
16 JAPAN	.	.	.	.	.	.	.	.	-	1575	2078	3500	5035	6486	6088
17 NETHERLANDS	.	.	.	.	.	.	2509	2488	2053	3069	3688	5239	6171	8754	8284
18 NEW ZEALAND	-	.	.	.	.	4998	3425	4561	2942	3594	5078	6354	7172	9100	10895
19 NORWAY	.	.	.	.	.	.	.	.	2196	1641	2085	3056	4077	5484	5431
20 POLAND	-	-	-	-	-	-	-	-	-	-	.	1280	2217	3478	3913
21 PORTUGAL	.	.	.	.	.	.	.	.	.	.	5340	2676	3797	5718	8756
22 ROMANIA	-	-	-	-	-	-	-	-	-	-	-	.	.	.	.
23 SPAIN	.	.	.	.	.	.	.	.	230	325	1544	1986	2769	4255	5375
24 SWEDEN	-	-	572	705	1114	1653	1748	2333	1258	2291	3640	4860	6315	6973	6537
25 SWITZERLAND	.	.	.	.	.	.	2971	2859	874	3134	5187	6303	7529	8828	9118
26 TURKEY	-	-	-	-	-	-	-	-	-	-	-	2942	3913	4808	4599
27 UK ENGLAND AND WALES	.	.	.	.	.	.	.	5122	4364	3464	3726	4820	5918	6133	6031
28 UK NORTHERN IRELAND	-	-	-	-	.	.	3341	3804	4326	2899	3448	3860	5825	6164	8411
29 UK SCOTLAND	.	.	440	1211	1815	4956	.	.	5015	4092	3992	4388	5727	6670	6801
30 USA	.	.	.	.	.	.	.	9561	7314	8376	9438	9167	10019	11410	9907
31 YUGOSLAVIA	-	-	-	-	-	-	-	-	-	-	.	.	.	5111	.

- NO MORTALITY DATA ARE AVAILABLE FOR EVEN A BROADER GROUP OF CAUSES FOR THIS DISEASE

. MORTALITY DATA ARE PRESENTED FOR A BROADER GROUP OF CAUSES FOR THIS DISEASE

0 VALUE<0.5

THE STANDARD MORTALITY RATIOS WERE DERIVED WITH A FACTOR OF 10000

SERIAL MORTALITY TABLES FOR VARIOUS COUNTRIES 1901-1975

TABLE 161 : ACCIDENTS - OTHER TRANSPORT : MALES

	1901-	1906-	1911-	1916-	1921-	1926-	1931-	1936-	1941-	1946-	1951-	1956-	1961-	1966-	1971-75
1 AUSTRALIA	-	.	.	.	.	.	.	.	6285	5441	5704	4457	3431	3041	2533
2 AUSTRIA	.	.	.	.	-	-	-	-	-	.	10134	6608	3617	3043	2343
3 BELGIUM	.	.	.	.	.	.	.	.	.	.	2113	1465	2787	1208	1091
4 BULGARIA	-	-	-	-	-	.	.	.	.	.	.	.	2583	3943	3753
5 CANADA	-	-	-	-	.	.	.	.	11546	6364	6509	5008	4324	3792	3614
6 CHILE	-	.	.	.	.	.	.	9565	7757	6540	10414	9121	6360	6021	3517
7 CZECHOSLOVAKIA	-	-	-	.	.	.	.	.	4466	5013	4805	4929	5035	4628	3937
8 DENMARK		.	.	.	.	.	.	.	.	.	5038	3456	2649	2740	1896
9 EIRE	-	-	-	-	.	.	.	2081	3176	2445	3080	2649	1847	2111	1773
10 FINLAND		.	.	.	.	.	.	.	.	.	4769	7754	7233	7250	7303
11 FRANCE	-	-	-	-	.	.	.	.	2324	2203	2354	1864	1667	1022	1006
12 GREECE	-	-	-	-	.	.	.	.	-	-	-	1279	1024	2117	1043
13 HUNGARY	-	-	-	.	.	.	.	.	.	.	6998	6598	6362	6357	5490
14 ICELAND	-	-	.	.	.	.	.	.	.	.	.	.	22373	18769	17465
15 ITALY	.	.	.	.	.	.	.	.	.	.	3093	2441	1963	1445	1149
16 JAPAN	.	.	.	.	.	.	.	.	-	6856	6766	5950	4711	3348	2463
17 NETHERLANDS	.	.	.	.	.	.	2904	3576	5267	4578	4522	3611	2959	2201	1056
18 NEW ZEALAND	-	.	.	.	.	8369	10513	14611	11737	7646	8445	5245	4982	5050	3828
19 NORWAY	.	.	.	.	.	.	.	.	2472	1860	11359	10753	9992	8728	8421
20 POLAND	-	-	-	-	-	-	-	-	-	-	.	5351	4947	5958	6279
21 PORTUGAL	.	.	.	.	.	.	.	.	.	.	4541	4385	4669	3544	2713
22 ROMANIA	-	-	-	-	-	-	-	-	-	-	-	.	.	.	.
23 SPAIN	.	.	.	.	.	.	.	.	2483	2225	1605	2092	1880	1297	1339
24 SWEDEN	-	-	3276	2798	1361	1596	3281	3353	4401	3519	5653	4980	4376	3475	2762
25 SWITZERLAND	.	.	.	.	.	.	6890	7249	8459	8017	6262	5159	3966	2714	2269
26 TURKEY	-	-	-	-	-	-	-	-	-	-	-	341	220	312	422
27 UK ENGLAND AND WALES	.	.	.	.	.	.	.	4541	4730	3230	3013	2244	1589	1261	1041
28 UK NORTHERN IRELAND	-	-	-	-	.	.	3366	2512	2590	1955	5145	2296	1013	958	1463
29 UK SCOTLAND	.	.	7623	6282	4167	4030	.	.	8681	4012	4255	3229	2072	1914	1797
30 USA	.	.	.	.	.	.	.	5545	9526	5649	4538	3636	3034	3068	2544
31 YUGOSLAVIA	-	-	-	-	-	-	-	-	-	-	.	.	.	3685	.

- NO MORTALITY DATA ARE AVAILABLE FOR EVEN A BROADER GROUP OF CAUSES FOR THIS DISEASE

. MORTALITY DATA ARE PRESENTED FOR A BROADER GROUP OF CAUSES FOR THIS DISEASE

0 VALUE<0.5

THE STANDARD MORTALITY RATIOS WERE DERIVED WITH A FACTOR OF 1000

SERIAL MORTALITY TABLES FOR VARIOUS COUNTRIES 1901-1975

TABLE 161 : ACCIDENTS - OTHER TRANSPORT : FEMALES

	1901-	1906-	1911-	1916-	1921-	1926-	1931-	1936-	1941-	1946-	1951-	1956-	1961-	1966-	1971-75
1 AUSTRALIA	-	.	.	.	.	.	.	.	12440	9600	7927	6094	4478	4522	4504
2 AUSTRIA	.	.	.	.	-	-	-	-	-	.	24597	15857	8306	7504	7115
3 BELGIUM	.	.	.	.	.	.	.	.	.	.	4104	3407	6673	3228	4452
4 BULGARIA	-	-	-	-	-	.	.	.	.	.	.	.	7201	11737	11264
5 CANADA	-	-	-	-	.	.	.	.	11315	8488	6215	6341	4285	4901	4588
6 CHILE	-	.	.	.	.	.	.	9253	8827	13514	12564	11947	9842	8370	5573
7 CZECHOSLOVAKIA	-	-	-	.	.	.	.	.	11416	10176	8294	10454	11039	10523	9835
8 DENMARK	.	.	.	.	.	.	.	.	.	.	9273	10045	4851	3931	2571
9 EIRE	-	-	-	-	.	.	.	3571	7638	4675	5005	3122	3037	4742	2193
10 FINLAND	.	.	.	.	.	.	.	.	.	.	10351	10816	11055	7365	10231
11 FRANCE	-	-	-	-	.	.	.	.	5788	4172	3623	4287	3974	2450	3031
12 GREECE	-	-	-	-	.	.	.	.	-	-	-	2212	1978	4797	2305
13 HUNGARY	-	-	-	.	.	.	.	.	.	.	19234	14298	14812	13212	12410
14 ICELAND	-	-	.	.	.	.	.	.	.	.	.	.	6897	3125	11429
15 ITALY	.	.	.	.	.	.	.	.	.	.	5592	4546	3985	2582	2381
16 JAPAN	.	.	.	.	.	.	.	.	-	17271	16471	13158	10727	7693	6032
17 NETHERLANDS	.	.	.	.	.	.	6163	7891	15779	11752	9267	5908	5646	4927	2416
18 NEW ZEALAND	-	.	.	.	.	16484	28310	33650	11892	11925	20571	5055	5890	6770	3507
19 NORWAY	.	.	.	.	.	.	.	.	3626	4565	6034	5486	7041	4498	8686
20 POLAND	-	-	-	-	-	-	-	-	-	-	.	11426	11191	12123	12813
21 PORTUGAL	.	.	.	.	.	.	.	.	.	.	7685	8178	8127	7230	5027
22 ROMANIA	-	-	-	-	-	-	-	-	-	-	-	.	.	.	.
23 SPAIN	.	.	.	.	.	.	.	.	5337	3946	3248	4199	4177	2531	3186
24 SWEDEN	-	-	4361	6607	2677	3366	7740	8094	10555	7667	7378	5562	5603	4180	4394
25 SWITZERLAND	.	.	.	.	.	.	10502	11700	16750	15289	11149	9197	7760	5080	5378
26 TURKEY	-	-	-	-	-	-	-	-	-	-	-	2415	724	890	1351
27 UK ENGLAND AND WALES	.	.	.	.	.	.	.	6069	6251	4738	3664	3025	2193	2429	2033
28 UK NORTHERN IRELAND	-	-	-	-	.	.	7207	6388	6369	3814	10187	3901	1202	969	954
29 UK SCOTLAND	.	.	7735	10136	5543	5805	.	.	9154	7738	5223	3927	1393	1125	1805
30 USA	.	.	.	.	.	.	.	5918	7312	6359	4443	4064	4037	4304	4238
31 YUGOSLAVIA	-	-	-	-	-	-	-	-	-	-	.	.	.	9677	.

\- NO MORTALITY DATA ARE AVAILABLE FOR EVEN A BROADER GROUP OF CAUSES FOR THIS DISEASE

. MORTALITY DATA ARE PRESENTED FOR A BROADER GROUP OF CAUSES FOR THIS DISEASE

0 VALUE<0.5

THE STANDARD MORTALITY RATIOS WERE DERIVED WITH A FACTOR OF 10000

SERIAL MORTALITY TABLES FOR VARIOUS COUNTRIES 1901-1975

TABLE 162 : ACCIDENTS - ALL TRANSPORT : MALES

	1901-	1906-	1911-	1916-	1921-	1926-	1931-	1936-	1941-	1946-	1951-	1956-	1961-	1966-	1971-75
1 AUSTRALIA	-	.	.	.	.	.	.	.	19993	26985	34458	32863	32384	34982	33466
2 AUSTRIA	.	.	.	.	-	-	-	-	-	.	19512	38500	30756	38547	41747
3 BELGIUM	.	.	.	.	.	.	.	.	.	.	15105	19655	25800	29537	29511
4 BULGARIA	-	-	-	-	-	.	.	.	.	.	.	.	10756	19102	18464
5 CANADA	-	-	-	-	.	.	.	.	25797	23871	28802	29284	30986	32292	32517
6 CHILE	-	.	.	.	.	.	.	11500	9103	7947	16606	18219	14831	26739	22458
7 CZECHOSLOVAKIA	-	-	-	.	.	.	.	.	14120	13546	14804	19523	22067	27363	25617
8 DENMARK	.	.	.	.	.	.	.	.	.	.	19392	20949	22503	26838	22499
9 EIRE	-	-	-	-	.	.	.	8643	6077	7445	10477	11704	13014	17442	22953
10 FINLAND	.	.	.	.	.	.	.	.	.	.	16077	24669	31392	32342	30997
11 FRANCE	-	-	-	-	.	.	.	.	4515	6081	18187	23736	26246	28156	26682
12 GREECE	-	-	-	-	.	.	.	.	-	-	-	7013	11239	15339	16371
13 HUNGARY	-	-	-	.	.	.	.	.	8835	.	13761	15366	17011	20384	25212
14 ICELAND	-	-	.	.	.	.	.	.	.	.	.	.	32901	31250	29427
15 ITALY	.	.	.	.	.	.	.	.	.	.	19206	23127	27570	28038	28420
16 JAPAN	.	.	.	.	.	.	.	.	-	10943	13276	18496	23903	25232	21695
17 NETHERLANDS	.	.	.	.	.	.	11404	12007	10829	13677	17672	21021	23384	26320	23314
18 NEW ZEALAND	-	.	.	.	.	27820	16114	21341	22417	21760	27330	23974	24736	28448	29437
19 NORWAY	.	.	.	.	.	.	.	.	8403	6276	18070	20510	21509	22166	22126
20 POLAND	-	-	-	-	-	-	-	-	-	-	.	11527	14246	18363	19665
21 PORTUGAL	.	.	.	.	.	.	.	.	.	.	13520	14159	19587	26334	38546
22 ROMANIA	-	-	-	-	-	-	-	-	-	-	-	.	.	.	.
23 SPAIN	.	.	.	.	.	.	.	.	3430	3428	6189	9753	13302	15408	17626
24 SWEDEN	-	-	6429	5647	5562	8768	9691	11696	8672	11767	20075	19991	21425	19588	17474
25 SWITZERLAND	9432	9432	9221	9221	10380	17922	21208	18561	12337	20922	26358	30368	30259	28623	28396
26 TURKEY	-	-	-	-	-	-	-	-	-	-	-	10901	13513	15289	13838
27 UK ENGLAND AND WALES	11637	10123	.	.	.	.	.	22008	19351	13794	14794	16116	16971	15685	14372
28 UK NORTHERN IRELAND	-	-	-	-	.	.	13418	13241	14675	10836	17364	15108	14909	18657	24686
29 UK SCOTLAND	12996	10859	9096	9094	9993	16896	.	.	26269	14743	16239	16785	17936	18896	19032
30 USA	.	.	.	.	.	.	.	34827	34108	31884	31921	29008	28614	32163	28200
31 YUGOSLAVIA	-	-	-	-	-	-	-	-	-	-	.	.	.	20545	.

- NO MORTALITY DATA ARE AVAILABLE FOR EVEN A BROADER GROUP OF CAUSES FOR THIS DISEASE

. MORTALITY DATA ARE PRESENTED FOR A BROADER GROUP OF CAUSES FOR THIS DISEASE

0 VALUE<0.5

THE STANDARD MORTALITY RATIOS WERE DERIVED WITH A FACTOR OF 10000

SERIAL MORTALITY TABLES FOR VARIOUS COUNTRIES 1901-1975

TABLE 162 : ACCIDENTS - ALL TRANSPORT : FEMALES

	1901-	1906-	1911-	1916-	1921-	1926-	1931-	1936-	1941-	1946-	1951-	1956-	1961-	1966-	1971-75
1 AUSTRALIA	-	.	.	.	.	.	.	.	5025	5466	7562	8839	9666	11337	10816
2 AUSTRIA	.	.	.	.	-	-	-	-	-	.	4460	8420	7981	10609	11741
3 BELGIUM	.	.	.	.	.	.	.	.	.	.	3533	5034	6897	9696	10263
4 BULGARIA	-	-	-	-	-	.	.	.	.	.	.	.	2783	4877	5013
5 CANADA	-	-	-	-	.	.	.	.	5335	6153	7990	8758	9768	10783	10972
6 CHILE	-	.	.	.	.	.	.	1072	1047	1546	2560	3043	2553	4960	4401
7 CZECHOSLOVAKIA	-	-	-	.	.	.	.	.	4383	3282	2649	3909	5024	6909	7455
8 DENMARK	.	.	.	.	.	.	.	.	.	.	5000	6203	7608	9623	8556
9 EIRE	-	-	-	-	.	.	.	2018	1595	1899	2196	2972	3590	5203	6311
10 FINLAND	.	.	.	.	.	.	.	.	.	.	4173	5656	7861	9277	9288
11 FRANCE	-	-	-	-	.	.	.	.	1197	1341	3871	5728	7496	8822	8421
12 GREECE	-	-	-	-	.	.	.	.	-	-	-	1829	2611	4115	5073
13 HUNGARY	-	-	-	.	.	.	.	.	2472	.	3050	2931	3427	4813	6439
14 ICELAND	-	-	.	.	.	.	.	.	.	.	.	.	6109	3913	6507
15 ITALY	.	.	.	.	.	.	.	.	.	.	3250	4082	5665	6290	7206
16 JAPAN	.	.	.	.	.	.	.	.	-	3108	3493	4462	5608	6608	6082
17 NETHERLANDS	.	.	.	.	.	.	2873	3028	3425	3932	4238	5304	6121	8391	7728
18 NEW ZEALAND	-	.	.	.	.	6170	4094	5315	3842	4421	6584	6230	7051	8880	10196
19 NORWAY	.	.	.	.	.	.	.	.	2337	1931	2474	3292	4358	5392	5733
20 POLAND	-	-	-	-	-	-	-	-	-	-	.	2300	3114	4325	4770
21 PORTUGAL	.	.	.	.	.	.	.	.	.	.	2695	3217	4218	5864	8400
22 ROMANIA	-	-	-	-	-	-	-	-	-	-	-	.	.	.	.
23 SPAIN	.	.	.	.	.	.	.	.	736	683	1713	2205	2907	4087	5166
24 SWEDEN	-	-	934	1273	1266	1820	2339	2907	2189	2828	4012	4928	6247	6709	6338
25 SWITZERLAND	1603	1603	1380	1380	1855	2726	3738	3759	2483	4350	5779	6588	7551	8469	8764
26 TURKEY	-	-	-	-	-	-	-	-	-	-	-	2891	3602	4430	4288
27 UK ENGLAND AND WALES	1559	1515	.	.	.	.	.	5218	4554	3591	3720	4648	5567	5790	5665
28 UK NORTHERN IRELAND	-	-	-	-	.	.	3727	4060	4530	2989	4099	3864	5389	5679	7719
29 UK SCOTLAND	1304	1049	1165	2103	2188	5041	.	.	5427	4453	4113	4344	5313	6151	6339
30 USA	.	.	.	.	.	.	.	9192	7314	8173	8942	8671	9449	10740	9374
31 YUGOSLAVIA	-	-	-	-	-	-	-	-	-	-	.	.	.	5564	.

- NO MORTALITY DATA ARE AVAILABLE FOR EVEN A BROADER GROUP OF CAUSES FOR THIS DISEASE

. MORTALITY DATA ARE PRESENTED FOR A BROADER GROUP OF CAUSES FOR THIS DISEASE

0 VALUE<0.5

THE STANDARD MORTALITY RATIOS WERE DERIVED WITH A FACTOR OF 10000

SERIAL MORTALITY TABLES FOR VARIOUS COUNTRIES 1901-1975

TABLE 163 : ACCIDENTS - POISONING : MALES

	1901-	1906-	1911-	1916-	1921-	1926-	1931-	1936-	1941-	1946-	1951-	1956-	1961-	1966-	1971-75
1 AUSTRALIA	-	1961	2868	2088	1225	1586	761	700	759	718	1100	1162	1271	1025	555
2 AUSTRIA	.	.	.	.	-	-	-	-	-	.	2229	1951	1782	1100	694
3 BELGIUM	.	.	.	.	.	.	.	.	.	.	719	1031	1047	1275	1110
4 BULGARIA	-	-	-	-	-	.	.	.	.	.	.	.	1310	1767	2296
5 CANADA	-	-	-	-	1949	1746	1749	1254	1187	1245	1537	1269	1416	1834	2086
6 CHILE	-	984	1882	1905	2518	3871	3753	2783	2908	1889	1778	1084	1269	1267	309
7 CZECHOSLOVAKIA	-	-	-	892	762	755	819	824	808	970	1997	1718	2301	2765	3033
8 DENMARK	3043	2147	1611	1481	837	1298	970	973	1415	1779	1569	1471	1208	1000	853
9 EIRE	-	-	-	-	385	321	288	264	331	324	362	308	470	408	606
10 FINLAND	.	.	.	.	.	.	.	.	5198	4378	4626	4589	4624	5915	5934
11 FRANCE	-	-	-	-	.	.	.	.	2743	1753	1369	1323	1239	968	673
12 GREECE	-	-	-	-	.	1303	1257	1203	-	-	-	725	711	598	431
13 HUNGARY	-	-	-	.	.	.	1468	1505	1320	.	1376	1090	928	1124	1379
14 ICELAND	-	-	.	.	.	.	.	.	.	.	.	.	1556	1020	2870
15 ITALY	.	.	.	.	.	.	.	.	.	.	519	562	570	541	444
16 JAPAN	1069	925	1098	1144	1405	1590	1911	1993	-	1556	1236	1177	932	867	605
17 NETHERLANDS	774	712	582	706	593	433	412	377	1097	582	547	519	531	477	452
18 NEW ZEALAND	-	1379	1301	907	1109	1315	1089	872	531	722	804	780	1084	874	695
19 NORWAY	1080	1156	1638	2142	1648	.	.	.	3389	2230	1324	1227	986	1101	1413
20 POLAND	-	-	-	-	-	-	-	-	-	-	3763	2584	3517	4367	4515
21 PORTUGAL	.	.	.	.	.	.	.	.	.	.	884	788	651	975	896
22 ROMANIA	-	-	-	-	-	-	-	-	-	-	-	.	.	.	.
23 SPAIN	2722	1843	1136	1331	1389	1339	1031	1177	3329	4297	634	559	452	388	474
24 SWEDEN	-	-	11	14	24	39	6	3	11	18	842	788	1146	1539	1584
25 SWITZERLAND	2254	2254	1683	1683	1641	1461	612	317	1122	860	985	1146	1309	1020	457
26 TURKEY	-	-	-	-	-	-	-	-	-	-	-	2394	2733	2474	2236
27 UK ENGLAND AND WALES	1545	1457	3298	1974	693	679	525	595	612	657	923	1159	1501	1025	723
28 UK NORTHERN IRELAND	-	-	-	-	1278	1109	610	768	663	639	791	930	1387	849	1639
29 UK SCOTLAND	1712	1637	1355	1072	1018	765	677	780	1241	1904	2343	2310	3185	1114	615
30 USA	10055	6294	4916	4693	3206	3108	2184	1723	1566	1508	1122	1001	1132	1429	1750
31 YUGOSLAVIA	-	-	-	-	-	-	-	-	-	-	.	.	.	1555	.

- NO MORTALITY DATA ARE AVAILABLE FOR EVEN A BROADER GROUP OF CAUSES FOR THIS DISEASE

. MORTALITY DA‾A ARE PRESENTED FOR A BROADER GROUP OF CAUSES FOR THIS DISEASE

0 VALUE<0.5

THE STANDARD MORTALITY RATIOS WERE DERIVED WITH A FACTOR OF 1000

SERIAL MORTALITY TABLES FOR VARIOUS COUNTRIES 1901-1975

TABLE 163 : ACCIDENTS - POISONING : FEMALES

	1901-	1906-	1911-	1916-	1921-	1926-	1931-	1936-	1941-	1946-	1951-	1956-	1961-	1966-	1971-75
1 AUSTRALIA	-	12578	16853	10799	4646	8626	4409	3982	3911	4615	5859	7180	9762	7320	3862
2 AUSTRIA	.	.	.	.	-	-	-	-	-	.	20589	16712	14000	5915	3138
3 BELGIUM	.	.	.	.	.	.	.	.	.	.	5545	6240	8213	11273	9570
4 BULGARIA	-	-	-	-	-	.	.	.	.	.	.	.	4042	3194	4164
5 CANADA	-	-	-	-	10124	8947	6539	5259	6230	6487	6745	6204	7230	9719	10400
6 CHILE	-	10526	18977	19768	29207	36058	26916	24596	20227	16167	5754	6443	10115	7562	826
7 CZECHOSLOVAKIA	-	-	-	4846	4040	3848	4431	3983	5506	6134	10235	9904	14866	18418	19439
8 DENMARK	8660	6705	6745	5426	5288	6166	5456	7874	13599	15004	12061	9160	7386	6312	4416
9 EIRE	-	-	-	-	413	1255	1244	977	2333	2415	2408	2278	3778	2864	3767
10 FINLAND	.	.	.	.	.	.	.	.	10417	9790	6500	6763	6028	5995	6095
11 FRANCE	-	-	-	-	.	.	.	.	24235	13971	10674	10493	9161	7081	4336
12 GREECE	-	-	-	-	.	8697	7740	8875	-	-	-	4990	4465	3273	2898
13 HUNGARY	-	-	-	.	.	.	8820	10054	9964	.	6969	6239	4483	5346	4623
14 ICELAND	-	-	.	.	.	.	.	.	.	.	.	.	3093	12150	10169
15 ITALY	.	.	.	.	.	.	.	.	.	.	2756	2894	3209	2983	2516
16 JAPAN	3308	3428	5892	6667	10282	11251	12403	11469	-	6186	5074	5618	4988	4721	3216
17 NETHERLANDS	3882	4267	3435	4798	4246	3569	2484	2724	7743	4129	3988	3630	4508	4393	3092
18 NEW ZEALAND	-	6944	5779	3905	6004	6291	4741	4238	3321	4772	4309	4694	7555	8355	3820
19 NORWAY	2946	3551	4391	3302	3902	.	.	.	8043	4712	2476	1994	1442	1519	2269
20 POLAND	-	-	-	-	-	-	-	-	-	-	16592	11657	15690	16136	14097
21 PORTUGAL	.	.	.	.	.	.	.	.	.	.	4500	3774	3081	4217	3761
22 ROMANIA	-	-	-	-	-	-	-	-	-	-	-	.	.	.	.
23 SPAIN	11527	7803	4008	4219	4388	4729	4020	4626	20589	27222	3046	2407	1961	1849	2661
24 SWEDEN	-	-	129	62	209	86	82	26	50	47	2807	2755	3970	5522	3019
25 SWITZERLAND	9770	9770	7574	7574	5909	5952	2326	1798	7038	5258	5103	10369	11915	7524	1992
26 TURKEY	-	-	-	-	-	-	-	-	-	-	-	13542	17672	17648	16709
27 UK ENGLAND AND WALES	6790	6246	21853	11872	3023	3743	2421	2897	4046	5937	8386	10942	13946	9248	5450
28 UK NORTHERN IRELAND	-	-	-	-	8140	10233	3443	3930	3782	4558	4688	7407	11246	5335	12437
29 UK SCOTLAND	8619	6530	6132	4979	5090	5157	3540	4838	8004	15141	20262	20648	21782	8696	4418
30 USA	66050	37892	27430	23710	15356	13717	9008	8019	8384	7957	5244	4700	5420	6045	6602
31 YUGOSLAVIA	-	-	-	-	-	-	-	-	-	-	.	.	.	5145	.

- NO MORTALITY DATA ARE AVAILABLE FOR EVEN A BROADER GROUP OF CAUSES FOR THIS DISEASE

. MORTALITY DATA ARE PRESENTED FOR A BROADER GROUP OF CAUSES FOR THIS DISEASE

0 VALUE<0.5

THE STANDARD MORTALITY RATIOS WERE DERIVED WITH A FACTOR OF 10000

SERIAL MORTALITY TABLES FOR VARIOUS COUNTRIES 1901-1975

TABLE 164 : ACCIDENTS - FALLS : MALES

	1901-	1906-	1911-	1916-	1921-	1926-	1931-	1936-	1941-	1946-	1951-	1956-	1961-	1966-	1971-75
1 AUSTRALIA	-	.	.	.	.	.	.	.	1916	1720	1496	1305	1128	1165	1217
2 AUSTRIA	.	.	.	.	-	-	-	-	-	.	1400	2199	2341	2469	2480
3 BELGIUM	.	.	.	.	.	.	.	.	.	.	822	927	1208	1390	1513
4 BULGARIA	-	-	-	-	-	.	.	.	.	.	.	.	569	883	952
5 CANADA	-	-	-	-	.	.	.	.	2047	1931	1491	1342	1165	1152	1191
6 CHILE	-	.	.	.	.	.	.	6028	5500	4022	464	760	1622	1830	2445
7 CZECHOSLOVAKIA	-	-	-	.	.	.	.	.	.	.	1353	1531	1679	1809	1840
8 DENMARK	5956	4682	3333	3721	2665	3041	.	.	.	.	1493	1326	1368	1081	1026
9 EIRE	-	-	-	-	.	.	.	.	.	.	718	793	834	1002	1155
10 FINLAND	9233	7934	7758	6546	.	.	.	.	.	.	1723	1753	1681	1594	1777
11 FRANCE	-	-	-	-	.	.	.	.	303	338	927	1236	1305	1670	1765
12 GREECE	-	-	-	-	.	.	.	.	-	-	-	1230	1461	1438	1312
13 HUNGARY	-	-	-	.	.	.	.	.	.	.	1083	1172	1425	1662	2156
14 ICELAND	-	-	.	.	.	.	.	.	.	.	.	.	1865	1738	1659
15 ITALY	3069	12853	7154	4453	4355	5018	5247	4527	2072	1511	1583	1719	1655	1536	1609
16 JAPAN	.	225	233	231	263	.	.	.	-	1681	1598	1564	1438	1341	1094
17 NETHERLANDS	.	.	.	.	.	.	.	.	.	1120	1004	1064	1231	1386	1234
18 NEW ZEALAND	-	.	.	.	.	.	.	1247	1219	980	1064	1072	1175	1447	1915
19 NORWAY	.	.	.	.	.	.	.	.	.	.	1404	1355	1417	1303	1530
20 POLAND	-	-	-	-	-	-	-	-	-	-	.	398	674	1137	1049
21 PORTUGAL	.	.	.	.	.	.	.	.	.	.	2342	1920	1809	1812	1623
22 ROMANIA	-	-	-	-	-	-	-	-	-	-	-	.	.	.	.
23 SPAIN	.	.	.	.	.	.	.	.	1272	1277	1042	892	728	1007	1084
24 SWEDEN	-	-	.	.	.	.	.	.	.	.	1077	1141	1038	998	1324
25 SWITZERLAND	6918	6918	5812	5812	3994	4386	4161	3606	3709	2967	2794	2410	2566	2173	1897
26 TURKEY	-	-	-	-	-	-	-	-	-	-	-	585	345	204	137
27 UK ENGLAND AND WALES	2094	1569	.	.	.	.	.	2400	1580	1083	1093	1093	1005	904	814
28 UK NORTHERN IRELAND	-	-	-	-	.	.	1342	1749	1450	1444	919	849	1084	931	1195
29 UK SCOTLAND	1752	1380	.	.	.	.	.	.	.	1442	1470	1402	1338	1245	1424
30 USA	.	.	.	.	.	.	.	2801	2483	2143	1760	1466	1319	1171	963
31 YUGOSLAVIA	-	-	-	-	-	-	-	-	-	-	.	.	.	1137	.

- NO MORTALITY DATA ARE AVAILABLE FOR EVEN A BROADER GROUP OF CAUSES FOR THIS DISEASE

. MORTALITY DATA ARE PRESENTED FOR A BROADER GROUP OF CAUSES FOR THIS DISEASE

0 VALUE<0.5

THE STANDARD MORTALITY RATIOS WERE DERIVED WITH A FACTOR OF 1000

SERIAL MORTALITY TABLES FOR VARIOUS COUNTRIES 1901-1975

TABLE 164 : ACCIDENTS - FALLS : FEMALES

	1901-	1906-	1911-	1916-	1921-	1926-	1931-	1936-	1941-	1946-	1951-	1956-	1961-	1966-	1971-75
1 AUSTRALIA	-	.	.	.	.	.	.	.	16138	16005	14858	13078	11048	10874	9876
2 AUSTRIA	.	.	.	.	-	-	-	-	-	.	11734	15879	17066	18976	19685
3 BELGIUM	.	.	.	.	.	.	.	.	.	.	4519	6332	10866	13797	16591
4 BULGARIA	-	-	-	-	-	.	.	.	.	.	.	.	1958	3634	4086
5 CANADA	-	-	-	-	.	.	.	.	21794	20761	13218	11995	10231	8652	7733
6 CHILE	-	.	.	.	.	.	.	11238	9103	7043	963	1847	3445	4245	7258
7 CZECHOSLOVAKIA	-	-	-	.	.	.	.	.	.	.	11889	13323	14508	15084	15652
8 DENMARK	8527	8226	6560	5936	5559	7979	.	.	.	.	22159	22755	24047	14281	10957
9 EIRE	-	-	-	-	.	.	.	.	.	.	9172	9079	10951	12532	15070
10 FINLAND	17390	15134	15666	16623	.	.	.	.	.	.	14044	18838	17745	13015	10881
11 FRANCE	-	-	-	-	.	.	.	.	713	1510	7435	11647	13573	17720	19340
12 GREECE	-	-	-	-	.	.	.	.	-	-	-	6493	11444	12683	11205
13 HUNGARY	-	-	-	.	.	.	.	.	.	.	10466	11853	15364	17727	20896
14 ICELAND	-	-	.	.	.	.	.	.	.	.	.	.	14894	13627	15483
15 ITALY	10730	93698	41286	10858	10534	12101	11545	9847	5914	4806	6465	9422	10914	11310	13411
16 JAPAN	.	350	443	512	418	.	.	.	-	2699	2695	3324	3389	3424	3297
17 NETHERLANDS	.	.	.	.	.	.	.	.	.	9659	10215	12654	15813	19360	16586
18 NEW ZEALAND	-	.	.	.	.	.	.	10447	10960	12919	11247	13916	15565	16387	22815
19 NORWAY	.	.	.	.	.	.	.	.	.	.	16951	17601	18248	16303	17128
20 POLAND	-	-	-	-	-	-	-	-	-	-	.	896	2804	5268	5032
21 PORTUGAL	.	.	.	.	.	.	.	.	.	.	7965	6981	6406	6092	6089
22 ROMANIA	-	-	-	-	-	-	-	-	-	-	-	.	.	.	.
23 SPAIN	.	.	.	.	.	.	.	.	2449	2580	6682	3583	3254	3958	6525
24 SWEDEN	-	-	.	.	.	.	.	.	.	.	13422	13407	12319	10604	13205
25 SWITZERLAND	17250	17250	16948	16948	11834	15735	17434	18178	16810	14670	16256	15996	18063	17390	16297
26 TURKEY	-	-	-	-	-	-	-	-	-	-	-	2098	1095	741	540
27 UK ENGLAND AND WALES	16252	12581	.	.	.	.	.	19380	12555	10181	10835	11434	10362	9939	8765
28 UK NORTHERN IRELAND	-	-	-	-	.	.	11430	17730	14798	12655	11293	10588	12469	11259	14552
29 UK SCOTLAND	4648	3324	.	.	.	.	.	.	.	15410	14771	13621	13793	11568	11878
30 USA	.	.	.	.	.	.	.	30362	25831	21884	15703	12326	10264	8363	6019
31 YUGOSLAVIA	-	-	-	-	-	-	-	-	-	-	.	.	.	4810	.

- NO MORTALITY DATA ARE AVAILABLE FOR EVEN A BROADER GROUP OF CAUSES FOR THIS DISEASE

. MORTALITY DATA ARE PRESENTED FOR A BROADER GROUP OF CAUSES FOR THIS DISEASE

0 VALUE<0.5

THE STANDARD MORTALITY RATIOS WERE DERIVED WITH A FACTOR OF 10000

SERIAL MORTALITY TABLES FOR VARIOUS COUNTRIES 1901-1975

TABLE 165 : ACCIDENTS - "FIRE AND HEAT" : MALES

	1901-	1906-	1911-	1916-	1921-	1926-	1931-	1936-	1941-	1946-	1951-	1956-	1961-	1966-	1971-75
1 AUSTRALIA	-	.	4715	4242	3867	4128	3036	2970	2484	1971	2132	1934	1630	1736	1238
2 AUSTRIA	.	.	.	.	-	-	-	-	-	.	1413	1541	1438	816	795
3 BELGIUM	.	.	.	.	.	.	.	.	.	.	615	1100	845	693	980
4 BULGARIA	-	-	-	-	-	.	.	.	.	.	.	.	1315	1124	800
5 CANADA	-	-	-	-	4732	4465	4162	3738	3672	3384	3223	3121	2952	2931	3022
6 CHILE	-	8426	7066	6982	5591	4438	4749	4490	3833	2201	2712	2328	3046	3332	3160
7 CZECHOSLOVAKIA	-	-	-	2675	2780	3117	2943	2210	4045	1667	1537	1212	1248	1017	1044
8 DENMARK	2831	2355	2000	2069	1878	1633	1398	1420	986	899	771	635	766	762	791
9 EIRE	-	-	-	-	3644	3652	3383	3180	2338	1812	1331	1402	1333	1301	1479
10 FINLAND	.	.	.	.	.	.	.	.	3008	2654	2436	2217	2081	2538	2570
11 FRANCE	-	-	-	-	.	.	.	.	2332	1734	1446	1257	1128	1139	1112
12 GREECE	-	-	-	-	.	3173	3483	2743	-	-	-	1415	1145	892	819
13 HUNGARY	-	-	-	.	.	.	1500	915	1652	.	1749	1311	1163	1078	1252
14 ICELAND	-	-	.	.	.	.	.	.	.	.	.	.	1324	1781	2564
15 ITALY	5061	5499	4893	3904	3745	3703	3217	2950	3290	1875	1411	1139	1088	687	518
16 JAPAN	.	6032	5419	4937	11228	4550	4308	4485	-	2971	2514	2260	2687	1999	1521
17 NETHERLANDS	2762	2413	2284	2302	2155	2269	1596	1355	2245	1337	605	525	557	586	521
18 NEW ZEALAND	-	3710	4625	3681	3342	3630	2018	2016	2276	1780	1868	1452	1386	1387	1081
19 NORWAY	2084	1747	1745	2184	2133	2438	.	.	1907	1207	1044	1141	1184	1233	1239
20 POLAND	-	-	-	-	-	-	-	-	-	-	.	1080	1348	1110	857
21 PORTUGAL	.	.	.	.	.	.	.	.	.	.	3974	3271	2445	2197	1709
22 ROMANIA	-	-	-	-	-	-	-	-	-	-	-	.	.	.	.
23 SPAIN	4305	3914	3364	2847	2486	2023	1909	2353	1333	1190	1526	1192	932	608	714
24 SWEDEN	-	-	.	.	.	.	.	.	.	.	1388	1438	1453	1441	1155
25 SWITZERLAND	3881	3881	3502	3502	2926	2491	1515	1303	1213	943	1455	1071	1107	809	570
26 TURKEY	-	-	-	-	-	-	-	-	-	-	-	5572	4393	2944	2133
27 UK ENGLAND AND WALES	5634	5077	4718	4425	3352	2927	2404	2298	1962	953	1027	921	1072	962	888
28 UK NORTHERN IRELAND	-	-	-	-	4760	4783	4328	3869	2803	1573	1304	1340	1138	1439	1777
29 UK SCOTLAND	5970	5986	6684	6284	5444	4708	3923	3666	2594	1455	1582	1951	1779	2063	2079
30 USA	9093	7332	7612	7315	5683	5848	5264	5129	4941	4364	3665	3281	3305	3109	2668
31 YUGOSLAVIA	-	-	-	-	-	-	-	-	-	-	.	.	.	733	.

- NO MORTALITY DATA ARE AVAILABLE FOR EVEN A BROADER GROUP OF CAUSES FOR THIS DISEASE

. MORTALITY DATA ARE PRESENTED FOR A BROADER GROUP OF CAUSES FOR THIS DISEASE

0 VALUE<0.5

THE STANDARD MORTALITY RATIOS WERE DERIVED WITH A FACTOR OF 1000

SERIAL MORTALITY TABLES FOR VARIOUS COUNTRIES 1901-1975

TABLE 165 : ACCIDENTS - "FIRE AND HEAT" : FEMALES

	1901-	1906-	1911-	1916-	1921-	1926-	1931-	1936-	1941-	1946-	1951-	1956-	1961-	1966-	1971-75
1 AUSTRALIA	-	.	7316	5328	4951	3664	2582	2031	1575	1345	1340	1219	1203	1045	700
2 AUSTRIA	.	.	.	.	-	-	-	-	-	.	1063	917	759	554	380
3 BELGIUM	.	.	.	.	.	.	.	.	.	.	471	422	578	434	504
4 BULGARIA	-	-	-	-	-	.	.	.	.	.	.	.	835	721	578
5 CANADA	-	-	-	-	5016	4361	3626	3075	2921	2672	2399	2145	1867	1706	1648
6 CHILE	-	10533	9525	7816	5749	4278	4298	4938	3306	2235	2579	2647	2798	2749	2117
7 CZECHOSLOVAKIA	-	-	-	2701	2527	3229	2724	2188	1554	1027	1250	1060	945	733	633
8 DENMARK	1971	1717	941	1572	1325	1065	1425	944	965	753	638	593	442	489	546
9 EIRE	-	-	-	-	4601	4458	5039	4519	3608	2649	2070	1575	1622	1522	1544
10 FINLAND	.	.	.	.	.	.	.	.	2781	1618	1193	991	621	797	567
11 FRANCE	-	-	-	-	.	.	.	.	1647	1327	1215	984	822	662	600
12 GREECE	-	-	-	-	.	3468	3436	3121	-	-	-	1650	1615	1162	960
13 HUNGARY	-	-	-	.	.	.	1621	1190	1605	.	1332	1132	879	792	610
14 ICELAND	-	-	.	.	.	.	.	.	.	.	.	.	541	375	588
15 ITALY	7179	7373	6512	5000	4277	3965	3540	2956	2662	1512	1204	929	782	423	291
16 JAPAN	.	5662	4556	3906	10082	3552	3197	3176	-	1964	1662	1513	1482	1283	938
17 NETHERLANDS	2690	2667	2380	2511	2343	1918	1553	1160	1792	953	450	523	425	393	259
18 NEW ZEALAND	-	5000	4334	2727	2419	2266	1353	1455	2004	1741	1205	1056	858	868	638
19 NORWAY	1930	1602	1567	1677	1511	1528	.	.	1203	771	588	600	430	482	424
20 POLAND	-	-	-	-	-	-	-	-	-	-	.	700	719	508	257
21 PORTUGAL	.	.	.	.	.	.	.	.	.	.	4991	4651	3366	1990	1410
22 ROMANIA	-	-	-	-	-	-	-	-	-	-	-	.	.	.	.
23 SPAIN	5045	4958	3973	3685	2653	2041	2052	2021	1305	1272	951	636	519	356	419
24 SWEDEN	-	-	.	.	.	.	.	.	.	.	611	525	571	477	390
25 SWITZERLAND	4886	4886	3758	3758	2792	2423	918	954	778	665	836	672	567	297	270
26 TURKEY	-	-	-	-	-	-	-	-	-	-	-	6230	4802	3122	1997
27 UK ENGLAND AND WALES	7133	6708	5822	5652	3582	3132	2823	2826	2301	1387	1227	1117	1123	924	786
28 UK NORTHERN IRELAND	-	-	-	-	6006	5425	5280	4501	3518	2115	1594	1208	1203	1050	1302
29 UK SCOTLAND	7045	7259	7270	6938	5262	4348	4269	3922	3284	1886	1774	1478	1462	1363	1412
30 USA	12262	9698	9019	8806	6997	5825	4910	4257	3971	3139	2618	2347	2126	1793	1377
31 YUGOSLAVIA	-	-	-	-	-	-	-	-	-	-	.	.	.	698	.

- NO MORTALITY DATA ARE AVAILABLE FOR EVEN A BROADER GROUP OF CAUSES FOR THIS DISEASE

. MORTALITY DATA ARE PRESENTED FOR A BROADER GROUP OF CAUSES FOR THIS DISEASE

0 VALUE<0.5

THE STANDARD MORTALITY RATIOS WERE DERIVED WITH A FACTOR OF 1000

SERIAL MORTALITY TABLES FOR VARIOUS COUNTRIES 1901-1975

TABLE 166 : ACCIDENTS - FIREARMS : MALES

	1901-	1906-	1911-	1916-	1921-	1926-	1931-	1936-	1941-	1946-	1951-	1956-	1961-	1966-	1971-75
1 AUSTRALIA	-	.	2799	2822	2005	2409	1728	1474	1202	1253	1774	1545	1173	753	557
2 AUSTRIA	.	.	.	.	-	-	-	-	-	.	876	545	502	408	223
3 BELGIUM	.	.	.	.	.	.	.	.	.	.	183	183	197	187	199
4 BULGARIA	-	-	-	-	-	.	.	.	.	.	.	.	571	419	383
5 CANADA	-	-	-	-	3040	2008	1883	1434	1290	1478	1582	1477	1213	985	690
6 CHILE	-	.	5585	6024	507	2972	2045	814	816	864	2965	2202	2450	1393	72
7 CZECHOSLOVAKIA	-	-	-	7026	1544	1103	883	654	22580	6526	1317	837	538	451	265
8 DENMARK	258	788	361	308	593	555	408	285	1090	635	556	331	205	139	71
9 EIRE	-	-	-	-	3774	533	495	590	490	515	545	495	474	429	452
10 FINLAND	.	.	.	.	.	.	.	.	4465	2260	924	894	1006	500	364
11 FRANCE	-	-	-	-	.	.	.	.	3048	1234	884	746	679	449	267
12 GREECE	-	-	-	-	.	1283	1419	917	-	-	-	2058	1018	824	573
13 HUNGARY	-	-	-	.	.	.	670	749	1250	.	1498	1078	554	331	130
14 ICELAND	-	-	.	.	.	.	.	.	.	.	.	.	667	714	500
15 ITALY	.	.	.	.	.	.	.	.	.	.	712	528	484	350	319
16 JAPAN	.	229	162	174	156	111	134	116	-	374	289	204	121	68	34
17 NETHERLANDS	.	.	460	1502	429	268	165	185	4127	492	157	148	103	41	47
18 NEW ZEALAND	-	2000	2378	2400	1886	1878	3885	1811	1558	1477	1182	838	729	915	644
19 NORWAY	.	.	.	.	.	.	.	.	1252	1105	1692	1157	902	411	284
20 POLAND	-	-	-	-	-	-	-	-	-	-	.	370	394	363	236
21 PORTUGAL	.	.	.	.	.	.	.	.	.	.	744	694	671	527	804
22 ROMANIA	-	-	-	-	-	-	-	-	-	-	-	.	.	.	.
23 SPAIN	.	2574	2660	2623	2278	1345	1216	3731	1508	1186	895	653	417	170	315
24 SWEDEN	-	-	.	.	.	.	.	.	.	.	771	642	567	290	140
25 SWITZERLAND	996	996	1057	1057	1030	642	.	.	972	453	690	621	353	358	182
26 TURKEY	-	-	-	-	-	-	-	-	-	-	-	1740	348	295	414
27 UK ENGLAND AND WALES	.	.	418	473	300	282	241	298	437	265	309	253	218	116	82
28 UK NORTHERN IRELAND	-	-	-	-	1515	643	651	674	814	444	489	630	375	204	769
29 UK SCOTLAND	.	.	819	669	388	488	224	266	424	424	600	282	371	168	129
30 USA	6684	3170	3116	3169	3185	3113	2975	2523	2287	2161	1956	1818	1592	1602	1451
31 YUGOSLAVIA	-	-	-	-	-	-	-	-	-	-	.	.	.	454	.

- NO MORTALITY DATA ARE AVAILABLE FOR EVEN A BROADER GROUP OF CAUSES FOR THIS DISEASE

. MORTALITY DATA ARE PRESENTED FOR A BROADER GROUP OF CAUSES FOR THIS DISEASE

0 VALUE<0.5

THE STANDARD MORTALITY RATIOS WERE DERIVED WITH A FACTOR OF 100

SERIAL MORTALITY TABLES FOR VARIOUS COUNTRIES 1901-1975

TABLE 166 : ACCIDENTS - FIREARMS : FEMALES

	1901-	1906-	1911-	1916-	1921-	1926-	1931-	1936-	1941-	1946-	1951-	1956-	1961-	1966-	1971-75
1 AUSTRALIA	-	.	3057	3567	1765	1902	1205	1261	1044	1077	1434	1115	1281	1007	621
2 AUSTRIA	.	.	.	.	-	-	-	-	-	.	884	402	241	357	308
3 BELGIUM	.	.	.	.	.	.	.	.	.	.	680	403	454	497	360
4 BULGARIA	-	-	-	-	-	.	.	.	.	.	.	.	818	418	410
5 CANADA	-	-	-	-	3510	2537	1750	1201	1471	1442	1311	1127	1135	1013	658
6 CHILE	-	.	6723	7734	1087	5238	2342	1930	1467	957	5024	3953	4433	2163	229
7 CZECHOSLOVAKIA	-	-	-	11304	2442	1643	1164	1019	28588	13073	1318	530	495	276	157
8 DENMARK	556	769	0	217	593	403	465	0	1324	791	208	263	124	60	118
9 EIRE	-	-	-	-	4375	400	200	202	300	408	316	538	215	417	98
10 FINLAND	.	.	.	.	.	.	.	.	5790	1985	780	267	494	419	473
11 FRANCE	-	-	-	-	.	.	.	.	4547	1769	1189	906	671	485	309
12 GREECE	-	-	-	-	.	2740	2017	1565	-	-	-	1563	1288	864	629
13 HUNGARY	-	-	-	.	.	.	1218	1167	1288	.	599	1261	283	191	136
14 ICELAND	-	-	.	.	.	.	.	.	.	.	.	.	0	0	1429
15 ITALY	.	.	.	.	.	.	.	.	.	.	631	588	507	295	286
16 JAPAN	.	484	379	408	364	423	279	191	-	462	225	166	76	52	21
17 NETHERLANDS	.	.	748	1509	560	260	315	264	5886	183	87	80	49	69	22
18 NEW ZEALAND	-	1667	2059	1842	1628	851	4200	566	926	446	1077	1507	964	860	291
19 NORWAY	.	.	.	.	.	.	.	.	952	755	463	877	163	0	149
20 POLAND	-	-	-	-	-	-	-	-	-	-	.	229	380	249	245
21 PORTUGAL	.	.	.	.	.	.	.	.	.	.	974	571	779	599	1424
22 ROMANIA	-	-	-	-	-	-	-	-	-	-	-	.	.	.	.
23 SPAIN	.	3650	3031	3302	1892	1297	1377	5048	1037	492	770	423	419	195	169
24 SWEDEN	-	-	.	.	.	.	.	.	.	.	302	41	193	75	37
25 SWITZERLAND	1245	1245	1123	1123	1793	1088	.	.	735	503	422	503	457	144	370
26 TURKEY	-	-	-	-	-	-	-	-	-	-	-	2500	863	1097	853
27 UK ENGLAND AND WALES	.	.	467	476	228	244	186	331	573	225	148	151	144	141	67
28 UK NORTHERN IRELAND	-	-	-	-	2500	682	454	217	851	426	426	417	0	588	577
29 UK SCOTLAND	.	.	592	682	509	398	170	222	710	449	341	283	225	226	222
30 USA	9087	4100	4652	5459	5008	4721	4264	3543	3276	3211	2617	2446	2286	2577	2264
31 YUGOSLAVIA	-	-	-	-	-	-	-	-	-	-	.	.	.	1027	.

- NO MORTALITY DATA ARE AVAILABLE FOR EVEN A BROADER GROUP OF CAUSES FOR THIS DISEASE

. MORTALITY DATA ARE PRESENTED FOR A BROADER GROUP OF CAUSES FOR THIS DISEASE

0 VALUE<0.5

THE STANDARD MORTALITY RATIOS WERE DERIVED WITH A FACTOR OF 1000

SERIAL MORTALITY TABLES FOR VARIOUS COUNTRIES 1901-1975

TABLE 167 : ACCIDENTS - DROWNING AND SUBMERSION : MALES

	1901-	1906-	1911-	1916-	1921-	1926-	1931-	1936-	1941-	1946-	1951-	1956-	1961-	1966-	1971-75
1 AUSTRALIA	-	1243	1396	1015	917	916	524	528	525	535	536	453	371	310	333
2 AUSTRIA	.	.	.	.	-	-	-	-	-	.	417	408	362	332	274
3 BELGIUM	.	.	.	.	.	.	.	.	.	.	309	295	249	253	206
4 BULGARIA	-	-	-	-	-	.	.	.	.	.	.	.	440	430	427
5 CANADA	-	-	-	-	1066	1037	1018	882	653	615	624	537	435	433	375
6 CHILE	-	1029	1904	1800	1563	1864	1747	1624	1687	1393	1494	1292	1131	543	79
7 CZECHOSLOVAKIA	-	-	-	591	554	614	456	435	214	225	425	406	405	392	376
8 DENMARK	1131	1152	899	723	711	577	521	479	589	567	219	195	171	185	137
9 EIRE	-	-	-	-	478	469	409	339	421	416	406	401	372	328	247
10 FINLAND	.	.	.	.	.	2149	1952	1617	1640	1575	1188	733	651	630	674
11 FRANCE	-	-	-	-	.	.	.	.	627	648	630	541	511	421	269
12 GREECE	-	-	-	-	.	428	393	434	-	-	-	351	282	254	240
13 HUNGARY	-	-	-	.	.	.	451	561	507	.	377	332	350	339	297
14 ICELAND	-	-	10235	7784	11026	5310	4659	4702	1440	0	.	.	551	524	494
15 ITALY	488	446	454	447	395	413	400	384	378	315	321	319	296	248	224
16 JAPAN	.	1477	1473	1475	1332	1170	1101	1104	-	957	845	711	613	493	393
17 NETHERLANDS	1474	1314	1319	1163	951	829	720	697	755	574	425	377	334	291	217
18 NEW ZEALAND	-	1688	1329	1298	1184	1128	735	818	476	443	489	461	328	340	263
19 NORWAY	2410	2379	2178	1886	1926	2083	1887	2279	1090	903	670	543	492	442	449
20 POLAND	-	-	-	-	-	-	-	-	-	-	.	386	463	460	508
21 PORTUGAL	.	.	.	.	.	.	.	.	.	.	803	664	690	648	571
22 ROMANIA	-	-	-	-	-	-	-	-	-	-	-	.	.	.	.
23 SPAIN	525	598	617	640	552	560	494	579	488	425	339	274	259	294	304
24 SWEDEN	-	-	1897	1725	1288	1048	991	852	834	792	457	383	321	285	286
25 SWITZERLAND	950	950	818	818	668	671	556	408	558	446	431	411	387	300	220
26 TURKEY	-	-	-	-	-	-	-	-	-	-	-	363	309	302	269
27 UK ENGLAND AND WALES	818	710	769	657	475	431	231	256	397	267	220	205	169	129	100
28 UK NORTHERN IRELAND	-	-	-	-	457	301	210	265	395	370	277	263	217	190	159
29 UK SCOTLAND	1258	1189	1227	1214	794	650	678	749	607	508	399	387	354	274	204
30 USA	1893	1336	1143	810	724	730	673	572	470	401	352	310	288	314	334
31 YUGOSLAVIA	-	-	-	-	-	-	-	-	-	-	.	.	.	459	.

- NO MORTALITY DATA ARE AVAILABLE FOR EVEN A BROADER GROUP OF CAUSES FOR THIS DISEASE

. MORTALITY DATA ARE PRESENTED FOR A BROADER GROUP OF CAUSES FOR THIS DISEASE

0 VALUE<0.5

THE STANDARD MORTALITY RATIOS WERE DERIVED WITH A FACTOR OF 100

SERIAL MORTALITY TABLES FOR VARIOUS COUNTRIES 1901-1975

TABLE 167 : ACCIDENTS - DROWNING AND SUBMERSION : FEMALES

	1901-	1906-	1911-	1916-	1921-	1926-	1931-	1936-	1941-	1946-	1951-	1956-	1961-	1966-	1971-75
1 AUSTRALIA	-	22804	24347	25181	20349	18345	10958	9705	13221	10894	10532	10753	9600	7589	7967
2 AUSTRIA	.	.	.	.	-	-	-	-	-	.	11759	10755	9580	7758	6401
3 BELGIUM	.	.	.	.	.	.	.	.	.	.	8129	9356	8189	7125	7975
4 BULGARIA	-	-	-	-	-	.	.	.	.	.	.	.	7431	8414	7459
5 CANADA	-	-	-	-	19544	14128	15255	13212	11462	10803	9681	9797	8552	8679	7652
6 CHILE	-	31900	40195	41800	37123	41008	41353	40041	36743	33835	35928	32424	28815	13364	2186
7 CZECHOSLOVAKIA	-	-	-	21531	18931	21912	14491	14500	7392	7413	12646	9849	8811	9144	8233
8 DENMARK	8600	7289	7563	6178	10738	8394	7118	6117	9412	9451	4688	3575	3097	3366	3173
9 EIRE	-	-	-	-	11052	11588	8441	8594	11765	10389	11421	10256	10491	10764	4464
10 FINLAND	.	.	.	.	.	47595	41050	38345	40671	33857	22547	16499	11615	10426	9250
11 FRANCE	-	-	-	-	.	.	.	.	20914	19218	19290	14958	13031	9956	5879
12 GREECE	-	-	-	-	.	15152	13701	12100	-	-	-	9639	6365	6098	5864
13 HUNGARY	-	-	-	.	.	.	11188	11025	10734	.	8126	6587	5890	5832	4610
14 ICELAND	-	-	47222	18421	26829	47727	34783	20833	15686	0	.	.	10390	8434	3488
15 ITALY	19779	16697	16584	13692	13162	12446	11230	10706	9188	8640	7159	6185	5725	4653	4447
16 JAPAN	.	92292	90051	88454	83588	69075	63255	58813	-	47604	38170	27974	21242	17111	14137
17 NETHERLANDS	44494	41347	41258	39680	29812	24633	16780	15650	22910	15036	10651	8951	7756	6748	5020
18 NEW ZEALAND	-	34247	20972	30575	25156	18762	16790	17073	12804	12868	13973	13412	9456	8971	6639
19 NORWAY	32338	29042	32500	27147	30596	24043	23030	23116	18818	18820	14264	9993	8993	7959	6038
20 POLAND	-	-	-	-	-	-	-	-	-	-	.	9410	11126	10939	9290
21 PORTUGAL	.	.	.	.	.	.	.	.	.	.	26084	21247	19782	20330	15968
22 ROMANIA	-	-	-	-	-	-	-	-	-	-	-	.	.	.	.
23 SPAIN	14350	18066	17240	16791	14606	13496	12405	15280	11732	10568	9355	8000	9661	8214	7921
24 SWEDEN	-	-	27926	26096	21521	19375	16917	14673	12365	11950	8277	6473	5132	5038	4829
25 SWITZERLAND	20973	20973	18271	18271	13522	14485	11153	7423	8481	6772	7406	7935	6963	6499	4042
26 TURKEY	-	-	-	-	-	-	-	-	-	-	-	10611	8419	7361	5650
27 UK ENGLAND AND WALES	15144	13572	14377	12873	10054	9080	3103	4316	6887	6230	5621	5685	4655	3350	2527
28 UK NORTHERN IRELAND	-	-	-	-	10670	9325	5800	6471	7224	7011	6360	6563	4463	2047	3411
29 UK SCOTLAND	21490	21083	21503	21692	17329	16359	14775	12595	13672	13090	11420	9202	6722	4496	2626
30 USA	19128	13595	16167	11329	10202	10772	10067	8642	7823	6805	6215	5599	5754	6082	6366
31 YUGOSLAVIA	-	-	-	-	-	-	-	-	-	-	.	.	.	11551	.

- NO MORTALITY DATA ARE AVAILABLE FOR EVEN A BROADER GROUP OF CAUSES FOR THIS DISEASE

. MORTALITY DATA ARE PRESENTED FOR A BROADER GROUP OF CAUSES FOR THIS DISEASE

0 VALUE<0.5

THE STANDARD MORTALITY RATIOS WERE DERIVED WITH A FACTOR OF 10000

SERIAL MORTALITY TABLES FOR VARIOUS COUNTRIES 1901-1975

TABLE 168 : ACCIDENTS - OTHER THAN MOTOR VEHICLE : MALES

	1901-	1906-	1911-	1916-	1921-	1926-	1931-	1936-	1941-	1946-	1951-	1956-	1961-	1966-	1971-75
1 AUSTRALIA	-	.	.	.	.	.	.	.	26823	24688	24211	21228	18684	18092	17082
2 AUSTRIA	.	.	.	.	-	-	-	-	-	40513	36405	27948	24982	24042	23590
3 BELGIUM	29234	29821	33476	36314	.	.	.	.	.	.	25251	22547	18808	17823	17137
4 BULGARIA	-	-	-	-	-	.	.	.	.	.	.	.	26360	22055	23316
5 CANADA	-	-	-	-	.	.	.	.	36499	30379	28863	25530	22537	22104	23510
6 CHILE	-	.	.	.	.	.	.	63410	63472	63763	80220	68925	73067	60443	71948
7 CZECHOSLOVAKIA	-	-	-	.	.	.	.	.	54467	27999	30649	26575	26475	25481	24284
8 DENMARK	.	.	.	.	.	.	.	.	32519	21420	17055	13961	13566	12411	12260
9 EIRE	-	-	-	-	.	.	.	18429	17444	15888	13119	12432	12225	14386	15505
10 FINLAND	.	.	.	.	.	.	.	.	.	.	35493	32467	31352	33433	36547
11 FRANCE	-	-	-	-	.	.	.	.	47139	33968	28335	25156	25492	27123	27113
12 GREECE	-	-	-	-	.	.	.	.	-	-	-	18530	17008	16611	15119
13 HUNGARY	-	-	-	.	.	.	.	.	.	.	24572	21059	20732	21798	23583
14 ICELAND	-	-	.	.	.	.	.	.	.	.	36000	31194	34292	30922	35878
15 ITALY	.	.	.	.	.	.	.	.	.	.	17195	16629	16380	14095	13632
16 JAPAN	.	35508	37186	38602	37803	.	.	.	-	36066	32906	29931	25722	22150	17778
17 NETHERLANDS	.	.	.	.	.	.	.	.	45291	19092	16695	13332	13308	12996	10911
18 NEW ZEALAND	-	.	.	.	.	.	.	27073	28547	23126	23352	19926	18871	20545	20652
19 NORWAY	35288	34482	.	.	.	.	.	.	32712	23817	26062	23029	22007	20351	21943
20 POLAND	-	-	-	-	-	-	-	-	-	-	.	30204	31074	33007	34560
21 PORTUGAL	.	.	.	.	.	.	.	.	.	.	9505	24449	23930	23137	22155
22 ROMANIA	-	-	-	-	-	-	-	-	-	-	-	.	.	.	.
23 SPAIN	.	.	.	.	.	.	.	.	33682	28879	19534	18898	18458	18389	17728
24 SWEDEN	-	-	.	.	.	.	22120	21971	24513	20424	17584	16456	15850	15506	18692
25 SWITZERLAND	.	.	.	.	.	.	45766	39497	44306	34933	29258	25435	25664	22776	19061
26 TURKEY	-	-	-	-	-	-	-	-	-	-	-	30055	23996	23394	18523
27 UK ENGLAND AND WALES	.	.	.	.	.	.	.	25649	21238	14799	13965	13037	12336	11481	10210
28 UK NORTHERN IRELAND	-	-	-	-	.	.	.	15590	14202	13079	14663	12638	11688	10686	14471
29 UK SCOTLAND	61863	56350	57547	51713	.	.	.	.	31362	23211	22376	20428	19885	18179	18233
30 USA	.	.	.	.	.	.	.	36912	38620	30823	25059	21753	20331	21801	21108
31 YUGOSLAVIA	-	-	-	-	-	-	-	-	-	-	.	.	.	23981	.

- NO MORTALITY DATA ARE AVAILABLE FOR EVEN A BROADER GROUP OF CAUSES FOR THIS DISEASE

. MORTALITY DATA ARE PRESENTED FOR A BROADER GROUP OF CAUSES FOR THIS DISEASE

0 VALUE<0.5

THE STANDARD MORTALITY RATIOS WERE DERIVED WITH A FACTOR OF 10000

SERIAL MORTALITY TABLES FOR VARIOUS COUNTRIES 1901-1975

TABLE 168 : ACCIDENTS - OTHER THAN MOTOR VEHICLE : FEMALES

	1901-	1906-	1911-	1916-	1921-	1926-	1931-	1936-	1941-	1946-	1951-	1956-	1961-	1966-	1971-75
1 AUSTRALIA	-	.	.	.	.	.	.	.	11271	10914	10578	9765	8998	8894	8011
2 AUSTRIA	.	.	.	.	-	-	-	-	-	16597	13917	13134	12708	12977	13358
3 BELGIUM	6925	6974	6538	8740	.	.	.	.	.	.	11328	11699	11472	13358	13957
4 BULGARIA	-	-	-	-	-	.	.	.	.	.	.	.	7520	6463	6427
5 CANADA	-	-	-	-	.	.	.	.	14485	13913	11137	10475	9313	8759	8894
6 CHILE	-	.	.	.	.	.	.	19019	15830	15710	17956	15394	16772	15813	18127
7 CZECHOSLOVAKIA	-	-	-	.	.	.	.	.	10740	7438	12003	11346	11940	12388	12737
8 DENMARK	.	.	.	.	.	.	.	.	14363	13257	13202	13160	13572	9400	8415
9 EIRE	-	-	-	-	.	.	.	10840	10453	9668	8401	7519	8605	10028	11195
10 FINLAND	.	.	.	.	.	.	.	.	.	.	11379	12744	11325	9747	9247
11 FRANCE	-	-	-	-	.	.	.	.	17104	11414	11808	13091	14125	15823	16227
12 GREECE	-	-	-	-	.	.	.	.	-	-	-	7453	9341	9558	9001
13 HUNGARY	-	-	-	.	.	.	.	.	.	.	9355	9221	10419	11824	13582
14 ICELAND	-	-	.	.	.	.	.	.	.	.	7956	7978	8932	9729	12659
15 ITALY	.	.	.	.	.	.	.	.	.	.	5497	6422	7544	7190	8227
16 JAPAN	.	19389	18760	18565	17669	.	.	.	-	12152	10506	9258	7166	6516	5672
17 NETHERLANDS	.	.	.	.	.	.	.	.	18182	8489	8992	7868	9495	11295	9813
18 NEW ZEALAND	-	.	.	.	.	.	.	9788	9586	10585	9948	10103	10669	11448	13465
19 NORWAY	7340	6465	.	.	.	.	.	.	12340	11096	10780	10851	11221	10378	10664
20 POLAND	-	-	-	-	-	-	-	-	-	-	.	7785	8819	9743	9271
21 PORTUGAL	.	.	.	.	.	.	.	.	.	.	5718	9688	8645	7973	7006
22 ROMANIA	-	-	-	-	-	-	-	-	-	-	-	.	.	.	.
23 SPAIN	.	.	.	.	.	.	.	.	9597	9378	6997	5116	5653	5189	6586
24 SWEDEN	-	-	.	.	.	.	9334	10482	10178	8629	8483	8409	8216	7779	9870
25 SWITZERLAND	.	.	.	.	.	.	14288	13684	13321	11856	11386	11615	12791	11839	10884
26 TURKEY	-	-	-	-	-	-	-	-	-	-	-	12545	10524	9948	7624
27 UK ENGLAND AND WALES	.	.	.	.	.	.	.	13122	9835	8269	8536	9010	8860	8527	7686
28 UK NORTHERN IRELAND	-	-	-	-	.	.	.	10533	9805	8141	8932	8227	8714	7834	10715
29 UK SCOTLAND	20243	19073	18165	15932	.	.	.	.	13307	12397	12950	11955	11949	10420	10706
30 USA	.	.	.	.	.	.	.	18640	17755	15516	11938	10245	9370	8968	7900
31 YUGOSLAVIA	-	-	-	-	-	-	-	-	-	-	.	.	.	7299	.

- NO MORTALITY DATA ARE AVAILABLE FOR EVEN A BROADER GROUP OF CAUSES FOR THIS DISEASE

. MORTALITY DATA ARE PRESENTED FOR A BROADER GROUP OF CAUSES FOR THIS DISEASE

0 VALUE<0.5

THE STANDARD MORTALITY RATIOS WERE DERIVED WITH A FACTOR OF 10000

SERIAL MORTALITY TABLES FOR VARIOUS COUNTRIES 1901-1975

TABLE 169 : ACCIDENTS - ALL FORMS : MALES

	1901-	1906-	1911-	1916-	1921-	1926-	1931-	1936-	1941-	1946-	1951-	1956-	1961-	1966-	1971-75
1 AUSTRALIA	-	31052	35637	28921	28204	31571	25286	29358	22003	24359	27251	25313	24062	25134	24135
2 AUSTRIA	18712	19831	26705	21630	-	-	-	-	-	27843	25861	30835	26943	29803	31174
3 BELGIUM		.	.	.	.	.	.	.	.	.	21146	21683	21293	22875	22524
4 BULGARIA	-	-	-	-	-	.	.	.	.	.	.	.	18579	19974	20522
5 CANADA	-	-	-	-	30460	30380	26551	26877	27966	26016	27287	26109	25288	25902	26997
6 CHILE	-	66094	57474	58236	58162	52240	46069	53507	36065	36478	47440	43370	45914	44369	49424
7 CZECHOSLOVAKIA	-	-	-	19902	16009	18269	16512	16380	35922	17998	19010	22459	23413	25400	24216
8 DENMARK	22308	20991	17079	15873	13685	14521	14025	14155	21279	17097	16639	16028	16774	17785	16182
9 EIRE	-	-	-	-	13456	11861	12426	12241	11408	11521	11339	11605	12307	15372	18498
10 FINLAND	.	.	.	.	.	26774	23102	27469	32553	29945	25656	26669	29422	31051	32136
11 FRANCE	-	-	-	-	.	.	.	.	27262	22252	24217	24833	26178	28259	27628
12 GREECE	-	-	-	-	.	18169	15277	14091	-	-	-	13615	14801	15877	15821
13 HUNGARY	-	-	-	18546	17507	15655	13420	15310	16205	20168	18415	16517	17161	19331	22942
14 ICELAND	-	-	75387	58095	74671	43590	38500	38960	.	.	26019	23119	25840	24619	27389
15 ITALY	15946	32721	21686	16712	16043	17312	17319	16656	25804	17036	17484	19157	21082	20037	19992
16 JAPAN	20686	21554	.	.	30480	21966	22495	23750	-	22121	21521	22765	23753	23090	19277
17 NETHERLANDS	17297	16117	16451	16385	14406	14905	14448	14555	29100	15450	15896	15673	16941	18317	16227
18 NEW ZEALAND	-	32604	32318	27908	26383	28722	24632	24518	21900	20261	22485	20296	20093	22740	23876
19 NORWAY	21364	20954	20512	19511	18968	21069	18465	27109	22603	16644	19145	18607	18730	18477	19516
20 POLAND	-	-	-	-	-	-	-	-	-	-	28057	20277	22201	24701	27190
21 PORTUGAL	.	.	.	.	.	.	.	.	.	.	14257	18744	20949	24034	29232
22 ROMANIA	-	-	-	-	-	-	-	-	-	-	-	.	.	.	.
23 SPAIN	18679	19097	17046	16933	15655	15265	15221	27925	19669	17086	13450	14630	16165	17318	17870
24 SWEDEN	-	-	22218	20936	16306	16557	16145	16957	16857	16168	16992	16542	17012	16399	17867
25 SWITZERLAND	34622	34622	32475	32475	30178	33438	32892	28095	27780	26659	26516	26431	27058	25116	22890
26 TURKEY	-	-	-	-	-	-	-	-	-	-	-	21921	19932	20417	16916
27 UK ENGLAND AND WALES	26103	22409	25974	28106	17968	20489	19586	20651	19385	13621	13623	13930	14143	13211	11947
28 UK NORTHERN IRELAND	-	-	-	-	15721	15557	15669	16466	18476	14703	14297	13259	13107	14098	18888
29 UK SCOTLAND	34499	31502	33006	30457	24460	25475	22302	26554	26460	18727	18874	18384	19022	18444	18586
30 USA	73698	57583	48044	42905	37830	40749	37937	37062	33921	30146	27119	24201	23417	25859	24005
31 YUGOSLAVIA	-	-	-	-	-	-	-	-	-	-	.	.	.	21770	.

- NO MORTALITY DATA ARE AVAILABLE FOR EVEN A BROADER GROUP OF CAUSES FOR THIS DISEASE

. MORTALITY DATA ARE PRESENTED FOR A BROADER GROUP OF CAUSES FOR THIS DISEASE

0 VALUE<0.5

THE STANDARD MORTALITY RATIOS WERE DERIVED WITH A FACTOR OF 10000

SERIAL MORTALITY TABLES FOR VARIOUS COUNTRIES 1901-1975

TABLE 169 : ACCIDENTS - ALL FORMS : FEMALES

	1901-	1906-	1911-	1916-	1921-	1926-	1931-	1936-	1941-	1946-	1951-	1956-	1961-	1966-	1971-75
1 AUSTRALIA	-	10345	10064	8436	7981	8911	7879	9555	8427	8617	9438	9533	9445	10057	9282
2 AUSTRIA	6384	6226	5537	8642	-	-	-	-	-	11300	9552	11194	11087	12300	12984
3 BELGIUM	.	.	.	.	.	.	.	.	.	.	8524	9462	9929	12349	12925
4 BULGARIA	-	-	-	-	-	.	.	.	.	.	.	.	5276	5582	5631
5 CANADA	-	-	-	-	10385	10212	9884	11036	10458	10714	9999	9921	9704	9763	9927
6 CHILE	-	15856	13622	16390	18325	13596	11417	20874	9017	9018	10722	9777	10564	11132	12187
7 CZECHOSLOVAKIA	-	-	-	5970	4878	6315	5396	5361	7811	5233	6668	8286	9112	10228	10752
8 DENMARK	5764	5184	5244	5529	5053	5976	6996	7386	9335	9287	9968	10466	11525	9688	8673
9 EIRE	-	-	-	-	5668	5767	6427	6757	6565	6436	6061	5920	6897	8368	9630
10 FINLAND	.	.	.	.	.	6317	5367	7347	9364	7858	7944	9788	9850	9645	9224
11 FRANCE	-	-	-	-	.	.	.	.	10685	7687	9073	10679	12063	13757	13924
12 GREECE	-	-	-	-	.	6975	6602	6015	-	-	-	5247	6862	7561	7751
13 HUNGARY	-	-	-	6881	6041	5210	4305	4798	5252	5646	6064	6328	7322	8920	10806
14 ICELAND	-	-	6638	5622	4472	5734	6177	5030	.	.	6542	6375	7872	7611	10215
15 ITALY	8011	23141	12764	6020	5594	5814	5471	4892	6842	4437	4517	5514	6923	7013	8051
16 JAPAN	10618	10820	.	.	20314	10154	9811	9081	-	7634	6927	6829	6280	6504	5835
17 NETHERLANDS	5841	5874	5565	6042	5164	5356	5158	5486	11636	6325	6949	6878	8260	10366	9266
18 NEW ZEALAND	-	7974	7313	6762	6401	8161	8336	7751	6920	7889	8142	8744	9406	10592	12499
19 NORWAY	4528	4006	4152	3783	3942	4202	3903	6292	8641	7726	7727	8158	8754	8713	8849
20 POLAND	-	-	-	-	-	-	-	-	-	-	7064	5209	6217	7279	7807
21 PORTUGAL	.	.	.	.	.	.	.	.	.	.	5569	6973	6825	7139	7646
22 ROMANIA	-	-	-	-	-	-	-	-	-	-	-	.	.	.	.
23 SPAIN	6709	6967	6109	5754	4734	4265	4491	6615	5776	5733	4861	3929	4589	4849	6150
24 SWEDEN	-	-	4705	4863	4733	5660	6457	7421	6880	6329	6748	7157	7553	7506	8784
25 SWITZERLAND	9778	9778	9200	9200	8015	8900	9651	9361	8482	8562	9088	9688	10894	10772	10277
26 TURKEY	-	-	-	-	-	-	-	-	-	-	-	8509	7774	7809	6352
27 UK ENGLAND AND WALES	10721	9489	9247	8281	6739	7898	8317	9071	7792	6544	6856	7594	7881	7744	7157
28 UK NORTHERN IRELAND	-	-	-	-	7996	8148	8358	9517	8770	6706	6924	6660	7685	7248	9914
29 UK SCOTLAND	11801	11107	10782	9811	8710	9570	9408	9956	10113	9308	9683	9271	9785	9150	9407
30 USA	22257	16271	15048	14840	14529	15420	15284	15403	13530	12740	11004	9852	9605	9846	8609
31 YUGOSLAVIA	-	-	-	-	-	-	-	-	-	-	.	.	.	6440	.

- NO MORTALITY DATA ARE AVAILABLE FOR EVEN A BROADER GROUP OF CAUSES FOR THIS DISEASE

. MORTALITY DATA ARE PRESENTED FOR A BROADER GROUP OF CAUSES FOR THIS DISEASE

0 VALUE<0.5

THE STANDARD MORTALITY RATIOS WERE DERIVED WITH A FACTOR OF 10000

SERIAL MORTALITY TABLES FOR VARIOUS COUNTRIES 1901-1975

TABLE 170 : SUICIDE AND SELF-INFLICTED INJURY : MALES

	1901-	1906-	1911-	1916-	1921-	1926-	1931-	1936-	1941-	1946-	1951-	1956-	1961-	1966-	1971-75
1 AUSTRALIA	-	25577	29047	23020	23470	26757	23359	19718	12611	16045	17992	19780	22966	21214	19810
2 AUSTRIA	41092	47649	45344	31295	-	-	-	-	-	34104	33711	34844	33498	35086	35889
3 BELGIUM	27437	27944	29227	25764	.	.	.	.	.	.	20619	21079	21046	22104	22142
4 BULGARIA	-	-	-	-	-	30359	32624	31828	31867	21888	14434	11850	12912	15800	17900
5 CANADA	-	-	-	-	16105	16588	17968	16061	11703	14094	13592	15042	15565	18584	22188
6 CHILE	-	5817	8025	7233	7692	11014	16276	11913	8867	8707	13038	18492	11879	15828	15516
7 CZECHOSLOVAKIA	-	-	-	43957	50066	54199	57517	47592	37867	32051	32944	34178	33880	38667	37700
8 DENMARK	64245	55858	50599	32759	27645	32508	32007	30811	27040	35036	35342	31443	26409	26917	32214
9 EIRE	-	-	-	-	4994	6215	6414	5295	4794	4580	4060	4684	4110	3893	6149
10 FINLAND	13172	17171	21740	20007	27611	39896	44218	45266	36172	36425	39046	44124	41046	41146	44294
11 FRANCE	-	-	-	-	34036	32819	35700	31494	19076	22676	26306	27135	25773	25423	24736
12 GREECE	-	-	-	-	5049	9404	10907	10741	-	-	-	6071	5669	5304	4435
13 HUNGARY	-	-	-	45085	53797	54796	58440	50284	45121	39850	37019	37272	42121	49797	56753
14 ICELAND	-	-	18621	16561	15294	12500	16418	23288	16116	19403	23630	14286	20680	27415	17548
15 ITALY	13814	16386	17010	13319	16887	19383	17788	13622	8915	10706	10995	10433	8680	8596	8636
16 JAPAN	30993	29472	33574	30853	35605	39042	41275	42901	-	36368	38141	39722	25358	20872	23642
17 NETHERLANDS	14545	14709	13370	13633	12681	13190	15415	14500	26619	10966	9813	9583	9823	10351	11970
18 NEW ZEALAND	-	22872	26415	23399	25504	28143	26261	19388	15338	15692	16348	16652	14804	16438	15018
19 NORWAY	13009	11269	12831	8983	12941	14115	13364	12572	10447	12005	12074	12355	12279	12170	14319
20 POLAND	-	-	-	-	-	-	-	-	-	-	-	16961	19614	22823	23740
21 PORTUGAL	9965	11616	16470	13776	14783	15369	25615	25394	20487	20482	9303	18671	18632	18337	15950
22 ROMANIA	-	-	-	-	-	-	-	-	-	-	-	.	.	.	.
23 SPAIN	4787	7366	11509	11986	11825	11817	11731	11996	11468	11171	10965	9520	8991	7927	7320
24 SWEDEN	-	-	36695	24935	29349	29686	30808	28057	23787	24099	27425	28769	27129	30460	27920
25 SWITZERLAND	51523	51526	46881	46881	47107	48689	50136	44249	40304	39080	35560	33342	29042	29009	30995
26 TURKEY	-	-	-	-	-	-	-	-	-	-	-	3479	3613	3415	2281
27 UK ENGLAND AND WALES	22576	21481	19599	15066	18870	21346	22269	18668	13337	14601	14551	14870	14263	11503	9685
28 UK NORTHERN IRELAND	-	-	-	-	9351	11217	10085	8635	6987	6950	6016	5854	7839	8149	5411
29 UK SCOTLAND	13793	12437	11902	8929	12708	17694	18115	14741	11068	9142	8929	11935	11448	10048	10400
30 USA	43378	38073	34973	24074	23491	27044	30637	26757	18879	19946	18649	19225	19704	19456	21011
31 YUGOSLAVIA	-	-	-	-	-	-	-	-	-	-	.	.	.	25026	.

- NO MORTALITY DATA ARE AVAILABLE FOR EVEN A BROADER GROUP OF CAUSES FOR THIS DISEASE

. MORTALITY DATA ARE PRESENTED FOR A BROADER GROUP OF CAUSES FOR THIS DISEASE

0 VALUE<0.5

THE STANDARD MORTALITY RATIOS WERE DERIVED WITH A FACTOR OF 10000

SERIAL MORTALITY TABLES FOR VARIOUS COUNTRIES 1901-1975

TABLE 170 : SUICIDE AND SELF-INFLICTED INJURY : FEMALES

	1901-	1906-	1911-	1916-	1921-	1926-	1931-	1936-	1941-	1946-	1951-	1956-	1961-	1966-	1971-75
1 AUSTRALIA	-	6315	7589	5977	5602	6207	6285	5897	5126	5438	6053	7018	10820	10479	9063
2 AUSTRIA	11319	14867	14418	14347	-	-	-	-	-	14399	14114	13714	12569	12773	13215
3 BELGIUM	6400	6622	7715	8435	.	.	.	.	.	.	7029	7820	8040	9377	9693
4 BULGARIA	-	-	-	-	-	10282	13696	13548	11944	8272	6355	5517	6302	7110	7383
5 CANADA	-	-	-	-	5474	4886	5322	5253	4518	4418	4228	4023	4721	6708	8142
6 CHILE	-	982	2740	1487	3453	4126	6253	4579	3175	2941	3080	4195	2904	3987	3115
7 CZECHOSLOVAKIA	-	-	-	16301	15561	17502	18275	17296	16498	12468	12087	12984	12701	13534	12208
8 DENMARK	12674	11162	11349	10171	9149	10297	12396	13220	19280	20125	16115	14499	13610	13789	17813
9 EIRE	-	-	-	-	1443	1512	1596	1725	1297	1088	1022	1336	1007	1117	2185
10 FINLAND	2612	4304	5806	5101	6283	7269	7361	7807	6980	6771	8283	10579	9852	9963	10201
11 FRANCE	-	-	-	-	9229	9420	9408	9557	6789	6768	7187	8482	7534	8196	8718
12 GREECE	-	-	-	-	1671	2779	4134	4458	-	-	-	2980	2619	2177	1974
13 HUNGARY	-	-	-	21514	20887	22703	24398	22200	19844	15573	14436	14349	16488	18346	20789
14 ICELAND	-	-	10227	6417	4523	4225	5727	5328	4962	7042	6536	6344	4709	6616	6557
15 ITALY	3523	4911	6122	5252	5738	6048	5550	4438	2971	3905	4004	3976	3350	3328	3512
16 JAPAN	18772	18248	19736	18995	22134	23311	24137	23999	-	21917	23275	25382	17337	14836	15941
17 NETHERLANDS	3824	4416	4047	5131	4159	5520	6270	7018	7819	5287	5128	5923	5577	5794	7580
18 NEW ZEALAND	-	4502	5900	5853	6701	7205	6576	6456	6732	5859	5591	6191	6927	7869	7032
19 NORWAY	2585	2548	2317	2162	2702	2715	3046	3260	2918	2726	3417	3059	3396	3816	4559
20 POLAND	-	-	-	-	-	-	-	-	-	-	-	3377	3973	4307	4456
21 PORTUGAL	3422	3713	6297	4644	4870	4159	6907	6947	6455	5661	2936	4467	4435	4566	4193
22 ROMANIA	-	-	-	-	-	-	-	-	-	-	-	.	.	.	.
23 SPAIN	1141	1923	3078	3669	3254	3403	3242	3098	3728	3358	3322	3102	2705	2401	2355
24 SWEDEN	-	-	7635	6528	6596	6359	6784	7316	7153	7515	8102	8590	9206	11171	10725
25 SWITZERLAND	10167	10167	12059	12059	11262	12916	13474	11789	14219	13342	11582	10764	10191	9869	11626
26 TURKEY	-	-	-	-	-	-	-	-	-	-	-	1661	1761	1606	1285
27 UK ENGLAND AND WALES	6810	6420	6291	5643	6379	7958	8524	8070	6059	7220	7239	8423	8947	7189	5924
28 UK NORTHERN IRELAND	-	-	-	-	3259	2570	2586	2605	1499	2152	2005	2957	3899	5063	3200
29 UK SCOTLAND	4159	3879	3576	3213	4452	6690	6595	6397	4994	3934	4123	5708	6321	5696	6454
30 USA	14085	12036	11372	8920	7677	8433	8707	8140	6627	6059	4966	5247	6377	6901	7281
31 YUGOSLAVIA	-	-	-	-	-	-	-	-	-	-	.	.	.	8484	.

\- NO MORTALITY DATA ARE AVAILABLE FOR EVEN A BROADER GROUP OF CAUSES FOR THIS DISEASE

. MORTALITY DATA ARE PRESENTED FOR A BROADER GROUP OF CAUSES FOR THIS DISEASE

0 VALUE<0.5

THE STANDARD MORTALITY RATIOS WERE DERIVED WITH A FACTOR OF 10000

SERIAL MORTALITY TABLES FOR VARIOUS COUNTRIES 1901-1975

TABLE 170 : SUICIDE AND SELF-INFLICTED INJURY : PERSONS

	1901-	1906-	1911-	1916-	1921-	1926-	1931-	1936-	1941-	1946-	1951-	1956-	1961-	1966-	1971-75
1 AUSTRALIA	-	16736	19080	14963	14901	16828	15033	12900	8891	10756	11969	13320	16784	15729	14305
2 AUSTRIA	25671	30664	29312	22510	-	42693	44861	41135	-	23153	22738	22948	21660	22423	23018
3 BELGIUM	16845	17200	18333	16953	.	.	.	.	.	.	13517	14114	14169	15350	15514
4 BULGARIA	-	-	-	-	-	20400	23242	22737	21914	15061	10380	8613	9537	11371	12531
5 CANADA	.	3791	6454	5236	11148	11106	11988	10907	8242	9374	8976	9588	10129	12552	14988
6 CHILE	-	3375	5349	4315	5533	7497	11155	8167	5949	5731	7868	11068	7203	9642	9003
7 CZECHOSLOVAKIA	-	-	-	29228	31690	34663	36657	31515	26504	21630	21825	22873	22569	25230	24028
8 DENMARK	35269	30741	28487	20033	17929	20897	21815	21730	23046	27370	25448	22699	19786	20099	24718
9 EIRE	-	-	-	-	3241	3893	4050	3550	3058	2846	2551	3007	2543	2486	4130
10 FINLAND	7717	10538	13503	12272	16533	22927	24788	25248	20389	20176	22036	25631	23900	24024	25574
11 FRANCE	28446	24652	22725	15014	20755	20296	21586	19613	12361	13980	15878	17004	15913	16138	16154
12 GREECE	-	-	-	-	3327	6018	7442	7526	-	-	-	5506	5182	4634	3875
13 HUNGARY	-	-	-	32856	36708	38114	40699	35603	31877	26812	24895	24962	28345	32889	37409
14 ICELAND	-	-	14019	11047	9485	8060	10748	13823	10317	13043	14883	10260	12605	16881	11981
15 ITALY	8574	10508	11416	9182	11151	12452	11391	8815	5793	7121	7301	7024	5858	5796	5909
16 JAPAN	24881	23866	26659	24917	28807	31066	32568	33285	-	28808	30365	32210	21148	17698	19579
17 NETHERLANDS	9019	9408	8577	9271	8317	9269	10748	10687	17021	8057	7410	7699	7630	7991	9687
18 NEW ZEALAND	-	14556	16989	15119	16457	17956	16589	12938	10954	10677	10896	11329	10778	12029	10901
19 NORWAY	7420	6578	7178	5329	7474	8047	7898	7667	6505	7175	7592	7553	7696	7845	9242
20 POLAND	-	-	-	-	-	-	-	-	-	-	-	8384	11092	12776	13288
21 PORTUGAL	6392	7283	10872	8737	9316	9207	15340	15260	12803	12418	5813	10901	10863	10751	9465
22 ROMANIA	-	-	-	-	-	-	-	.	-	.	-	.	.	.	.
23 SPAIN	2887	4520	7104	7657	7352	7398	7236	7238	7334	6985	6843	6067	5607	4955	4667
24 SWEDEN	-	-	21266	15196	17364	17462	18301	17338	15231	15596	17527	18437	17944	20564	19059
25 SWITZERLAND	29944	29944	28491	28491	27995	29595	30556	26909	26352	25277	22713	21250	18960	18800	20675
26 TURKEY	-	-	-	-	-	-	4776	4356	3552	2186	2356	2582	2703	2543	1806
27 UK ENGLAND AND WALES	14340	13611	12558	10033	12184	14175	14898	12934	9175	10594	10595	11382	11399	9181	7662
28 UK NORTHERN IRELAND	-	-	-	-	6138	6658	6144	5463	4049	4419	3885	4306	5734	6496	4233
29 UK SCOTLAND	8640	7868	7477	5879	8303	11815	11960	10274	7799	6329	6321	8545	8651	7667	8238
30 USA	28783	25461	23610	16715	15781	17943	19835	17496	12726	10325	11625	11989	12735	12805	13690
31 YUGOSLAVIA	-	-	-	-	.	.	.	.	-	-	.	.	.	16219	.

- NO MORTALITY DATA ARE AVAILABLE FOR EVEN A BROADER GROUP OF CAUSES FOR THIS DISEASE

. MORTALITY DATA ARE PRESENTED FOR A BROADER GROUP OF CAUSES FOR THIS DISEASE

0 VALUE<0.5

THE STANDARD MORTALITY RATIOS WERE DERIVED WITH A FACTOR OF 10000

SERIAL MORTALITY TABLES FOR VARIOUS COUNTRIES 1901-1975

TABLE 171 : ACCIDENTS - ALL NON-TRAFFIC AND SUICIDE : MALES

	1901-	1906-	1911-	1916-	1921-	1926-	1931-	1936-	1941-	1946-	1951-	1956-	1961-	1966-	1971-75
1 AUSTRALIA	-	.	.	.	.	.	.	.	20428	20697	20976	20080	19827	18995	18051
2 AUSTRIA	.	.	.	.	-	-	-	-	-	.	33288	29222	27979	28026	28269
3 BELGIUM	.	.	.	.	.	.	.	.	.	.	24560	23051	19636	19995	19555
4 BULGARIA	-	-	-	-	-	.	.	.	.	.	.	.	21241	19543	21281
5 CANADA	-	-	-	-	.	.	.	.	24389	23927	22751	21579	19898	20739	23035
6 CHILE	-	.	.	.	.	.	.	45897	46476	47559	65656	53209	56582	48221	58010
7 CZECHOSLOVAKIA	-	-	-	.	.	.	.	.	50284	28558	31409	28800	28602	29799	28907
8 DENMARK	.	.	.	.	.	.	.	.	.	.	22061	19154	17533	16744	18702
9 EIRE	-	-	-	-	.	.	.	.	.	.	9776	9727	9792	11250	12945
10 FINLAND	.	.	.	.	.	.	.	.	.	.	37555	34906	33324	34900	38360
11 FRANCE	-	-	-	-	.	.	.	.	39226	31588	28688	26849	26733	28155	27923
12 GREECE	-	-	-	-	.	.	.	.	-	-	-	15208	14090	13095	12290
13 HUNGARY	-	-	-	.	.	.	38066	37380	31343	.	26015	24996	26684	30182	34293
14 ICELAND	-	-	-	-	-	-	-	-	.	.	.	.	21094	22474	23968
15 ITALY	.	.	.	.	.	.	.	.	.	.	14793	14555	14058	12620	12438
16 JAPAN	-	37827	39364	39526	37753	29064	29103	.	-	35159	33448	32398	24990	21655	20026
17 NETHERLANDS	.	.	.	.	.	.	.	.	.	13512	13368	11302	11724	12047	11567
18 NEW ZEALAND	-	.	.	.	.	.	.	.	.	19706	18583	17790	16506	18191	18351
19 NORWAY	.	.	.	.	.	.	.	.	.	.	17852	16157	15795	15162	17025
20 POLAND	-	-	-	-	-	-	-	-	-	-	-	25040	26799	28703	29931
21 PORTUGAL	.	.	.	.	.	.	.	.	.	.	26263	22021	21547	21499	20406
22 ROMANIA	-	-	-	-	-	-	-	-	-	-	-	.	.	.	.
23 SPAIN	.	.	.	.	.	.	.	.	27432	23910	17320	16081	15753	15674	14961
24 SWEDEN	-	-	.	.	.	.	.	.	.	.	19547	19486	18740	19936	21758
25 SWITZERLAND	.	.	.	.	.	.	.	.	30272	26274	30586	27555	26815	25308	23445
26 TURKEY	-	-	-	-	-	-	-	-	-	-	-	24141	19580	19080	14891
27 UK ENGLAND AND WALES	35178	30475	.	.	.	.	.	21769	17798	14276	13758	13580	13176	11757	10307
28 UK NORTHERN IRELAND	-	-	-	-	.	.	15514	15220	12211	11678	10444	10312	10855	10222	11920
29 UK SCOTLAND	.	.	19376	17350	.	.	.	.	.	17118	17326	17503	17534	15882	16098
30 USA	87419	63223	.	.	.	.	.	33095	29447	26535	22563	20794	20183	21195	21430
31 YUGOSLAVIA	-	-	-	-	-	-	-	-	-	-	.	.	.	24294	.

- NO MORTALITY DATA ARE AVAILABLE FOR EVEN A BROADER GROUP OF CAUSES FOR THIS DISEASE

. MORTALITY DATA ARE PRESENTED FOR A BROADER GROUP OF CAUSES FOR THIS DISEASE

0 VALUE<0.5

THE STANDARD MORTALITY RATIOS WERE DERIVED WITH A FACTOR OF 10000

SERIAL MORTALITY TABLES FOR VARIOUS COUNTRIES 1901-1975

TABLE 171 : ACCIDENTS - ALL NON-TRAFFIC AND SUICIDE : FEMALES

	1901-	1906-	1911-	1916-	1921-	1926-	1931-	1936-	1941-	1946-	1951-	1956-	1961-	1966-	1971-75
1 AUSTRALIA	-	.	.	.	.	.	.	.	9385	9428	9520	9326	10009	9812	8698
2 AUSTRIA	.	.	.	.	-	-	-	-	-	.	14197	13556	13166	13443	13867
3 BELGIUM	.	.	.	.	.	.	.	.	.	.	10538	11118	10900	12900	13424
4 BULGARIA	-	-	-	-	-	.	.	.	.	.	.	.	6726	6598	6699
5 CANADA	-	-	-	-	.	.	.	.	11726	11468	9492	8954	8411	8558	9109
6 CHILE	-	.	.	.	.	.	.	15693	12659	12192	14565	12546	13436	13084	14597
7 CZECHOSLOVAKIA	-	-	-	.	.	.	.	.	12986	9161	12560	12263	12566	13179	13030
8 DENMARK	.	.	.	.	.	.	.	.	.	.	14734	14098	14333	11226	11637
9 EIRE	-	-	-	-	.	.	.	.	.	.	6524	6066	6862	7951	9296
10 FINLAND	.	.	.	.	.	.	.	.	.	.	10840	12468	11159	10210	9780
11 FRANCE	-	-	-	-	.	.	.	.	14299	10521	11015	12388	12959	14590	15085
12 GREECE	-	-	-	-	.	.	.	.	-	-	-	6452	7796	7688	7376
13 HUNGARY	-	-	-	.	.	.	14126	13892	12169	.	10853	11015	12580	14254	16306
14 ICELAND	-	-	-	-	-	-	-	-	.	.	.	.	8032	9384	11289
15 ITALY	.	.	.	.	.	.	.	.	.	.	5139	5874	6553	6374	7245
16 JAPAN	-	21059	20727	20329	23461	17597	16948	.	-	15430	14702	14770	10667	9525	9323
17 NETHERLANDS	.	.	.	.	.	.	.	.	.	6778	7953	7549	8696	10196	9723
18 NEW ZEALAND	-	.	.	.	.	.	.	.	.	9329	8320	9412	10056	10904	12340
19 NORWAY	.	.	.	.	.	.	.	.	.	.	8942	8926	9280	8921	9152
20 POLAND	-	-	-	-	-	-	-	-	-	-	-	6308	7293	8063	7737
21 PORTUGAL	.	.	.	.	.	.	.	.	.	.	9449	8325	7565	7146	6396
22 ROMANIA	-	-	-	-	-	-	-	-	-	-	-	.	.	.	.
23 SPAIN	.	.	.	.	.	.	.	.	8137	7920	6168	4644	4932	4571	5598
24 SWEDEN	-	-	.	.	.	.	.	.	.	.	8635	8814	8851	9148	10562
25 SWITZERLAND	.	.	.	.	.	.	.	.	11930	10367	11778	11760	12529	11831	11609
26 TURKEY	-	-	-	-	-	-	-	-	-	-	-	10094	8693	8232	6290
27 UK ENGLAND AND WALES	1557[illegible]	13599	.	.	.	.	.	11941	8974	8305	8551	9300	9367	8576	7579
28 UK NORTHERN IRELAND	-	-	-	-	.	.	9184	10219	7800	6837	6922	7009	7804	7503	9198
29 UK SCOTLAND	.	.	7405	6875	.	.	.	.	.	10968	10749	10619	10950	9636	10077
30 USA	31641	22482	.	.	.	.	.	16206	14985	13241	10359	9233	8943	8789	8076
31 YUGOSLAVIA	-	-	-	-	-	-	-	-	-	-	.	.	.	7775	.

- NO MORTALITY DATA ARE AVAILABLE FOR EVEN A BROADER GROUP OF CAUSES FOR THIS DISEASE

. MORTALITY DATA ARE PRESENTED FOR A BROADER GROUP OF CAUSES FOR THIS DISEASE

0 VALUE<0.5

THE STANDARD MORTALITY RATIOS WERE DERIVED WITH A FACTOR OF 10000

SERIAL MORTALITY TABLES FOR VARIOUS COUNTRIES 1901-1975

TABLE 172 : HOMICIDE AND INJURY PURPOSELY INLICTED BY OTHER PERSONS (NOT IN WAR) : MALES

	1901-	1906-	1911-	1916-	1921-	1926-	1931-	1936-	1941-	1946-	1951-	1956-	1961-	1966-	1971-75
1 AUSTRALIA	-	.	316	341	267	308	327	282	215	191	254	272	255	255	357
2 AUSTRIA	424	511	375	505	-	-	-	-	-	489	222	242	181	203	283
3 BELGIUM	401	375	426	861	.	.	.	.	.	.	99	108	98	139	199
4 BULGARIA	-	-	-	-	-	.	2633	1913	2964	1527	633	583	470	570	634
5 CANADA	-	-	-	-	271	287	316	236	202	231	197	209	242	327	499
6 CHILE	-	.	5487	4620	6587	3034	4677	4237	3824	3391	1060	1181	668	1182	945
7 CZECHOSLOVAKIA	-	-	-	607	438	567	498	367	25405	673	384	229	234	256	245
8 DENMARK	71	84	74	89	96	116	95	88	137	140	134	80	70	81	104
9 EIRE	-	-	-	-	2169	200	158	122	117	76	56	35	57	71	140
10 FINLAND	979	1392	1263	5193	.	2572	1938	1173	1548	975	660	537	515	510	710
11 FRANCE	-	-	-	-	.	.	218	210	1259	242	127	448	292	152	178
12 GREECE	-	-	-	-	.	1511	1469	1100	-	-	-	305	261	167	148
13 HUNGARY	-	-	-	2271	1215	848	1086	994	621	1077	397	630	406	427	408
14 ICELAND	-	-	-	-	-	-	-	-	190	42	.	.	65	121	257
15 ITALY	1035	998	873	1039	1472	631	516	367	3261	688	333	314	215	185	265
16 JAPAN	-	116	123	109	113	99	107	109	-	408	412	419	325	280	242
17 NETHERLANDS	.	.	68	75	40	58	98	81	574	98	54	57	68	93	135
18 NEW ZEALAND	-	111	246	146	160	123	196	115	200	170	175	142	159	185	200
19 NORWAY	100	169	109	105	134	171	139	88	3192	112	61	87	88	126	138
20 POLAND	-	-	-	-	-	-	-	-	-	-	-	236	197	218	205
21 PORTUGAL	.	.	.	.	.	.	672	596	530	398	291	262	261	223	313
22 ROMANIA	-	-	-	-	-	-	-	-	-	-	-	.	.	.	.
23 SPAIN	.	266	256	259	177	116	324	17562	3236	480	92	104	27	59	81
24 SWEDEN	-	-	272	212	163	154	160	132	139	110	112	123	118	155	208
25 SWITZERLAND	511	511	370	370	287	295	309	225	260	133	191	130	107	116	155
26 TURKEY	-	-	-	-	-	-	-	-	-	-	-	1206	1097	1462	849
27 UK ENGLAND AND WALES	153	132	118	106	95	88	77	70	76	63	72	80	94	119	164
28 UK NORTHERN IRELAND	-	-	-	-	2401	153	188	125	192	37	82	95	53	168	2303
29 UK SCOTLAND	67	69	40	107	55	80	75	106	110	80	94	108	178	228	300
30 USA	1024	1592	1755	1945	1925	2065	2319	1760	1322	1388	1133	1061	1185	1811	2471
31 YUGOSLAVIA	-	-	-	-	-	-	-	-	-	-	.	.	.	850	.

\- NO MORTALITY DATA ARE AVAILABLE FOR EVEN A BROADER GROUP OF CAUSES FOR THIS DISEASE

. MORTALITY DATA ARE PRESENTED FOR A BROADER GROUP OF CAUSES FOR THIS DISEASE

0 VALUE<0.5

THE STANDARD MORTALITY RATIOS WERE DERIVED WITH A FACTOR OF 100

SERIAL MORTALITY TABLES FOR VARIOUS COUNTRIES 1901-1975

TABLE 172 : HOMICIDE AND INJURY PURPOSELY INLICTED BY OTHER PERSONS (NOT IN WAR) : FEMALES

	1901-	1906-	1911-	1916-	1921-	1926-	1931-	1936-	1941-	1946-	1951-	1956-	1961-	1966-	1971-75
1 AUSTRALIA	-	.	2409	2112	2046	2417	1754	1364	1340	1350	1582	1664	1901	1886	1967
2 AUSTRIA	1869	1710	1550	2459	-	-	-	-	-	2508	1578	1500	1308	1607	1899
3 BELGIUM	1472	1980	2143	3389	.	.	.	.	.	.	1188	987	1083	1373	1453
4 BULGARIA	-	-	-	-	-	.	5437	5388	3568	3862	2392	1543	1826	1761	1785
5 CANADA	-	-	-	-	1267	1890	1666	1550	1313	1264	1212	1339	1492	1912	2696
6 CHILE	-	.	4643	4873	6479	4300	5442	4802	3672	3771	1097	1762	945	1600	1305
7 CZECHOSLOVAKIA	-	-	-	2497	2617	3361	3622	2260	80866	2533	1781	1355	1368	1593	1602
8 DENMARK	286	692	690	1000	883	730	689	649	1413	1608	1460	1156	1026	1031	1388
9 EIRE	-	-	-	-	1833	1231	673	611	682	445	366	290	425	457	620
10 FINLAND	2353	2495	3127	4514	.	3458	3481	3827	3481	2504	2851	2458	2231	2054	2513
11 FRANCE	-	-	-	-	.	.	1425	1267	2584	1050	791	910	974	991	1027
12 GREECE	-	-	-	-	.	2847	3211	2529	-	-	-	1130	891	642	582
13 HUNGARY	-	-	-	4127	3223	2997	3405	3108	2430	3636	1786	2046	1943	2441	2629
14 ICELAND	-	-	-	-	-	-	-	-	476	435	.	.	667	0	1176
15 ITALY	1743	1850	1803	1954	2538	1976	1754	1441	3943	1644	1141	1167	892	853	960
16 JAPAN	-	1028	1148	941	973	1096	1047	1046	-	2645	2294	2082	1577	1509	1521
17 NETHERLANDS	.	.	229	304	226	375	435	548	984	439	407	341	376	483	680
18 NEW ZEALAND	-	938	2035	957	1456	1773	1535	871	1346	1144	1220	1213	1307	1358	1253
19 NORWAY	409	399	384	729	556	835	917	635	6641	510	429	622	797	541	798
20 POLAND	-	-	-	-	-	-	-	-	-	-	-	794	946	1048	1043
21 PORTUGAL	.	.	.	.	.	.	1274	1026	903	1003	991	837	850	819	820
22 ROMANIA	-	-	-	-	-	-	-	-	-	-	-	.	.	.	.
23 SPAIN	.	300	428	517	477	334	562	6611	1324	472	252	314	114	220	357
24 SWEDEN	-	-	1583	1296	1299	1052	1129	972	979	1069	1051	1142	1046	1114	1442
25 SWITZERLAND	2421	2421	1874	1874	1444	1886	2271	1725	2068	1565	1690	969	1288	1010	1311
26 TURKEY	-	-	-	-	-	-	-	-	-	-	-	2923	2593	3455	2220
27 UK ENGLAND AND WALES	1436	1204	1241	1093	933	846	862	718	685	662	654	805	853	1025	1289
28 UK NORTHERN IRELAND	-	-	-	-	4192	1154	821	524	1000	177	398	614	509	571	2172
29 UK SCOTLAND	663	586	433	663	684	741	766	488	630	667	670	926	915	1461	1472
30 USA	3248	4552	4685	4714	4762	5259	5394	4535	3472	3852	3457	3551	3864	5032	6595
31 YUGOSLAVIA	-	-	-	-	-	-	-	-	-	-	.	.	.	2589	.

- NO MORTALITY DATA ARE AVAILABLE FOR EVEN A BROADER GROUP OF CAUSES FOR THIS DISEASE

. MORTALITY DATA ARE PRESENTED FOR A BROADER GROUP OF CAUSES FOR THIS DISEASE

0 VALUE<0.5

THE STANDARD MORTALITY RATIOS WERE DERIVED WITH A FACTOR OF 1000

SERIAL MORTALITY TABLES FOR VARIOUS COUNTRIES 1901-1975

TABLE 173 : WAR INJURY : MALES

	1901-	1906-	1911-	1916-	1921-	1926-	1931-	1936-	1941-	1946-	1951-	1956-	1961-	1966-	1971-75
1 AUSTRALIA	-	.	.	.	53	35	29	25	16	0	24	19	27	23	8
2 AUSTRIA	.	.	.	.	-	-	-	-	-	.	0	0	0	0	0
3 BELGIUM	.	.	.	.	.	.	.	.	.	.	31	16	3	2	0
4 BULGARIA	-	-	-	-	-	.	.	.	.	.	.	.	0	0	0
5 CANADA	-	-	-	-	0	0	0	0	20	3	11	9	7	6	3
6 CHILE	-	.	.	.	.	.	.	131	3	0	0	0	0	0	0
7 CZECHOSLOVAKIA	-	-	-	374	7	0	0	0	16865	1343	0	1	0	17	0
8 DENMARK	.	.	.	.	.	.	.	.	.	.	3	3	0	0	2
9 EIRE	-	-	-	-	37	32	26	39	72	31	25	16	9	1	0
10 FINLAND	.	.	.	.	.	.	.	38802	87677	116	10	0	17	21	19
11 FRANCE	-	-	-	-	.	.	.	.	15369	68	40	29	9	7	8
12 GREECE	-	-	-	-	.	.	.	.	-	-	-	36	38	2	6
13 HUNGARY	-	-	-	.	.	.	1	4	177	7	0	1050	0	0	0
14 ICELAND	-	-	-	-	-	-	-	-	5300	7550	.	.	0	0	0
15 ITALY	.	.	.	.	.	.	.	.	.	.	127	34	22	9	4
16 JAPAN	-	0	0	0	0	0	1	0	-	6	3	7	4	3	2
17 NETHERLANDS	.	.	.	.	0	0	.	.	8998	874	74	6	7	1	0
18 NEW ZEALAND	-	.	.	.	.	0	0	0	31	0	0	4	22	34	20
19 NORWAY	.	.	.	.	.	.	.	.	3027	0	0	0	2	0	0
20 POLAND	-	-	-	-	-	-	-	-	-	-	-	177	28	1	3
21 PORTUGAL	.	.	.	.	.	.	.	.	.	.	0	2	2	16	2
22 ROMANIA	-	-	-	-	-	-	-	-	-	-	-	.	.	.	.
23 SPAIN	.	.	.	.	.	.	163	24228	5387	1639	203	200	0	0	0
24 SWEDEN	-	-	.	.	.	.	0	283	659	0	0	1	5	3	1
25 SWITZERLAND	0	0	21	21	18	18	.	.	69	0	3	2	1	0	1
26 TURKEY	-	-	-	-	-	-	-	-	-	-	-	0	0	0	0
27 UK ENGLAND AND WALES	3	1	.	.	55	49	50	1338	2208	61	51	38	20	6	5
28 UK NORTHERN IRELAND	-	-	-	-	21	75	44	65	.	18	21	7	39	50	1527
29 UK SCOTLAND	.	.	382	887	118	60	41	513	4130	88	37	23	5	2	6
30 USA	.	.	.	.	3	1	1	0	21	2	5	5	4	8	2
31 YUGOSLAVIA	-	-	-	-	-	-	-	-	-	-	.	.	.	0	.

- NO MORTALITY DATA ARE AVAILABLE FOR EVEN A BROADER GROUP OF CAUSES FOR THIS DISEASE

. MORTALITY DATA ARE PRESENTED FOR A BROADER GROUP OF CAUSES FOR THIS DISEASE

0 VALUE<0.5

THE STANDARD MORTALITY RATIOS WERE DERIVED WITH A FACTOR OF 10

SERIAL MORTALITY TABLES FOR VARIOUS COUNTRIES 1901-1975

TABLE 173 : WAR INJURY : FEMALES

	1901-	1906-	1911-	1916-	1921-	1926-	1931-	1936-	1941-	1946-	1951-	1956-	1961-	1966-	1971-75
1 AUSTRALIA	-	.	.	.	0	0	0	0	26	0	0	0	0	0	0
2 AUSTRIA	.	.	.	.	-	-	-	-	-	.	0	0	0	0	0
3 BELGIUM	.	.	.	.	.	.	.	.	.	.	10	18	11	13	7
4 BULGARIA	-	-	-	-	-	.	.	.	.	.	.	.	0	0	0
5 CANADA	-	-	-	-	0	0	0	0	0	0	0	0	0	0	0
6 CHILE	-	.	.	.	.	.	.	0	0	0	0	0	0	0	0
7 CZECHOSLOVAKIA	-	-	-	0	0	0	0	0	53857	3813	0	0	0	22	0
8 DENMARK	.	.	.	.	.	.	.	.	.	.	9	0	0	0	0
9 EIRE	-	-	-	-	0	0	0	44	257	0	0	0	0	0	0
10 FINLAND	.	.	.	.	.	.	.	5987	7203	12	0	0	0	0	0
11 FRANCE	-	-	-	-	.	.	.	.	48221	27	18	13	3	3	1
12 GREECE	-	-	-	-	.	.	.	.	-	-	-	28	40	4	0
13 HUNGARY	-	-	-	.	.	.	0	0	100	5	0	1436	0	0	3
14 ICELAND	-	-	-	-	-	-	-	-	16000	21333	.	.	0	0	0
15 ITALY	.	.	.	.	.	.	.	.	.	.	84	25	17	6	0
16 JAPAN	-	0	0	0	0	0	0	0	-	0	13	14	6	2	3
17 NETHERLANDS	.	.	.	.	0	0	.	.	39130	45	18	4	0	13	0
18 NEW ZEALAND	-	.	.	.	.	0	0	0	0	0	0	0	0	0	0
19 NORWAY	.	.	.	.	.	.	.	.	3319	0	0	0	0	0	0
20 POLAND	-	-	-	-	-	-	-	-	-	-	-	365	64	0	10
21 PORTUGAL	.	.	.	.	.	.	.	.	.	.	0	0	0	0	0
22 ROMANIA	-	-	-	-	-	-	-	-	-	-	-	.	.	.	.
23 SPAIN	.	.	.	.	.	.	92	14050	768	260	140	52	1	0	0
24 SWEDEN	-	-	.	.	.	.	0	52	146	0	0	0	0	0	0
25 SWITZERLAND	0	0	21	21	12	0	.	.	313	0	0	0	0	6	0
26 TURKEY	-	-	-	-	-	-	-	-	-	-	-	0	0	0	0
27 UK ENGLAND AND WALES	0	0	.	.	0	1	0	9815	15436	19	3	4	1	0	0
28 UK NORTHERN IRELAND	-	-	-	-	0	0	0	0	.	0	0	0	0	0	1341
29 UK SCOTLAND	.	.	0	55	0	0	0	387	7423	0	0	0	0	0	6
30 USA	.	.	.	.	0	0	0	0	2	0	0	0	0	0	0
31 YUGOSLAVIA	-	-	-	-	-	-	-	-	-	-	.	.	.	0	.

- NO MORTALITY DATA ARE AVAILABLE FOR EVEN A BROADER GROUP OF CAUSES FOR THIS DISEASE

. MORTALITY DATA ARE PRESENTED FOR A BROADER GROUP OF CAUSES FOR THIS DISEASE

0 VALUE<0.5

THE STANDARD MORTALITY RATIOS WERE DERIVED WITH A FACTOR OF 100

SERIAL MORTALITY TABLES FOR VARIOUS COUNTRIES 1901-1975

TABLE 174 : HOMICIDE AND WAR INJURY : MALES

	1901-	1906-	1911-	1916-	1921-	1926-	1931-	1936-	1941-	1946-	1951-	1956-	1961-	1966-	1971-75
1 AUSTRALIA	-	.	.	.	291	311	323	279	209	170	253	263	256	252	327
2 AUSTRIA	.	.	.	.	-	-	-	-	-	.	184	207	155	174	244
3 BELGIUM	.	.	.	.	.	.	.	.	.	.	128	116	89	122	172
4 BULGARIA	-	-	-	-	-	.	.	.	.	.	.	.	401	497	549
5 CANADA	-	-	-	-	248	262	285	212	201	210	187	196	225	300	448
6 CHILE	-	.	.	.	5994	2843	.	4095	3566	3156	1535	1099	622	1099	875
7 CZECHOSLOVAKIA	-	-	-	914	402	512	450	333	40588	2143	258	203	204	245	213
8 DENMARK	.	.	.	.	.	.	85	78	.	.	121	73	61	70	92
9 EIRE	-	-	-	-	1954	215	171	157	194	106	80	51	61	64	123
10 FINLAND	.	.	.	.	.	2351	1758	37257	82298	993	608	483	478	476	647
11 FRANCE	-	-	-	-	.	.	.	.	22736	300	160	427	266	141	165
12 GREECE	-	-	-	-	.	1378	1040	.	-	-	-	311	275	149	136
13 HUNGARY	-	-	-	.	.	.	979	895	745	968	352	1818	352	366	352
14 ICELAND	-	-	-	-	-	-	-	-	4783	5846	103	31	57	108	231
15 ITALY	.	.	.	.	.	.	.	.	.	.	437	316	216	173	235
16 JAPAN	-	106	112	100	104	91	99	100	-	381	381	388	298	255	220
17 NETHERLANDS	.	.	.	.	37	53	.	.	9767	981	130	58	68	84	119
18 NEW ZEALAND	-	.	.	.	150	111	174	102	213	149	156	132	166	202	201
19 NORWAY	.	.	.	.	.	.	.	.	6216	99	54	76	79	108	118
20 POLAND	-	-	-	-	-	-	-	-	-	-	-	372	205	195	186
21 PORTUGAL	.	.	.	.	.	.	.	.	.	.	3148	238	236	215	277
22 ROMANIA	-	-	-	-	-	-	-	-	-	-	-	.	.	.	.
23 SPAIN	.	.	.	.	.	.	447	39350	8223	2053	288	304	24	52	72
24 SWEDEN	-	-	.	.	.	.	141	462	953	96	97	107	108	135	177
25 SWITZERLAND	465	465	355	355	276	283	.	.	321	117	171	116	95	101	136
26 TURKEY	-	-	-	-	-	-	-	-	-	-	-	1130	1023	1361	790
27 UK ENGLAND AND WALES	143	122	.	.	141	132	127	1769	3441	136	130	121	108	110	148
28 UK NORTHERN IRELAND	-	-	-	-	2165	218	216	193	.	20	97	92	93	207	3835
29 UK SCOTLAND	.	.	372	916	166	134	112	692	5066	177	128	123	162	199	266
30 USA	.	.	.	.	1752	1870	2085	1571	1198	1234	1008	943	1054	1610	2179
31 YUGOSLAVIA	-	-	-	-	-	-	-	-	-	-	.	.	.	760	.

- NO MORTALITY DATA ARE AVAILABLE FOR EVEN A BROADER GROUP OF CAUSES FOR THIS DISEASE

. MORTALITY DATA ARE PRESENTED FOR A BROADER GROUP OF CAUSES FOR THIS DISEASE

0 VALUE<0.5

THE STANDARD MORTALITY RATIOS WERE DERIVED WITH A FACTOR OF 100

SERIAL MORTALITY TABLES FOR VARIOUS COUNTRIES 1901-1975

TABLE 174 : HCMICIDE AND WAR INJURY : FEMALES

	1901-	1906-	1911-	1916-	1921-	1926-	1931-	1936-	1941-	1946-	1951-	1956-	1961-	1966-	1971-75
1 AUSTRALIA	-	.	.	.	187	219	157	121	121	119	139	146	167	166	173
2 AUSTRIA	.	.	.	.	-	-	-	-	-	.	126	125	108	133	156
3 BELGIUM	.	.	.	.	.	.	.	.	.	.	102	86	92	117	123
4 BULGARIA	-	-	-	-	-	.	.	.	.	.	.	.	155	152	153
5 CANADA	-	-	-	-	116	173	151	140	118	113	109	120	134	170	238
6 CHILE	-	.	.	.	582	402	.	422	341	350	196	163	88	148	120
7 CZECHOSLOVAKIA	-	-	-	223	234	300	324	202	13688	696	144	117	116	138	136
8 DENMARK	.	.	.	.	.	.	61	57	.	.	128	99	87	87	117
9 EIRE	-	-	-	-	161	108	59	59	93	39	32	25	37	40	54
10 FINLAND	.	.	.	.	.	313	311	993	1110	224	252	215	194	177	213
11 FRANCE	-	-	-	-	.	.	.	.	7863	93	70	79	82	84	87
12 GREECE	-	-	-	-	.	259	260	.	-	-	-	103	83	56	50
13 HUNGARY	-	-	-	.	.	.	305	276	226	320	156	373	165	205	221
14 ICELAND	-	-	-	-	-	-	-	-	2042	2500	143	97	59	0	105
15 ITALY	.	.	.	.	.	.	.	.	.	.	110	104	79	74	82
16 JAPAN	-	93	104	86	89	100	96	95	-	242	210	189	142	135	135
17 NETHERLANDS	.	.	.	.	20	34	.	.	4301	44	38	30	33	44	59
18 NEW ZEALAND	-	.	.	.	119	161	137	77	118	100	108	107	116	120	110
19 NORWAY	.	.	.	.	.	.	.	.	993	44	37	53	68	46	67
20 POLAND	-	-	-	-	-	-	-	-	-	-	-	110	91	91	92
21 PORTUGAL	.	.	.	.	.	.	.	.	.	.	992	74	75	71	71
22 ROMANIA	-	-	-	-	-	-	-	-	-	-	-	.	.	.	.
23 SPAIN	.	.	.	.	.	.	60	2084	202	71	39	34	10	19	31
24 SWEDEN	-	-	.	.	.	.	99	91	104	92	90	96	88	93	120
25 SWITZERLAND	218	218	170	170	130	167	.	.	208	135	145	83	110	87	111
26 TURKEY	-	-	-	-	-	-	-	-	-	-	-	271	240	319	205
27 UK ENGLAND AND WALES	132	109	.	.	83	75	75	1421	2344	59	56	68	71	86	107
28 UK NORTHERN IRELAND	-	-	-	-	372	103	73	52	.	39	35	53	44	49	379
29 UK SCOTLAND	.	.	53	65	61	66	67	92	1047	57	57	79	77	123	124
30 USA	.	.	.	.	434	477	486	405	309	341	304	312	338	438	571
31 YUGOSLAVIA	-	-	-	-	-	-	-	-	-	-	.	.	.	228	.

- NO MORTALITY DATA ARE AVAILABLE FOR EVEN A BROADER GROUP OF CAUSES FOR THIS DISEASE

. MORTALITY DATA ARE PRESENTED FOR A BROADER GROUP OF CAUSES FOR THIS DISEASE

0 VALUE<0.5

THE STANDARD MORTALITY RATIOS WERE DERIVED WITH A FACTOR OF 100

SERIAL MORTALITY TABLES FOR VARIOUS COUNTRIES 1901-1975

TABLE 175 : ACCIDENTS - ALL VIOLENCE EXCLUDING SUICIDE : MALES

	1901-	1906-	1911-	1916-	1921-	1926-	1931-	1936-	1941-	1946-	1951-	1956-	1961-	1966-	1971-75
1 AUSTRALIA	-	3359	3546	2898	2823	3156	2546	2932	2197	2418	2721	2534	2410	2513	2434
2 AUSTRIA	1922	2051	2689	2225	-	-	-	-	-	2817	2571	3062	2670	2954	3103
3 BELGIUM	.	.	.	.	.	.	.	.	.	.	2097	2147	2103	2266	2242
4 BULGARIA	-	-	-	-	-	2060	1990	1824	5874	2739	2340	1860	1908	2064	2130
5 CANADA	-	-	-	-	3031	3027	2660	2674	2854	2655	2708	2595	2522	2600	2740
6 CHILE	-	6432	6976	6841	6811	5565	5690	6311	4485	4411	5033	4519	4636	4617	5046
7 CZECHOSLOVAKIA	-	-	-	2169	1662	1911	1725	1682	13426	2474	2292	2241	2334	2538	2415
8 DENMARK	2189	2064	1681	1567	1356	1442	1390	1401	2106	1699	1654	1584	1655	1756	1604
9 EIRE	-	-	-	-	1779	1209	1254	1232	1160	1150	1127	1147	1218	1518	1837
10 FINLAND	2940	2820	2714	8845	3260	2844	.	12114	24366	3177	2658	2722	2988	3145	3291
11 FRANCE	-	-	-	-	2553	2571	2516	3219	4741	2242	2403	2523	2619	2795	2739
12 GREECE	-	-	-	-	1835	1922	1816	1615	-	-	-	1402	1509	1586	1577
13 HUNGARY	-	-	-	2324	1984	1720	1554	1714	1763	2203	1882	2041	1757	1971	2321
14 ICELAND	-	-	-	-	-	-	-	-	5801	3094	2564	2265	2538	2430	2729
15 ITALY	1793	3417	2311	1859	1886	1828	1803	1705	3215	1808	1809	1944	2109	1998	2007
16 JAPAN	-	.	.	.	.	.	2370	2346	-	2256	2197	2318	2391	2315	1934
17 NETHERLANDS	1651	1570	1619	1614	1414	1466	1431	1438	5248	1750	1583	1545	1672	1810	1613
18 NEW ZEALAND	-	3203	3206	2753	2616	2835	2446	2418	2189	2014	2232	2013	2001	2268	2379
19 NORWAY	2108	2082	2026	1928	1881	2094	1833	2668	3609	1649	1884	1837	1851	1832	1935
20 POLAND	-	-	-	-	-	-	-	-	-	-	-	2073	2216	2457	2698
21 PORTUGAL	1264	1244	1722	1840	1806	2138	2166	2161	2025	1883	2097	1887	2101	2397	2920
22 ROMANIA	-	-	-	-	-	-	-	-	-	-	-	.	.	.	.
23 SPAIN	1820	1873	1721	1710	1566	1514	1597	12585	3961	2175	1383	1501	1584	1704	1763
24 SWEDEN	-	-	2227	2089	1627	1649	1610	1760	1858	1602	1683	1642	1689	1634	1786
25 SWITZERLAND	3493	3493	3255	3255	3013	3332	3276	2790	2782	2631	2630	2610	2667	2478	2269
26 TURKEY	-	-	-	-	-	-	-	-	-	-	-	2457	2229	2366	1861
27 UK ENGLAND AND WALES	2579	2215	2557	2763	1787	2031	1942	2435	2650	1362	1361	1389	1407	1316	1201
28 UK NORTHERN IRELAND	-	-	-	-	.	.	1684	1787	2310	1443	1420	1317	1302	1425	2705
29 UK SCOTLAND	.	.	3257	3204	2426	2517	2203	2759	3786	1871	1874	1825	1896	1848	1876
30 USA	7421	5988	5097	4640	4139	4446	4217	3998	3598	3238	2886	2582	2527	2880	2816
31 YUGOSLAVIA	-	-	-	-	-	-	-	-	-	-	.	.	.	2311	.

- NO MORTALITY DATA ARE AVAILABLE FOR EVEN A BROADER GROUP OF CAUSES FOR THIS DISEASE

. MORTALITY DATA ARE PRESENTED FOR A BROADER GROUP OF CAUSES FOR THIS DISEASE

0 VALUE<0.5

THE STANDARD MORTALITY RATIOS WERE DERIVED WITH A FACTOR OF 1000

SERIAL MORTALITY TABLES FOR VARIOUS COUNTRIES 1901-1975

TABLE 175 : ACCIDENTS - ALL VIOLENCE EXCLUDING SUICIDE : FEMALES

	1901-	1906-	1911-	1916-	1921-	1926-	1931-	1936-	1941-	1946-	1951-	1956-	1961-	1966-	1971-75
1 AUSTRALIA	-	11672	10391	8728	8261	9240	8071	9616	8513	8692	9537	9644	9598	10190	9444
2 AUSTRIA	6646	6456	5747	8979	-	-	-	-	-	11510	9626	11218	11082	12316	13029
3 BELGIUM	.	.	.	.	.	.	.	.	.	.	8557	9445	9916	12337	12914
4 BULGARIA	-	-	-	-	-	6559	5850	5342	12956	7552	6384	4901	5498	5783	5834
5 CANADA	-	-	-	-	10417	10390	10013	11107	10929	11057	10020	9970	9786	9918	10206
6 CHILE	-	15448	14399	17163	18848	13827	12473	21509	9684	9704	10958	9947	10517	11227	12182
7 CZECHOSLOVAKIA	-	-	-	6366	5327	6890	6053	5722	39116	6867	8336	8359	9164	10299	10806
8 DENMARK	5687	5210	5268	5612	5119	5988	6976	7348	9404	9392	10028	10455	11470	9670	8727
9 EIRE	-	-	-	-	5906	5882	6415	6738	6626	6378	6002	5853	6835	8283	9548
10 FINLAND	7345	6914	7115	9878	6944	5797	.	9491	11741	8201	8347	10052	10055	9812	9470
11 FRANCE	-	-	-	-	6735	7067	7176	12316	16966	7718	9033	10628	11995	13666	13840
12 GREECE	-	-	-	-	5947	7016	7146	6412	-	-	-	5359	6893	7521	7699
13 HUNGARY	-	-	-	7641	6615	5751	4946	5344	5659	6260	6280	7009	7510	9147	11021
14 ICELAND	-	-	-	-	-	-	-	-	7589	7389	6702	6447	7829	7452	10221
15 ITALY	8208	22979	12850	6299	6006	6100	5714	5077	7484	4663	4661	5619	6943	7020	8053
16 JAPAN	-	.	.	.	.	.	10229	9121	-	8065	7284	7119	6465	6663	6006
17 NETHERLANDS	5433	5729	5479	5962	5088	5308	5127	5472	21662	6279	6878	6795	8155	10245	9200
18 NEW ZEALAND	-	7997	7626	6816	6568	8329	8467	7750	7035	7937	8200	8786	9452	10621	12467
19 NORWAY	4509	3996	4137	3843	3964	4271	3991	6277	10511	7659	7646	8102	8716	8638	8809
20 POLAND	-	-	-	-	-	-	-	-	-	-	-	5351	6284	7319	7835
21 PORTUGAL	5306	4875	5996	6109	5880	9368	8749	8011	7207	6391	7409	6982	6839	7139	7634
22 ROMANIA	-	-	-	-	-	-	-	-	-	-	-	.	.	.	.
23 SPAIN	6539	6805	6053	5727	4723	4234	4526	11316	6106	5764	4839	3918	4513	4789	6088
24 SWEDEN	-	-	4905	5004	4874	5734	6527	7457	6953	6388	6793	7205	7575	7538	8837
25 SWITZERLAND	10083	10083	9391	9391	8162	9108	9889	9488	8762	8667	9201	9659	10896	10732	10292
26 TURKEY	-	-	-	-	-	-	-	-	-	-	-	9017	8207	8447	6722
27 UK ENGLAND AND WALES	10786	9526	9296	8318	6777	7888	8299	11962	12500	6531	6831	7579	7868	7758	7216
28 UK NORTHERN IRELAND	-	-	-	-	.	.	8653	9615	12975	6586	6852	6633	7620	7202	10444
29 UK SCOTLAND	.	.	10613	9732	8649	9500	9347	9938	12153	9234	9603	9243	9746	9207	9459
30 USA	22443	16918	15757	15562	15266	16228	16097	16001	13934	13230	11440	10314	10107	10511	9507
31 YUGOSLAVIA	-	-	-	-	-	-	-	-	-	-	.	.	.	6807	.

- NO MORTALITY DATA ARE AVAILABLE FOR EVEN A BROADER GROUP OF CAUSES FOR THIS DISEASE

. MORTALITY DATA ARE PRESENTED FOR A BROADER GROUP OF CAUSES FOR THIS DISEASE

0 VALUE<0.5

THE STANDARD MORTALITY RATIOS WERE DERIVED WITH A FACTOR OF 10000

SERIAL MORTALITY TABLES FOR VARIOUS COUNTRIES 1901-1975

TABLE 176 : HOMICIDE, SUICIDE AND WAR INJURY : MALES

	1901-	1906-	1911-	1916-	1921-	1926-	1931-	1936-	1941-	1946-	1951-	1956-	1961-	1966-	1971-75
1 AUSTRALIA	-	.	.	.	1617	2713	2409	2036	1325	1612	1858	2031	2318	2153	2086
2 AUSTRIA	4086	4752	4433	3255	-	-	-	-	-	3469	3270	3386	3220	3379	3505
3 BELGIUM	.	.	.	.	.	.	.	.	.	.	2007	2042	2019	2141	2179
4 BULGARIA	-	-	-	-	-	.	5057	5093	5091	3083	1756	1496	1497	1827	2053
5 CANADA	-	-	-	-	1688	1744	1888	1649	1239	1467	1403	1544	1617	1954	2402
6 CHILE	-	.	.	.	7252	4115	6226	5283	4554	4106	2781	2819	1738	2615	2310
7 CZECHOSLOVAKIA	-	-	-	4804	4922	5394	5642	4633	35643	4649	3238	3311	3287	3762	3648
8 DENMARK	5870	5120	4657	3051	2598	3065	3010	2900	2589	3330	3361	2971	2495	2548	3058
9 EIRE	-	-	-	-	2014	743	725	610	593	505	437	472	427	409	664
10 FINLAND	.	.	.	.	.	6654	5567	36357	75273	4206	4098	4448	4160	4166	4586
11 FRANCE	-	-	-	-	.	.	3446	3053	8389	2320	2554	2828	2583	2458	2413
12 GREECE	-	-	-	-	.	2277	2230	1888	-	-	-	813	738	603	510
13 HUNGARY	-	-	-	5888	5862	5668	6179	5351	4747	4434	3688	4827	4162	4887	5523
14 ICELAND	-	-	-	-	-	-	-	-	5623	6939	2243	1328	1933	2595	1802
15 ITALY	2115	2312	2254	2029	2683	2266	2029	1527	3247	1483	1358	1206	966	925	973
16 JAPAN	-	3063	3145	2885	3310	3603	3813	3961	-	3654	3814	3964	2574	2126	2351
17 NETHERLANDS	.	.	.	.	1186	1248	1484	1389	10709	1845	1007	928	958	1019	1196
18 NEW ZEALAND	-	2169	2606	2251	2456	2672	2557	1868	1580	1564	1629	1636	1496	1675	1544
19 NORWAY	1263	1165	1255	903	1287	1423	1329	1219	5828	1185	1158	1201	1197	1207	1414
20 POLAND	-	-	-	-	-	-	-	-	-	-	-	1883	1969	2254	2332
21 PORTUGAL	.	.	.	.	.	.	2899	2812	2305	2189	3146	1912	1905	1860	1687
22 ROMANIA	-	-	-	-	-	-	-	-	-	-	-	.	.	.	.
23 SPAIN	.	.	.	.	.	.	1469	35439	8105	2767	1246	1124	846	771	731
24 SWEDEN	-	-	3562	2443	2812	2841	2954	2940	2896	2306	2618	2755	2604	2932	2724
25 SWITZERLAND	5107	5107	4589	4589	4549	4704	4836	4240	3951	3705	3420	3175	2757	2759	2973
26 TURKEY	-	-	-	-	-	-	-	-	-	-	-	1595	1466	1825	1076
27 UK ENGLAND AND WALES	2178	2063	.	.	1848	2070	2154	3020	3558	1453	1444	1468	1402	1147	1004
28 UK NORTHERN IRELAND	-	-	-	-	2670	1211	1103	932	780	668	631	612	795	916	3581
29 UK SCOTLAND	1304	1185	1236	1622	1304	1734	1756	1902	4923	979	922	1196	1180	1078	1158
30 USA	4783	4761	4602	3750	3902	4233	4523	3708	2678	2813	2519	2527	2666	3074	3635
31 YUGOSLAVIA	-	-	-	-	-	-	-	-	-	-	.	.	.	2937	.

- NO MORTALITY DATA ARE AVAILABLE FOR EVEN A BROADER GROUP OF CAUSES FOR THIS DISEASE

. MORTALITY DATA ARE PRESENTED FOR A BROADER GROUP OF CAUSES FOR THIS DISEASE

0 VALUE<0.5

THE STANDARD MORTALITY RATIOS WERE DERIVED WITH A FACTOR OF 1000

SERIAL MORTALITY TABLES FOR VARIOUS COUNTRIES 1901-1975

TABLE 176 : HOMICIDE, SUICIDE AND WAR INJURY : FEMALES

	1901-	1906-	1911-	1916-	1921-	1926-	1931-	1936-	1941-	1946-	1951-	1956-	1961-	1966-	1971-75
1 AUSTRALIA	-	.	.	.	377	756	706	638	566	593	666	761	1128	1095	970
2 AUSTRIA	1179	1491	1438	1500	-	-	-	-	-	1485	1406	1364	1246	1280	1337
3 BELGIUM	.	.	.	.	.	.	.	.	.	.	724	787	812	953	986
4 BULGARIA	-	-	-	-	-	.	1672	1952	1350	1022	742	612	698	768	793
5 CANADA	-	-	-	-	606	604	620	600	513	501	480	472	546	755	936
6 CHILE	-	.	.	.	916	803	1102	877	637	622	477	544	352	512	400
7 CZECHOSLOVAKIA	-	-	-	1680	1620	1852	1943	1753	11683	1670	1226	1289	1263	1355	1230
8 DENMARK	1179	1073	1092	1007	904	999	1190	1265	1877	1968	1588	1418	1328	1345	1740
9 EIRE	-	-	-	-	260	225	193	205	191	130	119	142	121	133	243
10 FINLAND	.	.	.	.	.	1171	929	1512	1523	802	962	1141	1055	1051	1096
11 FRANCE	-	-	-	-	.	.	960	964	2733	693	717	844	758	821	872
12 GREECE	-	-	-	-	.	531	639	608	-	-	-	354	304	242	218
13 HUNGARY	-	-	-	2286	2158	2306	2490	2263	2006	1679	1452	1598	1649	1849	2088
14 ICELAND	-	-	-	-	-	-	-	-	2168	2742	719	663	481	605	688
15 ITALY	462	597	701	630	717	703	640	511	548	471	453	444	367	361	383
16 JAPAN	-	1833	1886	1801	2085	2201	2272	2260	-	2214	2307	2483	1708	1473	1575
17 NETHERLANDS	.	.	.	.	397	534	607	684	4236	521	502	570	540	569	746
18 NEW ZEALAND	-	491	717	613	729	796	715	655	712	618	600	656	731	820	735
19 NORWAY	268	264	241	254	289	309	344	344	1002	285	344	321	362	387	470
20 POLAND	-	-	-	-	-	-	-	-	-	-	-	401	438	467	480
21 PORTUGAL	.	.	.	.	.	.	729	714	659	593	919	470	467	476	440
22 ROMANIA	-	-	-	-	-	-	-	-	-	-	-	.	.	.	.
23 SPAIN	.	.	.	.	.	.	348	2006	506	365	336	312	258	237	241
24 SWEDEN	-	-	815	692	697	657	701	744	738	763	816	866	918	1105	1080
25 SWITZERLAND	1118	1118	1247	1247	1140	1320	1395	1202	1471	1335	1178	1059	1025	979	1159
26 TURKEY	-	-	-	-	-	-	-	-	-	-	-	437	411	485	334
27 UK ENGLAND AND WALES	740	682	.	.	653	792	845	1727	2121	713	713	832	883	728	623
28 UK NORTHERN IRELAND	-	-	-	-	599	319	295	276	206	211	211	313	393	505	573
29 UK SCOTLAND	433	401	361	349	459	668	661	660	1211	406	424	586	642	614	685
30 USA	1547	1470	1420	1200	1242	1291	1202	1072	852	824	695	726	849	967	1089
31 YUGOSLAVIA	-	-	-	-	-	-	-	-	-	-	.	.	.	960	.

- NO MORTALITY DATA ARE AVAILABLE FOR EVEN A BROADER GROUP OF CAUSES FOR THIS DISEASE

. MORTALITY DATA ARE PRESENTED FOR A BROADER GROUP OF CAUSES FOR THIS DISEASE

0 VALUE<0.5

THE STANDARD MORTALITY RATIOS WERE DERIVED WITH A FACTOR OF 1000

SERIAL MORTALITY TABLES FOR VARIOUS COUNTRIES 1901-1975

TABLE 177 : ACCIDENTS AND VIOLENCE - ALL FORMS : MALES

	1901-	1906-	1911-	1916-	1921-	1926-	1931-	1936-	1941-	1946-	1951-	1956-	1961-	1966-	1971-75
1 AUSTRALIA	-	3198	3415	2772	2739	3052	2500	2720	1990	2239	2520	2414	2386	2431	2338
2 AUSTRIA	2384	2626	3081	2417	-	-	-	-	-	2952	2752	3155	2816	3072	3206
3 BELGIUM	1933	1966	2160	2275	2078	2234	2083	2188	2781	1900	1907	2138	2104	2254	2236
4 BULGARIA	-	-	-	-	-	2258	2257	2116	5284	2615	2132	1711	1772	1956	2052
5 CANADA	-	-	-	-	2734	2744	2479	2447	2497	2394	2431	2376	2333	2453	2634
6 CHILE	-	5403	5876	5735	5712	4754	4943	7088	11676	11055	4196	4019	4004	4064	4389
7 CZECHOSLOVAKIA	-	-	-	2637	2368	2653	2576	2330	11294	2610	2478	2501	2569	2832	2712
8 DENMARK	3040	2771	2377	1919	1641	1817	1773	1765	2237	2091	2062	1919	1864	1953	1943
9 EIRE	-	-	-	-	1502	1082	1119	1077	1011	1000	980	1011	1058	1296	1597
10 FINLAND	2616	2600	2605	7451	3157	3308	3055	10512	19972	3275	2923	3086	3229	3356	3546
11 FRANCE	-	-	-	-	2744	2730	2753	3203	4102	2248	2453	2564	2610	2742	2684
12 GREECE	-	-	-	-	1577	1732	1677	1511	-	-	-	1238	1312	1363	1339
13 HUNGARY	-	-	-	3818	2887	2624	2467	2430	2364	2597	2285	2416	2308	2645	3065
14 ICELAND	-	-	-	-	-	-	-	-	4967	2866	2524	2099	2445	2490	2543
15 ITALY	1710	3060	2188	1751	1846	1850	1798	1634	2732	1653	1658	1750	1843	1754	1760
16 JAPAN	-	2264	2358	2360	2820	2506	2598	2732	-	2527	2519	2659	2421	2266	2028
17 NETHERLANDS	1612	1551	1563	1564	1384	1436	1454	1440	4703	1614	1458	1424	1532	1654	1529
18 NEW ZEALAND	-	3015	3090	2667	2602	2831	2485	2311	2043	1917	2108	1943	1898	2143	2198
19 NORWAY	1961	1909	1922	1756	1814	1969	1734	2379	3072	1554	1739	1709	1719	1704	1828
20 POLAND	-	-	-	-	-	-	-	-	-	-	-	1994	2162	2420	2629
21 PORTUGAL	1212	1228	1708	1749	1742	2020	2243	2236	2030	1917	1858	1883	2052	2280	2638
22 ROMANIA	-	-	-	-	-	-	-	-	-	-	-	1739	2035	2201	2221
23 SPAIN	1547	1640	1603	1603	1487	1446	1510	10220	3372	1952	1322	1385	1439	1511	1545
24 SWEDEN	-	-	2506	2168	1889	1920	1920	1986	1972	1781	1919	1915	1912	1938	2001
25 SWITZERLAND	3836	3836	3559	3559	3384	3674	3668	3163	3068	2920	2838	2770	2718	2569	2448
26 TURKEY	-	-	-	-	-	-	-	-	-	-	-	2068	1883	1997	1567
27 UK ENGLAND AND WALES	2514	2201	2431	2490	1809	2054	2007	2304	2343	1385	1382	1411	1411	1280	1150
28 UK NORTHERN IRELAND	-	-	-	-	1825	1476	1542	1589	1965	1284	1253	1169	1197	1301	2264
29 UK SCOTLAND	2983	2714	2831	2715	2179	2355	2117	2474	3192	1660	1658	1687	1733	1665	1695
30 USA	6774	5527	4757	4164	3758	4073	3966	3707	3222	2967	2667	2444	2414	2692	2671
31 YUGOSLAVIA	-	-	-	-	-	-	-	-	-	-	1964	1880	2045	2312	2485

- NO MORTALITY DATA ARE AVAILABLE FOR EVEN A BROADER GROUP OF CAUSES FOR THIS DISEASE

. MORTALITY DATA ARE PRESENTED FOR A BROADER GROUP OF CAUSES FOR THIS DISEASE

0 VALUE<0.5

THE STANDARD MORTALITY RATIOS WERE DERIVED WITH A FACTOR OF 1000

SERIAL MORTALITY TABLES FOR VARIOUS COUNTRIES 1901-1975

TABLE 177 : ACCIDENTS AND VIOLENCE - ALL FORMS : FEMALES

	1901-	1906-	1911-	1916-	1921-	1926-	1931-	1936-	1941-	1946-	1951-	1956-	1961-	1966-	1971-75
1 AUSTRALIA	-	10647	9840	8170	7799	8596	7686	8806	7775	7990	8803	9101	9843	10247	9370
2 AUSTRIA	7633	8242	7588	10119	-	-	-	-	-	12179	10655	11770	11398	12410	13066
3 BELGIUM	4710	4871	4928	6272	4720	5305	5107	5800	10076	5175	6681	9097	9526	11736	12276
4 BULGARIA	-	-	-	-	-	7292	7453	7063	12740	7709	6377	5035	5672	6069	6177
5 CANADA	-	-	-	-	9440	9307	9073	9912	9609	9697	8853	8794	8805	9298	9808
6 CHILE	-	12941	12342	14341	16058	12070	11335	34392	80803	75193	8769	8885	9137	9912	10469
7 CZECHOSLOVAKIA	-	-	-	8486	7520	9170	8673	8192	34072	7971	8937	9378	9933	10985	11096
8 DENMARK	7107	6421	6531	6560	5936	6881	8123	8616	11554	11726	11352	11324	11919	10514	10540
9 EIRE	-	-	-	-	4967	4963	5385	5659	5483	5247	5010	4967	5717	6925	8169
10 FINLAND	6393	6392	6852	8908	6809	6805	6258	9135	10724	7896	8334	10166	10012	9844	9629
11 FRANCE	-	-	-	-	7285	7585	7669	11707	14726	7512	8647	10192	11118	12632	12904
12 GREECE	-	-	-	-	5118	6200	6561	6029	-	-	-	4860	6007	6409	6531
13 HUNGARY	-	-	-	12480	10476	10023	9138	9037	8806	8367	8116	8649	9509	11157	13101
14 ICELAND	-	-	-	-	-	-	-	-	7086	7328	6675	6428	7246	7294	9544
15 ITALY	7250	19297	11476	6083	5950	6089	5680	4943	6528	4501	4519	5266	6182	6256	7125
16 JAPAN	-	12851	12682	12389	17259	12731	12633	12045	-	10773	10444	10834	8735	8403	8146
17 NETHERLANDS	5119	5472	5197	5797	4901	5351	5365	5799	18728	6070	6511	6614	7631	9359	8881
18 NEW ZEALAND	-	7302	7281	6619	6596	8089	8052	7462	6968	7488	7665	8274	8969	10098	11410
19 NORWAY	4150	3726	3829	3538	3744	3981	3802	5665	8948	6630	6756	7046	7622	7671	7941
20 POLAND	-	-	-	-	-	-	-	-	-	-	-	4930	5790	6681	7133
21 PORTUGAL	4927	4643	6056	5814	5676	8324	8381	7798	7056	6243	6488	6462	6348	6614	6929
22 ROMANIA	-	-	-	-	-	-	-	-	-	-	-	5791	6819	7225	7488
23 SPAIN	5416	5793	5438	5302	4422	4065	4264	9627	5615	5262	4521	3747	4138	4298	5328
24 SWEDEN	-	-	5438	5305	5220	5862	6581	7427	6997	6634	7080	7505	7921	8284	9214
25 SWITZERLAND	10101	10101	9961	9961	8839	9953	10696	10011	10002	9711	9726	9897	10749	10555	10561
26 TURKEY	-	-	-	-	-	-	-	-	-	-	-	7644	7017	7212	5746
27 UK ENGLAND AND WALES	9962	8883	8666	7741	6690	7904	8350	11075	11043	6683	6920	7758	8089	7645	6966
28 UK NORTHERN IRELAND	-	-	-	-	7536	7007	7378	8100	10478	5630	5856	5888	6875	6783	9038
29 UK SCOTLAND	10175	9542	9177	8379	7764	8897	8746	9161	10584	8082	8418	8490	9032	8495	8865
30 USA	20724	15917	14859	14201	13697	14601	14530	14308	12358	11697	10079	9276	9365	9808	9081
31 YUGOSLAVIA	-	-	-	-	-	-	-	-	-	-	6422	6330	6566	7034	7567

- NO MORTALITY DATA ARE AVAILABLE FOR EVEN A BROADER GROUP OF CAUSES FOR THIS DISEASE
. MORTALITY DATA ARE PRESENTED FOR A BROADER GROUP OF CAUSES FOR THIS DISEASE
0 VALUE<0.5
THE STANDARD MORTALITY RATIOS WERE DERIVED WITH A FACTOR OF 10000

SERIAL MORTALITY TABLES FOR VARIOUS COUNTRIES 1901-1975

TABLE 177 : ACCIDENTS AND VIOLENCE - ALL FORMS : PERSONS

	1901-	1906-	1911-	1916-	1921-	1926-	1931-	1936-	1941-	1946-	1951-	1956-	1961-	1966-	1971-75
1 AUSTRALIA	-	21935	22589	18295	17849	19807	16493	18067	13834	15139	16792	16365	16539	16892	15933
2 AUSTRIA	15470	16936	18770	16886	-	21035	20742	19081	-	19956	18139	20426	18623	20170	21005
3 BELGIUM	11926	12158	13038	14240	12564	13672	12775	13625	18703	11886	12507	14814	14831	16657	16804
4 BULGARIA	-	-	-	-	-	14887	14982	14063	32534	16751	13652	10895	11497	12577	13091
5 CANADA	21146	41098	18220	15303	18735	18706	17177	17387	17448	16912	16612	16285	15997	16706	17670
6 CHILE	-	33105	35141	35457	36179	29396	29922	52184	98276	92285	24729	23821	23855	24558	26374
7 CZECHOSLOVAKIA	-	-	-	16912	15135	17354	16737	15332	71156	16484	16358	16660	17174	18872	18297
8 DENMARK	17383	15816	14095	12103	10917	12269	12735	12977	16797	16189	15855	15134	15148	14790	14695
9 EIRE	-	-	-	-	9992	7889	8305	8242	7791	7622	7400	7503	8084	9842	11914
10 FINLAND	15976	15903	16112	40409	18693	19402	17738	53886	97917	19208	17728	19457	20005	20441	21093
11 FRANCE	16771	17231	20404	16956	16564	16674	16776	20913	26493	14178	15704	17002	17676	19044	18916
12 GREECE	-	-	-	-	10328	11633	11569	10510	-	-	-	9952	11724	12121	12097
13 HUNGARY	-	-	-	24851	19339	17854	16625	16376	15919	16615	15001	15850	15757	18135	21033
14 ICELAND	-	-	-	-	-	-	-	-	27010	17443	15524	13434	15582	15821	17236
15 ITALY	12119	24843	16564	11682	12065	12112	11618	10432	16492	10241	10246	11043	11899	11442	11887
16 JAPAN	-	17709	18096	17954	22655	18783	19167	19507	-	17671	17452	18284	16029	15111	13832
17 NETHERLANDS	10449	10338	10269	10596	9269	9763	9865	10027	32633	11004	10460	10332	11358	12806	11907
18 NEW ZEALAND	-	19583	19871	17109	16613	18445	16592	15300	13555	13205	14244	13695	13770	15457	16387
19 NORWAY	11425	10929	11037	10114	10504	11365	10174	14206	19219	10848	11830	11845	12180	12090	12779
20 POLAND	-	-	-	-	-	-	-	-	-	-	-	11995	13002	14629	15762
21 PORTUGAL	8249	8155	11097	11137	11022	13735	14779	14416	13077	12136	11959	12039	12691	13792	15481
22 ROMANIA	-	-	-	-	-	-	-	21082	-	14168	-	11227	13141	14119	14363
23 SPAIN	10281	10887	10503	10426	9389	8982	9341	52464	18623	11844	8505	8372	8815	9226	9955
24 SWEDEN	-	-	14678	13039	11689	12192	12597	13391	13129	12042	12940	13131	13299	13560	14264
25 SWITZERLAND	23731	23731	22097	22097	20511	22431	22784	20061	19584	18685	18296	18051	18265	17447	16829
26 TURKEY	-	-	-	-	-	-	8976	9763	9909	11226	13159	14277	13016	13796	10928
27 UK ENGLAND AND WALES	17302	15219	16015	15698	11962	13744	13753	16516	16257	9888	10013	10573	10740	9885	8921
28 UK NORTHERN IRELAND	-	-	-	-	12602	10674	11193	11809	14772	9065	8994	8593	9230	9627	15226
29 UK SCOTLAND	19349	17748	18093	17050	14248	15673	14502	16363	20383	11968	12110	12247	12715	12054	12342
30 USA	44067	35903	31536	28051	25760	27784	27127	25616	22143	16380	18068	16513	16331	17726	17074
31 YUGOSLAVIA	-	-	-	-	12685	13331	14043	15993	-	-	12631	12171	13050	14545	15642

\- NO MORTALITY DATA ARE AVAILABLE FOR EVEN A BROADER GROUP OF CAUSES FOR THIS DISEASE

. MORTALITY DATA ARE PRESENTED FOR A BROADER GROUP OF CAUSES FOR THIS DISEASE

0 VALUE<0.5

THE STANDARD MORTALITY RATIOS WERE DERIVED WITH A FACTOR OF 10000

SERIAL MORTALITY TABLES FOR VARIOUS COUNTRIES 1901-1975

TABLE 178 : ALL CAUSES : MALES

	1901-	1906-	1911-	1916-	1921-	1926-	1931-	1936-	1941-	1946-	1951-	1956-	1961-	1966-	1971-75
1 AUSTRALIA	-	22051	22777	21737	18879	17489	15397	15278	14540	13903	13460	12961	12877	13201	12564
2 AUSTRIA	36748	34476	30785	30933	-	-	-	-	-	15772	14315	14009	13482	13647	13032
3 BELGIUM	29096	27580	26682	24121	21409	20637	18408	18724	18451	14968	13333	12819	12752	12982	12599
4 BULGARIA	-	-	-	-	-	25572	24159	22500	26043	23332	18664	12581	10967	11253	12055
5 CANADA	-	-	-	-	19140	19107	16333	15542	14584	11063	12548	12156	11497	11236	11119
6 CHILE	-	62446	61883	69397	69284	58747	56540	53431	45571	38894	30850	28275	25239	20808	18907
7 CZECHOSLOVAKIA	-	-	-	34210	29235	27661	22686	20385	25480	17715	14768	13119	13115	13865	14110
8 DENMARK	31670	29737	24797	25083	16870	15972	15015	14151	12799	11353	10469	10312	10645	10500	10372
9 EIRE	-	-	-	-	19159	18240	17629	17619	17673	15825	13526	12456	12438	12494	12367
10 FINLAND	35118	32186	29852	39030	25668	24214	22190	27873	33535	20977	16948	15611	15561	15375	14610
11 FRANCE	-	-	-	-	23306	22070	20716	21385	19926	15776	14319	13287	12722	12185	11323
12 GREECE	-	-	-	-	27827	26922	25723	21974	-	-	-	10155	9956	9687	8985
13 HUNGARY	-	-	-	38947	35374	28455	25535	22133	21443	19390	15986	13770	12809	13042	13522
14 ICELAND	-	-	25438	23910	23502	17827	17121	15700	14178	11102	10187	9516	9627	9716	9288
15 ITALY	34366	32644	29716	32016	25808	23953	20787	20072	20930	14874	13308	12672	12352	11976	11417
16 JAPAN	36892	36485	34916	40796	41776	39665	37848	37717	-	22785	17899	15448	13523	12010	10376
17 NETHERLANDS	27418	24133	21350	22961	16823	15691	13714	13347	17681	11494	9975	9768	9990	10266	10278
18 NEW ZEALAND	-	19453	18269	19917	15766	15245	13424	13851	13538	12529	12243	12070	12246	12577	12403
19 NORWAY	16790	16123	16997	18510	15689	14629	13226	12764	12944	10405	9406	9537	9947	10074	10457
20 POLAND	-	-	-	-	-	-	-	-	-	-	21894	15595	14003	13204	13112
21 PORTUGAL	34509	35062	35598	47891	36932	31437	29887	27651	26929	22228	19544	17943	16006	15378	14470
22 ROMANIA	-	-	-	-	-	-	-	-	-	-	-	15556	13138	13527	12645
23 SPAIN	43754	41277	38168	41790	34780	31057	28224	33657	25278	19305	15060	13273	11628	11161	10969
24 SWEDEN	-	-	18290	18935	15229	14752	13724	13443	11829	11023	10261	9956	9881	9710	9699
25 SWITZERLAND	30109	30109	26735	26735	21280	19940	18579	16966	15451	13847	12744	11991	11788	11187	10326
26 TURKEY	-	-	-	-	-	-	-	-	-	-	-	29249	22177	17926	15705
27 UK ENGLAND AND WALES	33264	26200	27796	26035	20934	19470	17973	17331	15164	13718	13574	13011	13031	12737	12238
28 UK NORTHERN IRELAND	-	-	-	-	22211	20845	19702	19206	18196	16305	13357	12952	12930	12849	13594
29 UK SCOTLAND	34917	32064	30161	27895	24017	22034	20121	19764	17848	15780	14887	14524	14625	13968	13793
30 USA	47167	34467	28468	27307	21180	20775	18790	17863	15867	14312	13298	12970	12733	12662	12048
31 YUGOSLAVIA	-	-	-	-	-	-	-	-	-	-	21450	17040	14783	13852	13258

- NO MORTALITY DATA ARE AVAILABLE FOR EVEN A BROADER GROUP OF CAUSES FOR THIS DISEASE

. MORTALITY DATA ARE PRESENTED FOR A BROADER GROUP OF CAUSES FOR THIS DISEASE

0 VALUE<0.5

THE STANDARD MORTALITY RATIOS WERE DERIVED WITH A FACTOR OF 10000

SERIAL MORTALITY TABLES FOR VARIOUS COUNTRIES 1901-1975

TABLE 178 : ALL CAUSES : FEMALES

	1901-	1906-	1911-	1916-	1921-	1926-	1931-	1936-	1941-	1946-	1951-	1956-	1961-	1966-	1971-75
1 AUSTRALIA	-	19019	18890	17946	15455	14123	9983	11747	11298	10110	8988	8330	7978	7985	7473
2 AUSTRIA	30303	28680	24361	25886	-	-	-	-	-	11313	10032	9189	8593	8551	8062
3 BELGIUM	24151	22949	21322	19883	18012	17396	15244	14676	13940	11731	9502	8792	8429	8342	7883
4 BULGARIA	-	-	-	-	-	21180	19380	17186	17429	15918	13021	9920	8555	8499	8895
5 CANADA	-	-	-	-	17632	17574	14637	13471	12108	10592	9165	8437	7638	6976	6456
6 CHILE	-	51927	53691	61823	60716	51130	47802	45315	37544	31232	23805	20352	17726	14329	12365
7 CZECHOSLOVAKIA	-	-	-	29441	23841	22480	18029	16035	16833	13127	10851	9215	8608	8627	8587
8 DENMARK	20138	19949	17238	18173	15108	14495	13644	12630	11488	9976	8916	8278	7891	7313	6754
9 EIRE	-	-	-	-	17407	17047	16195	16144	15704	13658	11220	9964	9435	9085	8753
10 FINLAND	28178	25532	23343	25292	19397	18151	16076	16552	15191	12954	10859	9805	9520	8829	7847
11 FRANCE	-	-	-	-	17026	16164	14525	14584	13125	10565	9324	8353	7700	7126	6552
12 GREECE	-	-	-	-	23905	23442	22513	19153	-	-	-	8100	7743	7354	6741
13 HUNGARY	-	-	-	34658	30638	24755	21631	18308	17262	14446	12046	10337	9282	8995	8910
14 ICELAND	-	-	17231	16753	15297	13279	12339	10932	10522	8700	7596	7516	6942	6766	6094
15 ITALY	32733	30775	27885	30797	23382	21117	17828	16828	16321	12012	10246	9199	8454	7826	7270
16 JAPAN	32387	33075	31352	36445	35388	32384	30125	29712	-	17280	13299	10829	9152	7930	6823
17 NETHERLANDS	22711	20558	18415	20098	15209	14370	12620	11859	13489	9874	8360	7664	7085	6864	6488
18 NEW ZEALAND	-	17960	16186	17109	13650	12837	11365	11233	10819	9616	8932	8402	8158	7977	7862
19 NORWAY	14178	13685	14013	15065	12915	12172	11077	10302	9433	8508	7646	7375	7275	6789	6807
20 POLAND	-	-	-	-	-	-	-	-	-	-	14440	10056	8910	8141	7714
21 PORTUGAL	26286	26515	26702	36201	26542	22536	20980	19063	18483	15457	13165	12046	10611	10053	9395
22 ROMANIA	-	-	-	-	-	-	-	-	-	-	-	11600	9960	9886	9238
23 SPAIN	39308	35806	32464	35839	28327	24278	21522	20749	17017	13454	10850	9483	8231	7712	7436
24 SWEDEN	-	-	15034	15563	13097	12872	12118	11709	10224	9645	8652	7956	7396	6873	6336
25 SWITZERLAND	24809	24809	21275	21275	16900	15398	14207	12856	11557	10450	9270	8383	7838	7322	6517
26 TURKEY	-	-	-	-	-	-	-	-	-	-	-	21908	16653	13744	12461
27 UK ENGLAND AND WALES	28581	22439	20843	19200	15882	14610	13466	12545	10563	9607	9004	8361	8153	7756	7519
28 UK NORTHERN IRELAND	-	-	-	-	20348	19003	17428	17020	15399	13688	10482	9518	9050	8549	8533
29 UK SCOTLAND	26391	24519	22864	20930	18507	17032	15697	14752	12746	11645	10606	9821	9294	8680	8265
30 USA	38912	28563	23809	23678	18654	17662	15271	13860	11729	10055	8879	8380	7980	7578	6916
31 YUGOSLAVIA	-	-	-	-	-	-	-	-	-	-	16797	13206	11098	9955	9264

- NO MORTALITY DATA ARE AVAILABLE FOR EVEN A BROADER GROUP OF CAUSES FOR THIS DISEASE

. MORTALITY DATA ARE PRESENTED FOR A BROADER GROUP OF CAUSES FOR THIS DISEASE

0 VALUE<0.5

THE STANDARD MORTALITY RATIOS WERE DERIVED WITH A FACTOR OF 10000

SERIAL MORTALITY TABLES FOR VARIOUS COUNTRIES 1901-1975

TABLE 178 : ALL CAUSES : PERSONS

	1901-	1906-	1911-	1916-	1921-	1926-	1931-	1936-	1941-	1946-	1951-	1956-	1961-	1966-	1971-75
1 AUSTRALIA	-	20650	20958	19931	17227	15846	12717	13496	12872	11920	11047	10421	10144	10243	9643
2 AUSTRIA	33334	31411	27372	28251	-	19482	17767	16443	-	13222	11835	11156	10529	10509	9920
3 BELGIUM	26504	25142	23822	21842	19611	18933	16739	16587	16071	13258	11213	10561	10298	10303	9827
4 BULGARIA	-	-	-	-	-	23291	21672	19704	21446	19313	15566	11153	9667	9766	10351
5 CANADA	21211	15832	17574	15841	18410	18363	15507	14532	13372	10831	10853	10271	9505	8966	8536
6 CHILE	-	56934	57612	65466	64826	55274	51947	49153	41325	34824	27091	23963	21144	17277	15304
7 CZECHOSLOVAKIA	-	-	-	31607	26283	24817	20117	17977	20696	15169	12583	10918	10513	10804	10839
8 DENMARK	24817	23920	20310	20982	15919	15179	14283	13344	12108	10630	9653	9237	9166	8753	8347
9 EIRE	-	-	-	-	18255	17625	16896	16873	16672	14722	12348	11167	10852	10670	10410
10 FINLAND	31349	28570	26292	31489	22224	20876	18762	21413	22920	16251	13310	12129	11926	11410	10474
11 FRANCE	31070	23447	21252	18169	19780	18742	17193	17460	15940	12690	11335	10304	9658	9071	8378
12 GREECE	-	-	-	-	25811	25125	24070	20529	-	-	-	11472	12817	12233	11548
13 HUNGARY	-	-	-	36725	32912	26522	23481	20104	19210	16674	13799	11848	10808	10717	10834
14 ICELAND	-	-	20620	19715	18718	15176	14343	12933	12086	9756	8748	8423	8177	8121	7560
15 ITALY	33541	31697	28785	31395	24565	22481	19234	18353	18464	13328	11639	10755	10163	9596	9009
16 JAPAN	34517	34708	33061	38527	38389	35763	33684	33386	-	19742	15351	12871	11079	9727	8375
17 NETHERLANDS	24917	22237	19799	21454	15978	15003	13147	12575	15506	10652	9133	8663	8442	8415	8161
18 NEW ZEALAND	-	18799	17340	18626	14766	14084	12415	12546	12157	11030	10503	10103	10000	9995	9828
19 NORWAY	15375	14795	15362	16613	14158	13274	12040	11405	11006	9361	8448	8363	8490	8257	8411
20 POLAND	-	-	-	-	-	-	-	-	-	-	17555	13254	10999	10201	9877
21 PORTUGAL	29936	30289	30600	41268	31009	26338	24743	22644	22000	18301	15771	14455	12823	12217	11454
22 ROMANIA	-	-	-	-	-	-	-	45554	-	24864	-	13326	11341	11463	10719
23 SPAIN	41452	38391	35135	38623	31310	27354	24509	26398	20615	15968	12628	11083	9676	9174	8925
24 SWEDEN	-	-	16492	17077	14058	13723	12851	12508	10970	10291	9406	8889	8542	8160	7827
25 SWITZERLAND	27266	27266	23735	23735	18838	17400	16128	14660	13261	11927	10775	9932	9514	8941	8086
26 TURKEY	-	-	-	-	-	-	23686	25554	27356	21287	20522	25324	19238	15770	14073
27 UK ENGLAND AND WALES	30822	24229	23940	22220	18108	16742	15431	14612	12506	11349	10895	10241	10085	9691	9341
28 UK NORTHERN IRELAND	-	-	-	-	21205	19850	18477	18037	16687	14901	11780	11036	10738	10372	10623
29 UK SCOTLAND	30068	27772	26012	23941	20907	19220	17641	16944	14953	13423	12429	11781	11457	10761	10387
30 USA	42941	31504	26148	25500	19923	19226	17025	15832	13740	9676	10958	10496	10121	9793	9064
31 YUGOSLAVIA	-	-	-	-	32755	33624	30322	27633	-	-	18853	14875	12692	11644	10992

- NO MORTALITY DATA ARE AVAILABLE FOR EVEN A BROADER GROUP OF CAUSES FOR THIS DISEASE

. MORTALITY DATA ARE PRESENTED FOR A BROADER GROUP OF CAUSES FOR THIS DISEASE

0 VALUE<0.5

THE STANDARD MORTALITY RATIOS WERE DERIVED WITH A FACTOR OF 10000

TABLE 179 STANDARD MORTALITY RATES/1,000,000 POPULATION USED TO GENERATE STATISTICAL TABLES BY CAUSE AND AGE

CAUSE \ AGE	0-	5-	10-	15-	20-	25-	30-	35-	40-	45-	50-	55-	60-	65-	70-	75-	80+
1	4	1	1	7	24	44	59	64	73	89	114	140	174	206	209	193	139
2	13	4	3	4	2	2	2	1	1	1	1	1	1	1	1	1	0
3	1	0	0	0	1	1	1	1	1	1	1	1	2	2	3	3	3
4	0	0	0	0	0	1	1	1	1	2	2	2	3	4	6	6	6
5	2	1	1	2	2	3	3	4	6	8	10	12	15	19	21	23	26
6	16	4	4	6	5	6	7	8	10	13	14	17	21	26	30	33	35
7	20	5	5	13	29	50	66	72	83	102	128	158	195	232	239	226	175
8	0	0	0	0	0	0	0	0	0	0	1	3	5	8	9	8	5
9	0	0	0	0	0	0	0	1	1	2	3	5	6	7	6	5	2
10	0	0	0	0	0	0	0	1	1	2	3	5	8	11	11	10	6
11	0	0	0	0	0	0	1	2	4	7	13	25	39	59	77	90	92
12	1	0	0	0	0	1	2	3	5	9	16	30	47	70	88	100	98
13	8	0	0	0	1	1	1	1	1	2	2	2	2	1	1	0	1
14	1	0	0	0	0	1	2	3	5	9	16	31	47	71	89	102	99
15	2	5	8	13	14	13	13	13	11	11	11	10	10	10	5	3	2
16	2	1	1	1	2	1	2	2	2	2	3	3	4	3	3	2	3
17	4	5	9	14	15	14	15	15	13	14	15	13	13	13	8	5	4
18	77	87	55	103	189	238	227	261	217	285	277	315	340	283	305	.	.
19	1	1	1	4	4	4	5	6	5	7	7	8	10	10	12	8	8
20	3	1	0	1	2	3	4	5	5	4	6	7	8	9	13	16	9
21	121	75	25	11	8	6	6	5	3	2	2	1	1	1	1	0	0
22	33	1	3	4	5	6	8	12	14	22	31	40	55	71	101	145	201
23	9	1	1	1	1	1	1	1	1	2	2	3	3	4	4	5	6
24	464	369	85	16	7	5	4	5	4	4	5	5	5	3	4	4	3
25	-	-	-	-	-	-	-	-	-	-	-	-	-	-	-	-	-
26	32	2	1	2	1	1	1	0	1	1	1	1	1	2	2	1	1
27	-	-	-	-	-	-	-	-	-	-	-	-	-	-	-	-	-
28	0	0	0	0	0	0	0	1	1	1	1	1	2	2	2	2	1
29	5	4	5	5	3	3	3	3	3	3	4	5	6	4	4	2	1
30	2	1	1	2	1	1	2	2	3	4	4	4	6	6	6	5	4

\- STANDARD RATES NOT USED FOR THIS CAUSE

. STANDARD RATES ARE FOR BROADER AGE GROUP FROM ADJACENT YOUNGER AGE

0 VALUE < 0.5/1,000,000

TABLE 179 STANDARD MORTALITY RATES/1,000,000 POPULATION USED TO GENERATE STATISTICAL TABLES BY CAUSE AND AGE

CAUSE \ AGE	0-	5-	10-	15-	20-	25-	30-	35-	40-	45-	50-	55-	60-	65-	70-	75-	80+
31	15	7	4	5	5	7	8	7	8	9	8	9	9	8	7	7	3
32	456	54	18	25	31	32	45	47	44	37	35	25	16	4	7	4	3
33	17	4	1	0	0	0	0	0	0	0	0	0	0	0	0	0	0
34	-	-	-	-	-	-	-	-	-	-	-	-	-	-	-	-	-
35	4	2	1	2	2	2	3	3	4	5	7	8	8	11	11	14	22
36	1	1	.	0	.	1	.	0	.	1	.	0	.	0	.	0	.
37	3	3	3	8	8	7	9	10	12	14	7	13	13	0	0	0	0
38	51	17	12	15	15	15	24	22	20	20	24	28	32	36	42	41	46
39	0	1	1	1	2	2	3	4	4	5	5	6	5	6	6	5	4
40	7	3	3	3	4	7	9	16	14	16	27	44	82	120	155	193	116
41	130	25	14	25	40	63	82	90	105	132	170	219	276	343	374	386	382
42	0	1	1	1	1	2	3	6	10	19	33	53	80	122	178	260	360
43	0	0	0	0	0	1	2	4	11	24	46	80	131	194	281	397	526
44	0	0	0	0	2	5	13	30	65	128	242	423	676	1030	1467	1967	2386
45	0	1	1	1	3	8	18	40	86	171	321	557	888	1346	1926	2624	3272
46	0	0	0	1	2	6	13	28	53	94	160	272	426	668	1021	1523	2264
47	0	0	0	0	1	3	6	14	29	53	96	165	262	412	607	860	1206
48	0	0	0	1	3	9	19	42	82	147	256	437	689	1080	1628	2383	3470
49	1	1	1	2	6	17	37	82	168	318	577	994	1576	2426	3554	5007	6741
50	0	0	0	0	0	0	1	2	4	9	17	31	46	66	87	102	110
51	0	0	0	1	3	8	21	56	144	339	691	1209	1797	2258	2355	2114	1465
52	0	0	0	1	3	8	22	58	147	348	708	1240	1843	2325	2442	2215	1575
53	0	0	0	0	2	15	58	142	297	495	655	788	900	1026	1172	1386	1924
54	0	0	0	0	2	8	25	57	105	155	192	205	227	243	267	299	315
55	0	0	0	0	2	3	3	6	17	36	71	119	166	201	235	270	303
56	0	0	0	0	3	11	28	63	121	191	263	323	392	444	501	569	619
57	1	1	1	4	10	26	79	182	336	530	727	845	1002	1104	1186	1245	1087
58	0	0	0	0	0	0	0	1	2	8	28	86	236	576	1235	2274	3680
59	0	0	0	1	3	5	7	11	14	17	22	26	34	48	74	109	221
60	3	3	8	13	9	6	6	7	9	13	18	27	38	52	65	89	103

- STANDARD RATES NOT USED FOR THIS CAUSE
. STANDARD RATES ARE FOR BROADER AGE GROUP FROM ADJACENT YOUNGER AGE
0 VALUE < 0.5/1,000,000

TABLE 179 STANDARD MORTALITY RATES/1,000,000 POPULATION USED TO GENERATE STATISTICAL TABLES BY CAUSE AND AGE

CAUSE \ AGE	0-	5-	10-	15-	20-	25-	30-	35-	40-	45-	50-	55-	60-	65-	70-	75-	80+
61	45	29	26	37	52	88	174	356	725	1357	2319	3695	5409	7445	9544	11877	14460
62	38	32	21	21	18	19	20	26	32	39	52	74	107	146	197	248	289
63	3	6	5	7	10	10	9	11	11	12	16	22	23	26	27	24	13
64	6	7	8	14	22	28	29	33	42	56	80	113	159	206	239	260	250
65	89	68	55	72	92	135	222	415	799	1452	2451	3882	5674	7796	9981	12385	14998
66	13	6	6	7	7	8	11	16	25	36	45	56	68	78	82	98	145
67	102	74	61	79	98	143	234	430	823	1489	2496	3938	5743	7874	10063	12484	15142
68	0	0	0	0	0	0	0	0	0	1	1	1	2	3	4	6	9
69	0	0	0	0	0	1	1	2	3	4	7	11	18	27	32	35	26
70	2	2	3	4	5	7	10	13	17	24	39	76	154	285	483	719	916
71	2	0	0	0	0	0	1	1	1	2	3	4	5	8	13	20	50
72	5	2	2	3	3	3	3	4	5	8	12	22	41	82	160	307	616
73	34	8	12	16	20	21	26	32	45	63	87	127	173	232	274	303	304
74	48	14	16	20	23	26	35	44	61	88	130	214	350	581	907	1342	1896
75	0	0	0	2	4	4	4	5	7	9	11	19	28	44	82	177	509
76	12	3	2	2	2	2	1	1	1	1	1	1	1	1	1	1	2
77	12	3	2	3	5	5	5	6	8	10	12	20	29	45	83	178	510
78	8	3	7	10	17	26	46	81	154	312	603	1101	2108	4061	7765	14045	29089
79	47	3	2	2	2	1	2	2	3	4	5	7	9	12	12	14	17
80	0	0	0	1	2	5	11	19	28	36	42	44	41	39	29	20	11
81	13	7	8	15	19	18	17	17	16	16	14	15	15	16	16	16	21
82	5	1	1	1	1	0	0	1	0	1	1	2	3	7	10	14	24
83	18	1	1	2	2	2	2	2	2	3	3	3	4	4	4	4	4
84	18	1	1	2	2	2	2	2	2	3	3	4	5	6	8	12	16
85	130	26	28	41	50	61	88	135	223	399	713	1251	2313	4376	8228	14700	29950
86	142	28	30	45	55	66	94	141	231	409	725	1271	2342	4421	8312	14878	30460
87	1	2	4	3	2	1	2	2	2	2	2	3	4	4	4	5	6
88	0	1	4	9	18	31	54	85	125	173	230	293	361	445	527	652	859
89	2	1	1	3	7	19	61	179	440	926	1750	3086	5300	8813	14355	23164	46624
90	13	4	8	20	34	62	130	287	599	1156	2081	3571	6041	9994	16370	26716	55821

\- STANDARD RATES NOT USED FOR THIS CAUSE

. STANDARD RATES ARE FOR BROADER AGE GROUP FROM ADJACENT YOUNGER AGE

0 VALUE < 0.5/1,000,000

TABLE 179 STANDARD MORTALITY RATES/1,000,000 POPULATION USED TO GENERATE STATISTICAL TABLES BY CAUSE AND AGE

CAUSE \ AGE	0-	5-	10-	15-	20-	25-	30-	35-	40-	45-	50-	55-	60-	65-	70-	75-	80+
91	14	6	12	23	36	64	132	289	601	1157	2083	3574	6045	9998	16374	26721	55827
92	0	0	0	1	3	6	12	24	44	86	157	284	514	929	1622	2719	4380
93	1	0	1	3	4	5	7	11	19	33	63	130	275	579	1277	2782	8502
94	4	1	2	5	11	17	26	48	84	156	281	515	971	1807	3389	6216	13999
95	16	5	10	25	45	79	157	335	683	1312	2362	4087	7012	11801	19759	32932	69821
96	25	8	17	35	62	106	202	416	838	1624	2965	5188	9120	15862	27523	46977	98910
97	17	7	14	28	47	81	159	337	685	1313	2364	4090	7016	11805	19763	32936	69827
98	72	2	1	1	1	1	1	2	2	4	5	9	16	26	48	78	225
99	15	3	5	7	7	7	10	12	18	29	44	74	127	215	359	579	1198
100	31	2	3	4	5	6	8	12	20	33	52	84	136	206	321	497	927
101	500	20	13	15	13	14	18	26	41	68	118	223	438	849	1763	3627	10022
102	63	3	2	3	3	4	4	5	7	11	17	27	45	75	118	213	471
103	525	22	17	21	21	22	29	42	68	111	186	337	629	1218	2488	5018	14389
104	99	3	2	2	2	2	3	5	7	12	20	38	75	138	263	516	1353
105	33	3	2	3	3	6	10	23	56	142	340	734	1400	2201	3150	4404	6539
106	168	8	7	9	9	11	15	31	64	153	343	726	1383	2261	3364	4765	7365
107	39	33	13	9	10	9	7	8	10	11	12	15	19	19	19	24	27
108	3	0	0	0	1	1	1	1	2	3	4	6	9	12	16	19	23
109	0	0	0	0	0	0	0	0	0	1	1	2	3	5	9	14	26
110	744	39	32	42	43	48	66	104	180	341	656	1274	2351	3991	6610	10885	23974
111	16	3	2	3	4	5	6	7	10	13	16	18	23	27	27	27	33
112	1	0	0	0	1	2	4	7	13	26	42	71	112	176	275	403	638
113	1	0	0	0	2	4	6	11	18	31	48	73	110	165	241	328	439
114	2	0	0	1	2	5	8	15	27	49	77	123	190	301	467	675	1066
115	1	0	0	0	0	0	0	0	1	1	1	1	2	3	6	12	34
116	3	0	0	1	3	5	8	15	28	49	78	125	192	304	473	686	1100
117	7	6	6	5	4	4	4	4	6	8	12	15	22	33	45	63	88
118	59	2	2	2	2	3	4	7	11	18	29	50	88	152	265	441	834
119	130	3	2	5	7	7	10	11	15	19	29	45	68	117	186	286	512
120	132	3	2	5	7	8	10	12	16	20	30	46	70	121	194	300	554

- STANDARD RATES NOT USED FOR THIS CAUSE
. STANDARD RATES ARE FOR BROADER AGE GROUP FROM ADJACENT YOUNGER AGE
0 VALUE < 0.5/1,000,000

TABLE 179 STANDARD MORTALITY RATES/1,000,000 POPULATION USED TO GENERATE STATISTICAL TABLES BY CAUSE AND AGE

CAUSE \ AGE	0-	5-	10-	15-	20-	25-	30-	35-	40-	45-	50-	55-	60-	65-	70-	75-	80+
121	3	1	1	1	2	2	5	9	18	30	48	66	84	100	109	109	93
122	0	0	0	0	1	2	6	7	13	24	45	78	116	160	205	278	334
123	0	0	0	0	0	1	1	2	4	6	12	22	39	69	123	205	386
124	3	1	1	2	2	3	6	11	22	36	60	88	123	169	232	314	479
125	228	16	13	17	21	27	39	59	97	155	245	377	577	899	1396	2073	3511
126	3	1	2	2	2	2	2	2	3	3	3	5	7	9	12	16	25
127	5	5	7	14	20	22	27	35	45	57	77	104	136	189	264	385	613
128	8	6	8	16	22	24	29	37	48	60	80	109	143	198	276	401	638
129	7	1	2	2	3	5	6	8	12	18	28	44	72	117	193	331	662
130	15	8	10	18	26	29	35	45	60	78	108	153	214	315	469	731	1300
131	0	0	0	0	0	1	1	2	3	4	6	10	13	19	29	41	54
132	0	0	0	0	0	0	0	0	0	1	8	29	91	271	707	1594	3907
133	22	9	11	20	28	32	40	53	72	95	132	197	302	509	886	1538	2996
134	0	0	0	1	4	6	5	4	2	0	0	0	0	0	0	0	0
135	0	0	0	2	8	10	9	8	4	1	0	0	0	0	0	0	0
136	0	0	0	1	3	6	6	5	3	0	0	0	0	0	0	0	0
137	0	0	0	2	6	7	7	6	2	0	0	0	0	0	0	0	0
138	0	0	0	7	31	41	41	36	17	3	1	0	0	0	0	0	0
139	3	0	0	0	0	1	1	1	1	2	2	3	5	7	12	18	39
140	0	0	0	0	0	1	1	2	3	7	14	27	51	86	140	231	438
141	0	0	0	0	0	0	0	0	2	3	4	10	23	49	88	141	225
142	1	0	0	0	0	0	0	1	1	1	1	2	2	3	5	5	9
143	1	0	0	0	0	0	0	0	1	1	1	2	2	3	4	6	11
144	2	1	1	1	1	1	2	3	5	9	17	31	56	93	151	245	462
145	10	1	3	7	4	4	4	6	7	10	14	19	29	43	76	138	361
146	13	2	4	8	5	5	6	9	12	19	31	50	85	136	227	383	823
147	-	-	-	-	-	-	-	-	-	-	-	-	-	-	-	-	-
148	385	22	16	16	13	12	11	11	11	13	12	14	15	16	14	13	11
149	938	36	26	24	20	18	17	20	23	30	31	33	34	37	35	40	42
150	-	-	-	-	-	-	-	-	-	-	-	-	-	-	-	-	-

- STANDARD RATES NOT USED FOR THIS CAUSE

. STANDARD RATES ARE FOR BROADER AGE GROUP FROM ADJACENT YOUNGER AGE

0 VALUE < 0.5/1,000,000

TABLE 179 STANDARD MORTALITY RATES/1,000,000 POPULATION USED TO GENERATE STATISTICAL TABLES BY CAUSE AND AGE

CAUSE \ AGE	0-	5-	10-	15-	20-	25-	30-	35-	40-	45-	50-	55-	60-	65-	70-	75-	80+
151	-	-	-	-	-	-	-	-	-	-	-	-	-	-	-	-	-
152	-	-	-	-	-	-	-	-	-	-	-	-	-	-	-	-	-
153	-	-	-	-	-	-	-	-	-	-	-	-	-	-	-	-	-
154	-	-	-	-	-	-	-	-	-	-	-	-	-	-	-	-	-
155	-	-	-	-	-	-	-	-	-	-	-	-	-	-	-	-	-
156	3149	36	26	24	20	18	17	20	23	30	31	33	34	37	35	40	42
157	0	0	0	0	0	0	0	0	0	0	0	0	0	8	111	600	4886
158	40	1	0	1	2	2	2	2	3	4	5	6	10	14	30	56	172
159	40	1	0	1	2	2	2	2	3	4	5	6	10	22	141	656	5058
160	62	74	53	227	214	124	90	81	83	90	101	122	145	173	238	346	426
161	3	5	8	17	24	19	16	15	14	15	16	18	18	13	13	17	17
162	65	78	60	244	238	142	106	96	97	105	117	140	164	186	251	363	443
163	10	1	2	8	13	12	13	17	21	25	30	34	39	46	69	117	212
164	16	6	8	10	14	14	14	17	19	25	33	47	75	139	324	807	2884
165	31	10	4	4	4	5	5	6	7	8	10	11	16	25	46	91	193
166	0	1	2	3	2	1	1	1	1	1	1	1	1	1	1	1	1
167	26	26	15	17	13	9	8	8	9	11	12	15	17	21	23	26	27
168	235	61	55	88	107	97	96	103	116	132	152	182	227	300	538	1140	3467
169	297	135	108	315	321	220	185	184	199	222	253	304	372	473	776	1486	3893
170	0	0	1	24	56	72	81	97	119	146	174	200	214	225	228	221	179
171	229	56	43	91	132	144	155	177	213	252	299	350	408	496	735	1326	3608
172	15	4	2	7	9	8	7	6	6	5	5	4	4	4	4	5	6
173	0	0	0	0	0	0	0	1	1	1	1	3	4	5	4	4	1
174	15	4	3	7	9	8	8	7	6	5	6	7	8	9	9	8	7
175	312	139	111	322	330	228	193	191	205	227	259	311	381	482	784	1494	3901
176	15	4	4	30	65	80	89	103	125	151	180	207	223	234	236	229	186
177	312	139	112	345	386	301	274	288	324	373	433	511	595	707	1012	1715	4079
178	4947	390	333	657	785	832	1067	1594	2625	4447	7420	12179	19682	31326	49727	79316	158194

- STANDARD RATES NOT USED FOR THIS CAUSE
. STANDARD RATES ARE FOR BROADER AGE GROUP FROM ADJACENT YOUNGER AGE
0 VALUE < 0.5/1,000,000

TABLE 180 POPULATION ESTIMATES (THOUSANDS) FOR AUSTRALIA BY AGE,SEX AND QUINQUENNIA

AGE	0-	5-	10-	15-	20-	25-	30-	35-	40-	45-	50-	55-	60-	65-	70-	75-	80+	NO. YRS DATA
MALE																		
1901-	-	-	-	-	-	-	-	-	-	-	-	-	-	-	-	-	-	
1906-	1059	872	834	926	951	796	649	580	570	535	417	258	180	150	115	77	48	4
1911-	1402	1238	1151	1165	1156	1044	925	817	763	690	578	405	295	220	152	97	65	5
1916-	1485	1406	1271	1172	1124	1096	1055	920	818	712	641	509	387	256	162	98	70	5
1921-	1523	1531	1386	1234	1163	1168	1160	1012	897	772	709	595	472	306	188	109	77	5
1926-	1488	1565	1486	1387	1316	1272	1207	1075	1015	899	780	627	521	377	249	140	87	5
1931-	1461	1572	1577	1542	1468	1384	1263	1145	1130	1034	862	672	572	454	323	178	101	5
1936-	1460	1414	1572	1612	1502	1488	1368	1241	1140	1102	979	796	619	477	361	213	126	5
1941-	1673	1478	1559	1573	1547	1602	1472	1367	1228	1168	1060	885	702	524	390	235	152	5
1946-	2088	1728	1553	1473	1615	1728	1570	1519	1396	1241	1111	936	823	601	418	248	177	5
1951-	2450	2184	1695	1476	1601	1826	1760	1635	1579	1379	1174	997	898	695	464	268	210	5
1956-	2686	2556	2284	1781	1630	1772	1937	1828	1669	1584	1342	1105	898	758	541	313	224	5
1961-	2942	2776	2645	2366	1924	1765	1854	1980	1847	1657	1537	1266	996	760	588	369	259	5
1966-	2971	3090	2901	2735	2504	2087	1879	1934	2017	1843	1602	1441	1139	848	581	392	297	5
1971-	3232	3103	3213	2984	2861	2678	2205	1959	1977	2006	1787	1503	1288	967	660	385	322	5
FEMALE																		
1901-	-	-	-	-	-	-	-	-	-	-	-	-	-	-	-	-	-	
1906-	1022	843	819	910	884	722	592	520	473	417	312	195	149	137	101	64	42	4
1911-	1343	1180	1113	1141	1126	989	848	739	656	570	451	310	240	193	136	87	60	5
1916-	1419	1339	1220	1146	1150	1096	985	851	737	629	529	404	317	220	149	95	70	5
1921-	1470	1479	1330	1182	1193	1192	1111	968	833	704	616	507	405	260	171	108	82	5
1926-	1437	1513	1424	1321	1294	1234	1148	1063	957	824	700	567	474	334	227	137	98	5
1931-	1404	1532	1517	1478	1404	1277	1183	1161	1095	964	794	633	550	428	302	173	116	5
1936-	1400	1400	1519	1556	1450	1398	1268	1188	1146	1084	922	747	612	488	365	218	147	5
1941-	1536	1381	1500	1541	1480	1525	1374	1249	1198	1158	1035	867	693	548	422	264	186	5
1946-	1911	1611	1494	1433	1520	1614	1486	1410	1307	1167	1099	954	825	636	477	302	227	5
1951-	2345	2087	1629	1411	1482	1680	1672	1587	1469	1248	1133	1062	971	777	560	353	305	5
1956-	2561	2446	2179	1698	1518	1605	1783	1746	1621	1479	1234	1105	1014	890	668	431	356	5
1961-	2801	2646	2529	2247	1814	1650	1703	1849	1780	1622	1461	1207	1059	940	775	524	443	5
1966-	2825	2941	2765	2621	2384	1954	1769	1797	1895	1787	1593	1421	1166	988	812	602	547	5
1971-	3089	2950	3051	2856	2749	2542	2074	1860	1849	1904	1761	1535	1368	1094	864	634	649	5

- NO MORTALITY STATISTICS ARE PRESENTED FOR THIS QUINQUENNIA

TABLE 180 POPULATION ESTIMATES (THOUSANDS) FOR AUSTRIA BY AGE,SEX AND QUINQUENNIA

AGE	0-	5-	10-	15-	20-	25-	30-	35-	40-	45-	50-	55-	60-	65-	70-	75-	80+	NO. YRS DATA
MALE																		
1901-	1182	1065	1029	945	999	858	771	702	657	540	510	435	366	252	177	96	57	3
1906-	786	732	734	622	658	572	534	488	424	388	346	288	240	188	124	68	38	2
1911-	1200	1152	1146	969	1011	879	843	771	654	600	531	441	375	291	192	105	57	3
1916-	2000	1920	1910	1615	1685	1465	1405	1285	1090	1000	885	735	625	485	320	175	95	5
1921-	-	-	-	-	-	-	-	-	-	-	-	-	-	-	-	-	-	
1926-	508	505	611	478	593	549	518	456	409	391	355	316	256	193	131	58	41	2
1931-	1204	1342	1502	1026	1469	1448	1407	1175	1017	980	913	829	670	511	352	149	112	5
1936-	456	569	591	351	582	611	611	484	404	393	375	348	282	217	152	62	49	2
1941-	-	-	-	-	-	-	-	-	-	-	-	-	-	-	-	-	-	
1946-	1063	1051	1117	879	1003	933	695	831	943	978	881	703	588	483	355	205	128	4
1951-	1286	1288	1467	1127	1174	1133	963	819	1151	1229	1186	948	754	625	466	295	183	5
1956-	1360	1258	1282	1458	1088	1129	1099	934	793	1112	1172	1100	845	633	479	310	214	5
1961-	1574	1347	1253	1279	1435	1071	1111	1080	912	777	1069	1095	980	707	486	319	236	5
1966-	1600	1567	1344	1244	1263	1427	1058	1096	1061	893	742	1002	981	818	536	321	248	5
1971-	1396	1612	1580	1379	1303	1251	1361	1049	1096	1049	868	708	911	828	621	351	253	5
FEMALE																		
1901-	1179	1050	1044	987	1014	885	807	717	681	564	555	465	414	285	210	117	69	3
1906-	782	734	742	656	676	612	562	506	436	410	364	316	264	214	142	80	48	2
1911-	1194	1152	1158	1023	1038	939	888	798	672	633	558	483	411	333	222	126	75	3
1916-	1990	1920	1930	1705	1730	1565	1480	1330	1120	1055	930	805	685	555	370	210	125	5
1921-	-	-	-	-	-	-	-	-	-	-	-	-	-	-	-	-	-	
1926-	496	497	600	477	604	591	566	533	482	457	399	358	291	225	157	92	57	2
1931-	1173	1310	1469	1026	1487	1495	1473	1377	1228	1179	1054	965	768	599	429	254	160	5
1936-	444	553	575	352	585	605	613	569	501	487	445	415	325	255	187	111	71	2
1941-	-	-	-	-	-	-	-	-	-	-	-	-	-	-	-	-	-	
1946-	1019	1016	1082	852	1001	1180	895	1050	1150	1117	1034	909	775	641	485	300	191	4
1951-	1232	1237	1414	1088	1142	1339	1306	1073	1436	1437	1366	1217	1030	876	665	434	282	5
1956-	1305	1207	1230	1394	1047	1106	1304	1280	1048	1402	1394	1312	1147	933	736	490	362	5
1961-	1506	1294	1202	1229	1377	1035	1095	1291	1256	1037	1369	1346	1241	1046	796	554	440	5
1966-	1536	1501	1293	1196	1222	1379	1029	1086	1276	1245	1007	1323	1277	1136	896	606	515	5
1971-	1330	1540	1506	1328	1276	1219	1335	1035	1095	1274	1223	987	1266	1178	980	683	584	5

1901-19 DATA FOR 7 PROVINCES IN AUSTRO-HUNGARIAN EMPIRE

- NO MORTALITY STATISTICS ARE PRESENTED FOR THIS QUINQUENNIA

TABLE 180 POPULATION ESTIMATES (THOUSANDS) FOR BELGIUM BY AGE,SEX AND QUINQUENNIA

AGE	0-	5-	10-	15-	20-	25-	30-	35-	40-	45-	50-	55-	60-	65-	70-	75-	80+	NO. YRS DATA
MALE																		
1901-	701	650	617	598	557	517	463	412	361	317	257	233	191	152	107	64	38	3
1906-	1922	1882	1811	1700	1573	1495	1368	1240	1083	937	758	656	534	447	313	179	112	5
1911-	1019	1090	1095	1050	973	903	836	782	697	609	500	420	339	274	190	111	68	3
1916-	557	664	707	720	674	589	546	530	490	441	373	308	247	181	125	77	44	2
1921-	1394	1642	1584	1761	1732	1563	1446	1363	1269	1179	1030	861	691	495	339	202	117	5
1926-	1593	1715	1346	1667	1770	1750	1610	1411	1302	1247	1128	972	785	578	392	215	130	5
1931-	1672	1666	1295	1632	1777	1775	1612	1463	1369	1322	1196	1035	852	649	447	241	147	5
1936-	1659	1541	1355	1635	1764	1688	1505	1519	1464	1404	1241	1059	899	708	505	279	170	5
1941-	1645	1426	1418	1638	1751	1604	1405	1577	1564	1492	1287	1084	949	774	571	324	196	5
1946-	1661	1383	1492	1631	1707	1540	1358	1626	1613	1544	1335	1128	1006	834	629	370	228	5
1951-	1776	1632	1363	1473	1613	1708	1575	1298	1591	1604	1503	1249	1006	842	653	426	275	5
1956-	1870	1786	1640	1369	1476	1614	1700	1553	1277	1552	1538	1405	1124	858	661	448	320	5
1961-	1973	1891	1799	1657	1401	1519	1642	1657	1485	1219	1460	1412	1243	943	666	451	358	5
1966-	1925	1999	1908	1818	1705	1451	1541	1642	1637	1454	1171	1364	1263	1043	726	451	369	5
1971-	1759	1946	2011	1928	1871	1718	1435	1523	1617	1598	1391	1097	1222	1058	794	485	375	5
FEMALE																		
1901-	694	627	589	581	544	500	439	388	346	316	259	246	206	161	119	76	49	3
1906-	1918	1813	1729	1659	1540	1441	1299	1165	1034	921	754	698	585	481	349	218	147	5
1911-	1110	1124	1097	1028	947	901	835	764	676	589	484	432	363	312	223	136	95	3
1916-	621	696	717	706	660	610	563	528	479	427	359	312	262	212	152	96	64	2
1921-	1322	1615	1708	1796	1716	1551	1425	1359	1267	1157	1003	853	717	543	391	255	162	5
1926-	1453	1652	1469	1712	1728	1651	1540	1428	1317	1231	1101	952	794	608	439	272	181	5
1931-	1631	1691	1272	1626	1727	1744	1648	1499	1369	1306	1200	1057	877	688	500	293	205	5
1936-	1633	1585	1296	1615	1709	1680	1558	1535	1445	1388	1274	1115	944	760	564	333	227	5
1941-	1606	1464	1354	1615	1689	1593	1445	1566	1529	1477	1347	1168	1012	836	635	383	252	5
1946-	1580	1353	1415	1615	1668	1512	1340	1597	1618	1571	1423	1222	1085	920	716	440	279	5
1951-	1704	1578	1334	1453	1595	1643	1518	1275	1591	1630	1582	1410	1192	1012	805	551	413	5
1956-	1787	1719	1587	1341	1461	1602	1648	1516	1268	1573	1597	1530	1334	1086	858	602	492	5
1961-	1880	1812	1728	1599	1365	1488	1619	1651	1500	1245	1525	1529	1435	1208	921	644	562	5
1966-	1837	1910	1833	1749	1633	1395	1507	1627	1646	1484	1219	1476	1451	1314	1034	703	623	5
1971-	1672	1859	1925	1850	1783	1636	1396	1506	1618	1626	1444	1183	1400	1333	1133	795	699	5

- NO MORTALITY STATISTICS ARE PRESENTED FOR THIS QUINQUENNIA

TABLE 180 POPULATION ESTIMATES (THOUSANDS) FOR BULGARIA BY AGE,SEX AND QUINQUENNIA

AGE	0-	5-	10-	15-	20-	25-	30-	35-	40-	45-	50-	55-	60-	65-	70-	75-	80+	NO. YRS DATA
MALE																		
1901-	-	-	-	-	-	-	-	-	-	-	-	-	-	-	-	-	-	
1906-	-	-	-	-	-	-	-	-	-	-	-	-	-	-	-	-	-	
1911-	-	-	-	-	-	-	-	-	-	-	-	-	-	-	-	-	-	
1916-	-	-	-	-	-	-	-	-	-	-	-	-	-	-	-	-	-	
1921-	-	-	-	-	-	-	-	-	-	-	-	-	-	-	-	-	-	
1926-	248	211	232	251	277	216	172	157	153	125	98	95	76	54	37	21	20	4
1931-	295	298	330	267	366	302	258	230	193	175	154	117	96	72	49	26	25	5
1936-	228	234	270	234	319	243	222	213	181	160	136	99	89	63	40	23	20	4
1941-	222	218	266	279	350	234	230	245	223	185	143	106	109	70	42	25	21	4
1946-	273	268	321	382	458	302	312	329	324	270	202	153	156	96	58	37	27	5
1951-	278	290	305	345	432	345	358	304	324	307	250	187	155	101	74	42	28	5
1956-	674	712	703	594	590	660	672	636	396	508	480	392	286	189	154	105	70	2
1961-	1667	1692	1794	1662	1448	1535	1634	1668	1379	1064	1231	1105	847	587	373	273	213	5
1966-	1619	1647	1716	1766	1624	1422	1544	1629	1654	1356	1032	1178	1023	747	473	263	241	5
1971-	1710	1596	1631	1699	1741	1597	1403	1528	1604	1618	1314	979	1086	890	594	372	189	5
FEMALE																		
1901-	-	-	-	-	-	-	-	-	-	-	-	-	-	-	-	-	-	
1906-	-	-	-	-	-	-	-	-	-	-	-	-	-	-	-	-	-	
1911-	-	-	-	-	-	-	-	-	-	-	-	-	-	-	-	-	-	
1916-	-	-	-	-	-	-	-	-	-	-	-	-	-	-	-	-	-	
1921-	-	-	-	-	-	-	-	-	-	-	-	-	-	-	-	-	-	
1926-	240	203	236	258	238	207	170	164	153	125	97	83	73	52	42	22	27	4
1931-	284	288	339	275	309	282	248	226	192	180	145	113	97	69	55	29	34	5
1936-	219	226	278	240	268	227	213	203	175	160	126	104	93	63	47	26	29	4
1941-	213	210	274	287	296	222	221	230	208	174	131	123	115	75	52	30	31	4
1946-	262	258	332	393	389	286	301	306	295	244	182	180	169	112	77	45	43	5
1951-	267	280	315	357	369	325	346	288	296	275	220	197	169	126	100	56	47	5
1956-	645	684	679	577	587	653	663	638	395	495	470	395	313	232	201	128	90	2
1961-	1584	1622	1725	1610	1421	1533	1613	1655	1382	1058	1206	1102	892	673	492	361	281	5
1966-	1537	1567	1644	1701	1585	1411	1528	1602	1641	1366	1026	1177	1060	815	569	368	337	5
1971-	1621	1517	1550	1631	1690	1565	1399	1520	1588	1617	1342	991	1124	969	690	492	283	5

1927-55 DATA FOR TOWNS ONLY
- NO MORTALITY STATISTICS ARE PRESENTED FOR THIS QUINQUENNIA

TABLE 180 POPULATION ESTIMATES (THOUSANDS) FOR CANADA BY AGE,SEX AND QUINQUENNIA

AGE	0-	5-	10-	15-	20-	25-	30-	35-	40-	45-	50-	55-	60-	65-	70-	75-	80+	NO. YRS DATA
MALE																		
1901-	502	586	600	586	532	446	398	376	340	284	240	191	166	132	96	60	50	5
1906-	363	593	645	614	560	480	444	421	392	329	280	228	193	157	114	73	65	5
1911-	262	599	693	645	589	516	495	472	452	380	326	272	225	186	136	89	85	5
1916-	190	606	745	677	620	556	552	529	520	441	380	324	261	222	161	107	111	5
1921-	1875	1878	1620	1417	1266	1316	1332	1351	1125	922	760	569	484	341	224	133	105	5
1926-	2727	2927	2694	2570	2245	1949	1757	1744	1736	1591	1273	907	713	554	415	230	159	5
1931-	2703	2813	2726	2664	2370	2124	1901	1831	1738	1617	1382	1065	840	642	464	266	189	5
1936-	2679	2704	2758	2762	2503	2315	2055	1922	1739	1644	1501	1250	990	743	519	308	225	5
1941-	2956	2811	2801	2794	2609	2503	2233	2080	1832	1715	1604	1394	1136	871	599	360	267	5
1946-	3809	3279	2860	2721	2667	2673	2443	2354	2080	1860	1672	1443	1255	1036	723	428	314	5
1951-	4700	3929	3144	2755	2752	2881	2693	2620	2369	2061	1781	1516	1321	1153	857	517	369	5
1956-	5421	4871	4062	3215	2977	3105	3136	2913	2709	2412	2027	1691	1365	1173	953	611	443	5
1961-	5818	5485	5001	4088	3166	2987	3170	3197	2926	2633	2327	1918	1528	1219	971	690	570	5
1966-	5211	5915	5619	4977	4147	3417	3193	3256	3206	2862	2543	2192	1743	1331	1005	707	640	5
1971-	4575	5370	5998	5657	4956	4397	3615	3236	3246	3112	2777	2378	2020	1554	1099	708	690	5
FEMALE																		
1901-	488	571	582	582	563	472	409	375	330	269	232	186	163	122	90	55	47	5
1906-	352	577	627	608	582	508	455	418	376	311	268	221	188	147	107	68	63	5
1911-	254	583	676	635	601	548	507	466	429	360	309	263	218	177	128	85	86	5
1916-	183	589	728	664	621	590	564	520	489	416	356	312	253	213	153	105	117	5
1921-	1829	1831	1573	1378	1279	1250	1160	1106	914	747	633	494	419	298	207	132	116	5
1926-	2673	2864	2634	2514	2148	1755	1611	1600	1451	1266	1039	765	629	511	387	221	177	5
1931-	2639	2751	2667	2610	2301	1977	1771	1679	1520	1356	1158	898	735	585	437	261	210	5
1936-	2605	2642	2699	2710	2466	2227	1946	1762	1593	1451	1292	1053	859	669	493	310	244	5
1941-	2861	2735	2735	2746	2610	2488	2170	1935	1728	1566	1425	1203	993	780	573	366	285	5
1946-	3667	3161	2775	2685	2713	2747	2472	2271	1970	1709	1547	1324	1129	932	696	431	336	5
1951-	4500	3760	3029	2681	2747	2951	2782	2604	2277	1910	1677	1461	1250	1063	826	522	431	5
1956-	5190	4695	3887	3120	2918	2975	3126	2938	2649	2276	1878	1614	1358	1158	957	630	521	5
1961-	5556	5239	4780	3928	3173	2952	3067	3198	2958	2594	2245	1841	1522	1278	1055	756	675	5
1966-	4942	5659	5376	4816	4142	3423	3115	3160	3206	2911	2548	2173	1772	1452	1183	867	843	5
1971-	4353	5128	5731	5446	4940	4367	3499	3118	3119	3133	2872	2464	2106	1716	1326	978	1095	5

1901-20 DATA FOR ONTARIO ONLY

1901-30 DATA FOR REGISTRATION AREA ONLY

\- NO MORTALITY STATISTICS ARE PRESENTED FOR THIS QUINQUENNIA

TABLE 180 POPULATION ESTIMATES (THOUSANDS) FOR CHILE BY AGE, SEX AND QUINQUENNIA

AGE	0-	5-	10-	15-	20-	25-	30-	35-	40-	45-	50-	55-	60-	65-	70-	75-	80+	NO. YRS DATA
MALE																		
1901-	-	-	-	-	-	-	-	-	-	-	-	-	-	-	-	-	-	
1906-	264	212	194	174	129	126	99	105	72	80	59	43	35	27	16	10	13	1
1911-	1271	1134	1025	903	717	679	537	549	407	401	290	225	170	129	78	49	61	5
1916-	1213	1236	1095	947	820	743	596	578	478	402	282	241	165	122	75	47	56	5
1921-	1270	1298	1141	1015	910	795	651	609	520	423	296	251	175	127	77	47	56	5
1926-	1414	1331	1171	1103	990	839	702	644	540	458	328	257	198	139	82	47	58	5
1931-	1501	1418	1279	1180	1043	903	769	692	585	494	366	281	226	149	92	51	60	5
1936-	1546	1549	1454	1249	1077	985	850	750	654	529	410	322	261	159	107	56	61	5
1941-	1660	1690	1548	1304	1159	1023	889	802	715	565	464	353	293	177	123	63	65	5
1946-	1466	1474	1264	1079	903	824	718	679	617	482	422	300	258	163	113	57	57	4
1951-	1618	1606	1290	1116	1134	830	724	719	665	514	482	318	283	188	130	65	62	4
1956-	2478	2414	2027	1732	1630	1292	1154	1075	978	780	698	491	423	278	189	98	93	5
1961-	3121	2745	2346	1992	1616	1395	1367	1121	1000	871	763	578	483	342	215	125	107	5
1966-	3416	3114	2710	2300	1872	1553	1435	1262	1121	928	802	652	541	402	258	142	114	5
1971-	3262	3026	2940	2587	2106	1836	1577	1337	1173	1051	854	709	578	429	289	222	83	5
FEMALE																		
1901-	-	-	-	-	-	-	-	-	-	-	-	-	-	-	-	-	-	
1906-	260	209	192	172	126	133	110	98	72	79	55	45	36	27	18	12	17	1
1911-	1252	1115	1002	916	716	719	580	524	405	398	278	237	181	134	86	56	78	5
1916-	1194	1207	1056	989	842	790	618	567	471	404	279	252	180	129	83	52	69	5
1921-	1253	1269	1100	1070	942	855	657	613	511	425	297	268	189	134	88	52	68	5
1926-	1400	1307	1135	1159	1020	918	697	662	530	459	328	285	207	147	100	57	72	5
1931-	1485	1390	1248	1221	1091	991	758	723	571	491	368	303	241	156	115	62	76	5
1936-	1522	1510	1429	1262	1159	1074	838	795	631	520	417	323	291	165	134	68	80	5
1941-	1634	1650	1526	1318	1261	1118	894	863	689	565	473	349	332	186	153	77	87	5
1946-	1446	1450	1245	1108	1115	906	746	743	598	498	430	306	293	177	138	71	76	4
1951-	1600	1591	1270	1165	1233	917	777	801	648	548	481	334	322	209	156	82	84	4
1956-	2451	2386	1999	1796	1773	1423	1217	1181	963	820	711	509	480	306	230	125	156	5
1961-	3093	2726	2316	2081	1746	1524	1442	1208	1039	927	782	610	541	382	262	160	178	5
1966-	3358	3090	2687	2376	2004	1671	1515	1352	1177	998	849	703	602	458	313	180	190	5
1971-	3177	3022	2919	2630	2231	1929	1668	1411	1223	1118	930	787	650	521	363	328	138	5

- NO MORTALITY STATISTICS ARE PRESENTED FOR THIS QUINQUENNIA

TABLE 180 POPULATION ESTIMATES (THOUSANDS) FOR CZECHOSLOVAKIA BY AGE,SEX AND QUINQUENNIA

AGE	0-	5-	10-	15-	20-	25-	30-	35-	40-	45-	50-	55-	60-	65-	70-	75-	80+	NO. YRS DATA
MALE																		
1901-	-	-	-	-	-	-	-	-	-	-	-	-	-	-	-	-	-	
1906-	-	-	-	-	-	-	-	-	-	-	-	-	-	-	-	-	-	
1911-	-	-	-	-	-	-	-	-	-	-	-	-	-	-	-	-	-	
1916-	1000	1374	1705	1483	1262	939	802	770	726	692	626	511	433	310	199	106	60	2
1921-	2817	3566	3519	3609	3323	2645	2262	2034	1861	1753	1588	1343	1123	812	540	290	163	5
1926-	1267	1481	1156	1405	1400	1189	1019	859	763	711	645	565	465	341	234	128	71	2
1931-	3106	3160	1661	2684	3060	2913	2503	1889	1592	1454	1322	1232	989	741	539	300	166	4
1936-	903	829	323	648	818	847	729	507	411	370	337	328	259	197	150	84	47	1
1941-	568	459	450	523	534	389	424	510	463	408	308	246	208	164	120	72	43	1
1946-	3053	2481	2187	2456	2534	2286	1695	2475	2365	2132	1669	1275	1055	832	605	375	230	5
1951-	3328	2991	2430	2162	2411	2485	2203	1691	2371	2247	2004	1512	1130	883	652	398	280	5
1956-	3188	3304	2981	2420	2146	2390	2462	2178	1665	2316	2158	1871	1352	953	677	438	311	5
1961-	2825	3175	3328	3002	2441	2154	2358	2424	2125	1646	2263	2050	1671	1137	715	439	310	5
1966-	2822	2801	3154	3305	2971	2408	2125	2322	2382	2067	1581	2119	1836	1393	861	472	337	5
1971-	3012	2796	2764	3116	3246	2908	2337	2048	2247	2281	2012	1419	1891	1528	1050	560	346	5
FEMALE																		
1901-	-	-	-	-	-	-	-	-	-	-	-	-	-	-	-	-	-	
1906-	-	-	-	-	-	-	-	-	-	-	-	-	-	-	-	-	-	
1911-	-	-	-	-	-	-	-	-	-	-	-	-	-	-	-	-	-	
1916-	971	1367	1694	1514	1346	1102	950	884	814	758	680	557	510	371	256	136	86	2
1921-	2741	3530	3477	3659	3459	2960	2603	2341	2119	1955	1761	1483	1311	969	689	377	240	5
1926-	1236	1458	1136	1415	1422	1272	1140	992	883	807	730	631	539	404	297	168	107	2
1931-	3041	3082	1616	2671	2982	2876	2665	2188	1895	1702	1551	1406	1130	870	675	401	260	4
1936-	887	803	312	639	772	788	748	589	499	443	406	381	293	230	186	115	75	1
1941-	549	447	440	515	556	398	447	523	482	443	366	299	259	204	154	92	63	1
1946-	2943	2409	2140	2419	2606	2380	1774	2552	2445	2265	1934	1555	1330	1062	790	490	332	5
1951-	3166	2899	2371	2124	2406	2574	2303	1775	2468	2375	2181	1838	1435	1183	865	546	397	5
1956-	3023	3146	2893	2366	2117	2396	2560	2286	1756	2429	2318	2099	1728	1290	981	623	460	5
1961-	2690	3037	3189	2909	2375	2133	2375	2528	2251	1747	2394	2234	1977	1565	1090	712	539	5
1966-	2687	2673	3023	3175	2892	2360	2118	2355	2500	2213	1705	2310	2111	1797	1325	813	643	5
1971-	2876	2669	2641	2991	3128	2847	2313	2066	2306	2435	2200	1599	2181	1926	1530	997	738	5

- NO MORTALITY STATISTICS ARE PRESENTED FOR THIS QUINQUENNIA

TABLE 180 POPULATION ESTIMATES (THOUSANDS) FOR DENMARK BY AGE,SEX AND QUINQUENNIA

AGE	0-	5-	10-	15-	20-	25-	30-	35-	40-	45-	50-	55-	60-	65-	70-	75-	80+	NO. YRS DATA
MALE																		
1901-	281	249	230	210	205	188	166	143	140	111	97	71	61	42	31	18	11	5
1906-	303	268	248	226	221	202	178	154	151	120	105	76	65	46	33	19	12	5
1911-	298	285	266	229	232	223	207	181	158	126	122	95	78	54	39	23	15	5
1916-	325	310	289	249	253	242	225	196	171	137	133	103	84	59	43	25	17	5
1921-	847	845	846	789	705	617	566	524	477	417	359	300	267	205	152	98	67	5
1926-	802	845	834	811	758	675	622	560	507	461	412	342	287	219	172	107	73	5
1931-	793	815	813	825	786	730	684	613	555	503	452	383	319	243	186	115	79	5
1936-	805	768	786	832	796	783	755	681	618	543	482	423	361	276	196	122	87	5
1941-	881	820	783	805	782	799	782	730	678	594	526	461	396	310	220	137	98	5
1946-	1013	949	795	758	752	789	777	766	736	654	581	499	423	345	258	160	113	5
1951-	994	1086	884	766	723	744	783	761	777	713	632	550	455	377	283	185	129	5
1956-	953	978	1080	876	737	696	731	771	746	760	690	601	509	403	311	207	159	5
1961-	967	947	977	1075	861	729	696	730	766	735	739	658	554	448	329	225	180	5
1966-	1035	963	947	978	1068	858	730	696	726	755	714	703	604	484	362	237	199	5
1971-	942	1034	963	957	1001	1071	849	729	696	722	735	682	647	525	389	259	222	5
FEMALE																		
1901-	281	248	234	234	247	223	201	170	168	133	118	96	82	65	46	32	23	5
1906-	303	267	253	253	266	240	217	184	181	144	128	103	88	70	49	35	25	5
1911-	297	283	275	266	284	272	247	209	187	159	152	124	106	81	61	38	30	5
1916-	323	308	299	290	309	295	269	228	204	173	165	135	116	88	67	41	32	5
1921-	828	833	833	789	755	671	618	565	510	440	393	333	305	240	182	114	92	5
1926-	786	827	817	811	794	727	679	604	549	492	440	366	319	254	202	125	98	5
1931-	775	795	793	820	809	768	732	653	599	538	480	405	346	274	216	135	104	5
1936-	782	748	766	820	806	798	780	711	659	578	515	451	384	299	226	142	112	5
1941-	850	794	761	789	785	807	796	751	711	628	564	494	421	334	248	157	123	5
1946-	969	913	771	739	753	802	788	779	756	686	624	537	459	377	281	180	139	5
1951-	945	1037	852	743	717	760	802	773	788	737	671	596	498	418	314	204	157	5
1956-	902	934	1031	842	727	707	751	791	761	775	719	648	565	456	357	238	189	5
1961-	924	900	933	1022	831	723	704	747	785	751	759	697	618	521	395	274	226	5
1966-	983	922	901	932	1013	825	721	702	742	775	736	736	665	571	454	310	273	5
1971-	895	984	920	903	947	1005	813	717	700	738	758	714	703	616	502	363	336	5

1901-20 DATA FOR TOWNS ONLY

- NO MORTALITY STATISTICS ARE PRESENTED FOR THIS QUINQUENNIA

TABLE 180 POPULATION ESTIMATES (THOUSANDS) FOR EIRE BY AGE,SEX AND QUINQUENNIA

AGE	0-	5-	10-	15-	20-	25-	30-	35-	40-	45-	50-	55-	60-	65-	70-	75-	80+	NO. YRS DATA
MALE																		
1901-	-	-	-	-	-	-	-	-	-	-	-	-	-	-	-	-	-	
1906-	-	-	-	-	-	-	-	-	-	-	-	-	-	-	-	-	-	
1911-	-	-	-	-	-	-	-	-	-	-	-	-	-	-	-	-	-	
1916-	-	-	-	-	-	-	-	-	-	-	-	-	-	-	-	-	-	
1921-	573	568	594	574	503	429	369	354	340	341	335	273	225	211	152	133	25	4
1926-	716	711	742	717	628	536	461	443	425	426	418	341	281	264	189	166	31	5
1931-	694	692	726	700	656	554	466	468	421	411	402	362	318	286	198	172	27	5
1936-	686	681	701	685	645	566	485	472	428	397	387	360	335	303	218	179	26	5
1941-	717	678	671	662	598	548	512	468	434	407	366	338	316	301	243	194	27	5
1946-	776	696	669	638	568	514	507	500	443	428	378	335	304	285	249	219	28	5
1951-	786	737	682	621	501	468	464	487	472	427	402	350	301	274	239	160	106	5
1956-	761	749	718	603	435	396	409	430	451	444	391	367	302	268	224	156	116	5
1961-	784	747	737	628	431	367	374	399	417	435	414	358	317	264	217	147	121	5
1966-	805	778	738	671	502	399	374	379	395	409	412	383	320	273	215	141	119	5
1971-	835	818	786	712	578	472	409	384	380	391	395	387	346	282	223	144	118	5
FEMALE																		
1901-	-	-	-	-	-	-	-	-	-	-	-	-	-	-	-	-	-	
1906-	-	-	-	-	-	-	-	-	-	-	-	-	-	-	-	-	-	
1911-	-	-	-	-	-	-	-	-	-	-	-	-	-	-	-	-	-	
1916-	-	-	-	-	-	-	-	-	-	-	-	-	-	-	-	-	-	
1921-	553	549	569	548	462	427	359	356	326	320	303	240	213	200	178	161	32	4
1926-	692	686	711	684	577	534	448	445	408	400	379	300	266	250	222	201	39	5
1931-	671	672	701	663	591	523	447	465	400	387	373	326	294	259	224	204	35	5
1936-	657	656	672	651	585	530	457	465	407	374	361	332	308	268	229	206	34	5
1941-	691	658	651	650	575	548	494	463	424	397	350	330	306	280	245	218	37	5
1946-	742	671	647	605	536	513	496	483	419	418	365	331	301	277	253	235	39	5
1951-	753	703	659	570	466	469	464	482	441	404	384	343	301	268	249	166	125	5
1956-	734	713	688	560	417	403	421	448	442	421	364	359	310	265	240	168	141	5
1961-	752	716	702	593	414	368	379	412	422	423	388	345	325	275	242	169	158	5
1966-	769	747	710	638	481	392	366	380	399	409	399	365	317	291	252	170	163	5
1971-	794	782	756	683	553	456	397	374	377	395	396	382	342	295	266	185	169	5

- NO MORTALITY STATISTICS ARE PRESENTED FOR THIS QUINQUENNIA

TABLE 180 POPULATION ESTIMATES (THOUSANDS) FOR FINLAND BY AGE, SEX AND QUINQUENNIA

AGE	0-	5-	10-	15-	20-	25-	30-	35-	40-	45-	50-	55-	60-	65-	70-	75-	80+	NO. YRS DATA
MALE																		
1901-	925	787	745	680	624	564	451	439	366	347	294	259	195	146	99	57	29	5
1906-	985	853	787	705	667	607	527	482	376	367	309	274	213	166	107	59	36	5
1911-	961	891	844	749	696	628	575	517	412	394	317	287	226	180	115	64	42	5
1916-	884	908	912	810	713	633	600	548	470	426	319	300	236	187	122	72	44	5
1921-	864	912	904	853	769	674	628	568	514	459	351	321	243	196	130	79	50	5
1926-	879	907	847	883	857	745	658	580	546	491	409	348	248	206	137	87	60	5
1931-	878	874	837	891	854	780	704	609	562	494	428	356	259	210	136	87	64	5
1936-	865	824	857	883	790	787	765	652	564	477	415	348	274	210	128	82	61	5
1941-	972	850	856	852	783	775	735	672	599	500	427	353	285	212	131	82	57	5
1946-	1188	931	841	807	813	750	651	674	659	553	457	365	292	214	141	84	52	5
1951-	1199	1139	878	804	799	769	663	624	682	617	510	396	305	230	152	89	53	5
1956-	1090	1189	1131	867	782	775	752	649	608	658	585	469	347	250	170	96	62	5
1961-	1015	1077	1180	1117	840	749	750	733	631	585	623	537	412	285	186	109	68	5
1966-	950	997	1067	1156	1059	796	720	733	713	606	553	571	472	338	211	118	75	5
1971-	801	937	991	1050	1113	1030	781	712	715	687	574	509	504	389	253	154	69	5
FEMALE																		
1901-	892	763	725	660	606	550	436	434	372	357	315	285	223	174	129	77	43	5
1906-	949	822	765	685	648	590	507	471	377	374	328	297	246	199	139	82	53	5
1911-	951	865	814	723	688	622	567	509	403	398	336	312	264	219	149	89	62	5
1916-	870	878	876	782	720	640	600	546	467	433	339	329	274	229	159	99	67	5
1921-	831	883	890	828	765	674	634	578	524	468	362	352	282	241	171	110	74	5
1926-	846	878	829	848	832	735	672	598	562	503	424	384	287	256	186	122	87	5
1931-	850	855	804	859	853	782	717	628	593	526	468	408	303	270	193	130	96	5
1936-	838	807	826	857	800	800	774	675	613	529	476	416	338	282	188	130	99	5
1941-	899	806	834	837	778	809	791	716	650	553	497	429	370	298	196	135	101	5
1946-	1095	876	819	795	798	807	746	743	717	615	542	451	394	318	225	147	104	5
1951-	1150	1091	847	780	780	791	758	722	765	702	604	502	417	351	255	164	112	5
1956-	1045	1142	1086	839	753	755	775	746	710	751	684	580	472	374	289	181	130	5
1961-	977	1035	1134	1075	810	716	729	760	733	696	731	658	546	425	310	208	147	5
1966-	912	960	1026	1103	1008	763	698	721	748	718	678	705	622	496	358	225	168	5
1971-	766	900	953	1006	1053	976	753	695	712	736	702	657	671	572	426	309	162	5

- NO MORTALITY STATISTICS ARE PRESENTED FOR THIS QUINQUENNIA

TABLE 180 POPULATION ESTIMATES (THOUSANDS) FOR FRANCE BY AGE,SEX AND QUINQUENNIA

AGE	0-	5-	10-	15-	20-	25-	30-	35-	40-	45-	50-	55-	60-	65-	70-	75-	80+	NO. YRS DATA
MALE																		
1901-	3192	3003	3014	3054	4183	3954	3662	3525	2622	2382	2225	2016	1216	956	732	428	273	5
1906-	8591	8322	8173	7956	7750	7627	7271	6809	6332	5862	5167	4550	3937	3173	2249	1292	781	5
1911-	7844	8185	8357	8102	7546	7306	7171	6877	6399	6049	5375	4681	3929	3211	2271	1305	792	5
1916-	6459	7773	8490	8453	7233	6579	6601	6566	6524	6251	5567	4942	4133	3239	2311	1330	797	5
1921-	1631	1219	1589	1731	1608	1542	1269	1277	1265	1269	1139	1028	879	682	476	274	170	1
1926-	8855	6937	7006	8303	8427	8479	7030	6349	6207	6167	5767	5245	4448	3513	2445	1407	864	5
1931-	8471	8762	6998	6923	8119	8738	8300	6864	6044	5837	5700	5350	4550	3620	2578	1494	888	5
1936-	7803	8149	8623	6161	7569	7636	8219	7782	6257	5922	5363	5167	4574	3647	2672	1561	924	2
1941-	7282	7360	8100	7347	7940	6036	7383	7787	7202	6466	5162	4870	4353	3677	2727	1576	946	5
1946-	7684	7432	7536	7949	8154	5860	7105	6979	7743	6980	5506	5154	4212	3672	2756	1669	1023	5
1951-	10195	8800	6841	7429	8105	8127	7171	5462	7435	7509	6960	5250	4185	3598	2783	1931	1220	5
1956-	10092	10320	8927	6971	7609	8240	8206	7208	5441	7278	7184	6483	4732	3580	2818	1888	1426	5
1961-	10525	10379	10616	9197	7311	7955	8483	8371	7269	5420	7090	6787	5890	4102	2869	1966	1557	5
1966-	10772	10246	10508	10776	9539	7560	8048	8542	8368	7175	5271	6620	6143	5054	3323	2039	1719	5
1971-	10761	9752	10753	10586	11151	10206	7797	8092	8463	8162	7107	4776	6008	5323	4113	2432	1917	5
FEMALE																		
1901-	*	*	*	*	*	*	*	*	*	*	*	*	*	*	*	*	*	5
1906-	8502	8268	8081	8004	7940	7783	7308	6928	6423	6034	5505	4862	4368	3643	2701	1626	1157	5
1911-	7722	8120	8254	8102	7922	7768	7512	7123	6647	6236	5658	5018	4528	3709	2811	1705	1228	5
1916-	6327	7730	8404	8413	8104	7776	7555	7360	7000	6507	5897	5335	4715	3809	2955	1810	1288	5
1921-	1602	1195	1569	1707	1695	1636	1538	1511	1451	1384	1251	1127	993	819	620	385	282	1
1926-	8686	6772	6862	8137	8458	8369	7922	7607	7279	6996	6433	5769	5062	4233	3186	1991	1473	5
1931-	8309	8593	6814	6753	7940	8382	8262	7813	7314	7008	6624	6040	5252	4400	3374	2147	1591	5
1936-	7674	8053	8467	6046	7533	7554	8042	7993	7431	7071	6654	6210	5471	4561	3565	2308	1708	2
1941-	7087	7261	7967	7251	7953	6096	7437	7900	7675	7278	6714	6235	5653	4822	3747	2417	1808	5
1946-	7423	7282	7390	7852	8111	5905	7226	7028	7748	7453	6895	6370	5822	5072	3966	2626	1990	5
1951-	9817	8482	6654	7276	7819	7919	7134	5505	7499	7607	7309	6715	5978	5312	4292	3063	2371	5
1956-	9716	9959	8593	6703	7296	7906	8026	7186	5527	7457	7453	7083	6369	5467	4562	3297	2867	5
1961-	10124	10001	10232	8809	6872	7493	8145	8237	7309	5607	7444	7328	6852	5959	4829	3623	3394	5
1966-	10327	9864	10138	10365	9042	7067	7632	8227	8283	7337	5580	7223	7064	6469	5349	3965	4075	5
1971-	10266	9353	10363	10237	10562	9423	7141	7634	8214	8210	7464	5245	6955	6653	5865	4456	4841	5

* PERSONS FIGURES INSERTED IN MALE TABLE
1901-05 DATA FOR TOWNS ONLY
\- NO MORTALITY STATISTICS ARE PRESENTED FOR THIS QUINQUENNIA

TABLE 180 POPULATION ESTIMATES (THOUSANDS) FOR GREECE BY AGE,SEX AND QUINQUENNIA

AGE	0-	5-	10-	15-	20-	25-	30-	35-	40-	45-	50-	55-	60-	65-	70-	75-	80+	NO. YRS DATA
MALE																		
1901-	-	-	-	-	-	-	-	-	-	-	-	-	-	-	-	-	-	
1906-	-	-	-	-	-	-	-	-	-	-	-	-	-	-	-	-	-	
1911-	-	-	-	-	-	-	-	-	-	-	-	-	-	-	-	-	-	
1916-	-	-	-	-	-	-	-	-	-	-	-	-	-	-	-	-	-	
1921-	1225	1284	1270	1177	890	778	616	645	583	587	500	388	326	244	175	98	95	4
1926-	1889	1624	1593	1681	1277	1233	918	877	767	791	687	538	458	351	245	147	132	5
1931-	1946	1800	1784	1717	1329	1356	1094	1008	856	800	708	591	511	385	272	160	167	5
1936-	1166	1186	1188	1031	811	860	753	679	564	480	431	381	333	246	178	101	122	3
1941-	-	-	-	-	-	-	-	-	-	-	-	-	-	-	-	-	-	
1946-	-	-	-	-	-	-	-	-	-	-	-	-	-	-	-	-	-	
1951-	-	-	-	-	-	-	-	-	-	-	-	-	-	-	-	-	-	
1956-	1931	1977	2083	1790	1484	1483	1329	1231	1064	870	758	666	575	435	321	184	214	5
1961-	1916	1757	1991	1914	1694	1463	1232	1223	1160	999	816	658	550	442	331	199	182	5
1966-	1872	1826	1755	1950	1853	1591	1266	1192	1210	1115	924	711	570	461	363	230	184	5
1971-	1908	1819	1806	1728	1878	1751	1498	1220	1160	1176	1078	880	660	511	387	277	218	5
FEMALE																		
1901-	-	-	-	-	-	-	-	-	-	-	-	-	-	-	-	-	-	
1906-	-	-	-	-	-	-	-	-	-	-	-	-	-	-	-	-	-	
1911-	-	-	-	-	-	-	-	-	-	-	-	-	-	-	-	-	-	
1916-	-	-	-	-	-	-	-	-	-	-	-	-	-	-	-	-	-	
1921-	1143	1202	1160	1227	981	880	713	732	628	542	481	352	354	239	197	97	116	4
1926-	1805	1543	1460	1721	1408	1302	993	1003	868	756	676	504	494	351	275	144	165	5
1931-	1864	1703	1672	1730	1421	1403	1133	1097	956	788	739	574	549	387	313	169	186	5
1936-	1115	1115	1135	1026	844	881	756	706	618	484	474	381	358	248	208	115	123	3
1941-	-	-	-	-	-	-	-	-	-	-	-	-	-	-	-	-	-	
1946-	-	-	-	-	-	-	-	-	-	-	-	-	-	-	-	-	-	
1951-	-	-	-	-	-	-	-	-	-	-	-	-	-	-	-	-	-	
1956-	1840	1853	2013	1778	1526	1537	1352	1265	1141	898	859	711	648	467	387	221	194	5
1961-	1815	1650	1914	1924	1769	1564	1329	1308	1232	1042	909	756	671	525	407	242	158	5
1966-	1748	1728	1669	1945	1924	1711	1402	1308	1303	1168	1004	820	713	582	454	283	252	5
1971-	1767	1701	1710	1652	1898	1873	1672	1375	1285	1278	1141	972	781	662	512	369	283	5

- NO MORTALITY STATISTICS ARE PRESENTED FOR THIS QUINQUENNIA

TABLE 180 POPULATION ESTIMATES (THOUSANDS) FOR HUNGARY BY AGE, SEX AND QUINQUENNIA

AGE	0-	5-	10-	15-	20-	25-	30-	35-	40-	45-	50-	55-	60-	65-	70-	75-	80+	NO. YRS DATA
MALE																		
1901-	-	-	-	-	-	-	-	-	-	-	-	-	-	-	-	-	-	
1906-	-	-	-	-	-	-	-	-	-	-	-	-	-	-	-	-	-	
1911-	-	-	-	-	-	-	-	-	-	-	-	-	-	-	-	-	-	
1916-	663	864	934	839	694	562	493	484	432	385	363	311	267	201	120	65	36	2
1921-	1828	2196	2042	2086	1844	1546	1371	1250	1111	1014	931	796	688	522	331	183	98	5
1926-	2101	2249	1683	2071	2010	1769	1596	1310	1156	1092	966	824	718	553	379	215	113	5
1931-	2152	2192	1698	2112	1875	1884	1783	1453	1285	1159	1004	874	749	580	416	241	132	5
1936-	1643	1663	1548	1746	1281	1530	1539	1317	1173	970	832	748	622	482	352	205	122	4
1941-	788	793	869	899	556	775	823	736	660	505	430	397	321	249	185	109	69	2
1946-	2033	1881	1843	1950	1941	1835	1094	1785	1686	1527	1205	909	816	648	442	259	156	5
1951-	1816	1592	1520	1479	1531	1523	1279	1067	1380	1257	1147	895	674	559	397	234	149	4
1956-	2288	2240	1967	1828	1699	1816	1845	1591	1264	1675	1509	1347	1019	723	544	334	214	5
1961-	1766	2266	2229	1946	1792	1664	1787	1814	1571	1224	1614	1419	1220	872	565	366	247	5
1966-	1727	1758	2263	2227	1934	1778	1651	1768	1787	1539	1183	1527	1289	1043	679	382	276	5
1971-	1929	1724	1759	2276	2220	1918	1759	1640	1743	1742	1484	1115	1384	1091	801	449	289	5
FEMALE																		
1901-	-	-	-	-	-	-	-	-	-	-	-	-	-	-	-	-	-	
1906-	-	-	-	-	-	-	-	-	-	-	-	-	-	-	-	-	-	
1911-	-	-	-	-	-	-	-	-	-	-	-	-	-	-	-	-	-	
1916-	645	865	931	853	808	679	590	549	477	395	367	304	279	205	134	69	45	2
1921-	1787	2182	2020	2123	2052	1757	1583	1431	1250	1074	971	798	719	534	366	196	126	5
1926-	2067	2209	1647	2110	2097	1848	1749	1519	1338	1208	1051	856	752	566	414	237	146	5
1931-	2116	2143	1660	2133	1924	1909	1873	1619	1466	1317	1135	946	807	610	455	268	171	5
1936-	1608	1626	1520	1741	1333	1557	1563	1375	1289	1119	972	843	699	525	388	231	158	4
1941-	768	775	857	886	587	792	812	725	701	590	516	464	375	280	206	123	89	2
1946-	1954	1829	1810	1941	2025	2054	1251	1964	1820	1609	1462	1138	1045	805	550	313	213	5
1951-	1741	1535	1483	1463	1541	1605	1425	1203	1516	1359	1250	1097	868	731	520	310	203	4
1956-	2177	2151	1909	1830	1777	1879	1959	1777	1425	1853	1651	1498	1279	971	749	463	305	5
1961-	1673	2160	2145	1898	1816	1760	1859	1934	1763	1388	1805	1589	1408	1155	809	543	378	5
1966-	1629	1666	2157	2142	1891	1806	1751	1847	1915	1737	1356	1745	1505	1282	977	601	465	5
1971-	1820	1624	1666	2155	2138	1874	1789	1738	1826	1883	1694	1304	1651	1369	1090	732	544	5

- NO MORTALITY STATISTICS ARE PRESENTED FOR THIS QUINQUENNIA

TABLE 180 POPULATION ESTIMATES (THOUSANDS) FOR ICELAND BY AGE, SEX AND QUINQUENNIA

AGE	0-	5-	10-	15-	20-	25-	30-	35-	40-	45-	50-	55-	60-	65-	70-	75-	80+	NO. YRS DATA
MALE																		
1901-	-	-	-	-	-	-	-	-	-	-	-	-	-	-	-	-	-	
1906-	-	-	-	-	-	-	-	-	-	-	-	-	-	-	-	-	-	
1911-	27	24	23	22	19	18	12	10	10	9	8	10	6	5	3	2	1	5
1916-	28	26	25	23	20	19	14	12	11	10	9	9	7	6	3	2	2	5
1921-	30	27	26	24	21	20	16	14	12	11	10	9	7	6	4	2	2	5
1926-	32	29	27	25	23	21	18	17	13	11	10	9	8	7	4	3	2	5
1931-	31	31	29	27	24	22	20	19	15	13	11	9	8	7	5	3	2	5
1936-	30	31	31	29	26	23	22	20	17	16	12	10	9	7	5	4	3	5
1941-	34	33	31	30	28	25	23	21	19	18	14	12	10	7	6	4	3	5
1946-	43	36	30	31	30	28	25	23	21	19	16	14	11	8	6	5	4	5
1951-	50	43	32	30	31	29	27	24	22	20	18	16	13	10	7	5	4	5
1956-	57	50	43	33	29	31	29	27	24	21	20	17	15	12	8	5	5	5
1961-	60	56	50	42	32	29	31	29	27	23	21	19	16	14	10	6	5	5
1966-	58	59	56	50	42	32	29	30	28	26	22	20	17	14	12	8	6	5
1971-	54	57	59	55	49	41	30	28	30	28	25	21	18	16	12	9	7	5
FEMALE																		
1901-	-	-	-	-	-	-	-	-	-	-	-	-	-	-	-	-	-	
1906-	-	-	-	-	-	-	-	-	-	-	-	-	-	-	-	-	-	
1911-	25	24	22	20	20	19	13	10	12	11	11	11	8	7	4	3	3	5
1916-	26	25	23	21	20	19	15	12	13	12	11	11	9	8	5	3	3	5
1921-	28	27	24	23	21	20	16	15	13	12	11	11	9	8	6	4	3	5
1926-	30	28	26	25	22	20	19	17	14	12	12	11	10	9	6	5	4	5
1931-	30	29	28	26	23	21	20	19	15	14	12	11	10	9	7	5	4	5
1936-	29	30	30	28	25	23	21	19	17	16	13	11	10	9	7	6	5	5
1941-	33	31	30	29	27	25	22	20	19	18	15	13	11	9	8	6	6	5
1946-	41	35	29	30	29	26	24	22	20	19	17	15	12	10	8	6	7	5
1951-	47	40	31	29	31	28	26	23	22	20	18	17	14	11	8	7	7	5
1956-	53	47	40	32	29	30	28	26	23	21	19	17	16	13	9	6	8	5
1961-	57	53	47	40	31	28	29	27	25	23	21	19	16	15	12	8	8	5
1966-	55	56	53	47	39	31	28	29	27	25	22	20	18	15	13	10	9	5
1971-	51	54	56	52	45	38	30	27	28	27	24	22	19	17	14	11	11	5

- NO MORTALITY STATISTICS ARE PRESENTED FOR THIS QUINQUENNIA

TABLE 180 POPULATION ESTIMATES (THOUSANDS) FOR ITALY BY AGE,SEX AND QUINQUENNIA

AGE	0-	5-	10-	15-	20-	25-	30-	35-	40-	45-	50-	55-	60-	65-	70-	75-	80+	NO. YRS DATA
MALE																		
1901-	10785	9157	8714	7539	6611	5414	5003	4739	4460	4085	3844	3346	2862	2130	1521	872	494	5
1906-	10910	9404	9082	7701	6830	5564	5073	4686	4435	4175	3956	3411	3021	2286	1612	902	543	5
1911-	10575	9702	9566	8098	7186	5822	5288	4808	4552	4327	4060	3532	3181	2425	1718	954	588	5
1916-	9606	10078	10234	8888	7767	6259	5741	5210	4897	4578	4150	3743	3338	2527	1845	1043	623	5
1921-	9536	10519	10093	9544	8402	6777	6168	5510	5162	4779	4266	3908	3442	2665	1968	1134	668	5
1926-	10806	11056	8797	9925	9104	7416	6526	5625	5282	4891	4423	3993	3460	2861	2080	1223	727	5
1931-	11418	11253	9244	9171	9687	8344	7112	6052	5438	5037	4607	4110	3541	2967	2215	1331	810	5
1936-	11091	10891	11103	8094	9949	9247	7573	6828	5876	5377	4883	4279	3717	3003	2349	1442	907	5
1941-	11092	10501	10948	8843	10087	9456	7311	7387	6721	5967	5257	4454	3891	3166	2435	1526	977	5
1946-	11094	10125	10796	9661	10226	9670	7058	7991	7686	6621	5660	4637	4072	3338	2525	1615	1052	5
1951-	10678	10427	10296	10238	10126	9769	8176	7155	8478	7373	6188	4963	4223	3513	2642	1724	1137	5
1956-	10531	10497	10284	10102	9933	9798	9557	8021	7073	8280	7097	5837	4537	3676	2836	1857	1341	5
1961-	11214	10290	10389	10092	9927	9666	9511	9307	7833	6857	7940	6652	5264	3895	2945	2012	1558	5
1966-	11831	10955	10147	10245	9941	9773	9485	9286	9044	7566	6534	7416	5980	4459	3051	2060	1725	5
1971-	11216	11788	10998	10129	10204	9775	9542	9291	9132	8838	7236	6233	6794	5242	3649	2148	1852	5
FEMALE																		
1901-	10359	8838	8500	7772	6853	5836	5359	4950	4651	4188	4025	3399	2998	2164	1553	856	522	5
1906-	10497	9063	8834	8138	7314	6271	5588	5037	4703	4322	4128	3471	3159	2306	1664	899	582	5
1911-	10173	9345	9279	8547	7780	6727	5944	5274	4861	4487	4212	3590	3319	2441	1786	958	643	5
1916-	9215	9716	9900	9017	8232	7201	6508	5759	5189	4699	4267	3784	3471	2561	1920	1045	702	5
1921-	9145	10153	9751	9458	8718	7645	7011	6219	5578	4986	4415	3978	3595	2736	2068	1157	774	5
1926-	10402	10690	8509	9836	9242	8018	7374	6607	6059	5395	4712	4164	3669	3004	2235	1310	866	5
1931-	11016	10910	8980	9047	9652	8624	7727	7047	6462	5824	5094	4396	3794	3187	2411	1486	993	5
1936-	10682	10561	10828	7928	9830	9322	7847	7528	6845	6245	5547	4734	4069	3326	2583	1652	1142	5
1941-	10637	10126	10650	8677	9969	9622	7666	7989	7464	6662	5943	5151	4475	3645	2745	1775	1252	5
1946-	10592	9708	10474	9495	10110	9931	7489	8478	8139	7106	6367	5605	4922	3995	2917	1907	1373	5
1951-	10190	9968	9939	10039	10049	9985	8752	7609	8803	7711	6764	6073	5279	4394	3184	2074	1504	5
1956-	10094	10054	9879	9828	9810	9812	9787	8577	7497	8610	7487	6521	5720	4783	3698	2370	1824	5
1961-	10685	9846	9962	9773	9710	9626	9623	9614	8421	7341	8395	7228	6178	5227	4112	2795	2264	5
1966-	11376	10499	9737	9801	9574	9656	9538	9480	9442	8239	7118	8069	6821	5636	4496	3186	2800	5
1971-	10672	11307	10490	9741	9800	9537	9540	9429	9383	9310	8018	6978	7717	6411	5056	3542	3307	5

- NO MORTALITY STATISTICS ARE PRESENTED FOR THIS QUINQUENNIA

TABLE 180 POPULATION ESTIMATES (THOUSANDS) FOR JAPAN BY AGE,SEX AND QUINQUENNIA

AGE	0-	5-	10-	15-	20-	25-	30-	35-	40-	45-	50-	55-	60-	65-	70-	75-	80+	NO. YRS DATA
MALE																		
1901-	14596	12830	11830	11115	10309	8840	8558	6721	7001	5914	5590	4559	3350	2601	1605	925	558	5
1906-	15780	14320	12744	11354	10487	9865	9263	7367	7251	5654	5852	4937	3938	2758	1590	991	687	5
1911-	17080	15652	13725	12481	11160	10183	9473	8215	7836	6051	6044	4788	4208	3018	1841	1060	771	5
1916-	18501	16910	14833	13785	11935	10435	9587	9029	8402	6612	6198	4618	4343	3251	2122	1119	808	5
1921-	20118	17339	16378	14629	12606	11020	9601	8938	8234	7367	6151	4806	3950	3093	2063	1087	589	5
1926-	21191	18295	17775	15583	13302	11794	10113	9273	8432	7787	6323	5131	4020	3094	2029	1068	522	5
1931-	21854	19776	19038	16706	14043	12695	11022	10033	8974	7939	6677	5526	4470	3244	2049	1067	554	5
1936-	4452	4143	3967	3483	2901	2653	2321	2103	1863	1606	1380	1155	952	667	412	213	115	1
1941-	-	-	-	-	-	-	-	-	-	-	-	-	-	-	-	-	-	
1946-	5719	4825	4400	4318	3836	2822	2360	2376	2199	2019	1719	1379	1110	796	540	268	124	1
1951-	26870	25369	23453	21929	20441	17252	12607	11694	11477	10284	9320	7575	5909	4259	2844	1585	761	5
1956-	21028	26612	25324	23211	21263	19994	17128	12476	11450	11157	9828	8718	6796	4911	3196	1812	1033	5
1961-	20236	20888	26448	24936	22227	20560	19921	16974	12295	11151	10705	9225	7888	5726	3765	2084	1237	5
1966-	21513	20065	20706	26048	23868	21840	20792	19891	16744	11948	10728	10055	8381	6706	4451	2483	1488	5
1971-	24953	21752	20372	20839	25465	23889	22175	20945	19697	16496	11725	10202	9329	7350	5400	3114	1932	5
FEMALE																		
1901-	14224	12496	11569	10845	10077	8674	8234	6422	6570	5598	5314	4472	3474	2841	1922	1203	787	5
1906-	15353	13893	12445	11002	10248	9742	8947	7044	6841	5383	5581	4845	4004	2978	1884	1273	858	5
1911-	16650	15243	13382	12043	10865	9916	9121	7919	7433	5774	5794	4728	4278	3268	2157	1348	939	5
1916-	18089	16547	14444	13267	11573	9998	9175	8759	8028	6334	5989	4603	4448	3554	2484	1427	982	5
1921-	19793	17028	15956	14148	12185	10467	9044	8552	8027	7193	6098	4898	4195	3505	2563	1512	771	5
1926-	20860	17976	17349	15180	12922	11273	9531	8820	8213	7600	6311	5313	4375	3601	2625	1562	732	5
1931-	21436	19402	18629	16407	13785	12319	10519	9556	8602	7635	6613	5783	4926	3840	2705	1588	819	5
1936-	4358	4062	3888	3437	2866	2598	2231	2005	1769	1531	1360	1217	1057	798	551	321	175	1
1941-	-	-	-	-	-	-	-	-	-	-	-	-	-	-	-	-	-	
1946-	5487	4697	4300	4250	3890	3363	2842	2672	2284	1986	1669	1370	1194	975	741	418	247	1
1951-	25759	24493	22893	21517	20457	18358	15542	13642	12617	10423	9181	7501	6204	4999	3861	2470	1479	5
1956-	20070	25524	24451	22774	21290	20135	18113	15357	13384	12333	10107	8778	7038	5487	4120	2810	2038	5
1961-	19359	20051	25486	24226	22431	20860	19843	17913	15119	13109	11970	9680	8297	6344	4614	3031	2479	5
1966-	20482	19296	19977	25415	23919	22226	20847	19734	17634	14829	12776	11438	9133	7492	5398	3477	2846	5
1971-	23687	20795	19546	20140	25422	24053	22439	20897	19623	17516	14773	12416	11089	8565	6665	4302	3511	5

- NO MORTALITY STATISTICS ARE PRESENTED FOR THIS QUINQUENNIA

TABLE 180 POPULATION ESTIMATES (THOUSANDS) FOR NETHERLANDS BY AGE,SEX AND QUINQUENNIA

AGE	0-	5-	10-	15-	20-	25-	30-	35-	40-	45-	50-	55-	60-	65-	70-	75-	80+	NO. YRS DATA
MALE																		
1901-	1746	1542	1432	1287	1151	989	899	798	690	632	524	488	397	313	222	134	83	5
1906-	1843	1663	1534	1378	1218	1069	986	862	765	681	563	511	401	343	245	139	93	5
1911-	1906	1759	1645	1501	1319	1164	1061	940	848	746	624	556	429	362	257	152	102	5
1916-	1959	1848	1765	1644	1439	1270	1134	1028	941	823	698	612	468	378	266	168	111	5
1921-	2025	1957	1846	1753	1565	1395	1235	1120	1020	900	783	674	525	417	287	184	122	5
1926-	2103	2083	1899	1836	1699	1539	1362	1219	1091	981	879	745	598	475	317	199	135	5
1931-	2146	2123	1970	1939	1792	1661	1496	1343	1190	1070	960	819	677	534	359	223	149	5
1936-	2163	2103	2055	2060	1854	1766	1639	1492	1316	1169	1031	897	763	594	412	256	164	5
1941-	2497	2123	2077	2095	1931	1812	1711	1585	1431	1258	1110	960	821	645	458	274	174	5
1946-	2966	2214	2140	2101	2003	1826	1739	1644	1525	1347	1205	1027	872	698	505	293	192	5
1951-	2930	2838	2233	2053	2021	1923	1838	1671	1618	1513	1341	1168	972	793	592	387	266	5
1956-	2903	2898	2811	2219	2013	1950	1878	1810	1645	1588	1475	1286	1089	871	663	437	332	5
1961-	3054	2892	2896	2804	2205	1999	1944	1871	1797	1623	1553	1413	1192	966	726	492	395	5
1966-	3073	3048	2897	2900	2810	2250	2031	1961	1866	1774	1581	1480	1301	1044	787	531	458	5
1971-	2862	3093	3073	2918	2927	2866	2287	2048	1947	1835	1725	1505	1361	1132	842	564	503	5
FEMALE																		
1901-	1712	1520	1410	1281	1182	1041	943	827	709	645	547	511	432	346	257	166	110	5
1906-	1803	1630	1510	1368	1244	1116	1035	904	796	699	584	532	436	374	280	174	122	5
1911-	1854	1719	1614	1483	1341	1207	1109	982	885	771	649	579	461	394	290	184	134	5
1916-	1890	1801	1724	1615	1457	1311	1180	1065	980	855	730	639	496	412	297	195	145	5
1921-	1946	1900	1797	1722	1587	1440	1285	1161	1060	934	817	705	551	451	316	209	156	5
1926-	2016	2013	1842	1813	1733	1591	1418	1269	1131	1012	910	775	627	506	343	224	166	5
1931-	2054	2040	1904	1905	1806	1702	1554	1399	1234	1107	992	849	709	565	386	249	180	5
1936-	2069	2008	1979	2001	1823	1782	1696	1551	1368	1218	1065	927	797	628	445	285	198	5
1941-	2378	2027	1993	2025	1903	1830	1764	1649	1494	1323	1155	998	858	682	495	306	209	5
1946-	2814	2120	2046	2028	1999	1853	1786	1714	1598	1426	1267	1081	918	743	548	331	230	5
1951-	2770	2696	2136	1973	1974	1949	1890	1721	1690	1596	1428	1250	1040	849	643	426	317	5
1956-	2758	2747	2676	2128	1942	1922	1918	1867	1702	1669	1569	1392	1196	962	735	493	394	5
1961-	2913	2753	2752	2679	2105	1908	1908	1907	1859	1688	1646	1533	1337	1114	846	578	486	5
1966-	2927	2912	2760	2761	2663	2082	1902	1904	1901	1844	1664	1609	1475	1249	984	676	599	5
1971-	2734	2949	2937	2790	2793	2666	2090	1910	1906	1891	1821	1627	1552	1384	1114	797	728	5

\- NO MORTALITY STATISTICS ARE PRESENTED FOR THIS QUINQUENNIA

TABLE 180 POPULATION ESTIMATES (THOUSANDS) FOR NEW ZEALAND BY AGE,SEX AND QUINQUENNIA

AGE	0-	5-	10-	15-	20-	25-	30-	35-	40-	45-	50-	55-	60-	65-	70-	75-	80+	NO. YRS DATA
MALE																		
1901-	-	-	-	-	-	-	-	-	-	-	-	-	-	-	-	-	-	
1906-	59	53	46	45	49	53	47	38	30	24	20	17	13	11	8	5	3	1
1911-	307	283	247	234	248	264	246	208	170	133	111	88	68	57	44	27	15	5
1916-	321	316	285	258	244	237	241	234	205	165	134	100	78	64	43	28	20	5
1921-	336	338	323	291	260	237	234	250	236	204	161	118	90	70	47	29	24	5
1926-	336	338	344	323	300	272	238	248	240	231	187	148	106	79	55	32	26	5
1931-	313	332	345	332	324	301	264	252	226	232	213	182	132	97	62	37	28	5
1936-	323	330	337	335	313	305	283	263	228	233	224	206	159	119	73	44	31	5
1941-	385	333	313	326	253	271	288	284	255	236	209	207	184	146	91	53	34	5
1946-	380	302	262	251	224	242	245	250	232	206	174	160	153	131	90	52	34	4
1951-	623	534	433	355	357	386	365	346	342	306	261	208	186	169	133	81	54	5
1956-	697	631	546	440	367	386	405	376	354	342	300	249	191	161	133	93	69	5
1961-	780	709	647	551	447	385	402	415	385	352	337	285	228	165	127	93	77	5
1966-	767	789	719	644	532	448	388	403	415	378	341	316	261	198	128	86	79	5
1971-	778	775	805	720	626	550	472	398	408	407	373	321	291	227	157	103	61	5
FEMALE																		
1901-	-	-	-	-	-	-	-	-	-	-	-	-	-	-	-	-	-	
1906-	57	51	45	44	46	46	41	32	26	20	16	12	10	8	6	3	2	1
1911-	297	274	240	228	235	240	220	180	150	114	91	69	56	46	32	18	12	5
1916-	310	305	276	251	243	243	233	214	186	143	114	83	67	52	35	22	17	5
1921-	323	326	312	281	258	251	244	242	221	180	140	104	81	60	40	26	21	5
1926-	321	325	330	310	286	269	253	251	235	214	167	132	99	73	49	29	25	5
1931-	298	319	332	320	313	292	263	254	237	226	198	165	123	92	60	36	28	5
1936-	308	318	323	324	331	311	279	266	243	236	219	193	150	117	74	44	32	5
1941-	370	324	299	318	332	320	309	290	255	241	220	205	179	147	93	57	38	5
1946-	366	291	252	242	261	266	262	252	225	202	183	168	156	135	95	58	38	4
1951-	595	512	417	342	341	364	364	351	333	292	255	223	204	185	147	93	69	5
1956-	668	605	522	422	353	361	378	374	357	332	287	246	214	190	159	113	91	5
1961-	747	679	617	527	426	370	376	389	382	356	329	278	236	203	166	125	113	5
1966-	733	757	687	614	516	438	378	383	393	379	351	318	269	223	177	130	130	5
1971-	744	742	771	687	599	540	459	387	387	387	376	338	310	255	199	168	116	5

- NO MORTALITY STATISTICS ARE PRESENTED FOR THIS QUINQUENNIA

TABLE 180 POPULATION ESTIMATES (THOUSANDS) FOR NORWAY BY AGE,SEX AND QUINQUENNIA

AGE	0-	5-	10-	15-	20-	25-	30-	35-	40-	45-	50-	55-	60-	65-	70-	75-	80+	NO. YRS DATA
MALE																		
1901-	720	683	635	565	450	365	318	292	267	248	222	194	159	145	115	85	64	5
1906-	720	706	670	590	450	365	341	305	269	253	235	209	174	145	108	85	72	5
1911-	729	715	690	622	489	401	367	322	288	265	243	220	186	152	111	85	74	5
1916-	744	715	697	659	559	470	397	342	321	283	248	227	196	165	121	85	71	5
1921-	703	714	708	678	596	515	441	379	348	299	267	239	205	173	131	89	74	5
1926-	632	711	720	683	606	540	496	432	371	314	297	254	212	178	141	97	82	5
1931-	631	678	680	664	621	573	541	479	407	349	331	275	227	190	153	103	89	5
1936-	676	628	611	631	639	614	577	523	455	402	370	302	248	208	166	107	97	5
1941-	725	581	549	598	658	658	616	570	510	464	412	331	270	228	181	112	105	5
1946-	787	618	530	550	627	675	650	615	562	515	460	377	302	245	197	125	112	5
1951-	789	788	595	518	554	621	672	635	606	544	499	436	346	270	205	148	123	5
1956-	790	784	780	594	518	551	617	667	629	598	530	479	407	310	227	155	143	5
1961-	790	786	782	782	591	505	533	601	655	617	582	508	446	366	264	173	153	5
1966-	834	788	786	780	779	583	500	530	595	645	600	555	471	395	301	194	166	5
1971-	822	836	790	786	782	781	585	499	525	584	627	573	515	417	404	174	144	5
FEMALE																		
1901-	694	655	610	555	493	421	373	343	308	291	259	221	184	168	134	100	86	5
1906-	691	680	645	580	498	431	396	348	313	301	274	242	199	173	131	100	96	5
1911-	699	690	665	612	532	460	418	364	332	311	283	257	215	184	137	102	100	5
1916-	714	690	672	649	590	506	441	390	362	321	288	270	233	199	150	104	100	5
1921-	675	689	683	665	617	544	478	423	388	338	306	281	245	211	162	112	104	5
1926-	606	686	695	665	619	576	529	463	411	361	333	291	252	221	175	125	112	5
1931-	604	654	656	645	626	606	565	501	445	397	365	311	269	234	188	135	123	5
1936-	646	606	589	613	635	634	591	539	490	445	401	339	293	251	201	142	136	5
1941-	692	561	529	583	644	662	618	580	538	500	440	370	319	269	216	150	151	5
1946-	747	591	510	532	604	662	645	612	580	545	490	412	350	290	235	162	162	5
1951-	745	745	570	500	530	596	665	631	604	565	531	469	387	318	250	182	169	5
1956-	753	741	737	569	496	526	592	658	625	598	555	517	449	361	282	199	189	5
1961-	750	750	740	742	563	487	517	584	650	618	588	541	496	419	318	224	212	5
1966-	787	749	750	739	731	556	485	515	581	645	609	575	522	466	374	257	244	5
1971-	782	791	752	752	735	729	557	486	511	575	636	596	556	493	541	243	228	5

- NO MORTALITY STATISTICS ARE PRESENTED FOR THIS QUINQUENNIA

TABLE 180 POPULATION ESTIMATES (THOUSANDS) FOR POLAND BY AGE, SEX AND QUINQUENNIA

AGE	0-	5-	10-	15-	20-	25-	30-	35-	40-	45-	50-	55-	60-	65-	70-	75-	80+	NO. YRS DATA
MALE																		
1901-	-	-	-	-	-	-	-	-	-	-	-	-	-	-	-	-	-	
1906-	-	-	-	-	-	-	-	-	-	-	-	-	-	-	-	-	-	
1911-	-	-	-	-	-	-	-	-	-	-	-	-	-	-	-	-	-	
1916-	-	-	-	-	-	-	-	-	-	-	-	-	-	-	-	-	-	
1921-	-	-	-	-	-	-	-	-	-	-	-	-	-	-	-	-	-	
1926-	-	-	-	-	-	-	-	-	-	-	-	-	-	-	-	-	-	
1931-	-	-	-	-	-	-	-	-	-	-	-	-	-	-	-	-	-	
1936-	-	-	-	-	-	-	-	-	-	-	-	-	-	-	-	-	-	
1941-	-	-	-	-	-	-	-	-	-	-	-	-	-	-	-	-	-	
1946-	-	-	-	-	-	-	-	-	-	-	-	-	-	-	-	-	-	
1951-	6756	4743	4352	4751	4738	4366	3210	2644	3390	3096	2482	1782	1284	950	607	367	252	4
1956-	9126	8534	6192	5280	5799	5872	5374	4055	3198	4051	3725	2928	2025	1362	896	508	337	5
1961-	7959	9012	8487	6125	5186	5676	5863	5189	3991	3148	3912	3520	2670	1734	1014	596	383	5
1966-	6737	7798	8955	8381	6037	5158	5605	5815	5105	3890	3039	3699	3196	2273	1346	719	473	5
1971-	6953	6634	7710	8854	8291	6040	4975	5445	5620	4968	3757	2842	3284	2705	1770	907	560	5
FEMALE																		
1901-	-	-	-	-	-	-	-	-	-	-	-	-	-	-	-	-	-	
1906-	-	-	-	-	-	-	-	-	-	-	-	-	-	-	-	-	-	
1911-	-	-	-	-	-	-	-	-	-	-	-	-	-	-	-	-	-	
1916-	-	-	-	-	-	-	-	-	-	-	-	-	-	-	-	-	-	
1921-	-	-	-	-	-	-	-	-	-	-	-	-	-	-	-	-	-	
1926-	-	-	-	-	-	-	-	-	-	-	-	-	-	-	-	-	-	
1931-	-	-	-	-	-	-	-	-	-	-	-	-	-	-	-	-	-	
1936-	-	-	-	-	-	-	-	-	-	-	-	-	-	-	-	-	-	
1941-	-	-	-	-	-	-	-	-	-	-	-	-	-	-	-	-	-	
1946-	-	-	-	-	-	-	-	-	-	-	-	-	-	-	-	-	-	
1951-	6491	4621	4268	4698	4874	4706	3630	3185	3853	3479	2995	2296	1779	1393	929	596	478	4
1956-	8705	8174	6020	5195	5742	5985	5848	4658	3824	4651	4248	3612	2741	2032	1469	846	685	5
1961-	7534	8619	8160	5967	5095	5641	5945	5804	4609	3738	4514	4097	3408	2509	1639	1083	810	5
1966-	6389	7444	8586	8089	5959	5107	5619	5894	5726	4529	3622	4369	3880	3111	2137	1312	1031	5
1971-	6611	6342	7377	8506	8036	5936	4970	5487	5751	5603	4451	3509	4112	3577	2718	1673	1291	5

- NO MORTALITY STATISTICS ARE PRESENTED FOR THIS QUINQUENNIA

TABLE 180 POPULATION ESTIMATES (THOUSANDS) FOR PORTUGAL BY AGE, SEX AND QUINQUENNIA

AGE	0-	5-	10-	15-	20-	25-	30-	35-	40-	45-	50-	55-	60-	65-	70-	75-	80+	NO. YRS DATA
MALE																		
1901-	1332	1289	1210	1033	885	748	664	582	586	482	499	350	372	215	174	90	78	4
1906-	1742	1718	1579	1352	1143	960	864	761	747	613	631	452	475	285	231	117	102	5
1911-	1037	1064	988	853	704	591	530	472	454	382	379	278	284	178	142	72	62	3
1916-	1585	1746	1713	1502	1192	1010	877	803	763	678	623	475	460	303	228	120	101	5
1921-	742	759	667	663	579	476	394	368	336	297	280	225	200	139	100	58	43	2
1931-	1998	1997	1759	1741	1533	1306	1103	1006	892	784	735	598	527	374	264	156	116	5
1936-	2088	2095	1956	1829	1563	1432	1265	1107	947	834	760	621	558	400	279	166	126	5
1941-	2168	2103	2037	1910	1667	1540	1329	1211	1045	911	802	659	587	429	337	180	132	5
1946-	2240	2051	2032	1988	1831	1635	1319	1319	1181	1012	857	709	618	461	445	198	134	5
1951-	2300	2082	1979	2007	1929	1771	1449	1296	1282	1114	931	764	635	503	349	215	133	5
1956-	2324	2223	2048	1907	1856	1773	1622	1341	1255	1223	1047	865	682	548	389	216	153	5
1961-	2418	2185	2123	1960	1655	1599	1520	1429	1284	1145	1156	982	794	583	426	262	186	5
1966-	2299	2212	2057	1957	1745	1394	1354	1331	1277	1164	1050	1050	867	667	443	280	187	5
1971-	2041	2080	2103	1915	1623	1272	1132	1237	1289	1242	1129	991	955	748	519	295	194	5
FEMALE																		
1901-	1289	1248	1169	1089	1023	862	782	676	683	565	607	423	467	266	233	114	113	4
1906-	1691	1664	1522	1422	1348	1144	1035	888	870	724	775	545	600	356	309	147	153	5
1911-	1009	1031	951	894	833	715	644	557	535	450	469	338	362	224	191	92	96	3
1916-	1543	1687	1649	1568	1382	1204	1082	965	923	789	773	582	590	385	316	162	160	5
1921-	726	732	640	678	624	556	469	430	402	354	340	274	252	181	142	82	75	2
1926-	1815	1830	1599	1695	1561	1391	1172	1075	1006	884	849	684	629	453	354	204	188	2
1931-	1939	1921	1690	1765	1601	1474	1267	1165	1058	938	896	736	669	496	379	229	210	5
1936-	1997	2009	1890	1843	1586	1531	1396	1281	1116	996	941	781	719	541	405	254	238	5
1941-	2065	2019	1974	1922	1673	1607	1432	1371	1209	1083	993	837	770	593	439	283	260	5
1946-	2143	1977	1971	2002	1840	1698	1402	1441	1333	1197	1051	903	823	651	482	316	278	5
1951-	2195	2019	1923	1990	1954	1819	1526	1394	1418	1298	1137	973	850	724	527	351	272	5
1956-	2224	2121	1996	1901	1940	1854	1718	1439	1370	1370	1245	1084	903	770	600	349	312	5
1961-	2295	2094	2055	2005	1798	1770	1667	1586	1406	1268	1308	1182	1018	803	632	419	375	5
1966-	2182	2111	1988	1940	1826	1593	1593	1537	1483	1322	1199	1223	1095	911	669	424	408	5
1971-	1962	2031	2051	1938	1792	1504	1354	1447	1468	1419	1282	1144	1157	1009	769	459	425	5

- NO MORTALITY STATISTICS ARE PRESENTED FOR THIS QUINQUENNIA

TABLE 180 POPULATION ESTIMATES (THOUSANDS) FOR ROMANIA BY AGE,SEX AND QUINQUENNIA

AGE	0-	5-	10-	15-	20-	25-	30-	35-	40-	45-	50-	55-	60-	65-	70-	75-	80+	NO. YRS DATA
MALE																		
1901-	-	-	-	-	-	-	-	-	-	-	-	-	-	-	-	-	-	
1906-	-	-	-	-	-	-	-	-	-	-	-	-	-	-	-	-	-	
1911-	-	-	-	-	-	-	-	-	-	-	-	-	-	-	-	-	-	
1916-	-	-	-	-	-	-	-	-	-	-	-	-	-	-	-	-	-	
1921-	-	-	-	-	-	-	-	-	-	-	-	-	-	-	-	-	-	
1926-	-	-	-	-	-	-	-	-	-	-	-	-	-	-	-	-	-	
1931-	-	-	-	-	-	-	-	-	-	-	-	-	-	-	-	-	-	
1936-	1001	838	587	785	711	662	490	416	398	394	285	253	200	166	100	59	32	1
1941-	-	-	-	-	-	-	-	-	-	-	-	-	-	-	-	-	-	
1946-	969	835	634	783	762	729	578	401	464	471	372	315	236	185	123	65	36	1
1951-	-	-	-	-	-	-	-	-	-	-	-	-	-	-	-	-	-	
1956-	1839	1855	1524	1392	1582	1599	1515	1232	723	1092	1008	863	618	442	305	181	102	2
1961-	4052	4618	4495	3534	3596	3925	3939	3559	2602	1995	2644	2295	1854	1234	833	503	299	5
1966-	4338	4013	4701	4392	3431	3526	3948	3872	3522	2488	1969	2486	2113	1572	947	546	363	5
1971-	5270	4249	3987	4686	4369	3401	3482	3904	3807	3451	2411	1846	2271	1822	1239	641	428	5
FEMALE																		
1901-	-	-	-	-	-	-	-	-	-	-	-	-	-	-	-	-	-	
1906-	-	-	-	-	-	-	-	-	-	-	-	-	-	-	-	-	-	
1911-	-	-	-	-	-	-	-	-	-	-	-	-	-	-	-	-	-	
1916-	-	-	-	-	-	-	-	-	-	-	-	-	-	-	-	-	-	
1921-	-	-	-	-	-	-	-	-	-	-	-	-	-	-	-	-	-	
1926-	-	-	-	-	-	-	-	-	-	-	-	-	-	-	-	-	-	
1931-	-	-	-	-	-	-	-	-	-	-	-	-	-	-	-	-	-	
1936-	974	821	563	836	681	685	518	502	436	443	292	300	211	189	104	61	37	1
1941-	-	-	-	-	-	-	-	-	-	-	-	-	-	-	-	-	-	
1946-	935	811	612	816	739	734	620	482	524	508	380	364	280	234	150	85	50	1
1951-	-	-	-	-	-	-	-	-	-	-	-	-	-	-	-	-	-	
1956-	1755	1779	1474	1359	1603	1585	1513	1374	878	1228	1058	907	769	599	448	270	162	2
1961-	3848	4419	4324	3425	3584	3929	3914	3644	3003	2392	2926	2422	2103	1638	1209	760	497	5
1966-	4132	3821	4508	4215	3333	3513	3929	3850	3652	2928	2363	2828	2363	1880	1343	842	627	5
1971-	5031	4055	3799	4501	4204	3313	3483	3902	3806	3601	2872	2268	2678	2151	1586	980	738	5

- NO MORTALITY STATISTICS ARE PRESENTED FOR THIS QUINQUENNIA

TABLE 180 POPULATION ESTIMATES (THOUSANDS) FOR SPAIN BY AGE, SEX AND QUINQUENNIA

AGE	0-	5-	10-	15-	20-	25-	30-	35-	40-	45-	50-	55-	60-	65-	70-	75-	80+	NO. YRS DATA
MALE																		
1901-	3365	3269	3014	2350	2239	2048	1892	1673	1669	1363	1375	1029	1010	607	452	222	194	3
1906-	5872	5747	5174	4170	3837	3454	3230	2829	2816	2394	2319	1765	1752	1106	783	377	288	5
1911-	3527	3523	3237	2692	2400	2131	2002	1729	1743	1482	1419	1105	1165	694	490	236	167	3
1916-	2286	2350	2268	1944	1684	1477	1387	1178	1213	1005	970	776	898	471	340	168	113	2
1921-	5927	6075	5779	5128	4568	4006	3662	3102	3142	2606	2509	2021	2231	1248	893	453	298	5
1926-	6415	6422	5769	5321	5057	4468	3911	3333	3240	2736	2609	2091	2008	1358	940	493	321	5
1931-	6326	6679	6081	5641	5207	4694	4195	3628	3393	2891	2712	2181	1980	1446	983	541	348	5
1936-	5862	6871	6643	6063	5113	4741	4513	3981	3589	3067	2817	2287	2076	1516	1024	596	381	5
1941-	5943	6734	6571	6353	5501	5053	4609	4175	3878	3354	2988	2421	2172	1600	1096	643	416	5
1946-	6398	6387	6083	6546	6284	5578	4550	4250	4249	3741	3213	2581	2271	1697	1194	682	455	5
1951-	6870	6436	6169	6474	6369	5863	4883	4579	4359	3950	3487	2866	2431	1835	1316	748	520	5
1956-	7363	6753	6647	6231	5966	5969	5535	5118	4280	4025	3806	3267	2644	2011	1459	839	612	5
1961-	8026	7430	6871	6302	5543	5220	5461	5424	4899	4088	3902	3617	3084	2379	1611	1010	738	5
1966-	8148	7968	7406	6636	6031	5215	5156	5580	5410	4779	3988	3748	3325	2684	1831	1081	857	5
1971-	8328	8256	7972	7144	6500	5883	5095	5397	5772	5354	4535	3710	3434	2887	2030	1214	928	5
FEMALE																		
1901-	3298	3148	2977	2507	2493	2230	2042	1783	1810	1495	1509	1102	1129	652	496	237	208	3
1906-	5747	5263	5141	4455	4247	3776	3536	3066	3037	2551	2547	1917	1990	1194	871	413	373	5
1911-	3464	3248	3221	2884	2656	2344	2201	1885	1888	1576	1554	1197	1241	763	559	266	239	3
1916-	2260	2265	2252	2091	1869	1636	1520	1282	1329	1086	1056	829	851	531	402	193	168	2
1921-	5834	5938	5970	5445	4979	4385	3971	3372	3422	2826	2734	2189	2170	1422	1074	544	463	5
1926-	6244	6237	6373	5513	5336	4776	4172	3621	3467	2956	2862	2334	2202	1551	1142	625	524	5
1931-	6145	6504	6624	5810	5588	5112	4459	3955	3644	3153	2972	2469	2315	1705	1220	709	597	5
1936-	5718	6749	6767	6285	5764	5411	4819	4366	3923	3405	3070	2597	2491	1884	1308	797	683	5
1941-	5693	6655	6594	6550	6006	5643	5012	4635	4169	3660	3233	2732	2620	2021	1412	881	752	5
1946-	6050	6187	6046	6715	6451	5920	5119	4880	4508	4059	3560	2946	2763	2181	1593	1004	837	5
1951-	6561	6121	5970	6572	6348	6131	5425	5188	4749	4411	3944	3313	3008	2412	1822	1157	978	5
1956-	7067	6470	6377	6184	5752	6196	5848	5457	4794	4574	4249	3735	3284	2643	2019	1285	1138	5
1961-	7649	7065	6392	6287	5818	5482	6022	5746	5446	4665	4454	4123	3569	3001	2236	1458	1347	5
1966-	7764	7628	6991	6439	6160	5642	5612	5976	5760	5229	4577	4344	3903	3317	2530	1612	1552	5
1971-	7893	7881	7623	6981	6429	5888	5240	5569	5948	5566	4943	4379	4151	3632	2824	1860	1691	5

- NO MORTALITY STATISTICS ARE PRESENTED FOR THIS QUINQUENNIA

TABLE 180 POPULATION ESTIMATES (THOUSANDS) FOR SWEDEN BY AGE,SEX AND QUINQUENNIA

AGE	0-	5-	10-	15-	20-	25-	30-	35-	40-	45-	50-	55-	60-	65-	70-	75-	80+	NO. YRS DATA
MALE																		
1901-	-	-	-	-	-	-	-	-	-	-	-	-	-	-	-	-	-	
1906-	-	-	-	-	-	-	-	-	-	-	-	-	-	-	-	-	-	
1911-	1524	1417	1358	1258	1096	908	770	745	669	613	553	499	424	373	282	198	122	5
1916-	1564	1462	1388	1288	1124	966	861	770	659	653	593	514	439	378	284	203	145	5
1921-	1537	1474	1432	1334	1178	1026	929	814	704	685	607	542	465	389	292	207	160	5
1926-	1467	1464	1487	1391	1254	1089	979	875	792	710	602	579	500	404	305	209	167	5
1931-	1349	1421	1473	1417	1319	1154	1040	935	860	756	647	611	517	429	327	217	175	5
1936-	1208	1359	1413	1419	1376	1222	1111	995	913	819	733	639	519	461	357	230	182	5
1941-	1149	1241	1309	1389	1390	1288	1206	1082	986	885	803	686	562	490	370	245	192	5
1946-	1139	1098	1182	1339	1372	1353	1325	1193	1077	956	861	748	637	515	370	263	205	5
1951-	1250	1169	1140	1235	1297	1370	1374	1279	1184	1048	936	815	702	559	405	284	217	5
1956-	1465	1405	1147	1104	1190	1352	1371	1347	1308	1162	1027	885	757	619	471	309	230	5
1961-	1453	1601	1296	1086	1110	1250	1397	1345	1379	1270	1127	969	810	675	506	339	246	5
1966-	1357	1453	1601	1302	1114	1139	1257	1393	1335	1359	1240	1080	902	722	559	369	290	5
1971-	1358	1360	1454	1608	1342	1145	1143	1251	1380	1314	1324	1187	1005	803	595	407	325	5
FEMALE																		
1901-	-	-	-	-	-	-	-	-	-	-	-	-	-	-	-	-	-	
1906-	-	-	-	-	-	-	-	-	-	-	-	-	-	-	-	-	-	
1911-	1466	1370	1322	1211	1079	936	833	822	758	692	636	578	504	450	350	251	176	5
1916-	1501	1413	1342	1246	1129	999	908	824	738	740	681	590	519	457	357	261	207	5
1921-	1473	1423	1378	1292	1182	1061	976	862	772	763	691	621	549	472	366	268	225	5
1926-	1406	1410	1426	1347	1237	1124	1039	928	848	768	676	666	592	492	376	273	232	5
1931-	1295	1368	1413	1370	1294	1188	1098	993	917	807	711	690	604	519	400	281	241	5
1936-	1164	1308	1360	1370	1351	1253	1156	1058	983	873	784	697	594	551	435	291	251	5
1941-	1108	1193	1264	1341	1358	1299	1229	1134	1050	940	854	737	628	570	446	307	261	5
1946-	1095	1052	1145	1294	1331	1332	1314	1219	1121	1011	922	802	696	577	438	327	271	5
1951-	1197	1117	1103	1195	1265	1338	1347	1281	1204	1095	996	874	765	618	469	343	282	5
1956-	1397	1341	1108	1071	1178	1325	1342	1327	1300	1194	1076	952	835	686	533	355	295	5
1961-	1374	1523	1244	1056	1110	1235	1370	1319	1351	1280	1163	1028	896	758	577	390	315	5
1966-	1280	1375	1524	1258	1097	1126	1239	1367	1312	1337	1257	1130	979	824	652	440	366	5
1971-	1286	1284	1379	1540	1290	1105	1126	1236	1358	1298	1314	1223	1080	908	718	506	428	5

- NO MORTALITY STATISTICS ARE PRESENTED FOR THIS QUINQUENNIA

TABLE 180 POPULATION ESTIMATES (THOUSANDS) FOR SWITZERLAND BY AGE,SEX AND QUINQUENNIA

AGE	0-	5-	10-	15-	20-	25-	30-	35-	40-	45-	50-	55-	60-	65-	70-	75-	80+	NO. YRS DATA
MALE																		
1901-	1966	1841	1736	1703	1519	1457	1324	1188	1016	872	749	634	520	412	281	156	86	10
1906-	.	.	.	.	.	.	.	.	.	.	.	.	.	.	.	.	.	
1911-	1820	1892	1924	1860	1604	1474	1372	1290	1181	1051	870	710	563	419	285	166	96	10
1916-	.	.	.	.	.	.	.	.	.	.	.	.	.	.	.	.	.	
1921-	829	905	929	938	850	753	685	653	624	569	489	415	317	224	150	87	52	5
1926-	826	887	850	911	892	821	738	665	614	584	532	450	347	260	167	89	54	5
1931-	811	858	820	889	883	845	790	711	646	605	553	478	382	294	187	101	60	5
1936-	789	821	820	871	840	835	842	783	709	630	557	501	420	328	210	121	69	5
1941-	831	841	811	851	820	838	854	833	775	677	587	527	450	360	239	143	81	5
1946-	986	952	789	829	834	857	804	842	842	763	659	557	464	385	278	165	98	5
1951-	1061	1065	872	807	880	886	854	811	859	828	737	612	493	401	301	189	114	5
1956-	1104	1059	1071	912	938	948	901	858	790	853	805	695	557	424	317	207	141	5
1961-	1234	1115	1127	1197	1115	1035	974	908	859	789	832	758	632	480	339	222	167	5
1966-	1329	1234	1140	1174	1268	1185	1075	992	921	860	772	789	695	549	384	238	186	5
1971-	1185	1303	1243	1168	1197	1318	1203	1071	986	911	837	736	726	608	444	275	209	5
FEMALE																		
1901-	1955	1836	1731	1673	1574	1441	1334	1201	1061	927	839	719	626	498	342	191	106	10
1906-	.	.	.	.	.	.	.	.	.	.	.	.	.	.	.	.	.	
1911-	1788	1881	1914	1873	1734	1570	1456	1334	1237	1111	960	811	684	525	377	221	136	10
1916-	.	.	.	.	.	.	.	.	.	.	.	.	.	.	.	.	.	
1921-	807	891	921	960	935	843	764	708	670	603	537	470	382	283	208	123	79	5
1926-	802	869	837	928	960	901	825	738	677	626	585	505	412	326	230	128	87	5
1931-	786	835	804	896	925	903	870	787	721	661	616	537	452	367	254	145	98	5
1936-	764	794	802	864	855	866	904	853	793	706	634	567	499	405	279	175	111	5
1941-	801	809	790	839	835	862	898	893	858	765	676	605	540	443	314	205	131	5
1946-	943	915	765	826	888	907	834	887	906	846	759	658	565	476	367	233	161	5
1951-	1012	1019	844	823	941	930	880	841	912	896	833	722	604	502	398	268	188	5
1956-	1054	1013	1025	915	979	965	939	903	825	904	881	807	685	552	428	299	235	5
1961-	1186	1073	1093	1170	1096	1020	990	963	901	823	897	859	772	633	480	331	283	5
1966-	1269	1186	1100	1148	1249	1147	1042	1003	971	901	814	877	825	719	555	377	330	5
1971-	1124	1244	1196	1135	1214	1292	1151	1038	1000	965	888	796	844	774	640	448	396	5

. 1901 AND 1906 DATA ARE FOR 10 YEARS

\- NO MORTALITY STATISTICS ARE PRESENTED FOR THIS QUINQUENNIA

TABLE 180 POPULATION ESTIMATES (THOUSANDS) FOR TURKEY BY AGE,SEX AND QUINQUENNIA

AGE	0-	5-	10-	15-	20-	25-	30-	35-	40-	45-	50-	55-	60-	65-	70-	75-	80+	NO. YRS DATA
MALE																		
1901-	-	-	-	-	-	-	-	-	-	-	-	-	-	-	-	-	-	
1906-	-	-	-	-	-	-	-	-	-	-	-	-	-	-	-	-	-	
1911-	-	-	-	-	-	-	-	-	-	-	-	-	-	-	-	-	-	
1916-	-	-	-	-	-	-	-	-	-	-	-	-	-	-	-	-	-	
1921-	-	-	-	-	-	-	-	-	-	-	-	-	-	-	-	-	-	
1926-	-	-	-	-	-	-	-	-	-	-	-	-	-	-	-	-	-	
1931-	1133	1469	.	1009	.	913	.	570	.	341	.	253	.	151	.	70	.	5
1936-	1044	1766	.	992	.	938	.	707	.	383	.	262	.	138	.	66	.	5
1941-	394	803	.	392	.	382	.	328	.	166	.	108	.	52	.	25	.	2
1946-	426	702	.	508	.	336	.	333	.	239	.	111	.	52	.	19	.	1
1951-	2695	4134	.	3471	.	2216	.	1710	.	1398	.	709	.	306	.	108	.	5
1956-	2676	4406	.	3052	.	2547	.	1524	.	1391	.	888	.	339	.	111	.	4
1961-	3994	7221	.	4550	.	3801	.	2606	.	1903	.	1493	.	616	.	198	.	5
1966-	4981	9292	.	6151	.	4209	.	3694	.	2121	.	1850	.	941	.	293	.	5
1971-	4512	8722	.	6273	.	3874	.	3466	.	2187	.	1562	.	961	.	323	.	4
FEMALE																		
1901-	-	-	-	-	-	-	-	-	-	-	-	-	-	-	-	-	-	
1906-	-	-	-	-	-	-	-	-	-	-	-	-	-	-	-	-	-	
1911-	-	-	-	-	-	-	-	-	-	-	-	-	-	-	-	-	-	
1916-	-	-	-	-	-	-	-	-	-	-	-	-	-	-	-	-	-	
1921-	-	-	-	-	-	-	-	-	-	-	-	-	-	-	-	-	-	
1926-	-	-	-	-	-	-	-	-	-	-	-	-	-	-	-	-	-	
1931-	861	1146	.	720	.	878	.	617	.	441	.	307	.	147	.	81	.	5
1936-	899	1484	.	835	.	988	.	744	.	521	.	369	.	169	.	82	.	5
1941-	371	710	.	371	.	429	.	338	.	234	.	167	.	74	.	33	.	2
1946-	350	538	.	485	.	311	.	277	.	213	.	144	.	68	.	25	.	1
1951-	2215	3213	.	2740	.	2005	.	1473	.	1222	.	847	.	402	.	155	.	5
1956-	2359	3703	.	2550	.	2364	.	1409	.	1227	.	919	.	450	.	192	.	4
1961-	3523	6131	.	3869	.	3646	.	2357	.	1690	.	1446	.	752	.	340	.	5
1966-	4332	7783	.	5090	.	4094	.	3245	.	1868	.	1690	.	974	.	452	.	5
1971-	3898	7283	.	5179	.	3574	.	3121	.	1879	.	1422	.	930	.	431	.	4

1931-75 DATA FOR VARING NUMBER OF PROVINCES (SEE TEXT 2.3.26)

. DATA ARE FOR BROADER AGE GROUP FROM ADJACENT YOUNGER AGE

- NO MORTALITY STATISTICS ARE PRESENTED FOR THIS QUINQUENNIA

TABLE 180 POPULATION ESTIMATES (THOUSANDS) FOR UK: ENGLAND AND WALES BY AGE,SEX AND QUINQUENNIA

AGE	0-	5-	10-	15-	20-	25-	30-	35-	40-	45-	50-	55-	60-	65-	70-	75-	80+	NO. YRS DATA
MALE																		
1901-	9365	8821	8449	8096	7398	6788	6037	5431	4694	3995	3337	2618	2132	1509	1026	583	361	5
1906-	9367	8859	8453	8247	8272	7631	6631	5832	5004	4284	3631	2912	2478	1844	1330	794	561	5
1911-	9662	9308	8810	8321	7577	7170	6901	6439	5706	4779	4029	3207	2506	1912	1246	674	407	5
1916-	8627	9171	9169	8404	7380	6812	6609	6456	6125	5394	4506	3644	2789	2100	1303	732	441	5
1921-	8999	8179	9057	8871	7661	6733	6545	6258	6226	5803	5168	4056	3202	2316	1534	815	486	5
1926-	8119	8654	8124	8809	8426	7483	6812	6316	6135	5909	5524	4635	3594	2671	1757	932	554	5
1931-	7413	7879	8616	7960	8497	8386	7785	6563	6198	5903	5607	5033	4116	3046	2004	1088	617	5
1936-	7207	7305	7887	8412	6955	7973	8120	7548	6411	6053	5673	5241	4507	3475	2295	1242	715	5
1941-	7542	7095	7237	6288	2601	3380	5100	6380	6733	6098	5785	5301	4656	3759	2655	1472	882	5
1946-	9154	7440	7060	5908	6086	7714	7474	8297	8134	7204	6104	5386	4691	3903	2933	1763	1096	5
1951-	8823	9052	7379	6724	6931	7735	8163	7550	8232	7997	7006	5637	4772	3913	2973	1907	1243	5
1956-	8721	8707	9008	7247	6930	7280	7703	8071	7471	8089	7685	6551	5063	4001	2987	1953	1424	5
1961-	9990	8666	8785	9099	7532	7463	7550	7815	8158	7436	7772	7208	5933	4222	3045	1948	1498	5
1966-	10570	9888	8616	8779	9085	7735	7516	7523	7734	7985	7154	7301	6450	4925	3182	1992	1541	5
1971-	9492	10276	9835	8790	8838	8942	7478	7165	7177	7454	7594	6671	6638	5493	3763	2116	1670	5
FEMALE																		
1901-	9566	9109	8662	8230	7475	7126	6621	6046	5186	4461	3708	2929	2322	1740	1141	624	387	5
1906-	9502	9127	8678	8370	8342	7975	7249	6492	5573	4805	4029	3236	2657	2104	1512	882	623	5
1911-	9561	9295	8899	8495	8194	7982	7592	6934	6148	5163	4371	3553	2864	2286	1640	981	683	5
1916-	8507	9107	9186	8793	8381	7996	7712	7353	6706	5843	4851	3999	3201	2523	1774	1068	756	5
1921-	8770	8077	8978	8955	8586	8211	7723	7287	7062	6336	5528	4415	3606	2772	2017	1221	863	5
1926-	7935	8468	8033	8851	8840	8444	7957	7450	7095	6757	6026	5086	4030	3203	2280	1385	990	5
1931-	7215	7739	8449	7967	8854	8820	8315	7734	7284	6895	6429	5641	4643	3632	2613	1595	1117	5
1936-	6949	7138	7762	8476	7974	8794	8732	8234	7663	7182	6700	6134	5231	4127	2970	1832	1307	5
1941-	7227	6868	7106	7510	7675	7798	8699	8606	8035	7454	6926	6373	5683	4633	3410	2163	1616	5
1946-	8709	7153	6838	7083	7629	8414	7964	8672	8418	7889	7181	6499	5845	5031	3890	2518	1981	5
1951-	8405	8641	7101	6917	7229	7800	8336	7815	8464	8281	7667	6886	6149	5337	4297	2936	2296	5
1956-	8280	8313	8603	7164	7056	7232	7744	8282	7739	8328	8088	7395	6521	5598	4555	3268	2787	5
1961-	9475	8242	8370	8759	7539	7206	7264	7710	8196	7703	8200	7810	6983	5961	4823	3510	3238	5
1966-	10043	9395	8195	8530	8994	7560	7150	7207	7645	8083	7533	7935	7407	6400	5172	3772	3699	5
1971-	8992	9765	9317	8374	8656	8783	7253	6949	7104	7534	7923	7195	7511	6846	5636	4051	4191	5

\- NO MORTALITY STATISTICS ARE PRESENTED FOR THIS QUINQUENNIA

TABLE 180 POPULATION ESTIMATES (THOUSANDS) FOR UK: NORTHERN IRELAND BY AGE,SEX AND QUINQUENNIA

AGE	0-	5-	10-	15-	20-	25-	30-	35-	40-	45-	50-	55-	60-	65-	70-	75-	80+	NO. YRS DATA
MALE																		
1901-	-	-	-	-	-	-	-	-	-	-	-	-	-	-	-	-	-	
1906-	-	-	-	-	-	-	-	-	-	-	-	-	-	-	-	-	-	
1911-	-	-	-	-	-	-	-	-	-	-	-	-	-	-	-	-	-	
1916-	-	-	-	-	-	-	-	-	-	-	-	-	-	-	-	-	-	
1921-	249	248	227	235	208	178	157	138	133	127	129	110	89	70	56	33	14	4
1926-	311	311	284	294	260	223	196	172	167	159	161	138	111	88	70	41	18	5
1931-	295	293	304	277	278	240	210	187	165	159	149	148	121	90	63	45	24	5
1936-	290	288	300	296	253	248	219	205	182	157	147	138	131	111	78	46	22	5
1941-	319	283	286	302	224	241	218	206	191	158	152	135	132	113	82	47	21	5
1946-	358	315	283	289	273	277	228	208	192	161	150	138	135	118	85	49	21	5
1951-	353	343	297	282	248	227	227	213	219	198	184	153	124	106	87	64	43	5
1956-	361	343	333	304	253	213	205	212	201	210	188	171	136	105	82	58	48	5
1961-	391	350	334	323	249	209	203	210	217	200	203	177	151	119	86	58	49	5
1966-	415	388	347	324	274	221	206	202	208	211	193	188	160	128	92	58	48	5
1971-	386	405	384	343	303	263	228	210	201	202	201	180	168	135	98	60	45	5
FEMALE																		
1901-	-	-	-	-	-	-	-	-	-	-	-	-	-	-	-	-	-	
1906-	-	-	-	-	-	-	-	-	-	-	-	-	-	-	-	-	-	
1911-	-	-	-	-	-	-	-	-	-	-	-	-	-	-	-	-	-	
1916-	-	-	-	-	-	-	-	-	-	-	-	-	-	-	-	-	-	
1921-	240	242	222	236	224	209	187	160	154	140	137	113	92	76	67	45	20	4
1926-	300	302	278	295	280	261	233	200	193	175	171	141	115	95	84	56	25	5
1931-	284	284	295	270	278	261	247	222	191	183	163	157	124	95	70	56	36	5
1936-	278	278	289	293	265	269	244	232	208	179	166	151	138	117	90	56	30	5
1941-	305	272	277	296	280	287	257	232	221	187	179	150	142	123	98	61	28	5
1946-	342	300	271	281	287	285	257	231	219	191	174	152	145	125	100	62	28	5
1951-	334	328	286	268	257	248	241	226	235	215	203	175	152	130	108	79	59	5
1956-	339	325	320	278	249	235	232	229	216	227	206	192	162	135	108	79	68	5
1961-	370	332	316	314	254	219	218	226	228	212	218	196	180	154	117	82	74	5
1966-	389	366	330	311	281	229	213	215	222	221	207	206	187	166	131	88	82	5
1971-	361	379	361	319	271	250	222	209	211	215	213	195	195	173	142	98	88	5

- NO MORTALITY STATISTICS ARE PRESENTED FOR THIS QUINQUENNIA

TABLE 180 POPULATION ESTIMATES (THOUSANDS) FOR UK: SCOTLAND BY AGE,SEX AND QUINQUENNIA

AGE	0-	5-	10-	15-	20-	25-	30-	35-	40-	45-	50-	55-	60-	65-	70-	75-	80+	NO. YRS DATA
MALE																		
1901-	1341	1254	1201	1152	1044	907	773	685	610	515	433	340	283	192	137	76	51	5
1906-	1339	1274	1223	1152	1026	907	820	741	652	549	470	373	295	212	152	82	51	5
1911-	1019	1090	1095	1050	973	903	836	782	697	609	500	420	339	274	190	111	68	3
1916-	1193	1249	1237	1143	986	860	798	770	744	672	556	456	360	257	163	92	57	5
1921-	1170	1189	1201	1170	1019	876	783	744	719	695	605	500	395	294	185	102	61	5
1926-	1105	1163	1119	1123	1025	911	801	729	689	666	623	548	434	322	212	114	65	5
1931-	1048	1099	1144	1047	1060	967	869	736	690	645	631	581	485	358	237	132	69	5
1936-	1022	1019	1088	1122	1010	1017	932	845	712	661	609	581	515	404	265	142	79	5
1941-	1059	1043	1040	1079	1067	940	978	907	837	700	640	572	520	439	316	174	92	5
1946-	1134	1007	989	939	951	950	865	933	891	807	655	574	499	427	335	196	115	5
1951-	1137	1107	975	848	830	900	895	816	894	856	760	596	498	411	321	213	131	5
1956-	1146	1106	1082	880	780	845	860	856	785	859	812	698	524	410	307	208	150	5
1961-	1229	1113	1072	1006	825	797	800	817	820	752	812	748	610	428	304	197	154	5
1966-	1199	1183	1079	990	906	775	755	764	785	783	713	747	660	498	316	195	154	5
1971-	1055	1172	1160	1036	935	871	746	727	739	757	743	659	661	545	368	202	155	5
FEMALE																		
1901-	1322	1230	1167	1131	1107	994	842	746	651	557	479	396	351	257	198	118	92	5
1906-	1317	1261	1197	1136	1090	1009	894	797	695	596	516	421	351	277	223	131	94	5
1911-	1110	1124	1097	1028	947	901	835	764	676	589	484	432	363	312	223	136	95	3
1916-	1171	1232	1232	1186	1098	999	933	873	799	702	593	500	405	315	230	147	112	5
1921-	1148	1173	1183	1177	1119	1018	921	867	808	742	641	538	441	346	254	157	118	5
1926-	1085	1147	1102	1129	1094	1015	931	864	796	749	677	584	477	381	282	170	121	5
1931-	1027	1086	1130	1040	1082	1038	963	879	811	758	712	635	522	419	305	192	126	5
1936-	995	1002	1077	1120	1009	1053	1008	936	853	784	726	667	577	453	335	206	146	5
1941-	1026	1008	1020	1086	1037	943	1030	1005	944	854	773	698	616	514	383	248	174	5
1946-	1089	976	963	976	980	964	913	992	955	900	802	714	634	538	422	265	204	5
1951-	1083	1062	948	926	931	933	942	882	948	913	855	749	651	554	435	297	221	5
1956-	1094	1054	1038	916	875	875	887	908	855	919	879	811	698	580	457	315	256	5
1961-	1169	1063	1021	990	864	825	828	850	877	827	885	838	755	625	483	337	288	5
1966-	1135	1125	1027	964	906	792	780	798	823	847	795	843	788	681	524	362	334	5
1971-	998	1113	1104	1002	927	863	759	757	776	800	817	758	791	716	581	401	378	5

- NO MORTALITY STATISTICS ARE PRESENTED FOR THIS QUINQUENNIA

TABLE 180 POPULATION ESTIMATES (THOUSANDS) FOR USA BY AGE,SEX AND QUINQUENNIA

AGE	0-	5-	10-	15-	20-	25-	30-	35-	40-	45-	50-	55-	60-	65-	70-	75-	80+	NO. YRS DATA
MALE																		
1901-	5444	9846	.	9591	.	9202	.	7499	.	5211	.	3244	.	1808	.	744	.	5
1906-	10406	18474	.	19024	.	18029	.	14535	.	10382	.	6141	.	3379	.	1336	.	5
1911-	15414	27485	.	27069	.	25807	.	20989	.	15605	.	9351	.	4996	.	1985	.	5
1916-	20993	38736	.	32860	.	31941	.	27690	.	21021	.	12989	.	6692	.	2638	.	5
1921-	25700	48316	.	41364	.	39285	.	34121	.	25485	.	16559	.	8706	.	3257	.	5
1926-	27628	56209	.	49571	.	43760	.	39765	.	30376	.	20022	.	10856	.	4030	.	5
1931-	10582	23561	.	21411	.	18233	.	17132	.	13421	.	8725	.	4878	.	1849	.	2
1933-	16898	17934	18059	17728	16306	15180	14286	14103	12785	11671	10140	7998	6380	4809	3305	1859	1272	3
1936-	27447	28061	29785	30268	27593	26232	24769	23636	21857	20508	18158	14530	11566	8987	6085	3457	2426	5
1941-	30834	29098	29308	29372	27824	27600	26114	24819	23086	21547	19361	16021	12941	10242	6893	4025	2898	5
1946-	38133	32574	28780	27373	27859	29147	27597	26789	24753	22393	20307	17554	14551	11583	7811	4733	3486	5
1951-	45040	38830	31911	26265	24384	28860	29303	28270	26412	24036	21100	18820	16089	13053	9005	5523	4195	5
1956-	50077	45745	39290	30549	25185	27332	29580	29829	27865	26101	22809	19948	16914	14229	10454	6403	4929	5
1961-	52627	50799	46205	38896	29936	26829	27725	29873	29606	27445	24998	21544	17928	14404	11351	7427	5757	5
1966-	47290	52640	51277	45986	36541	30915	27163	27655	29636	28898	26311	23229	19335	15103	11226	7917	6751	5
1971-	42386	46401	53015	51591	45095	38237	31672	27413	28066	28905	28308	24426	21175	16936	11885	7855	7465	5
FEMALE																		
1901-	5358	9755	.	10074	.	9018	.	7055	.	4956	.	3296	.	1912	.	852	.	5
1906-	10194	18226	.	18855	.	16473	.	13098	.	9349	.	5840	.	3423	.	1501	.	5
1911-	15058	27048	.	26811	.	23730	.	18905	.	13802	.	8591	.	4934	.	2216	.	5
1916-	20497	38096	.	34526	.	31651	.	25331	.	18505	.	11810	.	6498	.	2977	.	5
1921-	24903	47660	.	42118	.	39286	.	31540	.	23086	.	15229	.	8409	.	3631	.	5
1926-	26773	55120	.	50357	.	43980	.	37489	.	27878	.	18379	.	10470	.	4438	.	5
1931-	10281	23004	.	21838	.	18505	.	16392	.	12362	.	8117	.	4731	.	2032	.	2
1933-	16390	17461	17631	17803	17061	15749	14445	13925	12220	10926	9327	7409	6054	4695	3274	1943	1526	3
1936-	26591	27279	29020	30336	29159	27591	25323	23785	21400	19574	16904	13613	11158	8970	6169	3695	2930	5
1941-	29800	28211	28448	29387	29446	29151	27001	25385	23035	21026	18520	15348	12684	10500	7215	4435	3586	5
1946-	36746	31482	27808	27353	29311	30653	28812	27710	24987	22319	20121	17288	14446	12196	8462	5385	4461	5
1951-	43416	37414	30776	26558	27683	30473	30925	29480	27094	24450	21343	19145	16580	14070	10105	6484	5617	5
1956-	48373	44179	37945	30576	26921	28383	30933	31327	28940	26863	23371	20713	18283	15905	12094	7847	6941	5
1961-	50650	49149	44674	38350	31256	27739	28788	31324	31208	28697	26114	22814	19722	16934	13968	9590	8463	5
1966-	45384	50720	49595	45192	39025	31965	28254	29032	31331	30846	28137	25240	21782	18225	14919	11191	10604	5
1971-	40640	44650	51013	50369	45925	39073	32758	28923	29467	30834	30506	26739	24192	21167	16224	11870	13553	5

1901-32 DATA FOR EXPANDING REGISTRATION AREA

. DATA ARE FOR BROADER AGE GROUP FROM ADJACENT YOUNGER AGE GROUP

- NO MORTALITY STATISTICS ARE PRESENTED FOR THIS QUINQUENNIA

TABLE 180 POPULATION ESTIMATES (THOUSANDS) FOR YUGOSLAVIA BY AGE,SEX AND QUINQUENNIA

AGE	0-	5-	10-	15-	20-	25-	30-	35-	40-	45-	50-	55-	60-	65-	70-	75-	80+	NO. YRS DATA
MALE																		
1901-	-	-	-	-	-	-	-	-	-	-	-	-	-	-	-	-	-	
1906-	-	-	-	-	-	-	-	-	-	-	-	-	-	-	-	-	-	
1911-	-	-	-	-	-	-	-	-	-	-	-	-	-	-	-	-	-	
1916-	-	-	-	-	-	-	-	-	-	-	-	-	-	-	-	-	-	
1921-	1454	1535	1378	1261	1118	860	766	676	618	526	500	412	389	262	195	101	98	2
1926-	4326	4178	3093	3186	3161	2550	2177	1749	1590	1412	1277	1041	968	705	515	267	245	5
1931-	4899	4466	2983	3331	3485	2870	2342	1890	1715	1563	1321	1069	975	758	537	284	244	5
1936-	1890	1770	1318	1416	1380	1100	881	823	748	672	543	441	397	309	213	117	97	2
1941-	-	-	-	-	-	-	-	-	-	-	-	-	-	-	-	-	-	
1946-	-	-	-	-	-	-	-	-	-	-	-	-	-	-	-	-	-	
1951-	5153	3998	4121	4445	4320	3410	2396	1829	2564	2422	2019	1438	1066	898	621	351	255	5
1956-	5151	4942	3904	3933	4304	4219	3310	2355	1731	2431	2276	1869	1268	886	678	419	308	5
1961-	4803	5022	4879	3857	3859	4204	4105	3235	2302	1667	2326	2130	1693	1071	677	459	373	5
1966-	4742	4787	4991	4866	3815	3740	4003	3958	3159	2244	1603	2222	1955	1499	815	458	383	5
1971-	4633	4689	4788	4997	4817	3638	3577	3942	3882	3076	2168	1512	2025	1670	1164	532	394	5
FEMALE																		
1901-	-	-	-	-	-	-	-	-	-	-	-	-	-	-	-	-	-	
1906-	-	-	-	-	-	-	-	-	-	-	-	-	-	-	-	-	-	
1911-	-	-	-	-	-	-	-	-	-	-	-	-	-	-	-	-	-	
1916-	-	-	-	-	-	-	-	-	-	-	-	-	-	-	-	-	-	
1921-	1397	1463	1306	1266	1173	934	917	774	738	566	558	416	413	249	202	96	105	2
1926-	4181	3987	2936	3189	3152	2644	2443	1968	1925	1561	1479	1085	1055	691	545	261	264	5
1931-	4752	4272	2840	3322	3412	2934	2523	2092	2050	1761	1581	1176	1106	790	588	294	271	5
1936-	1830	1696	1258	1410	1409	1173	970	908	859	753	650	507	465	342	241	128	113	2
1941-	-	-	-	-	-	-	-	-	-	-	-	-	-	-	-	-	-	
1946-	-	-	-	-	-	-	-	-	-	-	-	-	-	-	-	-	-	
1951-	4950	3836	3957	4308	4258	3894	2894	2185	2809	2506	2213	1765	1426	1230	850	485	365	5
1956-	4865	4717	3741	3787	4175	4146	3762	2849	2089	2677	2384	2085	1604	1238	984	611	479	5
1961-	4552	4753	4665	3696	3737	4097	4061	3690	2794	2023	2589	2280	1952	1414	998	710	599	5
1966-	4466	4563	4773	4665	3704	3683	4002	3990	3621	2747	1937	2529	2173	1830	1128	725	645	5
1971-	4381	4473	4561	4793	4584	3531	3571	3945	3922	3552	2709	1877	2408	1958	1526	799	693	5

- NO MORTALITY STATISTICS ARE PRESENTED FOR THIS QUINQUENNIA

Numerical index to cause of death tables

Table number	*Cause*	*Tabulation by sex**	*Source of standard rates***	*Page number*
1	Tuberculosis – respiratory system	M, F, P	E & W, 1951-75	113
2	Tuberculosis – meninges and central nervous system	M, F	E & W, 1951-75	116
3	Tuberculosis – "alimentary"	M, F	E & W, 1951-75	118
4	Tuberculosis – bones and joints	M, F	E & W, 1951-75	120
5	Tuberculosis – all other forms	M, F	E & W, 1951-75	122
6	Tuberculosis – non-respiratory	M, F	E & W, 1951-75	124
7	Tuberculosis – all forms	M, F, P	E & W, 1951-75	126
8	Tabes dorsalis	M, F	E & W, 1951-67	129
9	General paralysis of the insane	M, F	E & W, 1951-67	131
10	Syphilis – CNS	M, F	E & W, 1951-75	133
11	Syphilis – all other	M, F	E & W, 1951-75	135
12	Syphilis – all forms	M, F	E & W, 1951-75	137
13	"Gonococcal infection"	M, F	E & W, 1921-30	139
14	"Venereal disease"	M, F	E & W, 1951-75	141
15	Typhoid fever	M, F	E & W, 1921-30	143
16	Paratyphoid fever and other Salmonella infections	M, F	E & W, 1921-30	145
17	Typhoid and paratyphoid	M, F	E & W, 1921-30	147
18	Cholera	M, F	Japan, 1902	149
19	Brucellosis (undulant fever)	M, F	Italy, 1926-35	151
20	Dysentery – all forms	M, F	E & W, 1921-30	153
21	Scarlet fever	M, F	E & W, 1921-30	155
22	Erysipelas	M, F	E & W, 1921-30	157
23	Septicaemia/Pyaemia	M, F	E & W, 1951-67	159
24	Diphtheria	M, F, P	E & W, 1921-30	161
25	Whooping cough	M, F	Rate/1000 persons 0-4	164
26	Meningococcal infections	M, F	E & W, 1951-75	166
27	Plague	M, F, P	Absolute numbers	168
28	Leprosy	M, F	Japan, 1950-59	171
29	Tetanus	M, F	E & W, 1921-30	173
30	Anthrax	M, F	Italy, 1926-35	175
31	Poliomyelitis and infectious encephalitis including late effects	M, F	E & W, 1951-67	177
32	Smallpox	M, F, P	Japan, 1908	179
33	Measles	M, F	E & W, 1951-75	182

*M = Male, F = Female, P = Persons. * *E & W = England and Wales

Table number	*Cause*	*Tabulation by sex**	*Source of standard rates***	*Page number*
34	Yellow fever	M, F	Absolute numbers	184
35	Hepatitis, infectious	M, F	E & W, 1951-75	186
36	Rabies	M, F	US, 1921-30	188
37	Typhus and other rickettsial diseases	M, F	Spain, 1905-12	190
38	Malaria	M, F	Italy, 1926-35	192
39	Hydatid disease	M, F	Italy, 1926-35	194
40	Ankylostomiasis	M, F	Japan, 1950	196
41	Infections – all forms	M, F, P	E & W, 1951-75	198
42	Malignant neoplasm – buccal cavity and pharynx	M, F	E & W, 1951-75	201
43	Malignant neoplasm – oesophagus	M, F	E & W, 1951-75	203
44	Malignant neoplasm – stomach	M, F	E & W, 1951-75	205
45	Malignant neoplasm – buccal cavity, pharynx, oesophagus and stomach	M, F	E & W, 1951-75	207
46	Malignant neoplasm – intestine excluding rectum	M, F	E & W, 1951-75	209
47	Malignant neoplasm – rectum	M, F	E & W, 1951-75	211
48	Malignant neoplasm – intestine and rectum	M, F	E & W, 1951-75	213
49	Malignant neoplasm – "alimentary tract"	M, F	E & W, 1951-75	215
50	Malignant neoplasm – larynx	M, F	E & W, 1951-75	217
51	Malignant neoplasm – trachea, bronchus and lung, not specified as secondary	M, F	E & W, 1951-75	219
52	Malignant neoplasm – larynx, trachea, bronchus and lung	M, F	E & W, 1951-75	221
53	Malignant neoplasm – breast	F	E & W, 1951-75	223
54	Malignant neoplasm – cervix uteri	F	E & W, 1951-75	224
55	Malignant neoplasm – uterus, other and unspecified	F	E & W, 1951-75	225
56	Malignant neoplasm – uterus	F	E & W, 1951-75	226
57	Malignant neoplasm – female genital organs	F	E & W, 1921-30	227
58	Malignant neoplasm – prostrate	M	E & W, 1951-75	228
59	Malignant neoplasm – skin	M, F	E & W, 1951-75	229
60	Malignant neoplasm – bone and connective tissue	M, F	E & W, 1951-75	231
61	Malignant neoplasm – all solid tumours	M, F	E & W, 1951-75	233
62	Leukaemia and aleukaemia	M, F	E & W, 1951-75	235
63	Hodgkin's disease	M, F	E & W, 1921-30	237
64	Lymphosarcoma and other neoplasms of lymphatic and haematopoietic system	M, F	E & W, 1951-75	239
65	Malignant neoplasm – all forms	M, F	E & W, 1951-75	241
66	Neoplasm – benign and unspecified	M, F	E & W, 1951-75	243
67	Neoplasm – all forms	M, F, P	E & W, 1951-75	245
68	Goitre – non-toxic	M, F	E & W, 1951-75	248
69	Thyrotoxicosis with or without goitre	M, F	E & W, 1951-75	250
70	Diabetes mellitus	M, F	E & W, 1951-75	252
71	Avitaminosis and other deficiency states	M, F	E & W, 1951-75	254
72	Anaemias	M, F	E & W, 1951-75	256
73	Allergic disorders, all other endocrine, metabolic and blood diseases	M, F	E & W, 1951-75	258
74	Allergic disorders, endocrine, metabolic and blood diseases	M, F	E & W, 1951-75	260
75	Mental illness	M, F	E & W, 1951-75	262
76	Mental deficiency	M, F	E & W, 1951-75	264

*M = Male, F = Female, P = Persons. * *E & W = England and Wales

Table number	*Cause*	*Tabulation by sex**	*Source of standard rates***	*Page number*
77	Mental illness – all forms	M, F	E & W, 1951-75	266
78	Vascular lesions affecting central nervous system	M, F, P	E & W, 1951-75	268
79	Meningitis – non-meningococcal	M, F	E & W, 1951-75	271
80	Multiple sclerosis	M, F	E & W, 1951-75	273
81	Epilepsy	M, F	E & W, 1951-75	275
82	Organs of vision – all diseases	M, F	E & W, 1921-30	277
83	Otitis media and mastoiditis	M, F	E & W, 1951-75	279
84	Eye and ear – all diseases	M, F	E & W, 1951-75	281
85	Nervous system and sense organs – all diseases	M, F	E & W, 1951-75	283
86	Mental illness and diseases of the nervous system	M, F	E & W, 1951-75	285
87	Rheumatic fever	M, F	E & W, 1951-75	287
88	Heart disease – chronic rheumatic	M, F	E & W, 1951-75	289
89	Heart disease – arteriosclerotic and degenerative	M, F	E & W, 1951-75	291
90	Heart – all diseases	M, F, P	E & W, 1951-75	293
91	Heart disease and acute rheumatism	M, F	E & W, 1951-75	296
92	Hypertensive disease	M, F	E & W, 1951-75	298
93	Arteries – all diseases	M, F	E & W, 1951-75	300
94	Circulatory system – all diseases	M, F	E & W, 1951-75	302
95	Cardio-vascular disease	M, F	E & W, 1951-75	304
96	Cardio-vascular disease and vascular lesions affecting central nervous system	M, F	E & W, 1951-75	306
97	Circulatory disease and acute rheumatism	M, F	E & W, 1951-75	308
98	Respiratory infections – acute upper	M, F	E & W, 1951-75	310
99	Influenza	M, F	E & W, 1951-75	312
100	Pneumonia – lobar	M, F	E & W, 1951-67	314
101	Broncho-pneumonia	M, F	E & W, 1951-67	316
102	Pneumonia – primary atypical, other and unspecified	M, F	E & W, 1951-67	318
103	Pneumonia – all forms	M, F, P	E & W, 1951-75	320
104	Bronchitis – acute	M, F, P	E & W, 1951-67	323
105	Bronchitis – chronic and unqualified	M, F, P	E & W, 1951-67	326
106	"Bronchitis" – all forms	M, F	E & W, 1951-75	329
107	Tonsils and adenoids – hypertrophy	M, F	E & W, 1921-30	331
108	Empyema and lung abscess	M, F	E & W, 1951-75	333
109	Pleurisy	M, F	E & W, 1951-67	335
110	Respiratory disease – all forms	M, F, P	E & W, 1951-75	337
111	Teeth and supporting structures – all diseases	M, F	E & W, 1921-30	340
112	Stomach – ulcer	M, F, P	E & W, 1951-67	342
113	Duodenum – ulcer	M, F	E & W, 1951-67	345
114	Peptic ulcer	M, F	E & W, 1951-75	347
115	Gastritis and duodenitis	M, F	E & W, 1951-75	349
116	Stomach and duodenum – all diseases	M, F	E & W, 1951-75	351
117	Appendicitis	M, F	E & W, 1951-75	353
118	Intestinal obstruction and hernia	M, F	E & W, 1951-75	355
119	Gastro-enteritis and colitis excluding diarrhoea of the newborn	M, F	E & W, 1951-67	357
120	Gastritis, duodenitis, enteritis and colitis	M, F	E & W, 1951-67	359
121	Cirrhosis of liver	M, F, P	E & W, 1951-75	361
122	Biliary calculi	M, F	E & W, 1921-30	364
123	Cholelithiasis and cholecystitis	M, F	E & W, 1951-75	366

*M = Male, F = Female, P = Persons. * *E & W = England and Wales

Table number	Cause	Tabulation by sex*	Source of standard rates**	Page number
124	Liver and biliary passages – all diseases	M, F	E & W, 1951-75	368
125	Alimentary disease – all forms	M, F, P	E & W, 1951-75	370
126	Nephritis – acute	M, F	E & W, 1951-75	373
127	Nephritis – chronic, other and unspecified	M, F	E & W, 1951-75	375
128	Nephritis and nephrosis	M, F, P	E & W, 1951-75	377
129	Kidney – infections	M, F	E & W, 1951-75	380
130	Kidney – all diseases excluding calculi	M, F	E & W, 1951-75	382
131	Urinary system – calculi	M, F	E & W, 1951-75	384
132	Prostrate – "hyperplasia"	M	E & W, 1951-75	386
133	Genito-urinary system – all diseases	M, F	E & W, 1951-75	387
134	Pregnancy, childbirth and the puerperium – sepsis	F	Rate/1000 live births	389
135	Pregnancy and the puerperium – toxaemias	F	Rate/1000 live births	390
136	Pregnancy and childbirth – haemorrhage	F	Rate/1000 live births	391
137	Abortion	F	Rate/1000 live births	392
138	Pregnancy, childbirth and the puerperium – complications	F	Rate/1000 live births	393
139	Skin and subcutaneous tissue – infections	M, F	E & W, 1951-75	394
140	Arthritis and spondylitis	M, F	E & W, 1951-75	396
141	Rheumatism – muscular and unspecified	M, F	E & W, 1921-30	398
142	Osteomyelitis and periostitis	M, F	E & W, 1951-75	400
143	Ankylosis and acquired musculoskeletal deformities	M, F	E & W, 1951-75	402
144	Bones and joints – all diseases	M, F	E & W, 1951-75	404
145	Skin diseases	M, F	E & W, 1951-75	406
146	Skin, musculoskeletal system and connective tissue – all diseases	M, F	E & W, 1951-75	408.
147	Congenital malformations – spina bifida and meningocele	M, F	Rate/1000 live births	410
148	Congenital malformations – "cardio-vascular"	M, F	E & W, 1951-75	412
149	Congenital malformations – all forms	M, F	E & W, 1951-75	414
150	Newborn – birth injuries	M, F	Rate/1000 live births	416
151	Newborn – post-natal asphyxia and atelectasis	M, F	Rate/1000 live births	418
152	Newborn – birth injuries, post-natal asphyxia and atelectasis	M, F	Rate/1000 live births	420
153	Newborn – infections	M, F	Rate/1000 live births	422
154	Newborn – haemolytic disease	M, F	Rate/1000 live births	424
155	Newborn – all diseases	M, F	Rate/1000 live births	426
156	Newborn – diseases and congenital malformations	M, F	E & W, 1951-75	428
157	Senility without mention of psychosis	M, F	E & W, 1951-75	430
158	Ill-defined and unknown causes of mortality	M, F	E & W, 1951-75	432
159	Senility, ill-defined, and unknown causes of mortality	M, F, P	E & W, 1951-75	434
160	Accidents – motor vehicle	M, F	E & W, 1951-75	437
161	Accidents – other transport	M, F	E & W, 1951-75	439
162	Accidents – all transport	M, F	E & W, 1951-75	441
163	Accidents – poisoning	M, F	E & W, 1951-75	443
164	Accidents – falls	M, F	E & W, 1951-75	445
165	Accidents – "fire and heat"	M, F	E & W, 1951-75	447
166	Accidents – firearms	M, F	E & W, 1951-75	449
167	Accidents – drowning and submersion	M, F	E & W, 1951-75	451
168	Accidents – other than motor vehicle	M, F	E & W, 1951-75	453
169	Accidents – all forms	M, F	E & W, 1951-75	455

*M = Male, F = Female, P = Persons. * *E & W = England and Wales

Table number	Cause	Tabulation by sex*	Source of Standard rates* *	Page number
170	Suicide and self-inflicted injury	M, F, P	E & W, 1951-75	457
171	Accidents – all non-traffic and suicide	M, F	E & W, 1951-75	460
172	Homicide and injury purposely inflicted by other persons (not in war)	M, F	E & W, 1951-75	462
173	War injury	M, F	E & W, 1951-75	464
174	Homicide and war injury	M, F	E & W, 1951-75	466
175	Accidents – all violence including suicide	M, F	E & W, 1951-75	468
176	Homicide, suicide, and war injury	M, F	E & W, 1951-75	470
177	Accidents and violence – all forms	M, F, P	E & W, 1951-75	472
178	All causes	M, F, P	E & W, 1951-75	475
179	Standard mortality rates by cause			478
180 (1)	Australia – Population estimates			484
180 (2)	Austria – Population estimates			485
180 (3)	Belgium – Population estimates			486
180 (4)	Bulgaria – Population estimates			487
180 (5)	Canada – Population estimates			488
180 (6)	Chile – Population estimates			489
180 (7)	Czechoslavakia – Population estimates			490
180 (8)	Denmark – Population estimates			491
180 (9)	Eire – Population estimates			492
180 (10)	Finland – Population estimates			493
180 (11)	France – Population estimates			494
180 (12)	Greece – Population estimates			495
180 (13)	Hungary – Population estimates			496
180 (14)	Iceland – Population estimates			497
180 (15)	Italy – Population estimates			498
180 (16)	Japan – Population estimates			499
180 (17)	Netherlands – Population estimates			500
180 (18)	New Zealand – Population estimates			501
180 (19)	Norway – Population estimates			502
180 (20)	Poland – Population estimates			503
180 (21)	Portugal – Population estimates			504
180 (22)	Romania – Population estimates			505
180 (23)	Spain – Population estimates			506
180 (24)	Sweden – Population estimates			507
180 (25)	Switzerland – Population estimates			508
180 (26)	Turkey – Population estimates			509
180 (27)	UK England and Wales – Population estimates			510
180 (28)	UK Northern Ireland – Population estimates			511
180 (29)	UK Scotland – Population estimates			512
180 (30)	USA – Population estimates			513
180 (31)	Yugoslavia – Population estimates			514

*M = Male, F = Female, P = Persons. * *E & W = England and Wales

Alphabetical Index to Cause of Death Tables

Cause	*Table number*	*Page number*
Abortion	137	392
Accidents – All forms	169	455
Accidents – All non-traffic and suicide	171	460
Accidents – All transport	162	441
Accidents – All violence excluding suicide	175	468
Accidents – Drowning and submersion	167	451
Accidents – Falls	164	445
Accidents – "Fire and Heat"	165	447
Accidents – Firearms	166	449
Accidents – Motor vehicle	160	437
Accidents – Other than motor vehicle	168	453
Accidents – Other transport	161	439
Accidents – Poisoning	163	443
Accidents and violence – All forms	177	472
Alimentary disease – All forms	125	370
Allergic disorders, all other endocrine, metabolic and blood diseases	73	258
Allergic disorders, endocrine, metabolic and blood diseases	74	260
Anaemias	72	256
Ankylosis and acquired musculoskeletal deformities	143	402
Ankylostomiasis	40	196
Anthrax	30	175
Appendicitis	117	353
Arteries – All diseases	93	300
Arthritis and spondylitis	140	396
Avitaminosis and other deficiency states	71	254
Benign and unspecified neoplasms	66	243
Biliary calculi	122	364
Bones and Joints – All diseases	144	404
Bronchitis – Acute	104	323
"Bronchitis" – All forms	106	329
Bronchitis – Chronic and unqualified	105	326
Broncho-pneumonia	101	316
Brucellosis (undulant fever)	19	151
Cardio-vascular disease	95	304
Cardio-vascular disease and vascular lesions affecting Central Nervous System	96	306
Cholelithiasis and cholecystitis	123	366
Cholera	18	149
Circulatory disease and acute rheumatism	97	308
Circulatory system – All diseases	94	302
Cirrhosis of liver	121	361
Congenital malformations – All forms	149	414

Cause	*Table number*	*Page number*
Congenital malformations – Cardio-vascular	148	412
Congenital malformations – Spina bifida and meningocele	147	410
Diabetes mellitus	70	252
Diphtheria	24	161
Duodenum – Ulcer	113	345
Dysentery – All forms	20	153
Empyema and lung abscess	108	333
Epilepsy	81	275
Erysipelas	22	157
Eye and ear – All diseases	84	281
Gastritis and duodenitis	115	349
Gastritis, duodenitis, enteritis and colitis	120	359
Gastro-enteritis and colitis excluding diarrhoea of the newborn	119	357
General paralysis of the insane	9	131
Genito-urinary system – All diseases	133	387
Goitre – Non-toxic	68	248
"Gonococcal infection"	13	139
Heart – All diseases	90	293
Heart disease and acute rheumatism	91	296
Heart disease – Arteriosclerotic and degenerative	89	291
Heart disease – Chronic rheumatic	88	289
Hepatitis, infectious	35	186
Hodgkin's Disease	63	237
Homicide and injury purposely inflicted by other persons (not in war)	172	462
Homicide, suicide and war injury	176	470
Homicide and war injury	174	466
Hydatid disease	39	194
Hypertensive disease	92	298
Ill-defined and unknown causes of mortality	158	432
Infections – All forms	41	198
Influenza	99	312
Intestinal obstruction and hernia	118	355
Kidney – Infection	129	380
Kidney and urethra – All diseases excluding calculi	130	382
Leprosy	28	171
Leukaemia and Aleukaemia	62	235
Liver and biliary passages – All diseases	124	368
Lymphosarcoma and other neoplasms of lymphatic and haematopoietic system	64	239
Malaria	38	192
Malignant neoplasm – "Alimentary tract"	49	215
Malignant neoplasm – All forms	65	241
Malignant neoplasm – All solid tumours	61	233
Malignant neoplasm – Bone and Connective Tissue	60	231
Malignant neoplasm – Breast	53	223
Malignant neoplasm – Buccal cavity and pharynx	42	201
Malignant neoplasm – Buccal cavity, pharynx, oesophagus and stomach	45	207
Malignant neoplasm – Cervix uteri	54	224
Malignant neoplasm – Female genital organs	57	227
Malignant neoplasm – Intestine and rectum	48	213
Malignant neoplasm – Intestine excluding rectum	46	209

Cause	*Table number*	*Page number*
Malignant neoplasm – Larynx	50	217
Malignant neoplasm – Larynx, trachea, bronchus and lung	52	221
Malignant neoplasm – Lung	51	219
Malignant neoplasm – Oesophagus	43	203
Malignant neoplasm – Prostate	58	228
Malignant neoplasm – Rectum	47	211
Malignant neoplasm – Skin	59	229
Malignant neoplasm – Stomach	44	205
Malignant neoplasm – Trachea, bronchus and lung, not specified as secondary	51	219
Malignant neoplasm – Uterus	56	226
Malignant neoplasm – Uterus, other and unspecified	55	225
Measles	33	182
Meningitis – Non-meningococcal	79	271
Meningococcal infections	26	166
Mental deficiency	76	264
Mental illness	75	262
Mental illness – All forms	77	266
Mental illness and diseases of the nervous system	86	285
Multiple sclerosis	80	273
Neoplasms – All forms	67	245
Nephritis – Acute	126	373
Nephritis – Chronic, other and unspecified	127	375
Nephritis and nephrosis	128	377
Nervous system and sense organs – All diseases	85	283
Newborn – All diseases	155	426
Newborn – Birth injuries	150	416
Newborn – Birth injuries, postnatal asphyxia atelectasis	152	420
Newborn – Diseases and congenital malformations	156	428
Newborn – Haemolytic disease	154	424
Newborn – Infections	153	422
Newborn – Postnatal asphyxia and atelectasis	151	418
Organs of Vision – All diseases	82	277
Osteomyelitis and periostitis	142	400
Otitis media and mastoiditis	83	279
Paratyphoid fever and other Salmonella infections	16	145
Peptic ulcer	114	347
Plague	27	168
Pleurisy	109	335
Pneumonia – All forms	103	320
Pneumonia – Lobar	100	314
Pneumonia – Primary atypical other and unspecified	102	318
Poliomyelitis and infectious encephalitis including late effects	31	177
Pregnancy and childbirth – Haemorrhage	136	391
Pregnancy, childbirth and puerperium – Complications	138	393
Pregnancy, childbirth and the puerperium – Sepsis	134	389
Pregnancy and the puerperium – Toxaemias	135	390
Prostate – "Hyperplasia"	132	386
Rabies	36	188
Respiratory diseases – All forms	110	337
Respiratory infections – Acute upper	98	310

Cause	*Table number*	*Page number*
Rheumatic fever	87	287
Rheumatism – Muscular and unspecified	141	398
Scarlet fever	21	155
Senility, ill-defined, and unknown causes of morality	159	434
Senility without mention of psychosis	157	430
Septicaemia/Pyaemia	23	159
Skin diseases	145	406
Skin, musculoskeletal system and connective tissue – All diseases	146	408
Skin and subcutaneous tissue – Infections	139	394
Smallpox	32	179
Stomach – Ulcer	112	342
Stomach and Duodenum – All diseases	116	351
Suicide and self-inflicted injury	170	457
Syphilis – All forms	12	137
Syphilis – All other	11	135
Syphilis – CNS	10	133
Syphilis – General paralysis of the insane	9	131
Syphilis – Tabes Dorsalis	8	129
Tabes Dorsalis	8	129
Teeth and supporting structures – All diseases	111	340
Tetanus	29	173
Thyrotoxicosis with or without Goitre	69	250
Tonsils and adenoids – Hypertrophy	107	331
Tuberculosis – "Alimentary"	3	118
Tuberculosis – All forms	7	126
Tuberculosis – All other forms	5	122
Tuberculosis – Bones and joints	4	120
Tuberculosis – Meninges and Central Nervous System	2	116
Tuberculosis – Non-respiratory	6	124
Tuberculosis – Respiratory system	1	113
Tyhoid fever	15	143
Typhoid and paratyphoid	17	147
Typhus and other rickettsial diseases	37	190
Urinary system – Calculi	131	384
Vascular lesions affecting Central Nervous System	78	268
"Venereal Disease"	14	141
War injury	173	464
Whooping cough	25	164
Yellow fever	34	184